AN ILLUSTRATED MANUAL OF CALIFORNIA SHRUBS

BY HOWARD E. McMINN

Berkeley, Los Angeles, London
UNIVERSITY OF CALIFORNIA PRESS

UNIVERSITY OF CALIFORNIA PRESS
BERKELEY AND LOS ANGELES, CALIFORNIA

UNIVERSITY OF CALIFORNIA PRESS, LTD.
LONDON, ENGLAND

First published by J. W. Stacey, Incorporated, 1939
PRINTED IN THE UNITED STATES OF AMERICA
ISBN: 0-520-00847-2

7 8 9

TO THE

SANTA BARBARA BOTANIC GARDEN

OF SANTA BARBARA, CALIFORNIA

IN RECOGNITION OF ITS WORK

IN PROMOTING

THE KNOWLEDGE OF NATIVE

CALIFORNIAN PLANTS

CONTENTS

PREFACE

The object of this volume is to present a systematic and descriptive account of the shrubs of California which will serve as a working manual for their identification by the forester, ranger, traveler, vacationist, teacher, landscape designer, gardener, and student of nature. While primarily planned for the use of the general public, the book has been written to serve also the professional botanist who is interested in the native shrubs of California.

The author has included all of those vegetative forms* classified as woody perennials and semi-woody plants except trees and the succulent-stemmed shrubs of the Cactus Family. About 800 species and 200 varieties of native shrubs, woody vines, subshrubs, woody cushion plants, and halfshrubs have been recognized. Fourteen species of introduced shrubs which have become naturalized have also been included. Many of the larger shrubs included often have a single trunk for a short distance from the ground and are often arborescent in form and stature. It is not possible that critics will approve the recognition accorded to some species or denied others. Where difference of opinion has arisen, the author has attempted to maintain a conservative position.

The collecting of material has taken place over a period of twenty years. During this time the author has botanized most of the shrub areas of California, where the shrubs have been studied in their native habitats. Over 300 species have been transplanted to the trial gardens at Mills College where they have been under observation for structural variations.

Type specimens and other specimens have been examined at the following herbaria and botanical gardens: University of California, Vegetative Type Map, and Graduate Students' herbaria, Berkeley; Dudley Herbarium, Stanford University; California Academy of Sciences, San Francisco; Southern California Academy of Sciences, Los Angeles; Pomona College, Claremont; Santa Barbara Botanic Garden and Museum of Natural History, Santa Barbara; Santa Ana Rancho Botanic Garden, Santa Ana Canyon, Orange County; Natural History Museum, San Diego; Mills College, Oakland; Notre Dame University, South Bend, Indiana; National Herbarium, Washington, D. C.; Philadelphia Academy of Sciences; New York Botanical Gardens; Gray Herbarium, Boston, Massachusetts; Royal Botanic Gardens at Kew and the British Museum, London, England; Cambridge University, England; Jardin des Plantes, Paris, France; Geneva, Switzerland; Berlin-Dahlem, Germany; Royal Botanic Garden, Edinburgh, Scotland.

The botanical descriptions and notes on distribution have been prepared from living material and herbarium specimens, after comparison with original diagnoses, type specimens, and published descriptions in monographs, special papers, and floras on Californian plants, all of which are listed in the general bibliography or in the citations of species given after the botanical descriptions. Double citation has been employed if the name of the species or variety used in this book did not originate with the author of the first published description of the plant, as in *Physocarpus capitatus* (Pursh) Ktze., the species name having been transferred by Kuntze from *Spiraea capitata* of Pursh, or in *Physocarpus alternans* (Jones) J. T. Howell, the species name having been transferred by J. T. Howell from *Neillia monogyna* var. *alternans* of Jones.

*See Ecological Classification of Plants page 1.

The author has endeavored to follow the International Rules of Botanical Nomenclature. The sequence of families, with slight modification, is that used by Engler and Prantl in their *Natürliche Pflanzenfamilien* and in Engler's *Syllabus*.

Most of the pen and ink drawings have been prepared, under direction of the author, by Emily Patterson Thompson. The others have been drawn by Marjory DeJean, Edna Russell, Evelyn Maino, Dorothy Harris, Ruth Rossbach, Dixie Lee Ray, and M. Sörensen. Photographs for the half-tone illustrations, figures 113, 137, 150, 176, 184, 206, 228, 234, 235, 263, 308, 314, 330, 335, 344, 359, 378, 409, 427, 428, 439, 448, 537, 578, 614, 628, 629, 641, and 730 were taken by Paul W. Hollingshead. Such clearness as they possess is due to his painstaking work. Photographs for figures 8, 82, 83, 122, 625, 636, and 648 were taken by Wm. Mathews, photographer at the University of California, and for figures 21, 22, 23, and 719 by the author.

ACKNOWLEDGMENTS

To the many persons who have given valuable assistance during the progress of this study I wish to make grateful acknowledgment. I am especially indebted to Willis Linn Jepson for suggestions and inspiration during the entire period of study. His publications on the native plants of California, especially the *Flora of California,* have been of inestimable value.

For friendly courtesies enabling me to extend my field and herbarium observations I take this opportunity to thank Miss Persis Coleman, Mr. Linden Naylor, Mrs. Lora J. Knight, Dr. W. B. Stephens, Mr. Frank J. McCoy, and Dr. George Piness.

Among the directors and members of the staffs of the botanical gardens, herbaria, and botanical departments of educational institutions previously mentioned the following have been helpful: Dr. H. L. Mason, Dr. Lincoln Constance, Miss Ethel Crum, Miss Annetta Carter, Mrs. H. P. Bracelin, Miss Alice Eastwood, Mr. John T. Howell, Dr. Leroy Abrams, Dr. Ira Wiggins, Mrs. Roxana Ferris, Mr. A. E. Wieslander, Miss Beryl Schreiber, Mr. Maunsell Van Rensselaer, Dr. P. A. Munz, Dr. Carl Epling, Dr. Carl Wolf, Mr. Milo S. Baker, Dr. Theodor Just, Dr. Francis Pennell, Dr. H. A. Gleason, Dr. W. H. Camp, Dr. M. L. Fernald, Dr. Ivan Johnston, Mr. Louis Wheeler, Mr. N. Y. Sandwith, Dr. John Ramsbottom, Dr. B. P. G. Hochreutiner, and Dr. C. Baehni.

My friend, Herbert L. Mason, with whom I have spent many pleasant and profitable hours in the field, herbarium, and home discussing the taxonomy and distribution of the California native shrubs, has made many valuable suggestions during the preparation of the manuscript. Dr. Rimo Bacigalupi has furnished field notes on the distribution and growth habits of several species. He has also read the greater part of the manuscript. Dr. David Keck has given aid on the species of *Penstemon*. Dr. Carlton Ball identified questionable specimens of the genus *Salix*.

It has been a pleasure to work with the artist, Emily Patterson Thompson, because of her aptitude for perceiving and delineating the essential characteristics of the species.

The granting of a leave of absence from academic duties by President Aurelia Henry Reinhardt and the Board of Trustees of Mills College made it possible for the author to visit herbaria and botanical libraries in the United States and Europe.

To my wife, Helen R. McMinn, for her untiring assistance given throughout the preparation of the manuscript and the reading of the proof I am especially indebted.

Finally, the author wishes to follow the advice of Epictetus who said that every author should say to the critics of his work, "That if they who find some faults in it were as intimate with it as I am, they would find a great many more."

HOWARD E. McMINN

Mills College, California

October 4, 1939

INTRODUCTION

The Classification and Naming of Plants

Plants may be grouped or classified according to their systematic position, that is, their genetic relationship, or according to habitat responses. The former is known as phylogenetic classification, the latter as ecological classification.

PHYLOGENETIC CLASSIFICATION

The forms of plant life are classified according to an established system composed of categories of varying ranks. Individuals which are most alike are grouped into species or subdivisions of the species called varieties or subspecies. Thus all individuals of Pinemat Manzanita are of one species, the Pinemat or *nevadensis* species of manzanita, and all individuals of the Whiteleaf Manzanita belong to the Whiteleaf or *viscida* species. Species which are most alike are brought together into a category called a genus. Thus all species of manzanita belong to the genus *Arctostaphylos,* and all species of huckleberry belong to the genus *Vaccinium.* Genera which are closely related are grouped into families. Further steps in classification are the groupings of related families into orders, related orders into classes (or subclasses), and related classes into divisions or phyla. The plant kingdom is made up of four phyla, Thallophytes (seaweeds, pondscums, mushrooms, molds, etc.), Bryophytes (mosses and liverworts), Pteridophytes (ferns and scouring-rushes), and Spermatophytes (seed plants). The phylum Spermatophytes is composed of two classes, Gymnosperms (naked-seed plants, as pines, firs, etc.) and Angiosperms (covered-seed plants, as manzanitas, apples, beans, etc.).

The scientific name of a plant consists of the name of the genus followed by that of the species. The name or the abbrevation of the name of the person who properly applied the scientific name to the plant is written after the species. For example, the scientific name of Pinemat Manzanita is *Arctostaphylos nevadensis* Gray. The genus is always written with a capital letter, and in this book, the species, in accordance with the International Rules of Nomenclature, is uncapitalized, except in those species whose names were derived from names of persons or from other genera. The ending *ii* instead of *i* is used for certain species named after persons, as *Berberis Fremontii* and *Ceanothus Jepsonii.* However, if the person's name ends in *er* or *y,* a single *i* is added, as *Salix Coulteri* and *Ceanothus Parryi.*

The hyphen is used in the common name whenever the last part of the name refers to the common name of another genus, as in Poison-oak, the common name of *Rhus diversiloba,* and in Oregon-grape, the common name of *Berberis aquifolium.* The genus for oak is *Quercus* and the genus for grape is *Vitis.*

ECOLOGICAL CLASSIFICATION

Various attempts have been made to classify plants according to their habitats or environments, and according to their responses to the environment. This type of classification assumes that every plant or community of plants responds to the factors of the habitat and consequently exhibits forms, known as habitat forms, which clearly bear the impress of the environment. The factors which exert their influences upon plant life, either directly or indirectly, are usually grouped into four general divisions: climatic, such as moisture, temperature, and light; physiographic, those factors associated with land surface, such as slope and other topographic factors; edaphic, those that have to do with the chemical and physical character of the soil; and biotic, those that are associated with animals and plants. Water is usually considered the most important single factor in the habitats of plants, and upon the basis of water relation these habitat forms are classified as: hydrophytes, plants which can endure large amounts of water, either wholly or partially submerged; mesophytes, plants which live in habitats with a medium water supply; and xerophytes, plants which grow in places with small amounts of water, as deserts, sandhills, and alpine peaks. Xerophytes which grow in soil which is physiologically dry because of excess soil salts are known as halophytes and those which grow in soil physically dry for a part or most of the year in consequence of a dry climate, may be classified either as drymophytes (chaparral and deciduous shrubs) or eremophytes (desert plants). Drymophytes have a discontinuous water supply due to a long dry period alternating with a wet season, and eremophytes lack water most of the year.

Upon the basis of the above ecological classification most of the Californian shrubs are drymophytes and eremophytes, a few are halophytes and mesophytes, and none is strictly a hydrophyte.

Another ecological classification is based upon length of life and character of the plant and upon methods of preservation and increase of the vegetative shoots. Such a classification refers to the vegetative or growth forms of plants. These forms are less dependent than habitat forms upon the habitat and hence their ecologic responses are less evident. They are grouped as follows:

1. *Annuals.* Living one year; passing the unfavorable season in seed form.
2. *Biennials.* Living two or parts of two years; passing one unfavorable season in seed form and the next in some form of a vegetative propagule, such as a bulb or fleshy root.
3. *Herbaceous perennials.* Living several to many years; passing each unfavorable season as seeds and propagule forms.
4. *Woody perennials.* Usually living many years; passing each unfavorable season as seeds and aerial shoots, and often as propagules also.
    a. *Trees.* Usually developing a main trunk.
    b. *Shrubs.* Usually not developing a main trunk, with the stem branched from the base either below or above the ground.
        (1) *Long-shoot shrubs.* The crown built up mainly by long shoots with elongated internodes. The great majority of shrubs belong here.
            (a) *Aeroxylic.* Without underground ramification of the stem.
            (b) *Geoxylic.* With a well developed underground ramification of the stem, often with a root-crown from which aerial stems arise.
        (2) *Rosette-shrubs.* The crown built up by shoots with very short internodes and the leaves crowded into rosettes on the ends of the short branches.
    c. *Succulent-stemmed shrubs.* The Cactus Family.
    d. *Dwarfshrubs or subshrubs.* Less than 2½ feet high, not forming cushions.
    e. *Woody cushion plants.* With all the branches tightly grouped together into a compact cushion-like mass.
    f. *Woody vines or climbing shrubs.* Supported by other plants, rocks, etc.
5. *Semi-woody plants or halfshrubs (suffruticose perennials).* Only the lower part of the stem woody and perennial, the upper part herbaceous and annual.

Another useful classification based upon the texture of the stems and leaves is briefly summarized:

1. Stems herbaceous.
   a. Grasses.
   b. Herbs, including annuals, biennials, and perennials.
2. Stems woody.
   a. Shrubs, including dwarfshrubs, woody cushion plants, and woody vines.
   b. Trees.
3. Stems succulent, i.e., fleshy and usually watery.
   a. Succulents, such as cacti.

Composition of the Shrub Areas of California

VEGETATION UNITS

The total of all the plants in an area is known as the vegetation of that area. The vegetation, however, is more than just an assemblage of individual plants. It is the aggregation of individuals which require the same type of environment, and often, as a response to the environment, it exhibits a common growth form, as desert shrub or tree; or it may exhibit two or more growth forms, as the under growth of annuals, herbaceous perennials, and shrubs which form layer societies in a forest. These assemblages or plant communities have been given various names, depending upon the importance of the community in a larger association of plants.

The major units of vegetation, as forest and grassland, are commonly known as plant formations. Since these communities are considered products of the climate and are controlled by it they are known also as climaxes. Weaver and Clements state that, "Each formation is the highest type of vegetation possible under its particular climate, and this relation makes the term climax especially significant, as it is derived from the same root as climate." The names of the formations are taken from the dominant growth form exhibited by the vegetation community, as grassland, chaparral, and coniferous forest. No single formation is uniform throughout its entire area because the various portions differ somewhat in their climatic and edaphic factors. Such major divisions of a formation are known as associations, as the Redwood *(Sequoia sempervirens)* and Douglas Fir *(Pseudotsuga taxifolia)* associations of the Pacific conifer formation. The names of the associations are taken from the dominant species in the vegetation area.

The larger vegetation areas or communities (formations, climaxes, climax-formations) in California may be classified as forest and woodland, grassland, shrub, mixed, and alpine. A study of them reveals that they are often composed of different types or elements, as conifer and broad-sclerophyll forest, or chaparral and desert shrub.

SHRUB TYPES OR ELEMENTS

The shrub types or elements which compose the shrub areas or formations in California may be classified as desert shrub, Great Basin sagebrush, coastal sagebrush, deciduous shrub, chaparral, succulent, and alpine. These types will be described with the discussion of shrub areas. They are represented by such growth forms given in the ecological classification of plants as long-shoot shrubs, rosette-shrubs, succulent-stemmed shrubs, dwarfshrubs or subshrubs, woody cushion plants, woody vines or climbing shrubs, and halfshrubs or suffruticose perennials.

SHRUB AREAS IN CALIFORNIA

The major shrub areas in California are coextensive with the shrub formations or climaxes. These are desert shrub, sagebrush, and chaparral. Lesser areas occur, such as the layer communities in the forest and woodland formations, shrub "islands" in the grassland formation, shrub in the mixed formation, alpine shrub in the alpine formation, and a small littoral area confined to the immediate vicinity of the ocean.

Desert Shrub Formation

This formation occurs in California on the Colorado and Mohave deserts and in the Death Valley region, extending up the lower slopes of the mountains in and adjacent to these regions. The desert shrub area has the lowest rainfall, the greatest evaporation, and the highest mean temperature of all California shrub areas, therefore, the shrub elements are the most xerophytic of all shrub species. Occurring as they do in a region with 2 to 10 inches of rainfall, they have many characteristics, such as reduced leaf-size, deep root system, and water storage cells, which enable them to secure and conserve the small amount of available water. The shrubs are usually spaced from 10 to 30 feet apart, a characteristic which sets off this formation from the chaparral and sagebrush formations. During the early spring, many low annuals occur in the intervals between the shrubs.

The desert shrubs consist of many species of different families not at all uniform in external characters. The cacti and *Fouquieria* have succulent stems. Some are small-leaved shrubs, some are thorny, and a few, as the Creosote Bush (*Larrea divaricata*), resemble somewhat species of chaparral. In respect to their systematic relationship the desert shrubs are less homogeneous than either chaparral or sagebrush. The dominant genera such as *Larrea, Prosopis, Ephedra, Franseria,* and *Atriplex* belong to different families.

Two vegetation belts or zones of desert shrubs are usually evident in most of the desert areas. The Upland Belt consists of Juniper and Yucca with associated species of *Salvia, Tetradymia,* and *Senecio.* The Creosote Belt dominated by the Creosote Bush lies below the Upland Belt. *Franseria dumosa* is probably the second most abundant shrub of this belt. Species of *Suaeda, Atriplex,* and *Allenrolfea* occur in the lower saline areas. These species have succulent stems or leaves.

An airplane view of the desert shrub area reveals distinct color-tones due to the hue of the foliage, stems, and branches of the plants. The Creosote Bush gives a brownish green or bronze aspect. On the high alluvial fans of the Mohave Desert, *Grayia spinosa, Salazaria,* and *Coleogyne* occur in such abundance as to give a blue-gray tone. The canyon floors and flood plains appear a vivid green because of the presence of *Prosopis, Acacia,* and *Cercidium.*

Sagebrush Formation

The sagebrush formation consists of two distinct associations, the Great Basin sagebrush and the coastal sagebrush. The Great Basin sagebrush association as a climax is confined mainly to the central part of the Great Basin, from eastern Oregon and southern Idaho to northeastern California, Nevada, and central Utah. This association extends in all directions from the climax area to adjacent formations, and hence the limits are difficult to place. In California, it occurs chiefly east of the Sierra Nevada crest, but tongues of sagebrush extend westerly over the crest into the Sierran montane forest (*Pinus-Abies association*) and woodland formations (*Pinus-Juniperus association*) and southward into southern California where it comes in contact with the desert shrub, the eastern extension of the coastal sagebrush, and occasionally with outlying extensions of chaparral.

This area has from 5 to 15 inches of rainfall and is nearly as hot as the desert shrub area. The shrubs are of the Great Basin sagebrush element and are primarily xerophytic in character. They have a more uniform superficial ecological character than desert shrub and exhibit a more or less single growth form of low shrubs or bushes not as distantly placed as in the desert shrub area. They are typically deep-rooted shrubs, with reduced leaf-surface and gray hairy epidermis which gives a gray color-tone to this area. Some authors consider them shrubby adaptations of herbaceous families.

The Great Basin sagebrush is more homogeneous than desert shrub in respect to systematic relationship. There are many species represented in the area, but not so many families as in the desert shrub area. Clements gives 17 dominant species for the sagebrush formation (Great Basin sagebrush and coastal sagebrush associations), 11 of which belong to Asteraceae, 4 to Chenopodiaceae, 1 to Polygonaceae, and 1 to Menthaceae. *Artemisia tridentata* is the most outstanding dominant as well as one of the most widespread. Other important dominants are *Atriplex confertifolia, A. canescens, Gutierrezia Sarothrae, Grayia spinosa, Chrysothamnus nauseosus, Tetradymia spinosa,* and *Eurotia lanata*. Several of the dominants can withstand considerable alkali and hence are sometimes associated with the more halophytic species of the area, as *Sarcobatus vermiculatus* (Greasewood) and *Atriplex Nuttallii* var. *falcata* (Moundscale), but are never found in the same association with the more alkali tolerant *Allenrolfea* and *Suaeda*.

The coastal sagebrush area or association occupies the lower dry foothills of the Coast Ranges from the San Francisco Bay region southward to San Diego County and into Lower California. It extends eastward along the foothills of the San Bernardino Mountains to the desert shrub and southwestern edge of the Great Basin sagebrush association. It usually lies between grassland and *Adenostoma* of the chaparral but may occur in southern California between *Larrea* desert shrub and *Adenostoma*.

The main portion or climax area receives annually from 10 to 18 inches of rainfall but the extra-associational communities of southern California receive from 5 to 10 inches. The coastal sagebrush elements have gray herbage for the most part, and hence give to the association much the same color-tone as the Great Basin sagebrush. The major dominant is *Artemisia californica* (Coast Sagebrush). It often forms pure communities in the coast hills but is more commonly associated with *Eriogonum fasciculatum* (California-buckwheat) and *Salvia mellifera* (Black Sage). Other important associated species are *Salvia apiana* (White Sage), *S. leucophylla* (Purple Sage), *Senecio Douglasii* (Bush Senecio), *Lotus scoparius* (Deerweed), and *Solanum umbelliferum* (Blue Witch). *Eriogonum fasciculatum* gives way to the variety *polifolium* in the drier areas approaching the desert.

Chaparral Formation

The term chaparral is derived from the Spanish "chaparra," meaning scrub oak. In California, it is usually applied to the dominant mostly evergreen shrubby vegetation which inhabits the region of "California climate," that is, the region west of the Sierra Nevada and the Colorado and Mohave deserts. This type of shrubby vegetation is known as broad-sclerophyll. It is characterized by thick, stiff, hard, usually flat, and evergreen leaves and by dense rigid branching. Much of the broad-sclerophyll vegetation in California is composed of trees, as *Arbutus Menziesii, Quercus agrifolia,* and *Q. Wislizenii,* which constitute the broad-sclerophyll forest formation. The broad-sclerophyll shrub or chaparral element is the most important type in the chaparral formation.

Broad-sclerophyll communities are generally found in regions where the total annual rainfall is less than 30 inches and the summer precipitation is less than 20 per cent of the total. Considerable areas of sclerophyllous vegetation are found in parts of Australia and in the Mediterranean region where the shrub type is known as "macchie" and "garigue." Some areas are found also in South Africa, in South America on the west slope of the Chilean Andes, and in Mexico. In the United States, broad-sclerophyll vegetation occurs from southern California northward in the mountains and foothills to Oregon, a few species extending as far north as British Columbia.

The chaparral formation, as previously pointed out, is composed chiefly of the chaparral element, but a few species of the deciduous element occur, as *Rhus diversiloba, Quercus dumosa* (semi-deciduous), *Prunus virginiana* var. *demissa, Cercocarpus betuloides, Holodiscus discolor,* and *Amelanchier alnifolia.* This formation, as here treated, is referable to Cooper's Climax Chaparral Association.

The chaparral element which often forms associations in the conifer forest, I prefer to classify into communities of the conifer forest formation rather than of the chaparral formation as given by some authors. These communities are mentioned in the discussion of the lesser shrub areas. In California the chaparral formation has its best development in the mountains of southern California, the South Coast Ranges, and the foothills of the central and southern Sierra Nevada. In the North Coast Ranges the chaparral formation gives way more and more to its closest ecological relative, the broad-sclerophyll forest formation, in which occur small communities of the chaparral element. Around the northern end of the Sacramento Valley it disappears entirely as a dominant formation. In the northern Sierra Nevada it occupies discontinuous areas separated by tongues of the Sierran conifer forests which often reach down the foothills to the valley floor.

The chaparral consists of many species of genera which, although unrelated phylogenetically, have a definite ecological type. The exceptions to this type are few, but oddly enough, one of the most important if not the most important species, *Adenostoma fasciculatum,* has short needle-like leaves instead of the broader sclerophyllous leaf-type. The species of chaparral are more mesophytic than desert shrub, sagebrush, or grassland, but more xerophytic than broad-sclerophyll or conifer forest. Among the more important shrubs of the chaparral formation are *Adenostoma fasciculatum, Ceanothus cuneatus, Prunus ilicifolia, Pickeringia montana, Dendromecon rigida, Photinia arbutifolia,* and various species of *Arctostaphylos, Rhus, Quercus, Rhamnus, Garrya,* and *Eriodictyon.*

THE LESSER SHRUB AREAS

Of the lesser shrub areas of California three are of sufficient importance to deserve special mention. However, since the species that compose them are not the dominant species of the larger community, and since they do not constitute the prominent growth form, the areas are not classified as formations or associations.

In the forest and woodland formations there occur a great number of species of shrubs which are constituents of the layer societies common to such formations. Many shrubs of the deciduous element, such as species of *Ribes, Prunus, Acer,*

Rubus, Lonicera, and *Amelanchier,* occur in the more mesophytic areas. Other deciduous species, as *Cephalanthus occidentalis, Calycanthus occidentalis, Rhododendron occidentale,* and species of *Salix,* usually occur along streams, either in the forest or in more open communities. It is not uncommon to find in the forest and woodland formation species of the chaparral element, such as *Arctostaphylos patula, A. nevadensis, Ceanothus cordulatus, C. prostratus, C. velutinus, Quercus vaccinifolia, Rhododendron macrophyllum, Gaultheria shallon,* and *Vaccinium ovatum.* Occasionally a few species of the desert shrub, coastal sagebrush, and Great Basin sagebrush invade open spaces in adjacent woodland and forest formations.

In the alpine and subalpine areas of the California mountains there occur species of dwarfshrubs and woody cushion plants. These often form patch communities of various extent on old rock slides, in decomposed granite, on rocky slopes, and in bogs surrounding alpine mountain meadows and lakes. The brilliant color and profusion of their flowers and the flowers of their herbaceous perennial associates can scarcely be matched elsewhere. Among the more striking species of these dwarf subshrubs are *Phlox Douglasii, Leptodactylon pungens, Cassiope mertensiana, Phyllodoce Breweri, Lupinus Lyallii* var. *Lobbii, L. Breweri, Vaccinium caespitosum,* and *Salix petrophila* var. *caespitosa.* The woody cushion plant growth form is represented by *Eriogonum ovalifolium* and *E. incanum.*

A few shrubs and subshrubs occur in a narrow area within the immediate influence of the ocean. These may occur on the sand dunes, in the salt marshes, or on the bluffs above the ocean. Among the more important species of this littoral area are *Suaeda californica, Eriogonum parvifolium, Atriplex lentiformis* var. *Breweri, Haplopappus ericoides, H. Eastwoodae, Eriophyllum staechadifolium, Lupinus Chamissonis, L. arboreus, Senecio Blochmanae, Baccharis pilularis,* and *Grindelia humilis.*

Explanation of Terms*

For the guidance of readers not familiar with botanical terminology the following account will serve as an introduction to the study of those plant organs the characters of which are used in the keys and descriptions. The information in this account and that given in the Glossary should give sufficient preparation for the successful use of this manual.

THE STEM

The stem is the part of the plant that grows upward from the root and bears the other organs. At definite places on the stem, called nodes, the leaves arise. The parts of the stem between the nodes are called internodes. In the axils of the leaves arise the branches from which flowers and fruits are produced. In trees the stem is a single woody trunk and does not branch for some distance above the ground. In shrubs the woody trunks branch at or near the ground and the stems and branches grow to form bush-like plants. Many shrubs grow to heights of twenty feet or more and their stems become six inches or more in diameter. These then are arborescent shrubs.

The characteristics of stems used in the classification of plants are mostly internal. In most stems the woody part occurs in annual concentric layers, known as annual rings, surrounding a small central pith and protected by a separable bark on the outside. Such stems are characteristic of Gymnosperms (pines) and

*Reprinted from *An Illustrated Manual of Pacific Coast Trees,* by permission of the University of California Press, Berkeley, California.

Dicotyledonous-Angiosperms (oaks) and are called exogenous (outside-growing). They normally produce leaves with netted venation. In the stems of palms and palm-like plants there is no separable bark and the woody part is much reduced and occurs in threads or bundles which are scattered throughout the abundant pithy material. This type of stem is called endogenous (inside-growing) and is characteristic of Monocotyledonous-Angiosperms. They produce leaves with parallel veins. Terms applying to the external characteristics of stems are included in the Glossary and can be learned when met in the keys and descriptions.

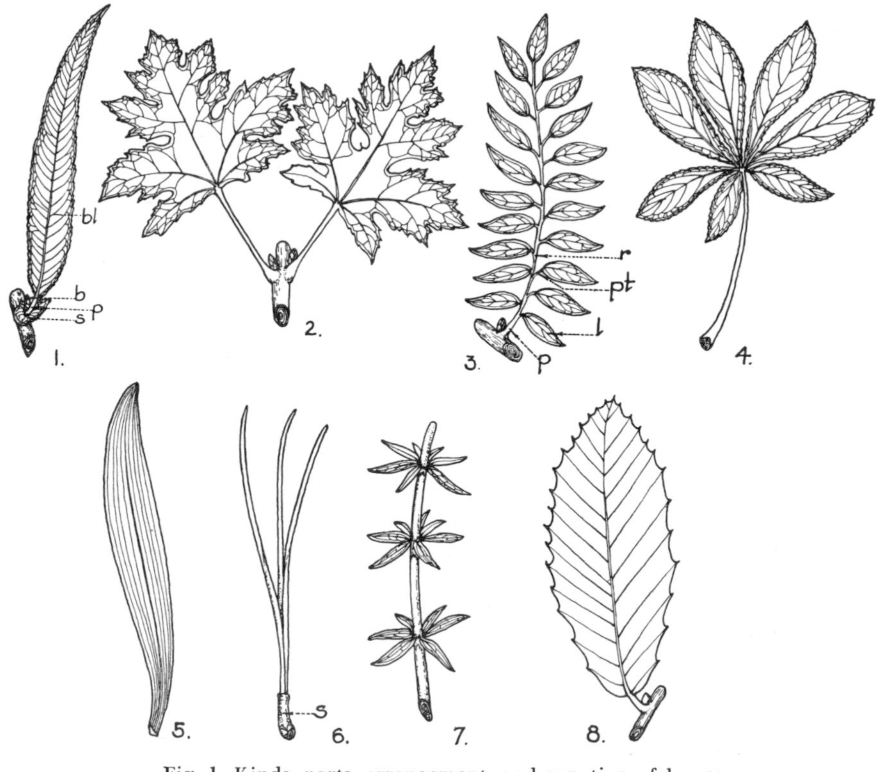

Fig. 1. Kinds, parts, arrangement, and venation of leaves.
1. Simple, alternate leaf with netted venation; b, bud; bl, blade; p, petiole; s, stipule. 2. Simple, opposite, palmately veined and lobed leaves. 3. Pinnately compound, alternate leaf. 4. Palmately compound leaf. 5. Simple leaf with parallel veins. 6. Simple leaves in a fascicle; s, sheath. 7. Whorled arrangement of simple leaves. 8. Simple, alternate leaf with straight veins. *(From Pacific Coast Trees, Univ. of Calif. Press.)*

THE LEAF

Leaves are usually green expansions growing out laterally from the stems or branches. In the axil formed by the leaf and branch occurs a bud which produces a new branch. In determining the leaf it is very important that the bud be located because confusion often occurs in distinguishing the leaflets of a compound leaf from simple leaves. Buds are not found at the bases of leaflets. The leaves of Gymnosperms and some Angiosperms are very small, often scale-like or needle-like, and the axillary buds are usually apparently absent. Therefore their structural nature is learned only by practice.

The simple leaf.—The most common kind of leaf is a simple leaf. It usually consists of an expanded part, the blade, and a slender stalk, the petiole, which attaches the blade to the branch. If the blade is directly attached to the branch then the leaf is sessile. Outgrowths, called stipules, often occur at the base of the

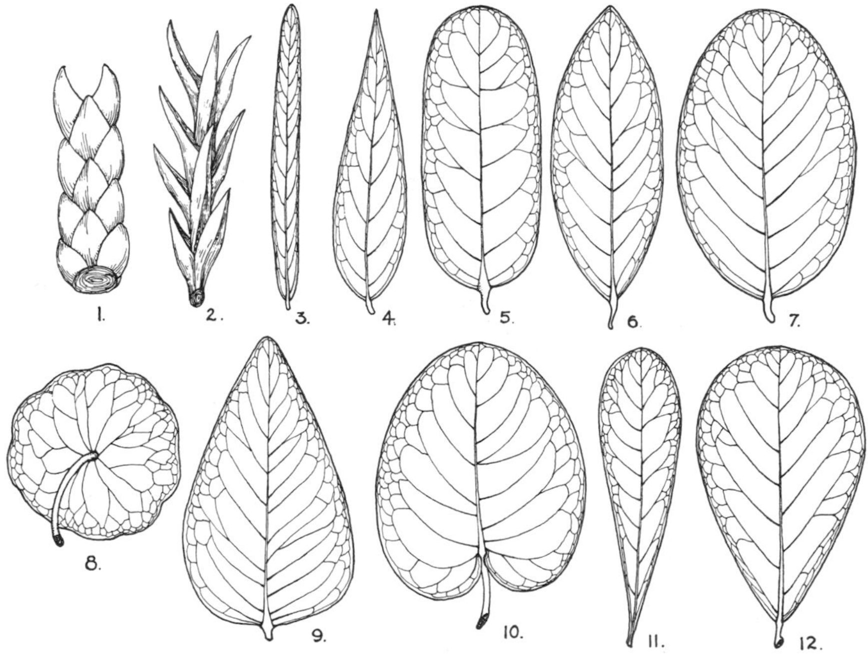

Fig. 2. Shapes of leaves.
1. Scale-like. 2. Awl-shaped. 3. Linear. 4. Lanceolate. 5. Oblong. 6. Elliptic. 7. Oval. 8. Orbicular. 9. Ovate. 10. Cordate. 11. Oblanceolate. 12. Obovate. *(From Pacific Coast Trees, Univ. of Calif. Press.)*

petiole. They may be very small and scale-like, thorn-like, or leaf-like. The midrib extends from the summit of the petiole to the apex of the blade. Along the side of or extending from the midrib are veins which divide into veinlets.

The compound leaf.—Whenever a leaf is divided to the midrib into separate parts it is a compound leaf. The separate parts are called leaflets. These may be sessile or petiolulate. If the leaflets are arranged laterally along the common stalk or rachis the leaf is pinnately compound. In bipinnately compound leaves the pinnae are divided to their main veins. When there is a single leaflet at the end of the rachis the leaf is odd-pinnate. If two leaflets terminate the rachis the leaf is even-pinnate. If all the leaflets arise from the apex of the petiole, like the fingers from the palm of the hand, the leaf is palmately compound.

Arrangement of leaves.—When only one leaf occurs at a node the arrangement is alternate, and if two leaves oppose each other at a node the arrangement is opposite. If three or more leaves are arranged around the stem at a node, like the spokes of a wheel, the arrangement is called whorled or cyclic. Leaves are fascicled when two or more leaves are bundled together and surrounded at the base by a sheath, as in the pines. If no sheath is present the bundled arrangement is called clustered, as are some of the leaves of the Deodar.

Venation.—The arrangement of the veins in the leaf-blades is called venation. Leaves are parallel-veined when several main veins run parallel to one another.

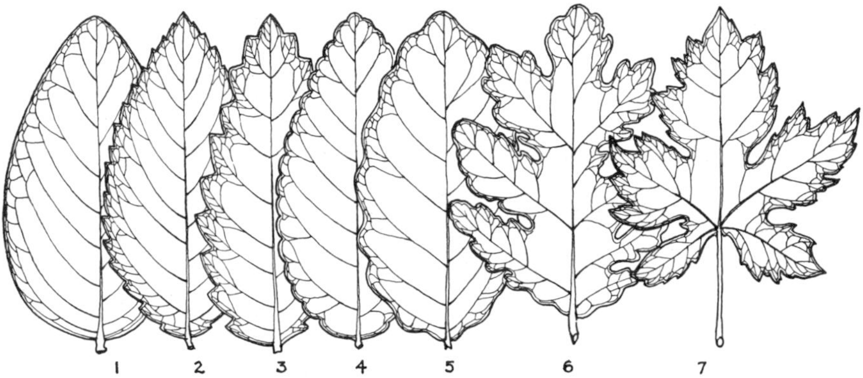

Fig. 3. Margins of leaves.
1. Entire. 2. Serrate. 3. Dentate. 4. Crenate. 5. Sinuate. 6. Pinnately lobed. 7. Palmately lobed. *(From Pacific Coast Trees, Univ. of Calif. Press.)*

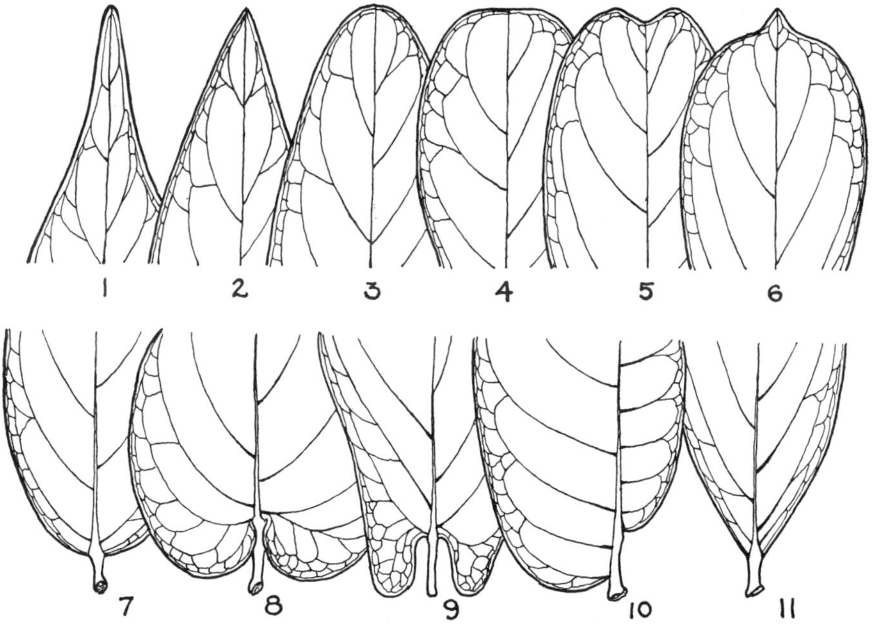

Fig. 4. Tips and bases of leaves.
1. Acuminate. 2. Acute. 3. Obtuse. 4. Truncate. 5. Emarginate. 6. Mucronate. 7. Rounded. 8. Cordate or heart-shaped. 9. Auriculate. 10. Oblique or unequal. 11. Cuneate or wedge-shaped. *(From Pacific Coast Trees, Univ. of Calif. Press.)*

When three or more main veins arise from the summit of the petiole and radiate from one another the venation is palmate. If the secondary veins all branch from the midrib the venation is pinnate and if the secondary veins are very distinct and run straight and parallel to one another the leaves are straight-veined.

Shapes, margins, tips, bases, surface, texture, and duration of leaves.—The terms used in describing these leaf characters may be understood by referring to the diagrams which follow and to the Glossary.

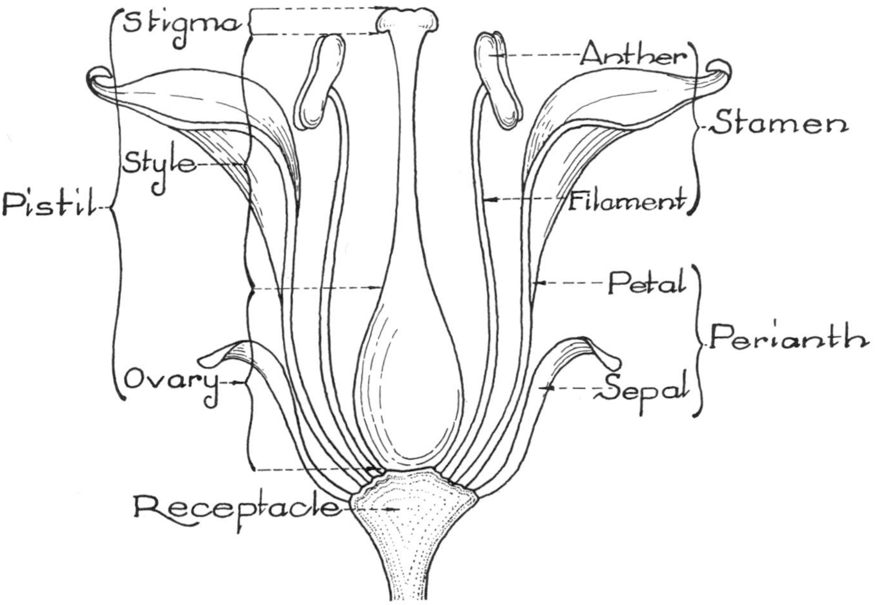

Fig. 5. Structure of a complete flower. *(From Pacific Coast Trees, Univ. of Calif. Press.)*

THE FLOWER

The flower is that organ of a plant which has to do with the production of seeds. A complete flower is composed of four whorls or cycles of parts borne upon the receptacle. The outermost whorl is the calyx. The individual parts of the calyx are called sepals. The next whorl is the corolla, which is composed of petals. The stamens comprise the next whorl and the pistils form the innermost whorl.

The calyx and corolla taken collectively compose the perianth or floral envelopes. If only one set of floral envelopes is present it is called the calyx and the flower is then apetalous. If the petals are joined to one another so as to form a single structure the flower is sympetalous, and if the petals are distinct then the flower is choripetalous or polypetalous.

The stamens and pistils comprise the essential organs. The stamen is made up of a stalk or filament supporting a terminal sac or anther which usually bears a yellow powdery substance called pollen. The pollen contains the male elements, sperms, which unite with the female elements, eggs, within the ovules located in the ovary of the pistil. The transference of the pollen from the anther to the stigma of the pistil is called pollination. This may be accomplished by insects, wind, water, gravity, and other agencies. If the stamens are united into one group they are called monadelphous, and if into two groups, diadelphous. The ovary is the swollen basal part of the pistil which bears one or more ovules. It continues into the style, which terminates in the stigma, the part that receives the pollen. The flower is called bisexual (perfect) if both stamens and pistils are present, staminate if only the stamens are present, and pistillate if only the pistils occur. When the staminate and pistillate flowers are borne upon separate plants, as in the willows,

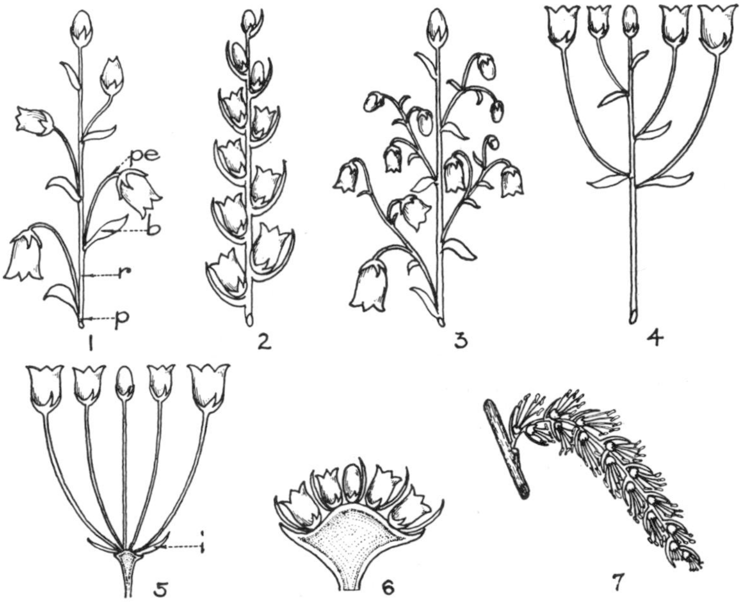

Fig. 6. Kinds of Inflorescence.
1. Raceme; p, peduncle; pe, pedicel; b, bract; r, rachis. 2. Spike. 3. Panicle. 4. Corymb. 5. Umbel; i, involucre. 6. Head. 7. Catkin. *(From Pacific Coast Trees, Univ. of Calif. Press.)*

the plants are dioecious, and when they are borne upon the same plants, as in the alders, the plants are monoecious. Pistils may be simple or compound according to the number of carpels involved. The carpel is generally considered a modified leaf bearing ovules. The simple pistil consists of a single carpel; a compound pistil, of two or more united carpels. If the ovary is not adherent to the calyx it is superior; if it is adherent, it is inferior.

THE ARRANGEMENT OF THE FLOWERS (INFLORESCENCE)

The name inflorescence is given to the arrangement of flowers upon the stems and branches. Flowers are terminal when borne at the ends of the stems or branches and axillary when they arise in the axils of leaves. They may be borne singly or in clusters of varying shapes and sizes. The stalk of a solitary flower or the main stalk of a cluster is called the peduncle. The individual stalklets supporting the flowers of a cluster are called pedicels. Whenever the flowers are without stalklets they are said to be sessile. The simplest type of inflorescence is the raceme, in which the central and indefinite axis bears lateral flowers upon pedicels of nearly equal lengths. If the flowers are sessile upon the elongated axis they form a spike. When the central axis branches and the divisions bear two or more flowers each, the inflorescence is a panicle. If the raceme or panicle is very compact and consists of unisexual flowers, it is called a catkin or ament. When the lower divisions of a panicle or the pedicels of a raceme become elongated, a corymb is formed. When the pedicels or divisions of a raceme or panicle arise from a common base, a simple or compound umbel is formed. Frequently the central axis becomes much shortened and bears sessile flowers in a close cluster known as a head. Small modified leaves, called bracts, often occur in a flower-cluster at the base of the pedicels and below the sepals. If several bracts encircle a flower-cluster as in an umbel or a head they constitute an involucre. The involucral bracts may be scale-like or larger, leaf-like, and often colored. The diagrams (fig. 6) show the common types of inflorescence.

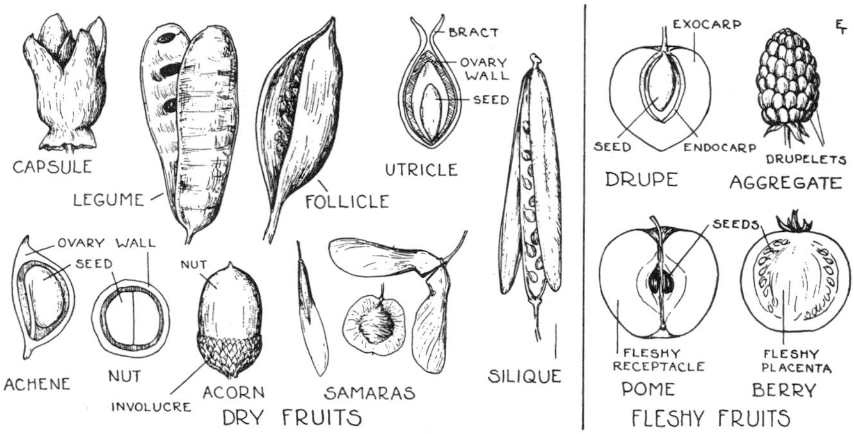

Fig. 7. Kinds of fruits.

THE FRUIT AND SEED

The fruit is the matured ovary and any adjacent part that may develop with it. The seed is a matured ovule. The union (fertilization) of the egg within the ovule with the sperm from the germinated pollen grain forms the embryonic plant, stimulates growth of the surrounding tissues, and causes the subsequent ripening of the ovule and ovary.

The kinds of fruits take their names from their texture, origin, and manner of escape of the seeds. The following outline gives the main kinds of fruits used in the keys and descriptions.

A. Kinds of fruits according to texture.

1. Dry.

   a. *Pod.* A term loosely used for any dry dehiscent fruit. More specifically, a fruit with one carpel splitting along two sutures, as the legume.

   b. *Capsule.* From a compound ovary, splitting along two or more lines.

   c. *Legume.* From a simple ovary, splitting along two lines.

   d. *Follicle.* From a simple ovary, splitting along one line.

   e. *Achene.* A one-seeded fruit from a simple or compound ovary which does not open.

   f. *Utricle.* An achene with a loose involucral covering.

g. *Nut.* A one-seeded hard fruit from a compound ovary which does not open.

h. *Acorn.* A nut partly surrounded by a fibrous or woody cup (involucre).

i. *Samara.* A winged nut, achene, or any other dry indehiscent usually one-seeded fruit, as that of the ash, maple, or hop-tree.

j. *Cone.* A collection of carpels on a common receptacle, as in pines and firs, also less appropriately applied to the fruits of alders, birches, and similar plants.

2. Fleshy.

a. *Drupe.* Usually from a simple ovary, with a fleshy outside (exocarp) surrounding a hard stone or pit (endocarp) which encloses the usually single seed.

b. *Pome.* From an inferior compound ovary with papery or cartilaginous carpels surrounded by a fleshy receptacle and calyx.

c. *Berry.* From a compound, superior or inferior ovary, fleshy throughout, with the seeds embedded in the fleshy pulp. The orange, lemon, and other citrus fruits are berries with leathery rinds, called hesperidia (singular, hesperidium).

B. Kinds of fruits according to origin.

1. *Simple.* From a single, simple or compound ovary.

2. *Aggregate.* From a collection of ovaries of a single flower ripening into a single mass, as in the blackberry.

3. *Multiple.* From the ovaries of several flowers massed together on or in a common receptacle, as in the mulberry and fig.

4. *Accessory.* From ovaries with adjacent parts such as the calyx and the receptacle developing with them.

C. Kinds of fruit according to manner of escape of seeds.

1. *Dehiscent.* Splitting open.

2. *Indehiscent.* Not splitting open.

How to Use the Keys

The shrubs of California may be identified by the use of the Key to the Genera or the Key to the Families. In both keys the first choice must be made between I and II. Having made that choice, continue to choose between contrasted subheads, indicated by indentation of lines upon the page or by letters, numbers, or other symbols, until one leads to the name of a genus or of a family. If a genus contains two or more species or a family two or more genera, a key follows which will identify the species or genus.

Abbreviations Other Than Citations of Literature and Authors' Names

acc. According to.
Bibl. Bibliography.
Herb. Herbarium.
Ms. Manuscript.
n. comb. New combination.
n. var. New variety.
vars. Varieties.
V. T. M. Vegetative Type Map Herbarium of the California Forest and Range Experiment Station.
♀ Female; pistillate.
♂ Male; staminate.

KEY TO THE GENERA

I. Semi-parasitic subshrubs growing on trees or shrubs. . . . PHORADENDRON, p. 89

II. Independent plants (autophytes).

Plants leafless or apparently so, often succulent or cactus-like. . . . . . . A, p. 15

Leafy shrubs, subshrubs, woody vines, or coarse palm-like perennials.

1. Plants with long linear or lanceolate parallel-veined leaves 8 inches to 3½ feet long arising from a basal rosette or from the summit of the main stem or its divisions.
   - Flowers 1¼ to 3½ inches long; fruit not winged. . . . . YUCCA, p. 49
   - Flowers 1/16- to ¼-inch long; fruit winged. . . . . NOLINA, p. 54
2. Woody vines or climbing shrubs. . . . . A, p. 16
3. Erect shrubs and subshrubs including prostrate diffuse woody plants and low acaulescent plants with woody bases.
   - Gymnospermous plants (seeds borne upon open scales).
     - Leaves needle-like, in fascicles of 5; fruit a woody cone. PINUS ALBICAULIS, p. 39
     - Leaves scale-like or awl-shaped.
       - Fruit a berry-like cone; staminate and ovulate flowers usually on separate plants. . . . . JUNIPERUS, p. 42
       - Fruit a small woody cone; staminate and ovulate flowers on the same plant . . . . CUPRESSUS, p. 41
   - Angiospermous plants (seeds borne within closed ovaries).
     - Leaves compound or apparently so.
       - Leaves opposite. . . . . A, p. 17
       - Leaves alternate.
         - Plants with thorny, spiny, or prickly stems, branches, or leaf-rachises . . . . B, p. 17
         - Plants without spiny or thorny stems and branches. . . . . . . A, p. 18
     - Leaves simple.
       - Leaves opposite or whorled and often apparently fascicled. A, p. 20
       - Leaves alternate or spirally arranged. . . . . A, p. 24

A. PLANTS LEAFLESS OR APPARENTLY SO

Plants succulent or with several thick cane-like stems from the base.
- Stems and branches spiny or thorny; plants somewhat cactus-like, with 4 to 40 mostly simple stems 6 to 20 feet high. . . . . FOUQUIERIA, p. 361
- Stems and branches not spiny; branchlets jointed, fleshy, green. ALLENROLFEA, p. 103

Plants neither succulent nor cactus-like.
- Plants with spiny or thorny branches or leaf-rachises.
  - Flowers distinctly irregular.
    - Flowers yellow. . . . . ULEX, p. 218
    - Flowers purplish or reddish.
      - Calyx glandular-dotted; stamens monadelphous. . . . . DALEA, p. 218
      - Calyx not glandular-dotted; stamens diadelphous. . . . . ALHAGI, p. 225

Flowers regular or nearly so.
Flowers white or greenish white; fruit not a legume.
Flowers dioecious; petals 7 or 8; fruit drupe-like, in clusters on the branched thorns............................HOLACANTHA, p. 261
Flowers bisexual; petals 5, 4, or none; fruit a drupe; stamens opposite the petals..................................CONDALIA, p. 321
Flowers yellow; fruit a legume.
Branchlets either ending in a spine or thorn or armed with one or with a pair of axillary thorns; small trees or large shrubs.
CERCIDIUM, p. 225
Branchlets not spiny or thorny; leaf-rachis terminated by a short spine; small or medium-sized shrubs......................CASSIA, p. 228
Plants not thorny.
Flowers in composite heads, i.e. on the enlarged summit of the common peduncle (receptacle), surrounded by an involucre of few to numerous bracts.
Branchlets 4-angled and striate............BACCHARIS SAROTHROIDES, p. 580
Branchlets not 4-angled.
Pappus none; "fruit" a prickly bur; receptacle with slender bracts; ray-flowers none.................................OXYTENIA, p. 604
Pappus present; achenes not enclosed in a prickly bur.
Receptacle with scarious bracts; ray-flowers present, yellow.
BEBBIA, p. 595
Receptacle naked; ray-flowers none..........LEPIDOSPARTUM, p. 617
Flowers not in composite heads.
Stems jointed; leaves present as opposite or whorled scales at the joints.
EPHEDRA, p. 44
Stems not jointed.
Flowers unisexual, either monoecious or dioecious, apetalous.
ATRIPLEX, p. 109
Flowers bisexual.
Flowers very irregular, yellowish; fruit a pod.
Branchlets angled; erect shrubs 3 to 6 feet high....CYTISUS, p. 233
Branchlets terete; usually subshrubs less than 3 feet high, decumbent to half erect.................................LOTUS, p. 240
Flowers neither very irregular nor yellowish.
Branchlets opposite, grayish; corolla tubular, 1 to 1½ inches long, dull red.............................BELOPERONE, p. 519
Branchlets alternate.
Branchlets covered with minute scale-like leaves; flowers small, numerous, lavender or pink, in long spike-like clusters.
TAMARIX, p. 357
Branchlets leafless, greenish yellow; flowers ¼- to ⅓-inch long, dark purple........................THAMNOSMA, p. 259

A. WOODY VINES OR CLIMBING SHRUBS

Leaves compound.
Leaves opposite; plants climbing by aid of twisting petioles....CLEMATIS, p. 115
Leaves alternate.

Plants usually prickly, without aerial roots . . . . RUBUS, p. 175
Plants not prickly, climbing by aerial roots . . . . RHUS, p. 263
Leaves simple.
Leaves opposite or whorled.
Leaves 4 to 6 at a node; stems usually square and mostly herbaceous, woody at base . . . . GALIUM, p. 523
Leaves 2 at a node, often with smaller ones in their axils.
Leaves palmately lobed; fruit a 2-winged samara . . . . ACER, p. 276
Leaves not lobed.
Leaves 3-veined from the base; flowers with petals distinct. WHIPPLEA, p. 167
Leaves 1-veined from the base; flowers with petals united. LONICERA, p. 536
Leaves alternate or spirally arranged.
Leaves palmately lobed or toothed, opposite the tendrils or flower-clusters. VITIS, p. 333
Leaves neither lobed nor toothed.
Leaves ovate-cordate, tomentose on both surfaces; plants climbing by twining stems . . . . ARISTOLOCHIA, p. 92
Leaves broadly ovate, glabrous on both surfaces; plants climbing by coiled tendril-like appendages of the petioles . . . . SMILAX, p. 48

A. LEAVES OPPOSITE

Leaves with 2 leaflets appearing as a single 2-lobed leaf; herbage resinous and heavy-scented . . . . LARREA, p. 257
Leaves with 3 or more leaflets (or with 2 leaflets or simple in *Fraxinus*).
Leaflets 3 (rarely 2 or 1).
Leaflets about ¼- to ½-inch long, entire, sessile . . . . FAGONIA, p. 258
Leaflets ½-inch or more long.
Branchlets 4-angled; fruit a single-winged samara . . . . FRAXINUS, p. 435
Branchlets terete; fruit a 3-celled bladder-like capsule . . . STAPHYLEA, p. 275
Leaflets 5 to 9.
Leaves palmately compound . . . . AESCULUS, p. 277
Leaves pinnately compound.
Branchlets 4-angled; leaflets not unequal at base; fruit a single-winged samara . . . . FRAXINUS, p. 435
Branchlets terete; leaflets commonly unequal at base; fruit a berry-like drupe . . . . SAMBUCUS, p. 525

B. PLANTS WITH THORNY, SPINY, OR PRICKLY STEMS, BRANCHES, OR LEAF-RACHISES

Leaves 2 or 3 times pinnate.
1. Flowers very small, in small globular heads . . . . ACACIA FARNESIANA, p. 229
2. Flowers in cylindrical spikes.
Leaves with 2 or 4 pinnae; spines not hooked, borne only at the base of the petioles . . . . PROSOPIS, p. 231
Leaves usually with 4 pinnae (or 2 or 6); spines hooked, borne along the branchlets . . . . ACACIA, p. 229
3. Flowers in racemes . . . . CERCIDIUM, p. 225

Leaves once-pinnate.
Leaves palmately 1- or 3-foliolate, nearly sessile; branchlets spinose. PICKERINGIA, p. 227
Leaves pinnately compound; leaflets 3 to 27.
Leaflets 11 to 27; branchlets and leaf-rachises with prickle-like glands. AMORPHA, p. 239
Leaflets 3 to 9, rarely 11.
Branchlets terminating in sharp stiff spines.
Flowers in spikes or racemes; fruit a pod................. DALEA, p. 218
Flowers in heads; "fruit" a prickly bur............... FRANSERIA, p. 600
Branchlets not terminating in stiff spines.
Branchlets not prickly or thorny over the surface; leaf-rachises terminated by a spine............................... CASSIA ARMATA, p. 229
Branchlets prickly or thorny over the surface; leaf-rachises not terminated by a spine.
Leaves 3-foliolate (sometimes simple or with 5 or 7 leaflets); fruit an aggregation of drupelets......................... RUBUS, p. 175
Leaves usually with 5 or 7 leaflets (rarely 3, 9, or 11); fruit, i.e. achenes, enclosed in an urn-shaped receptocalyx-tube or "hip"; base of petiole winged on either side..................... ROSA, p. 179

A. PLANTS WITHOUT SPINY OR THORNY STEMS AND BRANCHES

1. LEAVES 2 OR 3 TIMES PINNATE OR PINNATELY DISSECTED.

Leaves pinnately dissected into linear or filiform divisions; flowers in composite heads.
Main stem thick and fleshy; flowers yellow.................. COREOPSIS, p. 591
Main stems not fleshy but becoming woody at base; flowers white or purple-tinged .... MALACOTHRIX, p. 551
Leaves distinctly twice- or thrice-pinnately compound.
Leaves thrice-pinnate, heavy-scented.................... CHAMAEBATIA, p. 173
Leaves twice-pinnate.
Leaves with 2 to 8 pinnae.
Flowers purplish red, in heads; stamens numerous; pinnae 2, 4, 6, or 8, each with 10 to 18 leaflets...................... CALLIANDRA, p. 243
Flowers yellow, in racemes; stamens 10; pinnae 2 or 3.
Pinnae 2, each with 4 or 6 leaflets.................. CERCIDIUM, p. 225
Pinnae 3, each with more than 6 leaflets; stems numerous and rush-like. HOFFMANSEGGIA, p. 244
Leaves with 20 to 40 pinnae, very aromatic; leaflets numerous, very minute. CHAMAEBATIARIA, p. 172

2. LEAVES ONCE-COMPOUND OR DEEPLY PINNATIFID.

a. *Leaves pinnatifid.*

(1). FLOWERS IN COMPOSITE HEADS.

(a). *Fruit a bur; ray-flowers none.*

Leaves 1½ to 3 inches long, 3- to 5-parted into filiform divisions.. OXYTENIA, p. 604
Leaves usually less than 1 inch long, once- to thrice-pinnately parted into few short obtuse lobes....................... .... FRANSERIA, p. 600

(b). *Fruit not a bur.*

Receptacle with chaffy bracts.............................. HYMENOCLEA, p. 603
Receptacle naked.
Plants with milky juice; heads with ray-flowers only...... MALACOTHRIX, p. 551
Plants without milky juice; heads with ray- and disk-flowers or of disk-flowers only.
Herbage with odor of sage............................. ARTEMISIA, p. 604
Herbage without odor of sage.
Involucral bracts not well imbricated.
Pappus of soft capillary bristles; achenes terete.......... SENECIO, p. 615
Pappus of hyaline paleae; achenes usually 4- or 5-angled.
ERIOPHYLLUM, p. 597
Involucral bracts well imbricated; pappus of capillary scabrous bristles.
HAPLOPAPPUS, p. 558

(2). FLOWERS NOT IN COMPOSITE HEADS.

Flowers yellow; stamens 6.................................. STANLEYA, p. 134
Flowers white; stamens very numerous....................... ROMNEYA, p. 129

b. *Leaves distinctly once-compound; flowers not in composite heads.*

(1). LEAFLETS WITH PRICKLY OR SPINOSE MARGINS............. BERBERIS, p. 119

(2). LEAFLETS NOT PRICKLY OR SPINOSE.

(a). *Leaves palmately compound.*

Leaflets 5 to 17.. LUPINUS, p. 235
Leaflets usually 3.
Petals 4; fruit-pods inflated.............................. ISOMERIS, p. 132
Petals 5; fruit-pods not inflated.......................... CYTISUS, p. 233

(b). *Leaves pinnately compound.*

†. LEAFLETS 2 TO 7, OR RARELY 9.

Leaflets toothed; flowers not yellow.
Leaflets usually 3 (rarely reduced to 1 and irregularly lobed); base of petiole not laterally winged.
Leaflets punctate, regularly crenate........................ PTELEA, p. 259
Leaflets not punctate, irregularly lobed or toothed............. RHUS, p. 263
Leaflets usually 5 to 9; base of petiole laterally winged............ ROSA, p. 179
Leaflets entire.
Flowers yellowish or orange-colored.
Branchlets densely leafy, silky-hairy when young; leaflets white-silky beneath; flowers regular, ½-inch to 1 inch broad............. POTENTILLA, p. 185
Branchlets sparsely leafy or apparently leafless; fruit a legume or pod.
Flowers regular or nearly so.
Leaves even-pinnate; petals 5.................... CASSIA COVESII, p. 228
Leaves irregularly pinnatifid; petals 4................ STANLEYA, p. 134
Flowers irregular; petals 5; leaflets usually 3 to 5........... LOTUS, p. 240
Flowers blue, pinkish or purplish.......................... DALEA, p. 218

††. LEAFLETS 9 TO 35.

Leaflets entire.
Leaflets about ¼-inch or less long.
Flowers regular; stamens distinct........................ BURSERA, p. 263
Flowers irregular; stamens monadelphous.................... DALEA, p. 218

Leaflets ½-inch to 1½ inches long; fruit a pod. . . . . AMORPHA, p. 239
Leaflets serrate.
Foliage heavy-scented; flowers monoecious; fruit a nut with a dry husk.
JUGLANS, p. 85
Foliage not heavy-scented; flowers bisexual; fruit a small berry-like pome.
SORBUS, p. 186

A. LEAVES OPPOSITE OR WHORLED AND OFTEN APPARENTLY FASCICLED

1. PLANTS WITH THORNY OR SPINESCENT BRANCHLETS.

Leaves linear to narrowly oblanceolate, less than ⅝-inch long, apparently fascicled and sessile; flowers without petals and with numerous stamens; fruit an achene . . . . COLEOGYNE, p. 187
Leaves broader.
Leaves ¼-inch or less long, petioled; flowers with 5 hooded petals; fruit a 3-celled capsule . . . . ADOLPHIA, p. 321
Leaves ¼-inch to 2 inches long.
Flowers bisexual, irregular; fruit of 4 nutlets enclosed in an inflated bladder-like calyx . . . . SALAZARIA, p. 465
Flowers dioecious; fruit not enclosed in a bladder-like calyx.
Leaves silvery-scurfy beneath, entire . . . . SHEPHERDIA, p. 365
Leaves not silvery-scurfy beneath, serrulate above the base or entire.
FORESTIERA, p. 439

2. PLANTS WITHOUT THORNY OR SPINESCENT BRANCHLETS.

Leaves with 3 to 7 linear palmate divisions or lobes, usually much fascicled in the axils.
Leaves prickly pointed . . . . LEPTODACTYLON, p. 447
Leaves not prickly pointed . . . . LINANTHUS, p. 445
Leaves without linear divisions.
Leaves 3 or more at a node.
Leaves 4 to 6 at a node.
Plants vine-like, with square stems, woody at base . . . . GALIUM, p. 523
Plants not vine-like, without square stems . . . . FRANKENIA, p. 357
Leaves usually 3 at a node.
Leaves ¾-inch to 2 inches long; flowers irregular, in long racemes.
PENSTEMON TERNATUS, p. 505
Leaves 2 to 5 inches long; flowers regular, in long-peduncled heads.
CEPHALANTHUS, p. 521
Leaves 2 at a node.
Leaves lobed.
Leaves very glutinous and rank-smelling, appearing simple and divergently 2-lobed, less than ½-inch long . . . . LARREA, p. 257
Leaves not glutinous or rank-smelling.
Leaves palmately lobed . . . . ACER, p. 276
Leaves pinnately lobed or more often entire . . . . . SYMPHORICARPOS, p. 531
Leaves not lobed.
**Leaves variously toothed.* (See p. 22 for **.)
Leaves spine-tipped or with spinose teeth.

Herbage strongly aromatic; fruit of 4 nutlets . . . . SALVIA, p. 469
Herbage not aromatic; fruit a 3-celled capsule . . . . CEANOTHUS, p. 278
Leaves finely or coarsely toothed but not spinose.
Herbage aromatic, usually with odor of mint or sage; fruit of 4 or 2 nutlets.
1. Flowers solitary or 2 to 4 in axils of the leaves.
Leaves 3/8- to 3/4-inch long; flowers creamy-white, usually 2 to 4 in the leaf-axils . . . . SATUREIA, p. 467
Leaves 2 to 4 inches long; flowers white or pink- or purple-tinted, solitary in the axils of the reduced upper leaves, forming a leafy raceme. SPHACELE, p. 468
2. Flowers in heads; subshrubs . . . . MONARDELLA, p. 464
3. Flowers in axillary clusters, often forming whorls which form terminal racemes or spikes.
Nutlets 4; ovary lobed.
Fertile stamens 2; calyx 2-lipped . . . . SALVIA, p. 469
Fertile stamens 4; calyx-teeth subequal . . . . HYPTIS, p. 467
Nutlets 2; ovary not lobed . . . . LIPPIA, p. 461
Herbage without odor of mint or sage.
Flowers in composite heads, i.e. as in the Aster Family.
Petioles more than 2 times the length of the blades; the blades with a few small teeth . . . . HOFMEISTERIA, p. 610
Petioles less than 2 times the length of the blades; the blades crenate-serrate. BRICKELLIA, p. 611
Flowers not in composite heads, may be in head-like clusters but without involucres as in the Aster Family.
Leaves 3- or 5-veined from the base.
Plants trailing, scarcely woody . . . . WHIPPLEA, p. 167
Plants not trailing, distinctly woody.
Flowers about 1/4-inch broad; corolla 5-lobed; fruit a drupe. VIBURNUM, p. 529
Flowers 1/2-inch or more broad; corolla of 4 separate petals; fruit a capsule . . . . PHILADELPHUS, p. 136
Leaves 1-veined from the base, or rarely with the sub-basal lateral pair slightly prominent in *Jamesia*.
Herbage usually glandular or glutinous; leaves often revolute. DIPLACUS, p. 495
Herbage not glandular or glutinous.
Flowers usually dioecious, inconspicuous . . . . FORESTIERA, p. 439
Flowers bisexual, usually conspicuous.
a. FLOWERS IRREGULAR; FRUIT A 2-CELLED CAPSULE . . PENSTEMON, p. 501
b. FLOWERS REGULAR.
Leaves densely tomentose on both surfaces . . . . BUDDLEIA, p. 440
Leaves not tomentose on both surfaces.
1. Flowers red-brown; the ultimate branches square.
Petals 5; leaves 1 1/2 to 3 1/2 inches long . . . . EUONYMUS, p. 273
Petals 4; leaves 1/2-inch to 1 1/4 inches long . . . . PACHYSTIMA, p. 273
2. Flowers pink, in terminal clusters; leaves deciduous, densely hairy beneath. JAMESIA, p. 135
3. Flowers white or blue; leaves evergreen.

Flowers small, less than $\frac{1}{2}$-inch broad, in showy clusters; stamens 5; leaves less than 2 inches long. . . . . CEANOTHUS, p. 278

Flowers large, over $1\frac{1}{2}$ inches broad; stamens numerous; leaves 2 to 5 inches long . . . . CARPENTERIA, p. 139

*****Leaves entire, or some finely denticulate.***

Flowers borne in composite heads, i.e. the heads subtended by an involucre, as in the family Asteraceae; ovary inferior.

Ray-flowers present. . . . . VIGUIERA, p. 593

Ray-flowers absent. . . . . BRICKELLIA, p. 611

Flowers not in composite heads, but sometimes in other types of heads.

1. FLOWERS WITHOUT PETALS (OR WITH 1 OR 2 IN *Forestiera*). *(Apetalous.)*

Leaves linear; fruit a 4-lobed capsule. TETRACOCCUS, p. 252

Leaves broader.

Flowers in catkins 1 to 6 inches long; leaves leathery, $\frac{1}{2}$-inch or more wide. GARRYA, p. 367

Flowers not in catkins.

Leaves white-scurfy, only the lower ones opposite. . . . . ATRIPLEX, p. 109

Leaves not scurfy.

a. Leaves round-ovate; fruit a single-winged samara. . . . . FRAXINUS, p. 435

b. Leaves spatulate-oblong or elliptic, some finely serrulate; fruit a drupe. FORESTIERA, p. 439

c. Leaves elliptic to oblong-ovate, thick, all entire; fruit an ovoid leathery capsule with a single large seed. . . . . SIMMONDSIA, p. 262

2. FLOWERS WITH PETALS.

a. *Petals not united. (Choripetalous.)*

Leaves 3-veined from the base.

Petals 5; low trailing plants, scarcely woody. . . . . WHIPPLEA, p. 167

Petals 4; distinctly woody shrubs. . . . . PHILADELPHUS, p. 136

Leaves 1-veined from the base.

a. Flowers scarlet, 1 inch or more long; stamens 8. . . . . ZAUSCHNERIA, p. 366

b. Flowers yellow; stems numerous, 1 foot or less high, wiry, from a woody base. HYPERICUM, p. 351

c. Flowers white, blue, reddish, or purplish.

Herbage aromatic when crushed.

Leaves less than $\frac{1}{4}$-inch wide; flowers white. . . . . CNEORIDIUM, p. 259

Leaves 1 inch or more wide; flowers reddish. . . . . CALYCANTHUS, p. 118

Herbage not aromatic.

Leaves almost terete; low seacoast subshrubs. . . . . FRANKENIA, p. 357

Leaves not terete; distinctly woody shrubs.

Flowers large, white, with numerous stamens; leaves oblong, 2 to $4\frac{1}{2}$ inches long, often somewhat revolute. . . . . CARPENTERIA, p. 139

Flowers small, with 5 or fewer stamens.

Petals and stamens 5; leaves evergreen, thick and leathery; fruit a 3-lobed capsule. . . . . CEANOTHUS, p. 278

Petals and stamens 4; leaves deciduous, thin; fruit a drupe. CORNUS, p. 374

b. *Petals united. (Sympetalous.)*

(1). FLOWERS REGULAR.

Leaves scale-like, thickly covering the branches; low heather-like subalpine plants. CASSIOPE, p. 380

Leaves not scale-like; plants not heather-like.

Leaves prickly to the touch, linear or narrowly lanceolate; fruit a 3-celled capsule; low caespitose plants slightly woody at base.

Expanded part of corolla spreading at right angles to the narrow cylindrical tube .... PHLOX, p. 441

Expanded part of corolla spreading upward and outward from the funnel-shaped tube .... LEPTODACTYLON, p. 447

Leaves not prickly to the touch.

Leaves with revolute margins.

Leaves ½-inch to 1 inch long; plants 2 feet or less high.

Herbage glabrous................................ KALMIA, p. 380

Herbage tomentose .... BUDDLEIA, p. 440

Leaves 1 to 3 inches long; plants 2 to 3½ feet high; herbage usually densely woolly at least on the young branches and inflorescences. TRICHOSTEMA, p. 465

Leaves without revolute margins.

Herbage aromatic; fruit of 4 nutlets; flowers in heads.. MONARDELLA, p. 464

Herbage not aromatic; fruit a berry or capsule.

Stamens 5.

Ovary inferior; fruit a berry.

Corolla swollen on one side at base; berry red, yellow, or black. LONICERA, p. 536

Corolla not swollen on one side at base; berry white. SYMPHORICARPOS, p. 531

Ovary superior; fruit a capsule.................. LINANTHUS, p. 445

Stamens 2 or 3.................................... MENODORA, p. 437

(2). FLOWERS IRREGULAR.

Ovary superior; fruit dry, never a berry.

Fruit of 4 nutlets; herbage aromatic.

Fertile stamens 4................................ TRICHOSTEMA, p. 465

Fertile stamens 2.. SALVIA, p. 469

Fruit a capsule; herbage not aromatic.

Herbage usually glutinous; leaves commonly revolute....... DIPLACUS, p. 495

Herbage not glutinous.

Stems soon leafless, rush-like; flowers dull red; stamens 2. BELOPERONE, p. 519

Stems leafy, not rush-like; stamens 4 or 5.

Stamens 4, all anther-bearing, a fifth present as a rudiment.

Leaves linear, 3 to 6 inches long; flowers whitish or pinkish. CHILOPSIS, p. 520

Leaves ovate or oval to oblong, ¾-inch to 2 inches long; flowers scarlet .... ANTIRRHINUM, p. 494

Stamens 5, only 4 with anthers.................... PENSTEMON, p. 501

Ovary inferior; fruit a berry............................ LONICERA, p. 536

A. LEAVES ALTERNATE OR SPIRALLY ARRANGED

1. Plants with spiny or thorny branches or branchlets.

(See p. 25 for 2.)

a. *Leaves lobed or varying from coarsely toothed to minutely serrulate.*

Flowers inconspicuous, monoecious or dioecious.
  Leaves pinnately parted; flowers monoecious; fruit a spiny bur. FRANSERIA, p. 600
  Leaves only slightly lobed or toothed, usually many of them entire; flowers dioecious; fruit a utricle enclosed by 2 appressed bracts... ATRIPLEX, p. 109
Flowers showy, bisexual.
  Leaves palmately 3- to 5-lobed or veined; fruit a berry............ RIBES, p. 140
  Leaves pinnately veined.
    Leaves doubly serrate above the middle, often lobed; fruit a pome. CRATAEGUS, p. 201
    Leaves finely serrate to entire.
      Fruit a 3-celled capsule.............................. CEANOTHUS, p. 278
      Fruit a drupe... PRUNUS, p. 195

b. *Leaves entire.*

Flowers yellow and in composite heads; principal leaves modified into spines with small secondary ones in their axils..................... TETRADYMIA, p. 618
Flowers not borne in composite heads.
  Flowers without petals *(Apetalous.)*
    Flowers monoecious or dioecious.
      Leaves more or less fleshy, linear-oblanceolate, 1/3-inch to 1 1/2 inches long; fruiting bracts present.
        Leaves flattened.................................. GRAYIA, p. 106
        Leaves rounded on lower side..................... SARCOBATUS, p. 105
      Leaves not fleshy.
        Fruit a 3-lobed capsule; leaves obovate, 1/4-inch or less long, usually fascicled in the axils...................... HALLIOPHYTUM, p. 249
        Fruit a utricle surrounded by a pair of foliaceous bracts.. ATRIPLEX, p. 109
    Flowers bisexual; leaves 3/8-inch or less long.
      Leaves strongly revolute......................... CERCOCARPUS, p. 205
      Leaves plane........................... CONDALIA SPATULATA, p. 324
  Flowers with petals.
    Petals united into a funnelform tube.
      Stamens 2; fruit a deeply 2-parted capsule.............. MENODORA, p. 437
      Stamens 5 or 4; fruit a berry.......................... LYCIUM, p. 479
      Stamens 10 to 17; fruit a capsule..................... FOUQUIERIA, p. 361
    Petals not united into a tube.

**Flowers regular.*

Sepals purplish, petal-like; fruit a globose prickly pod.......... KRAMERIA, p. 244
Sepals not purplish; fruit not prickly.
  Stamens 15 or more; fruit a fleshy drupe..................... PRUNUS, p. 195
  Stamens 10 or less.
    Stamens usually 6 to 10, not opposite the petals; leaves 1/4-inch or less long; fruit an ovoid follicle......................... GLOSSOPETALON, p. 271
    Stamens 5 or 4, opposite the petals.

Calyx-lobes petal-like; fruit a 3-celled capsule; leaves ovate to elliptic-ovate . . . . CEANOTHUS, p. 278
Calyx-lobes not petal-like; leaves elliptical or ovate to obovate.
Fruit drupe-like, broad, with 1 stone or nutlet. . . . . CONDALIA, p. 321
Fruit a 3-celled capsule; petals sessile, hooded. . . . . COLUBRINA, p. 320

***Flowers irregular.*

Fruit a globose prickly pod; sepals purplish, petal-like. . . . . KRAMERIA, p. 244
Fruit not prickly.
Petals 3; stamens 8, monadelphous; fruit a capsule. . . . . POLYGALA, p. 247
Petals 5; stamens 10; fruit a legume.
Flowers yellow, crowded at the ends of the branches; stamens monadelphous. ULEX, p. 218
Flowers not yellow.
Calyx and fruit-pods glandular-dotted. . . . . DALEA, p. 218
Calyx and fruit-pods not glandular-dotted.
Flowers solitary; some leaves palmately 3-foliolate; stamens distinct. PICKERINGIA, p. 227
Flowers in axillary racemes; all leaves simple; stamens diadelphous. ALHAGI, p. 225

2. PLANTS WITHOUT SPINY BRANCHES OR BRANCHLETS.

Flowers in composite heads; fruit an achene. . . . . Family ASTERACEAE, p. 545
Flowers not in composite heads.

a. LEAVES LINEAR OR SCALE-LIKE, 2 INCHES OR LESS LONG. (See p. 26 for b.)

(1). *Flowers without petals. (Apetalous.)*

Flowers unisexual.
Flowers dioecious.
Leaves revolute. . . . . EUROTIA, p. 105
Leaves plane.. . . . . ATRIPLEX, p. 109
Flowers monoecious; stamens 2; fruit a 3-lobed capsule. . . . . . . STILLINGIA, p. 254
Flowers bisexual and pistillate.
Leaves usually fleshy; calyx fleshy; stamens 5. . . . . SUAEDA, p. 106
Leaves not fleshy; calyx surrounding the fruit.
Calyx developing 5 horizontal wings in fruit; low perennial herbs, woody only at base. . . . . KOCHIA, p. 108
Calyx not developing wings in fruit; flowers borne in an involucre. ERIOGONUM, p. 93

(2). *Flowers with petals.*

(a). PETALS DISTINCT. *(Choripetalous.)*

Tall shrubs; flowers small, in clusters.
Flowers white.. . . . . ADENOSTOMA, p. 194
Flowers pink.. . . . . TAMARIX, p. 357
Low shrubs or subshrubs, woody at base.
Flowers bisexual.
Stamens 5; herbage scabrous. . . . . PETALONYX LINEARIS, p. 363
Stamens more than 5; herbage not scabrous.
1. Flowers white; fruit a flat pod, about as broad as long, notched at apex. LEPIDIUM, p. 133
2. Flowers yellow. . . . . HELIANTHEMUM, p. 358
3. Flowers red or scarlet; stamens 8. . . . . ZAUSCHNERIA, p. 366

Flowers unisexual; herbage silvery-hairy; leaves ½-inch to 1½ inches long; plants monoecious....................ARGYTHAMNIA, p. 255

(b). PETALS UNITED. *(Sympetalous.)*

Flowers regular.
Stamens 2....................MENODORA, p. 437
Stamens 5 to 10.
Leaves with revolute margins....................PHYLLODOCE, p. 381
Leaves not revolute.
1. Flowers white; fruit of 4 nutlets....................CRYPTANTHA, p. 459
2. Flowers blue; fruit a 3-celled capsule....................HUGELIA, p. 446
3. Flowers scarlet; fruit a 3-celled capsule....................LOESELIA, p. 446
Flowers irregular....................CASTILLEIA, p. 492

b. LEAVES NOT LINEAR OR SCALE-LIKE, OR IF LINEAR THEN OVER 2 INCHES LONG.

(1). *Leaves lobed or variously toothed.* (See p. 29 for (2).)

(a). LEAVES DIVIDED OR DISTINCTLY LOBED.

Leaves palmately lobed or divided.
Leaves divided into 3 to 9 linear sharp-pointed divisions; flowers with petals united....................LEPTODACTYLON, p. 447
Leaves not divided into linear divisions.
Flowers large, all over ½-inch wide.
Flowers yellow or orange; sepals petal-like; petals none..FREMONTIA, p. 352
Flowers pink or rose-color; sepals not petal-like; petals 5.
Petals 1 inch or more long; anthers scattered along the outside of the filament-tube....................LAVATERA, p. 334
Petals less than 1 inch long; anthers borne in a cluster at the summit of the filament-tube.
Carpels differentiated into 2 parts, upper and lower.
SPHAERALCEA, p. 351
Carpels not differentiated into 2 parts....................MALVASTRUM, p. 337
Flowers small, less than ½-inch wide.
Leaves 4 to 10 inches broad, 3- to 11-lobed; plants monoecious.
RICINUS, p. 251
Leaves less than 4 inches broad; plants with bisexual flowers.
Stamens 20 or more; ovary superior....................PHYSOCARPUS, p. 191
Stamens 10 or fewer; ovary inferior....................RIBES, p. 140
Leaves pinnately lobed or divided.
Leaves twice- or thrice-parted into linear lobes; decumbent subalpine plants.
LUETKEA, p. 187
Leaves once-parted or lobed.
Leaf-lobes with revolute margins; fruit an achene.
Pistil one; style not plumose....................PURSHIA, p. 202
Pistils 5 or more (rarely 2 or 3); styles long-plumose.
Calyx-lobes with supplementary foliaceous bracts......FALLUGIA, p. 204
Calyx-lobes without foliaceous bracts....................COWANIA, p. 204
Leaf-lobes without revolute margins.
Lobes short-subulate and spinulose, usually near the base of the leaves.
HUGELIA, p. 446
Lobes larger, not spinulose.

Flowers regular.
Flowers yellow, in long terminal racemes............STANLEYA, p. 134
Flowers white.
1. Flowers about ¼-inch or less broad; stamens 6...LEPIDIUM, p. 133
2. Flowers ¾-inch to 1 inch broad; stamens numerous; fruit a pome. PYRUS, p. 216
3. Flowers 3 to 5 inches broad; stamens numerous; fruit a capsule. ROMNEYA, p. 129
Flowers irregular.................................CASTILLEIA, p. 492

(b). LEAVES NEITHER LOBED NOR DIVIDED BUT DISTINCTLY AND VARIOUSLY TOOTHED.

† *Flowers without petals. (Apetalous.)*

Flowers borne in catkins.
Fruit an acorn; leaves usually coriaceous.....................QUERCUS, p. 79
Fruit not an acorn; leaves deciduous.
Fruit a nut enclosed in a foliaceous involucre; leaves pubescent on both surfaces, cordate at base...............................CORYLUS, p. 70
Fruit a cone of many nutlets; leaves not cordate at base.
Cones woody; cone-scales persistent.......................ALNUS, p. 74
Cones not woody; cone-scales deciduous..................BETULA, p. 71
Flowers not borne in catkins.
Flowers bisexual or polygamous.
Leaves equal at base.
Stamens numerous; fruit a tailed achene............CERCOCARPUS, p. 205
Stamens 4 or 5; fruit berry-like, of 2 or 3 seed-like nutlets..RHAMNUS, p. 324
Leaves unequal at base; fruit a drupe.......................CELTIS, p. 88
Flowers unisexual.
Flowers monoecious.
Plants herbaceous, woody only at base; herbage with stinging hairs. TRAGIA, p. 254
Plants distinctly shrubby; herbage without stinging hairs.
Leaves grayish beneath, prominently veined, ¼- to ⅜-inch (or to 1½ inches) long...............................BERNARDIA, p. 251
Leaves greenish on both surfaces, ½-inch to 1¼ inches long. ACALYPHA, p. 251
Flowers dioecious; leaves white-scurfy, undulate and with coarse teeth. ATRIPLEX, p. 109

††*Flowers with petals.*

*PETALS DISTINCT, OR RARELY UNITED AT BASE. *(Choripetalous.)*

(See p. 28 for **.)

Herbage covered with stinging hairs and barbed pubescence; petals united at base. EUCNIDE, p. 364
Herbage without stinging hairs.
Stamens united into a tube.
Fertile stamens 5; leaves ½-inch or less long.................AYENIA, p. 352
Fertile stamens numerous; leaves ½-inch or more long.
Anthers scattered along the outside of the stamen-tube.....HIBISCUS, p. 335
Anthers borne at the summit of the stamen-tube.
Carpels of 2 parts, the upper dehiscent, the lower indehiscent. SPHAERALCEA, p. 351

Carpels not differentiated into 2 parts.............MALVASTRUM, p. 337
Stamens not united into a tube.
Flowers monoecious; low subshrubs ½-foot or less high..ARGYTHAMNIA, p. 255
Flowers bisexual.
Ovary superior or half inferior in *Amelanchier*.
Stamens 5 or 4.
Stamens opposite the petals.
Sepals petal-like; fruit a 3-celled capsule.........CEANOTHUS, p. 278
Sepals not petal-like; fruit berry-like, of 2 or 3 seed-like nutlets. RHAMNUS, p. 324
Stamens alternate with the petals; sepals not petal-like; fruit a dry berry-like drupe..............................RHUS, p. 263
Stamens 10 or more.
Fruit fleshy.
Fruit a subglobose drupe..........................PRUNUS, p. 195
Fruit a pome; ovary half inferior.............AMELANCHIER, p. 216
Fruit dry.
Fruit an achene.................................PURSHIA, p. 202
Fruit of 1 to 5 follicles.
Flowers white or cream-colored; follicles 1-seeded. HOLODISCUS, p. 211
Flowers pink or purplish; follicles 2- to several-seeded. SPIRAEA, p. 189
Ovary inferior.
Perennial herbs or low shrubs.
Herbage rough-pubescent; stamens 5..............PETALONYX, p. 361
Herbage pubescent or nearly glabrous, but not rough; stamens 8. ZAUSCHNERIA, p. 366
Large woody shrubs or small trees; stamens numerous.
Leaves with prickly teeth along the margins, evergreen. PHOTINIA, p. 213
Leaves without prickly teeth; deciduous.
Leaves mostly elliptic, usually serrate only on upper half or near the apex..............................AMELANCHIER, p. 216
Leaves mostly ovate in outline, toothed except near the base. PYRUS, p. 216

**PETALS UNITED. (*Sympetalous.*)

Herbage covered with bristles; fruit a capsule..................EUCNIDE, p. 364
Herbage not bristly.
Fertile stamens 5.
Flowers ½-inch or more broad, wheel-shaped, with scarcely any tube. SOLANUM, p. 486
Flowers less than ½-inch broad, funnelform or campanulate.
Plants distinctly shrubby; leaves 2 to 6 inches long; capsule 4-valved. ERIODICTYON, p. 451
Plants more or less herbaceous, woody only at base; leaves ¼-inch to 2 inches long.
Leaves ½-inch or less long; flowers brownish...........AYENIA, p. 352

Leaves over ½-inch long; flowers purple. . . . . NAMA, p. 456
Fertile stamens 10 or 8; flowers white or pink.
Ovary superior.
Stamens 8; corolla 4-toothed or lobed. . . . . MENZIESIA, p. 423
Stamens 10; corolla 5-toothed.
Sepals distinct; anthers awnless.
Fruit a capsule; leaves glabrous beneath. . . . . LEUCOTHOE, p. 424
Fruit berry-like, red; leaves white-tomentose beneath.
COMAROSTAPHYLIS, p. 421
Sepals united at base; calyx tubular, becoming fleshy in fruit.
GAULTHERIA, p. 424
Ovary inferior; leaves ovate-elliptic to elliptical. . . . . VACCINIUM, p. 429

(2). *Leaves entire or some very finely serrulate or with 1 or 2 coarse teeth on one or both margins.*

(a). FLOWERS WITHOUT PETALS. *(Apetalous.)*

Some or all of the flowers in catkins or spikes.
Plants dioecious; leaves deciduous.
Fruit a nutlet; leaves fragrant, resinous-dotted. . . . MYRICA HARTWEGII, p. 88
Fruit a 1-celled capsule; leaves not fragrant or resinous-dotted. . . SALIX, p. 55
Plant monoecious or rarely dioecious.
Perennial herbs, woody only at base; fruit a capsule. . . . . STILLINGIA, p. 254
Shrubs or small trees.
Fruit a waxy nutlet. . . . . MYRICA CALIFORNICA, p. 87
Fruit an acorn.
Leaves straight-veined; acorn-cup with slender spreading scales.
LITHOCARPUS, p. 77
Leaves not straight-veined; acorn-cup with closely appressed scales.
QUERCUS, p. 79
Fruit a nut, 2 to 5 enclosed in a prickly involucre. . . . . . CASTANOPSIS, p. 75
None of the flowers in catkins.
Flowers bisexual.
Foliage, when crushed, with an odor of bay rum. . . . . UMBELLULARIA, p. 119
Foliage without odor of bay rum.
Flowers small, few to many borne in an involucre; calyx 6-parted or -cleft.
ERIOGONUM, p. 93
Flowers not borne in an involucre; calyx 4- or 5-toothed or -parted.
Flowers yellow; leaves not revolute, over ⅜-inch wide.
Flowers ¾-inch to 1¼ inches broad; leaves evergreen, densely pubescent at least beneath. . . . . FREMONTIA, p. 352
Flowers less than ½-inch broad; leaves deciduous, glabrous.
DIRCA, p. 364
Flowers not yellow; leaves ⅜-inch or less wide. . . . . . CERCOCARPUS, p. 205
Flowers unisexual (monoecious or dioecious).
Fruit a capsule.
Leaves ¾-inch to 1½ inches long, oblong to elliptic. . . . . CROTON, p. 255
Leaves ½-inch or less long, obovate-roundish. . . . . EUPHORBIA, p. 254
Fruit an achene or utricle surrounded by 2 appressed bracts.
Bracts totally united to form a sac with a small hole at apex. . GRAYIA, p. 106
Bracts never totally united. . . . . ATRIPLEX, p. 109

(b). FLOWERS WITH PETALS.

†*Petals distinct. (Choripetalous.)* (See p. 31 for ††.)

*FLOWERS REGULAR. (See page 31 for **.)

1. Flowers blue (rarely white); stamens 5, opposite the petals... CEANOTHUS, p. 278
2. Flowers purplish; stamens 15 to 20.......................... CROSSOSOMA, p. 169
3. Flowers salmon-color; stamens numerous, monadelphous.... HORSFORDIA, p. 335
4. Flowers yellow or yellowish.
Flowers ¾-inch or more broad; petals 4; stamens numerous. DENDROMECON, p. 131
Flowers less than ¾-inch broad.
Herbage roughish; flowers greenish yellow; stamens 5..... PETALONYX, p. 361
Herbage smooth.
Flowers deep yellow; stamens 6.......................... STANLEYA, p. 134
Flowers pale yellow; stamens 5.......................... COLUBRINA, p. 320
5. Flowers white, pink, pale rose, or greenish.
Herbage roughish; stamens 5.............................. PETALONYX, p. 361
Herbage not roughish.
Petals 4.
Stamens 6.. LEPIDIUM, p. 133
Stamens 4 or 5... RHAMNUS, p. 324
Petals 5.

‡*Ovary superior.*

Stamens 5; flowers bisexual or polygamous.
Leaves ½-inch or less long, oval, thick and scabrous; capsule 1-celled; rare. MORTONIA, p. 271
Leaves over ½-inch long, not scabrous.
Stamens opposite the petals.
Sepals petal-like; fruit a 3-celled capsule............... CEANOTHUS, p. 278
Sepals not petal-like; fruit berry-like, of 2 or 3 stony nutlets. RHAMNUS, p. 324
Stamens alternate with the petals; fruit a flattened drupe........ RHUS, p. 263
Stamens 10 to 50.
Flowers bisexual.
Leaves ¼-inch or less long; plants 2 feet or less high.
Leaves glabrate, with 1 longitudinal vein tipped by a spine. GLOSSOPETALON PUNGENS, p. 273
Leaves densely silky, without a spine-tipped longitudinal midvein. SPIRAEA CAESPITOSA, p. 191
Leaves ¼-inch or more long; plants over 2 feet high.
Stamens 10; fruit a 5-celled capsule......................... LEDUM, p. 425
Stamens 15 to 50.
Fruit a drupe.. PRUNUS, p. 195
Fruit a follicle... CROSSOSOMA, p. 169
Flowers unisexual.
Plants monoecious; stamens 10 to 15; fruit a 3-celled densely hairy capsule. ARGYTHAMNIA, p. 255
Plants dioecious; stamens 15; fruit a drupe.............. OSMARONIA, p. 213

‡‡Ovary inferior.

Leaves serrate at apex; flowers in racemes................AMELANCHIER, p. 216
Leaves entire all around or minutely serrulate; flowers solitary or 2 or 3 in an umbel ....PERAPHYLLUM, p. 215

**FLOWERS IRREGULAR.

Leaves round, cordate; flowers red-purple.......................CERCIS, p. 233
Leaves not round or cordate.
Flowers yellow ....LOTUS, p. 240
Flowers blue, purple, or white...........................POLYGALA, p. 247

††Petals united. (Sympetalous.)

Flowers regular.
1. Flowers whitish or pinkish.
Ovary superior.
Stamens 5.
Fruit of 4 nutlets; low prostrate plants...............COLDENIA, p. 459
Fruit a berry; erect or sprawling plants...............SOLANUM, p. 486
Stamens 8 to 16.
Leaves strongly revolute, white-tomentose beneath..XYLOCOCCUS, p. 421
Leaves not revolute.
Filaments united for part of their length; flowers ½-inch or more broad ....STYRAX, p. 434
Filaments not united.
Fruit a capsule; anthers not awned.............LEUCOTHOE, p. 424
Fruit berry-like; anthers awned or rarely awnless.
Calyx of distinct dry sepals.............ARCTOSTAPHYLOS, p. 382
Calyx of united sepals, fleshy and surrounding the pod when mature ....GAULTHERIA, p. 424
Ovary inferior.
Herbage rough-pubescent; petals only apparently joined; fruit a capsule. PETALONYX, p. 361
Herbage not rough-pubescent; petals definitely joined; fruit a berry. VACCINIUM, p. 429
2. Flowers yellowish.
Herbage rough-pubescent; leaves usually with 1 or more teeth. PETALONYX, p. 361
Herbage not rough-pubescent.
Leaves over 1 inch long; corolla 1 to 1½ inches long; tall shrubs or small trees ....NICOTIANA, p. 485
Leaves less than 1 inch long; corolla-tube ½-inch or less long; low bushes. MENODORA, p. 437
3. Flowers blue or purplish.
Stamens 5.
Leaves 6 to 10 inches long, viscid-pubescent, ill-scented; fruit a capsule. NAMA, p. 456
Leaves less than 4 inches long, not ill-scented; fruit a berry. SOLANUM, p. 486
Stamens 8; flowers greenish purple; leaves obovate, 1 to 3 inches long, rusty-pubescent above...............................MENZIESIA, p. 423

Flowers irregular or only slightly so in *Rhododendron*.
Leaves linear, 3 to 6 inches long; flowers pinkish, 1 to 1¾ inches long. CHILOPSIS, p. 520
Leaves usually not linear, if linear then less than 3 inches long.
Flowers over ½-inch broad; fertile stamens 5 or 10; tall shrubs. RHODODENDRON, p. 427
Flowers less than ½-inch broad; fertile stamens 4; subshrubs.
Corolla-tube with a sac at base........ANTIRRHINUM GLANDULOSUM, p. 494
Corolla-tube without a sac at base.....................CASTILLEIA, p. 492

KEY TO THE FAMILIES

I. Gymnosperms. (Seeds naked.)

Trees and shrubs with the seeds borne upon open scales instead of within closed ovaries. Leaves needle-like, scale-like, narrowly linear, or awl-shaped. Flowers unisexual, borne on the same or different plants.

Leaves needle-like, in fascicles.............................. PINACEAE, p. 39

Leaves awl- or scale-like, opposite or whorled.

Leaves thickly covering the ultimate branchlets; cones woody or berry-like. CUPRESSACEAE, p. 40

Leaves scattered, inconspicuous, 2 or 3 at a node and more or less sheathing the branches; shrubs with fluted jointed stems............ GNETACEAE, p. 44

II. Angiosperms. (Seeds enclosed.)

Trees, shrubs, and herbs with the seeds borne within closed ovaries. Flowers bisexual or unisexual.

A. MONOCOTYLEDONS. (Seed-leaves one.) Leaves mostly parallel-veined (netted-veined in *Smilax*). Parts of the flower in threes, never in fives.

Trees or shrubs; leaves linear or lanceolate, arising from the summit of the trunk or crowded in a rosette at the ground; flowers showy, bisexual, in terminal clusters.................................. LILIACEAE, p. 48

Climbing plants; leaves ovate, subcordate, alternate, not clustered; flowers small, unisexual, in axillary umbels.......... *Smilax* in LILIACEAE, p. 48

B. DICOTYLEDONS. (Seed-leaves two.) Leaves mostly netted-veined. Parts of the flowers in fours or fives.

1. APETALOUS SECTION. (Corolla none.) (See p. 35 for 2.)

Semi-parasitic subshrubs, upon native trees............ LORANTHACEAE, p. 89

Independent shrubs, subshrubs, or vines.

a. *Flowers in catkins.*

Leafless shrubs with jointed stems; flowers bisexual. *Allenrolfea* in CHENOPODIACEAE, p. 103

Leafy shrubs.

Leaves opposite or the upper leaves in some species alternate, evergreen; plants dioecious, i.e. male and female flowers on different plants.

(1). Fruit an achene or utricle; leaves usually white-scurfy, only the lower leaves opposite.................... *Atriplex* in CHENOPODIACEAE, p. 109

(2). Fruit a berry; leaves not scurfy; flowers in cup-like bracts; catkins pendent, 1 to 5 inches long...................... GARRYACEAE, p. 367

(3). Fruit a 3-valved, 1-celled, 1-seeded capsule............ BUXACEAE, p. 261

Leaves alternate.

Leaves once-pinnately compound; fruit a nut with dry husk. JUGLANDACEAE, p. 85

Leaves simple.

Flowers dioecious; ovary 1-celled.

(1). Fruit a 2- to 4-valved capsule; calyx none; leaves deciduous, neither resinous nor fragrant........................ SALICACEAE, p. 55

(2). Fruit a small nutlet; calyx none; leaves deciduous, resinous and fragrant. . . . . *Myrica Hartwegii* in MYRICACEAE, p. 88

(3). Fruit an achene or utricle; calyx in the staminate flowers 4- or 5-parted (absent in *Sarcobatus*); calyx in pistillate flowers absent (present in *Sarcobatus*); leaves evergreen, usually white-scurfy (green in *Grayia*). . . . . CHENOPODIACEAE, p. 102

Flowers monoecious.

Only the staminate flowers in catkins.

Fruit a nut surrounded by a leafy involucre; leaves deciduous. *Corylus* in BETULACEAE, p. 70

Fruit a nut in a scaly cup or bur; leaves deciduous or evergreen. FAGACEAE, p. 75

Both the staminate and pistillate flowers in catkins.

Leaves aromatic, evergreen, resinous; fruit a waxy-coated berry. *Myrica californica* in MYRICACEAE, p. 87

Leaves without decided aromatic odor; fruit an achene, capsule, or nutlet.

Ovary 1-celled; fruit an achene or utricle. . . CHENOPODIACEAE, p. 102

Ovary 2- to 5-celled.

Fruit a 3-valved capsule; ovary 3-celled; catkins or spikes less than ½-inch long. . . . . EUPHORBIACEAE, p. 248

Fruit a nutlet, many in small woody cones; ovary 2-celled; catkins ½-inch to 4 inches long. . . . . BETULACEAE, p. 70

b. *Flowers not in catkins.*

Leaves opposite or basal.

Leaves usually compound.

Climbing woody vines; all leaves compound; fruit a tailed achene. *Clematis* in RANUNCULACEAE, p. 115

Shrubs or small trees; leaves compound or simple; fruit a single-winged samara . . . . *Fraxinus* in OLEACEAE, p. 435

Leaves simple.

Flowers bisexual.

Plants spiny. . . . . *Coleogyne* in ROSACEAE, p. 187

Plants not spiny. . . . . *Eriogonum* in POLYGONACEAE, p. 93

Flowers unisexual, dioecious or polygamous.

(1). Stamens 2 to 4. . . . . OLEACEAE, p. 435

(2). Stamens 6 to 8.

Plants spiny; leaves silvery-scurfy below. *Shepherdia* in ELAEAGNACEAE, p. 365

Plants not spiny; fruit a 4-celled capsule. *Tetracoccus* in EUPHORBIACEAE, p. 252

(3). Stamens 10 to 12; fruit a 3-valved capsule. . . . . BUXACEAE, p. 261

Leaves alternate.

(1). Low spreading or prostrate subshrubs; leaves evergreen, linear; fruit a triangular achene. . . . . POLYGONACEAE, p. 93

(2). Low twining vines; leaves deciduous, cordate; fruit a 6-angled capsule. ARISTOLOCHIACEAE, p. 92

(3). Erect shrubs or small trees.

Leaves with odor of bay rum; fruit a drupe. . . . . LAURACEAE, p. 119

Leaves without bay rum odor.
Flowers bisexual.
Stamens 5, monadelphous; sepals large, yellow, petal-like.
Fremontia in STERCULIACEAE, p. 352
Stamens free from each other.
(a). Stamens numerous; fruit a hairy-tailed achene.
Cercocarpus in ROSACEAE, p. 205
(b). Stamens 8; fruit a drupe; stems very pliable.
Dirca in THYMELAEACEAE, p. 364
(c). Stamens 5 or less.
Fruit an achene or utricle................CHENOPODIACEAE, p. 102
Fruit a drupe....................*Condalia* in RHAMNACEAE, p. 321
Flowers unisexual (monoecious or dioecious) or polygamous.
Ovary 1-celled.
Flowers typically dioecious (sometimes monoecious or polygamous); fruit an achene or utricle...............CHENOPODIACEAE, p. 102
Flowers monoecious or polygamous; fruit a drupe.
Celtis in ULMACEAE, p. 88
Ovary 2- to 5-celled; fruit not an achene.
Flowers typically monoecious (dioecious in *Halliophytum*); fruit a capsule ..............................EUPHORBIACEAE, p. 248
Flowers typically polygamous; fruit a drupe or berry.
Rhamnus crocea in RHAMNACEAE, p. 330

2. CHORIPETALOUS SECTION. (Petals present and distinct.) (See p. 37 for 3.)

a. *Ovary superior, sometimes incompletely surrounded by a disk.*
(See p. 37 for b.)

(1). STAMENS MORE THAN 10.

Stamens united by their filaments into a tube around the pistil; leaves palmately veined ....MALVACEAE, p. 334
Stamens distinct, or at least not united into one tube.
Leaves opposite, simple.
Stamens somewhat united by their filaments into 3 clusters, inserted on a flattened disk ................................HYPERICACEAE, p. 351
Stamens all distinct.
Stamens inserted on a cup-like hollow receptacle...CALYCANTHACEAE, p. 118
Stamens inserted on the calyx.....................SAXIFRAGACEAE, p. 135
Leaves alternate; stamens all distinct.
Leaves compound.
Leaves bipinnately or tripinnately compound.
Branchlets with spines; fruit a legume; flowers yellow.
Acacia in FABACEAE (Leguminosae), p. 229
Branchlets without spines; fruit an achene or partially dehiscent pod; flowers white..................................ROSACEAE, p. 170
Leaves once-pinnately compound.....................ROSACEAE, p. 170
Leaves simple.
Sepals 2; petals 4; fruit a capsule..................PAPAVERACEAE, p. 129
Sepals more than 2; petals 5.
Stamens hypogynous.............................CISTACEAE, p. 358

Stamens perigynous.
Stamens borne on the calyx........................ROSACEAE, p. 170
Stamens borne on a disk lining the calyx....CROSSOSOMATACEAE, p. 168

(2). STAMENS 10 OR LESS.

(a). *Flowers regular or only slightly irregular.* (See p. 37 for (b).)

†FLOWERS CRUCIFEROUS, I.E., WITH 4 SEPALS, 4 PETALS, AND 6 STAMENS.

Leaves simple ..............................BRASSICACEAE (Cruciferae), p. 133
Leaves palmately compound, with 3 to 5 leaflets...........CAPPARIDACEAE, p. 131

††FLOWERS NOT CRUCIFEROUS.

**Plants thorny and leafless or the leaves reduced to mere scales.*

Flowers dioecious........................*Holacantha* in SIMARUBACEAE, p. 261
Flowers bisexual.
Petals, sepals, and stamens 5..................*Condalia* in RHAMNACEAE, p. 321
Petals and sepals 4; stamens 8................*Thamnosma* in RUTACEAE, p. 259

***Plants with leaves, with or without thorns.*

‡LEAVES COMPOUND.

Leaves palmately compound and opposite..*Aesculus* in HIPPOCASTANACEAE, p. 277
Leaves pinnately compound.
Leaves alternate.
Leaflets holly-like; petals and sepals 6, similar.........BERBERIDACEAE, p. 119
Leaflets not holly-like; petals 5, unlike the sepals.
Fruit a legume; stamens 7 to 10...........FABACEAE (Leguminosae), p. 217
Fruit not a legume.
Leaflets 3.
Fruit a winged samara...................*Ptelea* in RUTACEAE, p. 259
Fruit drupaceous, not winged................ANACARDIACEAE, p. 263
Leaflets numerous.............................BURSERACEAE, p. 262
Leaves opposite.
Petals 2; stamens 1 to 4; fruit a samara..*Fraxinus dipetala* in OLEACEAE, p. 436
Petals 5; stamens 5 or 10.
Stamens 5; fruit a 3-celled capsule.................STAPHYLEACEAE, p. 275
Stamens 10; fruit a 5-celled pod breaking up into separate carpels.
ZYGOPHYLLACEAE, p. 255

‡‡LEAVES SIMPLE.

Leaves opposite.
Leaves palmately veined and lobed........................ACERACEAE, p. 276
Leaves pinnately veined.
Stamens 4 to 7.
Petals strongly hooded; capsules 3-celled.............RHAMNACEAE, p. 278
Petals not hooded.
Leaves serrate or serrulate, branchlets angled......CELASTRACEAE, p. 269
Leaves entire; branchlets terete.................FRANKENIACEAE, p. 356
Stamens 8 to 12.
Petals 4............................*Cneoridium* in RUTACEAE, p. 259
Petals 5.......................................SAXIFRAGACEAE, p. 135
Leaves alternate.
Leaves linear, numerous and covering the branchlets, heather-like.
TAMARICACEAE, p. 357

Leaves broader, not heather-like.
Leaves palmately veined; vines . . . . VITACEAE, p. 333
Leaves pinnately veined; shrubs.
Stamens united into a tube . . . . *Ayenia* in STERCULIACEAE, p. 352
Stamens distinct.
Petals hooded; stamens opposite the petals . . . . RHAMNACEAE, p. 278
Petals not hooded; stamens alternate with the petals.
Leaves less than $\frac{1}{2}$-inch long; plants spinescent.
Stamens 6 to 10; sepals not petal-like.
Glossopetalon in CELASTRACEAE, p. 271
Stamens 4, all on one side of the flower; sepals petal-like.
KRAMERIACEAE, p. 244
Leaves more than $\frac{1}{2}$-inch long; plants not spiny.
Leaves $\frac{3}{8}$- to $\frac{3}{4}$-inch wide; fruit a capsule; stamens 10.
Ledum in ERICACEAE, p. 425
Leaves $\frac{3}{4}$-inch to 2 inches wide; fruit drupaceous; stamens 5.
ANACARDIACEAE, p. 263

(b). *Flowers irregular.*

Leaves opposite, palmately compound . . . . . *Aesculus* in HIPPOCASTANACEAE, p. 277
Leaves alternate, simple or pinnately compound.
Petals 5.
Stamens 10; fruit a legume . . . . FABACEAE (Leguminosae), p. 217
Stamens 4, all on one side of the flower . . . . KRAMERIACEAE, p. 244
Petals 3; stamens 8; fruit a capsule . . . . POLYGALACEAE, p. 247

b. *Ovary inferior, i.e. completely adnate to the calyx.*

Stamens 10 or more.
Leaves alternate.
Plants with rough or stinging hairs . . . . *Eucnide* in LOASACEAE, p. 364
Plants without rough or stinging hairs . . . . ROSACEAE, p. 170
Leaves opposite . . . . *Whipplea* in SAXIFRAGACEAE, p. 167
Stamens less than 10.
Stamens 8 . . . . ONAGRACEAE, p. 366
Stamens 4 or 5.
Petals 4; leaves opposite . . . . CORNACEAE, p. 374
Petals 5; leaves alternate.
Style 1; leaves sessile, not lobed; fruit a capsule . . . . LOASACEAE, p. 361
Styles 2; leaves petioled, palmately lobed; fruit a berry.
Ribes in SAXIFRAGACEAE, p. 140

3. SYMPETALOUS SECTION. (Petals united.)
Stamens 8 or more.
Flowers regular.
Stamens united into a tube.
Petals 6; leaves pinnately veined . . . . STYRACACEAE, p. 434
Petals 5; leaves palmately veined . . . . MALVACEAE, p. 334
Stamens not united into a tube.
Styles 3; spiny cactus-like desert shrubs . . . . FOUQUIERIACEAE, p. 361
Style 1.
Fruit a legume . . . . FABACEAE (Leguminosae), p. 217
Fruit a capsule or berry . . . . ERICACEAE, p. 379

Flowers irregular.
Stamens 8; petals 3. . . . . Polygalaceae, p. 247
Stamens 10; petals 5.
Fruit a legume. . . . . Fabaceae (Leguminosae), p. 217
Fruit a capsule. . . . . Ericaceae, p. 379
Stamens 5 or less.
Ovary superior.
Corolla regular.
Stamens 2. . . . . *Menodora* in Oleaceae, p. 437
Stamens 4 or 5.
Flowers in coiled racemes; ovary apparently 2-celled.
Hydrophyllaceae, p. 450
Flowers not in coiled racemes.
Style 3-cleft; ovary 3-celled. . . . . Polemoniaceae, p. 440
Style entire, rarely 2-lobed or -cleft; ovary 2- or 4-celled.
Flowers in dense heads; fruit a capsule. . . . . . Loganiaceae, p. 440
Flowers not in heads.
Fruit a berry or capsule; ovary 2-celled. . . . . Solanaceae, p. 479
Fruit of 3 or 4 nutlets; ovary 4-celled. . . . . Boraginaceae, p. 459
Corolla irregular.
Fertile stamens 5. . . . . . . *Rhododendron occidentale* in Ericaceae, p. 429
Fertile stamens 4 or 2.
Sepals petal-like; fruit spiny. . . . . Krameriaceae, p. 244
Sepals not petal-like; fruit not spiny.
Fruit a capsule.
Capsule 4 to 8 inches long; seeds with hairy appendages.
Bignoniaceae, p. 520
Capsule less than 1 inch long; seeds not hairy.
Stems nearly leafless and rush-like. . . . . Acanthaceae, p. 519
Stems leafy and not rush-like. . . . . Scrophulariaceae, p. 492
Fruit of 4 or 2 nutlets; leaves opposite.
Herbage usually with mint- or sage-like odor; stems usually square; ovary lobed. . . . . Menthaceae (Labiatae), p. 463
Herbage without mint-like odor; ovary not lobed.
Verbenaceae, p. 461
Ovary inferor.
Flowers in composite heads surrounded by involucres; stamens united by their anthers. . . . . Asteraceae (Compositae), p. 545
Flowers not in heads surrounded by involucres; stamens distinct.
Leaves opposite or whorled.
Leaves 3 or more at a node. . . . . Rubiaceae, p. 521
Leaves 2 at a node. . . . . Caprifoliaceae, p. 525
Leaves atlernate. . . . . *Vaccinium* in Ericaceae, p. 429

DESCRIPTIVE ACCOUNT OF THE SHRUBS

I. GYMNOSPERMAE. CONE-BEARING SHRUBS AND THEIR ALLIES

Pinaceae. Pine Family

The Pine Family includes 8 genera and about 150 species, well scattered over the world, often forming great forests in the temperate regions. The firs, hemlocks, spruces, false hemlocks, true cedars, larches, and pines belong to this family. Five genera and 30 species are represented in our Californian native flora. Only one species occurs sometimes as a shrub.

1. **Pinus** L. PINE

(The classical name of the pine tree.)

The genus *Pinus* contains about 80 species, widely scattered over the northern hemisphere, extending from the Arctic region southward to southern Europe and Asia, the West Indies, the mountains of western America, Mexico, Central America, northern Africa, the Canary Islands, the Philippines, and the Malayan Archipelago. The pines are among the most valuable forest trees for timber, turpentine, rosin, pitch, and tar.

1. **Pinus albicaulis** Engelm. WHITEBARK PINE. Fig. 8.

Usually a subalpine tree growing up to 40 feet high but frequently with 2 or 3 main trunks from the base and only 2 to 6 feet high. Leaves evergreen, persisting from 4 to 8 years, in fascicles of 5, needle-like, 1 to 2½ inches long, rigid, blunt, clustered at the ends of the branches. Staminate cones subglobose, about ⅜-inch long, reddish purple. Ovulate cones oval to subglobose, 1 to 3 inches long, dark purple when young, varying to yellowish brown when matured in August of the second year, remaining closed on the plant and eventually breaking up to disperse the seeds; scales broad and thick at apex, scarcely overlapping, usually armed with a short stout point. Seeds obovoid, ⅜- to ½-inch long, very hard, with a very narrow wing which usually remains on the scale. Flowering period, July and August.

Whitebark Pine is characteristic of the Hudsonian Life Zone. In California it extends from Warner Peak, Modoc County and the Mount Shasta region, Siskiyou County, southward along the high Sierra Nevada to the Kings River and the Little Kern River sources, and on Mount Whitney. It ranges northward through Oregon, Washington, and British Columbia and eastward into the Rocky Mountains of Montana. In its shrub form it inhabits the rocky draws, depressions, and ridges of the highest mountain ranges where it is exposed to the severe weather conditions of the timber-line region. These dwarf pines form broad flat-topped crowns 6 to 8 feet wide and only 2 to 4 feet high.

Pinus albicaulis Engelm. Trans. St. Louis Acad. 2:209 (1863). Type locality: In the Cascade Mountains of Oregon. Collected by *Newberry*.

Cupressaceae. Cypress Family

The Cypress Family consists of about 10 genera and 70 species of evergreen trees and shrubs, widely scattered over the world. Five genera and 15 species are native to California, but only 5 of these are shrubs or shrub-like.

Fig. 8. WHITEBARK PINE. *Pinus albicaulis* Engelm.

KEY TO THE GENERA

Mature cones woody; staminate and ovulate flowers on the same plant. 1. CUPRESSUS.

Mature cones fleshy or fibrous, berry-like; staminate and ovulate flowers usually on separate plants. . . . . 2. JUNIPERUS.

1. **Cupressus** L. Cypress

(The ancient Latin name of the cypress.)

Leaves opposite, scale-like, covering the branchlets, or some awl-shaped on young plants and vigorous shoots. Flowers unisexual, both kinds in cones on the same plant; the staminate cones terminal on the branchlets, yellowish, with shield-shaped scales bearing 3 to 5 pollen-sacs; the young ovulate cones inconspicuous, borne upon short lateral branchlets, composed of 6 or 8 small opposite scales, each with several erect ovules at base. Fruiting cones globose or slightly oblong, maturing the second year; the scales woody and shield-shaped, closely fitted together, spreading apart when mature. Seeds numerous, with very narrow margins.

About 14 species of cypresses have been described from the north temperate zone in Asia, southern Europe, the southwestern United States, and Mexico. Six species are native to California, 3 of which are sometimes shrub-like.

KEY TO THE SPECIES

Leaves usually pale green or glaucous, very fragrant, with conspicuous resin-pits on their backs....................................1. *C. Macnabiana.*

Leaves light or dark green or yellowish green, with inconspicuous closed resin-pits or some without pits.

Cones usually ¾-inch to 1 inch long; seeds reddish brown, with thin margins. 2. *C. Sargentii.*

Cones usually ½- to ¾-inch long; seeds black, scarcely margined. 3. *C. Goveniana.*

1. **Cupressus Macnabiana** Murr. Macnab Cypress. Fig. 9.

A small open spreading tree, 20 to 60 feet high, or sometimes bushy or a low shrub, with smooth gray bark. Leaves bluish green, very aromatic, with conspicuous dorsal resin-pits. Cones globose, ½- to ¾-inch in diameter, reddish brown, with 6 or 8 scales, the uppermost pair often with conical or hooked projections.

Macnab Cypress inhabits the dry hills and flats of the inner North Coast Range from Napa County north to Siskiyou County, east to Modoc County, and south in scattered locations on the lower western slope of the Sierra Nevada to the south fork of the Consumnes River in Amador County near Aukum.

Cupressus Macnabiana Murr. Edinb. New Phil. Jour. 1:293 pl. 11 (1855). Type locality: Near Whiskeytown, Shasta County. Collected by *Macnab.*

2. **Cupressus Sargentii** Jepson. Sargent Cypress. Fig. 10.

A small tree, 10 to 40 feet high, but sometimes branching from near the ground and thus becoming shrub-like, with thickish obscurely squarish branchlets. Leaves not glandular or some with closed resin-pits. Cones ¾-inch to 1 inch in diameter. Seeds reddish brown, with thin margins.

Sargent Cypress occurs in small groves or as isolated plants on the dry slopes and in the valleys of the Santa Lucia and Santa Cruz mountains and in Marin, Sonoma, Napa, Lake, Colusa (Cooks Springs) and Mendocino (Red Mountain) counties.

Cupressus Sargentii Jepson, Fl. Calif. 1:61 (1909). Type locality: Mayacamas Range, Napa County. Collected by *Jepson. C. Goveniana* Engelm. in Bot. Calif., in part, not Gord.

3. **Cupressus Goveniana** Gord. Gowen Cypress. Fig. 11.

A small bushy tree, or sometimes shrub-like, with squarish branchlets and light to dark green foliage. Leaves not glandular or a few with closed resin-pits. Cones ½- to ¾-inch diameter. Seeds black.

Gowen Cypress occurs on the Monterey peninsula and the Mendocino "White Plains" east of Fort Bragg and Mendocino City, California.

On the "White Plains" this cypress often grows no higher than 2 to 10 feet and forms a "pigmy forest." The trees usually have a whip-like leading shoot, whereas the plants at Monterey are more bush-like.

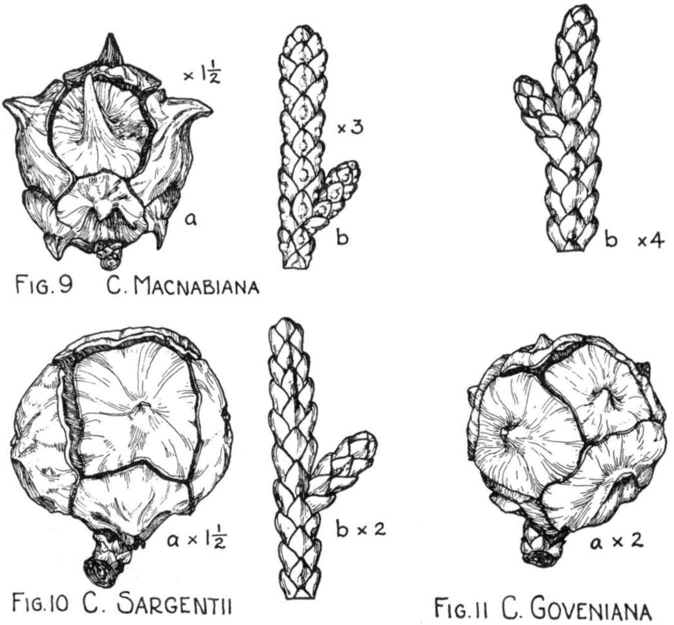

CUPRESSUS. a, Fruiting cone. b, Branchlet with scale-like leaves.
(From Pacific Coast Trees, Univ. of Calif. Press.)

Cupressus Goveniana Gord. Jour. Hort. Soc. Lond. 4:295 (1849). Type locality: "The pine barrens of Huckleberry Hill," Monterey, California. Collected by *Hartweg*. *Cupressus pygmaea* Sarg.

2. **Juniperus** L. JUNIPER

(The classical name of the juniper.)

Aromatic evergreen trees or shrubs. Leaves simple, in cycles of 2 or 3, of 2 kinds—short-linear to linear-lanceolate and extending radially, or scale-like and closely appressed and covering the cord-like branchlets. Flowers small, usually dioecious; the staminate in small axillary catkins consisting of many stamens; the ovulate consisting of few opposite pairs of fleshy scales, each scale with 1 or 2 ovules. Fruit an ovoid berry-like cone, usually with coalesced fleshy scales, maturing the first, second, or third year.

There are about 35 species of junipers widely distributed in the northern hemisphere from the Arctic Circle to the mountains of northern Africa, southern Japan,

China, the West Indies, and Mexico. Four species are native to California, one of which is always a low nearly prostrate shrub and one sometimes shrub-like.

KEY TO THE SPECIES

Low prostrate shrubs; leaves short-linear or linear-lanceolate, sharp-pointed at apex, in whorls of 3, spreading from the branchlets. . . . . 1. *J. sibirica.*
Erect shrubs or more often small trees; leaves scale-like, opposite or in whorls of 3, closely appressed to the branchlets . . . . 2. *J. californica.*

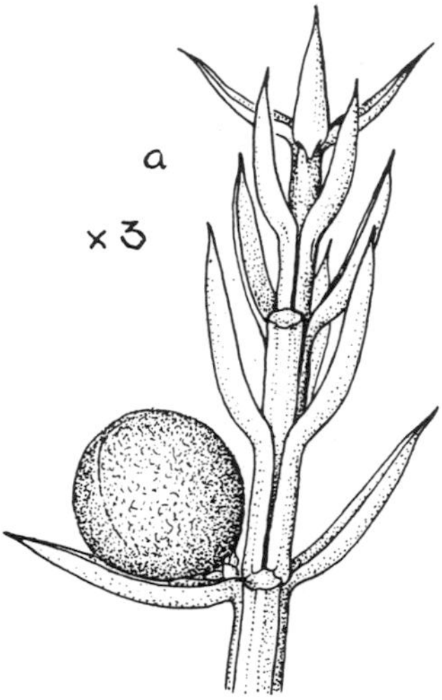

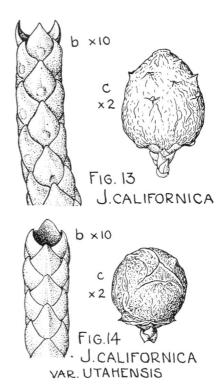

FIG. 12 J. SIBIRICA

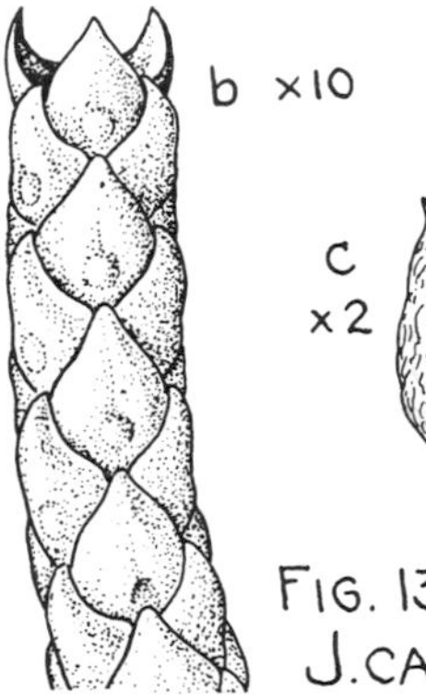

FIG. 13
J. CALIFORNICA

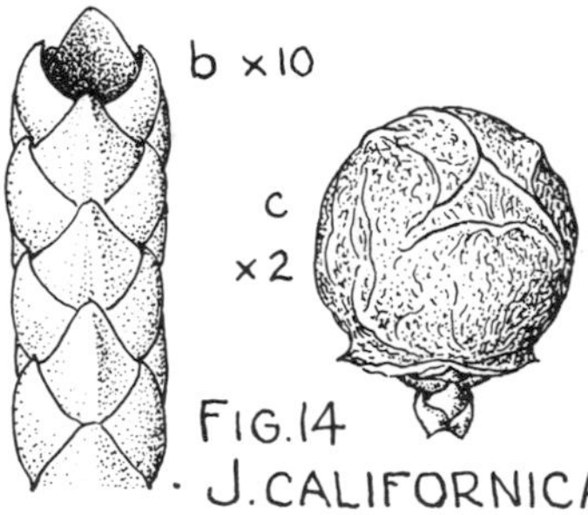

FIG. 14
J. CALIFORNICA
VAR. UTAHENSIS

JUNIPERUS. a, Branchlet with leaves and fruit. b, Branchlet with scale-like leaves. c, Fruit. *(From Pacific Coast Tress, Univ. of Calif. Press.)*

1. **Juniperus sibirica** Burgsd. DWARF JUNIPER. Fig. 12.

A low or almost prostrate shrub, forming patches several feet in width. Leaves short-linear or linear-lanceolate, ¼- to ½-inch long, in whorls of 3, spreading from the branchlets, sharp-pointed at apex, jointed at the base, dark green, shining, and keeled or strongly convex on the lower (outer) surface, deeply grooved and with a broad white band on the upper (inner) surface. Fruit globose, ¼- to ⅜-inch in diameter, blue, covered with a white bloom, fleshy and sweet, ripening in the fall of the third year. Seeds 1 to 3.

Dwarf Juniper is a rare shrub in California. It occurs in the Sierra Nevada from Mono Pass northward in scattered localities of the Hudsonian and Arctic-alpine Life Zones to Siskiyou County and westward to Del Norte County (above Gasquets). Beyond California it has a wide distribution in the Arctic and Alpine regions of the northern hemisphere.

Juniperus sibirica Burgsd. Anleit. Holz. no. 272 (1787). Type locality: Siberia. *Juniperus communis* var. *montana* Ait.

2. **Juniperus californica** Carr. California Juniper. Fig. 13.

A much branched arborescent shrub, 3 to 15 feet high, or often tree-like and up to 40 feet high. Leaves scale-like, closely appressed to the branchlets, usually in whorls of 3, distinctly glandular-pitted on the back, bluntly pointed. Juvenile leaves usually short-linear and very glaucous. Fruit oblong-ovoid, about ½-inch long, at first bluish with a dense bloom, at maturity reddish brown beneath the bloom, nearly smooth or with few small projections (umbos of the fleshy cone-scales), the pulp firm, dry, and sweetish. Seeds 1 to 3.

California Juniper occurs on dry hills and lower mountain slopes from Tehama County southward in the inner Coast Ranges to the Tehachapi Mountains, eastward to the base of the Sierra Nevada in Kern and Tulare counties, and thence north as far as the Merced River. In southern California it is abundant on the desert slopes of the Sierra Liebre, Sierra Madre, and San Bernardino mountains where it inhabits the lower edge of the Piños Pine belt and where it is associated with sagebrush *(Artemisia tridentata)* and the Joshua Tree *(Yucca brevifolia).*

2a. Var. **utahensis** Engelm. Utah Juniper. Fig. 14.

Usually more compact and tree-like than *J. californica.* Leaves in 2's or rarely in 3's, usually not glandular on the back. Fruit globose to narrowly ellipsoid, about ¼-inch long, reddish brown beneath a bluish bloom, the pulp dry and sweetish. Seeds 1 or rarely 2.

This variety occurs in the desert mountain ranges of eastern San Bernardino County and in Mono and Inyo counties. It extends eastward into Nevada, Utah, Arizona, New Mexico, Colorado, and Wyoming.

Juniperus californica Carr. Rev. Hort. IV, 3:352 (1854). Type locality: "California," locality not known.

Var. utahensis Engelm. Trans. St. Louis Acad. 3:588 (1877). Type locality: Not Known. *J. utahensis* (Engelm.) Lemmon.

Gnetaceae. Ephedra or Gnetum Family

This family consists of 3 genera and about 45 species of shrubs, small trees, and semi-woody perennials, usually of tropical or desert regions. Only the genus *Ephedra* is native to California.

1. **Ephedra L.** Ephedra

(From the Greek *ephedra,* the name used for the horse-tails.)

Desert shrubs with long-fluted jointed opposite or whorled branches resembling the scouring-rushes or horse-tails of our streams. Leaves simple, scale-like (hence referred to as leaf-scales), opposite or in whorls of 3 at a node. Flowers unisexual, the male and female appearing on separate plants, with decussate persistent bracts, borne in catkins. Staminate catkins composed of 6 to 10 decussate imbricated bracts, each pair of bracts enclosing 2 staminate flowers; the flowers consisting of 2 more or less connate scales (perianth) enclosing the stamen-tube, perhaps better considered as 1 stamen with 2 to several anthers. Ovulate catkins 2 to 6 at each node, each catkin composed of 4, 5, or more pairs of whorls of bracts, the terminal pair subtending 1 or 2 erect ovules invested by the hardened perianth-segments. The integuments elongated at apex into a style-like process. Seeds nut-like, surrounded by the hardened perianth, the whole called a fruit which is wholly or partially enclosed by the large and chaffy or rarely fleshy fruiting bracts forming the so-called cone.

This genus contains about 40 species of the arid regions of North and South America and the Mediterranean region. Five species are native to California.

KEY TO THE SPECIES

Branchlets spinosely tipped; leaf-scales in 3's; fruits solitary, elongate-acuminate, scarcely exserted.

Leaf-scales becoming shreddy in age; fruit linear-lanceolate, about ½-inch long; fruiting bracts thin and membranous, rounded-cordate, usually entire, ¼- to ½-inch in diameter.................................1. *E. trifurca.*

Leaf-scales not becoming shreddy; fruit pyramidal, about ¼-inch long; fruiting bracts firm, contracted at base into a claw, the margins slightly crenulate. 2. *E. funerea.*

Branchlets not spinosely tipped.

Leaf-scales usually in 3's (sometimes in 2's and 3's on the same plant), about ¼-inch long...................................3. *E. californica.*

Leaf-scales usually in 2's.

Branches numerous, slender, erect, broom-like, green or bright yellowish green.......................................4. *E. viridis.*

Branches stout, spreading, gray or brownish green.........5. *E. nevadensis.*

1. **Ephedra trifurca** Torr. THREE-FORK EPHEDRA. Fig. 15.

An erect much branched shrub, 2 to 4 feet high, with pale or yellowish green straight stiff branches, usually spinosely tipped. Leaf-scales in 3's, ¼- to ⅜-inch long, at first distinctly joined and sheathing the stem to about ½ their length, becoming distinct and shreddy in age, persistent. Staminate catkins solitary, on very short pedicels or sessile, ⅛- to 3/16-inch long. Ovulate catkins 1-flowered, with numerous thin membranous bracts. Fruiting bracts round or somewhat kidney-shaped, ¼- to ½-inch in diameter, with distinct brown stalks. Fruits usually solitary, included within the bracts, linear-lanceolate, about ½-inch long, usually 4-angled, tapering to a prominent beak. Flowering period, February to April.

Three-fork Ephedra is rare in California, being known from near Flowing Well, Coyote Wells, and between Holtville and the sandhills in Imperial County, at Daggett along the Mohave River, and from the Superstition Mountains in the Colorado Desert. It occurs mainly in the Lower Sonoran Life Zone of Arizona, New Mexico, and southern Colorado, and eastward to western Texas, southward into Sonora, Mexico and Lower California.

Ephedra trifurca Torr. in Emory's Notes Mil. Rec. 152 (1848). Type locality: "Between the Del Norte and Gila Rivers," New Mexico. Collected by *Emory*.

2. **Ephedra funerea** Cov. & Morton. DEATH VALLEY EPHEDRA. Fig. 16.

An intricately branched shrub, 2 to 4 feet high, with pale green spinosely tipped branchlets. Leaf-scales in 3's, about ¼-inch long. Ovulate spikes sessile, solitary or 2 at a node, about ⅜-inch long. Bracts pale green, borne in about 3 series, about 3/16-inch broad, firm, contracted at base into a claw, the margins slightly crenulate. Fruits solitary, elongate-acuminate, about ⅜-inch long, scarcely exserted beyond the bracts. Flowering period, April and May.

This species occurs in the mountains surrounding Death Valley, Inyo County (Furnace Creek Canyon, *Coville* & *Gilman;* Warm Springs Canyon, Panamint

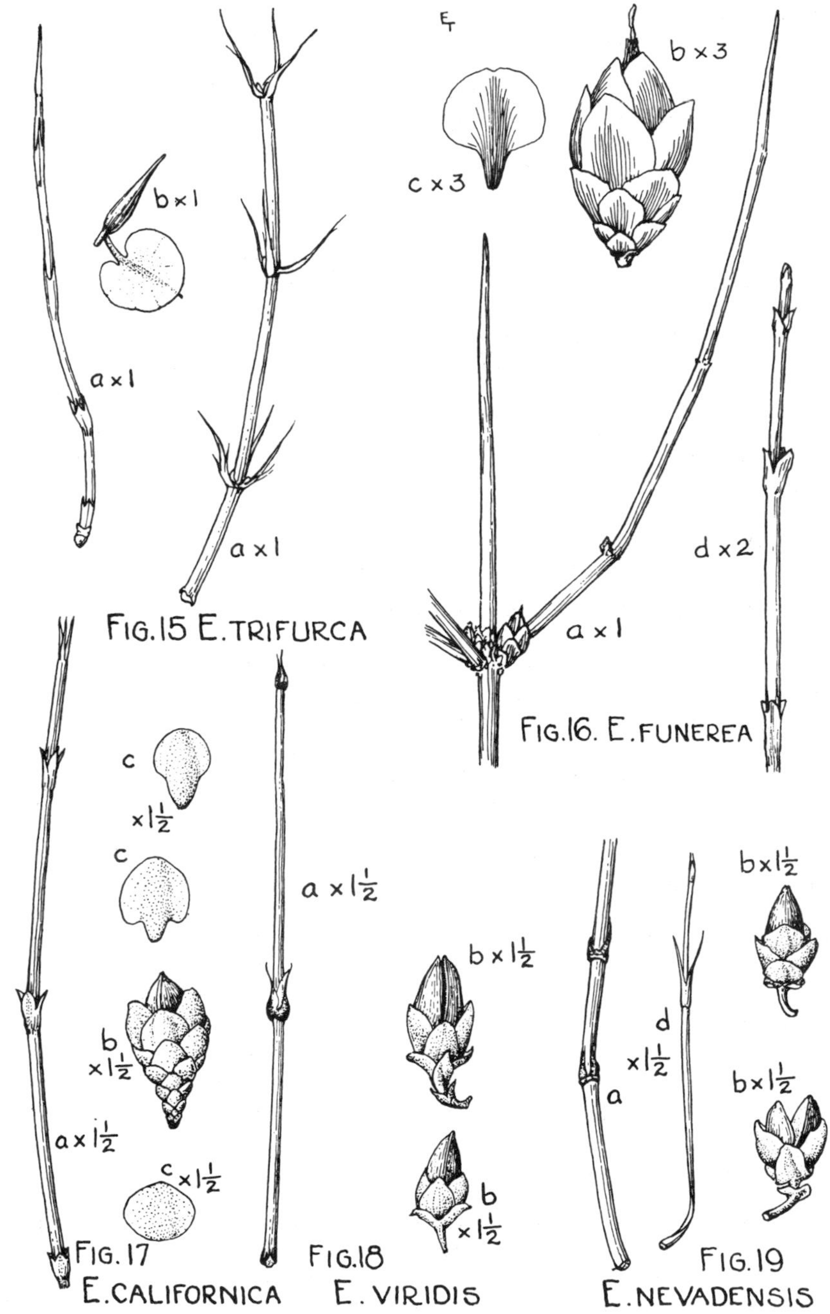

EPHEDRA. a, Branchlet with leaves. b, Fruit. c, Single bract.
d, Young branchlet with scale-like leaves.

Mountains, *Coville* & *Gilman;* Boundary Canyon, alt. about 3200 ft., *Coville* & *Gilman;* Dante's View, *McMinn;* Funeral Mountains, slope of Salsberry Pass, *Charles Brown;* east of Bradbury Well, *J. T. Howell*). It is closely related to *Ephedra californica* but differs in its long acuminate fruits. *Ephedra californica* is not known from the Death Valley region.

Ephedra funerea Cov. & Morton, Jour. Wash. Acad. Sci. 25:307 (1935). Type locality: Furnace Creek Canyon, alt. about 3200 ft. Collected by *Coville* and *Gilman*.

3. **Ephedra californica** Wats. CALIFORNIA EPHEDRA. DESERT TEA. Fig. 17.

A low spreading or suberect shrub, 1 to 3 feet high, with numerous opposite or whorled pale green or glaucous branches. Leaf-scales in 3's (rarely in 2's), 1/4-inch or less long, at first joined and sheathing the steam to about 1/2 or 3/4 their length, soon splitting and becoming recurved, turning black in age, then falling. Staminate catkins solitary, almost sessile. Ovulate catkins solitary, with 8 or more semi-membranous bracts. Fruiting bracts round to kidney-shaped, about 1/4-inch in diameter, sessile or with a very short broad stalk. Fruits solitary, ovoid, about 1/4-inch long (rarely 1/2-inch), exserted from the bracts, somewhat-4-angled, abruptly pointed at apex. Flowering period, February to April.

California Ephedra occurs on dry plains of the Mohave and Colorado deserts, southward to Lower California, westward to the coast near San Diego, and northward, in the Cuyama Valley, Santa Barbara County, in western Fresno County (25 miles south of Dos Palos, on the Panoche-Dos Palos road, *Roxana Ferris*), and to Big Panoche Pass in San Benito County (12 miles east of Llanada, *D. Keck*), mainly in the Upper Sonoran Life Zone.

Ephedra californica Wats. Proc. Am. Acad. 14:300 (1879). Type locality: Promontory near San Diego and Jamul Valley, California. Collected by *Dr. E. Palmer*.

4. **Ephedra viridis** Cov. GREEN EPHEDRA. Fig. 18.

An erect shrub, 1 to 3 feet high, with numerous bright green or yellowish green broom-like slender branches. Leaf-scales usually in 2's, their free tips falling away from the brown bases. Staminate catkins 1 or sometimes 2 on each side at the nodes, usually sessile. Ovulate catkins 2 at a node (rarely more), almost sessile or on short scaly pedicels. Bracts 6, 8, or 10, round-ovate, about 1/4-inch long, with scarious entire margins. Fruits solitary and angled or often 2 in a cone and with flat faces and convex or ridged backs, 1/4- to 1/2-inch long, well exserted from the bracts. Flowering period, March to May.

Green Ephedra inhabits the desert mountain slopes of the juniper belt in the Upper Sonoran Life Zone. It extends from the lava beds of eastern Lassen County southward into Mono and Inyo counties and to the mountain slopes bordering the Mohave Desert of Kern, Ventura, Los Angeles, and San Bernardino counties. It occurs also in Nevada, Arizona, Utah, and New Mexico.

Ephedra viridis Cov. Contr. U. S. Nat. Herb. 4:220 (1893). Type locality: Above Crystal Spring, Coso Mts., Inyo County, California. Collected by *Coville* and *Funston*.

5. **Ephedra nevadensis** Wats. NEVADA EPHEDRA. Fig. 19.

An erect shrub, 1/2-foot to 3 feet high, with pale green or grayish somewhat scabrous spreading branches. Leaf-scales usually in 2's, their free tips falling in age. Staminate catkins solitary or several in a cluster, usually sessile. Ovulate catkins 2 to 6 at a node, sessile or on short scaly pedicels. Fruiting bracts 6 to 12, round-ovate, about 1/4-inch long, with scarious entire margins. Fruits solitary and 3-angled or in pairs and with flat faces and convex-ridged backs, well exserted from the bracts. Flowering period, March to May.

Nevada Ephedra usually occurs at lower elevations than Green Ephedra. It inhabits the upper Larrea belt and lower juniper belt of the Lower and Upper Sonoran Life Zones in Modoc, Inyo, San Bernardino, Riverside, San Diego, and Kern counties. It extends eastward to Nevada, Utah, and Arizona and southward to Lower California.

Ephedra nevadensis Wats. Proc. Am. Acad. 14:298 (1879). Type locality: "Pah Ute Mountains, Nevada, altitude 5000 ft., and Carson City, Nevada."

II. ANGIOSPERMAE. TRUE-FLOWERING SHRUBS

Liliaceae. Lily Family

The Lily Family contains about 200 genera and about 2500 species of caulescent and acaulescent perennial herbs, rarely shrubs and trees, distributed in all parts of the world. Thirty genera and about 155 species are native to California, 7 of which contain woody tissue.

KEY TO THE GENERA

Plants climbing by means of tendrils; leaves less than 6 inches long; fruit a berry. 1. SMILAX.

Plants not climbing; leaves usually over 6 inches long; fruit a fleshy or dry capsule, indehiscent or dehiscent.

Flowers 3/4-inch to 3 inches long; fruit not winged..................2. YUCCA.

Flowers less than 1/2-inch long; fruit winged.....................3. NOLINA.

1. **Smilax** L. GREENBRIER

(From the Greek *Smilax,* the name perhaps not originally applied to these plants.)

This genus contains about 200 species of usually woody climbers, but a few are herbaceous, growing chiefly in the tropical and temperate regions of Asia and America. Only one is native to California.

Although the greenbriers are quite useful for winter greens and outdoor planting, their ornamental value seems to have been largely forgotten. However, *S. lanceolata* of Florida is shipped extensively from the southern to the northern states for use in decorations.

1. **Smilax californica** (A. DC.) Gray. CALIFORNIA SMILAX. Fig. 20.

A woody vine, climbing by means of paired tendrils at the bases of the petioles, 3 to 6 (or even 14) feet in length, with terete or somewhat angled stems, these smooth or sometimes covered with slender spreading brownish prickles, arising from a large tuberous rootstock. Leaves simple, alternate, deciduous, the lower ones reduced to scales, the upper entire or lobed. Flowers small, greenish, dioecious, borne in axillary umbels on peduncles 2 to 3 times longer than the petioles. Fruit a globose black berry about 1/4-inch in diameter. Flowering period, April to June.

California Smilax grows along stream banks, climbing bushes and small trees, in the Upper Sonoran and Transition Life Zones from Butte County northward to Siskiyou County and thence west and south to Trinity County. It is found outside of California only in southern Oregon. This species is near *S. hispida* of the Atlantic states, but the leaves of the latter are less acuminate and more cordate.

Smilax californica (A. DC.) Gray; Bot. Calif. 2:186 (1880). *S. rotundifolia* var. *californica* A. DC. Type locality: Near Chico, California. Collected by *Hartweg*.

2. **Yucca** L. Spanish Bayonet

(Yucca, native name for the Manihot, a cassava, erroneously applied to the present plants.)

Acaulescent to tall palm-like plants with a simple or branched woody caudex. Leaves simple, crowded, fibrous, thick, rigid, sword-shaped, and evergreen with smooth or serrulate or filamentous margins. Flowers bisexual, in large terminal panicles, opening at night; perianth-segments 6, many-nerved, distinct, nearly equal; stamens 6, adnate to the base of the segments, filaments enlarged above; ovary superior, 3-celled, the stigmas usually sessile but sometimes borne on a short persistent style. Fruit a capsule, more or less fleshy and indehiscent, or dry and dehiscent.

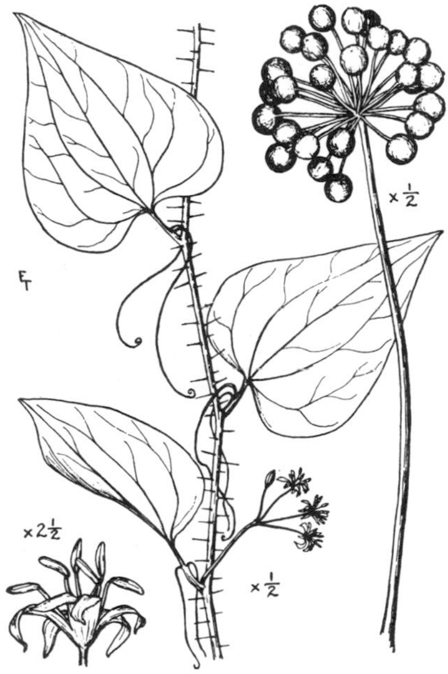

FIG. 20 SMILAX CALIFORNICA

This genus consists of about 30 species, confined to North America and the West Indies, being most abundant in the southwestern United States and northern Mexico. The four species of yuccas growing in California have a woody caudex.

One of the most interesting facts about the yuccas is that pollination occurs only through the aid of a little white *Pronuba* moth which is found wherever yuccas occur wild on the continent. At night the female moth deliberately gathers pollen from one plant and places it on the stigmatic surface of another so that the larvae that hatch from the eggs which she has laid in the ovary will have developing seeds upon which to feed.

The trunks of the arborescent species are often used for stockades, and the Indians have used the leaves for thatching. Paper can be made from the fiber of the trunks and leaves. Cattle eat the flower panicles and in times of severe drought the leaves are of some importance as forage. The yuccas play a very important part in binding the sand of the Southwest, for their roots are often 40 feet long.

KEY TO THE SPECIES

Leaves with free marginal fibers, concave above; fruit fleshy, eventually pendent.

Leaves pale bluish green, in a rosette on the ground or from a very short unbranched stem; perianth-segments 2¼ to 3½ inches long. . . . 1. *Y. baccata*.

Leaves yellowish green, in rosettes at the ends of simple or branched trunks 3 to 12 feet high; perianth-segments less than 2 inches long. . 2. *Y. schidigera*.

Leaves without marginal fibers, plane; fruit spongy or dry, spreading.
Leaves 1 foot or less long . . . . 3. *Y. brevifolia.*
Leaves more than 1 foot long, grayish green . . . . 4. *Y. Whipplei.*

1. **Yucca baccata** Torr. SPANISH BAYONET. Fig. 21.

Plants usually single, sometimes forming small open clumps with 2 to 6 short procumbent stems and heads of leaves. Leaves pale bluish green, 1 to 3 feet long,

Fig. 21. SPANISH BAYONET. *Yucca baccata* Torr.

in a rosette on the ground or from a very short unbranched stem, the margins bearing coarse recurved threads. Flowers borne on a scape 2 to 3¼ feet high; perianth-segments 2¼ to 4 inches long, appressed to the style above the ovary and then open-campanulate; the base of the filaments papillate; style ¾-inch to 1½ inches long. Fruit conical, often up to 6¼ inches long. Flowering period, March to June, varying with the latitude.

Spanish Bayonet occurs occasionally with the variety *vespertina* on the east slope of the Providence Mountains of San Bernardino County. It extends eastward to Nevada, southwestern Utah, Arizona, southwestern Colorado, New Mexico, and southwestern Texas and southward to Mexico.

1a. Var. **vespertina** McKelvey. Plants usually clustered in larger colonies, with many heads of leaves.

This variety is the common form in the New York, Clark, and Providence mountains in the eastern Mohave Desert. It extends eastward in southern Nevada, southwestern Utah, and Arizona.

Yucca baccata Torr. Bot. Mex. Bound. 221 (1859). Type locality: "Parras, Coahuila, Mexico." Collected by *Thurber*.

Var. vespertina McKelvey, Yuccas sw. U. S. Part I, 45 (1938). Type locality: "East of Peach Spring, Mohave County, Arizona." Collected by *McKelvey*.

2. **Yucca schidigera** Roezl ex Ortgies. SPANISH DAGGER. Fig. 22.

Trunk simple or shortly branched, 3 to 15 feet high, or sometimes with almost no caudex, often clothed to the ground with living leaves. Leaves light yellowish green, concave, 1¼ to 3½ feet long, 1 to 1½ inches wide, with a stout sharp-pointed apex, the margins with long pale filaments. Flowers with creamy-white perianth-segments, or the outer surface often purplish, ¾-inch to 1¾ inches long, borne in dense sessile or short-stalked panicles 1 to 1⅔ feet long; filaments more or less hairy and somewhat clavate at apex, nearly as long as the pistil; style less than ¼-inch long with a 3-lobed stigma, each lobe notched at the apex. Fruit fleshy, 2½ to 4 inches long and about half as broad. Flowering period, April to June.

Fig. 22. SPANISH DAGGER.
Yucca schidigera Roezl ex Ortgies.
(From Pacific Coast Trees, Univ. of Calif. Press.)

Spanish Dagger grows in the Lower Sonoran Life Zone throughout the Mohave Desert and in the San Bernardino Valley, and southward through the San Jacinto and Santa Rosa mountains and west to the coast near San Diego. Outside of California it is found in northern Lower California, Arizona, and southern Nevada.

The fibers of the leaves were used by the Coahuila Indians of California for weaving and making sandals and saddle mats. The green fruits were roasted and eaten, while the ripe fruit was eaten raw.

Yucca schidigera Roezl ex Ortgies, Gartenflora 20:110 (1871). Type locality: Near San Diego, California. Collected by *Roezl*. *Y. mohavensis* Sarg.

3. **Yucca brevifolia** Engelm. JOSHUA TREE. Fig. 23.

Commonly a tree growing up to 30 feet in height and becoming much branched and forming a rounded open head, the trunk growing to be 1 to 3½ feet in diameter; young trees unbranched until 6 to 9 feet in height and covered nearly to the ground with spreading or reflexed leaves. Leaves 1 foot or less long, ⅜- to ⅝-inch wide, more or less 3-sided, forming tufts and spreading in all directions from the ends of the branches, the margins denticulate, without fibers. Flowers greenish white, borne in a sessile panicle 8 to 14 inches long; perianth-segments

Fig. 23. Joshua Tree. *Yucca brevifolia* Engelm.

thick and fleshy, 1 to 1½ inches long; stamens ½ the length of the pistil. Fruit ovoid, 2 to 4 inches long, dry and spongy, indehiscent. Flowering period, April and May.

Joshua Tree grows in the Lower Sonoran Life Zone in the Mohave Desert, west to Antelope Valley and to Upper Piru Creek along the highway from Gorman to Castaic, Los Angeles County, and north to eastern Kern and Inyo counties. It extends eastward to Arizona, Nevada, and Utah.

3a. Var. **Jaegeriana** McKelvey.

Plants usually 9 to 12 feet or rarely to 18 feet high, with a short stout stem branching at about 3 feet above the ground. Leaves usually about 4 inches long, not exceeding 9 inches.

This variety occurs in northeastern San Bernardino County, where it is "plentiful in the region of the Shadow and New York Mts.," *McKelvey*. It extends eastward to northwestern Arizona, New Mexico, southwestern Colorado, and southwestern Texas.

Yucca brevifolia Engelm. Bot. King Expl. 496 (1871). Type locality: Eastern Mohave Desert. Collected by *Bigelow*. *Y. draconis* var. *arborescens* Torr. *Y. arborescens* (Torr.) Trel.

Fig. 24. CHAPARRAL YUCCA. *Yucca Whipplei* Torr.
(Photograph by Lustin E. Martindale.)

Var. Jaegeriana McKelvey, Jour. Arn. Arb. 16:269 (1935). Type locality: "Vicinity of the Shadow Mts." Collected by *McKelvey.*

4. **Yucca Whipplei** Torr. CHAPARRAL YUCCA. SPANISH BAYONET. QUIXOTE PLANT. OUR LORD'S CANDLE. Fig. 24.

An acaulescent plant with the leaves in a dense basal rosette and with a flowering stem 6 to 14 feet high. Leaves 1 to 1¾ feet long, ⅓- to ⅔-inch wide, linear-subulate from a broad base, attenuate to a sharp triangular brown spine, grayish green, deeply concave near the apex, the margins finely serrulate. Flowers creamy-white, open-campanulate, pendulous, 1 to 2 inches long, borne in panicles 3 to 6 feet long. Fruit a globose-obovate capsule 1 to 2 inches long. Flowering period, April to June.

Chaparral Yucca grows on the chaparral-covered slopes and mesas of the mountains of southern California and extends northward in the inner South Coast Ranges to San Benito and Monterey counties and in the southern Sierra Nevada to the Kings River region. It extends southward into Lower California.

After the plant flowers and produces seeds it dies and the new generation comes about either through the rooting stolons or the germination of the seeds. In the case of the other woody species of *Yucca,* only the scape dies after the fruit matures.

Yucca Whipplei Torr. Bot. Mex. Bound. 222 (1859). Type locality: "near San Pasqual, California." Collected by *Schott. Hesperoyucca Whipplei* (Torr.) Baker.

Fig. 25. PARRY NOLINA. *Nolina Parryi* Wats. *(Photograph by Hugh P. Dearing.)*

3. **Nolina** Michx.

(Named in honor of C. P. Nolin, a French scientist of the 18th century.)

Palm-like plants with a thick woody basal caudex or short trunk, often much dilated from the base. Leaves narrowly linear, rigid, borne in clusters at the summit of the short stalk or at the ground. Flowers whitish, polygamo-dioecious, borne on a stout nearly naked stem in a much congested compound panicle. Pedicels jointed near the base and subtended by minute scarious bracts. Perianth-segments 6, distinct, elliptic to lanceolate, persistent. Stamens 6, usually abortive in the fertile flowers; filaments very short, slender. Ovary superior, deeply 3-lobed, 3-celled, with 2 ovules in each cell; style very short or none; stigmas 3, recurved. Fruit a capsule with 3 broad wings, usually bursting irregularly.

This genus consists of about 24 species confined to the southern United States and Mexico. Only 2 are native to California.

KEY TO THE SPECIES

Leaves strongly serrulate; style present.......................... 1. *N. Parryi*.
Leaves entire or scarcely serrulate; style absent.................. 2. *N. Bigelovii*.

1. **Nolina Parryi** Wats. PARRY NOLINA. Fig. 25.

Stems unbranched, 3 to 6 feet high, with a crown of leaves at the summit spreading in all directions. Leaves thick, concave, rigid, 2 to 3½ feet long, ¾-inch to 1¼ inches wide, serrulate. Flowering stalk erect, 1½ to 2 feet long. Pedicels and branches of the inflorescences stout. Flowers about ¼-inch long. Capsule thin-walled, notched at both ends, about ½-inch long and about as broad, the seeds light brown in color and with very thin irregularly wrinkled seed-coats. Flowering period, May and June.

Parry Nolina grows in the Lower Sonoran Life Zone along the desert side of the San Bernardino Mountains, south through the San Jacinto Mountains, and on the western interior hills of Riverside and San Diego counties. Outside of California it is found in Arizona and in Lower California.

Nolina Parryi Wats. Proc. Am. Acad. 14:247 (1879). Type locality: "near Whitewater, desert slopes of the San Bernardino Mountains." Collected by *Parry*.

2. **Nolina Bigelovii** (Torr.) Wats. BIGELOW NOLINA.

Stems stout, 2 to 3 feet high. Leaves flat, 2½ to 4 feet long, about ¾-inch wide above the dilated base, the margins entire or scarcely serrulate, shredding into brown fibers. Flowering stalk 2 to 3½ feet long. Branchlets of the compound panicle slender, 1 to 2 inches long, jointed near the middle. Perianth-segments oblong-linear, ⅛-inch or less long. Capsule ¼-inch long and about as broad, the walls very thin, the seeds whitish gray, distinctly wrinkled. Flowering period, May and June.

Bigelow Nolina grows in the Lower Sonoran Life Zone in the mountains bordering the western Colorado Desert and in the Old Woman Mountains on the eastern Mohave Desert (acc. *Munz*). Outside of California it is found in Lower California and western Arizona.

Nolina Bigelovii (Torr.) Wats. Proc. Am. Acad. 14:247 (1879). *Dasylirion Bigelovii* Torr. Type locality: "mountain sides, Williams River, Arizona." Collected by *Bigelow*.

Salicaceae. Willow Family

The Willow Family contains 2 genera, *Populus* and *Salix*, with many species, widely distributed but most abundant in the north temperate and subarctic regions. Only the genus *Salix* has shrubby species native to California.

1. **Salix** L. WILLOW

(The ancient Latin name of the willow.)

Creeping or low shrubs or tall trees. Leaves simple, alternate, deciduous, usually with short petioles and persistent or deciduous stipules (or these absent). Winter bud-scales single, yellow, brown, or black. Flowers unisexual, male and female borne in catkins on separate plants (dioecious), appearing before, with, or after the leaves. Each flower subtended by a small scale (or bract), without sepals or petals, and with 1 or 2 small glands at the base of the scale; stamens 1 to many (usually 2 in ours), the filaments distinct or united at base, glabrous or hairy below; ovary 1-celled, 2-valved, sessile or short-pedicelled, glabrous or hairy; style evident or obsolete; stigmas entire or divided. Fruit a capsule, dehiscent by 2 valves, glabrous or hairy, sessile or pedicelled, with numerous small seeds with tufts of hairs at base.

The willows are among the most commonly recognized trees and shrubs that grow along water courses, around lakes, in wet meadows, and along seashores. The genus *Salix* is easily distinguished from other genera but the variation in leaf size and shape, the apparent intergrading of many forms, and the hybridization of the forms render this genus a very difficult one to separate into definite species. Over 300 species of willows have been described, mostly from the north temperate and arctic zones. About 30 species occur in California, 27 of which are shrubs or often shrub-like.

The excellent collection of *Salix* specimens at the University of California, annotated by Dr. C. R. Ball, and the text prepared by Dr. Ball for *An Illustrated Flora of the Pacific States* by Dr. LeRoy Abrams have been most useful in the preparation of the following key and diagnoses.

KEY TO THE SPECIES

[Leaf size refers to the leaves of fruiting branches.]

Low prostrate creeping shrubs, sometimes ascending to 2½ feet; capsule hairy.
- Leaves broadly oblong, obovate, or almost round, usually ½-inch or less long, glabrous; plants creeping, about 1 inch high . . . . 1. *S. nivalis.*
- Leaves elliptic to obovate or broadly elliptic-ovate, usually ½-inch or more long; plants creeping or ascending and erect, up to 2½ feet high.
  - Leaves hairy on the margins and usually on the upper surface; plants 2 to 4 inches high . . . . 2. *S. petrophila* var. *caespitosa.*
  - Leaves glabrous; plants 4 inches or up to 3½ feet high . . . . 3. *S. monica.*

Erect or spreading shrubs, 3 feet or more high.
- Petioles glandular at summit . . . . 4. *S. caudata* var. *Bryantiana.*
- Petioles not glandular at summit.
  1. Leaves linear to linear-lanceolate, or narrowly elliptical to oblanceolate, often 5 or more times longer than wide; filaments 2, distinct, pubescent or woolly below.
     - Capsules white-hairy; leaves usually silvery-hairy but varying to almost glabrous; style evident but very short; stigmas linear, 3 to 4 times longer than broad . . . . 5. *S. Hindsiana.*
     - Capsules glabrous; leaves pubescent to glabrous; style obsolete; stigmas less than 1/32-inch long.
       - Plants gray in appearance.
         - Leaves ⅛- to ⅜-inch wide; mostly east of the Sierra Nevada and in southern California . . . . 6. *S. exigua.*
         - Leaves ⅜- to ¾-inch wide; Humboldt and Del Norte counties. 7. *S. Parksiana.*

Plants green in appearance; mostly west side of the Sierra Nevada and in the Great Valley and Coast Ranges..........8. *S. melanopsis.*

2. Leaves broader in relation to the length, rarely more than 5 times longer than wide.

a. *Leaves less than ½-inch wide, entire.*

Filaments pubescent or long-hairy below.

Leaves glaucous below, not hairy; filaments almost distinct; styles evident or nearly obsolete; stigmas lobed.......9. *S. Lemmonii.*

Leaves silky-hairy on both surfaces, at least when young.

Filaments distinct; styles evident................27. *S. orestera.*

Filaments united at base; styles obsolete.
10. *S. Geyeriana* var. *argentea.*

Filaments glabrous.

Capsules hairy, sessile or the pedicels less than ¹⁄₁₆-inch long.

Leaves oblanceolate, usually obtuse at apex; capsules with very short pedicels............................11. *S. Jepsonii.*

Leaves lanceolate to oblong, acute at both ends; capsules sessile.................................12. *S. Breweri.*

Capsules glabrous.

Leaves glaucous below....................13. *S. Mackenziana.*

Leaves green below, or if pale not glaucous. 14. *S. pseudomyrsinites.*

b. *Leaves typically ½-inch or more wide.*

(1) *Filaments glabrous.*

(a) Stamen 1 (rarely 2); leaves silvery- or white-hairy beneath.

Leaves oblong-obovate or oblanceolate, silvery- or satiny-pubescent beneath; anthers purple..............16. *S. sitchensis.*

Leaves generally more oblong-elliptic, densely white-tomentose beneath; anthers yellow...................15. *S. Coulteri.*

(b) Stamens 2.

Filaments united at base; leaves glabrous above, glaucous (or white-tomentose in *S. Hookeriana*) beneath.

Leaves rather thin, pale or somewhat glaucescent beneath, glandular-serrate to entire, ovate to ovate-lanceolate.

Branchlets brown or greenish; leaves narrowly to broadly lanceolate, dark green above, serrulate to entire; catkins on short peduncles.
13. *S. Mackenziana.*

Branchlets yellow; leaves lanceolate to ovate-lanceolate, yellowish green above, glandular-serrulate; catkins sessile or very short-peduncled.
17. *S. lutea.*

Leaves thicker, very glaucous or white-hairy beneath, elliptic, obovate to oblanceolate, or broadly oval.

Leaves hairy beneath, broadly oval or broadly lanceolate; style less than ¹⁄₁₆-inch long.....................................18. *S. Hookeriana.*

Leaves not hairy beneath (except in some specimens of *S. lasiolepis*), usually broadly elliptical to oblanceolate or obovate.

Filaments united for ⅓ of their length; Humboldt and Del Norte counties.

Leaves 2¼ to 5 inches long............................19. *S. Piperi.*

Leaves 1⅛ to 2¼ inches long.........................20. *S. Tracyi.*

Filaments united at base but for much less than 1/3 their length; common in the hill and valley country. . . . . 21. *S. lasiolepis.*

Filaments free at base.

Styles none or not evident.

Scales of catkins black, long-hairy; common in Sierra Nevada and along the north coast. . . . . 22. *S. Scouleriana.*

Scales of catkins yellowish; rare, doubtfully in California. . . . 23. *S. Bebbiana.*

Styles evident.

Leaves densely hairy at maturity, at least below (sparsely hairy in some specimens of *S. Breweri* var. *delnortensis*).

Capsules glabrous or finely pubescent; catkins appearing with the leaves; leaves silky-pubescent to glabrate, not much paler beneath than above;

Capsules hairy.

Modoc and Siskiyou counties. 24. *S. commutata.*

Branchlets always covered with a bloom; leaves silvery-pubescent beneath. . . . . 25. *S. subcoerulea.*

Branchlets without a bloom; leaves densely hairy beneath.

Leaves linear-lanceolate; anthers yellow. . . . . 12. *S. Breweri.*

Leaves obovate-oblong or oblong-ovate; anthers purple.

12a. *S. Breweri* var. *delnortensis.*

Leaves not hairy at maturity.

Leaves green below, or scarcely paler than above. . 14. *S. pseudomyrsinites.*

Leaves glaucous beneath. . . . . 13. *S. Mackenziana.*

(2) *Filaments hairy below;* leaves hairy on both sides when young.

Styles evident.

Leaves elliptical to elliptic-obovate, green and gray-tomentose on both sides, glandular-serrate; catkins leafy-peduncled; 8000 to 9000 feet in the Sierra Nevada. . . . . 26. *S. Eastwoodiae.*

Leaves lanceolate to oblanceolate; green above and glaucous beneath, entire or nearly so, without marginal glands; catkins subsessile; high mountain slopes Sierra Nevada, 9000 to 12,000 feet. . . . . 27. *S. orestera.*

Styles obsolete. . . . . 7. *S. Parksiana.*

1. **Salix nivalis** Hook. Snow Willow. Fig. 26.

A dwarfed creeping subshrub, with branches about 1 inch high from buried stems. Leaf-blades oblong-obovate or almost round, 1/4- to 1/2-inch long, 1/8- to 3/8-inch wide, dark green and shining above, glaucous and prominently reticulately veined beneath, entire and somewhat revolute; petioles 1/16- to 1/4-inch long. Catkins appearing after the leaves, less than 1/2-inch long; scales yellowish, nearly glabrous; stamens 2; filaments glabrous, distinct; ovary and capsule tomentose or almost glabrous; style evident but very short.

Snow Willow is very rare in California, being known only from Mono County in the vicinity of Mount Dana east of the Sierra Crest. (North side of Mt. Dana, *Mrs. Bracelin;* between Parker Peak and Koip Peak, below the Koip Glacier, at 11,500 feet elevation, *Vernon Bailey;* Tioga Crest, *H. L. Mason;* Dora Plateau, *K. Sharsmith.*) It is known from the Arctic-alpine Zone in British Columbia and Alberta, southward in the Cascade and Rocky mountains to Washington, Colorado, and northern New Mexico.

Salix nivalis Hook. Fl. Bor. Am. 2:152 (1839). Type locality: "near the summits of the peaks in the Rocky Mountains, . . . Alberta or British Columbia."

2. **Salix petrophila** var. **caespitosa** (Kennedy) Schn. ALPINE WILLOW. Fig. 27.

A low creeping subshrub, with erect branches 2 to 4 inches high, from horizontal rooting stems. Leaf-blades elliptical to obovate, 1/4- to about 3/4-inch long, 1/8- to 3/8-inch wide, dark green and sparsely hairy above, paler and almost glaucous beneath, the margins entire and hairy; petioles 1/8-inch or less long. Catkins appearing with the leaves, on erect leafy peduncles; the staminate 3/8- to 3/4-inch long; the pistillate 3/4-inch to 1 3/4 inches long; scales brown to black, hairy within and without; filaments 2, glabrous, distinct; ovary and capsule gray-tomentose, almost sessile; styles evident.

Alpine Willow inhabits the higher mountain peaks of the Sierra Nevada from Mount Lassen southward to Mount Whitney and adjacent Nevada, at 8500 to 12,000 feet elevation in the Arctic-alpine Life Zone. This is the common willow which forms the carpet-like masses along the banks of streams leading from the melting snow.

Salix petrophila var. caespitosa (Kennedy) Schn. Bot. Gaz. 66:136 (1918). *S. caespitosa* Kennedy. Type locality: "Mount Rose, Washoe County, Nevada." *S. petrophila* Rydb. of Jepson's Manual.

3. **Salix monica** Bebb. MONO WILLOW. Fig. 28.

A low semi-prostrate or erect shrub, 1/2-foot to 3 feet high, with yellowish green or brownish red twigs and branches. Leaf-blades ovate to obovate, 3/8-inch to 1 1/4 inches long, 1/4- to 1/2-inch wide, glabrous and bright green above, a little paler beneath, entire or remotely serrulate; petioles 1/8- to 1/4-inch long. Catkins appearing with the leaves, 3/8-inch to 1 1/4 inches long, almost sessile; scales brownish to nearly black, with long yellowish white hairs; filaments 2, glabrous, united at base; ovary and capsule pubescent, short-pedicelled; styles evident.

Mono Willow occurs in the high Sierra Nevada of Tuolumne and Mono counties. Specimens have been examined from Upper Gaylor Lake, from between Mount Dana and Mount Gibbs, the Soda Springs of Tuolumne County, and near Mono Pass, Mono County. It occurs in the Hudsonian and Arctic-alpine Life Zones from 8500 to 13,000 feet elevation.

Salix monica Bebb; Bot. Calif. 2:90 (1880). Type locality: "Mono Pass Summit," Mono County, California. *S. phylicifolia* var. *monica* (Bebb) Jepson.

4. **Salix caudata** var. **Bryantiana** Ball & Bracelin. BRYANT WILLOW. Fig. 29.

An erect shrub, 3 to 15 feet high, with several stems from a clustered base. Twigs and branches brownish red, glabrous, shining. Leaf-blades lanceolate, 2 1/4 to 5 1/2 inches long, 1/2-inch to 1 1/4 inches wide, dark green and glabrous above, green or paler but not glaucous beneath, glandular-serrulate; petioles 1/8- to 1/4-inch long, glabrous, glandular at summit. Catkins appearing with the leaves; scales yellow, glabrate or glabrous; the staminate catkins 3/4-inch to 1 1/2 inches long; stamens 3 to 9; filaments hairy below; pistillate catkins 1 to 2 inches long; ovary and capsule glabrous; styles evident.

Bryant Willow occurs occasionally along mountain streams and in wet meadows from 6000 to 7500 feet altitude from the San Bernardino Mountains (Bear Valley, *S. B. Parrish*) northward in the Sierra Nevada of Tulare, Placer, Nevada (lower end of Donner Lake, *Heller*), Sierra, Plumas, and Modoc counties. It extends northward east of and rarely in the Cascades of Oregon, Washington, and British

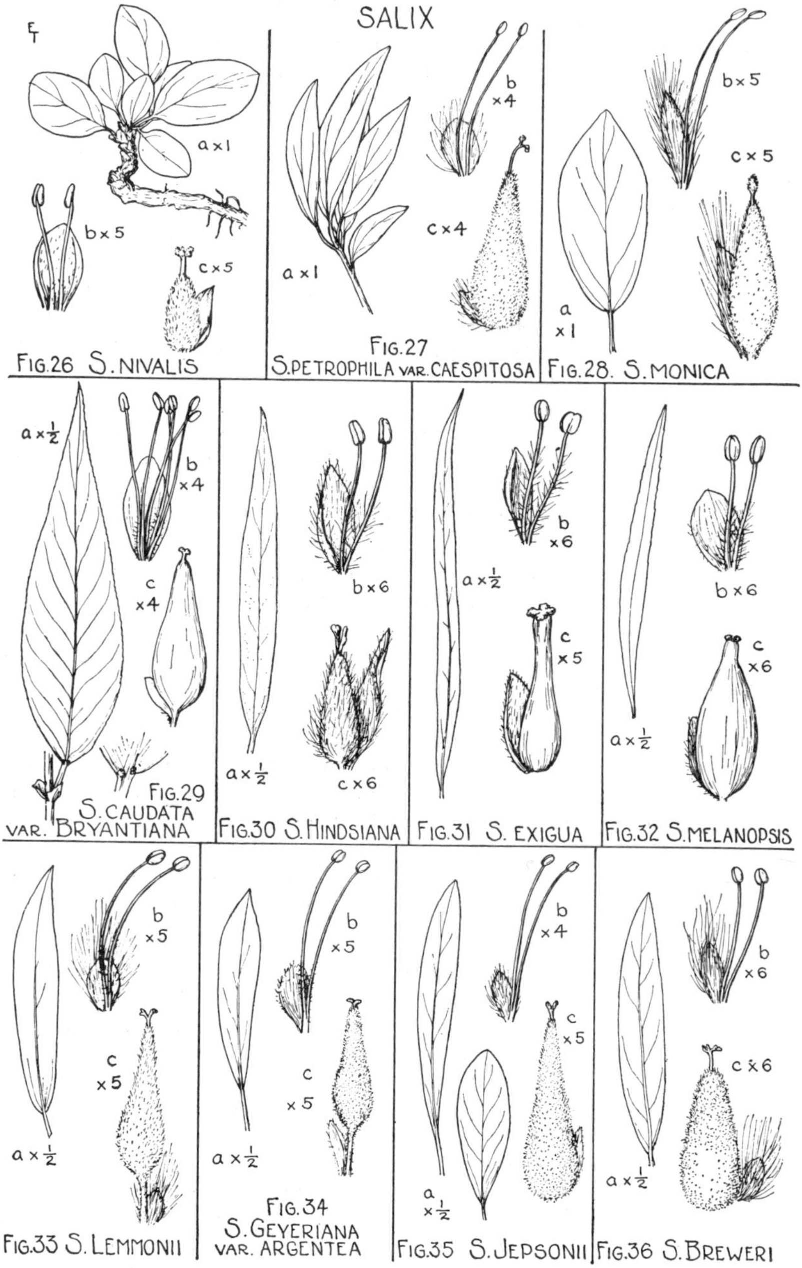

SALIX. a, Leaf. b, Staminate flower. c. Pistillate flower.

Columbia, eastward throughout the Rocky Mountains to the Black Hills of South Dakota.

Salix caudata var. Bryantiana Ball & Bracelin, Jour. Wash. Acad. Sci. 28:445 (1938). Type locality: Snow Valley, Ormsby County, Nevada. Collected by *C. F. Baker*.

5. **Salix Hindsiana** Benth. SANDBAR WILLOW. VALLEY WILLOW. Fig. 30.

An erect shrub or small tree, 6 to 25 feet high, with slender gray stems, the young stems densely gray-tomentose. Leaf-blades linear to linear-lanceolate, tapering to both ends, 1½ to 3¼ inches long, ⅛- to ⅜-inch wide, thinly gray-villous or green and glabrate or densely villous and silky, especially on young and sterile shoots, entire or rarely slightly denticulate; petioles less than ⅛-inch long or the blades tapering to a petiole-like base. Catkins appearing after the leaves, on leafy peduncles; the staminate ⅜-inch to 1 inch long; stamens 2; filaments pubescent, distinct; the pistillate ½-inch to 1 inch long; ovary sessile, silky; styles evident; stigmas divided; capsules silky-villous or becoming almost glabrous.

Sandbar Willow is one of our most common willows occurring along stream and river banks of the Great Valley, the Coast Ranges, southern California, and the Sierra Nevada foothills up to about 3000 feet elevation. It extends northward to southern Oregon and southward to Lower California. It spreads very rapidly by underground stems and often becomes a real nuisance in irrigation ditches in the Great Valley.

The plants from Ventura and Kern counties southward to San Diego County have been considered by some authors to constitute the variety **S. Hindsiana leucodendroides** (Rowl.) Ball. The leaves are usually larger and more denticulate than those of the northern specimens. A form with very narrow leaves from San Luis Obispo, Ventura, Los Angeles, Orange, and Riverside counties is known by the variety name, **S. Hindsiana Parishiana** (Rowl.) Ball. The capsules are thinly hairy at first but become glabrate in age.

Salix Hindsiana Benth. Pl. Hartw. 335 (1857). Type locality: Along the Sacramento River. *S. sessilifolia* var. *Hindsiana* (Benth.) Anderss. *S. argophylla* Nutt., acc. Jepson, in part.

6. **Salix exigua** Nutt. NARROWLEAF WILLOW. SLENDER WILLOW. Fig. 31.

A tall shrub, 6 to 15 feet high, with grayish appearance. Leaf-blades linear to oblanceolate, 2 to 5 inches long, ⅛- to ⅜-inch wide, more or less pubescent or silky on both surfaces, or often glabrate above, entire or remotely glandular-serrulate, almost sessile. Catkins appearing after the leaves on leafy peduncle-like branchlets, ¾-inch to 2 inches long; scales yellowish, more or less hairy; stamens 2; filaments distinct, hairy below; ovary glabrous, sessile; styles obsolete; stigmas divided; capsules glabrous, short-pedicelled.

Narrowleaf Willow inhabits wet places and banks of mountain streams east of the Sierra Nevada from Modoc County southward to southern California, in the Upper Sonoran and Transition Life Zones. It extends northward to British Columbia and eastward to New Mexico and Texas.

Salix exigua Nutt. Sylva 1:75 (1843). Type locality: "probably 'on the banks of Lewis River of the Shoshone' (the Snake River, in Idaho)."

7. **Salix Parksiana** Ball. SMITH RIVER WILLOW.

A low to medium-sized shrub, 3 to 8 feet high, with gray bark and pilose brown branchlets. Leaf-blades usually narrowly to broadly elliptical, acute at both ends,

1¾ to 4½ inches long, ⅜- to ¾-inch wide, densely to thinly gray-pilose on both surfaces, irregularly and sometimes remotely glandular-denticulate, sessile except on vigorous shoots. Catkins appearing with the leaves, solitary or in clusters of 2 to 4, 1½ to 3 inches long; scales yellowish, thinly pilose, becoming glabrate; stamens 2; filaments distinct, densely hairy on their basal ½ or ⅔; ovary glabrous or thinly pilose; styles obsolete; stigmas very short, divided; capsules glabrous, sessile or subsessile.

Smith River Willow occurs on gravel bars and in sandy beds or banks of streams along a narrow coastal area about 100 miles long in Humboldt and Del Norte counties, California.

Salix Parksiana Ball, Univ. Calif. Publ. Bot. 17:400 (1934). Type locality: Staminate specimen from gravel bars of the Smith River, near Roosevelt Highway Bridge, Del Norte County. Pistillate specimen from gravel beds along the Van Duzen River, between Alton and Carlotta, Humboldt County. Collected by *H. E. Parks.*

8. **Salix melanopsis** Nutt. Dusky Willow. Longleaf Willow. Fig. 32.

A tall shrub or small tree, 6 to 15 feet high, with dark green appearance. Leaf-blades linear-lanceolate to oblanceolate, tapering to both ends, 1½ to 3 (rarely 5) inches long, ¼- to ⅝-inch wide, dark green and glabrous above, somewhat paler beneath, denticulate with sharp-pointed teeth or almost entire; petiole very short or almost absent. Catkins appearing after the leaves, ¾-inch to 1½ inches long; scales yellowish, more or less hairy; stamens 2; filaments distinct, hairy below; ovary glabrous; styles obsolete; stigmas very short; capsules glabrous, subsessile.

Dusky Willow inhabits stream beds and banks in the valleys and foothills of the North Coast Range in Sonoma and Lake counties and extends northward to Glenn, Tehama, Trinity, Humboldt, and Del Norte counties, eastward into Siskiyou, Shasta, and Modoc counties, thence southward in the foothills and lower slopes of the Sierra Nevada to Tulare and Kern counties. Specimens have been collected also from the San Antonio and Argus mountains of southern California. This species extends northward to the Rocky Mountains of British Columbia and Alberta and eastward to northern Utah, Montana, and Wyoming.

Salix melanopsis Nutt. Sylva 1:78 (1843). Type locality: "Fort Hall, on the alluvial lands of Lewis River of the Shoshone" (the Snake River of southeastern Idaho). *S. melanopsis* var. *Bolanderiana* Schn.

9. **Salix Lemmonii** Bebb. Lemmon Willow. Fig. 33.

A rounded shrub, 4 to 12 feet high, with many ascending stems from a clustered base. Twigs and branches yellowish green or brown, shining and usually glabrous. Leaf-blades lanceolate, oblanceolate, or narrowly elliptic-lanceolate, 1½ to 3½ inches long, ⅜- to ⅝-inch wide, deep green and shining above, glabrate beneath and usually glaucescent, finely denticulate or entire; petioles about ¼-inch long. Catkins appearing with the leaves, ½-inch to 1 inch long, on short peduncles with 2 or 3 foliaceous bracts; scales black, hairy on both sides; stamens 2; filaments almost distinct, pubescent at base; ovary pedicellate, pubescent; styles very short or almost obsolete; stigmas lobed; capsules pedicellate, silky-pubescent.

Lemmon Willow is common in swampy meadows where it often covers large areas in the Sierra Nevada from 5000 to 10,000 feet elevation. It extends from southern Siskiyou (Mt. Eddy) and Modoc counties southward through the Sierra Nevada to Tulare County, and reappears in the San Bernardino Mountains (banks of Dollar Lake, *P. A. Munz*) of southern California, in the Canadian and Hudsonian Life Zones. It extends northward to Oregon and eastward to Nevada.

Salix Lemmonii Bebb; Bot. Calif. 2:88 (1880). Type locality: Sierra County, California.

10. **Salix Geyeriana** var. **argentea** (Bebb) Schn. SILVER WILLOW. Fig. 34.

A slender shrub, 5 to 16 feet high, with several stems clustered from the base. Twigs and branchlets pubescent or white-glaucous. Leaf-blades lanceolate or linear-oblanceolate, 1 to 2½ inches long, ¼- to ½-inch wide, entire, silky-hairy on both surfaces or becoming green and glabrous above, permanently silky beneath; petioles ⅛- to ¼-inch long. Catkins appearing with the leaves on short peduncles with 2 or 3 foliaceous bracts; the staminate ⅓- to ½-inch long; the pistillate subglobose, about ⅓-inch long; fruiting catkins ½- to ¾-inch long, the scales yellowish, often tipped with red; stamens 2; filaments united at base, densely hairy below; ovary and capsule pedicelled, pubescent; styles almost obsolete.

Silver Willow occurs in the Warner Mountains of Modoc County and extends southward in the Sierra Nevada through Tehama, Butte, Plumas, Sierra, Eldorado, Alpine, Mono, and eastern Tulare counties, from about 7500 to 9000 feet elevation, in the Canadian Life Zone.

Salix Geyeriana var. argentea (Bebb) Schn. Jour. Arn. Arb. 2:74 (1920). *S. macrocarpa* var. *argentea* Bebb. Type locality: "Sierra County, Plumas County," California.

11. **Salix Jepsonii** Schn. JEPSON WILLOW. Fig. 35.

An erect shrub, 3 to 6 feet high, with chestnut to dark purple twigs and branchlets. Leaf-blades linear to oblanceolate, usually obtuse at apex, 1¼ to 3 inches long, ¼- to almost ½-inch wide, entire, somewhat silky above, densely silky-tomentose beneath; petioles ⅛- to ¼-inch long. Catkins appearing before or with the leaves; the staminate almost sessile, ⅜- to ¾-inch long; the pistillate ¾ inch to 1½ inches long, on bracted peduncles; scales brown, densely pilose; stamens 2; filaments glabrous, distinct or sometimes united at the base or even almost to the middle; ovary very short-pedicelled, pubescent; styles evident; capsules densely silky-pubescent.

Jepson Willow has been confused with various forms of *S. sitchensis* Sanson and *S. commutata* Bebb. It has a much wider distribution than has been recorded in the various publications to date. This willow occurs at elevations from 5500 to 10,000 feet in the North Coast Range and in the central Sierra Nevada. Specimens have been examined from the South Fork Mountains of Humboldt and Trinity counties, the Klamath Mountains, Yosemite Valley (Nevada Falls), and from Mariposa, Placer, Eldorado, Tuolumne, Mono, Fresno, and Tulare counties.

Salix Jepsonii Schn. Jour. Arn. Arb. 1:89 (1919). Type locality: "high mountains near Donner Pass, Placer County, California." *S. sitchensis* var. *angustifolia* Bebb. *S. sitchensis* var. *Ralphiana* Jepson.

12. **Salix Breweri** Bebb. BREWER WILLOW. Fig. 36.

A low spreading shrub, 1 to 2½ feet high, with slender dark brown branchlets. Leaf-blades linear-lanceolate to oblong, 1 to 2½ inches long, ¼- to ½-inch wide, entire, dull green and puberulent above, paler beneath with a gray tomentum thickly covering the reticulated raised veins; petioles less than ⅛-inch long or almost none. Catkins appearing before or with the leaves; scales yellowish, long-hairy; the staminate ½- to ¾-inch long; stamens 2; filaments glabrous, distinct;

the pistillate ¾-inch to 1½ inches long; ovary and capsule hairy, sessile; styles evident.

Brewer Willow usually occurs in dry ravines of the Upper Sonoran Life Zone in the inner Coast Ranges of San Luis Obispo, San Benito, Santa Clara, Napa, Lake, and Colusa counties.

12a. Var. **delnortensis** (Schn.) Jepson.

Similar to the species except the leaves usually obovate and the anthers purple.

This variety is known only from near Gasquets on the Smith River, Del Norte County, California.

Salix Breweri Bebb; Bot. Calif. 2:89 (1880). Type locality: "on San Carlos Mountain, in a dry ravine, at 3500 feet elevation, San Benito County, California."

Var. delnortensis (Schn.) Jepson, Man. 267 (1925). *S. delnortensis* Schn. Type locality: "Gasquets, Del Norte County, California."

13. **Salix Mackenziana** (Hook.) Barr. MACKENZIE WILLOW. Fig. 37.

An erect shrub or small tree, 6 to 25 feet high, with dark brown or yellowish branchlets. Leaf-blades lanceolate or oblong-lanceolate, rounded to somewhat heart-shaped at base, 2 to 4 inches long, ¾-inch to 1½ inches wide, green and glabrous above, paler and glaucous beneath, glandular-serrate or entire; petioles ⅛- to ⅜-inch long. Catkins appearing with the leaves on short peduncles with 2 or 3 foliaceous bracts; scales black, hairy; the staminate catkins ¾-inch to 1½ inches long; stamens 2; filaments distinct or united at the very base, glabrous; the pistillate catkins 1 to 2¼ inches long; styles evident; ovary and capsule pedicelled, glabrous.

Mackenzie Willow is rare in California, having been collected, to my knowledge, only in Sequoia National Park, Tulare County, in the Yosemite Valley, Mariposa County, and in Siskiyou and Modoc counties. It extends northward to Oregon, Washington, and British Columbia and eastward to Nevada, Utah, and Montana.

Salix Mackenziana (Hook.) Barr.; Anderss. Svensk. Vet. Akad. Handl. (Monogr. Sal.) 6:160 (1867). *S. cordata* var. *Mackenziana* Hook. Type locality: "Great Slave Lake and Mackenzie River." *S. cordata* Muhl. of Jepson's Manual.

14. **Salix pseudomyrsinites** Anderss. FIRMLEAF WILLOW.

Characters of the key.

I have seen no specimens from California that answer to the description of this species. According to Ball it occurs in the high Sierras of California and in southern British Columbia through Washington and Oregon, east of the Cascade Mountains, and east to Saskatchewan and south in the Rockies to New Mexico.

Salix pseudomyrsinites Anderss.; Oefv. Svensk. Vet. Akad. Förh. 15:129 (1858). *S. pseudocordata* of authors, in part.

15. **Salix Coulteri** Anderss. VELVET WILLOW. COULTER WILLOW. Fig. 38.

An erect shrub or small tree, 6 to 20 feet high, with stoutish brown-pubescent or tomentose branchlets. Leaf-blades variable, somewhat thick and leathery, oblanceolate or obovate, 1¾ to 5 inches long, ¾-inch to 2 inches wide, entire or nearly so, dark green and almost glabrous, with impressed veins above, densely white silky-tomentose beneath; petioles ⅛- to ½-inch long. Catkins appearing with the leaves, on very short peduncles with 2 or 3 leafy bracts; scales brownish, with long white silky hairs; staminate catkins 1¼ to 2¾ inches long; stamen 1; filament glabrous; anthers yellow; pistillate catkins 1 to 2½ inches long; fruiting catkins 2 to 5 inches long; ovary and capsule pedicelled and silky-tomentose; styles evident.

Velvet Willow inhabits stream banks and draws of the outer Coast Range from San Luis Obispo County northward along the coast to Humboldt and Del Norte counties. It extends northward to Washington. This willow can be distinguished by the very silky tomentum of the lower leaf-surface and by the single stamen.

Salix Coulteri Anderss.; Oefv. Svensk. Vet. Akad. Förh. 15:119 (1858). Type locality: "in California, probably Monterey." *S. sitchensis* var. *Coulteri* (Anderss.) Jepson.

16. **Salix sitchensis** Sanson. SITKA WILLOW. Fig. 39.

This willow is very closely related to *Salix Coulteri* Anderss. and by some writers the two are considered the same. Ball, in his descriptions of the two species in the *Illustrated Flora of the Pacific States* by LeRoy Abrams, brings out the following differences. In *S. sitchensis,* the branchlets are slender, glabrous or rarely pubescent and in *S. Coulteri* they are stoutish, pubescent to densely tomentose. Specimens annotated by Ball in the University of California Herbarium and filed as *S. sitchensis* were collected at the foot of Mount Hood, Sonoma County; Independence Creek, Siskiyou County; Trinity Summit, Humboldt County; and at Gasquet, Del Norte County. It extends northward to Alaska.

Salix sitchensis Sanson; Bongard, Mem. Acad. Sci. St. Petersb. 7, 2:162 (1833). Type locality: "Indian River, near Sitka, Alaska."

17. **Salix lutea** Nutt. YELLOW WILLOW. Fig. 40.

An erect shrub, 6 to 15 feet high, with yellow or reddish brown glabrous twigs. Leaf-blades oblong-lanceolate or ovate-lanceolate to narrowly lanceolate, rather thin, 1½ to 3½ inches long, ⅝-inch to 1½ inches wide, yellowish green above, paler and glaucescent beneath, finely serrulate to entire; petioles ⅛- to ¼-inch long. Catkins appearing before and with the leaves, ¾-inch to 1½ inches long, on very short leafy peduncles; scales brown, thinly hairy; stamens 2; filaments glabrous, united at base; ovary and capsule glabrous, pedicelled.

Yellow Willow occurs along streams and in wet places in the high mountains in the Transition and Canadian Life Zones from the San Bernardino and San Jacinto mountains northward on the east side of the Sierra Nevada to Kern, Inyo, and Modoc counties. It extends northward to Washington and northern Alberta and east to Arizona and Colorado.

Salix lutea Nutt. Sylva 1:63 (1843). Type locality: "Rocky Mountains westward to the Oregon" (Columbia River). *S. lutea* var. *Watsonii* (Bebb) Jepson.

18. **Salix Hookeriana** Barr. COAST WILLOW. Fig. 41.

An erect shrub or small tree, 6 to 25 feet high, with rough dark gray bark. Leaf-blades rather thick, broadly elliptical or broadly lanceolate, 1¼ to 5 inches long, ½-inch to 1½ inches wide, dark green and glabrous above, densely white-hairy beneath, finely serrulate or crenulate to entire; petioles ¼- to ⅜-inch long. Catkins appearing before the leaves, on short leafy peduncles; scales black, long-hairy; staminate catkins 1¾ to 2 inches long; stamens 2; filaments glabrous, united at base; pistillate catkins 1½ to 2¾ inches long; ovary and capsule glabrous, short-pedicelled; styles evident.

Coast Willow occurs at the mouths of rivers and in lagoons along the seashore of Mendocino, Humboldt, and Del Norte counties. It extends northward to Vancouver Island.

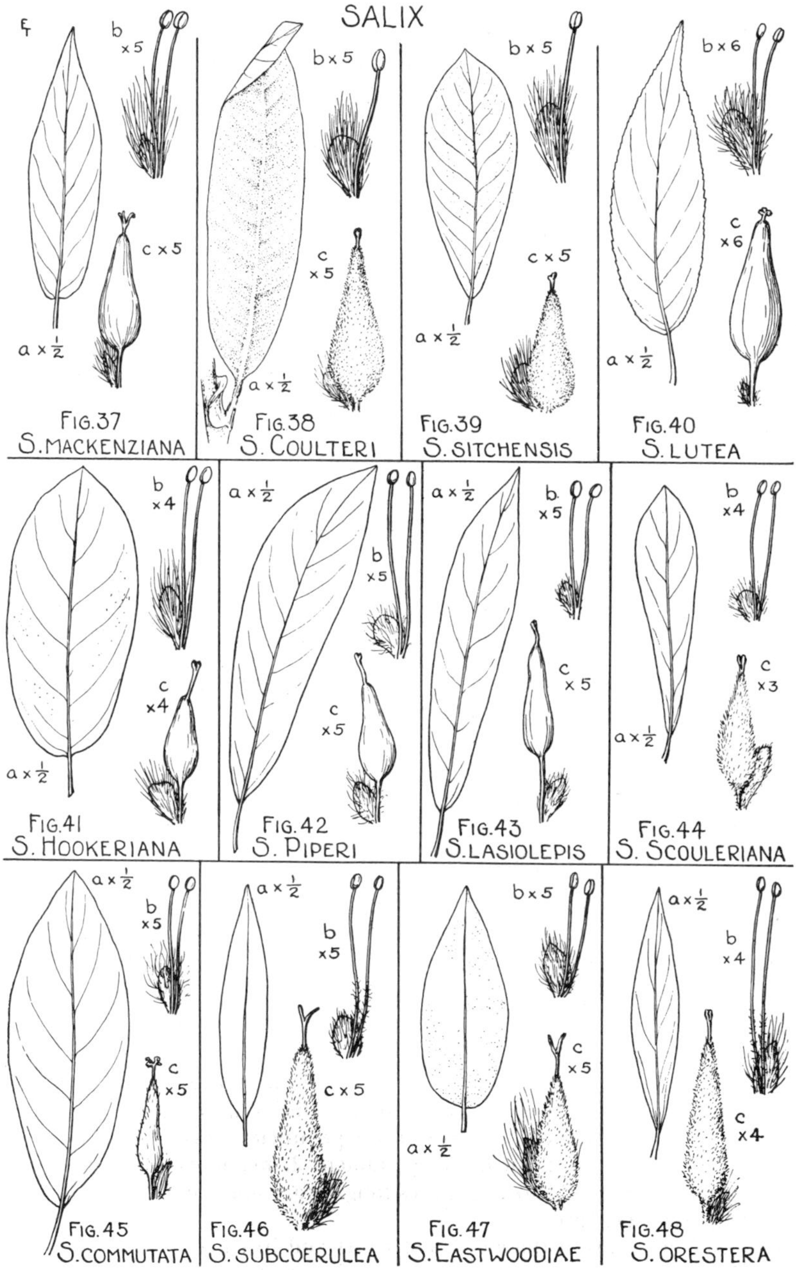

SALIX. a, Leaf. b, Staminate flower. c, Pistillate flower.

A form with tomentose capsules has been collected at the mouth of the Caspar River, Mendocino County and on the sand dunes near Samoa, Humboldt County. It has been described as **S. Hookeriana** var. **tomentosa** Henry.

Salix Hookeriana Barr.; Hook. Fl. Bor. Am. 2:145 (1839). Type locality: "N. W. Coast of America."

19. **Salix Piperi** Bebb. PIPER WILLOW. DUNE WILLOW. Fig. 42.

An erect large shrub, 12 to 20 feet high, with stout shining glabrous branchlets. Leaf-blades rather thick, broadly elliptical or oblanceolate, 2¼ to 5 inches long, 1¾ to 2 inches wide, dark green and glabrous above, glaucous beneath, serrulate to entire; petioles ⅛- to ½-inch long. Catkins appearing before or with the leaves on short leafy peduncles, scales brown, long-hairy; staminate catkins 1 to 2 inches long; stamens 2; filaments glabrous, united for about ⅓ their lengths; pistillate catkins 1½ to 4 inches long; ovary and capsule glabrous, pedicelled; styles evident.

Piper Willow is rare in California, occurring intermingled with *S. Hookeriana* at the mouth of the Caspar River in Mendocino County and at a few other scattered localities along the coast of Humboldt and Del Norte counties. It extends north to Washington.

The glaucous lower leaf-surfaces and general habit of growth cause it to be confused with the large-leaf forms of *S. lasiolepis*.

Salix Piperi Bebb, Gard. & For. 8:482 (1895). Type locality: "Lake Washington, Seattle, Washington."

20. **Salix Tracyi** Ball. TRACY WILLOW.

A slender shrub or small tree, 6 to 15 feet high, with smooth grayish green trunks and slender grayish yellow to brownish glabrous branchlets. Leaf-blades oblanceolate, elliptical-oblanceolate, or narrowly obovate, 1⅛ to 2¼ inches long, ⅝- to ¾-inch wide, or up to 5 inches long and 1¼ inches wide on vigorous shoots, green above, glaucous beneath, entire or crenate-serrulate on vegetative shoots; petioles ⅛- to ¼-inch long or longer on vegetative shoots. Catkins appearing before or with the leaves on the shoots of the previous season, ¾-inch to 2 inches long; stamens 2; filaments glabrous, united at base for about ⅓ of their lengths; ovary and capsule glabrous, long-pedicelled; styles evident; stigmas about equalling the styles, entire or notched. Flowering period, late April and throughout May.

Tracy Willow inhabits sand and gravel bars of the rivers and streams of northwestern California and adjacent Oregon. It is closely related to *S. lasiolepis* but differs in its more slender branchlets, thinner and less veiny leaves, and later flowering period.

Salix Tracyi Ball, Univ. Calif. Publ. Bot. 17:403 (1934). Type locality: Smith River, Del Norte County, California. Collected by *Tracy, Parks,* and *Ball.*

21. **Salix lasiolepis** Benth. ARROYO WILLOW. Fig. 43.

An erect shrub or small tree, 6 to 20 or rarely up to 30 feet high, with smooth bark and brownish or yellowish branchlets. Leaf-blades variable, narrowly to broadly oblanceolate, or oblong-obovate, or rarely almost linear, 2 to 5 inches long, ⅜-inch to 1 inch or more wide, dark green and glabrous above, paler and glaucous or pubescent beneath; obscurely finely serrulate or apparently entire, often somewhat revolute, petioles ⅛- to ½-inch long. Catkins appearing before the leaves, apparently sessile; the staminate ¾-inch to 1½ inches long; stamens 2; filaments glabrous, united at base; the pistillate ¾-inch to 1¼ inches long; fruiting catkins 1 to 2¼ inches long; scales dark brown to almost black, densely hairy; ovary and capsule glabrous or puberulent, pedicelled; styles evident. Flowering period, February to April.

Arroyo Willow is one of the most common willows of the valleys and foothills throughout California. It inhabits dry or living stream banks and beds of the Upper Sonoran and Transition Life Zones, from sea level up to 5000 feet elevation. It extends northward to Washington and Idaho, eastward to Nevada and Arizona, and southward to Mexico.

21a. Var. **Sandbergii** (Rydb.) Ball.

"Differs from the species in the more broadly oblanceolate to obovate leaves and the much denser and more permanent pubescence of all the vegetative organs, namely, branchlets, budscales, and leaves."

This variety occurs in the Coast Ranges and in the Sierra Nevada of northern California. It extends northward into Oregon, Washington, and western Idaho.

21b. Var. **Bigelovii** (Torr.) Bebb.

Leaf-blades broadly cuneate-oblanceolate to obovate, often densely pubescent beneath, entire. Catkins peduncled.

This variety occurs occasionally with the species in the San Francisco Bay region.

Salix lasiolepis Benth. Pl. Hartw. 335 (1857). Type locality: Along the Salinas and Carmel rivers, California.

Var. Sandbergii (Rydb.) Ball, Jour. Wash. Acad. Sci. 448 (1938). *S. Sandbergii* Rydb. Type locality: Northern Idaho.

Var. Bigelovii (Torr.) Bebb; Bot. Calif. 2:86 (1880). Type locality: "near San Francisco," California. *S. Bigelovii* Torr.

22. **Salix Scouleriana** Barr. NUTTALL WILLOW. SCOULER WILLOW. Fig. 44.

A shrub or small tree, 3 to 30 feet tall, usually with many stems spreading from the base. Branches commonly with whitish bark. Leaf-blades variable, usually oblanceolate or obovate, 1¼ to 4 inches long, ½-inch to 1½ inches wide, green and glabrous above, silvery-pubescent or glabrate to glaucous beneath; entire or very shallowly dentate; petioles about ¼- to ½-inch long. Catkins appearing before the leaves, ½-inch to 1 inch long, almost sessile; scales obovate, black, hairy; stamens 2, long-exserted; filaments glabrous, distinct; ovary and capsule white-hairy, pedicelled; styles none (or very short); stigmas linear, often divided.

Nuttall Willow occurs in the Sierra Nevada from Modoc and Siskiyou counties southward to Tulare County at 4000 to 10,000 feet elevation, in the Coast Ranges near the coast from Del Norte County southward to Alameda and Monterey counties, and in the San Antonio, San Jacinto, and San Bernardino mountains of southern California, in the Transition and Canadian Life Zones. It extends northward to Alaska and eastward to the Rocky Mountains.

Salix Scouleriana Barr; Hook. Fl. Bor. Am. 2:145 (1839). Type locality: Along the Columbia River. *S. flavescens* Nutt.

23. **Salix Bebbiana** Sarg. BEBB WILLOW.

Characters of the key.

It is very doubtful that this willow occurs in California. No specimens are filed at the University of California Herbarium. According to Ball, it occurs in the "Boreal zones; Alaska and Yukon south to Central California, Arizona and New Mexico, east to Labrador, Newfoundland and New Jersey. Rare west of the Cascades."

Salix Bebbiana Sarg. Gard. & For. 8:463 (1895). Type locality: "wooded country from lat. 54° to 64° north," Northwest Territory, Canada.

24. **Salix commutata** Bebb. MOUNTAIN WILLOW. Fig. 45.

Characters of the key.

This species occurs in the Warner Mountains of Modoc County and in Siskiyou County. It extends northward to Alaska and eastward to Wyoming and Montana.

Salix commutata Bebb as described in the *Manual of Flowering Plants of California* by Jepson is here assigned in most part to *S. Eastwoodiae* Ckl.

Salix commutata Bebb, Bot. Gaz. 13:110 (1888). Type locality: "Eagle Creek (or Wallowa) Mountains, Wallowa County, Oregon."

25. **Salix subcoerulea** Piper. BLUISH WILLOW. Fig. 46.

Characters of the key.

Bluish Willow occurs locally in the high mountains of Fresno, Inyo, and Tulare counties. One specimen was seen from "the borders of stream in Onion Valley, 1/2-mile north of end of road, elevation 9400 feet, Inyo County." It extends northward to eastern Oregon and Washington and eastward to Utah and New Mexico.

Salix subcoerulea Piper, Bull. Torr. Club 27:400 (1900). Type locality: "Powder River Mountains, Wallowa County, Oregon."

26. **Salix Eastwoodiae** Ckl. EASTWOOD WILLOW. Fig. 47.

A low shrub, 2 to 6 feet high, with usually dark brown tomentose branchlets. Leaf-blades elliptical or elliptical-obovate, 1 to 2 1/2 inches long, 1/2-inch to 1 inch wide, gray-tomentose on both sides or green and glabrate in age, very finely glandular-serrulate; petioles about 1/4-inch long. Catkins appearing with the leaves, on leafy peduncles; the staminate 3/8-inch to 1 inch long; the pistillate 3/4-inch to 1 3/4 inches long; scales brown, hairy; stamens 2; filaments distinct, hairy at base; styles evident; ovary and capsule gray-tomentose; pedicels less than 1/16-inch long.

Eastwood Willow is one of the more common broad- and gray-leaved willows of the high Sierra Nevada, occurring in the Canadian and Hudsonian Life Zones from 8000 to 10,000 feet elevation. It extends from the Warner Mountains of Modoc County south through the Sierra Nevada to Tulare County, northward to Washington and Idaho, and eastward to Nevada. This willow is easily confused with *S. orestera* Schn., from which it differs in the leafy-pedunculate catkins and broader glandular-serrulate leaves.

Salix Eastwoodiae Ckl.; Heller, Cat. N. Am. Pl. ed. 2, 89 (1910). *S. californica* Bebb. *S. commutata* Bebb, of Jepson's Manual.

27. **Salix orestera** Schn. GRAYLEAF SIERRA WILLOW. Fig. 48.

A spreading or erect shrub, 3 to 8 feet high, with brown tomentose branchlets. Leaf-blades lanceolate to oblanceolate, 1 1/2 to 2 1/2 inches long, 3/8- to 3/4-inch wide, thinly silky-villous on both surfaces, green above, glaucous beneath, densely tomentose on both sides when young, entire; petioles 1/4-inch or less long. Catkins appearing with the leaves on very short leafy peduncles or sessile; the staminate 1/2-inch to 1 inch long; fruiting catkins 3/4-inch to 2 inches long; scales dark brown, hairy; stamens 2; filaments usually distinct, hairy below; styles evident; ovary and capsule silky-villous; pedicels 1/16-inch or more long.

Grayleaf Sierra Willow occurs in the Sierra Nevada in the Canadian, Hudsonian, and Arctic-alpine Life Zones from 8000 to 12,000 feet elevation. It extends from Tulare County northward to Lassen County and eastward to Elko County, Nevada.

The entire and less tomentose leaves, almost sessile catkins, and longer pedicels separate this species from *S. Eastwoodiae*.

Salix orestera Schn. Jour. Arn. Arb. 1:164 (1920). Type locality: "Mount Goddard, Fresno County, California." *S. glauca* var. *orestera* (Schn.) Jepson. *S. glauca* var. *villosa* of Calif. authors, not Anderss.

Betulaceae. Birch Family

The Birch Family contains 6 genera and about 80 species of trees and shrubs mostly in the north temperate zone of both hemispheres, but a few species extend south into the south temperate zone in the Andes. Three genera and 7 species are native to California, 5 of which are shrubby.

KEY TO THE GENERA

Leaves typically pubescent on both surfaces, cordate at base; fruit a nut enclosed in a leafy involucre; pistillate flowers borne in a small oval scaly or bracted cluster, with protruding red stigmas..........................1. CORYLUS.

Leaves rarely pubescent on both surfaces, not cordate at base; fruit a cone containing many nutlets; pistillate flowers borne in small catkins.

Pistillate catkins solitary, cylindrical in fruit; fruiting scales thin and 3-lobed, falling away at maturity and releasing the nutlets.............2. BETULA.

Pistillate catkins in short clusters, short-ellipsoidal in fruit; fruiting scales woody and obscurely toothed, persistent, the whole falling as a woody cone. 3. ALNUS.

1. **Corylus** L. HAZEL. HAZELNUT

(From the Greek *korys,* a hood or helmet, in reference to the involucre covering the nut.)

This genus contains about 15 species of shrubs and trees of the northern hemisphere in Europe, Asia, and North America. Only one is native to California.

Many varieties of hazelnuts are grown in Europe and a few in America for their edible nuts and ornamental value. The nuts of the species in Europe are usually called filberts but are so similar to the nuts of the American species that all may be called hazelnuts. In early spring the staminate flowers shed a considerable amount of pollen which may be a factor in causing hay-fever.

1. **Corylus rostrata** var. **californica** A. DC. CALIFORNIA HAZELNUT. Fig. 49.

An open spreading shrub, 5 to 12 feet high, with numerous ascending stems, smooth bark, and hairy or glandular-pubescent branchlets usually becoming glabrous in age. Leaves simple, alternate, deciduous; the blades rounded to obovate, more or less oblique and cordate at base, 1½ to 3 inches long, ¾-inch to 2½ inches wide, doubly serrate and sometimes slightly 3-lobed, glandular-hairy in spring and early summer, becoming more or less glabrous in age, paler beneath; petioles ¼- to ⅝-inch long. Flowers unisexual, monoecious; the staminate very small and numerous, borne in elongated drooping cylindrical catkins sessile on the ends of the branchlets of the previous year, appearing before the leaves, each flower solitary in the axil of the catkin-scales and composed of 4 stamens or apparently 8 because of the extremely cleft filaments, without sepals or petals; the pistillate fewer and borne in small rounded scaly buds, 1, 2, or 3 flowers borne on a bract, sepals very minute and adnate to the 2-celled inferior ovary, petals none, styles short and branching into 2 bright red stigmas which protrude when mature from between the bracts. Fruit an oval or subglobose nut, 3/8- to 5/8-inch long, with a very hard shell, surrounded by 2 or 3 united usually hispid bracts which form an envelope or involucre extending beyond the nut 1/2-inch to 1 1/4 inches into a fringed tube, the involucre often becoming glabrous in age. Flowering period, January to April.

California Hazelnut inhabits moist wooded canyons in the Humid Transition Life Zone from the Santa Cruz Mountains northward along the coast to Del Norte County, eastward through Siskiyou County, and south in the Sierra Nevada to the Kaweah River in Tulare County. Outside of California it is found in Oregon, Washington, and British Columbia. Eastward it is replaced by *Corylus rostrata,* Beaked Hazelnut. Cattle and sheep on some ranges browse extensively upon the foliage of this species.

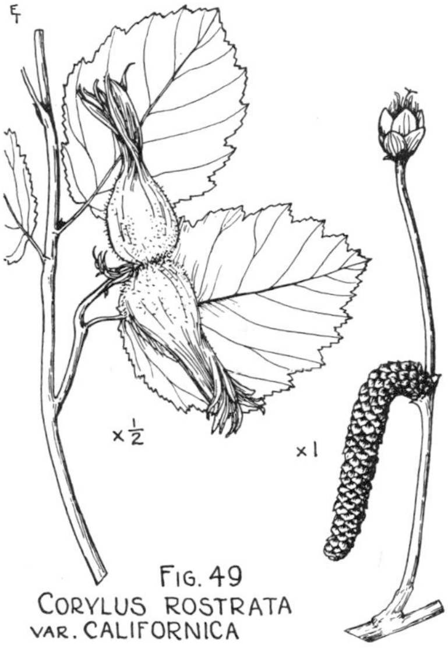

FIG. 49
CORYLUS ROSTRATA
VAR. CALIFORNICA

1a. Var. **Tracyi** Jepson.

Leaves less hairy than in the species, often nearly glabrous. Involucral tube extending beyond the nut only 1/8- to 1/2-inch.

This variety occurs on Grouse Mountain *(Tracy)* and near Eureka, Humboldt County, near Comptche, Mendocino County *(H. A. Walker),* on Mount Shasta, and occasionally southward in the Sierra Nevada (acc. *Jepson*).

Corylus rostrata var. californica A. DC. Prodr. 16:133 (1864). Type locality: Woods near Santa Cruz, California. Collected by *Hartweg.*

Var. Tracyi Jepson, Man. 271 (1923). Type locality: Grouse Mountain, Humboldt County. Collected by *Tracy.*

2. **Betula** L. Birch

(The Latin name of the birch.)

Trees or shrubs with smooth aromatic bark having prominent longitudinal lenticels. Leaves simple, alternate, deciduous, variously toothed. Flowers unisexual, monoecious; the staminate usually borne in 3's in the axils of the bracts of pendulous catkins, calyx membranous, 2- or 4-lobed, petals none, stamens 2, with divided filaments, each division with an anther; the pistillate borne in 3's in the axils of the bracts of erect catkins, sepals and petals none, ovary sessils, style branched, each branch with an elongated stigma. Fruits small compressed nutlets, winged on the margins, borne on the scales of the cones, the scales breaking away from the cones at maturity.

About 30 species of birches are now recognized, 13 of which are found in North America, 2 being native to California. They inhabit the subarctic and cooler parts of the north temperate zone, extending from the Arctic Circle to Texas in America, and to southern Europe, the Himalayas, China, and Japan.

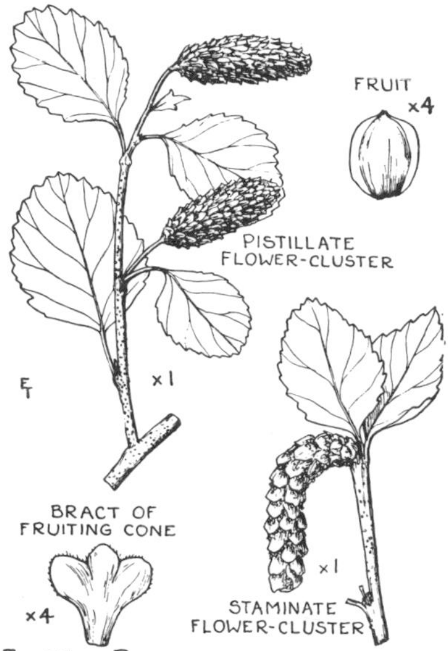

FIG. 50 BETULA GLANDULOSA

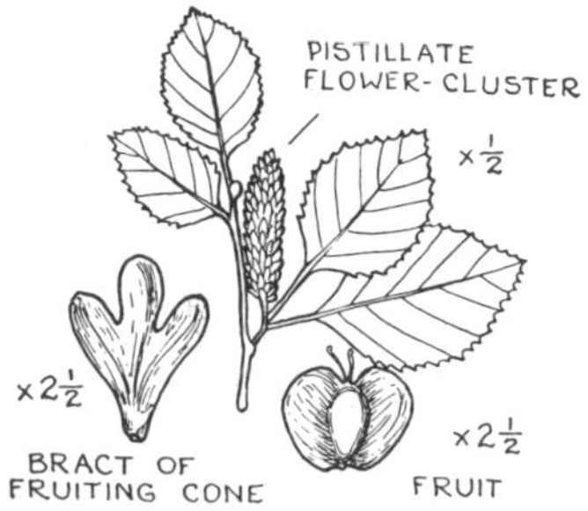

FIG. 51 BETULA FONTANALIS

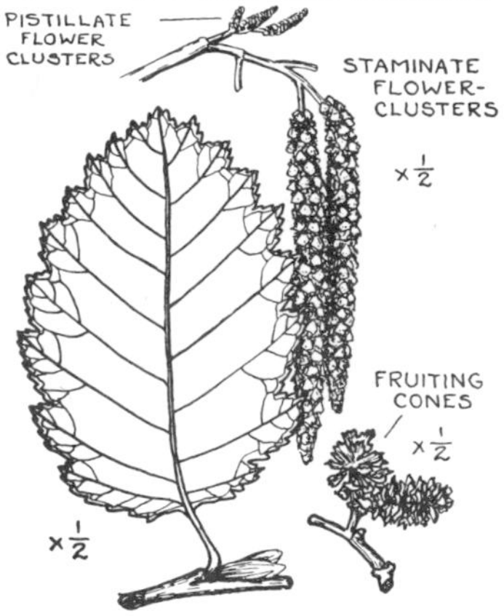

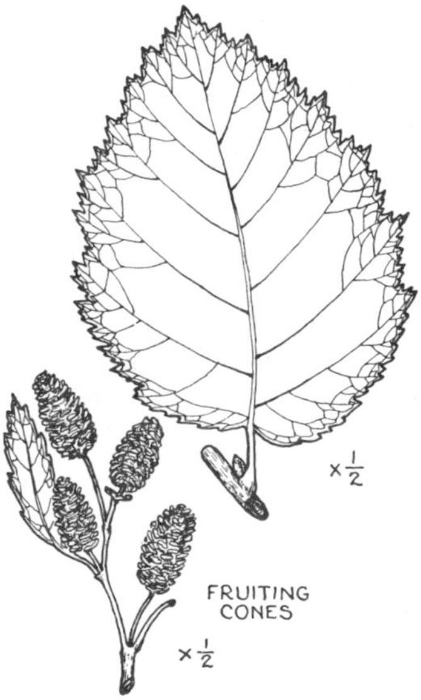

FIG. 53. ALNUS TENUIFOLIA FIG. 52 ALNUS SINUATA

(Figs. 51 and 52 from Pacific Coast Trees, Univ. of Calif. Press.)

A few of the species furnish excellent wood for cabinet making and for interior finishing. Many small articles such as Indian clubs, spools, lasts, boxes, etc., are manufactured from the hard durable wood. The bark of some species peels off in thin layers and is extensively used for basketry and in making canoes in the northern United States and Canada. Considerable starch is stored in the inner bark, furnishing food for browsing animals in times of lessened food supply. A volatile oil is obtained from the bark of an eastern species which is an inexpensive imitation of the oil of wintergreen. The wood is excellent for fuel and the manufacture of charcoal. The sap of some species is used as a beverage.

The species of birches with white bark have been extensively planted in public and private grounds in the cooler climates. A few weeping and cut-leaved varieties have been produced by nurserymen. The windblown pollen may be a factor in causing hay-fever.

KEY TO THE SPECIES

Leaves firm, usually less than 1 inch long, regularly crenate.....1. *B. glandulosa.*
Leaves thin, ½-inch to 3 inches long, irregularly sharply serrate..2. *B. fontanalis.*

1. **Betula glandulosa** Michx. Resin Birch. Fig. 50.

A small shrub, 1 to 6 feet high, sometimes procumbent in exposed situations, with smooth dark brown bark and glandular warty branchlets. Leaf-blades firm, broadly ovate or roundish, usually wedge-shaped or rounded at base, rounded at apex, ½-inch to 1½ inches long, ⅜-inch to 1 inch wide, 1- or 3-veined from the base, rather coarsely crenate or round-dentate, glabrous on both surfaces, dark green above, rather paler and glandular-dotted beneath; petioles reddish, ⅛- to ¼-inch long. Staminate catkins usually solitary near the ends of the shoots, cylindrical, about 1 inch long when mature, with closely overlapping ciliate scales. Pistillate catkins sessile or short-pedicelled, about ¾-inch long at maturity; scales smooth, divided above the middle into 3 nearly equal divisions. Nutlets oval, about ⅛-inch long, with narrow thin lateral wings. Flowering period, April and May.

Resin Birch is found in California only in the high mountain regions of the northern part, in the Canadian Life Zone. It has been collected from the Warner Range, Modoc County at an elevation of 7000 feet, from near Lassen Peak and Big Meadows, Plumas County, from near Colby, Butte County, and from Bridge Creek, Lassen County. It extends northward to Oregon, Washington, and Alaska, eastward to the Rocky Mountains, the Great Lakes region, and the New England states.

Betula glandulosa Michx. Fl. 2:180 (1803). Type locality: Lake Mistassini, Labrador. Collected by *Michaux.*

2. **Betula fontanalis** Sarg. Water Birch. Red Birch. Fig. 51.

A tall shrub or small tree, 10 to 25 feet high, usually with several stems from a common base, with gray or dark brown shining bark. Leaf-blades broadly ovate, mostly acute at apex, ½-inch to 2 inches long, ½-inch to 1¼ inches wide, 1-veined from the base, the margins sharply serrate, nearly entire at the base, surfaces at maturity smooth or with a few glandular dots beneath, resinous-glandular on upper surface when young; petioles about ½-inch or less long, flattened above. Staminate catkins cylindrical, clustered near the ends of the branchlets, 2 inches or more long when flowering, scales brown and sharp-pointed. Pistillate catkins solitary or rarely 2, about ¾-inch long, with protruding bright red stigmas from between the green scales; fruiting catkins 1½ to 2 inches long, scales with 3 unequal points, all fringed with small hairs. Nutlets pale brown, 2 or 3 borne on each scale, the body obovate with persistent stigmas, the wings lateral and almost as broad as or broader than the nutlets. Flowering period, April and May.

Water Birch occurs in California in a few localities in the Sierra Nevada from Tulare, Inyo (Lone Pine Creek; Cottonwood Creek; Silver Canyon, east of Laws; Round Mt.) and Fresno (Wood Creek, near S. Fk. Kings River) counties, northward to Butte and Modoc counties, and westward in Siskiyou County (Mt. Shasta; near Callahan; Salmon Mts.; Mill Creek, near Etna Mills; Mt. Eddy) to Humboldt County (Grouse Creek). It extends eastward to the Rocky Mountains and northward to British Columbia.

Betula fontanalis Sarg. Bot. Gaz. 31:239 (1901). Type locality: Sweetwater River, Wyoming, one of the branches of the Platte River. Collected by *Nuttall.*

3. **Alnus** Hill. Alder

(The ancient Latin name of the alder.)

Trees or shrubs. Leaves simple, alternate, deciduous, short-petioled, the margins dentate or serrate. Flowers unisexual, monoecious; the staminate borne in 3's, in the axils of the bracts of drooping catkins, calyx 4-parted, petals none, stamens 1 to 7, their filaments undivided; the pistillate borne in 2's in the axils of the bracts of erect spike-like catkins, calyx and corolla none; ovary single, 2-celled, stigmas 2. Fruits small flat nutlets borne on the somewhat woody scales of the small ovoid cone, the scales persistent on the cone at maturity.

This genus contains 15 to 30 species, widely scattered throughout the temperate regions of the northern hemisphere and southward to the Andes in South America. Four species grow in California, 2 of which are shrubby or have shrubby forms.

The alders have a limited economic value. A few have been planted in landscaping. Charcoal and gunpowder are made from the wood. The astringent bark and woody cones are used in tanning leather and in medicine.

KEY TO THE SPECIES

Leaves thin, the margins finely but unevenly serrate; flowers appearing with the leaves on the twigs of the new season; fruiting peduncles and their divisions slender, as long as or longer than the cones. . . . . 1. *A. sinuata.*

Leaves firm, the margins coarsely toothed and often again finely serrate; flowers appearing before the leaves on the twigs of the past season; fruiting peduncles and their divisions stout, shorter than the cones. . . . . 2. *A. tenuifolia.*

1. **Alnus sinuata** (Regel) Rydb. Sitka Alder. Thinleaf Alder. Fig. 52.

A slender shrub or small tree, 5 to 40 feet high, with brown or grayish bark, shining when young. Leaf-blades thin, ovate, 2 to 6 inches long, 1½ to 3½ inches wide, yellowish to bright green and glabrous above, paler and nearly glabrous beneath, white-hairy along the midrib and in the axils of the main veins beneath, very gummy when young, doubly and unevenly glandular-serrate; petioles ¼- to ¾-inch long, grooved above. Staminate catkins 1 inch or more long, 2 to 4 in a cluster, appearing with the leaves; stamens 5, 6, or 7 to a scale. Pistillate catkins ovate, ½- to ¾-inch long, 3 to 5 in a cluster, on slender pedicels; peduncles leafy at base, their divisions ½-inch to 1 inch long. Nutlets oval, pale brown, about as wide as the wings. Flowering period, May to July.

Sitka Alder occurs in California in the extreme northern part where it is known from Del Norte County (1 mile southeast and 2 miles north of Crescent City), Humboldt County (at Trinity Summit at about 6000 feet elevation, in dense thickets, *Tracy*), and in Siskiyou County (Hancock Lake on trail to Marble Mt., elevation 7000 ft.; Rattlesnake Meadow, trail to Preston Peak, elevation 5000 ft.; Mt. Shasta, 6500 ft. elevation). It extends northward to Alaska and eastward to Alberta and the Rocky Mountains of western Montana and Wyoming.

Alnus sinuata (Regel) Rydb. Bull. Torr. Club 24:190 (1897). *Alnus viridis* var. *sinuata* Regel. Type locality: Kamtchatka, peninsula off Siberia.

2. **Alnus tenuifolia** Nutt. MOUNTAIN ALDER. Fig. 53.

A shrub or small tree, 6 to 25 feet high, with smooth gray or reddish brown bark. Leaf-blades ovate-oblong to roundish, 1½ to 4 inches long, 1 to 2½ inches wide, dark green and nearly glabrous above (pubescent when young), pale yellowish green or finely pubescent beneath, coarsely toothed and again finely serrate; petioles ¼-inch to 1 inch long. Staminate catkins 1 to 3 inches long, 3 or 4 in a cluster, appearing before the leaves on the twigs of the past season; stamens 4 to each scale. Pistillate catkins ovate, ¼- to ½-inch long, 3 to 7 in a cluster near the ends of the branchlets, sessile or very short-pedicelled. Fruiting cones 5/16- to 5/8-inch long, on stout leafless pedicels shorter than the cones. Nutlets nearly circular, surrounded by a very narrow thin membranous border. Flowering period, April to June.

Mountain Alder inhabits borders of moist mountain meadows and lake shores from 5000 to 8000 feet elevation in the Sierra Nevada from Tulare County northward to Modoc County and westward in Siskiyou, Trinity, and Shasta counties to Humboldt County (Sphagnum bog near Bald Mt., 3000 ft. elevation; Trinity Summit). It extends north to Alaska and eastward to the Rocky Mountains.

Alnus tenuifolia Nutt. Sylva 1:32 (1842). Type locality: Rocky Mountains and the Blue Mountains. Collected by *Nuttall*.

Fagaceae. Beech or Oak Family

The Oak Family contains 5 genera and approximately 400 species of trees and shrubs, mostly of the subtropical and north temperate zones. Three genera with 18 species are native to California.

KEY TO THE GENERA

Fruit a spiny bur enclosing 1 to 3 nuts; leaves evergreen, entire, yellowish gray or rusty-tomentose beneath . . . . 1. CASTANOPSIS.

Fruit an acorn.

- Leaves with prominent parallel lateral veins, evergreen; staminate flowers in erect catkins, some with pistillate flowers at base; the cup-like involucre usually covered with many stiff linear scales . . . . 2. LITHOCARPUS.
- Leaves without prominent parallel lateral veins (except in *Quercus Sadleriana*); staminate flowers in drooping catkins, none with pistillate flowers at base; the cup-like involucre scaly, but scales not stiff and linear . . . . . 3. QUERCUS.

1. **Castanopsis** Spach. CHINQUAPIN

(From the Greek *kastanea,* chestnut, and *opsis,* resemblance, in allusion to its resemblance to the chestnut tree.)

Leaves simple, alternate, evergreen. Flowers unisexual, the staminate and pistillate borne on the same plant; petals absent. Staminate flowers in groups of 3 in the axils of bracts forming densely flowered erect cylindrical catkins 1 to 3 inches long; calyx 5- or 6-parted; stamens 6 to 17; rudimentary ovary sometimes present. Pistillate flowers 1 to 3 in an involucre usually at the base of the staminate catkins or borne in short separate catkins; calyx 6-cleft, with abortive stamens on its lobes; ovary inferior, 3-celled; styles 3. Fruit a spiny bur enclosing 1 to 3 bitter nuts, maturing the autumn of the second year.

This genus contains about 30 species, mostly of Asia. Two occur in California.

KEY TO THE SPECIES

Leaves tapering or long-pointed at apex, commonly trough-like by infolding upward.................................1. *C. chrysophylla* var. *minor*.
Leaves more commonly obtuse at apex, mostly plane.........2. *C. sempervirens*.

1. **Castanopsis chrysophylla** var. **minor** (Benth.) A. DC. GOLDEN CHINQUAPIN. Fig. 54.

An evergreen shrub or small tree, 3 to 15 feet high. Leaf-blades oblong or oblong-lanceolate, 1½ to 3 inches long, ½-inch to 1½ inches wide, tapering at both ends, usually acute or long-pointed at apex, commonly trough-like because of upward infolding along the midrib, dark green and shining above, golden-tomentose beneath; petioles about ¼-inch long. Burs chestnut-like, 3 to 5 in a cluster, with 1 or 2 nuts. Flowering period, June to September.

Golden Chinquapin is found most commonly in the Humid Transition and Upper Sonoran Life Zones near the coast from the Pecho Mountains of San Luis Obispo County northward in the Santa Lucia Mountains of Monterey County to the "White Plains" of Mendocino County, thence northward into Humboldt, Del Norte, Trinity, and Siskiyou counties. It also occurs sparingly on the western slope of the Sierra Nevada (Gaddis Creek, Eldorado County, *C. M. Belshaw*).

It apparently is a shrubby form of Giant Chinquapin *(Castanopsis chrysophylla)*. It is found at higher elevations and in more xerophytic habitats of the range of the species. In certain localities one can find a series of plants varying from typical shrubs to large trees. In Thornhill Gulch near Oakland, small trees are found on the mesophytic slopes, and on the dry exposed Moraga Ridge, not far distant, the plants are more shrubby. In habit of growth the shrubby form resembles Bush Chinquapin, *Castanopsis sempervirens,* but retains its characteristic leaf differences. It sends up numerous stump-sprouts after fire or cutting.

Castanopsis chrysophylla var. minor (Benth.) A. DC. Prodr. 16:110 (1864). *Castanea chrysophylla* var. *minor* Benth. Type locality: Santa Cruz Mountains. Collected by *Hartweg*.

2. **Castanopsis sempervirens** (Kell.) Dudley. BUSH CHINQUAPIN. SIERRA CHINQUAPIN. Fig. 55.

A low spreading round-topped evergreen shrub, 1 to 8 feet high, with smooth brown or gray bark. Leaf-blades oblong or oblong-lanceolate, commonly obtuse at apex, 1 to 3 inches long, ½-inch to 1 inch wide, mostly plane, entire, yellowish or gray-green above, golden or pale rusty-tomentose beneath; petioles ⅛- to ¼- (or ½-) inch long. Burs chestnut-like, 2 to 7 in a cluster. Flowering period, July and August.

Bush Chinquapin usually forms thickets on dry mountain ridges or in rocky places of open forests in the Transition and Canadian Life Zones. It extends from the San Jacinto and San Bernardino mountains northward through the Sierra Nevada of California and adjacent Nevada to southern Oregon, westward in the mountains of Siskiyou, Trinity, and Humoldt counties, and south into Mendocino and Lake counties, at elevations from 1500 to 12,500 feet. It stump-sprouts readily after fires and cutting.

Castanopsis sempervirens (Kell.) Dudley; Merriam, N. Am. Fauna 16:142 (1899). *Castanea sempervirens* Kell. Type locality: Near Mariposa, California. Collected by *L. Ransom.*

2. **Lithocarpus** Bl.

(From the Greek *lithos,* rock, and *karpos,* fruit, in allusion to the hard stone-like acorn.)

This genus possesses characters of the chestnut, *Castanea,* and of the oak, *Quercus,* and may be considered intermediate between the two. The erect elongated catkins, parallel lateral veins of the leaves, pistillate flowers at the base of the staminate catkins, and bur-like character of the involucre or cup are chestnut characters. The habit of growth, the acorn cup instead of a closed bur, the 3-celled ovary, the single pistillate flower in an involucre, and the bitter taste of the true acorns are oak characters.

There are about 100 species, all of which are confined to southeastern Asia except the single Californian species.

1. **Lithocarpus densiflora** var. **echinoides** (R. Br.) Abrams. SHRUB TAN-OAK. DWARF TANBARK. Fig. 56.

A low evergreen shrub, 1 to 10 feet high. Leaves simple, alternate; the blades oblong or oblong-ovate, rounded at both ends, 1 to 3 inches long, ½-inch to 1¼ inches wide, leathery, densely covered with a whitish or yellowish stellate pubescence when young, almost glabrous above in age, pale and lead-colored beneath, entire or inconspicuously toothed; the lateral veins nearly parallel; petioles ¼- to ½-inch long. Flowers unisexual, the staminate and pistillate on the same plant; petals absent. Staminate flowers numerous, in erect ill-smelling tomentose catkins 2 to 4 inches long. Pistillate flowers solitary in the axils of involucral bracts; the involucres about 3 to 6 at the base of some of the staminate catkins; ovary inferior, 3-celled; styles 3. Fruit an acorn, maturing in the autumn of the second year. The nut 1-seeded, surrounded at base by a bur-like cup with subulate or very narrow recurving scales. Flowering period, June to August.

This shrubby variety of Tan-oak occurs in the Transition and Canadian Life Zones around Mount Shasta, thence westward to the Salmon and Klamath mountains, northward through the Siskiyou Mountain region into southern Oregon, and in a few locations on the west slope of the Sierra Nevada (BUTTE COUNTY: Near Sterling, *Heller.* SIERRA COUNTY: ½ mi. e. of Texas Hill, *N. French;* 2 mi. n. of Poverty Hill, *A. Lewis.* PLUMAS COUNTY: 1¼ mi. s.w. Mt. Ararrat, *G. T. Nordstrom.* PLACER COUNTY: Mosquito Ridge, Colfax Quad., *N. French.* ELDORADO COUNTY: ½-mi. s. of Bolis Cabin, Pyramid Peak Quad., *P. L. Johannsen.* MARIPOSA COUNTY: 5½ mi. e. of Jerseydale, Yosemite Quad., *W. A. Peterson.* TUOLUMNE COUNTY: Crocker Ridge, el. 6000 ft., *N. French;* 2 mi. n.e. of Mt. Lewis, Big Trees Quad., *B. Bolt*). The plants of the Sierra Nevada are often intermediate between the species and this variety.

Lithocarpus densiflora var. echinoides (R. Br.) Abrams, Illus. Fl. Pacif. States 1:516 (1923). *Quercus echinoides* R. Br. (of Campster). Type locality: Mount Shasta and Siskiyou regions.

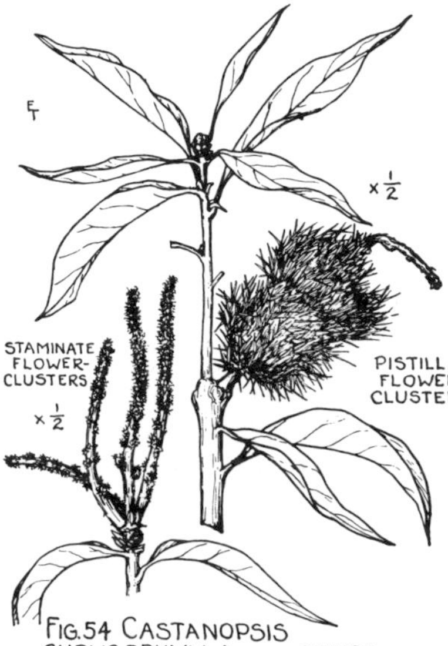

FIG. 54 CASTANOPSIS CHRYSOPHYLLA VAR. MINOR

FIG. 55 CASTANOPSIS SEMPERVIRENS

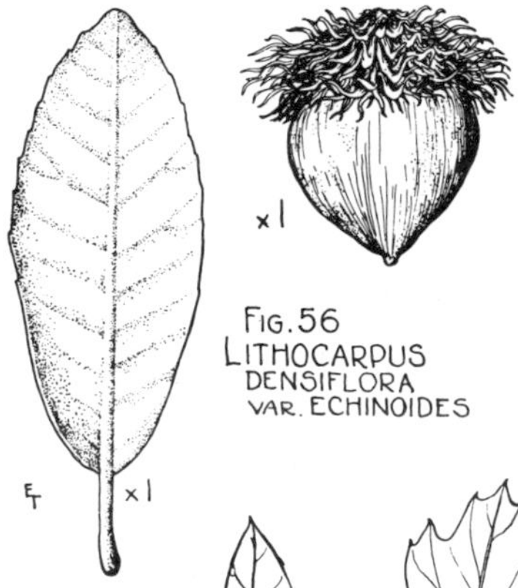

FIG. 56 LITHOCARPUS DENSIFLORA VAR. ECHINOIDES

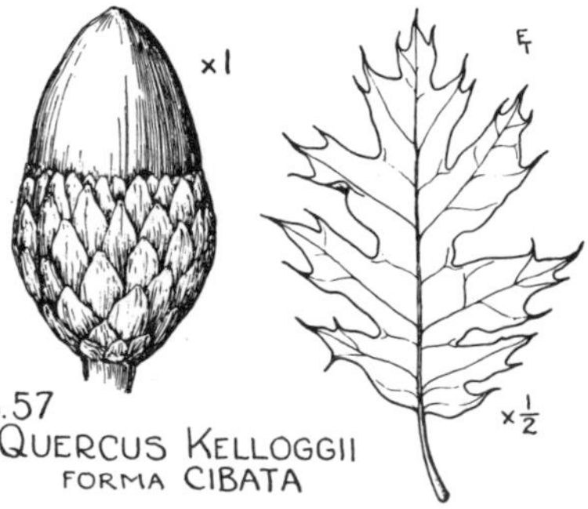

FIG. 57 QUERCUS KELLOGGII FORMA CIBATA

FIG. 58. QUERCUS MOREHUS

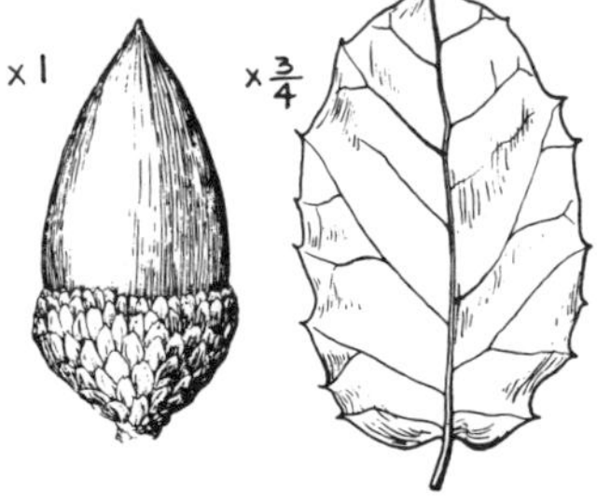

FIG. 59 QUERCUS AGRIFOLIA VAR. FRUTESCENS

3. **Quercus** L. Oak

(An ancient Latin name, probably from the Celtic *quer,* fine, and *cuez,* a tree, signifying a beautiful tree.)

Leaves simple, alternate, evergreen or deciduous, lobed, dentate, crenate, irregularly toothed, or entire. Flowers small, apetalous, green or yellowish, unisexual, the staminate and pistillate borne on the same plant. Staminate flowers numerous, in pendulous slender catkins; calyx usually 6-lobed; stamens 5 to 10. Pistillate flowers solitary, subtended by an early falling bract and 2 bractlets, borne in short or elongated few-flowered clusters from the axils of the leaves of the present season; calyx urn-shaped, adnate to the 3-celled inferior ovary; styles 3 or rarely 4, short. Fruit consisting of the more or less imbricated and united bracts of the cup-like involucre which partially encloses the hard 1-seeded nut, maturing in 1 or 2 years.

The genus *Quercus* contains approximately 300 species, widely scattered in the temperate regions of the northern hemisphere and the mountainous regions of the tropics. About 15 species with several varieties and forms are native to California.

The oaks are usually trees, but in California, at least 10 species and varieties are distinctly shrubby. These usually occur in the dry chaparral areas and often constitute an important element of these communities.

Many oaks produce tannin in their leaves and bark, which is important in the tanning of leather. The hard wood is used extensively in the manufacturing of furniture and many other household products. The abundant wind-blown pollen is a factor in causing hay-fever. Some of the species are used in landscaping.

KEY TO THE SPECIES

Leaves usually glabrous and light green beneath.
  Leaves pinnately lobed or deeply and coarsely toothed, the lobes tipped with bristle-like teeth.
    Lobes extending halfway or more to midrib; leaves deciduous.
      1. *Q. Kelloggii* forma *cibata.*
    Lobes extending less than halfway to midrib; leaves evergreen or nearly so.
      2. *Q. Morehus.*
  Leaves not lobed, the margins spiny- or prickly-toothed or entire.
    Leaves often convex above, typically roundish, usually with axillary tufts of hairs beneath; acorns maturing the first year.
      3. *Q. agrifolia* var. *frutescens.*
    Leaves usually plane and oblong; acorns maturing the second year.
      Nuts ½- to ¾-inch thick. . . . . 4. *Q. Wislizenii* var. *frutescens.*
      Nuts about ¼-inch thick, narrow-cylindrical. . 4a. *Q. Wislizenii* var. *extima.*

Leaves pale gray or lead-color, or some golden-fuzzy beneath.
  Leaves distinctly lobed, deciduous; acorns maturing the first year; winter buds ⅜- to ½-inch long, densely tomentose. . . . . 5. *Q. Garryana* var. *Breweri.*
  Leaves entire or variously toothed, rarely lobed, evergreen; winter buds less than ⅜-inch long.
    Leaves with prominent and parallel lateral veins, resembling leaves of the chestnut tree, 2½ to 4 inches long. . . . . 6. *Q. Sadleriana.*
    Leaves without prominent and parallel lateral veins, ½-inch to 2 inches long.

Acorns maturing the first year; the cup-scales evident and usually tuberculate; the nut glabrous on the inner surface.

Leaves convex and usually finely tomentose above, entire or irregularly toothed..7. *Q. durata.*

Leaves plane or occasionally undulate, typically glabrous above, the margins varying from entire to irregularly or regularly toothed. 8. *Q. dumosa.*

Acorns maturing the second year; the cup-scales not tuberculate, usually covered by a fine pubescence or tomentum; the nut tomentose on the inner surface.

Leaves wavy-spinose, often holly-like, or some nearly entire, the young leaves often with golden fuzz; acorn-cups 2 times broader than deep...9. *Q. Palmeri.*

Leaves mostly entire.

Young leaves without golden fuzz; branches slender. 10. *Q. vaccinifolia.*

Young leaves usually with golden fuzz; branches more rigid. 11. *Q. chrysolepis* var. *nana.*

1. **Quercus Kelloggii** forma **cibata** Jepson. DWARF BLACK OAK. Fig. 57.

A low or semi-prostrate shrub. Leaf-blades deeply pinnately lobed, 3 to 6 inches long, 2 to 4 inches wide, finely tomentose, the lobes often toothed and tipped by fine bristle-like teeth.

Black Oak is usually a large deciduous tree but in certain exposed situations it is reduced to a shrub-like habit. It was described by Jepson from material collected on the Yollo Bolly Mountains from 5000 to 8000 feet altitude. This shrub form may be expected at the higher altitudes within the range of the species, which occurs on the lower and middle mountain slopes and the foothills from southwestern Oregon south in the Coast Ranges and the Sierra Nevada to the mountains of southern California.

Quercus Kelloggii forma cibata Jepson, Silva Calif. 233 (1910). Type locality: Yollo Bolly Mountains, California.

2. **Quercus Morehus** Kell. ORACLE OAK. Fig. 58.

Usually a small nearly evergreen tree, 20 to 40 feet high, but sometimes shrub-like. Leaf-blades oblong to elliptic, 2 to 4 inches long, 1 to 2 inches wide, with shallow spinose-tipped lobes or coarsely and deeply toothed, glabrous, dark green and glossy above, paler beneath; petioles ¼- to ½-inch long. Acorns maturing the second year.

Oracle Oak occurs in scattered localities on the lower slopes and foothills of the Sierra Nevada, the Coast Ranges, and the San Bernardino Mountains of southern California. It is nowhere abundant.

Quercus Morehus Kell. Proc. Calif. Acad. 2:36 (1863). Type locality: Near Clear Lake, Lake County, California. Collected by *A. A. Veatch.*

3. **Quercus agrifolia** var. **frutescens** Engelm. DWARF COAST LIVE OAK. Fig. 59.

An evergreen shrub, 3 to 5 feet high. Leaf-blades oval, elliptic or rounded, usually 1 to 2 inches long, ½-inch to 1 inch wide, firm and leathery, most commonly with spine-tipped teeth or rarely almost entire, often convex above, glabrous on both surfaces except for small tufts of axillary hairs beneath; petioles ⅛- to ¼-inch long. Staminate catkins 1 to 2 inches long, yellowish or reddish.

Pistillate flowers in the upper axils of the leaves on the present season's growth. Acorns borne singly or 2 to 4 in a cluster, maturing the first autumn; the cup ⅓- to ½-inch deep, silky-pubescent within, the scales thin and pointed at apex; the nut slender, about 1 inch long. Flowering period, February to April.

Dwarf Coast Live Oak occurs in the chaparral or on exposed hill and valley slopes within the range of the species from Mendocino County southward in the Coast Ranges to southern California, in the Upper Sonoran and Transition Life Zones. Many of the apparent shrub-clusters are stump-sprouts from old trees which have been cut or burned. The leaves from these sprouts are very holly-like.

Quercus agrifolia var. frutescens Engelm.; Bot. Calif. 2:98 (1880). Type locality: Near Mendocino, California. Collected by *Bolander*.

4. **Quercus Wislizenii** var. **frutescens** Engelm. DWARF INTERIOR LIVE OAK. Fig. 60.

An evergreen shrub, 3 to 8 (or to 15) feet high, with very stout stiff branches. Leaf-blades ovate or oblong, ¾-inch to 2 inches long, ½-inch to 1 inch wide, very stiff and brittle, entire or irregularly to regularly spiny-toothed, flat or slightly undulate, dark green glabrous and shining above, paler and glabrous beneath; petioles ⅛- to ¼-inch long. Acorns maturing the second summer; the cup ½- to ¾-inch wide and about as deep, its scales thin, long, much overlapping, and sometimes ciliate; the nut oblong-ovate, abruptly pointed at apex, ¾-inch to 1¼ inches long. Flowering period, April and May.

Dwarf Interior Live Oak inhabits the climax chaparral regions of the inner Coast Ranges, the mountains of southern California, and occasionally the foothills of the Sierra Nevada. It is easily confused with the shrub form of *Quercus agrifolia* but differs in having more open branching and the leaves are usually not convex above. The ability to stump-sprout after fire saves this species from complete destruction in burned-over regions.

4a. Var. **extima** Jepson. Fig. 61.

Nuts slender-cylindrical, ¾-inch to 1 inch long, about ¼-inch broad.

This variety occurs occasionally in the foothills of the Sierra Nevada (near Ione, Amador County, *McMinn;* Kaweah River, *Fry*).

Quercus Wislizenii var. frutescens Engelm.; Bot. Calif. 2:99 (1880). Type locality: Not given.

Quercus Wislizenii var. extima Jepson, Man. 276 (1923). Type locality: Kaweah River Basin. Collected by *Walter Fry*.

5. **Quercus Garryana** var. **Breweri** (Engelm.) Jepson. BREWER OAK. Fig. 62.

A spreading deciduous shrub, 3 to 15 feet high, with smooth gray bark. Leaf-blades oblong, 1½ to 3 or rarely 4 inches long, ½-inch to 1¼ inches wide, lobed to near the middle or some only slightly if at all lobed, the lobes entire or toothed, acute or obtuse, at first finely pubescent above, becoming glabrous and shiny, grayish and often soft-pubescent beneath; petioles ¼- to ½-inch long. Acorns maturing the first year; the cup somewhat tuberculate, ½- to ¾-inch broad; the nut oval, ¾-inch to 1⅜ inches long. Flowering period, April and May.

Brewer Oak occurs on mountain slopes from southern Oregon southward in Siskiyou and Trinity counties to Mendocino (Covelo, *H. S. Yates*) and Lake (Snow Mt.) counties in the North Coast Ranges, on the western slope of the Sierra Nevada from Lassen County to Tulare County, and on the western border of the Liebre Mountains *(A. D. Gifford)* in Kern and Los Angeles counties. In the northern part of its range it inhabits the Transition and Canadian Life Zones and

QUERCUS

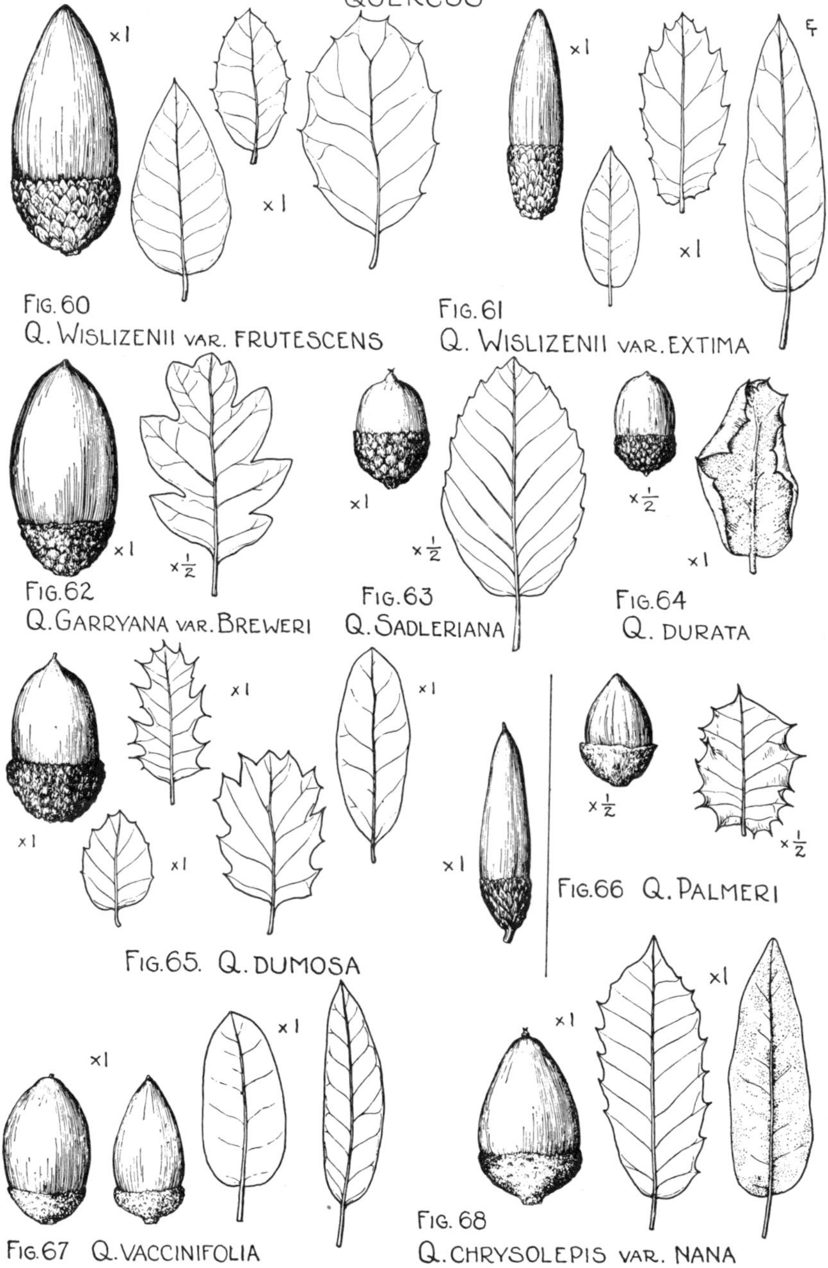
×1
×1
×1
×1
×1
FIG. 60
Q. WISLIZENII VAR. FRUTESCENS
FIG. 61
Q. WISLIZENII VAR. EXTIMA
×1
×½
FIG. 62
Q. GARRYANA VAR. BREWERI
×1
×½
FIG. 63
Q. SADLERIANA
×½
×1
FIG. 64
Q. DURATA
×1
×1
×1
×1
×1
×1
FIG. 65. Q. DUMOSA
×½
×½
FIG. 66 Q. PALMERI
×1
×1
FIG. 67 Q. VACCINIFOLIA
×1
×1
FIG. 68
Q. CHRYSOLEPIS VAR. NANA

in the Sierra Nevada and the southern part of its range it occurs in the Upper Sonoran and Arid Transition Life Zones. Some authors separate the southern Sierra Nevada material with scarcely tuberculate cup-scales into the variety *semota* Jepson. Examination of a series of specimens collected by the V. T. M. shows the cup-scales to be too variable for use in separating this species into varieties.

Quercus Garryana var. Breweri (Engelm.) Jepson, Fl. Calif. 1:354 (1909). *Q. Breweri* Engelm. Type locality: "mountains west of Shasta." Collected by *Brewer*.

6. **Quercus Sadleriana** R. Br. of Campster. DEER OAK. SADLER OAK. Fig. 63.

An evergreen shrub, 2 to 8 feet high, with many slender flexible stems from the base. Leaf-blades chestnut-like, oblong-ovate, 2 to 4 inches long, 1 to 2 inches wide, the lateral veins parallel and very prominent, nearly glabrous above, pale gray or lead-color beneath, coarsely serrate; petioles 1/4- to 3/4-inch long; stipules oblanceolate, densely silky. Acorns solitary or rarely several and crowded in the axils of the upper leaves, maturing the first autumn; the cup about 3/4-inch broad, somewhat tomentose without, silky-pubescent within; the nut ovoid, 1 to 1 1/2 inches long. Flowering period, April and May.

Deer Oak is limited in its distribution in California to the Transition and Canadian Life Zones on Trinity Summit, Humboldt County and in the Salmon and Siskiyou mountains of Trinity, Del Norte, and Siskiyou counties. It extends northward to the Siskiyou and Rogue River mountains of southwestern Oregon.

Quercus Sadleriana R. Br. of Campster, Ann. & Mag. Nat. Hist. IV, 7:249 (1871). Type locality: "Crescent City trail between Sailors' Diggings, Oregon and Smith Creek, California." Collected by *John Jeffrey*.

7. **Quercus durata** Jepson. LEATHER OAK. Fig. 64.

An evergreen shrub, 2 to 8 feet high, with stout rigid branches; the young branchlets and leaves densely tomentose. Leaf-blades oval, oblong, or elliptic, 1/2-inch to 1 inch or rarely 2 inches long, 3/8- to 3/4-inch wide, decidedly convex above, leathery, dark dull green and pubescent above (in age often almost glabrous and shiny), pale and tomentose beneath; usually with prickly teeth but varying from entire to irregularly toothed; petioles 1/8- to 1/4-inch long. Acorns 2 or 3 in a cluster, usually 1 or 2 much larger, maturing the first year; the cup 1/2- to 3/4-inch wide, 1/4- to 3/8-inch deep, its scales usually tuberculate; the nut ovoid, thick, about 3/4-inch long, abruptly pointed, about 1/3 enclosed by the cup, glabrous on the inner surface. Flowering period, April and May.

Leather Oak occurs on the chaparral-covered hills and lower mountain slopes of the middle and inner Coast Ranges from Trinity County southward in Tehama, Glenn, Mendocino, Sonoma, Lake, Napa, Contra Costa, Alameda, San Mateo, Santa Clara, Santa Cruz, Monterey, San Benito, and San Luis Obispo counties, in the foothills of the Sierra Nevada in Nevada, Placer, and Eldorado counties, and in the San Gabriel Mountains of Los Angeles County (1/2-mi. e. Palmer Canyon, alt. 2000 ft., *L. Wheeler* 323; San Antonio Canyon near Claremont and the San Anita Canyon Trail). It is often associated with *Quercus dumosa*, from which it can be distinguished by the convex upper leaf-surfaces and the more compact growth of leaves at the ends of the branches.

Quercus durata Jepson, Fl. Calif. 1:356 (1909). *Q. dumosa* var. *bullata* Engelm. Type locality: Santa Lucia Mountains. Collected by *Brewer*.

8. **Quercus dumosa** Nutt. CALIFORNIA SCRUB OAK. Fig. 65.

An evergreen or tardily deciduous shrub, 2 to 6 feet high, or sometimes a tree to 30 feet high. Branches stout, rigid; the very young branchlets densely tomentose. Leaf-blades quite variable but typically oblong to roundish, 1/2-inch to 1 inch long, 1/4- to 3/4-inch wide, brittle, plane or undulate, shiny and glabrous but not convex above, pale and pubescent beneath; spinose-serrate or somewhat sinuately lobed; petioles about 1/8-inch long. Staminate catkins loosely flowered, 1 to 2 inches long. Pistillate flowers usually 2 or 3 in the axils of the upper leaves of the present season's growth. Acorns usually in clusters of 2 or 3, maturing the first autumn; the cup either shallow or deep, about 1/2- to 3/4-inch broad, enclosing about 1/2 the nut, its scales ovate or united and tuberculate, especially near the base; the nuts ovoid, rounded or acute at apex, 1/2-inch to 1 inch long. Flowering period, March to May.

California Scrub Oak is an important constituent of the chaparral in the mountains of southern and Lower California. It extends northward in the Coast Ranges and the western middle slopes of the Sierra Nevada to Tehama County, in the Upper Sonoran Life Zone. It is the most variable of our shrubby oaks in foliage and fruit characters. Leaves with entire, irregularly toothed, and nearly regularly toothed margins occur throughout the range of the species and often on the same plant. In the inner South Coast Ranges from the San Carlos Range to the San Emigdio Mountains of Kern County this species apparently hybridizes with *Q. Douglasii,* and in the mountains of southern California it hybridizes with *Q. Engelmanii.*

Several varieties of this species have been described, but the characters used in attempting to distinguish them fail when specimens collected throughout the range of this polymorphic species are examined.

Quercus dumosa Nutt. Sylva 1:7 (1842). Type locality: Santa Barbara, California. Collected by *Nuttall. Q. Alvordiana* Eastw. *Q. dumosa* var. *Alvordiana* (Eastw.) Jepson. *Q. turbinella* Greene. *Q. dumosa* var. *turbinella* (Greene) Jepson. *Q. dumosa* var. *elegantula* (Greene) Jepson. *Q. Macdonaldii* var. *elegantula* Greene.

9. **Quercus Palmeri** Engelm. PALMER OAK. Fig. 66.

An evergreen shrub, 6 to 15 feet high, with stout rigid branches; the young branchlets covered with a yellowish deciduous tomentum. Leaf-blades elliptic to round-ovate, abruptly acute at apex, 1/2-inch to 1 1/2 inches long, 3/8- to 3/4-inch wide, undulate, dull green above, lead-color beneath or when young densely white- or yellow-tomentose, coarsely and very irregularly spinose-toothed or some almost entire, petioles 1/8- to 1/4-inch long. Staminate catkins 1 to 4 inches long, 4 to 10 in a dense cluster. Acorns maturing the second autumn; the cup shallow, about 3/4-inch broad and 1/4-inch deep, its walls thin, its scales densely covered with a fine tomentum; the nut ovoid, 3/4-inch to 1 inch long, acutely pointed, tomentose on the inner surface. Flowering period, April and May.

Palmer Oak occurs in the chaparral areas of the Upper Sonoran Life Zone from the San Jacinto Range southward in the mountains of San Diego County and Lower California and along the Peachy Canyon road, San Luis Obispo County at an elevation of 1100 feet (*Nordstrom* in V. T. M. Herb.). In foliage characteristics this species resembles somewhat the stump-sprouts of *Q. chrysolepis,* but is easily distinguished from the shrub form (var. *nana*) of that species which has smaller and usually entire leaves.

Quercus Palmeri Engelm. Trans. St. Louis Acad. 3:393 (1877). Type locality: East of San Diego, California. Collected by *Palmer*.

10. **Quercus vaccinifolia** Kell. HUCKLEBERRY OAK. Fig. 67.

A low often prostrate evergreen shrub, 1 to 4 feet high, with slender pliable branchlets. Leaf-blades oblong-ovate, rounded or abruptly acute at apex, ½-inch to 1¼ inches long, ⅜- to ⅝-inch wide, dull gray-green and glabrous above, pale and finely tomentose beneath, mostly entire, some with few small irregular spinose teeth; petioles ¼-inch or less long. Acorns maturing the second autumn; the cup shallow, about ½-inch wide, finely pubescent within, its scales covered with a fine whitish tomentum; the nut round-ovoid, about ½-inch long, tomentose on the inner surface. Flowering period, May to July.

Huckleberry Oak is a small compact shrub inhabiting mountain ridges and rocky situations in the Canadian Life Zone. It extends from southern Oregon south in the Siskiyou, Scott, Klamath, Trinity, and Salmon mountains, eastward and southward in the Sierra Nevada to the Yosemite National Park region. It has been collected also from Mount Sanhedrin *(A. Shelton)* and Red Mountain *(Tracy)*, Mendocino County.

Quercus vaccinifolia Kell. Proc. Calif. Acad. ed. 2, 1:106 (1873). Type locality: "Trinity, Scott, and Siskiyou Mountains." Collected by *M. F. Beardsley*.

11. **Quercus chrysolepis** var. **nana** Jepson. DWARF CANYON OAK. Fig. 68.

A compactly branched evergreen shrub, 2 to 6 feet high, with stout stiff branches. Leaf-blades oblong or ovate, ¾-inch to 1½ inches long, ½- to ¾-inch wide, pale green above, yellow or lead-color beneath with a fine fuzzy powder, usually entire but sometimes variously toothed; petioles ⅛- to ¼-inch long. Acorns maturing the second autumn; the cup shallow, with very thick walls, silky within, its scales covered with a dense coat of rusty-tomentum; the nut oval or oblong, ½-inch to 1¼ inches long and almost as broad, rounded at apex, tomentose on the inner surface. Flowering period, May and June.

This shrubby form of *Quercus chrysolepis* inhabits the higher chaparral slopes and higher Coast Range summits from Trinity County southward to the mountains of southern California and rocky declivities in the canyons of the Sierra Nevada (Alpine County near Markleville; Emerald Bay, Eldorado Co., *McMinn*).

Quercus chrysolepis, although widely distributed, rarely forms a large forest but is scattered in isolated patches or as individual trees or shrubs. Many leaf variations are evident, and often entire, irregularly toothed, and regularly spinose-toothed leaves can be found on the same specimen. The stump-sprouts have very spinose undulate holly-like leaves. The yellow fuzz on the young leaves and branchlets, the lead-color on the lower surface of the adult leaves, and the dense coat of tomentum on the acorn-cups distinguish this species from the other oaks.

Quercus chrysolepis var. nana Jepson, Man. 275 (1923). Type locality: Summit of Mount St. Helena. Collected by *Jepson*.

Juglandaceae. Walnut Family

The Walnut Family is comprised of 6 genera and 35 species, mostly of the north temperate regions.

1. **Juglans** L. WALNUT

(From the Latin *Jovis*, Jupiter, and *glans*, nut.)

About 10 species of walnuts have been described from temperate North Ameri-

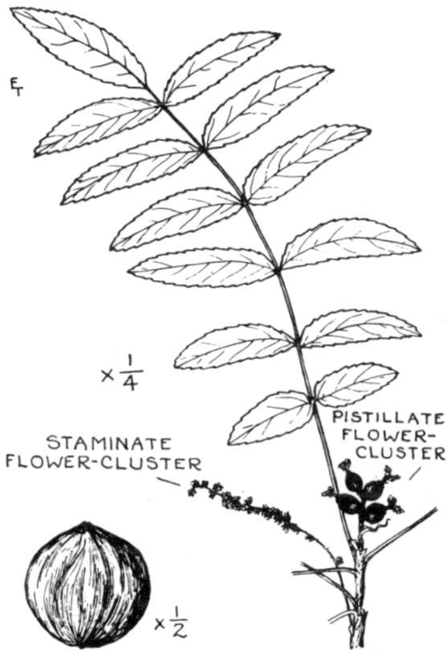

FIG. 69 JUGLANS CALIFORNICA

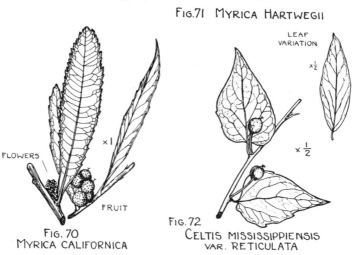

FIG. 71 MYRICA HARTWEGII

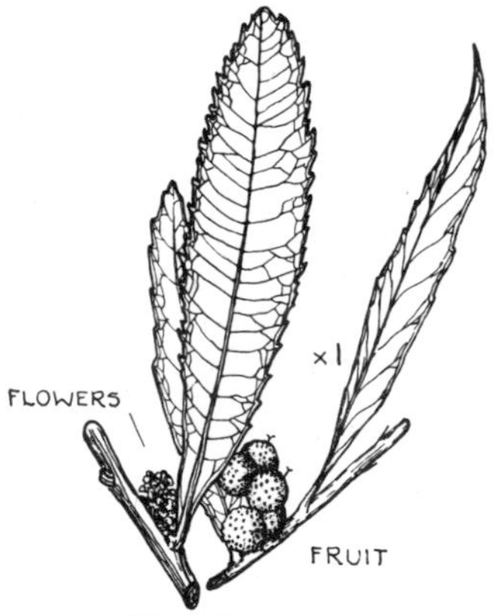

FIG. 70
MYRICA CALIFORNICA

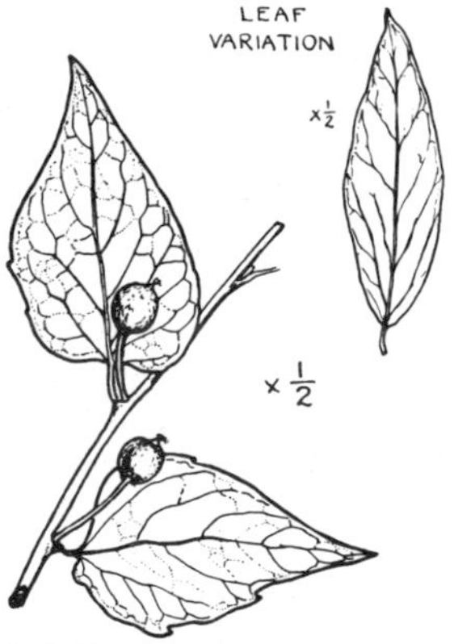

FIG. 72
CELTIS MISSISSIPPIENSIS
VAR. RETICULATA

ca, the West Indies, South America (from Venezuela to Peru), Persia, northwestern India, northern China, Manchukuo, and Japan. Two species are native to California. The following is often more shrub-like than tree-like.

1. **Juglans californica** Wats. SOUTHERN CALIFORNIA BLACK WALNUT. Fig. 69.

An arborescent shrub or small tree, 15 to 30 feet high, commonly with several stems from the ground or the single stem branching within 1 to 4 feet of the ground, forming a shrub-like growth often as broad as high. Leaves odd-pinnately compound, alternate, deciduous, 6 to 12 inches long; leaflets 9 to 19, oblong-lanceolate, 1½ to 3 inches long, ⅓- to ¾-inch wide, often long-pointed, coarsely serrate except at base, glabrous above and below, sometimes with tufts of hairs in the axils of the veins beneath, sessile. Flowers monoecious, apetalous; the staminate in catkins 2 to 5 inches long, each flower with 20 to 40 stamens, calyx-lobes very minute; the pistillate flowers 1 to several in a cluster, each flower with bracts, bracteoles, and a 4-lobed calyx, pistil with 2 styles and 2 recurved stigmas, the ovary inferior, 1- or incompletely 2- to 4-celled. Fruit a globose nut, ¾-inch to 1¼ inches in diameter, consisting of a single seed surrounded by a smooth shell with a few longitudinal depressions, enclosed in a semi-fleshy or fibrous husk. Flowering period, March and April.

Southern California Black Walnut inhabits dry hillsides and valleys of the Upper Sonoran Life Zone in the coastal mountains of San Luis Obispo, Santa Barbara, and Ventura (Ojai Valley) counties, southward to the Santa Monica Mountains (Cahuenga Pass), thence along the Sierra Madre and San Bernardino foothills (Waterman Canyon) as far east as the highway from San Bernardino to the Cajon Pass, and south to La Brea Canyon in the Santa Ana Mountains.

Juglans californica Wats. Proc. Am. Acad. 10:349 (1875). Type locality: Not indicated.

Myricaceae. Sweet Gale Family

The Sweet Gale Family contains 2 genera with about 40 species of trees or shrubs, widely distributed over subtropical and temperate regions. Only one genus occurs in California.

1. **Myrica** L.

(From the Greek *murike,* probably originally applied to the tamarisk.)

Small trees or shrubs with simple alternate deciduous or evergreen leaves. Flowers unisexual, the male and female flowers on the same or separate plants, apetalous, in catkins. Ovary superior, 1-celled, subtended by 2 to 4 short bractlets. Fruit a nut or nutlet.

This genus contains about 30 species, only 2 of which are native to California.

KEY TO THE SPECIES

Leaves evergreen; plants monoecious........................1. *M. californica.*
Leaves deciduous; plants dioecious..........................2. *M. Hartwegii.*

1. **Myrica californica** C. & S. PACIFIC WAX-MYRTLE. Fig. 70.

A large evergreen shrub or small tree, 10 to 35 feet high, with slender ascending branches and smooth gray or light brown bark. Leaf-blades oblong to oblanceolate, 2 to 4½ inches long, ½- to ¾-inch wide, glabrous, dark green and glossy above, slightly paler beneath, remotely serrate or almost entire, narrowed at the base to a petiole ⅛- to ⅜-inch long. Staminate and pistillate catkins borne on the same plant; the staminate catkins ½-inch to 1 inch long; the pistillate catkins ¼- to ½-inch long, in the leaf-axils above those bearing the staminate catkins. Pistillate and staminate flowers sometimes borne in the same catkin. Fruit a globose papillate brownish purple nut, ⅙- to ¼-inch in diameter, covered with a thin coat of whitish wax, berry-like in appearance. Flowering period, March and April.

Pacific Wax-myrtle occurs in canyons and on moist hill slopes of the coastal region from the Santa Monica Mountains of Los Angeles County northward to Del Norte County, and north to Washington.

The evergreen glossy foliage and bushy habit make this plant desirable for cultivation. It thrives best in semi-moist habitats.

Myrica californica C. & S. Linnaea 6:535 (1831). Type locality: San Francisco, California. Collected by *Chamisso*.

2. **Myrica Hartwegii** Wats. SIERRA WAX-MYRTLE. SIERRA-BAY. Fig. 71.

A low diffuse shrub, 3 to 6 feet high, with rather slender pubescent branches becoming glabrous and dark red-brown in age. Leaves deciduous, aromatic, appearing after the flowers; the blades oblanceolate, 1½ to 3 inches long, ½-inch to 1 inch wide, thin, light green and minutely pubescent or glabrate above, paler and permanently pubescent beneath, serrate above the attenuated entire base; petioles ⅜-inch or less long. Staminate and pistillate catkins borne on separate plants; the staminate catkins cylindric, ½- to ¾-inch long; the pistillate catkins subglobose, about ⅙-inch long, becoming nearly ½-inch long in fruit. Fruit a laterally compressed nutlet, about ⅛-inch long, shorter than the bracts which enclose it. Flowering period, June and July.

Sierra Wax-myrtle occurs occasionally along stream banks and on hill slopes of the Transition Life Zone in the Sierra Nevada from Yuba County south to Fresno County.

Myrica Hartwegii Wats. Proc. Am. Acad. 10:350 (1875). Type locality: Probably on the San Joaquin River or on the Yuba River. Collected by *Hartweg*.

Ulmaceae. Elm Family

This family consists of about 13 genera and 140 species of trees and shrubs, widely distributed in temperate and tropical regions. A single genus with one variety is native to California.

1. **Celtis** L. HACKBERRY

(Name of an African *Lotus* tree, given by Pliny but later adopted by Tournefort for the hackberry.)

This genus contains about 60 species, widely distributed in the tropical and temperate regions of both hemispheres.

1. **Celtis mississippiensis** var. **reticulata** (Torr.) Sarg. WESTERN HACKBERRY. Fig. 72.

A low densely branched shrub or a small spreading tree, 10 to 30 feet high. Leaves simple, alternate, deciduous; the blades ovate or ovate-lanceolate, unequal at the slightly heart-shaped base, 1 to 3½ inches long, ¾-inch to 1½ inches wide, somewhat 3-veined from the base, thick, leathery, very veiny, deep green above, lighter and pubescent on the veins beneath, very rough to the touch, the margins serrulate to coarsely serrate or entire; petioles ¼-inch or less long, slightly pubescent. Flowers inconspicuous, monoecious or polygamo-monoecious, appearing with or before the leaves on branches of the season; the staminate flowers in clusters at the base of the season's shoot, the pistillate flowers solitary or few in clusters in the axils of the upper leaves; calyx deeply 4- to 6-lobed, greenish yellow; corolla none; stamens 4 to 6 in both the staminate and bisexual flowers, the filaments exserted; ovary superior, usually 1-celled, with a short sessile style. Fruit a globose drupe about 1/4-inch in diameter, dark brown or orange-red when mature, on pubescent peduncles 1/4- to 3/8-inch long. Flowering period, March or April.

Western Hackberry occurs occasionally in gravelly washes and canyons in the mountain ranges bordering the deserts of southern California, in the Upper Sonoran Life Zone. The known localities in California are in Hackberry Canyon, a tributary of Caliente Creek and in a canyon about 3 miles above Caliente, Kern County; Eureka Valley and near Independence, Inyo County; about 1/4-mile up the canyon from the reservoir on Arthur Gilman's ranch near Banning, Riverside County; Thing's Valley about 15 miles north of Campo, San Diego County; and in the Clark and New York mountains in eastern San Bernardino County. It extends eastward to Arizona, New Mexico, and Texas and northward to Idaho and eastern Oregon and Washington. The plants in San Diego County usually have coarsely serrate leaves, and the pubescence on the lower surface is confined to the veins. The leaves of the Inyo County plants are usually hirsutulous between the veins as well as on the veins beneath, and their margins vary from serrulate to entire. The leaves of the Kern County plants are pubescent only on the veins beneath, and their margins are nearly entire.

Celtis mississippiensis var. reticulata (Torr.) Sarg. Silva N. Am. 7:72 (1895). *Celtis reticulata* Torr. Type locality: The Rocky Mountains. *Celtis Douglasii* Planch.

Loranthaceae. Mistletoe Family

The Mistletoe Family contains 21 genera and about 600 species of semi-parasitic evergreen shrubs or herbs, mostly tropical or subtropical, a few extending into the temperate zone.

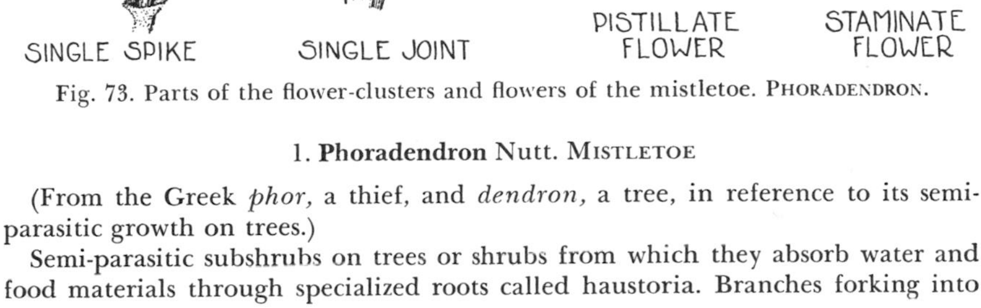

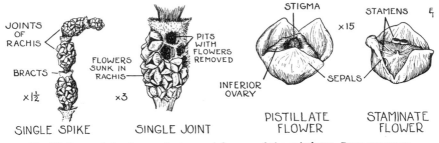

Fig. 73. Parts of the flower-clusters and flowers of the mistletoe. PHORADENDRON.

1. **Phoradendron** Nutt. MISTLETOE

(From the Greek *phor,* a thief, and *dendron,* a tree, in reference to its semi-parasitic growth on trees.)

Semi-parasitic subshrubs on trees or shrubs from which they absorb water and food materials through specialized roots called haustoria. Branches forking into

2 nearly equal divisions (dichotomous). Leaves simple, opposite, entire, often reduced to scales. Flowers usually unisexual, the staminate and pistillate on separate plants, or rarely bisexual, solitary or in clusters; sepals 2 to 5, in the pistillate flowers united at base with the receptacle to form a receptocalyx; petals none; stamens as many as the sepals and inserted on their bases; ovary inferior, 1-celled. Fruit a 1-seeded berry.

About 100 species of mistletoes have been described from North and South America. Eight species are native to California. These plants are well known to

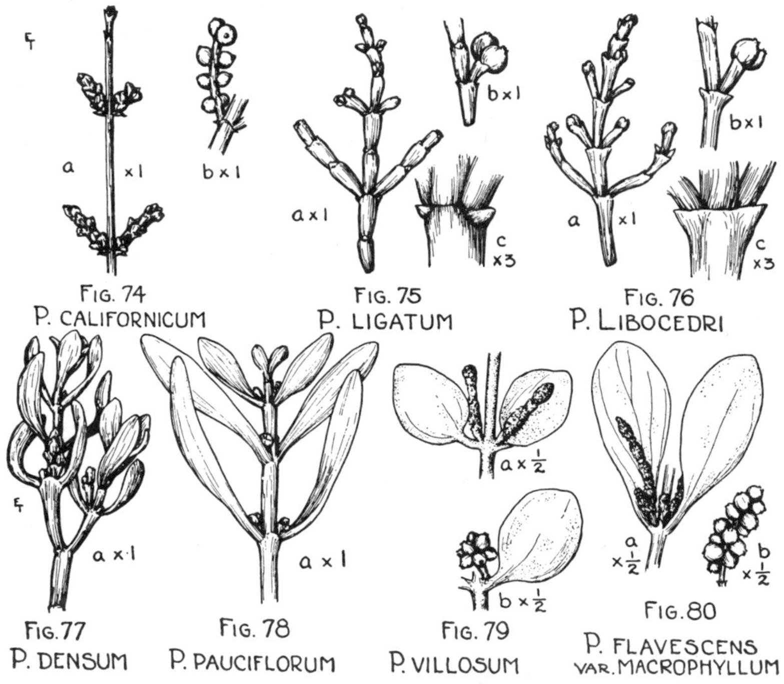

PHORADENDRON. a, Branchlet with leaves and flowers. b, Fruit.

most people since they are used extensively for Christmas decorations in the United States. The plants grow in such abundance in some localities that they ultimately kill their hosts. The fruits are eaten by birds and it is largely by this agency that the plants are dispersed from one host to another.

KEY TO THE SPECIES

Parasitic on broad-leaved trees or shrubs, never on coniferous trees.

Leaves scale-like; pistillate flowers 2 at each joint; fruit red, or white in one variety..1. *P. californicum.*

Leaves foliaceous; pistillate flowers 6 or more at the joints of the rachis; fruit white or pink-tinged.

Parasitic on Prosopis; leaves essentially glabrous; joints of staminate spikes 20- to 30-flowered.................................2. *P. coloradense.*

Parasitic chiefly on oaks; leaves villous-pubescent, ¾-inch to 1½ inches long; joints of staminate spikes about 12-flowered............*3. P. villosum.*

Parasitic on soft-wood trees (willow, poplar, buckeye, ash, sycamore, walnut, etc.); leaves densely pubescent when young, nearly glabrous in age, 1 to 3 inches long; joints of staminate spikes 20- to 30-flowered. 4. *P. flavescens* var. *macrophyllum.*

Parasitic on coniferous trees.

Leaves scale-like.

Scale-like leaves distinctly constricted-grooved at base; parasitic on junipers. 5. *P. ligatum.*

Scale-like leaves not distinctly constricted at base; parasitic on Incense-cedar. 6. *P. Libocedri.*

Leaves foliaceous.

Parasitic on firs; leaves usually about 1 inch long.........7. *P. pauciflorum.*

Parasitic on junipers, pines, and cypresses; leaves usually less than ¾-inch long......................................8. *P. densum.*

1. **Phoradendron californicum** Nutt. MESQUITE MISTLETOE. CALIFORNIA MISTLETOE. Fig. 74.

Mesquite Mistletoe is parasitic on various trees and shrubs of the Mohave and Colorado deserts, east to Arizona, and south to Sonora and Lower California. It has been seen growing on *Prosopis chilensis, P. pubescens, Acacia Greggii, Olneya tesota, Condalia lycioides, C. spatulata,* and *Larrea divaricata.*

A form with elongated fruiting spikes in which the fruit is arranged in distinctly separated whorls has been described by Trelease as **P. californicum** var. **distans.** Another form with white berries found at Twenty-nine Palms and at Andreas Canyon, Riverside County, has been described by Trelease as **P. californicum** forma **leucocarpum.**

Phoradendron californicum Nutt. Jour. Phil. Acad. ser. 2, 1:185 (1848). Type locality: Southern California. Collected by *Gambel.*

2. **Phoradendron coloradense** Trel. COLORADO DESERT MISTLETOE.

This mistletoe is parasitic on *Prosopis.* It has been reported from Needles, San Bernardino County, Laguna, San Diego County and eastward to Arizona.

Phoradendron coloradense Trel. Monogr. Phoradendron 39 (1916). Type locality: Fort Yuma, Arizona.

3. **Phoradendron villosum** Nutt. COMMON MISTLETOE. Fig. 79.

Common Mistletoe is parasitic chiefly on oaks but has been found growing on *Umbellularia, Aesculus, Arctostaphylos, Castanopsis, Fraxinus,* and *Adenostoma.* It occurs from Oregon south in the Coast Ranges and foothills of the Sierra Nevada to southern and Lower California.

Phoradendron villosum Nutt. Jour. Phil. Acad. ser. 2, 1:185 (1848). Type locality: Willamette Valley, Oregon.

4. **Phoradendron flavescens** var. **macrophyllum** Engelm. BIGLEAF MISTLETOE. Fig. 80.

This species occurs upon a number of soft-wood trees of the Sacramento and San Joaquin valleys, in southern California, and east to Arizona and probably to Texas. Known host trees are *Populus Fremontii, Salix laevigata, S. fluvitalis, S. nigra, Juglans Hindsii, J. californica, Alnus rhombifolia, Umbellularia californica, Platanus racemosa, Fraxinus oregona, F. dipetala,* and *Aesculus californica.*

Phoradendron flavescens var. macrophyllum Engelm. Bot. Wheeler Exp., Rep.

U. S. Surv. 100th Merid. 6:252 (1878). Type locality: Gila and Bonita rivers, Arizona. *Phoradendron longispicum* Trel.

5. **Phoradendron ligatum** Trel. CONSTRICTED MISTLETOE. Fig. 75.

This mistletoe is parasitic upon junipers. It is very close to *P. juniperinum* Engelm. of the Rocky Mountains, and might easily be included in that species since the character, constricted bases of the scale-like leaves, is quite a variable one. It has been collected near Mount Bidwell, northeastern Modoc County *(Mrs. M. H. Manning)*.

Phoradendron ligatum Trel. Monogr. Phoradendron 24 (1916). Type locality: Crook County, Oregon.

6. **Phoradendron Libocedri** (Engelm.) Howell. INCENSE-CEDAR MISTLETOE. Fig. 76.

This mistletoe grows on the Incense-cedar *(Libocedrus decurrens)* and occurs sparingly throughout the range of that species. It is closely related to *Phoradendron juniperinum* and *P. ligatum*.

Phoradendron Libocedri (Engelm.) Howell, Fl. N. W. Am. 1:618 (1902). *P. juniperinum* var. *Libocedri* Engelm. Type locality: Duffield's Ranch, Sierra Nevada, California.

7. **Phoradendron pauciflorum** Torr. FIR MISTLETOE. Fig. 78.

Fir Mistletoe occurs on the White Fir *(Abies concolor)* in the Sierra Nevada southward to Lower California. In the Sierra San Pedro Martir it grows on *Cupressus (I. L. Wiggins)*.

Phoradendron pauciflorum Torr. Pacif. R. Rep. 4:134 (1857). Type locality: Duffield's Ranch, Sierra Nevada, California.

8. **Phoradendron densum** Torr. CYPRESS MISTLETOE. Fig. 77.

This mistletoe grows on *Cupressus Macnabiana, C. Sargentii, Juniperus californica, J. occidentalis,* and *Pinus monophylla* (Lockwood Creek canyon, Mount Piños region). This species is referred by some authors to *Phoradendron bolleanum* Eichler which is native to Mexico and has very narrow almost linear leaves.

Phoradendron densum Torr.; Trel. Monogr. Phoradendron 27 (1916). Type locality: Mount Shasta, California.

Aristolochiaceae. Birthwort Family

The Birthwort Family consists of 5 genera and about 200 species, widely distributed in the warmer parts of the world, being most abundant in South America. Two genera, *Asarum* and *Aristolochia,* with 4 species are native to California, only one of which is woody.

1. **Aristolochia** L. BIRTHWORT. DUTCHMAN'S PIPE

(From the Greek *aristos,* best, and *locheia,* parturition, because of its supposed efficacy in childbirth.)

This genus contains about 180 species of perennial herbs or twining woody vines, widely distributed in tropical and temperate regions. They are interesting because of their odd flowers which often have a disagreeable odor. Many forms are grown in botanical collections.

1. **Aristolochia californica** Torr. CALIFORNIA DUTCHMAN'S PIPE. Fig. 81.

A semi-woody climber, 6 to 12 feet long, woody at base, with slender stems more or less covered with short silky hairs. Leaves simple, alternate, deciduous; the blades ovate-cordate, 1½ to 5 inches long, 1 to 3 inches wide, pubescent on both surfaces, palmately veined, entire; petioles ½-inch to 2 inches long. Flowers pipe-shaped, solitary, axillary, pendulous, greenish purple, about 1 inch long, doubled on themselves near the middle, each composed of 3 united petal-like sepals; petals none; stamens usually 6, without filaments, the anthers in pairs, adnate to the short style or stigma; ovary 6-celled, attached to the calyx-tube. Fruit a 6-valved and 6-angled capsule, 1 to 2½ inches long, with numerous seeds. Flowering period, March and April.

California Dutchman's Pipe is found usually in the lower foothills of the middle and inner Coast Ranges from Santa Clara, San Mateo, Marin, and Solano counties northward around the head of the Sacramento Valley, thence southward along the Sierra Nevada foothills to Sacramento County, in the Upper Sonoran Life Zone. It is said also to occur sparingly near the coast in Monterey County.

Aristolochia californica Torr. Pacif. R. Rep. 4:128 (1857). Type locality: "Corte Madera, Marin County." Collected by *Bigelow*.

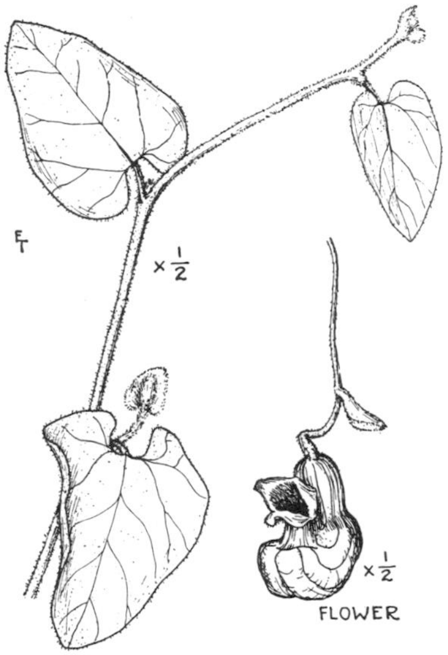

FIG. 81 ARISTOLOCHIA CALIFORNICA

Polygonaceae. Buckwheat Family

The Buckwheat Family consists of 30 genera and about 700 species, mostly in the temperate zones. Ten genera and about 150 species are native to California. Only the genus *Eriogonum*, in California, has species distinctly shrubby.

1. **Eriogonum** Michx. WILD-BUCKWHEAT

(From the Greek *erion*, wool, and *gonu*, knee or joint, in reference to the hairy joints and stems of some species.)

Mostly annual or herbaceous perennial plants, some species woody at the base, and a few shrubby throughout. Leaves simple, alternate, basal, whorled, or fascicled, entire, usually reduced to bracts on the flower-bearing stalks, without stipules. Flowers usually bisexual, borne in an involucre, usually exserted on recurved stalklets when mature; sepals 6, usually colored and united at their bases, sometimes tapering at base into a narrow stalk (stipe) continuous with the pedicel; petals none; stamens usually 9; pistil 1, with 3 styles, 3 stigmas, and a superior, 3-carpelled, 1-celled ovary. Involucres sessile or stalked, borne in heads, umbels, or solitary along the branches or sometimes terminal at the ends of leafless stems arising from the ground. Fruit an achene, usually triangular and surrounded by the persistent bases of the calyx.

This genus contains about 160 species, mostly of the western United States and a few in Mexico. About 100 species and varieties have been described from California and the islands off the coast, only 6 of which are distinctly shrubby.

The wild-buckwheats are among our most interesting and ornamental native shrubs and subshrubs. Their white, cream-colored, pink, reddish, yellow, or sulphur-colored flowers and commonly gray or white-tomentose leaves make them very attractive in their native habitats as well as in cultivation. Several of the dwarf varieties should make fine rock garden plants.

Under different habitat conditions, considerable variation occurs in all parts of the plants, but the variation in the size of the plants and the amount of branching

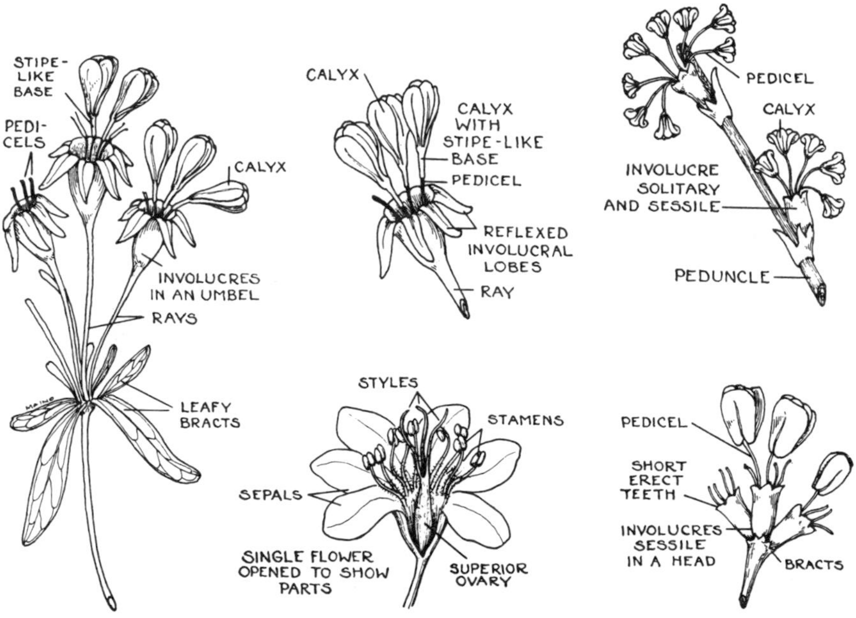

Parts of the flower-clusters and flowers of ERIOGONUM.

of the flower-bearing stalks is most noticeable. Simple or branched stalks with simple or compound umbels are found on the same plant, or the umbels are reduced to a sessile head in the axil of two or more branches of the flower-bearing stalks. The bracts, involucres, calyces, and their supporting stalks furnish important "key" characters and anyone hoping to identify the wild-buckwheats should become acquainted with these characters before attempting to use the following key.

KEY TO THE SPECIES

I. Plants distinctly shrubby.

Plants usually leafless for most of the year; involucres solitary or rarely 2 at a node; leaf-blades ovate, about $\frac{1}{4}$-inch long, not revolute; petioles $\frac{1}{4}$-inch or less long; calyx yellow, villous; Colorado Desert........1. *E. deserticola.*

Plants with leaves throughout the year; involucres 2 to many in heads, umbels, or cymes.

Margins of leaves revolute; involucres in head-like clusters.

Leaves $\frac{1}{2}$-inch to $1\frac{1}{2}$ inches long, linear or narrowly oblong, crowded on the ends of the branchlets; the head-like clusters of involucres in compound cymes; island species......................2. *E. arborescens.*

Leaves 1/8- to 2/3-inch long, usually crowded or fascicled; the head-like clusters of involucres terminal or in racemes or umbels; chiefly mainland species.

Leaves round-ovate or oblong-lanceolate, truncate or subcordate at base, the margins commonly undulate................3. *E. parvifolium.*

Leaves oblong, linear or oblanceolate, tapering to a narrow base, the margins not undulate; involucres with short erect teeth.
4. *E. fasciculatum.*

Margins of leaves not revolute; leaf-blades ovate.

Leaf-blades 1 to 2½ inches long, densely white-tomentose on both surfaces or rarely glabrate above; petioles ½-inch to 1 inch long; involucres in dense compound cymes; island species..............5. *E. giganteum.*

Leaf-blades ½-inch to 1 inch long; thinly gray-tomentose beneath; petioles ¼- to ½-inch long; involucres in heads, these in racemes or umbels; coastal mainland species...........................6. *E. cinereum.*

II. Plants not distinctly shrubby but with short stems woody at base, often mat-like and less than 1 foot high; the herbaceous flowering stems sometimes 2 to 4 feet high. (The following species are "keyed out" but not described.)

A. Leaves distinctly round or round-ovate.

1. Leaves densely white-tomentose on both surfaces (rarely glabrate above).

Leaf-blades ½-inch to 1 inch long and about as broad; calyx prolonged into a stipe-like base.

Peduncles lying flat upon the ground, 3 to 8 inches long; leaves densely silvery-tomentose, the blades and petioles about 1 inch long; involucres in umbels or heads; calyx white, soon changing to pink.
7. *E. Lobbii.* GRANITE-BUCKWHEAT.

Peduncles erect, naked, 4 to 12 inches high.

Involucres solitary, scattered along the branches of the peduncle; petioles 1/8- to ¼-inch long; calyx glabrous, white or pale yellow.
8. *E. saxatile.* HOARY-BUCKWHEAT.

Involucres in a terminal head on an unbranched peduncle; petioles 1/3-inch to 1 inch long; calyx appressed-hairy at base, white.
9. *E. latens.* INYO-BUCKWHEAT.

Leaf-blades usually ½-inch or less broad; subalpine dwarfs, usually 1 to 3 inches high, or sometimes as much as 12 inches high.

a. Involucres solitary on the leafless flowering stem; bracts borne near the middle of the stem; calyx yellow, prolonged into a stipe-like base.
10. *E. alpinum.* ALPINE-BUCKWHEAT.

b. Involucres crowded into a single head at the top of the naked stem which bears 3 or 4 short bracts just below the head; calyx white or reddish, not prolonged into a stipe-like base.
11. *E. ovalifolium.* SUBALPINE-BUCKWHEAT.

c. Involucres in umbels or rarely reduced to heads; peduncle without bracts; calyx yellow or changing to red, prolonged into a stipe-like base....................13. *E. marifolium.* MOUNTAIN-BUCKWHEAT.

2. Leaves usually glabrate above in age; involucres in heads or umbels; calyx prolonged into a stipe-like base; peduncles leafless, arising from a densely leafy basal stem.

Peduncles 2 to 3½ inches tall; bracts 2, elongated; umbels with 1 to 3 involucres on stalks (rays) about ⅙-inch long, sessile and head-like; leaf-blades 1 inch long or less; petioles usually as long as the blades; calyx villous or hairy, red.........12. *E. pyrolaefolium.* SHASTA-BUCKWHEAT.

Peduncles 2 to 12 inches tall.

Bracts usually inconspicuous or absent; umbels with 3 to 6 rays ½-inch to 2½ inches long, or the umbels reduced to heads; leaf-blades and petioles ¼- to ¾-inch long; calyx glabrous, yellowish, varying to red in age....................13. *E. marifolium.* MOUNTAIN-BUCKWHEAT.

Bracts very conspicuous, subtending the rays of the umbels; calyx glabrous.

Involucral lobes reflexed........14. *E. umbellatum.* SULPHUR FLOWER.

Involucral lobes or teeth erect......15. *E. ursinum.* BEAR-BUCKWHEAT.

B. Leaves not round.

1. Involucres solitary or few at the nodes, sessile and scattered along the branches of the inflorescence or rarely congested.

a. Peduncles unbranched (sometimes branched in *E. sphaerocephalum*), 3 to 6 inches high, bearing a solitary involucre; calyx stipe-like at base; plants often dwarfed and matted; leaf-blades ¼- to rarely ¾-inch long.

Peduncles naked; leaves densely white-tomentose; involucral lobes reflexed; calyx yellow to reddish..16. *E. caespitosum.* MAT-BUCKWHEAT.

Peduncles with 3 to several bracts near their middle or the bracts subtending the 2- to 4-rayed umbel; the rays with bracts near the middle.

Bracts 3, leaf-like; involucral teeth erect; calyx white or pinkish.
17. *E. Kelloggii.* MENDOCINO-BUCKWHEAT.

Bracts 4 or more; involucral lobes reflexed, as long as or longer than the tube.

Leaf-blades about ¼-inch long, oval; calyx yellow or rarely cream-colored; dwarf matted plants.
18. *E. Douglasii.* DOUGLAS-BUCKWHEAT.

Leaf-blades ½-inch or more long, oblanceolate or oblong, the margins often revolute; calyx white or rarely yellow; plants much branched, with short leafy branches.
19. *E. sphaerocephalum.* ROCK-BUCKWHEAT.

b. Peduncles branched, forming compound inflorescences, with many involucres which are scattered or congested; calyx not stipe-like at base.

Plants usually 4 to 12 (16) inches high.

Peduncles branched near the summit into 3 or more forks, the forks again once- (or more-) divided; involucres congested at the ends of the forks; leaves usually glabrate above.
20. *E. microthecum.* NUTTALL-BUCKWHEAT.

Peduncles irregularly branched, usually with only 2 or 3 forks, these rarely again forked; involucres scattered along the peduncle or forks.

Leaves white-tomentose on both surfaces; flowers white or pink.
21. *E. Wrightii.* WRIGHT-BUCKWHEAT.

Leaves glabrate above; flowers white or pink.
22. *E. taxifolium.* PINE-BUCKWHEAT.

Plants 1 to 3 feet tall.

Inflorescences intricately branched, commonly paniculate; flowers few, mostly terminal.

Flowering branchlets glabrous, somewhat spinescent; forks of the panicle straight; involucral teeth or lobes glabrous, scarious-margined............23. *E. Heermannii.* MOHAVE-BUCKWHEAT.

Flowering branches densely tomentulose, not spinescent; forks of the panicle somewhat curved; involucral teeth or lobes pubescent, not scarious-margined....24. *E. plumatella.* YUCCA-BUCKWHEAT.

Inflorescences racemose, with slender elongated branches often again di vided; leaves ½-inch to 1½ inches long.

Involucres sessile along one side of short lateral branchlets, or some pedicellate and in the axils of the forks; leaves white-woolly beneath, not undulate.....25. *E. nodosum.* SONORAN-BUCKWHEAT.

Involucres remotely scattered along the elongated stems or branches, or sometimes congested near the ends; leaves undulate, silvery-tomentose on both surfaces or glabrate above.
26. *E. elongatum.* SILVER-BUCKWHEAT.

2. Involucres 2 to several in heads or umbels, rarely solitary; plants usually 2 to 16 inches tall (often taller in *E. nudum*).

Calyx not stipe-like at base.

Plants dwarfed, 2 to 8 inches high; leaves densely white-tomentose on both surfaces.

Calyx yellow; leaves ¾-inch to 1¼ inches long; involucres in a head-like cluster, the lobes 6 to 8, erect.
27. *E. ochrocephalum.* WOOLLY-BUCKWHEAT.

Calyx white, pink, or reddish; leaves less than ½-inch long; peduncles with a single head.

Stems 3 to 8 inches tall; leaves revolute; calyx-segments similar; desert species.............28. *E. Kennedyi.* KENNEDY-BUCKWHEAT.

Stems 1 to 3 inches tall; leaves not revolute; involucres woolly; the head subtended by 3 or 4 small bracts; calyx-segments dissimilar; high mountain species. 11. *E. ovalifolium.* SUBALPINE-BUCKWHEAT.

Plants ½-foot to 3 (rarely 5) feet high; leaves 1 to 2½ inches long.

Involucres glabrous or nearly so, nearly ¼-inch long; stems often hollow, usually branching into several forks.

Flowers white or rarely yellowish or pale rose.

Plants 1 to 3 feet high; chiefly mainland.
34. *E. nudum.* NAKED-BUCKWHEAT.

Plants 3 to 5 feet high; Santa Barbara Islands.
34a. *E. nudum* var. *grande.*

Flowers red or deep rose-pink; low procumbent plants; Santa Barbara Islands................35. *E. rubescens.* RED-BUCKWHEAT.

Involucres tomentose, in terminal and sessile capitate clusters; stems usually not hollow, usually branching into 2 or 4 forks or simple and with a single large head..36. *E. latifolium.* COAST-BUCKWHEAT.

Calyx stip-like at base.

Leaves erect, the blades 1½ to 4½ inches long, triangular-ovate or oblong-ovate, cordate at base; petioles 2 to 5 inches long; umbels 6- to 10-rayed, each with a head-like cluster of 1 to 5 involucrés.
29. *E. compositum.* NORTHERN-BUCKWHEAT.

Leaves spreading, the blades and petioles less than 2 inches long.
Leaf-blades glabrous, about 1 inch long.
30. *E. Torreyanum.* DONNER-BUCKWHEAT.
Leaf-blades white-tomentose, at least beneath.
Peduncles bearing a solitary involucre.
a. Peduncles without bracts; involucral teeth erect; calyx white.
9. *E. latens.* INYO-BUCKWHEAT.
b. Peduncles with 2 linear bracts beneath the head; calyx red.
12. *E. pyrolaefolium.* SHASTA-BUCKWHEAT.
c. Peduncles with a whorl of bracts near the middle; involucral lobes reflexed; calyx yellow.
31. *E. siskiyouensis.* SISKIYOU-BUCKWHEAT.
Peduncles bearing 2 to 10 rays, each ray with 1 to many involucres or the rays almost absent and the inflorescence head-like.
Leaves ¼-inch or less wide, the margins revolute; peduncles with a 3-rayed umbel; rays 3 to 5 inches long, bearing a whorl of bracts at the middle; involucral lobes reflexed; calyx yellow, densely hairy............32. *E. tripodum.* LAKE-BUCKWHEAT.
Leaves ¼-inch or more wide.
Bracts of the peduncles and rays inconspicuous or absent.
Involucres in umbels, rarely in heads; the umbels with 3 to 6 rays ½-inch to 3 inches long, the central involucre sometimes sessile; leaves white-woolly above or glabrous in age; peduncles 3 to 12 inches tall, from loosely branching bases........13. *E. marifolium.* MOUNTAIN-BUCKWHEAT.
Involucres usually in head-like clusters or the rays of the umbel less than ½-inch long; leaves white-tomentose on both surfaces, or glabrate above in age; peduncles 1 to 4 inches long, from compact bases.
33. *E. incanum.* SIERRA-BUCKWHEAT.
Bracts of the peduncles and rays conspicuous.
Bracts 2, linear or spatulate; umbels small, with 1 to 3 involucres on very short rays, or head-like; calyx red, villous; leaf-blades about 1 inch long, ovate or roundish.
12. *E. pyrolaefolium.* SHASTA-BUCKWHEAT.
Bracts 3 to many, subtending the umbels and secondary umbels or near the middle of the peduncles and rays; calyx glabrous.
Involucral lobes reflexed; peduncles 3 to 5 (or 8) inches tall; umbels simple or compound; rays 1 to 9, ½-inch to 3 inches long; calyx sulphur-yellow; leaf-blades ¼-inch to 1 inch long, ovate.
14. *E. umbellatum.* SULPHUR FLOWER.
Involucral teeth erect; peduncles 4 to 12 inches high; umbels usually compound, 3- to 10-rayed or reduced to head-like clusters; calyx white or yellow; leaf-blades ⅓- to ¾-inch long, ovate..15. *E. ursinum.* BEAR-BUCKWHEAT.

1. **Eriogonum deserticola** Wats. DESERT-BUCKWHEAT.

An erect or spreading almost leafless shrub, 2 to 4½ feet high and sometimes 8 feet wide, with tomentulose branches becoming glabrate in age. Branches forking by twos, the older ones often spreading along the surface of the ground. Leaves few, alternate, often clustered; the blades ovate or spatulate, about ¼-inch long, less than ¼-inch wide, obtuse or acute at apex, rounded at base or tapering to

Fig. 82. SANTA CRUZ ISLAND-BUCKWHEAT. *Eriogonum arborescens* Greene.

Fig. 83. SAINT CATHARINE'S LACE. *Eriogonum giganteum* Wats.

the petiole, gray-tomentose on both sides or glabrate above in age; petioles ¼-inch or less long. Involucres solitary at the nodes, nearly sessile, densely tomentose without, 4-toothed at summit, bearing 2 or 3 flowers. Calyx yellow, densely villous without, slightly villous at the base within, about ⅛-inch long, the segments almost equal, nearly distinct; filaments hairy at base. Flowering period, June to August.

Desert-buckwheat occurs on the sand flats and small shifting dunes in Imperial County between Holtville, California, and Yuma, Arizona, in the Lower Sonoran Life Zone. Collections were made by the writer in 1925 from about 40 miles west of Yuma to within 15 miles east of Holtville. Mr. I. T. Weeks, of Imperial Valley, has made a rather thorough study of its distribution and concludes that it is "pre-eminently a species of the shifting sand-dune country—in the eastern Colorado Desert." It may extend southward into Lower California.

Eriogonum deserticola Wats. Proc. Am. Acad. 25:125 (1891). Type locality: Southwestern part of the Colorado Desert. Collected by *C. R. Orcutt.*

2. **Eriogonum arborescens** Greene. SANTA CRUZ ISLAND-BUCKWHEAT. Fig. 82.

An erect or spreading shrub, 2 to 8 feet high, with the main stem often 4 inches thick. Leaves linear or linear-oblong, sessile, crowded on the ends of the branchlets, ½-inch to 1½ inches long, ⅛- to ¼-inch wide, gray and glabrous or tomentulose above, white-tomentose beneath, the margins strongly revolute. Peduncles stout, 2 to 8 inches long, bearing compound flower-clusters in which the terminal or central flowers bloom first. Involucres in head-like clusters, toothed at the summit. Calyx pink or rose-colored, densely white-hairy at base. Flowering period, May to September.

Santa Cruz Island-buckwheat occurs on the islands of Santa Cruz, Santa Rosa, and Anacapa off the coast of southern California, but has never been collected on

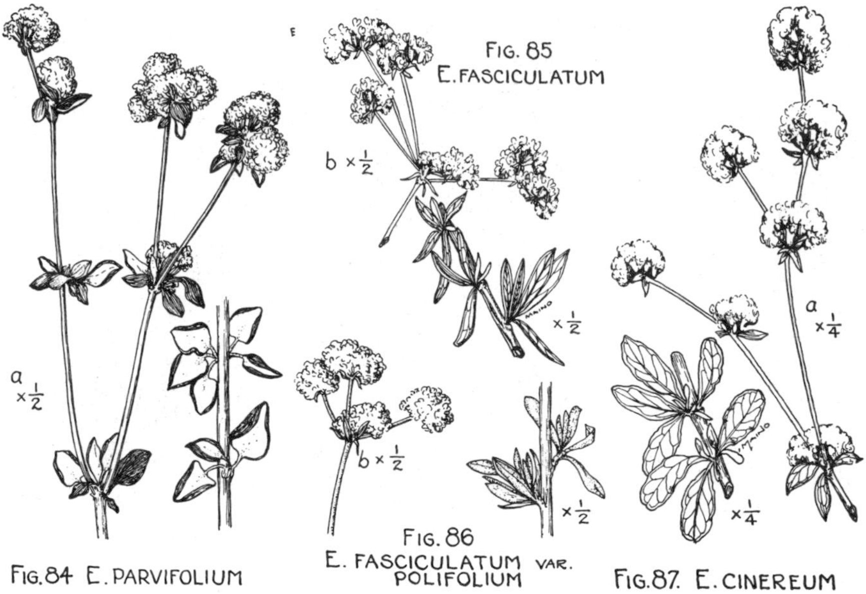

ERIOGONUM. a, Branchlet with flower-clusters. b, An umbel of flower-clusters.

the mainland. Its compact and spreading habit of growth when in cultivation, the dense masses of pinkish flowers in the summer, the grayish evergreen foliage, and its adaptability to dry soil make this plant desirable for ornamental planting. It seeds abundantly and the seeds germinate easily without special treatment.

Eriogonum arborescens Greene, Bull. Calif. Acad. 1:11 (1884). Type locality: Santa Cruz Island. Collected by *Kellogg* and *Harford*.

3. **Eriogonum parvifolium** Smith. SEACLIFF-BUCKWHEAT. Fig. 84.

A spreading shrub, 1 to 4 feet high, or sometimes woody only at the base, with numerous branches densely covered with clustered leaves. Leaf-blades roundish to deltoid-ovate or oblong-lanceolate, truncate or subcordate at base, acute at apex, ⅛- to ½-inch long, ⅛- to ¼- (rarely ⅜-) inch wide, densely white-tomentose beneath, dark green and usually glabrate above, the margins strongly revolute and often undulate; petioles ⅛-inch or less long. Peduncles simple or 2- or 3-branched, bearing few compact terminal or scattered heads of involucres or the heads sessile in the axils of the branches of the inflorescence. Calyx white and glabrous. Flowering period, May to September.

Seacliff-buckwheat occurs on the sand flats and hills from north of Seaside, Monterey County and extends southward along the coast to San Diego County. The triangular-shaped leaves, often thickly clothing the stems, are very distinctive and aid in field identification. The clusters of pink or white flowers furnish nectar for bees.

Eriogonum parvifolium Smith, Rees Cycl. 13 (1819). Type locality: Probably at Monterey, California. Collected by *Menzies*.

4. **Eriogonum fasciculatum** Benth. CALIFORNIA-BUCKWHEAT. Fig. 85.

KEY TO THE SPECIES AND VARIETIES

Upper surface of leaves glabrous. . . . . *E. fasciculatum*.

Upper surface of leaves pubescent or tomentose.

Upper surface of leaves green and pubescent. . . . . 4a. var. *foliolosum*.

Upper surface of leaves gray. . . . . 4b. var. *polifolium*.

Semi-erect bushes, 1 to 3 feet high and often 2 to 4 feet broad, with numerous slender flexible branches. Outer bark thin and exfoliating in thin strips. Leaves sessile, evergreen, in alternate fascicles, oblong-elliptic to linear or oblong-lanceolate, tapering at both ends, ½- to ¾-inch or rarely 1 inch long, less than ¼-inch wide, glabrous or white-tomentose above, white-tomentose beneath, the margins entire, usually more or less revolute. Peduncles terminating the branches, 3 to 10 inches long, bearing 4 to 9 unequal simple or branched rays in an umbel. Involucres sessile or short-stalked, with short acute teeth, borne in dense or open head-like clusters at the ends of the rays or sessile in their forks. Bracts linear or lanceolate, subtending the umbel and umbellets or heads, sometimes also on the rays below the flower-clusters. Calyx white or pinkish, glabrous or hairy, not stipe-like at base; anthers pink. Flowering period, May to October.

California-buckwheat inhabits the lower mountain slopes and flats from northern Santa Clara County southward to San Diego County and the desert slopes of the mountains of southern California, in the Lower and Upper Sonoran Life Zones.

The typical form with glabrous upper leaf-surfaces and flowers is confined to the coastal region. Two forms growing on the interior mountain slopes and flats have pubescent upper leaf-surfaces and flowers. They are given varietal rank. All the forms are considered good bee-plants.

4a. Var. **foliolosum** Stokes. Leaves more revolute, green and pubescent above, white-tomentose beneath. Peduncles 5 to 10 inches long.

This variety occurs in the Mount Hamilton Range, southward on the chaparral slopes in Monterey County, and on the lower mountain slopes of southern California. When transplanted it retains its distinctive characters. The spreading habit and long flowering period (May to October) make it suitable for ornamental planting, especially since it requires no watering during the dry summer months.

4b. Var. **polifolium** (Benth.) T. & G. Fig. 86. Foliage distinctly grayish. Leaves less revolute than in the preceding variety. Calyx conspicuously villous or hairy outside.

This variety occurs on the desert slopes of all the mountains of southern California and occasionally on the more arid exposures of the interior coastal slopes from Monterey County to San Diego County.

Several other forms are listed in the literature and herbaria, but all may be identified as belonging to the species and varieties as herein described.

Eriogonum fasciculatum Benth. Trans. Linn. Soc. 17:411 (1837). Type locality: "Upper California." Collected by *Menzies, Douglas,* and others.

Var. foliolosum Stokes; Abrams, Bull. N. Y. Bot. Gard. 6:351 (1910). *E. rosmarinifolium* Nutt. Type locality: Santa Barbara, California. Collected by *Nuttall.*

Var. polifolium (Benth.) T. & G. Proc. Am. Acad. 8:169 (1870). *E. polifolium* Benth. Type locality: "In Sierra Nevada, California," probably near Tehachapi. Collected by *Fremont.*

5. **Eriogonum giganteum** Wats. SAINT CATHARINE'S LACE. Fig. 83.

A freely branching shrub, 3 to 8 feet high, with tomentose or glabrate branches, a trunk often 4 inches in diameter, and rough bark. Leaves alternate; the blades rather thick and leathery, ovate, obtuse at apex, truncate or subcordate or rarely tapering at base, 1 to 2½ inches long, ½-inch to 2 inches wide, white-tomentose on both surfaces or glabrate above, the margins plane; petioles ½-inch to 1½ inches long. Peduncles much branched. Involucres densely white-tomentose without, sessile or very short-pedicelled, clustered near the ends of the numerous forks of the peduncle, the whole forming a compound cyme. Bracts foliaceous, subtending the forks of the inflorescence and the involucres. Calyx white or pinkish, densely white-hairy near the base, not stipe-like at base. Flowering period, April to October.

Saint Catharine's Lace occurs on Santa Catalina and San Clemente islands. It has not been found on the mainland.

Eriogonum giganteum Wats. Proc. Am. Acad. 20:371 (1885). Type locality: Santa Catalina Island. Collected by *W. S. Lyon.*

6. **Eriogonum cinereum** Benth. ASHYLEAF-BUCKWHEAT. Fig. 87.

A freely branched shrub, 2 to 6 feet high, with tomentulose branchlets. Leaves alternate, often with smaller ones in their axils; the blades ovate or somewhat triangular, acute or tapering at apex, tapering or sharply abrupt at base, ½-inch to 1 inch long, ⅜- to ¾-inch wide, glabrate above, white-tomentose beneath; petioles ¼- to ½-inch long. Peduncles commonly forking by twos, 6 to 18 inches long, finely tomentose. Involucres white-tomentose without, sessile, in head-like clusters, these in racemes or umbels. Bracts foliaceous, subtending the forks and heads. Calyx white or pink, not stipe-like at base. Flowering period, May to December.

Ashyleaf-buckwheat occurs in the canyons of the foothills and on the bluffs along the coast from Santa Barbara County southward to Los Angeles County, in the Upper Sonoran Life Zone.

Eriogonum cinereum Benth. Bot. Voy. Sulph. 45 (1844). Type locality: San Pedro, California. Collected by *Hinds.*

Chenopodiaceae. Goosefoot or Saltbush Family

The Goosefoot Family consists of about 75 genera and 550 species, mostly herbaceous annuals, biennials, or perennials, and a few shrubs, scattered throughout the world, commonly in alkaline or salty soils. Fifteen genera and about 60 species are found in California. Eighteen of these species are woody.

KEY TO THE GENERA

Leaves reduced to alternate scales on the fleshy jointed branches and branchlets . . . . 1. ALLENROLFEA.

Leaves not reduced to scales; branches not jointed.
Leaves revolute, linear; fruit densely white-hairy.................2. EUROTIA.
Leaves not revolute; fruit not white-hairy.
Leaves fleshy.
Plants thorny or spinescent, sometimes not thorny in *Grayia;* flowers unisexual.
Leaves about 1/8-inch wide; pistillate flowers with calyx but bractless; fruit with a broad circular horizontal wing from near the middle. 3. SARCOBATUS.
Leaves about 1/4-inch wide; pistillate flowers without calyx but with a membranous sac composed of 2 united bracts completely enclosing the ovary; fruit completely surrounded by reddish or whitish orbicular thin bracts.....................................4. GRAYIA.
Plants not thorny or spinescent; flowers bisexual or some pistillate.
Calyx in fruit not transversely winged.....................5. SUAEDA.
Calyx in fruit transversely winged........................6. KOCHIA.
Leaves not fleshy or only slightly so.
Plants subshrubby, less than 1 foot high; leaves linear, terete; flowers bisexual...6. KOCHIA.
Plants distinctly shrubby, over 1 foot high; flowers unisexual; pistillate flowers enclosed by 2 closely appressed bracts.
Leaves usually glabrate; bracts wholly united into a sac......4. GRAYIA.
Leaves more or less covered with a mealiness; bracts never wholly united to apex.......................................7. ATRIPLEX.

1. **Allenrolfea** Ktze.

(Named for Allen Rolfe, a botanist at Kew Gardens, England.)

This is a small genus of 3 species, only one of which grows in the United States.

1. **Allenrolfea occidentalis** (Wats.) Ktze. BUSH PICKLEWEED. KERN-GREASEWOOD. IODINE BUSH. Fig. 88.

A much branched erect succulent shrub, 2 to 4 feet high. Branches and branchlets green, jointed, and very fleshy. The main stems and branches woody. Leaves reduced to alternate broadly triangular scales. Flowers bisexual, small, crowded, arranged spirally by threes in the axils of fleshy subsessile bracts, forming a spike, the spikes numerous, cylindrical, 1/2-inch to 1 inch long; calyx of 4 or 5 concave, carinate, imbricate sepals, more or less united; petals none; stamens 1 or 2, filaments slender, exserted from between the bracts of the spike; ovary superior, 1-celled; styles 2 or 3, distinct. Fruit an achene with a membranous pericarp surrounded at maturity by the fleshy calyx. Flowering period, June to August.

Bush Pickleweed is found in strongly alkaline soils from near Byron Springs, Contra Costa County and the Altamont Pass southward through the Great Valley to the Mohave and Colorado deserts of southern California, in the Lower and Upper Sonoran Life Zones. Beyond our borders, it is found in the Great Basin region and southward to western Texas and into Mexico.

The stems when crushed leave a dark brown stain resembling an iodine stain, hence the name Iodine Bush. To the people of the desert almost any shrub may be called greasewood and since this plant is abundant south of Bakersfield in Kern County it also has been called Kern-greasewood. This plant sheds an abundance of light wind-blown pollen which may be a cause of hay-fever.

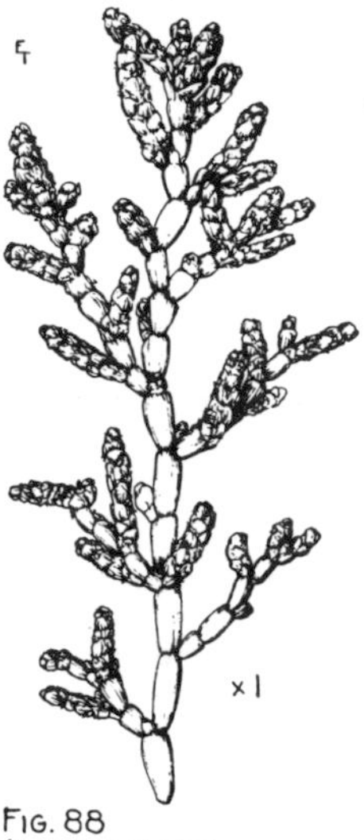

Fig. 88
Allenrolfea occidentalis

Fig. 89
Eurotia lanata

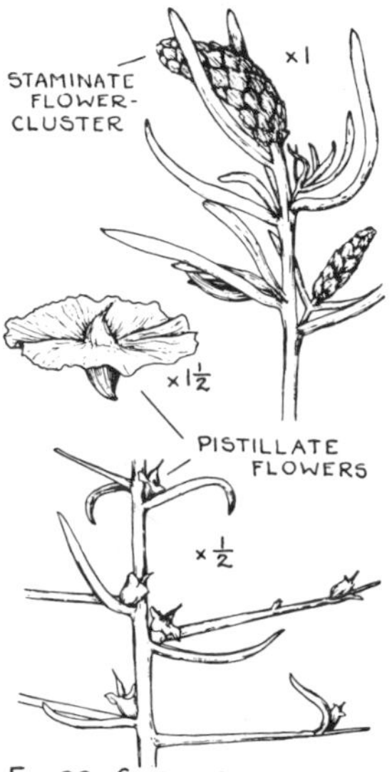

Fig. 90 Sarcobatus vermiculatus

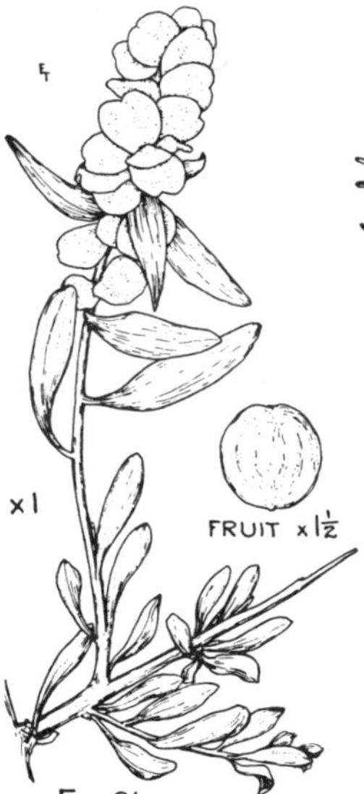

Fig. 91
Grayia spinosa

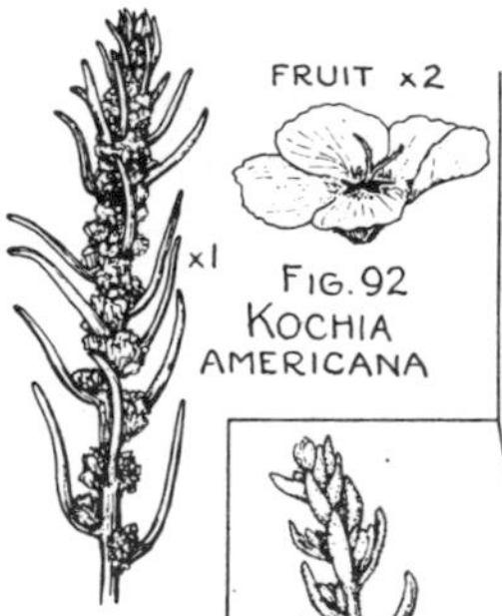

Fig. 92
Kochia americana

Fig. 93 Kochia californica

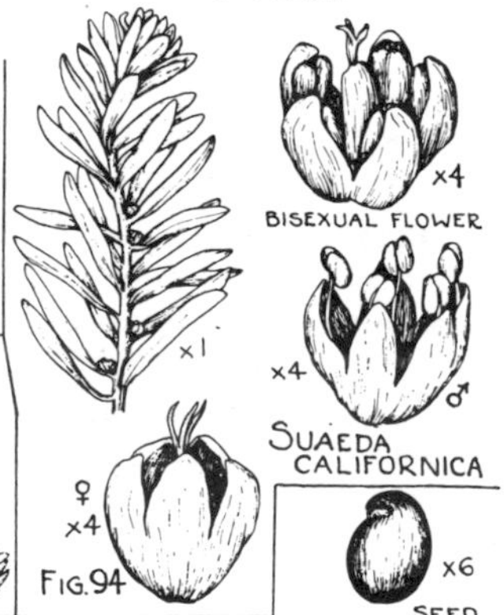

Fig. 94
Suaeda californica

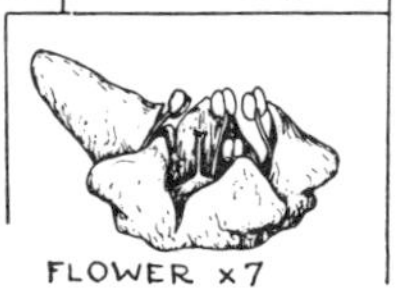

Fig. 95 Suaeda fruticosa

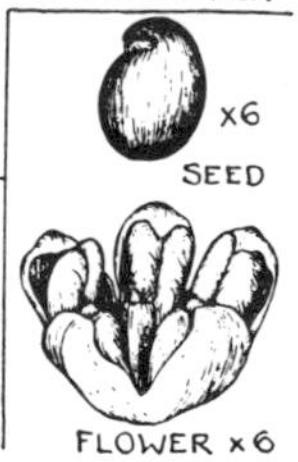

Fig. 96 Suaeda Torreyana

Allenrolfea occidentalis (Wats.) Ktze. Rev. Gen. Pl. 2:546 (1891). *Holostachys occidentalis* Wats. Type locality: "About Great Salt Lake and in alkaline valleys westward to the sinks of the Carson and Humboldt Rivers, where it grows luxuriantly in large tracts that would be otherwise destitute of vegetation." *Spirostachys occidentalis* Wats.

2. **Eurotia** Adans.

(From the Greek *euros,* mould, referring to the hairy covering of the plant.)

This is a small genus of 2 species, one from Europe and Asia and one from western United States and Mexico.

1. **Eurotia lanata** (Pursh) Moq. WINTER FAT. Fig. 89.

An erect or spreading shrub, 1 to 3 feet high, with ascending or spreading slender branches sometimes becoming more or less spinescent in age. The whole plant covered with a dense coating of star-shaped and unbranched hairs often intermingled, white when young, becoming rusty in age. Leaves simple, alternate or apparently fascicled, sessile, linear to linear-oblong, ½-inch to 1¾ inches long, the axillary and apparently fascicled ones less than ½-inch long, the margins strongly revolute, entire. Flowers unisexual, monoecious or dioecious, in dense paniculate clusters along the upper portions of the branches. The staminate flowers without bracts; sepals 4; petals none; stamens 4, opposite the sepals. The pistillate flowers with 2 bracts united to their summits and covered by long silky hairs; sepals none; petals none; ovary superior, 1-celled; styles 2. Fruit a utricle surrounded by 2 persistent bracts about ¼-inch long, covered by silvery white hairs, and beaked above by 2 short horns. Flowering period, April to August.

Winter Fat usually occurs in subalkaline soils on mesas and flats above 2000 feet altitude in eastern Lassen County, Inyo County, the Mohave Desert region of Kern, Los Angeles, and San Bernardino counties, and at Sunset in the eastern foothills of the inner Coast Range in Kern County *(Heller).* It extends northward to eastern Oregon, Washington, Idaho, and Canada, eastward through the Great Basin and the Rocky Mountain States to New Mexico, western Texas, and Nebraska, and southward to Mexico. Livestock feed upon the herbage during the winter months when other browse is scarce.

Eurotia lanata (Pursh) Moq. Enum. Chenopod. 81 (1840). *Diota lanata* Pursh. Type locality: "On the banks of the Missouri, in open prairies." Collected by *Lewis. E. subspinosa* Rydb.

3. **Sarcobatus** Nees.

(From the Greek *sarkos,* fleshy, and *batos,* thorn, referring to the fleshy leaves and thorns on the stems.)

This genus contains a single species.

1. **Sarcobatus vermiculatus** (Hook.) Torr. GREASEWOOD. Fig. 90.

A much branched erect or spreading shrub, 3 to 6 feet high, with the ultimate branches transformed into thorns. Leaves simple, alternate, evergreen, fleshy, linear, ½-inch to 1½ inches long, entire, at first minutely hairy, later subglabrous or glabrous, flat on the upper side, rounded beneath, sessile. Flowers small, unisexual, the staminate and pistillate borne on the same or different plants. Staminate flowers in a terminal catkin-like spike ½-inch to 1 inch long; calyx none; stamens 2 to 5, under a stalked scale. Pistillate flowers usually solitary and axillary in the upper leaves; calyx sac-like, undivided or sometimes slightly 2-lipped, surrounding the superior 1-celled ovary; style 1; stigmas 2. The calyx in fruit expanded into a broad circular horizontal membranous wing about ½-inch wide. Flowering period, May to August.

Greasewood inhabits alkaline flats along the borders of Mono Lake, Mono County, east of Middle Lake and near Mount Bidwell in northeastern Modoc County, near Honey Lake, Lassen County, and about Owens Lake, Inyo County, in the Lower and Upper Sonoran Life Zones. It extends northward to eastern Oregon and Washington and east and south through the Great Basin region to Arizona and Texas.

A form with the leaf-blades covered with white branched hairs and with the staminate inflorescences ¼- to ⅜-inch long occurs in western Nevada east of the Death Valley region of California and may be expected in the latter and adjacent areas. It is known as **Sarcobatus Baileyi** Cov.

Sarcobatus vermiculatus (Hook.) Torr.; Emory, Notes Mil. Rec. 150 (1848). *Batis ? vermiculatus* Hook. Type locality: "Common on the barren grounds of the Columbia, and particularly near salt marshes." Collected by *Douglas.*

4. **Grayia** H. & A.

(Named in honor of Asa Gray, the distinguished American botanist.)

The genus *Grayia* consists of 2 species of the Great Basin and desert regions of western North America. Only the following species has been found in California.

1. **Grayia spinosa** (Hook.) Moq. Spiny Hop-sage. Fig. 91.

An erect diffusely branched spinescent shrub, 1 to 3 feet high. Leaves simple, alternate, evergreen; the blades linear-oblanceolate or obovate, ⅓-inch to 1¼ inches long, rather fleshy, entire, sessile or very short-petiolate. Flowers small, greenish, monoecious or dioecious. Staminate flowers clustered in the axils of bracts or leaves; calyx 4- or 5-parted, membranous; petals none; stamens 4 or 5. Pistillate flowers mostly in dense crowded terminal spikes; calyx none; petals none; pistil almost completely enclosed by a pair of bracts folded along their midribs and united almost to their summits. Bracts in fruit obovate or round, ¼- to ½-inch wide, sessile, entire, notched at apex, often tinged with red. Flowering period, April to June.

Spiny Hop-sage occurs in alkaline valleys on the Mohave Desert of Kern, San Bernardino, and Los Angeles counties, in the White, Argus, and Panamint mountains of Inyo County, in eastern San Diego County (road to Salton Sea, *A. B. Clayton*), and in Honey Lake Valley, Lassen County *(J. B. Davy)*. Its range extends northward in eastern Oregon and Washington, and east to Nevada, Utah, Colorado, and Wyoming. It is reported to be of some value as a forage plant.

Grayia spinosa (Hook.) Moq.; DC. Prodr. 13:119 (1849). *Chenopodium ? spinosum* Hook. Type locality: "Interior of North California." Collected by *Douglas. Grayia polygaloides* H. & A.

5. **Suaeda** Forsk. Sea Blite

(An Arabic name.)

Annual or perennial herbs or sometimes subshrubs or shrubs. Leaves simple, alternate, evergreen, fleshy, linear, subterete. Flowers small, bisexual or unisexual by abortion, solitary or clustered in the axils of leafy bracts; calyx fleshy, 5-lobed or -parted, enclosing the fruit in age; petals none; stamens 2, 3, or 5; ovary superior, 1-celled; styles 2 or 3. Fruit a utricle, enclosed by the calyx.

This genus contains about 40 species of world-wide distribution, growing along seashores and in alkaline valleys. Five species are native to California, 3 of which are somewhat shrubby. The light wind-blown pollens may be a factor in causing hay-fever.

KEY TO THE SPECIES

Flowers 1/8-inch or more broad; leaves on flowering branches very crowded. 1. *S. californica.*

Flowers less than 1/8-inch broad; leaves on flowering branches not crowded.

Branches of the inflorescence crowded and ascending; calyx parted nearly to the base, one lobe much larger than the others. . . . . .2. *S. fruticosa.*

Branches of the inflorescence open and divaricate or spreading; calyx parted to below the middle, the lobes equal. . . . . .3. *S. Torreyana.*

1. **Suaeda californica** Wats. CALIFORNIA SEASHORE BLITE. Fig. 94.

A spreading or decumbent subshrub, 2 to 7 feet across, woody only at the base. Leaves densely crowded, very fleshy, linear, 1/2-inch to 1 1/4 inches long, not much reduced in the inflorescence, glabrous or more or less pubescent, subterete, sessile. Flowers 1 to 3 in the axils of the leaves, 1/8-inch or more wide, when 3-flowered the central one bisexual and the 2 lateral ones smaller and pistillate; stamens 5, exserted. Flowering period, August to October or as early as May.

California Seashore Blite occurs in alkaline depressions and along sandy beaches around the San Francisco Bay and along the sea cliffs north of San Luis Obispo. Southward along the coast it is replaced by the variety *pubescens.*

1a. Var. **pubescens** Jepson.

Herbage tomentose or woolly-pubescent, otherwise like the species.

This variety is known along the coast from Santa Barbara southward to San Diego and Lower California, also on Santa Catalina, San Clemente, and Santa Cruz islands.

Suaeda californica Wats. Proc. Am. Acad. 9:89 (1874). Type locality: Salt marshes of San Francisco Bay. Collected by *Bolander* and *Kellogg.*

Var. pubescens Jepson, Fl. Calif. 1:447 (1914). Type locality: Del Mar, San Diego County. Collected by *Jepson.*

2. **Suaeda fruticosa** (L.) Forsk. ALKALI BLITE. Fig. 95.

A glabrous and glaucous perennial, shrubby at base, with stems 1 1/2 to 3 feet long, these much branched, ascending or erect. Branches of the inflorescence crowded and ascending. Leaves linear, 1/4- to 5/8-inch long, gradually reduced upward, sessile. Flowers less than 1/8-inch broad, several in a cluster; calyx parted nearly to the base, one lobe usually larger than the others. Flowering period, July to September.

Alkali Blite inhabits alkaline depressions and flats from Santa Clara County (near Milpitas) south in the San Joaquin Valley to southern California and Mexico. It extends northward to Alberta and is found also in the West Indies, Europe, Asia, and Africa.

Suaeda fruticosa (L.) Forsk. Fl. Aegypt.-Arab. 70 (1775). *Chenopodium fruticosum* L. Type locality: Seacoast of France. *S. Moquinii* Greene.

3. **Suaeda Torreyana** Wats. DESERT BLITE. Fig. 96.

A green mostly subglabrous erect branching suffrutescent perennial, 1 to 3 feet high, with sparsely leafy branches. Branches of the inflorescence open and spreading. Leaves linear-lanceolate, 3/8-inch to nearly 1 inch long, those of the inflorescence much shortened, flattened, sessile. Flowers less than 1/8-inch broad, 1 to 6 in each leaf-axil; calyx parted to below the middle, the lobes usually equal. Flowering period, May to September.

Desert Blite inhabits the alkaline valleys of southern California, northward to Inyo and Lassen counties, and in the San Joaquin Valley to the Altamont Pass. Its range extends to eastern Oregon, Arizona, New Mexico, Texas, and Mexico.

3a. Var. **ramosissima** (Standl.) Munz.

Stems and leaves densely and very finely pubescent throughout.

This variety occurs on the Mohave and Colorado deserts, eastward to Arizona, and southward to Lower California.

Suaeda Torreyana Wats. Proc. Am. Acad. 9:88 (1874). Type locality: "In alkaline soils from the North Fork of the Platte River *(Fremont)* to northern Nevada, and south to northern Mexico and southern California." *S. suffrutescens* Wats.

Var. ramosissima (Standl.) Munz, Man. S. Calif. Bot. 144 (1935). *Dondia ramosissima* Standl. Type locality: "Lees Ferry, Arizona." Collected by *E. W. Nelson.*

6. **Kochia** Roth

(Named in honor of W. D. J. Koch, German botanist of the last century.)

Ours perennial herbs, somewhat woody at base. Leaves simple, alternate, evergreen, linear, entire. Flowers bisexual or some pistillate, without petals, sessile, solitary or in small axillary heads; calyx 5-lobed, persistent over the fruit and with 5 horizontal wings developing in age; stamens 5; ovary superior, 1-celled; stigmas 2 or 3. Fruit a depressed globose utricle.

Kochia is a polymorphous genus of herbs which are often suffrutescent. About 30 or 40 species have been described, of which 2 are native to western United States and the others native to the Old World and Australia.

KEY TO THE SPECIES

Branches erect and virgate; leaves linear, 1/4-inch to 1 inch long, subterete; herbage nearly glabrous, at least in age . . . . 1. *K. americana.*

Branches spreading; leaves short-linear, 1/8- to nearly 1/2-inch long, flat; herbage densely tomentose . . . . 2. *K. californica.*

1. **Kochia americana** Wats. Green Molly. Fig. 92.

A low subshrub, 4 to 12 inches high, with many erect stems from a branching woody base. Flowering period, May to September.

Green Molly is rare in California, being known only from alkaline places in Inyo County (Cosos Mts. *Hall* & *Chandler;* 2 miles s. of Darwin, *P. A. Munz*), San Bernardino County (Barstow, *K. Brandegee*), and Lassen County (Honey Lake Valley, *J. B. Davy*). It extends eastward to Colorado, Wyoming, and New Mexico.

Kochia americana Wats. Proc. Am. Acad. 9:93 (1874). Type locality: Western Nevada. Collected by *Torrey, Watson,* and others. *K. vestita* (Wats.) Rydb. *K. americana* var. *vestita* Wats. *K. prostrata* Hook., not Schrad.

2. **Kochia californica** Wats. Rusty Molly. Fig. 93.

Closely related to the preceding but more spreading and branched above.

Rusty Molly is known from a few localities in alkaline flats of the desert region of Los Angeles (Lancaster, Antelope Valley), San Bernardino (Victorville; Rabbit Springs), Inyo (Shoshone, *Joseph Grinnell*) counties and near Bakersfield, Kern County *(R. R. Rogers).*

Kochia californica Wats. Proc. Am. Acad. 17:378 (1882). Type locality: Lancaster, Mohave Desert, *Parry,* and Rabbit Springs, Mohave Desert, *S. B.* & *W. F. Parish. K. americana* var. *californica* (Wats.) Jones.

7. **Atriplex** L. SALTBUSH. SCALEBUSH

(The ancient Latin name.)

Herbs and shrubs, more or less pubescent with bran-like hairs. Leaves simple, alternate or opposite. Flowers either staminate or pistillate, one or both kinds borne on the same plant, few in axillary clusters or in spikes or panicles. Staminate flowers without bracts; calyx 3- to 5-parted; stamens 3 to 5. Pistillate flowers each subtended by 2 foliaceous bracts, these distinct or united at least at the base and enclosing the fruit; ovary superior, 1-celled; styles 2. Fruit a small 1-seeded inflated carpel (utricle).

This genus contains about 130 species widely scattered over the earth, especially common in alkaline regions. Twenty-nine species and many varieties have been described from California, 13 of which are woody.

KEY TO THE SPECIES

Plants subshrubby, prostrate or up to 2 feet high.
- Leaves alternate, linear-spatulate, ¾-inch to 1½ inches long, short-petioled. 1. *A. Nuttallii* var. *falcata.*
- Leaves nearly all opposite, broadly elliptic to ovate.........2. *A. decumbens.*

Plants woody throughout.
- Leaves deeply and irregularly toothed, roundish or round-ovate, ½-inch to 1¼ inches long..................................3. *A. hymenelytra.*
- Leaves entire or some subhastate.
  - Leaves cordate or subcordate at base, sessile, round-ovate, ¼- to ½-inch long; plants spiny..4. *A. Parryi.*
  - Leaves not cordate at base.
    - Leaves short-petioled (or the upper ones sessile), not more than 2½ times longer than broad, cuneate or truncate at base.
      - Leaves 1- or 3-veined from the base, all strictly entire, round-ovate or broadly elliptic, ⅜- to ¾-inch long; plants 1 to 2½ feet high; fruiting bracts longer than broad, the body small.....5. *A. confertifolia.*
      - Leaves 1-veined from the base, entire or often subhastate, deltoid-ovate to ovate or elliptic to oblong.
        - Fruiting bracts round or broader than long; plants 3 to 10 feet high. 6. *A. lentiformis.*
        - Fruiting bracts longer than broad, the body large, contracted to a neck beneath the 2 free wings; plants 1 to 4 feet high, very spiny. 7. *A. spinifera.*
    - Leaves sessile, elliptic-oblong to linear or spatulate, thickish.
      - Leaves typically 5 or more times longer than wide (sometimes much reduced); fruiting bracts with 4 conspicuous longitudinal wings or crests..8. *A. canescens.*
      - Leaves typically less than 5 times longer than broad; fruiting bracts without longitudinal wings or crests, their margins fringed. 9. *A. polycarpa.*

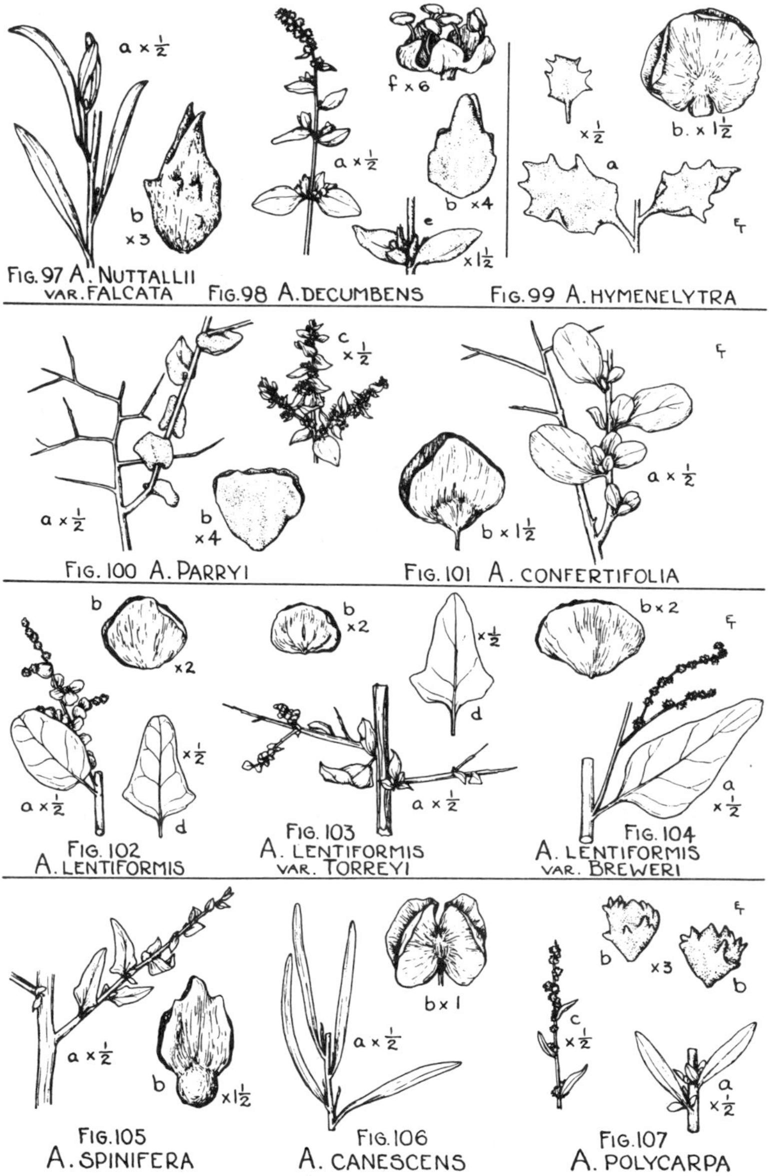

ATRIPLEX. a, Branchlet. b, Fruiting bracts. c, Flower-cluster. d, Leaf. e, Young fruits in leaf-axils. f, Staminate flower.

1. **Atriplex Nuttallii** var. **falcata** Jones. MOUNDSCALE. NUTTALL SALTBUSH. Fig. 97.

A diffuse subshrub, 1 to 2 feet high, woody only at the base, with rigid gray or whitish branches.

Moundscale has been found in California only in Lassen County on the dry hills near Willow Creek Valley *(J. B. Davy)* and west of Amedee *(M. E. Jones)*. It occurs outside of the state in Montana, Utah, Nevada, Idaho, Oregon, and Washington on interior desert plains, in the Upper Sonoran Life Zone.

Atriplex Nuttallii var. falcata Jones, Contr. West. Bot. 11:19 (1903). Type locality: Weiser, Idaho. *A. Nuttallii* Wats., in part.

2. **Atriplex decumbens** Wats. MATSCALE. DECUMBENT SALTBUSH. Fig. 98.

A prostrate perennial herb, slightly woody below, with many branches forming a tangled mass 3 to 9 feet broad. Stems and branches densely white-scurfy. Flowering period, April to July, or to September.

Matscale occurs along the coast from Santa Barbara County south to Lower California and on Santa Catalina, San Nicolas, and San Clemente islands. This species is of some value as a forage plant for cattle.

Atriplex decumbens Wats. Proc. Am. Acad. 12:275 (1877). Type locality: Near San Diego, California. Collected by *Palmer*. *A. Watsonii* A. Nels.

3. **Atriplex hymenelytra** (Torr.) Wats. DESERT-HOLLY. HOLLYSCALE. Fig. 99.

An erect compactly branched shrub, 1 to 3 feet high, with rounded outline when fully developed. Branches silvery-white with a dense persisting scurf. Leaves alternate, evergreen, very numerous; the blades roundish or round-ovate, abruptly subcordate or short-cuneate at base, obtuse at apex, 1/2-inch to 1 1/4 inches long and about as wide, 1-veined from the base, silvery-white with a dense smooth scurf on both surfaces, the margins undulate and deeply and irregularly toothed, thus somewhat holly-like; petioles 1/8- to 3/8-inch long. Flower-clusters in compound inflorescences, the staminate and pistillate borne on different plants. Fruiting bracts on a short club-shaped stalk, round kidney-shaped, strongly flattened except for the small convex body covering the seed, 1/4- to 1/2-inch broad, nearly distinct, the margins entire, smooth on both surfaces. Flowering period, February to April.

Desert-holly occurs in the desert regions of southern California, southern Nevada, southwestern Utah, and western Arizona. It extends southward to Sonora, Mexico and Lower California. It usually grows rather sparingly in the dry gravelly washes of the Lower Sonoran Life Zone.

This is one of the most interesting shrubs of the deserts. Its somewhat holly-like silvery-scurfy leaves make it much sought after for decorations. At Christmas time it is sent throughout the United States in great abundance under the name of Desert-holly.

Atriplex hymenelytra (Torr.) Wats. Proc. Am. Acad. 9:119 (1874). *Obione hymenelytra* Torr. Type locality: Hills and gravelly places on the Williams River, Arizona. Collected by *Fremont*.

4. **Atriplex Parryi.** Wats. PARRY SALTBUSH. Fig. 100.

A dense rigidly branched shrub, about 1 foot high, rounded in form, spiny, with slender straw-colored erect or ascending white-scurfy branches. Leaves alternate or at first clustered, early deciduous, round-ovate, cordate or subcordate at base, usually obtuse at apex, 1/4- to 1/2-inch long and as broad, 1- or 3-veined from the base, gray- or white-scurfy on both surfaces, entire, sessile. Flower-clusters axillary, the staminate and pistillate borne on separate plants; the staminate in the upper axils, forming dense leafy-bracted compound clusters; the pistillate 1 to several in each of the upper axils, forming small compound clusters. Fruiting bracts sessile or nearly so, rounded, or somewhat fan-shaped, about 1/8-inch across, entire, or with a few low teeth, the surface smooth, united to above the middle. Flowering period, May and June.

Parry Saltbush occurs on the Mohave Desert, in Los Angeles, Kern, San Bernardino, and Inyo counties, and also in western Nevada, in the Lower Sonoran Life Zone. It usually inhabits alkaline depressions, but sometimes associates with desert shrubs less tolerant of alkali.

Atriplex Parryi Wats. Proc. Am. Acad. 17:378 (1882). Type locality: "Lancaster, Mohave Desert, Calif." acc. to *Parish,* Zoe 5:113 (1901). Collected by *Parry.*

5. **Atriplex confertifolia** (Torr. & Fremont) Wats. SHADSCALE. SPINY SALTBUSH. Fig. 101.

An erect very rigidly branched spiny shrub, 1 to 3 feet high, usually compact and round in general form, with straw-colored branches. Leaves alternate, crowded, early deciduous from the branchlets which become modified into spines; the blades round-ovate, elliptic or round-obovate, rounded or cuneate at base, obtuse at apex, 1/4- to 3/4-inch long, 1/8- to 1/2-inch wide, 1- or 3-veined from the base, gray-scurfy on both surfaces, the margins entire; petioles 1/8-inch or less long. Flowers borne on separate plants, the staminate in globose axillary clusters on short lateral almost leafless branchlets, the pistillate solitary or several in each of the upper leaf-axils. Fruiting bracts sessile, broadly elliptic or rounded, 1/4- to 3/8-inch long, entire, the surfaces smooth, convex and joined over the seed. Flowering period, May and June.

Shadscale occurs on dry alkaline plains and slopes on the Mohave Desert in San Berdardino County and north into Inyo County, in the Lower Sonoran Life Zone. It grows abundantly in the Great Basin region from Montana to northern Mexico where it is a browse plant for sheep and cattle. The pollen from this species is a cause of hay-fever.

Atriplex confertifolia (Torr. & Fremont) Wats. Proc. Am. Acad. 9:119 (1874). *Obione confertifolia* Torr. & Fremont. Type locality: Borders of the Great Salt Lake. Collected by *Fremont.*

6. **Atriplex lentiformis** (Torr.) Wats. LENSCALE. QUAIL BRUSH. Fig. 102.

A wide-spreading much branched shrub, 3 to 10 feet high, and often 12 feet or more broad, with rigid and round or angled branches, sometimes spinescent. Leaves alternate, deciduous in desert forms and almost evergreen in coastal forms, triangular or ovate to oblong, truncate to wedge-shaped at base, obtuse and tipped with a short soft point at apex, 1/2-inch to 2 inches long, 1/4-inch to 1 1/2 inches wide, 1-veined from the base, bluish gray with a fine scurf, entire or subhastate, sessile or short-petioled. Flower-clusters (both staminate and pistillate) crowded along the branchlets, forming dense compound groups 4 to 8 inches long, borne upon the same or separate shrubs. Fruiting bracts sessile, roundish, 1/8- to 1/4-inch across, the surfaces smooth, united only near the base or to the middle, the free margins entire or obscurely crenulate. Flowering period, June to August.

Lenscale occurs in alkaline depressions, desert areas, dry and inland flats, and on coastal bluffs, from the upper San Joaquin and Salinas valleys southward to Lower California, in the Lower and Upper Sonoran Life Zones. It extends eastward into Nevada, Utah, and New Mexico.

This species yields abundant pollen which may be an important factor in causing hay-fever. At La Jolla the coastal form is used as a hedge. Its gray foliage and dense growth when trimmed make it very suitable for wind-breaks. Cattle are said to browse on the foliage in the desert areas.

Considerable variation occurs in this species. Some authors segregate 3 or more species based upon branch and fruiting-bract variations but here these variations are treated as one species and 2 varieties.

KEY TO THE SPECIES AND VARIETIES

(based on key to subspecies by H. M. Hall. See Bibl.)

Branchlets sharply angled by several raised longitudinal ridges, becoming spiny as the leaves and bracts are lost; bracts finely crenulate....... 6a. var. *Torreyi.*

Branchlets not sharply angled, roundish.

Mature bracts flattened, margins finely crenulate; sometimes spiny shrubs; interior and desert.. *A. lentiformis.*

Mature bracts usually convex, the margins entire; branches not becoming spiny; coastal.. 6b. var. *Breweri.*

A. lentiformis (Torr.) Wats. Mohave and Colorado deserts; San Joaquin and Salinas valleys.

6a. Var. **Torreyi** (Wats.) n. comb. Fig. 103. Mohave Desert region, north to Inyo County. TORREY LENSCALE.

6b. Var. **Breweri** (Wats.) n. comb. BREWER LENSCALE. Fig. 104.

Along the coast from Santa Barbara southward to Santa Monica and San Juan Capistrano; near Teal, Suisun Marshes *(Dudley);* south of Hollister in sandy creek bottoms *(Hall);* on Santa Catalina and San Clemente islands *(Blanche Trask).*

Atriplex lentiformis (Torr.) Wats. Proc. Am. Acad. 9:118 (1874). *Obione lentiformis* Torr. Type locality: "on the Colorado of California." Collected by *S. W. Woodhouse.*

Var. Torreyi (Wats.) McMinn. *Obione Torreyi* Wats. Type locality: Dry valleys along the Truckee and Carson rivers, Nevada. Collected by *Torrey. A. Torreyi* Wats.

Var. Breweri (Wats.) McMinn. *A. Breweri* Wats. Type locality: Santa Monica, California. Collected by *Fremont, Torrey, Brewer.*

7. **Atriplex spinifera** Macbr. SPINESCALE. Fig. 105.

An erect rigidly branched spiny shrub, 1 to 5 feet high, with white-scurfy or glabrate and very pale branches, the old bark splitting off in thin longitudinal strips. Leaves alternate, rather crowded, early deciduous from the branchlets which become modified into spines; the blades triangular-ovate or elliptic, wedge-shaped at base, obtuse at apex, 3/8-inch to 1 1/2 inches long, 1/4- to 1/2-inch wide (leaves on young branchlets much smaller), 1-veined from the base, gray- or white-scurfy on both surfaces, entire or some subhastate; petioles 1/8-inch or less long, or the leaves sessile. Flower-clusters borne on separate plants, the staminate in globose axillary clusters, the pistillate in small clusters or solitary. Fruiting bracts sessile, the body globose, the free margins developed above the body into rounded or oblong wings, the whole bract 1/4- to 1/2-inch long, entire, or the wings irregularly dentate. Flowering period, March and April.

Spinescale occurs on moderately alkaline plains from the western side of the San Joaquin Valley to the western part of the Mohave Desert, in the Upper Sonoran Life Zone.

Hall considers this a "far-western development from *A. confertifolia,* which it resembles in the spiny habit and in the general features of the inflorescence and fruiting bracts. . . . It forms open stands, often pure, but sometimes mixed with *A. polycarpa,* or in Antelope Valley with the closely related *A. confertifolia.*"

Atriplex spinifera Macbr. Contr. Gray Herb. n. s. 53:11 (1918). Type locality: Maricopa Hills, Kern County, California. Collected by *Eastwood.*

8. **Atriplex canescens** (Pursh) Nutt. WINGSCALE. FOURWING SALTBUSH. Fig. 106.

An erect roundish gray shrub, 1½ to 5 feet high, with stout round gray-scurfy or glabrate branches. Leaves alternate, evergreen, numerous, linear, broadly elliptic, or spatulate, usually obtuse at apex, narrowed at base, ½-inch to 2 inches long, 1⁄16- to ⅜-inch wide, 1-veined from the base, gray with a dense permanent scurf on both surfaces, the margins entire, sessile or nearly so. Flower-clusters borne on separate plants, the staminate clusters in dense spikes forming long terminal panicles, the pistillate in dense leafy spike-like panicles. Fruiting bracts sessile, forming a thick hard body united over the seed, projecting above into 2 free flat wings, a second pair of wings developing from the medial line of each exposed face, the four wings entire or fringed, the whole bract ¼- to ¾-inch long and about as broad. Flowering period, July and August.

Wingscale occurs rather abundantly in the Colorado and Mohave deserts of southern California, in Los Angeles County (at Burbank), and in San Diego and Orange counties, where it reaches the coast at Laguna Beach and San Diego, in the Lower and Upper Sonoran Life Zones. It is the most widely distributed of the shrubby species of the genus *Atriplex.* Outside of California it extends eastward to western Texas and Kansas, southward to Lower California, and northward to eastern Washington, Montana, and Alberta, Canada.

As a browse shrub it ranks among the best in the desert region. Great quantities of wind-blown pollen are produced by the flowers which causes hay-fever in some individuals.

Some variation occurs in the size of the wings on the fruiting bracts and in the size of the leaves. The following key will identify these variations, which are here considered the typical form of the species and 3 varieties.

KEY TO THE SPECIES AND VARIETIES

Leaves ⅛- to 5⁄16-inch wide.
  Wings of fruiting bracts ⅙- to ⅓-inch broad.
    Wings irregularly dentate . . . . *A. canescens.*
    Wings deeply laciniate . . . . 8a. var. *laciniata.*
  Wings of fruiting bracts less than ⅙-inch broad, coarsely dentate.
    8b. var. *macilenta.*
Leaves less than ⅛-inch wide . . . . 8c. var. *linearis.*

A. canescens (Pursh) Nutt. Rather common on the Colorado and Mohave deserts. Colorado Desert: Caleb, *Parish;* Salton Creek, *Brandegee.* Los Angeles County: Glendale to Burbank, *Braunton.* Orange County: Laguna Beach, *McMinn.*

8a. Var. **laciniata** Parish. Colorado Desert: Caleb, *Parish;* Dos Palmas, *Childs.* Mohave Desert: Barstow, *Jepson;* near Newberry, *Morefort.*

8b. Var. **macilenta** Jepson. In the southern part of the Colorado Desert: Holtville, *Parish.*

8c. Var. **linearis** (Wats.) Munz. Colorado Desert: Durmid, Salton Sea, *Parish.* South into Mexico, *Jepson.*

Atriplex canescens (Pursh) Nutt. Gen. Pl. 1:197 (1818). *Calligonum canescens* Pursh. Type locality: Plains of the Missouri River, near the Big Bend, South Dakota. Collected by *Lewis.*

Var. laciniata Parish; Jepson, Fl. Calif. 1:442 (1914). Type locality: Caleb, Colorado Desert, California. Collected by *Parish.*

Var. macilenta Jepson, Fl. Calif. 1:442 (1914). Type locality: Holtville, California. Collected by *Parish.*

Var. linearis (Wats.) Munz, Man. S. Calif. Bot. 141 (1935). *Atriplex linearis* Wats. Type locality: Alkaline soil about Guaymas, Sonora, Mexico.

9. **Atriplex polycarpa** (Torr.) Wats. ALLSCALE. Fig. 107.

An erect intricately branched shrub, 2 to 6 feet high, with gray or yellowish brown branches, the bark exfoliating in thin strips. Leaves alternate, crowded on the young twigs, early deciduous, elliptic-oblong or spatulate, narrowed at base, obtuse or acute at apex, $\frac{1}{8}$- to $\frac{1}{2}$-inch long, usually less than $\frac{1}{8}$-inch wide, on young sterile twigs as much as 1 inch long and with small leaves fascicled in their axils, 1-veined from the base, gray with a dense scurf on both surfaces, the margins entire, usually sessile. Flowers male or female, borne on separate plants; the staminate in axillary or terminal spikes; the pistillate forming diffuse panicles crowded along the numerous divergent branches. Fruiting bracts sessile, united to well above the middle or rarely distinct nearly to the base, roundish, about $\frac{1}{8}$-inch long and as broad, the thin margins shallowly to deeply and laciniately toothed above the base, the surfaces with 2 to several slender spreading appendages or rarely smooth. Flowering period, June to September.

Allscale inhabits the Colorado Desert, western Mohave Desert, the alkaline plains south of Bakersfield, and scattered alkaline localities in Fresno, Inyo, Merced, and San Luis Obispo counties, in the Lower and Upper Sonoran Life Zones. Outside the state it occurs in the desert areas of southern Nevada, Utah, Arizona, Sonora, Mexico, and Lower California. During the flowering period the abundant pollen is a cause of hay-fever. Like *A. canescens,* it is a very important browse plant for sheep and cattle.

Atriplex polycarpa (Torr.) Wats. Proc. Am. Acad. 9:117 (1874). *Obione polycarpa* Torr. Type locality: Valley of the Gila River, Arizona. Collected by *Parry, Fremont.*

Ranunculaceae. Buttercup Family

The Buttercup Family consists of 30 genera and about 1200 species, of worldwide distribution, but more abundant in the northern hemisphere. Sixteen genera and 70 species are found in California. Only one Californian genus contains woody plants.

1. **Clematis** L. CLEMATIS

(The ancient name of a climbing plant, from the Greek *klema,* a twig.)

Woody vines, climbing by bending or twining of the leaf-stalks, or sometimes erect perennial herbs. Leaves pinnately compound, opposite. Flowers solitary or in clusters, bisexual or unisexual; sepals 4, white or cream-colored, petal-like;

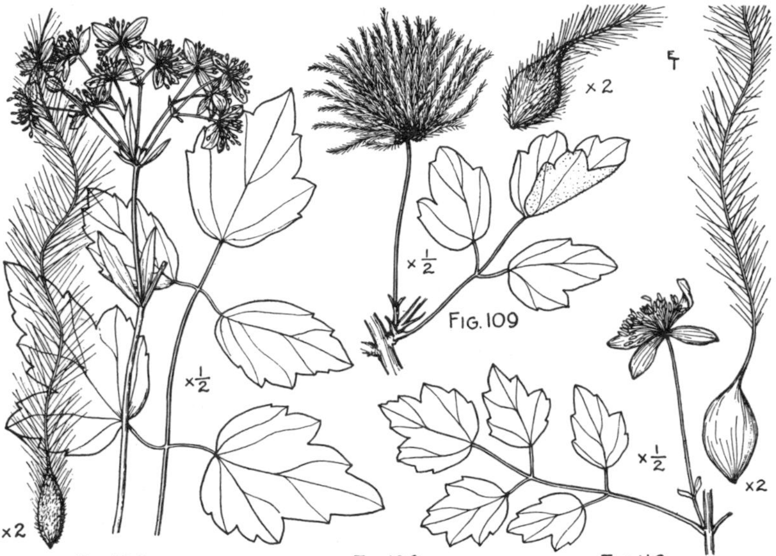

Fig. 108 Clematis ligusticifolia

Fig. 109 Clematis lasiantha

Fig. 110 Clematis pauciflora

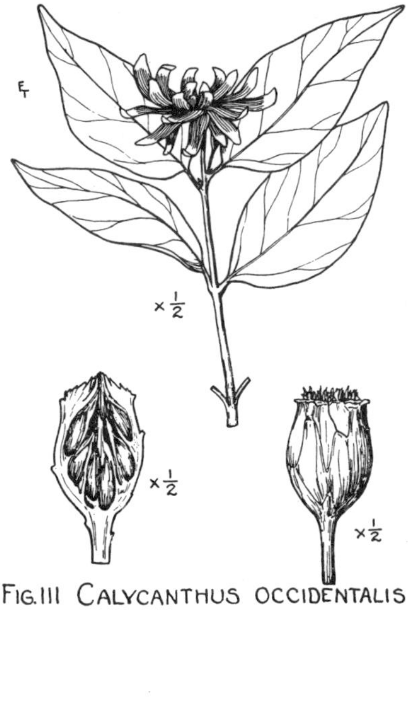

Fig. 111 Calycanthus occidentalis

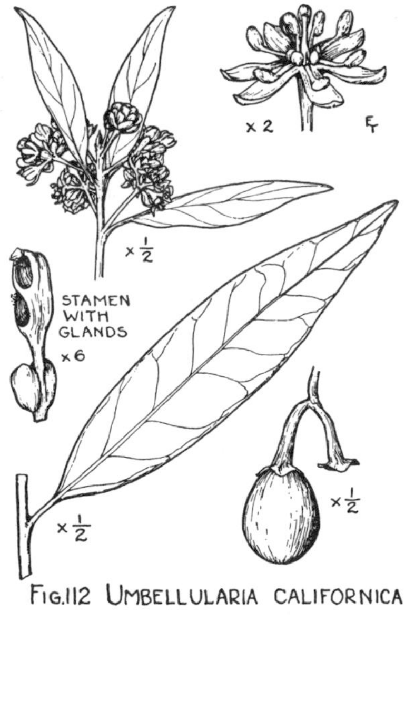

Fig. 112 Umbellularia californica

petals none; stamens distinct, numerous, in very conspicuous head-like clusters; pistils many, distinct; ovary superior, 1-celled. Fruit an achene.

This genus includes about 150 to 200 species of wide geographical distribution, mostly of temperate regions. About 25 species occur in North America, only 3 being native to California.

KEY TO THE SPECIES

Flowers many in a cluster; leaflets 5 to 7; achenes pubescent. . . 1. *C. ligusticifolia.*
Flowers 1 to 3 on each peduncle; peduncles with 2 bractlets below the middle.
Leaflets 3; achenes pubescent. . . . . .2. *C. lasiantha.*
Leaflets 5 to 9 (or 3); achenes glabrous. . . . . .3. *C. pauciflora.*

1. **Clematis ligusticifolia** Nutt. Western Clematis. Fig. 108.

A woody vine, climbing bushes or trees to a height of 40 feet, with gray and stringy bark on old stems, nearly glabrous except for the flower-clusters. Leaflets 5 to 7, the primary or basal ones commonly again divided, ovate, rounded or cordate at the base, acute or acuminate at the apex, 1 to 3 inches long, almost entire to coarsely toothed or sometimes slightly 3-lobed, glabrous above, sparingly hairy below; petioles long, twining like tendrils about twigs. Flowers numerous, polygamo-dioecious, about ½- to ¾-inch wide, borne in open long-stalked leafy panicles; peduncles 1 to 4 inches long, arising from the axils of the compound opposite leaves; sepals 4, greenish white, tomentulose, about ¼- to ½-inch long; stamens numerous, shorter than the sepals. Achenes ovoid, pubescent, with persistent hairy styles 1 to 2 inches long. Flowering period, March and April.

Western Clematis is found in the valleys, foothills, and mountains throughout the Coast Ranges, the Sierra Nevada, and southern California, in the Upper Sonoran and Transition Life Zones. This vine attracts the traveller's attention by its profusion of white flowers or hairy fruits which develop from May to August. However, it has little ornamental value except in large masses in its native habitat. The Spanish-Californians used an infusion of the herbage for healing sores on horses caused by thorn or wire cuts.

Clematis ligusticifolia Nutt.; T. & G. Fl. N. Am. 1:9 (1838). Type locality: "Plains of Rocky Mts." Collected by *Nuttall.*

2. **Clematis lasiantha** Nutt. Pipe-stem Clematis. Fig. 109.

A woody vine clambering over shrubs and low trees, with tomentose-pubescent branchlets. Leaflets 3, orbicular to elliptic-ovate, rounded or truncate at base, slightly tapering or obtuse at apex, 1 to 2 inches long, coarsely toothed and often more or less lobed, pubescent beneath; petioles twining. Flowers polygamous, 1½ to 2½ inches across, solitary (or 2 or 3); peduncles 2 to 6 inches long, with 2 leaf-like bracts below the middle; sepals 4, white, broadly oblong or oval, ¾-inch to 1 inch long, silky-pubescent without. Achenes pubescent, with plumose tails 1 inch or more long, in head-like clusters 2 inches wide. Flowering period, April and May.

Pipe-stem Clematis grows in the Coast Range valleys, the Sierra Nevada canyons, and the foothills of the mountains of southern California, in the Upper and Lower Sonoran and Transition Life Zones. Its profusion of white flowers gives a striking appearance to the brush on the valley slopes during April and May.

Clematis lasiantha Nutt.; T. & G. Fl. N. Am. 1:9 (1838). Type locality: San Diego, California. Collected by *Nuttall.*

3. **Clematis pauciflora** Nutt. Southern California Clematis. Fig. 110.

A slender slightly woody vine trailing over rocks and shrubs. Leaves more or less fascicled; leaflets 3 to 5, round-ovate, toothed or lobed, tapering or heart-shaped at base, acute at apex, ¾-inch to 1 inch long, the basal ones often replaced by 3 leaflets; the common petioles ½-inch to 1 inch long. Flowers polygamous, 1 or 3 on a peduncle about 1 inch long, about ¾-inch to 1 inch wide; sepals 4 (or 3), white, about ½-inch long. Achenes glabrous, with tails about 1 inch long. Flowering period, March and April.

Southern California Clematis inhabits the lower foothills of the mountain regions of southern California, extending from Santa Barbara County south to San Diego County, in the Lower and Upper Sonoran Life Zones.

Clematis pauciflora Nutt.; T. & G. Fl. N. Am. 1:9 (1838). Type locality: San Diego, California. Collected by *Nuttall.*

Calycanthaceae. Sweet Shrub Family

This is a small family containing 2 genera with 8 species of peculiar distribution, 2 in China and Japan, one in Queensland, 4 in the eastern United States, and one in California.

1. **Calycanthus** L. SWEET-SCENTED SHRUB. SPICE BUSH

(From the Greek *kalyx,* calyx or covering, and *anthos,* flower, in reference to the large conspicuous receptacle.)

This genus contains 5 species, all native to the United States, one of which is native to California.

1. **Calycanthus occidentalis** H. & A. SPICE BUSH. Fig. 111.

An erect bushy shrub, 4 to 12 feet high, with smooth brown bark. Leaves simple, opposite, deciduous, aromatic when crushed; the blades ovate to oblong-lanceolate, rounded at base, tapering at apex, 2 to 6 inches long, 1 to 2 inches wide, with 1 main vein from the base, glabrous but rough above, nearly glabrous and smooth beneath, entire; petioles about ¼-inch long. Flowers reddish brown, 1½ to 2½ inches across, solitary at the ends of the branches, sepals and petals similar, oblanceolate, oblong, or linear, about 1 inch long, the upper third turning dull brown in age; stamens numerous, the anthers as long as or longer than the filaments; pistils 15 to 20, enclosed in an urn-shaped receptacle, their ovaries superior, covered with soft white hairs. Fruit about 1 inch long, consisting of the large ovoid or urn-shaped receptacle containing the white-velvety brownish achenes. Flowering period, May to July.

Spice Bush is usually found along streams and on moist canyon slopes of the Humid Transition Life Zone in the North Coast Ranges from Sonoma and Napa counties north to Trinity County and in the Sierra Nevada foothills from Shasta County south to Tulare County at elevations ranging from 600 to 3500 feet. This shrub has been given a variety of common names because of the interesting flowers, fruits, and aromatic odor of the leaves. Wine-flower, Wild-poppy, California Calycanth, Strawberry Bush, Bubby Bush, Spice Wood, Vinegar Bush, Sweet Shrub, and California Sweet-scented Shrub are common names applied to this plant.

The flowers of *Calycanthus floridus,* a frequently cultivated species native to southeastern United States, give when crushed a very marked odor of ripe strawberries. Our Californian species possesses this characteristic to a less marked degree.

Spice Bush can be recommended for ornamental planting in moderately moist to wet soils. Propagation can be easily made from cuttings or from root-crown sections taken from the parent plant. It is a rapid grower and relatively free from scale and insect pests. Although it is reported that livestock seldom graze on the foliage of this plant, it is held, by stockmen, responsible for the death of many cattle.

Calycanthus occidentalis H. & A. Bot. Beechey 340 (1840). Type locality: California.

Lauraceae. Laurel Family

The Laurel Family consists of 40 genera and about 1000 species, mostly forest trees in tropical and subtropical regions. Many species are of economic value on account of the volatile oils which they contain. Cinnamon, camphor, sassafras, and avocados are obtained from members of this family. One genus with a single species is native to California.

1. **Umbellularia** Nutt.

(From the Latin *umbella,* a sunshade, referring to the arrangement of flowers.)

1. **Umbellularia californica** (H. & A.) Nutt. CALIFORNIA BAY. CALIFORNIA-LAUREL. Fig. 112.

Commonly a tree, 20 to 60 feet high, but sometimes shrub-like in exposed places and in the chaparral. Leaves simple, alternate, evergreen; the blades oblong-elliptic, 3 to 5 inches long, $\frac{3}{4}$-inch to 1 inch wide, glabrous, entire, with a pungent odor when crushed; petioles about $\frac{1}{4}$-inch long. Flowers small, yellowish, bisexual, 4 to 6 in simple peduncled umbels; sepals 6, distinct, petal-like; petals none; stamens 9, the 3 inner with a stipitate orange-colored gland on each side of the filament at base, these alternating with scale-like staminodia; ovary superior, 1-celled, 1-ovuled. Fruit a plum-like drupe, about 1 inch long, greenish to purplish. Flowering period, February to April.

California Bay usually occurs in canyons, on shaded slopes, or along streams from the Umpqua River, Oregon, southward in the Coast Ranges and on the western slope of the Sierra Nevada to San Diego County, California, extending from sea level to about 4000 feet elevation. In its shrub-form, *Umbellularia* inhabits draws and slopes in the chaparral. The wood is used for furniture, boat building, and stave timber. The dried leaves are used in flavoring meats and soups.

Umbellularia californica (H. & A.) Nutt. Sylva 1:87 (1842). *Tetranthera californica* H. & A. Type locality: Probably in the vicinity of San Francisco or Monterey, California. Collected by *Lay* or *Collie*.

Berberidaceae. Barberry Family

The Barberry Family contains about 20 genera and 150 species widely scattered throughout the north temperate zone, in the Andes, and parts of temperate South America. Three genera and 12 species are native to California, and of these, only the genus *Berberis* has woody species. Our species belong to the section Mahonia.

1. **Berberis** L. BARBERRY

(An Arabic name.)

Evergreen shrubs with yellow inner bark and wood. Leaves simple or in ours once-pinnately compound, alternate; leaflets 3 to many, prickly, glabrous, sessile; rachis jointed at the insertion of the leaflets; petioles somewhat clasping. Flowers perfect, yellow, borne in racemes which emerge from between the scales of the terminal buds; sepals 6, in 2 series, petal-like, distinct, falling early, subtended by 3 bractlets; petals 6, in 2 series, distinct, concave, each bearing 2 small glands on the upper side near the base; stamens 6, opposite the petals, usually with a pair of small divergent teeth near the apex of the filament; ovary superior, 1-celled, composed of 1 carpel; stigma sessile. Fruit a small berry, with few seeds, often becoming dry.

This genus contains about 100 species, widely distributed in North America, Europe, Asia, North Africa, and South America. The section Mahonia, to which our species belong, contains about 40 species which occur in China, central Asia, and western North America and Mexico, of which 9 species and 3 varieties are found in the Pacific Coast states. The compound leaves and the absence of spines on the stems and branches of the species of the section Mahonia are characters used to separate these from the other species of the genus *Berberis*. Our species are known as Mahonia, Oregon-grape, Hollygrape, and Barberry.

The handsome evergreen foliage, yellow flowers, and colored berries make our species highly desirable for ornamental planting. They may be propagated by seeds, or from suckers, cuttings, and by layering. Most of the species produce suckers rather freely but much care must be given to the transplanting of sucker material from the field because it does not adapt itself to the new conditions as readily as do most plants which are propagated by this method. Seeds should be sown soon after maturing in the late summer or treated by the stratification method. The mahonias thrive best in a semi-humid or humid habitat. All of the Pacific Coast species are practically resistant to the fungus *(Puccinia graminis)* which causes stem-rust of wheat.

KEY TO THE SPECIES

The dull or glossy leaf characters of some species seem to vary with the exposure to sun and shade as well as with the age of the foliage, and allowance must be made, therefore, in the identification of specimens.

Leaflets 11 to 23 (rarely 5 to 9), usually palmately veined; leaves 8 to 18 inches long, borne in a terminal cluster from a simple unbranched stem; bud-scales ¾-inch to 1½ inches long, persistent; filaments without teeth. . 1. *B. nervosa.*

Leaflets 3 to 11 (rarely to 15), usually pinnately veined; leaves 8 inches or less long; bud-scales less than ¼-inch long, deciduous; filaments with a pair of recurved appendages near the apex.

- Leaflets over ⅝-inch wide; raecmes densely many-flowered.
  - Leaflets with both surfaces green and usually glossy (sometimes becoming dull in the sun or in age); lower surface without evident microscopic papillae.
    - Leaflets crowded on the rachis and often overlapping, usually strongly undulate and shallowly sinuate-margined, with 10 to 20 bristle-tipped teeth on each side; the basal pair of leaflets usually close to base of the petiole. . . . . 2. *B. pinnata.*
    - Leaflets usually not crowded on the rachis, nearly plane or undulate, with 10 to 20 slender spines on each side; the basal pair of leaflets usually ¾-inch or more from base of the petiole. . . . . 3. *B. aquifolium.*
  - Leaflets dull and with microscopic papillae beneath, either dull or glossy above.
    - Leaflets with 8 to 20 bristle- or prickle-like (rarely spinose) teeth on each margin.

Leaflets bright green and shining above . . . . 4. *B. Sonnei.*
Leaflets dull above . . . . 5. *B. repens.*
Leaflets with 3 to 11 slender or stout spines on each margin.
Leaflets bright green and shining above, the margins tipped with slender spines . . . . 6. *B. Piperiana.*
Leaflets dull above, the margins with medium or stout spines.
Leaflets plane or some undulate, with medium-sized spinescent teeth; plants 6 to 16 inches high . . . . 7. *B. pumilia.*
Leaflets usually strongly undulate (often nearly plane in young growth and in the shade) and rigid, with stout spines often nearly as long as the body of the blade; plants 1 to 6 feet high. . . . . 8. *B. dictyota.*
Leaflets 5/8-inch or less wide, glaucescent on both surfaces; racemes loosely 5- to 9-flowered.
Leaflets with 2 to 4 stout spines on each margin; the terminal leaflet usually not much longer than the lateral ones; berries blue, drying brown or yellow, inflated, 1/4- to 1/2-inch in diameter . . . . 9. *B. Fremontii.*
Leaflets with 3 to 16 bristle-like or spinescent teeth on each margin; the terminal leaflet usually longer than the lateral ones; berries red. 1/4- to 3/8-inch in diameter . . . . 10. *B. Nevinii.*

1. **Berberis nervosa** Pursh. LONGLEAF MAHONIA. Fig. 114.

An erect shrub, 3/4-foot to 2 feet (rarely to 6 feet) high, with an unbranched stem bearing the leaves in a terminal cluster. Leaves 8 to 18 inches long; leaflets 11 to 23 (rarely, 5, 7, or 9), ovate to ovate-lanceolate, acute, 1 to 3 3/4 inches long, 3/4-inch to 1 3/4 inches wide, somewhat palmately veined, glossy-green above and beneath, the margins serrate with bristle-like teeth. Bud-scales 3/4-inch to 1 1/2 inches long. Racemes erect, 3 to 6 (or 10) inches long. Berries 1/4- to 1/3-inch in diameter, blue, with a gray bloom. Flowering period, April to June.

Longleaf Mahonia occurs in the forests from Vancouver Island and British Columbia southward in the Coast Ranges of Washington, Oregon, and California to Monterey and San Benito (Fremont Peak) counties, in the Humid Transition Life Zone; also in Shasta, Trinity, and Siskiyou counties, California and the Blue Mountains of eastern Oregon and Idaho.

Berberis nervosa Pursh, Fl. Am. Sept. 219, pl. 5 (1814). Type locality: The Cascades of the Columbia River. Collected by *Lewis.*

2. **Berberis pinnata** Lag. SHINYLEAF MAHONIA. CALIFORNIA BARBERRY. Fig. 115.

An erect stiffly branched shrub, 1 to 3 (or 6) feet high. Leaves 2 to 5 inches long; leaflets 5 to 9 (or to 17), much crowded on the rachis and usually overlapping, ovate or ovate-elliptical to oblong, 1 to 2 inches long, 3/4-inch to 1 1/2 inches wide, thin, glossy-green above, paler but glossy beneath, the margins strongly undulate and sinuate, with 10 to 20 bristle-tipped teeth on each margin, the basal pair of leaflets usually close to the base of the petiole. Racemes clustered, many-flowered, 1 to 2 1/2 inches long. Berries ovoid, about 1/4-inch long, blue-glaucous. Flowering period, late February to early May.

Shinyleaf Mahonia inhabits rocky outcroppings of hill summits and slopes in the outer and middle Coast Ranges from Curry County, Oregon, southward in the coastal counties of California to San Diego County, and in Box Canyon, Lower California (about 57 miles north of Ensenada, *Wiggins*); also on Santa Cruz and Santa Rosa islands. No specimens have been seen from Ventura and Orange coun-

Fig. 113. Oregon-grape. *Berberis aquifolium* Pursh.

ties, California. Some specimens in the northern part of California, in the portion where its overlapping in distribution with *B. aquifolium* occurs, approach specimens of the latter in characters of leaf-margins and arrangement of the leaflets on the rachis. In the San Gabriel Mountains of Los Angeles County, the leaflets often are thicker, duller, and have coarser teeth and in these characteristics they resemble the leaflets of *B. dictyota.* However, the absence of microscopic papillae on the lower surfaces distinguishes the leaflets from those of *B. dictyota.* On Santa Cruz Island some plants lean on and climb trees of *Quercus tomentella* and *Photinia abutifolia* to a height of 19 feet. Their leaflets are very thin and nearly entire.

Berberis pinnata Lag., Elench. Hort. Madr. 6 (1803). nom. nudum; l. c. 14 (1816). Type locality: Monterey, California. Collected by *Née.*

3. **Berberis aquifolium** Pursh. Oregon-grape. Hollyleaf Mahonia. Fig. 113.

Usually an erect freely branching shrub, 1 to 6 (or 10) feet high. Leaves 4 to 10 inches long; leaflets 5 to 9 (or to 13), oblong-ovate, 1 to 2½ inches long, ¾-inch to 1½ inches wide, thin but firm, glossy-green above and below, in exposed situations becoming duller in age, plane or somewhat undulate, the margins shallowly sinuate, with 10 to 20 slender spines on each margin, the basal pair of leaflets usually ¾-inch or more from base of the petiole. Berries globular, about ¼-inch in diameter, bluish. Flowering period, March to May.

Oregon-grape occurs in the wooded mountain regions of southern British Columbia and Vancouver Island southward in western Washington and Oregon to Trinity and Humboldt counties in northern California, in the Humid Transition Life Zone. Some specimens from the vicinity of Spokane, Washington, are referable to this species. In northern California this species apparently intergrades with *B. pinnata, B. repens,* and *B. Piperiana.*

This shrub is frequently used as an ornamental throughout the cooler parts of the Pacific Coast states. Its holly-like foliage is often used for Christmas decorations. It is the state flower of Oregon.

Berberis aquifolium Pursh, Fl. Am. Sept. 1:219 (1814). Type locality: Great Rapids of the Columbia River, Oregon. Collected by *Lewis.*

4. **Berberis Sonnei** (Abrams) n. comb. Truckee Mahonia. Truckee Barberry. Fig. 116.

A low shrub, ¾-foot to 2 feet high. Leaves 4 to 10 inches long; leaflets 5, ovate-lanceolate, 1½ to 3 inches long, tapering or rounded at base, somewhat palmately veined, bright green and glossy above, dull beneath with thinly scattered papillae, the margin with 12 to 20 bristle-tipped teeth on each side. Racemes densely flowered, 1½ to 2½ inches long. Berries ovoid, about ¼-inch long, blue-black. Flowering period, April and May.

Truckee Mahonia, to my knowledge, has been collected only from the rocky banks of the Truckee River, Nevada County, California. It seems very closely related to *B. repens* and perhaps is only a more upright form of that species.

Berberis Sonnei (Abrams) McMinn. *Mahonia Sonnei* Abrams. Type locality: Rocky bank of the Truckee River. Collected by *C. F. Sonne.*

5. **Berberis repens** Lindl. Creeping Mahonia. Creeping Barberry. Fig. 117.

A low prostrate subshrub, 4 to 8 inches high, with the stems ascending from creeping stolon-like bases. Leaves 3 to 10 inches long; leaflets 5 (rarely 3 or 7), broadly ovate or oblong-ovate, the base obliquely truncate to slightly subcordate, 1 to 2½ inches long, ⅝-inch to 1¾ inches wide, nearly plane, dull (or rarely

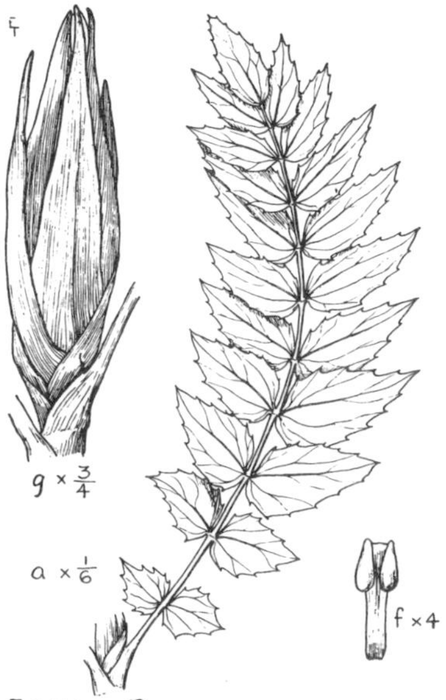

FIG. 114 B. NERVOSA

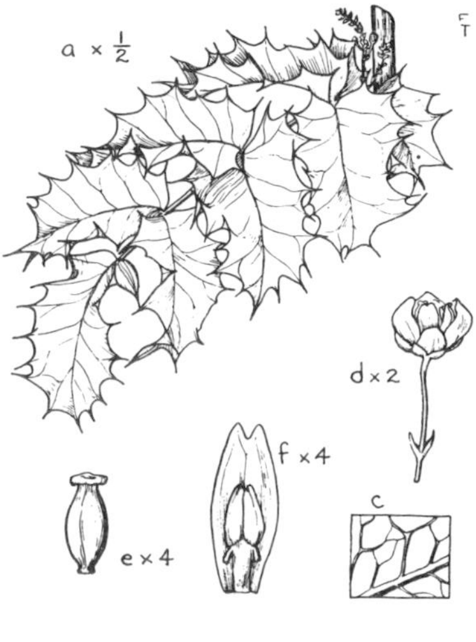

FIG. 115 B. PINNATA

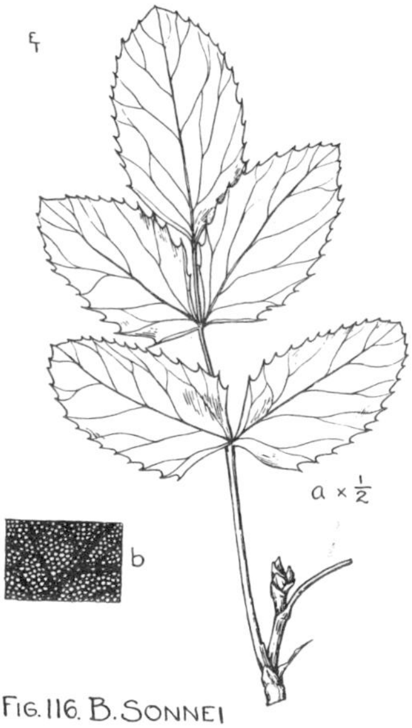

FIG. 116. B. SONNEI

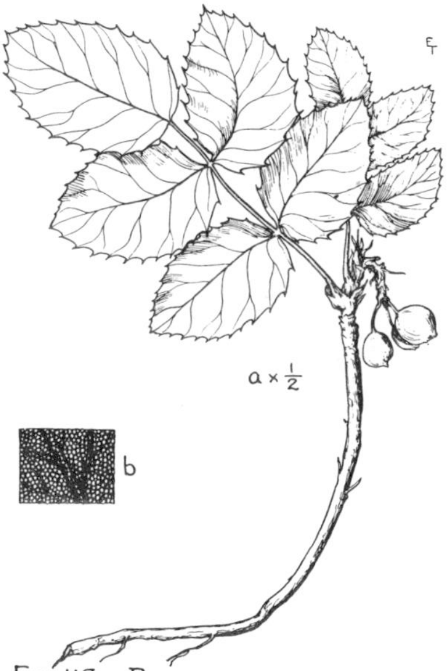

FIG. 117 B. REPENS

BERBERIS. a, Compound leaf. b, Papillae on lower surface of leaf. c, Venation on lower surface of leaf. d, Flower. e, Pistil. f, Petal and stamen. g, Terminal bud.

glossy) above, paler beneath with evident microscopic papillae, the margins slightly sinuate, with 8 to 20 bristle-like or somewhat spinose teeth on each margin. Berries ovoid, 1/8- to 1/4-inch long, blue-glaucous. Flowering period, April to June.

Creeping Mahonia occurs in the open pine woods of Modoc and Inyo (and probably Siskiyou) counties, California. It extends northward in the mountains of central and eastern Oregon to southeastern Washington and British Columbia, eastward into Idaho, the Rocky Mountain states, and the Black Hills region of the Dakotas, and southward to New Mexico and Texas.

Berberis repens Lindl. Bot. Reg. 14. pl. 1176 (1828). Type locality: "probably Montana." Collected by *Lewis.*

6. **Berberis Piperiana** (Abrams) n. comb. PIPER MAHONIA. Fig. 118.

An erect shrub, 8 inches to 2 feet high. Leaves 4 to 8 inches long; leaflets 5 to 9, ovate, 1 to 2 1/2 inches long, upper surface glossy green and finely reticulate, the lower surface gray-green and papillate, usually with 7 to 10 or rarely to 20 spinescent teeth on each margin. Racemes 1 1/4 to 2 3/4 inches long, densely or rather loosely fascicled. Berry ellipsoid-ovoid, about 1/4-inch long, blue black. Flowering period, March and April.

Piper Mahonia occurs on open wooded slopes in the Arid Transition Life Zone from northern Lake County northward in the North Coast Ranges to Trinity, Siskiyou, and Del Norte counties. It extends northward into Oregon. These plants have been considered by many botanists as belonging to *B. aquifolium,* but Abrams in placing them in this new species refers to the study of Charles V. Piper who stressed the importance of the papillae on the lower leaf-surface. The leaflets of *B. aquifolium* lack the evident papillae.

Berberis Piperiana (Abrams) McMinn. *Mahonia Piperiana* Abrams. Type locality: "Along the Pacific Highway, near the Siskiyou Summit, Jackson County, Oregon." Collected by *Abrams* and *Benson.*

7. **Berberis pumila** Greene. DWARF MAHONIA. DWARF BARBERRY. Fig. 119.

A low ascending or erect shrub, 6 to 16 inches high. Leaves 3 to 6 inches long; leaflets 3 to 9, broadly ovate to oblong-ovate, 1 1/2 to 2 1/2 inches long, 3/4-inch to 1 3/4 inches wide, often with 1 main vein and 2 sublateral ones, dull and strongly reticulate-veined above, paler beneath with evident microscopic papillae, the margins plane or slightly undulate, each margin with 3 to 10 medium-sized spinose teeth. Racemes dense, fascicled, many-flowered. Berries oblong-ovoid, 1/8- to 1/4-inch long, blue-black, with a bloom. Flowering period, late March to May.

Dwarf Mahonia occurs in scattered locations in the inner South Coast Range and the Siskiyou Mountains of Oregon and extends southward in the mountains of northern California, in the inner North Coast Range to Lake County, and in the Sierra Nevada to Mariposa County. It usually inhabits open pine woods in the Upper Sonoran and Arid Transition Life Zones. Some specimens from Tehama, Amador, Mariposa, and Shasta counties, California resemble specimens of *B. dictyota,* but lack the strongly undulate and spinose leaf-margins of that species. Specimens from the Cuyamaca Mountains of San Diego County are herein referred to *B. dictyota,* but are certainly somewhat intermediate in leaf-characters between that species and *B. pumila.*

Berberis pumila Greene, Pitt. 2:161 (1891). Type locality: Near Waldo, Oregon. Collected by *Howell.*

8. **Berberis dictyota** Jepson. CALIFORNIA MAHONIA. CALIFORNIA BARBERRY. Fig. 120.

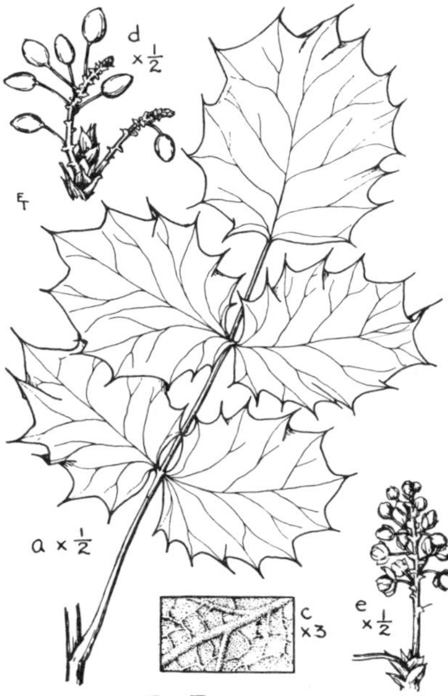

FIG. 118 B. PIPERIANA

FIG. 119 B. PUMILA

FIG. 120 B. DICTYOTA

FIG. 121 B. FREMONTII

BERBERIS. a, Compound leaf. b, Branchlet with leaves and fruit. c, Papillae on lower surface of leaf. d, Fruit. e, Flower-cluster.

An erect sparingly branched shrub, with stout stems 1½ to 6 feet (rarely 10 inches) high. Leaves 2 to 4 inches long; leaflets 5 (rarely 3 or 7), oblong to suborbicular in outline, ¾-inch to 2 inches long, ½- to ¾-inch wide, thick and stiff, dull above (sometimes glossy when young), paler and glaucous beneath, with evident microscopic papillae, prominently net-veined on both surfaces, the margins strongly undulate, with 3 to 8 stout or medium-sized spines on each margin. Berries ovoid, about ¼-inch long, blue-glaucous. Flowering period, April to early June.

California Mahonia inhabits the dry rocky foothills of the inner Coast Ranges, the mountains at the head of the Sacramento Valley, the Sierra Nevada foothills, Marysville Buttes, and the lower mountain slopes of southern California, in the Upper Sonoran Life Zone. Although this barberry has a wide distribution in California it is nowhere abundant and is seldom collected. Throughout its range, especially in the Cuyamaca region of San Diego County, specimens are found which grow about 1 foot high and have less undulate leaves and weaker spines. In these respects they resemble specimens of *B. pumila,* a closely related species. The young growth also closely resembles the foliage of that species. The type specimen collected by Jepson has the upper leaf-surfaces glossy. It apparently was a young specimen as the mature leaves of specimens from Marysville Buttes are typically dull above.

Berberis dictyota Jepson, Bull. Torr. Club 18:319 (1891). Type locality: Marysville Buttes, California. Collected by *Jepson. B. californica* Jepson.

9. **Berberis Fremontii** Torr. Desert Mahonia. Desert Barberry. Fig. 121.

An erect shrub, 3 to 12 feet high, usually with many stems from the base, or rarely tree-like to 15 feet high. Leaves 1½ to 3 inches long; leaflets 3 or 5, ovate to polyhedric in outline, ½-inch to 1 inch long, about ½-inch wide, thick and leathery, pale gray-green or yellowish gray on both surfaces, sinuately 1- to 4-toothed or 4-lobed on each margin, each lobe terminated by a stout spine, the terminal leaflet usually not much longer than the lateral ones. Racemes erect, 1 to 1½ inches long, terminating the numerous short spur-like branchlets, 3- to 9-flowered; the peduncles ½-inch to 2 inches long; the pedicels ¼- to ¾-inch long. Berries spherical when ripe, about ½-inch in diameter, dark blue to brown, dry, inflated. Flowering period, May and June.

Desert Mahonia occurs occasionally on desert mountain slopes and flats of the Upper Sonoran Life Zone in the eastern part of San Bernardino County (lower slopes of the New York Mountains, near Ivanpah and 3 miles s. of Barnwell with *Juniperus utahensis;* Cushenberry Springs, Mohave Desert, *M. E. Jones*) and in a few localities in the mountains of eastern San Diego County (canyon s. of Mistletoe Lodge, *M. L. Harris;* Walker's Ranch, near Jacumba, *Abrams;* Dripping Springs, *E. C. Jaeger*). It extends eastward to Arizona, Nevada, Utah, Colorado, and southward to Lower California and Sonora, Mexico. In Arizona it is more abundant and is usually associated with junipers and piñon pines.

Berberis Fremontii Torr. Bot. Mex. Bound. 30 (1859). Type locality: Southern Utah on the tributaries of the Virgin River, Utah. Collected by *Fremont.*

10. **Berberis Nevinii** Gray. Nevin Mahonia. Nevin Barberry. Fig. 122.

An erect much branched shrub, 3 to 6 feet high, with gray-glaucous foliage. Leaves 1½ to 3 inches long; leaflets 3 or 5 (or rarely 7), the lateral oblong or ovate, ½-inch to 1 inch long, ½-inch or less wide, the terminal leaflet broadly lanceolate, acuminate, 1 to 1½ inches long, all somewhat undulate but not markedly sinuate,

Fig. 122. Nevin Mahonia. *Berberis Nevinii* Gray.

with 5 to 16 bristle-like or slender spinose teeth on each margin. Racemes loosely 5- to 7-flowered, 1 to 2 inches long. Berries about 1/4-inch in diameter, yellowish red, or deep red when ripe, covered with a bloom, juicy. Flowering period, late March to May.

Nevin Mahonia is a rare species occurring in a few sandy washes of the San Fernando Valley, in San Francisquito Canyon *(Bacigalupi),* and in the Arroyo Seco, San Gabriel Mountains of Los Angeles County, California, in the Upper Sonoran Life Zone. This species is used as an ornamental in the coastal region of California. Its gray persistent spinescent foliage, yellow flowers, and colored berries make it one of the choicest of our native shrubs for single or group planting. It makes a fine hedge if properly pruned.

Berberis Nevinii Gray, Syn. Fl. 1:69 (1895). Type locality: Sandy wash in the San Fernando Valley, Los Angeles County, California. Collected by *J. C. Nevin.*

Papaveraceae. Poppy Family

The Poppy Family consists of about 23 genera and 200 species, chiefly herbs but some shrubs, widely distributed in the north temperate zone. Many species are grown as ornamentals. The opium of commerce is obtained from *Papaver somniferum.* Nine genera and 19 species are native to California, only one of which is definitely shrubby.

KEY TO THE GENERA

Leaves pinnatifid; flowers white..................................1. ROMNEYA.
Leaves not pinnatifid; flowers yellow........................2. DENDROMECON.

1. **Romneya** Harv. MATILIJA POPPY

(Named in honor of T. Romney Robinson, friend of Dr. Thos. Coulter, the discoverer of the genus.)

This is a genus of only a single species, native to California and Mexico.

1. **Romneya Coulteri** Harv. MATILIJA POPPY. Fig. 123.

KEY TO THE SPECIES AND VARIETY

Sepals glabrous, slightly beaked.................................*R. Coulteri.*
Sepals with short bristle-like hairs, beakless.................1a. var. *trichocalyx.*

A large glabrous suffruticose perennial, 3 to 8 feet high, with colorless bitter juice and leafy branching stems from a woody base. Leaves simple or almost compound, alternate, pinnatifid, 2 to 8 inches long. Fruit an ovoid or oblong coriaceous capsule, 1 to 1 1/2 inches long, strigose-hispid, with 7 to 12 placentae some of which meet in the axis and form partitions. Flowering period in the wild, June and July but for a longer time in cultivation.

Matilija Poppy occurs in washes and canyons below 4000 feet elevation in the coastal mountain area of southern California from Santa Barbara County south to San Diego County. It extends into Mexico. The large showy white flowers and divided gray-green leaves make this one of the most attractive plants of our native flora. It thrives in cultivation in almost any kind of soil.

1a. Var. **trichocalyx** (Eastw.) Jepson. Fig. 124. Like the species but the calyx with short bristle-like hairs and beakless.

The variety occurs occasionally with the species. An exceptionally fine colony

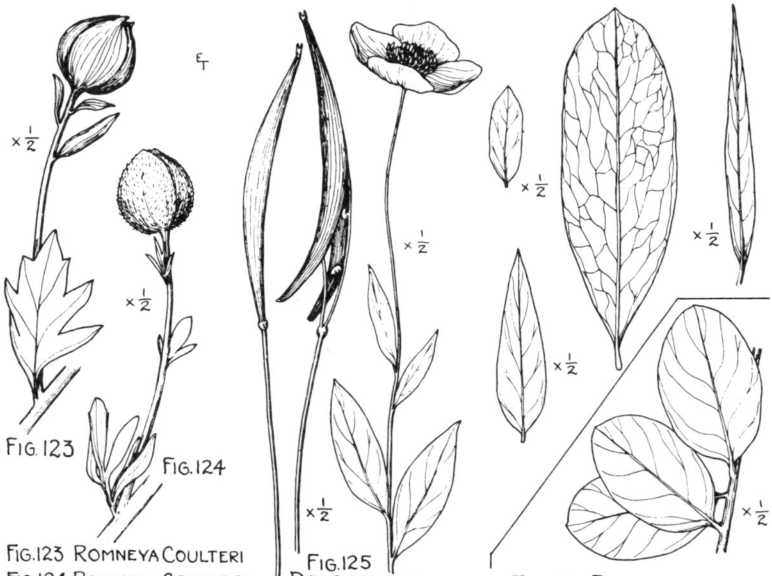

FIG. 123 ROMNEYA COULTERI
FIG. 124 ROMNEYA COULTERI VAR. TRICHOCALYX

FIG. 125 DENDROMECON RIGIDA

FIG. 126 DENDROMECON RIGIDA VAR. HARFORDII

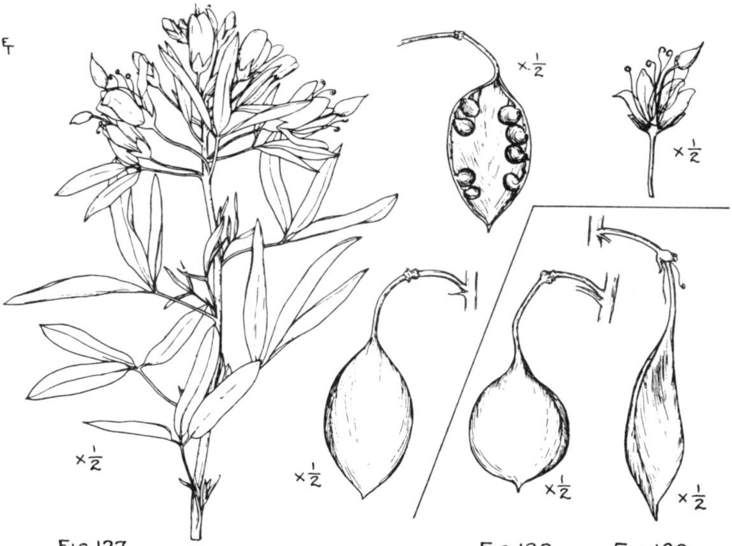

FIG. 127
ISOMERIS ARBOREA

FIG. 128
I. ARBOREA
VAR. GLOBOSA

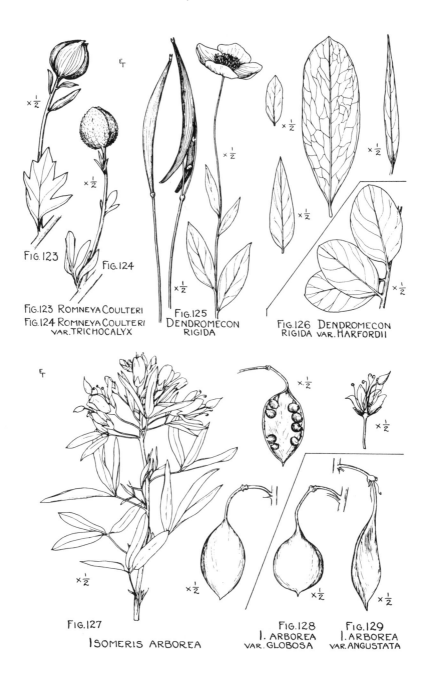

FIG. 129
I. ARBOREA
VAR. ANGUSTATA

of this variety was found by Dr. H. L. Mason and the writer in June 1923 in the upper Sespe Canyon of Ventura County.

Romneya Coulteri Harv.; Hook. Lond. Jour. Bot. 4:75 (1845). Type locality: California. Collected by *Coulter.*

Var. trichocalyx (Eastw.) Jepson, Fl. Calif. 1:563 (1922). *R. trichocalyx* Eastw. Based primarily upon cultivated plants.

2. **Dendromecon** Benth. Bush Poppy

(From the Greek *dendron,* tree, and *mecon,* poppy, in reference to the size of some plants.)

This genus contains a single polymorphic species native to the California mainland, the Santa Barbara Islands, and Santa Catalina Island.

1. **Dendromecon rigida** Benth. Bush Poppy. Fig. 125.

KEY TO THE SPECIES AND VARIETY

Leaf-blades linear-lanceolate to oblong or elliptical, finely denticulate. .*D. rigida.*
Leaf-blades broadly elliptic to oval, entire. . . . . 1a. var. *Harfordii.*

A glabrous freely branched evergreen shrub, 2 to 8 feet high, with yellowish gray or almost white shreddy bark on the stems and main branches. Leaves simple, alternate; the blades linear-lanceolate to oblong or elliptical, 1 to 4 inches long, 1/4-inch to 1 inch wide, coriaceous, gray or yellowish green, finely reticulate, apparently entire but finely denticulate; petioles 1/8-inch or less long. Flowers bisexual, regular, yellow, showy, solitary on peduncles 1 to 3 inches long; sepals 2, falling early; petals 4 (rarely 5), distinct, obovate or rounded, 3/4-inch to 1 1/4 inches long; stamens numerous, distinct, with short filaments and yellow linear anthers; ovary superior, 1-celled, 2-carpelled. Fruit a linear curved capsule, 2 to 4 inches long, its 2 valves separating incompletely from the 2 thread-like marginal placentae. Flowering period, April to June.

Bush Poppy usually inhabits the dry chaparral slopes of the Coast Ranges, the lower western slope of the Sierra Nevada, and the chaparral areas in the mountains of southern California, in the Upper Sonoran Life Zone. Several species and varieties have been segregated from this species but only one seems distinct enough to warrant recognition.

1a. Var. **Harfordii** (Kell.) K. Brandg. Island Bush Poppy. Fig. 126.

Large shrubs or sometimes becoming tree-like and attaining a height of 20 feet, with a stem 6 to 12 inches in diameter. Leaf-blades broadly elliptic to oval, 1 to 3 inches long (or much longer on crown-sprouts), entire, less reticulate than in the species.

This variety occurs on Santa Catalina, Santa Rosa, and Santa Cruz islands.

Dendromecon rigida Benth. Trans. Hort. Soc. Lond. II, 1:407 (1834). Type: Grown from seeds collected in California by *David Douglas.*

Var. Harfordii (Kell.) K. Brandg. Zoe 4:83 (1893). *D. Harfordii* Kell. Type locality: Santa Rosa Island. Collected by *W. G. Harford.*

Capparidaceae. Caper Family

The Caper Family consists of about 40 genera and 500 species inhabiting the warmer parts of the world. Six genera and 12 species are found in California, only one of which is a shrub.

1. **Isomeris** Nutt. Bladderpod

(From the Greek *isos,* equal, and *meris,* part.)

This genus contains one species and 2 varieties native to California and Mexico.

1. **Isomeris arborea** Nutt. Bladderpod. Fig. 127.

KEY TO THE SPECIES AND VARIETIES

Capsules oval to broadly elliptical . . . . *I. arborea.*
Capsules globose . . . . 1a. var. *globosa.*
Capsules narrowly oblong . . . . 1b. var. *angustata.*

An ill-scented widely branched shrub, 2 to 9 feet high, with hard yellow wood and puberulent branches. Leaves 3-foliolate, or simple below the flower-clusters, alternate, evergreen; leaflets oblong to lancolate, ½-inch to 1½ inches long, ¼-inch or less wide (or as much as ½-inch wide in Catalina Island material), soft-tipped at apex, rounded at base, greenish yellow or grayish, entire, short-petiolulate; the foliar petioles ½-inch to 1 inch long. Flowers bisexual, regular, large, yellow, in terminal bracteate racemes; sepals 4, united at base, persistent; petals 4, distinct, yellow, ½- to ¾-inch long; stamens 6, distinct, long-exserted; ovary superior, 1-celled, long-stipitate. Fruit an oval or broadly elliptical inflated capsule, 1 to 2 inches long, abruptly tapering at apex, gradually tapering into a stipe (½-inch to 1½ inches long) at base; seeds round, smooth, a little smaller than peas. Flowering period, February to May, or throughout most of the year.

Bladderpod is a rather common shrub on the bluffs and hills near the coast in San Diego, Orange, and Los Angeles counties, and on Santa Rosa and Santa Catalina islands. It extends eastward to the western side of the Mohave and Colorado deserts, and northward in the inner Coast Ranges through Santa Barbara County to Monterey County and southward to Lower California and Sonora, Mexico, in the Lower and Upper Sonoran Life Zones. This shrub shows considerable variation in shape and inflation of the fruit pods, as well as in vegetative characters. Upon the basis of some of these variations, 2 varieties are here included.

1a. Var. **globosa** Cov. Fig. 128.

Capsules globose, about 1 inch in diameter. This variety occurs along the coast in San Diego County and extends northward into Orange, Los Angeles (near Gorman Station, new Ridge Route, *J. A. Ewan*), western Kern, western Fresno, Ventura, Santa Barbara, and Monterey counties. It also occurs on Santa Catalina, Santa Rosa, and Cedros islands and in Lower California. It intergrades with the species.

1b. Var. **angustata** Parish. Fig. 129.

Capsules narrowly oblong, 1½ to 2 inches long, 3- to 5-seeded, not much inflated. This variety apparently occurs only on the Mohave and Colorado deserts and on Cedros Island. Specimens have been examined from Mopas Wash at the base of North Butte of the Mopas Mountains *(Roxana Ferris* & *Bacigalupi),* from near Beals Wells, Borrego Springs, west slope of the Chocolate Mountains, Palm Canyon, Twenty-nine Palms, Cottonwood Pass, Ironwood Springs, and Cedros Island.

Isomeris arborea Nutt.; T. & G. Fl. N. Am. 1:124 (1838). Type locality: San Diego. Collected by *Nuttall.*

Var. globosa Cov. Proc. Biol. Soc. Wash. 7:73 (1892). Type locality: Caliente Creek, Kern County. Collected by *Coville.*

Var. angustata Parish, Muhlenbergia 3:128 (1907). Type locality: Palm Springs, Riverside County. Collected by *Parish.*

Brassicaceae (Cruciferae). Mustard Family

The Mustard Family contains about 200 genera and 2000 species, found on all continents but chiefly in the temperate and frigid zones of the northern hemisphere. Four genera have a few woody or semi-woody species native to California. Many of the garden vegetables, such as turnip, rutabaga, kohlrabi, radish, cabbage, horse-radish, Brussels sprouts, broccoli, mustard, water cress, and cauliflower belong to this family.

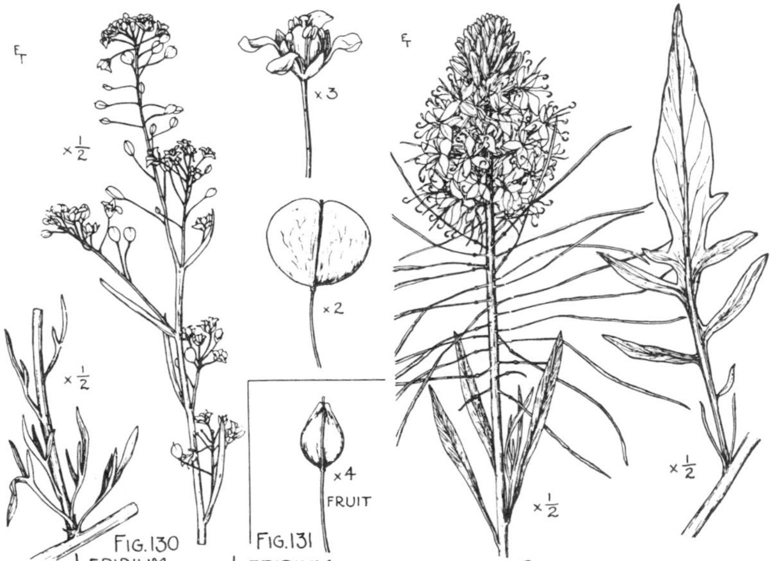

FIG. 130 LEPIDIUM FREMONTII FIG. 131 LEPIDIUM ALYSSOIDES FIG. 132 STANLEYA PINNATA

KEY TO THE GENERA

Flowers white, purplish, or pink; fruit-pods round or broadly elliptical, usually notched at apex . . . . 1. LEPIDIUM.
Flowers yellow or orange-colored; fruit-pods long-stipitate . . . . 2. STANLEYA.

1. **Lepidium** L. PEPPERGRASS

(From the Greek *lepidion,* a little scale, in reference to the flattened pods.) This genus contains about 100 species, widely distributed; only 2 of the 18 Californian species have woody tissue.

KEY TO THE SPECIES

Capsules orbicular, notched at apex; plants bushy and distinctly woody below. 1. *L. Fremontii.*

Capsules oval, not notched at apex; plants less bushy and scarcely woody at base. 2. *L. alyssoides.*

1. **Lepidium Fremontii** Wats. BUSH PEPPERGRASS. DESERT-ALYSSUM. Fig. 130.

A low rounded bushy subshrub, 1 to 3 feet high, with glabrous and glaucous stems and branches. Leaves simple, alternate, evergreen, nearly sessile, 1 to 2½ inches long, 1/8-inch or less wide, the lower leaves often pinnatifid, with linear divisions, the upper leaves linear, entire, somewhat fleshy and glaucous. Flowers bisexual, regular, white, fragrant, borne on slender pedicels in numerous racemes; sepals 4; petals 4, distinct, about 1/8-inch long, clawed; stamens 6, the 4 inner longer than the 2 outer; ovary superior, 2-celled. Fruit a rounded 2-celled capsule, about 1/4-inch in diameter, notched at apex. Flowering period, January to June.

Bush Peppergrass inhabits arid rocky ground below 4500 feet altitude on the north side of the Colorado Desert, the Mohave Desert, and north to Inyo County (White Mountains, *V. Duran;* near Laws, *Heller*). It extends eastward to Nevada, Arizona, Utah, and Colorado.

Lepidium Fremontii Wats. Bot. King. Expl. 30 (1871). Type locality: Mohave River. Collected by *Fremont.*

2. **Lepidium alyssoides** Gray. MESA PEPPERGRASS. Fig. 131.

Usually a many-stemmed perennial, rarely somewhat woody at base. Flowers white, smaller than in *L. Fremontii.* Capsules oval, about 1/8-inch long.

This species is rare in California, having been reported from the eastern Mohave Desert (New York Mountains, *J. Grinnell*). It extends eastward to Colorado and Texas.

Lepidium alyssoides Gray, Mem. Am. Acad. 4:10 (1849). Type locality: New Mexico. Collected by *Fendler.*

2. **Stanleya** Nutt.

(Named after Lord Stanley, English ornithologist.)

Large perennial or biennial glabrous herbs, sometimes woody at base. Leaves simple, usually pinnatifid, and alternate. Flowers large, yellow, numerous in showy elongated spike-like racemes; sepals 4, distinct; petals 4, distinct, clawed; stamens 6, equal, the filaments long-exserted; ovary superior, of 2 united carpels. Fruit a capsule, linear, long-stipitate.

This genus contains 5 species native to the arid regions of western North America, 2 of which occur in California.

KEY TO THE SPECIES

Petals much surpassing the sepals, bright yellow, their claws woolly. . 1. *S. pinnata.*
Petals scarcely surpassing the sepals, pale yellow, their claws glabrous. . 2. *S. elata.*

1. **Stanleya pinnata** Britt. DESERT PLUME. Fig. 132.

Coarse perennials 2 to 5 feet high, often woody at base, with erect nearly glabrous branches. Leaves glabrous and glaucous; the lower ones 2 1/2 to 8 inches long, commonly pinnatifid into lanceolate segments, long-petioled; the upper ones 1 1/4 to 2 1/2 inches long, usually lanceolate and subentire, short-petioled or nearly sessile. Racemes 1/2-foot to 2 feet long, many-flowered; petals bright yellow, 5/8- to 3/4-inch long, the claw woolly and as long as the oblong blade. Capsules linear, 1 1/2 to 2 1/2 inches long, widely spreading, curved as a sickle; stipe 1/2- to 3/4-inch long. Flowering period, May and June.

Desert Plume inhabits dry slopes and plains between 1000 and 5000 feet in the desert areas of Inyo (Panamint and White mountains), Kern, Santa Barbara, Ventura, Los Angeles, San Bernardino, and Riverside (eastern base of Mt. San Jacinto) counties. It extends eastward to Nebraska and Texas.

Stanleya pinnata (Pursh) Britt. Trans. N. Y. Acad. Sci. 8:62 (1888). *Cleome pinnata* Pursh. Type locality: "In Upper Louisiana," that is, the upper Mississippi Valley. Collected by *Bradbury. Stanleya pinnatifida* Nutt.

2. **Stanleya elata** M. E. Jones. PANAMINT PLUME.

Plants 2 to 6½ feet high, only occasionally with woody tissue at base. Leaf-blades lance-ovate, 4 to 8 inches long, entire or with a few small basal lobes, narrowed at base to a short petiole or in upper leaves the petiole half as long as the blade. Racemes 6 to 18 inches long; sepals petal-like, about ⅜-inch long; petals pale yellow, about as long as the sepals, the claws glabrous. Capsules narrow-linear, 3 to 4 inches long, the stipe about ½-inch long. Flowering period, May and June.

Panamint Plume is rare in California, being known only from the Panamint (alt. 5000 ft., *Roxana Ferris*), White (Black Canyon, alt. 5700 ft., *V. Duran*), and Argus (alt. 5000 ft., *M. E. Jones*) mountains of Inyo County. It extends eastward into Nevada.

Stanleya elata M. E. Jones, Zoe 2:16 (1891). Type locality: "Near Hawthorne, Mineral County, Nevada." Collected by *M. E. Jones.*

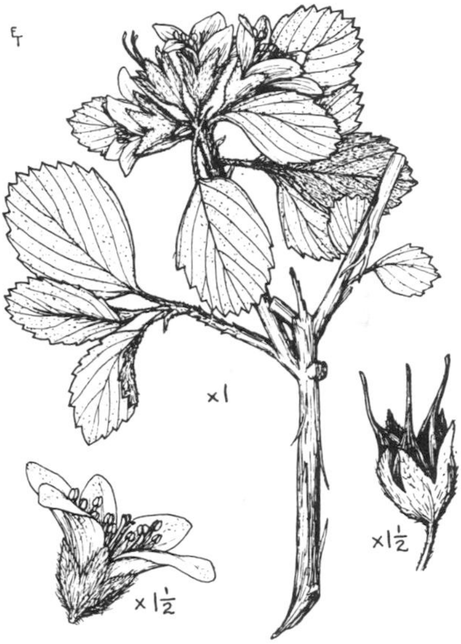

FIG. 133 JAMESIA AMERICANA

Saxifragaceae. Saxifrage Family

This family is a large and important family economically, consisting of about 75 genera and 700 species of mostly perennial herbs or shrubs and having their greatest development in the temperate regions. The gooseberries and currants are familiar examples. Eighteen genera and about 70 species are found in California, 33 species of which are shrubs or subshrubs.

KEY TO THE GENERA

Erect shrubs 1 foot or more high.
- Leaves opposite; fruit a dry pod.
  - Leaves coarsely serrate; stamens 10; flowers pink or rose-colored. . 1. JAMESIA.
  - Leaves entire or dentate; stamens 20 to numerous; flowers white or pale yellow.
    - Leaves 3-veined from the base, deciduous; stamens 20 to 40. 2. PHILADELPHUS.
    - Leaves 1-veined from the base, evergreen; stamens 150 to 250. 3. CARPENTERIA.
- Leaves alternate; fruit a more or less fleshy berry. . . . . .4. RIBES.

Low trailing or erect subshrubs less than 1 foot high; leaves opposite. . 5. WHIPPLEA.

1. **Jamesia** T. & G.

(Named for Dr. Edwin James, who discovered the plant, botanist and historian of Long's expedition to the Rocky Mountains in 1820.)

This genus consists of 2 species native to the region from the southern Rocky Mountain states to southeastern California. Only one species occurs in California.

1. **Jamesia americana** T. & G. CLIFFBUSH. Fig. 133.

A low deciduous much branched shrub, 1½ to 6 feet high, with somewhat shreddy grayish or reddish bark, the young branches pubescent. Leaf-blades oblong to round, ½-inch to 2 inches long, ⅜- to ¾-inch wide (3 inches long on young shoots), 1-veined from the base, green and pubescent above, paler and densely hairy beneath, coarsely toothed; petioles ⅛- to ¼-inch long, pubescent. Flowers bisexual, regular, few in terminal clusters; receptocalyx partially joined to the ovary, hairy, the tube flattish or turbinate, the lobes 5, acute or rarely obtuse, ⅛- to 3/16-inch long; petals 5, pink, obtuse, ¼- to ⅜-inch long; stamens 10, the alternate ones shorter; ovary about ½ inferior, conical, with 3 to 5 parietal placentae; styles 3 to 5. Fruit a many-seeded capsule almost ½-inch long. Flowering period, July and August.

Cliffbush occurs on rocky canyon walls in the southern Sierra Nevada of Fresno and Tulare counties, in the Panamint Mountains of Inyo County, and on Mono Pass, Mono County. (FRESNO COUNTY: Glenn Pass, 12,000 feet elevation, *Roxana Ferris* & *Bacigalupi;* Palisade Creek, acc. *Jepson.* TULARE COUNTY: White Chief Mine, Mineral King District, *Hall;* Kern-Kaweah Canyon, east of Rockslide Lake, elevation 9600 feet, *Bacigalupi;* Canyon Creek Falls, *Eastwood;* Volcano Creek Falls, *Hall;* Whitney Creek, *Culbertson.* INYO COUNTY: Panamint Mountains, acc. *Munz;* Pine Creek Canyon, *Roxana Ferris.* MONO COUNTY: Mono Pass, *Anita Noldeke.*) It extends eastward to Nevada, Arizona, Utah, New Mexico, Colorado, and Wyoming.

Jamesia americana T. & G. Fl. N. Am. 1:593 (1840). Type locality: Rocky Mountains of Colorado. Collected by *James. J. americana* var. *californica* (Small) Jepson. *Edwinia californica* Small.

2. **Philadelphus** L. MOCK ORANGE

(Named for Ptolemy Philadelphus, an ancient Egyptian king.)

Deciduous shrubs. Leaves simple, opposite, the blades entire or toothed. Flowers bisexual, regular, large, white, solitary or in terminal clusters; sepals 4 or 5, persistent; petals 4 or 5, distinct; stamens numerous, usually 20 to 60, distinct or more or less united below; ovary almost completely inferior, 4-celled; styles 4, usually distinct at apex. Fruit a capsule with numerous seeds.

This genus consists of about 40 species occurring in North America, central Europe, and Asia. Three species and one variety are native to California. Several species have been cultivated for their large and fragrant flowers, Much variation occurs in the genus, partially owing to hybridization, and as a result, the determination of species is often very difficult.

In California two distinct types are found. One type has very small almost sessile leaves and flowers solitary or 2 or 3 in a cluster. The other type has larger petiolate leaves and more numerous flowers, these usually 5 to 40 in terminal clusters. The type with smaller leaves occurs in the desert mountains of southeastern California, while that with larger leaves occurs in the North Coast Ranges and in the Sierra Nevada.

KEY TO THE SPECIES AND VARIETIES

Leaves not over ½-inch wide; flowers solitary or rarely 2 or 3 in a cluster. 1. *P. serpyllifolius.*

Leaves over ½-inch wide; flowers more than 3 in a cluster.

Leaves usually glabrous, typically entire; mainly Sierra Nevada and northern California . . . . 2. *P. Lewisii* var. *californicus.*

Leaves usually pubescent beneath, denticulate; North Coast Range and the Siskiyou Mountains. . . . . .2a. *P. Lewisii* var. *Gordonianus.*

1. **Philadelphus serpyllifolius** Gray. LITTLELEAF MOCK ORANGE. Fig. 134.

A low rigid shrub, 1 to 3 feet high, with spreading branches bent downward at the ends and exfoliating bark on the old stems. Leaf-blades oval to oblong-elliptic, 1/4- to 3/4-inch long, 3/16- to 3/8-inch wide, 3-veined from the base, sparsely pubescent above, silky-pubescent or -strigose beneath, entire; petioles less than 1/16-inch long.

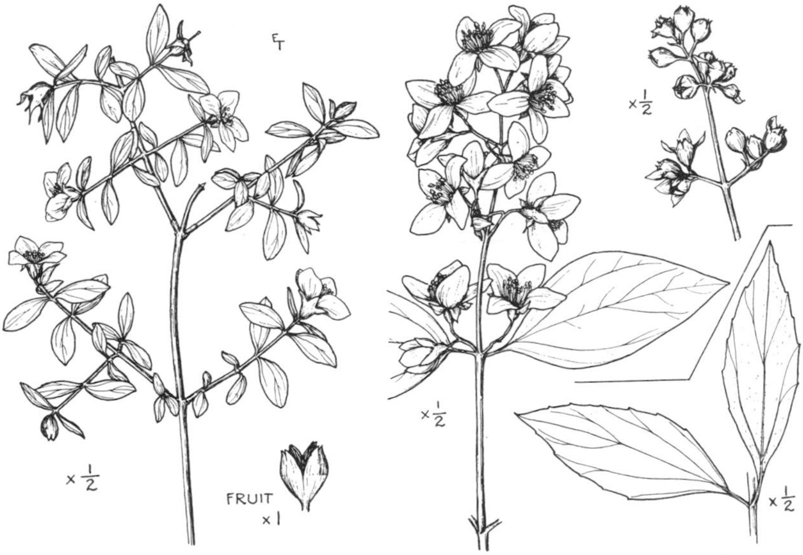

FIG. 134 PHILADELPHUS SERPYLLIFOLIUS

FIG. 135 PHILADELPHUS LEWISII VAR. CALIFORNICUS

FIG. 136 P. LEWISII VAR. GORDONIANUS

Flowers solitary (rarely 2 or 3), subsessile on very short branches with 1 or 2 pairs of leaves; receptocalyx silky-hispid; petals oval or rounded, about 3/8-inch long, white or yellowish white. Flowering period, July and August.

Littleleaf Mock Orange is known in California from the White Mountains of Mono County (Black Canyon, el. 5700 feet, *V. Duran;* White Mountains, el. 8500 feet, *W. H. Shockley*) and the San Jacinto Mountains of Riverside County (Dark Canyon, el. 7500 feet, *Munz* & *Johnston;* vicinity of Tamarack Valley, el. 8500 feet, *Hall;* Long Valley, el. 8000 feet, *Jaeger*). It is found eastward in Nevada, Arizona, New Mexico, and Texas.

This species is very closely related to *Philadelphus microphyllus* Gray but differs in its smaller leaves and flowers.

Philadelphus serpyllifolius Gray, Pl. Wright. 1:77 (1852). Type locality: Western Texas. Collected by *Wright. P. stramineus* Rydb. *P. pumilus* Rydb.

2. **Philadelphus Lewisii** var. **californicus** (Benth.) Gray. WILD MOCK ORANGE. Fig. 135.

A loosely branched shrub, 4 to 10 feet high, with reddish glabrous bark on young branches and brown exfoliating bark on the stems of the previous season, that of

Fig. 137. Carpenteria. *Carpenteria californica* Torr.

the old stems gray. Leaf-blades ovate or lanceolate-ovate, 1¼ to 3¼ inches long, ¾-inch to 1½ inches wide, 3- to 5-veined from the base or from near the base, usually entire or minutely denticulate, glabrous or nearly so on both surfaces; petioles about ⅜-inch long. Flowers white, ¾-inch to 1 inch broad, usually numerous, in panicles; receptocalyx glabrous; petals oblong, oval, elliptical, or obovate; styles united nearly to the summit or distinct for the upper half. Capsules about ⅜-inch long. Flowering period, May to July.

Wild Mock Orange is a beautiful flowering shrub occurring in the lower Sierra Nevada and foothills from Siskiyou and Trinity counties south to Tulare County. It is nowhere abundant but its large attractive flowers make it conspicuous. It transplants easily from root-sections and thrives in the cooler parts of California.

2a. **Philadelphus Lewisii** var. **Gordonianus** (Lindl.) Jepson. Fig. 136.

This variety is very closely related to the one above and seems to differ only in the more toothed and pubescent leaves and fewer racemose flowers. It occurs in Siskiyou, Trinity, Del Norte, Humboldt, Mendocino, and Lake counties. Plants growing in Siskiyou and Trinity counties are often intermediate, and thus it is very difficult to place them in either of the above varieties. It may be better to consider both varieties as one since the number of flowers, amount of pubescence, and leaf-margins are characters in which there is a considerable amount of variation.

Philadelphus Lewisii var. californicus (Benth.) Gray, Bot. Calif. 1:202 (1876). *P. californicus* Benth. Type locality: In the *Pinus ponderosa* belt, "on the headwaters of the Yuba . . . excursion to Bear Valley." Collected by *Hartweg*.

Var. Gordonianus (Lindl.) Jepson, Man. 466 (1925). *P. Gordonianus* Lindl. Type locality: Banks of the Columbia River. Collected by *Douglas*.

3. **Carpenteria** Torr.

(Named after Professor William M. Carpenter of Louisiana.)

This is a genus of a single species.

1. **Carpenteria californica** Torr. CARPENTERIA. BUSH-ANEMONE. Fig. 137.

An erect shrub, 3 to 7 feet high, with numerous clustered stems, the branches opposite and somewhat 4-angled, the bark light-colored and peeling in thin shreds, the young shoots often purplish. Leaves simple, opposite, evergreen; the blades thick, oblong-lanceolate, 2 to 4½ inches long, ¾-inch to 1¼ inches wide, tapering at both ends, 1-veined from the base, dark green and glabrous above, whitened beneath with a close pubescence, entire or sometimes slightly toothed; petioles ¼- to ¾-inch long. Flowers bisexual, regular, large, 1½ to 2½ inches broad, fragrant, few in open terminal clusters; sepals 5 to 7, ovate-lanceolate, persistent; petals 5 to 7, white, obovate or round-obovate, ¾-inch to 1¼ inches long; stamens very numerous (commonly about 150 to 250), distinct, the filaments of varying lengths; ovary 5- to 7-celled; style short, with a 5- to 7-lobed stigma. Fruit a leathery capsule, somewhat conical, about ½-inch long, 5- to 7-valved; seeds numerous. Flowering period, June to August.

Carpenteria occurs in the Sierra Nevada foothills in a few restricted localities between the Kings and San Joaquin rivers in Fresno County, in the Transition Life Zone between 1500 and 4000 feet elevation. It is one of the rarest of the endemic shrubs of California.

Carpenteria is a handsome evergreen shrub and very showy when in full bloom. It thrives best in well-drained soils and in a somewhat protected place. The freeze of 1932–33 did not kill the plants in the San Francisco Bay region. It suckers rather freely and can be propagated from suckers as well as from cuttings made from the younger stems.

Carpenteria californica Torr.. Pl. Frem. 12, pl. 7 (1853). Type locality: Sierra foothills of Fresno County, California. Collected by *Fremont.*

4. **Ribes** L. GOOSEBERRY. CURRANT

(An ancient Arabic name.)

Shrubs, either unarmed or with nodal spines and sometimes with additional internodal prickles or bristles. Leaves simple, alternate, commonly palmately lobed. Flowers bisexual, regular, in racemes or rarely solitary; pedicels with bractlets; sepals 5 (rarely 4), usually joined at base to form a tube, the basal portion of this adnate to the ovary; petals 5 (rarely 4), distinct, adnate to the throat of the calyx; stamens 5 (rarely 4), alternate with the petals and inserted on the throat of the calyx; ovary inferior, 1-celled; style 2-lobed or -divided. Fruit a 1-celled many-seeded berry.

There are about 150 species of the genus *Ribes* distributed in North and South America, Europe, Asia, and northern Africa. Some authors reserve the genus *Ribes* for the currants and place the gooseberries in the genus *Grossularia.*

KEY TO THE SPECIES

I. Stems and branches without nodal spines and without internodal prickles and bristles.

Leaves evergreen, leathery, sparingly toothed or lobed; calyx-tube very short, saucer-shaped . . . . 1. *R. viburnifolium.*

Leaves deciduous, all lobed or toothed.

Calyx-tube saucer-shaped, the lobes spreading from near the summit of the ovary; leaves thin, maple-like, 2 to 8 inches broad.

Ovary with stalked glands; flower-clusters 2 to 4 inches long, with 5 to 12 purplish flowers . . . . 2. *R. laxiflorum.*

Ovary with sessile glands; flower-clusters with 20 to 50 greenish white flowers.

Flower-clusters 4 to 10 inches long; sepals green; berry with bloom. 3. *R. bracteosum.*

Flower-clusters 2½ to 4½ inches long; sepals white; berry without bloom. 4. *R. petiolare.*

Calyx-tube cylindrical, bell-shaped, or rarely urn-shaped; leaves ½-inch to 3 inches broad.

Flowers yellow, often tinged with red; leaves usually glabrous, nearly alike on both surfaces, not heart-shaped at base except on young shoots. 5. *R. aureum.*

Flowers not yellow; leaves usually pubescent or glandular on one or both surfaces, heart-shaped at base.

Calyx-tube 2 to 4 times as long as broad, cylindrical, the lobes about 1/16-inch long; flowers white or cream-colored, or rarely slightly pinkish; leaves usually indistinctly and shallowly 3- or 5-lobed or not lobed . . . . 6. *R. cereum.*

Calyx-tube less than 2 times as long as broad; leaves distinctly 3- or 5-lobed.

Flowers 5/8- to 3/4-inch long, 3 to 12 in a loose cluster; calyx-tube nearly as broad as long, the lobes shorter than the tube. 7. *R. viscosissimum.*

Flowers 1/2-inch or less long, 10 to 50 in racemes.

Styles villous, at least at base.

Leaves usually rugose and with stalked glands above; calyx-tube broadly cylindrical; styles not divided more than 1/2 their lengths.

Flowers pink or rose-color, over 5/16-inch long. .8. *R. malvaceum.*

Flowers white, less than 5/16-inch long........9. *R. indecorum.*

Leaves not rugose above; calyx-tube urn-shaped, 1/16-inch or less high; styles divided to the base.........10. *R. canthariforme.*

Styles glabrous.

Flowers from base of ovary to tip of calyx-lobes 3/8-inch or less long; calyx-lobes erect when in full bloom, reddish. 11. *R. nevadense.*

Flowers from base of ovary to tip of calyx-lobes 3/8-inch or more long; calyx-lobes spreading or recurved when in full bloom, pink or rarely red.....................12. *R. sanguineum.*

II. Stems and branches with nodal spines, with or without internodal prickles and bristles (the spines sometimes very weak or absent at many nodes).

Calyx-tube not conspicuous, saucer-shaped, the lobes spreading or rotate; internodal prickles or bristles usually present on new growth.

Spines 5 to 9 at a node; leaves usually 1 to 2 inches (rarely 3/4-inch) broad, glabrous on both surfaces or rarely slightly pubescent, not glandular-sticky; racemes commonly 5- to 15-flowered...................13. *R. lacustre.*

Spines 3 at a node; leaves 1/2-inch to 1 inch broad, glandular-sticky and pubescent on both surfaces; racemes usually 3- to 7-flowered. 14. *R. montigenum.*

Calyx-tube evident, cylindric or bell-shaped.

Flowers with parts in 4's, red, fuchsia-like; petals as long as the erect sepals; stamens long-exserted; stems with internodal bristles and prickles. 15. *R. speciosum.*

Flowers with parts in 5's; petals shorter than the usually reflexed sepals which are commonly erect in age.

Ovary and berry without spines or prickles.

Styles villous, at least toward the base; calyx green without or reddish in the variety *Parishii*.........................16. *R. divaricatum.*

Styles glabrous; calyx yellow or whitish to rarely pinkish.

Ovary and fruit soft- or glandular-pubescent; calyx-tube as broad as long, slightly shorter than the lobes...........17. *R. velutinum.*

Ovary and fruit glabrous or rarely with a few scattered hairs; calyx-tube longer than broad.

Calyx-tube longer than the lobes. 18. *R. leptanthum* var. *lasianthum.*

Calyx-tube shorter than or only as long as the lobes. 19. *R. quercetorum.*

Ovary and berry with spines, prickles, or bristles.

Calyx-tube distinctly longer than broad or rarely only slightly longer in

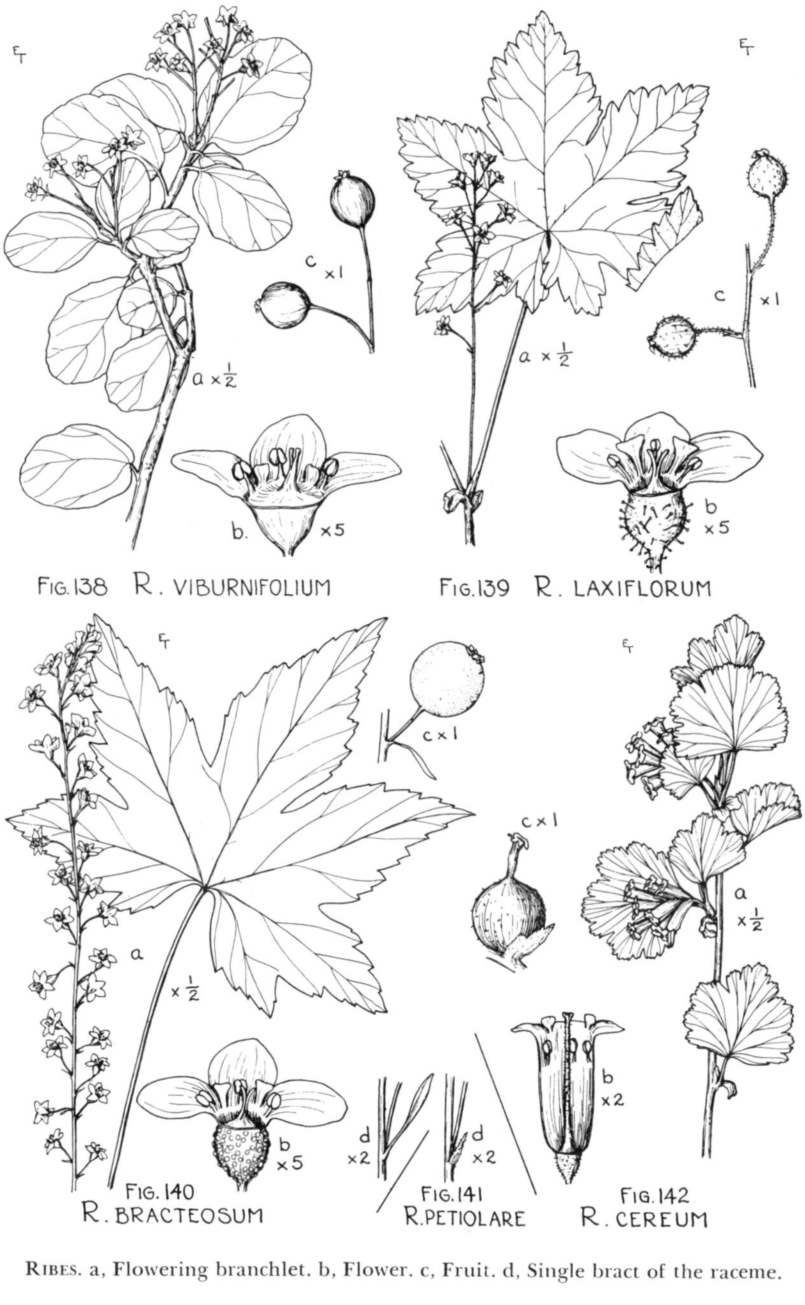

RIBES. a, Flowering branchlet. b, Flower. c, Fruit. d, Single bract of the raceme.

R. Roezlii var. *cruentum;* stems without internodal spines, prickles, or bristles.

Ovary and berry with all or nearly all the bristles gland-tipped.

Anthers nearly as broad as long, obtuse at apex; flowers nearly 1 inch long....................................20. *R. Lobbii.*

Anthers much longer than broad, lanceolate to linear, apiculate at apex; flowers usually less than ¾-inch long.....21. *R. amarum.*

Ovary and berry with long non-glandular spines and intermediate short gland-tipped bristles; bracts as long as or longer than the pedicels and often covering the ovary; anthers apiculate at apex. 22. *R. Roezlii.*

Calyx-tube as broad as long or nearly so.

Young stems usually without internodal prickles or bristles; leaves not glandular beneath or with only a few glands along the veins.

Calyx-lobes ½-inch long, 3 or 4 times the length of the tube, dark red; stamens 2 to 3 times as long as the petals; anthers obtuse at apex....................................23. *R. Marshallii.*

Calyx-lobes ¼- to ⅜-inch long, 2 or 2½ times as long as the tube, usually greenish white or rarely slightly reddish to purplish.

Leaves glabrous or nearly so on both surfaces; anthers apiculate at apex..............................24. *R. californicum.*

Leaves finely pubescent above and beneath; anthers obtuse at apex..............................25. *R. binominatum.*

Young stems usually with internodal prickles or bristles; leaves glandular beneath.

Calyx greenish white or white; anthers apiculate at apex. 26. *R. victoris.*

Calyx purplish or reddish.

Stamens nearly 3 times as long as the petals; anthers obtuse at apex; berry ⅔-inch to nearly 1 inch in diameter. 27. *R. sericeum.*

Stamens not more than 2 times longer than the petals; anthers apiculate at apex; berry normally not more than ½- to ⅝-inch in diameter............................28. *R. Menziesii.*

1. **Ribes viburnifolium** Gray. Evergreen Currant. Catalina Perfume Currant. Fig. 138.

A straggling evergreen unarmed shrub, 2 to 6 feet high, with resinous-glandular young stems and branches. Leaf-blades thick, ovate, obovate, or almost round, ¾-inch to 1½ inches long, 1-veined from the base or rarely obscurely 3-veined, dark green and glabrous above, paler and resinous-dotted beneath, entire or sparingly irregularly toothed or lobed; petioles ¼- to ¾-inch long. Flowers small, about ⅛-inch high and ¼-inch broad, rose-colored, few to several in erect racemes, 2 or 3 racemes from the same short branchlet; pedicels filiform, ¼- to ⅜-inch long; bracts lanceolate, shorter than the pedicels, falling early; ovary glabrous; calyx-tube saucer-shaped or wheel-shaped, expanding immediately above the ovary into 5 oval spreading and rose-colored lobes; petals 5, greenish, very small, about ¼ as long as the calyx-lobes. Berry almost globular, about ¼-inch in diameter, glabrous, red. Flowering period, February to April.

Evergreen Currant occurs in canyons on Santa Catalina Island and on the mainland of Lower California at All Saints Bay. In general outward character this shrub does not resemble any of the other species of our native currants or gooseberries. The almost entire non-lobed evergreen leaves with apparently only one vein from the base distinguish it from the other currants. Unless it be in fruit, one is likely to mistake it for an *Elaeagnus*, a *Rhus*, or any of several other shrubby genera not related to *Ribes*. In cultivation, it does well in sunny exposures.

Ribes viburnifolium Gray, Proc. Am. Acad. 17:202 (1882). Type locality: All Saints Bay, Lower California. Collected by *Parry, Pringle, Jones*.

2. **Ribes laxiflorum** Pursh. LOOSE-FLOWERING CURRANT. Fig. 139.

A spreading or decumbent shrub, with unarmed stems 3 to 8 feet long. Leaf-blades thin, nearly round in outline, heart-shaped at base, 2 to 4 inches broad, 5-veined from the base, deeply 5-lobed and sometimes with two extra sub-basal lobes, the lobes rather bluntly toothed, glabrous above, paler and sparingly pubescent beneath; petioles slender, 1½ to 3½ inches long; buds rather large, the scales thin and loosely overlapping, becoming larger with the opening of the bud and persisting as brown appendages at the bases of the petioles and peduncles. Flowers purplish, about ¼-inch broad, 5 to 12 in glandular-pubescent racemes 2 to 4 inches long; pedicels ¼- to ⅜-inch long, glandular-pubescent; bracts lanceolate, shorter than the pedicels; ovary with stalked glands; calyx-tube very short, spreading and saucer-shaped; petals fan-shaped, minute, red, ½ the length of the calyx-lobes. Berry globular, about ¼-inch or less in diameter, black, with few stalked glands, often covered with a bloom. Flowering period, April and May.

Loose-flowering Currant occurs in wet places and dense woods from sea level to 500 feet elevation in Humboldt County (Prairie Creek, *J. P. Tracy;* Humboldt Bay region, *H. P. Chandler*). It extends northward through British Columbia to Alaska, and thence westward to Siberia. It occurs also in the northern Rocky Mountains in Idaho and Alberta. The large thin persistent bud-scales at the base of the leaves and peduncles make this species easy to identify. It is known also as Coast Trailing Currant and Western Black Currant.

Ribes laxiflorum Pursh, Fl. Am. Sept. 731 (1814). Type locality: "North West Coast of America." Collected by *Menzies*.

3. **Ribes bracteosum** Dougl. STINK CURRANT. CALIFORNIA BLACK CURRANT. Fig. 140.

A tall shrub, 4 to 12 feet high, with ascending unarmed stems and sparingly pubescent herbage. Leaf-blades thin, maple-like, 2½ to 8 inches broad, heart-shaped at base, deeply 5-lobed, the lobes sharply doubly serrate, glabrous above, paler and resinous-dotted beneath; petioles slender, as long as or longer than the blades. Flowers greenish white, 20 or more in elongated racemes 5 to 8 inches long; pedicels ⅜-inch or less long, pubescent; bracts half as long or as long as the pedicels, the lower stalked and leaf-like; ovary with sessile glands; calyx-tube saucer-shaped; calyx-lobes green, spreading, ⅛-inch or more long; petals minute, white. Berry globular, about ⅜-inch in diameter, resinous-dotted, black and covered with a bloom when mature. Flowering period, May and June.

Stink Currant inhabits shady woods and creek banks in northern California from Mendocino County (vicinity of Ft. Bragg) northward to Del Norte County. It extends northward to Alaska. Its large thin maple-like leaves and long clusters of greenish white flowers easily distinguish this currant from the other Californian species of *Ribes*.

Ribes bracteosum Dougl.; Hook. Fl. Bor. Am. 1:233 (1834). Type locality: Mouth of the Columbia River. Collected by *Scouler* and *Douglas*.

4. **Ribes petiolare** Dougl. WESTERN BLACK CURRANT. Fig. 141.

An erect or spreading unarmed shrub, 3 to 6 feet high, with glabrous herbage. Leaf-blades thin, round-cordate, 1½ to 5 inches broad, 3- to 5-lobed, the lobes ovate-deltoid, coarsely doubly dentate, glabrous or sparingly pilose and resinous-dotted beneath; petioles slender, often longer than the blades. Flowers whitish, 20 to 50 in erect racems 2½ to 4½ inches long; pedicels ⅛- to ¼-inch long, longer than the bracts; ovary resinous-dotted; calyx-tube saucer-shaped, glandular-dotted; caylx-lobes whitish, ⅛- to ¼-inch long, ascending; petals white, about ½ the length of the calyx-lobes. Berry subglobose, about ⅜-inch in diameter, black, without bloom. Flowering period, May to July.

Western Black Currant has been noted in California about 9 miles south of the California-Oregon boundary on Shovel Creek in Siskiyou County (T47NR3W Sec. 35, Mt. Diablo Mer., *Root* & *Day*). It extends northward into Oregon, Washington, and British Columbia and eastward to Utah, Wyoming, and Montana. This species is considered to be the most susceptible of all the species of *Ribes* to blister rust, which is such a menace in the white pine forests.

Ribes petiolare Dougl. Trans. Hort. Soc. Lond. 7:514 (1830). Type locality: Western base of the Rocky Mountains. Collected by *Douglas*.

FIG. 143 RIBES AUREUM

5. **Ribes aureum** Pursh. WESTERN GOLDEN CURRANT. Fig. 143.

A rather tall deciduous unarmed shrub, 3 to 8 feet high, with smooth glabrous erect or ascending branches and with gray or brown bark. Leaf-blades rather firm and leathery, ¾-inch to 2 inches wide, inconspicuously 3- or 5-veined from the obtuse base (heart-shaped on young shoots), 3- or 5-lobed, the lobes rounded, entire or variously toothed, light green and almost glabrous on both surfaces; petioles ½-inch to 1½ inches long, usually glabrous. Flowers yellow, few to many, in racemes 1 to 2½ inches long, with or without odor; pedicels about ⅛-inch long; bractlets foliaceous, mostly longer than the pedicels; calyx yellow, its tube cylindric, ¼- to ½-inch long, the 5 lobes oval and spreading or erect, about ½ or ⅓ the length of the tube; petals 5, yellow, oblong, about ⅛-inch long, with irregular margins; ovary glabrous. Berry globular, about ¼-inch in diameter, yellow, orange, red, or black. Flowering period, February to June.

Western Golden Currant inhabits moist places in the foothills of the South Coast Ranges from Alameda County southward to Los Angeles and western Riverside and San Bernardino counties, in the White, Panamint, and Nelson ranges of Inyo County, and occurs northward in eastern Lassen and Modoc counties and westward to Siskiyou County. It extends eastward to the Rocky Mountains and northward to British Columbia.

In the South Coast Ranges and in southern California the flowers lack the spicy odor of the plants east of the Sierra Nevada and in the Rocky Mountains. Their

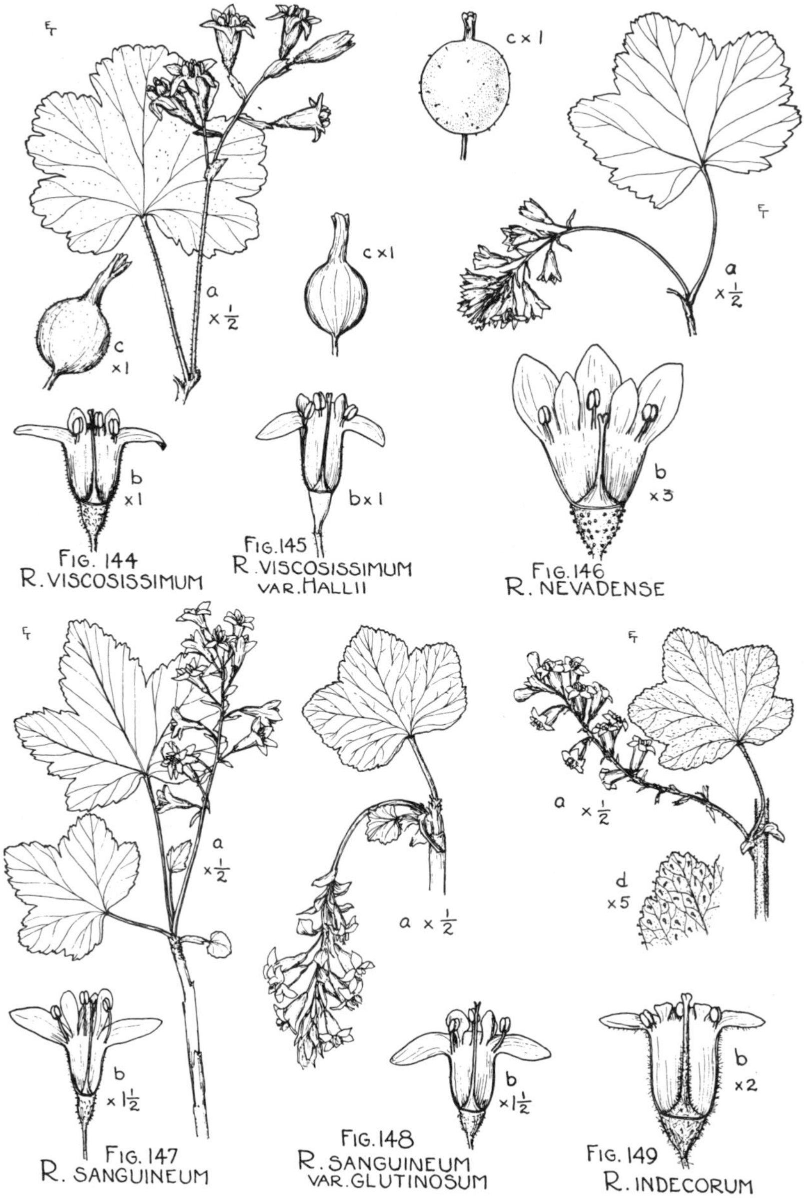

RIBES. a, Leaf and flower-cluster. b, Section of flower. c, Fruit. d, Stalked glands on leaf.

calyx-tubes are usually 2 or 3 times as long as their lobes while the calyx-tube of the flowers in northern and eastern California is usually only 1½ to 2 times as long as the lobes. Some authors segregate the coastal plants as the species *R. gracillimum* Cov. & Britt. Since considerable variation occurs in the relative lengths of calyx-tubes and calyx-lobes throughout the range of the species, it does not seem advisable upon the basis of this character to accept the species *R. gracillimum*. At best, it might be recognized as *R. aureum* var. *gracillimum* (Cov. & Britt.) Jepson.

Golden Currant, because of its clusters of bright yellow flowers, clean glossy foliage, clusters of red, orange, or black berries, and ease of propagation from cuttings and suckers, is very suitable for ornamental plantings whenever deciduous shrubs are not objectionable. The variation in fruit color is a most striking characteristic of this plant. Suckers taken from plants in the trial garden at Mills College have borne all black fruit during the early part of the season and all orange fruit during the later part of the season. The parent plant has produced ripe black, red, or orange fruits.

Ribes aureum Pursh, Fl. Am. Sept. 1:164 (1814). Type locality: Rocky Mountain region. Collected by *Lewis*. *R. aureum* var. *gracillimum* (Cov. & Britt.) Jepson.

6. **Ribes cereum** Dougl. Wax Currant. Squaw Currant. Fig. 142.

A low intricately branched shrub, 2 to 8 feet high (or rarely only 3 to 12 inches high), with smooth glabrous gray or brown bark on old branches and finely pubescent bark on young shoots, without spines or bristles. Leaves deciduous, rather heavily fragrant, clustered on short lateral branchlets, scattered on young shoots; the blades roundish, ½-inch to 1 inch broad (larger on young shoots), 3- to 5-veined from the base, obscurely 3- to 5-lobed, glossy green and with sessile glands above, finely puberulent and glandular beneath, the margins finely toothed; petioles ½- to ¾-inch long. Flowers white, cream-colored or pinkish, 2 to 8 in short drooping bracteate racemes; peduncles glandular-pubescent; bracts thin, pubescent, glandular, toothed; pedicels very short or almost obsolete; calyx white or cream-colored, rarely pinkish or greenish, the tube about ¼-inch long, cylindrical, the lobes about 1/16-inch long; petals white, nearly round, very minute, inserted near the top of the calyx-tube; stamens inserted about ¾ of the way up the calyx-tube, alternate with the petals; ovary smooth or slightly glandular; style pubescent. Berry bright red, about ½-inch in diameter, slightly glandular-hairy, becoming glabrous. Flowering period, June and July.

Wax Currant grows at the higher altitudes, 4800 to 12,300 feet, in the Sierra Nevada from Tulare County northward to Plumas County, on Mount Shasta, Siskiyou County, in the Warner Mountains, Modoc County, in the higher mountains of Mono and Inyo counties, on Mount Piños, Ventura County, and eastward and southward in the San Gabriel, San Bernardino, San Jacinto, and Santa Rosa mountains of southern California. It extends eastward to the Rocky Mountains and northward to Oregon, Washington, and British Columbia. Near timber-line this shrub assumes a very compact form usually not over 2 feet high. The tubular cream-colored flowers, fragrant glandular foliage, and leaves glossy above easily distinguish this currant from all others.

Ribes cereum Dougl. Trans. Hort. Soc. Lond. 7:512 (1830). Type locality: "Upper Columbia River." Collected by *Douglas*.

7. **Ribes viscosissimum** Pursh. Sticky Flowering Currant. Fig. 144.

Fig. 150. CHAPARRAL FLOWERING CURRANT. *Ribes malvaceum* Smith.

KEY TO THE SPECIES AND VARIETY

Ovary glandlar-hairy; calyx greenish or pinkish . . . . *R. viscosissimum.*
Ovary glabrous; calyx purplish . . . . 7a. var. *Hallii.*

An erect or spreading deciduous shrub, 1 to 4 feet high, with fragrant glandular foliage and without spines or bristles. Leaf-blades round in outline, heart-shaped at base, ¾-inch to 3 inches wide, 3- to 5-veined from the base, 3-lobed or sometimes 5-lobed, the lobes with rounded teeth, pubescent and glandular on both sides, paler beneath; petioles usually shorter than the blades, distinctly glandular and pubescent. Flowers greenish white or pinkish, including the ovary, about ⅝-inch long, 3 to 12 in a shortened cluster; pedicels ¼- to ½-inch long, glandular-pubescent; bracts thin, greenish, usually toothed at the apex, glandular-pubescent, shorter than or as long as the pedicels; ovary glandular-pubescent; calyx-tube greenish or pinkish, cylindric or bell-shaped, about ¼-inch long and about as wide; sepals greenish or pinkish, spreading or reflexed, ½ as long to as long as the tube, sparingly if at all glandular; petals erect, dull white, shorter than the sepals. Berry globular or ovoid, about ⅜- to ½-inch in diameter, black, more or less glandular-bristly. Flowering period, April to June.

Sticky Flowering Currant occurs in shady woods and in rocky places in the Sierra Nevada at 6000 to 9000 feet elevation from Tulare County north to Mariposa County. Northward it gives way to var. *Hallii* and some intermediate forms. It extends eastward to the Rocky Mountains and northward in eastern Modoc County to Washington and British Columbia.

7a. Var. **Hallii** Jancz. Fig. 145.

Flowers purplish; ovary glabrous. Fruit bluish white with a bloom.

This variety occurs in the Sierra Nevada from Mariposa County northward to Modoc County, thence westward to Mount Shasta, the Salmon Mountains, and to South Fork Mountain in Humboldt County. It extends northward to the Blue Mountains of Oregon and eastward to Nevada (Washoe County). Hall *(Yosemite Flora)* calls attention to a collection from Matterhorn Canyon (*Jepson,* #4498) which has flowers with glabrous and glandular-pubescent ovaries and purplish and pinkish calyces. I find that some specimens in Humboldt County have flowers with slightly glandular-pubescent ovaries instead of the glabrous ovaries normal for the variety *Hallii.* It would seem that this variety is founded upon rather unstable characters.

Ribes viscosissimum Pursh, Fl. Am. Sept. 1:163 (1814). Type locality: Bitter-root Mountains, Idaho. Collected by *Lewis.*

Var. Hallii Jancz. Mém. Soc. Genève 35:328, Fig. 62 (1907). Type locality: Lake Independence, Sierra County, California. Collected by *Hall* and *Babcock.*

8. **Ribes malvaceum** Smith. CHAPARRAL FLOWERING CURRANT. Fig. 150.

An erect deciduous shrub, 3 to 7 feet high, with 5 to 20 straight stout stems from the base. Young branches tomentose and glandular, the bark brown. Leaf-blades rather thick, rugose, more or less round in outline, ¾-inch to 3 inches wide, 3- to 5-veined from the heart-shaped base, 3- to 5-lobed, the lobes obtuse and doubly toothed, dull olive-green and rough above with numerous short-stalked glands, glandular and grayish pubescent beneath; petioles ½-inch to 2 inches long, glandular-pubescent. Flowers light pink or sometimes almost white, nearly ½-inch long, several in drooping racemes 2 to 4 inches long; pedicels about ⅛-inch long; bractlets lanceolate, glandular, longer than the pedicels; calyx pink or purplish, broadly cylindric, pubescent, the 5 lobes spreading, about 1/8-inch long, finely pubescent without; petals white, rounded, about 1/2 as long as the sepals; ovary densely white-hairy and with short glandular hairs; styles hairy. Berry globose or round-ovoid, about 1/4-inch in diameter, blue with a glaucous bloom, often somewhat hairy and glandular. Flowering period, December to April.

Chaparral Flowering Currant occurs on the open dry hill and lower mountain slopes of the inner North Coast Range from Tehama County south to Mount Diablo and in the outer Coast Range from Marin County southward to the foothills of southern and Lower California, in the Upper Sonoran Life Zone. Plants growing at Shingle Springs, Eldorado County apparently belong to this species.

The clusters of pink flowers usually begin to appear in December just before the new season's growth of leaves. The plants keep blooming rather profusely until March or April but in cultivation flowers may be found as late as June. This shrub is very hardy and grows well on dry slopes. It is easily propagated from seeds, cuttings, or by layering. It is often confused with its near relative *R. sanguineum* var. *glutinosum* from which it differs in having much thicker leaves with stalked rather than sessile glands on the upper surfaces.

Ribes malvaceum Sm.; Rees, Cycl. 30, no. 13 (1819). Type locality: California. Collected by *Menzies*. *R. malvaceum* var. *viridifolium* Abrams.

9. **Ribes indecorum** Eastw. WHITE FLOWERING CURRANT. Fig. 149.

An erect open deciduous shrub, 3 to 6 feet high, with dark brown shreddy bark on the older growth and with tomentose and glandular young growth. Leaf-blades round in outline, 3- to 5-lobed, 3/4-inch to 1 1/2 inches broad, thickish, stipitate-glandular, finely rugose and dark green above, whitish tomentose beneath, the lobes obtuse and crenate; petioles shorter than or equalling the blades. Flowers white, about 1/4-inch long, nearly sessile in compact glandular-pubescent racemes 1 to 2 inches long; bractlets somewhat foliaceous, glandular-pubescent; calyx white, cylindrical, about 1/4-inch or less long, pubescent, the 5 lobes spreading; petals white, orbicular, less than 1/16-inch wide; stamens as long as the petals; style villous near the base, 2-cleft at apex. Berry globose, about 1/4-inch long, viscid-pubescent and with some stalked glands. Flowering period, January to March.

White Flowering Currant occurs in the chaparral areas of the interior canyons of southern California from Santa Barbara County southward to San Diego County and to Lower California. It is very closely related to *R. malvaceum* and occasionally intermediate forms between the two species occur.

Ribes indecorum Eastw. Proc. Calif. Acad. ser. 3, 2:243 (1902). Type locality: Cajon Heights, near San Diego, California. Collected by *Eastwood*. *R. malvaceum* var. *indecorum* (Eastw.) Jancz.

10. **Ribes canthariforme** Wiggins. SAN DIEGO CURRANT. Fig. 151.

A much branched unarmed deciduous shrub, 3 to 6 feet high, with pubescent and capitate-glandular young branches. Leaf-blades suborbicular to reniform-orbicular in outline, 1 1/4 to 1 3/4 inches long, 1 1/2 to 2 1/2 inches wide, strongly heart-shaped at base, 3-lobed, the lobes rounded and crenate, 3- to 5-veined from the base, green and slightly villous above, rarely with a few stalked or nearly sessile glands, densely soft-pubescent beneath and with more numerous stalked glands, especially along the veins; petioles 1 to 1 1/2 inches long, villous-pubescent and with scattered stalked glands. Flowers rose-purple, nearly sessile, in drooping compact many-flowered racemes 1 to 2 1/2 inches long; peduncles villous and glandular-pubescent; ovary densely villous-pubescent with straight white hairs and some gland-tipped hairs; calyx-tube broadly urn-shaped, broader than high, villous- and glandular-pubescent; sepals broadly spatulate, rotately spreading, pink-purple or whitish with purple veins; petals purplish, less than ½ the length of the sepals; stamens directed inward from the rim of the calyx-tube at nearly a right angle to the style, the yellow anthers as broad as long; style short and stout, divided to the base, sparsely villous toward the base; berry globose to ovoid, about ¼-inch in diameter, purple to black, sparsely white-villous and with few stalked glands. Flowering period, March to May.

San Diego Currant is known from the vicinity of the Moreno Dam, San Diego County, California (*McMinn* 4021, 4023; *Wiggins* 2399). It is related to *R. malvaceum* and *R. indecorum* but differs from both in the broad urn-shaped calyx-tube, more compact racemes of subsessile flowers, non-rugose upper leaf surfaces, and style divided to the base.

Ribes canthariforme Wiggins, Contr. Dudley Herb. 1:101 (1929). Type locality: Slope below Moreno Dam, San Diego County. Collected by *Wiggins.*

11. **Ribes nevadense** Kell. MOUNTAIN PINK CURRANT. Fig. 146.

A slender spreading or erect deciduous shrub, 3 to 6 feet high, without spines or prickles. Leaf-blades thin, round in outline or broader than long, 1 to 3 inches wide, 3- to 5-veined from the heart-shaped base, 3- to 5-lobed, the lobes obtuse and bluntly toothed, finely pubescent or glabrous above and below; petioles ½-inch to 1¼ inches long, finely pubescent and somewhat glandular. Flowers pink, about ¼- (rarely ⅜-) inch long, including the ovary, 8 to 20 in erect spreading or drooping racemes 2 to 4 inches long; pedicels slender, about ⅛- to ¼-inch long; bracts thin, pink or greenish, about as long as the pedicels; ovary with stalked or nearly sessile glands; calyx-tube pink or rose-colored, bowl-shaped, about 1/12-inch long; sepals pink or reddish, erect, about 2 times as long as the tube; petals white, shorter than the sepals; styles glabrous. Berry globular, about 5/16-inch in diameter, blue-black, covered with a bloom, somewhat glandular. Flowering period, April to July.

Mountain Pink Currant occurs in moist places and along streams in the Sierra Nevada from Modoc and Shasta counties southward to Tulare County, in the North Coast Ranges of Humboldt (Trinity Summit), Trinity, and Siskiyou counties, on Mount Piños, Ventura County, and in the San Gabriel, San Antonio, San Jacinto, San Bernardino, and Palomar mountains of southern California. It occurs mainly between 4000 and 8000 feet elevation. Its numerous clusters of pink flowers make this shrub very attractive. It does not thrive when transplanted into the lower altitudes.

Ribes nevadense Kell. Proc. Calif. Acad. 1:63 (1855). Type locality: Above Placerville, California. Collected by *E. W. Garvett.*

12. **Ribes sanguineum** Pursh. PINK WINTER CURRANT. BLOOD CURRANT. Fig. 147.

KEY TO THE SPECIES AND VARIETY

Leaves densely tomentose or finely pubescent beneath; racemes erect or ascending; flowers deep pink to nearly red. . . . . *R. sanguineum.*

Leaves nearly glabrous beneath; racemes spreading or nodding; flowers pink. 12a. var. *glutinosum.*

An erect or spreading deciduous shrub, 4 to 12 feet high, with brownish shreddy bark and glandular herbage, without spines or prickles. Leaf-blades thin to moder-

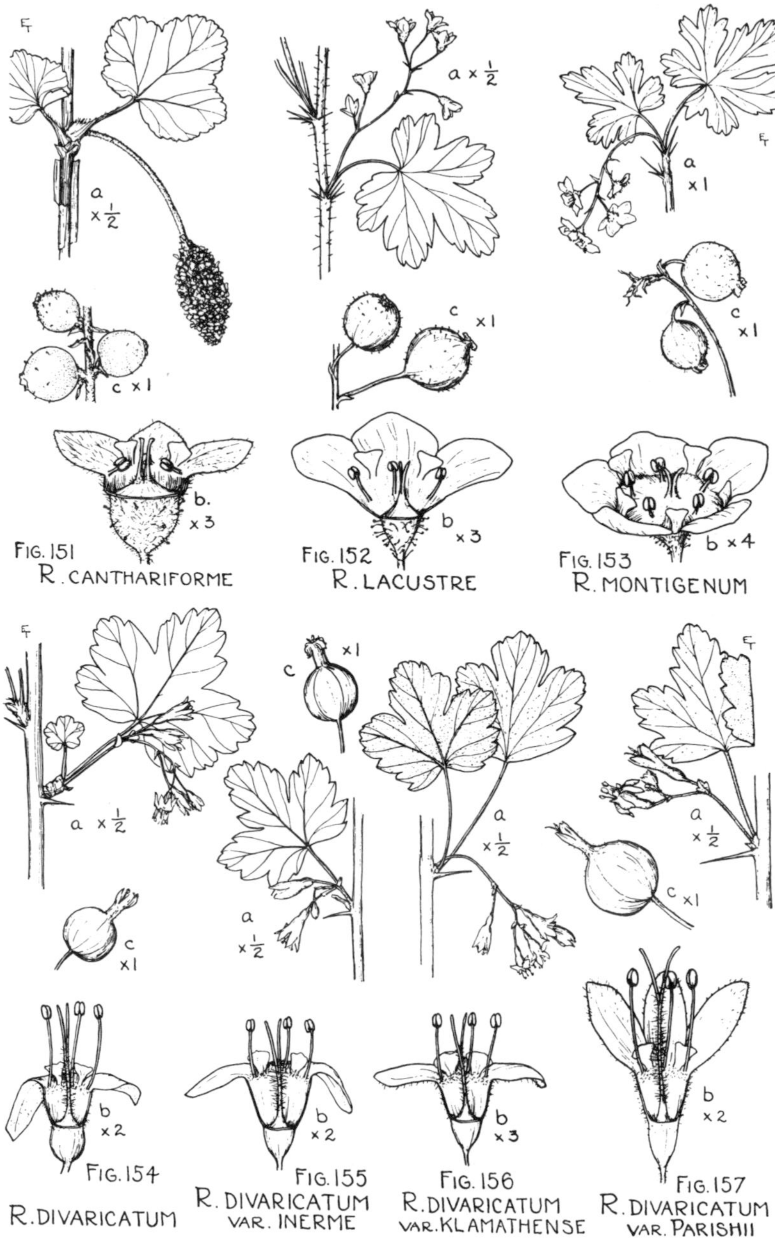

RIBES. a, Leaves and flower-cluster. b, Flower. c, Fruit.

ately thick, not rugose, round in outline or broader than long, heart-shaped at base, 1 to 2½ inches broad (sometimes as much as 6 inches broad in the shade), 3- to 5-veined from the base, 3- to 5-lobed, the lobes obtuse, irregularly toothed, green and slightly pubescent above or glabrous in age, finely pubescent or densely tomentose beneath, with sessile glands on both surfaces or with a few stalked glands beneath; petioles ¾-inch to 1½ inches long, glandular-pubescent and with a few longer hairs at base. Flowers deep pink to red, 10 to 15 (or to 30) in erect or ascending racemes 2 to 4 inches long including the peduncle; pedicels ⅛- to ⅜-inch long, glandular-pubescent; bracts crimson, usually longer than or only as long as the pedicels; ovary usually glabrous except for the stalked glands; calyx-tube funnelform, ⅛- to 3⁄16-inch long, commonly pubescent and with scattered short-stalked glands without, glabrous within; sepals elliptic, spreading, as long as or longer than the tube; petals white or pink, often changing to red, shorter than the sepals, longer than the stamens; styles glabrous. Berry globular or short-ellipsoidal, ¼- to ⅜-inch long, blue-black, covered with a whitish bloom. Flowering period, March to June.

Pink Winter Currant occurs on semi-moist mountain slopes and in canyons of the Coast Ranges from Del Norte and Siskiyou counties southward to Lake, Marin, and Santa Clara counties (probably in San Luis Obispo County). In the southern part of its range, it is often with difficulty distinguished from the variety *glutinosum*. It extends northward to British Columbia.

12a. Var. **glutinosum** (Benth.) Loud. PINK FLOWERING CURRANT. Fig. 148.

Leaves less pubescent or tomentose beneath, more glutinous, the terminal lobe usually broader than long. Flowers deep or pale pink or becoming reddish in age, 15 to 40 in nodding or spreading racemes; calyx-tube cylindric; calyx-lobes spreading or recurved, becoming erect in age. Berries blue-black or black, usually with a whitish bloom. Flowering period, January to March.

Pink Flowering Currant is the common currant on moist canyon slopes along the coast from San Luis Obispo County northward to the Smith River, Del Norte County. When crushed, its glutinous foliage emits an odor similar to that of black walnut leaves.

In dense shade and very moise places the plants sometimes attain a height of 15 feet. The leaves of such plants are thinner, and the flowers paler in color and fewer. By some authors these plants are classified as *R. deductum* Greene or *R. sanguinum* var. *deductum* (Greene) Jepson.

The numerous clusters of pink flowers appearing in late winter or early spring and the ease of its propagation from cuttings have made this currant one of the most widely used of the native shrubs.

Ribes sanguineum Pursh, Fl. Am. Sept. 1:164 (1814). Type locality: Columbia River. Collected by *Lewis*.

Var. glutinosum (Benth.) Loud. Arb. 988 (1838). *R. glutinosum* Benth. Type locality: California. Collected by *Douglas*. *R. sanguineum* var. *deductum* (Greene) Jepson. *R. sanguineum* var. *melanocarpum* (Greene) Jepson.

13. **Ribes lacustre** (Pers.) Poir. SWAMP GOOSEBERRY. Fig. 152.

A rather low spreading or prostrate deciduous shrub, 3 to 4 feet high, with 5 to 9 nodal spines and internodal prickles or the latter sometimes absent. Leaf-blades thin, nearly round in outline, heart-shaped at base, 1 to 2 inches broad, 3- to 5-veined from the base, deeply 3- or 5-lobed, the lobes deeply toothed, the sinuses open, dark green and glabrous above, paler and glabrous beneath or rarely pubescent; petioles slender, hairy and glandular, about as long as the blades. Flowers greenish white or purplish, about 1/4-inch long, 5 to 15 in axillary racemes 1 to 2 inches long; pedicels about 1/4-inch long; bracts thin, less than 1/2 the length of the pedicels; ovary with stalked glands; calyx-tube inconspicuous, bowl- or saucer-shaped, the lobes spreading, reddish tinged; petals smaller than the sepals. Berry globular, 1/4-inch in diameter, deep purple or black, with gland-tipped bristles. Flowering period, June and July.

Swamp Gooseberry occurs in wet woods and meadows in the mountains of Humboldt and Siskiyou counties (Trinity Summit, Marble and Salmon mountains) in the upper Transition Life Zone. It is a transcontinental species ranging from California northward to Alaska, eastward to Newfoundland, and southward to Michigan, Pennsylvania, Utah, and Colorado.

Ribes lacustre (Pers.) Poir.; Lam. Encyc. Suppl. 2:856 (1811). *R. oxyacanthoides* var. *lacustre* Pers. Type locality: Lake Mistassini, Canada. Collected by *Michaux*.

14. **Ribes montigenum** McCl. MOUNTAIN GOOSEBERRY. GOOSEBERRY CURRANT. Fig. 153.

A low straggling flexous much branched deciduous shrub, 1 to 2 1/2 feet high, the stems with 1 to 3 spines at the nodes and with bristly or sometimes almost naked internodes. Leaf-blades glandular-sticky, rounded in outline, heart-shaped at base, 1/2-inch to 1 inch wide, 5-lobed or -cleft, the lobes much incised and toothed, more or less densely hairy and glandular on both surfaces; petioles glandular-hairy, mostly shorter than the blades. Flowers reddish brown to greenish white, 3 to 7 in a short raceme; pedicels about 1/8-inch long; bracts nearly as long as the pedicels; ovary glandular-hairy and bristly; calyx saucer-shaped, about 1/4-inch broad, the lobes broad and veiny, greenish, becoming reddish in age; petals 5, reddish, about 1/3 to 1/2 the length of the calyx-lobes. Berry globular, up to 1/4-inch in diameter, red, usually glandular-bristly. Flowering period, July and August.

Mountain Gooseberry occurs in the higher altitudes of the Sierra Nevada from Tehama County southward to Tulare County (north in Siskiyou County?), at Pine Creek, Inyo County, Mount Piños, Ventura County, and in the San Jacinto, San Gabriel, and San Bernardino mountains of southern California. It inhabits the drier exposed slopes in the Canadian Life Zone from 7400 feet to 12,500 feet elevation. It ranges northward into British Columbia and eastward to Nevada, Utah, Colorado, Wyoming, Montana, Idaho, Arizona, and New Mexico.

The small very glandular-sticky leaves, saucer-shaped flowers, and low bushy form make this plant easily identified.

A specimen examined from Mount Stanford, Nevada County appears to be somewhat intermediate between *R. montigenum* and *R. lacustre*. It probably represents *R. lacustre* var. *molle* Gray.

Ribes montigenum McCl. Erythea 5:38 (1897). *R. nubigenum* McCl., not Phil. Type locality: Mount San Antonio. Collected by *McClatchie*.

15. **Ribes speciosum** Pursh. FUCHSIA FLOWERING GOOSEBERRY. Fig. 176 (p. 166).

A tall nearly evergreen shrub, 3 to 10 feet high, the stems with 3 very stout sharp spines at the nodes, the spines 3/8- to 3/4-inch long, often more or less densely bristly on the internodes. Leaf-blades rather thick and leathery, round, oblong, or obovate in outline, tapering or rounded at the base, about 3/4-inch to 1 1/2 inches long, inconspicuously 3- or 5-veined from the base, slightly 3- to 5-lobed or toothed at the apex, entire along the lower half, glabrous or sparingly glandular-hairy above, lighter beneath; petioles 1/4-inch to 1 inch long. Flowers deep crimson, 1 or 2 on drooping peduncles from the short lateral branchlets; pedicels slender, glandular-bristly, 1/4- to 3/4-inch long; bracts ovate-round, shorter than the pedicels; ovary densely glandular-bristly; calyx-tube deep red, glandular-bristly, less than 1/8-inch long, forming a swollen ring; sepals 4 (rarely 5), erect, 1/4- to 1/2-inch long, bright red; petals 4 (rarely 5), narrow, involute, about as long as the sepals; filaments much exserted, 2 to 4 times as long as the sepals. Berry ovoid, about 3/8- to 1/2-inch long, densely glandular-bristly, becoming dry. Flowering period, January to May, or in cultivation as early as November.

Fuchsia Flowering Gooseberry inhabits moist and semi-moist slopes along the coast from Santa Clara and Monterey counties southward to San Diego County, in the Upper Sonoran Life Zone. It is one of the most desirable native shrubs for cultivation. The numerous long drooping crimson flowers with exserted stamens resemble somewhat those of the *Fuchsia,* hence its common name. It is easily propagated from cuttings and stem-sections taken from near the base.

Ribes speciosum Pursh, Fl. Am. Sept. 731 (1814). Type locality: Probably near Monterey, California, although given as "Northwest coast." Collected by *Menzies.*

16. **Ribes divaricatum** Dougl. STRAGGLY GOOSEBERRY. Fig. 154.

KEY TO THE SPECIES AND VARIETIES

Calyx-tube and -lobes greenish or purple-tinged within; flowers not over 3/8-inch long.
  Stamens longer than the calyx-lobes, 3 to 4 times the length of the petals; calyx pilose, the lobes 2 to 2 1/2 times the length of the tube....... *R. divaricatum.*
  Stamens shorter than or just equalling the calyx-lobes, about 2 times the length of the petals; calyx-lobes as long as or slightly longer than the tube.
    Leaves glabrous on both surfaces or sparingly pubescent beneath; calyx glabrous.. 16a. var. *inerme.*
    Leaves villous; calyx thinly hairy or glabrous........ 16b. var. *klamathense.*
Calyx-tube and -lobes purplish red, pubescent, about 3/8-inch long; petals red; branchlets covered with a dense felt..................... 16c. var. *Parishii.*

A much branched deciduous shrub, 3 to 8 feet high, with long straggling and drooping branches. The main stems and branches with gray bark and with 1 to 3 spines at the nodes or the spines absent on parts of the branches. The young branches with brown bark and with 1 to 3 spines at the nodes, rarely with bristles on the internodes. Leaf-blades thin, roundish in outline, rounded or somewhat heart-shaped at base, 3/4-inch to 2 inches broad, 3- to 5-veined from the base, 3- to 5-lobed, the lobes coarsely toothed, finely pubescent or almost glabrous above, paler and often pubescent beneath; petioles 3/8-inch to 1 1/4 inches long, finely pubescent. Flowers greenish purple, 2 to 6 in drooping racemes; pedicels slender, 1/4- to 1/2-inch long; bracts at the base of the pedicels small and roundish; calyx greenish or purplish, the tube bowl-shaped and about 1/8-inch or less long, sparingly pubescent or glabrous, the lobes broadly oblong, greenish or rarely purplish, about 1/4-inch long, reflexed; petals white, plane, less than 1/2 as long as the sepals; ovary glabrous; style villous. Berry globular, 1/4- to 3/8-inch in diameter, smooth, black or dark purple. Flowering period, March to May.

Straggly Gooseberry inhabits shady canyons and moist flats from Shasta and Lassen counties westward to Trinity and Humboldt counties and southward in the Coast Ranges to Santa Barbara County, in the Transition Life Zone. It extends northward to Oregon, Washington, and British Columbia and eastward to Nevada and Colorado. The branches often bend over and root at the nodes in contact with moist ground. Some specimens growing in San Luis Obispo, Santa Barbara, and Ventura counties seem intermediate between the species and the variety *Parishii* of the San Bernardino Valley foothills.

16a. Var. **inerme** (Rydb.) n. comb. Fig. 155.

A spreading deciduous shrub, 2 to 5 feet high, with glabrous often simple stems, the branches mostly with 1 to 3 short nodal spines, usually without internodal prickles or bristles. Leaves round in outline, 3/4-inch to 1 1/2 inches broad, 3- or 5-lobed, the lobes sharply toothed, glabrous on both surfaces or with some scattered pubescence beneath; petioles about as long as the blades, often with a few bristles near the base. Flowers greenish or purplish, about 1/4-inch long, 1 to 4 on a nodding peduncle; pedicels 1/4-inch or less long; bracts small, much shorter than the pedicels; ovary glabrous; calyx glabrous, the tube about as long as the lobes; stamens about 2 times the length of the petals. Berry globular, a little over 1/4-inch in diameter, dark purple, glabrous, smooth. Flowering period, April to July.

This gooseberry inhabits wet places in the Sierra Nevada from Tulare and Inyo counties northward to Lassen and Modoc counties, westward in Siskiyou and Shasta counties, at 3500 to 10,000 feet elevation, and southward to Potter Valley in Mendocino County, in the Transition and Canadian Life Zones. It extends northward to Oregon, Washington, and British Columbia, and eastward to the Rocky Mountains. "The berries make an agreeable sharp sauce and are prized by the mountaineers." Jepson.

16b. Var. **klamathense** (Cov.) n. comb. KLAMATH GOOSEBERRY. Fig. 156.

This shrub is similar to the variety *inerme* but differs in having much more villous leaves and usually hairy calyces. The peduncles often bear 5 to 8 flowers. It occurs in shaded canyons in Humboldt, Siskiyou, and Shasta counties, California and extends northward into southern Oregon.

16c. Var. **Parishii** (Heller) Jepson. PARISH GOOSEBERRY. Fig. 157.

This variety differs from the species in having leaves more densely pubescent beneath, larger and more purplish flowers, and hairy pedicels, bracts, and calyces. The branches usually have a greater number of stouter nodal spines, which are often 1/2-inch or more in length. The stamens are as long as the sepals.

Parish Gooseberry is known from a few localities in the San Bernardino Valley. It inhabits moist ground and is usually associated with willows. Occasionally in moist canyons or flats in the foothills of San Luis Obispo, Santa Barbara, and Ventura counties plants are found which seem closer to the variety *Parishii* than to the species *R. divaricatum*.

Ribes divaricatum Dougl. Trans. Hort. Soc. Lond. 7:515 (1830). Type locality: "Northwest Coast of America." Collected by *Douglas*.

Var. inerme (Rydb.) McMinn. *R. inerme* Rydb. Type locality: "Slough Creek, Yellowstone Park." Collected by *Tweedy*.

Var. klamathense (Cov.) McMinn. *Grossularia klamathense* Cov. Type locality: Keno, Klamath County, Oregon. Collected by *Applegate*. *Ribes inerme* var. *klamathense* (Cov.) Jepson.

Var. Parishii (Heller) Jepson, Fl. Calif. 2:151 (1936). *R. Parishii* Heller. Type locality: "Warm Creek, San Bernardino Valley." Collected by *S. B.* and *W. F. Parish.*

17. **Ribes velutinum** Greene. PLATEAU GOOSEBERRY. Fig. 158.

KEY TO THE SPECIES AND VARIETY

Ovary and berry pubescent, rarely glandular, not bristly; leaves pubescent. *R. velutinum.*

Ovary and berry densely glandular-hairy and bristly; leaves glandular-hairy. 17a. var. *glanduliferum.*

A stout rigidly branched shrub, 2 to 6 feet high or sometimes lower and nearly creeping, with soft-pubescent but glandless herbage, usually with a single stout spine at each node, without internodal prickles. Leaf-blades round in outline, ⅜- to ¾-inch broad, deeply 5-cleft, the lobes often 3-cleft, densely soft-pubescent; the petioles shorter than the blades. Flowers yellowish or whitish or rarely pinkish, 1 to 4 on short deflexed peduncles; ovary soft-pubescent, either glandular or without glands; calyx-tube as broad as long, slightly shorter than the 5 lobes; style glabrous. Berry dark purple, velvety-pubescent but usually not glandular. Flowering period, May and June.

Plateau Gooseberry occurs on the dry interior mountain slopes of Trinity, Siskiyou, Lassen, and Modoc counties and southward on the eastern slopes of the Sierra Nevada to the mountains of Inyo and Kern counties. It extends eastward to Nevada, Arizona, and Utah.

17a. Var. **glanduliferum** (Heller) Jepson. Fig. 159.

Herbage glandular-puberulent. Ovary and fruit densely glandular-hairy and bristly.

This variety is known in California from the dry interior mountain area of Siskiyou County (Yreka, *Heller*), from the White Mountains *(Jepson)* and Argus Peak *(Purpus)* in Inyo County, Mount Piños, Ventura County *(Hall),* and from Mount San Antonio, Los Angeles County *(Pierson).* It probably occurs also on the eastern slopes of the Sierra Nevada and more generally in the mountains of Inyo County.

Ribes velutinum Greene, Bull. Calif. Acad. 1:83 (1885). Type locality: "Open grounds in the northern part of California and the region adjacent." *R. leptanthum* var. *brachyanthum* Gray.

Var. glanduliferum (Heller) Jepson, Man. 472 (1925). *R. glanduliferum* Heller. Type locality: Yreka, Siskiyou County. Collected by *Heller.*

18. **Ribes leptanthum** var. **lasianthum** (Greene) Jepson. ALPINE GOOSEBERRY. Fig. 161.

A stout intricately and rigidly branched shrub, 1 to 4 feet high, with white shreddy bark and with 1 to 3 straight spines at the nodes, rarely with internodal prickles. Leaves deciduous, apparently clustered at the ends of the short lateral branchlets; the blades round in outline, ⅜- to ¾-inch broad, 3- to 5-veined from the base, cleft into 3 to 5 blunt and toothed lobes, slightly glandular-puberulent above, minutely soft-pubescent to almost glabrous beneath; petioles ⅛- to ¼-inch long, glandular-puberulent, broadest near the base. Flowers lemon-yellow, 1 or 2 (sometimes 3 or 4) in short clusters near the ends of short lateral leafy branchlets;

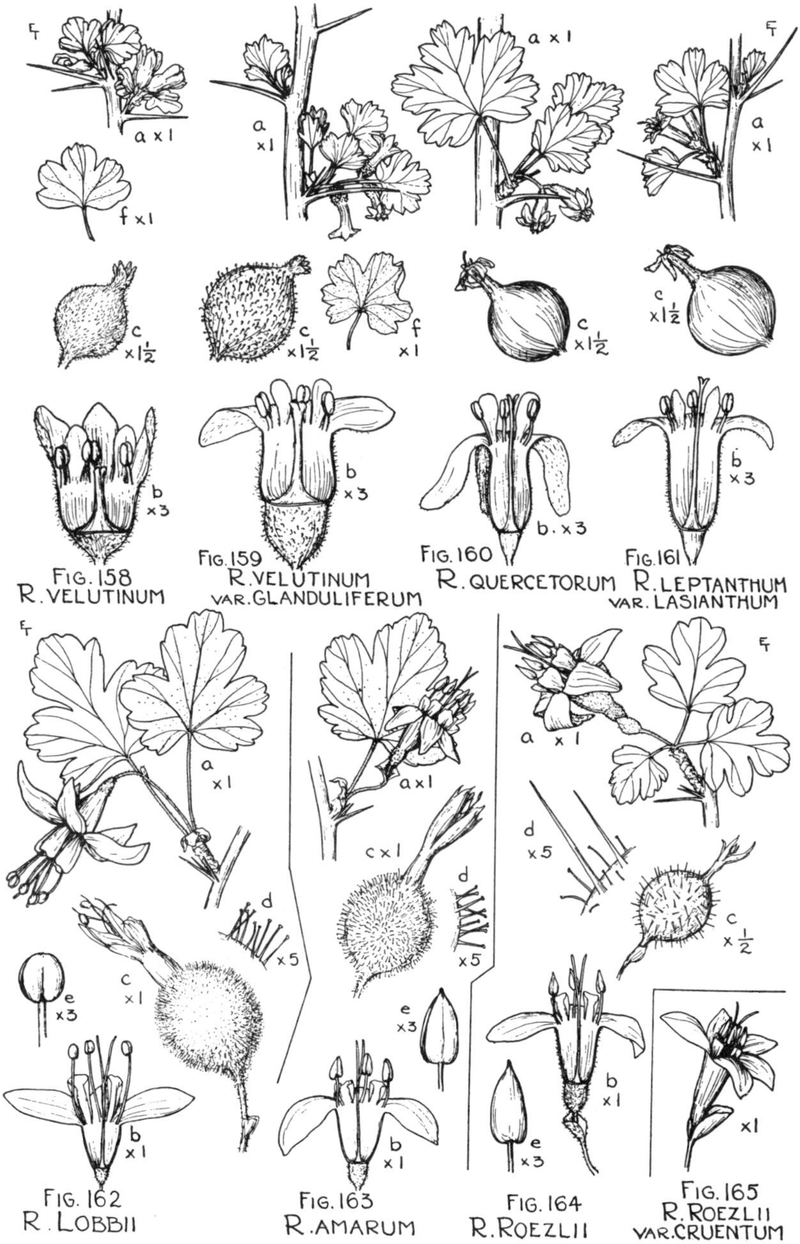

RIBES. a, Portion of branchlet with thorns, leaves, and flowers. b, Section of flower. c, Fruit. d, Bristles on fruit. e, Anther. f, Leaf.

ovary glabrous; calyx yellow, the tube cylindrical, almost 1/4-inch long, hairy-pubescent, the 5 lobes at first reflexed, later erect, shorter than the tube; petals yellow or nearly white, spatulate, shorter than the calyx-lobes, as long as the stamens; style glabrous, not divided. Berry globular, about 1/4-inch in diameter, glabrous, dark red. Flowering period, June to August.

Alpine Gooseberry occurs from 7000 to 10,000 feet elevation in the Sierra Nevada from Nevada County southward to Tulare County, in the Canadian and Hudsonian Life Zones. The plants are often gregarious, forming dense patches in rocky places.

Ribes leptanthum var. lasianthum (Greene) Jepson, Man. 472 (1925). *R. lasianthum* Greene. Type locality: Castle Peak, Nevada County, California. Collected by *Greene*.

19. **Ribes quercetorum** Greene. Rock Gooseberry. Fig. 160.

A low or medium-sized deciduous shub, 2 to 4 feet high, with spreading and often recurved branches and usually a single straight or slightly curved spine at the nodes, 3/8-inch or less long, without prickles or bristles on the internodes. Leaf-blades rather thin, almost round in outline, heart-shaped or truncate at the base, 3/8- to 3/4-inch wide, 3- to 5-veined from the base, deeply 3- to 5-cleft and -toothed, finely puberulent on both surfaces, sometimes minutely glandular; petioles as long as or shorter than the blades, puberulent. Flowers yellowish or whitish, 2 or 3 on short pubescent peduncles; pedicels about 1/16-inch long; bracts shorter than or as long as the pedicels; ovary glabrous; calyx-tube yellowish, short-cylindric, 1/8-inch or less long, slightly pubescent; calyx-lobes yellowish, about as long as the calyx-tube, slightly spreading; petals plane, yellow, shorter than the sepals, slightly longer than the stamens; style glabrous, not divided. Berry globular, about 1/4-inch in diameter, smooth, black. Flowering period, May and June.

Rock Gooseberry inhabits rocky slopes and oak-covered foothills of the Sierra Nevada from Tuolumne County southward to Kern County and in the inner and middle South Coast Ranges of Alameda, Santa Clara, Monterey, and San Luis Obispo counties, southward and eastward in the Tehachapi and Liebre mountains, and in the mountains bordering the western side of the Colorado Desert of Riverside and San Diego counties, in the Upper Sonoran Life Zone.

Ribes quercetorum Greene, Bull. Calif. Acad. 1:83 (1885). Type locality: Paso Robles, California. Collected by *Greene*.

20. **Ribes Lobbii** Gray. Gummy Gooseberry. Fig. 162.

A deciduous shrub, 2 to 6 feet high, with 3 spines at the nodes (rarely absent at some nodes), without internodal prickles or bristles. Leaf-blades thin but firm, round in outline, 3/4-inch to 2 inches broad, 3- or 5-lobed, crenately toothed, glabrous above, glandular-pubescent beneath, especially when young; petioles about as long as the blades, glandular-pubescent. Flowers 1 to 3 on glandular peduncles shorter than the leaves; bracts thin, round to ovate, shorter than the glandular pedicels; ovary glandular; calyx-tube longer than broad, the lobes crimson, not more than 2 times the length of the tube; petals pale yellow, involute, about 1/2 as long as the stamens; anthers broadly oval, nearly as broad as long, purple, obtuse at apex. Berries short-ellipsoidal, 1/2- to 5/8-inch long, densely covered with short gland-tipped bristles. Flowering period, April to June.

Gummy Gooseberry occurs in the high mountains of northern Lake (Snow Mt.), western Tehama, eastern Humboldt, Trinity, Shasta, and Siskiyou counties of northern California. Outside the state, it occurs in Oregon, Washington, and British Columbia.

The berries resemble those of *R. Menziesii.* That species, however, has internodal prickles and sagittate anthers.

Ribes Lobbii Gray, Am. Nat. 10:274 (1876). Type locality: Vancouver Island. Collected by *Wood.*

21. **Ribes amarum** McCl. Bitter Gooseberry. Fig. 163.

An erect deciduous shrub, 3 to 6 feet high, with nodal spines but without internodal prickles or bristles. Leaf-blades almost round in outline, heart-shaped at base, ¾-inch to 1½ inches broad, 3- to 5-lobed, the lobes crenately toothed, more or less glandular-puberulent on both surfaces; petioles shorter than or as long as the blades, glandular-pubescent. Flowers purplish, almost ¾-inch long, 1 to 3 on glandular-pubescent peduncles; pedicels glandular, ⅛- to ¼-inch long; bracts broadly ovate, often lobed, shorter than or equalling the pedicels; ovary densely glandular-bristly; calyx-tube purplish, about 2 times as long as broad; sepals broad, purplish red, reflexed, much shorter than the tube; petals pinkish white, involute, nearly as long as the filaments; anthers sagittate, over 1/16-inch long, apiculate at apex. Berry almost globular, about ½-inch in diameter, densely covered with short equal gland-tipped bristles. Flowering period, February to April.

Bitter Gooseberry inhabits shady canyon slopes in the chaparral belt of the mountains of southern California and it extends northward in the Coast Ranges to Monterey County *(Bacigalupi)* and in the Sierra Nevada to Eldorado County (northeast of Georgetown, *D. R. Miller* & *H. D. Jones*), in the Upper Sonoran Life Zone. Apparently it is rare in San Diego County.

It is similar to *R. Menziesii* in many characteristics but lacks the internodal prickles of that species.

Ribes amarum McCl. Erythea 2:79 (1894). Type locality: San Gabriel Mountains of Los Angeles County. Collected by *McClatchie.*

22. **Ribes Roezlii** Regel. Sierra Gooseberry. Fig. 164.

KEY TO THE SPECIES AND VARIETY

Ovary, calyx-tube, and usually the leaves pubescent . . . . *R. Roezlii.*
Ovary, calyx-tube, and leaves glabrous . . . . 22a. var. *cruentum.*

A stout shrub, 1 to 4 feet high, with many long spreading branches, short rigid branchlets, and 1 to 3 straight spines at the nodes, without internodal prickles. Leaves deciduous, clustered on the ends of the short lateral branchlets; the blades round in outline, ½-inch to 1 inch broad, 3- to 5-veined from the base, cleft into 3- to 5-toothed lobes, dark green and finely puberulent above, paler and finely pubescent beneath; petioles ¼- to ¾-inch long, finely pubescent. Flowers dull red, 1 or 2 on a peduncle near the ends of the short lateral leafy branchlets; peduncles ¼- to ½-inch long, finely pubescent; bractlets 1 or 2, thin, clasping; pedicels ¼- to ½-inch long, pubescent and glandular-hairy near the base of the ovary; calyx purplish or dull red, the tube about ¼-inch long, pubescent, often grayish, the 5 lobes lanceolate, ¼- to ⅜-inch long, finely pubescent without; petals 5, whitish, involute, about ½ as long as the calyx-lobes; stamens 5, the filaments about the length of the petals, the anthers apiculate at the apex; ovary usually densely white-hairy and somewhat bristly. Berry purple or sometimes pinkish or yellowish, ½-inch in diameter, beset with stout spines and usually with some short gland-tipped bristles. Flowering period, June and July.

Sierra Gooseberry is the common gooseberry found at middle altitudes in the canyons and on mountain slopes from 3500 to 8500 feet elevation in the Sierra Nevada from Tulare County to Modoc County, thence west to Humboldt County, and also in the mountains of southern California from the Tehachapi region through the Topatopa, San Gabriel, San Bernardino, San Jacinto, and Santa Ana mountains to the Cuyamaca, Laguna, and Palomar mountains of San Diego County. According to Bacigalupi (personal communication), this species occurs in the Santa Lucia Mountains of Monterey County.

22a. Var. **cruentum** (Greene) Rehd. Fig. 165.

This variety is apparently only a more glabrous form of *R. Roezlii.* The calyx, ovary, and leaves are distinctly glabrous.

This variety occurs in the North Coast Ranges from Napa (Upper Mill Creek Canyon, alt. 1700 feet, *H. B. Kaufner*) and Sonoma counties northward to Humboldt, Trinity, Siskiyou, and Del Norte counties and eastward to Modoc County, in the upper Transition Life Zone. It extends northward into southern Oregon.

Ribes Roezlii Regel, Gartenflora 28:226 (1879). Type locality: Probably the Sierra Nevada. Grown from seed collected by *Benito Roezl. R. Roezlii* var. *amictum* (Greene) Jepson.

Var. cruentum (Greene) Rehd.; Bailey Cyclop. Hort. 5:2962 (1916). *R. cruentum* Greene. Type locality: Probably from the mountains of Sonoma County.

23. **Ribes Marshallii** Greene. Hupa Gooseberry. Fig. 166.

A low spreading deciduous shrub, often forming colonies 3 to 7 feet across. Stems and branches with nodal spines but without internodal bristles. Leaf-blades thin, round in outline, heart-shaped at base, ¾-inch to 1¼ inches broad, 3- or 5-lobed, the lobes with rounded teeth, glabrous except for a few glandular hairs below on the veins; petioles about as long as the blades, glabrous or with a few glandular hairs. Flowers purplish, ½-inch to 1 inch long, borne singly on a pedicel ¼- to ½-inch long; bract at junction of pedicel and peduncle shorter than the pedicel; calyx-tube as broad as long, the lobes ½-inch or more long, crimson; ovary not glandular; stamens 2 or 3 times the length of the yellow petals; anthers oblong, obtuse at apex, yellow. Berry large, ovoid or pear-shaped, ½-inch or more long with long glandless spines, black when mature. Flowering period, June and July.

Hupa Gooseberry occurs at Trinity Summit, Humboldt County, and on ridges and meadows near Marble Mountain, Siskiyou County. It is to be expected that a wider range will be encountered for this species when that region is more thoroughly collected.

"Abundant scrub bush about 2 feet tall, forming thickets on exposed slopes 5,000 to 6,300 feet. Berries not glandular, of fine acid flavor, delicious, ovate, often somewhat pyriform, less often globose; turning red and finally dark blackish red when fully ripe. One of the important fruit crops in its region." *Joseph P. Tracy* 5229. Note in pocket on herbarium sheet no. 205482 U. C.

Ribes Marshallii Greene, West Am. Sci. 3:24 (Jan. 1887). Type locality: Trinity Summit, Humboldt County. Collected by *C. C. Marshall.*

24. **Ribes californicum** H. & A. Hillside Gooseberry. Fig. 167.

KEY TO THE SPECIES AND VARIETY

Filaments 2 to 3 times the length of the petals. . . . . *R. californicum.*
Filaments only slightly longer than the petals. . . . . 24a. var. *hesperium.*

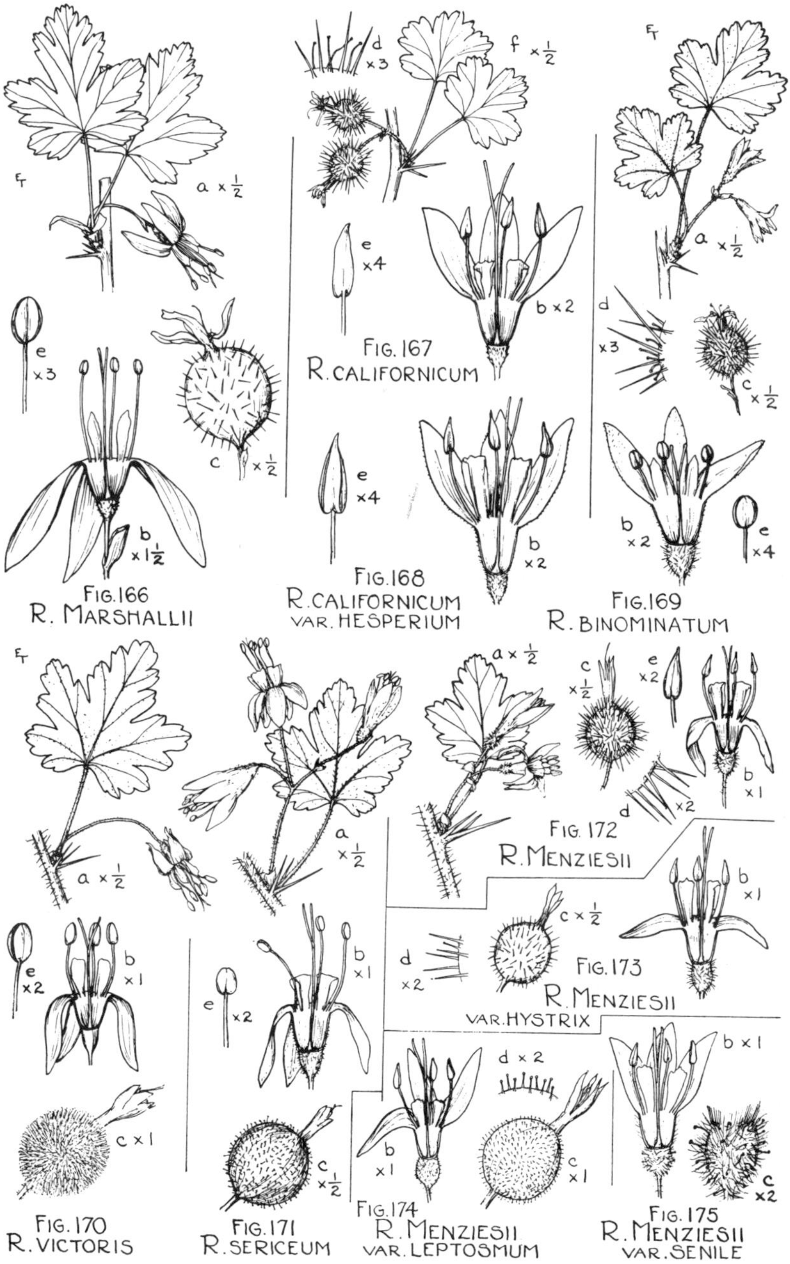

RIBES. a, Portion of branchlet with leaves, thorns, and flowers. b, Section of flower. c, Fruit. d, Bristles on fruit. e, Anther. f, Portion of branchlet with leaves, thorns, and fruit.

A compact intricately branched deciduous shrub, 2 to 4 feet high, with 3 rather stout spines at the nodes and usually without prickles (these sometimes present on young growth). Leaf-blades thin, almost round in outline, heart-shaped at base, ½-inch to 1½ inches wide, 3- to 5-veined from the base, usually with 5 lobes, the lobes coarsely and crenately toothed, glabrous or nearly so on both surfaces, deep green above, paler beneath; petioles ¼- to ¾-inch long, pubescent and often with longer hairs near the bases. Flowers greenish or purplish, 1 to 3 on peduncles about ¼- to ½-inch long; pedicels slender, about ¼-inch long, sparsely glandular, with 2 shallowly lobed bracts; ovary bristly and often with intermediate shorter gland-tipped bristles; calyx-tube very short, about 1/16-inch long, cylindric; sepals 5, green, dull white, or somewhat purplish, about ¼-inch long, reflexed, glabrous or pubescent, sometimes tipped with a few long soft spreading hairs; petals white, involute, about ⅛-inch long, much shorter than the stamens which equal the sepals; anthers apiculate at apex. Berry globular, about ⅜-inch in diameter, usually densely bristly or sparingly prickly, and with short-stalked intermediate glandular bristles. Flowering period, January to March.

Hillside Gooseberry is the common gooseberry found on the open hills and rocky canyons of the Coast Ranges from Monterey County northward to Mendocino County. Also from Amador County, "2¾ miles east of Ione on road to Jackson," *Belshaw*. Considerable variation occurs in the nature and abundance of the prickles, bristles, and glands on the ovaries and fruits.

Some specimens from Monterey County have berries with very few spines and these irregularly scattered. This form has been described as *R. oligacanthum* Eastw., *R. californicum* var. *oligacanthum* (Eastw.) Jepson. Since, however, the berries on a single plant show much variation in the abundance of spines, it seems best to include these plants in the species *R. californicum* as herein described.

24a. Var. **hesperium** (McCl.) Jepson. Fig. 168.

This gooseberry seems to be a variable entity. In most characters, the specimens examined resemble *R. californicum* but some are more like *R. Roezlii* and *R. Menziesii*. In what are judged to be typical specimens, the petals are almost as long as the filaments and the fruit is much more spiny than in *R. californicum*. The flowers are often purplish.

This variety occurs in the canyons of the chaparral region of Santa Barbara County southward to the Santa Monica, San Gabriel, and Santa Ana mountains.

Ribes californicum H. & A. Bot. Beechey 346 (1838). Type locality: "California." Collected by *Douglas*.

Var. hesperium (McCl.) Jepson, Man. 473 (1925). *R. hesperium* McCl. Type locality: Canyons of the San Gabriel mountains of southern California. Collected by *McClatchie*. *R. Menziesii* var. *hesperium* (McCl.) Jepson, Fl. Calif.

25. **Ribes binominatum** Heller. Trailing Gooseberry. Fig. 169.

A low deciduous shrub, with trailing stems 2 to 4 feet long and with 3 unequal nodal spines, usually without internodal prickles or bristles. Nodal spines ⅜-inch or less long. Leaf-blades thin, round or broadly round-ovate in outline, heart-shaped at base, ¾-inch to 2 inches broad, 3- to 5-veined from the base, deeply 3- or sometimes 5-lobed, the lobes with rounded teeth, finely pubescent above, densely pubescent beneath, usually without glands; petioles hairy, about as long as the blades. Flowers greenish white, 1 to 3 on short hairy peduncles; pedicels hairy, about ¼-inch long; bracts ovate-oblong, about as long as the pedicels; ovary bristly; calyx-tube short-cylindric, about as broad as long, pubescent; sepals greenish white, 2 times as long as the tube; petals white, ½ as long (or rarely nearly as long) as the sepals; stamens slightly exceeding the petals; anthers short-elliptic or oval, about 1⁄16-inch long, obtuse at apex; berry globular, about ⅜-inch in diameter, with long non-glandular prickles and some shorter gland-tipped bristles. Flowering period, May and June.

Trailing Gooseberry occurs in the higher mountains of Humboldt (Trinity Summit, *J. P. Tracy*) and Siskiyou (Scott Mountains, *Greene;* head of Shackelford Creek, *J. B. Davy*) counties. It extends northward into southern Oregon.

Ribes binominatum Heller, Cat. N. Am. Pl. ed. 2, 5 (1900). *R. ambiguum* Wats., not Maxim. Type locality: Scott Mountains, Siskiyou County. Collected by *Greene.*

26. **Ribes victoris** Greene. Victor Gooseberry. Fig. 170.

A deciduous shrub, 1 to 3 or rarely 5 feet high, the young stems usually very prickly, the slender old stems with 1 to 3 spines at the nodes. Leaf-blades ½-inch to 1½ inches broad, 3- or 5-lobed, the lobes crenately toothed, sparsely hairy and glandular on both surfaces or without glands above; petioles about as long as or shorter than the blades, glandular-hairy. Flowers whitish or greenish white, rarely tinged with purple, ½-inch or less long, 1 or 2 on a glandular peduncle; pedicels ⅛- to ¼-inch long, glandular-pubescent; bracts as long as or shorter than the pedicels; ovary glandular-pubescent; calyx-tube about as broad as long, glandular; sepals ¼- to ⅜-inch long, recurved; petals white, filaments shorter than or equalling the sepals, sometimes scarcely exceeding the petals. Berry oval, ½- to ¾-inch long, golden-yellow, densely and shortly glandular-bristly. Flowering period, March to May.

Victor Gooseberry occurs in shady canyons in Napa, Solano, Marin, and Sonoma counties, and probably also in Santa Clara County. Except for flower-color, this species may be easily confused with *R. Menziesii.*

Ribes victoris Greene, Pitt. 1:224 (1888). Type locality: Lake Lagunitas, Mount Tamalpais, Marin County. Collected by *V. K. Chestnut. R. victoris* var. *Greeneianum* (Heller) Jepson. *R. victoris* var. *minus* (Jancz.) Jepson.

27. **Ribes sericeum** Eastw. Silky Gooseberry. Lucia Gooseberry. Fig. 171.

A spreading deciduous shrub, 2 to 4 feet high, with nodal spines and with the stems and branches densely beset with internodal bristles. Leaf-blades round-ovate in outline, thin, ½-inch to 1½ inches broad, 3- to 5-lobed, the lobes sharply-toothed, glandular and villous-pubescent; petioles as long as or shorter than the blades, glandular-pubescent. Flowers purplish or greenish red, ½-inch to 1 inch long, borne in 3's on glandular-pubescent peduncles; pedicels glandular-pubescent, shorter than the peduncles; bracts roundish, glandular, shorter than the pedicels; ovary densely glandular-bristly and somewhat villous; calyx-tube bell-shaped, about ⅛-inch long, pubescent; sepals red or greenish, 2 to 3 times as long as the tube; petals white, involute; stamens 2 to 3 times the length of the petals, the anthers narrowly oblong, a little over 1⁄16-inch long, not apiculate. Berry globular, ½-inch to nearly 1 inch in diameter, densely glandular-bristly. Flowering period, April to June.

Silky Gooseberry is known only from the Santa Lucia Mountains of Monterey and San Luis Obispo counties. It usually occurs along the coast near sea level to 1000 feet elevation.

Ribes sericeum Eastw. Proc. Calif. Acad. ser. 3, 2:246 (1902). Type locality: Gorda, Santa Lucia Mountains. Collected by *R. A. Plaskett.*

28. **Ribes Menziesii** Pursh. CANYON GOOSEBERRY. Fig. 172.

KEY TO THE SPECIES AND VARIETIES

Leaves conspicuously glandular beneath and sometimes above.
  Ovary with both glandular and non-glandular bristles.
    Petals shorter than the filaments.
      Herbage not strongly aromatic; fruit up to nearly 1/2-inch in diameter. *R. Menziesii.*
      Herbage strongly aromatic; fruit 1/2-inch to nearly 1 inch in diameter. 28a. var. *ixoderme.*
    Petals as long as the filaments.......................... 28b. var. *hystrix.*
  Ovary evenly and densely covered with glandular bristles; petals 1/2 the length of the filaments................................ 28c. var. *leptosmum.*
Leaves softly villous-pubescent beneath, with few glandular hairs; ovary with a dense covering of white glandless hairs between the few glandular or glandless bristles.. 28d. var. *senile.*

An ascending loosely branched deciduous shrub, 4 to 8 feet high, the stems usually with 3 stout spreading spines at the nodes and numerous prickles on the internodes, especially on the young growth. Leaf-blades rather firm, ovate or roundish in outline, usually heart-shaped or truncate at base, 1/2-inch to 1 1/2 inches wide, rough with glandular hairs above or sometimes almost glabrous, distinctly stalked-glandular and velvety-pubescent beneath, 3- to 5-veined and lobed, the lobes with coarse rounded teeth; petioles slender, 1/2-inch to 1 inch long, glandular and pubescent. Flowers purplish 1 to 3 on a slender peduncle; pedicels glandular, 1/8- to 1/4-inch long; bracts thin, shorter than the pedicels; calyx-tube more or less glandular-hairy, cup-shaped and less than 1/8-inch long, the lobes oblong, 1/4- to 3/8-inch long, closely reflexed, purplish; petals 5, whitish, involute, shorter than the filaments; ovary pubescent and densely glandular-bristly. Berry globular, about 3/8-inch in diameter, densely glandular-bristly or glandular-spiny. Flowering period, January to March.

Canyon Gooseberry occurs in moist canyons, on bushy slopes, and moist flats in the outer Coast Range from Del Norte County southward to San Luis Obispo County, in the Transition Life Zone.

Considerable variation exists in the characters of the ovaries and fruits. In some instances the ovary may be bristly while in others almost prickly. These bristles or prickles are usually gland-tipped but sometimes the glands are more or less wanting. The stems also vary much as to the abundance and nature of the prickles and spines. Upon these variations several species or varieties have been described.

28a. Var. **ixoderme** Quick.

Herbage strongly aromatic; leaf-blades with hairs and stalked glands on both surfaces; young branches very bristly and glandular. Fruit 1/2-inch to nearly 1 inch in diameter, densely glandular-bristly, viscid and with a heavy odor.

This variety occurs in mixed chaparral below the "lower limit of yellow pine along the Sand Creek road to General Grant National Park in the foothills of the Sierra Nevada, Fresno County" and in Tulare County "along the Orosi-Badger road." *(Quick).*

Fig. 176. Fuchsia Flowering Gooseberry. *Ribes speciosum* Pursh.

28b. Var. **hystrix** (Eastw.) Jepson. Fig. 173.

"Stems thickly set with rigid horizontal yellow prickles, some gland-tipped." Petals as long as the broad filaments. Filaments dilated at base. Berry about ½-inch in diameter, purple, more or less covered with stiff spreading prickles.

This variety is known in the Santa Lucia Mountains of Monterey County from Point Lobos southward to Point Gorda.

28c. Var. **leptosmum** (Cov.) Jepson. Fig. 174.

This variety has fewer prickles on the stems than in the species. The ovary is evenly and densely covered with glandular bristles.

It has been collected from the canyons of Marin, San Mateo, Alameda, and Sonoma counties.

28d. Var. **senile** (Cov.) Jepson. Fig. 175.

The new growth is usually densely glandular-bristly and the leaves softly villous-pubescent beneath. The ovary has, in addition to the glandular or glandless bristles, a dense covering of white glandless hairs.

This variety has been collected in the foothills and coastal mountains of Santa Clara and Santa Cruz counties.

Ribes Menziesii Pursh, Fl. Am. Sept. 732 (1814). Type locality: Fort Trinidad, Humboldt County. Collected by *Menzies.*

Var. ixoderme Quick, Madroño 4:287 (1938). Type locality: "at 3000 feet altitude . . . along the San Creek road to General Grant National Park." Collected by *Quick.*

Var. hystrix (Eastw.) Jepson, Man. 473 (1925). *R. hystrix* Eastw. Type locality: Point Gorda, Santa Lucia Mountains. Collected by *R. A. Plaskett.*

Var. leptosmum (Cov.) Jepson, Man. 474 (1925). *Grossularia leptosma* Cov. Type locality: Bear Valley, Marin County. Collected by *Davy. Ribes subvestitum* H. & A.

Var. senile (Cov.) Jepson, Man. 474 (1925). *Grossularia senilis* Cov. Type locality: Saratoga, Santa Clara County. Collected by *Heller.*

5. **Whipplea** Torr.

(Named in honor of Lieut. A. W. Whipple, U. S. Army commander of a Pacific Railroad Expedition from the Mississippi River to Los Angeles.)

Small subshrubs. Leaves simple, opposite. Flowers bisexual, regular, small, in cymes on naked terminal peduncles; sepals 5 (rarely 4 or 6), united at base into a tube adnate to the lower part of the ovary; petals 5 (rarely 4 or 6), distinct, inserted on the calyx-tube; stamens 8 to 12, those alternate with the sepals longer, inserted at summit of the calyx-tube; ovary half inferior, 3- to 5-celled; styles 3 to 5, distinct. Fruit a 3- to 5-celled capsule.

This is a small genus of 3 species native to western North America. Two species occur in California.

KEY TO THE SPECIES

Trailing subshrubs; flowers in racemes or simple cymes; capsules globular. 1. *W. modesta.*

Erect low shrubs, 6 to 16 inches high; flowers in compound cymes; capsules oblong. 2. *W. utahensis.*

1. **Whipplea modesta** Torr. Western Whipplea. Fig. 177.

A low diffuse subshrub with reclining or trailing stems and branches 1 to 2½ feet long and with many short lateral leafy flowering branchlets. Flowering period, April to June.

Western Whipplea inhabits the forested regions of the Coast Ranges from Monterey County northward in the Redwood belt to Del Norte County and to Oregon. Outside the Redwood belt, it occurs in the wooded areas of Lake, Napa, and Solano counties. Very often this species occurs as a coarse perennial only slightly woody at the base.

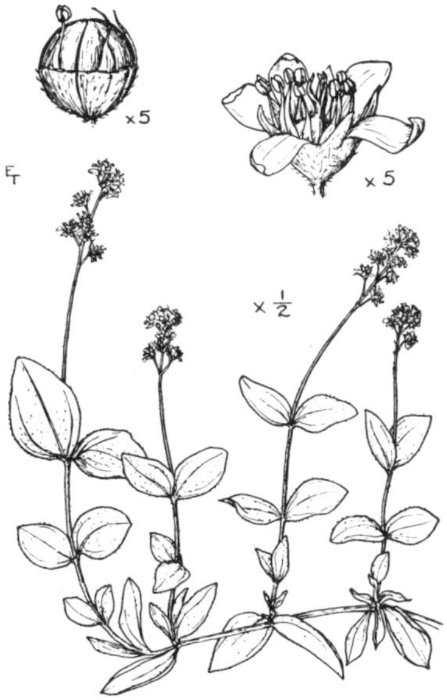

FIG. 177 WHIPPLEA MODESTA

FIG. 178 WHIPPLEA UTAHENSIS

Whipplea modesta Torr. Pacif. R. Rep. 4:90 (1857). Type locality: Marin County, California. Collected by *Bigelow*.

2. **Whipplea utahensis** Wats. UTAH WHIPPLEA. Fig. 178.

A low subshrub, 6 to 16 inches high, with hirsutulous herbage. Leaves deciduous; the blades ovate to oblong, ¼- to ½-inch long, 3-veined from the base, entire, nearly sessile. Flowers white, small, less than ⅛-inch long, in compound cymes. Capsules cylindric, about 3/16-inch long, usually 3-celled, with persistent styles. Flowering period, May to August.

Utah Whipplea has been collected in California in rocky canyons of Clark Mountain in the eastern Mohave Desert. It extends eastward to Arizona, Utah, and New Mexico.

Whipplea utahensis Wats. Am. Nat. 7:300 (1873). Type locality: Kanab, Utah. Collected by *E. P. Thompson*.

Crossosomataceae. Crossosoma Family

This family contains a single genus, *Crossosoma,* which is included by some authors in the family Rosaceae and by others in the Ranunculaceae.

1. **Crossosoma** Nutt. Crossosoma

(From the Greek *krossoi,* fringe, and *soma,* body, in reference to the appendage about the seed.)

Deciduous shrubs or small trees with rough bitter bark. Leaves simple, alternate, often crowded on short lateral spurs. Flowers bisexual, regular, solitary at the ends of short lateral branches; sepals 5, persistent; petals 5, distinct, deciduous, white or purplish; stamens 15 to 50, distinct, inserted on a thin disk lining the calyx-

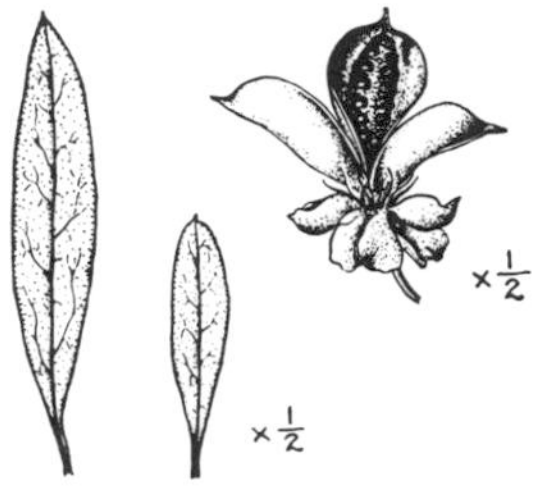

FIG. 179 CROSSOSOMA CALIFORNICUM

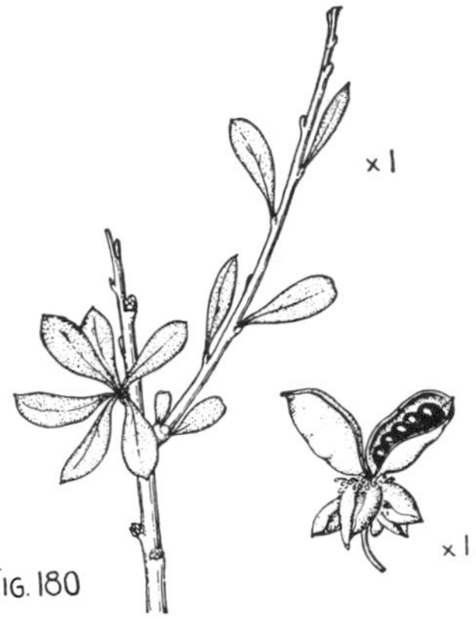

CROSSOSOMA BIGELOVII FIG. 180

tube; pistil of 3 to 5 stipitate carpels, ultimately distinct or nearly so, the ovary superior. Fruit a cluster of 2 to 9 follicles.

This genus contains 4 species occurring in southwestern North America, 2 of which are native to California.

KEY TO THE SPECIES

Leaves ¾-inch to 3½ inches long, usually scattered on the branches; fruits 15- to 25-seeded. . . . . .1. *C. californicum.*

Leaves ¼- to ¾-inch long, mostly clustered on short branchlets; fruits 2- to 5-seeded. . . . . .2. *C. Bigelovii*

1. **Crossosoma californicum** Nutt. California Crossosoma. Crabapple Bush. Fig. 179.

An erect shrub, rarely somewhat tree-like, 3 to 15 feet high, with rough scaly bark on the main stems and smooth grayish bark on the branches. Leaf-blades oblong, spatulate, or obovate, ¾-inch to 3½ inches long, ¼- to ¾-inch wide, commonly with a soft tip at apex, tapering at base, smooth and almost glabrous, entire, sessile or nearly so. Flowers numerous, about 1 inch broad, long-pedicelled; sepals round-ovate, less than ½-inch long; petals white, broadly oblong-obovate, ½- to ¾-inch long; stamens 40 to 50. Follicles 3 to 9 in a cluster, drooping, cylindrical, ½-inch to 1 inch long, each terminating in a curved or hooked beak, with 15 to 25 seeds in 2 rows. Flowering period, December to July.

California Crossosoma occurs on Santa Catalina, San Clemente, and Guadalupe islands.

Crossosoma californicum Nutt. Jour. Phil. Acad. ser. 2, 1:150 (1847). Type locality: Santa Catalina Island. Collected by *Gambel.*

2. **Crossosoma Bigelovii** Wats. Bigelow Crossosoma. Fig. 180.

An erect shrub, 3 to 4 feet high, with rigid irregularly much branched stems and often spinescent branches. Leaf-blades spatulate to obovate or elliptic, 1/4- to 3/4-inch long, 1/8- to 1/4-inch wide, acute or often with a soft tip at apex, smooth and glaucous, entire, sessile or nearly so. Flowers 1/2- to 3/4-inch broad, short-pedicelled; sepals suborbicular, less than 1/2-inch long; petals white, rose, or purplish, oblong to spatulate, about 1/2-inch long; stamens 15 to 30. Follicles 1 to 3 in a cluster, cylindrical, 1/4- to 1/2-inch long, each terminating in a short beak, with 2 to 5 seeds. Flowering period, January to April.

Bigelow Crossosoma occurs in the canyons of the lower mountain slopes on the west side of the Colorado Desert in Riverside County and at a few localities in southwestern San Bernardino County (Warren's Well, *Brandegee;* Ord Mts., *E. Jaeger*), in the Lower Sonoran Life Zone. It extends eastward to Arizona and southward into Sonora, Mexico and Lower California.

Crossosoma Bigelovii Wats. Proc. Am. Acad. 11:122 (1876). Type locality: "Near the mouth of Bill Williams River, Arizona." Collected by *Bigelow.*

Rosaceae. Rose Family

The Rose Family is a very large and economically important family containing 90 genera and about 1500 species of herbs, shrubs, climbing vines, and trees, distributed in all parts of the world but more abundant in temperate regions. Apples, pears, plums, peaches, cherries, prunes, apricots, strawberries, blackberries, roses, and hawthorns are familiar examples of this family. Thirty-one genera and about 125 species are native to California, of which about 50 species are shrubs or woody vines.

KEY TO THE GENERA

Leaves compound or apparently so, with 3 to numerous leaflets.
- Leaves fern-like, dissected into many small lobes, or twice- or thrice-pinnately compound; herbage heavy-scented.
  - Leaves twice-pinnately compound or the pinnae only deeply lobed; fruit consisting of 5 coriaceous dehiscent several-seeded pods. 1. CHAMAEBATIARIA.
  - Leaves thrice-pinnately compound or some secondary pinnae only deeply lobed; fruit an achene . . . . 2. CHAMAEBATIA.
- Leaves once-pinnately or palmately compound, not fern-like; herbage not heavy-scented.
  - Stems prickly.
    - Leaves usually 3-foliolate (sometimes simple or with 5 to 7 leaflets); pistils numerous, crowded on a cone-shaped receptacle; fruit an aggregate of drupelets, commonly called a "berry" . . . . 3. RUBUS.
    - Leaves usually 5- to 7-foliolate (leaflets sometimes 3, 9, or 11); pistils numerous, borne within an urn-shaped fleshy receptacle; fruit a collection of achenes within the ripened receptacle, the whole called a "hip." 4. ROSA.
  - Stems not prickly.
    - Leaflets 3 to 7, entire, 1/4-inch to 1 inch long . . . . 5. POTENTILLA.
    - Leaflets 7 to 15, serrate, 1 to 2 inches long . . . . 6. SORBUS.

Leaves simple.
- Leaves opposite but apparently fascicled; branches spinescent; petals none. 7. COLEOGYNE.

Leaves alternate.
  Plants very low, prostrate or creeping; fruit dehiscent along both sutures, at least for part of the distance.
    Leaves doubly 3-lobed; stamens united at base .... 8. LUETKEA.
    Leaves entire; stamens distinct .... 9. SPIRAEA CAESPITOSA.
  Plants erect, branching.
    Leaves palmately veined and lobed.
      Leaves 1 to 2 inches broad, usually 3-lobed .... 10. PHYSOCARPUS.
      Leaves 3 to 7 inches broad, usually 5-lobed .... 3. RUBUS PARVIFLORUS.
    Leaves not palmately veined and lobed.
      Leaves small, linear, entire, heather-like .... 11. ADENOSTOMA.
      Leaves broader, not heather-like.
        Plants thorny or spiny.
          Leaves revolute; petals absent; fruit a dry villous achene. 17. CERCOCARPUS INTRICATUS.
          Leaves not revolute; petals present; fruit fleshy.
            Leaves finely toothed or entire; ovary superior; fruit a drupe; fruiting calyx deciduous .... 12. PRUNUS, in part.
            Leaves coarsely toothed or slightly lobed; ovary inferior; fruit a pome; calyx persistent on fruit .... 13. CRATAEGUS.
        Plants without spines or thorns.
          Leaves 3- to 5-lobed, the lobes entire, usually fascicled and revolute.
            Pistil 1; fruit an oblong pubescent achene; style not plumose. 14. PURSHIA.
            Pistils 5 or more; styles long-plumose.
              Calyx-lobes with supplementary foliaceous bracts; pistils numerous; achenes pubescent .... 15. FALLUGIA.
              Calyx-lobes without supplementary bracts; pistils 5 to 10, rarely 2 or 3, densely villous .... 16. COWANIA.
          Leaves serrate or entire, or rarely lobed, the lobes toothed.
            Petals absent; calyx consisting of a slender tube expanded at summit; fruit a villous achene, with a twisted hairy style. 17. CERCOCARPUS.
            Petals present.
              Fruit consisting of 1 to 5 dry pods.
                Flowers white or cream-colored.
                  Flowers in corymbs; pods inflated, 2- to 4-seeded, dehiscent along both sutures .... 10. PHYSOCARPUS.
                  Flowers in panicles; pods not inflated, 1-seeded, tardily dehiscent or indehiscent .... 18. HOLODISCUS.
                Flowers pink or purplish .... 9. SPIRAEA.
              Fruit fleshy, indehiscent.
                Ovary superior; fruit a drupe.
                  Leaves entire; flowers dioecious; pistils 5 ... 19. OSMARONIA.
                  Leaves finely serrate or spiny-toothed; flowers bisexual; pistil 1 .... 13. PRUNUS.
                Ovary inferior or one-half inferior in *Amelanchier;* fruit a pome.
                  Leaves coriaceous, somewhat holly-like, evergreen. 20. PHOTINIA.

Leaves thinner, never holly-like, deciduous.
Leaves entire or nearly so, oblanceolate, mostly fascicled at the ends of short spurs........21. PERAPHYLLUM.
Leaves serrate, at least at the apex.
Leaves ovate, serrate almost to the base, 1 to 4 inches long; fruit about ½-inch in diameter...22. PYRUS.
Leaves broadly elliptic, normally serrate only near or at the apex, ¾-inch to 1½ inches long; fruit about ¼-inch in diameter...........23. AMELANCHIER.

1. **Chamaebatiaria** (Porter) Maxim.

(Named for its resemblance to *Chamaebatia.*)

This genus contains a single species native to the western United States.

1. **Chamaebatiaria millefolium** (Torr.) Maxim. FERN BUSH. DESERT SWEET. Fig. 181.

A stout densely branched shrub, 2 to 4 (rarely 6) feet high, with fern-like very fragrant foliage and densely glandular branchlets. Leaves bipinnately compound, alternate, deciduous, with numerous small segments or leaflets, oblong-lanceolate

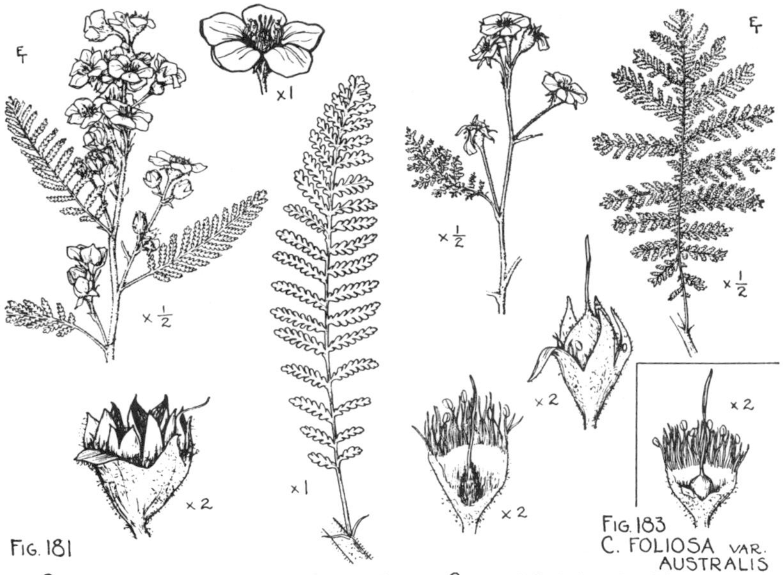

FIG. 181 CHAMAEBATIARIA MILLEFOLIUM FIG. 182 CHAMAEBATIA FOLIOSA FIG. 183 C. FOLIOSA VAR. AUSTRALIS

in outline, ¾-inch to 2 inches long, more or less clustered at the ends of the branchlets, soft-pubescent beneath, glabrous above, short-petioled, with stipules. Flowers bisexual, white, ½- to ¾-inch broad, in terminal compound leafy clusters (panicles) about 2 to 4 inches long; sepals 5, lanceolate, sharp-pointed, erect, united at the base with the receptacle to form a turban-like receptocalyx; petals 5, distinct, rounded, wavy and crenulate, ¼-inch or less long; stamens numerous, about as long as the petals, inserted on the margin of a disk lining the receptocalyx; pistils

5, more or less united below; ovaries superior, 1-celled. Fruit composed of 5 small smooth several-seeded pods, dehiscent down one side, ¼-inch or less long. Flowering period, June to August.

Fern Bush inhabits desert mountain slopes and rock-cracks of lava beds on the eastern side of the Sierra Nevada from Tulare and Inyo counties north to Shasta, Siskiyou, and Modoc counties. It extends northward into Oregon and Idaho and eastward to Wyoming, Arizona, and Nevada, in the Upper Sonoran and Transition Life Zones. It is nowhere abundant and usually occurs in scattered clumps.

Chamaebatiaria millefolium (Torr.) Maxim. Acta. Hort. Petrop. 6:225 (1879). *Spiraea millefolium* Torr. Type locality: Williams Mountains, Arizona. Collected by *Bigelow*.

2. **Chamaebatia** Benth.

(From the Greek *chamae*, dwarf, low, and *batos*, a bramble, in reference to its bramble-like flowers.)

This genus consists of a single species with one variety, native to California and Lower California.

KEY TO THE SPECIES AND VARIETY

Leaf-blades obovate or ovate in outline; ovary pubescent. . . . . 1. *C. foliolosa*.
Leaf-blades lanceolate in outline; ovary glabrous. . . . . 1a. var. *australis*.

1. **Chamaebatia foliolosa** Benth. SIERRA MOUNTAIN MISERY. KET-KET-DIZZE. Fig. 182.

A low glandular-pubescent heavy-scented shrub, with dissected fern-like foliage. Leaves 3 to several times pinnately dissected into minute crowded segments or lobes, alternate, evergreen, ½-inch to 3 inches long. Flowers bisexual, white, about ½-inch broad, in loose terminal clusters; sepals 5, persistent, lanceolate, united at the base with the calyx to form a turbinate-campanulate receptocalyx; petals 5, distinct, spreading; stamens very numerous, inserted in several rows on the throat of the receptocalyx; pistils solitary; ovary superior, 1-celled, 1-ovuled, pubescent. Fruit an achene, included in the persistent calyx. Flowering period, May to July.

Sierra Mountain Misery inhabits mountain slopes on the western side of the Sierra Nevada from Kern County northward to Sierra County in the Transition and lower Canadian Life Zones. In the open Yellow Pine forests of the lower and middle altitudes, this shrub is often gregarious, forming pure associations of great extent. During the heat of the day, the glutinous foliage gives off a characteristic odor suggestive of medicinal properties. Some people consider this odor very disagreeable. Other names applied to this plant are Bear-mat, Tarweed, Bear-clover, Running-oak, and Tobacco Plant.

1a. Var. **australis** Brandg. SAN DIEGO MOUNTAIN MISERY. Fig. 183.

Similar to the species but the leaves lanceolate in outline, the ultimate divisions oval or rounded. Ovary glabrous.

This variety occurs in southern San Diego County in the Tecate Mountain region. It extends southward into Lower California (east of Ensenada).

Chamaebatia foliolosa Benth. Pl. Hartw. 308 (1848). Type locality: "mountains of the Sacramento." Collected by *Hartweg*.

Var. australis Brandg. Bot. Gaz. 27:447 (1899). Type locality: La Grulla, Lower California. Collected by *Orcutt*.

Fig. 184. THIMBLEBERRY. *Rubus parviflorus* Nutt.

3. **Rubus** L. Bramble. Blackberry. Raspberry

(From the Latin *ruber,* red, perhaps in reference to its fruits.)

Perennial herbs, shrubs, or trailing vines, usually bearing scattered spines or bristles along the stems and leaf-stalks. Leaves simple or pinnately compound, alternate, with conspicuous stipules. Flowers large, bisexual, usually borne in clusters, sometimes solitary; sepals 5, green, united at the base to the slightly concave part of the receptacle forming a receptocalyx; petals 5, distinct; stamens numerous, inserted on the margin of the receptocalyx; pistils numerous, inserted on a cone-like portion of the receptacle which extends upward through the center of the flower. Fruit an aggregation of drupelets, usually known as blackberries or raspberries.

Rubus is one of the most common genera and its species have been extensively cultivated in all parts of the temperate zone. More than 3000 specific names have been given to various forms included in the genus, but probably 300 to 400 well marked species would include all the forms. Four species are native to California. Two species, *Rubus laciniatus* and *R. recurvans,* have escaped from cultivation in northern and central California and are included in the key and descriptions that follow.

KEY TO THE SPECIES

Leaves simple, palmately lobed; shrubs, not prickly............1. *R. parviflorus.*
Leaves compound; prickly shrubs or vines.
  Leaves pinnately compound; native species.
    Flowers red; fruit separating from the central receptacle when ripe.
      2. *R. spectabilis.*
    Flowers white or pale pink.
      Leaves white-tomentose beneath, 3-foliolate; fruit separating from the central receptacle when ripe.....................3. *R. leucodermis.*
      Leaves often pubescent beneath but not white-tomentose, 3- to 5-foliolate; fruit persistent upon the central receptacle when ripe..4. *R. vitifolius.*
  Leaves palmately compound; fruit persistent upon the central axis when ripe; introduced species.
    Leaflets cut into several oblong toothed divisions...........5. *R. laciniatus.*
    Leaflets not cut into oblong divisions.....................6. *R. recurvans.*

1. **Rubus parviflorus** Nutt. Thimbleberry. Fig. 184.

An erect unarmed shrub, 3 to 6 feet high, with gray bark which ultimately peels off in thin strips. Leaves simple, deciduous; the blades round in outline, 2 to 7 inches long and as broad, palmately 3- or 5-lobed, cordate at base, coarsely and unequally serrate, glabrous or sparingly hairy above, usually soft-pubescent beneath; petioles 1 to 2 inches long, usually bristly and more or less glandular. Flowers large, white (rarely pinkish), 1 to 2 inches across, about 4 to 7 in a terminal cluster; peduncle and pedicels glandular-hispid; sepals 5 (sometimes 6 or 7), tipped with a long slender appendage. Fruit flattened, hemispheric, ½- to ¾-inch wide, falling from the conical receptacle when ripe, red to deep scarlet, edible. Flowering period, April to June.

Thimbleberry is a common shrub near water courses in the Upper Sonoran, Transition, and lower Canadian Life Zones, extending from the San Jacinto and San Bernardino mountains of southern California northward in the Sierra Nevada and the Coast Range hills to northern California. It ranges from near sea level

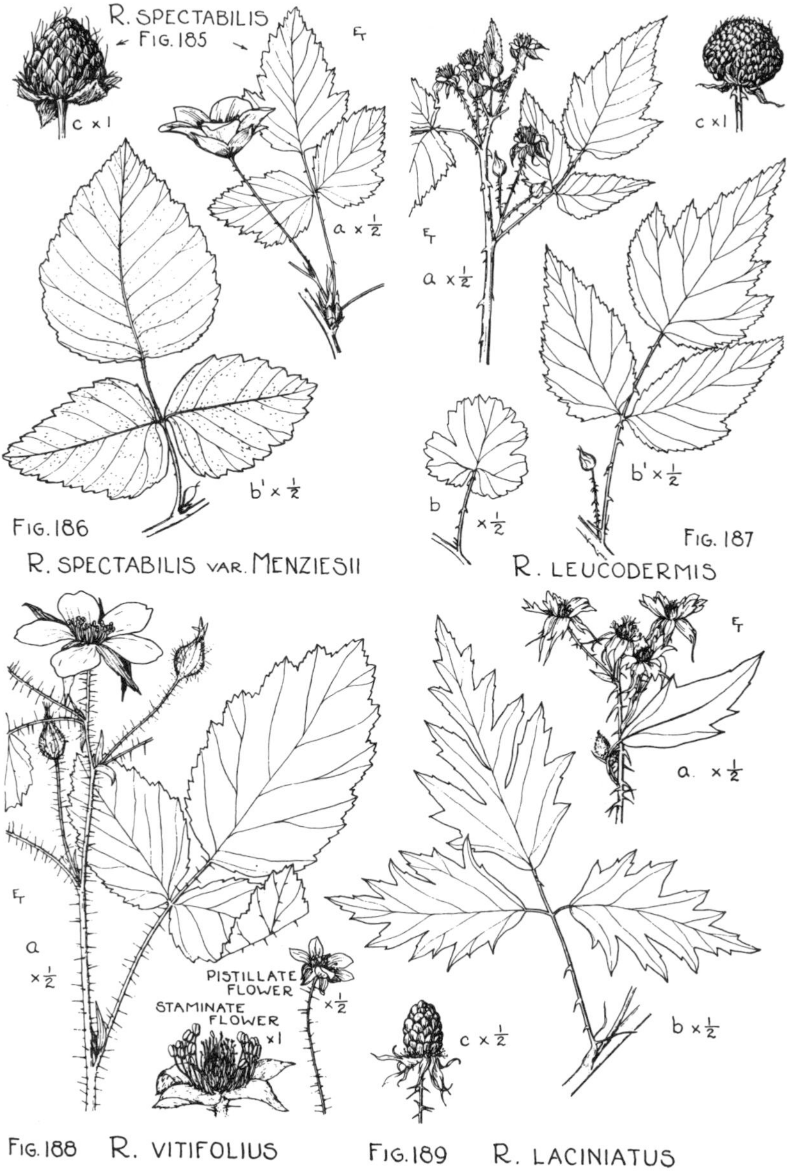

RUBUS. a, Branchlet with leaf and flowers. b, Simple leaf. b', Compound leaf. c, Fruit.

up to 9000 feet elevation. Outside the state it extends northward to Alaska, eastward to the Rocky Mountains and the Great Lakes, and southward to Mexico.

Rubus parviflorus Nutt. Gen. 1:308 (1878). Type locality: "On the island of Michilimackinac, Lake Huron." Collected by *Nuttall.*

2. **Rubus spectabilis** Pursh. SALMONBERRY. Fig. 185.

An erect or ascending shrub, 3 to 12 feet high, sometimes leaning on other plants, sparingly armed or the sterile shoots very prickly, with exfoliating reddish brown bark, the young shoots hairy but becoming glabrous in age. Leaves deciduous, usually 3-foliolate, sometimes incompletely divided; leaflets oblong-ovate in outline, 1 to 3 inches long, ½-inch to 1½ inches wide, long-pointed at apex, rounded at base, doubly toothed and more or less lobed, glabrous above, pubescent or only slightly hairy on the veins beneath; petioles shorter than the blades, slightly hairy. Flowers red, 1 to 1½ inches broad, solitary or 2 or 3 in a cluster; sepals hairy, sharply pointed; petals ovate or elliptic, ¾-inch to 1 inch long. Fruit red, salmon-colored, or yellow, ovoid or globose, ½-inch to almost 1 inch long, very juicy and edible; drupelets glabrous, bearing the persistent styles. Flowering period, March to July.

Salmonberry grows in moist ravines and draws along the borders of woods near the coast in the Transition Life Zone, extending from the Santa Cruz Mountains northward to Del Norte County. It ranges northward to Alaska and eastward in the Rocky Mountains to Idaho and Montana. The plants in the Santa Cruz Mountains and other localities in the southern part of its range usually have more pubescent leaves, especially beneath. This form is usually known as var. **Menziesii** Wats. Fig. 186.

When ripe, the fruits are usually light red but some plants have yellow-orange fruits. These are more globose than the red ones. In other characters the plants are similar.

Rubus spectabilis Pursh, Fl. Am. Sept. 1:348 (1814). Type locality: "On the banks of the Columbia." Collected by *Lewis.*

Var. Menziesii Wats. Bot. Calif. 1:172 (1876). Type locality: "near San Francisco and northward: Punta de los Reyes." Collected by *Bigelow.*

3. **Rubus leucodermis** Dougl. WESTERN RASPBERRY. Fig. 187.

A semi-erect shrub with two types of stems armed with stout recurved spines or prickles, the first-year stems usually erect, 3 to 6 feet high, bearing leaves with 5 to 7 leaflets, the second-year stems more straggling, usually covered with a pale bloom and bearing short leafy flowering branchlets with 3-foliolate leaves or these rarely simple and 3-lobed. Leaflets ovate in outline, 1 to 3 inches long, long-pointed at apex, rounded or cordate at base, doubly toothed, green and slightly pubescent above, white with dense tomentum beneath; petioles shorter than the blades, armed with recurved prickles. Flowers white, about ½-inch broad, few, in clusters, terminal on short lateral branches of the preceding year or sometimes axillary from the season's growth; peduncles prickly; sepals hairy, about ¼-inch long, long-acuminate; petals oblong, shorter than the sepals. Fruit red, dark purple, or black, about ½-inch in diameter, covered with a bloom, sweet and edible, separating from the conical receptacle when ripe. Flowering period, May and June.

Western Raspberry inhabits hill slopes, canyon flats, and stream banks in the Upper Sonoran and Transition Life Zones, extending from the Cuyamaca, Palomar, San Bernardino, and San Gabriel mountains of southern California northward in the Sierra Nevada to the Oregon line, and also near the coast in the Santa Cruz Mountains northward to Del Norte County. It ranges northward to British Columbia and Alaska and eastward to Montana, Utah, Wyoming, Nevada, and Arizona.

The fruit is of excellent quality, ripening from June to August, and is eaten by birds and other animals of the woods. Considerable variation occurs in the characters of the prickles, leaves, and pedicels but none seems sufficiently well defined to warrant the describing of new species or varieties.

Rubus leucodermis Dougl.; Hook. Fl. Bor. Am. 1:178 (1834), as a synonym. *R. occidentalis* β Hook. Fl. Bor. Am. 1:178 (1834). Type locality: "North West America." Collected by *Nuttall.*

4. **Rubus vitifolius** C. & S. CALIFORNIA BLACKBERRY. Fig. 188.

Usually a trailing or climbing shrub, often 15 to 20 feet long, with spiny or prickly foliage, stems, and branches. Leaves evergreen, pinnately 3- to 5-foliolate or rarely simple and lobed, 3 to 6 inches long; leaflets oblong-ovate to triangular in outline, 2 to 3 inches long, sharply and doubly serrate; midribs and lateral veins very prickly; petioles 1 to 2 inches long, very prickly; stipules falling early. Flowers white, 3/4-inch to 1 1/2 inches broad, functionally unisexual; staminate flowers with elliptical petals and several immature pistils; pistillate flowers smaller, with broadly oval petals and many reduced stamens. Fruit globose to oblong, about 1/2-inch long, black, sweet, persistent on the conical portion of the receptacle. Flowering period, January to May.

California Blackberry grows in valleys and foothills, mostly along streams, in the Upper Sonoran and Transition Life Zones, extending from southern California northward through the Coast Ranges, the San Joaquin-Sacramento Valley, and the lower Sierra Nevada to Oregon, Washington, and Birtish Columbia.

Rubus vitifolius C. & S. Linnaea 2:10 (1827). Type locality: San Francisco, California. Collected by *Chamisso. R. ursinus* C. & S.

5. **Rubus laciniatus** Willd. CUTLEAF BLACKBERRY. Fig. 189.

A very strong grower with angled thick trailing or climbing stems, 4 to 10 feet long, armed with flat hooked prickles. Leaves 3- or 5-foliolate, cut into several oblong toothed divisions. Flowers white or pinkish, about 1 inch broad, in prickly clusters; sepals white-tomentose, reflexed; petals obovate, about 3/8-inch long. Fruit globose, about 1/2-inch in diameter, black, persistent on the conical portion of the receptacle. Flowering period, April to June.

Cutleaf Blackberry has escaped from cultivation in several localities in the old mining districts of the Sierra Nevada foothills and in the Coast Range valleys near the early settlements.

Rubus laciniatus Willd. Hort. Berol. pl. 82 (1809). Native to Europe.

6. **Rubus recurvans** Blanch. YANKEE BLACKBERRY.

Stems at first erect, later recurving and often rooting at the tips, 3 to 8 feet long, armed with straight slightly retrorse prickles. Leaves of the sterile shoots with 5 (or 3) palmately arranged leaflets, 4 of these sessile or nearly so, the terminal one with a petiolule 1/2-inch to 1 1/4 inches long; leaflets 1 1/4 to 2 1/2 inches long, glabrate or sparsely pubescent above, densely and softly pilose beneath, coarsely and doubly serrate, or rarely lobed. Leaves of the flowering branches 3-foliolate or the upper unifoliolate. Flowers white, borne in a few-flowered corymb. Fruit elongate or globose, 3/8-to 3/4-inch long, the drupelets glabrous, sweet.

Yankee Blackberry has escaped from cultivation in a few localities in the lower Sierra Nevada (near Pine Grove, Amador County) and in logged-off areas in Humboldt County *(Tracy)*. It is native to northeastern North America.

Rubus recurvans Blanch. Rhod. 6:224 (1904). Type locality: Southern Vermont.

4. **Rosa** L. Rose

(The Latin name.)

Erect or sprawling shrubs, usually prickly. Leaves deciduous or rarely evergreen, pinnately compound, alternate, with serrate leaflets and persistent adnate stipules. Flowers bisexual, regular, showy, solitary or commonly in clusters of 2 to many; sepals 5, united at base with the fleshy cup-shaped receptacle to form a receptocalyx commonly called a hypanthium; petals 5 (rarely 6 to 10), distinct, inserted on the rim of the receptocalyx; stamens numerous, distinct, inserted with the petals; pistils few to numerous, inserted on the inner walls and on the bottom of the receptocalyx; ovaries superior, 1-celled. Fruit consisting of the ripened hypanthium enclosing the several hairy bony achenes, the whole called a "hip."

This large and variable genus contains from 100 to 4000 species. Most botanists recognize about 100 species, the other forms being minor variations of uncertain taxonomic rank. They occur in the north temperate regions of all continents and in the mountains of the tropics. One author lists 35 species of wild roses from California. These are herein reduced to 8 species and 2 varieties.

KEY TO THE SPECIES

Sepals, styles, and upper part of the hypanthium persistent on the fruit; pistils numerous.
- Hypanthium densely glandular or glandular-hispid or bristly.
  - Stems with stout (rarely slender) prickles ¼- to ½-inch long, usually straight, more or less flattened below, often ascending; petals ¾-inch to 1½ inches long. . . . . 1a. *R. nutkana* var. *hispida.*
  - Stems with few slender usually straight prickles, sometimes with many additional bristles; sepals without foliaceous tips; petals ½- to ¾-inch long. 2. *R. spithamea.*
- Hypanthium normally smooth and glabrous.
  - Stems with stout prickles, rarely slender and weak in some segregates of *R. californica;* sepals often prolonged into foliaceous appendages; plants 2 to 10 feet high.
    - Prickles straight or nearly so, more or less flattened below, often ascending; stipules, rachis, and leaflets glandular. . . . . 1. *R. nutkana.*
    - Prickles usually curved, or straight in some segregates of *R. californica.*
      - Pedicels glandular-hispid or bristly, the bristles often ⅛-inch long; sepals glandular-hispid, often pinnatifid. . . . . .3. *R. rubiginosa.*
      - Pedicels normally not glandular-hispid or bristly, sometimes glandular; sepals often villous, not pinnatifid but usually serrate. 4. *R. californica.*
  - Stems with slender straight (or nearly so) prickles.
    - Stipules, petioles, and rachises copiously glandular; leaflets with gland-tipped teeth. . . . . .5. *R. pinetorum.*
    - Stipules, petioles, and rachises not conspicuously glandular.
      - Sepals usually without broad foliaceous tips.
        - Sepals decidedly glandular. . . . . .6. *R. pisocarpa.*

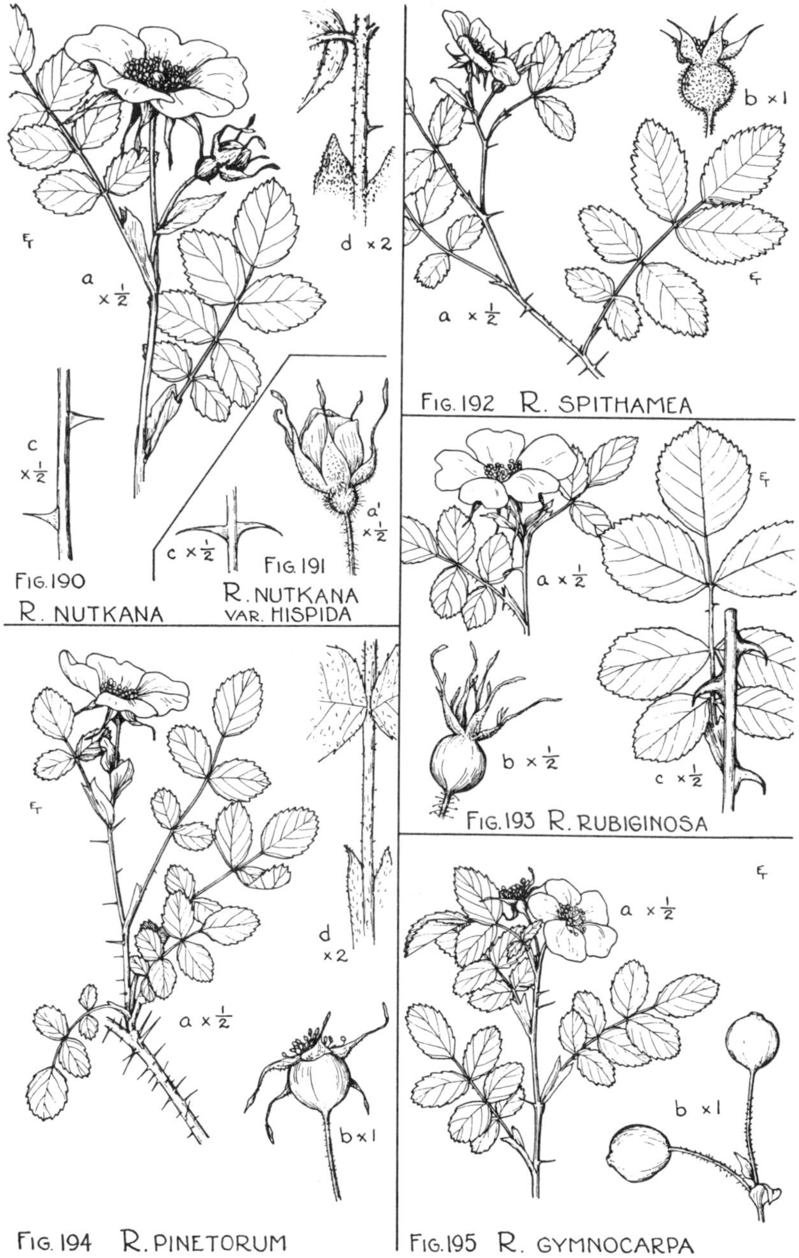

ROSA. a, Branchlet with leaves and flower. a', Single flower. b, Fruit. c, Thorns on branchlet. d, Portion of leaf-rachis with parts of stipules and leaflets.

Sepals not glandular.
Flowers usually several in a cluster; leaflets pubescent beneath. 7. *R. ultramontana.*
Flowers solitary or 2 or 3 in a cluster; leaflets glabrous on both surfaces, sometimes glaucous beneath...........8. *R. mohavensis.*
Sepals normally with broad foliaceous tips...4. *R. californica* segregates.
Sepals, styles, and upper part of the hypanthium not persistent on the fruit; pistils few...9. *R. gymnocarpa.*

1. **Rosa nutkana** Presl. NOOTKA ROSE. Fig. 190.

KEY TO THE SPECIES AND VARIETY

Hypanthium glabrous, without glandular prickles................*R. nutkana*
Hypanthium densely hairy or glandular-prickly................1a. var. *hispida.*

Stout shrub, 1 to 6 feet high, usually armed with stiff straight and ascending or recurved prickles, the flowering branches sometimes unarmed. Leaflets 5 to 9, usually 7, broadly oval or elliptical, ½-inch to 2 inches long, dark green and glabrous above, paler and somewhat glandular-pubescent beneath, doubly serrate with glandular points; petioles and rachises glandular and usually pubescent; stipules strongly glandular on the margins. Flowers rose-pink, usually solitary or rarely 2 to 4 together; pedicels glabrous or somewhat glandular-hairy or with gland-tipped bristles; sepals ½-inch to 1½ inches long, commonly prolonged into foliaceous appendages, glandular-margined, persistent on fruit; petals broadly obovate, ¾-inch to 1½ inches long; hypanthium in fruit globose, about ½-inch in diameter, glabrous. Flowering period, May to July.

Nootka Rose inhabits moist flats and mountain slopes in the Transition Life Zone of northern Mendocino, Humboldt, Del Norte, Siskiyou, and Trinity counties. It extends northward to Oregon, Washington, British Columbia, and Alaska and eastward to Idaho, Utah, and Montana.

1a. Var. **hispida** Fer. BRISTLY ROSE. Fig. 191.

Hypanthium densely hairy or glandular-prickly.

This variety occurs in the same clumps with the species near Alton, Humboldt County.

Rosa nutkana Presl. Epim. Bot. 203 (1849). Type locality: Nootka Sound, British Columbia. Collected by *Haenke*. *R. fraxinifolia* Hook., not Borkh.

Var. hispida Fer. Bot. Gaz. 19:335 (1894). Type locality: "Based on Rock Creek, Mont., *Watson* 124, and Pullman, Wash., *Piper* 1540."

2. **Rosa spithamea** Wats. GROUND ROSE. Fig. 192.

KEY TO THE SPECIES AND VARIETY

Leaflets thin, usually more than ⅝-inch long; stems with few slender straight prickles...*R. spithamea.*
Leaflets firm, less than ⅝-inch long, glaucous beneath; stems armed with numerous stoutish straight or recurved prickles..................2a. var. *sonomensis.*

A low sparingly branched shrub, ½-foot to 1 foot high, usually armed with bristles and slender straight prickles or sometimes almost unarmed. Leaflets 3 to 7, usually 5, oval or almost round, ¼-inch to 1¼ inches long, glabrous and green (or rarely slightly pubescent) above, sometimes almost green but usually paler and somewhat glandular-waxy and pubescent (or not glandular) beneath, doubly serrate with glandular teeth; petioles and rachises more or less glandular; stipules glandular on the margins. Flowers rose-pink, solitary or few to several in terminal clusters; pedicels with gland-tipped hairs; sepals 1/4- to 1/2-inch long, usually without foliaceous tips, glandular-hairy on the back, persistent on fruit; petals obcordate, 1/2-inch to rarely 1 inch long; hypanthium in fruit subglobose, 1/4- to 1/2-inch long, glandular-hairy or densely glandular-bristly. Flowering period, May to July.

Ground Rose occurs in open woods of the North Coast Ranges from Humboldt and Trinity counties southward to Mendocino and Lake counties where it becomes intermediate with the variety, and in the Sierra Nevada from Tulare County to Mariposa County, in the Transition Life Zone.

2a. Var. **sonomensis** (Greene) Jepson. SONOMA ROSE.

Stems armed with numerous slender or stout straight or recurved prickles. Leaflets firm, 1/2-inch or less long, glaucous beneath. Flowers usually several in a cluster.

Sonoma Rose inhabits dry slopes of the outer Coast Ranges from San Luis Obispo County northward to Mendocino County where it is replaced by the species.

Rosa spithamea Wats. Bot. Calif. 2:444 (1880). Type locality: Trinity River, California. Collected by *Rattan.*

Var. sonomensis (Greene) Jepson, Fl. W. Mid. Calif. 279 (1901). *R. sonomensis* Greene. Type locality: The Petrified Forest, Sonoma County, California. Collected by *Greene.*

3. **Rosa rubiginosa** L. SWEETBRIAR. Fig. 193.

A tall branched shrub, 3 to 6 feet high, armed with stout curved flattened prickles, sometimes also slightly bristly. Leaflets 5 to 7, broadly oval or roundish, 3/8-inch to 1 inch long, very aromatic, somewhat pubescent on both sides, distinctly glandular beneath, doubly serrate with gland-tipped teeth; petioles and rachis glandular-hairy and more or less prickly; stipules densely glandular beneath and on the margins. Flowers bright rose-color, varying to white, solitary or 2 to 4 together; pedicels glandular-hispid or bristly; sepals usually much lobed, glandular-hispid on the back, tardily deciduous in fruit; petals obovate or obcordate, 1/2- to 3/4-inch (rarely 1 inch) long; hypanthium in fruit pear-shaped, glabrous or rarely with few bristles near the base. Flowering period, March to July.

Sweetbriar, the Eglantine of Chaucer, Spenser, and Shakespeare, is native to Europe but has become naturalized in many places in the United States and Canada. In California it occurs in a few places along the roadsides in Humboldt and Siskiyou counties.

Rosa rubiginosa L. Mant. 2:564 (1771). Type locality: Southern Europe.

4. **Rosa californica** C. & S. CALIFORNIA WILD ROSE. Fig. 196.

Usually an erect stout diffusely branched shrub, 3 to 9 feet high, with straight or curved stout prickles or sometimes unarmed. Leaflets 5 to 7 (rarely 3 or 9), ovate to oblong, 1/2-inch to 1 1/2 inches long, glabrous or pubescent above, paler and finely pubescent or distinctly glandular or sometimes almost glabrous beneath, usually simply serrate and not glandular; petioles and rachises varying from glabrous to pubescent or glandular; stipules either with or without glands on the margins. Flowers rose-colored or light pink, few to 30 (rarely more) in a much branched cluster; pedicels not glandular-hispid or bristly (rarely slightly so); sepals either glandular or without glands, often tipped with foliaceous appendages, persistent on the matured fruit; petals obcordate, 3/4-inch to 1 inch long; hypanthium globose or ovoid, about ½- to ¾-inch long; glabrous or rarely pilose when young, never glandular, usually somewhat constricted below the calyx-lobes. Flowering period, May to November.

California Wild Rose is the most widely distributed, the most abundant, and the most variable of our native roses. It occurs most commonly along creek banks, near seepages, and in wet places along roadsides at the lower and middle elevations throughout California, in the Upper Sonoran and Transition Life Zones.

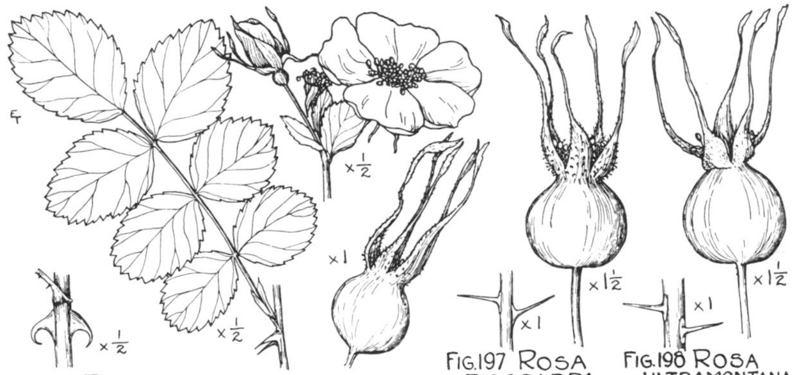

FIG. 196 ROSA CALIFORNICA FIG. 197 ROSA PISOCARPA FIG. 198 ROSA ULTRAMONTANA

Some of the numerous segregates or forms of this species extend northward to Oregon and Washington and eastward to the Rocky Mountain states.

In this species the characters of the spines, glands, glandular hairs, bristles, hypanthia, pedicels, sepals, petioles, stipules, rachises, and the leaflets show much variation and intergradation, and consequently some of the numerous forms have been described by various authors as varieties and species. Until more is known about the genetic fixity of these characters under controlled conditions, this species must remain a heterogeneous complex of forms of uncertain taxonomic rank.

Rosa californica C. & S. Linnaea 2:35 (1827). Type locality: San Francisco, California. Collected by *Chamisso*.

5. **Rosa pinetorum** Heller. PINE ROSE. Fig. 194.

A slender low sparingly branched shrub, ¾-foot to 2½ feet high, usually armed with numerous bristles and slender straight prickles. Leaflets 5 to 7, roundish or oval, ⅜-inch to 1¼ inches long, nearly glabrous above, slightly pubescent and glandular on the veins beneath, doubly or singly serrate with gland-tipped teeth; petioles and rachises usually glandular; stipules conspicuously glandular. Flowers usually solitary; pedicels glandular-hispid, bristly, or glabrous; sepals glandular on the back; petals obcordate, about ¾-inch long; hypanthium globose, not glandular-hispid or prickly. Flowering period, May to July.

Pine Rose occurs in the pine woods in the vicinity of Monterey Bay and in the Sierra Nevada from Tulare County northward to Shasta County, in the Transition and lower part of the Canadian Life Zones. In general habit of growth this species is easily confused with *R. gymnocarpa* from which it can be distinguished by the persistent calyx on the fruit.

Rosa pinetorum Heller, Muhlenbergia 1:53 (1904). Type locality: Pacific Grove, Monterey County, California. Collected by *Heller*.

6. **Rosa pisocarpa** Gray. CLUSTER ROSE. Fig. 197.

A slender shrub, 3 to 6 feet high, armed with few slender straight prickles, or rarely unarmed. Leaflets 5 or 7, oval, ½-inch to 1½ inches long, glabrous and green above, paler and finely puberulent or rarely glabrous beneath, finely serrate. Flowers in corymbs or rarely solitary, conspicuously leafy-bracted; pedicels glabrous; sepals prolonged into a slender terminal linear or lanceolate appendage, usually glandular-hispid; petals obcordate, ½- to ⅔-inch long; hypanthium globose, glabrous. Flowering period, June to August.

Cluster Rose occurs on shaded hill slopes of the North Coast Ranges from northern Lake and Mendocino counties northward to Del Norte, Trinity, and Siskiyou counties, in the Transition Life Zone. It extends northward to Oregon.

Rosa pisocarpa Gray, Proc. Am. Acad. 8:382 (1872). Type locality: "Oregon." Collected by *Elihu Hall*. *R. pisocarpa* var. *rivalis* (Eastw.) Jepson.

7. **Rosa ultramontana** (Wats.) Heller. MOUNTAIN ROSE. Fig. 198.

An erect shrub, 2 to 6 feet high, armed with slender usually straight prickles, or nearly unarmed. Leaflets 5 or 7, oval, glabrous above, puberulent and sometimes a little glandular beneath. Flowers usually several in a corymbose cluster; pedicels glabrous; sepals lanceolate, not glandular; petals obcordate, ½- to ¾-inch long; hypanthium globose, ⅜- to ½-inch long, glabrous. Flowering period, June and July.

Mountain Rose occurs chiefly on the eastern side and to the east of the Sierra Nevada from Modoc County southward to Inyo and Kern counties, at elevations from 3500 to 10,900 feet (Slate Creek Basin, Mono County, *J. Clausen*). It also occurs sparingly in the mountains bordering the western Mohave Desert. It extends northward to British Columbia and eastward to Nevada.

Rosa ultramontana (Wats.) Heller, Muhlenbergia, 1:107 (1904). *R. californica* var. *ultramontana* Wats. Type locality: Eastern side of the Sierra Nevada. *R. gratissima* Greene. *R. pisocarpa* var. *gratissima* (Greene) Jepson.

8. **Rosa mohavensis** Parish. DESERT ROSE.

Herbage nearly glabrous and without glands. Flowers solitary or 2 or 3 in a cluster. Otherwise very much like *R. ultramontana*.

Desert Rose occurs in moist places of the desert slopes of the San Bernardino and San Gabriel mountains and probably north to the mountains of Inyo County.

Rosa mohavensis Parish, Bull. S. Calif. Acad. 1:87 (1902). Type locality: North side of the San Bernardino Mountains at Cushenbury Springs. Collected by *S. B. Parish*.

9. **Rosa gymnocarpa** Nutt. WOOD ROSE. Fig. 195.

A slender shrub, 1 to 3 feet high, armed with long straight slender prickles and numerous bristles, or rarely nearly unarmed. Leaves 2 to 3½ inches long; the leaflets 5 or 7 (rarely 9), elliptic-ovate or roundish, ¾-inch to 1 inch long, ¼- to ½-inch wide, glabrous on both surfaces or rarely pubescent on one or both surfaces, dark green and shining above, green and a little paler beneath, doubly serrate with gland-tipped teeth; rachises and petioles more or less glandular-hispid; stipules glandular-ciliate and dentate on the margins. Flowers usually solitary or in clusters of 2 to 4; pedicels slender, ½-inch to 1½ inches long, glabrous or more or less glandular-hispid, commonly curving in fruit; sepals ovate, ¼- to ⅜-inch long, glabrous on the back or sometimes slightly puberulent, tomentose on the margins, deciduous with the styles and upper part of the hypanthium; petals obcordate, about ½-inch long. Hypanthium in fruit globose, ovoid, or ellipsoid, ¼- to ⅔-inch long. Flowering period, April to June.

Wood Rose occurs on moist wooded slopes and along shaded stream banks from Monterey County north in the Coast Ranges to Humboldt and Siskiyou counties, in the Sierra Nevada from Fresno County northward to Modoc County, and in the Palomar Mountains of San Diego County, in the Transition and Canadian Life Zones.

FIG. 199 POTENTILLA FRUTICOSA

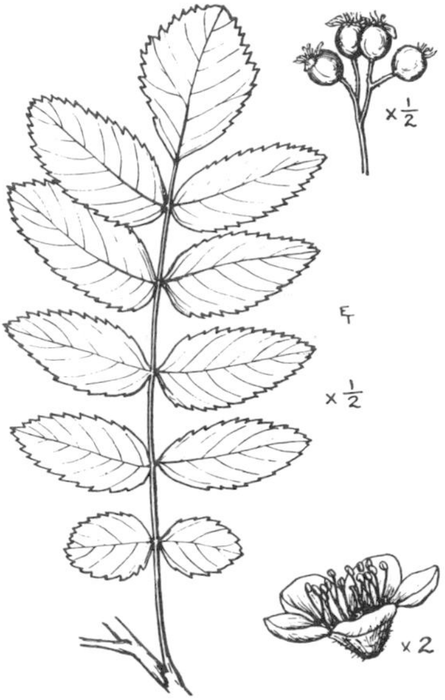

FIG. 200 SORBUS SITCHENSIS

Considerable variation occurs in the pubescence, glandulosity, and size of the leaflets. Some of these variations have been described as distinct species but no constant character has been found to warrant such treatment.

Rosa gymnocarpa Nutt.; T. & G. Fl. N. Am. 1:461 (1840). Type locality: "Oregon." Collected by *Nuttall.*

5. **Potentilla** L. CINQUEFOIL

(From the Latin diminutive of *potens,* powerful, in reference to the medicinal properties of some species.)

This is a large genus of over 350 species of perennial herbs, rarely annuals or shrubs, widely scattered in the north temperate and frigid zones, and a few in New Zealand and the Andes of South America.

As many as 48 species have been described as native to California, only one of which may be considered to be a shrub.

1. **Potentilla fruticosa** L. SHRUBBY CINQUEFOIL. Fig. 199.

An ascending or erect shrub, 1 to 3½ feet high, with shreddy reddish bark and very leafy branches. Leaves pinnately compound, alternate, almost deciduous, ½-inch to 1 inch long, and as broad or broader; leaflets 3 to 7 (usually 5), much crowded on the rachis, oblong, elliptic, or oblanceolate, 3/4-inch or less long, usually sharp-pointed, entire and often revolute, appressed-hairy above, white with a silky pubescence beneath; petioles 1/4- to 1/2-inch long. Flowers yellow, bisexual, 1/2-inch to 1 inch broad, in small loose clusters or solitary; sepals 5, triangular, alternating with 5 tooth-like foliaceous bracts, inserted on the margins of a slightly concave receptocalyx; petals 5, rounded, 1/4- to 1/2-inch long; stamens numerous, inserted with the petals on a thickened ring near the base of the receptocalyx; pistils numerous, hairy, simple, inserted on the conical portion of the receptacle. Fruit a small achene with long straight hairs. Flowering period, July to Sepember.

Shrubby Cinquefoil occurs near timber-line in meadows and in rocky habitats in the Sierra Nevada from Tulare County northward to Modoc County, westward to Mount Eddy, Siskiyou County, and in the White Mountains of Inyo County. It extends eastward to the Rocky Mountains and Minnesota, Illinois, and New Jersey and northward to Alaska and around the world in subarctic regions.

Potentilla fruticosa L. Sp. Pl. 495 (1753). Type locality: "Europe." *Dasiphora fruticosa* (L.) Rydb.

6. **Sorbus** L.

(The Latin name.)

This genus contains about 80 species of trees or shrubs restricted to the northern part of the northern hemisphere. A single species with one variety is native to California.

1. **Sorbus sitchensis** Roem. Western Mountain-ash. Fig. 200.

KEY TO THE SPECIES AND VARIETY

Pedicels glabrous. . . . . *S. sitchensis.*
Pedicels hairy. . . . . 1a. var. *densa.*

An erect deciduous many-stemmed shrub, 2 to 9 feet high. Leaves once-pinnately compound, alternate, 3 to 8 inches long; leaflets 7 to 15, oblong, 1 to 2 1/2 inches long, 1/2-inch to 1 inch wide, light green and glabrous above, paler beneath, serrate except near the base, sessile; petioles 1/2-inch to 1 1/2 inches long. Flowers white, bisexual, about 1/4-inch broad, in flat-topped clusters 2 to 3 inches broad; sepals 5, deciduous; petals 5, inserted on the urn-shaped receptocalyx; stamens about 20; ovary inferior, 2- to 5-celled. Fruit a small berry-like pome, about 1/4- to 1/3-inch in diameter, coral-red, with acrid pulp. Flowering period, June to August.

Western Mountain-ash occurs along stream banks and moist mountain slopes and flats of the Sierra Nevada from Tulare County north to Modoc County, thence west to Siskiyou, Trinity (Salmon Mountains), and Humboldt (Trinity Summit) counties, in the Canadian and Hudsonian Life Zones. It extends northward through Oregon and Washington to Alaska and eastward to the Rocky Mountain states.

1a. Var. **densa** Jepson.

Leaflets more crowded. Inflorescences hairy and denser than those in the species.

This variety occurs occasionally in the Sierra Nevada from Mariposa County northward to Modoc and Siskiyou counties (Emerald Bay, Eldorado County; between Sawyer's Bar and Etna Mills, Siskiyou County; Warner Mountains, Modoc County.)

Sorbus sitchensis Roem. Fam. Syn. Monogr. Rosifl. 3:139 (1847). Type locality: Sitka, Alaska. Collected by *Mertens.*

Var. densa Jepson, Man. 508 (1925). Type locality: Stubblefield Canyon, Yosemite National Park. Collected by *Jepson*.

7. **Coleogyne** Torr.

(From the Greek *koleos,* sheath, and *gune,* ovary, in reference to the tubular sheath which encloses the ovary.)

This genus contains a single species native to southern California, Arizona, Utah, southwestern Colorado, and Nevada.

1. **Coleogyne ramosissima** Torr. Black Bush. Fig. 202.

An erect densely branched spinescent shrub, 1 to 6 feet high, with divergent opposite branches and ashy-gray bark which turns black in age. Leaves simple, opposite, deciduous, apparently fascicled at the ends of the branches; the blades linear or club-shaped, 1/4- to 1/2-inch long, entire, flat above, 2- to 4-grooved beneath, apparently sessile or with very short persistent petioles; stipules small, scale-like, persistent with the petioles. Flowers bisexual, solitary, about 1/4- to 1/2-inch broad, terminating short branches, subtended by 2 to 4 small 3-lobed bracts; sepals 4, united at base, yellowish or brownish, about 1/4-inch long, persistent; petals none; stamens 20 to 40; filaments slender, distinct except at the very base where they are slightly attached to a tubular sheath-like prolongation of the receptacle which encloses the ovary; pistil 1; ovary superior, 1-celled, 1-ovuled; style attached laterally, very villous at base, bent and twisted. Fruit a glabrous achene. Flowering period, March to July.

Black Bush inhabits gravelly slopes, desert mesas, and foothills of the mountains in the western Colorado Desert and the eastern Mohave Desert, north to Inyo County, in the Lower and Upper Sonoran Life Zones.

Coleogyne ramosissima Torr. Pl. Frem. 8, pl. 4 (1853). Type locality: "Sources of the Mohave and Virgin Rivers, tributaries of the Colorado of the West, in the mountains of southern California." Collected by *Fremont*.

8. **Luetkea** Bong.

(Named in honor of Count F. P. Luetke, a Russian sea captain.)

This is a genus of a single species.

1. **Luetkea pectinata** (Pursh) Ktze. Partridge Foot. Fig. 203.

A low subshrub, 4 to 6 (or 12) inches high, with decumbent or creeping stolon-like branches forming a dense carpet-like undergrowth. Leaves simple, alternate, about 1/2- to 3/4-inch long, 2- or 3-lobed, the lobes twice- or thrice-parted into linear divisions, glabrous, grooved on the upper side, crowded along the lower parts of the ascending stems, reduced upward along the flowering stems to small entire bracts in the flower-clusters, short-petiolate or apparently sessile. Flowers white, bisexual, about 1/4-inch broad, borne at the tops of leafy stems in cylindrical clusters 2 inches or less long; sepals 5, joined at the base with the receptacle to form a hemispheric receptocalyx; petals 5, distinct, inserted on the margins of the receptocalyx; stamens about 20, inserted below the petals, united at base; pistils usually 5 (4 to 6), distinct; ovaries superior, 1-celled, with several ovules. Fruit composed of small smooth pods about 1/8- to 1/4-inch long, dehiscent along both sutures. Flowering period, July to September.

Partridge Foot occurs in the Mount Shasta region of Siskiyou County (above Cold Spring, W. Fk. Woolly Creek, *Geo. D. Butler*) and in the Salmon Mountains

Fig. 201. Douglas Spiraea. *Spiraea Douglasii* Hook.
(Photograph by Sidney Gulick.)

between Trinity and Siskiyou counties (Rocky Creek, Foxtail Ridge, *W. R. Dudley*). It extends northward to Alaska.

Luetkea pectinata (Pursh) Ktze. Rev. Gen. Pl. 1:217 (1891). *Saxifraga pectinata* Pursh. Type locality: "On the northwest coast." Collected by *Menzies*.

9. **Spiraea** L. SPIRAEA

(From the Greek *speira,* a band or wreath.)

Deciduous or rarely evergreen shrubs. Leaves simple, alternate, short-petioled, without stipules. Flowers bisexual, small, white, rose-colored, or pink, numerous, in terminal clusters; sepals 5, persistent, united with the receptacle to form a receptocalyx; petals 5, distinct, borne on the receptocalyx; stamens 10 to numerous, exserted, borne with the stamens; pistils usually 5, distinct and slightly joined; ovaries superior, 1-celled. Fruit a 1-celled dry pod, dehiscing along one suture and partially along the second, with a few to several seeds.

This genus contains from 40 to 75 species of the north temperate zone, extending south into Mexico and into the Himalayas of Asia. Three species are native to California. Several of the species are extensively cultivated as ornamentals. A great many of the horticultural varieties are of garden origin.

KEY TO THE SPECIES

Erect shrubs; flowers pink or rose-colored; leaves serrate at least at apex, not in rosettes.

Leaves white-tomentose beneath; flowers in dense elongated leafy panicles 2 to 6 inches long..1. *S. Douglasii.*

Leaves glabrous; flowers in compact roundish clusters about 1 inch broad. 2. *S. densiflora.*

Prostrate shrubs; flowers white, in cylindrical spikes; leaves entire, clustered in rosettes..3. *S. caespitosa.*

1. **Spiraea Douglasii** Hook. DOUGLAS SPIRAEA. Fig. 201.

An erect deciduous shrub, 2 to 4 feet high, with rather straight ascending branches, reddish brown bark on old stems, and pale brown pubescent branchlets. Leaf-blades oblong-ovate to elliptical, rounded at both ends, $1\frac{1}{2}$ to 3 inches long, $\frac{1}{2}$-inch to $1\frac{1}{4}$ inches wide, 1-veined from the base, green and glabrous above, white-tomentose beneath, the margins serrate above the middle or sometimes only at the apex; petioles $\frac{1}{8}$- to $\frac{1}{4}$-inch long. Flowers small, rose-colored or reddish, in terminal cylindrical panicles 2 to 5 inches long; calyx-segments blunt, mostly reflexed; petals ovate; stamens numerous, many times longer than the petals. Pods 5, glabrous, about $\frac{1}{8}$-inch long. Flowering period, June to August.

Douglas Spiraea grows in swales, along stream banks, and near seepages in the mountains of northern California from Plumas County northward to Modoc County, thence westward to Siskiyou, Shasta, Tehama, Butte, Trinity, Humboldt, and Del Norte counties, in the Transition Life Zone. It extends northward to British Columbia and eastward on the western slopes of the northern Rocky Mountains.

This spiraea was discovered by David Douglas, a Scottish botanical explorer, over 100 years ago. Its large panicles of rose-colored flowers make it one of the most desirable of our native shrubs for garden use. It grows readily in moist soils and is easily propagated from stem-sections.

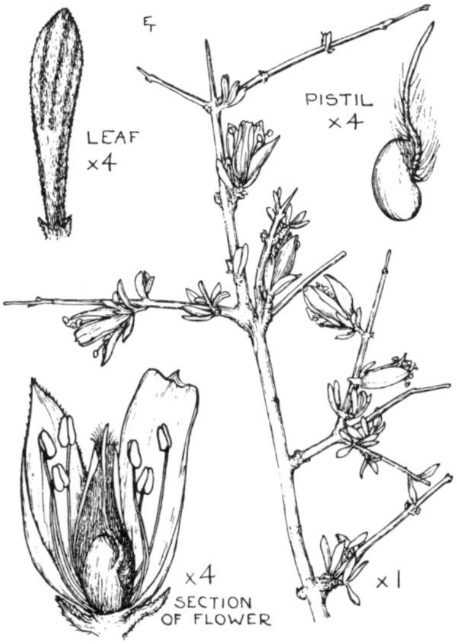

FIG. 202 COLEOGYNE RAMOSISSIMA

FIG. 203 LUETKEA PECTINATA

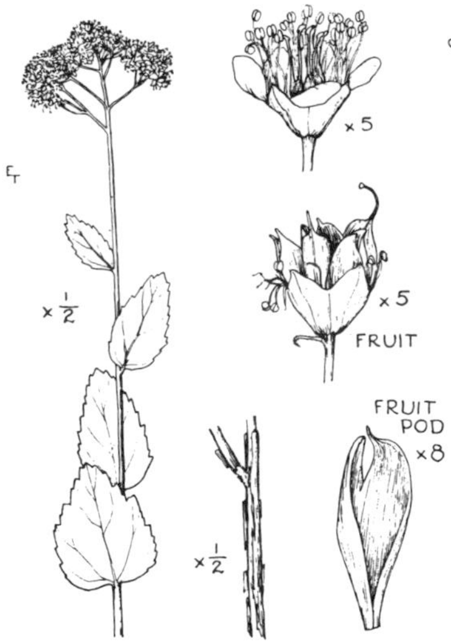

FIG. 204 SPIRAEA DENSIFLORA

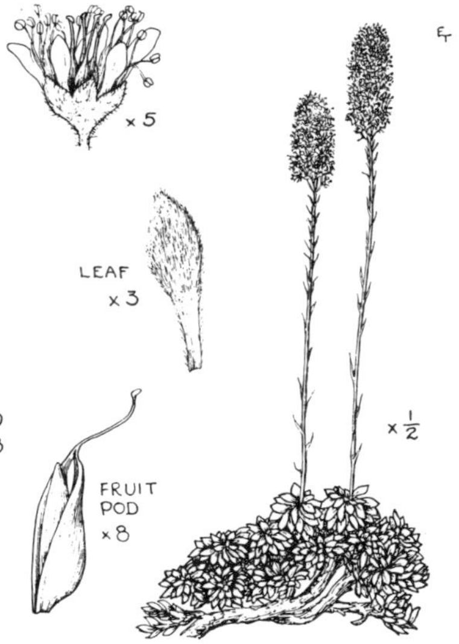

FIG. 205 SPIRAEA CAESPITOSA

Spiraea Douglasii Hook. Fl. Bor. Am. 1:172 (1834). Type locality: "Northwest Coast of America, about the Columbia and Straits of [Juan] de Fuca." Collected by *Douglas.*

2. **Spiraea densiflora** Nutt. MOUNTAIN SPIRAEA. Fig. 204.

An erect deciduous shrub, 1 to 3 feet high, with slender stems and gray or reddish brown bark. Leaf-blades elliptic to ovate, obtuse at apex, rounded or tapering at base, ½-inch to 1½ inches long, ¼- to ¾-inch wide, 1-veined from the base, sharply and unequally toothed above the entire base or sometimes almost entire, glabrous on both surfaces; petioles ¼-inch or less long. Flowers pink or rose-colored, about ⅛-inch broad, in rounded terminal compact clusters ½-inch to 1½ inches broad; sepals erect; petals rounded, with a short stalk; stamens numerous. Pods 5, glabrous, about ⅛-inch long. Flowering period, July and August.

Mountain Spiraea inhabits rocky moist soil, often in rocky clefts, from 5000 to 10,000 feet elevation, in the Transition, Canadian, and Hudsonian Life Zones. It extends from Tulare County in the Sierra Nevada northward to Lassen Peak and Mount Shasta, and to British Columbia, and eastward to Idaho, Montana, Wyoming, and Nevada.

Spiraea densiflora Nutt.; T. & G. Fl. N. Am. 1:414 (1840). Type locality: "Blue Mts. of Columbia." (Oregon). Collected by *Nuttall.*

3. **Spiraea caespitosa** Nutt. DWARF SPIRAEA. Fig. 205.

A low depressed evergreen subshrub with tufted branches clothed with numerous leaves spreading as in rosettes. Flowers white, in terminal compact spikes ¾-inch to 2 inches long. Flowering period, May to October.

Dwarf Spiraea occurs occasionally on rocky cliffs and exposed rocky areas in the Providence, Panamint, and Clark mountains and in the higher southern Sierra Nevada of Tulare County, in the Upper Sonoran and Arid Transition Life Zones. It extends eastward to the Rocky Mountains and the Black Hills of South Dakota. In Panamint Canyon in Inyo County at about 7000 feet elevation, H. M. Hall and H. P. Chandler found a plant about 3 feet in diameter spreading over the rocks.

Spiraea caespitosa Nutt.; T. & G. Fl. N. Am. 1:418 (1840). Type locality: Sources of the Platte River, Rocky Mountains. Collected by *Nuttall.*

10. **Physocarpus** Maxim. NINEBARK

(From the Greek *physa,* bellows, and *karpos,* fruit, in reference to the inflated fruit-pods.)

Deciduous shrubs with thin shreddy bark. Leaves simple, alternate. Flowers bisexual, white or rarely pinkish, in terminal clusters on lateral leafy branchlets; sepals 5, united at base with the receptacle to form a receptocalyx; petals 5, distinct; stamens numerous, inserted with the petals on the receptocalyx; pistils 1 to 5, commonly 3, with superior ovaries united at their bases. Fruit a small dry 1-celled inflated pod, dehiscing along both sutures, with 2 to 4 seeds.

Thirteen species of ninebarks have been described from North America and one from eastern Asia. Two species occur in California. Most of the North American species are closely related and could easily be reduced to 3 or 4 good species.

KEY TO THE SPECIES

Carpels 3 to 5; stamens similar . . . . 1. *P. capitatus.*
Carpel 1; stamens dissimilar . . . . 2. *P. alternans.*

Fig. 206. Western Ninebark. *Physocarpus capitatus* (Pursh) Ktze.

1. **Physocarpus capitatus** (Pursh) Ktze. WESTERN NINEBARK. Fig. 206.

An erect or spreading shrub, 3 to 8 feet high, often growing over neighboring plants. Leaf-blades of flowering branches round-ovate, 1 to 3 inches long, 3/4-inch to 1 1/2 inches wide, pinnately or often palmately veined, 3- or 5-lobed, irregularly doubly serrate, glabrous above, slightly to densely stellate-pubescent beneath; leaf-blades of the sterile shoots larger and more lobed and toothed; petioles 1/2-inch to 1 1/2 inches long. Flowers white or rarely pinkish, numerous, in corymbs 2 to 3 inches broad; petals about 1/6-inch long. Pods 1/4- to 1/3-inch long, divergent, reddish, becoming brown in age. Flowering period, April to June.

Western Ninebark occurs along streams and on moist hill slopes in the Coast Ranges from San Mateo and Santa Clara counties northward to Del Norte County, thence eastward into Trinity and Siskiyou counties and southward at scattered localities in the lower Sierra Nevada to Tulare County, in the Transition Life Zone. It extends northward to British Columbia and eastward to Idaho and Montana.

The masses of white flowers followed by the inflated reddish fruit-pods make this a very ornamental species. It is easily propagated by cuttings or from seeds.

Physocarpus capitatus (Pursh) Ktze. Rev. Gen. Pl. 1:219 (1891). *Spiraea capitata* Pursh. Type locality: "Northwest Coast of America." Collected by *Menzies.*

2. **Physocarpus alternans** (Jones) J. T. Howell. DWARF NINEBARK. Fig. 207.

KEY TO THE SPECIES AND VARIETY

Inner surface of receptocalyx glabrous. . . . . *P. alternans.*
Inner surface of receptocalyx with ring of hairs near the summit.
2a. var. *annulatus.*

A low densely branched shrub, 1 to 4 feet high, with stellate-pubescent and often glandular branchlets. Leaf-blades rounded to rhomboidal, 1/4- to 3/4-inch long, sparingly to densely pubescent above and below, doubly crenate or often 3-lobed. Flowers white, 3 to 6 in a terminal umbellate corymb. Receptocalyx glabrous within. Fruit a solitary pod, densely pubescent, about 3/16-inch long. Flowering period, June and July.

Dwarf Ninebark inhabits crevices of rocks in a few localities in the Panamint Range of Inyo County. It extends eastward into Nevada and the mountains of the Great Basin. Many of the plants in the Panamint Range have leaves predominantly pubescent above. These are sometimes classified as **P. alternans** var. **panamintensis** (J. T. Howell) Jepson. Fig. 208.

2a. Var. **annulatus** (J. T. Howell) Jepson. Fig. 209.

Receptocalyx with a conspicuous hairy ring just below the insertion of the stamens.

This variety is known only from the White Mountains of Inyo County (Marble Canyon of Black Canyon, *V. Duran*).

Physocarpus alternans (Jones) J. T. Howell, Proc. Calif. Acad. ser. 4, 20:130 (1931). *Neillia monogyna* var. *alternans* Jones. Type locality: Colorado. Collected by *Greene.*

Var. annulatus (J. T. Howell) Jepson, Fl. Calif. 2:164 (1936). *P. alternans* subsp. *annulatus* J. T. Howell. Type locality: "Wyman Creek, White Mts., el. 8500 ft., Inyo Co., Calif." Collected by *V. Duran.*

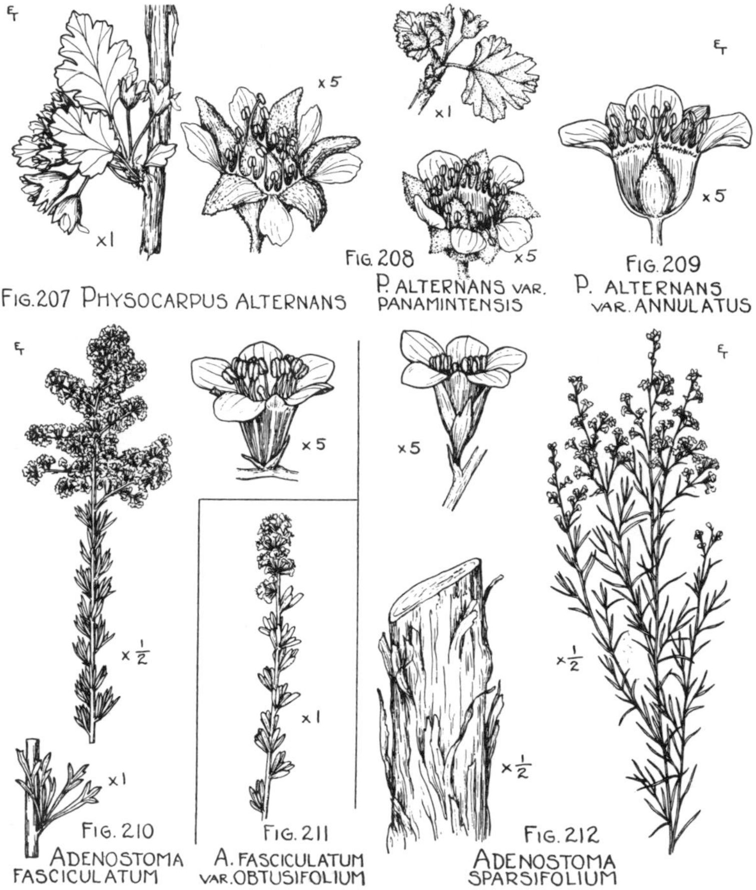

FIG. 207 PHYSOCARPUS ALTERNANS

FIG. 208 P. ALTERNANS VAR. PANAMINTENSIS

FIG. 209 P. ALTERNANS VAR. ANNULATUS

FIG. 210 ADENOSTOMA FASCICULATUM

FIG. 211 A. FASCICULATUM VAR. OBTUSIFOLIUM

FIG. 212 ADENOSTOMA SPARSIFOLIUM

11. **Adenostoma** H. & A.

(From the Greek *aden,* a gland, and *stoma,* mouth, in reference to the 5 glands at the mouth of the calyx.)

Erect evergreen shrubs with somewhat resinous heather-like foliage. Leaves simple, alternate, in clusters, linear, entire, and very numerous. Flowers bisexual, small, white or rarely pinkish, numerous, in terminal compound clusters; sepals 5, persistent, united at base with the receptacle to form a 10-ribbed receptocalyx; petals 5, distinct, roundish, white, spreading; stamens 10 to 15, inserted in 2's and 3's and alternating with the petals upon the margin of the receptocalyx; pistil 1; ovary superior, 1-celled. Fruit an achene, included in the hardened receptocalyx.

This genus consists of 2 species native to California and Lower California.

KEY TO THE SPECIES

Leaves in clusters or some single and alternate; flowers nearly sessile; bark gray or very dark on old stems. . . . . 1. *A. fasciculatum.*

Leaves scattered and alternate, a few rarely opposite; flowers pedicelled; bark reddish on old stems.................................2. *A. sparsifolium.*

1. **Adenostoma fasciculatum** H. & A. CHAMISE. "GREASEWOOD." Fig. 210.

A diffusely branched shrub, 2 to 12 feet high, with slender straight branches covered with numerous clusters of linear leaves. Leaves mostly fascicled or some single and alternate, linear, about 1/4-inch (rarely 1/2-inch) long, sharp-pointed, usually channeled on one side; leaves from seedlings and stump-sprouts usually pinnately divided into 2 to several linear lobes. Flowers white, almost sessile, in compact clusters 1 1/2 to 4 inches long. Flowering period, February to July.

Chamise is one of the most common shrubs of the California chaparral. It inhabits mountain slopes and ridges in the lower part of the Upper Sonoran Life Zone, often forming a distinct belt between the lower foothills and the Yellow Pine belt. It extends through the Coast Ranges, the mountains of southern California, the lower Sierra Nevada, and southward into Lower California. On the upper slopes of Mount Diablo, in the San Gabriel and San Bernardino mountains, and the mountains near Santa Barbara, it forms thickets almost impenetrable to man or pack animals.

1a. Var. **obtusifolium** Wats. Fig. 211.

Leaves very obtuse at apex, 1/8- to 1/4-inch long.

This variety occurs in the mountains of western San Diego County and in northern Lower California. Its status as a variety is weakened by intermediate forms with the species.

Adenostoma fasciculatum H. & A. Bot. Beechey 139 (1832). Type locality: Sandy plains about the Bay of Monterey, California. Collected by *Lay* and *Collie.*

Var. obtusifolium Wats. Bot. Calif. 1:184 (1876). *A. brevifolium* Nutt. Type locality: San Diego, California. Collected by *Nuttall.*

2. **Adenostoma sparsifolium** Torr. RED SHANKS. RIBBON WOOD. Fig. 212.

A shrub or small tree, 6 to 20 feet high, with yellowish green bark, becoming reddish on the old stems and peeling off in thin sheets. Leaf-bearing branchlets glandular and clustered near the ends of the branches. Leaves linear, 1/4- to almost 3/4-inch long, scattered, alternate or rarely opposite, glandular-dotted. Flowers white or rarely pinkish, fragrant, pedicelled, in loose clusters 3/4-inch to 2 1/2 inches long. Flowering period, July and August.

Red Shanks occurs mostly in the chaparral between 2000 and 6000 feet elevation from Santa Barbara County (Tepesquet Creek, *Wieslander*) southward to San Diego and western Imperial counties. It extends into Lower California.

Adenostoma sparsifolium Torr.; Emory, Notes Mil. Rec. 140 (1848). Type locality: In the mountains east of San Diego. Collected by *Emory.*

12. **Prunus** L. PLUM

(The Latin name of the plum.)

Trees and shrubs with bitter bark, leaves, and seeds. Leaves simple, alternate, deciduous or evergreen. Flowers bisexual, borne in clusters or rarely solitary, white or pink; sepals 5, united at base with the receptacle to form a cup-shaped receptocalyx; petals 5, distinct, spreading; stamens many, inserted with the petals on the receptocalyx; pistil 1; ovary superior, 1-celled. Fruit a drupe.

This genus contains about 175 species widely scattered but chiefly in the northern hemisphere. It includes the cherries, plums, prunes, peaches, apricots, and almonds. About 25 to 30 species are native to North America. Seven species with several varieties and many forms are native to California.

KEY TO THE SPECIES

Leaves evergreen, thick and leathery, spinosely toothed or entire.
  Leaves normally spinosely toothed, ¾-inch to 2 inches long......1. *P. ilicifolia.*
  Leaves mostly entire, 2 to 5 inches long........................2. *P. Lyonii.*
Leaves deciduous, never spinosely toothed.
  Branchlets stout and spur-like, usually thorny or spinescent.
    Leaves narrow, mostly fascicled.
      Leaves mostly entire; flowers white, sessile, ¼-inch or less broad. 3. *P. fasciculata.*
      Leaves minutely serrulate; flowers rose-colored, pedicelled, about ½-inch broad....................................4. *P. Andersonii.*
    Leaves broadly elliptic, roundish, or ovate, not fascicled.
      Flowers mostly solitary or in clusters of 2 to 10; ovary and fruit pubescent....................................5. *P. Fremontii.*
      Flowers in clusters of 2 to 4; ovary and fruit glabrous.....6. *P. subcordata.*
  Branchlets neither thorny nor spiny, except in *P. subcordata.*
    Flowers 2 to 10 in lateral clusters.
      Petioles ¼-inch or less long; drupe ovoid, ¼- to ½-inch long. 7. *P. emarginata.*
      Petioles ¼- to ¾-inch long; drupe oblong, ¾-inch to 1 inch long. 6. *P. subcordata.*
    Flowers numerous, in racemes...............8. *P. virginiana* var. *demissa.*

1. **Prunus ilicifolia** (Nutt.) Walp. HOLLYLEAF CHERRY. ISLAY. EVERGREEN CHERRY. Fig. 213.

A much branched evergreen shrub or small tree up to 30 feet high, with a compact crown of dark green foliage. Leaf-blades ovate to elliptic, acute or rounded at apex, truncate or tapering or rounded to subcordate at base, ¾-inch to 2 inches long, ¾-inch to 1½ inches wide, often somewhat holly-like, dark green, glabrous, and shining above, paler and glabrous beneath, the margins spiny-toothed or sometimes almost entire; petioles ¼- to ½-inch long. Flowers white, ¼-inch or less across, in racemes 1 to 2 inches long. Drupe dark red, purple, or black, about ½-inch in diameter, the pulp very thin and sweet when ripe. Flowering period, March to May.

Hollyleaf Cherry inhabits the dry foothills, lower mountain slopes, and rich valleys of the Coast Ranges from the Napa Range *(F. A. Leach)* southward to the western part of the Tehachapi Mountains and the mountains of southern California. It extends southward to Lower California.

This species is widely cultivated because of its dark green holly-like foliage. It is a good plant for hedges if kept properly pruned.

Prunus ilicifolia (Nutt.) Walp. Rep. 2:10 (1843). *Cerasus ilicifolia* Nutt. Type locality: Santa Barbara, California. Collected by *Nuttall.*

2. **Prunus Lyonii** (Eastw.) Sarg. CATALINA CHERRY. Fig. 214.

A large evergreen shrub or small tree, 10 to 45 feet high, resembling *P. ilicifolia.* Leaf-blades ovate to ovate-lanceolate, 2 to 5 inches long, dark green, glabrous, leathery, usually entire. Racemes 2 to 5 inches long. Drupe usually black, ½-inch to 1 inch long. Flowering period, March to May.

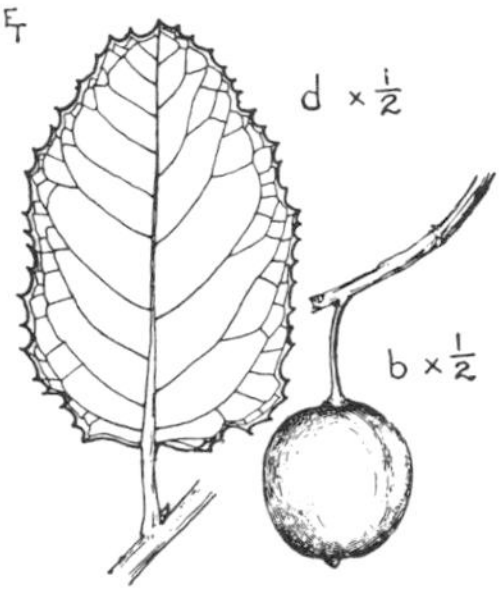

FIG. 213 P. ILICIFOLIA

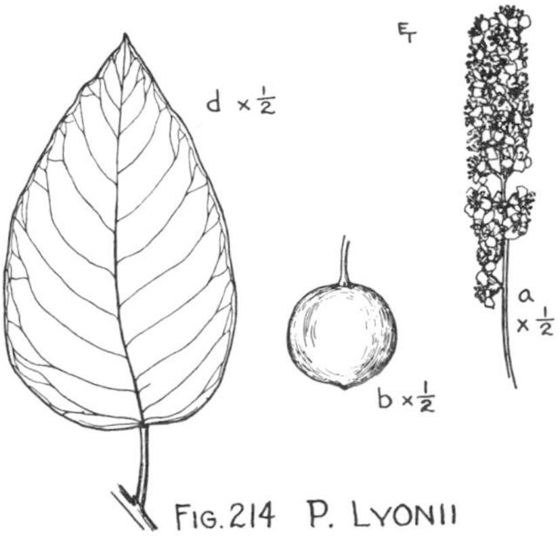

FIG. 214 P. LYONII

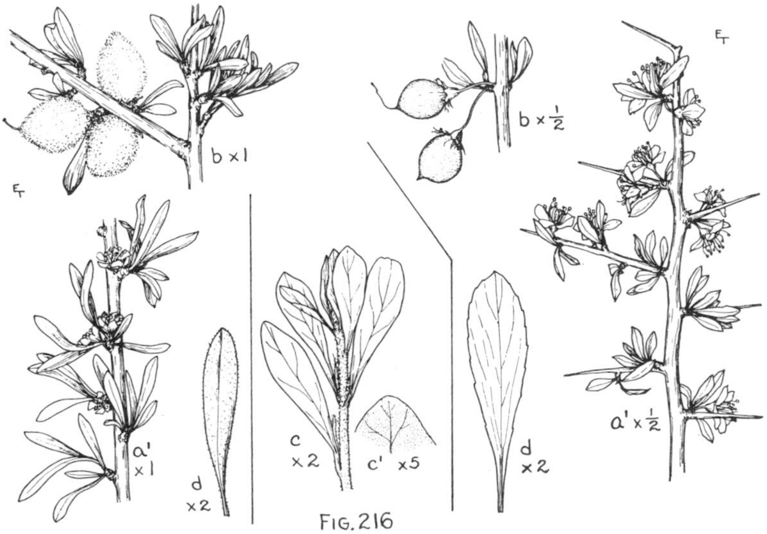

FIG. 215 P. FASCICULATA

FIG. 216 P. FASCICULATA VAR. PUNCTATA

FIG. 217 P. ANDERSONII

PRUNUS. a, Flower-cluster. a′, Branchlet with leaves and flowers. b, Fruit or fruiting branchlet. c, Young branchlet with pubescence. c′, Leaf-tip. d, Leaf.

Catalina Cherry occurs on Santa Catalina, San Clemente, Santa Cruz, and Santa Rosa islands.

Prunus Lyonii (Eastw.) Sarg. Pl. Wilsonianae 74 (1911). *Cerasus Lyonii* Eastw. Type locality: Santa Catalina Island. Collected by *Lyon*. *P. ilicifolia* var. *integrifolia* Sudw. *P. ilicifolia* var. *occidentalis* (Lyon) Brandg.

3. **Prunus fasciculata** (Torr.) Gray. DESERT ALMOND. Fig. 215.

KEY TO THE SPECIES AND VARIETY

Leaves minutely pubescent, not glandular-punctate . . . . *P. fasciculata*.
Leaves glabrous, glandular-punctate . . . . 3a. var. *punctata*.

A divaricately branched deciduous shrub, 2 to 6 (or rarely to 9) feet high, with short stiff often thorn-like branchlets. Leaves fascicled on short bud-like suppressed branchlets, spatulate or linear-oblanceolate, 1/4- to 1/2- (or 3/4-) inch long, 1/8- to 1/4-inch wide, finely pubescent, mostly entire, rarely with 1 or 2 teeth on each margin, tapering to a short petiole-like base. Flowers white, more or less dioecious, solitary or 2 or 3 together, 1/4-inch or less broad, sessile or nearly so. Fruit subglobose to ovoid, about 3/8-inch long, covered with a coat of light brown short bristly hairs. Flowering period, March to May.

Desert Almond inhabits dry desert mountain slopes, mesas, and washes from 2500 to 6500 feet elevation from the western and northern borders of the Colorado Desert northward through the Mohave Desert to Inyo County. It extends eastward to Arizona and Utah.

3a. Var. **punctata** Jepson. Fig. 216.

Young shoots very pubescent. Leaves glabrous, glandular-punctate.

This variety occurs in a few scattered locations on sandy mesas from northern Santa Barbara County to southern San Luis Obispo County (Nipomo Mesa).

Prunus fasciculata (Torr.) Gray, Proc. Am. Acad. 10:70 (1874). *Emplectocladus fasciculatus* Torr. Type locality: "Sierra Nevada of California; probably in the southern part of the range." Collected by *Fremont.*

Var. punctata Jepson, Fl. Calif. 2:230 (1936). Type locality: Bicknell Station, Santa Barbara County. Collected by *Jepson.*

4. **Prunus Andersonii** Gray. DESERT PEACH. NEVADA WILD ALMOND. Fig. 217.

A spreading diffusely branched deciduous shrub, 2 to 6 feet high, with short rigid or spinescent branches. Leaves fascicled on short lateral thorny branchlets, oblong or oblong-lanceolate, 1/2-inch to 1 inch long, 1/8- to 3/8-inch wide, finely serrulate, glabrous, almost sessile. Flowers solitary, about 1/2-inch broad, pedicelled, appearing with the leaves; petals rose-colored, about 1/4-inch long; stamens about 20. Fruit globose, compressed, about 1/2-inch long, covered with a dark brown pubescence. Flowering period, April and May.

Desert Peach occurs on arid desert mountain slopes and mesas on the eastern side of the Sierra Nevada from Modoc and Lassen counties southward to Inyo and Kern (Onyx, *Epling*) counties. It extends eastward to Nevada.

Prunus Andersonii Gray, Proc. Am. Acad. 7:337 (1868). Type locality: "Foothills of the eastern side of the Sierra Nevada, near Carson," (Nevada). Collected by *C. L. Anderson.*

5. **Prunus Fremontii** Wats. DESERT APRICOT. Fig. 218.

An intricately branched deciduous shrub or sometimes a small tree, 4 to 15 feet high, with numerous spinose branchlets. Leaves alternate, on short lateral spurs; leaf-blades rounded to ovate, truncate or subcordate at base, obtuse or acute at apex, 1/2- to 3/4-inch long, 3/4-inch or less wide, 1-veined from the base, glabrous on both surfaces, thin, finely serrulate; petioles 1/2-inch or less long. Flowers solitary or in clusters of 2 to 10, 1/2-inch or less broad, short-pedicelled; petals white. Fruit elliptic-ovoid, 1/3- to 1/2-inch long, minutely puberulent. Flowering period, February to April.

Desert Apricot inhabits the lower arid canyon slopes and flats of the mountains bordering the western side of the Colorado Desert in Riverside and San Diego counties, in the Lower Sonoran Life Zone. It extends southward into Lower California.

Prunus Fremontii Wats. Bot. Calif. 2:442 (1880). Type locality: Oriflamme Canyon, San Diego County. Collected by *Cleveland*. *P. eriogyna* S. C. Mason. *P. Fremontii* var. *pilulata* Jepson.

6. **Prunus subcordata** Benth. SIERRA PLUM. Fig. 219.

A deciduous shrub or sometimes a small tree, 6 to 20 feet high, with stiff crooked branches and short thorn-like branchlets. Leaf-blades ovate, elliptic, obovate, or almost round, subcordate or sometimes rounded or cuneate at base, ¾-inch to 2 inches long, ½-inch to 1½ inches wide, 1-veined from the base, finely serrulate; petioles ¼- to ¾-inch long, usually with a pair of glands near the base of the blade. Flowers white, ageing to pink, fragrant, about ½-inch across, 2 to 4 (or 5) in a cluster, on pedicels about ½-inch long; petals obovate, about ¼-inch long. Fruit oblong, pubescent or glabrous, usually bright red or sometimes yellow, ¾-inch to 1 inch long. Flowering period, March and April.

Sierra Plum inhabits moist or dry rocky slopes of the Coast Range foothills and middle altitudes of the Sierra Nevada, in the Transition Life Zone. It extends from the Santa Cruz Mountains northward to Siskiyou and Del Norte counties and in the Sierra Nevada from Kern and Tulare counties northward to Modoc County, thence into southern Oregon. In dry or gravelly soils this plant tends to be distinctly shrubby, but in more fertile soils it becomes much larger and often tree-like. In the northern part of its range the fruit is usually larger, more juicy, and quite edible but in the southern part it is much drier and scarcely edible, while around the San Francisco Bay region this species rarely sets mature fruits.

Considerable variation in the size and shape of the leaves, color of the flowers, and color and size of the fruits occurs in this species. A few of these variations have been described as varieties or species, but until more extensive field and garden studies can be carried on, these are best treated as minor variations of uncertain taxonomic rank. The plants from Sierra County to Mount Shasta with larger, yellow, more pulpy, and sweeter fruits are often known as **P. subcordata** var. **Kelloggii** Lemmon. The small shrubs in Modoc County with subglobose bright red fruits with very bitter pulp have been referred by some writers to **P. subcordata** var. **rubicunda** Jepson. In the Warner Mountains of Modoc County, this shrub has very fragrant pink flowers (*McMinn* 2480). The leaves are obovate and narrower than those on most plants in other locations. The glands are often absent from the petiole. This form is apparently **P. oregana** Greene or **P. subcordata** var. **oregana** Wight.

Prunus subcordata Benth. Pl. Hartw. 308 (1848). Type locality: Probably in the Sierra Nevada foothills of Butte County. Collected by *Hartweg*.

7. **Prunus emarginata** (Dougl.) Walp. BITTER CHERRY. Fig. 220.

A deciduous shrub, 4 to 12 feet high, or sometimes a small tree up to 30 feet high, with long very slender gray or reddish brown branches. Leaf-blades ovate, oblong, or oblong-obovate, rounded at apex, ¾-inch to 2 inches long, ⅜-inch to 1 inch wide, usually with 1 or 2 glands near the petiole on the wedge-shaped base, glabrous and dark green above, glabrous or woolly-pubescent beneath, finely serrulate or crenulate; petioles about ¼-inch long. Flowers white, about ½-inch wide, 3 to 10 in short corymbose clusters, appearing when the leaves are half grown; pedicels ¼- to ½-inch long; petals white or faintly tinged with green, obovate, rounded or notched at the apex. Fruit oval, ⅓- to ½-inch long, red at first but nearly black when mature, smooth, very bitter. Flowering period in

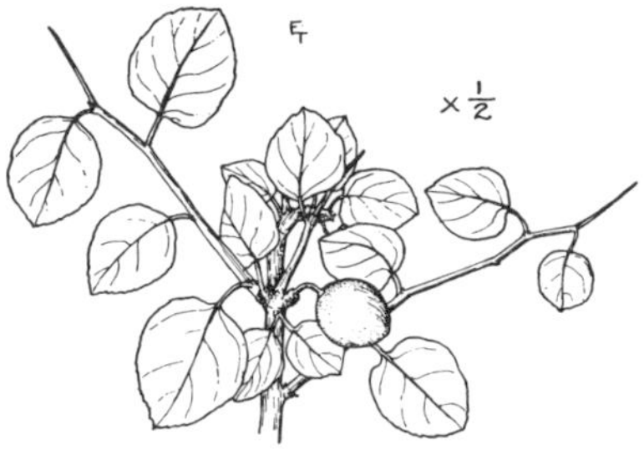

FIG. 218

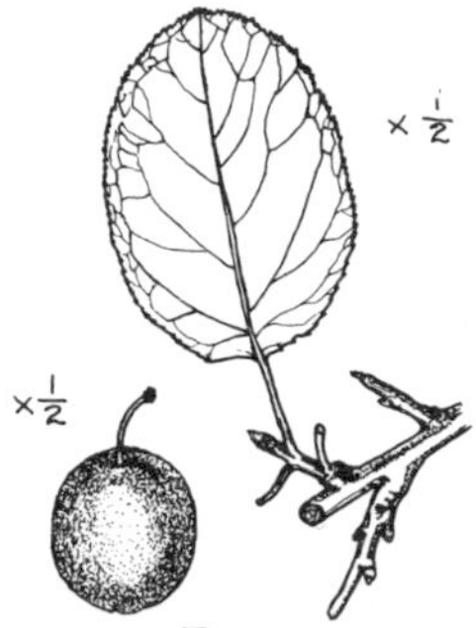

FIG. 219

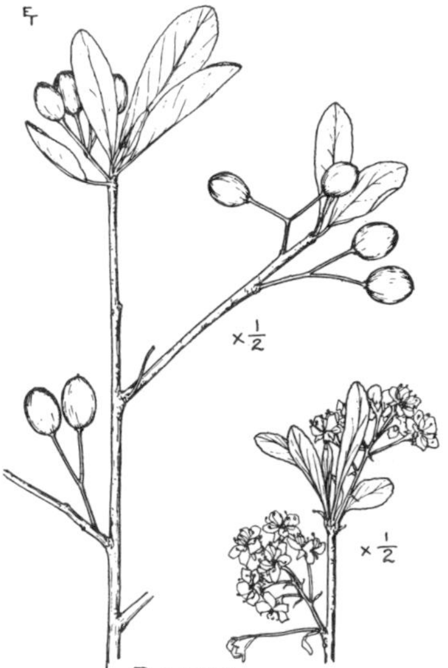

FIG. 220

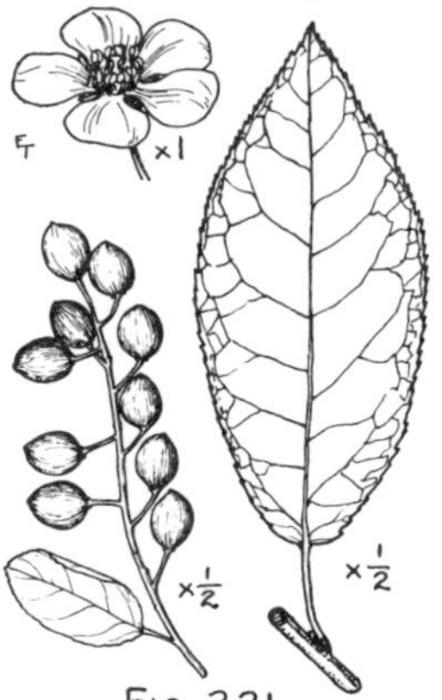

FIG. 221

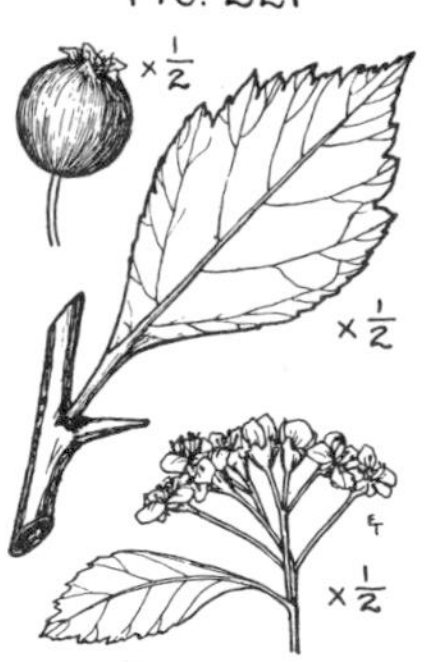

FIG. 222

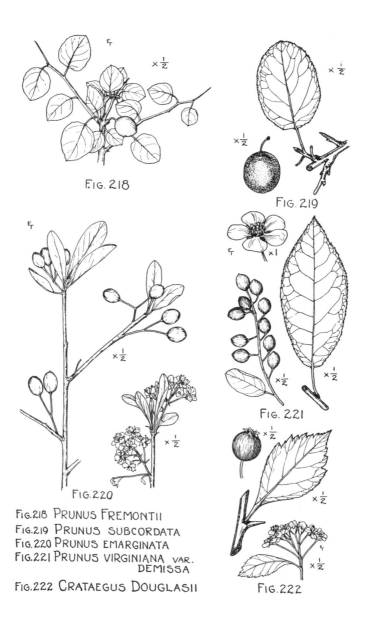

FIG. 218 PRUNUS FREMONTII
FIG. 219 PRUNUS SUBCORDATA
FIG. 220 PRUNUS EMARGINATA
FIG. 221 PRUNUS VIRGINIANA VAR. DEMISSA
FIG. 222 CRATAEGUS DOUGLASII

southern California and in the Coast Ranges, April and May, in the Sierra Nevada, June and July.

Bitter Cherry often forms extensive thickets on moist slopes and along stream banks in the Transition and Canadian Life Zones in the Coast Ranges, the mountains of southern California, and in the Sierra Nevada. It extends northward to Idaho and British Columbia and eastward to Nevada and Arizona.

Prunus emarginata (Dougl.) Walp. Rep. 2:9 (1843). *Cerasus emarginata* Dougl. Type locality: Upper part of the Columbia River. Collected by *Douglas.*

8. **Prunus virginiana** var. **demissa** (Nutt.) Torr. Western Choke-cherry. Fig. 221.

Usually an erect deciduous shrub, 3 to 12 feet high, but sometimes a small tree up to 20 feet high, with thin smooth or scaly dark red or brown bark and glabrous or pubescent young branchlets. Leaf-blades ovate or broadly elliptic, sometimes broader above the middle, abruptly taper-pointed at apex, rounded or slightly cordate at base, 1½ to 3½ inches long, ¾-inch to 2 inches wide, glabrous to slightly pubescent, finely serrate; petioles ⅜- to ¾-inch long, glabrous or pubescent, with 2 glands just below the attachment with the blades. Flowers white, ⅓- to ½-inch broad, numerous, in elongated cylindrical racemes 2 to 5 inches long terminating lateral leafy shoots; pedicels green, ¼- to ⅜-inch long. Fruit globose, ¼- to ½-inch in diameter, red to dark purple, bitter but edible. Flowering period, April and May.

Western Choke-cherry is widely distributed in moist places of the mountains throughout California, in the Upper Sonoran and Transition Life Zones. It extends from San Diego County northward in the Coast Ranges and in the Sierra Nevada to the mountains of northern California, thence northward to British Columbia and eastward to Nevada and Arizona.

Prunus virginiana var. demissa (Nutt.) Torr. Bot. Wilkes Exped. 248 (1874). *Cerasus demissa* Nutt. Type locality: "Plains of the Oregon [Columbia River] towards the sea, and at the mouth of the Wahlamet, *Nuttall;* Oregon, *Mr. Tolmie.*"

13. **Crataegus** L. Hawthorn

(From the ancient Greek *kratos,* strength, in reference to the hardness of the wood.)

This is a large genus of about 1000 species of the north temperate zone. Many are grown for their ornamental value. A single species is native to California.

1. **Crataegus Douglasii** Lindl. Black Hawthorn. Western Black Haw. Fig. 222.

A much branched shrub, 5 to 10 feet high, or a small tree, 15 to 30 feet high, with stout spreading or ascending branches armed with strong thorns. Leaves simple, alternate, deciduous; the blades obovate or ovate to broadly oval in outline, rounded or pointed at apex, wedge-shaped at base, 1 to 3 inches long, ¾-inch to 2 inches wide, 1-veined from the base, dark green and shining above, paler beneath, doubly serrate along the upper ⅔ of the margin or often lobed, entire at base; petioles ½-inch or less long, glabrous or often hairy, slightly margined by the extension of the bases of the leaf-blades. Flowers bisexual, white, heavy-scented, about ½-inch or less broad, in flat or convex clusters; sepals 5, sharp-pointed, united at base with the urn-shaped receptacle to form a receptocalyx-tube extending above the ovary; petals 5, distinct, roundish, about ⅛-inch or more long; stamens 10 to 20, inserted on the margin of the receptocalyx-tube; pistil 1, of 2 to 5 carpels embedded in the fleshy receptocalyx; ovary inferior, 2- to 5-celled; styles

2 to 5, distinct, surrounded by hairs at the base. Fruit drupe-like, ½-inch in diameter, sweet, black, with 1 to 5 bony nutlets or carpels, each containing a single seed. Flowering period, May to July.

Black Hawthorn inhabits canyon flats from Sonoma County north to Humboldt County, thence eastward to Trinity, Siskiyou, and Modoc counties, in the Transition Life Zone. It extends northward to British Columbia, eastward into Idaho, Montana, Wyoming, New Mexico, Colorado, and across the plains to Michigan.

There is some variation in the size of the fruit, in the leaf-margins, and in the size and number of thorns. Material collected by E. B. Copeland from Wildwood, Trinity County, altitude 3800 feet, has very small fruits and inconspicuous thorns. Some specimens from Humboldt County (*Joseph P. Tracy* 5977) have very stout thorns.

Crataegus Douglasii Lindl. Bot. Reg. t. 1810 (1836). *C. punctata* var. *brevispina* Dougl. Type locality: Northwest America. Collected by *Douglas*.

14. **Purshia** DC.

(Named after F. T. Pursh, author of the *Flora Americae Septentrionalis*.)

Diffusely branched shrubs. Leaves simple, alternate, deciduous or apparently evergreen, crowded and apparently fascicled, deeply 3-toothed or -lobed, with revolute margins. Flowers bisexual, solitary and terminal or few in the axils of the leaves, pale yellow or white; sepals 5, joined at base with the receptacle to form a receptocalyx; petals 5, distinct; stamens 18 to 30, inserted in one row with the petals on the margin of the receptocalyx-tube; pistils 1 or rarely 2; ovary superior, 1-celled. Fruit a leathery oblong pubescent achene, about ¼- to ½-inch long, tapering to the persistent style.

This is a western North American genus of 2 species, both native to California.

KEY TO THE SPECIES

Leaves without depressed glands, revolute only along the margins.
1. *P. tridentata*.

Leaves with distinct depressed glands, the blades rolled inwardly. 2. *P. glandulosa*.

1. **Purshia tridentata** (Pursh) DC. Bitterbrush. Antelope Brush. Fig. 223.

An erect widely branched silvery shrub, 2 to 8 feet high, with gray or brown bark, the young branches pubescent. Leaves wedge-shaped in outline, ¼- to ½-inch long or to 1 inch long on new growth, with 3 oblong lobes at the apex, green and finely pubescent above, white-tomentose beneath, the margins revolute, the base tapering to a very short petiole. Flowers about ⅔-inch broad, usually solitary and terminating short lateral branchlets; receptocalyx-tube often with numerous stalked resin glands; sepals persistent in fruit; petals pale yellow, obovate, ¼- to ⅓-inch long, with a slender claw or stalk. Flowering period, April to July.

Bitterbrush inhabits arid flats, valleys, slopes of the summits, and higher portions of the western slope and eastern side of the Sierra Nevada from Tulare and Inyo counties northward to the Warner Mountains of Modoc County, thence westward to Shasta, Siskiyou, Lassen, and northern Trinity counties, in the Upper Sonoran and Transition Life Zones. It extends northward to eastern Oregon and eastward throughout the Rocky Mountains.

This species is one of the most important browse plants of the West for game animals, sheep, and cattle.

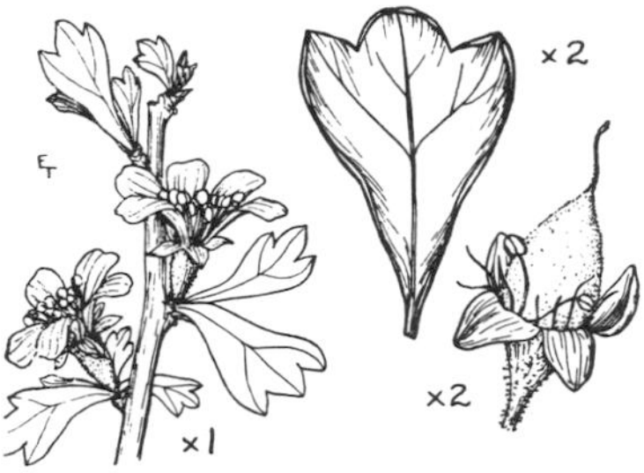

FIG. 223 PURSHIA TRIDENTATA

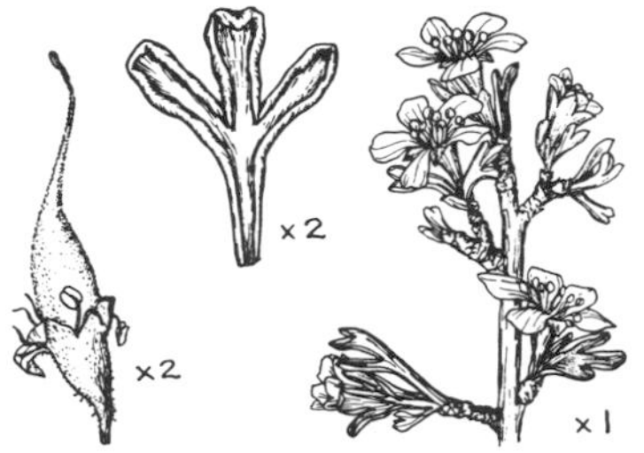

FIG. 224 PURSHIA GLANDULOSA

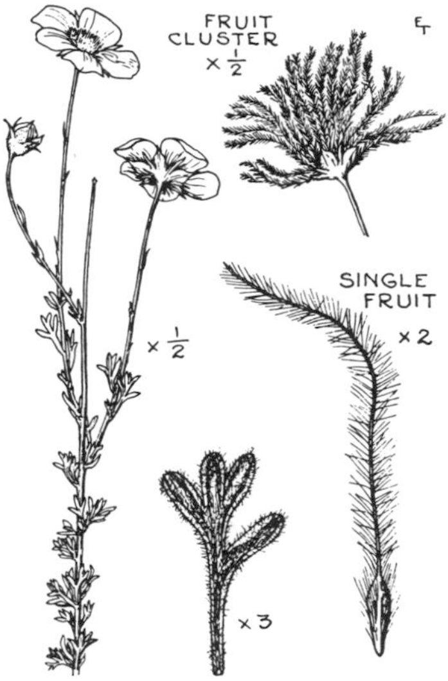

FIG. 225 FALLUGIA PARADOXA

FIG. 226 COWANIA MEXICANA VAR. STANSBURIANA

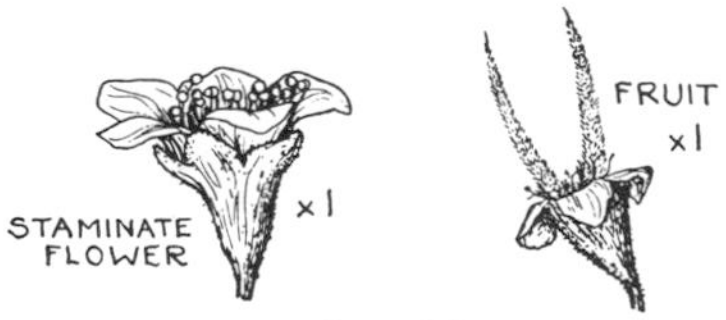

FIG. 227 COWANIA MEXICANA VAR. DUBIA

Purshia tridentata (Pursh) DC. Trans. Linn. Soc. 12:158 (1817). *Tigarea tridentata* Pursh. Type locality: "In the prairies of the Rocky-mountains (in Montana) and on the Columbia River." Collected by *Lewis*.

2. **Purshia glandulosa** Curran. WAXY BITTERBRUSH. Fig. 224.

An erect greenish shrub, 2 to 8 feet high, with grayish or dark brown bark. Leaves ¼- to ⅜-inch long, divided into 3 to 5 linear lobes or sometimes merely toothed, slightly hairy above when young but glabrate in age, depressed-glandular above and on the margins, the blades becoming revolute downward, the base tapering to a very short petiole. Flowers ½-inch or less wide, solitary and terminal on the short lateral leafy branchlets; receptocalyx-tube with or without glands, tomentulose; petals pale yellow or white. Fruit canescent. Flowering period, April to July.

Waxy Bitterbrush occurs in desert canyons and slopes of the mountains bordering the western part of the Colorado Desert and extends northward in the mountains of the Mohave Desert and westward to Mount Piños, Ventura County and northward to the desert mountains of Inyo and Mono counties, in the Upper Sonoran Life Zone. It extends eastward to Nevada.

Purshia glandulosa Curran, Bull. Calif. Acad. 1:153 (1885). Type locality: On the Mohave Desert side of the Tehachapi Pass. Collected by *Curran*.

15. **Fallugia** Endl.

(Named after Virgilio Fallugi, an Italian abbot and botanical writer.)

This genus contains a single species native to arid western North America.

1. **Fallugia paradoxa** (D. Don) Endl. APACHE PLUME. Fig. 225.

A much branched deciduous shrub, 1 to 5 feet high, with straw-colored branches and flaky bark. Leaves alternate and in clusters along the branchlets, pinnately dissected into 3 to 7 linear divisions with revolute margins, ½-inch to 1 inch long, the upper surface puberulent, rusty beneath. Flowers usually bisexual (rarely only staminate), large, white, 1 to 1½ inches across, solitary (or rarely 2 or 3) on long peduncles at the ends of the branches; sepals 5, joined at the base with the receptacle to form a short hemispherical receptocalyx-tube, alternating with 5 supplementary bractlets; petals 5, distinct, rounded, ½- to ¾-inch long, spreading, white or yellowish white; stamens numerous, inserted in 3 series on the margin of the receptocalyx; pistils numerous, villous, inserted on a conical portion of the receptacle; ovaries superior, 1-celled; styles slender, twisted, persistent in fruit. Fruit composed of numerous oblong villous achenes, ⅛-inch or less long, with long plumose persistent styles 1 to 1½ inches long. Flowering period, April and May.

Apache Plume occurs in the New York, Providence, Old Dad, and Clark mountains of eastern San Bernardino County, in the Lower Sonoran Life Zone. It extends eastward to Nevada, Arizona, southern Utah, Colorado, and to western Texas and southward to Mexico.

This handsome shrub should be brought into cultivation in the drier parts of California. It grows rapidly and produces numerous large white flowers which are followed by large clusters of plumose fruits, these at first greenish and later pink or reddish-tinged. In New Mexico and Arizona it is a valuable forage plant for cattle, sheep, and goats. The Hopi Indians of Arizona use an infusion of the leaves for washing the hair in order to promote its growth. It is reported to be an important erosion-control plant in the arid regions of the Southwest.

Fallugia paradoxa (D. Don) Endl.; Torr. in Emory, Notes Mil. Rec. 140 (1848). *Sieversia paradoxa* D. Don. Type locality: Mexico. Collected by *Mociño* and *Sesse*.

16. **Cowania** D. Don

(Named after James Cowan, an English merchant, who introduced many Peruvian and Mexican plants into England.)

This is a small genus of 2 to 6 species of shrubs from the southwestern United States and Mexico. Two varieties of one species are native to California.

KEY TO THE VARIETIES

Pistils 5 to 10; fruit with long plumose tails. . . . . 1. *C. mexicana* var. *Stansburiana*.
Pistils 2 or 3; fruit with short and hairy but not plumose tails.
1a. *C. mexicana* var. *dubia*.

1. **Cowania mexicana** var. **Stansburiana** (Torr.) Jepson. CLIFFROSE. Fig. 226.

A much branched evergreen shrub, 1 to 6 feet high, with gray shreddy bark.

Leaves simple, alternate, obovate in general outline, ¼- to ½-inch long, pinnately 3- to 5-divided or -lobed, the lobes revolute, glandular-dotted and green above, more or less white-tomentulose beneath. Flowers bisexual or rarely only staminate, ½- to ¾-inch broad, solitary and terminal on the short branchlets; peduncles ¼-inch or less long; sepals 5, persistent, united at the base with the receptacle to form a receptocalyx, without alternating supplementary bracts; petals 5, distinct, cream-colored or sulphur-yellow or rarely white, broadly ovate, about ¼-inch long; stamens numerous, in 2 series, inserted in the throat of the receptocalyx; pistils 5 to 10, distinct, densely villous-hirsute; ovaries superior, 1-celled. Fruit composed of oblong achenes, about ⅛-inch long, striate, nearly included in the receptocalyx-tube, tailed by elongated plumose styles 1 to 2 inches long. Flowering period, April to June.

Cliffrose occurs on dry canyon slopes in the Providence, Panamint, New York, Clark, Inyo, and White mountains of eastern Mohave Desert and Inyo County. It extends eastward to Nevada, Arizona, Utah, Colorado, and New Mexico and southward to Mexico. This variety is an important browse plant for cattle, sheep, and deer.

1a. Var. **dubia** Brandg. Fig. 227.

Pistils 2 or 3. Fruits with short tails, these densely hairy but not plumose.

To my knowledge, this variety has been collected only from the Providence Mountains of eastern San Bernardino County. Rydberg *(North American Flora)* suggests that this variety may be a hybrid between *Purshia tridentata* (Pursh) DC. and *Cowania Stansburiana* Torr.

Cowania mexicana var. Stansburiana (Torr.) Jepson, Man. 498 (1925). *C. Stansburiana* Torr. Type locality: Stansbury Island, Great Salt Lake, Utah. Collected by *Stansbury*.

Var. dubia Brandg. Zoe 5:149 (1903). Type locality: Providence Mountains. Collected by *T. S. Brandegee*.

17. **Cercocarpus** H. B. K. Mountain-mahogany. Hard-tack

(From the Greek *kerkis,* a shuttle, and *karpos,* fruit, in reference to the fruit with a twisted tail.)

Evergreen or deciduous shrubs or small trees with hard wood and short spur-like leaf-bearing branchlets. Leaves simple, alternate, with small early-falling stipules. Flowers bisexual, small, solitary or few to several in a cluster, axillary or terminal; sepals 5, united below with the tubular portion of the receptacle to form a narrow tubular receptocalyx which expands abruptly at the summit into 5 free segments, these soon deciduous; petals none; stamens numerous, inserted in 2 or 3 rows at different heights on the receptocalyx-tube; pistil 1; ovary superior, 1-celled; style elongated, hairy, persistent on the ovary. Fruit a hard villous achene, included within the persistent receptocalyx-tube, tipped by the twisted hairy persistent style.

This genus with about 20 species is strictly North American, confined mostly to the western United States and Mexico. Six species are native to California and the adjacent islands.

KEY TO THE SPECIES

Leaves entire, revolute; flowers sessile, solitary or rarely in pairs.

Leaves narrowly lanceolate or elliptical, ½-inch to 1 inch long, only slightly revolute; shrubs or small trees without spines. . . . . 1. *C. ledifolius.*

Fig. 228. Western Mountain-mahogany. *Cercocarpus betuloides* Nutt.

Leaves appearing linear, ½-inch or less long, strongly revolute; shrubs more or less spinescent. . . . . 2. *C. intricatus.*

Leaves more or less toothed, at least near the apex; flowers pedicelled, usually in clusters of 2 to several.

Leaves mostly obovate or elliptic, usually less than 1 inch long; flowers usually solitary or 2 or 3 in a cluster (up to 15 in one variety of *C. betuloides*).

Flowers about ¼-inch broad; leaves pubescent and more or less whitish beneath, usually obovate. . . . . 3. *C. betuloides.*

Flowers about ⅛-inch broad; leaves glabrous on both surfaces, yellowish green beneath, elliptic. . . . . 4. *C. minutiflorus.*

Leaves broadly elliptical or oval, usually over 1 inch long.

Under surface of leaves and receptocalyx subglabrous. . . . . 5. *C. alnifolius.*

Under surface of leaves and receptocalyx white-tomentose. . . . . 6. *C. Traskiae.*

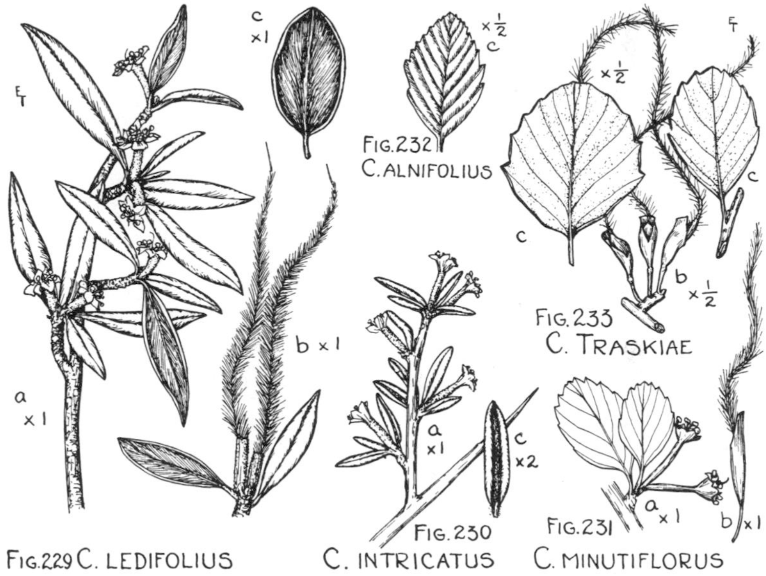

CERCOCARPUS. a, Flowering branchlet. b, Fruit. c, Leaf.

1. **Cercocarpus ledifolius** Nutt. DESERT MOUNTAIN-MAHOGANY. DESERT-MAHOGANY. CURLLEAF MOUNTAIN-MAHOGANY. Fig. 229.

An erect shrub, 6 to 12 feet high, or sometimes a small tree up to 30 feet high and with a trunk 2 feet in diameter, with stout contorted branches forming a spreading crown; bark gray, smooth on young branches, rough and furrowed on old stems. Leaf-blades elliptic to lanceolate, pointed at both ends, ½-inch to 1 inch long, about ¼-inch wide, leathery, somewhat resinous and glabrous above, white-hairy beneath, the margins entire and rolled toward the lower surface, the midrib very prominent; petioles about ⅓-inch or less long. Flowers commonly solitary, sessile, sometimes 2 to 8 in a cluster on the short leaf-bearing branchlets; receptocalyx-tube whitened by a villous tomentum, about ⅓-inch long in fruit. Fruit including the persistent twisted plumose style 2 to 3 inches long. Flowering period, April to June.

Desert Mountain-mahogany inhabits dry slopes and flats of the mountains bordering the Mohave and Colorado deserts and along the eastern slopes and ridges of the Sierra Nevada and adjacent desert mountains from Kern County northward to Modoc County and thence westward to Siskiyou County. It extends westward in the Tehachapi Mountains to San Emigdio Canyon in the Mount Piños region. Outside the state it ranges northward to Washington and eastward to Nevada, Utah, Colorado, Idaho, and Montana.

Cercocarpus ledifolius Nutt.; T. & G. Fl. N. Am. 1:427 (1840). Type locality: On the summits of the hills of Bear River, in the Rocky Mountains of Idaho. Collected by *Nuttall.*

2. **Cercocarpus intricatus** Wats. LITTLELEAF MOUNTAIN-MAHOGANY. Fig. 230.

An intricately branched more or less spinescent shrub, 2 to 4 feet high, with fissured ashy bark. Leaf-blades oblong to almost linear, ½-inch or less long, dark green and glabrous above in age, white-pubescent beneath, the margins strongly revolute and almost meeting over the midrib beneath, apparently sessile or very short-petiolate. Flowers solitary or in pairs, almost sessile; receptocalyx-tube hairy. Fruit including the persistent plumose style 1 to 1¾ inches long. Flowering period, March and April.

Littleleaf Mountain-mahogany occurs in the Panamint, White, Clark, and Providence mountains of eastern San Bernardino and Inyo counties. It extends eastward to Arizona, Nevada, southwestern Colorado, and Utah where, according to Tidestrom, it intergrades with *C. ledifolius.*

Cercocarpus intricatus Wats. Proc. Am. Acad. 10:346 (1875). *C. breviflorus* Wats., not Gray. Type locality: American Fork Canyon of the Wasatch Mountains, Utah. Collected by *Watson.*

3. **Cercocarpus betuloides** Nutt. WESTERN MOUNTAIN-MAHOGANY. HARD-TACK. Fig. 228.

KEY TO THE SPECIES AND VARIETIES

Flowers in clusters of 2 or 3.
  Leaves normally ½-inch to 1 inch long.......................*C. betuloides.*
  Leaves 1¼ to 2¼ inches long...........................3a. var. *macrourus.*
Flowers in clusters of 5 to 12; leaves 1 to 1½ inches long......3b. var. *multiflorus.*

A loosely spreading shrub, 5 to 12 feet high, or a small tree up to 20 feet high, with smooth gray or brown bark and spreading somewhat recurved branches. Leaves usually clustered on short lateral spur-like branchlets; leaf-blades usually obovate or broadly elliptical, ½-inch to 1 inch (or rarely up to 2 inches) long, ⅜-inch to 1 inch wide, wedge-shaped and entire below the middle, serrate above, dark green and glabrous on the upper surface, paler and prominently feather-veined beneath, glabrous or variably pubescent; petioles ⅛- to ¼-inch long. Flowers in clusters of 2 or 3, short-pedicelled; receptocalyx-tube at first hairy but becoming glabrous and reddish brown in age, splitting about halfway on one side in fruit. Fruit distinctly hairy, surmounted by a plumose twisted persistent style 2 to 3½ inches long; fruiting pedicel ¼-inch or less long. Flowering period, March to May.

Western Mountain-mahogany inhabits dry slopes of the foothills and lower mountain slopes in the Upper Sonoran Life Zone of the mountains of southern

California (west of the desert areas), the Coast Ranges, the western slope of the Sierra Nevada, and the Siskiyou Mountain area of northern California. It extends northward to Oregon, eastward to Nevada, and southward into Lower California.

This species is an important browse shrub for cattle, sheep, and deer. It crown-sprouts after fires or cutting and the young shoots and leaves are very palatable. The names Mountain Ironwood, Sweet Brush, and Birchleaf Mountain-mahogany are often applied to this shrub.

3a. Var. **macrourus** (Rydb.) Jepson.

Leaves 1¼ to 2¼ inches long.

This variety occurs on lava beds and rocky mountain slopes at about 4000 feet elevation in Modoc and Siskiyou counties, California and in Klamath County, Oregon (Barkley Spring, *Applegate*).

3b. Var. **multiflorus** Jepson.

Leaves 1 to 2½ inches long. Flowers 5 to 12 in a cluster.

This variety occurs in the Santa Ana Mountains (Claymine Canyon, *J. T. Howell*), the San Gabriel Mountains (Mount Wilson, *C. E. Hutchinson*), and on Santa Catalina Island.

Cercocarpus betuloides Nutt.; T. & G. Fl. N. Am. 1:427 (1840). Type locality: "Mountains of Santa Barbara." Collected by *Nuttall.*

Var. macrourus (Rydb.) Jepson, Man. 503 (1925). *C. macrourus* Rydb. Type locality: Modoc County, California. Collected by *M. S. Baker.*

Var. multiflorus Jepson, Man. 503 (1925). Type locality: Avalon, Santa Catalina Island. Collected by *Jepson.*

4. **Cercocarpus minutiflorus** Abrams. San Diego Mountain-mahogany. Fig. 231.

This is a small-flowered mountain-mahogany similar to *C. betuloides.* The leaves are usually elliptic, glabrous on both sides, and yellowish green beneath. The flowers are about ⅛-inch broad. It occurs on the chaparral covered hills and flats of southern San Diego County and in Lower California.

Cercocarpus minutiflorus Abrams, Bull. Torr. Club 37:149 (1910). Type locality: Hills near San Dieguito (Bernardo), San Diego County. Collected by *Abrams.*

5. **Cercocarpus alnifolius** Rydb. Alderleaf Mountain-mahogany. Fig. 232.

A large shrub or small tree, 8 to 20 feet high. Leaf-blades broadly elliptical, 1¼ to 2¼ inches long, thick and leathery, dark green and glabrous above, paler and subglabrous beneath. Flowering period, March and April.

Alderleaf Mountain-mahogany is very closely related to some of the forms of *C. betuloides* with larger leaves and perhaps should be treated as a variety of that species. It occurs on Santa Catalina and Santa Cruz islands.

Cercocarpus alnifolius Rydb. N. Am. Fl. 22:421 (1913). Type locality: Avalon, Santa Catalina Island. Collected by *Blanche Trask.*

6. **Cercocarpus Traskiae** Eastw. Catalina Hard-tack. Fig. 233.

This species is very similar to *C. alnifolius.* The leaves are densely white-tomentose beneath and the margins are distinctly revolute in age. It occurs on Santa Catalina and Santa Cruz islands, but is not common.

Cercocarpus Traskiae Eastw. Proc. Calif. Acad. ser. 3, 1:136 (1898). Type locality: Salta Verde, Santa Catalina Island. Collected by *Blanche Trask.*

Fig. 234. CREAMBUSH. *Holodiscus discolor* (Pursh) Maxim.

18. **Holodiscus** Maxim.

(From the Greek *holo,* whole, and *diskos,* a disk, referring to the entire disk of the flower.)

This is a small genus of 2 to 5 closely related species of spiraea-like shrubs occurring in western North America. A single species with 2 varieties is native to California.

1. **Holodiscus discolor** (Pursh) Maxim. CREAMBUSH. Fig. 234.

This species is composed of a complex of variations which are not easily separable because of numerous intergrades. The following key will identify the species and 2 more or less typical forms.

Leaves 5/8-inch to 3 inches long; erect shrubs 3 to 6 or 20 feet high; panicles much branched . . . . *H. discolor.*

Leaves usually less than 5/8-inch long; low diffusely spreading or nearly prostrate shrubs 1 to 4 feet high; panicles relatively simple.

Leaves white-tomentose beneath, not glandular-dotted. . . . . . . 1a. var. *dumosus.*

Leaves sparingly pubescent, conspicuously glandular-dotted.
1b. var. *glabrescens.*

Erect or spreading shrubs, 3 to 20 feet high, with light brown or ashy-gray bark, often shreddy on the older shoots. Leaves simple, alternate, deciduous; the blades ovate in outline, 5/8-inch to 3 inches long, 3/8-inch to 2 inches wide, broadly wedge-shaped and entire at base, coarsely toothed above, green and slightly pubescent and often impressed-veiny on the upper surface, more or less white-hairy and prominently veined beneath; petioles 1/8- to 3/4-inch long. Flowers bisexual, numerous, small, about 1/8-inch broad, creamy-white, in ample compound clusters terminating and somewhat drooping from the ends of the branchlets; sepals 5, persistent and erect in fruit; petals 5, distinct, elliptic; stamens 20, inserted on the ring-like entire disk lining the receptocalyx-tube; pistils 5, distinct; ovaries superior, 1-celled. Fruit small hairy 1-seeded almost indehiscent pods, 1/8-inch or less long. Flowering period, May to July.

This species inhabits moist hill slopes and canyons throughout the Coast Ranges from Orange County northward to Del Norte and Siskiyou counties and occasionally in the Sierra Nevada and on Santa Cruz Island, in the Transition Life Zone. It extends northward to British Columbia and eastward to the Rocky Mountains.

Creambush, also known as Ocean Spray, Meadow Sweet, and California-spiraea, is a very ornamental shrub when in full bloom. Its panicles are sometimes 12 inches long. It deserves a much wider use in landscaping in the coastal area of the Pacific slope. Propagation is easily made from cuttings.

1a. Var. **dumosus** (Nutt.) Dippel. ROCK-SPIRAEA.

A low often prostrate shrub, 1 to 3 feet high. Leaf-blades 5/8-inch or less long, soft-puberulent or white-tomentose beneath, subsessile. Panicles rather simple, 1 to 2 1/2 inches long. Petals often pinkish. Flowering period, June to August.

Rock-spiraea inhabits rocky ledges, cliffs, and rocky summits of the higher mountains of the North Coast Ranges, the Sierra Nevada, the Panamint, White, and Providence mountains, Mount Piños, and the mountains of southern California, from 6000 to 11,000 feet elevation.

1b. Var. **glabrescens** (Greenman) Jepson.

A diffusely branched shrub, 1 to 4 feet high. Leaf-blades 5/8-inch or less long,

Fig. 235. Oso Berry. *Osmaronia cerasiformis* (T. & G.) Greene.

sparingly hairy or nearly glabrous, conspicuously glandular-dotted, decurrent on the short petioles.

This variety occurs on rocky slopes and ridges from 4000 to 9500 feet elevation on Mount Shasta and other high mountains of Siskiyou County, in the Warner Mountains of Modoc County, on Lassen Peak, and southward on "easterly slopes or east side of the Sierra Nevada" *(Jepson)* to Placer County. It extends northward into the Cascades of Oregon and eastward to Utah.

Holodiscus discolor (Pursh) Maxim. Acta. Hort. Petrop. 6:254 (1879). *Spiraea discolor* Pursh. Type locality: "On the banks of the Kooskoosky." Clearwater River, Idaho. Collected by *Lewis*.

Var. dumosus (Nutt.) Dippel, Handb. Laubh. 3:508 (1893). *Spiraea dumosa* Nutt. Type locality: "Rocky Mountains." Collected by *Nuttall*. *Holodiscus dumosus* (Nutt.) Heller.

Var. glabrescens (Greenman) Jepson, Man. 479 (1925). *Spiraea discolor* var. *glabrescens* Greenman. Type locality: "Oregon, Stein's Mountains." Collected by *Cusick*.

19. **Osmaronia** Greene

(From the Greek *osme,* fragrant, and *Aronia,* a genus of the Rose Family proposed by Persoon.)

This genus contains a single species.

1. **Osmaronia cerasiformis** (T. & G.) Greene. Oso Berry. Fig. 235.

An erect shrub, 3 to 12 feet high, with rather straight slender stems, smooth gray or reddish brown bark, and light green foliage. Leaves simple, alternate, deciduous, scattered along the branches; the blades oblong-ovate, narrowed to each end, sometimes blunter at the apex, 1½ to 3½ inches long, ¾-inch to 1 inch wide, 1-veined from the base, glabrous, light green above, paler beneath, entire; petioles ¼- to ½-inch long. Flowers dioecious, white, fragrant, arranged in terminal clusters; sepals 5, united at the base with the receptacle to form a receptocalyx; petals 5, distinct, inserted upon the receptocalyx-tube, spreading in the staminate flowers, erect in the pistillate flowers, ¼-inch or less long; stamens 15, in 3 rows, 10 inserted with the petals, 5 inserted lower on the disk lining the receptocalyx-tube, abortive in the pistillate flowers; pistils 5, distinct; ovaries superior, 1-celled. Fruit consisting of 1 to 5 ovoid blue-black drupes about ⅜-inch long, the pulp very thin and bitter. Flowering period, January to April.

Oso Berry inhabits the moist slopes of canyons in the Transition Life Zone from Del Norte County south in the Coast Ranges to northern Santa Barbara County, mainly in the outer ranges, and in the Sierra Nevada from Shasta County southward to Tulare County at 1500 to 4500 feet elevation. It extends northward to British Columbia.

The light yellowish green foliage, clusters of white flowers, numerous green drupes changing from pink or red to blue-black, its freedom from garden pests, and ease of propagation by cuttings or from seeds make this a desirable plant for ornamental use. It grows best in moist habitats.

Osmaronia cerasiformis (T. & G.) Greene, Pitt. 2:191 (1891). *Nuttallia cerasiformis* T. & G. Type locality: Columbia River. Collected by *Nuttall*.

20. **Photinia** Lindl.

(From the Greek *photeinos,* shining, alluding to the shining foliage.)

This genus consists of about 25 species native to Europe, southern Asia, western

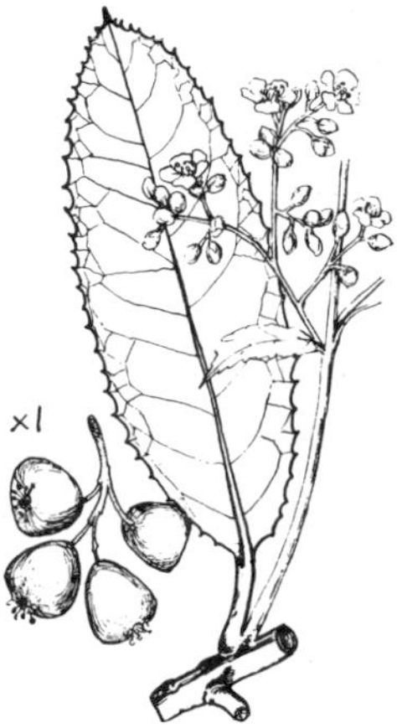

Fig. 236
PHOTINIA ARBUTIFOLIA

Fig. 237
PERAPHYLLUM RAMOSISSIMUM

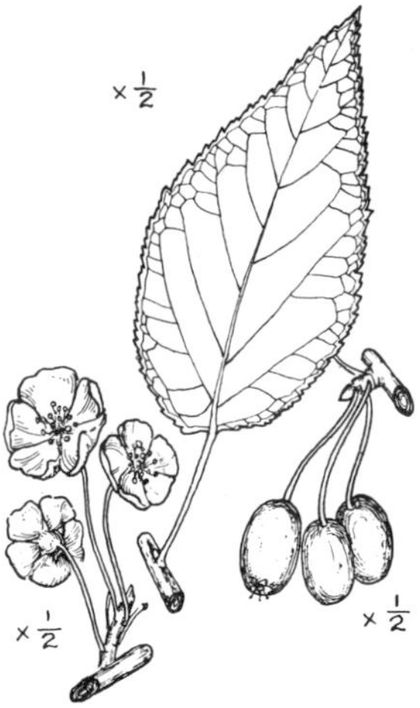

Fig. 238
PYRUS FUSCA
(from Pacific Coast Trees, Univ. of Calif. Press)

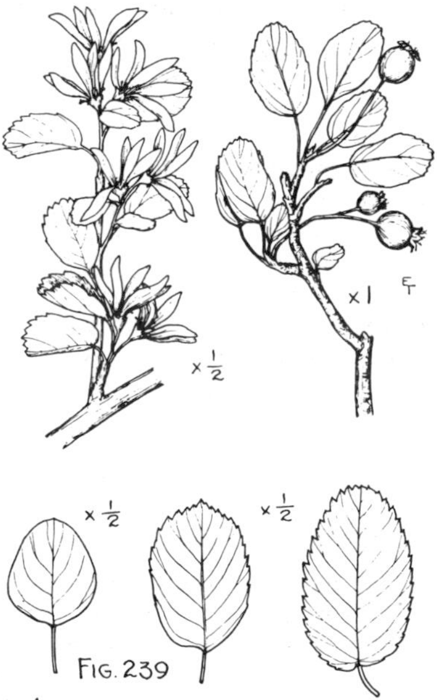

Fig. 239
AMELANCHIER ALNIFOLIA

North America, and Central America. One species is native to California.

1. **Photinia arbutifolia** (Ait.) Lindl. TOYON. CHRISTMAS BERRY. CALIFORNIA-HOLLY. Fig. 236.

A large erect bushy evergreen shrub or small tree, 6 to 10 feet high. Leaves simple, alternate, with minute early-falling stipules; the blades oblong or elliptical, acute at both ends, 2 to 4 inches long, 3/4-inch to 1 1/2 inches wide, 1-veined from the base, thick and leathery, dark glossy green above, lighter beneath, the margins regularly toothed and bristly pointed petioles 1/2-inch to 1 inch long. Flowers bisexual, small, white, in large terminal clusters; sepals 5, persistent, united at the base with the receptacle to form a receptocalyx; petals 5, distinct, spreading; stamens 10, in pairs opposite the calyx-lobes; pistils 2 or 3, at first only slightly united to the receptocalyx-tube, in age completely united and covered by the receptocalyx. Fruit bright or pale red, rarely yellowish, berry-like, 1/4-inch or more in diameter. Flowering period, June and July. Fruit, November to January.

Toyon inhabits rocky lower mountain slopes, foothills, and canyon bottoms in the lower Sierra Nevada from Shasta and Tehama counties southward to Tulare County, in the Coast Ranges from Humboldt County southward to the mountains of southern California, and on Santa Catalina and San Clemente islands. It extends southward to Lower California. On San Clemente and Santa Catalina islands, a form occurs with larger and rarely yellow berries. Yellow berries occur occasionally throughout the range of the species and the yellow color seems to be associated with a pathological condition of the leaves and fruits.

The large clusters of red berries against the deep green foliage make this one of the most handsome of the native shrubs. During the past fifteen years, it has been extensively planted in parks and gardens. The fruit and foliage are much used for Christmas decorations. With proper cutting of the branches the shrubs are not harmed and the quality of the berries is improved.

Photinia arbutifolia (Ait.) Lindl. Bot. Reg. 6, pl. 491 (1820). *Crataegus arbutifolia* Ait. Type specimen cultivated from seeds collected in California by *Menzies*. *P. arbutifolia* var. *cerina* Jepson. *P. arbutifolia* var. *macrocarpa* Munz.

21. **Peraphyllum** Nutt.

(From the Greek *pera,* excessively, and *phullon,* leaf, in reference to the crowded leaves.)

This genus consists of a single species native to the western United States.

1. **Peraphyllum ramosissimum** Nutt. SQUAW-APPLE. WILD CRAB. Fig. 237.

An intricately branched deciduous shrub, 2 to 6 feet high, with gray branches. Leaves simple, alternate, mostly clustered at the ends of the short branchlets; the blades oblanceolate, obtuse or acute at apex, narrowed at base, 1/2-inch to 2 inches long, 1/4- to 3/8-inch wide, 1-veined from the base, light green and glabrous or pubescent above, paler beneath with minute pubescence, the margins minutely serrate or almost entire, often tipped with deciduous glands; petioles 1/8-inch or less long. Flowers bisexual, solitary or 2 or 3 together, pale pink, fragrant; sepals 5, reflexed, persistent, united at the base to the urn-shaped receptacle and forming a receptocalyx which is adnate to the ovary; petals 5, distinct, roundish, spreading, about 1/4- to 1/3-inch long; stamens about 20, distinct, inserted on the margin of the receptocalyx; pistil 1, of 1 to 5 united carpels; ovary inferior, 2- to 4-celled; styles 2. Fruit a globose fleshy bitter pome, about 1/2-inch or less in diameter, greenish yellow when mature, not edible. Flowering period, April to May.

Squaw-apple inhabits moist slopes and ravines of the plateau area of Modoc, Lassen, and northeastern Shasta counties at about 4000 to 5000 feet elevation. It extends northward to southern Oregon and eastward to the Rocky Mountains.

Peraphyllum ramosissimum Nutt.; T. & G. Fl. N. Am. 1:474 (1840). Type locality: "Near the Blue Mountains of Oregon." Collected by *Nuttall.*

22. **Pyrus** L. Pear. Apple

(From the Latin name of the pear.)

This is a polymorphic genus of probably 60 species in the north temperate zone. Many are grown for ornamentals and some for their fruit. One species is native to California.

1. **Pyrus fusca** Raf. Oregon Crab Apple. Fig. 238.

A many-stemmed shrub or more commonly a tree, 10 to 50 feet high. Leaves simple, alternate, deciduous, with early-falling stipules; the blades ovate, pointed at apex, 1 to 3 inches long, ½-inch to 1½ inches wide, 1-veined from the base, usually serrate but some often slightly lobed, pale green above, eventually rusty-tomentose beneath; petioles ¼-inch to 1 inch long. Flowers bisexual, white, 4 to 12 in flat-topped clusters; sepals 5, united at the base with the receptacle to form an urn-shaped receptocalyx which surrounds the ovary and becomes fleshy in fruit; petals 5, distinct, elliptical, ¼- to ½-inch long; stamens about 20, inserted on the margin of the receptocalyx; pistil 1, of 3 to 5 united carpels; ovary inferior, 3- to 5-celled. Fruit an oblong or ovoid pome, about ½-inch long, yellowish, becoming brown or purplish black when ripe. Flowering period, April to June.

Oregon Crab Apple occurs occasionally in fertile valleys and canyons of the North Coast Range from Napa and Sonoma counties northward to Del Norte County, in the Transition Life Zone. It extends northward to Alaska.

Pyrus fusca Raf. Med. Fl. 2:254 (1830). Type locality not known. *P. diversifolia* Bong. *P. rivularis* Dougl.

23. **Amelanchier** Medic. June Berry. Service Berry

(The Savoy name of the Medlar.)

This genus consists of about 12 species native to the north temperate zone. A single polymorphic species is native to California.

1. **Amelanchier alnifolia** Nutt. Western Service Berry. Fig. 239.

An erect deciduous shrub, 4 to 15 feet high, with gray bark on the older stems and smooth and reddish brown bark on the younger stems and branches. Leaves simple, alternate, usually borne on short lateral branchlets; the blades mostly broadly oval or elliptic, ¾-inch to 1¾ inches long, ½-inch to 1 inch wide, 1-veined from the rounded to slightly cordate base, dark or pale green and glabrous or pubescent above, paler and slightly pubescent beneath, serrate above the middle or subentire to entire; petioles ¼- to ¾-inch long. Flowers bisexual, white, in racemes 1 to 2 inches long, or rarely solitary; sepals 5, joined at the base to the receptacle to form a receptocalyx which is adnate to the ovary, the free segments persistent on the fruit; petals 5, distinct, oblanceolate, ½- to ¾-inch long, falling early; stamens numerous, inserted on the receptocalyx-tube; pistil 1; ovary inferior, 5-celled; styles 5, united below. Fruit a bluish or purplish berry-like pome, about ¼-inch in diameter, juicy and edible. Flowering period, May and June.

Western Service Berry occurs in moist habitats of the mountain slopes throughout California. In the southern part of the state and in the Sierra Nevada it ranges from 2500 to 9000 feet elevation and in the Coast Ranges it approaches sea level. Outside the state, it extends as far north as Alaska, eastward throughout the Rocky Mountains, thence to Nebraska and Michigan. Its profuse white flowers and purplish fruit make it very attractive in cultivation. This species can be propagated from one-year old seeds or from cuttings. The Indians and early mountain settlers used the edible fruits for food.

Much variation occurs in the shape, size, amount of pubescence, and margins of the leaves and in the amount of pubescence on the calyx-lobes. These variations have furnished material for the descriptions of several species and many varieties. Until more knowledge is obtained concerning the constancy of these variations under known cultural conditions, it seems best to consider them as minor variations of the species. There seems to be much intergrading of characters throughout the range of distribution of this species.

Amelanchier alnifolia Nutt. Jour. Phil. Acad. 7:22 (1834). *Aronia alnifolia* Nutt. Type locality: Fort Mandan, North Dakota to the Rocky Mountains. Collected by *Wyeth*.

Fabaceae (Leguminosae). Pea Family

The Pea Family is the second largest family of true flowering plants, containing about 550 genera and 12,000 species of world-wide distribution. Twenty-six genera and about 250 species are native to California, of which 41 species are shrubs or subshrubs. Certain introduced shrubby species have become naturalized in a few localities and are here included.

KEY TO THE GENERA

Plants with spines or thorns.
  Branchlets ending in a spine or thorn.
    Stamens monadelphous or diadelphous.
      Stamens monadelphous.
        Flowers yellow; leaves spine-like or the branchlets leafless; pods flat, villous, about ½-inch long . . . . 1. ULEX.
        Flowers not yellow; leaves unequally pinnate or simple, not spine-like; pods thickish, ovate, 1- or 2-seeded, not constricted between the seeds, less than ½-inch long . . . . 2. DALEA.
      Stamens diadelphous; leaves simple; pods 1- or 2-seeded, usually constricted between the seeds . . . . 3. ALHAGI.
    Stamens distinct, 10.
      Flowers yellow, nearly regular, in racemes; leaves bipinnate. 4. CERCIDIUM MICROPHYLLUM.
      Flowers purple, irregular, solitary; leaves palmately 1- to 3-foliolate. 5. PICKERINGIA.
  Branchlets not ending in a spine.
    Leaf-rachis terminated by a blunt point or short spine; leaves once-pinnate; flowers large, nearly regular, in racemes . . . . 6. CASSIA ARMATA.
    Leaf-rachis not terminated by a spine; leaves twice-pinnate.
      Branches with short curved spines the shape of a cat's claw; stamens numerous . . . . 7. ACACIA.

Branches armed with solitary or paired axillary thorns; stamens 10, distinct.
Flowers small, sessile, in axillary cylindrical spikes..........8. PROSOPIS.
Flowers larger, on jointed pedicels in axillary racemes.
4. CERCIDIUM FLORIDUM.
Plants without spines or thorns.
Leaves simple, rounded to heart-shaped..........................9. CERCIS.
Leaves compound.
Leaves palmately compound.
Leaves with 3 leaflets or the branchlets leafless...............10. CYTISUS.
Leaves with more than 3 leaflets..........................11. LUPINUS.
Leaves pinnately compound.
Leaves once-pinnately compound.
Leaves even-pinnate; flowers nearly regular...........6. CASSIA COVESII.
Leaves odd-pinnate; flowers distinctly irregular.
Leaves 4 inches or more long, with 11 to 27 leaflets......12. AMORPHA.
Leaves less than 4 inches long.
Flowers yellow, solitary or in umbels...................13. LOTUS.
Flowers not yellow, in spikes or racemes................2. DALEA.
Leaves twice-pinnately compound.
Leaves equally pinnate with 2 to 4 (rarely 1) pairs of pinnae; flowers in dense heads; pods straight.......................14. CALLIANDRA.
Leaves with one pair of lateral pinnae and a terminal pinna twice as long as the lateral ones; flowers in racemes; pods crescent-shaped.
15. HOFFMANSEGGIA.

1. **Ulex** L. GORSE

(From the Latin name of some similar plant.)

This genus consists of about 20 species of woody plants in western and southern Europe and northern Africa. A single species has become naturalized in parts of California.

1. **Ulex europaeus** L. GORSE. FURZE. Fig. 240.

A densely spiny much branched shrub, 2 to 6 feet high, with dark green almost leafless branches terminated by spiny tips. Flowering period, April to September.

Gorse has become naturalized in a few localities in the Oakland Hills, and in San Mateo, San Francisco, Marin, Sonoma, and Mendocino counties. It spreads readily by means of numerous seeds.

Ulex europaeus L. Sp. Pl. 741 (1753).

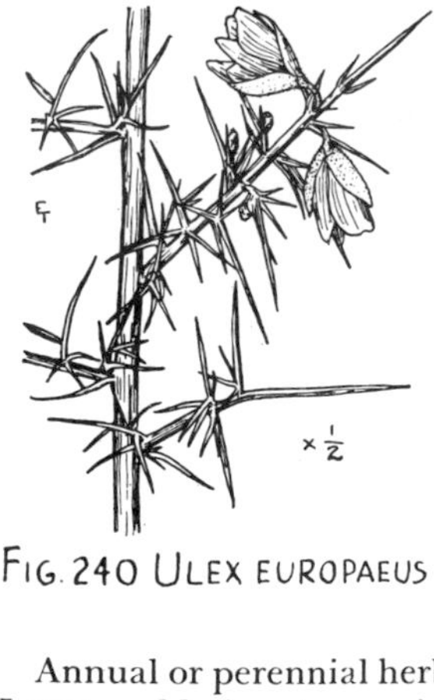

FIG. 240 ULEX EUROPAEUS

2. **Dalea** Juss.

(Named in honor of Samuel Dale, early English botanist.)

Annual or perennial herbs, shrubs, or small trees, with glandular-dotted herbage. Leaves odd-pinnate or simple, alternate. Flowers bisexual, irregular, borne in spikes or simple racemes, or rarely solitary; calyx 5-toothed; corolla of 5 petals, all with claws, the banner heart-shaped; stamens 10 (rarely 9), monadelphous; ovary superior, 1-celled. Fruit an ovate indehiscent pod, 1- or 2-seeded.

This is a large genus of nearly 150 species, chiefly Mexican, but extending into South America and into the southwestern part of the United States. Eight species and 4 varieties are native to California where they are very characteristic plants of the desert areas.

KEY TO THE SPECIES

Plants distinctly shrubby or tree-like.
  Leaves simple or the plants leafless.
    Plants leafless at time of flowering; large shrubs or small trees, very spinose, silver-gray . . . . 1. *D. spinosa.*
    Plants with leaves at time of flowering; shrubs, less spinose, herbage greenish. 2. *D. Schottii.*
  Leaves pinnately compound.
    Flowers ¼-inch or less long, in dense head-like spikes ¼- to ¾-inch long.
      Leaflets 3 to 7, rarely to 11, the terminal one much longer than the lateral ones; branches not conspicuously covered with reddish glands. 3. *D. Emoryi.*
      Leaflets usually 7 to 11 (5 to 17), the terminal one no longer than the lateral ones; branches thickly sprinkled with yellowish, brownish, or reddish glands . . . . 4. *D. polyadenia.*
    Flowers over ¼-inch long, mostly a little less than ½-inch long, in loose spikes or racemes.
      Plants densely villous-tomentose; leaflets ovate to obovate, densely silvery-canescent, more or less decurrent on the rachis. . . . . . 5. *D. arborescens.*
      Plants puberulent, canescent, or nearly glabrous; leaflets linear, oblong, or elliptic-oblong, usually distinct from the rachis. . . . . . . 6. *D. Fremontii.*
Plants herbaceous, sometimes woody at the base, not spiny.
  Flowers purple, in loose spike-like racemes; calyx-lobes not longer than the tube, somewhat canescent. . . . . 7. *D. Parryi.*
  Flowers pink, in dense hairy spikes ¾-inch to 1½ inches long; calyx-lobes longer than the tube, densely silky-pilose. . . . . 8. *D. mollis.*

1. **Dalea spinosa** Gray. SMOKE TREE. TREE-PEA. Figs. 241, 242.

An intricately branched nearly leafless shrub or small tree, 6 to 30 feet high, with yellowish green to ashy-gray spinose branchlets sparsely dotted with glands. Spines (reduced branchlets) 1 to 3 inches long. Leaves simple, few, early deciduous, linear-oblong to spatulate, ¼-inch to 1 inch long, 1/16- to ⅛-inch wide, with few glands, entire to irregularly dentate, almost sessile. Flowers dark blue and very fragrant, in short spike-like racemes ½-inch to 1 inch long; pedicels about 1/16-inch long; calyx densely hairy, the tube with a row of reddish glands; corolla ⅓- to ½-inch long. Fruit-pods ovate, canescent, glandular-dotted. Flowering period, June and July.

Smoke Tree is a familiar small tree or large shrub in dry washes of the Lower Sonoran Life Zone in the Colorado Desert. It extends eastward to Arizona and southward to Lower California. Its ashy-gray appearance at a distance gives the effect of smoke, hence the name Smoke Tree.

Dalea spinosa Gray, Mem. Am. Acad. n. ser. 5:315 (1855). Type locality: "Arroyos on the Gila; and on the California desert west of the Colorado." Collected by *Thurber, Fremont. Parosela spinosa* (Gray) Heller.

2. **Dalea Schottii** Torr. MESA DALEA. SCHOTT DALEA. Fig. 243.

Fig. 241. Smoke Tree. *Dalea spinosa* Gray.
(Photograph by Hugh P. Dearing.)

An intricately branched compact spinescent shrub, 3 to 9 feet high, with slender greenish glabrate nearly glandless branches. Leaves linear, 1/4-inch to 1 1/2 inches long, greenish gray, puberulent but soon glabrate, glandular-dotted along the thickened margins, nearly sessile. Flowers in loose racemes 1 1/2 to 4 inches long; pedicels 1/16-inch or less long; calyx about 3/16-inch long, sparsely hirsute, glabrate in fruit, glandular-dotted; corolla blue to deep purple. Fruit-pods obliquely ovate, conspicuously dotted with red glands, the body about 3/8-inch long and with 1 large seed, the beak 3/16-inch long. Flowering period, January to April.

Mesa Dalea occurs on the Colorado Desert of Imperial, Riverside, and eastern San Diego counties, in the Lower Sonoran Life Zone. It extends southward into Lower California and eastward to western Arizona.

2a. Var. **puberula** (Parish) Munz.

Young branches, leaves, and calyx white-pubescent or canescent.

This variety occurs on the western side of the Colorado Desert, south of the Santa Rosa Mountains.

Dalea Schottii Torr. Bot. Mex. Bound. 53 (1859). Type locality: "Banks of the Colorado." Collected by *Schott*. *Parosela Schottii* (Torr.) Heller.

Var. puberula (Parish) Munz, Man. S. Calif. Bot. 263 (1935). *Parosela Schottii* var. *puberula* Parish. Type locality: Colorado Desert. Collected by *T. S. Brandegee*.

3. **Dalea Emoryi** Gray. EMORY DALEA. WHITE DALEA. Fig. 244.

An intricately branched shrub, 1 to 5 feet high, with white-tomentose branches, often sprinkled with glands, without true spines. Leaves once-pinnately compound, 1/2-inch to 1 1/2 inches long; leaflets usually 5 or 7 (3 to 11), rarely reduced to 1, elliptic or obovate, 3/16- to 3/4-inch long, pubescent and sparsely glandular, the terminal one longer than the lateral ones. Flowers small, in short head-like spikes, 1/4- to 3/4-inch long; calyx silky-villous, about 1/4-inch long, densely dotted with orange glands; corolla dark blue or purple, little exceeding the calyx-teeth, about 1/4-inch long. Fruit-pods obliquely obovate, dotted with numerous red glands. Flowering period, April to June.

Emory Dalea occurs in the Lower Sonoran Life Zone of the Colorado Desert in Imperial, Riverside, and eastern San Diego counties. Specimens have been collected from near Indio, Palm Springs, San Felipe wash, Borrego Springs, Dixieland, Mecca, Salton Sea, Signal Mountain, and from Oasis, Mono County *(Curtis Ferris)*. It extends eastward to Arizona and southward to Sonora, Mexico and Lower California.

Dalea Emoryi Gray, Mem. Am. Acad. n. ser. 5:315 (1854). Type locality: "desert tablelands, Gila River, Ariz." Collected by *Emory*. *Parosela Emoryi* (Gray) Heller.

4. **Dalea polyadenia** Torr. NEVADA DALEA. Fig. 245.

KEY TO THE SPECIES AND VARIETY

Calyx-tube hairy . . . . *D. polyadenia*.
Calyx-tube glabrous . . . . 4a. var. *subnuda*.

A divaricately branched somewhat spinose shrub, 1 1/2 to 5 feet high, with conspicuously canescent and glandular branches, the glands saucer-shaped, red, brownish, or yellowish. Leaves once-pinnately compound, 3/8-inch to 1 inch long; leaflets 5 to 17 (usually 7 to 11), ovate, 1/16- to 3/16-inch long, densely short-villous, glandular. Flowers numerous, in globose or oblong spike-like clusters 1/3-inch to 1 inch long; calyx densely villous and glandular-dotted between the evident ribs; corolla rose-

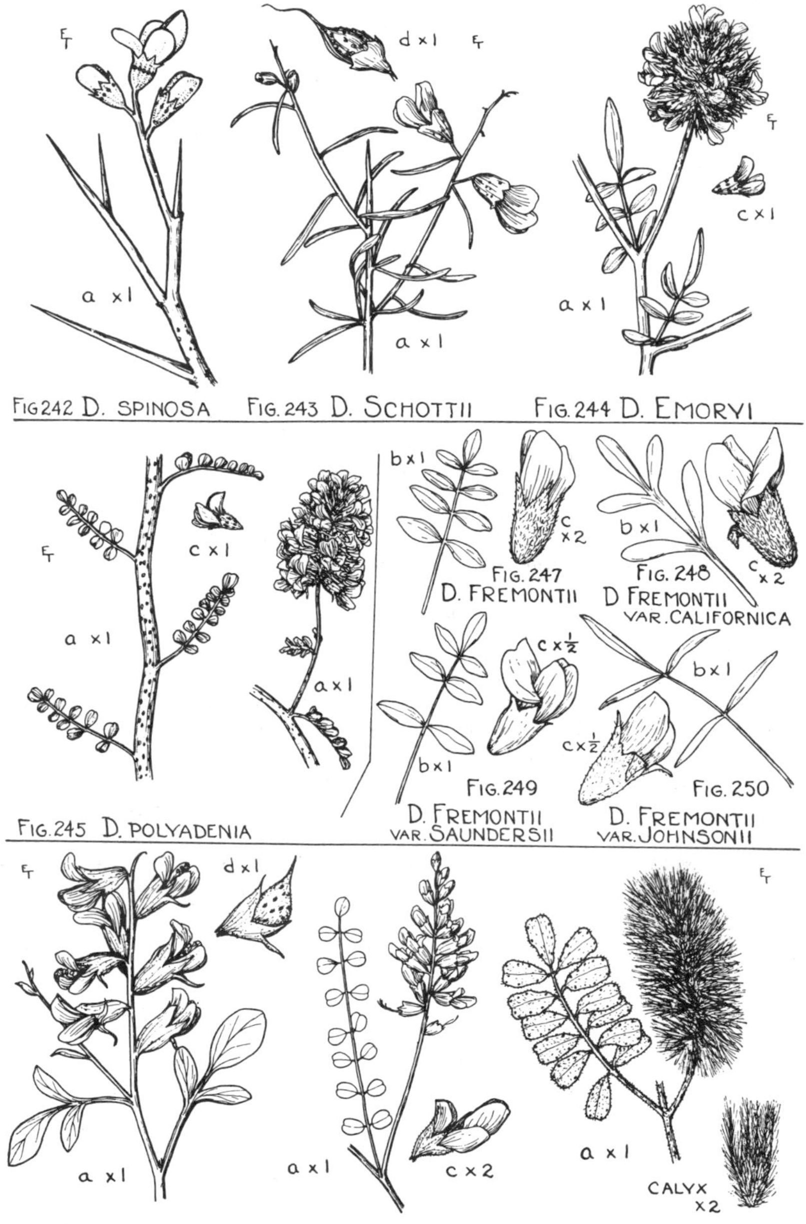

DALEA. a, Flowering branchlet. b, Compound leaf. c, Flower. d, Fruit.

pink to purple, about 1/4-inch long. Fruit-pods obliquely ovate, about 1/4-inch long, glabrous below, villous above. Flowering period, May and June.

This shrub is rare in California, having been found only on the sandy plains of the Owens Valley, Inyo County and in a few localities in the central Mohave Desert (Barstow, *Jepson*). It occurs also in western Nevada.

4a. Var. **subnuda** Wats.

Glabrous or nearly so. Calyx-tube glabrous, the teeth villous-ciliate.

This variety occurs with the species in Owens Valley, Inyo County and in Mono County.

Dalea polyadenia Torr.; Wats. Bot. King's Expl. 64, pl. 9 (1871). Type locality: "Border of Truckee Desert, Nevada." Collected by *W. W. Bailey*. *Parosela polyadenia* Heller.

Var. subnuda Wats. Bot. Calif. 2:441 (1880). Type locality: Owens Valley, California. Collected by *Matthews*. *Parosela polyadenia* var. *subnuda* (Wats.) Parish.

5. **Dalea arborescens** Torr. MOHAVE DALEA. Fig. 246.

A rather spiny shrub, 1 to 3 feet high, with villous-tomentose slender branches, the upper part of the branches with scattered bristle-like yellowish glands. Leaves once-pinnately compound, 3/4-inch to 1 1/2 inches long; leaflets 3 to 7, oval or obovate, 1/4- to 3/8-inch long, silvery-canescent, obscurely glandular-dotted, usually unequal, mostly sessile and decurrent on the rachis, the terminal one larger and sometimes 2- or 3-lobed. Flowers in racemes 3/4-inch to 2 inches long; calyx silky-pubescent, the linear teeth nearly as long as the tube; corolla blue, about 3/8-inch long. Fruit-pods obliquely ovate, villous and glandular-dotted, the body about 3/8-inch long, the beak about 1/4-inch long. Flowering period, April and May.

Mohave Dalea is known in California only from a few localities on the Mohave Desert in the Barstow region and in Mono County (Fishponds Station, *S. B. Parish;* near Daggett; Barstow, *Jepson;* Black's Ranch, 20 miles n.w. of Barstow, *Hall* & *Chandler;* Benton, Mono County, *Heller*).

Dalea arborescens Torr.; Gray, Mem. Am. Acad. n. ser. 5:316 (1855). Type locality: Probably near Barstow, Mohave Desert. Collected by *Fremont*. *Parosela arborescens* (Torr.) Heller.

6. **Dalea Fremontii** Torr. FREMONT DALEA. Fig. 247.

This species varies considerably in the size, shape, and pubescence of its leaflets. The following key will identify a few typical variants. Many specimens will be intermediates and consequently will not "key out" satisfactorily.

KEY TO THE SPECIES AND VARIETIES

Upper leaflets not confluent.
- Calyx densely pubescent or rarely nearly glabrous without.
  - Terminal leaflet not longer than the lateral ones; leaflets 3 or 5, usually ovate-oblong, 1/4-inch or less long .... *D. Fremontii*.
  - Terminal leaflet often longer than the lateral ones; leaflets 5 to 11, usually linear or linear-lanceolate, often more than 1/4-inch long. 6a. var. *Johnsonii*.
- Calyx glabrous without; terminal leaflet not longer than the lateral ones; foliage becoming glabrous and greenish in age........6b. var. *Saundersii*.

Upper leaflets often confluent, some often decurrent; calyx densely canescent without..6c. var. *californica*.

A low intricately branched shrub, 1 to 3 feet high, with nearly glabrous branches and leaves. Leaves once-pinnately compound, 3/4-inch to 1 5/8 inches long; leaflets usually 3 or 5, ovate-oblong or elliptic, 3/16- to 1/4-inch long, thinly canescent, not decurrent on the rachis. Flowers in loose racemes 3 to 5 inches long; calyx about 1/4-inch long, finely pubescent without and within, the teeth as long as the tube; corolla purple, about 3/8-inch long. Fruit-pods obliquely obovate, the body about 3/8-inch long, conspicuously glandular-dotted. Flowering period, April to June.

Fremont Dalea, in its typical form, occurs in the Owens Valley, California and in Nevada and Utah.

6a. Var. **Johnsonii** (Wats.) Munz. Fig. 250.

This variety inhabits dry slopes of the desert mountains of the Death Valley region of Inyo County, south in the Ord and Cottonwood mountains of the Mohave Desert, and occasionally in the northwestern part of the Colorado Desert. It extends eastward to Nevada, Arizona, and Utah.

6b. Var. **Saundersii** (Parish) Munz. Fig. 249.

This variety occurs in the eastern part of the Mohave Desert and north in Inyo County to Mono County.

6c. Var. **californica** (Wats.) n. comb. Fig. 248.

This variety occurs on the slopes of canyons in the desert mountains on the western part of the Colorado Desert (San Jacinto Valley; canyon of the San Jacinto River, *Hall;* 2 miles east of Banning; Palm Springs; Morongo wash; Byrnes Canyon, east end of the San Bernardino Mountains, *Parrish*).

Dalea Fremontii Torr.; Gray, Mem. Am. Acad. n. ser. 5:316 (1855). Type locality: "mountains of Pah-Ute Country [that is, Muddy River, s. Nev.]." Collected by *Fremont. Parosela Fremontii* (Torr.) Vail.

Var. Johnsonii (Wats.) Munz, Man. S. Calif. Bot. 262 (1935). *D. Johnsonii* Wats. Type locality: Near St. George, Virgin River, Utah. Collected by *J. E. Johnson, Palmer. Parosela Fremontii* var. *Johnsonii* (Wats.) Jepson.

Var. Saundersii (Parish) Munz, Man. S. Calif. Bot. 262 (1935). *D. Saundersii* Parish. Type locality: Victorville, Mohave Desert. *Parosela Fremontii* var. *Saundersii* (Parish) Macbr.

Var. californica (Wats.) McMinn. *Dalea californica* Wats. Type locality: San Bernardino Mountains. Collected by *Parry. Parosela Fremontii* var. *californica* (Wats.) Jepson. *Parosela californica* (Wats.) Vail.

7. **Dalea Parryi** T. & G. Parry Dalea. Fig. 251.

A diffusely spreading perennial, 6 inches to 2 feet tall, with slender somewhat woody stems, these finely puberulent or glabrous, dotted with small glands. Flowering period, April to June, or as early as December.

Parry Dalea occurs chiefly in Riverside County in the washes and mountains separating the Mohave and Colorado deserts and sparingly in Imperial, San Diego, and San Bernardino counties. It extends eastward into Arizona and southward into Lower California.

Dalea Parryi T. & G. Proc. Am. Acad. 7:397 (1868). *D. divaricata* var. *cinerea* Gray. Type locality: Gravelly hills near Fort Mohave, Arizona. Collected by *Cooper. Parosela Parryi* Heller.

8. **Dalea mollis** Benth. Hairy Dalea. Fig. 252.

An herbaceous perennial, 4 to 8 inches high, with several hairy-pubescent stems from a somewhat woody base, not spiny. Stems and leaves dotted with small brown or black saucer-shaped glands. Flowering period, April and May.

Hairy Dalea is a short-lived rank-smelling perennial which occurs rather commonly on the Colorado and Mohave deserts in the Lower Sonoran Life Zone. Specimens have been examined from Inyo, San Bernardino, Riverside, San Diego, and Imperial counties. It extends eastward to Nevada and Arizona.

Dalea mollis Benth. Pl. Hartw. 306 (1848). Type locality: Probably the Colorado Desert. "In vicinibus Monterey legit Coulter," must be an error. Collected by *Coulter*. *Parosela mollis* (Benth.) Heller.

3. **Alhagi** Desv.

(The Mauritanian name.)

This genus contains 3 species of shrubs native from the Mediterranean region to the Himalayas. One species has become naturalized in the Colorado Desert and lower San Joaquin Valley of California.

1. **Alhagi camelorum** Fisch. CAMEL THORN. Fig. 253.

A very spiny shrub, 1 to 2 feet high, the spines single, numerous, slender, 1/2-inch to 1 inch long. Leaves simple, alternate, deciduous; the blades elliptical to oblanceolate-oblong, 1/2- to 7/8-inch long, glabrous, entire; the petiole about 1/16-inch long. Flowers lavender-red, bisexual, irregular, few in racemes; stamens 10, diadelphous; ovary superior, 1-celled. Fruit an incompletely 2-celled linear pod 1/8- to 1/2-inch long, 1- to 3-seeded, constricted between the seeds, the sections globular. Flowering period, June and July.

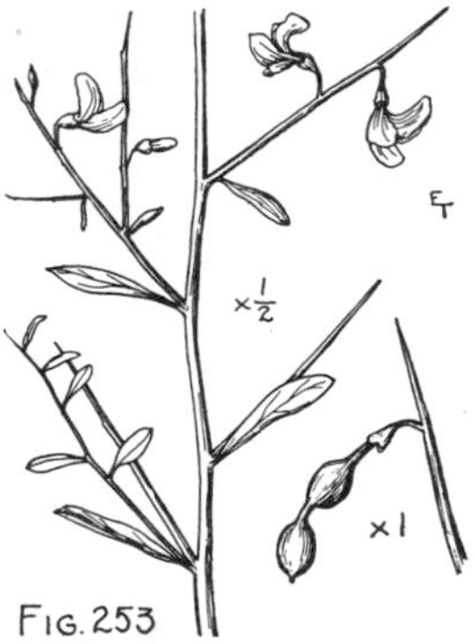

FIG. 253
ALHAGI CAMELORUM

Camel Thorn, a native of Asia Minor, has become naturalized at several localities on the Colorado Desert and in a few localities in the lower San Joaquin Valley. It was probably introduced into Imperial Valley with "packings of shipments of date cuttings from Africa or in impure alfalfa seed from Turkestan." W. L. Jepson, Fl. 2:395 (1936).

Alhagi camelorum Fisch. Hort. Gorenk. ed. 2, 72 (1812).

4. **Cercidium** Tul.

(From the Greek *kerkidion,* a weaver's shuttle, in reference to the fruit.)

Small trees or shrubs with green bark. Leaves bipinnate, alternate. Flowers yellow, bisexual, nearly regular, borne in axillary racemes; calyx bell-shaped, the 5 segments reflexed; petals obovate, clawed; stamens 10, distinct, the filaments hairy near the base; ovary superior, 1-celled. Fruit-pods linear or oblong, flattened or cylindric.

This genus contains about 10 species extending from the southwestern United States to Mexico and northwestern South America. Two species are native to California.

KEY TO THE SPECIES

Pinnae with 1 to 3 pairs of leaflets, the primary rachis evident; branches with short spines; pods flattish . . . . 1. *C. floridum*.

Pinnae with 4 to 12 pairs of leaflets, the primary rachis undeveloped and the leaves thus appearing once-pinnate; branches spinose at tip; pods cylindric, constricted between the seeds . . . . 2. *C. microphyllum*.

1. **Cercidium floridum** Benth. Palo Verde. Fig. 254.

A large shrub or small tree, 15 to 35 feet high, with slender glabrous yellowish green armed branches and gray foliage, or leafless for most of the year. Leaves with 2 or rarely 4 or 6 pinnae from an evident rachis $\frac{1}{4}$- to $\frac{3}{4}$-inch long, each pinna with 2 to 4 pairs of pale leaflets $\frac{1}{8}$- to $\frac{3}{8}$-inch long. Flowers $\frac{1}{2}$- to $\frac{3}{4}$-inch broad, on jointed pedicels, in axillary racemes 2 to $4\frac{1}{2}$ inches long. Fruit-pods oblong, 2 to 4 inches long, flattened but thickish, 1- to 8-seeded, sometimes constricted between the flat seeds. Flowering period, April to July.

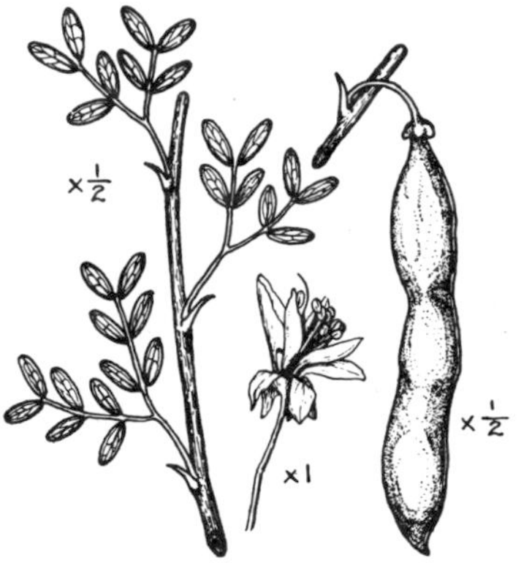

Fig. 254 Cercidium floridum

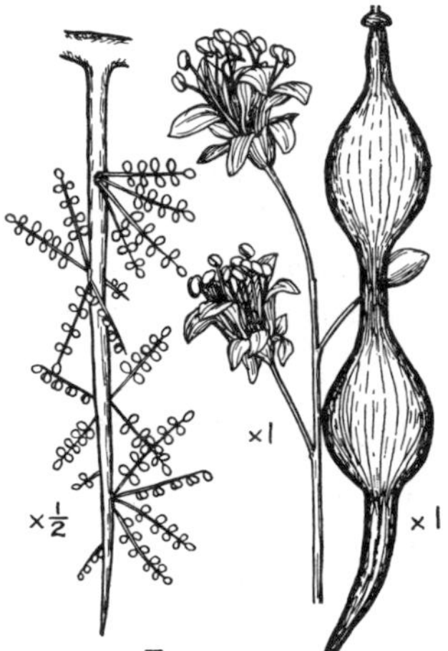

Fig. 255 Cercidium microphyllum

Palo Verde occurs chiefly on the Colorado Desert in sandy washes of the Lower Sonoran Life Zone. It is a common plant along the Colorado River in eastern Imperial and Riverside counties and it extends northward as far as Needles. Its range extends eastward to Arizona and southward to Lower California and Mexico. The common name Palo Verde is the Spanish-Mexican name referring to the smooth green bark which stands out in contrast to the gray of the desert. The pods occur in great abundance and they furnish a welcome source of stock food after ripening in July. The natives often grind the pods and seeds from which they prepare a very palatable meal. In a few places in southern California, this plant is being tried out as a roadside tree. Its habit of shedding leaves soon after March makes it less desirable than other trees which can stand the drought, for example, *Robinia*.

Cercidium floridum Benth.; Gray, Pl. Wright. 1, 58 (1852). Type locality: Northern Mexico between Monterey and Matamoras. Collected by *Coulter, Gregg*. *C. Torreyanum* (Wats.) Sarg.

2. **Cercidium microphyllum** (Torr.) Rose & Johnst. Littleleaf Palo Verde. Male Palo Verde. Fig. 255.

A large shrub or small tree, 5 to 25 feet high, with stiff spinose-tipped branchlets. Leaves with 1 or rarely 2 pairs of pinnae from a very short rachis or apparently sessile, thus appearing once-pinnate, each pinna $\frac{1}{2}$-inch to $1\frac{1}{4}$ inches long, with 9 to 17 elliptic entire leaflets about $\frac{1}{16}$-inch long. Flowers pale yellow, in loose racemes about 1 inch long. Fruit-pods linear-cylindric, 1 to 3 inches long, 1- to 3-seeded, constricted between the seeds. Flowering period, April and May.

Littleleaf Palo Verde is known in California only along the Colorado River (Whipple Mountains, San Bernardino County). It extends southward to Sonora, Mexico and Lower California and eastward to Arizona.

Cercidium microphyllum (Torr.) Rose & Johnst. Contr. Gray Herb. 70:66 (1924). *Parkinsonia microphylla* Torr. Type locality: Williams River, Arizona and along the banks of the Colorado River. Collected by *Bigelow*.

5. **Pickeringia** Nutt.

(Named in honor of Charles Pickering of the Wilkes Expedition, which visited California in 1841.)

This genus consists of a single species with one variety native to California.

KEY TO THE SPECIES AND VARIETY

Branchlets and leaves glabrous or nearly so .... 1. *P. montana*.
Branchlets and leaves pubescent .... 1a. var. *tomentosa*.

1. **Pickeringia montana** Nutt. CHAPARRAL-PEA. Fig. 256.

An erect shrub, 2 to 6 feet high, with very spinose branchlets and few leaves. Leaves simple or palmately 3-foliolate, alternate; the blades obovate, ¼- to ½-inch long, glabrous or merely puberulent, entire, sessile. Flowers rose-purple, bisexual, irregular, solitary in the leaf-axils near the ends of the branchlets or rarely in short racemes; calyx bell-shaped, with 5 low tooth-like lobes; corolla of 5 petals (1 banner, 2 wings, and 2 keel-petals), the banner with a yellowish spot near the base; stamens 10, distinct; ovary superior, 1-celled. Fruit a flat straight linear several-seeded pod 1½ to 2 inches long, on a short stipe. Flowering period, May and June.

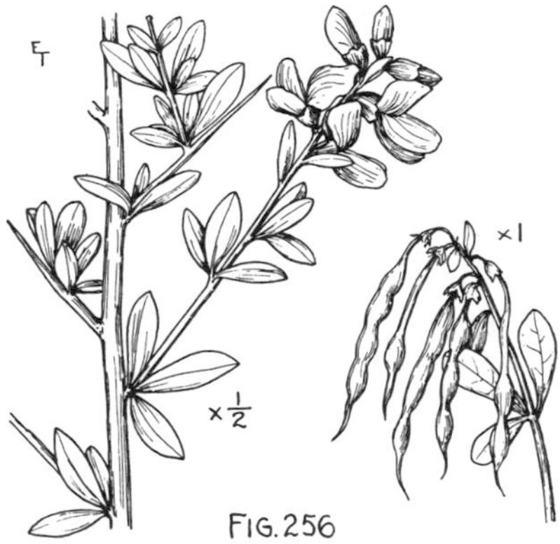

FIG. 256
PICKERINGIA MONTANA

Chaparral-pea is a shrub of the chaparral areas from Lake and Mendocino counties southward in the Coast Ranges to the Santa Monica and San Bernardino mountains of southern California. It occurs sparingly in the chaparral of the Sierra Nevada from Butte County south to Mariposa County and on Santa Cruz Island. It rarely matures fruit. It usually propagates by means of shoots from exposed roots.

1a. Var. **tomentosa** (Abrams) Johnst.

Branches and leaves pubescent. This variety occurs in the mountains of eastern San Diego County and sparingly in the San Bernardino Mountains, where it seems to merge with the species.

Pickeringia montana Nutt.; T. & G. Fl. N. Am. 1:389 (1840). Type locality: "Summits of the mountains in the vicinity of Santa Barbara." Collected by *Nuttall*.

Var. tomentosa (Abrams) Johnst. Contr. Gray Herb. 68:81 (1923). *Xylothermia montana* subsp. *tomentosa* Abrams. Type locality: Near El Nido, San Diego County. Collected by *Abrams*.

6. **Cassia** L. Senna

(Ancient Greek name.)

Shrubs, trees, or perennial herbs with even-pinnate leaves. Flowers bisexual, nearly regular, in racemes; sepals 5, nearly equal, distinct or nearly so; petals 5, spreading, distinct; stamens 5 to 10, some of the anthers abortive, fertile stamens in ours 7, sterile stamens 3 and represented by short filaments on the upper side of the flower; ovary superior, 1-celled. Fruit a several-seeded pod.

This is a large genus of about 450 species in the warmer parts of the world. Two species are native to California.

Fig. 257 Cassia Covesii

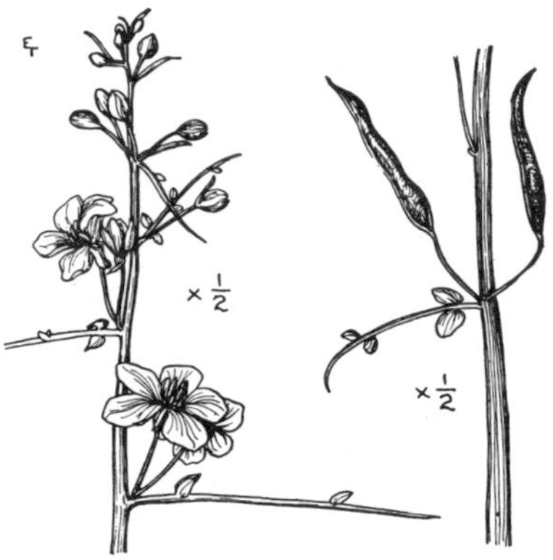

Fig. 258 Cassia armata

KEY TO THE SPECIES

Leaflets ½-inch to 1 inch long, pubescent; leaf-rachis not spinose-pointed; racemes axillary, few-flowered. . . . . 1. *C. Covesii.*

Leaflets ¼-inch or less long, glabrous; leaf-rachis ending in an enlarged pointed prickle or spine; racemes terminal, several flowered. . . . . 2. *C. armata.*

1. **Cassia Covesii** Gray. Hairy Senna. Fig. 257.

A low bush, 1 to 2 feet high, with velvety-pubescent herbage and linear early-falling stipules. Leaflets 4 or 6, oblong or elliptic, ½-inch to 1 inch long, pubescent, with a narrow gland between the lower pair of leaflets. Flowers few, in axillary racemes 1 to 2 inches long; sepals densely pubescent; petals oblong-ovate, about ½-inch long. Fruit-pods straight, compressed, ¾-inch to 1¼ inches long, about ¼-inch wide, sparingly pubescent, dehiscent along both sutures. Flowering period, April to June.

Hairy Senna is a rare plant in California. It occurs in sandy washes in a few localities on the Colorado Desert (Martinez Canyon in the Santa Rosa Mountains of Riverside County, *E. C. Jaeger;* Vallecito, *S. B. Parish* and Grapevine Grade, Sentenac Canyon, *Jepson,* in eastern San Diego County; Chuckawalla Mountains, Riverside County, *Munz* & *Keck*). It extends southward to Lower California and eastward to Arizona.

Cassia Covesii Gray, Proc. Am. Acad. 7:399 (1868). Type locality: South of Prescott, Arizona. Collected by *Coues, Palmer.*

2. **Cassia armata** Wats. Armed Senna. Fig. 258.

A much branched shrub, 2 to 6 feet high, with pale green glabrous or sparingly pubescent almost leafless branches. Leaves 1¾ to 2½ inches long; leaf-rachis enlarged at the apex into a sharp prickle or spine; leaflets 2 to 8, ovate to almost round, ¼-inch or less long, glabrate or pubescent. Flowers several, in terminal racemes 2 to 6 inches long; sepals about ¼-inch long; petals yellow to salmon-colored, ⅜- to ½-inch long. Fruit-pods linear, ¾-inch to 1¼ inches long, spinulose-tipped, curved, not compressed between the seeds. Flowering period, May to July.

Armed Senna is widely scattered over the Colorado and Mohave deserts and in Death Valley, growing in gravelly or sandy washes in the Lower Sonoran Life Zone. It has been collected in Inyo, Kern, San Bernardino, Riverside, Imperial, and San Diego counties. It extends eastward to Arizona and Nevada.

Cassia armata Wats. Proc. Am. Acad. 11:136 (1876). Type locality: Between Fort Mohave, Arizona and Cajon Pass, California, on the Mohave Desert. Collected by *Cooper*.

7. **Acacia** Willd. Acacia

(From the Greek *akakie*, a point, in reference to the prickles of some species.)

This is a large genus of about 500 species, chiefly of Australia and Africa, but dispersed throughout the tropical and subtropical parts of the world. A single species is native to California. Another species apparently has become naturalized in southern San Diego County.

KEY TO THE SPECIES

Spines short, hooked; flowers in spikes..........................1. *A. Greggii.*
Spines long, straight; flowers in heads.......................2. *A. Farnesiana.*

1. **Acacia Greggii** Gray. Catclaw. Fig. 259.

A straggling shrub, 4 to 8 feet high, or sometimes a small tree up to 12 feet high, usually with prickly branches. Prickles stout and curved, about ¼-inch long. Leaves bipinnately compound, deciduous, 1 to 2 inches long, with 4 or 6 pinnae; leaflets 8 to 12 on each pinna, oblong-ovate, ⅛- to ¼-inch long, pale green, entire. Flowers very small, numerous, bisexual, regular, yellow, in cylindrical spikes ¾-inch to 2 inches long; calyx 5-toothed; petals 5, distinct; stamens numerous, distinct, much exserted; ovary superior, 1-celled. Fruit-pods much flattened, 2 to 6 inches long, 2- to 11-seeded or sometimes 1-seeded and less than 1 inch long. Flowering period, April to July.

Catclaw is a common shrub of washes and desert hillslopes from 200 to 2000 feet elevation in the Colorado Desert to the southern Mohave Desert (Providence, Old Woman, and Ord mountains). It extends eastward to Texas and southward to Mexico.

Acacia Greggii Gray, Pl. Wright. 1:65 (1852). Type locality: Western Texas. Collected by *Wright*.

2. **Acacia Farnesiana** (L.) Willd. Sweet Acacia. Fig. 260.

This is an arborescent shrub which has recently been found near Otay, San Diego County. In all probability it has been introduced into this region by Indians. Standley states that in, "many parts of Mexico the plant is found chiefly about dwellings and seems naturalized, but in other regions it appears to be native." The Indians use the plant parts for many purposes.

Acacia Farnesiana (L.) Willd. Sp. Pl. 4:1083 (1806). *Mimosa Farnesiana* L.

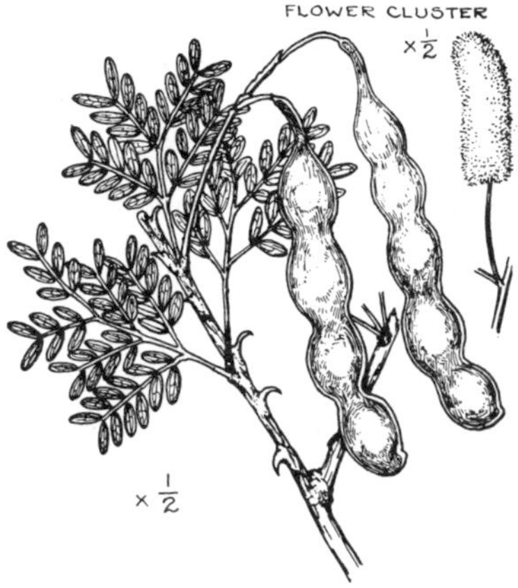

FIG. 259 ACACIA GREGGII

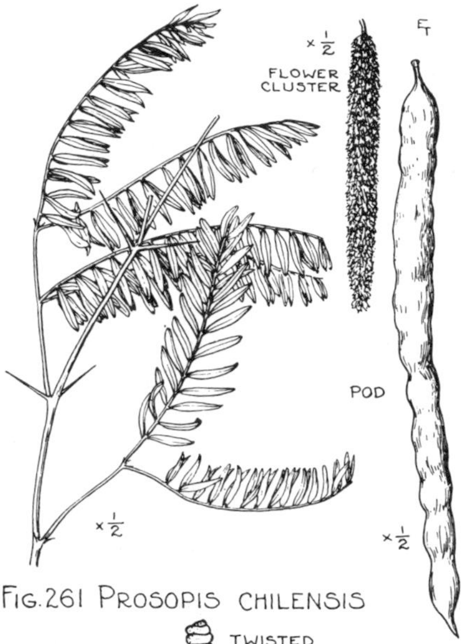

FIG. 261 PROSOPIS CHILENSIS

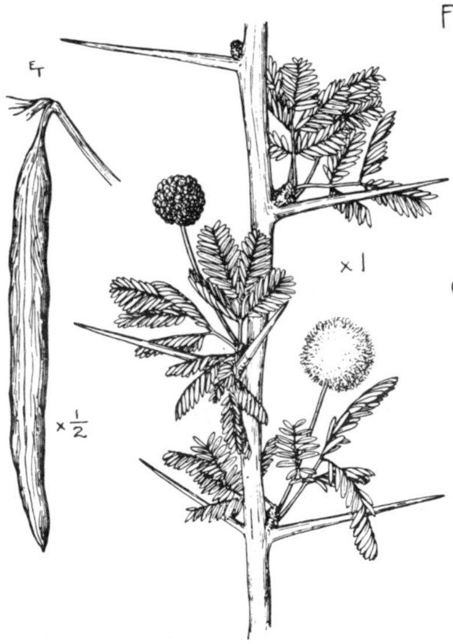

FIG. 260 ACACIA FARNESIANA

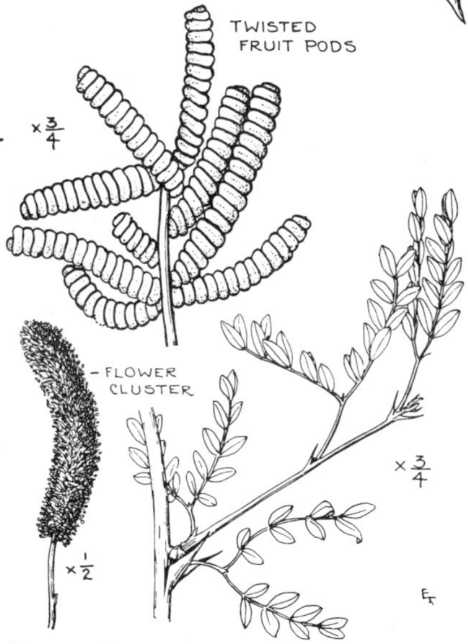

FIG. 262 PROSOPIS PUBESCENS

8. **Prosopis** L. Mesquite

(The Greek *prosopis,* the ancient name of the burdock, the reference obscure.) Shrubs or trees with the branches armed with spines or thorns. Leaves twice-pinnately compound, alternate, deciduous. Flowers small, numerous, bisexual, regular, sessile in axillary pedunculate cylindrical spikes; calyx bell-shaped, with 5 short teeth; petals 5, distinct; stamens 10, distinct, exserted; ovary superior, 1-celled, stipitate. Fruit an indehiscent many-seeded pod.

This genus contains about 25 species, native to tropical and subtropical regions of all the continents except Europe and Australia, though chiefly African. Two species are native to California.

KEY TO THE SPECIES

Leaflets 2 inches or more long; pinnae with 18 to 36 leaflets; pods straight or curving but not spirally coiled............................1. *P. chilensis.*
Leaflets less than 2 inches long; pinnae with 10 to 22 leaflets; pods spirally coiled into a cylindrical body..................................2. *P. pubescens.*

1. **Prosopis chilensis** (Molina) Stuntz. Honey Mesquite. Fig. 261.

A much branched shrub, 6 to 10 feet high, or a small tree, 15 to 20 feet high, with a short trunk dividing into many crooked branches. Thorns 1 or 2, axillary, 1/4-inch to 1 1/4 inches long, rarely absent. Leaves usually with 2 pinnae about 2 to 4 inches long, each pinna with 18 to 36 linear entire leaflets 3/8-inch to 1 inch long; petioles enlarged and glandular at base. Flowers greenish yellow, in slender cylindrical spikes 2 to 3 1/2 inches long; stamens twice as long as the petals. Fruit-pods linear, 3 to 8 inches long, 1/3- to 1/2-inch wide, curved, flat or becoming thickened, irregularly constricted between the seeds, in drooping clusters of 1 to 6. Seeds smooth, about 1/4-inch long. Flowering period, April to June, rarely December and January.

Honey Mesquite is a common shrub or small tree in washes and low places, usually below 3000 feet, in the southern Death Valley region, central and eastern Mohave Desert, and on the Colorado Desert. It is found locally in the upper San Joaquin Valley (Buena Vista Lake, *F. M. Anderson*) and occasionally on the western Mohave Desert and in cismontane southern California and even near the coast in San Diego County. It extends eastward to Texas and Louisiana and southward to Mexico, and occurs also in Chile and Peru.

Prosopis chilensis (Molina) Stuntz, U. S. Bur. Pl. Indust. Invent. 31:85 (1914) *Ceratonia chilensis* Molina. Type locality: Chile. *P. juliflora* var. *glandulosa* (Torr.) Ckll. *P. glandulosa* Torr.

2. **Prosopis pubescens** Benth. Screwbean Mesquite. Fig. 262.

A shrub or small tree, 10 to 30 feet high, with stout whitish stipular spines 1/4- to 1/2-inch long. Leaves puberulent, usually with 2 pinnae, each pinna with 10 to 22 oblong leaflets 1/8- to 7/16-inch long. Flowers yellowish, in slender cylindrical spikes 2 to 3 inches long. Fruit-pods coiled into a narrow cylindrical body 1 to 1 1/2 inches long, borne in clusters of 2 to 15. Seeds very small, less than 1/8-inch long. Flowering period, April to June.

Screwbean Mesquite occurs rather commonly along the Colorado River bottoms between Yuma, Arizona and Needles, California. It extends northwest into the Death Valley region where it is less common than along the river bottoms and westward in a few scattered locations on the Mohave and Colorado deserts to the

Fig. 263. WESTERN REDBUD. *Cercis occidentalis* Torr.

cismontane area near San Bernardino. Outside of California its range extends southward to Lower California and Mexico and eastward to Texas.

The pods and early spring growth furnish food for livestock. The Indians and Mexicans grind the seeds into a meal for baking. The plants crown-sprout after injury to the trunk or after cutting.

Prosopis pubescens Benth.; Hook. Lond. Jour. Bot. 5:82 (1846). Type locality: Probably along the Yuma-San Felipe Trail. Collected by *Coulter*.

9. **Cercis** L. REDBUD. JUDAS TREE

(From *Kerkis,* the Greek name of the Judas Tree.)

This genus contains about 6 species of Europe, Asia, and North America. A single species is native to California.

1. **Cercis occidentalis** Torr. WESTERN REDBUD. Figs. 263, 264.

A tall shrub or small tree, 8 to 20 feet high, usually with many long stems from the base. Leaves simple, alternate, deciduous; the blades round, 2 to 3½ inches wide, heart-shaped at base, somewhat palmately veined, glabrous on both surfaces, entire; petioles ½-inch to 1 inch long. Flowers red-purple, appearing before the leaves in simple umbel-like clusters at the alternate nodes; pedicels ¼- to ½-inch long, glabrous; calyx broadly bell-shaped, 5-toothed or -lobed, about ⅜-inch broad; petals 5, distinct, somewhat papilionaceous, about ½-inch long, the banner smaller than the wing-petals, the keel-petals larger than the wing-petals; stamens 10, distinct; ovary superior, 1-celled, oblong, glabrous. Fruit-pods oblong, 1½ to 3 inches long, ½- to ⅝-inch wide, flat, dull red when mature. Flowering period, February to April.

Western Redbud is a familiar shrub of the Sierra Nevada foothills from Tulare County northward to Shasta County, westward through Siskiyou and Trinity counties to Humboldt County, thence southward in the inner North Coast Range to Lake, Napa, and Solano counties. It occurs also in Kern and San Diego counties. Its range extends eastward to Texas.

This shrub is one of the most attractive native flowering species, especially when the numerous buds break into flower. After the first flowers appear, the young bronze-colored leaves develop and soon turn a glossy green. The numerous large clusters of reddish brown fruit-pods give color to the shrubs until the following spring.

Cercis occidentalis Torr.; Gray, Jour. Bost. Soc. Nat. Hist. 6:177 (1850). Type locality: "rocky plains of the upper Guadaloupe" in western Texas. Collected by *Lindheimer*.

10. **Cytisus** L.

(From the Greek *kutisus,* a kind of clover.)

Mostly shrubs, rarely small trees, with trifoliolate or unifoliolate alternate leaves. Flowers bisexual, irregular, yellow or white, axillary or in terminal heads or racemes; sepals 5, united into a campanulate tube 2-lipped at the apex; petals 5; stamens 10, monadelphous; ovary superior, 1-celled. Fruit a flat dehiscent several-seeded pod.

This genus contains about 50 species native to Europe, the Canary Islands, western Asia, and northern Africa. Three species have become naturalized in parts of California.

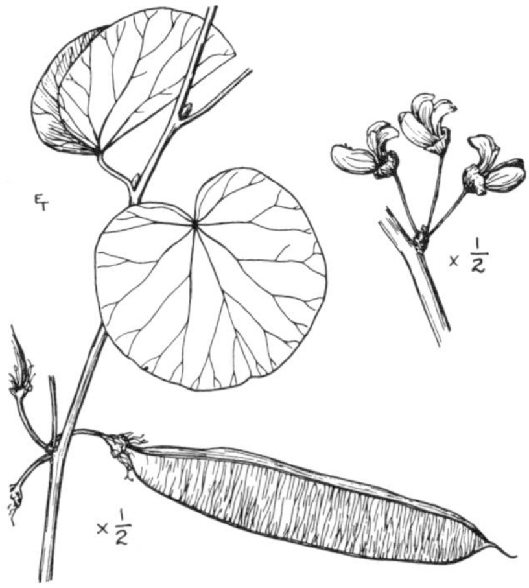

FIG. 264 CERCIS OCCIDENTALIS

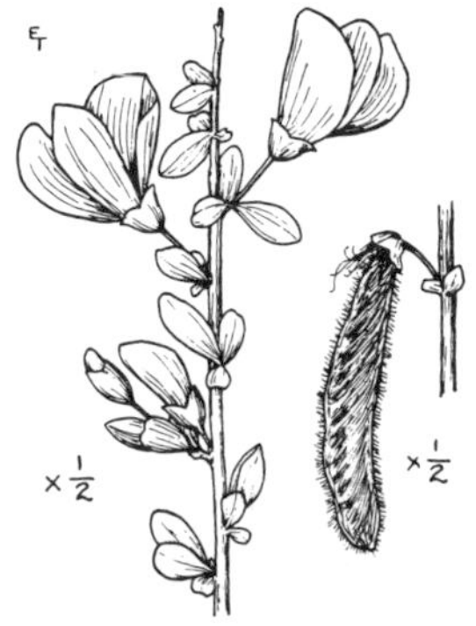

FIG. 265 CYTISUS SCOPARIUS

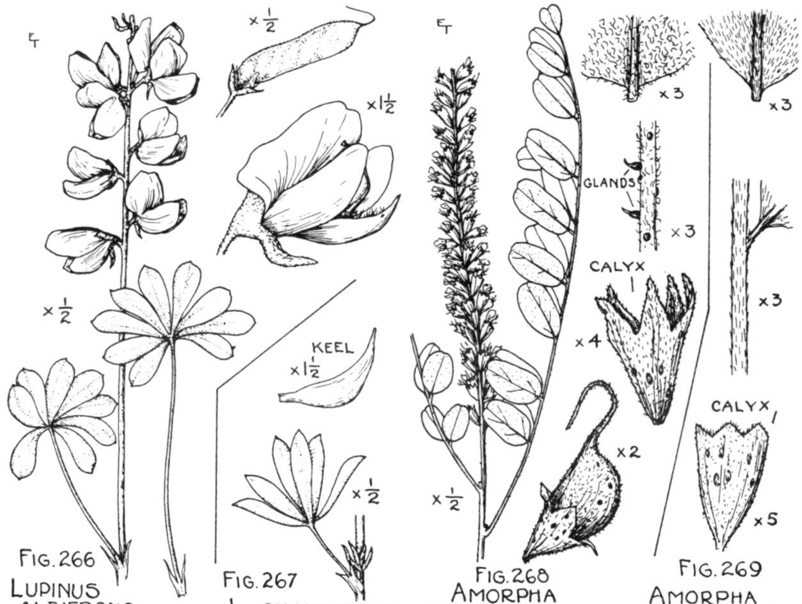

FIG. 266 LUPINUS ALBIFRONS

FIG. 267 L. CHAMISSONIS

FIG. 268 AMORPHA CALIFORNICA

FIG. 269 AMORPHA FRUTICOSA

KEY TO THE SPECIES

Foliage sparse; pods black, hairy only along the margins.........1. *C. scoparius.*
Foliage abundant; pods brown, finely hairy all over.
2. *C. monspessulanus* and *C. canariensis.*

1. **Cytisus scoparius** Link. SCOTCH BROOM. Fig. 265.

An erect shrub, 3 to 10 feet high, with slender angled branches and sparse foliage. Flowers solitary or in pairs in the leaf-axils, about 3/4-inch long, bright yellow. Flowering period, January to June.

Scotch Broom has become naturalized in several places along the coast from Santa Cruz County northward to Del Norte County and in the Sierra Nevada foothills of Amador, Eldorado, Placer, and Nevada counties.

Cytisus scoparius (L.) Link, Enum. Hort. Berol. 2:241 (1822). *Spartium scoparium* L. Type locality: Europe.

2. **Cytisus monspessulanus** L. SPANISH BROOM. FRENCH BROOM.

An erect evergreen shrub, 4 to 10 feet high, with villous-pubescent slightly angled branchlets and abundant foliage. Flowers 2 to 9 in very short or capitate racemes at the ends of short lateral branchlets, leafy at the base, about 1/2-inch long, bright yellow, fragrant. Flowering period, April to June.

Spanish Broom is extensively cultivated in California. It has escaped and become naturalized in several localities (Santa Cruz Mountains, Oakland, Eureka, and elsewhere).

Cytisus monspessulanus L. Sp. Pl. 740 (1753). Type locality: France.

Cytisus canariensis Ktze., with more numerous flowers in rather dense and short axillary or terminal racemes, may be found occasionally as an escape.

11. **Lupinus** L. LUPINE

(From the Latin *lupus,* a wolf, since the plants were thought to rob the soil of its fertility. We now know that they aid in restoring nitrogen to the soil.)

Herbs or shrubs, with alternate palmately compound leaves. Flowers bisexual, irregular, blue, white, or yellow, in racemes, often verticillate; calyx of 5 united sepals, 2-lipped, the lips entire or toothed; corolla of 5 petals (1 banner, 2 wings, and 2 keel-petals); stamens 10, monadelphous; ovary superior, 1-celled. Fruit a pod, dehiscent by both sutures, with 2 to 12 seeds.

This is a large and complex genus of about 100 species, chiefly of the western United States but occurring in all continents except Australia. About 50 species and many varieties are native to California, 5 of which are shrubs. Several others are sometimes woody at the base. So much variation occurs in habit of growth and in vegetative and floral characters that no satisfactory key for the identification of the numerous forms has yet been made. The following key is no exception to this statement.

KEY TO THE SPECIES

Plants distinctly shrubby.
Flowers yellow or rarely lilac, blue, or violet; keel ciliate on the upper margins; mainly sandy bluffs or beaches and dunes along the coast..1. *L. arboreus.*
Flowers blue, lilac, violet, or almost white, rarely yellowish.
Keel ciliate.
Flowers 1/2- to 3/4-inch long; petioles 1 1/2 to 4 inches long; leaflets greenish,

subsilky; Ventura and San Bernardino counties, southward to San Diego County . . . . 2. *L. longifolius.*

Flowers 1/3- to 1/2-inch long; leaflets densely silky.

Petioles 1/2-inch to 1 1/2 inches long; pedicels 1/8- to 1/3-inch long; of wide distribution . . . . 3. *L. albifrons.*

Petioles 1 to 3 1/2 inches long; pedicels about 1/6-inch long; Inyo County. 4. *L. excubitus.*

Keel not ciliate; petioles about 3/4-inch long; coastal and sand hills from Los Angeles County northward to San Francisco . . . . 5. *L. Chamissonis.*

Herbaceous perennials, usually 2 to 16 inches (or up to 2 feet) tall, sometimes woody at the base.

Plants prostrate, 2 to 6 inches high, forming mats.

Leaflets 5 or 6 (rarely 7); high alpine summits of the Sierra Nevada and the North Coast Ranges . . . . 6. *L. Lyallii* var. *Lobbii.*

Leaflets 6 to 10.

Flowers 1/2- to 3/8-inch long; high mountain summits . . . . 7. *L. Breweri.*

Flowers 1/2- to 3/4-inch long; hills about San Francisco Bay. 3. *L. albifrons* var. *collinus.*

Plants neither prostrate nor matted, 6 inches to 2 feet high.

Plants 1 to 2 feet high.

Basal petioles 4 to 7 inches long; Sierra Nevada, 2000 to 9000 feet elevation . . . . 8. *L. laxiflorus.*

Basal petioles 1 to 4 inches long; San Luis Obispo County. 9. *L. ludovicianus.*

Plants 6 to 18 inches high.

Petioles 3/4-inch to 1 3/4 inches long.

Flowers about 1/4-inch long; Sierra Nevada, 5000 to 9500 feet elevation . . . . 10. *L. meionanthus.*

Flowers about 1/2-inch long, blue, purple, pink, white or yellow; Monterey County to Mendocino County . . . . 11. *L. variicolor.*

Petioles 1 3/4 to 5 inches long.

Leaflets 6 or 7; flowers less than 1/2-inch long; Napa and Mayacamas ranges . . . . 12. *L. sericatus.*

Leaflets 5 to 9; flowers about 1/2-inch long; Sierra Nevada . . . 13. *L. Grayi.*

1. **Lupinus arboreus** Sims. TREE LUPINE.

A distinctly shrubby plant, 1 1/2 to 8 feet high, with short-petioled leaves; leaflets 6 to 11, usually appressed-silky on both surfaces or becoming glabrate above. Flowers usually bright yellow, rarely blue or violet, in long racemes; keel ciliate along the upper margin. Flowering period, April to September.

Tree Lupine occurs along the ocean shore from Santa Barbara County northward to Del Norte County, and locally at Three-mile Slough, lower Sacramento River *(Bacigalupi)*. Its long clusters of yellow flowers and usually distinct trunk which branches some distance above the ground easily distinguish this species from all others. It usually grows in sandy soils.

Lupinus arboreus Sims, Bot. Mag. t. 682 (1803). Type locality: Cultivated at Kensington, England, from seed gathered in California.

2. **Lupinus longifolius** (Wats.) Abrams. PAUMA LUPINE.

An erect stout shrub, 2 1/2 to 5 feet high, with greenish appressed-pubescent branches. Leaves mostly short-petioled; leaflets 6 to 9, the largest as much as 2 inches long, sparingly silky on both surfaces. Flowers bluish or rarely yellowish, scattered or somewhat whorled, in racemes 8 to 16 inches long; keel more or less ciliate above. Flowering period, January to July.

Pauma Lupine occurs in the foothills and in valleys away from the coast of Los Angeles, Orange, San Diego, and San Bernardino counties.

Lupinus longifolius (Wats.) Abrams, Fl. Los Angeles & Vicinity 209 (1904). *L. Chamissonis* var. *longifolius* Wats. Type locality: San Diego, California. Collected by *Cleveland.*

3. **Lupinus albifrons** Benth. Silver Lupine. Fig. 266.

A tall rounded much branched shrub, 2 to 6 feet high (or much smaller in varietal forms), with very leafy branches and appressed-silky herbage. Leaflets 7 to 10, ½-inch to 1¼ inches long, silvery-silky on both surfaces; petioles of the upper leaves about ½-inch long, those of the lower leaves up to 1½ inches long. Flowers blue or purple, the banner with a yellow center changing to violet, mostly in whorls on an elongated peduncle 3 to 12 inches long; keel ciliate or nearly glabrous in one variety. Flowering period, March to July.

Silver Lupine is a common plant of the dry hillsides and canyons of the Coast Ranges from Humboldt County south to Ventura County, in the lower Sierra Nevada from Shasta County to Tulare County, and occasionally in southern California where it segregates into several varietal forms.

On the hills of the San Francisco Bay region this plant is very low and nearly prostrate. The keel is nearly glabrous. This form is usually known as **L. albifrons** var. **collinus** Greene.

Lupinus albifrons Benth. Hort. Soc. ser. 2, 1:410 (1835). The type specimen was from a cultivated plant grown from seeds collected in California by *Douglas.*

4. **Lupinus excubitus** Jones. Inyo Lupine.

An erect bushy shrub, 2 to 4 feet high, and often 6 feet broad, with densely appressed-silky herbage. Leaflets 5 to 8, ¾-inch to 1½ inches long; petioles 1 to 4 inches long. Flowers very fragrant, blue, lavender or whitish, the banner with a central yellow area turning purplish; keel ciliate. Fruit-pods densely pubescent. Flowering period, May and June.

Inyo Lupine occurs in dry gravelly creek beds and on mesas of the desert area of Inyo County.

Lupinus excubitus Jones, Contr. West. Bot. 8:26 (1898). Type locality: Lone Pine, Inyo County, California. Collected by *Jones.*

5. **Lupinus Chamissonis** Esch. Dune Lupine. Fig. 267.

An erect much branched shrub, 1 to 3 feet high, with pubescent or tomentose herbage. Leaves short-petioled; leaflets 6 to 9, ½-inch to 1 inch long, silky on both surfaces. Flowers blue or lavender; the banner with a yellow center; keel usually not ciliate. Flowering period, April to July.

This is a common shrubby lupine, occurring on the sand hills and valleys along the coast from San Francisco to Los Angeles County, and locally at Three-mile Slough, lower Sacramento River *(Bacigalupi).*

Lupinus Chamissonis Esch. Mem. Acad. Sci. St. Petersb. 10:288 (1826). Type locality: Probably on the sand dunes of San Francisco. Collected by *Chamisso.*

6. **Lupinus Lyallii** var. **Lobbii** (Wats.) C. P. Sm. Alpine Lupine.

A low perennial, 6 inches or less high, arising from a somewhat woody base.

Alpine Lupine inhabits dry alpine summits of the Sierra Nevada from Tulare County northward to Nevada County and of the higher North Coast Ranges of eastern Mendocino, Humboldt, Trinity, and Siskiyou counties. It extends northward to Oregon and Washington.

Lupinus Lyallii var. Lobbii (Wats.) C. P. Sm.; Jepson, Man. 525 (1925). *L. aridus* var. *Lobbii* Wats. Type locality: "high Sierras of California." Collected by *Lobb.*

7. **Lupinus Breweri** Gray. MAT LUPINE.

A low prostrate plant, not over 6 inches high, much branched and matted, with appressed silvery-silky herbage. Leaflets 7 to 10, 1/4- to 3/4-inch long. Flowers violet, 1/4- to 3/8-inch long, the banner with a whitish or yellow center, in densely flowered racemes 1 to 2 inches long; keel not ciliate. Flowering period, June to August.

Mat Lupine occurs on rocky mountain summits of the San Bernardino, San Gabriel, and White mountains, on Mount Piños, in the Sierra Nevada from Tulare County to Lassen County, and in Siskiyou County.

Lupinus Breweri Gray, Proc. Am. Acad. 7:334 (1868). Type locality: Yosemite trail in Yosemite Valley, California. Collected by *Brewer.*

8. **Lupinus laxiflorus** Dougl. CREST LUPINE.

Plants 1 to 2 feet high with several stems from a woody base. Flowering period, May to July.

This species occurs in the northern Sierra Nevada from Mono and Tuolumne counties northward to Modoc and Siskiyou counties, mainly along the crest and on the eastern slopes, occasionally on the western slope from 2000 to 9500 feet elevation. It extends northward to Idaho and eastward to Utah.

Lupinus laxiflorus Dougl.; Lindl. Bot. Reg. t. 1140 (1828). Type locality: "great rapids of the Columbia River." Collected by *Douglas.*

9. **Lupinus ludovicianus** Greene. SAN LUIS OBISPO LUPINE.

Plants 1 to 1 1/2 feet high, with several leafy stems from a woody base. Flowering period, May and June.

This species is known only from dry canyons in western San Luis Obispo County, California.

Lupinus ludovicianus Greene, Bull. Calif. Acad. 1:184 (1885). Type locality: Near San Luis Obispo, California. Collected by *K. Curran.*

10. **Lupinus meionanthus** Gray. TAHOE LUPINE.

An erect or ascending perennial, 1/2-foot to 1 1/2 feet high, with dense subappressed silky stems, woody only at the base. Leaves short-petioled; leaflets 6 to 9, 1/2- to 3/4-inch long, silky-pubescent on both surfaces. Flowers blue or lilac, the banner with a yellow center; keel ciliate on the upper margin. Flowering period, July and August.

Tahoe Lupine occurs in the forests on the slopes of the Sierra Nevada from Madera County to Plumas County, from 5000 to 9500 feet altitude. It extends eastward to Nevada.

Lupinus meionanthus Gray, Proc. Am. Acad. 6:522 (1865). Type locality: Carson City, Nevada. Collected by *Anderson.*

11. **Lupinus variicolor** Steud. VARICOLORED LUPINE.

A low plant, 1/2-foot to 1 1/2 feet high, with several slender decumbent stems from a woody base. Flowering period, April to June.

Varicolored Lupine occurs near the coast on open grassy fields and sand dunes from Monterey County northward to Mendocino County.

Lupinus variicolor Steud. Nom. ed. 2, 2:78 (1841). *L. versicolor* Lindl., not Sweet. Type locality: Type from cultivated plants grown from seed collected in California.

12. **Lupinus sericatus** Kell. SATIN LUPINE.

Plants 5 to 12 inches high, with several decumbent stems from a slightly woody base. Flowering period, April and May.

Satin Lupine occurs on open wooded mountain slopes of the Napa and Mayacamas ranges of Lake, Sonoma, and Napa counties.

Lupinus sericatus Kell. Proc. Calif. Acad. 7:92 (1877). Type locality: Lake County. Collected by *Johanna Anderson.*

13. **Lupinus Grayi** Wats. SIERRA LUPINE.

Plants 5 to 12 inches high, with several ascending stems from a slightly woody base. Flowering period, June and July.

Sierra Lupine occurs chiefly in the open forests between 2400 and 6500 feet elevation on the western slope of the Sierra Nevada from Kern County northward to Plumas County.

Lupinus Grayi Wats. Proc. Am. Acad. 11:126 (1876). *L. Andersonii* var. *Grayi* Wats. Type locality: "near Clarks Ranch (Wawona), Mariposa Co." Collected by *Gray.*

12. **Amorpha** L. INDIGOBUSH

(From the Greek *amorphos,* deformed, in reference to the odd-shaped corolla which consists of a single petal.)

Deciduous shrubs with glandular-dotted herbage. Leaves odd-pinnate, alternate. Flowers bisexual, small, blue, purple, violet, or white, in long terminal spike-like racemes; calyx 5-toothed or -lobed; corolla consisting of 1 petal, this the banner which is folded around the stamens and style; stamens 10, united only at the base, exserted; ovary superior, 1-celled. Fruit a short 1- or 2-seeded pod, tardily dehiscent.

This genus is composed of about 20 species native to the United States and northern Mexico. Two species are native to California.

KEY TO THE SPECIES

Branchlets and rachis without prickle-like glands but with some sessile globose glands; calyx-lobes not more than 1/4 as long as the tube. . . . . . . 1. *A. fruticosa.*

Branchlets and rachis usually with prickle-like glands and with additional sessile globose glands; calyx-lobes 1/3 to 3/4 as long as the tube. . . . . 2. *A. californica.*

1. **Amorpha fruticosa** L. DESERT INDIGOBUSH. FALSE INDIGOBUSH. Fig. 269.

A slender shrub, 3 to 8 feet high, with straight appressed scattered pubescence. Leaves 4 to 8 inches long; leaflets 11 to 21, ovate to oblong, 1/2-inch to 1 1/2 inches long, 3/8- to 3/4-inch wide, sparsely hairy, short-petiolulate; rachis with few sessile glands. Flowers dark purple, about 1/4-inch long, in racemes 3 to 9 inches long; calyx hairy or nearly glabrous, glandular, the teeth short-triangular and not more than 1/4 as long as the tube. Fruit-pods about 1/4-inch long, conspicuously glandular. Flowering period, May to July.

Desert Indigobush occurs in the foothills of the San Bernardino and San Jacinto mountains southward in the lower mountain valleys of San Diego County, in the Upper Sonoran Life Zone. It extends southward to Lower California and eastward to Texas and the Atlantic coast. According to Dayton, the early settlers used this shrub as a substitute for true indigo.

Amorpha fruticosa L. Sp. Pl. 713 (1753). Type locality: Carolina. *A. occidentalis* Abrams.

2. **Amorpha californica** Nutt. CALIFORNIA INDIGOBUSH. MOCK LOCUST. Fig. 268.

A slender shrub, 4 to 9 feet high, with prickle-like glands on the pubescent branchlets and leaf-rachises, and curled and erect pubescence. Leaves 4 to 10 inches long; leaflets 11 to 27, broadly oval to elliptic, 3/8-inch to 1 1/8 inches long, 1/4- to 5/8-inch wide, often with a short straight point at the retuse apex, softly hairy on both surfaces, short-petiolulate; petioles 3/8-inch to 1 inch long, pubescent, with prickle-like stalked glands scattered among the sessile ones. Flowers about 1/4-inch long, reddish purple, in racemes 2 to 8 inches long; calyx densely hairy, glandular or without glands, the teeth from 1/3 the length of to as long as the tube. Fruit-pods about 1/4-inch long, with conspicuous circular depressed glands. Flowering period, May to July.

California Indigobush occurs in wooded canyons of the Upper Sonoran and Transition Life Zones in the Coast Ranges from Sonoma and Napa counties southward to the San Gabriel, San Bernardino, San Jacinto, Santa Rosa, and Santa Ana mountains of southern California, also sparingly on the Marysville Buttes, near Kennett, Shasta County *(Bacigalupi),* and in the foothills of the Sierra Nevada in Shasta (Montgomery Creek, *Wieslander*), northern Placer, and Eldorado counties.

A subglabrous form, **A. californica** var. **napensis** Jepson, occurring on Howell Mountain in the Napa Range has racemes 1 to 1 1/4 inches long and lacks the glands usually found on the rachis. The calyx-teeth are very short.

Amorpha californica Nutt.; T. & G. Fl. N. Am. 1:306 (1838). Type locality: "St. Barbara, California; near the coast." Collected by *Nuttall.*

13. **Lotus** L. BIRD'S-FOOT TREFOIL

(An ancient Greek plant name.)

Herbs or subshrubby plants, with alternate pinnately compound leaves; leaflets 1 to many, entire. Flowers bisexual, irregular, solitary or umbellate, axillary, usually leafy-bracteate; calyx cylindrical, with subequal teeth; corolla with 5 distinct petals, yellow to nearly white, often marked with red, rose, or purple; stamens 10, diadelphous; ovary superior, 1-celled. Fruit a pod, 1- to many-seeded, straight or curved.

The genus *Lotus* is comprised of about 125 species which have been assigned to several genera by various authors. Ottley, in her revision of the Californian species of *Lotus,* states, "Therefore, since characters of generic importance are lacking in inflorescence, flower, and fruit, and since the distinctive leaf characters in addition to being merely vegetative are weakened by the presence of exceptions and intergrades, we have remanded the American species to the Old World genus *Lotus* in its broadest sense." About 30 species occur in California, 7 of which are subshrubby or slightly woody at the base.

KEY TO THE SPECIES

Fruit-pods dehiscent, 3/4-inch to 2 inches long, not beaked; flowers 1/2- to 3/4-inch long . . . . 1. *L. rigidus.*

Fruit-pods indehiscent, 1/2-inch or less long, beaked; flowers less than 1/2-inch long.

Herbage glabrous or nearly so; stems wiry or rush-like, usually ascending or diffuse-spreading.

Umbels sessile or rarely short-peduncled, numerous and rather crowded on the branches; calyx-teeth short-triangular, stiffly erect. . . . 2. *L. scoparius.*

Umbels peduncled.

Umbels few, 2- to 5-flowered; calyx-teeth short-triangular. . . . 3. *L. junceus.*

Umbels numerous, 5- to 11-flowered; the peduncles commonly longer than the leaves; calyx-teeth awl-shaped, lax or recurved, never stiffly erect. 4. *L. Benthamii.*

Herbage silvery-canescent or woolly; stems usually trailing or decumbent.

Umbels 12- to 20-flowered, peduncled. 5. *L. ornithopus.*

Umbels 1- to 8-flowered, sessile or subsessile.

Leaflets 3; umbels 1- to 3-flowered, bractlets none. . . . . 6. *L. leucophyllus.*

Leaflets 3, 4, or 5; umbels 3- to 8-flowered, bractlets usually present. 7. *L. argophyllus.*

1. **Lotus rigidus** (Benth.) Greene. Broom Lotus. Fig. 270.

An erect suffrutescent perennial, 1 to 2½ feet high, with many rigid rush-like stems. Flowering period, March to June.

Broom Lotus occurs on arid slopes and in washes from the Death Valley region of Inyo County southward in the eastern part of the Mohave Desert to the Colorado Desert and adjacent mountain canyons. It extends eastward to Arizona and Utah and southward to Lower California.

Lotus rigidus (Benth.) Greene, Pitt. 2:142 (1890). *Hosackia rigida* Benth. Type locality: Probably on the Colorado Desert. Collected by *Coulter.*

2. **Lotus scoparius** (Nutt.) Ottley. Deerweed. Fig. 271.

A spreading bushy subshrub, 1½ to 4 feet high, with long slender greenish branches and glabrous or sparingly pubescent herbage. Flowering period, February to October.

Deerweed is a common subshrubby perennial of the foothills in the Coast Ranges from Humboldt County southward to San Diego County and in the lower Sierra Nevada foothills of Amador County southward to Kern County. It extends southward to Lower California. This species varies much in size, habit of growth, and number of flowers. Ottley describes 1 variety from the mainland and 3 varieties from the coastal islands.

2a. Var. **brevialatus** Ottley.

Flowers ¼- to ⅜-inch long; banner short; keel extending noticeably beyond the wings. Southern California.

2b. Var. **Veatchii** (Greene) Ottley.

Plants decumbent, herbage more pubescent than in the species. Umbels 5- to 8-flowered. San Miguel Island and Lower California.

2c. Var. **dendroideus** (Greene) Ottley.

Erect, more woody than the species, 4 to 7 feet high. Umbels 7- to 12-flowered. Santa Cruz, Santa Rosa, and Santa Catalina islands.

2d. Var. **Traskiae** (Eastw.) Ottley.

Erect plants. Umbels 3-flowered, pedunculate with or without a bract of one leaflet. Claws of petals conspicuously exserted. Calyx-teeth short, subulate-triangular. Santa Catalina and San Clemente islands.

Lotus scoparius (Nutt.) Ottley, Univ. Calif. Publ. Bot. 10:227 (1923). *Hosackia scoparia* Nutt. Type locality: Santa Barbara, California. Collected by *Nuttall.*

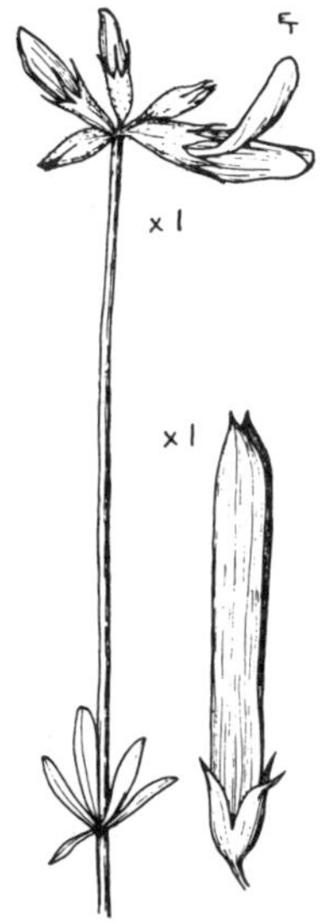

FIG. 270
LOTUS RIGIDUS

FIG. 271
LOTUS SCOPARIUS

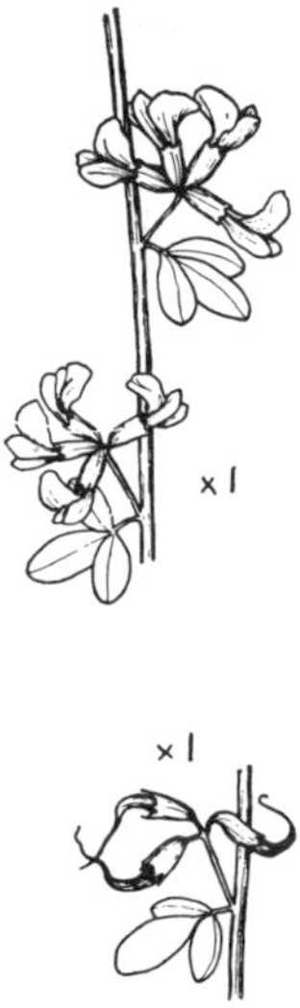

FIG. 272
LOTUS JUNCEUS

FIG. 273
LOTUS BENTHAMII

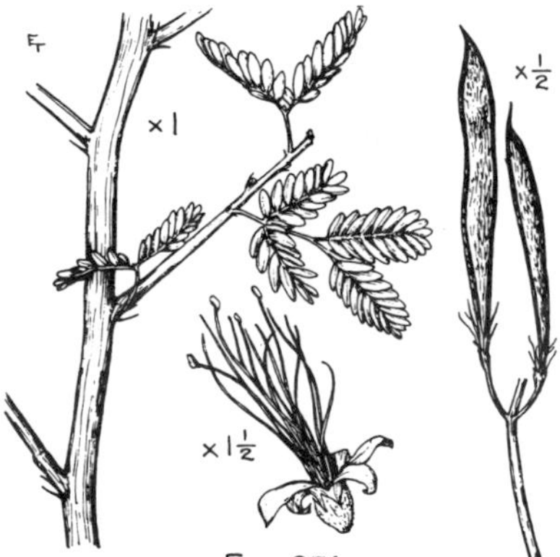

FIG. 274
CALLIANDRA ERIOPHYLLA

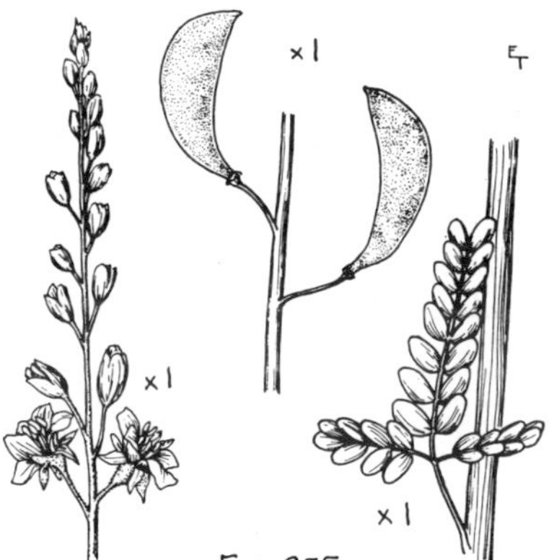

FIG. 275
HOFFMANSEGGIA MICROPHYLLA

Var. brevialatus Ottley, l. c. 229. Type locality: Little Tujunga wash, Los Angeles County. Collected by *Ottley.*

Var. Veatchii (Greene) Ottley, l. c. 228. *Hosackia Veatchii* Greene. Type locality: "Elide [Lower California], opposite Cedros Island." Collected by *Veatch.*

Var. dendroideus (Greene) Ottley, l. c. 228. *Syrmatium dendroideum* Greene. Type locality: Santa Cruz Island. Collected by *Greene.*

Var. Traskiae (Eastw.) Ottley, l. c. 229. *Syrmatium Traskiae* Eastw. Type locality: Mosquito Harbor, San Clemente Island. Collected by *Trask.*

3. **Lotus junceus** (Benth.) Greene. RUSH LOTUS. Fig. 272.

An erect or decumbent much branched subshrub, ¾-foot to 2 feet high, with brownish wiry stems and sparingly hairy herbage, becoming glabrate in age. Flowering period, April to July.

Rush Lotus occurs on the dry hills of the outer Coast Ranges from near Fort Bragg, Mendocino County southward to San Luis Obispo County.

Lotus junceus (Benth.) Greene, Pitt. 2:148 (1890). *Hosackia juncea* Benth. Type locality: California. Collected by *Douglas*. *L. Biolettii* Greene. *L. junceus* var. *Biolettii* (Greene) Ottley.

4. **Lotus Benthamii** Greene. SONOMA LOTUS. Fig. 273.

A much branched decumbent or suberect perennial, with many brownish rush-like stems from a woody base. Flowering period, April to October.

This low suffrutescent plant occurs along the coast of Sonoma County and extends southward to Santa Barbara County, in the lower part of the Transition Life Zone. It is very closely related to *L. scoparius*.

Lotus Benthamii Greene, Pitt. 2:148 (1890). *Hosackia cytisoides* Benth. Type locality: California. Collected by *Douglas*.

5. **Lotus ornithopus** Greene. CATALINA LOTUS.

A much branched perennial, 1 to 3 feet high, woody at the base, with densely silky-pubescent herbage. Flowering period, April and May.

Catalina Lotus occurs on Santa Catalina, San Clemente, Guadalupe, Santa Barbara, and San Nicholas islands.

Lotus ornithopus Greene, Pitt. 2:149 (1890). *Hosackia ornithopus* Greene. Type locality: Guadalupe Island. Collected by *Greene*. *L. argophyllus* var. *ornithopus* (Greene) Ottley.

6. **Lotus leucophyllus** Greene. HOAR LOTUS.

A much branched decumbent or prostrate silky-canescent perennial, slightly woody at the base. Flowering period, April to July.

Hoar Lotus occurs on dry sandy soil in the foothills and on mountain slopes in the Upper Sonoran and Transition Life Zones from San Benito and Monterey counties southward to the San Gabriel and San Bernardino mountains and east to Inyo County.

Lotus leucophyllus Greene, Pitt. 2:149 (1890). *Hosackia sericea* Benth. Type locality: California. Collected by *Douglas*.

7. **Lotus argophyllus** (Gray) Greene. SILVER LOTUS.

A decumbent, silvery-canescent perennial, with many slender stems 2 to 6 feet long from a woody base. Flowering period, March to July.

Silver Lotus occurs in the foothills and on the plains from central California to southern California and on the adjacent islands. It is a variable species and several of the variations have been given the rank of varieties.

Lotus argophyllus (Gray) Greene, Pitt. 2:149 (1890). *Hosackia argophylla* Gray. Type locality: Santa Isabel. Collected by *Thurber*.

14. **Calliandra** Benth.

(From the Greek *kallos,* beautiful, and *andra,* stamen, in reference to the colorful stamens.)

This is a large genus of about 100 species native to the tropical and subtropical Americas and a few to India. A single species occurs in California.

1. **Calliandra eriophylla** Benth. FALSE MESQUITE. Fig. 274.

A densely branched bush, ½-foot to 3 feet high, with unarmed gray branches.

Leaves equally bipinnate, alternate, with 1 to 4 pairs of pinnae; leaflets 5 to 12 pairs, oblong, about 1/8-inch or less long. Flowers bisexual, regular, showy, borne in dense heads, these terminal on axillary peduncles; calyx 5-toothed, reddish brown; corolla of 5 dark red petals joined at base; stamens numerous, pink to deep red, 1/2-inch to 1 inch long, joined at base; ovary superior, 1-celled. Fruit a flat straight pod 2 to 2 1/2 inches long, silvery-pubescent, with dark red thickened margins. Flowering period, March to May.

False-mesquite occurs in small gullies in a few localities in the desert areas of eastern San Diego (Blair Valley, Vallecito Mts., *Florence Youngberg*), Imperial ("5 mi. s. of Midway Well on the Blythe-Glamis Road," *Roxana Ferris;* 20 mi. n. of Ogilby and in small gullies near Tumco, Cargo Muchacho Mts., *Munz* & *Hitchcock;* Mammoth wash n.e. of Calipatria, *Ethel Rockwell*), and Riverside (Mesquite Canyon, *S. B. Parish*) counties. It extends eastward to Texas and southward to Mexico and Lower California.

Calliandra eriophylla Benth. Lond. Jour. Bot. 3:105 (1844). Type locality: "Chila in the district of Pueblo, Mexico." Collected by *Andrieux*.

15. **Hoffmanseggia** Cav.

(Named in honor of J. Centurius, Count of Hoffmansegg, a botanist of the last century.)

This genus consists of about 25 species of herbs or small shrubs native to the southwestern United States, western Mexico, South America, and South Africa. Two species occur in California, one of which is a shrub.

1. **Hoffmanseggia microphylla** Torr. Littleleaf Rushpea. Fig. 275.

A broad rounded shrub, 2 to 6 feet high, with many pubescent rush-like stems. Leaves bipinnate, alternate, with 3 pinnae; the terminal pinna 1/2-inch to 1 1/4 inches long, with 14 to 26 leaflets; the lateral pinnae about 1/2 as long as the terminal one, with 8 to 18 leaflets about 1/8-inch or less long. Flowers yellow, bisexual, slightly irregular, about 3/8-inch long, borne in racemes 4 to 6 inches long; calyx bell-shaped, pubescent, 5-lobed; petals 5, distinct, nearly equal, not much longer than the calyx; stamens 10, distinct, pubescent; ovary superior, 1-celled. Fruit a flat oblong to crescent-shaped pod about 3/4-inch long, pubescent and usually glandular. Flowering period, April and May.

Littleleaf Rushpea occurs in canyons and washes in the Colorado Desert in the Lower Sonoran Life Zone of Riverside and Imperial counties and also near Independence, Inyo County, *Pierson,* acc. *Jepson*. It extends eastward to Arizona and southward to Lower California and Sonora, Mexico.

Hoffmanseggia microphylla Torr. Bot. Mex. Bound. 58 (1859). Type locality: "Sandy desert of the Colorado, California." Collected by *Schott*.

Krameriaceae. Krameria Family

This is a family with a single genus native to North and South America.

1. **Krameria** Loefl.

(Named in honor of J. G. Kramer, Austrian army physician.)

Shrubs or perennial herbs, with alternate simple (rarely 3-foliolate) and entire leaves. Flowers large, purplish, bisexual, irregular, solitary and axillary or in terminal racemes; sepals 5 (or 4), unequal, often petal-like; petals 5, the 3 upper ones with long claws and small blades, the 2 lower ones much smaller and often reduced to broad thick fleshy scales; stamens 4 (or 3), in 2 unequal pairs, usually all on the upper side of the flower; ovary superior, 1-celled, 2-ovuled. Fruit a globose spiny 1-seeded indehiscent pod.

This genus contains about 14 species, all of North and South America. Two species and one variety occur in California. Dayton states that "the genus is of pharmaceutical interest as the source of ratany root *(Krameria radix),* which is a powerful astringent, useful in the treatment of chronic diarrhea and other disorders. The Mexicans use several of the ratanies in dyeing wool and hides yellowish, brownish, or reddish, and the roots have been employed in the manufacture of ink."

KEY TO THE SPECIES

Fruiting spines barbed only at apex; upper petals distinct to the base. . 1. *K. Grayi.*
Fruiting spines usually barbed along the upper part of the spine; upper petals joined by their claws at base . . . . 2. *K. parvifolia.*

1. **Krameria Grayi** Rose & Painter. GRAY KRAMERIA. WHITE RATANY. Fig. 276.

A much branched thorny shrub, 1 to 2 feet high, with white or gray tomentose branchlets. Leaves linear or lanceolate to oblong, 1/8- to 1/2-inch long, silky, sessile. Peduncles gray-tomentose, mostly longer than the leaves, with a pair of leaf-like bracts at or above the middle; sepals 3/8- to 1/2-inch long, purple, spreading or reflexed; petals red-purple, the upper ones spatulate, distinct, about 1/4-inch long, with slender yellowish claws. Fruit subglobose, about 1/4-inch in diameter, the body densely woolly and armed with many slender spines barbed only at apex. Flowering period, April and May to September.

Gray Krameria occurs on stony and sandy areas on the Colorado and southern Mohave deserts, in the Lower Sonoran Life Zone. It extends eastward to New Mexico and Texas and southward to Lower California and Mexico. According to Thornber this plant is browsed in Arizona, almost to the point of extinction, by all classes of livestock, especially in the spring and early summer.

Krameria Grayi Rose & Painter, Contr. U. S. Nat. Herb. 10:108 (1906). *K. canescens* Gray, not Willd. Type locality: Prairies near the Pecos River, Texas. Collected by *Wright.*

2. **Krameria parvifolia** Benth. LITTLELEAF KRAMERIA. PIMA RATANY. Fig. 277.

KEY TO THE SPECIES AND VARIETY

Peduncles and sepals not glandular . . . . *K. parvifolia.*
Peduncles and sepals stipitate-glandular . . . . 2a. var. *glandulosa.*

A low intricately branched spiny shrub, 1 to 2 feet high. Leaves linear, 1/8- to almost 1/2-inch long, sessile. Peduncles silky, slender, 3/8- to 5/8-inch long, not glandular, with 2 or 3 pairs of opposite leaf-like bracts; sepals 1/4- to 7/16-inch long, silky, not glandular, ascending; the 3 upper petals united below into a short claw. Fruit subglobose, the body 1/4- to 3/8-inch in diameter, densely stiff-hairy and spiny, the spines strongly barbed nearly throughout or only on upper part, or rarely only spinose at apex and with 1 or 2 additional barbs. Flowering period, April and May.

Littleleaf Krameria occurs in the mountains bordering the southern part of the Mohave Desert and western Colorado Desert, in San Bernardino, Riverside, and San Diego counties, in the Lower Sonoran Life Zone. It extends eastward to Utah,

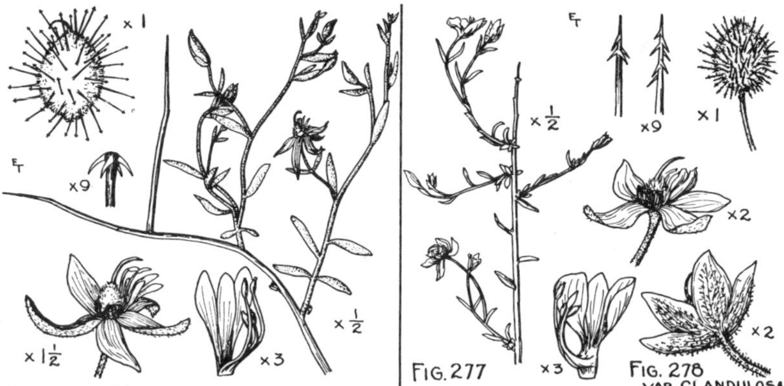

FIG. 276 KRAMERIA GRAYI FIG. 277 FIG. 278 VAR. GLANDULOSA KRAMERIA PARVIFOLIA

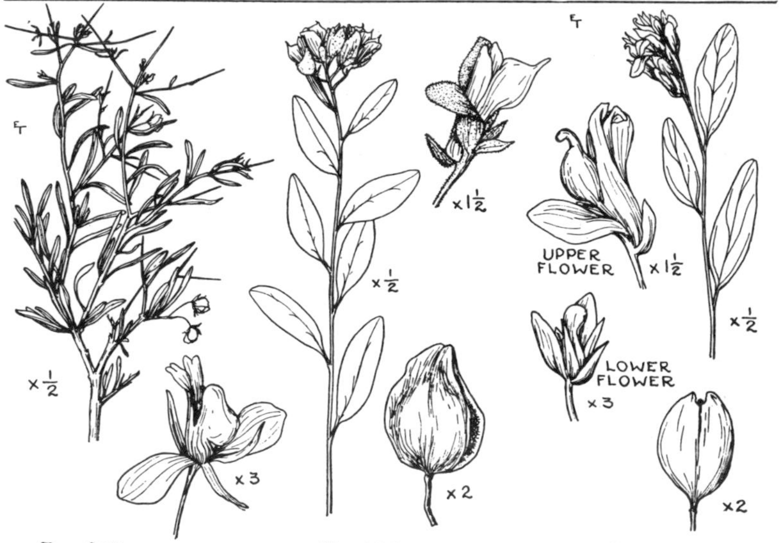

FIG. 279 POLYGALA ACANTHOCLADA FIG. 280 POLYGALA CORNUTA FIG. 281 POLYGALA CALIFORNICA

Nevada, Arizona, and New Mexico and southward into Mexico. The foliage is browsed by cattle.

2a. Var. **glandulosa** (Rose & Painter) Macbr. STICKY KRAMERIA. HEART-NUT. RANGE RATANY. Fig. 278.

Peduncles and the outer sepals stipitate-glandular. Fruit globular, densely beset with straight stiff hairs and bristle-like spines, these mostly barbless or with a few barbs near the apex.

Sticky Krameria occurs in California in a few localities in eastern San Bernardino County (near Ivanpah, New York Mountains) and in the desert canyons of the Santa Rosa Mountains of San Diego and Riverside counties. It extends eastward to New Mexico and Texas and southward to Mexico.

Krameria parvifolia Benth. Bot. Voy. Sulph. 6, pl. 1 (1844). Type locality: Magdalena Bay, Lower California. Collected by *Hinds*. *K. parvifolia* var. *imparata* Macbr.

Var. glandulosa (Rose & Painter) Macbr. Contr. Gray Herb. 56:52 (1918). *K. glandulosa* Rose & Painter. Type locality: El Paso, Texas. Collected by *Rose*.

Polygalaceae. Milkwort Family

The Milkwort Family contains 10 genera with about 680 species of wide distribution, occurring in all parts of the world except in the Arctic regions of North America and Asia, and New Zealand and Polynesia. Only 3 species of a single genus are native to California.

1. **Polygala** L. MILKWORT

(From the Greek *polus,* much, and *gala,* milk, referring to the milky juice which was reputed to be a stimulant to lactation.)

Herbs or shrubs, the stems often with milky juice. Leaves simple, alternate, evergreen. Flowers bisexual, irregular, in racemes, resembling the flowers of the sweet pea; sepals 5, distinct, unequal, the 2 large lateral ones (wings) white or colored, the 2 lower ones smaller, the upper keeled and about the size of the lower ones; petals 3, unequal, the lower one (the keel) boat-shaped, often beaked or crested and enclosing the stamens and pistil, the 2 upper ones usually ligulate and more or less united at base; stamens 8, the filaments united into a tube usually split on the upper side and adnate at the base to the petals; ovary superior, 2-celled, with 2 united carpels. Fruit a 2-celled, thin-walled, 2-seeded capsule.

This genus contains about 450 species occurring on all the continents, 3 of which are native to California.

KEY TO THE SPECIES

Plants distinctly shrubby, with spinescent branchlets; leaves ¼- to ¾-inch long, sessile . . . . 1. *P. acanthoclada*.

Plants woody only below, the branchlets not spinescent; leaves ½-inch to 1¼ inches long, petioled.

  Flowers all with petals; sepals pubescent . . . . 2. *P. cornuta*.

  Flowers of two kinds, those in basal racemes without petals, the others with petals; sepals glabrous . . . . 3. *P. californica*.

1. **Polygala acanthoclada** Gray. THORN POLYGALA. Fig. 279.

An intricately branched spinescent shrub, ½-foot to 3 feet high, with gray-pubescent branches. Leaves oblanceolate to linear-lanceolate, ¼- to ½- (or ¾-) inch long, 1/16- to ⅛-inch wide, finely pubescent on both surfaces, entire, sessile. Flowers few, small, about ¼-inch long, in axillary or terminal clusters, the flower-bearing branchlets produced into stout spines; petals yellowish white, the 2 lateral ones purple-tipped, the keel neither beaked nor ciliate. Capsule oval or round, 3/16-inch in diameter, notched at the apex. Flowering period, May to July.

Thorn Polygala occurs sparingly in the eastern part of the Mohave Desert (Cottonwood Springs, *Jaeger;* Barnwell, *T. S. Brandegee*). It extends eastward into Nevada, northern Arizona, Utah, and southwestern Colorado.

Polygala acanthoclada Gray, Proc. Am. Acad. 11:73 (1876). Type locality: San Juan River, southeastern Utah. Collected by *T. S. Brandegee*.

2. **Polygala cornuta** Kell. HORNED POLYGALA. Fig. 280.

A slender sparingly branched subshrub, 1 to 4 feet high, with numerous usually glabrous stems, woody at base. Flowering period, May to August.

Horned Polygala occurs on thinly wooded slopes and in canyons, at elevations from 1500 to 5000 feet, from Humboldt County north and east to Siskiyou and Shasta counties, thence southward in the Sierra Nevada to Fresno and northeastern Inyo counties.

2a. Var. **Fishiae** (Parry) Jepson.

A spreading bushy plant, 2 to 4 feet high, with long slender branches often climbing over other shrubs. Lateral or wing-sepals purple, finely ciliolate but only rarely puberulent.

This variety is very closely related to the species in morphological characters and perhaps should be included therein. It occupies a distinctly different geographical range, occurring in the mountains below 3000 feet in Santa Barbara, Ventura, Los Angeles, Riverside, and San Diego counties. It extends into Lower California.

Polygala cornuta Kell. Proc. Calif. Acad. ed. 2, 1:63 (1873). ("The Pacific." 1855.) Type locality: Placerville, Eldorado County. Collected by *Kellogg*.

Var. Fishiae (Parry) Jepson, Man. 594 (1925). *Polygala Fishiae* Parry. Type locality: Sauzal, Todos Santos Bay, Lower California. Collected by *Fanny E. Fish*.

3. **Polygala californica** Nutt. CALIFORNIA POLYGALA. Fig. 281.

A low perennial, 2 to 12 inches high, with several spreading stems from a woody base. Flowering period, May to July.

California Polygala inhabits forest floors and chaparral areas of the lower mountain slopes of the outer and middle Coast Ranges from northern San Luis Obispo County northward to Oregon.

Polygala californica Nutt.; T. & G. Fl. N. Am. 1:671 (1840). Type locality: "In the woods at Monterey." Collected by *Hartweg*.

Polygala subspinosa Wats. is a rare perennial, sometimes subshrubby, occurring in the lower mountains of southeastern Inyo County (Chloride Cliff, Death Valley, acc. *P. A. Munz*). It has spinose-tipped branches and yellowish flowers 1/3- to 1/2-inch long.

Euphorbiaceae. Spurge Family

This is a large and extremely variable family of about 220 genera and 4000 species of herbs, shrubs, and trees with acrid and often milky juice, of wide geographic distribution but chiefly tropical and subtropical. Ten genera and 34 species occur in California, 11 of which are woody at least at the base. The Castor-bean and Poinsettia belong to this family.

KEY TO THE GENERA

Plants distinctly shrubby.
- Branchlets spinescent; leaves small, crowded on short blunt branchlets which give the branches a rough appearance after the leaves fall; capsule 3-celled. .... 1. HALLIOPHYTUM.
- Branches not spinescent.
  - Leaves broad and palmately 7- to 11-lobed or -cleft.............. 2. RICINUS.
  - Leaves not lobed.
    - Leaves distinctly toothed.

Leaves greenish, broadly ovate or somewhat heart-shaped, often with 3 or 5 veins from the base; staminate flowers in spikes ½- to ¾-inch long .... 3. ACALYPHA.
Leaves grayish at least beneath, ovate to obovate, never heart-shaped, all 1-veined from the base; staminate flowers in racemes about ¼-inch long.. 4. BERNARDIA.
Leaves entire.
Leaves linear, opposite or some alternate; capsule 4-celled. 5. TETRACOCCUS.
Leaves round-ovate or obcordate, mostly alternate; capsule 3-celled; flowers in a single flower-like involucre............. 6. EUPHORBIA.
Plants herbaceous, woody only at base.
Herbage glabrous.
Stems rush-like; corolla none................................ 7. STILLINGIA.
Stems not rush-like; corolla present..................... 10. ARGYTHAMNIA.
Herbage pubescent or hirsute.
Leaves coarsely and sharply serrate, hirsute with stinging hairs.... 8. TRAGIA.
Leaves entire or nearly so, without stinging hairs.
Petioles ¼-inch to 1 inch long; petals absent................ 9. CROTON.
Petioles ⅛-inch or less long; petals present............ 10. ARGYTHAMNIA.

1. **Halliophytum** Johnst.

(Named in honor of H. M. Hall, a California botanist, and from the Greek *phyton,* plant.)

This is a genus with a single species and one variety.

1. **Halliophytum fasciculatum** var. **Hallii** (Brandg.) n. comb. CHUCKAWALLA BUSH. Fig. 282.

A rigid divaricately branched spinescent shrub, 2 to 6 feet high, with alternate very short knob-like or blunt spur-like leaf-bearing branchlets. Leaves simple, alternate or clustered on the short branchlets, deciduous; the blades oblanceolate or ovate, about ¼-inch long, nearly glabrous, entire, sessile. Flowers minute, apetalous, unisexual, the staminate and pistillate on different plants; staminate flowers on slender pedicels in axillary umbellate clusters, sepals 4 to 6, stamens 4 to 6, alternating with the lobes of a fleshy disk; pistillate flowers solitary, on short stout pedicels, the ovary superior, 3-celled. Fruit a globose 3-celled capsule, about ¼-inch in diameter, depressed at base, with 1 seed in each cell. Flowering period, January to May.

This spiny shrub occurs on dry benches and slopes of the mountains on the north side of the Colorado Desert in Imperial, Riverside, and San Bernardino counties. (Cottonwood Springs, *Parish;* Beals Well, *E. Jaeger;* Chuckawalla Bench, *Hall;* 5 mi. s. of Cottonwood Springs, *C. L. Hitchcock;* between Eagle Mts. and Cottonwood Mts. along road from Pinto Basin to Mecca, and 10 mi. s. of Ivanpah, *McMinn*). It extends eastward into Arizona (Kofa Mts., Yuma County, *Wiggins*).

Halliophytum fasciculatum var. Hallii (Brandg.) McMinn. *Tetracoccus Hallii* Brandg. Type locality: Colorado Desert, between Canyon Springs and Chuckawalla Springs. Collected by *Hall. Halliophytum Hallii* (Brandg.) Johnst. *Securinega fasciculatum* var. *Hallii* Jepson.

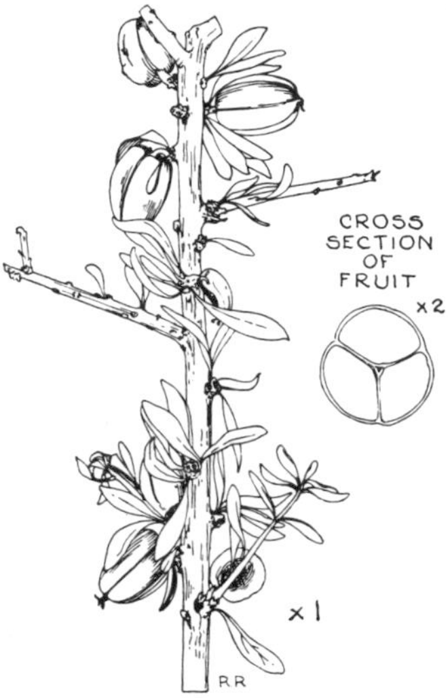

FIG. 282
HALLIOPHYTUM FASCICULATUM VAR. HALLII

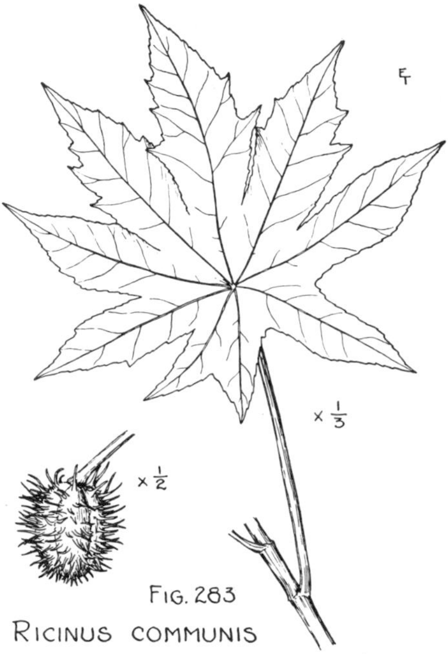

FIG. 283
RICINUS COMMUNIS

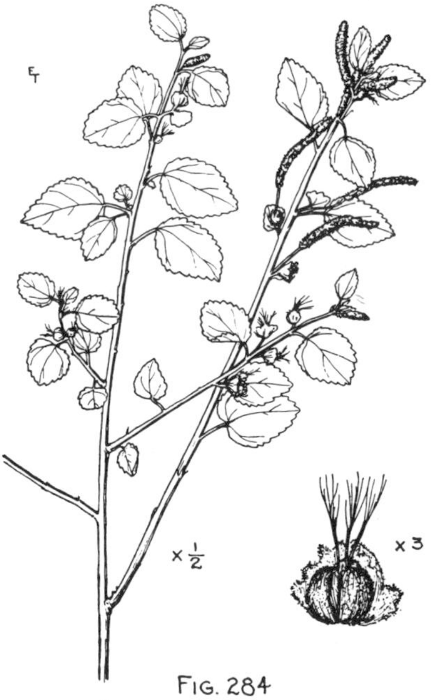

FIG. 284
ACALYPHA CALIFORNICA

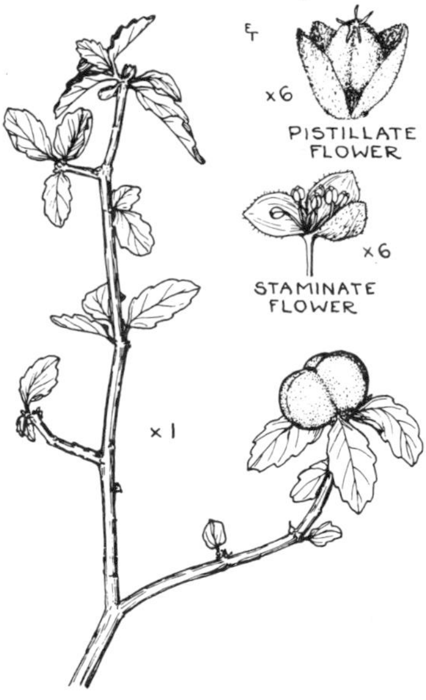

FIG. 285
BERNARDIA MYRICAEFOLIA

2. **Ricinus** L.

(From the Latin name of a genus of ticks, in reference to the resemblance of the seed of this plant to the tick. This genus consists of one species with many horticultural forms, and is probably native to Africa.)

1. **Ricinus communis** L. CASTOR-BEAN. CASTOR OIL PLANT. Fig. 283.

A large perennial herb or shrub, 4 to 8 feet high, with glabrous round often red stems.

Castor-bean is an introduced plant but is cultivated throughout California. The large glossy leaves, reddish stems, and resistance to insect enemies and fungus diseases make the plants very suitable for ornamental use. In southern California, it has escaped from cultivation and has become naturalized, especially in and around the Mexican settlements bordering the arroyos.

Ricinus communis L. Sp. Pl. 1007 (1753).

3. **Acalypha** L.

(From the Greek *akalyphes,* a nettle, in reference to the hispid herbage of some species.)

This genus contains about 230 species of herbs and shrubs, chiefly tropical or subtropical. A single species is native to California.

1. **Acalypha californica** Benth. CALIFORNIA COPPERLEAF. Fig. 284.

A slender rigidly branched shrub, 1 to 2 feet high. Leaves simple, alternate; the blades ovate to cordate, ½-inch to 1¼ inches long and about as wide, 1- or 3- to 5-veined from the base, glandular-pubescent to almost glabrous in age, brown beneath, finely toothed; petioles ⅛- to ¾-inch long. Flowers small, unisexual, the staminate and pistillate on the same plant, apetalous; the staminate flowers in peduncled spikes ½-inch to 1¼ inches long with one or more pistillate flowers at the base, calyx 4-parted, stamens usually 8, distinct; pistillate flowers solitary and few or in short spikes, calyx 3- to 8-lobed; ovary superior, 3-celled. Fruit a 3-celled, 3-seeded capsule, often surrounded by an enlarged bract. Flowering period, May and June.

This rare shrub is known in California only from San Diego County where it occurs on the dry hills between Jamul and Jamacha, also near Ramona, Bernardo, Foster, Lakeside, and Poway. It extends southward to Lower California on the islands in the Gulf of California, and Cedros Island.

Acalypha californica Benth. Bot. Voy. Sulph. 51 (1844). Type locality: Magdalena Bay, Lower California. Collected by *Hinds.*

4. **Bernardia** Houst. ex. P. Br.

(Named for P. F. Bernard, a French botanist.)

This is a genus of about 20 subtropical or tropical American species. A single species is native to the United States.

1. **Bernardia myricaefolia** (Scheele) Wats. BERNARDIA. Fig. 285.

An irregularly branched shrub, 3 to 8 feet high, with a grayish green fine dense star-shaped pubescence. Leaves simple, alternate, semi-deciduous; the blades thick, oblong to ovate, ¼-inch to 1½ (or 2) inches long, prominently net-veined, serrate or crenate; petioles ⅛-inch or less long. Flowers small, apetalous, unisexual, staminate and pistillate on the same plant or rarely on separate plants; staminate flowers in axillary raceme-like clusters, calyx 3- to 5-parted, stamens 4 to 8, alternating with minute glands; pistillate flowers terminal, sessile, calyx usually 6- (sometimes 3- or 9-) parted, ovary 3-celled and tomentulose. Fruit a globose capsule about ½-inch in diameter, whitened by a dense but close stellate tomentum, 2- or 3-lobed. Flowering period, April to November.

Bernardia is a rare shrub in California, occurring in dry rocky canyons of the mountains on the north and west sides of the Colorado Desert (Eagle Mts.; San Felipe; northern end of Santa Rosa Mts.; along Palms to Pines Highway; Cottonwood Spring; about 17 mi. s.e. Warner's Ranch, *Jaeger;* Whitewater) and in the southern Mohave Desert (Pinyon Wells). It extends eastward in Arizona and New Mexico to Texas, and southward to Lower California and Tamaulipas, Mexico.

Bernardia myricaefolia (Scheele) Wats. Bot. Calif. 2:70 (1880). *Tyria myricaefolia* Scheele. Type locality: "Neubraunfels, Texas." Collected by *Lindheimer.*

5. **Tetracoccus** Engelm.

(From the Greek *tetra,* four, and *coccus,* fruit, in reference to the 4-lobed fruit.)

Evergreen shrubs. Leaves simple, opposite or some alternate. Flowers small, reddish, unisexual, the staminate and pistillate flowers borne on separate plants, apetalous. Staminate flowers few to many, in clusters; sepals 6 to 10, joined at base; stamens 6 to 9, surrounding a circle of disk-glands. Pistillate flowers solitary; the peduncle about ¼-inch long; sepals 6 to 12, joined at base; ovary superior, 4-celled; styles 4, distinct. Fruit a 4-lobed and 4-celled capsule.

This genus contains 2 species native to California and adjacent Lower California.

KEY TO THE SPECIES

Leaves linear, entire . . . . 1. *T. dioicus.*
Leaves ovate-lanceolate to ovate, with 2 to 6 teeth on each margin.
2. *T. ilicifolius.*

1. **Tetracoccus dioicus** Parry. SAN DIEGO TETRACOCCUS. Fig. 286.

An erect spreading shrub, 1½ to 5 feet high, with rather slender grayish glabrous branches. Leaf-blades linear, ½-inch to 1¼ inches long, about ⅛-inch wide, glabrous, dull green above, brownish beneath, entire; petioles about 1/16-inch long. Peduncles and sepals of pistillate flowers glabrous. Capsules about ¼-inch in diameter, usually 4-seeded. Flowering period, April and May.

This shrub is known in California only from San Diego County (Red Mt. grade near Fallbrook, *Munz* & *Johnston;* near Temecula just south of Riverside County line, *McMinn;* near Jamacha, *Alice Murphy*). It extends southward into Lower California.

Tetracoccus dioicus Parry, West Am. Sci. 1:13 (1885). Type locality: Table Mountain, Lower California. Collected by *Parry.*

2. **Tetracoccus ilicifolius** Cov. & Gilman. HOLLYBUSH. HOLLYLEAF TETRACOCCUS. Fig. 287.

An openly branched shrub, 1 to 4½ feet high, with gray stems from an enlarged base. Leaves opposite; the blades ovate-lanceolate to ovate, ½-inch to 1¼ inches long, ¼- to ½-inch wide, thick, holly-like, pinnately veined, villous with pale brownish hairs on both surfaces when young, becoming glabrous, with as many as 6 teeth on each margin; petioles about 1/16-inch long. Peduncles and sepals of pistillate flowers with pale brownish hairs. Capsules oblong-orbicular, about ¼-

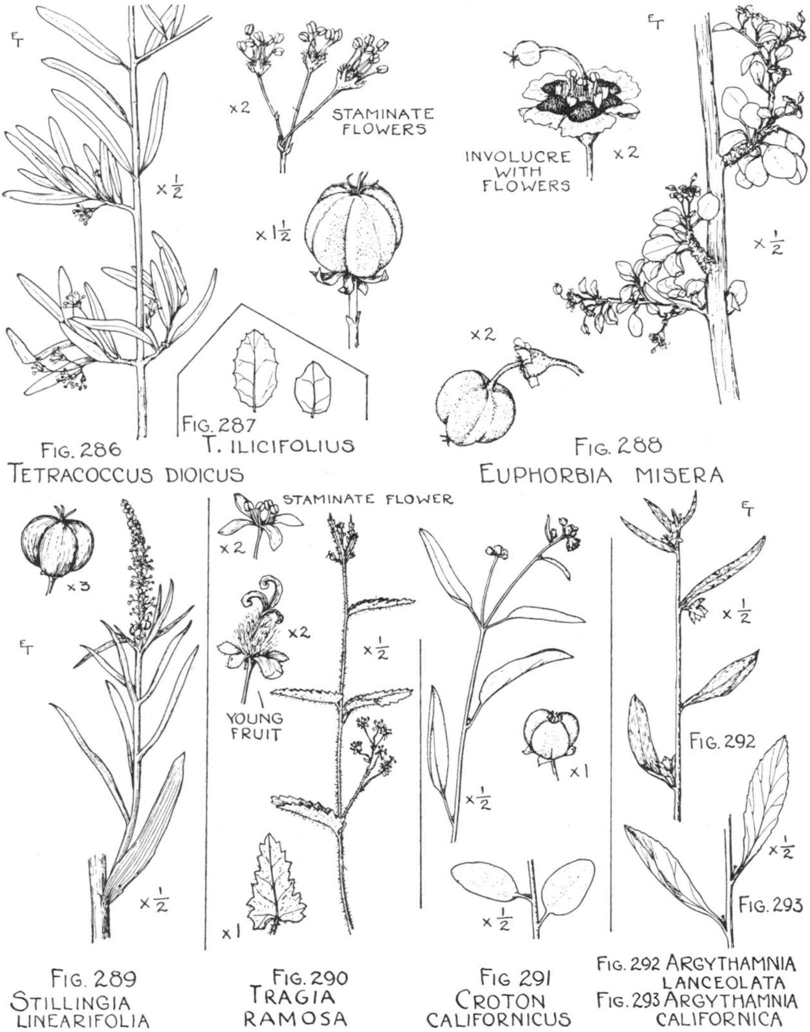

inch long, 4-celled, with usually 2 seeds in each cell. Flowering period, April and May.

Hollybush is known only from a large canyon north of Titus Canyon, on the west slope of the Grapevine Mountains in Death Valley, Inyo County, California. It was first collected in May 1936 by M. F. Gilman. According to Coville and Gilman only 15 plants had been discovered up to August 2, 1936.

Tetracoccus ilicifolius Cov. & Gilman, Jour. Wash. Acad. Sci. 26:531 (1936). Type locality: Grapevine Mountains, Inyo County, California. Collected by *M. F. Gilman.*

6. **Euphorbia.** L. Spurge

(Said by Pliny to be named in honor of Euphorbus, King Juba's physician.)

This is a large genus of about 1000 species of herbs, shrubs, and trees, most abundant in warm temperate and tropical regions. Many of the species are fleshy and are grown with cacti in succulent and cactus gardens. About 20 species are native to California, only one being a shrub.

1. **Euphorbia misera** Benth. Cliff Spurge. Bush Euphorbia. Fig. 288.

A much branched straggling shrub, 2 to 5 feet high, with glabrate or pubescent gray or brownish branches. Leaves simple, alternate or rarely opposite, often clustered on short spur-like branchlets; the blades round-ovate or obcordate, 1/4- to 1/2-inch long and as broad, often notched at apex, usually pubescent or scabrous, entire; petioles 1/8-inch or less long. Flowers small, apetalous, unisexual, the several staminate and single pistillate included in the same calyx-like involucre. Involucres hemispherical, less than 1/8-inch long, solitary and terminal on the short seasonal branchlets; the lobes 4 or 5, with as many purple glands in their sinuses; the glands usually with white crenulate appendages or margins. Pistillate flowers consisting of a single pistil on a pedicel which soon pushes the pistil beyond the involucral cup; calyx minute; ovary superior, 3-celled; styles 3, bifid. Staminate flowers consisting of a single stamen, jointed upon a short pedicel, usually with a minute bract or scale at base. Fruit a 3-celled, 3-seeded capsule about 1/4-inch long, with 3 rounded lobes, somewhat pubescent and warty. Flowering period, December to August.

Cliff Spurge occurs occasionally on the sea-bluffs in Orange and San Diego counties, on the Colorado Desert near Palm Springs *(E. C. Jaeger),* and on Santa Catalina Island. It extends southward into Lower California and on Cedros and Guadalupe islands.

Euphorbia misera Benth. Bot. Voy. Sulph. 51 (1844). Type locality: San Diego, California. Collected by *Hinds.*

7. **Stillingia.** A. Garden

(Named in honor of Benjamin Stillingfleet, an English botanist.)

A small genus of about 15 species of herbs, rarely woody at base, occurring in North and South America and on the Pacific islands.

1. **Stillingia linearifolia** Wats. Desert Stillingia. Fig. 289.

A slender erect perennial herb, 1 to 2 feet high, sometimes woody at base, with glaucous and glabrous herbage. Flowering period, February and March.

This rush-like perennial occurs occasionally on sandy and rocky hills and mesas between 1000 and 3000 feet altitude in cismontane interior valleys of southern California and extends southward to Lower California.

Stillingia linearifolia Wats. Proc. Am. Acad. 14:297 (1879). Type locality: "Boundary Monument, San Diego." Collected by *Palmer.*

8. **Tragia** L.

(Named in honor of Hieronymus Bock, a German botanist, Tragus being the Latin name of Bock.)

This genus contains about 100 species of herbs and shrubs, widely distributed in the subtropics and tropics of all continents except Europe. A single species is native to California.

1. **Tragia ramosa** Torr. TRAGUS BUSH. Fig. 290.

A small perennial herb, sometimes woody at base, 6 to 12 inches high, with several erect slender stems bearing stinging hairs. Flowering period, March and April.

This is a rare species in California, occurring on the east slope of the Providence Mountains and on Clark Mountain *(E. C. Jaeger)* in northeastern San Bernardino County, above 3000 feet altitude. It extends eastward to Missouri and Texas.

Tragia ramosa Torr. Ann. Lyc. N. Y. 2:245 (1828). Type locality: Probably northern New Mexico. Collected by *James*.

9. **Croton** L.

(From the Greek *kroton,* a tick, the seeds resembling that insect.)

This is a large genus of about 600 species, mostly herbs but some shrubs and a few trees, of the warm temperate and tropical regions. A single species is native to California.

1. **Croton californicus** Muell. Arg. CROTON. Fig. 291.

A low perennial, often slightly woody at the base, 2½ feet or less high, with gray-scurfy or hoary herbage. Flowering period, March to October.

This species occurs in sandy washes and on dry slopes below 3000 feet altitude from Contra Costa County (near Antioch) southward in the coastal region to southern California and thence eastward to the Colorado and Mohave deserts. Much variation occurs in the habit of growth, size and shape of leaves, and other characters.

Croton californicus Muell. Arg.; DC. Prodr. 15^2:691. (1866). *Hendecandra procumbens* Esch. Type locality: San Francisco, California. Collected by *Chamisso*.

10. **Argythamnia** P. Br.

(From the Greek *arguros,* silver, and *thamnos,* bush, in reference to the silvery coating of hairs in most of the species.)

This is a genus of about 35 species, chiefly of tropical America. Four species are native to California, one of which is often slightly woody at base.

1. **Argythamnia lanceolata** (Benth.) n. comb. SILVER BUSH. Fig. 292.

A low much branched subshrub, ½-foot to 2 feet high, with silvery-strigose herbage. Flowering period, March to May.

Silver Bush is known from the northern and western borders of the Colorado Desert. It extends eastward into Arizona and southward into Lower California.

Argythamnia lanceolata (Benth.) McMinn. *Serophyton lanceolatum* Benth. Type locality: Magdalena Bay, Lower California. Collected by *Hinds. Argythamnia sericophylla* Gray. *Ditaxis lanceolata* (Benth.) Pax. & Hoffm.

Argythamnia californica Brandg. occasionally has stems from a slightly woody base. Fig. 293. The herbage is glabrous instead of hairy-strigose as in *A. lanceolata.*

Zygophyllaceae. Caltrops Family

This family consists of about 25 genera and 160 species of perennial herbs, shrubs, or rarely trees of the warmer parts of the world especially in desert regions. Four genera, with 4 species, are native to California, only 2 of which are woody.

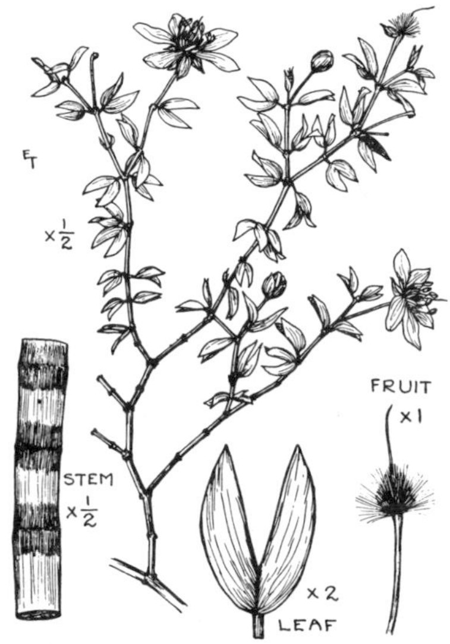

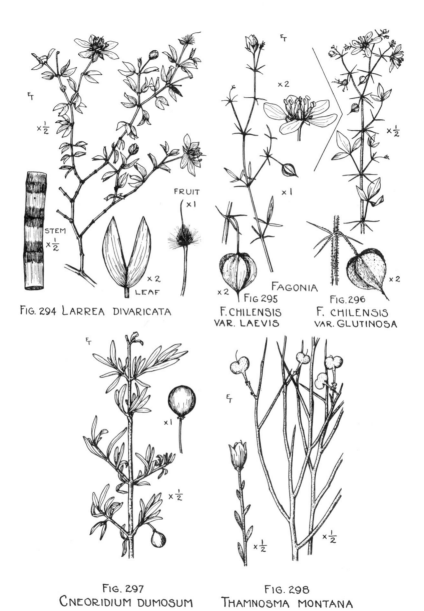

FIG. 294 LARREA DIVARICATA

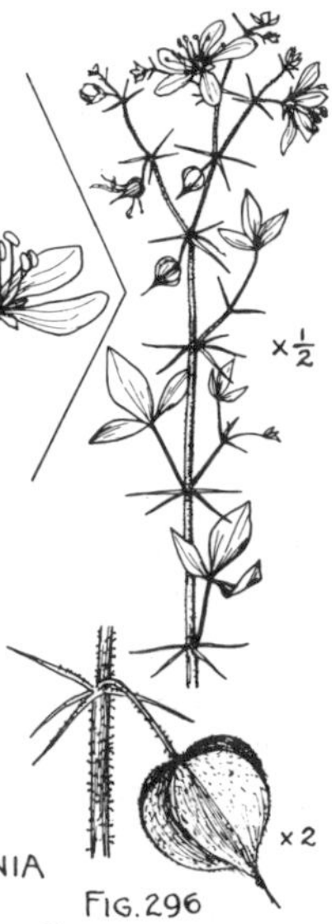

FAGONIA

FIG 295
F. CHILENSIS
VAR. LAEVIS

FIG. 296
F. CHILENSIS
VAR. GLUTINOSA

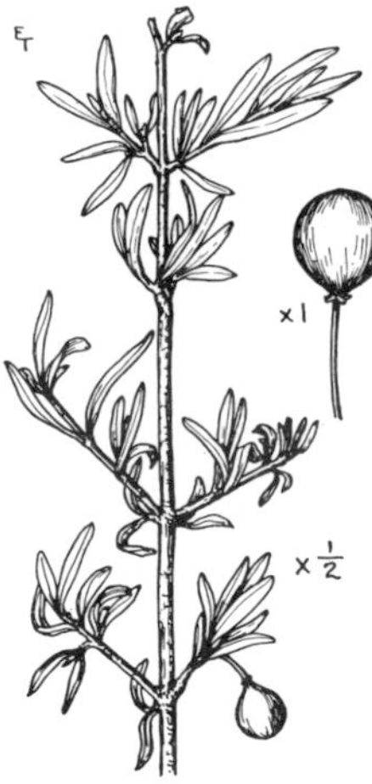

FIG. 297
CNEORIDIUM DUMOSUM

FIG. 298
THAMNOSMA MONTANA

KEY TO THE GENERA

Leaflets 2; flowers yellow. . . . . 1. LARREA.
Leaflets 3; flowers purplish. . . . . 2. FAGONIA.

1. **Larrea** Cav.

(Named for J. A. de Larrea, a Spanish promoter of science.)

This is a small genus of 3 or 4 species of the southwestern United States, Mexico, and the dry regions of South America.

1. **Larrea divaricata** Cav. CREOSOTE BUSH. Fig. 294.

An erect diffusely branched evergreen shrub, 2 to 9 feet high, with strong-scented resinous foliage and brittle branches with dark glutinous or corky rings at the nodes. Leaves opposite, consisting of a pair of sessile leaflets which appear as a single bilobed simple leaf; leaflets obliquely lanceolate to oblong, somewhat sickle-shaped, 3/8-inch or less long, indistinctly 3-veined from the base, finely silky-pubescent, becoming glabrate, entire; petioles about 1/8-inch long. Flowers bisexual, regular or nearly so, yellow, solitary and terminal on the short lateral branchlets; sepals 5, early deciduous; petals 5, distinct, about 1/4-inch long, often turned about halfway and cupped inwardly; stamens 10, inserted on a 10-lobed disk; ovary superior, 5-celled, short-stipitate. Fruit a globose capsule, 1/4-inch or less long, composed of 5 carpels eventually separating into 1-seeded nutlets, densely white- or rusty-hairy, tipped by the persistent style. Flowering period, November to May.

Creosote Bush is the most common and widely distributed shrub of the Lower Sonoran Life Zone in the desert regions of southern California where it often forms pure associations making a distinct belt of vegetation known as the *Larrea (Covillea)* belt. A few bushes occur on the bank of Poso Creek about 200 yards north of the bridge on the road between Woody and Bakersfield, Kern County. It extends eastward through Nevada, Arizona, and New Mexico to Texas and southward into Mexico. It also occurs in Argentina, South America. The North American plants may prove, upon further research, to be distinct from those of Argentina, but at present there seem to be no known valid morphological characters for separating them.

Paul C. Standley, in *Trees and Shrubs of Mexico,* gives the following account of the economic importance of Creosote Bush. "The flower buds, pickled in vinegar, are said to be eaten like capers. The plant is much used in domestic medicine, especially for rheumatism, a decoction of the leaves being employed for baths or fomentations. The decoction is said, also, to have remarkable antiseptic properties, and is applied to bruises and sores. It is taken internally for gastric disturbances and for venereal diseases. A reddish brown lac is often deposited upon the branches by a small scale insect. This lac is used in some parts of Mexico for dyeing leather red, and the Coahuilla Indians of California employ it as a cement. The same Indians use a decoction of the plant for intestinal complaints and for tuberculosis. The Pima Indians of Arizona drink a decoction of the leaves as an emetic, and apply the boiled leaves as poultices to wounds and sores."

Larrea divaricata Cav. Anal. Hist. Nat. 2:119 (1800). Type locality: "Between Mendoza and Buenos Aires, Argentina." *Larrea glutinosa* Engelm. *Larrea tridentata* Cov. *Covillea glutinosa* Rydb. *Larrea tridentata* var. *glutinosa* (Rydb.) Jepson.

2. Fagonia L.

(Named in honor of G. C. Fagon, a French botanist of the 17th century.)

This genus contains about 18 species native to the Mediterranean region, southwest Africa, Chile, the southwestern United States, and Mexico. A single woody species, represented by 2 varieties, is native to California.

KEY TO THE VARIETIES

Leaflets linear-oblong, less than 1/8-inch wide; branchlets, peduncles, and petioles glabrous, not glandular.......................... 1. *F. chilensis* var. *laevis*.

Leaflets rhombic-obovate to obliquely ovate, 1/8- to 3/8-inch wide; branchlets, peduncles, and petioles glandular.............. 2. *F. chilensis* var. *glutinosa*.

1. **Fagonia chilensis** var. **laevis** (Standl.) Johnst. CALIFORNIA FAGONIA. Fig. 295.

A low much branched subshrub, 1/2-foot to 2 feet high, with stems round or obscurely angled below, angled and channeled above, minutely spinulose or scabrous on the angles, not glandular. Leaves 3-foliolate, opposite, with small spiny stipules. Flowers small, crimson or rose-purple, bisexual, in open clusters terminating the branches. Fruit dry, about 3/16-inch long, deeply 5-lobed, the 5 one-seeded carpels separating from the axis and dehiscing along the inner edge. Flowering period, March to May.

This variety is the prevailing form found on the dry slopes of the hills and on the lower mountain slopes of the Colorado Desert and adjacent areas in Imperial, Riverside, and San Diego counties. It extends southward into Lower California.

Fagonia chilensis var. laevis (Standl.) Johnst. Proc. Calif. Acad. ser. 4, 12:1051 (1924). *Fagonia laevis* Standl. Type locality: Yuma, Arizona. Collected by *M. E. Jones*. *Fagonia californica* Benth., in part.

2. **Fagonia chilensis** var. **glutinosa** (Vail) Johnst. STICKY FAGONIA. Fig. 296.

Branches, peduncles, and petioles viscid with yellow glands.

This variety occurs occasionally on the Colorado Desert (Split Mountain, San Diego Co., *T. S. Brandegee;* etc.). It extends southward into Sonora, Mexico and Lower California.

Fagonia chilensis var. glutinosa (Vail) Johnst. Proc. Calif. Acad. ser. 4, 12:1051 (1924). *Fagonia californica* var. *glutinosa* Vail. Type locality: Sonora, Mexico. Collected by *Pringle*. *Fagonia californica* var. *Barclayana,* acc. Jepson in Fl., not Benth. *Fagonia viscosa* Rydb.

Rutaceae. Rue Family

The Rue Family contains about 120 genera and 900 species, widely distributed in the tropics and subtropics, especially abundant in Africa and Australia. The citrus fruits belong to this family. Three genera are represented in California, each by a single species.

KEY TO THE GENERA

Leaves opposite, usually clustered near the ends of the branches; fruit drupe-like. 1. CNEORIDIUM.

Leaves alternate.

Leaves simple; fruit a 2-lobed coriaceous capsule............. 2. THAMNOSMA.

Leaves trifoliolate; fruit a samara, with the wing all around........ 3. PTELEA.

1. **Cneoridium** Hook.

(Like *Cneorum,* a south European and north African genus.)
This genus contains a single species.

1. **Cneoridium dumosum** (Nutt.) Hook. f. BERRYRUE. BUSHRUE. Fig. 297. A strong-scented much branched glabrous shrub, 2 to 3 feet high. Leaves simple, opposite, often crowded at the ends of the short lateral branchlets, linear or spatulate, rounded at the apex, tapering to the base, 1/2-inch to 1 inch long, a little less than 1/8-inch wide, glandular-dotted especially on the lower surfaces and margin, yellowish green, entire, sessile. Flowers bisexual, 1 to 3 on short axillary or terminal peduncles, the peduncles solitary or clustered; sepals 4, very small, persistent; petals 4, white, obovate, about 1/6-inch long, spreading; stamens 8, those opposite the petals shorter than the others; filaments dilated and inserted around the base of a disk; ovary superior, globose, 1-celled, seated on a flat cushion-like disk; stigma capitate. Fruit drupe-like, globose, about 1/4-inch in diameter, 1- or 2-seeded, reddish brown, glabrous. Flowering period, January to April.

Berryrue is a common shrub in the chaparral belt of the Upper and Lower Sonoran Life Zones in San Diego County. It extends eastward to the desert slopes of the Cuyamaca and San Jacinto mountains. It also occurs in Lower California and in Arizona.

Cneoridium dumosum (Nutt.) Hook. f.; Baillon, Hist. Pl. 4:498 (1873). *Pitavia dumosa* Nutt. Type locality: San Diego, California. Collected by *Nuttall.*

2. **Thamnosma** Torr. & Frem.

(From the Greek *thamnos,* a bush, and *osme,* scent or bad smell.)
This genus consists of 2 species of shrub-like plants of the arid southwestern United States and northern Mexico. Only the following species has been found in California.

1. **Thamnosma montana** Torr. & Frem. TURPENTINE BROOM. Fig. 298.
A strong-scented glandular shrub, 1 to 2 feet high, with rigid often spinose branchlets and yellowish green bark. Leaves simple, alternate, soon deciduous, oblanceolate, 1/4- to 1/2-inch long, entire, sessile. Flowers 1/4- to 1/2-inch long, black-purple, in short racemes or solitary and scattered along the branchlets; sepals 4, united at base; petals 4, ovate or oblong, 1/4- to 1/2-inch long, purple, erect, scarcely spreading in age; stamens distinct, 4 long and 4 short; ovary superior, 2-celled, stipitate; style exserted. Fruit a 2-lobed coriaceous stipitate capsule. Flowering period, March to May.

Turpentine Broom inhabits the dry hills of the Colorado and Mohave deserts, in the Lower Sonoran Life Zone. It extends north into Inyo County, south into northern Mexico, and eastward to Nevada, Utah, and Arizona. According to Paul C. Standley, the Indians of Arizona make a tonic and blood purifier from a decoction of the plant.

Thamnosma montana Torr. & Frem.; Frem. Rep. 313 (1845). Type locality: "Virgin River, s. Utah." Collected by *Fremont.*

3. **Ptelea** L.

(Greek name of the elm, transferred to this genus on account of its similar fruit.)
This genus shows great variability and consists of 3 to 7 (1 to 60, in the opinion of some botanists) species, native to the United States and Mexico.

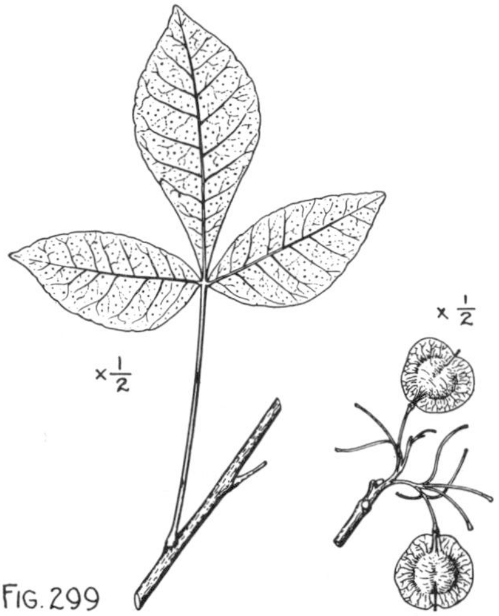

FIG. 299
PTELEA BALDWINII VAR. CRENULATA

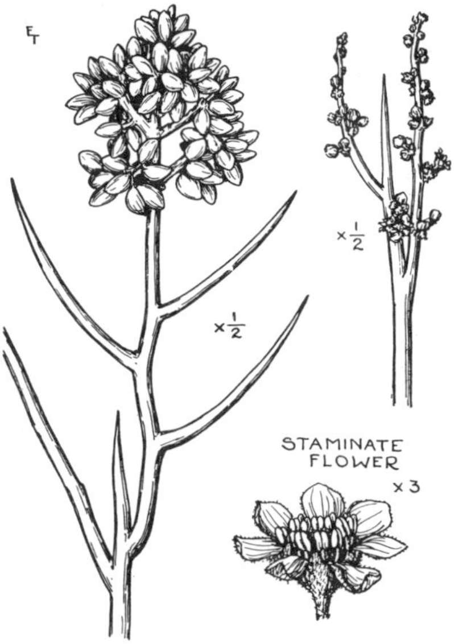

FIG. 300 HOLACANTHA EMORYI

FIG. 301 SIMMONDSIA CHINENSIS

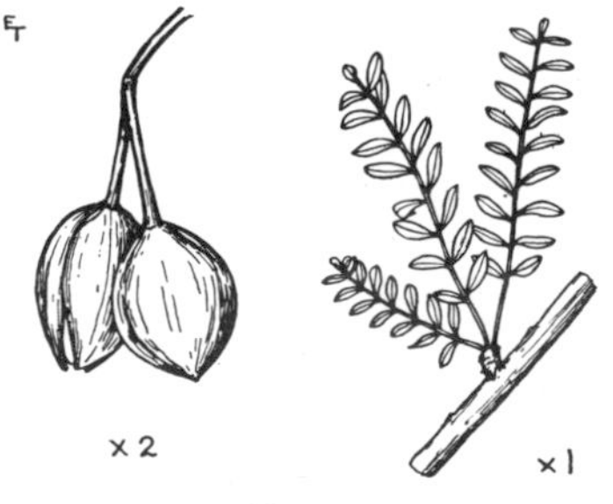

FIG. 302
BURSERA MICROPHYLLA

(Fig. 299 from Pacific Coast Trees, Univ. of Calif. Press)

1. **Ptelea Baldwinii** var. **crenulata** (Greene) Jepson. WESTERN HOP-TREE. Fig. 299. A shrub or small tree, 6 to 15 feet high, with glandular young twigs, smooth brown bitter bark, and often ill-smelling foliage. Leaves trifoliolate, alternate, deciduous; leaflets ovate, elliptical, lanceolate, oblong-ovate, or obovate, acute to somewhat acuminate or rounded at apex, cuneate to obliquely rounded at base, ¾-inch to 3 inches long, ½-inch to 1½ inches wide, crenulate or almost entire, glandular-dotted, glabrous above, somewhat pubescent beneath, sessile or the terminal one with a short petiole; the common petioles ¾-inch to 2½ inches long.

Flowers polygamous or dioecious, small, greenish white, in axillary clusters; sepals 4 or 5, very small; petals 4 or 5, about 1/4-inch long, surpassing the sepals, distinct; stamens 4 or 5, hairy toward the base, distinct, abortive in the pistillate flowers; ovary superior, 2-celled, inserted on a disk, sessile. Fruit a 2-celled samara, winged all around, commonly obricular, 1/2- to 2/3-inch in diameter, retuse at both ends, tipped by the persistent style. Flowering period, March to May.

Western Hop-tree inhabits moist canyons and flats in the foothills of the inner Coast Range from Contra Costa County (Mount Diablo) north to Shasta County, and in the foothills of the Sierra Nevada from Tehama County southward to Calaveras County, in the Upper Sonoran Life Zone. It occurs also in Santiago Canyon, Orange County *(W. G. Watkins).*

This shrub because of its glossy green foliage and light green fruits which turn brown in age should be introduced into more California gardens. It thrives in moist shady locations. It can be propagated from stem-cuttings, seeds, and root-crown sections taken during the winter months. The fruits, leaves, and bark emit, when bruised, a strong odor somewhat resembling hops, as a substitute for which the fruits have been used in brewing.

Ptelea Baldwinii var. crenulata (Greene) Jepson, Fl. W. Mid. Calif. 249 (1901). *P. crenulata* Greene. Type locality: "Clear Lake and on Mt. Diablo." *P. angustifolia* Brew. & Wats., not Benth.

Simarubaceae. Quassia Family

This family contains about 30 genera and 150 species of shrubs and trees distributed in the warmer parts of the world. One genus with a single species is native to California.

1. **Holacantha** Gray

(From the Greek *holos,* complete, and *akantha,* thorn or thorn-bush, in reference to the thorny branchlets.)

1. **Holacantha Emoryi** Gray. CRUCIFIXION THORN. Fig. 300.

A much branched very thorny shrub, 5 to 9 feet high, with spinose or spur-like branchlets and green, yellowish, or brownish bark. Leaves reduced to small alternate deciduous scales. Flowers dioecious, small, usually clustered on the ends of the divided thorny branchlets; sepals 5 to 8, united at base; petals 7 or 8, much longer than the sepals; stamens in staminate flowers 12 to 16, in pistillate flowers 6 to 8, and sterile; pistils 5 to 10, slightly joined or distinct; ovary superior, 1-celled. Fruit of 5 to 10 small drupes, about 1/4-inch long, soon becoming dry and nut-like, borne in large dense clusters. Flowering period, June and July.

Crucifixion Thorn grows in a few localities of the desert regions of southeastern California, Arizona, and northern Mexico, in the Lower Sonoran Life Zone. It has been collected in the vicinity of Amboy, Ludlow, Goffs, and Daggett on the Mohave Desert and near Hayfields, Chuckawalla Valley on the northern border of the Colorado Desert.

Holacantha Emoryi Gray, Mem. Am. Acad. ser. 2, 5:310 (1854). Type locality: "On the desert between the Gila River and Tucson."

Buxaceae. Box Family

The Box Family is a small family consisting of 6 genera and about 30 species, mainly of tropical and subtropical distribution. Only a single genus is native to

California. The Old World box, *Buxus sempervirens,* is often grown in California as a hedge plant.

1. **Simmondsia** Nutt.

(Named for the naturalist, F. W. Simmonds.)
This is a genus with a single species.

1. **Simmondsia chinensis** (Link) Schneider. GOATNUT. JOJOBA. Fig. 301.
A rigid spreading shrub, 3 to 10 feet high, with yellowish green pubescent twigs branching by 2's. Leaves simple, opposite, evergreen; the blades thick and leathery, oblong-ovate, rounded at both ends, 1 to 2 inches long, 5/8-inch to 1 inch wide, 1- or rarely 3-veined from the base, pale green or yellowish, minutely puberulent on both surfaces, entire; petioles 1/16-inch or less long. Flowers unisexual, dioecious, apetalous; staminate flowers about 1/6-inch long, in sessile or short-peduncled head-like clusters, sepals 5, distinct and somewhat unequal, stamens 10 to 12; pistillate flowers about 1/2-inch long, solitary on short peduncles, sepals 5, unequal, increasing in size as the fruit develops, styles 3, ovary superior, 3-celled, becoming 1-celled by abortion. Fruit a smooth cylindrical capsule, about 3/4-inch long, somewhat resembling an acorn, tipped by a short point, the calyx persisting. Seeds smooth, brown to black. Flowering period, March to May.

Goatnut is limited in California to the arid rocky hills and mountains below 5000 feet elevation in San Diego, Imperial, and Riverside counties. It extends eastward to Arizona and southward to Lower California and Sonora, Mexico, and is also found on San Clemente and Cedros islands. *Simmondsia chinensis* has a number of common or folk names. Among the most important are Goatnut, Jojoba, Pignut, Lemonleaf, Sheepnut, Quinine Plant, Wild-Hazel, and Deernut.

The scientific name *Simmondsia californica* Nutt. seems more appropriate for this plant but because of a confusion between material collected in China and California, the Californian plants, thought to have been collected in China, were originally named *Buxus chinensis* by Link. At a later date Hooker described the Californian material collected by Nuttall as *Simmondsia californica.* Schneider, in 1907, having discovered the mistaken source of the original herbarium material and recognizing that it was not *Buxus,* assigned it to the genus *Simmondsia* and, following the international rules of nomenclature, retained the earlier species name *chinensis.*

The leaves and young twigs of Goatnut are much browsed by sheep and cattle. The fruits have a nutty flavor with a slight bitterness similar to that of chestnuts or hazelnuts and are the source of food supply among certain Indians of Mexico and southern California. A beverage used as a substitute for chocolate and coffee is prepared from the seeds by roasting and grinding them with the yolks of hard boiled eggs and then boiling the mass with sugar and milk. The seeds are rather rich in oil which is reportedly used in the manufacture of a hair tonic.

Simmondsia chinensis (Link) Schneider, Ill. Handb. Laubholz K. 2:141 (1907). *Buxus chinensis* Link. "Hab. in China."? Type locality: Probably near San Diego, California. *Simmondsia californica* Nutt.

Burseraceae. Torchwood Family

This is a tropical and subtropical family containing about 15 genera and 400 species of shrubs and trees. A single genus with one species is native to California.

1. **Bursera** Jacq.

(Named for Joachim Burser, a botanist of the 16th century.)

This genus consists of about 40 species, chiefly of Mexico, Central and South America, and the West Indies.

1. **Bursera microphylla** Gray. ELEPHANT TREE. Fig. 302.

A small tree or large shrub, 4 to 15 feet high (to 30 feet in Mexico), with reddish or grayish branchlets. Leaves once-pinnate, alternate, deciduous, 1 to 2 inches long, grouped near the ends of the lateral branchlets; leaflets 11 to 35, oblong-linear, about 1/4-inch long, obtuse, glabrous, entire, sessile. Flowers polygamous, in clusters of 1 to 4; sepals 5, united below around a disk; petals 5, distinct, about 1/8-inch long; stamens 10, distinct, shorter than the petals, inserted under the disk; ovary superior, 3-celled. Fruit a glabrous and globular dryish drupe, about 1/4-inch in diameter, 3-angled, the outer part splitting when mature into 3 valves, 1-celled and 1-seeded by abortion. Flowering period, usually June and July. The fruits usually remain until the following spring.

Elephant Tree has a very restricted distribution in California, occurring at a few stations on the western side of the Colorado Desert (near the Palms in San Diego County, about 20 miles north of the Mexican line, *Martha P. King;* "between Fish Creek and Carrizo Creek" *Jepson*). It extends into southern Arizona, Lower California, and Sonora, Mexico. Mr. Edward H. Davis of Mesa Grande, California, in a letter filed in the herbarium at the University of California, states that he found 50 to 75 scattered trees about 30 to 50 miles north of the Mexican boundary along the western side of the Colorado Desert. They were associated with Ocotillo, Creosote Bush, several kinds of cacti, and vegetation common to that region. He says, "The trees grow isolated—no groves like ironwood or mesquite. The bark is yellowish-green with outside skin almost as thin as tissue paper. Cutting out a section of bark the edge shows a dark red color almost like blood and some kind of oil exudes which smells like strong turpentine or varnish. This makes an oil spot on the paper but is not inflammable, will not burn when a match is applied. . . . The seeds are yellow."

Bursera microphylla Gray, Proc. Am. Acad. 5:155 (1861). Type locality: Sierra Tule, Sonora, Mexico. Collected by *Schott* (a small fragment). Probably also #21 *L. J. Xanthus,* from Cape St. Lucas and Lower California, was used in drawing up the original description.

Anacardiaceae. Sumac Family

The Sumac Family consists of about 60 genera with nearly 500 species of trees or shrubs with resin passages in the bark. They are chiefly tropical in their distribution but many extend into southern Europe, temperate Asia, and America. A single genus with 5 species is native to California.

1. **Rhus** L. Sumac

(From the Greek *rhous,* sumac.)

Shrubs or trees with resinous, acrid, or milky sap. Leaves simple or compound, alternate. Flowers small, regular, in axillary or terminal panicles or spikes, either bisexual or polygamous; sepals 5, usually joined at base; petals 5, distinct, spreading; stamens 5, inserted between the lobes of the disk which lines the base of the calyx; ovary superior, 1-celled; styles 3. Fruit a small dry or semi-fleshy drupe.

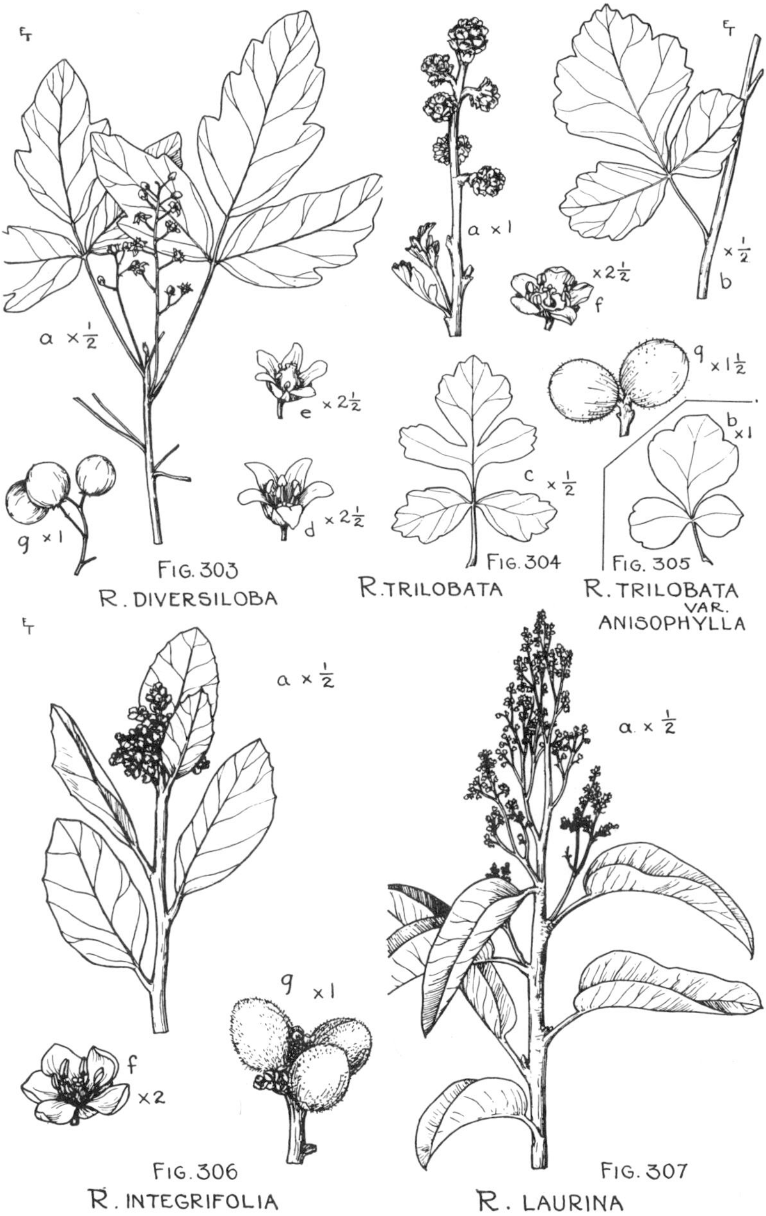

RHUS. a, Flowering branchlet. b, Compound leaf. c, Leaf variation. d, Staminate flower. e, Pistillate flower. f, Bisexual flower. g, Fruit.

About 150 species of sumacs have been described from the temperate and subtropical regions of the northern and southern hemispheres. Tannin is secured from some species and is used in the southern European countries for tanning of leather. Several species yield wax for candles. A fine lacquer is obtained from *Rhus verniciflua* in China and Japan. In South Africa a few of the sumacs grow large enough to be used for timber. All the species of *Rhus* have handsome foliage and many are suitable for ornamental planting.

KEY TO THE SPECIES

Leaves compound.
  Terminal leaflet 2 to 4 inches long, with a distinct petiole.....1. *R. diversiloba.*
  Terminal leaflet 3/4-inch to 2 inches long, without a distinct petiole. 2. *R. trilobata.*

Leaves simple.
  Leaf-blades usually flat, rounded or abruptly acute at apex; petioles 1/8- to 3/8-inch long..3. *R. intergrifolia.*
  Leaf-blades often trough-like above, more or less acuminate to acute at apex; petioles 3/8-inch to 1 inch long.
    Leaves always entire; drupe whitish and glabrous.............4. *R. laurina.*
    Leaves entire or some irregularly toothed; drupe red, pubescent and often waxy-coated..5. *R. ovata.*

1. **Rhus diversiloba** T. & G. POISON-OAK. Fig. 303.

An erect or spreading shrub, 2 to 6 feet high, or sometimes a woody vine climbing trees by adventitious roots. Leaves typically trifoliolate, rarely simple, deciduous, 3 to 6 inches long; leaflets variously toothed, lobed, or rarely entire, 1 to 4 inches long; terminal leaflet usually larger than the lateral ones, distinctly petiolate; common petiole 1/2-inch to 4 inches long. Flowers greenish white, in axillary usually pendulous panicles, appearing with the leaves. Fruit a brown or whitish smooth dry drupe, about 1/4-inch in diameter, falling early after maturing. Flowering period, April and May.

Poison-oak is not a true oak but is closely related to Poison Ivy of the eastern states. It is one of the most widely distributed shrubs of California, inhabiting the Great Valley and mountain slopes, foothills, and stream banks throughout the Coast Ranges, the Sierra Nevada, and southern California. It extends northward into Oregon and Washington, eastward into Arizona, and southward into Lower California. This shrub seldom extends above 5000 feet elevation in the mountains and is rare among the redwoods. In the fall the brilliant red foliage makes it very attractive on many brush-covered slopes throughout California. Unfortunately Poison-oak secretes a non-volatile juice highly poisonous to many people; therefore, it cannot be recommended for planting. One must come in contact with the oil-particles either directly on the plants or indirectly on clothes or other articles which have brushed against the foliage in order to acquire the skin irritation caused by the oils. There is even evidence that smoke may carry the oil-particles. Poison-oak is a fair browse-plant for cattle. Considerable variation occurs in the size, pubescence, and serration of the leaflets which has resulted in the description of many new species and varieties. However, most of the characters which have been used have proved to be too variable for use in distinguishing species in this genus.

Rhus diversiloba T. & G. Fl. N. Am. 1:218 (1838). Type locality: "Borders of woods, etc., in Oregon." Collected by *Douglas, Nuttall.* Also in California by *Beechey, Nuttall.*

2. **Rhus trilobata** Nutt. SQUAW BUSH. Fig. 304.

A diffusely branched spreading shrub, 3 to 5 feet high and sometimes 8 feet across, with smooth brown bark. Leaves deciduous, typically glabrous, trifoliolate or sometimes apparently 3- to 5-parted, usually 3 inches or less long; the terminal leaflet ¾-inch to 2 inches long, tapering at base to point of attachment with the lateral round-ovate and smaller leaflets, distinctly 3-lobed, the lobes variously toothed; the petiole ½-inch to 1 inch long. Flowers pale yellow, appearing before the leaves in terminal clustered spikes ½-inch to 1 inch long. Fruit a fleshy berry-like reddish drupe about ¼-inch in diameter, covered with a viscid secretion. Flowering period, March and April.

Squaw Bush inhabits canyon bottoms or flats in the middle and inner Coast Ranges, in the Sierra Nevada foothills, and in southern California. It extends northward to Oregon, southward into Lower California, and eastward to the Rocky Mountains and Texas.

The spreading habit, colored fruits, and ease of propagation from stem-cuttings and root-sections recommend this plant for mixed plantings of native shrubs. The Indians in early days prepared from the fruits a drink which resembled pink lemonade. The pliable stems were much used in basket-making.

Considerable variation occurs in the size and lobation of the leaflets and in the amount of pubescence on the leaflets and branchlets. Several of these variations have been described by various authors as distinct varieties or species. The three following are worthy of note.

2a. Var. **anisophylla** (Greene) Jepson. Fig. 305.

A dwarfed stout short-branched shrub, with puberulent twigs becoming glabrous in age. Foliage about one-half grown at flowering time. Leaves small, distinctly trifoliolate; the lateral leaflets on type specimen unequal and less than one-half the size of the terminal leaflet which is slightly 3-lobed. Spikes of flowers short, almost head-like.

This variety has been collected in the Panamint, New York, and Cottonwood mountains. It may be expected in other mountains of the Mohave Desert.

2b. Var. **malacophylla** (Greene) Munz.

Leaflets pubescent on both surfaces.

This variety appears more abundantly in southern California but occurs sporadically in other parts of the state. Its status even as a variety is very doubtful.

Rhus trilobata Nutt.; T. & G. Fl. N. Am. 1:219 (1838). Type locality: Rocky Mountains. Collected by *Nuttall.*

Var. anisophylla (Greene) Jepson, Man. 608 (1925). *Schmaltzia anisophylla* Greene. Type locality: Surprise Canyon near Brewery Springs in the Panamint Mountains, Inyo County. Collected by *A. K. Fisher* with *Coville* and *Funston* on the Death Valley Expedition.

Var. malacophylla (Greene) Munz, Man. S. Calif. Bot. 292 (1935). *Schmaltzia malacophylla* Greene. Type locality: Griffith Park, Los Angeles County. Collected by *E. Braunton.*

3. **Rhus integrifolia** (Nutt.) Benth. & Hook. LEMONADE-BERRY. MAHOGANY SUMAC. Fig. 306.

A medium-sized evergreen shrub, 3 to 10 feet high, or sometimes more or less depressed, or rarely tree-like and up to 30 feet tall. Leaves simple, rarely ternate, or with 1 or 2 lateral basal lobes; the blades elliptical or ovate to nearly orbicular, 1 to 2¼ inches long, ¾-inch to 1½ inches wide, rounded at both ends or rarely acute at apex, stiff and leathery, dark green and shining above in age, paler and prominently veined beneath, usually flat, rarely convex above, entire or irregularly toothed; petioles ⅛- to ⅜-inch long. Flowers white or pinkish, sessile, in ashy-puberulent panicles. Fruit a pubescent reddish somewhat flattened drupe, about ¼- to ½-inch long, usually covered with a waxy secretion. Flowering period, February and March, or sometimes from January to July.

Lemonade-berry inhabits bluffs and mesas along the coast of southern California from Santa Barbara County to San Diego County and northern Lower California. It extends inland to the Cahuenga Pass region of Los Angeles County, to the Cucamonga wash east of Uplands, and into the foothills east of San Diego. Specimens have been examined also from the islands of Santa Catalina, Santa Cruz, San Clemente, Cedros, and San Miguel. A few specimens collected by Blanche Trask on Santa Catalina Island have some leaves ternate. She states that the ternate leaves are of common occurrence, a condition, however, rarely found on the mainland plants.

This species is used to some extent as an ornamental from San Diego north to San Francisco. Its pinkish buds in late winter, the evergreen leaves, and resistance to frost recommend it for planting singly or in masses. It is not so desirable, however, as *Rhus ovata,* Sugarbush. A cooling but acrid drink is made from the fruits by the natives of Lower California.

Rhus integrifolia (Nutt.) Benth. & Hook.; Bot. Calif. 1:110 (1876). *Styphonia integrifolia* Nutt. Type locality: "On the margins of cliffs, and near the sea, around San Diego and Santa Barbara." Collected by *Nuttall.*

4. **Rhus laurina** Nutt. LAUREL SUMAC. Fig. 307.

A very leafy almost arborescent shrub, 6 to 12 feet high, with smooth brown or reddish bark. Leaves simple, evergreen, exhaling an aromatic odor; the blades oblong-lanceolate or ovate to elliptical, 2 to 4 inches long, ¾-inch to 2 inches wide, obtuse at base, acute or obtuse at apex, tipped with a fine soft point, thick and leathery, glabrous on both surfaces, the margins entire and often pinkish; petioles ⅝-inch to 1 inch long. Flowers white, very small and numerous in dense terminal nearly glabrous panicles. Fruit a whitish glabrous drupe, about ⅛-inch in diameter. Flowering period, May to July, or to December.

Laurel Sumac is usually confined to valley flats and mesas of the foothills in southern California. It occurs from Santa Barbara County south to San Diego County and northern Lower California, occupying about the same area as *Rhus integrifolia.* It extends inland to the Mount Piños region and to the hills at the head of Lake Elsinore. It also inhabits the islands of San Clemente, Santa Catalina, and Cedros.

The dense mass of evergreen foliage, reddish branchlets, pink leaf-margins and petioles, and relative freedom from garden pests make this species desirable for ornamental planting. It grows rapidly, can be trimmed, but cannot endure as low a temperature as *Rhus integrifolia* and *Rhus ovata.* During the cold winter of 1936–1937 many of the plants of this species growing in the wild had their leaves completely seared while those of the other two species were not hurt. The plant

Fig. 308. SUGARBUSH. *Rhus ovata* Wats.

exhales an odor of bitter almonds, the seeds yield a pungent oil, and the flowers furnish honey ingredients.

Rhus laurina Nutt.; T. & G. Fl. N. Am. 1:219 (1838). Type locality: Santa Barbara. Collected by *Nuttall*.

5. **Rhus ovata** Wats. SUGARBUSH. SUGAR SUMAC. Fig. 308.

An erect or spreading evergreen shrub, 2½ to 10 feet high, with smooth (or rough in age) brown or reddish bark. Leaves simple, rarely ternate; the blades ovate or elliptical to orbicular, 1½ to 3 inches long, ¾-inch to 1½ inches wide, acute or sometimes rounded at apex, thick and leathery, commonly trough-like above and thus folded inward along the midrib when pressed, glabrous and shining on both surfaces, entire or irregularly and sharply serrate, rarely a few lobed or ternate; petioles ⅜-inch to 1 inch long, reddish. Flowers white or pinkish, in dense puberulent or glabrate panicles of short spikes. Fruit a reddish pubescent drupe, about ¼-inch in diameter, usually coated with a sugary or waxy secretion. Flowering period, March to May.

Sugarbush inhabits the chaparral belt of the foothills and lower mountain slopes, usually away from the immediate coast, in southern California from the Santa Ynez Mountains of Santa Barbara County southward to San Diego County and northern Lower California. It extends eastward to the desert slopes of the Tehachapi, San Gabriel, San Bernardino, and Laguna Mountains and to Arizona. It occurs also on Santa Catalina Island.

This species of sumac is the most desirable of the Californian species for ornamental use because of its evergreen glossy foliage, clusters of pink flower-buds during late winter and early spring, spreading habit of growth, clusters of grayish to reddish velvety-appearing fruits, freedom from pests, and adaptability to varying soil and climatic conditions. It is planted in gardens from the San Francisco Bay area south to southern California. In order to insure an abundance of fruit it is necessary to grow the plants in mass effect since many of the flowers are unisexual and are therefore not self-pollinated. Fruit rarely sets in any quantity in the San Francisco Bay area.

Rhus ovata Wats. Proc. Am. Acad. 20:358 (1885). Type locality: "On hills and mountains, away from the coast, from San Diego to Los Angeles County, the Cantillas Mountains in Lower California, and in southern Arizona; also on Santa Catalina Island *(W. H. Lyon)*." Collected by *Orcutt*.

Celastraceae. Staff-tree Family

This family contains about 40 genera and 350 species of shrubs, climbing woody vines, and trees, widely distributed except in the polar regions. Four genera and 5 species are native to California.

KEY TO THE GENERA

Leaves alternate; fruit 1-celled.

Leaf-blades very thick, the margins usually revolute or thickened; stamens 5. 1. MORTONIA.

Leaf-blades thin, the margins not revolute or thickened; stamens usually 10. 2. GLOSSOPETALON.

Leaves opposite.

Plants nearly prostrate; leaves ¾-inch or less long, almost sessile . 3. PACHYSTIMA.

Plants erect; leaves 1½ to 4 inches long, distinctly petiolate . . . . . . 4. EUONYMUS.

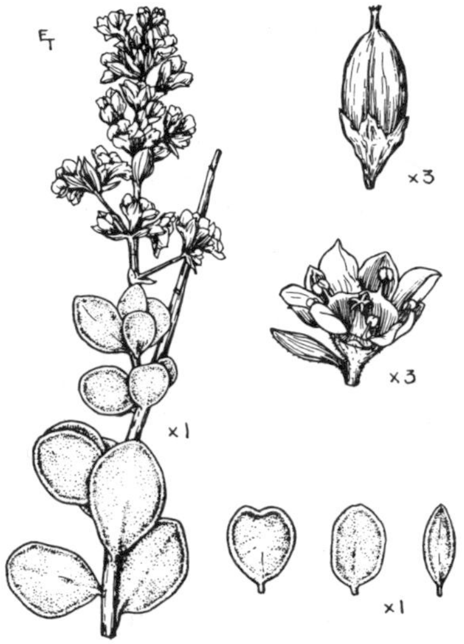

FIG. 309 MORTONIA UTAHENSIS

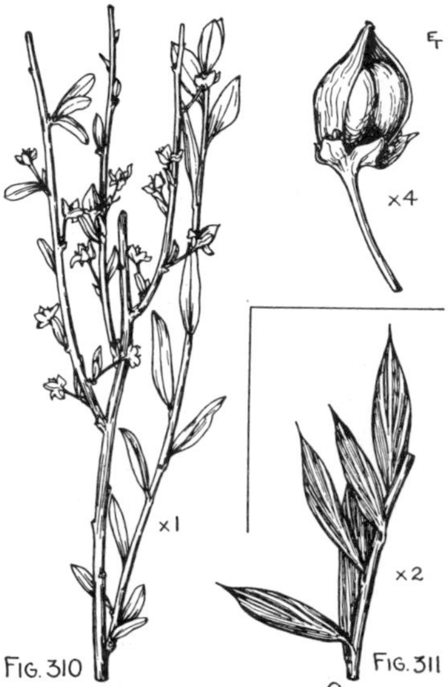

FIG. 310 GLOSSOPETALON SPINESCENS FIG. 311 G. PUNGENS

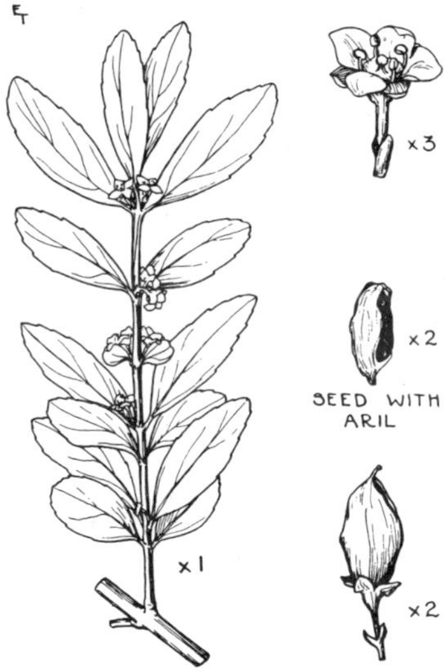

FIG. 312 PACHYSTIMA MYRSINITES

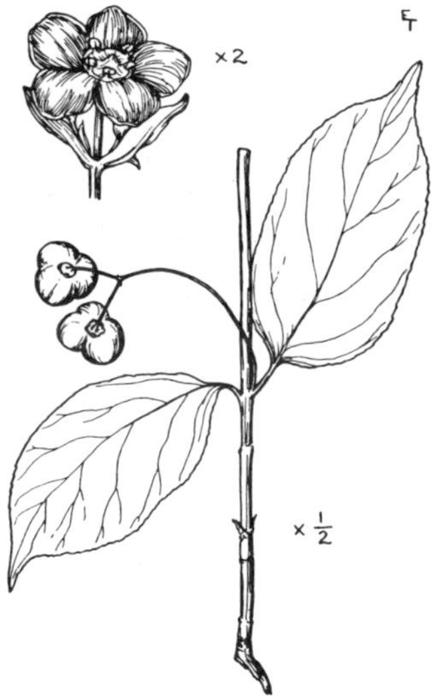

FIG. 313 EUONYMUS OCCIDENTALIS

1. **Mortonia** Gray

(Named in honor of Dr. S. G. Morton, once president of the Philadelphia Academy of Sciences.)

This is a small genus of about 6 species native to southwestern United States and northern Mexico. Only one species has been found in California.

1. **Mortonia utahensis** (Cov. ex Trel.) A. Nels. UTAH MORTONIA. Fig. 309.

An intricately branched low shrub, 1 to 3 feet high, with scabrous-hispidulous branches and yellowish bark. Leaves simple, alternate, evergreen; the blades very thick, oval or rarely elliptical or nearly orbicular, 1/4- to 1/2-inch long, 1/8- to 1/4-inch wide, scabrous-hispidulous, nearly sessile, the margins entire and fleshy-thickened, appearing as if bordered with cartilage. Flowers bisexual, regular, borne in narrow raceme-like panicles 1 1/4 to 2 inches long; sepals 5; petals 5, distinct, white, about 1/8-inch long, inserted under the free margin of the fleshy disk which lines the calyx; stamens 5, inserted on the disk; ovary superior, 5-celled; stigma 5-lobed. Fruit a dry oblong capsule, 1-celled and 1-seeded by abortion. Flowering period, March to May.

Utah Mortonia is a rare shrub in California. known only from the Panamint Mountains, Inyo County *(M. F. Gilman)* and from near Kingston, eastern Mohave Desert, San Bernardino County *(Jaeger)*. It extends eastward to Nevada, Utah, and Arizona.

Mortonia utahensis (Cov. ex Trel.) A. Nels. Bot. Gaz. 47:427 (1909). *M. scabrella* var. *utahensis* Cov. ex Trel. Type locality: "Utah and Nevada."

2. **Glossopetalon** Gray

(From the Greek *glossa,* tongue, and *petalon,* petal, referring to the shape of the petals.)

Small deciduous shrubs with greenish angled branches. Leaves simple, alternate. Flowers bisexual, nearly regular; sepals 5 (rarely 4 or 6); petals 5 (rarely 4 or 6), distinct, longer than the sepals, inserted under the fleshy disk lining the calyx; stamens usually 10, sometimes 5 or 4 inserted on the disk; carpels 1 to 3, distinct; ovary superior, 1-celled. Fruit an ovoid coriaceous follicle, with 1 or 2 seeds.

This is a small genus of 3 or 4 species in western North America. Two are native to California.

KEY TO THE SPECIES

Leaves merely tipped with a short soft point.................. 1. *G. spinescens.*
Leaves tipped with a spine.................................. 2. *G. pungens.*

1. **Glossopetalon spinescens** Gray. SPINY GREASEBUSH. Fig. 310.

An intricately branched spinescent shrub, 1 to 2 feet high. Leaf-blades oblong or oblanceolate to obovate, about 1/4-inch long, glaucous, glabrous, entire, nearly sessile. Flowers small, white, solitary in the leaf-axils, on slender pedicels about 1/4-inch long; carpels solitary. Fruit about 1/8-inch long. Flowering period, February to May.

Spiny Greasebush inhabits the dry mountain ravines of the desert ranges in Mono, Inyo, and San Bernardino counties of southwestern California (n. slope of San Bernardino Mts.; White Mts., *V. Duran;* Providence Mts.; Panamint Mts.). Its range extends northward to eastern Oregon and Washington, eastward to Nevada, Arizona, Utah, New Mexico, Oklahoma, and Texas.

Fig. 314. Western Burning Bush. *Euonymus occidentalis* Nutt.

Glossopetalon spinescens Gray, Pl. Wright. 2:29. t. 12B (1853). Type locality: In a mountain ravine near Frontera, New Mexico. Collected by *Wright.*

2. **Glossopetalon pungens** Brandg. DWARF GREASEBUSH. Fig. 311.

A low caespitose subshrub with stems 2 to 4 inches long. Leaf-blades oblong-elliptic or oblanceolate, 1/4- to 5/16-inch long, glabrate, tipped with a spine, entire, nearly sessile. Flowers small, terminal; carpels 2 or 3. Follicles leathery, about 1/8-inch long. Flowering period, February to April.

This subshrub is apparently limited in its distribution to a few localities on Clark Mountain of the eastern Mohave Desert, California *(Jaeger)* and in the Sheep Mountains of Nevada *(C. A. Purpus).*

Glossopetalon pungens Brandg. Bot. Gaz. 27:445 (1889). Type locality: Sheep Mountains, Nevada. Collected by *C. A. Purpus.*

3. **Pachystima** Raf.

(From the Greek *pachus,* thick, and *stima,* stigma, in reference to the slightly thickened stigma.)

This genus consists of 4 species native to North America. Only one is native to California.

1. **Pachystima myrsinites** (Pursh) Raf. MYRTLE BOXLEAF. OREGON BOXWOOD. Fig. 312.

A low densely branched very leafy evergreen shrub, 1 to 3 feet high, or sometimes nearly prostrate, with 4-angled twigs and brown bark. Leaves simple, opposite; the blades oval or elliptical, rounded at apex, narrowed or rounded at base, 1/4-inch to 1 inch long, 1/8- to 1/2-inch wide, leathery, smooth, glabrous, entire or more commonly serrulate above the base; petioles 1/16-inch or less long. Flowers bisexual, regular, numerous, small, clustered or single in the leaf-axils; sepals 4, united at base, green; petals 4, ovate, greenish or purplish, inserted beneath the fleshy disk lining the calyx; stamens 4, filaments twice as long as the anthers, inserted on the disk; ovary superior, 2-celled; style very short; stigma obscurely 2-lobed. Fruit a 2-celled capsule, about 1/4-inch long; seeds 1 or 2, surrounded by a white aril. Flowering period, April to June.

Myrtle Boxleaf inhabits mountain slopes and moist shady woods in scattered localities from Mariposa County to Modoc County, thence westward in Siskiyou and Humboldt counties. It extends northward into Oregon and Washington and occurs in the Rocky Mountains from Alberta southward to New Mexico. This plant is known also as Myrtlebush and Falsebox.

Pachystima myrsinites (Pursh) Raf. Fl. Tellur. 42 (1838). *Ilex myrsinites* Pursh. Type locality: Hungry Creek in northern Idaho. Collected by *Lewis.*

4. **Euonymus** L. BURNING BUSH

(From the Greek *eu,* good, and *onoma,* a name.)

This is a large genus of about 120 species of the north temperate zone. Many of the species have ornamental foliage and fruit. Only one species, with one variety, is native to California.

1. **Euonymus occidentalis** Nutt. WESTERN BURNING BUSH. Figs. 313, 314.

A large erect shrub or sometimes tree-like, 6 to 20 feet high, with greenish gray bark and slender 4-angled branchlets. Leaves simple, opposite, deciduous; the blades elliptical, ovate, or oblanceolate, acuminate at apex, rounded or tapering

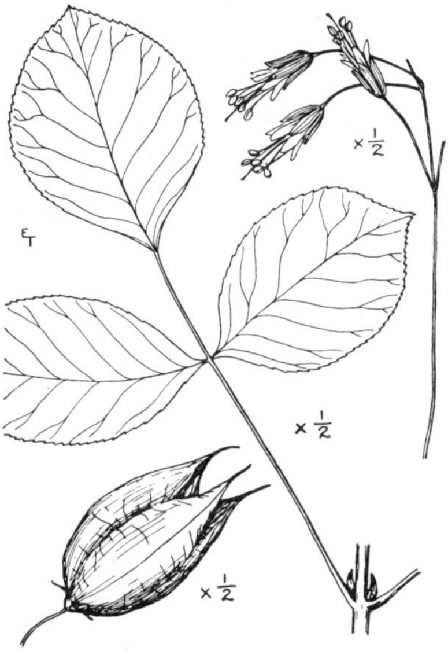

FIG. 315 STAPHYLEA BOLANDERI

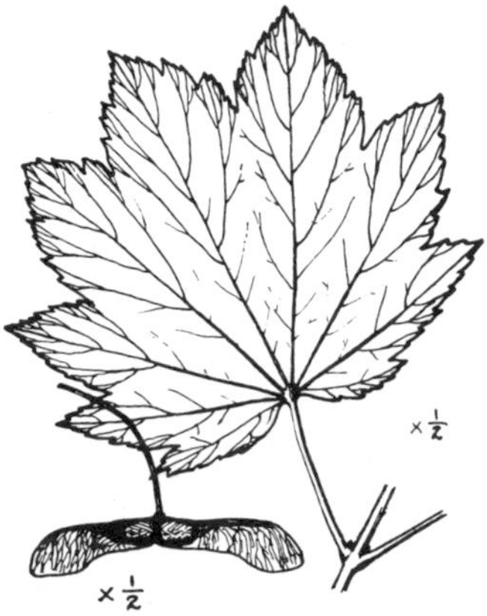

FIG. 316 ACER CIRCINATUM

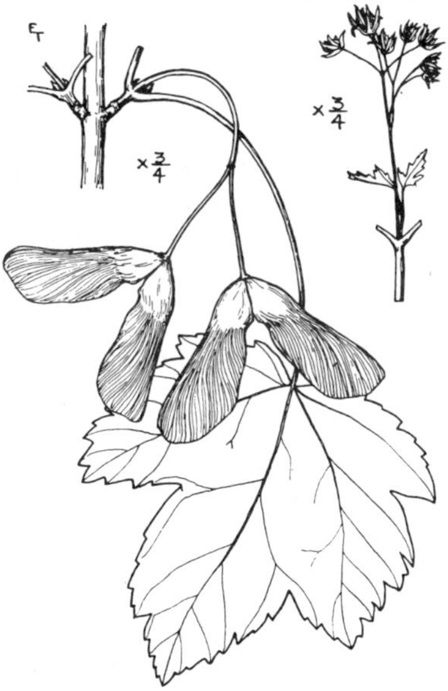

FIG. 317 ACER GLABRUM

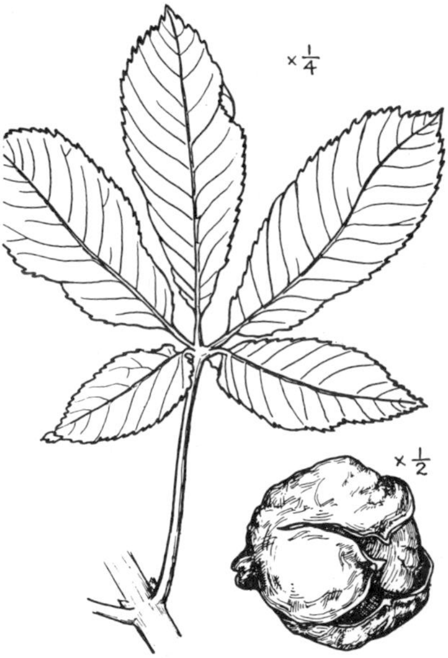

FIG. 318 AESCULUS CALIFORNICA

at base, 1½ to 4 inches long, ½-inch to 1½ inches wide, thin, glabrous, finely serrulate; petioles ¼- to ½-inch long. Flowers bisexual, regular, 1 to 7 in axillary clusters, purplish, rather inconspicuous, less than ½-inch across; peduncles ¾-inch to 3 inches long; sepals 5, united at base; petals 5, brownish purple, round, finely dotted, about ⅛-inch in diameter, their margins whitish; stamens 5, inserted on a 5-lobed fleshy disk; ovary superior, 3-celled. Fruit a distinctly 3-lobed capsule, smooth, ¼- to ½-inch wide; seeds surrounded by a red fleshy outgrowth (aril). Flowering period, May to July.

Western Burning Bush inhabits moist ravines and woods near the coast from Santa Cruz County northward through the outer Coast Ranges to Del Norte and Siskiyou counties, in the Transition Life Zone. It also occurs in Plumas County (*Mrs. K. M. Austin,* specimen collected in 1877 and filed in the Gray Herbarium). It extends northward into Oregon and Washington and eastward into Nevada.

This shrub is easily propagated from cuttings or by transplanting entire plants during the rainy season. It thrives best in moist ground.

1a. Var. **Parishii** (Trel.) Jepson. PARISH BURNING BUSH.

Bark on branches gray or whitish. Leaf-blades usually obtuse at apex. Similar to the species in other characters.

This variety occurs infrequently between 4500 and 6500 feet altitude, along streams in the Cuyamaca, Palomar, and San Jacinto mountains of San Diego and western Riverside counties. There seem to be no valid differences for separating this variety from the species. The length of peduncles and number of flowers, characters used in various manuals for separating the two forms, are unreliable characters.

Euonymus occidentalis Nutt.; Torr. Pacif. R. Rep. 4:74 (1857), based on *E. atropurpureus* var. β., T. & G. Fl. N. Am. 1:258 (1838). Type locality: Oregon, in dark woods. Collected by *Douglas, Nuttall.*

Var. Parishii (Trel.) Jepson, Man. 610 (1925). *E. Parishii* Trel. Type locality: San Jacinto Mountains. Collected by *S. B.* and *W. F. Parish.*

Staphyleaceae. Bladdernut Family

This family consists of 5 genera with about 22 species distributed throughout the north temperate zone, northern South America, and the Malay region.

1. **Staphylea** L. BLADDERNUT

(From the Greek *staphule,* a cluster, in reference to the clusters of flowers and fruits.)

There are 11 species in the temperate regions of the northern hemisphere, only one of which is native to California.

1. **Staphylea Bolanderi** Gray. SIERRA BLADDERNUT. Fig. 315.

An erect glabrous shrub, 6 to 10 feet high, or rarely a small slender tree up to 20 feet high. Leaves pinnately trifoliolate, opposite, deciduous; leaflets round-ovate or orbicular, 1 to 2½ inches long, ¾-inch to 1½ inches wide, glabrous, crenate or serrulate, the terminal leaflet with a stalk ¼-inch to 1 inch long, the lateral leaflets nearly sessile; petiole ¾-inch to 2½ inches long. Flowers white, bisexual, regular, in drooping terminal clusters; sepals 5, joined at the base; petals 5, distinct, nearly ½-inch long; stamens 5, distinct, much exserted; ovary superior, 3-celled; style much exserted. Fruit a 3-celled bladdery capsule, 1 to 2 inches long, each cell with 1 to 4 globose seeds and terminated by a horn-like projection. Flowering period, April and May.

Sierra Bladdernut is a rare shrub occurring on canyon slopes in the Sierra Nevada from Tulare County (near Cedar Creek Camp, Sequoia Nat. Forest, *Jepson*) northward to Shasta and Siskiyou counties.

This species because of its attractive green foliage and clusters of white flowers is suitable for ornamental planting. It grows rapidly in almost any kind of soil, but prefers full sunlight. Propagation is easily made from cuttings, by layering, or by taking root-shoots which the plants produce abundantly. Sierra Bladdernut can be grown throughout the Pacific Coast under coastal or lower mountain climatic conditions.

Staphylea Bolanderi Gray, Proc. Am. Acad. 10:69 (1874). Type locality: McCloud River, Shasta County. Collected by *Bolander*.

Aceraceae. Maple Family

The Maple Family consists of 2 genera and about 120 species, mostly of the north temperate zone, being especially well represented in the eastern part of the United States. The genus *Pipteronia* with a single species is native to central China. Only the genus *Acer* occurs on the Pacific Coast.

1. **Acer** L. Maple

(The classical name of the Maple.)

Trees or shrubs with simple or compound opposite deciduous leaves. Flowers small, bisexual or unisexual, apetalous or choripetalous, borne in drooping clusters; sepals 4 or 5; petals if present, 4 or 5; stamens 3 to 10; pistil 1, with 2 separate styles inserted between the lobes of the superior 2-celled ovary. Fruit a schizocarp of 2 (rarely 3 or 4) 1-seeded single-winged samaras.

This genus consists of about 120 species, 4 of which are native to the Pacific Coast. Two of these are usually shrubs and one is often vine-like.

KEY TO THE SPECIES

Leaves 5- to 11-lobed, 2 to 6 inches broad; wings of fruit extending in a nearly straight line..1. *A. circinatum*.

Leaves 3- or rarely 5-lobed, 1 to 3 inches broad, very pale beneath; wings of fruit diverging at an oblique angle............................2. *A. glabrum*.

1. **Acer circinatum** Pursh. Vine Maple. Fig. 316.

A reclining or vine-like shrub, or rarely a small tree, 5 to 35 feet high. Leaves simple; the blades thin, 2 to 6 inches long and as broad, cordate, glabrous, light to dark green above, paler beneath, palmately 5- to 11-lobed, the lobes triangular-ovate, acute and sharply serrate, the basal pair of lobes smaller; petioles 1 to 2 inches long, grooved. Flowers reddish purple, 2 to 10 or rarely more in peduncled umbel-like clusters, appearing with the leaves, choripetalous, most of them staminate, the cluster often setting but a single fruit. Samaras glabrous, the wings ½-inch to 1 inch long, spreading in a nearly straight line, reddish when ripe. Flowering period, April and May.

Vine Maple inhabits stream banks in deep shade from the coastal mountains of British Columbia southward in western Washington and Oregon to the mountains of northern California in Del Norte, Humboldt, Mendocino, Siskiyou, Shasta,

Trinity, Butte ("9 miles southwest of Butte Meadows along the road from Chico to Butte Meadows." *Bacigalupi*), and Yuba (2 miles west of Challenge, *F. Schumacher*) counties from near sea level to 5000 feet elevation.

This species is very ornamental in the fall when its foliage turns a rich scarlet. It is cultivated in the eastern part of the United States and in Europe because of its handsome foliage, purplish twigs, and reddish flowers with yellow stamens. Sheep and cattle browse upon the abundant and palatable herbage.

Acer circinatum Pursh, Fl. Am. Sept. 1:267 (1814). Type locality: "On the great rapids [Cascades] of the Columbia River." Collected by *Lewis*.

2. **Acer glabrum** Torr. Dwarf Maple. Mountain Maple. Fig. 317.

A shrub or small tree, 5 to 15 feet high, with smooth gray bark on the main stems and branches; the branchlets slender and with smooth reddish bark. Leaves simple or rarely compound; the blades round in outline, 1 to 3 inches long and about as broad, wedge-shaped to rounded or cordate at base, glabrous, paler and grayish beneath, palmately 3-lobed, often with 2 supplementary lobes at base, the lobes unequally and sharply toothed; petioles 1 to 5 inches long. Flowers greenish yellow, borne in branching clusters about 1 inch long, appearing with the leaves; the clusters with bisexual or unisexual flowers, or the plants dioecious; the staminate flowers without rudiments of pistils and the pistillate with short stamens. Samaras straw-color or reddish, glabrous, 2 to several in a cluster, the wings ½-inch to 1 inch long, diverging at an oblique angle. Flowering period, May to July.

Dwarf Maple inhabits moist rocky mountain slopes of the San Bernardino and San Jacinto mountains of southern California, the Sierra Nevada, and the higher mountains of northern California at elevations from 5000 to 9000 feet in the Canadian and Hudsonian Life Zones. It extends northward through Oregon, Washington, and British Columbia to Alaska and eastward to the Rocky Mountains. Specimens from the Rincon Mountains of Arizona *(J. C. Blumer),* the Mogollon Mountains of New Mexico *(Wolf),* and Amador County (Hidden Lake, *McMinn*), California have simple and compound leaves on the same branches. A careful search among specimens growing in the more shady and moister places usually will reveal a few compound leaves. The young foliage is browsed by deer, sheep, and cattle.

Acer glabrum Torr. Ann. Lyc. N. Y. 2:172 (1828). Type locality: "Rocky Mountains, 1000 ft. el. from the plain." Probably in Colorado. Collected by *Edwin James* on Long's expedition.

Hippocastanaceae. Horse-chestnut Family

This family consists of 2 genera and 22 species of trees and shrubs native to the north temperate zone. A single species is native to California.

1. **Aesculus** L. Horse-chestnut. Buckeye

(A name given by Pliny to an oak having edible acorns.)

This genus contains about 15 species of deciduous trees or shrubs, native to America, southeastern Europe, and Asia.

1. **Aesculus californica** (Spach) Nutt. California Buckeye. Fig. 318.

Usually a tree, 15 to 40 feet high, but sometimes shrub-like, with smooth gray bark and a broad open crown. Leaves palmately compound, opposite, long-petioled, early deciduous; leaflets usually 5, oblong-lanceolate, 3 to 6 inches long, nearly glabrous, serrate, on stalks 3/8-inch to 1 inch long. Flowers large, bisexual, irregular, pinkish white, in large cylindrical erect or rarely drooping clusters 6 to 10 inches long. Fruit a large somewhat pear-shaped 3-valved capsule 1 1/2 to 2 inches long, with 1 or 2 large glossy brown seeds. Flowering period, May to July.

California Buckeye inhabits canyon slopes and low dry hills of the Sierra Nevada and the Coast Ranges from Siskiyou and Shasta counties southward to the Tehachapi and Liebre mountains of Kern and Los Angeles counties, in the Upper Sonoran Life Zone.

Aesculus californica (Spach) Nutt.; T. & G. Fl. N. Am. 1:251 (1838). *Calothyrsus californica* Spach. Type locality: California, locality not given. Collected by *Botta*.

Rhamnaceae. Buckthorn Family

This family contains about 50 genera and 550 species, mostly shrubs but some small trees or rarely herbs, of world-wide distribution. Five genera and about 50 species, with many varieties, are native to California.

KEY TO THE GENERA

Fruit a 3-celled capsule.
  Leaves usually 1/2-inch to 3 inches long; branchlets usually not spinose, or if so alternate; receptocalyx-tube partially united to ovary.
    Sepals petal-like; petals hooded and with long stalks or claws. . 1. CEANOTHUS.
    Sepals not petal-like; petals sessile. . . . . .2. COLUBRINA.
  Leaves 1/4-inch or less long, soon deciduous; branchlets spinose, opposite; receptocalyx-tube not united with ovary; petals hooded. . . . .3. ADOLPHIA.
Fruit drupaceous or berry-like.
  Spinescent shrubs; leaves, if present, usually 1/2-inch or less long; fruit with 1 stone . . . . .4. CONDALIA.
  Shrubs without spines; leaves usually over 1/2-inch long (1/4- to 1/2-inch in *Rhamnus crocea*); fruit with 2 to 4 stones. . . . . .5. RHAMNUS.

1. **Ceanothus** L.

(The Greek name *Keanothus* was used by Theophrastus for some prickly plant.)

Shrubs or sometimes small trees. Leaves simple, alternate or opposite, deciduous or evergreen. Flowers small, bisexual, regular, borne in clusters (racemes, panicles, or umbels); sepals 5, somewhat petal-like, united at base with the urn-shaped receptacle to form a receptocalyx, this filled with a glandular disk in which the ovary is immersed; petals 5, distinct, scoop-shaped (hooded), and stalked; stamens 5, opposite the petals, with elongated filaments; ovary 3-celled, 3-lobed, with a short 3-cleft style. Fruit a 3-lobed capsule, separating at maturity into 3 parts. Seeds smooth, convex on one side.

This genus contains about 60 species, all natives of North America, but almost all limited to the Pacific Coast, 40 being native to California. Several of the species are cultivated for their ornamental leaves and flower-clusters. The flowers when crushed and rubbed in water give a foamy lather which may be used as a poor substitute for soap. From an eastern species *Ceanothus americanus* known as "New Jersey Tea," the Indians made a beverage which resembled tea. During the Revolutionary War the leaves were used in making a beverage as a substitute for Chinese tea.

Considerable hybridization occurs among the species in nature and among cultivated plants in nurseries and gardens. Most of the hybridization occurs between species of the same section of the genus but occasionally hybrids are found such as *Ceanothus serrulatus,* which appear to have originated from parents belonging to the sections Cerastes and Euceanothus.

KEY TO THE SPECIES

I. Leaves alternate. (Fruits without horns but often with ridges or crests on the lobes of the cells; stipules thin and early deciduous; stomata on lower epidermis, never in sunken pits.—Section Euceanothus. Two species, *C. megacarpus* and *C. verrucosus,* with alternate leaves, belong to the Section Cerastes which normally has opposite leaves.)

A. Leaves normally with 3 distinct veins from the base. In some species the venation is variable, with some leaves apparently 3-veined, and others with one main vein or midrib and 2 rather prominent equally or unequally inserted lateral veins, or else definitely pinnate-veined. These species are "keyed out" under B.

Plants distinctly spinose, with glaucous grayish leaves and grayish or greenish bark.

Low and rather round-topped shrubs, 1 to 4 feet high; leaves $\frac{1}{4}$-inch to 1 inch long, entire or denticulate to serrulate; usually high montane. 1. *C. cordulatus.*

Taller and more erect shrubs, 4 to 15 feet high; at elevations usually below 4000 feet, rarely up to 6000 feet.

Leaves normally $\frac{1}{4}$-inch to $1\frac{1}{4}$ inches long; fruit globose, not crested; usually in chaparral. . . . . .2. *C. leucodermis.*

Leaves normally 1 to $2\frac{1}{2}$ inches long; fruit triangular, verrucosely roughened; usually in coastal mountains. . . . . .3. *C. incanus.*

Plants not spinose; leaves not grayish glaucous.

Leaves entire.

Low shrubs 1 to $3\frac{1}{2}$ feet high, with slender arching branches; leaves oblong-elliptical, $\frac{1}{4}$-inch to 1 inch long; flowers blue, in nearly simple panicles 1 to $2\frac{1}{2}$ inches long. . . . . .4. *C. parvifolius.*

Taller shrubs 3 to 12 feet high; leaves commonly ovate, 1 to 3 inches long, or smaller and oblong-elliptical; flowers usually white, sometimes dark or pale blue, in branched panicles 2 to 6 inches long. 5. *C. integerrimus.*

Leaves glandular-denticulate, serrulate, or serrate.

Leaves deciduous, serrate, 1 to 4 inches long; flowers white; tall shrubs with reddish glabrous branchlets; Siskiyou County. .6. *C. sanguineus.*

Leaves evergreen.

Flowers white; leaves glabrous and usually varnished above, $1\frac{1}{2}$ to 3 inches long, emitting when crushed a strong but pleasant medicinal odor . . . . .7. *C. velutinus.*

Flowers varying from pale to dark blue, rarely nearly white.

Branchlets more or less rigid and divaricate, some subspinose; leaves $\frac{3}{8}$-inch to $1\frac{1}{2}$ inches long.

Leaves distinctly white (woolly-tomentose) beneath. 8. *C. tomentosus.*

Leaves varying from green and nearly glabrous to pale and grayish pubescent or hirsute but not woolly-tomentose beneath.

Branchlets distinctly hairy; leaves mostly pubescent or villous above, hirsute or pubescent beneath.....9. *C. oliganthus.*

Branchlets glabrate or slightly pubescent but not hairy; leaves usually glabrous and shining above, paler and pubescent beneath..............................10. *C. sorediatus.*

Branchlets flexible; leaves ¾-inch to 3 inches long.

Branchlets usually angled or ridged; leaves rarely over 1 inch wide.

Veins on underside of leaves very prominent and raised; branchlets not roughened with glandular secretions.
11. *C. thyrsiflorus.*

Veins of leaves not prominently raised beneath; branchlets roughened with numerous small glandular tubercles.
12. *C. cyaneus.*

Branchlets not angled or ridged; leaves over 1 inch wide; island species ....13. *C. arboreus.*

B. Leaves normally with 1 main vein from the base, some with the basal pair of lateral veins more prominent than the upper lateral ones.

1. Stipules inconspicuous, early deciduous.

Leaves entire or rarely denticulate at apex, glabrous.

Flowers white; fruit somewhat triangular, 3-lobed, ¼-inch or more broad, with conspicuous glandular crests; leaves firm and rather thick.
14. *C. Palmeri.*

Flowers white or blue; fruit less than ¼-inch broad.

Plants often with spinose branches; leaves thick; flowers pale blue; fruit globose, viscid..........................15. *C. spinosus.*

Plants never spinose; leaves thin.

Panicles simple, ½-inch to 1½ inches long; low rounded shrubs 1 to 3½ feet high, with slender arching branches; flowers blue.
4. *C. parvifolius.*

Panicles branched, rarely simple, 2 to 6 inches long; widely branched or erect shrubs 4 to 16 feet high; flowers white or blue.
5. *C. integerrimus.*

Leaves never strictly entire, usually pubescent at least beneath.

Inflorescences 3 to 8 inches long, often interrupted; leaves elliptical or ovate, ¼-inch to 2 inches long, densely villous beneath, 1- or 3-veined, the 2 sub-basal lateral veins often obscured by the revolute margins; large spreading shrubs or small trees with angular branchlets ....16. *C. Parryi.*

Inflorescences short, often almost globose, ½-inch to 2 inches long.

Leaves distinctly glandular-papillate on the upper surface, elliptical or oblong, ½-inch to 2 inches long...........17. *C. papillosus.*

Leaves not distinctly glandular-papillate on the upper surface but often glandular-denticulate, serrulate, or papillate on the margins, or sometimes the glands totally absent.

Leaves conspicuously revolute, distinctly 1-veined.

Leaves orbicular or broadly elliptic, ¼-inch to 1 inch long, the upper surface deeply furrowed over the midrib and lateral veins, the margins sometimes slightly glandular.
18. *C. impressus.*

Leaves elliptical or narrowly oblong, seemingly truncate at apex due to infolding, ⅛- to ½-inch long, sometimes glandular-papillate along the apparent margin; medium or low densely branched shrubs.........................19. *C. dentatus.*

Leaves not conspicuously revolute, some indistinctly 3-veined, often undulate.

Prostrate or trailing shrubs, 1 foot or less high, often forming a dense carpet under oaks and pines; young branches very villous; leaves ovate, orbicular, elliptical, broadly oblong, or obovate, ½-inch to 1½ inches long, finely villous, the margins denticulate, serrulate, or serrate but not persistently glandular...........................20. *C. diversifolius.*

Low or medium to tall spreading shrubs, commonly erect when in strict competition with other shrubs, ½-foot to 4 (rarely to 10) feet high.

Leaves plane, the margins finely serrulate and not persistently glandular; branches with grayish to nearly white bark.
21. *C. Lemmonii.*

Leaves usually undulate, the margins normally persistently glandular-serrulate; branches normally not whitish.
22. *C. foliosus.*

2. Stipules persistent, swollen and corky; flowers white, rarely bluish.

Leaves roundish-obovate or deltoid-obovate, ¼- to ½-inch long, generally truncate or retuse at apex, the margins denticulate, dentate, or entire; fruit without dorsal horns but sometimes with rudimentary lateral horns ....23. *C. verrucosus.*

Leaves cuneate-obovate or elliptical, ½-inch to 1¼ inches long, commonly retuse at apex, entire; juvenile leaves revolute, distantly and coarsely repand-dentate; fruit ¼- to ½-inch in diameter, with large dorsal or subdorsal horns (or hornless in the variety)........24. *C. megacarpus.*

II. Leaves opposite. (Fruit with dorsal or subdorsal horns, these often entirely lacking in some species; stipules persistent, swollen and corky; stomata in sunken pits on the lower leaf-surface.—Section Cerastes. *C. verrucosus* and *C. megacarpus,* although with alternate leaves and "keyed out" under I, belong to this section.)

Leaves densely white-tomentose beneath, mostly revolute (plane in the variety); southern California ....25. *C. crassifolius.*

Leaves not densely white-tomentose beneath, usually microscopically tomentulose, not revolute.

Fruit without horns or with short horns from near the middle of the capsule.

Prostrate or semi-prostrate shrubs; leaves narrow-obovate, ⅛- to ⅜-inch long, usually toothed near the apex................26. *C. fresnensis.*

Erect or spreading shrubs.

Flowers white; leaves in the Californian plants commonly cupped above; interior desert mountain shrubs..................29. *C. Greggii.*

Flowers blue; leaves not cupped; coastal species.
Branches inclined to arch, more lax; leaves usually rounded or truncate at apex, not crowded; flowers light blue, lavender, varying to nearly white . . . . 27. *C. ramulosus.*
Branches straight and intricate; leaves usually retuse at apex, crowded on short lateral branchlets; flowers dark or bright blue; Monterey . . . . 33. *C. rigidus.*
Fruit with distinct dorsal or subdorsal horns.
Fruit usually without wrinkled intermediate ridges, these if present inconspicuous.
Flowers usually white; plants 3 to 8 feet high.
All leaves on mature branches entire; fruit 1/4-inch or less broad.
28. *C. cuneatus.*
Many leaves on mature branches toothed; fruit 5/16- to 3/8-inch broad.
35. *C. Ferrisae.*
Flowers pale or dark blue to purple.
Plants erect or erect-spreading.
Leaves usually less than 1/2-inch long, less than 3/8-inch wide.
Leaves with 4 to 8 coarse nearly spinulose teeth.
30. *C. sonomensis.*
Leaves dentate, more commonly toothed toward the apex and entire below, or sometimes quite entire.
Branches inclined to arch, more lax; leaves usually rounded or truncate at apex, not crowded; flowers usually lavender or light blue varying to nearly white . . . . 27. *C. ramulosus.*
Branches straight and intricate; leaves usually retuse at apex, crowded on short lateral branchlets; flowers dark or bright blue . . . . 33. *C. rigidus.*
Leaves usually 1/2-inch to 1 1/2 inches long.
Leaves distinctly spinulose.
Leaves often convex above, the margins rarely undulate, often revolute; horns erect . . . . 32. *C. divergens.*
Leaves usually concave or "troughed" above, the margins undulate but not revolute . . . . 36. *C. purpureus.*
Leaves dentate, not spinulose; stipules 3/16-inch long.
34a. *C. gloriosus* var. *exaltatus.*
Plants prostrate.
Leaves with few strong spinulose teeth; the horns on fruit strongly divergent; Mt. St. Helena northward . . . . 31. *C. confusus.*
Leaves with numerous small teeth; horns erect . . . . . 34. *C. gloriosus.*
Fruit with large and conspicuous wrinkled dorsal horns and wrinkled intermediate ridges, or rarely without ridges; flowers blue or purple, varying to white.
Plants erect or drooping, rarely prostrate; leaves coarsely toothed or spinulose all around.
Leaves with 4 or 5 teeth on a side, coarsely spinulose, with one row of epidermal cells at right angles to the surface; North Coast Ranges.
37. *C. Jepsonii.*

Leaves with 6 to 8 teeth on a side, rather more coarsely toothed than spinulose, with two rows of epidermal cells parallel to the surface; southern Sierra Nevada....................38. *C. pinetorum.*

Plants prostrate or rarely semi-erect and drooping; leaves usually few and coarsely toothed near apex, or more finely toothed and with 4 to 7 teeth on each side, or sometimes entire...........39. *C. prostratus.*

III. Leaves alternate and opposite; probably of hybrid origin....40. *C. serrulatus.*

1. **Ceanothus cordulatus** Kell. MOUNTAIN WHITETHORN. SNOW BUSH. Fig. 319.

A much branched spinescent shrub, 2 to 5 feet high, with glaucous leaves and branchlets, giving the plant a grayish or whitish appearance. Leaves alternate and evergreen; the blades ovate to elliptic, acute at apex, rounded at base, ½-inch to 1 inch long, ¼- to ½-inch wide, 3-veined from the base, light green and glaucous above, gray beneath, glabrous or slightly puberulent, the margins entire or rarely denticulate; petioles ¼-inch or less long. Flowers white, in short dense clusters ½-inch to 1½ inches long. Fruit triangular, usually distinctly lobed, slightly crested, 3/16-inch broad, slightly viscid when young; pedicels about ½-inch long. Flowering period, May to July.

Mountain Whitethorn inhabits rocky ridges and open pine forests from about 3500 to 9000 feet elevation in the Sierra Nevada, Panamint, San Gabriel, San Bernardino, and San Jacinto mountains, on Mount Piños, and in the high North Coast Ranges from Lake and Mendocino counties northward to Siskiyou County, in the Canadian and upper Transition Life Zones. It extends northward to Oregon, eastward to Nevada, and southward in Lower California. It is a very common shrub and is easily identified by its gray appearance, spiny branchlets, and its semi-erect habit of growth. Some plants growing singly have a diameter-spread of 12 feet or they may grow in colonies or form a continuous ground-cover over large areas. This procumbent spreading habit is in part due to the weight of the heavy winter snows. During the flowering period the masses of white flowers often give to the mountain slopes the appearance of being snow-covered. The flowers have a very heavy and penetrating odor. After fires the seeds germinate abundantly and like several other species of *Ceanothus* this species stump-sprouts after cutting.

Ceanothus cordulatus Kell. Proc. Calif. Acad. 2:124 (1861). Type locality: Washoe, Nevada. Collected by *J. A. Veatch.*

2. **Ceanothus leucodermis** Greene. CHAPARRAL WHITETHORN. Fig. 320.

A tall stout shrub, 5 to 12 feet high, with rigid divaricate spinose branches which are usually very gray or whitish in color. Leaves alternate and evergreen; the blades elliptical-oblong to ovate, rounded or subcordate at base, acute to obtuse at apex, ½-inch to 1½ inches long, ¼- to ½-inch wide, 3-veined from the base, usually glabrous and glaucous on both surfaces, or sometimes pubescent in certain variations, the margins entire, glandular-denticulate, or serrulate (serrate on young growth and stump-sprouts); petioles about ⅛-inch long. Flower-clusters usually simple, short and dense or longer and narrower, 1 to 3 inches long. Flowers usually pale blue, varying to white. Fruit globose, about ¼-inch or less wide, slightly depressed at the summit, not crested, viscid. Flowering period, April to June.

Chaparral Whitethorn inhabits dry rocky chaparral slopes of the lower elevations (below 5500 ft.) of the mountains of southern California (exclusive of the desert areas), extending northward in the inner Coast Range to Alameda County,

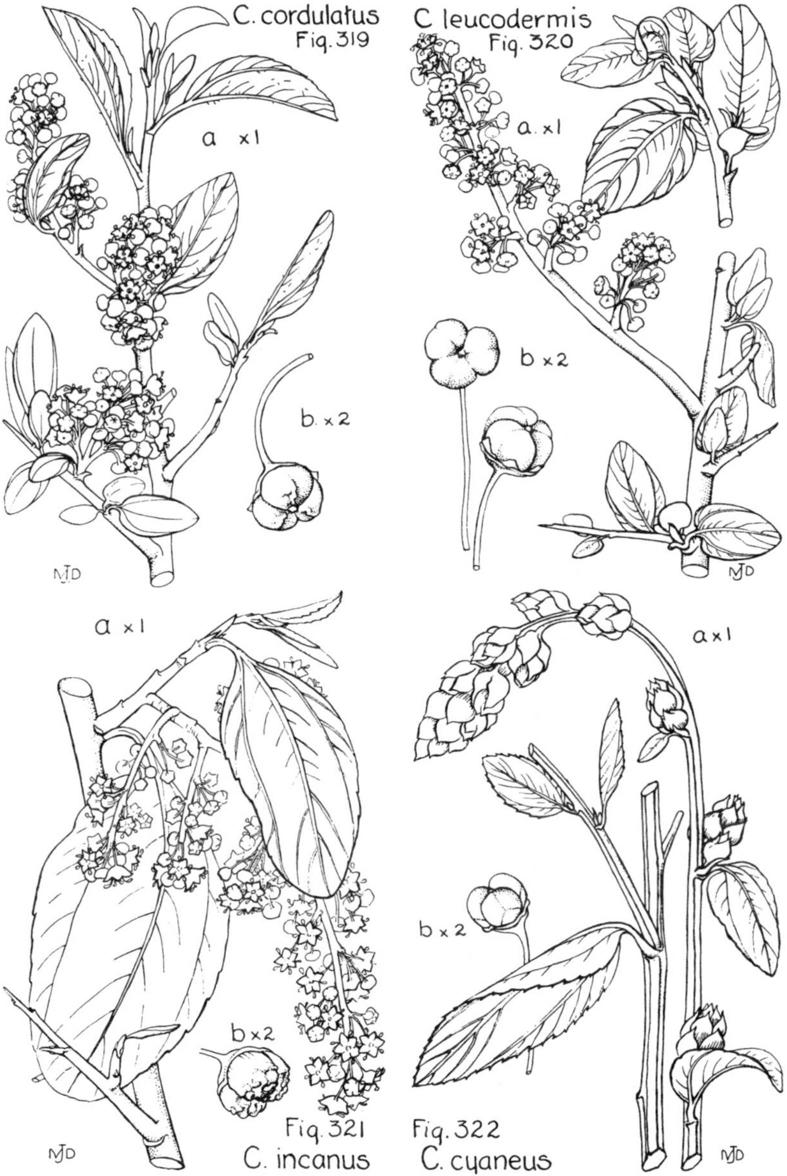

CEANOTHUS. a, Flowering branchlet. b, Fruit.

and in the Sierra Nevada foothills from Kern County to Mariposa County and at a few scattered locations northward to Shasta County, in the Upper Sonoran Life Zone. It extends southward to Lower California.

This species shows considerable variation in its leaves and flower-clusters. Most specimens from southern California have entire leaves, but plants are often found with serrulate, glandular-denticulate, and entire leaves. Specimens taken from San Luis Obispo, Monterey, Mariposa, and Alameda counties usually have serrulate leaves. Plants growing in draws and on the less exposed slopes on Cedar Mountain, Alameda County, have serrulate leaves, and those in more exposed and drier habitats have entire leaves.

The flower-clusters are usually simple and about 2 inches long but may be compound and almost 6 inches long (*C. divaricatus* var. *laetiflorus* Jepson in Man.). The leaves on vigorous stems and stump-sprouts are distinctly serrate (*C. divaricatus* var. *grosse-serratus* Torr.). In many places the plants form pure associations which, on account of the rigid spinescent branches, make almost impenetrable chaparral thickets.

Ceanothus leucodermis Greene, Kew Bull. 15 (1895). Type locality: California. Collected by *Lobb*. *C. divaricatus* B. & W., not Nutt. as given in many works. *C. divaricatus* var. *laetiflorus* Jepson, in Man. *C. divaricatus* var. *grosse-serratus* Torr.

3. **Ceanothus incanus** T. & G. COAST WHITETHORN. Fig. 321.

A tall shrub, 5 to 12 feet high, with numerous gray-glaucous branches and stout thorn-like branchlets, or the branchlets more slender on young and vigorous shoots. Leaves alternate and evergreen; the blades broadly ovate to elliptic, obtuse at apex, rounded or subcordate at base, 1 to 2½ inches long, ½-inch to 1 inch wide, 3-veined from the base, minutely pubescent or glabrate on both surfaces, dull grayish green above, lighter beneath, the margins entire or sometimes serrulate (serrate on stump-sprouts); petioles ⅛- to ½-inch long. Flower-clusters compound, short, dense, axillary, 1 to 3 inches long. Flowers white. Fruit triangular, shallowly lobed at the summit, verrucosely roughened, about ¼-inch broad. Flowering period, April and May.

Coast Whitethorn inhabits valley flats, moist slopes, and ridges of the Redwood belt from the Santa Cruz Mountains northward in San Mateo, San Francisco, Sonoma, Napa, Mendocino, Humboldt, western Lake, and southwestern Siskiyou counties. This species, although a member of the Redwood belt, does not occur in the shade of the redwoods but rather on the open ridges and in open flats, usually in logged-over areas. It stump-sprouts after cutting.

Ceanothus incanus T. & G. Fl. N. Am. 1:265 (1838). Type locality: Probably the Santa Cruz Mountains of California. Collected by *Douglas*.

4. **Ceanothus parvifolius** (Wats.) Trel. LITTLELEAF CEANOTHUS. Fig. 324.

A low spreading shrub, rarely over 3 feet tall, with slender flexible olive-green branches. Leaves alternate, deciduous; the blades oblong-elliptic or elliptic, narrowed at base, acute to obtuse at apex, ¼-inch to 1 inch long, ¼- to ½-inch wide, 3-veined from the base, glabrous and light green above, paler and rarely pubescent beneath, the margins entire, rarely denticulate at apex; petioles ¼-inch or less long. Flower-clusters simple, rarely compound, 1 to 3 inches long; peduncles 1 to 3 inches long or rarely longer, leafless. Flowers pale or deep blue. Fruit globose, less than ¼-inch in diameter, smooth and without crests on the backs of the carpels. Flowering period, June and July.

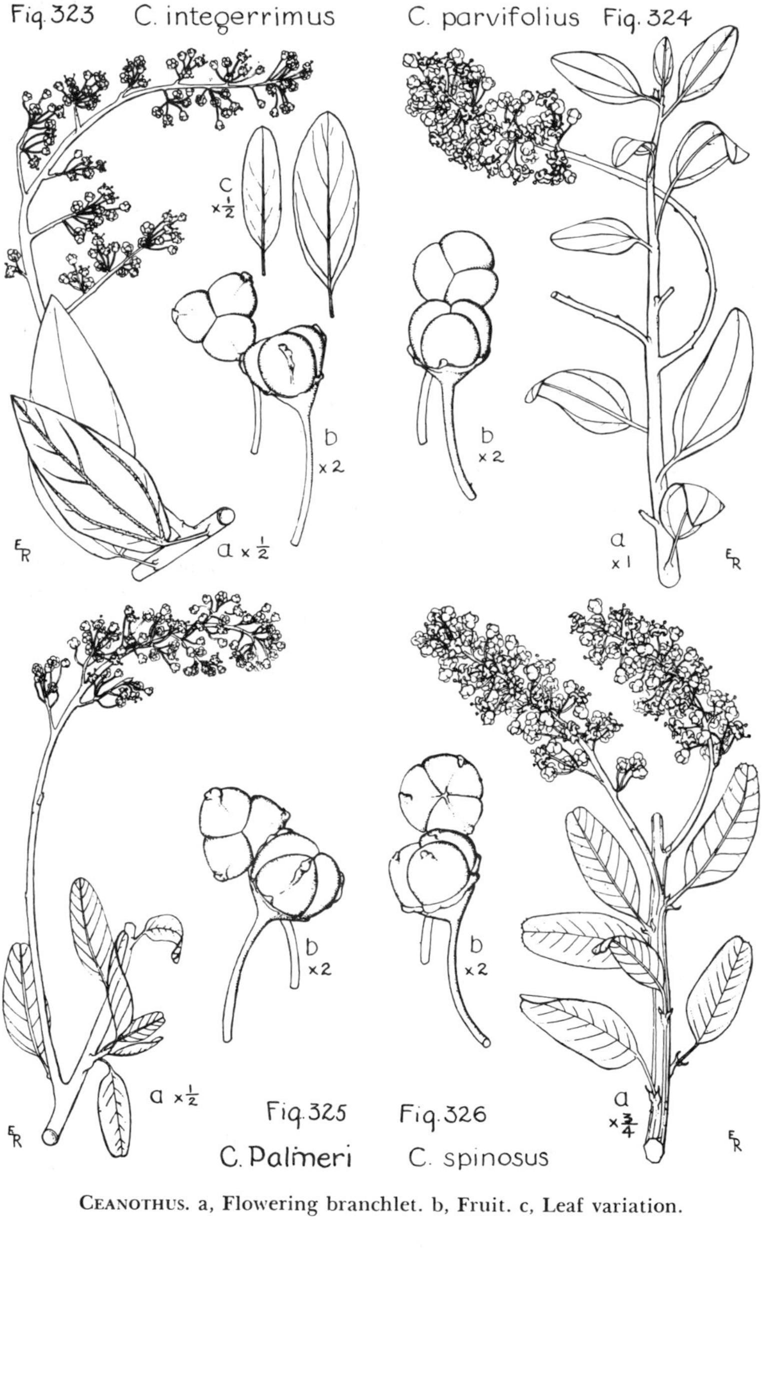

CEANOTHUS. a, Flowering branchlet. b, Fruit. c, Leaf variation.

Littleleaf Ceanothus is a very beautiful shrub inhabiting wooded mountain slopes and flats in the upper Transition and lower Canadian Life Zones, from Tulare County northward to Eldorado County (2 mi. s.w. of Big Hill Lookout, el. 5500 ft., *P. L. Johannsen*). Probably also in Plumas County (1 mi. s.w. of Mt. Jackson, *R. D. Roseberry*). Its flat-topped form, rotately-spreading flexible branches, small glabrous leaves, and attractive blue flowers in simple clusters are characteristics which enable one to recognize this species.

Ceanothus parvifolius (Wats.) Trel. Proc. Calif. Acad. ser. 2, 1:110 (1888). *C. integerrimus* var. *parvifolius* Wats. Type locality: California, in the Yosemite region. Collected by *Bridges, Brewer,* and others.

5. **Ceanothus integerrimus** H. & A. Deer Brush. Fig. 323.

A loosely branched shrub, 3 to 12 feet high, with green or yellowish branches which are often somewhat drooping. Leaves alternate, semi-deciduous or deciduous; the blades broadly elliptical to ovate or nearly oblong, rounded at the base, acute or obtuse at apex, 1 to 3 inches long, 3/8-inch to 1 1/2 inches wide, 3-veined from the base or less commonly pinnately veined, light green and puberulent to almost glabrous above, paler and usually pubescent on the veins beneath, the margins entire or sometimes denticulate at apex; petioles 1/2-inch or less long. Flower-clusters compound, rarely simple, 2 1/2 to 4 inches or even 6 inches long, 1 to 4 inches wide; peduncles 3 to 5 inches long, leafless. Flowers white or pale to dark blue, rarely pinkish. Fruit globose to triangular, 1/4-inch or less wide, slightly depressed at summit, viscid, often with very small lateral crests. Flowering period, May to July.

Deer Brush inhabits mountain slopes, ridges, and flats in the Transition Life Zone, extending from the Cuyamaca, San Jacinto, San Bernardino, and San Gabriel mountains of southern California northward in the Sierra Nevada from Kern County to Modoc County, thence westward through Siskiyou, Trinity, and Shasta counties to the Coast Ranges, southward in the North Coast Ranges, away from the coast, to Sonoma, Lake, and Napa counties and in the South Coast Ranges of Santa Cruz, San Benito, Monterey, western Fresno, San Luis Obispo, central Santa Barbara, Ventura, and southwestern Kern (San Emigdio Canyon) counties. On Figueroa Mountain in Santa Barbara County and in the Topatopa Mountains of Ventura County this species approaches the thinner leaf-form of *C. Palmeri* of San Diego County.

This species consists of a number of forms which seem to intergrade with one another not so much because of hybridization but because of adaptations to the amount of available water throughout the range of their distribution. Plants growing in well-watered situations have larger more ovate and distinctly 3-veined leaves, while those growing in drier and frequently burned-over areas have smaller more oblong-elliptic leaves with one main vein and the two basal lateral ones much obscured, thus being pinnately veined. The amount of pubescence on the leaf-surfaces varies but the greater number of plants have leaves with their upper surfaces glabrous and the lower surfaces with pubescence only along the veins. The leaf-margins are typically entire but specimens are not uncommon in which the blades are denticulate at the apex. The flowers on the majority of plants are white but blue-flowered plants are frequent in certain localities. The inflorescences vary from nearly simple to compound and from 1 1/2 to 6 inches long. All the forms stump-sprout after cutting.

One is tempted by the occurrence of these variations to recognize and describe several varieties of the species, but extensive field and herbarium studies have convinced the writer that until more extensive transplant studies can be carried out it is best to include the various forms in the single polymorphic species, *C. integerrimus* H. & A.

The following key will identify the more distinct variations.

Leaf-blades oblong to oblong-elliptical, typically pinna-veined or with the basal pair of lateral veins a little more prominent than the other lateral veins.
  Flowers white; Santa Cruz Mts. and South Coast Ranges. *C. integerrimus* H. & A.
  Flowers blue . . . . *Blue-flowering* form, common in Lake County.
Leaf-blades oblong-ovate to usually broadly ovate, distinctly 3-veined from the base.
  Leaf-blades typically glabrous above; branchlets glabrous or nearly so.
    Flowers white.
      Leaf-blades usually 1½ to 3 inches long, over ½-inch wide, not denticulate at apex; inflorescences compound . . . . . var. *californicus* (Kell.) Benson.
      Leaf-blades 1½ inches or less long, usually less than ½-inch wide, often denticulate at apex; inflorescences simple; Lake County.
      Lake County form.
    Flowers blue; leaf-blades usually less than 1½ inches long, often obtuse at apex . . . . *Blue-flowering* form, common in Lake County.
  Leaf-blades puberulent or pubescent above; branchlets pubescent or tomentose.
    Flowers white; veins not prominently raised beneath.
      Inflorescences broad and compound . . . . var. *puberulus* Abrams.
      Inflorescences narrow, nearly simple, 3 to 5 inches long.
      var. *peduncularis* Jepson.
    Flowers blue; veins prominently raised beneath; branchlets and leaf-blades tomentose; rare in vicinity of Mt. Shasta (Kennet, etc.) . . . . *Kennet* form.

Ceanothus integerrimus H. & A. Bot. Beechey 329 (1840). Type locality: Probably the Santa Cruz Mountains, California. Collected by *Douglas*. *C. Andersonii* Parry.

Var. californicus (Kell.) Benson, Contr. Dudley Herb. 2:120 (1930). *C. californicus* Kell. Type locality: Placerville, Eldorado County, California. Collected by *E. W. Garvitt*. *C. nevadensis* Kell.

Var. puberulus (Greene) Abrams, Bull. N. Y. Bot. Gard. 6:409 (1910). *C. puberulus* Greene. Type locality: San Bernardino Mountains of California. Collected by *Greene*.

Var. peduncularis (Greene) Jepson, Man. 620 (1925). *C. peduncularis* Greene. Type locality: "North side of Mount Hood, Oregon." Collected by *H. D. Langille*.

6. **Ceanothus sanguineus** Pursh. REDSTEM CEANOTHUS. OREGON TEA-TREE. Fig. 327.

A tall shrub, 5 to 10 feet high, with purple or reddish flexible glabrous branches. Leaves alternate and deciduous; the blades thin, broadly elliptical, varying to ovate or obovate, rounded or subcordate at base, obtuse to acute at apex, 1 to 4 inches long, ¾-inch to 1½ inches wide, 3-veined from the base, almost glabrous, the margins serrate; petioles ⅓-inch to 1 inch long. Flower-clusters compound, lateral, 2 to 4 inches long; peduncles usually 2 to 3 inches long. Flowers white. Fruit obovoid, about ⅙-inch wide, slightly lobed at the summit, with inconspicuous crests. Flowering period, May to July.

Redstem Ceanothus is rare in California, to my knowledge being found only in western Siskiyou County. It probably occurs also in Shasta County. It extends northward into Oregon, Washington, and British Columbia and eastward into Idaho and Montana.

Ceanothus sanguineus Pursh, Fl. Am. Sept. 167 (1814). Type locality: "Rocky Mountains on the banks of the Missouri." Collected by *Lewis*. Probably on Collins Creek, now Solo Creek, Idaho, acc. Piper, Contr. U. S. Nat. Herb. 11:387 (1906).

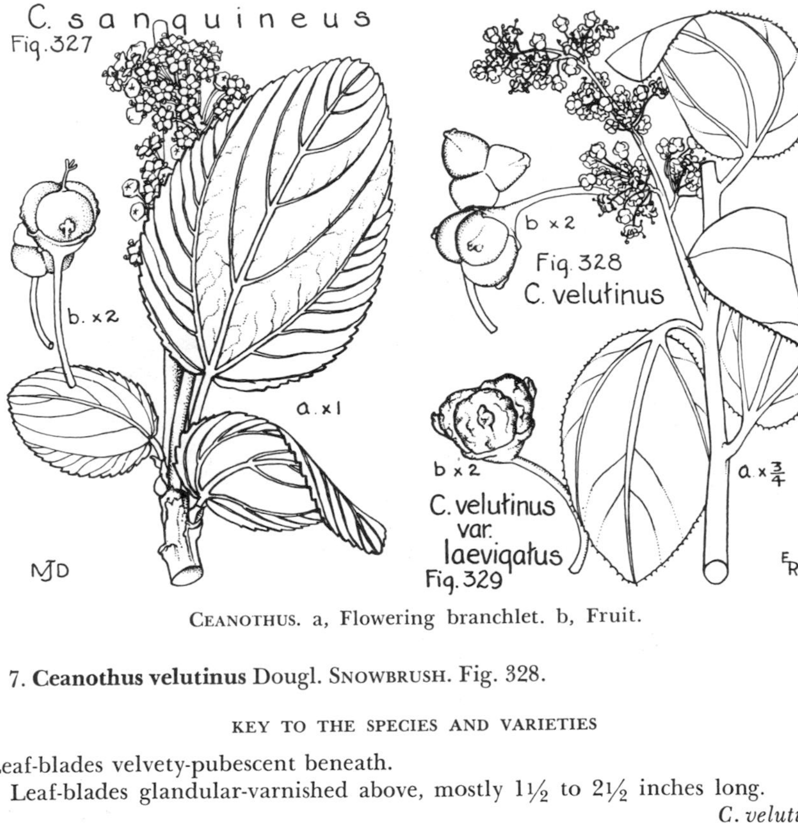

CEANOTHUS. a, Flowering branchlet. b, Fruit.

7. **Ceanothus velutinus** Dougl. SNOWBRUSH. Fig. 328.

KEY TO THE SPECIES AND VARIETIES

Leaf-blades velvety-pubescent beneath.
Leaf-blades glandular-varnished above, mostly 1½ to 2½ inches long. *C. velutinus.*
Leaf-blades scarcely glandular-varnished above, mostly 1 to 1¼ inches long. 7a. var. *Lorenzenii.*
Leaf-blades not velvety-pubescent beneath, at least not on the veins, highly glandular-varnished above............................7b. var. *laevigatus.*

Usually a diffusely spreading round-topped shrub, 2 to 5 feet high, or in one variety almost tree-like but with several stems from the ground, 6 to 20 feet high. Leaves alternate, evergreen, with a distinct walnut-, cinnamon-, or balsam-like odor; the blades broadly elliptical or elliptical-ovate, rounded or subcordate at base, obtuse or rounded at apex, mostly 1½ to 2½ inches long, ¾-inch to 1¼ inches wide, 3-veined from the base, dark green, glabrous and usually varnished

Fig. 330. HAIRY CEANOTHUS. *Ceanothus oliganthus* Nutt.

above, paler and finely canescent beneath, the margins finely serrate or glandular-serrulate; petioles ½- to ¾-inch long. Flower-clusters compound, 2 to 4 inches long, the peduncle somewhat angled, 1 to 2 inches long. Flowers white. Fruit subglobose to triangular, ⅛- to ⅙-inch wide, distinctly lobed at the summit, smooth or minutely roughened, commonly sticky-glandular, crestless or with very minute crests. Flowering period, May to August.

Snowbrush inhabits dry mountain slopes and ridges between 3500 and 10,000 feet elevation in the upper Transition, Canadian, and lower Hudsonian Life Zones, in the Sierra Nevada from Tulare County northward to Modoc County, thence westward to Shasta, Trinity, Siskiyou, and Humboldt counties. On the coast it gives way to the variety *laevigatus* T. & G. It extends northward to British Columbia and eastward to the northern Rocky Mountains and South Dakota. The large varnished leaves and strong balsamic odor easily identify this species of *Ceanothus* from all others. Other common names for this species are Mountain Balm, Sticky-laurel, Tobacco-brush, and Varnishleaf Ceanothus.

7a. Var. **Lorenzenii** Jepson.

Leaves and panicles smaller than in the species. Leaf-blades scarcely varnished above.

This variety occurs occasionally in the Sierra Nevada between 5900 and 8000 feet elevation from Kern Canyon northward to the Mount Shasta region of Siskiyou County. (Alpine County: 1.8 mi. n. of mouth of Golden Canyon; 3 mi. e. of Scotts Lake. Eldorado County: 1 mi. w. of Rubicon Point. Plumas County: 4¼ mi. n. of Hawks; Silver Creek. V. T. M.) It extends eastward into Washoe County, Nevada.

7b. Var. **laevigatus** T. & G. Fig. 329.

Tall shrubs or often tree-like, 6 to 20 feet high. Leaf-blades highly varnished above and without velvety pubescence beneath, thus appearing light green instead of gray as in the species. Fruit slightly crested and more roughened than in the species.

This variety occurs in the North Coast Ranges, usually near the coast, from Marin County northward to Del Norte County. It extends northward to Oregon, Washington, and British Columbia. It occurs locally on the south side of Mount Saint Helena, Napa County.

Ceanothus velutinus Dougl.; Hook. Fl. Bor. Am. 1:125 (1830). Type locality: "Subalpine hills near the source of the Columbia; and at Kettle Falls." Collected by *Douglas*.

Var. Lorenzenii Jepson, Man. 619 (1925). Type locality: Junction Meadow, Kern Canyon. Collected by *Jepson*.

Var. laevigatus (Hook.) T. & G. Fl. N. Am. 1:686 (1838). *C. laevigatus* Hook. Type locality: Nootka, Vancouver Island. Collected by *Menzies*.

8. **Ceanothus tomentosus** Parry. Woollyleaf Ceanothus. Fig. 333.

KEY TO THE SPECIES AND VARIETY

Leaf-blades glandular-serrate; central Sierra Nevada. . . . . *C. tomentosus*.
Leaf-blades glandular-denticulate; southern California. . . . . 8a. var. *olivaceus*.

A medium-sized to tall shrub, 2 to 8 feet high, with long and slender branches, gray or reddish bark, and rusty-tomentose young shoots. Leaves alternate and evergreen; the blades elliptical to round-ovate, commonly rounded at base and apex,

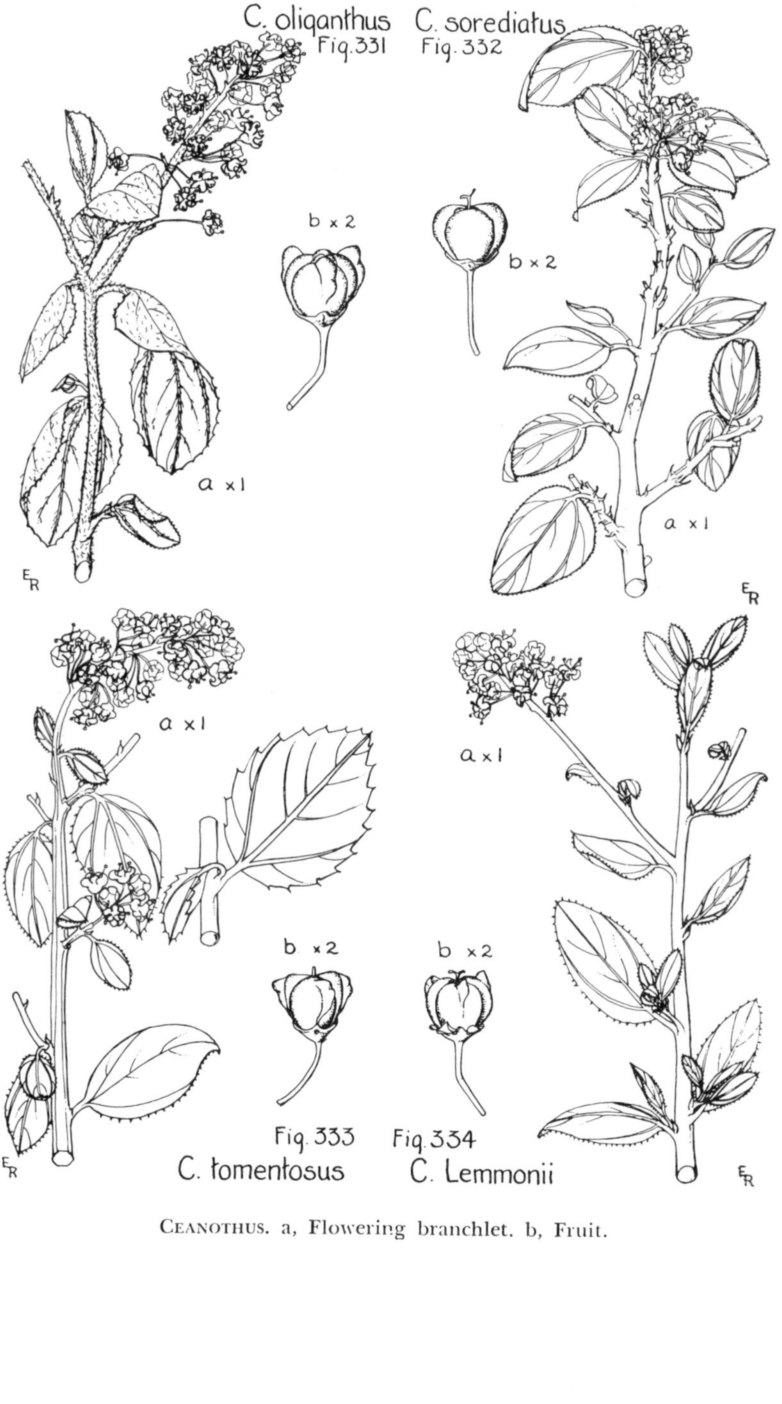

CEANOTHUS. a, Flowering branchlet. b, Fruit.

½-inch to 1 inch long, ¼- to ½-inch wide (longer and wider on suckers and on some plants in the San Bernardino Mountains), 3-veined or rarely apparently 1-veined from the base, dark green and finely pubescent above, whitish or brownish tomentose beneath, or sometimes only pubescent, the margins normally finely glandular-serrate; the petioles about ⅙-inch long. Flower-clusters compound, lateral or terminal, 1 to 2 inches long, loosely tomentose, the peduncles ½-inch to 1 inch long and usually with 1 or 2 small leaves at the base. Flowers azure-blue, varying to almost white. Fruit subglobose, about ⅙-inch wide, slightly lobed at the summit, somewhat laterally crested, viscid when developing. Flowering period, April and May.

Woollyleaf Ceanothus occurs in the foothills of the Sierra Nevada, nowhere abundant, from Mariposa County northward in Amador, Eldorado, and Placer counties, in the Upper Sonoran Life Zone. A nearly prostrate form sometimes occurs in the Ione area of Amador County. This species stump-sprouts.

8a. Var. **olivaceus** Jepson.

Leaf-blades normally glandular-denticulate. Flowering period, February to April.

This variety occurs in the chaparral of the low hills and mountains from near Redlands, San Bernardino County southward in western Riverside County and the Santa Ana Mountains to San Diego County. In the Santa Ana Mountains (Leach Canyon, *P. A. Munz*) and in certain localities in San Diego County this variety seems very much like *C. sorediatus* of central California.

Ceanothus tomentosus Parry, Proc. Davenp. Acad. 5:190 (1899). Type locality: Ione, Amador County. Collected by *Parry*.

Var. olivaceus Jepson, Man. 621 (1925). Type locality: Clevinger Canyon, Ramona, San Diego County. Collected by *Jepson*.

9. **Ceanothus oliganthus** Nutt. Hairy Ceanothus. Figs. 330, 331.

KEY TO THE SPECIES AND VARIETY

Flowers deep blue to purplish; capsules not villous-pubescent or strongly verrucose-roughened . . . . *C. oliganthus.*

Flowers pale blue; capsules villous-pubescent and strongly verrucose-roughened. 9a. var. *Orcuttii.*

A medium-sized to tall shrub, 4 to 10 feet high, often with a tree-like trunk and with many rather short and usually stiff but not spinescent branchlets. The younger branches and branchlets densely villous, more or less reddish and verrucose. Leaves alternate and evergreen; the blades ovate or oblong-ovate to elliptical, obtuse, rounded, or subcordate at base, obtuse, rounded or acute at apex, ½-inch to 1½ inches long, ¼-inch to 1 inch wide, typically 3-veined from the base, the upper surface dark green, beset with scattered rather long hairs, drying brownish, the lower surface paler, with scattered long hairs, especially along the veins, the margins glandular-denticulate; the petioles ⅛- to ¼-inch long, densely villous. Flower-clusters slightly puberulent, usually simple and rather loose, 1 to 2 inches long. Flowers deep or pale blue or purplish, varying to almost white. Fruit somewhat triangular, 3/16- to ¼-inch wide, somewhat depressed at the summit, smooth or verrucosely roughened, with subdorsal crests, usually viscid. Flowering period, March and April.

Hairy Ceanothus occurs in dry bushy woods and canyon slopes of the Upper Sonoran Life Zone in southern San Luis Obispo and Santa Barbara counties, southward and eastward in Ventura, Los Angeles, and western Riverside counties. In Trabuco and Bedford canyons of Riverside County it merges into *C. tomentosus.* In the Santa Ynez Mountains of Santa Barbara County and in San Luis Obispo County (1½ miles s.e. of Sycamore Springs, V. T. M.), it approaches *C. sorediatus* in characters of branchlets and leaves. In San Diego County this species merges into the variety *Orcuttii* (Parry) Jepson, which is of doubtful varietal rank.

9a. Var. **Orcuttii** (Parry) Jepson.

This variety is scarcely distinguishable from the species. The flowers are usually paler blue and the fruits are villous-pubescent and verrucosely roughened. It inhabits the interior mountains of the Upper Sonoran and Arid Transition Life Zones of San Diego County and extends northward to the Santa Ana Mountains of Orange County.

Ceanothus oliganthus Nutt.; T. & G. Fl. N. Am. 1:266 (1838). Type locality: "Bushy woods on the hills of Santa Barbara." Collected by *Nuttall.*

Var. Orcuttii (Parry) Jepson, Man. 621 (1925). *C. Orcuttii* Parry. Type locality: "High mountains east of San Diego." Collected by *Orcutt.*

10. **Ceanothus sorediatus** H. & A. JIM BRUSH. Fig. 332.

A medium-sized densely and rigidly branched shrub, 3 to 8 (rarely to 18) feet high, with gray-green or purplish and somewhat villous stiff nearly spinescent branchlets. Leaves alternate and evergreen; the blades elliptic to ovate, rounded at base, usually acute at apex, ⅓-inch to 1 inch long, ⅜- to ¾-inch wide, 3-veined from the base, dark glossy green and glabrous above, paler and usually appressed-silky (at least on the veins) beneath, the margins glandular-denticulate; petioles about ⅙-inch or less long. Flower-clusters short, dense, usually simple, ½-inch to 1¼ inches long. Flowers varying from pale to deep blue. Fruit smooth, globose, about ⅙-inch in diameter, scarcely lobed or crested, viscid with age. Flowering period, March and April.

Jim Brush inhabits canyon slopes and bushy woods in the Transition and Upper Sonoran Life Zones of the Coast Ranges from Humboldt County southward to the Santa Monica Mountains of Los Angeles County. In the southern part of its range, where it overlaps with that of *C. oliganthus,* as on La Cumbre Peak, Santa Barbara County, many specimens seem intermediate between the two species. Some specimens from the Santa Ana Mountains of Orange County which have been assigned to *C. tomentosus* have characters common to *C. sorediatus* and may very likely be intermediates between these two species.

This is the most common species of *Ceanothus* in the Oakland Hills. It is most abundant from the San Francisco Bay region southward in the inner Coast Range to San Luis Obispo County. It stump-sprouts after cutting.

Ceanothus sorediatus H. & A. Bot. Beechey 328 (1840). Type locality: California, probably near San Francisco or Monterey. Collected by *Douglas.*

11. **Ceanothus thyrsiflorus** Esch. BLUE BLOSSOM. Fig. 336.

This species varies greatly in its habit of growth, shape and size of leaves, and amount and type of pubescence on the under side of the leaves. Plants growing in fertile soil of the canyons of Mendocino County may attain heights of over 20 feet while on the bluffs above the sea they are prostrate and form dense mats several feet across. The two varieties "keyed out" below are of doubtful significance since they seem to intergrade with the species.

KEY TO THE SPECIES AND VARIETIES

Leaf-margins not revolute.

Leaf-blades 3/4-inch to 2 inches long; panicles normally over 3/4-inch long. *C. thyrsiflorus.*

Leaf-blades usually 3/4-inch or less long; panicles 3/4-inch or less long. 11a. var. *Chandleri.*

Leaf-margins revolute between the teeth; the blades usually silky beneath. 11b. var. *griseus.*

A low-growing or prostrate shrub in exposed places, but usually taller and ascending, 4 to 8 feet high, or a small tree up to 20 feet in the edges of deep forests, with green angled branchlets. Leaves alternate, evergreen; the blades oblong-ovate or broadly elliptical, rounded to acute at base, obtuse or acute at apex, 3/4-inch to 2 inches long, 1/2- to 3/4-inch wide, prominently 3-veined from the base, dark green and glabrous above, paler and glabrous except for a few coarse appressed hairs on the prominently raised veins beneath, the margins finely serrate or dentate, sometimes slightly revolute and then appearing entire; petioles 1/2-inch or less long. Flower-clusters compound, 1 to 3 inches long, the peduncles about as long and often somewhat leafy. Flowers light or deep blue, rarely varying to almost white. Fruit subglobose, about 1/6-inch wide, smooth, only slightly lobed at the summit, glandular-viscid and black in age. Flowering period, March to June.

Blue Blossom inhabits canyon slopes of the wooded hills and lower mountain slopes in the Transition Life Zone of the outer Coast Range from the vicinity of Cañada Honda, Santa Barbara County northward to Del Norte County, California and to Oregon.

This species has been in cultivation for many years for its dark green foliage and profuse clusters of blue flowers. In the nurseries it hybridizes with *C. arboreus* and *C. spinosus.*

11a. Var. **Chandleri** Jepson.

Branchlets more slender than in the species. Leaf-blades usually 3/4-inch or less long, puberulent beneath. Panicles subglobose, about 5/8-inch long on peduncles 2 to 3 3/4 inches long.

This variety occurs in its typical form in the Pajaro Hills of Monterey County (2 mi. s.e. of Elkhorn, *D. Axelrod*).

11b. Var. **griseus** Trel. Fig. 337.

Branchlets stout. Leaf-blades broadly ovate or roundish-ovate, obtuse at apex, gray-tomentulose or silky beneath with dense short hairs, the margins revolute between the teeth.

This variety occurs on the more open slopes at scattered locations from Santa Barbara County (Sulphur Ridge, Guadalupe Quadrangle, *G. E. Sindel*) northward in San Luis Obispo (1/2 mi. s. of Hollister Peak) and Monterey (Huckleberry Hill) counties to Mendocino County. Along the bluffs in Sonoma and Mendocino counties this form is often prostrate.

Ceanothus thyrsiflorus Esch. Mem. Acad. Sci. St. Petersb. ser. 6, 10:285 (1826). Type locality: Probably at San Francisco, California. Collected by *Eschscholtz.*

Var. Chandleri Jepson, Man. 619 (1925). Type locality: Pajaro Hills, Monterey County. Collected by *Chandler.*

Var. griseus Trel.; Gray, Syn. Fl. 1:415 (1897). Type locality: Monterey, California.

Fig. 335. Feltleaf Ceanothus. *Ceanothus arboreus* Greene.

12. **Ceanothus cyaneus** Eastw. SAN DIEGO CEANOTHUS. Fig. 322.

A tall erect shrub, 4 to 10 feet high, with angled branchlets and usually straight gray-green branches dotted with small brownish tubercles. Leaves alternate, evergreen; the blades ovate-elliptical, rounded at base, acute or obtuse at apex, 1 to 2 inches long, ½- to ¾-inch wide, 3-veined from the base, dark green and glabrous above, lighter and almost glabrous beneath, the margins finely glandular-denticulate, serrate, or almost entire; petioles about ⅛-inch long. Flower-clusters large, compound, 6 to 12 inches long, terminating the branches. Flowers very dark blue in bud and soon after opening, but becoming lighter in age. Fruit subglobose, about ⅙-inch wide, deeply lobed at the summit, slightly crested along the back of the lobes. Flowering period, May and June or in cultivation to November.

San Diego Ceanothus is a species local in the interior mountains of San Diego County. The known localities are: The Philbrook Ranch near Lakeside, el. about 1500 feet, *McMinn;* Mussey Grade to U. S. Highway 80 near Alpine, El Cajon Mountains, acc. *F. F. Gander;* and grade from Temecula to Pala, *McMinn.*

This is one of the most beautiful of all the species of *Ceanothus.* Its glossy green foliage and large compound clusters of deep blue flowers are not surpassed by those of any of the other species or varieties. Nurserymen have quickly recognized its beauty and now sell it extensively for ornamental planting. It grows very rapidly and blooms later and for a longer period than the other species of the genus. The name, *cyaneus,* referring to the deep clear blue or cornflower-color of the flowers, was well chosen. In the nurseries it readily hybridizes with *C. spinosus* and *C. thyrsiflorus,* and seeds gathered from nursery plants often produce plants inferior to those growing in nature.

Ceanothus cyaneus Eastw. Proc. Calif. Acad. 16:361 (1927). Type locality: Near Lakeside, San Diego County. Collected by *Myrtle Philbrook.*

13. **Ceanothus arboreus** Greene. FELTLEAF CEANOTHUS. Fig. 335.

A small tree, 15 to 25 feet high, or sometimes shrub-like, with soft-pubescent branchlets and smooth gray bark. Leaves alternate, evergreen; the blades broadly ovate or elliptical, rounded at base, acute to obtuse at apex, 1 to 3 inches long, ¾-inch to 1½ inches wide, 3-veined from the base, dark green, dull, and glabrous or slightly pubescent above, finely and densely white-tomentose beneath, the margins serrulate or serrate; petioles ⅓- to ¾-inch long. Flower-clusters compound, 2 to 6 inches long. Flowers pale blue. Fruit triangular, ¼- to ⅓-inch wide, roughened all over, crested on the back of the lobes or the crests almost absent, nearly black when ripe. Flowering period, February to May.

This species is the largest of the genus *Ceanothus.* It does not occur on the mainland but is found on Santa Rosa, Santa Catalina, and Santa Cruz islands. Under cultivation this species grows to a height of 30 feet with a trunk 16 inches in diameter. Its large masses of blue flowers in early spring make the plant very desirable for ornamental use. In cultivation it hybridizes with *C. thyrsiflorus* and *C. spinosus.*

On Santa Rosa Island a form with nearly glabrous leaves has been described as var. **glaber** Jepson.

Ceanothus arboreus Greene, Bull. Calif. Acad. 2:144 (1886). Type locality: Santa Cruz Island. Collected by *Greene.*

14. **Ceanothus Palmeri** Trel. PALMER CEANOTHUS. Fig. 325.

A tall spreading shrub, 4 to 12 feet high, with gray-green bark. Leaves alternate

CEANOTHUS. a, Flowering branchlet. b, Fruit. c, Single leaf. d, Cross section of leaf.

and semi-deciduous; the blades oblong to ovate-oblong, ½-inch to 1½ inches long, ⅜- to ⅝-inch wide, retuse or rounded at apex, rather firm and leathery, 1-veined from the base, on stump-sprouts and seedlings 3-veined, glabrous and light green above, paler beneath, entire; petioles about ⅛-inch long. Flower-clusters compound, 3 to 5 inches long, on leafy peduncles 1 to 2 inches long. Flowers white. Fruit somewhat triangular, ¼-inch or more broad, 3-lobed, with conspicuous glandular crests. Flowering period, May and June.

Palmer Ceanothus inhabits mountain slopes from about 4000 to 6000 feet elevation in the Transition Life Zone in the Palomar, Laguna, and Cuyamaca mountains of San Diego County and occasionally in the Santa Ana and San Jacinto mountains of Orange and Riverside counties. In the foothills of the Upper Sonoran Life Zone of Amador (northwest of Bishop Peak and along the Consumnes River south of Latrobe and elsewhere) and in Eldorado (near Dormoody's, *Wieslander*) counties occurs a *Ceanothus* that closely resembles *C. Palmeri* and probably should be classified as such. The leaves are not quite so thick nor are the fruits so large as those of typical *C. Palmeri.* The pinnate venation is a character common to both *C. Palmeri* and typical *C. integerrimus* of the Santa Cruz Mountains. However, the leaf-blades resemble in texture those of *C. Palmeri* more than those of *C. integerrimus. C. integerrimus* var. *californicus* is very abundant in the Arid Transition Life Zone of Amador and Eldorado counties but does not occur at the lower elevations in which the plants under discussion grow. Plants in the dry inner South Coast Range and in the San Rafael Mountains (Figueroa Mt.) of Santa Barbara County and in the Topatopa Mountains of Ventura County are undoubtedly very closely related to *C. Palmeri* but since their leaf-blades are typically thinner and the basal pair of lateral veins usually better developed it seems best to refer them to *C. integerrimus.* Extensive field and herbarium studies convince the writer that *C. Palmeri* has an intermediate position between *C. integerrimus* and *C. spinosus.*

This species stump-sprouts abundantly after cutting and the new shoots are eaten by browsing animals. During the winter when the snow is on the ground in the Cuyamaca Mountains cattle browse on the exposed shoots.

Ceanothus Palmeri Trel. Proc. Calif. Acad. ser. 2, 1:109 (1888). Type locality: In the mountains of San Diego County. Collected by *Palmer.*

15. **Ceanothus spinosus** Nutt. GREENBARK CEANOTHUS. RED-HEART. Fig. 326.

A tall shrub, or often arborescent, 8 to 20 feet high, with greenish yellow glabrous branchlets and branches, typically spinose (often without spines in favorable places and under cultivation). Leaves alternate and evergreen; the blades broadly elliptic or oblong, obtuse or emarginate at apex, rounded or tapering at base, ½-inch to 1¼ inches long, ⅝- to ¾-inch wide, thick and leathery, typically with 1 main vein from the base, glabrous and shining on both surfaces, the margins entire, rarely serrulate (on seedlings and young vigorous shoots the leaves are usually 3-veined from the base and distinctly serrate); petioles about ¼-inch long. Flower-clusters usually large and compound, rarely simple, 1½ to 6 inches long, usually leafy below. Flowers pale blue, varying to almost white. Fruit globose, about ¼-inch in diameter, viscid, scarcely lobed or crested. Flowering period, February to May.

This species inhabits the mountains of southern California, mostly near the coast, from San Luis Obispo County (Davis Canyon n.w. of Goldtree) southward to San Diego County (head of Cold Spring Canyon, *H. A. Jensen*), in the Upper

Sonoran Life Zone. It is particularly abundant on the lower mountain slopes and flats near Santa Barbara. The evergreen shining foliage and arborescent habit of growth make this species desirable for planting in large estates where a mass effect is desired. It stump-sprouts after cutting.

Ceanothus spinosus Nutt.; T. & G. Fl. N. Am. 1:267 (1838). Type locality: "Mountains of Santa Barbara." Collected by *Nuttall.*

16. **Ceanothus Parryi** Trel. PARRY CEANOTHUS. Fig. 338.

An erect rather large shrub, 6 to 18 feet high, with tomentose angled young branchlets. Leaves alternate and evergreen; the blades elliptic or oblong, rarely ovate, rounded at base, obtuse at apex, ½-inch to 2 inches long, ¼- to ¾-inch wide, typically 1-veined from the base (the two basal lateral veins usually not pronounced), dark green and glabrous above, lighter green and densely cobwebby beneath, the real margins denticulate but soon becoming slightly revolute and hence seemingly entire; petioles ¼-inch or less long. Flower-clusters usually simple, on leafy peduncles, the whole 3 to 8 inches long, drying brown. Flowers deep blue. Fruit subglobose, about ⅙-inch broad, very slightly depressed at the summit, smooth. Flowering period, April and May.

Parry Ceanothus inhabits wooded canyon slopes in the outer and middle North Coast Ranges of Marin, Sonoma, Napa, Lake, Mendocino, and Humboldt counties, in the Transition Life Zone. It usually grows farther inland than the closely related *C. thyrsiflorus*. The large clusters of deep blue flowers make it one of the most beautiful of all the species of *Ceanothus.*

Ceanothus Parryi Trel. Proc. Calif. Acad. ser. 2, 1:109 (1888). Type locality: "Cultivated at Calistoga, Napa County." Collected by *Parry.*

17. **Ceanothus papillosus** T. & G. WARTLEAF CEANOTHUS. Fig. 339.

KEY TO THE SPECIES AND VARIETY

Plants erect, 4 to 15 feet high . . . . *C. papillosus.*
Plants procumbent or nearly prostrate, 1 to 3 feet high . . . . . 17a. var. *Roweanus.*

A rather tall spreading and ofter straggly shrub, 4 to 15 feet high, with densely tomentose young branchlets and slightly roughened branches. Leaves alternate and evergreen, usually crowded on the branchlets; the blades elliptical, oblong, or narrowly linear, rounded or obtuse to truncate at apex, rounded at base, ½-inch to 2 inches long, ¼- to ½-inch wide, 1-veined from the base, the upper surface dark green, shining, slightly villous or hirsute and irregularly and closely glandular-papillate, the lower surface pale, usually densely felt-like and often hairy, the margins glandular-denticulate and usually strongly revolute; petioles about ⅛-inch long. Flower-clusters simple, dense, ½-inch to 2 inches long, on naked peduncles as long or longer. Flowers deep blue. Fruit triangular or subglobose, about ⅛-inch wide, distinctly 3-lobed at the summit, with low narrow subdorsal crests. Flowering period, March to May.

Wartleaf Ceanothus occurs on wooded mountain slopes and ridges near the coast from near sea level to about 3000 feet elevation in the South Coast Range from San Mateo County southward to San Luis Obispo County and at scattered locations in Ventura (Ocean View Trail above Matilija Ranger Station; ½-mi. n. of Long Valley), Orange (Trabuco Canyon; Los Piños Peak), and western Riverside (Sugarloaf Peak) counties, in the Transition Life Zone. Plants of the drier habitats and those not watered in the transplant garden at Mills College have very narrow linear leaves often truncate at the apex because of the strongly revolute margins. Specimens gathered throughout the range of the species show this character. In the Redwood area of the Santa Cruz Mountains the leaves are usually broader and often have fewer papillae on the upper surface. Hybrids between this species and *C. thyrsiflorus* have been observed in the Santa Cruz Mountains near Ben Lomond and on Kings Mountain, San Mateo County. Some specimens with reduced leaves and with few papillae on the upper surface are with difficulty distinguished from *C. dentatus.*

17a. Var. **Roweanus** McMinn. MOUNT TRANQUILLON CEANOTHUS.

A low spreading or procumbent shrub, 1 to 3 feet high, with a compact growth-form. Leaves usually narrower than those of the species.

This variety occurs on Mount Tranquillon, Santa Barbara County, California. When brought into cultivation it has a low spreading habit which makes it suitable for using as a ground-cover.

Ceanothus papillosus T. & G. Fl. N. Am. 1:268 (1838). Type locality: California. Collected by *Douglas. C. papillosus* var. *regius* Jepson.

Var. Roweanus McMinn, Madroño 5:13 (1939). Type locality: Mount Tranquillon, Santa Barbara County, California. Collected by *M. Van Rensselaer.*

18. **Ceanothus impressus** Trel. SANTA BARBARA CEANOTHUS. Fig. 340.

A low to tall shrub, 1 to 8 feet high and with a spread up to 20 feet. Leaves alternate and evergreen; the blades broadly elliptical to nearly round, 1/4-inch to 1 inch long, 1-veined from the base, loosely villous, especially on the veins below, upper surface deeply furrowed over the midrib and veins, the margin sometimes slightly glandular and very revolute, appearing crenate; petioles 1/8-inch or less long. Flower-clusters simple, 1/2-inch to 1 inch long. Flowers deep blue. Fruit subglobose, about 1/6-inch broad, with prominent lateral crests. Flowering period, February to April.

Santa Barbara Ceanothus occurs on dry sandy mesas and open slopes from the Nipomo Mesa of San Luis Obispo County southward in scattered locations to Burton Mesa, Santa Barbara County where it occurs in great abundance.

This species has until recently been little known and misunderstood by most authors. It is apparently at its best on the sandy mesa west of Nipomo where specimens occur up to 8 feet high and from 17 to 20 feet in diameter. In this region the species is invading the eucalyptus-planted areas. On Burton Mesa east of Purisima Point and south of Casmalia thousands of one- and two-year-old seedlings were observed in June 1938 growing in the oat fields which covered several hundred acres of the mesa. These seedlings had grown from seeds dispersed from nearby undisturbed natural stands of the species. Associated with this *Ceanothus* in undisturbed areas on both mesas is *Arctostaphylos rudis* Jeps. & Wies.

The Santa Barbara Botanic Garden at Santa Barbara has been very active in bringing this beautiful species into cultivation. It gives promise of being one of the most desirable of all the species of *Ceanothus* for garden use.

Ceanothus impressus Trel. Proc. Calif. Acad. ser. 2, 1:112 (1888). Type locality: Santa Barbara County. Collected by *Sara A. Plummer. C. dentatus* var. *impressus* Trel.

19. **Ceanothus dentatus** T. & G. CROPLEAF CEANOTHUS. Fig. 341.

A rather low densely branched shrub, 1 1/2 to 5 feet high, and often 4 feet broad, with hairy slightly roughened branchlets and rigid branches. Leaves evergreen,

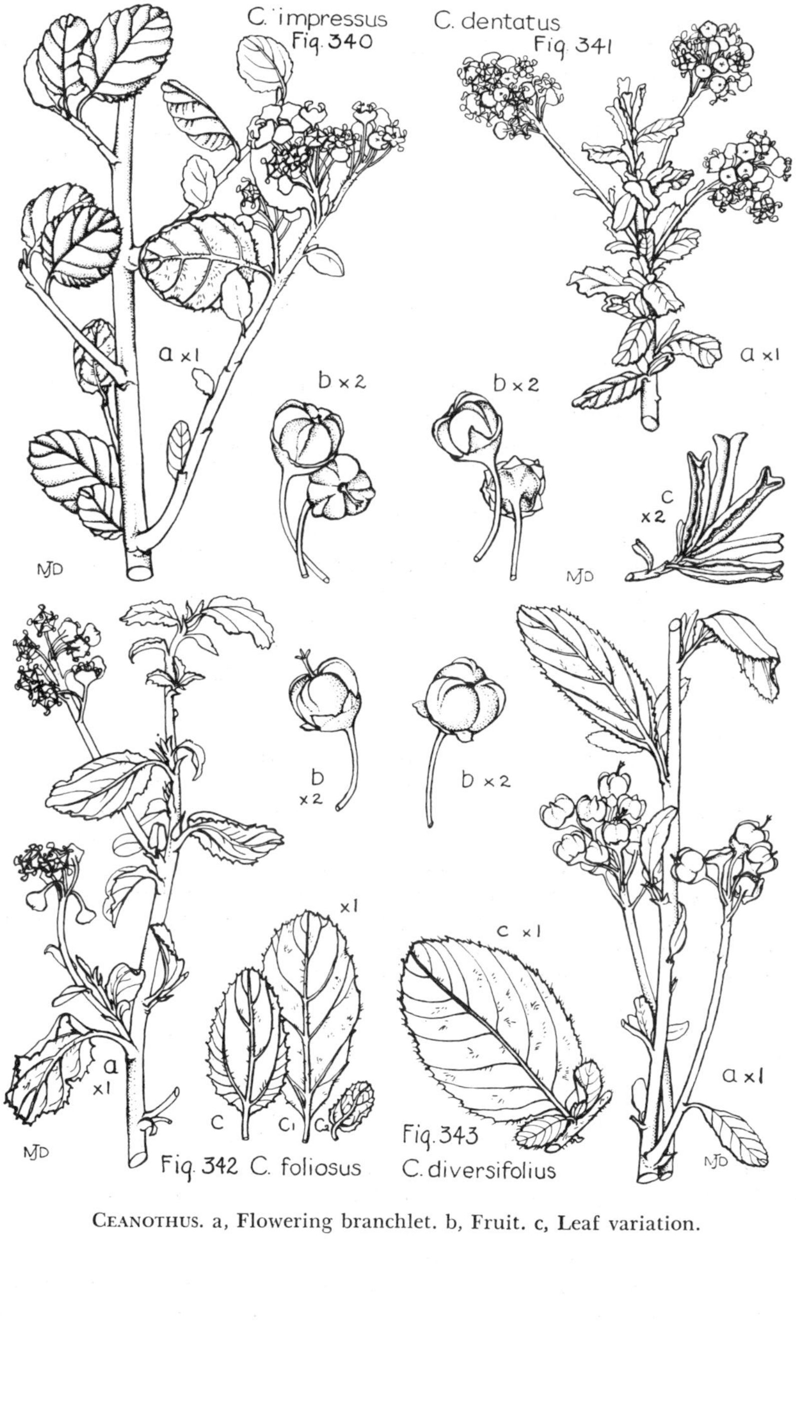

CEANOTHUS. a, Flowering branchlet. b, Fruit. c, Leaf variation.

much crowded, alternate but apparently fascicled; the blades elliptical or narrowly oblong to linear, rounded at base, usually truncate or retuse at apex owing to the infolding of the tip, 1/8- to 1/2-inch or rarely 1 inch long, 1/16- to 1/2-inch wide, 1-veined from the base, the upper surface dark green and waxen, usually hairy, often glandular-papillate along the apparent margin, the lower surface paler and densely matted-hairy, strongly revolute, the margins slightly or very densely glandular-papillate; petioles about 1/16-inch long. Flower-clusters simple, subglobose, 1/2-inch to 1 inch long, very tomentose, the peduncle with small leaves. Flowers deep blue. Fruit globose, about 1/6-inch in diameter, somewhat depressed at the summit, slightly laterally crested. Flowering period, March to June.

Cropleaf Ceanothus occurs on sandy flats, hills, and mountain slopes near the coast in southern Santa Cruz (2 mi. w. of Larkin Valley), Monterey (abundant on the sandy hills and flats n. of Monterey), and northern San Luis Obispo (San Simeon, *K. Brandegee*) counties. In the mountains away from the coast this species apparently intergrades with *C. foliosus* and *C. papillosus* (Chews Ridge Lookout, Monterey County). Occasionally bushes are found with numerous almost sessile flower-clusters and sparingly glandular-papillate leaves. According to some writers, this is *C. dentatus* var. *floribundus* Trel.

Ceanothus dentatus T. & G. Fl. N. Am. 1:268 (1838). Type locality: California, probably at Monterey. Collected by *Douglas*. *C. dentatus* var. *floribundus* Trel.

20. **Ceanothus diversifolius** Kell. TRAILING CEANOTHUS. Fig. 343.

A low trailing shrub, 1 foot or less high, 2 to 4 feet wide, with very villous flexible roughened branches, often forming a dense carpet under oaks and pines. Leaves alternate and evergreen; the blades ovate, orbicular, elliptical, broadly oblong, or obovate, obtuse or subacute at apex, rounded or tapering at base, 1/2-inch to 1 1/2 inches long, 1/4- to 3/4-inch wide, 1-veined from the base (sometimes 3-veined in the larger leaves), pale bluish green and finely villous above, paler and densely hairy-tomentose beneath, rather prominently pinnate-veined, the margins sparingly glandular-denticulate or serrate, sometimes undulate; petioles 1/8- to 1/2-inch long. Flower-clusters simple, few-flowered, axillary, small, about 1/2-inch long, on peduncles 1 inch or more long. Flowers blue, varying to almost white. Fruit subglobose, about 3/16-inch broad, smooth, distinctly crested at the apex and about 1/3 laterally. Flowering period, May and June.

Trailing Ceanothus inhabits the forest floor in draws and flats in the Transition Life Zone, from northern Lake County northward into Trinity County, thence eastward in Siskiyou County (Mt. Shasta, *F. H. Williams*), and southward in the Sierra Nevada from Shasta County to Kern County (Greenhorn Mts.). It is nowhere abundant, but easily identified by its prostrate habit and soft rather thin hairy leaves.

Ceanothus diversifolius Kell. Proc. Calif. Acad. 1:58 (1855). Type locality: Placerville, California. Collected by *E. W. Garvett*.

21. **Ceanothus Lemmonii** Parry. LEMMON CEANOTHUS. Fig. 334.

A low or medium-sized spreading shrub, 1 1/2 to 3 feet high, commonly erect when in competition with other shrubs, with long gray or whitish pubescent branches and branchlets. Leaves alternate and evergreen; the blades elliptic or oblong-elliptic (young leaves ovate), obtuse or acute at apex, rounded or tapering at base, 1/2-inch to 1 1/4 inches long, 1/4- to 3/4-inch wide, 1-veined or indistinctly 3-veined from the base, finely appressed-pubescent to nearly glabrous and dull and waxen above, paler and loosely but densely villous beneath, the margins glandular-denticulate or serrulate, the glands not usually persistent; petioles 1/8- to 1/4-inch long. Flower-clusters simple, several-flowered, 1/2-inch to 1 inch long, on peduncles as long as or slightly longer than the flower-clusters. Flowers pale blue. Fruit somewhat triangular, about 1/8-inch broad, distinctly depressed and lobed at the summit, conspicuously crested near the top, smooth. Flowering period, April and May.

Lemmon Ceanothus occurs on open wooded hill slopes or on burned-over areas in the Sierra Nevada foothills in the Upper Sonoran Life Zone, from Eldorado County (s. of Shingle Springs, *McMinn;* near Eggers, V. T. M.) northward to Shasta County and in the inner North Coast Range in Trinity and northern Lake (Bartlett Mt.) counties.

Ceanothus Lemmonii Parry, Proc. Davenp. Acad. 5:192 (1889). Type locality: "Johnson's Ranch, near Quincy, Plumas County." Collected by *Lemmon.*

22. **Ceanothus foliosus** Parry. Wavyleaf Ceanothus. Fig. 342.

A low spreading shrub, 1 to 3 feet high, or erect and up to 12 feet high when in competition with other shrubs, with diffuse straight slender branches and shortly villous and often somewhat glandular branchlets. Leaves alternate, evergreen, often with smaller ones clustered in their axils; the blades elliptical or oblong-elliptic to oblong, rarely obovate on young and vigorous shoots, 3/16- to 3/4-inch long (or rarely 1 inch long on young and vigorous shoots), 1/8- to 1/2-inch wide, obtuse at the base and apex, 1-veined or indistinctly 3-veined from the base (or prominently 3-veined on vigorous shoots), often infolded longitudinally, commonly undulate, dark green and microscopically hairy above or waxen and nearly glabrous in late summer and fall or on plants in severe dry habitats, greenish gray to whitish beneath and nearly glabrous to densely hairy on the veins, the margins minutely glandular-denticulate; petioles 1/8-inch or less long. Flower-clusters simple, subglobose to oblong, 1/4-inch to 1 inch long, or rarely compound and up to 4 inches long; peduncles naked or with 1 to few small leaves, 1/2-inch to 2 inches long; bud-scales glabrous to densely hirsute. Flowers pale to dark blue. Fruit subglobose, about 1/6-inch wide, smooth and glabrous, obscurely to distinctly lobed and crested. Flowering period, March to May.

Wavyleaf Ceanothus inhabits dry ridges and rocky brushy slopes from 200 to 5000 feet elevation in the Coast Ranges from Mendocino County southward to the Santa Cruz Mountains, and from Monterey (Chews Ridge Lookout, Santa Lucia Mts.) and Santa Clara (Ridge s. of Madrone Springs, Mt. Hamilton Range) counties southward in the Coast Ranges away from the coast to San Luis Obispo County (Cuesta Grade; 9 mi. e. of Pozo in Pozo Mts.); also in the Cuyamaca Mountains of San Diego County.

Considerable variation occurs in the size, viscidity, amount of pubescence, and undulations of the leaves and in growth form. Crested and non-crested capsules can be found on plants in the same colony and frequently upon the same plant, and consequently this character is of little value in the separation of forms.

Near the Vine Hill School in Sonoma County plants growing in deep soil along the road bank are semi-decumbent, their inflorescences are often compound, and the leaves on vigorous shoots are often obovate. This form may prove, after transplant studies, to be a distinct species or variety. It is one of the most desirable ceanothi for ornamental plantings. On the dry exposed slopes of Mount Tamalpais the plants are small of stature and their leaf-blades are usually much reduced in size and have a thick coat of glandular wax on their upper surfaces. This is especially evident in late summer and fall. Many plants of the southern Mount Hamilton Range and the eastern Santa Lucia Range have more oblong leaves which are densely hairy on the veins beneath. Some of these specimens seem closely related to *C. dentatus* but their leaves are not infolded at the apex, a character distinctive of *C. dentatus*.

The plants of the Cuyamaca Mountains of San Diego County are scarcely separable from many variants of *C. foliosus* occurring in the Coast Ranges of central California. Van Rensselaer in a personal communication states that the seedlings are distinct from those of *C. foliosus*.

Ceanothus foliosus Parry, Proc. Davenp. Acad. 5:172 (1898). Type locality: "Upper Napa Valley." Collected by *Parry*. *C. Lobbianus* Hook. *C. austromontanus* Abrams.

23. **Ceanothus verrucosus** Nutt. WARTYSTEM CEANOTHUS. Fig. 344.

A medium-sized to tall shrub, 3 to 8 (rarely to 12) feet high, with roughened (verrucose) rather rigid stems. Leaves alternate, evergreen, apparently crowded; the blades round-obovate or deltoid-obovate, tapering or rounded at base, obtuse or sometimes retuse at apex, 1/4- to 1/2-inch long, 1/8- to 3/8-inch wide, very thick and leathery, 1-veined from the base, green and glabrous above, paler and minutely canescent beneath, the margins entire, denticulate or dentate; petioles about 1/8-inch or less long. Flower-clusters axillary, few-flowered, 1/2- to 3/4-inch long. Flowers white with dark centers. Fruit globose, about 1/4-inch or less in diameter, without dorsal horns but sometimes with small lateral horns. Flowering period, January to April.

Wartystem Ceanothus occurs on the low hills and mesas along the coast of San Diego County and in northern Lower California.

Ceanothus verrucosus Nutt.; T. & G. Fl. N. Am. 1:267 (1838). Type locality: San Diego, California. Collected by *Nuttall*.

24. **Ceanothus megacarpus** Nutt. BIGPOD CEANOTHUS. Fig. 345.

KEY TO THE SPECIES AND VARIETY

Fruit with stout horns; leaves alternate........................*C. megacarpus*.
Fruit scarcely if at all horned; leaves often opposite...........24a. var. *insularis*.

A large shrub, 3 to 12 feet high, with long slender gray or brown branches. Leaves alternate, rarely opposite, evergreen, rather crowded; the blades cuneate-obovate or elliptical, wedge-shaped at base, truncate or usually notched at apex, 3/8-inch to 1 inch long, 1/4- to 1/2-inch wide, 1-veined from the base, thick and leathery, glabrous and dull above, microscopically canescent beneath, the margins entire (or the juvenile leaves repand, revolute, and distantly and coarsely toothed); petioles 1/8-inch or less long. Flower-clusters 1 to 5 on short lateral branchlets, about 1/2-inch long. Flowers white. Fruit large, globose, 3/8- to 1/2-inch in diameter, only 1 or 2 developing from a flower-cluster, with large dorsal or subdorsal horns, viscid, wrinkled at the summit when dry; peduncles 1/2- to 3/4-inch long. Flowering period, December to March.

Bigpod Ceanothus grows on the foothills and lower mountain slopes, especially near the coast, from Santa Barbara County southward in Ventura, Los Angeles (Santa Monica Mts.), Orange (Santa Ana Mts.; canyons s. of Laguna Beach, *Van Rensselaer*), and western Riverside (foothills on eastern side of Santa Ana Mts.) counties to San Diego County (near San Diego, *Mary Spencer*), and on Santa Catalina and Santa Cruz islands where it intergrades with the variety.

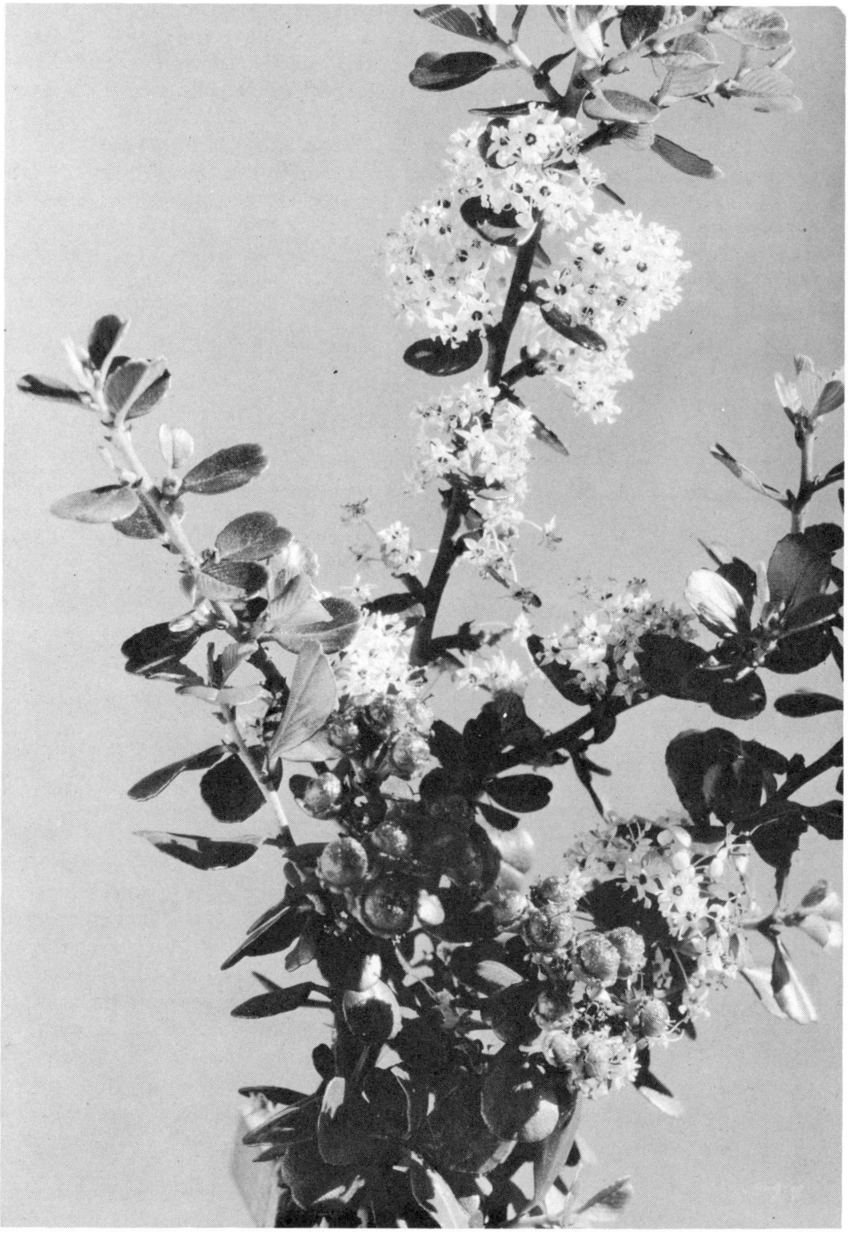

Fig. 344. Wartystem Ceanothus. *Ceanothus verrucosus* Nutt.

24a. Var. **insularis** (Eastw.) Munz.

Leaves alternate or opposite. Fruit usually without horns.

This variety occurs on Santa Catalina, Santa Cruz, and Santa Rosa islands.

Ceanothus megacarpus Nutt. N. Am. Sylva 2:46 (1846). *C. macrocarpus* Nutt., not Cav. Type locality: Mountains near Santa Barbara. Collected by *Nuttall.*

Var. insularis (Eastw.) Munz, Bull. S. Calif. Acad. 31:68 (1932). *C. insularis* Eastw. Type locality: Santa Cruz Island. Collected by *Mrs. Alonson Swain.*

25. **Ceanothus crassifolius** Torr. HOARYLEAF CEANOTHUS. Fig. 346.

A tall much branched shrub, 3 to 12 feet high, with gray, brown, white, or rusty-tomentose branches. Leaves opposite, evergreen; the blades broadly elliptic, rarely elliptic-obovate, wedge-shaped or rounded at base, rounded or obtuse at apex, 1/2-inch to 1 1/4 inches long, 3/8- to 3/4-inch wide, 1-veined from the base, thick and leathery, the upper surface dull green, glabrous, and somewhat minutely roughened, the lower surface distinctly white-tomentose, somewhat obscuring the veins (except in variations), the margins coarsely and pungently toothed or rarely almost entire, usually strongly revolute, rarely plane; petioles about 1/4-inch long. Flower-clusters umbel-like, almost sessile, 1/2- to 3/4-inch long. Flowers white. Fruit globose, 1/4- to 3/8-inch in diameter, viscid, with short subdorsal horns and no intermediate crests, roughened at the summit, the pedicels stout, about 3/8-inch long. Flowering period, January to April.

Hoaryleaf Ceanothus is a very common shrub in the chaparral of the Upper Sonoran Life Zone in the mountains of southern California. It occurs in the mountains near Santa Barbara and extends southward in the mountains of Ventura, Los Angeles, Orange, Riverside, San Bernardino, and San Diego counties. It extends southward into Lower California. The plants of Santa Barbara and Ventura counties have leaves less tomentose beneath and with almost plane margins. They have been described by Abrams as variety **planus.** The pedicels are shorter and stouter than in the typical form of the species. A close study of the field specimens shows intermediate forms between the variety and the species.

On Otay and San Miguel mountains of San Diego County occurs a form which appears intermediate between *C. crassifolius* and *C. Greggii* var. *vestitus.* The leaves are 1/4- to 3/8-inch long, very revolute, and their upper surfaces have the color of those of *C. Greggii* var. *vestitus.* The fruits are small and without dorsal horns. (San Miguel Mt., *Harley P. Chandler* 5221; Otay Mt., el. from 1600 to 3000 feet. Secs. 11, 23, & 28, *V. T. M.*)

Ceanothus crassifolius Torr. Pacif. R. Rep. 4:75 (1857). Type locality: "Mountains south of Los Angeles." Probably near Cajon Pass. Collected by *Bigelow.*

Var. planus Abrams, Bull. N. Y. Bot. Gard. 6:415 (1910). Type locality: Red Reef Canyon, Topatopa Mountains, Ventura County. Collected by *Abrams.*

26. **Ceanothus fresnensis** Dudley. FRESNO MAT. CREEPING CEANOTHUS. Fig. 347.

A low nearly prostrate shrub, with long creeping branches often forming mats 6 to 10 feet or rarely up to 20 feet across, or the branches semi-erect and arching to the ground. Leaves opposite, evergreen; the blades oblanceolate to elliptical, 1/8- to 1/2-inch long, coriaceous, dark green and apparently glabrous above, paler beneath with a whitish canescence, more or less toothed at the rounded or truncate apex, very short-petioled. Flowers blue, in small peduncled umbels. Fruit globose, about 3/16-inch in diameter, with slender subdorsal or lateral spreading horns; fruiting pedicels about 1/2-inch long. Flowering period, May and June.

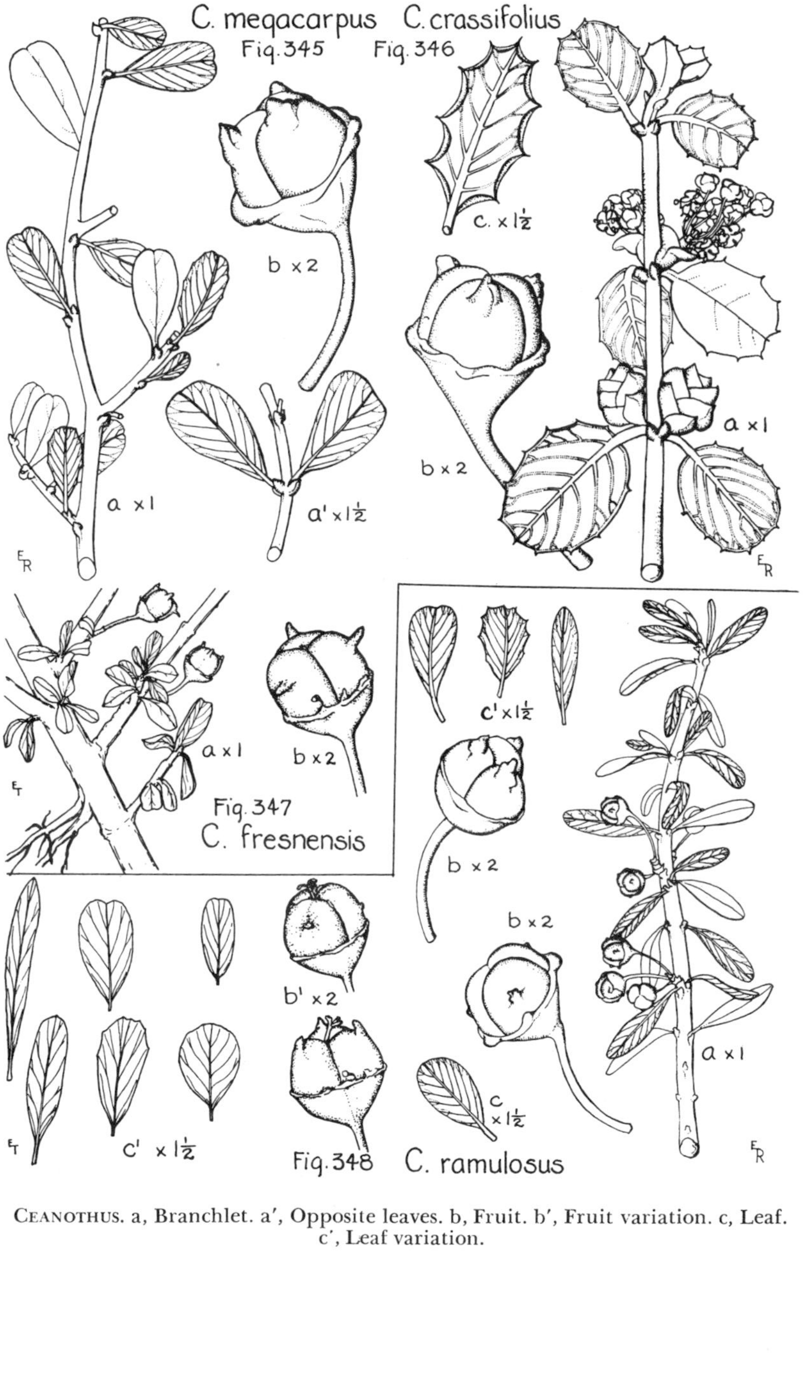

CEANOTHUS. a, Branchlet. a′, Opposite leaves. b, Fruit. b′, Fruit variation. c, Leaf. c′, Leaf variation.

Fresno Mat occurs on the western slope of the Sierra Nevada between 3000 and about 7000 feet elevation from Plumas County (3 mi. n. and 1 mi. w. of Silver Creek, Bidwell Bar Quad., el. 5100 ft., V. T. M.) southward in scattered locations to Fresno County (Pine Ridge, *Hall* & *Chandler;* Big Trees, *Hopping*). Specimens have been examined from Plumas, Nevada, Placer, Eldorado, Tuolumne, Mariposa, and Fresno counties.

Ceanothus fresnensis Dudley; Abrams Bot. Gaz. 53:68 (1912). Type locality: Pine Ridge, Fresno County. Collected by *Hall* and *Chandler*. *C. rigidus* var. *fresnensis* (Dudley) Jepson.

27. **Ceanothus ramulosus** (Greene) McMinn. COAST CEANOTHUS. Fig. 348.

A medium-sized shrub, 2 to 4 feet high, with spreading or arching branches, or sometimes procumbent. Leaves opposite and evergreen, usually not crowded on the branchlets; the blades quite variable in shape but typically obovate to oblanceolate, sometimes nearly round, 1/4- to 5/8-inch long, 1/8- to 3/8-inch wide, light to dark green above, paler beneath, usually toothed near the truncate or rounded apex, often entire, nearly sessile. Flowers lavender, blue, or nearly white, in small peduncled umbels. Fruit globose, about 3/16-inch in diameter, varying from prominently 3-horned to nearly hornless. Flowering period, February to April.

Coast Ceanothus occurs in dry rocky or sandy situations in the outer Coast Ranges near the coast from Santa Barbara County (La Purisima Hills and Burton Mesa near Lompoc) northward to southern Monterey County and in Santa Cruz and Marin counties. Around Monterey Bay it is replaced by *C. rigidus*.

This species seems to be intermediate between *C. rigidus* and *C. cuneatus* and perhaps should be considered a variety of one or the other. However, since the plants here included are intermediate and are not commonly associated geographically with either, it seems best for the time being to include them in the separate taxonomic unit *C. ramulosus*. The flower-color, varying from blue to nearly white, and the long arching branches are characters intermediate between *C. cuneatus* and *C. rigidus*. On the bluffs above Point Sal, Santa Barbara County, this species is procumbent to nearly prostrate. On Burton Mesa and on La Purisima Hills, Santa Barbara County, the plants have darker more compact foliage and in this respect are closer to *C. rigidus* than to *C. cuneatus*. The leaves, however, are more often cuneate-oblong and the fruits are often nearly hornless.

Plants grown from seeds taken from Marin County plants and observed in the trial garden at Mills College with *C. rigidus* show the distinct long arching type of branches and pale blue flowers characteristic of the parent plants. The Douglas specimen, taken as the type of *C. cuneatus,* from the Willamette River region in Oregon resembles the La Purisima plants in the prominent veins beneath the dark color of the leaves and in the obtuse or retuse or 3-toothed apices. The leaves are, however, much larger.

Ceanothus ramulosus (Greene) McMinn, Madroño 5:14 (1939). *C. cuneatus* var. *ramulosus* Greene. *C. rigidus* Nutt., as interpreted by Jepson, in part. Type locality: "In the Coast Range only, and from Santa Cruz Mts., *Greene,* to Marin and Napa counties, *Mrs. Curran, Dr. Parry*."

28. **Ceanothus cuneatus** (Hook.) Nutt. BUCK BRUSH. Fig. 349.

An erect medium-sized to tall shrub, 3 to 8 feet high, with rigid divaricate branches and stout short usually opposite unequal branchlets. Leaves opposite and evergreen, borne on spur-like branchlets; the blades spatulate to obovate-

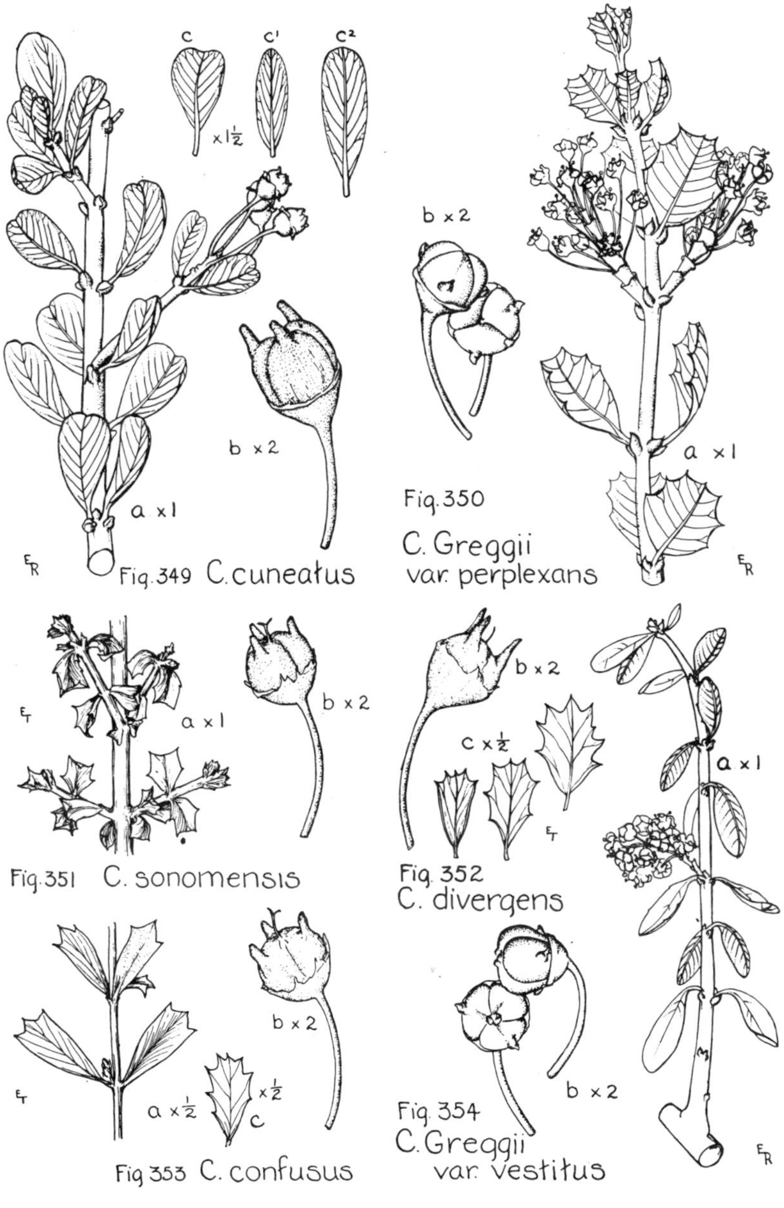

CEANOTHUS. a, Branchlet. b, Fruit. c, Leaf variation.

cuneate, or rarely elliptical, mostly obtuse or rounded at apex, or rarely retuse, wedge-shaped or rounded at base, 1/4-inch to 1 inch long, 3/16- to 1/4- or rarely 3/4-inch wide; 1-veined from the base, dull green and apparently glabrous but microscopically white-canescent above, much paler and with a fine white felt beneath, the margins typically entire; petioles 1/8-inch or less long. Flower-clusters umbellate, short-pedunculate, several-flowered. Flowers white, lavender, or sometimes blue. Fruit almost globose, 1/8- to 1/4-inch in diameter, with distinct dorsal or subdorsal horns and usually without intermediate crests or ridges. Flowering period, March to May.

Buck Brush is one of the main components of our California chaparral. It is the most widely distributed species of the genus in California, occurring on dry mountain slopes and ridges in the Coast Ranges, the Sierra Nevada, and in the mountains of southern California, in the Upper Sonoran Life Zone. It extends northward to Oregon and southward to Lower California. In many places this shrub forms dense thickets to the exclusion of all other shrubby species. When it is in full bloom the mountain slopes appear as if covered with snow.

Several varieties and species have been described from the numerous leaf-forms of this species but most of them are apparently minor ecological variations. In the Santa Cruz Mountains the plants are usually very vigorous growers and the leaves are larger than those on plants of drier habitats, as in the chaparral of the Sierra Nevada foothills.

The seeds germinate readily after chaparral fires and great colonies are often formed within a few years on burned-over areas. As in all species of the Cerastes section of *Ceanothus,* the seedling leaves of *C. cuneatus* are toothed.

Ceanothus cuneatus (Hook.) Nutt.; T. & G. Fl. N. Am. 1:267 (1838). *Rhamnus cuneatus* Hook. Type locality: "Near the sources of the Multonomak [Willamette] River, in sandy soils growing under the shade of *Pinus Lambertiana.*" Collected by *Douglas.*

29. **Ceanothus Greggii** Gray. GREGG CEANOTHUS. DESERT CEANOTHUS.

This species consists of a series of desert-mountain shrubs ranging from northern Mexico northward to New Mexico, Arizona, and southern California. The character of fruit and flowers and habit of growth are quite constant throughout the series but much variation occurs in the shape, size, color, and margins of the leaves. These leaf-variations seem to segregate into three more or less distinct and recognizable units which occupy different geographical areas and which seem to be adaptations to moisture conditions. These units are here considered as one species and two intergrading varieties.

Plants erect and rigidly and intricately branched, 2 to 6 feet high. Fruits globose, about 1/8- to 3/16-inch in diameter, without horns or with rudimentary horns from near the middle. Flowers white, borne in small peduncled umbels.

KEY TO THE SPECIES AND VARIETIES

Leaves only rarely concave above, grayish on both surfaces, entire or with 1 to 3 small teeth near the base, elliptic-oblong, 3/8- to nearly 5/8-inch long; Panamint Mts., Inyo Co. . . . . *C. Greggii*

Leaves commonly concave above (not all the leaves on a given plant show this character, but enough of them do to warrant the use of the character).

Leaves varying from entire to dentate all around, grayish green above, gray beneath, oblong-elliptical, round-ovate, or obovate to oblanceolate; dry interior mountain slopes bordering the Mohave Desert. . .29a. var. *vestitus.*

Leaves usually pungently low-toothed all around or only near the apex, or sometimes entire, yellowish green, roundish or broadly elliptical to broadly obovate, ⅜- to ¾-inch long; ranges bordering the western Colorado Desert. 29b. var. *perplexans.*

The typical forms of this species occur from northern Mexico northward to New Mexico and Arizona and westward to the Panamint Mountains of Inyo County, California and probably southward in the mountains bordering the Mohave Desert where it merges into var. *vestitus.*

29a. Var. **vestitus** (Greene) n. comb. Fig. 354.

This variety inhabits arid mountain slopes bordering the Mohave Desert, and is of rare occurrence northward and westward in Santa Barbara and San Luis Obispo counties, and in the mountains of Inyo County where it merges with *C. Greggii.* (SAN LUIS OBISPO COUNTY, Rinconado Creek, el. 2000 ft., V. T. M.; SANTA BARBARA COUNTY, 3 mi. s. of Little Pine Mts., el. 2500 ft., V. T. M.; VENTURA COUNTY, Mt. Piños and Frazier Mountain areas; desert mountain slopes in Kern, San Bernardino, Los Angeles, and Inyo counties.)

Sheet #22709 Herbarium Greeneanum at Notre Dame University contains two specimens collected by E. L. Greene, June 23, 1889, from the Tehachapi Mountains. The specimen on the right is a good match for *C. perplexans* Trel. and answers well to the description of *C. vestitus* Greene in Pitt. 2:101 (1890). The one on the left is apparently *C. cuneatus* Nutt. Since the specimen on the right answers to the original description of *C. vestitus* Greene it should be considered the type specimen. The leaves are more yellowish green and rounder than those normally occurring on plants of this region. However, after a wet season and on young vigorous shoots from plants in the more favored situations I have observed leaves of this type. They approximate those on the plants of San Diego County which I have here included rather reluctantly in the variety *perplexans.*

29b. Var. **perplexans** (Trel.) Jepson. CUPLEAF CEANOTHUS. Fig. 350.

This variety apparently grows in moister habitats than the variety *vestitus.* It occurs in the mountains of central and eastern San Diego County and extends northward to the San Jacinto, Santa Rosa, and the south slope of the Little San Bernardino and San Bernardino mountains. It extends southward into Lower California. Some leaves on specimens from the San Jacinto Mountains approximate those of var. *vestitus.*

Young plants taken in August 1926 from San Diego County and transplanted to the trial garden at Mills College lost the cupped condition of the leaves and the blades became much larger and grayer. One specimen was 7½ feet tall in 1938. The hornless fruit condition did not change. Upon the basis of leaf character alone one would consider the transplants different species from any of the *C. Greggii* forms found in nature. It would seem that the increased moisture of the San Francisco Bay region over a period of years was responsible for this leaf difference.

Ceanothus Greggii Gray, Pl. Wright. 2:228 (1853). Type locality: Based on specimens from the battlefield at Buena Vista, Mexico, collected by *Gregg,* and from Frontera, New Mexico, collected by *Fendler.*

Var. vestitus (Greene) McMinn. *C. vestitus* Greene. Type locality: "Borders of pine forests on mountains near Tehachapi, Kern County." Collected by *Greene*. *C. Greggii* Gray, as interpreted by Jepson in his Manual and Flora.

Var. perplexans (Trel.) Jepson, Man. 623 (1925). *C. perplexans* Trel. Type locality: Southwestern California. Collected by *Bigelow*. *C. vestitus* Greene, in part.

30. **Ceanothus sonomensis** J. T. Howell. SONOMA CEANOTHUS. Fig. 351.

An erect shrub, 1½ to 3 feet high, with nearly straight gray or brown stems bearing short lateral nearly spur-like opposite branchlets 1 to 3 inches long. Leaves opposite, evergreen; the blades cuneate-obovate to nearly orbicular, 3/16- to ½-inch long, ⅛- to ⅜-inch wide, glabrous and shining above, grayish tomentulose beneath, thick and somewhat holly-like, the margin with 4 to 8 coarse nearly spinose teeth, often undulate, short-petioled or apparently sessile. Flowers blue to lavender, in short-pedunculate or nearly sessile umbels. Fruit globose, about 3/16-inch in diameter, with 3 subdorsal horns, without prominent intermediate crests. Flowering period, March and April.

Sonoma Ceanothus occurs in the Hood Mountain Range of Sonoma County. Its gray bark and habit of growth suggest a relationship with *C. cuneatus*. The somewhat holly-like leaves are similar to but much smaller than those of *C. purpureus*.

Ceanothus sonomensis J. T. Howell, Leafl. West. Bot. 2:162 (1939). Type locality: "West Slope of Trinity Mt. 2 mi. e. Glen Ellen, Hood Mt. Range, Sonoma County, el. 1000 ft." Flowering specimen collected by *J. T. Howell*, fruiting specimen by *Henry Reents*.

31. **Ceanothus confusus** J. T. Howell. RINCON CEANOTHUS. Fig. 353.

A prostrate or decumbent shrub, 2 to 10 inches high, rooting at the nodes. Leaves opposite and evergreen; the blades obovate or elliptical, usually cuneate at base, ¼-inch to 1 inch long, ⅛- to ½-inch broad, dark green and glabrous above, grayish canescent beneath, coarsely denticulate to spinulose with 3 to 11 teeth. Flowers blue to purple, in subsessile umbels. Fruit globose, about 3/16-inch in diameter, with 3 lateral or subdorsal widely diverging horns, without prominent intermediate crests. Flowering period, March.

Rincon Ceanothus occurs in the middle North Coast Ranges of Napa, Sonoma, and Lake counties (Mt. Hood, Mt. St. Helena, Rincon Ridge, etc.). This species has long been confused with *C. divergens* Parry.

Ceanothus confusus J. T. Howell, Leafl. West. Bot. 2:160 (1939). Type locality: Rincon Ridge northeast of Santa Rosa, Sonoma County. Collected by *J. T. Howell*. *C. prostratus* var. *divergens* of many authors, not *C. divergens* Parry.

32. **Ceanothus divergens** Parry. MOUNT ST. HELENA CEANOTHUS. Fig. 352.

A scrambling or an erect shrub, 2 to 5 feet high, the "divergent branches inclined to support themselves on adjoining bushes, but never decumbent" (Parry). Leaves opposite, evergreen; the blades oblong to broadly elliptical or obovate, ½-inch to 1 inch long, ¼- to ⅝-inch wide, bright green and glabrous above, grayish tomentulose beneath, the margin with 5 to 8 coarse spinescent teeth or almost lobed, undulate and somewhat revolute, short-petioled or subsessile. Flowers blue, in small corymbs racemosely arranged along the branchlets. Fruit subglobose, about ¼-inch in diameter, with 3 prominent dorsal horns, without prominent intermediate crests. Flowering period, February and March.

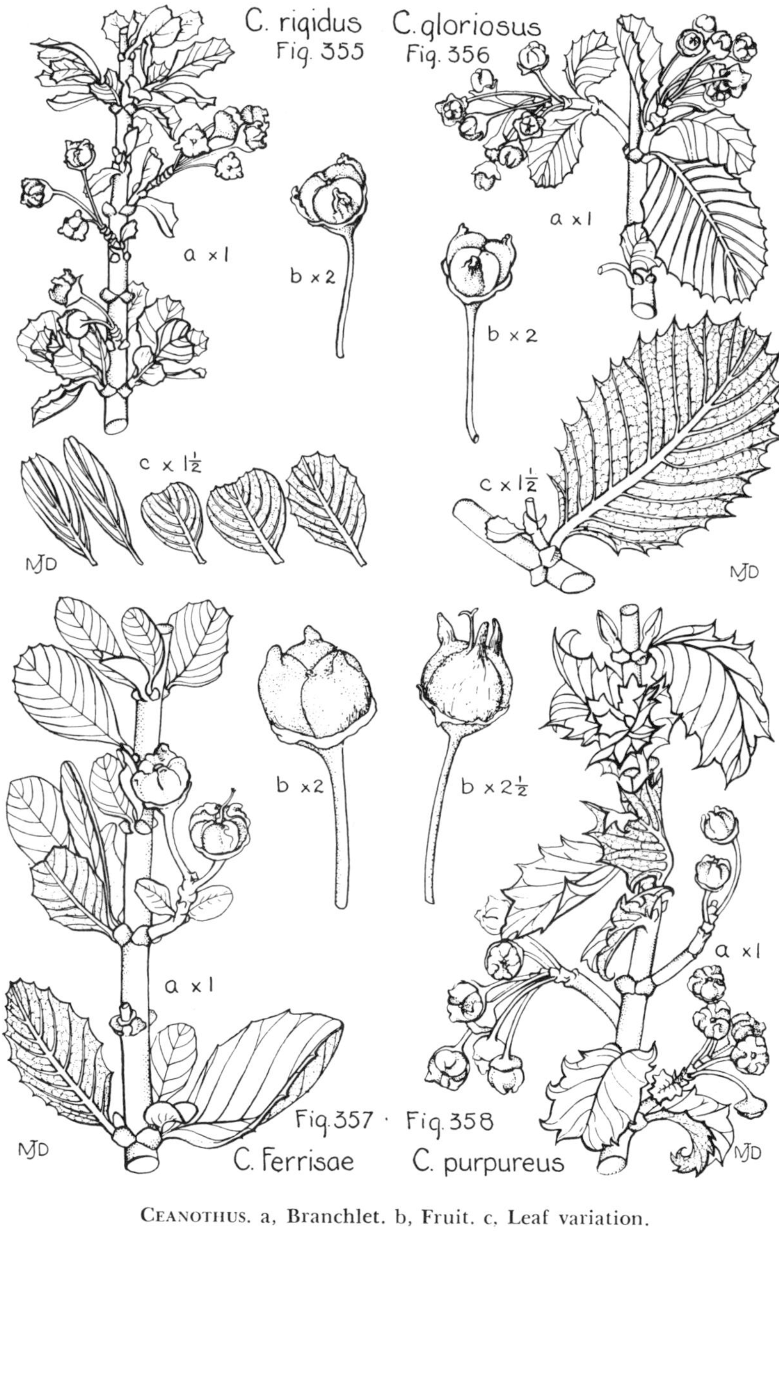

CEANOTHUS. a, Branchlet. b, Fruit. c, Leaf variation.

Mount St. Helena Ceanothus is a rare shrub known only from the Mount St. Helena region.

Ceanothus divergens Parry, Proc. Davenp. Acad. 5:173 (1889). Type locality: "Calistoga, California." Parry in 1881–8 (Herb. Gray).

33. **Ceanothus rigidus** Nutt. MONTEREY CEANOTHUS. Fig. 355.

A rather low or medium-sized shrub, 1 to 4 feet high, with numerous intricate branches. Leaves opposite, evergreen, mostly clustered on short lateral branchlets; the blades cuneate-obovate or rounded-obovate, 1/8- to 1/2-inch long, 1/8- to 3/8-inch wide, 1-veined from the base, thick and leathery, glabrous and shining above, paler beneath, the margins dentate all around or dentate only toward the apex, or rarely entire all around, often retuse at apex. Flower-clusters composed of several few-flowered sessile umbels. Flowers bright blue, varying to almost purple. Fruit globose, about 3/16-inch in diameter, viscid, with 3 dorsal horns, without intermediate crests. Flowering period, March and April.

Monterey Ceanothus occurs on the sand flats and hills bordering Monterey Bay. Northward and southward it is replaced by *C. ramulosus,* which is intermediate between *C. cuneatus* and *C. rigidus.* Plants grown in the trial garden at Mills College from seeds gathered from the Monterey plants have retained the dense intricate habit and small dark green leaves clustered on the short lateral branchlets. It is a very ornamental shrub when in full bloom.

Ceanothus rigidus Nutt.; T. & G. Fl. N. Am. 1:268 (1838). Type locality: Monterey, California. Collected by *Nuttall.*

34. **Ceanothus gloriosus** J. T. Howell. POINT REYES CEANOTHUS. Fig. 356.

A prostrate or decumbent shrub, 4 inches to 1 foot high, with long usually brownish or reddish stems and opposite branches. Leaves opposite and evergreen; the blades broadly elliptical, roundish, or broadly oblong, 1/2-inch to 1 1/2 inches long, 3/8-inch to 1 inch wide, 1-veined from the cuneate or obtuse base, rounded or truncate or retuse at apex, very thick and leathery, dark green and glabrous above, paler and microscopically canescent beneath, especially around the stomatal openings, the margins usually dentate or somewhat spinosely toothed with 15 to 30 teeth, or entire toward the base, rarely entire except at the apex; petioles 1/8-inch or less long. Flower-clusters composed of many sessile umbels on short axillary shoots. Flowers deep blue or sometimes almost purple. Fruit globose, about 1/8-inch or less in diameter, viscid, 3-horned at the summit, without intermediate crests. Flowering period, March to May.

Point Reyes Ceanothus usually occurs on the bluffs along the coast from Point Reyes northward to Point Arena. Plants growing on the brushy slopes and ridges and in valley flats away from the direct influence of the strong ocean winds have a more upright habit of growth.

34a. Var. **exaltatus** J. T. Howell.

Medium-sized to tall shrubs, 2 to 12 feet high, with widely spreading fastigiate-divaricate branches.

This variety seems to be only a more upright form of the species, occurring inland in the outer Coast Ranges from Marin County (Bolinas Ridge) northward to Mendocino County.

Ceanothus gloriosus J. T. Howell, Leafl. West. Bot. 2:43 (1937). *C. rigidus* var. *grandifolius* Torr. Type locality: Point Reyes, Marin County. Collected by *Bigelow. C. prostratus* var. *grandifolius* (Torr.) Jepson.

Fig. 359. Hollyleaf Ceanothus. *Ceanothus purpureus* Jepson.

Var. exaltatus J. T. Howell, Leafl. West. Bot. 2:44 (1937). Type locality: In an arroyo in the Vine Hill district north of Sebastopol, Sonoma County. Collected by *J. T. Howell*. *C. rigidus* var. *grandifolius* Torr., in part.

35. **Ceanothus Ferrisae** McMinn. COYOTE CEANOTHUS. Fig. 357.

An erect shrub, 2 to 6 feet high, with long stiff divergent or arching branches and numerous short lateral branchlets. Leaves opposite and evergreen; the blades orbicular to broadly elliptical, abruptly tapering or rounded at base, ½-inch to 1¼ inches long, ¼- to ¾-inch wide, 1-veined from the base, dark green and glabrous above, paler and microscopically canescent beneath, regularly to irregularly short-toothed or some leaves nearly or quite entire; petioles about ⅛-inch long. Flowers white, in umbels ½-inch to 1 inch long. Fruit globose, ¼- to ⅜-inch broad, with 3 dorsal or subdorsal horns, often roughened but without intermediate crests. Flowering period, January to March.

Coyote Ceanothus occurs locally on the hill slopes between 500 and 900 feet elevation along Coyote River east of Madrone Station in the Mount Hamilton Range, Santa Clara County, and occasionally in the Santa Cruz Mountains. In this locality, a few plants of *C. cuneatus* occur with one colony of *C. Ferrisae* but the former normally occurs higher on the chaparral slopes of the Mount Hamilton Range. In leaf character this species stands intermediate between the large leaf-form of *C. cuneatus* of the Santa Cruz Mountains and *C. gloriosus* of the North Coast Ranges. Leaves of young vigorous shoots on well-watered plants are quite similar to the adult leaves of *C. purpureus*.

In 1928 a set of 60 transplants was set out in the trial garden at Mills College. These plants in 1939 showed the same characteristic variation in leaf-margins as exhibited by the leaves of old plants in their native habitat. Several of the transplants not in competition with other shrubs showed a decided arching of the branches and the plants were semi-decumbent.

Ceanothus Ferrisae McMinn, Madroño 2:89 (1933). Type locality: Above Coyote Creek, Madrone Springs road, Mount Hamilton Range, Santa Clara County. Collected by *Abrams, Roxana Ferris*.

36. **Ceanothus purpureus** Jepson. HOLLYLEAF CEANOTHUS. Figs. 358, 359.

An erect or spreading shrub, 1½ to 4 feet high, with rather long rigid reddish brown branches. Leaves opposite and evergreen; the blades distinctly holly-like, roundish or broadly elliptical in outline, ½- to ¾-inch long, and about as wide, 1-veined from the base, often somewhat folded inwardly, dark green, glabrous, and shining above, paler and microscopically gray-canescent beneath, especially between the veins, the margins undulate and distinctly spinose-toothed all around; petioles very short or absent. Flower-clusters umbellate, several-flowered. Flowering buds globose, ¼- to ⅜-inch in diameter, with hairy purplish scales. Flowers deep blue to purple. Fruit globose, about 3/16-inch in diameter, with dorsal horns but without intermediate crests. Flowering period, February to April.

Hollyleaf Ceanothus is a local species of the southern Napa Range of Napa County. It occurs on the dry brush-covered slopes and summits. This species, because of its masses of deep blue to purple flowers, bright holly-like foliage, and spreading habit of growth, is one of the most attractive of the Californian native shrubs. It grows best in well-drained but moist soils.

In leaf character this species somewhat resembles the leaves of *C. Jepsonii*, but the fruits of the two are quite distinct. Those of *C. Jepsonii* are much larger and have wrinkled horns and intermediate crests.

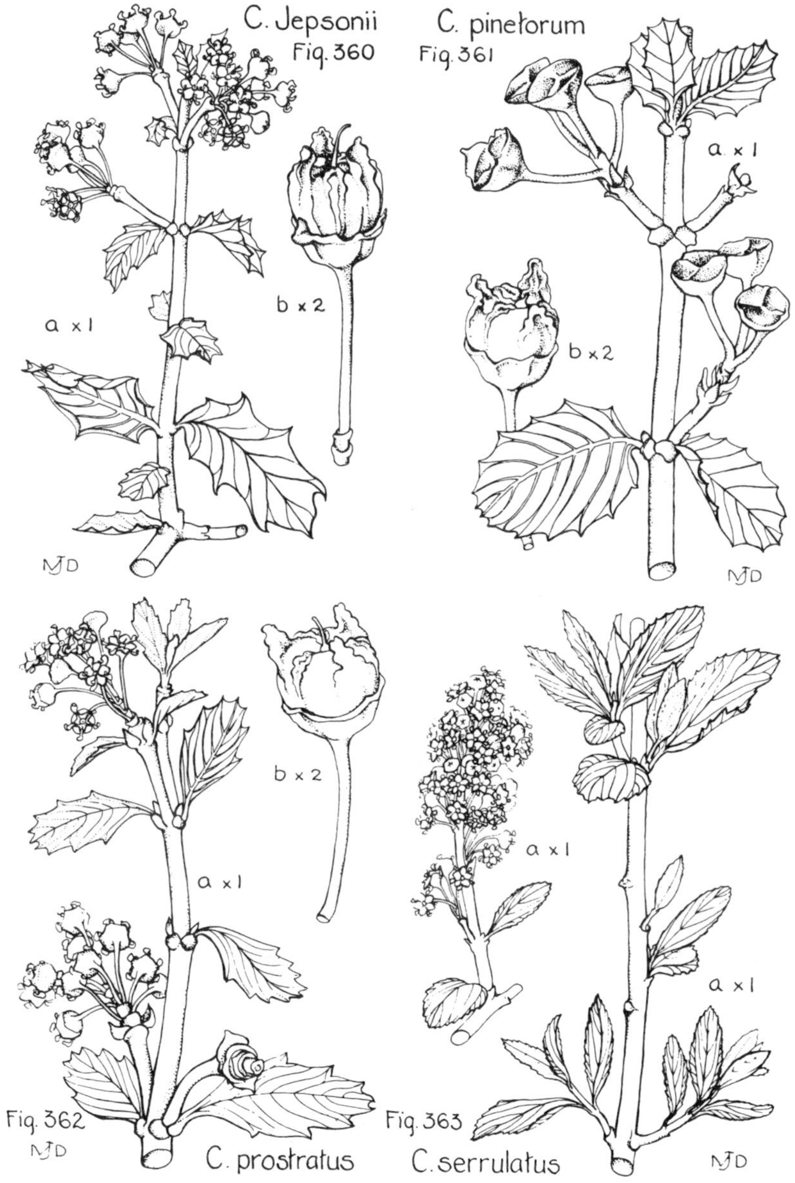

CEANOTHUS. a. Branchlet. b. Fruit.

Ceanothus purpureus Jepson, Fl. W. Mid. Calif. 258 (1901). Type locality: "Near Mt. George, Napa Co." Collected by *Jepson*. *C. Jepsonii* var. *purpureus* Jepson.

37. **Ceanothus Jepsonii** Greene. MUSKBRUSH. Fig. 360.

A low or medium-sized shrub, 2 to 4 feet high, with intricate stout short branches and branchlets with gray bark. Leaves opposite, evergreen, usually reflexed; the blades somewhat holly-like, elliptical, thick and leathery, rounded at apex and base, 3/8- to 3/4-inch long, 1/4- to 1/2-inch wide, 1-veined from the base, yellowish green and glabrous above, paler and microscopically white-canescent beneath, somewhat infolded longitudinally, the margins slightly revolute, undulate, and coarsely spinulose with 4 or 5 teeth on each margin; petioles 1/8-inch or less long. Flower-clusters simple, short-pedunculate, at the ends of the branchlets. Flowers blue, varying to almost white, giving off a musky odor. Fruit globose or somewhat oblong, about 1/4-inch broad, with large wrinkled dorsal horns and intermediate crests. Flowering period, March and April.

Muskbrush grows at many scattered localities on the open usually rocky hills and lower mountain slopes in Marin, Sonoma, southeastern Mendocino, Napa, Lake, and Tehama counties, in the Upper Sonoran Life Zone.

This species somewhat resembles *C. purpureus* in leaf characters but the fruits have large dorsal wrinkled horns and intermediate crests which are not characteristic of *C. purpureus.*

Ceanothus Jepsonii Greene, Man. S. F. Bay Region 78 (1894). Type locality: San Geronimo, Marin County. Collected by *Jepson*.

38. **Ceanothus pinetorum** Cov. KERN CEANOTHUS. Fig. 361.

An erect or semi-prostrate shrub, 1/2-foot to 4 feet high, with rigid divergent brown or often gray to almost white branches, the branches sometimes as much as 12 feet long and rooting at the nodes. Leaves opposite and evergreen, often clustered at the nodes; the blades broadly oblong, rounded, or elliptic, rounded at the apex and base, 1/2-inch to 1 inch long, 3/8- to 3/4-inch wide, with 1 main vein from the base, thick and leathery, glabrous and dark green above, microscopically canescent and paler beneath, the margins slightly revolute and with 6 to 9 teeth on a side, rather more coarsely toothed than spinulose. Flower-clusters umbellate, with 4 to 8 flowers, short-stalked. Flowers blue, varying to almost white. Fruit globose or slightly oblong, about 1/4-inch broad, with wrinkled dorsal horns and intermediate crests; fruiting pedicels about 1/2-inch or more long. Flowering period, June.

Kern Ceanothus occurs in the Upper Kern River Basin of the Sierra Nevada, in Kern and Tulare counties, between 6800 and 8800 feet elevation. Above Grouse Meadows, it occurs in the open Yellow Pine forest, growing in decomposed granite. Cattlemen of this region claim that bears and cattle eat the young buds in late fall.

Ceanothus pinetorum Cov. Contr. U. S. Nat. Herb. 4:80 (1893). Type locality: "Near Lyon Meadow, Sierra Nevada, Tulare County." Collected by *Coville*.

39. **Ceanothus prostratus** Benth. SQUAW CARPET. MAHALA MATS. Fig. 362.

A prostrate shrub, 2 to 6 inches (or to 1 1/2 feet) high, rooting at the nodes, often spreading and forming dense mats 2 to 8 feet across. Leaves opposite and evergreen; the blades obovate, spatulate, or broadly elliptical, usually wedge-shaped at base, thick and leathery, 1/4-inch to 1 inch long, 1/8- to 5/8-inch wide, 1-veined from the base, dark green and glabrous above, paler and microscopically canescent beneath, the margins usually with a few coarse teeth near the apex, or more finely toothed and with 4 to 7 teeth on each side, or rarely almost to quite entire; the petioles 1/8-inch or less long. Flower-clusters umbellate, with stout peduncles 1/4- to 1/2-inch long. Flowers deep or light blue, often becoming pinkish in age. Fruit subglobose or oblong, about 1/4-inch wide, with large wrinkled dorsal or subdorsal horns and wrinkled intermediate crests. Flowering period, April and May.

Squaw Carpet occurs as a prostrate plant in the higher mountains of the North Coast Ranges and extends eastward through the Siskiyou Mountains to Modoc County, thence southward in the Sierra Nevada to Calaveras County. It usually grows under the pines at elevations between 2100 and 7800 feet. At Tahoe Tavern on Lake Tahoe this species forms a beautiful dense carpet under the forest canopy. It extends northward to Washington and eastward into Nevada.

Much variation in the size of leaves, the dentation of the leaf-margins, and fruit characters occurs in this species throughout its range of distribution. Many varieties and a few species have been described from these variations.

Plants transplanted from the Sierra Nevada do not thrive in the San Francisco Bay area.

Ceanothus prostratus Benth. Pl. Hartw. 302 (1848). Type locality: "In montibus Sacramento." "At higher altitudes, in the *Pinus ponderosa* belt; about opposite Chico." Collected by *Hartweg*.

40. **Ceanothus serrulatus** McMinn. CASCADE LAKE CEANOTHUS. Fig. 363.

A low prostrate evergreen shrub, thickly matting the ground. Branches grayish or reddish, rooting from the lower surface when in contact with the ground. Leaves predominantly alternate, sometimes opposite near the ends of the younger branchlets; the blades narrowly to broadly elliptical, 1/2- to 3/4-inch long, 1/4- to 1/2-inch wide, thin but firm, prominently veined beneath, with 1 main vein and often with 2 sublateral veins from the base, pale green and ultimately glabrous above, paler and densely microscopically flocculent-canescent beneath, finely serrate except near the base; petioles about 1/8-inch long. Stipules small, early deciduous. Stomata in sunken pits on the lower surface of the leaves. Flower-clusters short-racemose, cylindrical or subglobose, 1/2-inch to 1 inch long, terminating short leafy lateral branchlets. Flowers white or pale blue. Fruit not known. Flowering period, May and June.

This species is known only from a shallow draw between Emerald Bay and Cascade Lake, Eldorado County, California, where it is associated with *C. prostratus, C. cordulatus,* and *C. velutinus*. It may have arisen as a hybrid between *C. prostratus* and *C. cordulatus*. The prostrate habit and the presence of sunken stomatal pits on the underside of the leaves relate it to *C. prostratus,* but the predominantly alternate, thinner, and finely serrate leaves, the small deciduous stipules, and short racemose clusters of white flowers separate it from that species. The plants during the past five years have not borne fruit.

Ceanothus serrulatus McMinn, Madroño 2:89 (1933). Type locality: Shallow draw between Emerald Bay and Cascade Lake, Eldorado County, California. Collected by *McMinn*.

2. **Colubrina** Rich.

(From the Latin *coluber*, a serpent, the application uncertain.)

This genus consists of 16 species of the warmer regions of America and other continents except Europe, also in the West Indies and the Hawaiian Islands. One species occurs in California.

1. **Colubrina californica** Johnst. CALIFORNIA COLUBRINA. Fig. 364.

An intricately branched shrub, 4 to 7 feet high, with short spreading usually gray-tomentose subspinescent branchlets, or sometimes almost glabrous. Leaves simple, alternate, deciduous, commonly fascicled, or single on the young branchlets; the blades oblong-ovate to obovate, 1/4- to almost 3/4-inch long, 1/4- to 3/8-inch wide, 1-veined from the base, grayish pubescent on both surfaces, especially on the lower veins and midrib, the margins entire or slightly serrulate; petioles 1/16- to 3/16-inch long. Flowers very small, bisexual, in axillary clusters, crowded on the younger twigs; pedicels very short, densely tomentose in flower; sepals 5, tomentose without, joined at the base with the receptacle to form a receptocalyx, the lobes tardily deciduous; the receptocalyx filled by a fleshy disk and joined to the ovary; petals 5, distinct, clawed, yellowish, less than 1/8-inch long; stamens 5, opposite the petals. Fruit a globose or obovoid 3-celled capsule, about 1/4-inch in diameter. Flowering period, May and June.

California Colubrina was first collected in California by I. M. Johnston, June 15, 1930, north of Mecca, along the washes, benches, and hillsides in the canyon at the southeastern end of the Eagle Mountains of Riverside County. It also occurs in southern Arizona and in the hills south of Las Animas Bay, Lower California.

Colubrina californica Johnst. Proc. Calif. Acad. ser. 4, 12:1085 (1924). Type locality: Las Animas Bay, Lower California. Collected by *I. M. Johnston.*

3. **Adolphia** Meisn.

(Named for Adolphe T. Brongniart, French botanist who monographed the family Rhamnaceae.)

This is a genus of 2 species, one of which is native to California.

1. **Adolphia californica** Wats. CALIFORNIA ADOLPHIA. Fig. 365.

A low or medium-sized rigidly branched shrub, 2 to 3 1/2 feet high, with divaricate spine-tipped opposite twigs, jointed at the base. Leaves simple, opposite, small, early deciduous; the blades spatulate to obovate, rounded at apex and tipped with a sharp but rather soft point, about 1/4-inch long or slightly longer, pale green and slightly pubescent, the margins entire; petioles about 1/16-inch long. Flowers bisexual, inconspicuous, 1 to 4 in axillary clusters; sepals 5, joined at base with the receptacle forming a cup-shaped receptocalyx, the lobes ovate, persistent, greenish white; petals 5, distinct, very small, white, hooded; stamens 5, opposite the petals; pistil 1, the ovary 3-celled, the lower part surrounded by but not adnate to the disk lining the receptocalyx, the style often jointed near the ovary. Fruit a dry 3-celled 3-lobed capsule about 1/4-inch broad; the pedicels 1/4-inch or more long. Flowering period, January to April.

California Adolphia occurs on dry canyon slopes and flats in western San Diego County and in adjacent Lower California, in the Lower Sonoran Life Zone.

Adolphia californica Wats. Proc. Am. Acad. 11:126 (1876). Type locality: Near San Diego at Soledad and Chollas Valley. Collected by *Parry, Cleveland.*

4. **Condalia** Cav.

(Named for Antonio Condal, a Spanish physician, who accompanied Peter Loefling, a Swedish botanist, on a journey up the Orinoco.)

Shrubs or small trees, usually with spinose branchlets. Leaves simple, alternate, deciduous, pinnately veined, usually entire, with minute stipules. Flowers bisexual,

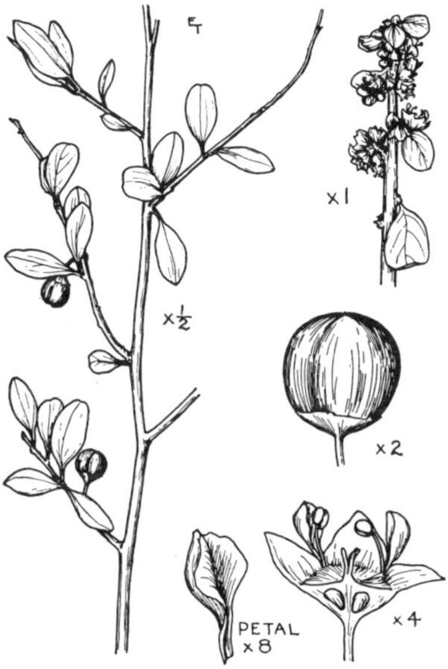

FIG. 364 COLUBRINA CALIFORNICA

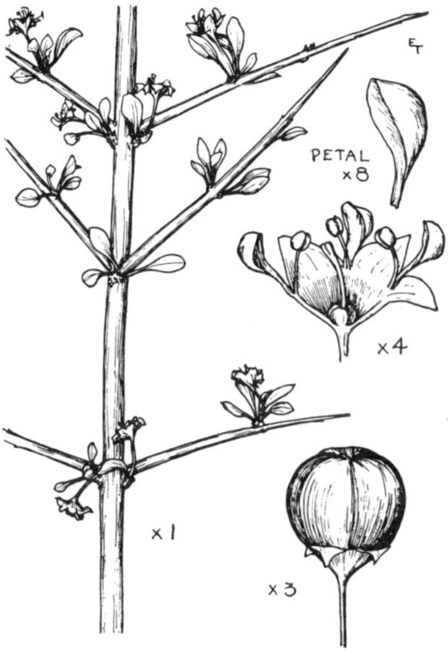

FIG. 365 ADOLPHIA CALIFORNICA

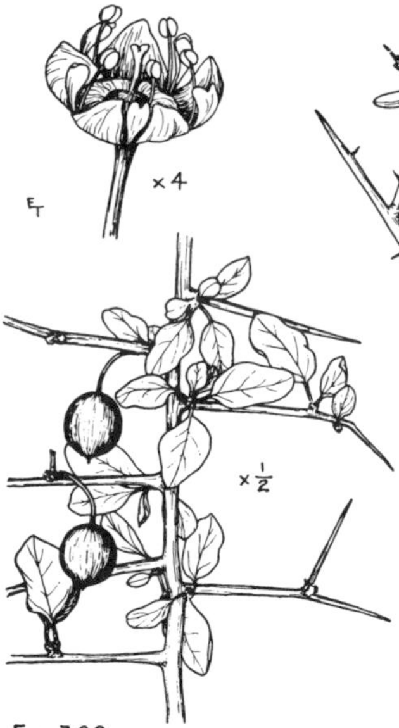

FIG. 366
CONDALIA PARRYI

FIG. 367
CONDALIA LYCIOIDES

FIG. 368
CONDALIA SPATULATA

in axillary clusters, or rarely solitary; sepals 5, joined at the base with the shallow cup-like receptacle to form a receptocalyx; petals 5, distinct, or none; stamens 5, opposite the petals, inserted on the receptocalyx below a fleshy disk; ovary free from the receptocalyx-tube, 1- or 2-celled. Fruit a 1-seeded drupe.

This genus consists of 10 species, native to the warmer parts of North and South America. Three species occur in California.

KEY TO THE SPECIES

Leaves usually elliptical or oblong-ovate, rarely obovate; petals present.
  Flower-clusters sessile; drupe about ½-inch long; branchlets glabrous. 1. *C. Parryi.*
  Flower-clusters peduncled; drupe about ⅓-inch long; branchlets puberulent. 2. *C. lycioides.*
Leaves spatulate or obovate; petals none....................3. *C. spatulata.*

1. **Condalia Parryi** (Torr.) Weberb. PARRY CONDALIA. Fig. 366.

A densely branched glabrous shrub, 3 to 6 or up to 10 feet high, with numerous slender gray or brown spinose branchlets. Leaves mostly fascicled; the blades oblong-elliptical or obovate, rounded at apex, ½- to ¾-inch long, ¼- to ½-inch wide, light green and glabrous on both surfaces, the margins entire; petioles about ¼-inch long. Flowers about 3/16-inch broad, borne singly or in sessile clusters of 2 to 6. Drupe oblong-ellipsoidal or ovoid, about ½-inch long, abruptly pointed at the summit; pedicels about ½- to ¾-inch long, recurved in fruit. Flowering period, March and April.

Parry Condalia inhabits the western and northern borders of the Colorado Desert, in the Lower Sonoran Life Zone. It extends southward into Lower California.

Paul C. Standley states that "The Coahuilla Indians of southern California pounded the fruit into a coarse meal which was mixed with water to make atole." Contr. U. S. Nat. Herb. 23:714 (1923).

Condalia Parryi (Torr.) Weberb.; Engler & Prantl, Nat. Pflzfam. 3:404 (1895). *Zizyphus Parryi* Torr. Type locality: San Felipe, eastern San Diego County. Collected by *Parry.*

2. **Condalia lycioides** Weberb. DESERT CONDALIA. Fig. 367.

A very rigid and spinose shrub, 3 to 6 feet high, with grayish green puberulent branchlets and foliage. Leaves early deciduous; the blades narrow-elliptic or oblong-ovate, obtuse at apex, ⅜- to ⅝-inch long, 1/16- to ¼-inch wide (or larger in Mexican specimens), 1-veined or obscurely 3-veined from the base, grayish on both surfaces, the margins entire or rarely slightly denticulate, very short-petioled. Flower-clusters short-peduncled, with 2 to 6 (rarely more) minute flowers. Fruit globose, ¼- to ⅓-inch in diameter, deep blue or black; the pedicels ¼-inch or less long. Flowering period, January and February.

Desert Condalia is not common in California. It has been collected from a few localities along the northern borders of the Colorado Desert (Purple Hills Pass, *Jepson;* Cottonwood Springs, *S. B. Parish;* Chuckawalla Mountains, *L. J. Childs;* and Mammoth Tank, *S. B. Parish*). It extends eastward into Arizona, New Mexico, and southwestern Texas and southward into Mexico. Its gray-pubescent spines and branches and smaller gray leaves distinguish it from the preceding species.

By some authors this gray Californian form has been treated as *C. lycioides* var.

canescens (Gray) Trel., the typical form being almost glabrous. Since considerable variation in amount of pubescence occurs in specimens examined from areas outside of California it seems best to consider the Californian plants as belonging to the species in the larger sense as herein described.

Condalia lycioides (Gray) Weberb.; Engler & Prantl, Pflzfam. 3:404 (1895). *Zizyphus lycioides* Gray. Type locality: Between Matamoras and Zapimi, Mexico. Collected by *Gregg*. *C. lycioides* var. *canescens* (Gray) Trel.

3. **Condalia spatulata** Gray. Knifeleaf Condalia. Fig. 368.

An intricately branched very leafy shrub, 2 to 6 feet high, with very slender spinose branchlets. Leaf-blades spatulate or obovate, 1/8- to 3/8-inch long, narrowed to very short petioles or sessile, gray-puberulent above, prominently veined beneath, the margins entire. Flower-clusters sessile, with 1 or 2 minute flowers, pedicels 1/8-inch or less long. Fruit ovoid, 1/6-inch long, with a very short beak, black or purplish. Flowering period, July and August.

To my knowledge Knifeleaf Condalia has been collected in California only from Mesquite Station on the Colorado Desert *(S. B. Parish)* and near Picacho Peak, Imperial County *(Roxana Ferris)*. It extends eastward to Texas and southward to Mexico.

Condalia spatulata Gray, Pl. Wright. 1:32 (1852). Type locality: "Rio Grande, Texas, and prairies on the San Felipe." Collected by *Wright*.

5. **Rhamnus** L. Coffeeberry. Buckthorn

(The ancient Greek name of the Buckthorn.)

Shrubs or small trees, usually not spiny. Leaves (in ours) alternate, pinnately veined, deciduous or evergreen. Flowers bisexual or with either stamens or pistils, in small axillary clusters; sepals 4 or 5, united at the base with a cup-shaped receptacle forming a receptocalyx, the upper portion falling after maturity, the lower portion remaining around the developing fruit; petals 4 or 5, distinct, or none, very small, inserted on the margin of a disk lining the receptocalyx; stamens 4 or 5; pistil 1, attached to the receptocalyx at the very base; ovary 3- or 4-celled. Fruit a berry-like drupe, with 2 to 4 nutlets.

The genus *Rhamnus* contains about 100 species, chiefly native to the temperate and warm regions of the northern hemisphere. Five species with many varieties are native to California.

KEY TO THE SPECIES

Leaves typically 1 to 3 (rarely 3/4-inch) inches long, never holly-like; fruit black when ripe.
  Leaves usually 3 to 8 (rarely 2) inches long, deciduous; petioles and midribs beneath brown-tomentulose; northern California........1. *R. Purshiana*.
  Leaves typically less than 3 inches long.
    Bark of branchlets cherry-red (rarely grayish); leaves usually 1/2-inch to 1 1/2 inches long, thin, glabrous or often puberulent beneath in one variety. 2. *R. rubra*.
    Bark of branchlets usually grayish or brownish.
      Leaves evergreen, not acuminate at apex; petals normally present. 3. *R. californica*.
      Leaves deciduous, acuminate at apex; petals none.........4. *R. alnifolia*.
Leaves typically less than 1 inch long or up to 2 inches in some varieties, firm and leathery, commonly brownish beneath, often holly-like in one variety; fruit red when ripe; petals none...............................5. *R. crocea*.

1. **Rhamnus Purshiana** DC. CASCARA SAGRADA. Fig. 369.

A large shrub or sometimes a small tree, 6 to 20 feet high, with smooth gray or brownish bark. Leaves deciduous, usually borne close together at the ends of the branchlets; the blades oblong-elliptic, 2 to 8 inches long, 3/4-inch to 2 1/2 inches wide, 1-veined from the base, rather thin, rounded to tapering or subcordate at base, abruptly acute or obtuse at apex, deep green and glabrous above, paler and brownish tomentulose on the midrib and veins beneath, the margins entire or finely serrulate; petioles 3/8- to 3/4-inch long, brownish tomentulose. Flowers greenish, small, numerous, in umbellate axillary clusters; peduncles 1/4-inch to 1 inch long; pedicels 1/8- to 1/2-inch long; sepals, petals, and stamens 5. Fruit globose, 1/4- to 1/2-inch in diameter, black, with 3 or rarely 2 nutlets. Flowering period, April to June.

Cascara Sagrada, often called Cascara, inhabits canyons and lower mountain slopes usually near the coast from Sonoma County northward in Mendocino, Humboldt, and Del Norte counties, thence eastward into Trinity, Siskiyou, and Shasta counties, thence southward in the Sierra Nevada in Plumas, Placer, and Butte counties, in the Transition Life Zone. Also on Snow Mountain, Lake County (acc. *G. T. Benson*). It extends northward to Washington and British Columbia and eastward to Idaho.

This species intergrades with *R. californica* and some specimens of the two are very difficult to distinguish. The Sierran form, often with obovate leaves and longer peduncles, sometimes passes under the name *R. anonaefolia* Greene. Cascara is well known because of the medicinal qualities of its bark.

Rhamnus Purshiana (Pursh) DC. Prodr. 2:25 (1825). *R. alnifolia* Pursh, not L'Her. Type locality: Kooskoosky River, Idaho, opposite Kamiah, Clearwater River. Collected by *Lewis*. *R. Purshiana* var. *anonaefolia* (Greene) Jepson. *R. anonaefolia* Greene.

2. **Rhamnus rubra** Greene. SIERRA COFFEEBERRY. MOUNTAIN PIGEONBERRY. Fig. 371.

KEY TO THE SPECIES AND VARIETIES

Blades with both surfaces glabrous to merely puberulent along the midrib and veins of the lower surface.
  Branchlets reddish; leaves scattered along the slender branchlets, not borne on stubby spurs.
    Leaves acute to obtuse at base and apex. . . . . *R. rubra*.
    Leaves obtuse to rounded at base and apex. . . . . 2a. var. *obtusissima*.
  Branchlets gray; leaves somewhat clustered at the tips of short stubby spurs. 2b. var. *modocensis*.
Blades with both surfaces covered with fine soft hairs. . . . . 2c. var. *yosemitana*.

An erect semi-deciduous shrub, 2 to 5 feet high, usually with deep reddish slender branchlets. Leaf-blades elliptical to oblanceolate, 1/2-inch to 1 1/2 inches long, pale or yellowish green, glabrous, finely serrulate; petioles about 1/4-inch long. Flowers greenish, inconspicuous, borne in sessile or very short-peduncled umbels. Fruit about 1/4-inch long, somewhat contracted at the base, black when ripe; pedicels 3/8- to 1/2-inch long. Flowering period, May to August.

Sierra Coffeeberry occurs in the Sierra Nevada from 2200 to 7200 feet elevation from Shasta and Modoc counties southward to Fresno County, and in Siskiyou County.

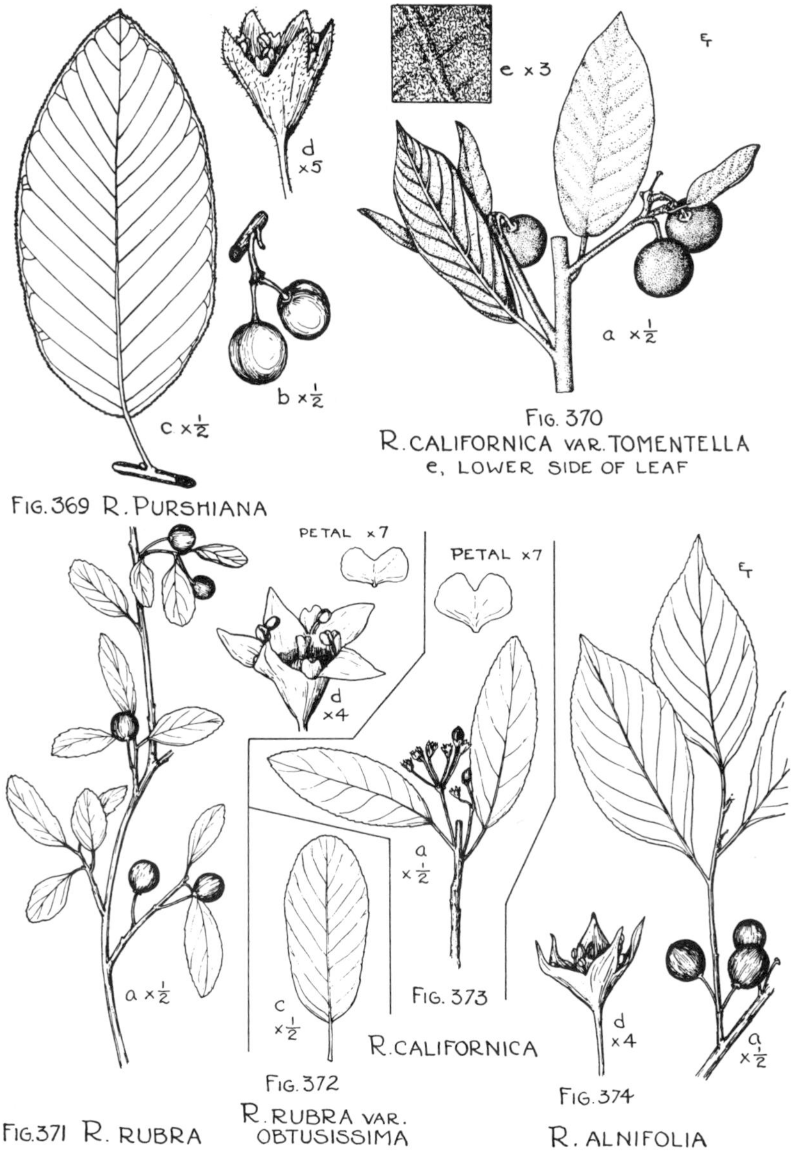

RHAMNUS. a, Branchlet. b, Fruit. c, Leaf. d, Flower.

2a. Var. **obtusissima** (Greene) Jepson. Fig. 372.

Leaf-blades broadly oblong-elliptic, very obtuse or rounded at the apex and base, 1 to 1¾ inches long, glabrous above, often puberulent beneath.

This variety occurs in the Sierra Nevada throughout the range of the species. In many situations it is very difficult to separate from the species and from *R. californica* which occurs in the Coast Ranges.

2b. Var. **modocensis** (Wolf) n. comb. MODOC COFFEEBERRY.

Leaves clustered at the ends of short spur-like branchlets; the blades narrowly or broadly elliptical, ⅝-inch to 1½ inches long, ¼- to ⅝-inch wide, obtuse or rounded at apex, obtuse at base, serrulate.

This variety occurs on dry pumice and sandy soil in the Yellow Pine forests or in open brush in Modoc, Siskiyou, and Shasta counties, in the Arid Transition Life Zone.

2c. Var. **yosemitana** (Wolf) n. comb. YOSEMITE COFFEEBERRY.

Leaves scattered along the branches; the blades elliptical to oblong, 1⅛ to 2⅞ inches long, ⅝-inch to 1 inch wide, obtuse or rounded at apex and base, green and very short-puberulent above, lighter and covered with soft hairs beneath, finely and sharply denticulate. Flowering period, June and July.

This variety occurs in open places and forest borders in the Arid Transition Life Zone at elevations of 4000 to 5000 ft., on the western slope of the Sierra Nevada in Tuolumne and Mariposa counties, and probably in Fresno and Tulare counties. It occurs also at about 6500 ft. on the eastern slope in Mono County.

Rhamnus rubra Greene, Pitt. 1:68, 160 (1887–1888). Type locality: Truckee, California. Collected by *Sonne*.

Var. obtusissima (Greene) Jepson, Fl. 2:459 (1936). *R. obtusissima* Greene. Type locality: Sisson, Siskiyou County, California. Collected by *E. B. Copeland*. *R. californica* var. *obtusissima* (Greene) Jepson, Man.

Var. modocensis (Wolf) McMinn. *R. rubra* subsp. *modcensis* Wolf. Type locality: "Seven miles southeast of Dry Lake, Modoc County." Collected by *Applegate*.

Var. yosemitana (Wolf) McMinn. *R. rubra* subsp. *yosemitana* Wolf. Type locality: "Yosemite National Park, Yosemite Valley, between the Church Bowl and W. B. Lewis Hospital, at about 4000 ft. elevation." Collected by *Wolf*.

3. **Rhamnus californica** Esch. CALIFORNIA COFFEEBERRY. COAST COFFEEBERRY. Fig. 373.

This species is extremely variable in leaf-form and in the amount of pubescence on the leaves. The size and texture of the leaves seem to be in direct relation to the habitats in which the plants grow. The leaves are usually small and thick in dry habitats and large and thin in moist shady situations. The various forms intergrade where their distributions overlap. The following key will identify the more typical common forms.

KEY TO THE SPECIES AND VARIETIES

Leaf-blades glabrous on both surfaces or only slightly puberulent beneath.

Leaf-blades dark green above, paler beneath, serrulate or nearly entire. *R. californica*.

Leaf-blades yellowish green, usually entire but sometimes serrulate. 3a. var. *occidentalis*.

Leaf-blades finely white-tomentose, white-velvety, or silvery beneath.
Leaf-margins entire or with blunt teeth; the blades pubescent with dense short white hairs.
Leaf-blades broadly elliptical, very thick and leathery, finely white-tomentulose on both surfaces............................3b. var. *crassifolia.*
Leaf-blades narrowly elliptical, thinner, finely tomentulose beneath with short dense hairs, nearly glabrous above.............3c. var. *tomentella.*
Leaf-margins sharply serrulate; the blades whitish beneath with short dense hairs and intermingled longer hairs.
Leaf-margins dentate.................................3d. var. *viridula.*
Leaf-margins serrate or rarely entire; mountains of eastern Mohave Desert. 3e. var. *ursina.*

Commonly a tall shrub, 4 to 6 (rarely up to 10 feet) high, with gray, brown, or reddish branches. Leaves evergreen, rarely tardily deciduous; the blades oblong-elliptic, 1 to 3 inches long, ½-inch to 1 inch wide, 1-veined from the base, the lateral veins curving somewhat upward, dark green and glabrous above, paler and glabrous beneath, the margins dentate or finely serrulate to nearly entire, often somewhat revolute and then apparently entire; petioles ¼- to ½-inch long, glabrous. Flowers inconspicuous, greenish, several in peduncled umbels; peduncles ¼-inch to 1 inch long; pedicels ⅛- to ½-inch long. Fruit subglobose, ¼- to ⅜-inch in diameter, at first green, then red, finally black when ripe, with 2 to 3 nutlets. Flowering period, April to June.

California Coffeeberry is one of the more common shrubs of the hills, canyons, and lower and middle mountain slopes of the Coast Ranges from Siskiyou and Trinity counties southward to the San Bernardino and San Jacinto mountains of southern California, in the Upper Sonoran and Transition Life Zones. It extends northward to southern Oregon (Klamath County, acc. *G. T. Benson*), eastward to Arizona, and southward to Lower California.

Along the coastal bluffs of central California the plants are often dwarfed or even prostrate and the leaf-blades are often glaucous beneath.

3a. Var. **occidentalis** (Howell) Jepson.

Branchlets glabrous. Leaf-blades yellowish green, oval or elliptic, obtuse or short-acute, 1½ to 2½ inches long, firm and leathery, glabrous, entire or obscurely denticulate.

This variety is local, occurring in the Upper Sonoran Life Zone of a few localities in Shasta, Siskiyou, Humboldt, and Del Norte counties, California and in Josephine and Curry counties, Oregon.

3b. Var. **crassifolia** Jepson. THICKLEAF COFFEEBERRY.

Branchlets white-tomentose. Leaf-blades oval or elliptical, obtuse or sometimes abruptly acute at apex, 1½ to 3 inches long, 1 to 2 inches broad, very thick and leathery, finely white-tomentulose above and beneath, the lateral veins beneath prominently parallel, the margins serrulate to nearly entire; petioles stout, white-tomentose.

This is a local form occurring in the Arid Transition Life Zone in a chaparral area of the inner North Coast Range foothills from the Napa-Lake County line northward to Trinity and Siskiyou counties.

3c. Var. **tomentella** Brew. & Wats. CHAPARRAL COFFEEBERRY. Fig. 370.

Leaf-blades oblong-elliptic to elliptical, rounded at base, acuminate or abruptly acute at apex, $1\frac{1}{2}$ to 3 inches long, white-tomentulose or silvery beneath, tomentulose or nearly to quite glabrous above, entire or obscurely serrulate.

This variety is widely distributed in the interior chaparral areas throughout California; in the Sierra Nevada from Shasta County southward to Kern County, on the Marysville Buttes, in the inner Coast Ranges from Trinity and Tehama counties southward to eastern San Luis Obispo and western Fresno counties, in the Mount Piños region and southward and eastward occasionally on the desert slopes of the San Gabriel and San Bernardino mountains, occasionally in the mountains of Mono and Inyo counties, and in the Santa Rosa Mountains and the mountains of eastern San Diego County. It extends southward to Lower California.

3d. Var. **viridula** Jepson.

Leaf-blades broadly elliptic, oval, or obovate, rounded at base and apex, $\frac{3}{4}$-inch to $2\frac{1}{4}$ inches long, $\frac{3}{8}$-inch to $1\frac{1}{8}$ inches wide, dark green and glabrous above, whitish beneath with short dense hairs and intermingled long coarse hairs, the margins sharply dentate with irregularly sized teeth.

This variety occurs on the desert slopes of the mountains of Inyo County, and on the desert slopes of the Tehachapi, San Gabriel, Providence, San Bernardino, Liebre, and San Jacinto mountains, in the Upper Sonoran and Arid Transition Life Zones; also in the vicinity of Poso Creek, Kern County, near Three Rivers, Tulare County, and at the summit of Santiago Peak, Orange County *(Wolf)*.

3e. Var. **ursina** (Greene) n. comb.

Leaf-blades elliptical or oval, $1\frac{1}{8}$ to $2\frac{1}{4}$ inches long, $\frac{3}{8}$-inch to $1\frac{1}{8}$ inches wide, dull or bright green and glabrous or pubescent above, white-tomentose beneath with both long and short hairs, serrate or rarely nearly entire. Flowering period, May to July.

This variety occurs in canyons and sheltered ravines in the Providence, New York, and Clark mountains in eastern San Bernardino County, in the Upper Sonoran Life Zone between 4000 and 7500 feet elevation. It extends eastward to Nevada, Arizona, and New Mexico.

Rhamnus californica Esch. Mem. Acad. Sci. St. Petersb. ser. 6, 10:285 (1823). Type locality: Along the coast of middle California. Collected by *Eschscholtz*.

Var. occidentalis (Howell) Jepson, Man. 615 (1925). *R. occidentalis* Howell. Type locality: "On gravelly hillsides and plains, along the eastern base of the Coast Mountains, near Waldo," Oregon. Collected by *Howell*.

Var. crassifolia Jepson, Man. 615 (1925). Type locality: Ridge west of Bear Valley, Colusa County, California. Collected by *Jepson*.

Var. tomentella (Benth.) Brew. & Wats. Bot. Calif. 1:101 (1876). *R. tomentella* Benth. Type locality: The Sierra Nevada foothills. Collected by *Hartweg*.

Var. viridula Jepson, Man. 615 (1925). *R. "virida"* by printer's error, acc. Jepson, Fl. 2:458 (1936). Type locality: Cottonwood Creek, Inyo County. Collected by *Jepson*. *R. cuspidata* Greene. Type locality: Tehachapi Mountains. Collected by *Greene*.

Var. ursina (Greene) McMinn. *R. ursina* Greene. Type locality: "On Bear Mt. near Silver City, New Mexico." Collected by *O. B. Metcalfe*.

4. **Rhamnus alnifolia** L'Her. Alderleaf Coffeeberry. Fig. 374.

A low deciduous shrub, 2 to 4 feet high, with gray or reddish brown branchlets. Leaf-blades ovate to elliptical, $1\frac{1}{2}$ to 3 inches long, $\frac{1}{2}$-inch to $1\frac{1}{2}$ (or 2) inches wide, 1-veined from the cuneate base, acuminate at apex, the lateral veins somewhat curving upward, glabrous above, glabrous or sometimes brownish tomentulose on the midrib and veins beneath, the margins distinctly crenate-serrate; petioles ¼- to ⅜-inch long. Flowers 2 to 5 in sessile axillary clusters; sepals and stamens 4 or 5; petals none. Fruit subglobose or obovoid, ⅜-inch or less in diameter, dark red to almost black, with 2 or 3 nutlets; pedicels ¼- to ⅜-inch long. Flowering period, May to July.

To my knowledge this shrub has been collected in California only at the lower end of Donner Lake, Nevada County, near Deer Park, Placer County *(Wolf),* on the road to Lake Tahoe on the Truckee River, near the Shingle Mill, Placer County *(C. F. Sonne),* and at Big Spring, Big Meadows, Plumas County *(Mrs. Austin).* It extends northward to Oregon and British Columbia and eastward to Maine and New Jersey.

Rhamnus alnifolia L'Her. Sert. Angl. 5 (1788). Type locality: "in America septentrionale."

5. **Rhamnus crocea** Nutt. REDBERRY. Fig. 378.

KEY TO THE SPECIES AND VARIETY

Leaves less than ½-inch long; branchlets very stiff and somewhat spinescent. *R. crocea.*

Leaves ½-inch to 1½ inches long; branchlets not spinescent.

  Leaves with long soft spreading hairs or at least pubescent......5a. var. *pilosa.*

  Leaves glabrous, thick, and firm.

    Leaves spinulose-toothed, rarely almost entire; mainland species. 5b. var. *ilicifolia.*

    Leaves usually entire, rarely spinulose; tree-like; island species. 5c. var. *insularis.*

A low densely spreading shrub, 2 to 3 feet high, with numerous short rigid or spinose branchlets. Leaves evergreen, often clustered; the blades nearly round to broadly ovate, ¼- to almost ½-inch long, almost as broad, 1-veined from the base, dark or pale green and glabrous above, glabrous and commonly brown or yellowish beneath, finely serrulate or glandular-denticulate; petioles ⅛-inch or less long. Flowers small, few in axillary sessile umbels; sepals and stamens 5; petals none or minute. Fruit globose, ¼-inch or less in diameter, red, glabrous, with 2 or 3 nutlets. Flowering period, February to May.

Redberry inhabits the dry lower slopes of the Coast Ranges from Sonoma, Lake, and Napa counties southward to San Diego County, in the Upper Sonoran Life Zone. It extends southward into Lower California. In central California it is nowhere abundant, usually occurring on decomposed serpentine outcroppings. In southern California it occurs in the lower part of the chaparral areas. Its glossy green foliage, clear globular bright red berries, and its habit of growth make it suitable for single or group planting. Plants brought from the hills and placed in a moderately well-watered place acquire a glossy foliage, the brown of the lower leaf-surface usually disappears, the habit of growth is less dense, and the plants sometimes attain a height of 5 feet. It seems to be free from all garden pests. The smooth bright red berries, partly hidden among the small leaves, give these shrubs a very striking appearance from August to October. Since the plants are polygamous, all do not set a heavy crop of fruit.

5a. Var. **pilosa** Trel. HAIRYLEAF REDBERRY.

Leaves 3/4-inch to 1 1/2 inches long, more or less covered with soft spreading hairs. Inflorescences strikingly gray-velvety.

This shrub usually occurs in the chaparral of the mountains and foothills east of San Diego, in the Upper Sonoran Life Zone.

5b. Var. **ilicifolia** (Kell.) Greene. HOLLYLEAF COFFEEBERRY. HOLLYLEAF REDBERRY. Fig. 375.

FIG 375 RHAMNUS CROCEA VAR. ILICIFOLIA

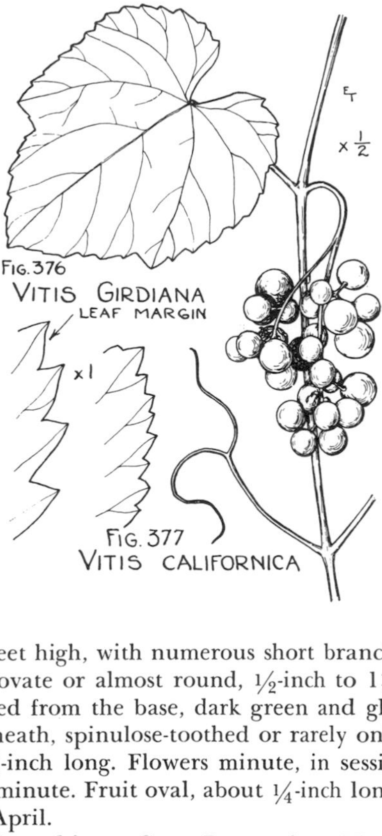

FIG. 376 VITIS GIRDIANA

FIG. 377 VITIS CALIFORNICA

A stout shrub or often tree-like, 3 to 15 feet high, with numerous short branchlets. Leaves evergreen; the blades broadly ovate or almost round, 1/2-inch to 1 1/4 inches long, 1/2-inch to 1 inch wide, 1-veined from the base, dark green and glabrous above, paler and often brownish beneath, spinulose-toothed or rarely only deeply serrate or entire; petioles 1/8- to 1/4-inch long. Flowers minute, in sessile umbels; petals none, or rarely present and minute. Fruit oval, about 1/4-inch long, bright red. Flowering period, February to April.

Hollyleaf Coffeeberry occurs in the middle and inner Coast Ranges from Humboldt, Siskiyou, and Trinity counties southward through the inner Coast Range to the foothills and mountains of southern California, where it is a common shrub of the chaparral in the Upper Sonoran Life Zone. It occurs also in the Sierra Nevada foothills from Shasta County southward to Tulare County and occasionally in the mountains of the Mohave Desert.

This variety intergrades with the species but in its typical form is larger and more open and spreading. The leaves are larger and more holly-like. The leaves from specimens taken in the southern Sierra Nevada usually lack the golden-brown color beneath.

Fig. 378. Redberry. *Rhamnus crocea* Nutt.

5c. Var. **insularis** (Greene) Sarg. ISLAND COFFEEBERRY. ISLAND REDBERRY.

Usually tree-like, 10 to 30 feet high. The leaves oblong-ovate, 1 to 2 inches long, scarcely toothed. Fruit larger than in the other varieties.

This variety is found on Santa Catalina, San Clemente, Guadalupe, and Santa Cruz islands.

Rhamnus crocea Nutt.; T. & G. Fl. N. Am. 1:261 (1838). Type locality: Monterey, California. Collected by *Nuttall.*

Var. pilosa Trel.; Curran, Proc. Calif. Acad. ser. 2, 1:251 (1888). Type locality: Santa Maria Valley east of San Diego, California. Collected by *K. Curran.*

Var. ilicifolia (Kell.) Greene, Fl. Fr. 79 (1891). *R. ilicifolia* Kell. Type locality: Vicinity of Clear Lake, Lake County. Collected by *Veatch.*

Var. insularis (Greene) Sarg. Gard. & For. 2:364 (1889). *R. insularis* Greene. Type locality: Santa Cruz Island. Collected by *Greene.*

Vitaceae. Grape Family

The Grape Family contains 11 genera and about 500 species of woody plants, usually climbing by tendrils, chiefly of tropical and subtropical distribution in all continents.

1. **Vitis** L. GRAPE

(The Latin name of the Vine.)

Woody vines, climbing by tendrils. Leaves simple, alternate, deciduous, palmately veined, opposite the flower-clusters and tendrils. Flowers mostly dioecious or polygamo-dioecious, small, in branched clusters; sepals 5 or 6, minute, joined into a 5- or 6-toothed or almost entire calyx-tube filled by a fleshy disk; petals usually 5 or 6, distinct, inserted on the disk, coherent in a cap, falling early without expanding; stamens as many as the petals and opposite them; ovary superior or partially inferior, 2-celled. Fruit a juicy berry.

This genus consists of about 25 species, 2 of which are native to California.

KEY TO THE SPECIES

Leaves thinnish, only thinly cobwebby-tomentose or pubescent beneath; berries purple, covered with a dense glaucous bloom; central and northern California . . . . 1. *V. californica.*

Leaves firm, densely cobwebby-tomentose beneath; berries black, only somewhat glaucous; southern California . . . . 2. *V. Girdiana.*

1. **Vitis californica** Benth. CALIFORNIA WILD GRAPE. Fig. 377.

A woody vine, 5 to 50 feet long, or sprawling and bush-like when not finding support. Young leaves and branches commonly densely white-tomentose. Leaf-blades roundish in outline, 1½ to 5 inches in diameter, cordate at base, the basal notch or sinus varying from deep and almost closed to shallow and very open, thinnish, 3- or 5-veined from the base, usually finely serrate and sometimes slightly 3- or 5-lobed, finely pubescent or thinly cobwebby-tomentose above, becoming nearly glabrous in age, thinly cobwebby-tomentose beneath; petioles 1 to 5 inches long. Tendrils opposite the leaves, at least once-branched and twisted. Flowers greenish, fragrant, numerous, in compound clusters. Berry globose, ¼- to ½-inch in diameter, purplish, covered with a whitish bloom. Flowering period, May to July.

California Wild Grape occurs along streams and in canyons of the Coast Ranges from San Luis Obispo County northward to Siskiyou County, in the Sacramento and San Joaquin valleys, and in the foothills of the Sierra Nevada from Kern County northward to Shasta County, in the Upper Sonoran Life Zone. It frequently climbs trees and when in full foliage completely covers them. The fragrant flowers are much frequented by bees.

Vitis californica Benth. Bot. Voy. Sulph. 10 (1844). Type locality: Lower Sacramento River. Collected by *Hinds.*

2. **Vitis Girdiana** Munson. DESERT WILD GRAPE. Fig. 376.

Similar to *V. californica* but usually with leaf-blades firmer and more coarsely toothed and denser and more permanently cobwebby-tomentose beneath. Berry globose, usually 1/8- to 1/4-inch in diameter, black, with little bloom. Flowering period, May and June.

Desert Wild Grape occurs along streams and in canyon bottoms of the mountains of southern California below 4000 feet elevation. It extends north into Inyo County and south into Lower California. It also occurs on Santa Catalina Island.

This species is very closely related to *V. californica* and might well be disposed of as a variety of that species. Specimens collected from southern California and grown for seven years in the trial garden at Mills College with specimens collected from northern California are now scarcely separable upon the basis of the characteristics given in the manuals.

Vitis Girdiana Munson, Proc. Soc. Prom. Agri. Sci. 8:59 (1887). Type locality: San Diego, California.

Malvaceae. Mallow Family

The Mallow Family consists of about 50 genera and about 1000 species of world-wide distribution, except in the colder regions. Such common plants as Tree Mallow *(Lavatera), Hibiscus, Abutilon,* Mallow *(Malva), Althaea,* and Cottonplant *Gossypium* belong to this family.

KEY TO THE GENERA

Arborescent shrubs with long-petioled maple-like leaves; flowers large and showy, axillary, subtended by a short 2- or 3-lobed involucel, the petals 1 inch or more long. . . . . 1. LAVATERA.

Shrubs or perennial herbs woody only at the base; petals less than 1 inch long.

  Anthers scattered along the outside of the stamen-tube; fruit a capsule of 5 cells splitting down their backs. . . . . 2. HIBISCUS.

  Anthers borne at the summit of the stamen-tube; fruit composed of a series of carpels around a central axis.

    Involucel-bractlets absent; carpels winged in upper part. . . . . 3. HORSFORDIA.

    Involucel-bractlets present; carpels not winged.

      Carpels not differentiated into upper and basal parts; plants shrubby, or sometimes woody only at base. 4. MALVASTRUM.

      Carpels of 2 parts, the lower part indehiscent and reticulated, the upper dehiscent and unreticulated; perennial herbs woody only at base. 5. SPHAERALCEA.

1. **Lavatera** L. TREE-MALLOW

(Named for two Lavater brothers, Swiss physicians and naturalists.)

This genus contains about 20 species, chiefly Mediterranean. A single species is native to the islands off the coast of southern California. It has been brought into cultivation at several places on the mainland.

1. **Lavatera assurgentiflora** Kell. CALIFORNIA TREE-MALLOW. Fig. 379.

An erect shrub, 3 to 8 feet high, or becoming tree-like and up to 15 feet high. Leaves simple, alternate, evergreen; the blades somewhat maple-like, palmately 5- to 7-lobed, 3 to 5 inches long and about as broad, the lobes coarsely toothed or lobed, glabrous on both surfaces; petioles 2 to 4 inches long. Flowering period, almost throughout the year but more abundantly from April to August.

California Tree-mallow occurs on the Santa Barbara Islands and on Santa Catalina Island. It has been widely planted throughout the coastal counties for hedges and wind-breaks as well as for ornamental purposes.

Lavatera assurgentiflora Kell. Proc. Calif. Acad. 1:14 (1854). Type locality: Anacapa Island.

2. Hibiscus L. ROSE-MALLOW

(The Greek name used by Dioscorides for Marsh Mallow.)

This is a large genus of about 150 species, widely distributed but chiefly in the tropics. Two species are native to California, one an annual and the other a suffrutescent perennial.

1. **Hibiscus denudatus** Benth. DESERT HIBISCUS. PALEFACE ROSE-MALLOW. Fig. 380.

A tufted suffrutescent plant, 1 to 2 feet high, with slender densely tomentose yellowish stems, often woody at the base. Leaves simple, alternate, evergreen; the blades ovate, rather thick, ½-inch to 1 inch long, densely and closely stellate-tomentose on both surfaces, serrulate; petioles ⅛- to ¼-inch long. Flowers bisexual, regular, showy, solitary on peduncles ¼- to ¾-inch long, borne along the somewhat naked ends of the branches; bractlets 3 to 7, bearing a bristle at the apex, about ⅛-inch long; calyx 5-parted, ½- to ¾-inch long, canescent, the segments about ⅜-inch long; petals ½- to ¾-inch long, white or pinkish, with a red or purplish claw and often with a narrow rose band on the center of the limb; anthers numerous and scattered along the outside of the stamen-tube. Fruit a glabrous capsule, about ¼-inch long, 5-celled, each cell dehiscent down the back to the base. Flowering period, March and April.

Desert Hibiscus grows on rocky slopes in dry canyons and desert valleys of the Colorado Desert below 2000 feet elevation. It extends eastward into Arizona, New Mexico, and Texas and southward into Lower California. Specimens have been examined from Hell Hole Canyon, near Borego *(Epling & Robison),* Palm Canyon, Chuckawalla Springs, Coyote Canyon *(Hall),* and at the north base of Signal Mountain *(Wolf).*

Hibiscus denudatus Benth. Bot. Voy. Sulph. 7 pl. 3 (1844). Type locality: Magdalena Bay, Lower California. Collected by *Hinds.*

3. Horsfordia Gray

(Named after F. H. Horsford, a New England botanical collector.)

Usually shrubs or subshrubs, the herbage yellowish, covered with a dense felty tomentum. Leaves simple, alternate, evergreen. Flowers bisexual, regular, solitary or 2 or 3 in axillary clusters, peduncled; bractlets absent; sepals 5, joined at the base; petals 5, distinct; anthers numerous, borne in a cluster at the summit of the stamen-tube; ovary superior, composed of several carpels which are crowded and

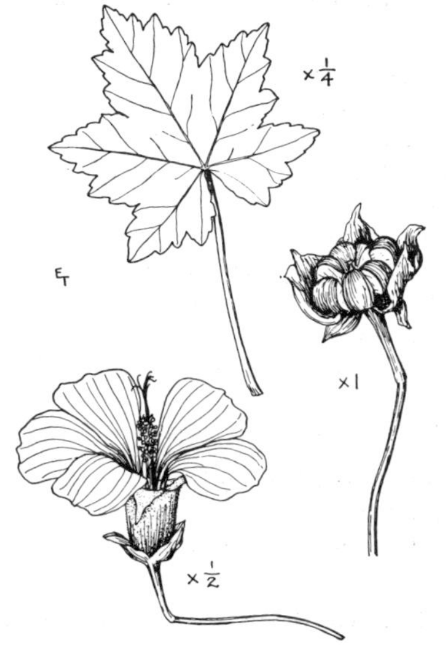

FIG. 379 LAVATERA ASSURGENTIFLORA

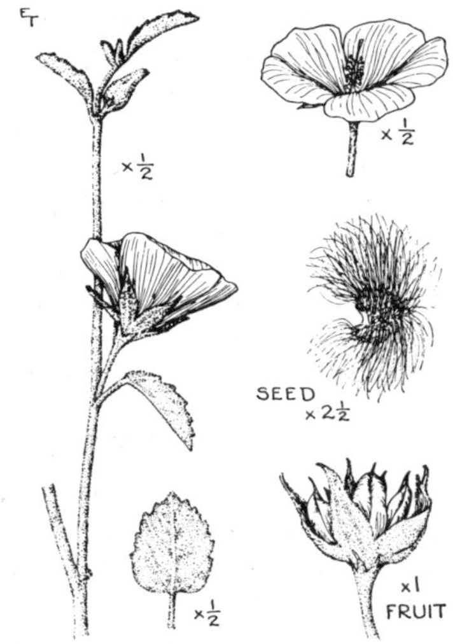

FIG. 380 HIBISCUS DENUDATUS

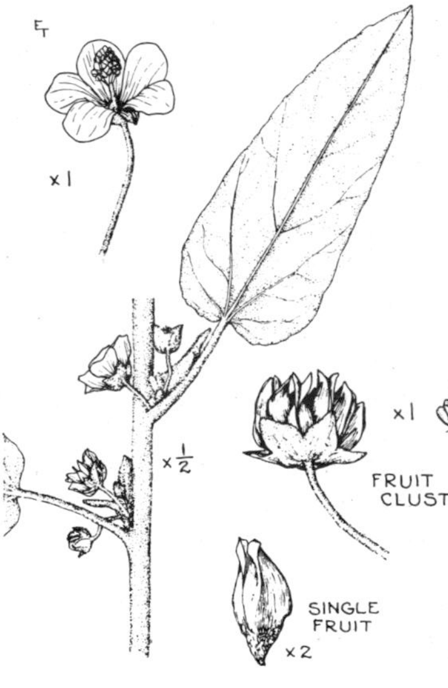

FIG. 381 HORSFORDIA NEWBERRYI

FIG. 382 HORSFORDIA ALATA

united around a central axis. Fruit dry, the 8 to 12 carpels separating at maturity, each carpel 2-valved above, with a pair of erect-spreading wings.

This is a small genus of 4 species native to Arizona, southern California, and northern Mexico.

KEY TO THE SPECIES

Flowers pink; leaves ovate..1. *H. alata.*
Flowers orange or salmon-yellow; leaves lanceolate............2. *H. Newberryi.*

1. **Horsfordia alata** (Wats.) Gray. TALL FALSE MALLOW. Fig. 382.

An erect sparingly branched shrub, 3 to 8 feet high. Leaf-blades broadly ovate-lanceolate, 3/4-inch to 2 1/2 inches long, 1 to 2 inches wide, truncate to cordate at base, densely stellate-tomentose, somewhat viscid, dentate or nearly entire; petioles 3/4-inch to 1 3/4 inches long. Flowers pink, 3/4-inch to 1 inch broad; peduncle jointed above the middle. Carpels 10 to 12, each 1-seeded, dehiscent at summit, the wings of the carpels 3 times as long as the lower seed-bearing part. Flowering period, March and April.

This shrub is rare in California, being known only from the Coachella Valley in a wash at Coral Reef Ranch *(Mrs. Clary).* It occurs also in Arizona (Gila Mts.) and in Sonora, Mexico and Lower California.

Horsfordia alata (Wats.) Gray, Proc. Am. Acad. 22:297 (1887). *Sida alata* Wats. Type locality: "State of Sonora, Mexico, 100 miles south of U. S. boundary and 30 miles from the Gulf of California. *Pringle.*"

2. **Horsfordia Newberryi** (Wats.) Gray. NEWBERRY FALSE MALLOW. Fig. 381.

An erect perennial, becoming shrubby, 3 to 8 feet high, with long slender stems covered with a fine dense yellowish stellate tomentum. Leaf-blades thick, lance-ovate or broadly lanceolate, cordate at base, 1 1/4 to 3 inches long, 3/4-inch to 1 1/4 inches wide, 3- to 5-veined from the base, greenish yellow to grayish, densely pubescent on both surfaces, finely toothed or entire; petioles 3/8-inch to 1 inch long. Flowers orange or salmon-yellow, 1/2-inch to 1 inch broad, in small axillary peduncled clusters or solitary. Carpels 8 or 9, each 2- or 3-seeded, the wings not much longer than the lower seed-bearing part. Flowering period, March and April.

Newberry False Mallow occurs occasionally in the canyons of the mountains along the western border of the Colorado Desert in San Diego and Imperial counties. It extends eastward to southern Arizona and southward to Sonora, Mexico and Lower California.

Horsfordia Newberryi (Wats.) Gray, Proc. Am. Acad. 22:297 (1887). *Abutilon Newberryi* Wats. Type locality: Canebrake Canyon on the lower Colorado River. Collected by *Newberry.*

4. **Malvastrum** Gray. GLOBEMALLOW

(A name dérived from *Malva,* a closely related genus.)

Herbs or shrubs, usually with white tomentum and star-shaped or branched hairs. Leaves simple, alternate, usually palmately veined and often lobed. Flowers bisexual, regular, mostly in terminal compound clusters or often reduced to axillary racemes or fascicles, each flower subtended by 1 to 3 bractlets; sepals 5, united at base; petals 5, distinct but often joined at their bases to the stamen-tube; stamens numerous, their filaments united into a tube surrounding the styles and carpels; ovary superior, composed of 5 to several carpels, each enclosing a single ovule. Fruit dry, composed of a cycle of united carpels which separate from each other at maturity; each carpel splitting open by 2 valves, 1-seeded.

The globemallows make up a large genus of beautiful flowering herbs or shrubs which occur in America and South Africa. Twelve species and several varieties native to California are either shrubs or have their herbaceous stems and branches arising from woody bases.

KEY TO THE SPECIES

I. Flowers in terminal congested heads or one or two heads below; heads subtended by conspicuous foliaceous bracts; calyx-segments about ½-inch long, hirsute . . . . 1. *M. Palmeri.*

II. Flowers in sessile axillary heads or rarely single and sessile in the axils, forming interrupted spikes, the basal flowers rarely in short lateral racemes.

Bractlets subtending the calyx broadly ovate, nearly ½-inch long, about ¼-inch wide; calyx-segments ovate, abruptly acuminate; buds pointed, distinctly angled . . . . 2. *M. aboriginum.*

Bractlets subtending the calyx filiform, linear or rarely lanceolate.

Calyx densely hispid, or densely long-pubescent or woolly and obscuring the segments.

Calyx densely woolly, the segments nearly or completely obscured.

Leaves usually very thick; bractlets nearly as long as the calyx, at least as long as the calyx-tube; buds subglobose . . . . 3. *M. Fremontii.*

Leaves relatively thin; bractlets shorter than the calyx, usually shorter than the calyx-tube . . . . 4. *M. orbiculatum.*

Calyx with long hispid hairs (or long-pubescent in *M. clementinum*).

Stems, branches, and leaves with greenish yellow aspect; calyx-segments and bractlets usually densely hispid; mainland species. 5. *M. marrubioides.*

Stems, branches, and lower surface of leaves with grayish white aspect; calyx-segments long-pubescent or slightly hispid; island species. 6. *M. clementinum.*

Calyx scabrous or short stellate-tomentose, not hispid.

Bractlets longer than the calyx-tube; leaves rather thick, usually distinctly rugose; San Francisco Bay region . . . . 7. *M. arcuatum.*

Bractlets shorter than the calyx-tube; typically southern California.

Herbage grayish . . . . 8. *M. fasciculatum.*

Herbage with yellowish green aspect. . 5a. *M. marrubioides* var. *viscidum.*

III. Flowers in an elongated branched inflorescence of sessile or pedunculate clusters or rarely 1 to 3 flowers peduncled in the axils, often some clusters sessile and axillary along the upper part of the flowering stem but the lower clusters at least racemose to paniculate.

A. Flower buds and calyx-segments densely soft-tomentose or woolly.

Leaves usually very thick.

Bractlets shorter than the calyx-tube; buds ovoid; calyx-segments densely stellate-tomentose without and villous near the apex within; southern California . . . . 9. *M. Davidsonii.*

Bractlets as long as the calyx-tube, usually as long as the calyx; buds globose, the segments densely woolly or stellate-tomentose and less woolly without; central and northern California. . . . . . 3. *M. Fremontii* vars.

Leaves relatively thin; calyx-segments long-pubescent to hirsute. 4. *M. orbiculatum.*

B. Flower buds and calyx-segments usually scabrous or short-canescent or closely stellate-tomentose.

Calyx 3/8- to 1/2-inch long, the segments long-acuminate; panicle open, the flowering branches distant............................10. *M. Abbottii.*

Calyx about 1/4-inch long.

Leaves cuneate to truncate at base, irregularly toothed, scarcely or not at all lobed, gray and nearly alike on both surfaces; flowers 1 to 3 on unequal peduncles in the upper axils........................11. *M. Jonesii.*

Leaves truncate to cordate or rarely rounded at base; flowers numerous.

Calyx-segments narrow-acuminate, purplish; branches of the inflorescence very slender...............................12. *M. gracile.*

Calyx-segments broad at base, ovate-acute, brownish or gray; branchlets of inflorescence thicker...................8. *M. fasciculatum* vars.

C. Flower buds, calyx-segments, and bractlets densely hispid.
5b. *M. marrubioides* var. *paniculatum.*

1. **Malvastrum Palmeri** Wats. CAMBRIA GLOBEMALLOW. Fig. 383.

KEY TO THE SPECIES AND VARIETY

Leaves stellate-pubescent on both surfaces.........................*M. Palmeri.*

Leaves glabrous on the upper surface....................1a. var. *involucratum.*

A coarse perennial, 4 to 8 feet high, with stout herbaceous stems, leafy to the summit, arising from a woody base. Leaf-blades broadly ovate or nearly round in outline, 1 to 3 inches long, nearly as broad, dark green, stellate-pubescent on both surfaces or becoming glabrous above in age, usually 3-lobed, crenate-dentate. Flowers few and sessile in a terminal head-like cluster or with 1 or 2 axillary clusters below, all clusters 1 to 2 inches wide and subtended by conspicuous foliaceous often lobed bracts; bractlets linear to ovate; calyx-lobes ovate-lanceolate, about 1/2-inch long, hirsute; petals rose-color, 3/4-inch to 1 inch long. Flowering period, May to July.

Cambria Globemallow has a limited distribution in the foothills of the Santa Lucia Mountains of San Luis Obispo and southern Monterey counties, in the vicinity of Cambria, Morro, and Atascadero.

1a. Var. **involucratum** (Rob.) n. comb.

Leaf-blades glabrous on the upper surface. Outer involucral bracts not lobed. Petals 1/2- to 3/4-inch long.

This variety has the habit and general appearance of the species and should perhaps be considered only a minor variation. It has been collected at Jolon *(T. S. Brandegee)* and between Jolon and King City, Monterey County *(Eastwood).*

Malvastrum Palmeri Wats. Proc. Am. Acad. 12:250 (1887). Type locality: "Cambria, 1 mile from the beach, San Luis Obispo County." Collected by *Palmer. Sphaeralcea Palmeri* (Wats.) Jepson.

Var. involucratum (Rob.) McMinn. *Malvastrum involucratum* Rob. Type locality: Monterey County, near Jolon. Collected by *T. S. Brandegee.*

2. **Malvastrum aboriginum** Rob. INDIAN GLOBEMALLOW. Fig. 384.

A coarse perennial, 1 to 2 1/2 feet high, with the stems and branches covered with a soft white felted tomentum and arising from a woody base. Leaf-blades broadly ovate, 1 to 2 inches long, and nearly as broad, 3- to 5-lobed, crenate-dentate, finely wrinkled and pale above, scarcely paler beneath; petioles about

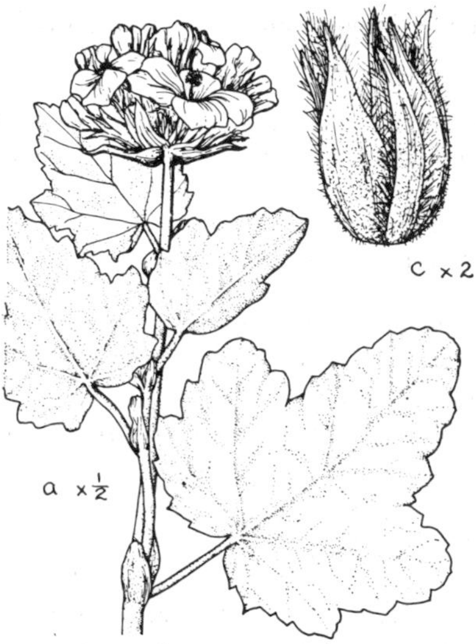

FIG. 383 M. PALMERI

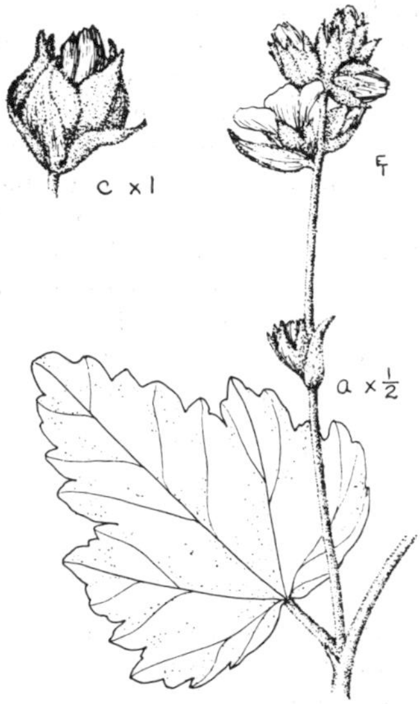

FIG. 384 M. ABORIGINUM

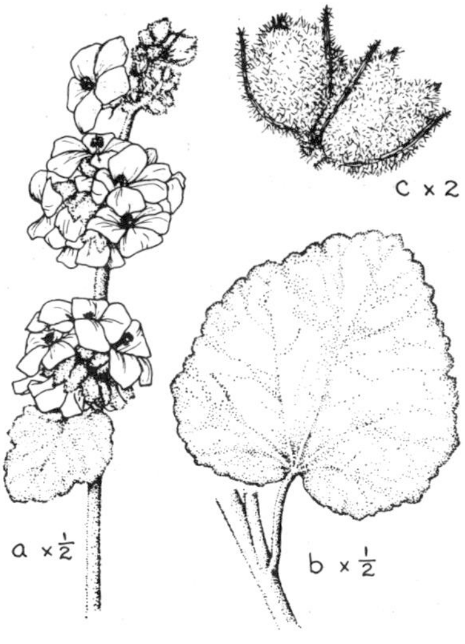

FIG. 385 M. FREMONTII

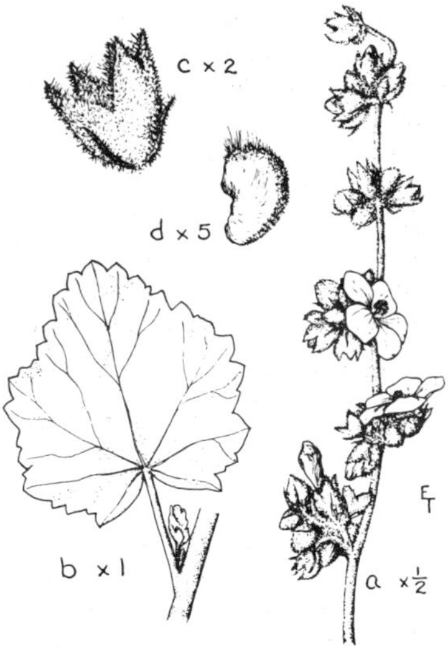

FIG. 386 M. ORBICULATUM

MALVASTRUM. a, Flowering branchlet. b, Leaf. c, Calyx. d, Carpel.

1 inch long. Flowers rose-color, sessile and in head-like clusters in the upper axils, forming elongated flexuous almost naked interrupted terminal inflorescences; bractlets 3, broadly ovate, nearly ½-inch long and about ¼-inch wide; calyx about ⅜-inch long, strongly plicate-angled in bud, canescent-tomentulose, its segments broader than long, abruptly acuminate. Flowering period, May to July.

Indian Globemallow occurs in the middle South Coast Range in San Benito and Monterey counties. It has been collected at Indian Valley, Monterey County *(K. Curran)*, near Bitterwood, Tres Piños, and the Pinnacles in San Benito County *(Eastwood)*, and at Bear Valley, San Benito County *(Jepson)*.

Malvastrum aboriginum Rob.; Gray, Syn. Fl. 1:311 (1897). Type locality: Indian Valley, southern Monterey County. Collected by *K. Curran*. *Sphaeralcea aboriginum* (Rob.) Jepson.

3. **Malvastrum Fremontii** T. & G. WHITE-COAT GLOBEMALLOW. FREMONT GLOBEMALLOW. Fig. 385.

An erect plant, 2 to 6 feet high, woody below, with densely white soft-tomentose herbage. Leaf-blades very thick, round-ovate, 1½ to 4½ inches long and about as broad, not lobed or shallowly 5- to 7-lobed, crenate, densely soft-tomentose above and below; petioles ½-inch to 1½ inches long. Flowers pink or rose-color in close head-like clusters in the axils, forming interrupted spikes at the summit of the stems; bractlets 3, linear-filiform, black, as long as the calyx or nearly so; calyx densely tomentose-woolly, nearly globose in bud, the segments obscured except for the small pointed tips; petals ½- to ¾-inch long, pink, becoming whitish in age. Flowering period, April to August.

White-coat Globemallow inhabits the foothills of the Sierra Nevada from Tulare County (Dry Creek, *M. S. Jussell*) north to Amador County and in a few localities in the inner central and North Coast Ranges (Mt. Diablo, Contra Costa County; Yollo Bolly foothills, Tehama County, *T. S. Brandegee*). It is nowhere abundant. Most of the specimens from the Sierra Nevada foothills have interrupted spicate inflorescences and are assigned to the species, while most from the Coast Range have paniculate inflorescences and are assigned to the varieties "keyed out" below.

KEY TO THE VARIETIES OF M. FREMONTII

Flowers numerous, definitely paniculate; buds and calyx densely woolly; bractlets as long as the calyx or nearly so; calyx-segments normally long-acuminate to attenuate-caudate.................................3a. var. *cercophorum*.

Flowers numerous, in short lateral racemose clusters or in heads in the upper axils; buds and calyx densely white-tomentose; bractlets about as long as the calyx-tube ....3b. var. *Helleri*.

Flowers few, 1 to 3 on unequal peduncles in the axils, the upper more paniculate; buds and calyx densely white-tomentose; bractlets green, as long as the calyx-tube or slightly longer..................................3c. var. *niveum*.

3a. Var. **cercophorum** Rob. Fig. 387.

This variety occurs more commonly in the inner dry North and central Coast Ranges, but is occasionally found in the lower Sierra Nevada foothills in Madera and Calaveras counties.

3b. Var. **Helleri** (Eastw.) n. comb. Fig. 388.

This variety occurs near Ladoga, Lake County, in the Yollo Bollys, and in western Yolo County.

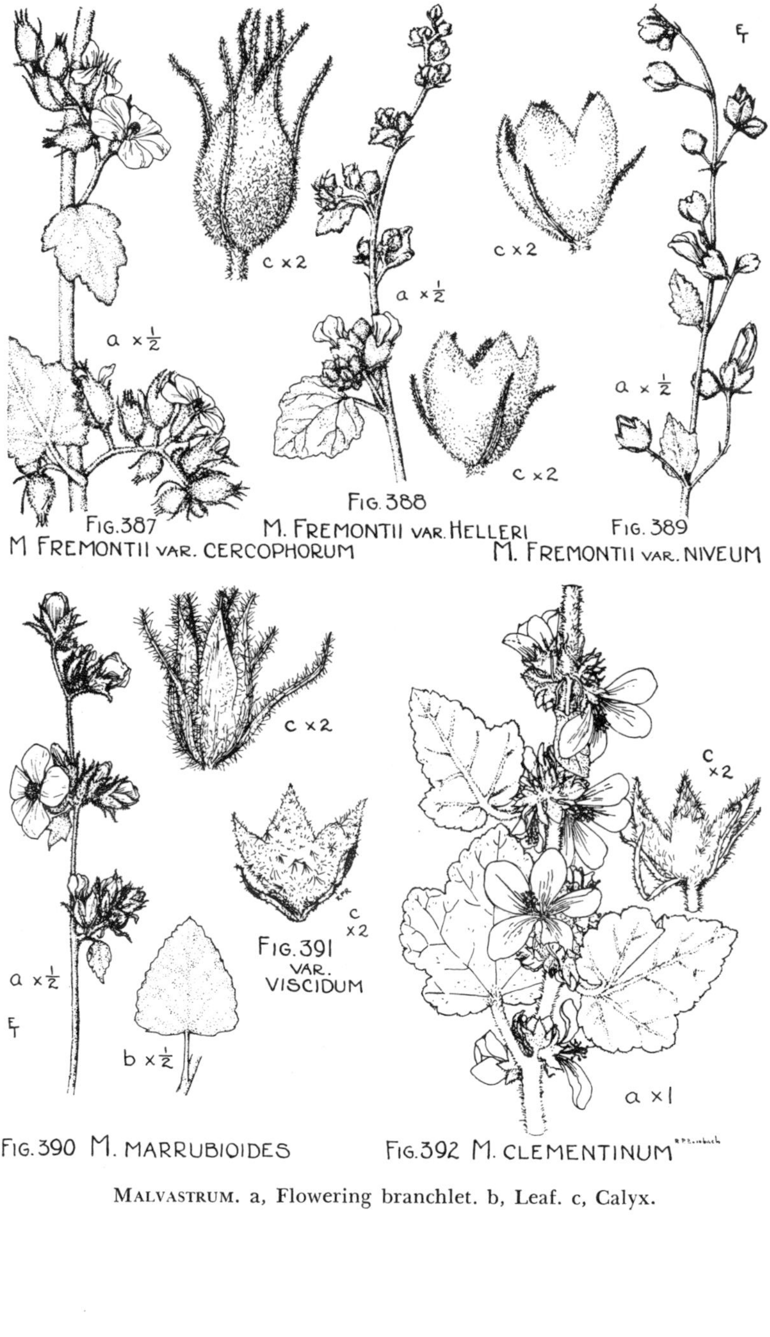

MALVASTRUM. a, Flowering branchlet. b, Leaf. c, Calyx.

3c. Var. **niveum** (Eastw.) n. comb. Fig. 389.

This is a beautiful variety with open panicles of few pink flowers. It has been collected in San Luis Obispo County (2 mi. north of the mouth of Morano Creek, *B. Bolt;* along the road to Pozo, *A. Eastwood;* Indian Creek, La Panza Mts., *Chester Dudley;* El Dorado School near Santa Margarita, *Mary E. Wall*).

Malvastrum Fremontii Torr. Pl. Fendl. in Gray, Mem. Am. Acad. 4:21 (1849). Type locality: "interior of California." Collected by *Fremont. Sphaeralcea Fremontii* (Torr.) Jepson.

Var. cercophorum Rob.; Gray, Syn. Fl. 1:311 (1897). Type locality: Arroyo del Valle, Alameda County, California. Collected by *Greene. Sphaeralcea Fremontii* var. *cercophorum* (Rob.) Jepson. *Malvastrum Howellii* Eastw. *M. Howellii* var. *cordatum* Eastw.

Var. Helleri (Eastw.) McMinn. *Malvastrum Helleri* Eastw. Type locality: Near Ladoga, Lake County, California. Collected by *Heller. Sphaeralcea Fremontii* var. *exfibulosa* Jepson.

Var. niveum (Eastw.) McMinn. *Malvastrum niveum* Eastw. *M. fragrans* Eastw., not Gray & Harv. Type locality: El Dorado School near Santa Margarita, San Luis Obispo County, California. Collected by *Mary E. Wall.*

4. **Malvastrum orbiculatum** Greene. TEHACHAPI GLOBEMALLOW. Fig. 386.

A subshrubby plant, 2 to 6 feet high, with erect stout and simple branches densely covered with soft stellate hairs. Leaf-blades almost round, rather thinnish, 1 to 2½ inches in diameter, sometimes obscurely 3-lobed, coarsely crenate, greenish and soft-pubescent above, paler and more densely pubescent beneath. Flowers rose-color, few in axillary sessile clusters terminating the almost naked stems, and more numerous in short lateral racemes below, the whole forming an interrupted spicate panicle; bractlets filiform, much shorter than the lanceolate-acuminate calyx-lobes; calyx somewhat hispid-hairy; petals about ½-inch long; carpels hairy-tufted and densely tomentulose at apex. Flowering period, June to August.

Tehachapi Globemallow occurs on dry slopes on the desert side of the San Bernardino and San Gabriel mountains, west to Mount Piños, and north to Inyo County, between 2000 and 9000 feet elevation. This species is closely related to *M. marrubioides* D. & H.

Malvastrum orbiculatum Greene, Fl. Fr. 109 (1891). Type locality: On the mountains south of Tehachapi, Kern County. Collected by *Greene. Sphaeralcea orbiculata* (Greene) Jepson.

5. **Malvastrum marrubioides** D. & H. HISPID GLOBEMALLOW. Fig. 390.

KEY TO THE SPECIES AND VARIETIES

Flowers in sessile axillary heads forming an interrupted leafy or naked spike.
- Calyx with long hispid hairs . . . . *M. marrubioides.*
- Calyx scabrous, not hispid . . . . 5a. var. *viscidum.*

Flowers in panicles . . . . 5b. var. *paniculatum.*

An erect perennial, 2 to 6 feet high, woody at base, with densely stellate-tomentose but greenish herbage. Leaf-blades broadly ovate to round in outline, ¾-inch to 1¾ inches long and about as broad, gray-green and shortly stellate-pubescent above, paler and more densely pubescent beneath, coarsely crenate-dentate or sometimes 3-lobed; petioles ½-inch to 1 inch long. Flowers rose-pink, numerous, in sessile clusters along the ends of the branches, forming an inter-

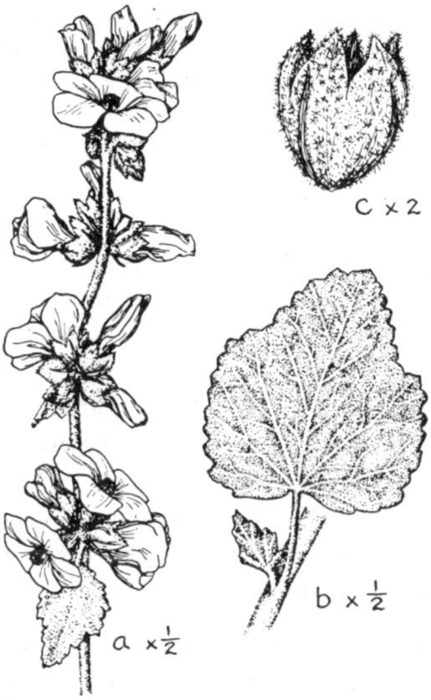

FIG. 393 M. ARCUATUM

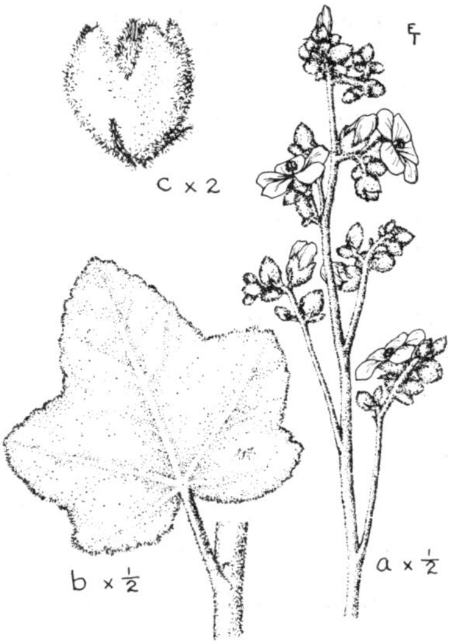

FIG. 394 M. DAVIDSONII

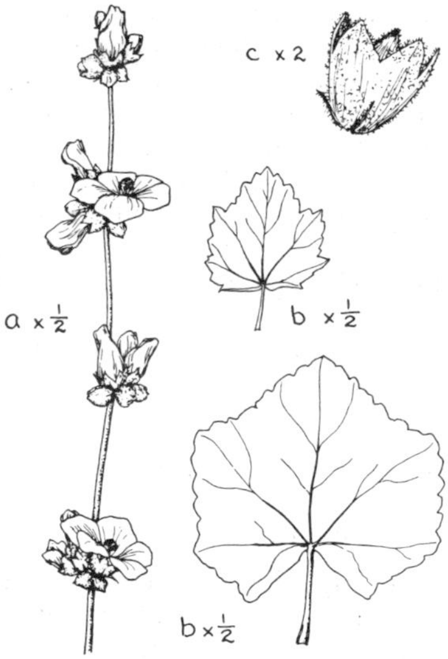

FIG. 395 M. FASCICULATUM

FIG. 396 M. FASCICULATUM VAR. NESIOTICUM

MALVASTRUM. a, Flowering branchlet. b, Leaf. c, Calyx.

rupted leafy or naked spike or sometimes with lateral spike-like branchlets; bractlets 3, nearly as long as the calyx, filiform, hispid; calyx 3/8- to 5/8-inch long, hispid-stellate, often papery-white in age, its segments lanceolate-acuminate, 1/4- to 3/8-inch long; petals 3/8- to 5/8-inch long. Flowering period, May to July.

Hispid Globemallow occurs on dry chaparral slopes and in adjacent valleys from San Diego County northward in the lower dry mountain areas of Orange, Riverside, Los Angeles, and Ventura counties. It is known also from the Mount Hamilton Range south of Livermore (*K. Curran* U. C. 109101) and in the Sierra Nevada foothills (Fort Miller, upper San Joaquin River). This species has long been confused with *Malvastrum densiflorum* Wats., which I consider identical to *M. marrubioides* D. & H. The type specimen at Paris and the material from the type collection at the U. S. Nat. Herb. very closely match the type of *M. densiflorum* Wats. collected by S. B. and W. F. Parish near Palm Springs, Riverside County.

5a. Var. **viscidum** (Abrams) n. comb. Fig. 391.

Calyx-segments 1/8- to 1/4-inch long, acute, scarcely hirsute; bractlets shorter than the calyx-tube, scarcely hirsute.

This variety occurs in southern San Diego County and in northern Lower California.

5b. Var. **paniculatum** Gray.

Inflorescence paniculate.

This variety is known in California only from the hills bordering Lake Elsinore, Riverside County. It is more common in Lower California.

Malvastrum marrubioides D. & H. Jour. Phil. Acad. ser. 2, 3:38 (1854). Type locality: Fort Miller, on the upper San Joaquin River. Collected by *Heermann*. *M. densiflorum* Wats. *M. gabrielense* Munz & Johnst. *Sphaeralcea densiflora* (Wats.) Jepson. *S. densiflora* var. *gabrielense* (Munz & Johnst.) Jepson.

Var. viscidum (Abrams) McMinn. *M. viscidum* Abrams. Type locality: El Nido, San Diego County, California. Collected by *Abrams*. *M. densiflorum* var. *viscidum* (Abrams) Estes. *Sphaeralcea densiflora* var. *viscida* (Abrams) Jepson.

Var. paniculatum Gray, Proc. Am. Acad. 22:290 (1887). Type locality: All Saints Bay, northern Lower California. Collected by *Orcutt*.

6. **Malvastrum clementinum** Munz & Johnst. San Clemente Globemallow. Fig. 392.

A rounded tufted shrub, 2 to 3 feet high, with many ascending densely stellate-tomentose branches. Leaf-blades round-ovate, often 3-lobed, or merely crenate, 1 to 2 1/2 inches wide, greenish above; flowers many, in subsessile heads or short lateral racemes, forming an interrupted elongated spike; bractlets linear, about 1/4-inch long and nearly equalling the calyx; calyx-segments broadly lanceolate, acute to acuminate, somewhat hispid-hairy. Flowering period, May to July.

San Clemente Globemallow occurs on rocky walls on San Clemente Island. It is very similar to *Malvastrum orbiculatum* Greene but can be distinguished by the bractlets which are nearly as long as the calyx.

Malvastrum clementinum Munz & Johnst. Bull. Torr. Club 51:296 (1924). Type locality: Lemon Tank, San Clemente Island. Collected by *P. A. Munz*. *Sphaeralcea orbiculata* var. *clementina* Jepson.

7. **Malvastrum arcuatum** (Greene) Rob. Canyon Globemallow. Fig. 393.

An erect subshrub, 2 to 5 feet high, with stems herbaceous above and woody

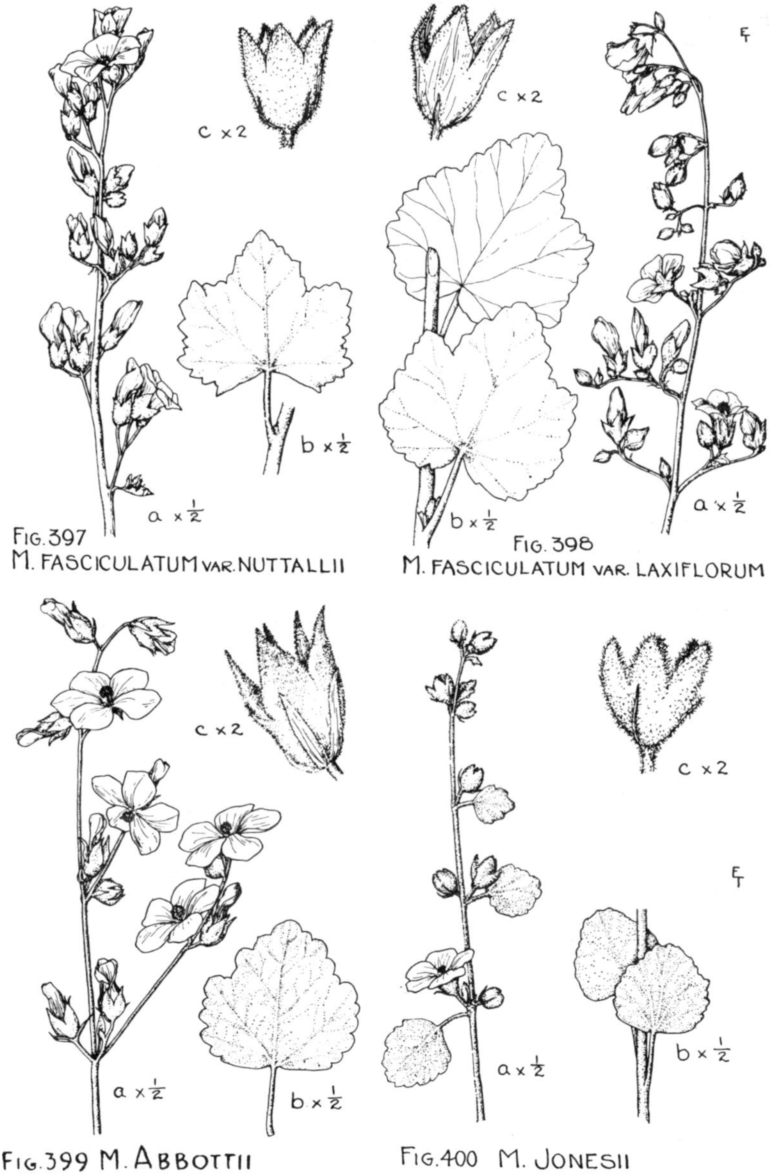

MALVASTRUM. a, Flowering branchlet. b, Leaf. c, Calyx.

below, covered with a dense white tomentum. Leaf-blades thickish and rugose, ovate or nearly round, ¾-inch to 2 inches long, ½-inch to 1½ inches wide, scarcely or not at all lobed, truncate or rounded at base, crenate-dentate, grayish or becoming green above, densely canescent-tomentose beneath; petioles ¼-inch to 1¼ inches long. Flowers rose-color, in dense head-like clusters sessile in the upper leaf-axils and forming at the ends of the branches interrupted spicate inflorescences; bractlets linear, shorter than or nearly equalling the rusty scabrous or tomentose calyx; petals ½- to ¾-inch long. Flowering period, May to July.

Canyon Globemallow occurs in the foothills of the eastern slope of the Coast Range in San Mateo, Santa Clara, and Santa Cruz counties. Specimens from the Mount Hamilton Range usually filed in the herbaria as *M. arcuatum* seem more closely related to the *M. fasciculatum* complex. Some specimens from the Marysville Buttes and from Lake County closely resemble this species but have been assigned to *M. Fremontii.*

Malvastrum arcuatum (Greene) Rob.; Gray, Syn. Fl. 1:311 (1897). *Malveopsis arcuata* Greene. Type locality: "eastern slopes of the Coast Ranges back of Belmont, San Mateo County." Collected by *Greene. Sphaeralcea arcuata* (Greene) Arthur.

8. **Malvastrum fasciculatum** (Nutt.) Greene. BUSH GLOBEMALLOW. MESA GLOBEMALLOW. Fig. 395.

KEY TO THE SPECIES AND VARIETIES

Inflorescences composed of head-like clusters of nearly sessile flowers forming an interrupted spike. . . . . *M. fasciculatum.*
Inflorescences paniculate.
  Leaves very thin but firm, distinctly lobed, green and apparently glabrous above; calyx canescent or tomentose.
    Branches of the rigid panicle numerous, long and ascending; calyx finely canescent. . . . . 8a. var. *nesioticum.*
    Branches of the panicle short, with more congested flower-clusters; calyx tomentose. . . . . 8b. var. *catalinense.*
  Leaves normally thicker; calyx scabrous.
    Leaves nearly alike on both surfaces. . . . . 8c. var. *Nuttallii.*
    Leaves distinctly unlike above and below. . . . . 8d. var. *laxiflorum.*

A tall shrub, 3 to 8 (or 15) feet high, with long slender wand-like branches herbaceous above and woody below, covered with a close soft tomentum. Leaf-blades round-ovate in outline, varying from not lobed to deeply 3- to 5-lobed, the lobes either obtuse or acute, crenate or crenate-dentate, ¾-inch to 3 inches long and about as broad, mostly truncate or subcordate at base, usually densely canescent below, less so above. Flowers pink, in sessile or short-pedunculate head-like clusters forming an interrupted spike-like inflorescence, or some flowers in short compact lateral racemes; bractlets filiform, much shorter than the calyx-tube; calyx about ¼-inch long, scabrous or sparsely stellate-pubescent, the segments triangular-ovate, acutely pointed or obtuse; petals ½- to ¾-inch long. Flowering period, May to August.

Bush Globemallow inhabits dry slopes and flats in the mountains from San Diego County northward through the mountains of southern California to Santa Barbara County where it intergrades with one or two varietal forms which extend northward in the inner Coast Ranges to the Mount Hamilton Range and to Mount Diablo, Contra Costa County.

Considerable variation occurs in the pubescence, character of the leaves, and the forms of the inflorescence. The following varieties represent the more striking variations. They all have paniculate inflorescences.

8a. Var. **nesioticum** (Rob.) n. comb. Fig. 396.

Known only from Santa Cruz Island. Very close to var. *laxiflorum.*

8b. Var. **catalinense** (Eastw.) n. comb.

Known only from Santa Catalina Island. Very close to var. *nesioticum.*

8c. Var. **Nuttallii** (Abrams) n. comb. Fig. 397.

Known from Ventura and Santa Barbara counties and probably Los Angeles County *(A. Davidson* #18790 U. C.).

8d. Var. **laxiflorum** (Gray) Munz & Johnst. Fig. 398.

This variety is the most widely distributed of all the paniculate forms. It occurs from San Diego County northward in the inner coastal mountains to Mount Diablo, Contra Costa County. In the Santa Ynez River region it is difficult to separate this variety from var. *Nuttallii*. Material collected from Mount Diablo has leaves somewhat less acutely angled than most of the leaves from material collected in southern California, but the other characters used by recent authors to separate the Mount Diablo plants into a new species or variety can be duplicated in southern California material.

Malvastrum fasciculatum (Nutt.) Greene, Fl. Fr. 108 (1891). *Malva fasciculata* Nutt. Type locality: Probably in the vicinity of San Diego, California. Collected by *Nuttall. Sphaeralcea fasciculata* (Nutt.) Arthur.

Var. nesioticum (Rob.) McMinn. *M. nesioticum* Rob. Type locality: Santa Cruz Island. Collected by *Greene. Sphaeralcea fasciculata* var. *nesiotica* (Rob.) Jepson.

Var. catalinense (Eastw.) McMinn. *M. catalinense* Eastw. Type locality: Near Avalon, Santa Catalina Island. Collected by *Eastwood, J. T. Carlson.*

Var. Nuttallii (Abrams) McMinn. *Malacothamnus Nuttallii* Abrams. Type locality: Casitas Pass, Ventura County, California. Collected by *Abrams. Malvastrum Nuttallii* (Abrams) Dav. & Mox. *Sphaeralcea fasciculata* var. *Nuttallii* (Abrams) Jepson.

Var. laxiflorum (Gray) Munz & Johnst. Bull. Torr. Club 51:296 (1924). *M. Thurberi* var. *laxiflorum* Gray. Type locality: Los Angeles County, California. Collected by *Wm. Wallace. M. splendidum* Kell. *M. Hallii* Eastw. *Sphaeralcea fasciculata* var. *laxiflora* (Gray) Jepson. *S. fasciculata* var. *Elmeri* Jepson.

9. **Malvastrum Davidsonii** Rob. Sand Globemallow. Fig. 394.

A tall robust tree-like shrub, 6 to 15 feet high, or less shrubby and 2 to 4 feet high, with stout flexuous branches and densely stellate-tomentose herbage. Leaf-blades very thick, round-cordate, 1 to 4 inches in diameter, 5-angled or shallowly 3- or 5-lobed, irregularly toothed, loosely and densely stellate-tomentose on both surfaces, the main veins on the lower surface very prominent; petioles ½-inch to 1½ inches long. Flowers numerous, clustered in the upper axils or shortly racemose, the racemes often branching and forming an interrupted panicle 10 to 18 inches long; bractlets 3, shorter than the calyx-tube; calyx densely stellate-tomentose, the segments ovate, acute; petals pink or rose-color, ½- to ¾-inch long, sometimes ageing yellow. Flowering period, May to August.

Sand Globemallow inhabits sandy washes and plains of the San Fernando Valley, Los Angeles County (Verdugo Hills and Little Tujunga wash). It also occurs in the Ojai Valley of Ventura County (*Peckham,* acc. *Jepson*).

This species is related to *M. Fremontii* of northern California but differs in having shorter bractlets, a less tomentose calyx, more deeply lobed cordate leaves, and carpels hairy-tufted and densely tomentulose at apex.

Malvastrum Davidsonii Rob.; Gray, Syn. Fl. 1:312 (1897). Type locality: San Fernando Valley. Collected by *A. Davidson*. *Sphaeralcea Davidsonii* (Rob.) Jepson.

10. **Malvastrum Abbottii** Eastw. SALINAS GLOBEMALLOW. Fig. 399.

An erect shrub, 3 to 6 feet high, with white-tomentose herbage. Leaf-blades broadly ovate, 1 to 2¼ inches long and nearly as broad, truncate at base, gray and densely soft-tomentose above, paler and more densely tomentose beneath, the margins crenate; petioles ⅜-inch to 1 inch long. Flowers rose-color, in large widely spreading panicles, the flowering branches very distant; bractlets narrowly lanceolate, as long as or longer than the calyx-tube; calyx ⅜- to ½-inch long, finely white-tomentose, the segments long-acuminate, nearly ¼-inch long; petals about ¾-inch long. Flowering period, June to October.

This is a beautiful large-flowered globemallow known only from the type locality in Monterey County. It is related to *Malvastrum fasciculatum* var. *laxiflorum*.

Malvastrum Abbottii Eastw. Leafl. West. Bot. 1:215 (1936). Type locality: Along the Salinas River, Monterey County. Collected by *E. K. Abbott*.

11. **Malvastrum Jonesii** Munz. SWEET GLOBEMALLOW. Fig. 400.

An erect shrub, 2 to 4 feet high, with rather slender and numerous branches. Leaf-blades firm, suborbicular, obscurely 3- to 5-lobed, coarsely and irregularly crenate-dentate, ½-inch to 1 inch long and about as wide, cuneate to truncate at base, pale green and closely velvety-pubescent above and below. Flowers pink or rose-color, solitary, or 2 to 4 in the upper axils forming a sparsely flowered interrupted spike-like inflorescence, or some of the flowers in short lateral pedunculate clusters; bractlets awl-shaped, about ⅛-inch long, stellate-pubescent; calyx about ⅜-inch long, loosely stellate-tomentose, the segments triangular-ovate, acute; petals about ½-inch long. Flowering period, May to July.

Sweet Globemallow is known only from San Luis Obispo County where it occurs on the dry slopes of Fern and Peachy canyons near Paso Robles and in the Santa Lucia Mountains *(J. H. Barber)*. It is closely related to *M. fasciculatum* (Nutt.) Greene.

Malvastrum Jonesii Munz, Bull. Calif. Acad. 24:88 (1925). Type locality: Paso Robles, San Luis Obispo County. Collected by *M. E. Jones*. *Malvastrum Dudleyi* Eastw. *Sphaeralcea fasciculatum* var. *Jonesii* (Munz) Jepson.

12. **Malvastrum gracile** Eastw. SLENDER GLOBEMALLOW. Fig. 401.

An erect tall slender shrub, 3 to 6 feet high. Leaf-blades ovate, often 3-lobed, ¾-inch to 2 inches long, truncate or obtuse at base, pale gray-green above, densely white-tomentose beneath, the margins crenate; petioles ¼- to ½-inch long. Flowers rose-color, in a widely spreading panicle, the branches of the panicle very slender; bractlets linear, as long as or shorter than the calyx-tube, purplish; calyx about ¼-inch long, reddish purple beneath the sparse glandular indument, the segments narrow-acuminate; petals about ½-inch long. Flowering period, May to August.

Slender Globemallow is a rare shrub known only from San Luis Obispo County, California.

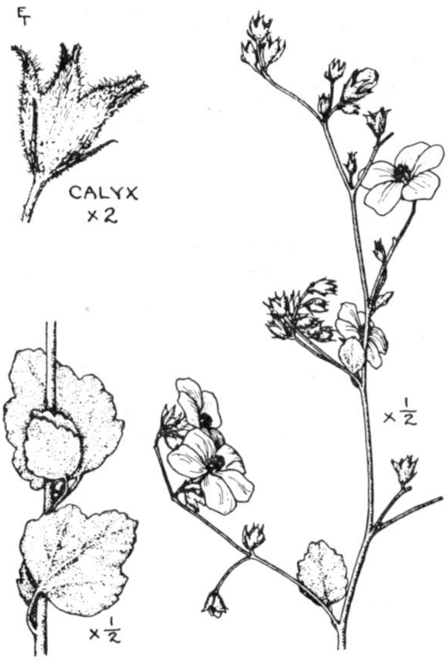

FIG. 401 MALVASTRUM GRACILE

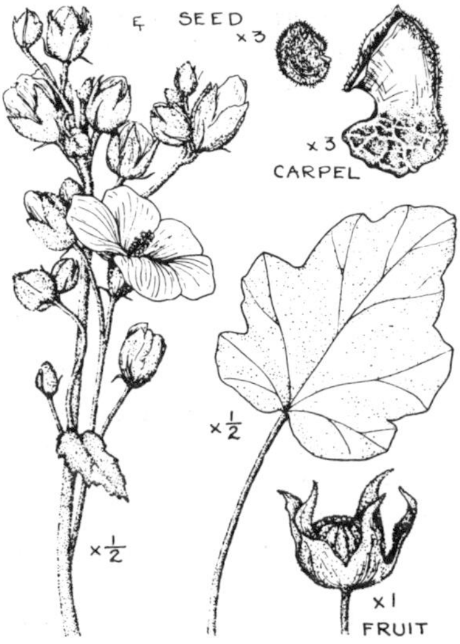

FIG. 402 SPHAERALCEA AMBIGUA

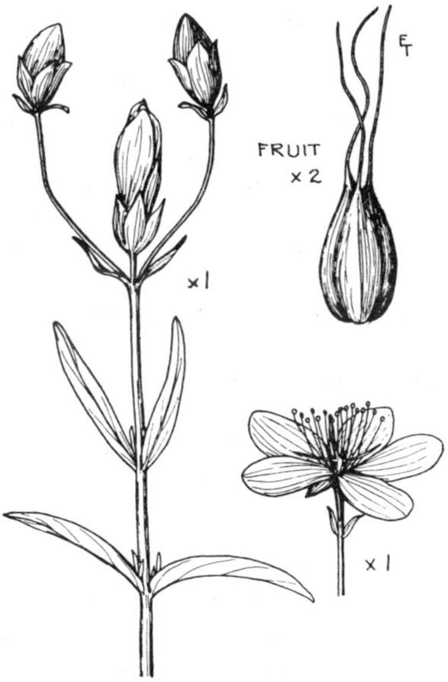

FIG. 403 HYPERICUM CONCINNUM

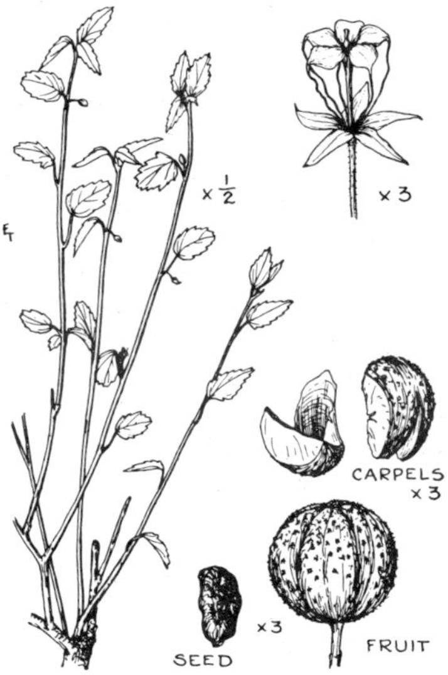

FIG. 404 AYENIA PUSILLA

Malvastrum gracile Eastw. Leafl. West. Bot. 1:219 (1936). Type locality: Between Arroyo Grande and Huasna, San Luis Obispo County, California. Collected by *Eastwood.*

5. **Sphaeralcea** St. Hil. BUSHMALLOW

(From the Greek *sphaera,* a sphere, and *alkea,* mallow, in reference to the spherical carpels.)

Perennial herbs, bushy suffruticose plants, shrubs, or rarely trees, usually with a close stellate tomentum. Leaves simple, alternate, with palmately lobed or dissected blades. Flowers bisexual, regular, in axillary clusters or terminal narrow panicles, each flower subtended by 2 or 3 bractlets; calyx 5-lobed; petals 5, distinct or partially united at base and slightly adnate to the stamen-tube; stamens numerous, joined by their filaments into a cylindrical tube surrounding the styles; pistils of several united carpels, the ovary superior. Fruit a collection of dry carpels which separate at maturity, each carpel composed of an upper dehiscent unreticulated part and a lower indehiscent reticulated part, 1- to 3-seeded.

This is a large genus of about 70 species, 4 or 5 of which are south African and the remainder from the warmer regions of North and South America. Our species are all perennial herbs, some slightly suffrutescent at base but hardly sufficiently woody to be considered shrubs. Two bush-like species and 3 varieties occur in the desert regions of southern California. They resemble the globemallows *(Malvastrum)* in general appearance. The most common species, **Sphaeralcea ambigua** Gray (Fig. 402), is known as Desert-mallow or Apricot-mallow. It is a bushy plant with many stems from the base which branch above into panicles of beautiful brick-red or rose-red flowers.

Hypericaceae. St. John's Wort Family

This family includes 8 or 10 genera and about 280 species of temperate and tropical regions. A single genus with 4 species is native to California, only one being woody at the base. Klamath Weed *(Hypericum perforatum)* a European introduction, has become a widely distributed weed throughout the valleys and hills of northern California.

1. **Hypericum** L. ST. JOHN'S WORT

(From the ancient Greek name, of obscure meaning.)

This is a genus of about 160 species, widely dispersed, but chiefly in the north temperate zone.

1. **Hypericum concinnum** Benth. GOLD-WIRE. Fig. 403.

A subshrub, with numerous wiry stems, forming a bushy plant ½-foot to 1½ feet high. Leaves simple, opposite, tardily deciduous; the blades linear to lanceolate, ½-inch to 1½ inches long, ⅛- to ¼-inch wide, acute at apex, commonly folded inward, with a few black dots, entire, usually inserted by a narrow but not clasping base. Flowers yellow, bisexual, regular, about 1 inch broad, in close clusters at the summit of the stems. Fruit a 3-lobed capsule, slightly less than ½-inch long. Flowering period, April to September.

Gold-wire is a very characteristic subshrub associated with the chaparral of the lower mountain slopes and foothills of the North Coast Ranges from Marin County north through Sonoma, Napa, and Lake counties to Mendocino County, and south in the Sierra Nevada from Shasta County to Mariposa County.

Hypericum concinnum Benth. Pl. Hartw. 300 (1848). Type locality: "In valle Sacramento." Collected by *Hartweg*, probably in Nevada County.

Sterculiaceae. Sterculia Family

This family is almost exclusively tropical, containing 58 genera and about 700 species of trees, shrubs, vines, and herbs. Two genera with 3 species are native to California.

KEY TO THE GENERA

Leaves serrate; flowers small; petals present........................1. AYENIA.
Leaves lobed to entire; flowers large; sepals yellow; petals none...2. FREMONTIA.

1. **Ayenia** Loefl.

(Named in honor of Duc d'Ayen.)

This is a small genus of about 15 closely related species of herbs or low shrubs native to the southwestern United States, Mexico, the West Indies, and South America. One species is native to California.

1. **Ayenia pusilla** L. AYENIA. Fig. 404.

A small subshrub, 6 to 12 inches high, with several slender stems from a woody base. Leaves simple, alternate, evergreen; the blades ovate to oblong-ovate or rarely lanceolate, 1/4- to 1/2-inch long, minutely pubescent, dentate-serrate; petioles 1/16- to 1/4-inch long. Flowers brownish, small, 1/8-inch or less broad, bisexual, regular. Fruit a globose capsule, 1/8- to 1/4-inch in diameter, with rough dark glands, splitting into 5 one-seeded carpels. Flowering period, February to April or rarely to July.

Ayenia is a rare subshrub in California, occurring occasionally along the eastern base of Mount San Jacinto in Riverside County and southward in San Diego County. (RIVERSIDE COUNTY: Lost Palms, canyon below Aushutz Well, *I. M. Johnston;* Tahquitz Canyon, Palm Springs, *Jaeger*. SAN DIEGO COUNTY: Borego Valley, *P. A. Munz;* Yaqui Well, Colorado Desert, *M. E. Jones;* Andreas Canyon, *P. A. Munz;* Hell Hole Canyon, *C. Epling* & *Robison;* San Felipe, *T. S. Brandegee;* Box Canyon, *Epling* & *Robison*.) Outside of California this species has a wide distribution in Mexico, southern Arizona to Texas, the West Indies, and Key West, Florida.

The plants show great variation in shape and pubescence of leaves. A number of these variations have been described as species but until further study can be made of the entire genus it seems best to consider these segregates as minor variations of the widely distributed species, *Ayenia pusilla* L.

Ayenia pusilla L. Syst. Nat. ed. 10, 1247 (1759). Type locality: Caribbean region. *A. compacta* Rose. *A. californica* Jepson. *A. microphylla* Gray.

2. **Fremontia** Torr.

(Named in honor of General John C. Fremont, who discovered the plant.)

Evergreen shrubs or small trees. Leaves simple, alternate, usually thick and with stellate pubescence. Flowers bisexual, regular, large and showy, solitary and axillary on the branchlets; sepals 5, petal-like, united at base; petals none; stamens 5, joined by their filaments for about 1/2 their length or sometimes almost to the anthers; ovary superior, 4- or 5-celled, surrounded by the base of the filament-tube;

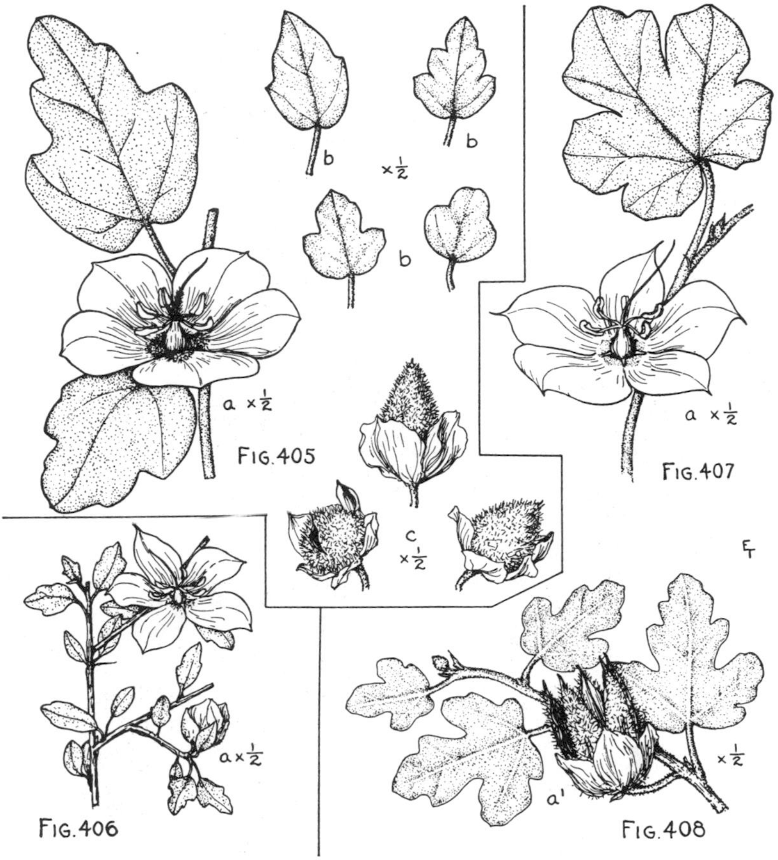

FREMONTIA. a, Flowering branchlet. a′, Fruiting branchlet. b, Leaf variation. c, Fruit. Fig. 405. F. CALIFORNICA. Fig. 406. F. CALIFORNICA var. NAPENSIS. Fig. 407. F. MEXICANA. Fig. 408. F. CRASSIFOLIA.

style exserted beyond the stamens. Fruit a broadly ovoid densely bristly-hairy capsule, 4- or 5-valved, dehiscent from the apex, persisting for many months; seeds 2 or 3 in each cell, brown or black.

This is a small genus of 2 species native to California and Lower California.

KEY TO THE SPECIES

Leaves distinctly palmately veined and lobed; glands at base of sepals usually not hairy; seeds black and shiny . . . . 1. *F. mexicana.*

Leaves entire to slightly lobed (or deeply lobed on rapid growing shoots); glands at base of sepals usually hairy; seeds brown, dull . . . . 2. *F. californica.*

1. **Fremontia mexicana** (Dav.) Macbr. SOUTHERN FREMONTIA. Figs. 407, 409.

A large shrub or small tree, 6 to 20 feet high. Leaf-blades distinctly 3- or 5-lobed, 1¼ to 3 inches long, thick, dark green and soft-pubescent and roughish above, becoming nearly glabrous in age, covered beneath with a dense whitish or brown-

Fig. 409. SOUTHERN FREMONTIA. *Fremontia mexicana (*Dav.) Macbr.

ish felt; petioles 1/2-inch to 1 inch long. Flowers 1 1/2 to 2 1/2 inches broad, yellow, often tinged with orange on the back of the sepals, the large gland at base of sepals usually without hairs; anthers reddish. Capsules conical, acuminate, 3/4-inch to 1 1/2 inches long, densely bristly hairy. Seeds black, shiny. Flowering period, March to June.

Southern Fremontia occurs in Woodwardia Canyon of Otay Mountain, near the eastern end of Otay Lake in San Diego County *(F. F. Gander)*, and probably elsewhere in San Diego County. Some specimens with hairless glands from the San Antonio Mountains are with hesitancy assigned to this species. It extends southward into Lower California. This is the common form seen in cultivation. It flowers during most of the growing season when in cultivation but more heavily from May to July.

Fremontia mexicana (Dav.) Macbr. Contr. Gray Herb. 53:14 (1918). *Fremontodendron mexicanum* Dav. Type locality: "15 miles from San Diego." #3234 S. Calif. Acad. Sci. Herb. Collected by *Kate Sessions,* June 1917. *F. californica* var. *mexicana* (Dav.) Jepson.

2. **Fremontia californica** Torr. FREMONTIA. FLANNEL BUSH. Fig. 405.

KEY TO THE SPECIES AND VARIETY

Leaf-blades 1/4-inch to 1 1/4 inches long; flowers 1 to 1 1/2 inches broad. *F. californica.*

Leaf-blades 1/4- to 3/4-inch long; flowers 3/4-inch to 1 1/4 inches broad. 2a. var. *napensis.*

A loosely branched shrub or small tree, 6 to 15 feet high, with long tough branchlets and short flower-bearing spurs covered with a stiff hairy pubescence. Leaf-blades round-ovate to elliptic-ovate, 1/4-inch to 1 1/2 inches long, often larger on sterile shoots, dark green and roughish above, densely stellate-pubescent beneath, entire to 3-lobed; petioles 1/4-inch to 1 inch long. Flowers lemon-yellow, 1 to 1 1/2 inches broad, the large gland at base of sepals usually with hairs. Capsules subglobose, 5/8-inch to 1 inch long, densely bristly hairy. Seeds brown, dull. Flowering period, May and June.

Fremontia inhabits dry foothills which are usually supplied with some seepage, of the western slope of the Sierra Nevada from Kern County northward to Tehama County, and southward in the inner and middle Coast Ranges in scattered locations from Lake County to San Luis Obispo County. In southern California it occurs on slopes of dry canyons in the Tehachapi Mountains, on the desert slopes of the San Gabriel and San Bernardino mountains and occasionally on the southern slopes of these mountains, in the Topatopa Mountains and the eastern slope of Mount Piños of Ventura County, in the San Jacinto Mountains, and rarely in San Diego County. It is an exceedingly variable shrub in the amount of hairy pubescence on the leaves and branchlets and in size and shape of the leaves. Some specimens from Loma Prieta, Santa Clara County, from the hills above Big Basin Park, Santa Cruz County, and other localities have very thick leaves and dense stellate-tomentose pubescence on the branches, petioles, fruits, and lower leaf-surface. These have been described by Alice Eastwood as **Fremontia crassifolia.** Fig. 408.

2a. Var. **napensis** (Eastw.) n. comb. NAPA FREMONTIA. Fig. 406.

Leaf-blades thin, 1/4- to 3/4-inch long, mostly pinnately veined or the larger ones palmately veined. Flowers small, 3/4-inch to 1 1/4 inches broad, the sepals widely

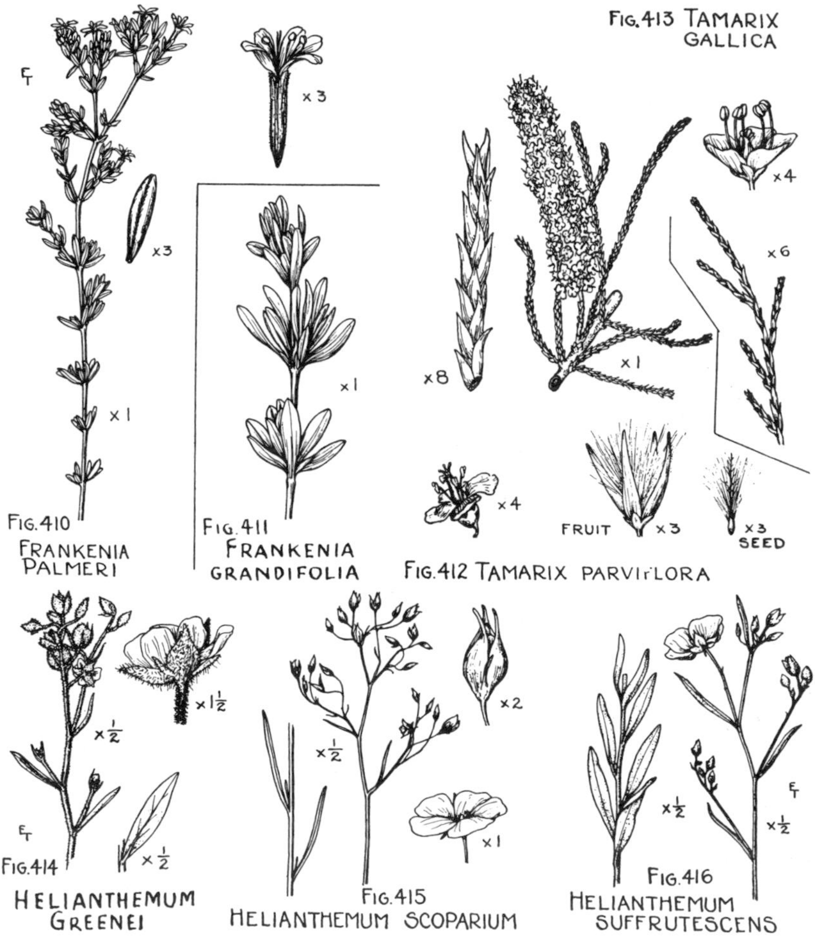

FIG. 410 FRANKENIA PALMERI
FIG. 411 FRANKENIA GRANDIFOLIA
FIG. 412 TAMARIX PARVIFLORA
FIG. 413 TAMARIX GALLICA
FIG. 414 HELIANTHEMUM GREENEI
FIG. 415 HELIANTHEMUM SCOPARIUM
FIG. 416 HELIANTHEMUM SUFFRUTESCENS

spreading forming a saucer-shaped calyx; gland hairy. Capsule subglobose to conical, ½- to ¾-inch long. Flowering period, May and June.

This variety occurs in a few localities in Napa County (near Knoxville; north side of Mt. St. Helena, *Mrs. Myron Hobson*).

Fremontia californica Torr. Pl. Frem. 6 (1850). Type locality: Mountains at the upper end of the Sacramento Valley. Collected by *Fremont*.

Var. napensis (Eastw.) McMinn. *F. napensis* Eastw. Type locality: Flowering specimen, Mt. St. Helena, Napa County. Collected by *Mrs. Myron Hobson*. Fruiting specimen, in the mountains of Napa County. Collected by *Cornelia S. Masters*.

Frankeniaceae. Frankenia Family

This family contains 4 genera and about 64 species of perennial herbs or subshrubs, widely distributed in temperate and subtropical regions.

1. **Frankenia** L. Frankenia

(Named for Johann Franke, professor at Upsala, the first author who treated of Swedish plants.)

Herbs or dwarf subshrubs. Leaves simple, opposite, usually with few to many additional ones clustered in their axils and thus appearing whorled, entire, nearly sessile. Flowers bisexual, regular; sepals 4 or 5, persistent, joined at base into a tube; petals 4 or 5, distinct, clawed, the claw with an appendage on the inner surface; stamens 4 to 7, exserted; pistil of 3 carpels united to form a 1-celled superior ovary. Fruit a linear 2- to 4-valved angled capsule.

This is a variable genus with 30 to 60 species of maritime plants, 2 of which occur in California.

KEY TO THE SPECIES

Leaves less than ¼-inch long, strongly revolute, nearly terete....... 1. *F. Palmeri.*
Leaves ¼- to nearly ½-inch long, narrowly oblanceolate to obovate. 2. *F. grandifolia.*

1. **Frankenia Palmeri** Wats. Palmer Frankenia. Fig. 410.

Palmer Frankenia occurs in California along the alkaline marshes in the vicinity of San Diego. It extends southward into Lower California and occurs on the islands in the Gulf of California (Tiburon Island, *I. M. Johnston*).

Frankenia Palmeri Wats. Proc. Am. Acad. 11:124 (1876). Type locality: "Lower California, on the Gulf side." Collected by *Palmer*.

2. **Frankenia grandifolia** C. & S. Alkali-heath. Fig. 411.

Alkali-heath inhabits salt marshes and sandy places along the seashore from Marin and Solano counties southward to San Diego County and Lower California, and on Anacapa, Santa Cruz, and Santa Catalina islands.

2a. Var. **campestris** Gray.

More tufted. Leaves narrowly spatulate to nearly linear, with revolute margins.

This variety occurs on alkaline flats away from the coast in the Great Valley, the South Coast Ranges, Inyo County *(S. B. Parish)*, and southern California.

Frankenia grandifolia C. & S., Linnaea 1:35 (1826). Type locality: San Francisco. Collected by *Chamisso*. First collected by *Haenke,* acc. Gray.

Var. campestris Gray, Syn. Fl. N. Am. 1:208 (1895). Type locality: "Plains near San Jacinto, southwestern California." Collected by *Parish*.

Tamaricaceae. Tamarisk Family

The Tamarisk Family consists of 5 genera and about 100 species of trees and shrubs of the northern hemisphere and Africa, mostly inhabitants of alkaline soils.

1. **Tamarix** L. Tamarisk

(From Tamaris, now Tambro, a river on the borders of the Pyrenees, in which region the Tamarisk abounds.)

This genus contains about 60 species native to Europe, Asia, and Africa. None is native to California but the following have escaped from plantings in some localities and may be mistaken for native plants.

KEY TO THE SPECIES

Racemes lateral on last year's branches; flowers with their parts in 4's. 1. *T. parviflora.*

Racemes in large terminal panicles; flowers with their parts in 5's. . . .2. *T. gallica.*

1. **Tamarix parviflora** DC. Smallflower Tamarisk. Fig. 412.

A deciduous shrub or small tree, 10 to 18 feet high, with numerous slender branches, gray- or red-brown bark, and green feathery branchlets.

This species has been planted in the warmer parts of California and it has escaped in a few localities (San Benito River bed, San Benito Co., Mission Valley, San Diego Co., etc.).

Tamarisk parviflora DC. Prodr. 3:97 (1828). Type locality: Southeastern Europe.

2. **Tamarix gallica** L. French Tamarisk. Fig. 413.

A densely branched bushy shrub or small tree, 5 to 20 feet high and often as broad, with numerous feathery branches. Flowering period, April to August.

French Tamarisk has been planted in many localities in California and has escaped from cultivation in several places. It serves as a windbreak in the hot interior valleys and on the Colorado Desert. The clusters of small pink flowers are on the plants for most of the year but more profusely from April to August.

Tamarix gallica L. Sp. Pl. 270 (1753). Type locality: "Gallia, Hispania, Italia."

Cistaceae. Rock-rose Family

The Rock-rose Family contains 7 genera and about 150 species of herbs and shrubs mostly native to the northern hemisphere. A single genus with 3 species is native to California.

1. **Helianthemum** Mill.

(From the Greek *helios,* sun, and *anthemum,* blossom, in reference to the flowers of some species opening only in sunshine.)

Leaves simple, alternate, deciduous, entire. Flowers bisexual, regular, yellow, opening but once; sepals 5, the 3 larger inside the 2 small or bract-like ones; petals 5, distinct, early deciduous; stamens numerous, distinct; ovary superior, 1-celled. Fruit a 3-valved capsule.

About 100 species belong to this genus. They are mostly found in the Mediterranean region but a few occur in North and South America. Three species and one variety occur in California.

KEY TO THE SPECIES

Inflorescences densely glandular-pubescent, corymbose or short-paniculate; Santa Cruz Island. . . . . .1. *H. Greenei.*

Inflorescences glabrous or stellate-pubescent, not glandular-pubescent, paniculate or racemose.

Leaves narrowly linear to linear-lanceolate, green, sparsely stellate-pubescent to glabrous, deciduous in summer. . . . . .2. *H. scoparium.*

Leaves linear-lanceolate to oblanceolate, densely stellate-pubescent, not deciduous in summer. . . . . .3. *H. suffrutescens.*

1. **Helianthemum Greenei** Rob. Island Rush-rose. Fig. 414.

A low tufted perennial, 6 to 12 inches high, often woody at base. Younger parts, except the inflorescence, densely white-woolly. Flowering period, March to May.

This species is known only from Santa Cruz and San Miguel islands off the coast of Santa Barbara County, California.

Helianthemum Greenei Rob.; Gray, Syn. Fl. N. Am. 1:191 (1895). *H. occidentale* Greene, not Nym. Type locality: Santa Cruz Island. Collected by *Greene*.

2. **Helianthemum scoparium** Nutt. RUSH-ROSE. Fig. 415.

KEY TO THE SPECIES AND VARIETY

Plants low and divaricate, with the ultimate twigs erect; inflorescences usually very leafy; flowers usually few............................*H. scoparium.*

Plants taller and rush-like; inflorescences sparsely leafy; flowers numerous. 2a. var. *Aldersonii.*

An herbaceous perennial, ½-foot to 1½ feet high, woody at base, with numerous erect or spreading tufted stems, green, slightly stellate-pubescent or glabrate. Flowering period, April to July.

This small somewhat woody perennial inhabits sandy flats, low hills, and ridges along the coast from Mendocino County southward to Santa Barbara County and on Santa Rosa and Santa Cruz islands.

2a. Var. **Aldersonii** (Greene) Munz.

Rush-like, 1 to 2½ feet high, with open branching and long inflorescences. Herbage sparsely stellate-pubescent or glabrous. Leaves deciduous in the summer, revolute. Petals from ¼- to ½-inch long. Calyx larger than in the species.

This variety is the common form on dry slopes and ridges in the chaparral belt of the Coast Ranges from Lake County southward to Santa Barbara County, in the Sierra Nevada from Mariposa County (near Baxter, *Nordstrom*) northward to Eldorado County, and in the cismontane region of southern California in Ventura, Los Angeles, Riverside, Orange, and San Diego counties, up to 5000 feet elevation.

Helianthemum scoparium Nutt.; T. & G. Fl. N. Am. 1:152 (1838). Type locality: Monterey, California. Collected by *Nuttall*.

Var. Aldersonii (Greene) Munz, Man. S. Calif. Bot. 316 (1935). *H. Aldersonii* Greene. Type locality: Mountains on the southern borders of San Diego County, California. Collected by *R. D. Alderson*. *H. scoparium* var. *vulgare* Jepson.

3. **Helianthemum suffrutescens** Schreiber. AMADOR RUSH-ROSE. Fig. 416.

An erect virgately branched shrub, 1 to 2½ feet high, with woody or herbaceous twigs covered with a stellate pubescence. Leaves linear-lanceolate to oblanceolate, ⅜-inch to 1¼ inches long, 1/16- to 5/16-inch wide, densely stellate-pubescent, shortly petioled or almost sessile. Flowers in leafy-bracteate panicles, the bracts ⅛-inch to 1 inch long, the lower foliaceous; sepals densely to lightly stellate-pubescent, hairs often tipped red, the 3 inner about 3/16-inch long, the 2 outer shorter; petals obovate, about ¼-inch long, erose at apex. Flowering period, April and May.

Amador Rush-rose is known only from Amador County, California in the Upper Sonoran Life Zone where it is associated with *Adenostoma fasciculatum, Lotus scoparius, Arctostaphylos manzanita* and other foothill species. The known localities are in the vicinity of Bisbee Peak *(Nordstrom)* and Michigan Bar *(Schreiber)*. Schreiber states that the seeds of this species are apparently fire resistant since it had reseeded itself on burned-over areas, whereas many species of other genera in the same vicinity had failed to do so.

Helianthemum suffrutescens Schreiber, Madroño 5:81 (1939). Type locality: On a dry slope 5.5 mi. w.sw. of Bisbee Peak, elevation 500 feet, Amador County, California. Collected by *Beryl Schreiber*.

Fig. 417. Ocotillo. *Fouquieria splendens* Engelm.
(Photograph on left by Hugh P. Dearing. On right by Lustin E. Martindale.)

Fouquieriaceae. Ocotillo Family

This is a small family of 2 genera and 8 species inhabiting the deserts of Mexico. One species extends into the southwestern United States.

1. **Fouquieria** H. B. K. Ocotillo

(Named for Professor P. E. Fouquier of Paris.)

Seven species have been described in this genus, one of which occurs in California.

1. **Fouquieria splendens** Engelm. Ocotillo. Fig. 417.

A spiny shrub, 6 to 20 feet high, with many slender branches from the base, leafless for most of the year. Leaves simple, of two kinds; the primary leaves alternate on the new shoots, the blades soon falling and their petioles developing into stout spines; the secondary leaves borne in the axils of the spines, the blades oblanceolate, 1/2-inch to 1 1/4 inches long, rounded or retuse at apex, fleshy, entire; petioles 1/8- to 1/4-inch long. Flowers bisexual, regular, showy, in terminal clusters; sepals 5, unequal, overlapping; corolla of 5 bright red petals, joined into a cylindrical tube 3/4-inch to 1 inch long, the lobes short and recurving; stamens 10 to 17, unequal, exserted. Ovary superior, incompletely 3-celled. Fruit a 3-valved capsule, about 3/4-inch long. Flowering period, in the summer after rains.

Ocotillo is a very striking and characteristic plant of the mesas of the Colorado Desert of California. It extends eastward in the desert areas of Arizona, New Mexico, and western Texas and southward in northern Mexico. The numerous cane-like stems are without leaves for most of the year, but after rains they are covered with bright green leaves, which, however, soon fall. The bright red flowers in terminal clusters are frequently photographed and are commonly seen on postal cards and paintings at desert stations along the highways and railways.

The stems are occasionally used on the desert for fences and for constructing huts, and also as walking sticks. The bark contains gums and wax. The Coahuila Indians of southern California used the fruiting capsules and flowers as a source of food.

Fouquieria splendens Engelm.; Wisliz. Mem. Tour. North. Mex. 98 (1848). Type locality: Jornade del Muerto, New Mexico. Collected by *Wislizenus*.

Loasaceae. Loasa Family

The Loasa Family consists of 13 genera and about 250 species of erect or climbing herbs or rarely shrubs and small trees, mostly native to South America, a few in western North America, and one in South Africa and Arabia.

Four genera and 20 species are native to California, 4 of which are somewhat shrubby at least at base.

KEY TO THE GENERA

Plants rough and pubescent but without stinging hairs; stamens 5. . 1. Petalonyx.
Plants with stinging hairs; stamens numerous. . . . . 2. Eucnide.

1. **Petalonyx** Gray

(From the Greek *petalon,* petal, and *onyx,* claw, in reference to the stalked, i.e. clawed, petal.)

FIG. 418
PETALONYX NITIDUS

FIG. 419
PETALONYX LINEARIS

FIG. 420
PETALONYX THURBERI

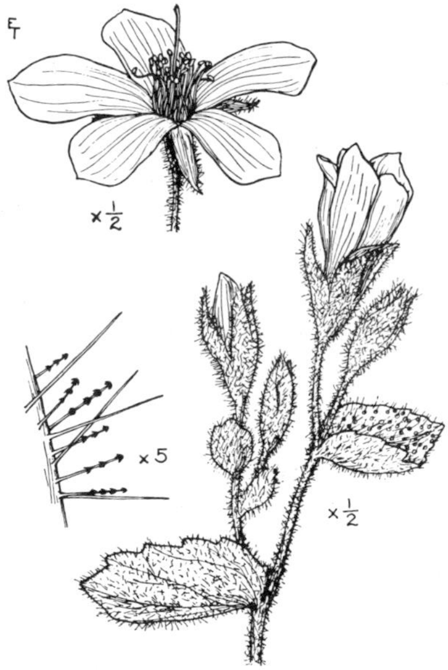

FIG. 421 EUCNIDE URENS

FIG. 422 DIRCA OCCIDENTALIS

Perennial herbs or low shrubs, with rough-pubescent herbage. Leaves simple, alternate, and evergreen. Flowers bisexual, regular, small, whitish or yellowish, in terminal heads or short spikes; sepals 5, united at base into a tube adnate to the ovary, the lobes linear, deciduous; petals 5, with long claws lightly joined and thus appearing as a 5-lobed tubular corolla; stamens 5, long-exserted; ovary inferior, 1-celled, with 1 ovule. Fruit a small oblong capsule, bursting irregularly.

This is a small genus of 5 species native to the southwestern United States and Mexico. Three species occur in California.

KEY TO THE SPECIES

Leaves distinctly petioled, irregularly toothed, broadly ovate, 3/8-inch to 1 inch wide..1. *P. nitidus.*

Leaves sessile or nearly so, 1/2-inch or less wide.

- Leaves all entire, narrowly elliptical to linear-oblong, about 1/4-inch wide, shining ....2. *P. linearis.*
- Leaves mostly entire but some toothed near the base, triangular-ovate or lance- to linear-ovate, usually attached by a broad base, dull.....3. *P. Thurberi.*

1. **Petalonyx nitidus** Wats. SMOOTH SANDPAPER PLANT. Fig. 418.

A low broad subshrub, 6 to 18 inches high, with pale gray branches. Leaf-blades broadly ovate to ovate-lanceolate, 3/4-inch to 1 1/4 inches long, 3/8-inch to 1 inch wide, scabrulose but shining, coarsely and irregularly toothed; petioles 1/6- to 1/4-inch long. Flowers yellowish, about 3/8-inch long, in dense paniculate clusters terminating the branches. Flowering period, May to August.

Smooth Sandpaper Plant occurs in a few localities in the desert mountains of Inyo County and adjacent San Bernardino County, at elevations between 3500 and 6500 feet. (INYO COUNTY: Silver Canyon, near Laws, very abundant, *K. Brandegee;* n.e. of Independence, *Mark Kerr;* Black Canyon, White Mountains, not uncommon, *V. Duran;* Surprise Canyon, Panamint Mountains, *Roxana Ferris;* Argus Mountains, *A. A. Purpus.* SAN BERNARDINO COUNTY: Cushenberry Springs and northern slopes of the San Bernardino Mountains, *S. B. Parish;* Arrastre Creek, Horsethief Flats, *F. R. Fosberg.*) It extends eastward to Nevada, Arizona, and southern Utah.

Petalonyx nitidus Wats. Am. Nat. 7:300 (1873). Type locality: Southern Nevada. Collected by *Wheeler.*

2. **Petalonyx linearis** Greene. NARROWLEAF SANDPAPER PLANT. Fig. 419.

An erect bushy shrub, 1 to 2 feet high, with numerous rough branches and scabrous herbage. Leaf-blades linear to linear-oblong, 1/2-inch to 1 inch long, 1/4-inch or less wide, greenish, entire, rounded at base, sessile. Flowers whitish, about 3/16-inch long, in dense head-like spikes 2 to 4 inches long; floral bracts orbicular-ovate, entire or crenate-toothed at the subcordate base. Flowering period, March and April.

Narrowleaf Sandpaper Plant occurs in canyons below 3000 feet in the Colorado Desert of Riverside and Imperial counties (Deep Canyon, east of Palm Springs, *F. W. Pierson;* Rockhouse Canyon, Santa Rosa Mountains, *E. C. Jaeger;* Painted Canyon, Mecca, *P. A. Munz & D. Keck;* Thousand Palms Canyon, *E. C. Jaeger;* Laguna Dam). It extends southward to Lower California and eastward to Arizona.

It has also been collected on Tortuga Island *(I. M. Johnston),* San Benito Island *(Anthony),* and on Cedros Island *(Greene).*

Petalonyx linearis Greene, Bull. Calif. Acad. 1:188 (1885). Type locality: Cedros Island. Collected by *Greene.*

3. **Petalonyx Thurberi** Gray. SANDPAPER PLANT. Fig. 420.

A perennial bush more or less shrubby at base, 1 to 3 feet high, 2 to 5 feet broad, with rough-pubescent branches and grayish foliage. Leaf-blades triangular-ovate or lance- to linear-ovate, ¼-inch to 1 inch long, thick, entire or few-toothed near the broad sessile base. Flowers white or yellowish, ⅛- to 3/16-inch long, in dense spike-like heads terminating the branchlets; floral bracts greenish, ovate, acuminate, toothed at base, about ¼-inch long. Flowering period, May to July.

Sandpaper Plant is a rather common bush on desert plains and dry sandy canyons of southern Indio County and on the Mohave and Colorado deserts below 4000 feet elevation. It extends eastward to southern Nevada and western Arizona and southward to Lower California.

Petalonyx Thurberi Gray, Mem. Am. Acad. n. ser. 2, 5:319 (1855). Type locality: Gila River Valley, Arizona. Collected by *Thurber.*

2. **Eucnide** Zucc.

(From the Greek *eu,* true, and *cnide,* seanettle.)

This is a small genus of 8 species native to Mexico and the southwestern United States.

1. **Eucnide urens** (Gray) Parry. ROCK NETTLE. Fig. 421.

A low bushy plant, 1 to 2 feet high, woody at the base, with stinging hairs and barbed pubescence, sometimes procumbent and 2 to 5 feet long; stems straw-colored. Flowers yellow, bisexual, mostly in terminal clusters. Fruit an obovoid capsule, ½-inch long, opening by 5 valves at summit. Flowering period, May to July.

Rock Nettle inhabits rocky places between 2000 and 4000 feet elevation in the desert ranges of the Death Valley region of Inyo County and adjacent San Bernardino County (Lone Willow Canyon, *S. B. Parish*). It extends eastward to Nevada, Arizona, and Utah and southward to Lower California.

Eucnide urens (Gray) Parry, Am. Nat. 9:144 (1875). *Mentzelia urens* Gray. Type locality: Western Arizona, along the Colorado River. Collected by *Bigelow.*

Thymelaeaceae. Leatherwood Family

The Leatherwood Family contains about 37 genera and 425 species, widely distributed over the earth, most abundant in Australia and South Africa. A single genus, with one species, is native to California.

1. **Dirca** L. LEATHERWOOD

(Named for a celebrated fountain in Thebes.)

1. **Dirca occidentalis** Gray. WESTERN LEATHERWOOD. Fig. 422.

An erect shrub, 2 to 6 feet high, with very pliable wood and leathery bark. Leaves simple, alternate, deciduous; the blades oval or obovate, rounded at apex and base, 1 to 2½ inches long, ½-inch to 1 inch wide, glabrous and light green above, slightly pubescent and lighter beneath, entire; petioles about ⅛-inch long. Flowers lemon-yellow, regular, bisexual, in clusters of 2 or 3, from lateral and terminal buds, deflexed, appearing before and with the first leaves, protected in

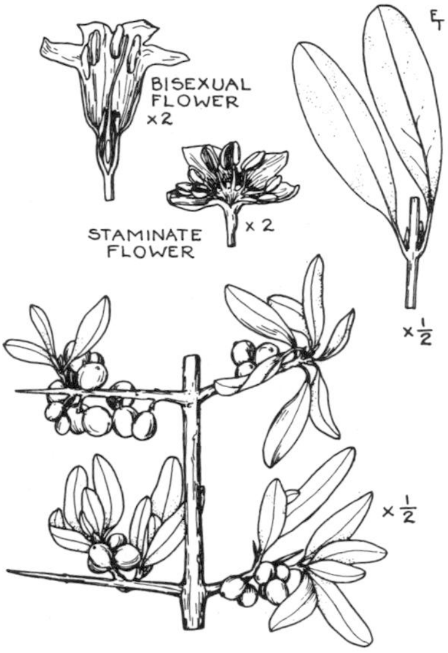

FIG. 423 SHEPHERDIA ARGENTEA. FIG. 424 Z. CALIFORNICA. FIG. 425 Z. LATIFOLIA. FIG. 426 Z. CANA. ZAUSCHNERIA

the bud by yellowish silky bud-scales which soon fall; sepals 4, united at base, corolla-like, about ⅓-inch long; petals none; stamens 8 (or 9 or 10), inserted upon the calyx-tube and longer than its lobes; ovary superior, 1-celled, nearly sessile; style filiform, exserted; stigma capitate. Fruit a red drupe-like berry, about ½-inch long. Flowering period, January to March.

Western Leatherwood is a rare shrub inhabiting wet slopes of rocky hills in the counties around San Francisco Bay, in the Transition Life Zone. Specimens have been collected from the Oakland, Berkeley, Stanford, San Leandro, and Marin County hills, also from the Santa Cruz Mountains in San Mateo County.

The yellow flowers appearing before the leaves make it a very attractive plant. A branch with buds placed in water will develop flowers and leaves which keep for many days. Because of the S-shaped arrangement of the lignified tissue in the fibrovascular bundles, the stems are so pliable that they can be tied into knots. The fruit is rarely found in this species.

Dirca occidentalis Gray, Proc. Am. Acad. 8:631 (1873). Type locality: Oakland Hills, Alameda County, California. Collected by *Bigelow*.

Elaeagnaceae. Oleaster Family

A family of 3 genera and about 30 species of shrubs and trees, chiefly native to southern Asia, Europe, and North America.

1. **Shepherdia** Nutt.

(Named for John Shepherd, an English botanist.)

This genus contains 3 species of which only the following is native to California.

1. **Shepherdia argentea** Nutt. SILVER BUFFALOBERRY. Fig. 423.

An erect spiny shrub or small tree, 4 to 20 feet high, with shaggy gray bark and brown or silvery-scurfy twigs and branchlets which terminate in stout thorns. Leaves simple, opposite, or some alternate, deciduous; the blades oblong-lanceolate or cuneate-oblong, 3/4-inch to 1 3/4 (or rarely 3) inches long, 1/4- to 5/8-inch (rarely 1 inch) wide, silvery-scurfy on both surfaces, paler beneath, entire; petioles 1/8- to 1/2-inch long. Flowers dioecious, apetalous, nearly sessile, in clusters at the nodes of the twigs or the pistillate sometimes solitary. Staminate flowers with 4 sepals joined at base; stamens 8, distinct, alternating with the processes of the thick disk. Pistillate flowers with 4 sepals, joined at base with the receptacle to form an urn-shaped receptocalyx which is adnate to the base of the superior 1-celled ovaries; and often with abortive stamens. Fruit drupe-like, consisting of a fleshy receptocalyx enclosing an achene or nut, ovoid, 1/4-inch or less long, red, sour, edible. Flowering period, April and May.

Silver Buffaloberry occurs along streams in a few localities in California. It has been collected in the Mount Piños region of Ventura and Kern counties, and in Mono, Alpine, Santa Barbara, San Bernardino (Mohave River bed, Rancho Verche, *F. R. Fosberg*) counties. It extends north to Oregon and east to the Rocky Mountains. Sometimes it is planted as an ornamental shrub.

Shepherdia argentea (Pursh) Nutt. Gen. Pl. 2:240 (1818). *Hippophae argentea* Pursh. Type locality: On the banks of the Missouri River. Collected by *Lewis*.

Onagraceae. Evening-Primrose Family

This family consists of about 30 genera and 470 species of mostly herbs, rarely shrubs, native chiefly to the temperate parts of the New World. Eleven genera occur in California, one of which occasionally has woody forms.

1. **Zauschneria** Presl. BALSAMEA. CALIFORNIA-FUCHSIA

(Named in honor of M. Zauschner, professor at Prague.)

Erect or decumbent perennials with scarlet fuchsia-like flowers 1 to 1 1/2 inches long. Flowering period, June to September.

This genus is represented in California by 3 species with numerous variable forms. They are usually perennial herbs but occasionally are somewhat woody at the base. These forms occur on dry slopes, rocky hillsides, cliffs, and in fields in the Coast Ranges, the mountains of southern California, the Sierra Nevada, and on the Santa Barbara Islands. Some forms extend northward into Oregon, eastward to Nevada, and southward into Lower California.

KEY TO THE SPECIES

Leaves linear to lanceolate, 1/2-inch to 1 1/2 inches long, usually less than 1/4-inch wide, entire or slightly denticulate, the lateral veins usually not evident.

- Herbage greenish pubescent or white-tomentose in the variety *villosa*, often glandular; leaves nearly 1/8- to 1/4-inch wide; petals longer than the calyx-lobes .... 1. *Z. californica*. Fig. 424.
- Herbage tomentose-canescent, not glandular; leaves about 1/16-inch wide, nearly filiform, densely fascicled in the axils; petals shorter than the calyx-lobes. 2. *Z. cana*. Fig. 426.

Leaves ovate to ovate-lanceolate or elliptical, 3/4-inch to 1 3/4 inches long, 1/3- to 5/8-inch wide, denticulate, the lateral veins evident; herbage green or white-villous, somewhat glandular to extremely viscid above. . 3. *Z. latifolia*. Fig. 425.

Garryaceae. Silktassel Family

This family consists of a single genus which is limited in its distribution to the western United States, Mexico, and the West Indies.

1. **Garrya** Dougl. SILKTASSEL. GARRYA

(Named for Nicholas Garry, secretary of the Hudson Bay Company and friend of David Douglas, an early botanical explorer of Pacific North America.)

Shrubs or small trees. Leaves simple, opposite, evergreen, usually thick and leathery, 1-veined from the base. Flowers small, apetalous, dioecious, borne in catkin-like clusters. Staminate flowers pedicelled, borne in groups of 6 to 10 in the axes of the opposite joined greenish cup-like bracts of the pendulous catkins; sepals 4; stamens 4; pistil rudimentary. Pistillate flowers sessile or nearly so, borne in pairs in the axes of the opposite joined bracts of the recurving catkins; sepals 2 or almost obsolete; stamens none; ovary inferior, 1-celled; styles 2, persistent. Fruit a berry, often drupe-like, at first fleshy, later the outer part becoming dry and separating from the dark juicy pulp which surrounds the 2, 3, or 4 horny seeds.

The genus *Garrya* contains about 15 species, 6 of which are native to the Pacific Coast states. The garryas, because of their thick leathery leaves, belong to that type of vegetation known as broad sclerophyll (hard-leaf), and are components of the chaparral or conifer forest chaparral associations. The bark, leaves, and fruits contain an alkaloid, garryine, which is used as a tonic. The bitter nature of this alkaloid has caused the name "quinine bush" to be applied to some of the species. Most of the species are worthy of cultivation for their evergreen foliage and showy pendulous flower-clusters. They can be propagated by seeds or by cuttings and layers. In propagating from seeds, it is advisable to treat the seeds with lye for 24 hours, then wash in running water. The seeds should then be planted in flats which should be kept moist in a cool lath-house or, if possible, at a temperature of about 45 degrees for three months, after which the flats should be removed to a higher temperature. A good germination should result from such treatment. *Garrya elliptica, G. Fremontii,* and *G. Veatchii* can be purchased in some of the California nurseries.

KEY TO THE SPECIES

Lower surface of leaves glabrous or sparingly pilose; leaves plane; fruit glabrous or pubescent when young. . . . . 1. *G. Fremontii.*

Lower surface of leaves covered with hairs (sometimes nearly glabrous in *G. flavescens* var. *pallida*).

- Lower surface of leaves more or less silky-pubescent with straight or wavy upwardly appressed hairs.
  - Leaf-margins usually plane.
    - Leaves bright green or yellowish to olive-green above; fruit glabrate; northern California . . . . 2. *G. buxifolia.*
    - Leaves yellowish gray or gray-green above; fruit densely appressed-pubescent; mostly southern California. . . . . 3. *G. flavescens* var. *pallida.*

Fig. 427. Fremont Silktassel. *Garrya Fremontii* Torr. Branchlet with pistillate flowers.

Leaf-margins more or less undulate; fruit densely pubescent; northern California .... 4. *G. Congdonii.*

Lower surface of leaves usually densely covered with curled or wavy hairs forming a woolly mat; fruit densely pubescent.

1. Leaf-margins usually strongly undulate; leaves widely elliptical to oval; upper leaf-surface usually dark green; along the coast, mostly northern California .... 5. *G. elliptica.*
2. Leaf-margins varying from slightly to strongly undulate; upper surface of leaves yellowish green; in the foothills of the interior Coast Ranges and of the Sierra Nevada, northern and central California...4. *G. Congdonii.*
3. Leaf-margins plane or rarely slightly undulate; leaves usually narrowly elliptical or ovate to lanceolate; mostly southern California. 6. *G. Veatchii.*

1. **Garrya Fremontii** Torr. Fremont Silktassel. Bear Brush. Figs. 427, 429.

An erect shrub, 4 to 10 feet high, usually yellowish green in appearance. Leaf-blades oblong-elliptical or oblong-ovate, 3/4-inch to 2 1/2 inches long, 1/2-inch to 1 1/2 inches wide, glabrous and shining above, usually yellowish green in age, paler and glabrous or sparingly pilose beneath, the margins plane and entire; petioles 1/4- to 1/2-inch long; young foliage often grayish pubescent with upwardly appressed hairs. Staminate catkins 3 to 8 inches long, yellowish, 2 to 5 in a cluster; pistillate catkins 1 1/2 to 2 inches long, or to 3 1/2 inches in fruit. Fruit about 1/4-inch in diameter, buff to purple or black, glabrous or rarely slightly pubescent. Flowering period, January to April.

Fremont Silktassel occurs in the chaparral or associated with the conifer forest from 2000 to 7500 feet elevation, in the Upper Sonoran and Transition Life Zones. It extends from the Cascades of Klickitat County, Washington southward in the Cascades of Oregon to the Siskiyou Mountains, the Sierra Nevada, the middle and inner Coast Ranges to Monterey County, California, and in the San Jacinto Mountains of Riverside County and the Laguna and Palomar mountains of San Diego County. In several localities (Cedar Mountain, Alameda County; Santa Lucia Mountains, Monterey County; Mt. Hamilton, Santa Clara County; Laguna and Palomar mountains, San Diego County) material of this species is somewhat pubescent on the lower leaf-surfaces and fruit, thus approaching *G. flavescens* var. *pallida*. Some specimens from Loma Prieta, Santa Clara County and Mount Tamalpais, Marin County have more or less undulate leaf-margins and few straight appressed hairs on the lower leaf-surfaces, thus showing relationship to *G. Congdonii*.

Fremont Silktassel is the most desirable of all the garryas for evergreen shrubberies because of its abundant glossy foliage, long pendulous staminate flower-clusters, and relative freedom from scale and other plant pests.

Garrya Fremontii Torr. Pacif. R. Rep. 4:136 (1857). Type locality: "On a small headwater of Cow Creek, Shasta County, California." Collected by *Fremont*.

2. **Garrya buxifolia** Gray. Boxleaf Silktassel. Fig. 430.

A low shrub, 2 to 5 (rarely to 10) feet high. Leaf-blades elliptic-ovate, 1/2-inch to 1 3/4 inches long, 1/2-inch to 1 inch wide, more or less acute at either end, glabrous above, silky-pubescent beneath with straight or slightly wavy upwardly appressed hairs, the margins plane and entire; petioles 1/8- to 1/4-inch long. Fruit glabrous, blue-black, about 3/16-inch in diameter. Flowering period, February to April.

Fig. 428. Coast Silktassel. *Garrya elliptica* Dougl. Branchlet with staminate flowers. Lower left, pistillate flowers.

Boxleaf Silktassel occurs on open mountain slopes and summits in the Humid Transition Life Zone from Red Mountain, Mendocino County northward in Humboldt, Siskiyou, and Del Norte counties to southwestern Oregon in Jackson, Josephine, and eastern Curry counties. Some specimens with little pubescence on the lower leaf-surfaces are very difficult to distinguish from *G. Fremontii,* a closely related species.

Garrya buxifolia Gray, Proc. Am. Acad. 7:349 (1867). Type locality: "on the Red Mountains, Mendocino County, California." Collected by *Bolander. G. flavescens* var. *buxifolia* Jepson.

3. **Garrya flavescens** var. **pallida** (Eastw.) Bacigalupi ex Ewan. PALE SILKTASSEL. Fig. 431.

An erect bushy shrub, 5 to 12 feet high, with grayish appearance. Leaf-blades ovate to elliptic-oblong, 1½ to 3 inches long, ¾-inch to 1¼ inches wide, gray-glaucous above, often with scattered appressed hairs, silky-pubescent beneath with straight or slightly wavy upwardly appressed hairs, the margins usually plane, entire; petioles ⅛- to ¼- (rarely ½-) inch long. Fruit ovoid, about ¼-inch long, densely pubescent or rarely glabrate. Flowering period, February to April.

Pale Silktassel inhabits the dry and semi-arid slopes of the foothills and mountains from 3000 to 7000 feet elevation in the Upper Sonoran and Arid Transition Life Zones. It occurs from San Diego County northward in Riverside, Orange, San Bernardino, Los Angeles, Ventura, Kern, Santa Barbara, Monterey, San Benito, Santa Clara, and Alameda (Cedar Mountain Ridge) counties, and in the Sierra Nevada in Tulare and Fresno counties. It occurs also in the Granite, Clark, and Providence mountains of San Bernardino County.

Pale Silktassel is very closely related to *G. Fremontii* and might well be considered a variety of that species. Some specimens on the Laguna and Palomar mountains of San Diego County and in the Mount Hamilton Range having a reduced amount of pubescence on the leaves and fruits are too close to *G. Fremontii* to separate with certainty. In general aspect, the foliage of *G. Fremontii* is yellowish green while that of *G. flavescens* var. *pallida* is glaucous-gray.

Garrya flavescens var. pallida (Eastw.) Bacigalupi ex Ewan, Bull. Torr. Club 64:519 (1937). *G. pallida* Eastw. Type locality: Kings River Canyon. Collected by *Eastwood.*

4. **Garrya Congdonii** Eastw. INTERIOR SILKTASSEL. Fig. 432.

An erect shrub, 3 to 6 feet high, with yellowish green aspect. Leaf-blades narrowly elliptic to oval, 1 to 1¾ inches long, ½-inch to 1½ inches wide, glabrous above, densely hairy beneath usually with long ascending and merely wavy hairs or sometimes with curly matted hairs, the margins more or less undulate, entire. Fruit densely pubescent or becoming glabrous in age. Flowering period, February to April.

Interior Silktassel inhabits the innermost South Coast Ranges, the inner North Coast Ranges from Napa County northward to Tehama County, and southward in scattered locations in the Sierra Nevada foothills to Mariposa County, in the Upper Sonoran and Arid Transition Life Zones. Its position taxonomically is difficult to determine because of the instability of the typical undulate leaf-margins and the hair characteristics on the lower leaf-surfaces. Some specimens in Tehama County with nearly plane leaves resemble specimens of *G. buxifolia* except for the glabrous fruit of that species. Other specimens with almost plane leaves and

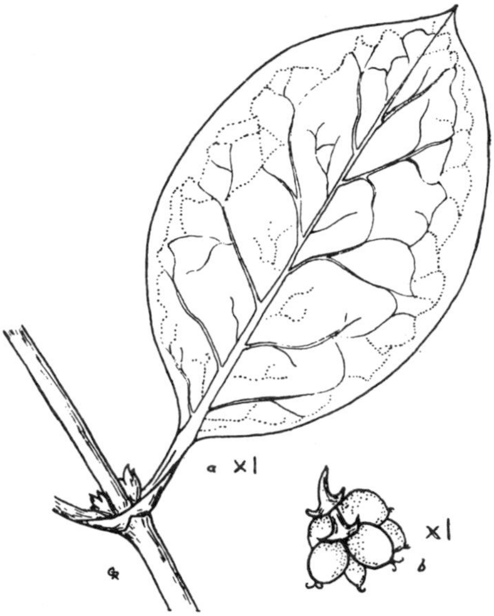

FIG. 429 G. FREMONTII

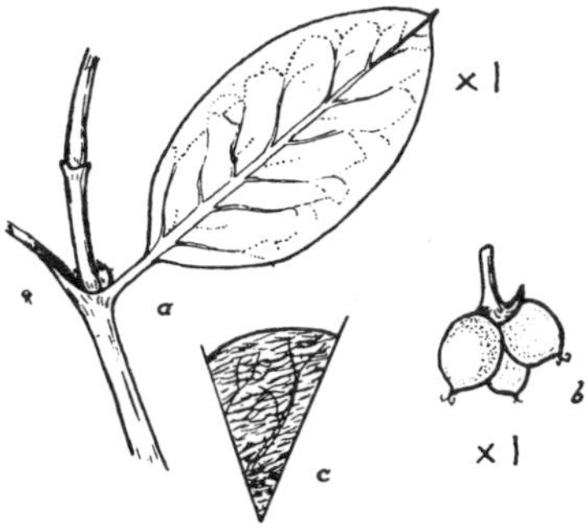

FIG. 430 G. BUXIFOLIA

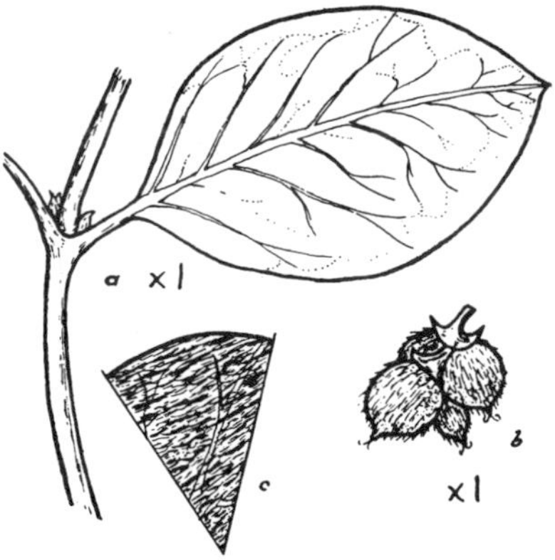

FIG. 431 G. FLAVESCENS

FIG. 432 G. CONGDONII

GARRYA. a, Leaf. b, Fruit. c, Pubescence on lower surface of leaf.

nearly straight appressed hairs on the lower leaf-surfaces are very close to *G. flavescens*. A few specimens from Sweetwater, Eldorado County have almost plane leaves, dark green above, covered beneath with a mat of curly wavy hairs and thus they resemble the leaves of *G. Veatchii*. To make the relationship seem nearly complete with all the Californian species of *Garrya,* some specimens from Napa and Lake counties are very close to *G. elliptica*. Some authors consider these specimens as the interior form of that species. Since this series of forms occupies a

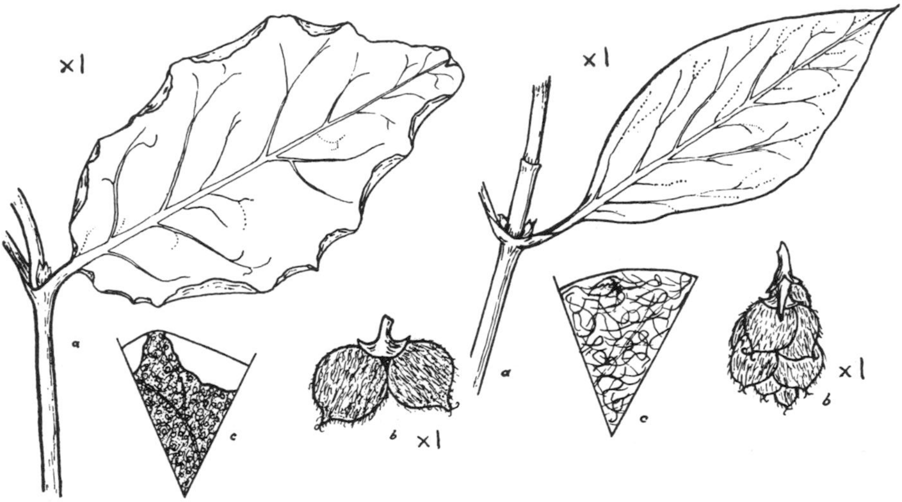

FIG. 433 G. ELLIPTICA FIG. 434 G. VEATCHII

GARRYA. a, Leaf. b, Fruit. c, Pubescence on lower surface of leaf.

rather definite geographical area it has seemed best to retain these as distinct under *G. Congdonii*.

Garrya Congdonii Eastw. Bot. Gaz. 36:459 (1903). Type locality: Near Coulterville, Mariposa County, California. Collected by *J. W. Congdon*. *G. flavescens* var. *venosa* Jepson.

5. **Garrya elliptica** Dougl. COAST SILKTASSEL. Figs. 428, 433.

An erect bushy shrub, 4 to 8 feet high, or rarely a small tree, 20 to 30 feet high. Leaf-blades elliptical or oval, 1½ to 2½ inches long, 1 to 1½ inches wide, dark green and nearly glabrous above, woolly or densely tomentose beneath with short curly or wavy hairs, the margins strongly undulate (rarely some almost plane), entire; petioles ¼- to ½-inch long. Catkins solitary or in clusters of 2 to 10; the staminate 3 to 8 inches long, pendulous, mostly from near the ends of the branches; the pistillate 2 to 3½ inches long, becoming as much as 6 inches long in fruit. Fruit globular, ½- to ⅜-inch in diameter, densely white-tomentose, becoming almost glabrous in age, the pulp very juicy when ripe, giving a purple stain when bruised. Flowering period, December to February.

Coast Silktassel inhabits the climax chaparral slopes and open spaces of the broad sclerophyll forest formation in the outer Coast Ranges from Lincoln County,

Oregon, southward to San Luis Obispo County and probably to Ventura and Los Angeles (Santa Monica Mountains) counties, California. It is nowhere abundant and usually occurs in small groups or as isolated shrubs in the Transition and Upper Sonoran Life Zones. Specimens collected in Trinity and western Tehama and Glenn counties, although having many characteristics of this species, are better referred to *G. Congdonii.*

Coast Silktassel has been brought into cultivation in many gardens and parks along the coast in central and northern California. It thrives best in well-drained soils of open sunny or semi-shady places. The long pendulous greenish yellow catkins of staminate flowers open from December to February. The fruit matures from June to September but may remain on the bushes until the following year. Goats and sheep are reported to browse upon the foliage to some extent.

Garrya elliptica Dougl.; Lindl. Bot. Reg. 7:1686 (1835). Type locality: Along the Umpqua River in Oregon about 20 miles from the ocean. Collected by *Douglas.*

6. **Garrya Veatchii** Kell. VEATCH SILKTASSEL. Fig. 434.

An erect shrub, 4 to 7 feet high. Leaf-blades narrowly elliptical, ovate to lanceolate or oval, usually short- to long-acuminate, 1 to 2½ inches long, ¾-inch to 1½ inches wide, dark green and glabrous above, densely covered beneath with curly or wavy hairs forming a felty mass, the margins plane or slightly undulate, entire; petioles ¼- to ¾-inch long. Catkins usually 2 to 4 in a cluster, rarely branched; the staminate 2 to 4 inches long; the pistillate 1½ to 3 inches long. Fruit ovoid to globose, about ¼-inch in diameter, densely pubescent. Flowering period, February and March.

Veatch Silktassel occurs chiefly on the dry chaparral slopes of the mountains of southern California, in the Upper Sonoran Life Zone, from San Diego County northward in the San Jacinto, San Bernardino (Cajon Pass), and San Gabriel mountains to Ventura and Santa Barbara counties. Specimens from La Cumbre Peak and Painted Cave regions of Santa Barbara County often have more undulate leaves than normal for the species and in this respect resemble specimens of *G. elliptica.* It occurs also on Cedros Island and in Lower California.

This species has been in the nursery trade of southern California for several years. It thrives along the coast from San Diego to Berkeley, California.

Garrya Veatchii Kell. Proc. Calif. Acad. 5:40 (1873). Type locality: Cedros Island. Collected by *Veatch. G. Veatchii* var. *Palmeri* Eastw. *G. flavescens* var. *Palmeri* Wats.

Cornaceae. Dogwood Family

This family contains about 10 genera and 100 species, mostly shrubs and trees, widely distributed but most abundant in the temperate regions of the northern hemisphere. A single genus is native to California.

1. **Cornus** L. DOGWOOD

(From the Latin *cornu,* a horn, referring to the hardness of the wood.)

Shrubs, trees, or rarely herbs. Leaves simple, usually opposite, deciduous or evergreen. Flowers small, bisexual, regular, in heads or open clusters; sepals 4, joined at base with the receptacle forming a bell-shaped receptocalyx, the free portion remaining as 4 small teeth or absent; petals 4, white or yellowish, distinct, inserted upon the receptocalyx; stamens 4, alternate with the petals; ovary inferior,

2-celled, with 1 ovule in each cell. Fruit an ovoid or globular drupe, the stone 2-celled and 2-seeded.

The genus *Cornus* contains from 25 to 50 species, native to the north temperate zone and one to Peru. Five species are native to California; 3 are shrubs, one a tree, and one an herb.

KEY TO THE SPECIES

Flowers in sessile umbels, appearing with or before the leaves; leaf-blades thin. 1. *C. sessilis.*

Flowers in compound stalked clusters, appearing after the leaves.

Leaf-blades lighter and puberulent or pubescent beneath, the veins prominent; branchlets purplish or deep red.

Leaf-blades beneath with straight short 2-branched (rarely single) usually appressed hairs....................................2. *C. stolonifera.*

Leaf-blades beneath with long curly or bent hairs, some single and some 2-branched, a few short, straight, and 2-branched. 2a. *C. stolonifera* var. *californica.*

Leaf-blades nearly alike on both sides, the veins not prominent; branchlets gray or yellowish brown, rarely reddish.......................3. *C. glabrata.*

1. **Cornus sessilis** Torr. Blackfruit Dogwood. Fig. 435.

A spreading shrub, 5 to 10 (20) feet high, with green bark. Leaves deciduous; the blades ovate or broadly elliptical, 1¾ to 4 inches long, ¾-inch to 1¾ (2¼) inches wide, short-acuminate, thin, with 3 to 5 pairs of prominent upward-curving nearly parallel lateral veins, some reaching almost to the apex, light green and glabrous above, pale and with scattered appressed pubescence beneath, entire; petioles ¼- to ½-inch long. Flowers yellowish, few to several in sessile umbels, appearing with or before the leaves, subtended by 4 small early-falling bracts; pedicels about ¼-inch long, densely hairy. Mature fruit ovoid or ellipsoidal, about ⅝-inch long, shiny, black; pedicels in fruit about ¾-inch long. Flowering period, April to June.

Fig.435 Cornus sessilis

Blackfruit Dogwood occurs in moist ravines of the foothills of the mountains in northern California from 1800 (rarely 500) to 4000 feet elevation in the Transition Life Zone. Its range extends from Amador County (Carpenter's Gulch near Barton's Flat) northward in the Sierra Nevada through Eldorado, Placer, Butte, eastern Tehama, and Shasta counties, thence westward into Trinity and Humboldt counties.

The fruit in maturing passes through an interesting set of color changes, at first greenish white, followed by yellow, then red, and finally when mature a shiny black.

Cornus sessilis Torr.; Dur. Jour. Phil. Acad. ser. 2, 3:89 (1855). Type locality: Deer Creek, near Nevada City, California. Collected by *Pratten*.

2. **Cornus stolonifera** Michx. American Dogwood. American Dog-berry. Figs. 436-A, -B, -C.

An erect but spreading shrub, 6 to 15 feet high, with smooth reddish or purplish branches. Leaves deciduous; the blades oval to elliptical, acute at apex, rounded

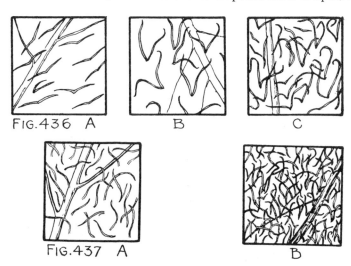

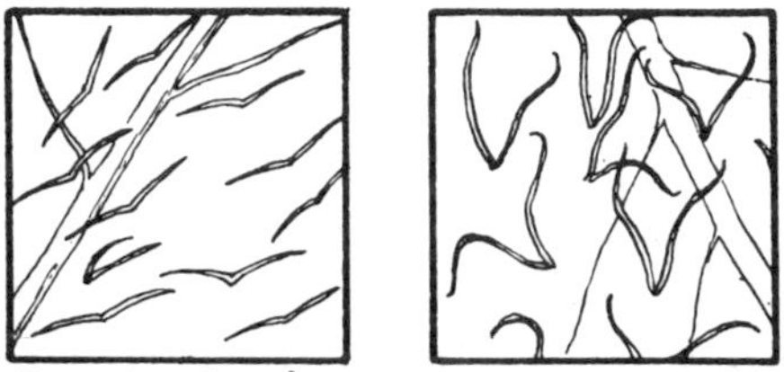

FIG.436 A B C

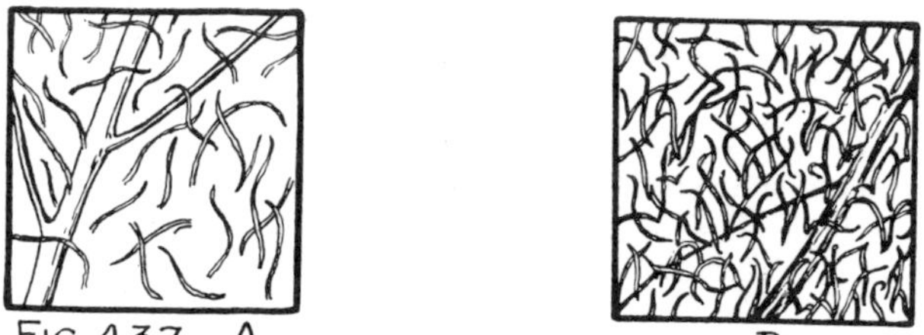

FIG.437 A B

Cornus. Fig. 436. Cornus stolonifera. A, Straight, 2-branched hairs on leaf. Eldorado County. B, Bent, 2-branched hairs on leaf. Siskiyou County. C, Straight and bent, 2-branched hairs on leaf. Del Norte County. Fig. 437. Cornus stolonifera var. californica. A, Curled, single hairs on leaf. San Luis Obispo County. B, Short, bent, 2-branched and single hairs on leaf. San Bernardino County.

at base, $1\frac{1}{2}$ to $3\frac{1}{2}$ inches long, $\frac{3}{4}$-inch to 2 (rarely 3) inches wide, the lateral veins prominent and curving upward, apparently glabrous but microscopically puberulent above, paler beneath with few to numerous straight usually appressed 2-branched hairs, petioles $\frac{1}{4}$- to $\frac{3}{8}$-inch long. Flowers small, numerous, in branched round-topped clusters (cymes) about 2 inches across; peduncle and branches of the cyme sparsely or rarely densely pubescent; petals $\frac{1}{8}$-inch or less long. Fruit almost spherical, about $\frac{1}{4}$-inch in diameter, white or blue, smooth; the stone somewhat compressed, furrowed on the edges. Flowering period, April to November.

American Dogwood inhabits canyons and mountain slopes in the Transition and Canadian Life Zones, from Humboldt County (Trinity Summit) eastward to the Warner Mountains of Modoc County, southward in the Sierra Nevada, usually above 5000 feet altitude, to Tulare County (Giant Forest), and occasionally in the San Bernardino Mountains of southern California (Pine Knot P. O., Bear Lake, el. 6700 ft., *L. Wheeler*). Along the west fork of the Carson River near Woodfords and along the Silver King Fork of the Carson River in Alpine County, specimens occur with leaves having a mixture of long curled and short 2-branched hairs. This species extends northward to Alaska and eastward to the Rocky Mountains and to Nova Scotia and Virginia.

2a. Var. **californica** (C. A. Mey.) n. comb. CREEK DOGWOOD. Figs. 437-A, -B, 439.

Leaf-blades beneath usually with numerous long, bent, curled, or straight hairs, some single and some 2-branched from the base (sometimes with a few short straight 2-branched appressed hairs). Inflorescence commonly sparsely pubescent or rarely densely shaggy-pubescent.

Creek Dogwood inhabits stream banks and moist flats from near sea level to 6000 feet altitude in the mountains of northern California, southward in the

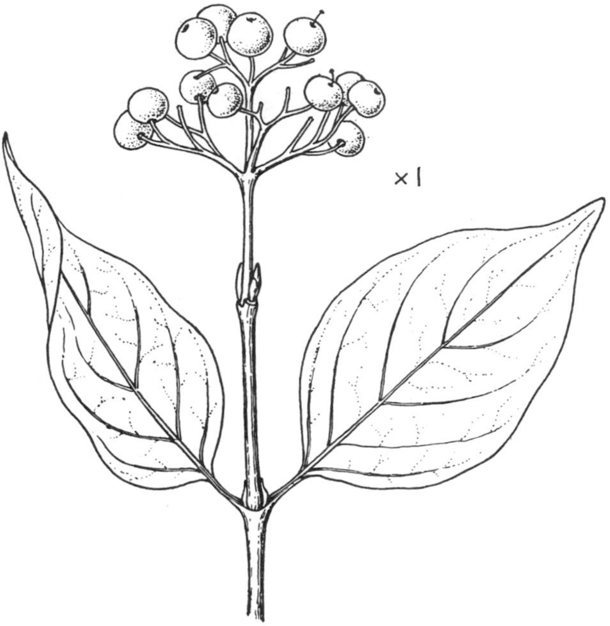

FIG. 438 CORNUS GLABRATA

Coast Ranges, the lower slopes of the Sierra Nevada, and along the streams of the Great Valley to southern California, where it occurs occasionally along streams and on the lower mountain slopes up to 7000 feet altitude. It occurs also on Santa Catalina Island. Three specimens examined from Lake County, Minnesota have the leaf-pubescence more like that of this variety than of the species which one normally expects there.

Cornus stolonifera Michx. Fl. 1:92 (1803). Type locality: Along rivers and brooks, Canada and New England. Probably collected by *Michaux*.

Var. californica (C. A. Mey.) McMinn. *C. californica* C. A. Mey. Type locality: "California." *C. californica* var. *pubescens* (Nutt.) Macbr. *C. pubescens* Nutt.

3. **Cornus glabrata** Benth. SMOOTH DOGWOOD. BROWN DOGWOOD. Fig. 438.

An erect or spreading shrub, 4 to 15 feet high, with long usually glabrous and smooth branches, these often bending over and trailing on the ground. Leaves deciduous; the blades ovate to elliptical, abruptly tapering at each end, 1 to 2 (3) inches long, ½-inch to 1¼ inches wide, light green and obscurely puberulent on

Fig. 439. Creek Dogwood. *Cornus stolonifera* var. *californica* (C. A. Mey.) McMinn.

both surfaces, thin, entire; petioles 1/4- to rarely 1/2-inch long. Flowers small, numerous, in open flat-topped compound stalked clusters; the main stalk and branches of flower-clusters slightly pubescent, glabrate in age; petals 1/8-inch or less long. Fruit globose, about 1/4-inch in diameter, bluish but white when mature. Flowering period, May to July.

Smooth Dogwood inhabits stream banks and moist flats, where it often forms dense thickets, in the lower foothills of the Coast Ranges, infrequently in the Sierra Nevada, and occasionally in the mountains of southern California, in the Upper Sonoran and Transition Life Zones. It extends from Siskiyou and Humboldt counties southward in the middle and inner Coast Ranges to Santa Barbara and Ventura counties. In the Sierra Nevada it is known in Eldorado County (Consumnes River) and has been reported from a few scattered localities southward to Tulare County. In southern California it occurs in the Mount Piños region, the San Jacinto Mountains (Hemet Valley), and the mountains of eastern San Diego County (Warner's Hot Springs; Mountain Springs grade). It has also been collected on Santa Catalina Island *(Blanche Trask).*

This species thrives when transplanted to semi-moist situations where it sends out long drooping branches which often touch the ground and continue trailing for several feet. After the fall of the leaves in late autumn the numerous clusters of bluish or white fruit borne upon reddish pedicels make the plants very colorful. The plants are easily propagated from cuttings or by layering.

Cornus glabrata Benth. Bot. Voy. Sulph. 18 (1844). Type locality: "San Francisco." Collected by *Hinds.*

Ericaceae. Heather Family

The Heather Family consists of about 90 genera and 1400 species distributed throughout the temperate and cold regions of the world. Twenty-three genera and about 75 species are native to California, of which 58 species are shrubs or subshrubs.

KEY TO THE GENERA

Leaves opposite.

Leaves scale-like, less than 1/4-inch long, thickly clothing the stems in 4 rows. 1. CASSIOPE.

Leaves linear to oblong, 1/4-inch to 1 inch long, with revolute margins. 2. KALMIA.

Leaves alternate.

Leaves linear, revolute; alpine heather-like shrubs.............3. PHYLLODOCE.

Leaves broader; plants not heather-like.

Leaves serrulate or serrate or some entire.

Stems usually smooth and red beneath the exfoliating bark or the bark sometimes shreddy and persistent; fruit brown or reddish, berry-like, with 2 to several distinct or more or less united nutlets; sepals distinct. 4. ARCTOSTAPHYLOS.

Stems not red.

Leaves thin and deciduous, 2 to 3 inches long, with rusty hairs on the upper surface.................................7. MENZIESIA.

Leaves thicker and evergreen, or if deciduous 2 inches or less long, glabrous above.

Ovary superior.
Fruit a capsule; leaves ½-inch to 1 inch wide........8. LEUCOTHOE.
Fruit berry- or drupe-like.
Sepals distinct; leaves usually white-pubescent beneath.
6. COMAROSTAPHYLIS.
Sepals united; leaves not white-pubescent beneath.9. GAULTHERIA.
Ovary inferior; fruit a berry with the remains of the calyx at summit.
12. VACCINIUM.
Leaves entire.
Flowers less than ½-inch long.
Flowers urn-shaped or globular, not more than ⅜-inch broad.
Ovary superior.
Leaves not revolute; bark of stems usually smooth and red or sometimes fibrous or shreddy.................4. ARCTOSTAPHYLOS.
Leaves revolute, tomentose beneath; bark of stems gray, persistent.
5. XYLOCOCCUS.
Ovary inferior; stems not red.......................12. VACCINIUM.
Flowers rotate, ⅜-inch or more broad; petals nearly distinct..10. LEDUM.
Flowers more than 1 inch long......................11. RHODODENDRON.

1. **Cassiope** D. Don

(Named for Cassiope, wife of Cepheus and mother of Andromeda.)

This genus consists of about 10 species of the northern hemisphere extending southward along the high mountain ranges in Europe, Asia, and North America. A single species is native to California.

1. **Cassiope Mertensiana** (Bong.) D. Don. WHITE-HEATHER. LOVE-HEATHER.

A diminutive subshrub, usually 4 to 12 inches high, with rigid ascending branches densely clothed with heather-like leaves. Flowering period, July and August.

White-heather inhabits rocky ridges and ledges near timber-line in the Sierra Nevada from Fresno County northward to Nevada County and in Siskiyou County, in the Hudsonian Life Zone. It extends northward to Alaska and eastward in the northern Rockies to Montana. The perennial wiry stems thickly clothed with heather-like leaves often form dense mats in the granite ledges.

Cassiope Mertensiana (Bong.) D. Don, Gen. Hist. 3:829 (1834). *Andromeda Mertensiana* Bong. Type locality: Sitka, Alaska.

2. **Kalmia** L.

(Named for Peter Kalm, early North American explorer, and pupil of Linnaeus.)

This genus contains about 7 species native to North America and the West Indies. A single species is native to California.

1. **Kalmia polifolia** var. **microphylla** (Hook.) Rehd. ALPINE-LAUREL. Fig. 440.

A low spreading subshrub, 2 to 6 (or rarely to 12) inches high. Flowering period, June to August.

Alpine-laurel inhabits borders of lakes, meadows, and swampy places in the Sierra Nevada, at elevations from 6500 to 12,000 feet, from Kern County northward to Modoc County and westward in Siskiyou County to Humboldt County

(Trinity Summit; Bald Meadow, el. 3500 ft.). It extends northward to Alaska and eastward to the Rocky Mountains. This species is reported very poisonous to sheep and cattle.

Kalmia polifolia var. microphylla (Hook.) Rehd. Cycl. Am. Hort. 2:854 (1900). Appears as a new variety as no synonym was cited. In 1914 Rehder cited as a synonym *K. glauca* var. *microphylla* Hook. Type locality: "Swamps in the Rocky Mountains." Collected by *Drummond*.

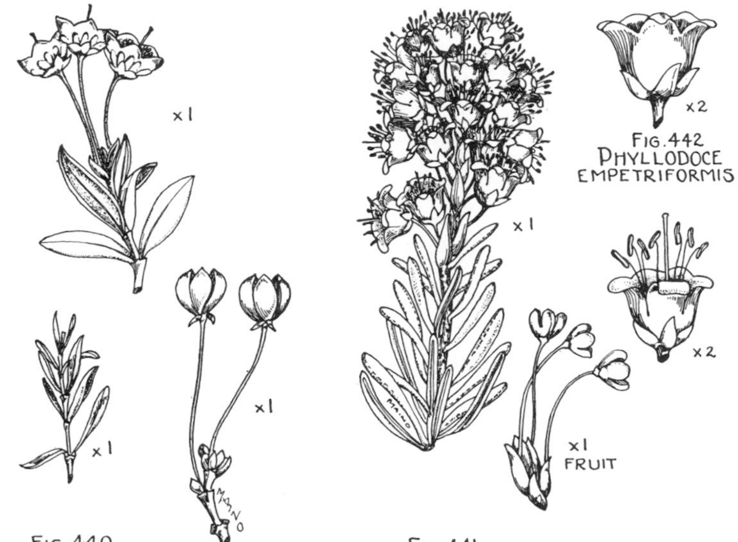

FIG. 442 PHYLLODOCE EMPETRIFORMIS

FIG. 440 KALMIA POLIFOLIA VAR. MICROPHYLLA

FIG. 441 PHYLLODOCE BREWERI

3. **Phyllodoce** Salisb.

(From the Greek *Phyllodoce,* a sea nymph mentioned by Virgil.)

Small heather-like shrubs. Leaves simple, alternate, evergreen, crowded, linear, revolute. Flowers bisexual, in short crowded terminal racemes; sepals 5; petals 5, joined to the middle or for most of their length; stamens 7 to 10, distinct; ovary superior, 5-celled. Fruit a globose capsule, splitting along the walls of the 5 cells.

This genus contains about 7 species inhabiting the high mountain ranges of the northern hemisphere. Two species occur in California. They are usually known as mountain-heathers.

KEY TO THE SPECIES

Stamens 7 to 10, exserted. . . . . 1. *P. Breweri.*
Stamens 5 to 9, included. . . . . 2. *P. empetriformis.*

1. **Phyllodoce Breweri** (Gray) Heller. RED MOUNTAIN-HEATHER. Fig. 441.

A low tufted diminutive heather-like subshrub, 1 foot or less high. Flowering period, June to August.

Red Mountain-heather occurs in swampy meadows or other wet acid soils in the Hudsonian and Arctic-alpine Life Zones in the Sierra Nevada from Tulare

County northward to Lassen Peak, Shasta County, westward to Mount Shasta and Marble Mountain, Siskiyou County, and in the San Bernardino Mountains, from 6500 to 12,000 feet elevation.

Phyllodoce Breweri (Gray) Heller, Muhlenbergia 1:1 (1900). *Bryanthus Breweri* Gray. Type locality: "High Sierras of California." Probably, "Woods Peak, Eldorado Co." Collected by *Brewer*.

2. **Phyllodoce empetriformis** (Smith) D. Don. NORTHERN MOUNTAIN-HEATHER. Fig. 442.

A low tufted plant, 4 to 10 inches high. Flowering period, June to August.

Northern Mountain-heather occurs in a few localities in the higher mountains of Siskiyou and northeastern Trinity counties (Mt. Shasta, Mt. Eddy, Salmon Mountains, Marble Mt., Craggy Peak, Shackleford Creek). It extends northward to Alaska and eastward to Wyoming and Montana.

Phyllodoce empetriformis (J. E. Smith) D. Don, Edinb. New Phil. Jour. 17:160 (1834). *Menziesia empetriformis* J. E. Smith. Type locality: "On the west coast of North America." Collected by *Menzies*.

4. **Arctostaphylos** Adans. MANZANITA

(From the Greek *arktos*, a bear, and *staphule*, a grape, in reference to the feeding of bears upon the berry-like fruits.)

Woody plants varying from low prostrate shrubs to small trees, usually with crooked branches and smooth reddish brown or purplish red bark on old stems and branches or the bark sometimes rough and shreddy. Leaves simple, alternate, and evergreen. Flowers bisexual, white or pinkish, in terminal simple or compound clusters, on slender pedicels bracteate at base; calyx 4- or 5-parted, the lobes broad; corolla small, urn-shaped or bell-shaped, with 4 or 5 small lobes at the summit, the lobes usually recurved; stamens 10, rarely 8, included within the corolla; anthers with 2 recurved appendages on the back, opening by round terminal pores; ovary superior, 4- to 10-celled, surrounded at the base by a 10-lobed disk. Fruit berry- or drupe-like, consisting of several stony nutlets surrounded by a soft pulp; the nutlets distinct or irregularly united in 2's or 3's, or sometimes coalesced into a single solid stone.

There are about 50 species of manzanitas distributed in North and Central America, chiefly on the Pacific Coast. One species is circumpolar. Thirty-eight species with several varieties and numerous forms are native to California.

The genus *Arctostaphylos* is easily recognized but the classification and identification of the various forms are rather difficult. The Californian manzanitas vary in growth-form from prostrate mat-forming shrubs to small trees. Some crown-sprout after fires or after cutting while others are completely destroyed by fires. The foliage varies from dark glossy green to gray or whitish in hue. Much variation occurs in the amount and character of pubescence and glandulosity of the vegetative and floral structures. Many intermediate and perplexing forms, probably of hybrid origin, occur in regions where several species overlap in their distribution.

KEY TO THE SPECIES

I. Plants prostrate or procumbent and often rooting from the branches when in contact with the ground, usually less than 2½ feet high; leaves 1 inch or less long, dark green and glabrous above, except in the form of *A. columbiana*.

A. Leaves petioled, not auriculate or heart-shaped at base.

1. Leaves dark or bright green above or on both surfaces, ½- (or ⅝-) inch or less wide.
   Young branchlets pubescent and bristly-hairy; fruit ⅛- to 3/16-inch long, greenish, breaking up early into 2 to 4 one-seeded nutlets, the pericarp thin.
      Bark of older branches covered with a whitish bloom; parts of the flower in 5's; Ione Hills, Amador Co. ....1. *A. myrtifolia.*
      Bark of older branches without a whitish bloom; parts of the flower in 4's; coastal mts. ....2. *A. nummularia.*
   Young branchlets not bristly-hairy; pericarp thicker.
      Lower surface of leaves paler than upper; leaves typically broadest beyond the middle; Monterey.....................4. *A. pumila.*
      Both surfaces of leaves alike.
         Leaves rounded or retuse at apex; bark rough or shreddy; fruit pink or red at maturity; coastal from Marin Co. north.....5. *A. Uva-ursi.*
         Leaves abruptly acute or obtuse and mucronate or pointed; bark smooth; mature fruit brown.
            Branchlets and peduncles not glandular.
               Flower-clusters usually simple.
                  Leaves broadest at or below the middle, shortly acute at apex.
                     Coastal species...........................6. *A. Hookeri.*
                     Mt. Tamalpais species.............14. Form of *A. pungens.*
                  Leaves broadest above the middle.
                     Chiefly Sierra Nevada...................7. *A. nevadensis.*
                     Coastal species...................5a. *A. Uva-ursi,* hybrid?
               Flower-clusters branched, rather dense, with numerous flowers; Sonoma Co. ....8. *A. densiflora.*
            Branchlets and peduncles glandular-pubescent; chiefly Sierra Nevada ....17. *A. patula,* hybrid?
2. Leaves pale on both surfaces; ½-inch to 1 inch wide; branchlets and petioles usually with dense pubescence and additional bristle-like hairs.
   26. *A. columbiana,* hybrid?

B. Leaves sessile or nearly so, auriculate or heart-shaped at base; chiefly La Purisima Hills ....35. Form of *A. viridissima.*

II. Plants usually erect, 2½ to 10, or 20 feet high.
   A. Bracts of the inflorescence usually subulate, not foliaceous.
      1. Leaves dark to light or yellowish green.
         a. Plants not crown-sprouting.
            (1). Some or all the nutlets separable.
               (a). Branchlets and petioles bristly-hirsute; parts of the flower in 4's; coastal region.................2a. *A. nummularia* var. *sensitiva.*
               (b). Branchlets not bristly-hirsute; parts of the flower in 5's.

Young branchlets not glandular-hairy.
   Branchlets glabrous.
      Fruit viscid; chiefly Lake Co.........,....................9. *A. elegans.*
      Fruit not viscid.
         Leaves tapering or rounded at base, acute at apex, pedicels glabrous; mainland species.
            Flowers pink; chiefly Napa and Lake counties......10. *A. Stanfordiana.*

Flowers white; Mt. Diablo . . . . 12. *A. manzanita,* hybrid?
Leaves obtuse or usually subcordate at base, obtuse to rounded at apex; pedicels usually glandular-hairy; island species . . . . . . 13. *A. insularis.*
Branchlets pubescent or white-downy, only slightly pubescent in some forms of *A. manzanita.*
Leaves obtuse or subcordate at base, obtuse or rounded at apex; pedicels glandular-hairy; island species . . . . 13a. *A. insularis* var. *pubescens.*
Leaves tapering or rounded at base, acute to obtuse at apex; pedicels not glandular-hairy.
Ovary glabrous; bracts not at all foliaceous.
Rachises not thickened upward.
Leaves 1 to 2½ inches long.
Flowers ¼- to 5/16-inch long; N. Coast Ranges and lower Sierra Nevada . . . . 12. *A. manzanita.*
Flowers 3/16-inch long; Mt. Diablo . . . . 12. *A. manzanita,* hybrid?
Leaves ½-inch to 1 inch long . . . . 14. Form of *A. pungens.*
Rachises often thickened upward and bearing a congested flower-cluster at summit; leaves ¾-inch to 1 inch long; s. coast. and s. Calif. 14. *A. pungens.*
Ovary pubescent or white-hairy; bracts somewhat foliaceous; n. coast. 25. *A. cinerea.*
Young branchlets and inflorescences glandular-pubescent or glandular.
Rachises slender; leaves dark or yellowish green; flowers pinkish.
Leaves rounded or tapering at base, acute at apex.
Plants erect, 3 to 8 feet high, n. coast . . . . 11. *A. hispidula.*
Plants spreading, 2 to 3 feet high; s. Calif. . 15a. *A. Parryana* var. *pinetorum.*
Leaves obtuse or subcordate at base, obtuse or rounded at apex; Santa Cruz Island . . . . 13a. *A. insularis* var. *pubescens.*
Rachises stout; leaves yellowish green or pallid; flowers white; Sierra Nevada. 20a. *A. mariposa* var. *bivisa.*
(2). Most of the nutlets united into a solid stone; young branchlets and rachises densely pubescent; spreading shrubs; chiefly s. Calif. 15. *A. Parryana.*
b. Plants crown-sprouting.
Bark rough and shreddy; leaves 1¼ inches or less long; Santa Barbara and San Luis Obispo counties . . . . 16. *A. rudis.*
Bark smooth; leaves 1¼ to 2½ inches long; Sierra Nevada.
Leaves bright or yellowish green; branchlets glandular or canescent. 17. *A. patula.*
Leaves pale or grayish green; branchlets glabrous or puberulent, not glandular . . . . 18. *A. mewukka.*
2. Leaves grayish or whitish or rarely yellowish green, often glaucous.
Plants crown-sprouting; pedicels glabrous; Sierra Nevada . . 18. *A. mewukka.*
Plants not crown-sprouting; pedicels glandular.
Branchlets not glandular-hairy, rarely pubescent or glandular.
Bracts of inflorescences ascending; ovary glabrous, pubescent, or glandular; fruit ⅓-inch or less in diameter, the nutlets usually separable; Sierra Nevada and N. Coast Ranges . . . . . 19. *A. viscida.*
Bracts of inflorescences stiff and spreading at right angles to the peduncle and rachis; ovary glandular-pubescent; fruit about ½-

inch in diameter, very viscid, the nutlets united into a solid stone; inner s. coast and s. Calif. . . . . .24. *A. glauca.*

Branchlets glandular-hairy.

Nutlets not united into a solid stone; bracts inconspicuous; central Sierra Nevada . . . . .20. *A. mariposa.*

Nutlets united into a solid stone; s. Calif. or inner S. Coast Ranges.

Pedicels ½- to ¾-inch long; bracts pink, membranous, deciduous. 21. *A. Pringlei* var. *drupacea.*

Pedicels about ¼-inch long; bracts stiff, persistent, spreading at right angles to the peduncle and rachis. 24a. *A. glauca* var. *puberula.*

B. Bracts of the inflorescences usually foliaceous or the upper ones reduced.

1. Leaves distinctly petiolate.

a. Plants not crown-sprouting.

Bark fibrous, rough, reddish brown.

Leaves truncate or subcordate or rarely rounded at base, densely tomentose beneath; San Luis Obispo Co. . . . . .36. *A. morroensis.*

Leaves obtuse or rounded at base, puberulent or nearly glabrous; Eldorado Co. . . . . .3. *A. nissenana.*

Bark smooth, deep red or red-brown.

Stems and branches canescent, pubescent, or glandular-hairy, but without long bristly hairs or only with a few scattered ones.

Branchlets white-canescent or pubescent, not glandular; petioles, bracts, and pedicels pubescent or rarely glabrous.

Leaves green; pedicels not reflexed in fruit.

Leaves 1 to 1½ inches long; bracts lanceolate, only the lowest foliaceous. . . . . .25. *A. cinerea.*

Leaves 1¼ to 2½ inches long; bracts leafy, lanceolate, all longer than the pedicels. . . . . . .26a. *A. columbiana* var. *Tracyi.*

Leaves pale, white-tomentulose on both surfaces.

Ovary densely hairy; leaves typically ovate; pedicels reflexed or spreading in fruit. . . . . .27. *A. canescens.*

Ovary glabrous or only slightly hairy.

Leaves rounded-cuneate at base. . . . . .22. *A. silvicola.*

Leaves truncate or heart-shaped at base. . . .23. *A. obispoensis.*

Branchlets glandular-hairy; petioles, bracts, pedicels, sepals, and ovary glandular.

Leaves elliptic to oblong, ½-inch to 1⅜ inches long; San Diego Co. . . . . .37. *A. otayensis.*

Leaves narrow-ovate to lanceolate, 1½ to 2¼ inches long; north coast. . . . . .26b. *A. columbiana* var. *virgata.*

Stems and branches with long or short bristly hairs, some often gland-tipped, or the hairs rarely sparse or lacking.

Leaves 1 to 2½ inches long; ovary densely white-hairy; fruit not striped. . . . . .26. *A. columbiana.*

Leaves ¾-inch to 1¾ inches long; ovary usually glabrous; fruit usually with blue-black stripes. . . . . .38. *A. pilosula.*

b. Plants crown-sprouting.

(1). Leaves usually truncate or subcordate at base (sometimes obtuse or

Fig. 443. Littleberry Manzanita. *Arctostaphylos nummularia* var. *sensitiva* (Jepson) McMinn.
(Photograph by Sidney Gulick.)

only slightly subcordate), more or less unlike above and beneath, with stomata only on the lower surface.....(*A. tomentosa* complex).

Branchlets, bracts, and pedicels glandular-hairy; leaves bright green.

Leaves thin; bracts lanceolate, as long as or longer than the pedicels; flowers few, in congested clusters; ovary pubescent, not glandular; chiefly adjacent to Monterey Bay........28. *A. bracteosa.*

Leaves thick; bracts oblong, shorter than the pedicels; flowers numerous, in dense panicles; ovary glandular-pubescent; Santa Rosa Island............................29. *A. confertiflora.*

Branchlets, bracts, and pedicels not glandular-hairy.

Pedicels glabrous; leaves pale green and glabrous but dull above, tomentulose, pubescent, or nearly glabrous beneath; branchlets usually with a few straight hairs; vicinity of Monterey Bay.
30b. *A. tomentosa* var. *hebeclada.*

Pedicels pubescent.

Lower surface of leaves usually densely white-tomentose; all bracts normally foliaceous.....................30. *A. tomentosa.*

Lower surface of leaves usually glabrous or only slightly tomentulose; upper bracts usually subulate or deltoid.31. *A. crustacea.*

(2). Leaves usually tapering or rounded at base, rarely truncate to subcordate, usually alike on both surfaces, with stomata on both surfaces.......................................32. *A. glandulosa.*

2. Leaves sessile or nearly so (very short-petioled in *A. pechoensis*), cordate or auriculate at base; plants not crown-sprouting.

Ovary and pedicels glandular-hairy or pubescent and not glandular; Contra Costa Co. s. to Monterey Co. ....33. *A. Andersonii.*

Ovary and pedicels glabrous.

Leaves pale gray-green, cordate at base, sessile or very short-petioled; branchlets sparsely tomentose; San Luis Obispo Co.
34. *A. pechoensis.*

Leaves dark green, glabrous, sessile, auriculate at base; branchlets tomentulose and with spreading bristly hairs; chiefly La Purisima Hills and Santa Cruz Island........................35. *A. viridissima.*

1. **Arctostaphylos myrtifolia** Parry. Ione Manzanita. Fig. 444.

An erect or spreading shrub, 1 to 2½ feet high, with shreddy exfoliating bark on the smaller branches and dark reddish-brown bark which is usually covered with a whitish bloom on the older branches. The branchlets glandular-pubescent and with additional straight stiff hairs. Leaf-blades firm and leathery, narrowly ovate or elliptic, ¼- to ½- (rarely ¾-) inch long, 3/16- to 5/16-inch wide, rounded or acute at base, acute and cuspidate at apex, bright green glabrous and microscopically glandular-papillate on both surfaces, the margins entire. Flowers white, about ⅛-inch long, in short simple or few-branched clusters; peduncle and rachis glandular-pubescent; pedicels glabrous; ovary densely hairy. Fruit globose, ¼-inch or less in diameter, smooth, greenish, separating into 4 one-seeded nutlets. Flowering period, January and February.

Ione Manzanita is confined to a small area in the Sierra Nevada foothills east of Ione, Amador County, where it forms nearly pure stands on the low exposed ridges. The plants do not crown-sprout after fires.

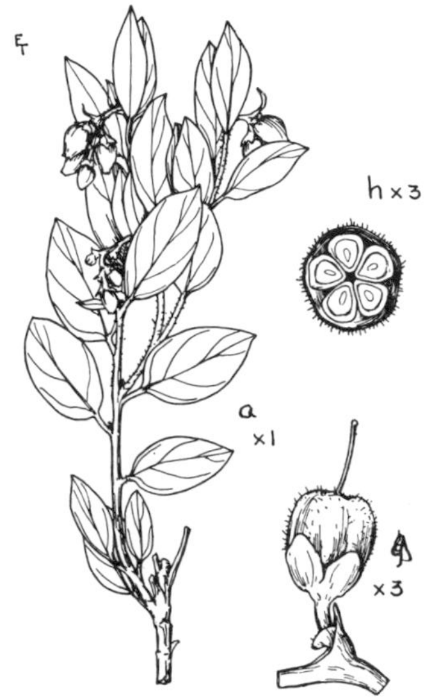

FIG. 444 A. MYRTIFOLIA

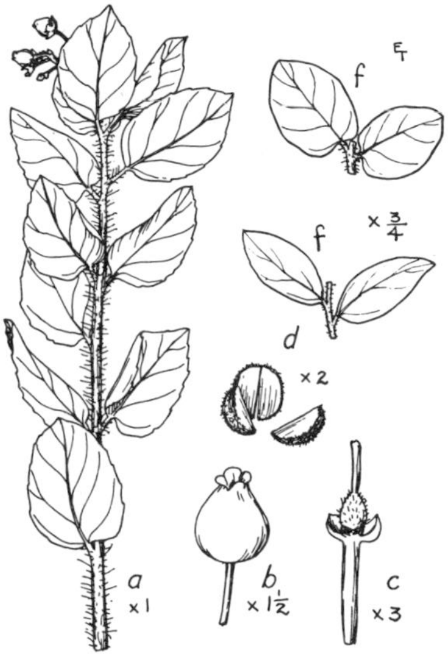

FIG. 445 A. NUMMULARIA

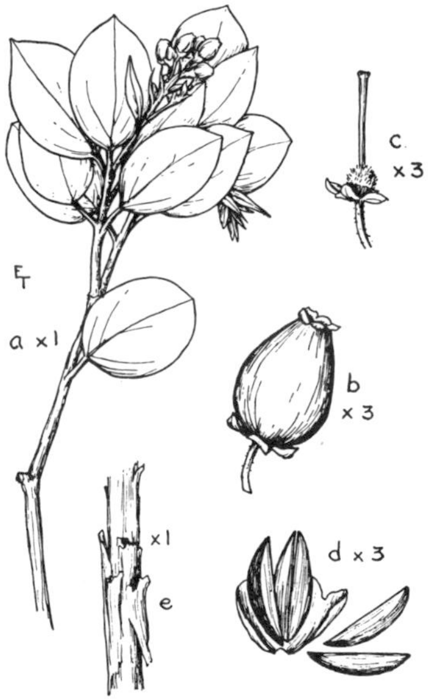

FIG. 446 A. NISSENANA

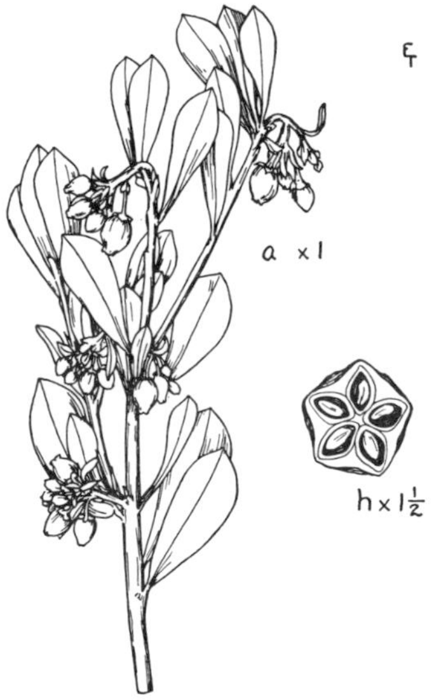

FIG. 447 A. PUMILA

ARCTOSTAPHYLOS. a, Flowering branchlet. b, Flower. c, Pedicel and pistil. d, Separable nutlets of fruit. e, Shreddy bark. f, Leaf variation. g, Fruit. h, Cross section of fruit.

Arctostaphylos myrtifolia Parry, Pitt. 1:34 & 35 (1887). Type locality: Ridges east of Ione, Amador County. Collected by *K. Curran.*

2. **Arctostaphylos nummularia** Gray. GLOSSYLEAF MANZANITA. FIRE MANZANITA. Fig. 445.

KEY TO THE SPECIES AND VARIETY

Plants normally prostrate or decumbent.......................*A. nummularia.*
Plants erect, 2 to 5 feet high...................................2a. var. *sensitiva.*

A low decumbent or often prostrate shrub, 6 inches to 2 feet high, or rarely erect and up to 7 feet high, with ascending or spreading stems, bristly-hairy branchlets, and exfoliating brown or reddish bark. Leaves thickly clothing the branchlets; the blades thin, narrowly elliptic or ovate to nearly orbicular, 3/8- to 3/4-inch long, 3/16- to 1/2-inch wide, obtuse or rounded or rarely acute and mucronate at apex, obtuse or truncate or somewhat heart-shaped at base, dark green glabrous and glossy above, paler and microscopically glandular-papillate beneath, the margins entire or ciliate and often distinctly revolute; petioles about 1/16-inch long, glandular-pubescent and stiff-hairy. Flowers white, 4-merous, 3/16-inch or less long, in short terminal simple or branched racemes; pedicels glabrous; ovary densely pubescent. Fruit oblong, about 3/16-inch long, greenish when ripe, falling early and separating into 2 to 4 one-seeded nutlets. Flowering period, March and April.

Glossyleaf Manzanita occurs on coastal plains of Mendocino County and occasionally in Sonoma County where it grows as a prostrate or dwarf shrub associated with stunted forms of *Pinus contorta, P. muricata,* and *Cupressus Goveniana.* The plants growing away from the immediate vicinity of the coast or not on the "pine flats" become more erect and form characteristic mounds. Near Fort Bragg I have observed specimens varying from prostrate to nearly 7 feet tall. This species does not crown-sprout after fires or cutting but often roots from the stem when in contact with the ground.

2a. Var. **sensitiva** (Jepson) n. comb. LITTLEBERRY MANZANITA. Fig. 443.

An erect dense shrub, 2 to 5 feet high. Leaf-blades broadly elliptical to nearly round, 1/2- to 3/4-inch long. This variety occurs on Mount Tamalpais and Bolinas Ridge, Marin County, northward to Mendocino County, and in the Santa Cruz Mountains of Santa Cruz County. In foliage, floral, and fruit characters this variety is similar to the species. Its denser more compact and erect habit of growth, however, seems to set it off from the species. Like the species it is killed outright by fire.

Arctostaphylos nummularia Gray, Proc. Am. Acad. 7:366 (1868). Type locality: Mendocino Plains, Mendocino County. Collected by *Bolander.*

Var. sensitiva (Jepson) McMinn. *A. sensitiva* Jepson. Type locality: Mount Tamalpais, Marin County. Collected by *Jepson.*

3. **Arctostaphylos nissenana** Merriam. ELDORADO MANZANITA. Fig. 446.

An erect shrub, 2 to 6 feet high, with reddish brown fibrous bark and slender hispid to nearly glabrous branchlets. Leaf-blades elliptic to oblong or somewhat obovate, 3/8-inch to 1 inch long, 1/4- to 3/4-inch wide, light or gray-green, puberulent or nearly glabrous, acute or obtuse and mucronate at apex, obtuse at base; petioles 1/8-inch or less long, villous-pubescent. Flowers pale pink, 5-merous, about 1/4-inch long, in small dense racemes; lower bracts foliaceous, often longer than the pedicels, the upper bracts reduced, more or less villous-pubescent, not glandular; pedicels subglabrous or glabrous; ovary glabrous or slightly hairy. Fruit globu-

Fig. 448. Stanford Manzanita. *Arctostaphylos Stanfordiana* Parry.

lar or angled, about 3/16-inch in diameter, thinly pubescent or glabrous, with 5 nutlets enclosed by a thin flesh, soon separating at maturity. Flowering period, December to February.

Eldorado Manzanita occurs in a few scattered locations in the lower Sierra Nevada foothills of Eldorado County (slopes at head of Spanish Ravine, *W. G. Watkins;* ridge at mouth of Brush Creek, el. 3200 ft., in dense chaparral, *H. A. Jensen;* Diamond Springs, el. 1800 ft., *Wieslander;* 2¼ mi. w.sw. Volcanoville on a ridge n. of Otter Creek, el. 2500 ft., *Belshaw*). It does not crown-sprout.

This species apparently hybridizes with *A. viscida,* the common species of this region. The hybrid has received from *A. viscida* the smooth dark red bark, glabrous peduncles, stipitate-glandular pedicels, and non-foliaceous bracts, and from *A. nissenana* the villous-pubescent branchlets and petioles, smaller and somewhat pubescent leaves, and densely pubescent ovaries *(Eastwood* & *Howell* #1935).

Arctostaphylos nissenana Merriam, Proc. Biol. Soc. Wash. 31:102 (1918). Type locality: About 2½ miles north of Louisville, Eldorado County, California. Collected by *C. H. Merriam.*

4. **Arctostaphylos pumila** Nutt. SANDMAT MANZANITA. DUNE MANZANITA. Fig. 447.

A low decumbent or prostrate shrub, or rarely more erect, forming dense mats or mounds 2 to 4 feet across, with erect branches, reddish brown exfoliating bark, and finely pubescent branchlets. Leaf-blades narrowly obovate to spatulate, ⅜- to ¾-inch long, ¼- to rarely ½-inch wide, rounded to acute and somewhat mucronate at apex, dull green and slightly pubescent above, becoming glabrous, distinctly paler and usually permanently pubescent beneath, entire; petioles ⅛-inch or less long. Flowers white or pink, about 3/16-inch long, in short simple or few-branched racemes; peduncles tomentose; pedicels glandular-pubescent or nearly glabrous; ovary glabrous. Fruit globose, slightly depressed, about ⅛-inch in diameter, glabrous, brown, with 5 separable nutlets. Flowering period, February to May.

Sandmat Manzanita is confined to the sandy flats and hills bordering Monterey Bay, where it is often associated with *A. Hookeri, Ceanothus rigidus,* and *C. dentatus.* It does not crown-sprout but roots readily from the prostrate branches.

Arctostaphylos pumila Nutt. Trans. Am. Phil. Soc. ser. 2, 8:266 (1843). Type locality: Monterey, California. Collected by *Nuttall.*

5. **Arctostaphylos Uva-ursi** (L.) Spreng. BEARBERRY. SANDBERRY. Fig. 449.

A prostrate shrub, with rooting branches, rough or shreddy reddish brown bark, and glabrous or sparsely tomentose branchlets. Leaf-blades spatulate to obovate or ovate, ½-inch to 1 inch long, ¼- to ½-inch wide, rounded or retuse at apex, bright green and glabrous on both surfaces or somewhat paler beneath, entire; petioles about ⅛-inch long. Flowers white or pinkish, about ¼-inch long, in short few-flowered racemose clusters; pedicels about ⅛-inch long, glabrous; ovary glabrous. Fruit globose, ¼- to 5/16-inch in diameter, bright red or pink, glabrous; nutlets separable, 1- or rarely 3-nerved on the back. Flowering period, March to May.

Bearberry occurs along the coast from Inverness Ridge and Point Reyes Peninsula, Marin County northward in Sonoma, Mendocino, Humboldt, and Del Norte counties. It extends northward to Alaska and around the world in the northern latitudes of both hemispheres. In the Rocky Mountain region it is commonly known as Kinnikinnick.

This species apparently hybridizes in California with *A. columbiana* and with *A. nummularia.* I have observed both of these hybrid forms on the bluffs near

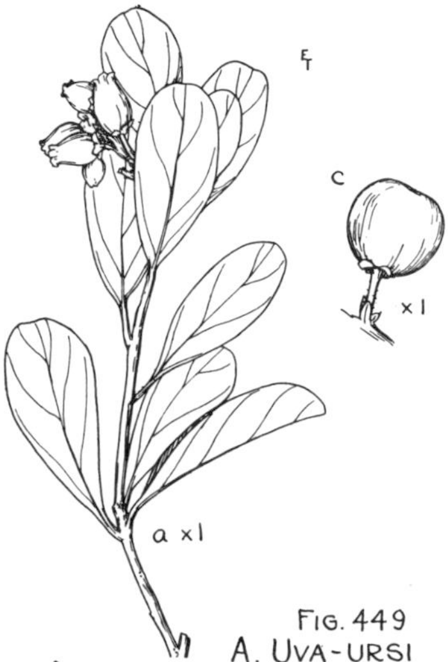

FIG. 449 A. UVA-URSI

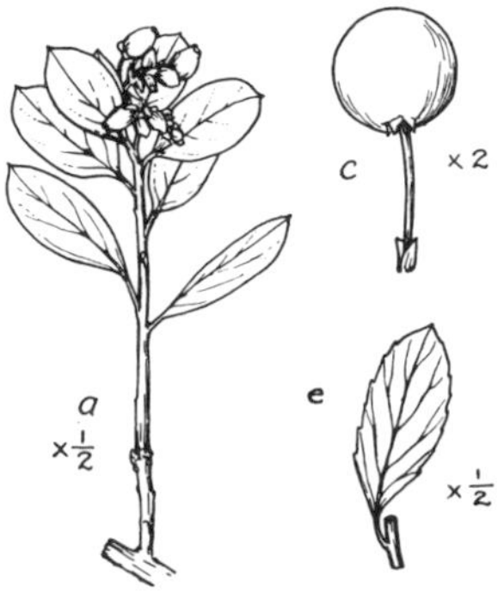

FIG. 450 A. HOOKERI

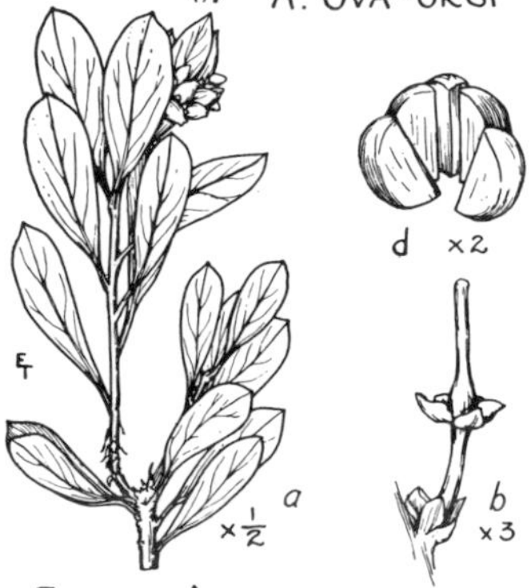

FIG. 451 A. NEVADENSIS

FIG. 452
A. DENSIFLORA

FIG. 455
A. HISPIDULA

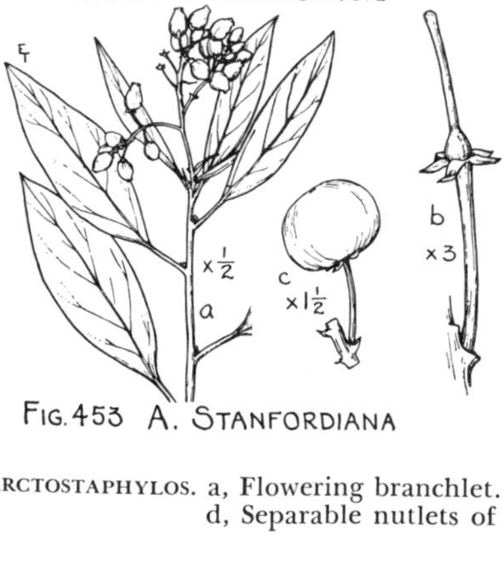

FIG. 453 A. STANFORDIANA

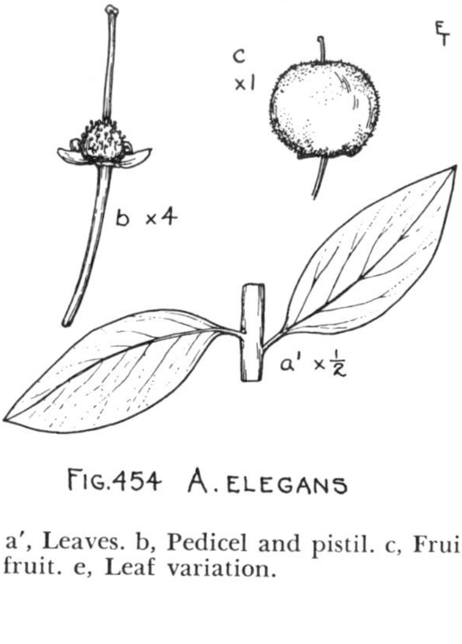

FIG. 454 A. ELEGANS

ARCTOSTAPHYLOS. a, Flowering branchlet. a′, Leaves. b, Pedicel and pistil. c, Fruit. d, Separable nutlets of fruit. e, Leaf variation.

Sail Rock, Mendocino County. A form with somewhat puberulent and larger leaves has been described as **A. media** Greene. It was first collected by Chas. V. Piper in Mason County, Washington. Some specimens along the Mendocino coast are referable to this form. It may be a hybrid between *A. Uva-ursi* and *A. columbiana,* resembling more the former parent.

Arctostaphylos Uva-ursi (L.) Spreng. Syst. Veg. 2:287 (1825). *Arbutus Uva-ursi* L. Type locality: Northern Europe and Canada.

6. **Arctostaphylos Hookeri** G. Don. Hooker Manzanita. Fig. 450.

A low, erect, or almost procumbent shrub, ½-foot to 3 feet high, with smooth very dark reddish brown or deep purplish bark and puberulent peduncles and branchlets. Leaf-blades elliptic or ovate to obovate, ½- to ¾-inch (or to 1 inch) long, ⅜- to ½-inch wide, bright green shining and glabrous on both surfaces, entire; petioles ⅛- to ¼-inch long. Flowers pink, usually a little more than ⅛-inch long, in short almost head-like racemes; pedicels about ⅛-inch long, glabrous; ovary glabrous. Fruit globose, slightly depressed, about 3⁄16-inch broad, reddish brown, glabrous; nutlets separable or irregularly united, ridged and roughened on the back. Flowering period, February to April.

Hooker Manzanita forms conspicuous mounds on sandy flats and in the open pine woods in the vicinity of Monterey Bay. It occurs also on serpentine in Laurel Hill Cemetery and on Mount Davidson, San Francisco. Eastwood has described the plants of San Francisco as *A. franciscana.* Specimens from Pacheco Peak, San Benito County although assigned to *A. pungens,* resemble the taller erect mound-like shrubs of *A. Hookeri.* The technical characters separating *A. Hookeri, A. pungens,* and *A. nevadensis* are often difficult to apply. *A. Hookeri* does not crown-sprout.

Arctostaphylos Hookeri G. Don, Gen. Syst. 3:836 (1834). Type locality: Monterey, California. Collected by *Lay* and *Collie. A. Franciscana* Eastw.

7. **Arctostaphylos nevadensis** Gray. Pinemat Manzanita. Fig. 451.

A low sprawling or prostrate shrub, ½-foot to 1½ feet high, with smooth reddish brown bark exfoliating in thin paper-like pieces and slightly tomentose branchlets. Leaf-blades thick and leathery, elliptic or obovate to oblanceolate, ¾-inch to 1½ inches long, ¼- to ¾-inch wide, mucronate, bright green, shining and glabrous on both surfaces or sparsely pubescent when young, entire; petioles ⅛- to ¼-inch long, glabrous or puberulent. Flowers white or sometimes pink, about ¼-inch long, in short racemes; pedicels about ⅛-inch long, glabrous or rarely puberulent; ovary glabrous. Fruit globose, about ¼-inch in diameter, glabrous, dark brown; nutlets easily separable or rarely fused into a single stone, roughened on the back. Flowering period, May and June.

Pinemat Manzanita is a common shrub in the Sierra Nevada from Tulare County northward to Shasta County and in the high North Coast Ranges from northern Lake County to Siskiyou County at altitudes from 6000 (rarely 4000) to 10,000 feet. It extends northward to Oregon and eastward to western Nevada. It usually occurs in the open pine and Red Fir forests where it often forms dense carpet-like mats covering many square feet. Although never an erect shrub it often sprawls over granite rocks to heights of 4 to 6 feet. It roots freely from the prostrate stems but does not crown-sprout. In certain regions where this species associates with *A. patula* intermediate forms occasionally occur. The plants are procumbent to erect and intermediate in size between the two parents. The leaves are also intermediate in size. The petioles and branchlets are either glandular or canescent. This variation is rather common also in *A. patula*. The bushy rather erect plants of Del Norte County may be hybrids between these two parents. They have been described as **A. parvifolia** Howell.

Arctostaphylos nevadensis Gray, Syn. Fl. 2:27 (1878). Type locality: "Sierra Nevada, California, common at 8000 to 10,000 feet."

8. **Arctostaphylos densiflora** Baker. SONOMA MANZANITA. Fig. 452.

A low spreading nearly prostrate shrub with numerous slender crooked and blackish branches, freely rooting. Leaf-blades elliptic to oblong-elliptic, or rarely oblanceolate or ovate, 1/2-inch to 1 1/4 inches long, 1/4- to 5/8-inch wide, bright green and glabrous except for a minute pubescence along the margins and veins, entire; petioles 3/16-inch or less long, pubescent. Flowers rosy or white, about 3/16-inch long, in short dense many-flowered panicles; pedicels glabrous, very slender; ovary glabrous. Fruit flattened-globular, about 1/4-inch in diameter, glabrous, with separable nutlets. Flowering period, February and March.

Sonoma Manzanita is apparently a relic endemic confined to a small area in the Vine Hill region of Sonoma County. M. S. Baker in Leafl. West. Bot. 1:32 (1932) states, "The known plants of this rare species will scarcely number one hundred and all but a half dozen of these are confined to the banks of a single road for a distance of scarcely 500 feet."

This species has apparently hybridized with *A. Stanfordiana*, its nearest relative, and with *A. manzanita*. Plants on Rincon Ridge east of Santa Rosa appear to be intergrades between this species and *A. Stanfordiana*. Baker states, "that it seems to have hybridized with *A. manzanita* of this locality and to have produced a most vigorous but variable descendant that is already the dominant manzanita of a section many miles in extent."

Arctostaphylos densiflora Baker, Leafl. West. Bot. 1:31 (1932). Type locality: "Roadside just west of Vine Hill Schoolhouse, about ten miles westerly from Santa Rosa, Sonoma County, California." Collected by *M. S. Baker*.

9. **Arctostaphylos elegans** Jepson. KONOCTI MANZANITA. Fig. 454.

Similar to *A. Stanfordiana* and *A. manzanita*, but distinguished from both of these species by the glandular ovary and large stipitate-glandular fruit. The flowers are usually white and larger than those of *A. Stanfordiana* and the branchlets are thicker.

This species occurs on the obsidian slopes south of Mount Konocti, on Snow Mountain, and on Mount St. Helena, Lake County. It also occurs occasionally in Napa and Sonoma counties. It does not crown-sprout after fires.

Arctostaphylos elegans Jepson, Erythea 1:15 (1893). Type locality: South of Mount Konocti, Lake County, California. Collected by *Jepson*.

10. **Arctostaphylos Stanfordiana** Parry. STANFORD MANZANITA. MYACOMA MANZANITA. Figs. 448, 453.

An erect branching shrub, 3 to 7 feet high, with relatively straight and slender glabrous stems and branches and smooth reddish brown bark. Leaf-blades thick, elliptic or ovate to oblanceolate, usually acute at both ends, 1 to 1 3/4 inches long, 1/2-inch to 1 inch wide, bright green, glabrous and shining on both surfaces, entire; petioles about 1/4-inch long. Flowers pinkish, about 1/4-inch long, in profuse loose drooping panicles; peduncles and rachises not glandular-pubescent, very slender;

pedicels glabrous; ovary glabrous. Fruit depressed-globose or somewhat irregular, about 1/4-inch wide and 1/8-inch high, red or reddish brown, glabrous; the nutlets irregularly united or some distinct. Flowering period, March and April.

Stanford Manzanita occurs on mountain ridges, slopes, and valleys in Lake, Mendocino, Sonoma, and Napa counties. It is one of the most ornamental of our native shrubs. Its clusters of pinkish urn-shaped flowers and dark green glossy foliage make it a very desirable shrub for single or group planting. It thrives in heavy or light soil and it needs very little water. The plants do not crown-sprout after fires. In Sonoma County in the Rincon Ridge and Vine Hill districts this species often becomes much reduced in size and often has a sprawling habit. It apparently hybridizes with *A. manzanita* and *A. densiflora* producing individuals difficult to assign to either parent.

Arctostaphylos Stanfordiana Parry, Bull. Calif. Acad. 2:493 (1887). Type locality: Calistoga, Napa County, California. Collected by *Parry*.

11. **Arctostaphylos hispidula** Howell. HOWELL MANZANITA. Fig. 455.

Old stems with black-purple smooth bark. Young growth and inflorescence glandular-hispidulous. Leaf-blades dull green and rough to the touch; petioles glandular-hairy.

Howell Manzanita occurs on a serpentine area in Sonoma County (2 mi. e. of Occidental; near Camp Meeker, *Adams*) and in the vicinity of Gasquet, Del Norte County. It extends northward into southern Oregon.

This species closely resembles *A. Stanfordiana* in habit, stature, slender inflorescences, shape and texture of the leaves, and in flower-characters. The glandular-hispidulous character of the branchlets and inflorescences and slight roughness of the leaves of this species distinguish it from *A. Stanfordiana*.

Arctostaphylos hispidula Howell, Fl. N. W. Am. 415 (1903). Type locality: Gasquet, Del Norte County, California.

12. **Arctostaphylos manzanita** Parry. COMMON MANZANITA. Fig. 456.

An erect tall shrub or becoming almost tree-like, 6 to 22 feet high, with dark reddish brown bark, long crooked branches, and puberulent branchlets or glabrous in a few forms. Leaf-blades thick and firm, elliptic to oblong or broadly ovate to suborbicular, rarely obovate, abruptly acute or mucronate at apex, 1 to 1 3/4 inches long, 3/4-inch to 1 1/2 inches wide, pale or dark green, usually puberulent when young, becoming nearly or quite glabrous in age, entire; petioles 1/8- to 1/4-inch long, glabrous or puberulent. Flowers white or pale pink, about 1/4-inch long, in drooping rather open panicles; rachis and branches of the panicles pubescent or rarely almost glabrous; pedicels glabrous, about 1/8-inch long; ovary glabrous. Fruit globose, sometimes depressed, 5/16- to 7/16-inch in diameter, glabrous, white in early summer, becoming deep reddish brown in late summer and fall; nutlets irregularly united or distinct, roughened or ridged on the back. Flowering period, February to April.

Common Manzanita occurs chiefly in the middle and inner North Coast Ranges from Mount Diablo, Contra Costa County northward to Tehama, Trinity, and Shasta counties, thence southward in the Sierra Nevada foothills to Mariposa County. It usually inhabits the low hills and valley-flats of the Digger Pine belt or rarely extending into the Yellow Pine belt. North of Lakeport, Lake County (Dr. Barclay Stephens' ranch) this species forms an almost impenetrable low forest, some specimens measuring 20 feet in height with trunks 8 inches in diameter 2 feet

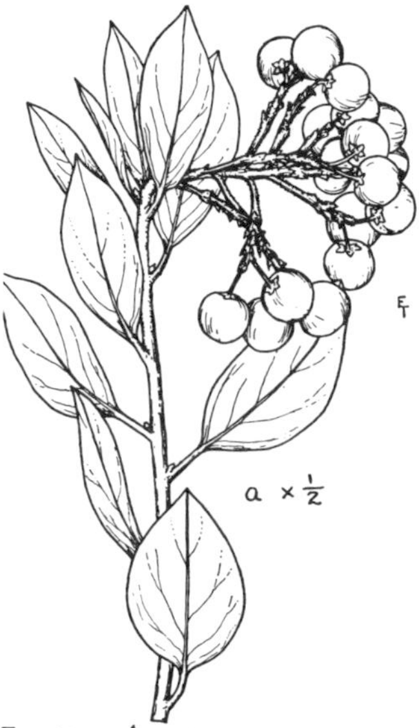

FIG. 456 A. MANZANITA

FIG. 457 A. INSULARIS VAR. PUBESCENS

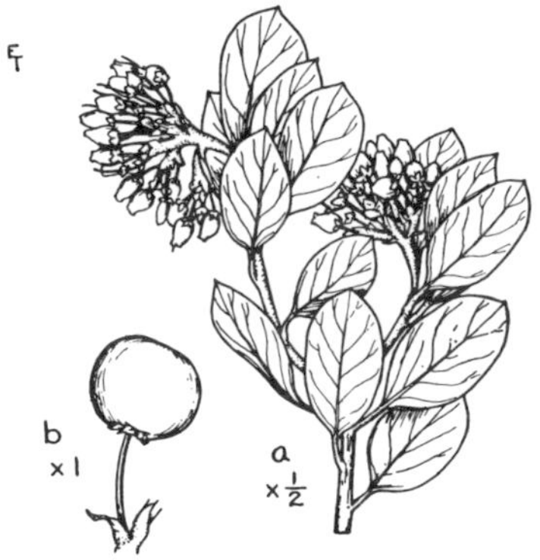

FIG. 458 A. PUNGENS

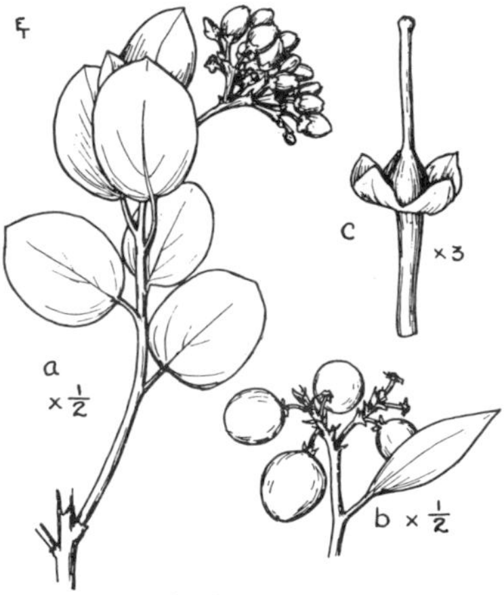

FIG. 459 A. PARRYANA

ARCTOSTAPHYLOS. a, A branchlet. b, Fruit. c, Pedicel and pistil.

above the ground. Considerable variation in the hue of the foliage exists in such colonies, some plants appearing grayish green, others bright green.

This species does not crown-sprout after cutting or fires. It propagates readily from seeds and it is not uncommon to find abandoned orchards and fields invaded by a solid stand of seedlings and young plants. In areas where this species grows with *A. Stanfordiana* plants occur which appear to be intermediate between the two. On Mount Diablo near Rock City plants occur which seem more closely related to *A. manzanita* than to *A. Stanfordiana.* The leaves, however, are more like those of *A. Stanfordiana,* being elliptic or lanceolate, acute at both ends and shining on both surfaces. These plants have been described as **A. laevigata** Eastw. Typical plants of *A. Stanfordiana* and *A. manzanita* do not occur on Mount Diablo. Adams suggests, "that the absence of either parent and rather long isolation have permitted a relative stabilization of the form." On the northeast lower slopes of Mount St. Helena, Lake County I have observed both parents, the Mount Diablo form, and intermediates.

Arctostaphylos manzanita Parry, Bull. Calif. Acad. 2:491 (1887). Type locality: In the Napa Range, near Calistoga, Napa County. Collected by *Parry.*

A. laevigata Eastw.: Probably a hybrid between *A. manzanita* & *A. Stanfordiana.*

13. **Arctostaphylos insularis** Greene. ISLAND MANZANITA.

KEY TO THE SPECIES AND VARIETY

Branchlets glabrous . . . . *A. insularis.*
Branchlets glandular-hispid . . . . 13a. var. *pubescens.*

An erect much branched shrub, 3 to 8 feet high, or sometimes arborescent, with smooth dark reddish brown or gray-glaucous bark and glabrous branchlets. Leaf-blades ovate to elliptical, 1 to 1¾ inches long, ½-inch to 1 inch wide, bright green and glossy above, glabrous or minutely puberulent beneath, rounded or truncate or subcordate at base, obtuse to acute at apex, entire; petioles about ¼-inch long. Flowers white, about ¼-inch long, in large spreading panicles; pedicels glandular-hairy; bracts minute; sepals with fimbriate to nearly entire glandular margins; ovary glabrous. Fruit depressed-globose, ¼- to ⅜-inch broad, nearly glabrous, light brown; the nutlets irregularly united, ridged on the back. Flowering period, February and March.

Island Manzanita occurs on Santa Cruz, Santa Rosa, and Santa Catalina islands. It does not crown-sprout after fires but seedlings spring up in great abundance often forming pure thickets in the chaparral.

13a. Var. **pubescens** Eastw. Fig. 457.

Branchlets glandular-hispid; bracts and rachises pubescent; ovary pubescent. This is the most common form of manzanita on the coast of Santa Cruz Island.

Arctostaphylos insularis Greene; Parry, Bull. Calif. Acad. 2:494 (1887). Type locality: Santa Cruz Island. Collected by *Greene.*

Var. pubescens Eastw. Leafl. West. Bot. 1:62 (1933). Type locality: Santa Cruz Island. Collected by *Greene.*

14. **Arctostaphylos pungens** H. B. K. MEXICAN MANZANITA. POINTLEAF MANZANITA. Fig. 458.

An erect or spreading shrub (or rarely decumbent), 2 to 10 feet high, with smooth reddish brown bark and canescent or white-tomentulose branchlets. Leaf-blades elliptic to oblong or roundish or obovate to oblanceolate, ¾-inch to 1 or rarely 1¼ inches long, ⅜- to ⅝-inch (rarely 1 inch) wide, usually abruptly acute and mucronate at apex, dull green, glabrous, and more or less glossy, finely tomentulose when young; petioles about ⅛-inch long. Flowers white or rarely pinkish, about ¼-inch long, in short compact simple or branched racemes, the rachises often distinctly thickened and club-shaped at tip; bracts short-deltoid; pedicels glabrous; ovary glabrous. Fruit depressed-globose, 3/16- to 5/16-inch broad, chestnut-brown, glabrous; nutlets separable or irregularly united, ridged on the back. Flowering period, January to March.

Mexican Manzanita occurs on dry slopes of the mountains of eastern San Diego County, in the San Jacinto, San Bernardino, and San Gabriel mountains, and northward in scattered locations in the inner South Coast Range to Mount Tamalpais, Marin County. It extends southward to Mexico and eastward to Texas.

On Mount Tamalpais this species sometimes occurs as a low spreading shrub often rooting where the branches touch the ground. The rachises are usually not swollen at the summit. This form is *A. montana* Eastw. Intermediate forms, however, occur between this and the erect form. The leaves on some specimens from Mount Tamalpais and Pacheco Peak, San Benito County are smaller than in most typical specimens of southern California. These specimens are difficult to separate from the more erect forms of *A. Hookeri* unless the inflorescences are present. The usually enlarged club-shaped rachises are distinct enough to identify this species from all other species of manzanita. It is very closely related to *A. manzanita* and like that species it does not crown-sprout after fires.

Arctostaphylos pungens H. B. K. nov. Gen. & Sp. 3:278 (1819). Type locality: On the Mexican Plateau in the vicinity of Mexico City. *A. montana* Eastw.

15. **Arctostaphylos Parryana** Lemmon. PARRY MANZANITA. PARDNERS MANZANITA. Fig. 459.

KEY TO THE SPECIES AND VARIETY

Branchlets, petioles, and inflorescences canescent. . . . . *A. Parryana*.
Branchlets, petioles, and inflorescences usually glandular-pubescent.
15a. var. *pinetorum*.

A diffuse widely spreading shrub, 3 to 7 feet high, with the lateral branches often decumbent and rooting in contact with the ground. Bark smooth, dark red or reddish brown. Branchlets lightly whitish tomentose or nearly glabrous. Leaf-blades thick and firm, ovate, elliptic, broadly oval, or rarely obovatish, ¾-inch to 1⅜ inches long, ½- to ¾-inch wide, bright green, shining, glabrous, entire; petioles ¼- to ⅜-inch long. Flowers white, about ¼-inch long, in simple racemes or few-branched panicles; rachises puberulent; pedicels about ¼-inch long, glabrous; ovary glabrous or puberulent. Fruit ovoid, ⅜- to ⅝-inch long, dark reddish brown, glabrous; the nutlets normally fused into a solid stone. Flowering period, February and March.

Parry Manzanita occurs in the Mount Piños region of Ventura County, in the Tehachapi Mountains, and southward in the San Gabriel and San Antonio mountains from 4000 to 7000 feet elevation, in the Upper Sonoran and Transition Life Zones. It does not crown-sprout after fires.

This species, in leaf-shape and puberulent branchlets, resembles *A. manzanita*. The more spreading habit of growth and normally coalesced nutlets distinguish it from that species. The hue of foliage is normally a lighter green than that of *A. manzanita*.

15a. Var. **pinetorum** (Rollins) Wies. & Schreib. Fig. 460.

Branchlets, petioles, and inflorescences glandular-pubescent. Nutlets usually separable.

This variety occurs in the mountains of southern California between 5000 and 8000 feet elevation, in the Transition and Canadian Life Zones where it is associated with *Pinus Jeffreyi, P. Lambertiana, Abies concolor, Ceanothus cordulatus,*

Fig. 460. *Arctostaphylos Parryana* var. *pinetorum* (Rollins) Wies. & Schreib. Killed after fire.

(Photograph by A. E. Wieslander, courtesy California Forest and Range Experiment Station, U. S. Forest Service.)

and *Castanopsis sempervirens.* Some known locations in California are: Los Angeles County.—Table Mountain, *J. Ewan.* San Bernardino County.—Big Bear, *A. Lewis;* Summit Camp Baldy, *J. S. Horton;* Lytle Creek, *R. St. John;* Silver Creek, *D. I. Axelrod;* Cucamonga Peak, *I. M. Johnston.* Riverside County.—Tahquitz Valley, *H. A. Jensen.* It extends eastward to Utah (Uinta Mts., *Payson*) and Colorado (Uncompahgre Plateau, *Rollins;* Buckeye Basin, Montrose Co., *Walker*).

This variety is similar to *A. patula* in characters of leaves and inflorescences but differs from that species in the absence of an enlarged root-crown or burl.

Arctostaphylos Parryana Lemmon, Pitt. 2:68 (1890). Type locality: Tehachapi Mountains, near Keene Station. Collected by *Lemmon.*

Var. pinetorum (Rollins) Wies. & Schreib. Madroño 5:46 (1939). *A. pinetorum* Rollins. Type locality: "3 miles west of Cold Spring Ranger Station, Uncompahgre Plateau, Mesa Co." Collected by *Rollins.*

16. **Arctostaphylos rudis** Jeps. & Wies. Shagbark Manzanita. Figs. 461, 462.

A low shrub, 2 to 5 (or rarely to 8) feet high, with rough and shreddy reddish brown bark and finely gray-puberulent branchlets. Leaf-blades broadly elliptic to oval or rarely ovate, 3/4-inch to 1 1/4 inches long, 5/16- to 5/8-inch wide, rounded at base, apiculate or obtuse at apex, bright green, glabrous or minutely puberulent, petioles 1/8- to 1/4-inch long, puberulent. Flowers pinkish, about 1/4-inch long, in short dense racemes; bracts mostly scale-like; pedicels glabrous; ovary glabrous. Fruit globose, about 3/8-inch in diameter, glabrous, light brown or reddish; the nutlets separable. Flowering period, late October to February.

Fig. 461. SHAGBARK MANZANITA. *Arctostaphylos rudis* Jeps. & Wies. Shreddy bark and burl formation at base.
(Photograph by A. E. Wieslander, courtesy California Forest and Range Experiment Station, U. S. Forest Service.)

Shagbark Manzanita occurs in sandy areas from near Oceano and Nipomo Mesa, San Luis Obispo County southward on Burton and Lompoc mesas, Santa Barbara County. This species forms burls at the base of the stem from which stems arise after fire or cutting. (Fig. 461.) In the summer of 1938 the writer observed in a cultivated field of oats thousands of small plants of this manzanita growing with seedlings of *Ceanothus impressus*.

Arctostaphylos rudis Jeps. & Wies. Erythea 8:100 (1938). Type locality: Corralillos Canyon, Santa Barbara County, California. Collected by *Wieslander*.

17. **Arctostaphylos patula** Greene. GREENLEAF MANZANITA. Fig. 463.

An erect much branched shrub, 3 to 7 feet high, with several stout stems from a usually swollen base. Bark smooth and reddish brown on old stems and branches. Branchlets finely glandular-puberulent with yellowish green glands, or often finely canescent and not glandular. Leaf-blades broadly ovate to nearly round, 1 to 1 3/4 inches long, 3/4-inch to 1 1/2 inches wide, rounded or somewhat heart-shaped at base, rounded to obtuse or broadly acute at apex, bright green or yellow-green and glabrous; petioles 3/8- to 5/8-inch long, glandular-puberulent or rarely glabrous. Flowers pinkish, about 1/4-inch long, in dense corymbose panicles; peduncles, branches of the inflorescences, and bracts glandular-puberulent; pedicels glabrous; ovary glabrous. Fruit globose, depressed, 1/4- to 1/2-inch broad, dark chestnut-brown to nearly black, glabrous; the nutlets irregularly joined, usually 3 distinct and 2 united. Flowering period, May and June.

Greenleaf Manzanita occurs usually in the open pine forests from 2000 to 5000 (or up to 8200) feet elevation in the Sierra Nevada from Siskiyou County southward to Kern County and in the higher inner North Coast Ranges from Snow Mountain and Mount Hull, Lake County northward to Trinity Summit, Humboldt County. It extends northward to Oregon and eastward to Nevada. In the mountains of southern California associated with such species as Jeffrey Pine *(Pinus Jeffreyi),* Mountain Whitethorn *(Ceanothus cordulatus),* and Canyon Oak *(Quercus chrysolepis)* occurs a manzanita which has long been known as *A. patula.* This manzanita differs, however, from *A. patula* in its response to fires and cutting. *A. patula* forms a globose swelling or burl just below the surface of the ground which sends up new shoots after fires or cutting, while the southern Californian plant is killed outright by fires. This latter manzanita is here identified as *A. Parryana* var. *pinetorum* (Rollins) Wies. & Schreib.

At the higher altitudes Greenleaf Manzanita sometimes is weighted down by snow, and the branches when in contact with the ground root freely, thus aiding in forming dense colonies. In the Sierra Nevada it usually occupies a vegetation belt higher than that in which *A. viscida* and *A. mariposa* occur. Where the species overlap in their distribution intermediates are often found which seem to be of hybrid origin. It is not unusual in the Sierra Nevada to find a form with finely gray-canescent branchlets, rachises, and peduncles instead of the normal glandular-puberulent ones. These two forms are often found associated in the same colonies (Alpine Highway from Jackson to Silver Lake). In the upper limits of its range where it associates with *A. nevadensis* intermediate forms occur which appear to be of hybrid origin. These forms, usually intermediate in stature, may have either glandular or canescent branchlets and peduncles.

Arctostaphylos patula Greene, Pitt. 2:171 (1891). Type locality: Central Sierra Nevada of California.

18. **Arctostaphylos mewukka** Merriam. INDIAN MANZANITA. Fig. 464.

An erect shrub, 3 to 8 feet high, with open crooked branches, deep red or purplish bark, and puberulent or glabrous branchlets. Leaf-blades narrowly oblong-elliptical or oblong-lanceolate or some obovate, 1 to 1 1/2 (or 2) inches long, 1/2- to 7/8-inch wide, glabrous and glaucous on both surfaces, pale green with a bluish or grayish hue; petioles 1/4- to 3/8-inch long, glabrous. Flowers white, about 1/4-inch long, in loose panicles; peduncles, rachises, and pedicels glabrous or puberulent, usually dark red; ovary glabrous or slightly pubescent at apex. Fruit globose, 3/8- to 5/8-inch broad, deeply depressed, glabrous and glossy, dark red to reddish brown, the pulp mealy; the nutlets separable or irregularly united, sometimes fused into a single stone. Flowering period, March and April.

Indian Manzanita inhabits the upper dry chaparral slopes of the lower Sierra Nevada from Tulare County northward to Plumas and Butte counties in a vegetation belt between that of *A. patula* and *A. viscida* or *A. mariposa.* The usually gray-green foliage, large smooth glabrous fruits in loose clusters, and glabrous pedicels distinguish this species from the other gray-leaved manzanitas. Some

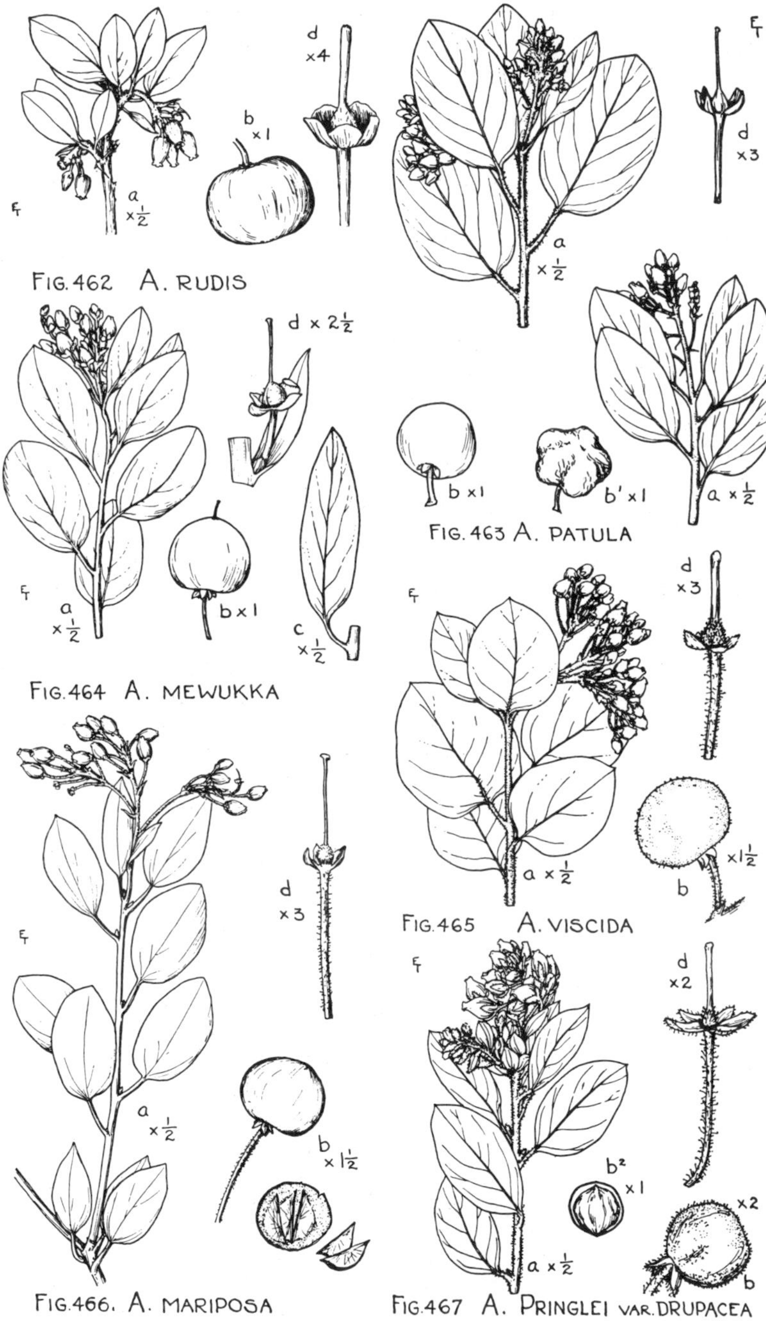

ARCTOSTAPHYLOS. a, Flowering branchlet. b, Fruit. b′, Dry fruit. b², Fruit with solid stone. c, Leaf. d, Pedicel and pistil.

specimens in the region of the overlap of distribution of *A. patula* and *A. viscida* seem very closely related to this species and it may be that *A. mewukka* is a rather stable form of hybrid origin. Like *A. patula* this species develops a swollen root-crown which sprouts after fires or cutting.

Arctostaphylos mewukka Merriam, Proc. Biol. Soc. Wash. 31:101 (1918). Type locality: "Ridge between N. Fk. American River and Bear River, near Colfax, California." Collected by *C. H. Merriam*. *A. pastillosa* Jepson.

19. **Arctostaphylos viscida** Parry. Whiteleaf Manzanita. Fig. 465.

KEY TO THE SPECIES AND VARIETY

Ovary glabrous or glandular.......................................*A. viscida*.
Ovary white-pubescent...............................19a. var. *oblongifolia*.

An erect shrub, 4 to 12 feet high, with several crooked stems from the base, crooked branches with deep red smooth bark, grayish foliage, and slender usually glabrous and glaucous branchlets and peduncles, or the branchlets sometimes sparsely glandular-pubescent or -hairy in some forms. Leaf-blades ovate or oblong-elliptic to round-ovate, 1 to 2 inches long, 3/4-inch to 1 1/2 inches wide, white-glaucous and glabrous on both surfaces; petioles 1/4- to 1/2-inch long. Flowers rosy to white, about 3/8-inch long, in open panicles or simple racemes; pedicels slender, 3/8- to 1/2-inch long, glandular-hairy; bracts small, ovate-lanceolate; calyx-lobes reflexed over the summit of the pedicels; ovary glabrous, pubescent, or glandular. Fruit globose, often depressed at summit, 1/4- to 3/8-inch in diameter, varying from light brown to deep red, commonly glandular, or glabrous; nutlets usually separable, or 3 separate and 2 united, sharply angled on the back. Flowering period, February to April.

Whiteleaf Manzanita is a very common and characteristic shrub of the Sierra Nevada foothills from Shasta County southward to Amador County where intermediate forms with *A. mariposa* occur, and then occasionally southward to Tuolumne County and in Tulare and northern Kern counties. From Calaveras County to Tulare County this species is practically replaced by the closely related species *A. mariposa*. It extends around the head of the Sacramento Valley to Tehama County and southward in the inner North Coast Range to Lake and Napa counties. Most of the shrubs in the North Coast Range have glandular fruits while those of the Sierra Nevada usually have glabrous fruits.

19a. Var. **oblongifolia** (Howell) Adams Ms.

Branchlets usually gray-pubescent. Leaf-blades oblong to oblong-ovate, somewhat pubescent. Inflorescences clothed with a fine white-pubescence. Ovary sparsely white-pubescent. Fruit finely pubescent.

This variety is known in California from northern Del Norte County (summit between Crescent City and Grants Pass, Ore., *Eastwood* & *Howell*). It is widely distributed in Josephine County, southern Oregon. Some specimens from northern Trinity County and from Shasta County apparently belong to this variety.

Arctostaphylos viscida Parry, Bull. Calif. Acad. 2:492 (1887). Type locality: Ione, Amador County, California. Collected by *Parry*.

Var. oblongifolia (Howell) Adams ex McMinn. *A. oblongifolia* Howell. Type locality: Near Waldo, Oregon.

20. **Arctostaphylos mariposa** Dudley. Mariposa Manzanita. Fig. 466.

KEY TO THE SPECIES AND VARIETY

Foliage white-glaucous; fruit glandular-viscid. *A. mariposa.*
Foliage greener; fruit glabrous or sparsely pubescent. . . . . 20a. var. *bivisa.*

An erect compactly branched shrub, 4 to 8 feet high, with very white-glaucous foliage, smooth reddish brown bark, and glandular-hairy branchlets. Leaf-blades thick, rough to the touch, broadly oval to elliptic, 1 to 2 inches long, 3/4-inch to 1 inch wide, shortly acute or mucronulate at apex, very pale grayish green or white-glaucous on both surfaces, glabrous or glandular-villous, entire or serrulate; petioles 1/4- to 3/8-inch long, glandular-pubescent. Flowers white or pinkish, about 1/4-inch long, in a many-flowered compact panicle; pedicels slender, about 1/4-inch long, glandular-hairy; ovary glandular-hairy or rarely glandular and glabrous. Fruit subglobose, somewhat depressed at summit, about 3/8-inch in diameter, red, glandular-viscid; nutlets irregularly separable. Flowering period, February to April.

Mariposa Manzanita occupies a narrow belt in the middle foothills of the Sierra Nevada from Amador County southward to Kern County. Considerable variation occurs in the nature of the pubescence and glandulosity of the branchlets. In the central part of its distribution the branchlets are glandular-hairy while in the northern and southern parts of its range where it associates with *A. viscida* the branchlets vary from glandular-hairy and glandular-pubescent to nearly glabrous. This species does not crown-sprout after fires or cutting.

20a. Var. **bivisa** Jepson.

Similar in habit and stature to the species. Foliage darker green, not as glaucous. Ovary glabrous. Fruit glabrous or very faintly pubescent, whitish or somewhat lucent.

This variety occurs locally in a few places in Mariposa and Tuolumne counties. It seems to the writer that this variety may represent one of the several intermediate forms btween *A. patula* and *A. mariposa* or *A. viscida.*

Arctostaphylos mariposa Dudley; Eastw. Sierra Club Publ. 27:52 (1902). Type locality: Millwood and Kings River Canyon, Fresno County, California. Collected by *Eastwood.*

Var. bivisa Jepson, Madroño 1:79 (1922). Type locality: Hetch-Hetchy, Tuolumne County, California. Collected by *Jepson. A. Jepsonii* Eastw.

21. **Arctostaphylos Pringlei** var. **drupacea** Parry. PINKBRACT MANZANITA. Fig. 467.

An erect shrub, 3 to 8 (or to 15) feet high, with spreading branches, smooth reddish brown bark, and densely glandular-pubescent branchlets. Leaf-blades ovate or broadly oblong-elliptic or almost orbicular, rarely obovate, 1 to 2 inches long, 1/2-inch to 1 1/4 inches wide, grayish green and minutely glandular-pubescent on both surfaces or becoming nearly glabrous, usually somewhat rough to the touch; petioles 1/8- to 1/4-inch long, glandular-hairy. Flowers rosy to white, in simple or branched nearly sessile racemes with glandular-hairy rachises and small lanceolate pink membranaceous deciduous bracts; pedicels slender, 3/8- to 5/8-inch long, reddish, glandular-hairy; ovary glandular or glandular-pubescent. Fruit ovoid or globular, 1/4- to 1/2-inch long, dark red, glandular-pubescent; nutlets united into a solid stone. Flowering period, February and March.

Pinkbract Manzanita occurs in the Transition Life Zone of the coniferous forests in the San Bernardino and San Jacinto mountains and in the mountains of San Diego County. It extends southward into Lower California. This variety differs from the species *A. Pringlei,* which occurs in Arizona and Lower California, in the complete union of the nutlets into a single solid stone.

Arctostaphylos Pringlei var. drupacea Parry, Bull. Calif. Acad. 2:495 (1887). Type locality: In the mountains east of San Diego, California. Collected by *Orcutt*. *A. drupacea* (Parry) Macbr.

22. **Arctostaphylos silvicola** Jeps. & Wies. SILVERLEAF MANZANITA. Fig. 468.

An erect silver-gray shrub, 6 to 8 feet high, with smooth dark red bark and densely gray-canescent branchlets. Leaf-blades elliptic to oblong-elliptic, 5/8-inch to 1 1/2 inches long, round-cuneate at base, gray-canescent or glabrate on both surfaces; petioles 1/8- to 5/16-inch long. Flowers white, about 1/4-inch long, in few-branched panicles; bracts foliaceous, densely canescent; pedicels glabrous or nearly so; ovary glabrous or rarely pubescent. Fruit globose, slightly depressed at the summit, 1/4- to 3/8-inch in diameter, light brown, glabrous; the nutlets separable. Flowering period, February and March.

Silverleaf Manzanita occurs on marine sand deposits in the Mount Hermon region of the Santa Cruz Mountains (about 2 mi. e. Ben Lomond to Zayante, *McMinn;* Mount Hermon, *Wieslander;* near Bonnie Doon, *H. S. Yates;* Glenwood, *Horace Davis;* Big Trees, *C. W. Hanks;* near Tuxido, *W. R. Dudley;* Scott's Valley, *Abrams*). This manzanita does not crown-sprout after fires, but seedlings appear in great abundance. These develop into nearly pure stands of chaparral as a fire type replacement of *Pinus ponderosa.*

This species appears closely related to *A. canescens* but differs from that species in having elliptical leaves and usually glabrous ovaries.

Arctostaphylos silvicola Jeps. & Wies. Erythea 8:101 (1938). Type locality: Near Felton Big Trees. Collected by *Wieslander*.

23. **Arctostaphylos obispoensis** Eastw. SERPENTINE MANZANITA. Fig. 469.

An erect grayish shrub, 3 to 7 feet high, with black-purple smooth branches and gray-tomentulose branchlets. Leaf-blades ovate or ovate-lanceolate, 3/4-inch to 1 1/2 inches long, round or truncate to subcordate at base, grayish tomentulose on both surfaces or rarely glabrate; petioles about 1/4-inch long. Flowers pinkish white, about 1/4-inch long, in subsessile panicles; bracts foliaceous, lanceolate-acuminate; pedicels nearly glabrous; ovary glabrous. Fruit globose, about 3/8-inch in diameter, glabrous; the nutlets separable. Flowering period, February and March.

Serpentine Manzanita occurs on serpentine areas from 500 to 3000 feet elevation in the mountains to the northeast, east, and southeast of Morro Bay, San Luis Obispo County. Some locations are: Chorro Creek, *Eastwood;* Pine Mt., *R. St. John;* Cuesta Pass, *McMinn;* Santa Lucia Range, Burnett Camp, Burnett Peak, and Morro Creek, *Wieslander.* This species does not crown-sprout after fires or cutting. Some specimens from the Morro Creek area have leaves subcordate, and in this respect approach the closely related species *A. pechoensis.*

Arctostaphylos obispoensis Eastw. Leafl. West. Bot. 2:8 (1937). Type locality: A serpentine area up Chorro Creek, near San Luis Obispo, California. Collected by *Eastwood.*

24. **Arctostaphylos glauca** Lindl. BIGBERRY MANZANITA. Fig. 470.

KEY TO THE SPECIES AND VARIETY

Branchlets glabrous and glaucous . . . . *A. glauca.*
Branchlets glandular-pubescent . . . . 24a. var. *puberula.*

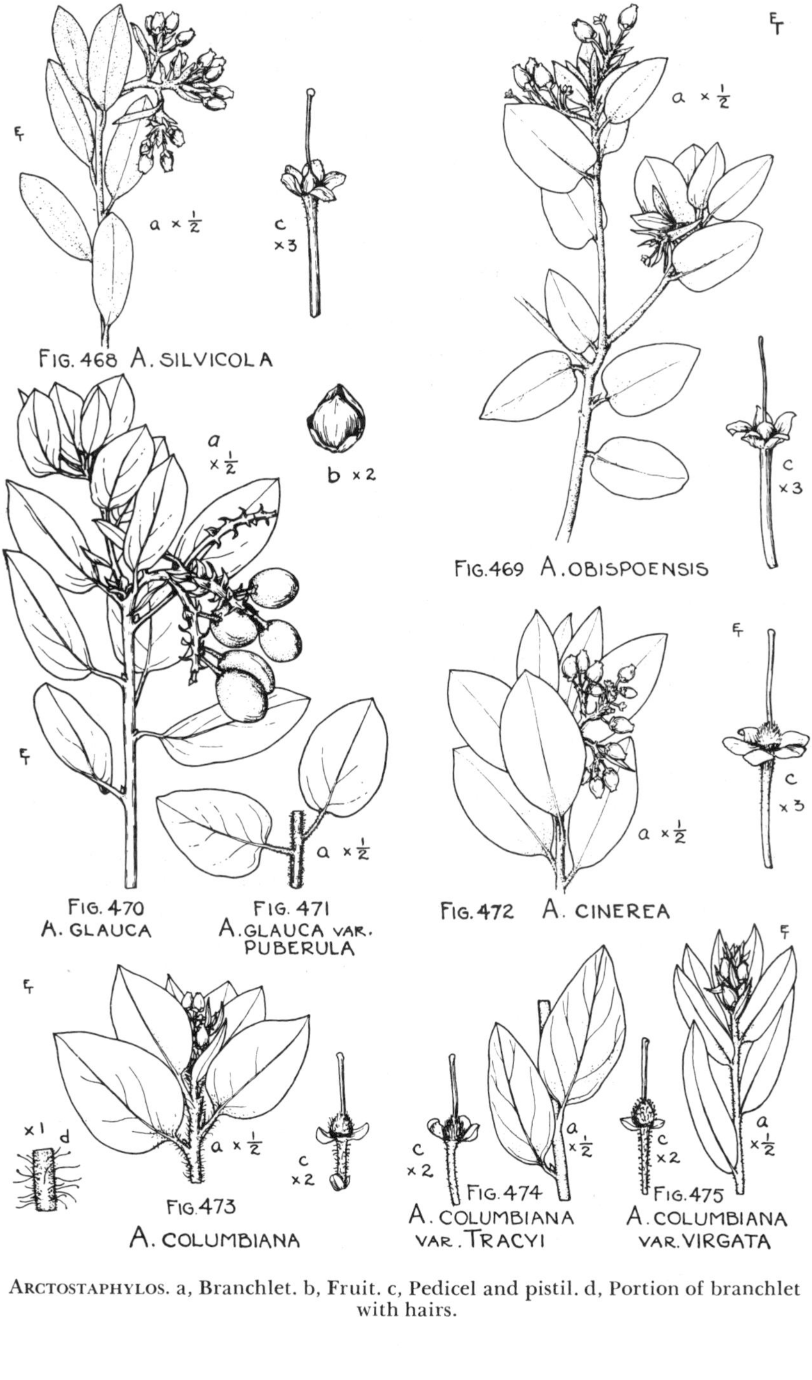

ARCTOSTAPHYLOS. a, Branchlet. b, Fruit. c, Pedicel and pistil. d, Portion of branchlet with hairs.

A large erect shrub, 6 to 10 feet high or often a small tree up to 25 feet high, with a distinct but short trunk. Bark smooth, reddish brown. Branchlets pale green, glaucous, and glabrous. Leaf-blades ovate or oblong-elliptic, 1 to 1¾ inches long, ½-inch to 1¼ inches wide, mostly truncate or subcordate at base or sometimes rounded to acute, pale grayish green, glaucous and glabrous on both surfaces, entire or on young shoots serrate; petioles ¼- to ½-inch long. Flowers white or tinged with pink, about ⅜-inch long, in short terminal panicles usually broader than long; peduncles and rachises usually glabrous and glaucous; pedicels glandular, stout; bracts short, spreading, broadly ovate; ovary glandular. Fruit globose to ovoid, about ½-inch long, light brown when mature, very glandular-viscid; nutlets united into a solid stone prominently apiculate. Flowering period, February to April.

Bigberry Manzanita is a common shrub or small tree of the lower and middle elevations of the mountains of southern California. It extends northward in the inner South Coast Range to Mount Hamilton and Mount Diablo and southward to Lower California. Its white-glaucous leaves and large viscid fruits with solid stones easily distinguish this species from all other manzanitas. It does not crown-sprout after fires or cutting.

24a. Var. **puberula** J. T. Howell. Fig. 471.

Branchlets glandular-pubescent to glandular-hirsute or finely pubescent.

This variety occurs on the northern slope of the Santa Ynez Mountains of Santa Barbara County (San Marcos Pass), in the inner South Coast Ranges of San Benito County and adjacent Monterey County, on the eastern slopes of Mount Hamilton, in the San Antonio Valley of Santa Clara County (acc. *Adams*), and in the Mount Piños region of Ventura County. It often grades off into the species in these localities.

Arctostaphylos glauca Lindl. Bot. Reg. 21, pl. 1791 (1836). Type locality: California. Collected by *Douglas*.

Var. puberula J. T. Howell, Leafl. West. Bot. 2:70 (1938). Type locality: "4 miles northwest of Hernandez, San Benito County, California." Collected by *J. T. Howell.*

25. **Arctostaphylos cinerea** Howell. Del Norte Manzanita. Fig. 472.

A decumbent shrub with semi-erect branches from the base. Branchlets and young growth clothed with a fine white pubescence. Leaf-blades oblong-elliptic or obovate, 1 to 1⅜ inches long, ⅜- to ¾-inch wide, pale and ashy green, becoming darker green in age, glabrous; petioles about ⅛-inch long, stout, flattish, and pubescent. Flowers rosy to white, nearly ¼-inch long, in spreading panicles with pubescent rachises and acuminate bracts, the lowest bracts sometimes foliaceous; pedicels pubescent; ovary densely pubescent. Fruit globose, ¼- to ⅜-inch in diameter, deep reddish brown; the nutlets variously separable. Flowering period, March and April.

Del Norte Manzanita occurs in the mountains along the boundary separating Del Norte County, California from Oregon and in Douglas County, Oregon. Specimens have been seen from French Hill, near Adams Station; Shelly Creek and near Gasquet, *Eastwood.*

Arctostaphylos cinerea Howell, Fl. N. W. Am. 416 (1901). Type locality: "Rocky hillsides along eastern base of Coast Mountains near Waldo, Oregon." Collected by *Howell.*

26. **Arctostaphylos columbiana** Piper. Hairy Manzanita. Fig. 473.

KEY TO THE SPECIES AND VARIETIES

Plants erect.
Branchlets with long stiff hairs............................*A. columbiana.*
Branchlets without long stiff hairs or rarely with a few scattered hairs.
Branchlets stout, white-canescent, not glandular; petioles, bracts, pedicels, sepals, and ovary pubescent, not glandular............26a. var. *Tracyi.*
Branchlets slender, with short dark glandular hairs; petioles, bracts, pedicels, sepals, and ovary glandular.........................26b. var. *virgata.*
Plants decumbent to nearly prostrate.......................26c. Hybrid form.

An erect shrub, 3 to 10 feet high, with the branchlets covered with a dense tomentum and long white bristly hairs, these sometimes gland-tipped. Leaf-blades ovate or oblong-ovate to broadly elliptical, 1 to 2½ inches long, ½-inch to 1¼ inches wide, obtuse or rounded-truncate at base, pale grayish green and sparingly pubescent to nearly glabrous on both surfaces; petioles ⅛- to ¼-inch long, densely long-hairy and pubescent, frequently glandular. Flowers white, about ¼-inch long, in short rather dense panicles; bracts foliaceous, lanceolate, usually hispid-ciliate; pedicels pubescent, or often glandular-hairy; ovary densely white-hairy. Fruit depressed-globose, about ¼-inch broad, light to deep chestnut-brown, sparingly pubescent or glabrous, often viscid; the nutlets irregularly separable. Flowering period, March and April.

Hairy Manzanita occurs in the low mountains near the coast from San Mateo County northward to Del Norte County. It extends northward to Oregon, Washington, and British Columbia. This species does not crown-sprout after fires.

26a. Var. **Tracyi** (Eastw.) Adams Ms. Fig. 474.

An erect shrub, 4 to 8 feet high, with tomentulose branchlets, without hispid hairs. Leaf-blades nearly glabrous, bright green.

This variety occurs with the species along the coast of Humboldt and Mendocino counties. Some plants with few hispid hairs on the branchlets are intermediate between this variety and the species.

26b. Var. **virgata** (Eastw.) McMinn. Bolinas Manzanita. Fig. 475.

A tall shrub, 6 to 15 (or to 20) feet high, with erect branches clothed with a dark glandular close pubescence. Leaf-blades narrow-ovate to lanceolate, 1½ to 2¼ inches long, ¾-inch to 1 inch wide, acute at apex, obtuse at base. Pedicels, bracts, sepals, and ovary glandular-hairy.

This variety occurs in Marin County usually near the redwoods. It is rather common on the south slopes of Mount Tamalpais near Muir Woods. The erect and non-sprouting habit of this plant ally it with *A. columbiana* rather than with *A. glandulosa* as given by some authors.

26c. Hybrid form. A low decumbent or nearly prostrate shrub with pale gray-green leaves smaller than in the species. Branchlets and petioles clothed with the long bristle-like hairs and soft pubescence characteristic of the species.

This form occurs along the bluffs near Sail Rock and Point Arena, Mendocino County and around Humboldt Bay, Humboldt County. It is associated with *A. Uva-ursi* and may be a hybrid between that species and *A. columbiana* which occurs in adjacent areas.

Arctostaphylos columbiana Piper, Fl. N. W. Coast 279 (1915). Type locality: Near Union City, Mason Co., Washington. Collected by *Piper. A. setosissima* Eastw.

Var. Tracyi (Eastw.) Adams ex McMinn. *A. Tracyi* Eastw. Type locality: Big Lagoon, Humboldt County, California. Collected by *Tracy*.

Var. virgata (Eastw.) McMinn; Jepson, Fl. Calif. 3:49 (1939). *A. virgata* Eastw. Type locality: Bootjack Trail, Mount Tamalpais, Marin County, California. Collected by *Eastwood*. *A. glandulosa* var. *virgata* (Eastw.) Jepson, in Manual.

27. **Arctostaphylos canescens** Eastw. HOARY MANZANITA. Fig. 476.

KEY TO THE SPECIES AND VARIETY

Leaf-blades broadly ovate to broadly oval or oblong-ovate or sometimes obovate, 1¼ to 2 inches long.......................................*A. canescens*.

Leaf-blades ovate-lanceolate to elliptic, ¾-inch to 1¼ inches long. 27a. var. *sonomensis*.

An erect or spreading shrub, 1 to 3 (or to 6) feet high, with smooth dark red-brown bark and densely soft white-pubescent branchlets, leaves, and peduncles. Leaf-blades variable, typically ovate to roundish, 1¼ to 2 inches long, ½-inch to 1¼ inches wide, pale green and gray-pubescent or canescent on both surfaces; petioles ⅛- to ¼-inch long, canescent. Flowers white or pinkish, about ¼-inch long, in short racemes or panicles; bracts large and foliaceous; pedicels ¼- to ⅜-inch long, pubescent or glandular-pubescent, reflexed in fruit; ovary densely white-tomentose. Fruit depressed-globular, ¼- to ⅜-inch broad, usually pubescent, sometimes slightly glandular or glabrate and glaucous; the nutlets irregularly separable. Flowering period, December to February.

Hoary Manzanita occurs in the North Coast Ranges from Marin County northward in Sonoma, Napa, Lake, Mendocino, Tehama, and Humboldt counties and in the Santa Cruz Mountains of Santa Cruz County. It extends northward into Oregon. In the northern part of its range it shows considerable variation in the hue of the foliage and amount of pubescence on the leaves, peduncles, and rachises. On Mount Tamalpais it is usually a low dense shrub while in the northern areas in competition with other shrubs it becomes much taller. It does not crown-sprout after fire.

27a. Var. **sonomensis** (Eastw.) Adams Ms.

Leaf-blades ovate-lanceolate to elliptic, ¾-inch to 1¼ inches long, ⅜- to ¾-inch broad, acute at apex, sparsely tomentose. Flowers white; pedicels pubescent or glandular-pubescent. Fruit pubescent or glandular.

This variety occurs locally on Rincon Ridge near Santa Rosa, Sonoma County.

Arctostaphylos canescens Eastw. Proc. Calif. Acad. ser. 3, 1:84 (1897). Type locality: South slopes of Mount Tamalpais, Marin County, California. Collected by *Eastwood*. *A. strigosa* Howell. *A. bracteata* Howell.

Var. sonomensis (Eastw.) Adams ex McMinn. *A. sonomensis* Eastw. Type locality: Rincon Ridge, Sonoma County, California. Collected by *M. S. Baker*.

28. **Arctostaphylos bracteosa** (DC.) Abrams. MONTEREY MANZANITA. Fig. 477.

An erect shrub, 2½ to 5 feet high, with dark shreddy bark on the old stems or sometimes smooth and with glandular-hairy branchlets. Leaf-blades broadly ovate to elliptic, ¾-inch to 1½ inches long, ½-inch to 1 inch wide, obtuse or acute and mucronate at apex, obtuse or slightly cordate at base, bright green, thin, slightly glandular-hairy or usually glabrate above, glandular-tomentulose or glabrate beneath; petioles short, pubescent and glandular-hairy, the hairs extending up the midrib and lower leaf-surface. Flowers usually white, about ¼-inch long, in small

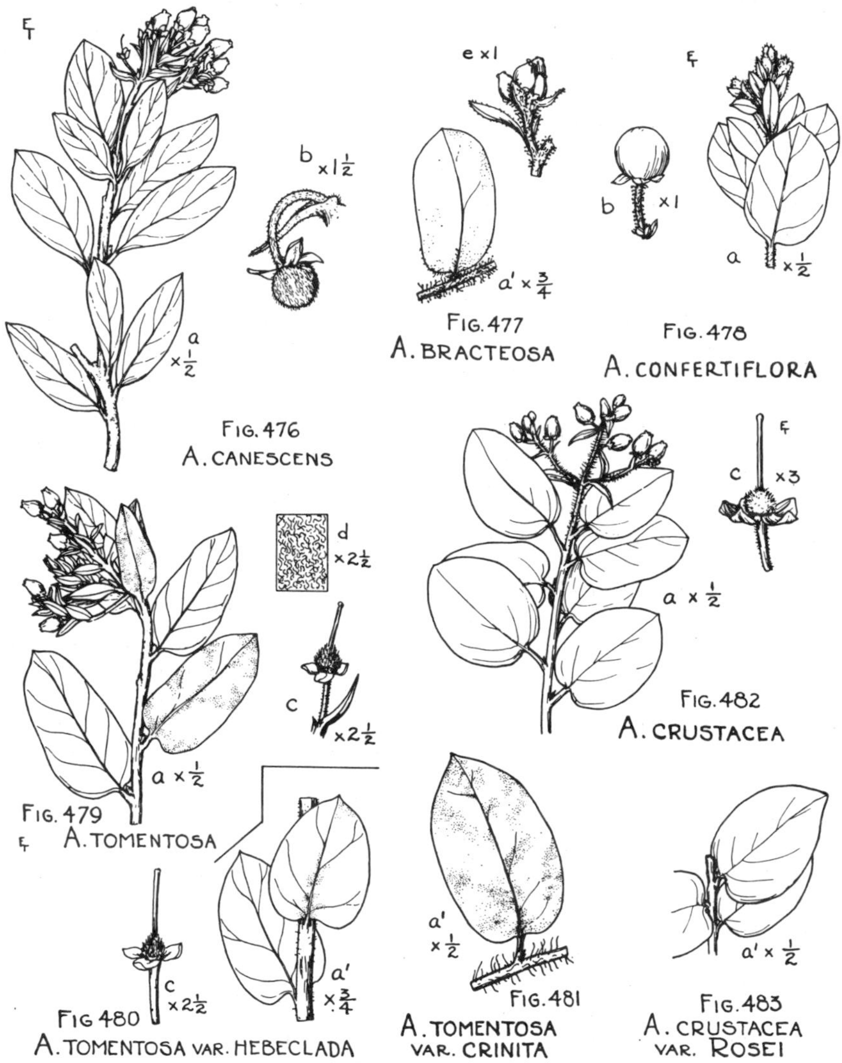

ARCTOSTAPHYLOS. a, Flowering branchlet. a′, Portion of branchlet with leaves. b, Fruit. c, Pedicel and pistil. d, Lower surface of leaf with curved hairs. e, Flower-cluster with bracts.

few-flowered congested clusters; bracts foliaceous, glandular-hairy; pedicels glandular-hairy; ovary pubescent to white-hairy, not glandular. Fruit depressed-globular, reddish brown, sparsely hairy, not glandular; nutlets separable. Flowering period, February to April.

Monterey Manzanita is common in the hills and lower mountain slopes adjacent to the Monterey Bay. On Santa Cruz Island a form occurs with smooth dark chocolate-brown bark on the old stems. This form has been described as *A. subcordata* Eastw. *A. bracteosa* crown-sprouts after fires or cutting. In this character it resembles *A. glandulosa* and *A. tomentosa*. In most characters except glandulosity this species resembles *A. tomentosa* and it is with great difficulty that some specimens in the Monterey area can be identified. This species and *A. crustacea* appear to be connecting links between the polymorphic species *A. tomentosa* and *A. glandulosa*.

Arctostaphylos bracteosa (DC.) Abrams, Leafl. West. Bot. 1:84 (1934). *Andromeda ? bracteosa a. trichoclada* DC. *Andromeda ? bracteosa* DC. Type locality: "Nova California." Collected by *Douglas*. *A. subcordata* Eastw.

29. **Arctostaphylos confertiflora** Eastw. Santa Rosa Island Manzanita. Fig. 478.

An erect tall shrub, 3 to 8 feet high, or depressed in exposed situations, with smooth dark red-purple bark and densely glandular-hairy branchlets, bracts, and pedicels. Leaf-blades usually broadly oval, 1¼ to 1¾ inches long, ½-inch to 1¼ inches wide, rounded at apex, subcordate or truncate at base, bright green, thick, glabrate or with few scattered hairs on the midrib and leaf-blade near the base. Flowers numerous in dense panicles with oblong glandular-hairy foliaceous bracts. Fruit flattened globular, reddish brown, the nutlets separable. Flowering period, December to February.

This species is apparently limited to Santa Rosa Island. It seems very closely related to *A. bracteosa* and with that species related to the *A. tomentosa* complex. It crown-sprouts after fire.

Arctostaphylos confertiflora Eastw. Leafl. West. Bot. 1:122 (1934). Type locality: "On Santa Rosa Island in a sheltered dell south of Black Mountain." Collected by *Ralph Hoffmann*.

30. **Arctostaphylos tomentosa** (Pursh) Lindl. Woollyleaf Manzanita. Explorers Manzanita. Fig. 479.

This species includes a number of forms occupying a region in the coastal mountains from San Mateo County southward to northern San Luis Obispo County and one or two forms along the coast in San Diego County and on Santa Cruz Island. A few of these forms appear very closely related to *A. crustacea* and *A. bracteosa* which seem to have an intermediate position between *A. tomentosa* and *A. glandulosa*. It seems probable that the numerous intermediate forms found in nature have resulted from hybridization. As here interpreted there is no glandulosity on any of the structures of the forms of *A. tomentosa*. The leaves are typically subcordate or truncate at base and are dissimilar above and below. In the forms of *A. glandulosa* the leaves are typically rounded or obtuse at base and nearly or quite similar on both surfaces. All the forms of this complex group of plants crown-sprout after fires.

The following key is an attempt to identify the more outstanding variations encountered.

KEY TO THE SPECIES AND VARIETIES

Branchlets with a close white tomentum, without bristle-like hairs or rarely with a few scattered ones, not glandular.
- Pedicels pubescent.
  - Leaves dark or bright green and usually glabrous and shining above, densely white-tomentose beneath . . . . *A. tomentosa.*
  - Leaves pallid or dull green and glabrate above, tomentulose or glabrescent beneath . . . . 30a. var. *crassifolia.*
- Pedicels glabrous; leaves pale green, glabrous but dull above, tomentulose, puberulent, or nearly glabrous beneath . . . . 30b. var. *hebeclada.*

Branchlets with a close white tomentum and with additional long bristle-like hairs. 30c. var. *crinita.*

An erect loosely branched shrub, 4 to 8 feet high, with shreddy usually persistent bark on old stems and densely white-tomentose branchlets. Leaf-blades oblong-ovate to round-ovate or broadly elliptic, 1 to 1¾ inches long, ½-inch to 1 inch wide, truncate or subcordate at base, acute and apiculate at apex, glabrous and shining above, typically densely white-tomentose beneath; petioles 1⁄16- to ¼-inch long, densely tomentulose. Flowers white, about ¼-inch long, in short spreading sessile panicles; bracts foliaceous, lanceolate, tomentulose; pedicels pubescent, not glandular; ovary densely white-hairy. Fruit depressed-globose, ¼- to ⅜-inch broad, sparsely pubescent or glabrous; the nutlets variously separable. Flowering period, February and March.

Woollyleaf Manzanita in its typical form occurs in the hills around Monterey Bay and southward to San Simeon Bay, northern San Luis Obispo County.

30a. Var. **crassifolia** Jepson.

Bark smooth, dark red. Branchlets tomentulose or rarely with longer soft white hairs. Leaves dull green or pallid or somewhat shining above, tomentulose or glabrescent beneath.

This variety occurs on the sandy mesas along the coast from Oceanside to San Diego in San Diego County. It seems very closely related to *A. glandulosa* var. *Cushingiana* but the more truncate leaf-bases, the usually more tomentulose lower leaf-surfaces, and distribution seem sufficient to maintain it as a variety of *A. tomentosa.*

30b. Var. **hebeclada** (DC.) Adams Ms. Fig. 480.

Bark more or less shreddy and persistent. Branchlets tomentose and usually with a few longer bristle-like hairs. Leaves glabrous or nearly so above, tomentulose, puberulent, or nearly glabrous beneath. Pedicels glabrous.

This variety occurs in the pine woods and adjacent open areas around Monterey Bay. It is quite similar in aspect to *A. bracteosa* but lacks the glandulosity characteristic of that species.

30c. Var. **crinita** Adams Ms. n. var. Fig. 481.

Bark smooth and dark purple. Branchlets with long spreading bristle-like hairs. Leaves varying from densely white-tomentose beneath to nearly glabrous, usually glabrous and shining above. ("A specie differt: ramis junioribus tomentosis et albo-divaricato-crinitis; corticis levigatis.")

This variety occurs from southern San Mateo County southward in the Santa Cruz Mountains to Monterey Bay. Adams states, "this variety appears as a possible intermediate step between *A. glandulosa* subsp. *crustacea (A. crustacea)* and *A. tomentosa*."

Arctostaphylos tomentosa (Pursh) Lindl. Bot. Reg. 21 (1836). *Arbutus tomentosa* Pursh. Type locality: Monterey, California. Collected by *Menzies*. *Arctostaphylos cordifolia* Lindl. *A. vestita* Eastw.

Var. crassifolia (Jepson) Jepson, Man. 749 (1925). *A. glandulosa* var. *crassifolia* Jepson. Type locality: Del Mar, San Diego County. Collected by *Jepson*.

Var. hebeclada (DC.) Adams ex McMinn. *Andromeda bracteosa* var. *hebeclada* DC. Type locality: "Nova California." Probably Monterey. *Arctostaphylos bracteosa* var. *hebeclada* (DC.) Eastw.

Var. crinita Adams ex McMinn. Type locality: Bonnie Doon Ridge, Santa Cruz County. Collected by *Adams*.

31. **Arctostaphylos crustacea** Eastw. BRITTLELEAF MANZANITA. Fig. 482.

KEY TO THE SPECIES AND VARIETY

Branchlets normally with hispid hairs.......................... *A. crustacea*.
Branchlets normally without hispid hairs...................... 31a. var. *Rosei*.

An erect branching shrub, 2½ to 6 feet high, with smooth dark purple bark on old stems and densely white-downy young stems and branchlets with additional long white hairs, not glandular. Leaf-blades oblong-ovate to roundish, or broadly lanceolate, ¾-inch to 1½ inches long, ½-inch to 1¼ inches wide, obtuse, truncate, or subcordate at base, bright green, thin or thick, brittle, glabrous and rather shining above, glabrous or slightly tomentulose, entire or serrulate; petioles about ¼-inch long, pubescent and villous. Flowers rosy or white, in nearly sessile panicles, the lowest bracts foliaceous, the upper usually deltoid-acuminate; pedicels pubescent; ovary densely or sparsely white-hairy or rarely glabrous, not glandular. Fruit depressed-globose, about ¼-inch broad, reddish brown, sparsely pubescent or glabrate. Flowering period, February and March.

Brittleleaf Manzanita occurs on the brushy hills of the South Coast Ranges from Contra Costa and Alameda counties southward in scattered locations to Santa Barbara County. It is the most common manzanita on the hills of Alameda and Contra Costa counties. Specimens from the southern part of the range have much thicker leaves than those from the northern locations. This species seems to connect the two polymorphic species *A. glandulosa* and *A. tomentosa*. According to Adams this species and *A. tomentosa* and its varieties have stomata distributed only on the lower surface while in *A. glandulosa* and its varieties the stomata are about equally distributed on both surfaces. The subcordate leaf-bases more closely relate the species to *A. tomentosa*.

31a. Var. **Rosei** (Eastw.) n. comb. Fig. 483.

Similar to the species except the branchlets are normally without hispid hairs and the leaves are longer and narrower.

This variety apparently is limited in its distribution to the hills bordering Lake Merced, San Francisco, California.

Arctostaphylos crustacea Eastw. Leafl. West. Bot. 1:74 (1933). Type locality: Kings Mountain, San Mateo County, California. Collected by *Mr.* and *Mrs. Seale*. *A. glandulosa* Eastw. in part, by various authors.

Var. Rosei (Eastw.) McMinn. *A. Rosei* Eastw. Type locality: Lake Merced, San

Francisco, California. Collected by *L. S. Rose*. *A. glandulosa* Eastw. in part, by various authors.

32. **Arctostaphylos glandulosa** Eastw. EASTWOOD MANZANITA. CROWN MANZANITA. Figs. 484, 486.

This is a variable species including many forms differing in amount and type of pubescence and glandulosity. In various areas within the range of the species variations occur which seem to intergrade with each other and with the species.

Fig. 484. EASTWOOD MANZANITA. *Arctostaphylos glandulosa* Eastw. Formation of burl. *(Photograph by A. E. Wieslander, courtesy California Forest and Range Experiment Station, U. S. Forest Service.)*

Several of these forms appear to be fairly constant and occupy distinct local areas. A few of the forms have recently been described as species but it seems best to include them here as varieties of the polymorphic species *A. glandulosa*. All the forms crown-sprout after fires and cutting and according to Adams have stomata on both leaf-surfaces.

KEY TO THE SPECIES, VARIETIES, AND FORMS

Branchlets usually glandular-hairy; bracts and pedicels glandular-hairy.
  Leaves dark to light green . . . . *A. glandulosa*.
  Leaves very pallid and scabrous . . . . 32a. var. *zacaensis*.
Branchlets not glandular-hairy.
  Inflorescences and ovary glandular-hispid; fruit viscid; leaves pale yellowish green . . . . 32b. var. *Howellii*.
  Inflorescences and ovary not glandular-hispid.
    Leaves dark green; pedicels glabrous . . . . 32c. glabrate form.
    Leaves pale or yellowish green; pedicels pubescent or glandular-hairy.

Branchlets with long soft or bristly hairs; pedicels pubescent, not glandular . . . . .32d. var. *Campbellae*.

Branchlets pubescent, without long bristly hairs.

Pedicels glandular-pubescent. . . . . .32e. var. *Cushingiana*.

Pedicels pubescent, not glandular . . . . .32f. Form of var. *Cushingiana*.

A spreading shrub, 2 to 4 feet high (rarely up to 8 feet), with several smooth reddish crooked stems from an enlarged woody base and coarse glandular-hairy

Fig. 485. Otay Manzanita. *Arctostaphylos otayensis* Wies. & Schreib. Plant by white stake killed by fire. Plants in foreground sprouting from burls after fire are *Arctostaphylos glandulosa*.

(Photograph by A. E. Wieslander, courtesy California Forest and Range Experiment Station, U. S. Forest Service.)

branchlets. Leaf-blades elliptic-ovate or lanceolate, 1 to 1¾ inches long, ½-inch to 1 inch wide, acute or obtuse and mucronate at apex, obtuse or rounded at base, dark to light green and more or less glandular-pubescent on both surfaces, or becoming glabrate in age; petioles about ¼-inch long, glandular-hairy. Flowers white, about ¼-inch long, in short spreading panicles; bracts foliaceous, lanceolate, glandular-hairy; peduncle and rachises glandular-hairy; pedicels glandular; ovary glandular-hairy. Fruit subglobose, about ⅜-inch wide, reddish brown when ripe, usually viscid; the nutlets variously separable. Flowering period, February and March.

Eastwood Manzanita is a common shrub of the lower mountain slopes and foothills in the Coast Ranges from Del Norte County southward to the mountains of southern California. Throughout its range sporadic variations occur which clearly belong to the species but differ in hue of foliage or in the amount, character, and distribution of the glandular pubescence.

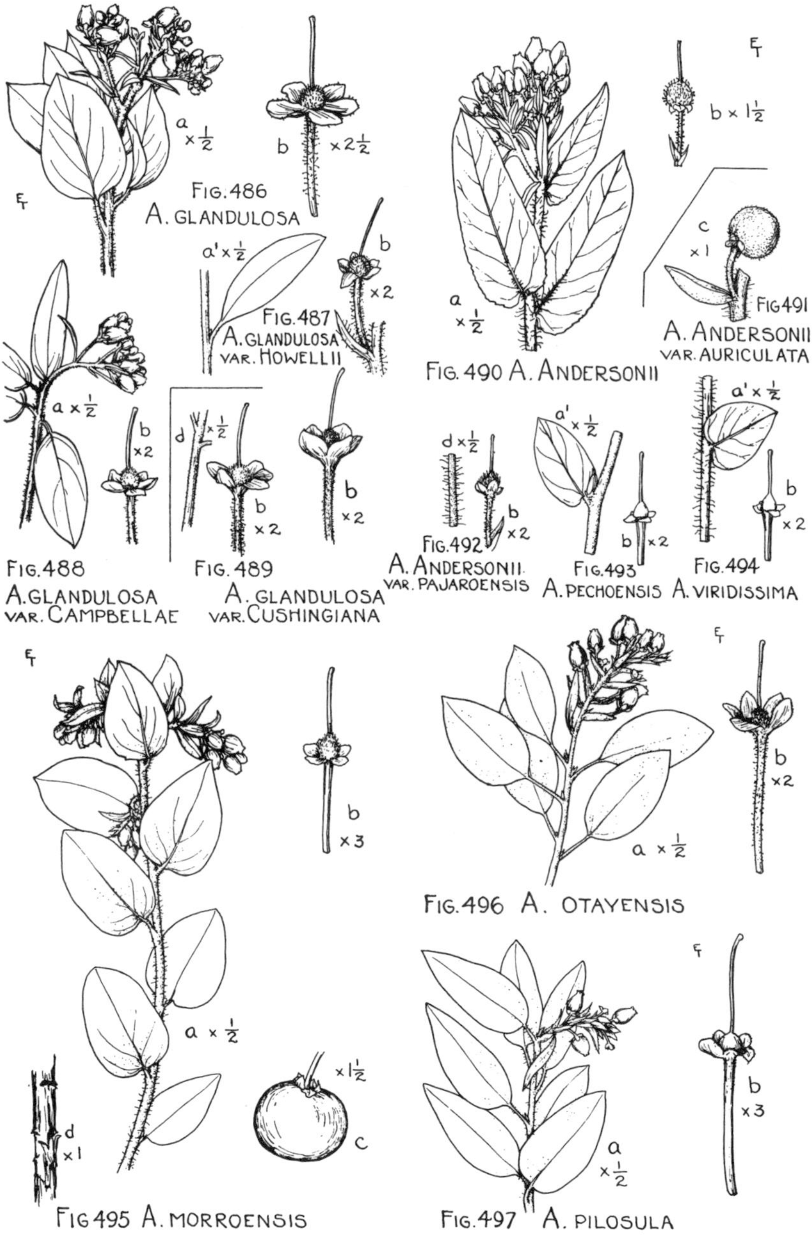

ARCTOSTAPHYLOS. a, Flowering branchlet. a', Portion of branchlet with leaf. b, Pedicel and pistil. c, Fruit. d, Portion of branchlet.

32a. Var. **zacaensis** (Eastw.) Adams Ms.

Young stems densely glandular-hairy. Leaves pale grayish green. Panicles nearly sessile.

This variety occurs in the mountains around Zaca Lake, Santa Barbara County. Many of the plants of San Diego County are close to this variety in color of foliage.

32b. Var. **Howellii** (Eastw.) Adams Ms. Fig. 487.

Branchlets white-pubescent, not glandular. Leaves pale yellowish green, elliptic to nearly orbicular, pubescent on both surfaces. Inflorescences very glandular. Ovary glandular. Fruit viscid.

This variety apparently is limited in its distribution to the Arroyo Seco and Vaquero Canyon areas of Monterey County.

32c. Glabrate form.

Branchlets pubescent, not glandular-hairy. Leaves dark green, nearly glabrous above. Inflorescences pubescent to nearly glabrous, not glandular-hispid. Pedicels glabrous. Ovary pubescent, not glandular.

This form occurs on the chaparral slopes and ridges of La Purisima Hills (Harriston Grade) of Santa Barbara County.

32d. Var. **Campbellae** (Eastw.) Adams Ms. Fig. 488.

Branchlets with a dense pubescence and additional long soft or bristly hairs, not glandular. Leaves light or yellowish green, pubescent or glabrate above in age. Pedicels pubescent. Ovary white-hairy, not glandular.

This variety occurs on Mount Hamilton and in the seaward mountains of Santa Barbara (Santa Ynez Mts.), Ventura, and Los Angeles (San Gabriel Mts.) counties. It is to be expected in the areas between these localities.

32e. Var. **Cushingiana** (Eastw.) Adams Ms. Fig. 489.

Branchlets with a close pubescence, not glandular. Leaves pale green with a bloom, becoming bright green in age. Peduncle and rachises pubescent, not glandular. Pedicels glandular-hairy. Ovary densely white-hairy, not glandular.

This variety occurs on the chaparral slopes on the south side of Mount Tamalpais, Marin County and extends northward in Marin, Napa, and Sonoma counties.

32f. Form of var. **Cushingiana.**

Similar to the preceding variety but the pedicels are pubescent, not glandular. It occurs with the preceding.

Arctostaphylos glandulosa Eastw. Proc. Calif. Acad. ser. 3, 1:82 (1897). Type locality: Mount Tamalpais, Marin County, California. Collected by *Eastwood*. *A. intricata* Howell.

Var. zacaensis (Eastw.) Adams ex McMinn. *A. zacaensis* Eastw. Type locality: Hills above Zaca Lake, Santa Barbara County, California. Collected by *Eastwood*.

Var. Howellii (Eastw.) Adams ex McMinn. *A. Howellii* Eastw. Type locality: Arroyo Seco River canyon, Santa Lucia Mountains, Monterey County, California. Collected by *J. T. Howell*.

Var. Campbellae (Eastw.) Adams ex McMinn. *A. Campbellae* Eastw. Type locality: Mount Hamilton, Santa Clara County, California. Collected by *Mrs. W. W. Campbell*.

Var. Cushingiana (Eastw.) Adams ex McMinn. *A. Cushingiana* Eastw. Type locality: South side of Mount Tamalpais, Marin County, California. Collected by *Eastwood*.

33. **Arctostaphylos Andersonii** Gray. HEARTLEAF MANZANITA. Fig. 490.

KEY TO THE SPECIES AND VARIETIES

Pedicels glandular-hairy; ovary glandular.
  Leaves bright green.
    Leaves 1¼ to 2¾ inches long; corolla ¼-inch long . . . . *A. Andersonii.*
    Leaves ¾-inch to 1¼ inches long; corolla about ⅛-inch long. 33a. var. *imbricata.*
  Leaves pale green . . . . 33b. var. *pallida.*
Pedicels and ovary pubescent, not glandular.
  Leaves densely white-downy; pedicels usually reflexed in fruit; Mt. Diablo. 33c. var. *auriculata.*
  Leaves glabrous, ¾-inch to 1¼ inches long . . . . 33d. var. *pajaroensis.*

A large erect or spreading shrub, 4 to 12 feet high, with a distinct trunk or branching from the base. Bark smooth, dark reddish brown. Branchlets densely clothed with a short pubescence and additional stiff hairs, these often with apical glands. Leaf-blades ovate or oblong-ovate, 1¼ to 2¾ inches long, ½-inch to 1¼ inches wide, pale to dark green, nearly or quite glabrous above, tomentulose or glabrous or sometimes glandular-hairy beneath, heart-shaped or usually auriculate at base, entire or serrulate near the base, sessile or very short-petioled. Flowers white or rosy, about ¼-inch long, in large compact panicles; bracts mostly foliaceous, ⅛- to ½-inch long, usually densely glandular-pubescent or glandular-hispid; peduncle and rachises pubescent or slightly glandular-hairy; pedicels glandular-hairy; ovary densely glandular. Fruit depressed-globose, about ¼-inch broad, viscid-pubescent, reddish brown; the nutlets separable. Flowering period, January to March.

Heartleaf Manzanita occurs in the Santa Lucia and Santa Cruz mountains and in the mountains of San Mateo County.

33a. Var. **imbricata** (Eastw.) Adams Ms.

Leaves bright green, ¾-inch to 1¼ inches long, much imbricated, glabrous except on the midrib toward the base. Pedicels glandular-hairy. Corolla about ⅛-inch long, white. Ovary glandular-pubescent.

This variety occurs locally in the San Bruno Hills of San Mateo County.

33b. Var. **pallida** (Eastw.) Adams Ms.

Leaves pale green, glabrous, imbricated, 1¼ to 2 inches long. Bracts nearly glabrous. Pedicels glandular-hairy. Corolla white. Ovary glandular-hairy.

This variety occurs on the chaparral areas in the hills of Alameda and Contra Costa counties where it associates with *A. crustacea.*

33c. Var. **auriculata** (Eastw.) Jepson. Fig. 491.

Leaves densely covered with a white pubescence. Pedicels and ovary pubescent, not glandular.

This variety is apparently local on Mount Diablo and in the hills near Nortonville, Contra Costa County.

33d. Var. **pajaroensis** Adams Ms. n. var. Fig. 492.

Leaves glabrous, ¾-inch to 1¼ inches long, auriculate-clasping at the base. Pedicels pubescent or rarely glabrate. Ovary densely white-hairy. ("Frutex erectus, dense; ramis junioribus pubescentibus et setosis; foliis ovatis, glabris, viridibus vel subpallidis, sessilibus, apice acutis, basi auriculatis, angulatis vel serrulatis, 2–3 cm. longis; bracteis foliaceis, viridibus, glabratis; pedicellis pubescentibus, saepe glabratis; corolla alba, 5-6 mm. longa; ovario dense albo-villosa; drupa parce pubescenti, non-glandulosa.")

This variety occurs in northern Monterey County in the hills south of Pajaro River.

Arctostaphylos Andersonii Gray, Proc. Am. Acad. 11:83 (1876). Type locality: Ben Lomond, near Santa Cruz, California. Collected by *Anderson. A. regismontana* Eastw.

Var. imbricata (Eastw.) Adams ex McMinn. *A. imbricata* Eastw. Type locality: San Bruno Hills, San Mateo County, California. Collected by *Mrs. Campbell.*

Var. pallida (Eastw.) Adams ex McMinn. *A. pallida* Eastw. Type locality: East Oakland Hills, Alameda County, California. Collected by *W. W. Carruth.*

Var. auriculata (Eastw.) Jepson, Madroño 1:88 (1922). *A. auriculata* Eastw. Type locality: "Trail above Boyd Ranch, Mt. Diablo, California." Collected by *Eastwood.*

Var. pajaroensis Adams ex McMinn. Type locality: Sandy hills west of Prunedale, Monterey County, California. Collected by *Adams.*

34. **Arctostaphylos pechoensis** Dudley. PECHO MOUNTAIN MANZANITA. Fig. 493.

A bushy shrub, 3 to 6 (or to 10) feet high, with smooth dark red-brown bark and somewhat white-tomentulose branchlets. Leaf-blades ovate to ovate-oblong, 5/8-inch to 1 1/4 inches long, 1/2- to 3/4-inch wide, acute and mucronate at the apex, auriculate or heart-shaped at base, pale gray-green, finely and sparsely tomentulose, sessile or with a very short petiole. Flowers white or pinkish, about 1/4-inch long, in short few-flowered panicles; bracts foliaceous, spreading, puberulent; pedicels nearly or quite glabrous; ovary glabrous or sparsely hairy at the summit. Fruit depressed-globose, glabrous; the nutlets irregularly separable. Flowering period, February and March.

Pecho Mountain Manzanita occurs in the low mountains from 500 to 2600 feet elevation in western central San Luis Obispo County. Some locations are: Head of Water Canyon, *H. A. Jensen;* 2 mi. s.sw. of Hollister Peak, *Wieslander;* Morro Creek and east of Cuesta Pass, *McMinn;* 1 1/4 mi. n. of Santa Manuela School and 1 3/4 mi. n.ne. of Slide Hill, *H. C. Lee;* 1 1/4 mi. w. of Gay Mt., *B. Bolt.*

This species does not crown-sprout after fires or cutting. The compact sessile inflorescences and nearly sessile auriculate leaves relate this species with *A. Andersonii* and perhaps the former would be better classified as a variety of the latter.

Arctostaphylos pechoensis Dudley; Abrams, N. Am. Fl. 29:98 (1914). Type locality: Head of Wild Cherry Canyon, Pecho Mountains, San Luis Obispo County, California. Collected by *W. R. Dudley. A. Andersonii* var. *pechoensis* (Dudley) Jepson.

35. **Arctostaphylos viridissima** (Eastw.) n. comb. LOMPOC MANZANITA. Fig. 494.

An erect shrub, 3 to 8 feet high, or sometimes procumbent and spreading over rocky ledges. Branchlets pubescent or tomentose and with bristly hairs. Leaf-blades broadly ovate, 1/2-inch to 1 inch long, 3/8- to 3/4-inch wide, rounded or acute and mucronate at apex, auriculate or heart-shaped at base, dark green, glabrous, entire or serrulate near the base, subsessile. Flowers white, about 3/16-inch long, in a dense sessile panicle; rachises pubescent; bracts foliaceous, glabrous but ciliate; pedicels glabrous or rarely sparsely pubescent; ovary glabrous. Fruit globose, about

1/4-inch in diameter, reddish brown, glabrous; the nutlets separable. Flowering period, April and May.

Lompoc Manzanita occurs on the brushy hills and flats of the coastal mountains in northwestern Santa Barbara County (Burton Mesa; La Purisima Hills; Casmalia Hills), in southern San Luis Obispo County (near Morro Bay, *Sinsheimer*), and on Santa Cruz Island. On the rocky cliffs between Casmalia and Burton Mesa this species is usually a low spreading shrub not more than 2 feet high. On Burton Mesa it associates with *Ceanothus ramulosus* and *Arctostaphylos rudis.* The auriculate leaves and short sessile flower-clusters relate this species to *A. Andersonii.* It does not crown-sprout after fires.

Arctostaphylos viridissima (Eastw.) McMinn. *A. pechoensis* var. *viridissima* Eastw. Type locality: China Harbor, Santa Cruz Island. Collected by *J. T. Howell.*

36. **Arctostaphylos morroensis** Wies. & Schreib. MORRO MANZANITA. Fig. 495.

An erect grayish or yellowish green shrub, 5 to 7 feet high, with red- or gray-brown rough and shreddy bark and appressed-pubescent branchlets, these usually with dense short or long bristly hairs. Leaf-blades oblong to oblong-elliptic, 1/2-inch to 1 1/4 inches long, truncate or subcordate or rarely rounded at base, glabrous or sparingly pubescent above, densely gray-tomentose beneath; petioles about 1/8-inch long. Flowers white or often tinged with pink, about 1/4-inch long, in mostly pendulous short panicles clustered in the upper leaves; bracts foliaceous, lanceolate, finely pubescent, often coarsely bristly; pedicels glabrous; ovary densely pubescent. Fruit globose or slightly flattened, about 3/8-inch in diameter, orange-brown when ripe; the nutlets separable. Flowering period, January to March.

Morro Manzanita occurs on the sandy hills south of Morro Bay, San Luis Obispo County, from 100 to 500 feet elevation. It does not crown-sprout.

Arctostaphylos morroensis Wies. & Schreib. Madroño 5:42 (1939). Type locality: Flowering specimen 0.4 mi. north of Hazard Canyon, el. 200 ft., *B. Bolt.* Fruiting specimen Hazard Canyon, south of Morro Bay, el. 250 ft., *Wieslander.*

37. **Arctostaphylos otayensis** Wies. & Schreib. OTAY MANZANITA. Figs. 485, 496.

An erect shrub, 3 to 8 feet high, with smooth dark red bark and glandular-hairy branchlets. Leaf-blades elliptic to oblong, 1/2-inch to 1 3/8 inches long, 3/8- to 3/4-inch wide, acute or apiculate at apex, rounded or rarely truncate at base, gray-green or yellowish green, finely pubescent above and beneath and finely glandular; petioles about 1/4-inch long. Flowers white, about 1/4-inch long, in open panicles or simple racemes; pedicels glandular-hairy; bracts leafy, lanceolate, 1/8- to 1/2-inch long, glandular-hairy; ovary glandular-hairy or with few glandular hairs. Fruit globose, 3/16- to 3/8-inch in diameter, pale brown, glabrous, sparsely hairy, or microscopically glandular; nutlets separable or coalesced into a solid stone. Flowering period, January to March.

Otay Manzanita occurs locally in the chaparral on Otay Mountain, San Diego County from 1800 to 3600 feet elevation. According to Wieslander it is associated with *Arctostaphylos glandulosa, Adenostoma fasciculatum, Rhus laurina, Ceanothus crassifolius, Xylococcus bicolor, Comarostaphylis diversifolia, Cercocarpus betuloides,* and *Chamaebatia foliolosa* var. *australis. Arctostaphylos otayensis* does not crown-sprout after fire. This characteristic distinguishes it from the species *A. glandulosa* which it resembles.

Arctostaphylos otayensis Wies. & Schreib. Madroño 5:43 (1939). Type locality: Otay Mountain, San Diego County. Collected by *H. A. Jensen* and *Wieslander.*

38. **Arctostaphylos pilosula** Jeps. & Wies. STRIPEDBERRY MANZANITA. Fig. 497.

An erect shrub, 3½ to 10 feet high, with smooth dark red bark and pubescent branchlets, these usually with short or long bristly hairs. Leaf-blades oblong-elliptic to ovate, ⅝-inch to 1¾ inches long, truncate or rounded at the base or rarely subcordate, yellow- or glaucous-green, glabrous or sparingly pubescent on both surfaces, young leaves densely silvery-tomentose; petioles about ¼-inch long. Flowers white or tinged with pink, about ¼-inch long, in short few-branched panicles, bracts foliaceous, lanceolate, finely pubescent to glabrous and usually bristly-ciliate; pedicels glabrous or slightly hairy; ovary usually glabrous. Fruit depressed-globose, ¼- to ⅜-inch wide, glabrous, light brown or red-brown, usually with blue-black vertical stripes when mature; the nutlets separable. Flowering period, February and March.

Stripedberry Manzanita occurs as a dominant component of the chaparral areas in San Luis Obispo County from 200 to 3600 feet elevation.

Representative specimens: 3 mi. e. of Pozo, el. 1850, *A. D. Gifford* V. T. M. 19625; 2.5 mi. s.w. of La Panza, el. 2300, *D. Axelrod* V. T. M. 17467. This species does not crown-sprout after fires.

Arctostaphylos pilosula Jeps. & Wies. Erythea 8:101 (1938). Type locality: American Canyon, La Panza Range, San Luis Obispo County. Collected by *Wieslander*.

5. Xylococcus Nutt.

(From the Greek *xylos*, wood, and *kokkos*, berry, in reference to the hard stone of the berry-like fruit.)

This genus contains a single species native to southern California, Lower California, and Santa Catalina Island.

1. **Xylococcus bicolor** Nutt. MISSION-MANZANITA. Fig. 498.

A densely branched shrub, 3 to 8 feet high, with grayish brown usually persistent bark and ash-colored tomentulose branchlets. Leaves simple, alternate, evergreen; the blades thick and leathery, ovate to oval or oblong-elliptic, ¾-inch to 2½ inches long, ½-inch to 1 inch wide, or apparently narrower due to enrolling of the margins, dark green and glabrous above, white-tomentose beneath, the margins revolute and entire; petioles about ¼-inch long. Flowers bisexual, white or pinkish, about ⅜-inch long, in dense few-flowered terminal panicles; peduncle tomentulose; pedicels stout, ⅛- to ¼-inch long; calyx red, the 5 lobes reflexed at maturity; corolla urn-shaped, the 5 lobes very small; stamens 10, rarely 8; ovary superior, 5- or rarely 4-celled, pubescent. Fruit dry, drupe-like, globular, ¼- to ⅜-inch in diameter, purplish red, with a smooth pericarp and a thin pulp; the nutlets united into a solid stone. Flowering period, January to March.

Mission-manzanita occurs in the chaparral of the foothills and mesas of western San Diego County, in the Verdugo Range of Los Angeles County, and on Santa Catalina Island. It crown-sprouts after fires.

Xylococcus bicolor Nutt. Trans. Am. Phil. Soc. 2, 8:259 (1843). Type locality: Monterey, California according to the type sheet, but this is certainly an error as the plant does not occur in the Monterey region. Probably San Diego, California. Collected by *Nuttall*. *Arctostaphylos bicolor* (Nutt.) Gray.

6. Comarostaphylis Zucc.

(From the Greek *komaros*, the Arbutus, and *staphule*, a grape, referring to the cluster of edible fruit.)

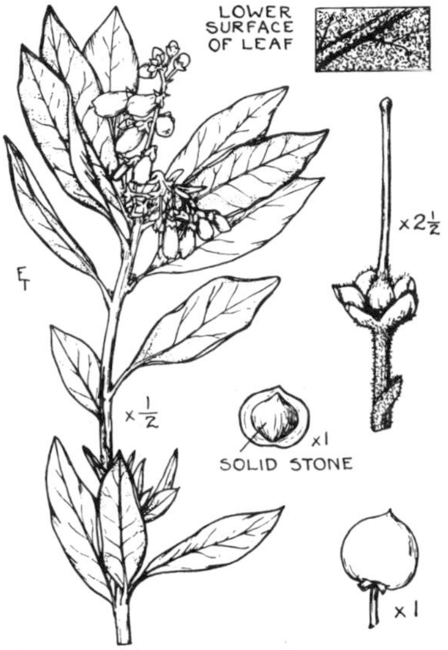

FIG. 498 XYLOCOCCUS BICOLOR

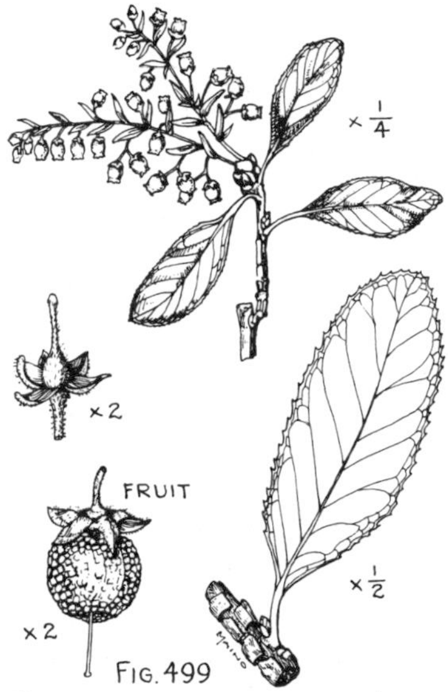

FIG. 499 COMAROSTAPHYLIS DIVERSIFOLIA

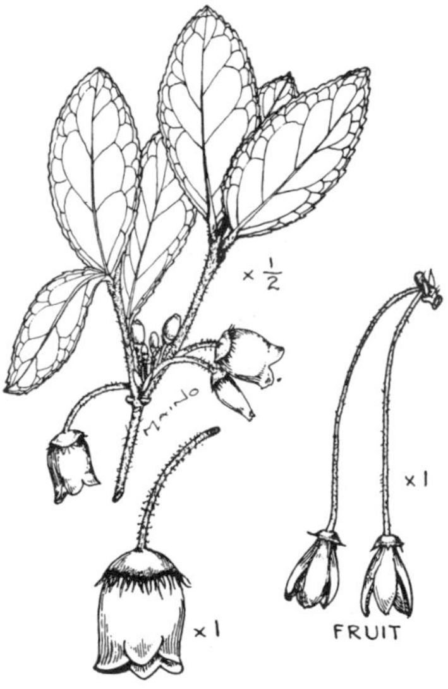

FIG 500 MENZIESIA FERRUGINEA

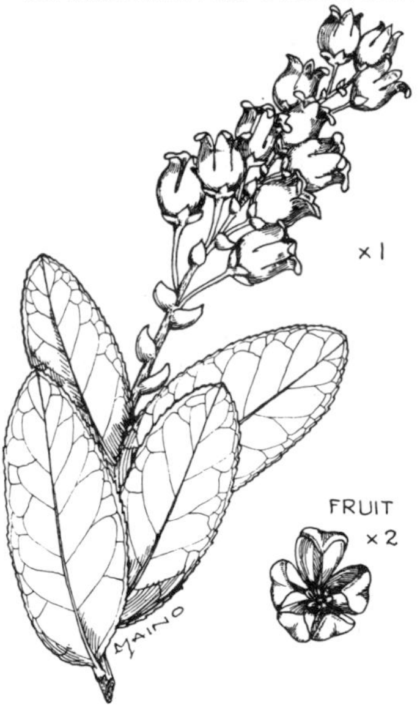

FIG. 501 LEUCOTHOE DAVISIAE

This genus contains about 25 species native to Mexico and California. A single species is native to California.

1. **Comarostaphylis diversifolia** (Parry) Greene. SUMMER-HOLLY. MOCK ARBUTE. Fig. 499.

An erect evergreen shrub or small tree, 6 to 18 feet high, with canescent-tomentulose twigs and alternate usually numerous thick and leathery leaves. Leaf-blades elliptic or oblong-ovate to ovate, 3/4-inch to 3 1/2 inches long, 1/2-inch to 2 inches wide, dark green, shining and glabrous above, whitish pubescent beneath, serrate; petioles about 1/4-inch long. Flowers bisexual, white, numerous in loose racemose panicles 2 to 5 inches long; calyx, pedicels, and peduncles tomentose; calyx 5-lobed, about 1/4-inch wide; corolla urn-shaped, about 1/4-inch long, 5-lobed, the lobes short and usually recurved; stamens 10, included; each anther-sac with a slender awn; ovary superior, 5-celled, pubescent. Fruit a globular red fleshy drupe-like berry, about 3/16-inch in diameter, consisting of a solid stone covered with the fleshy warty or papillose pericarp. Flowering period, April and May.

Summer-holly occurs along the coast of southern California from Santa Barbara County (Nojoqui Park) southward in the Santa Monica Mountains of Los Angeles County to San Diego County and on Santa Catalina, Santa Cruz, and Santa Rosa islands. It extends southward to Lower California. In flower characters this shrub resembles the flowers of manzanita but it differs from the manzanitas in having fleshy papillose or warty drupe-like berries and tomentose calyces.

Comarostaphylis diversifolia (Parry) Greene, Bull. Calif. Acad. 2:406 (1887). *Arctostaphylos arguta* var. *diversifolia* Parry. Type locality: Jamul Valley, San Diego County, California. Collected by *O. N. Sanford, Parry, Orcutt.*

7. **Menziesia** Smith

(Named in honor of Archibald Menzies, surgeon and botanist of the Vancouver Expedition.)

This genus contains about 7 species native to Asia and boreal America. A single species occurs in California.

1. **Menziesia ferruginea** Smith. RUSTYLEAF. MOCK AZALEA. Fig. 500.

A straggling or erect slender shrub, 6 to 15 feet high, with sparingly fine-pubescent twigs. Leaves simple, alternate, deciduous; the blades thin, elliptic-oblong to obovate, 1 1/4 to 2 3/4 inches long, 1/2-inch to 1 inch wide, deep green above, paler beneath, strigose on both surfaces with scattered rusty hairs but usually more so above, serrulate; petioles 1/4-inch or less long, long-hairy. Flowers bisexual, yellow or greenish purple, appearing with the leaves, borne in clusters terminating the branches; pedicels nodding, glandular-pubescent, 3/4-inch to 1 inch long, erect in fruit; calyx small, flat or saucer-shaped, bristly-ciliate, usually 4- (rarely 5-) lobed; corolla oblong-ovoid, becoming cylindrical, 1/4- to 1/2-inch long, 4-toothed or -lobed; stamens 8, included; ovary superior, 4-celled. Fruit an ovoid woody 4-celled capsule about 1/4-inch long, glabrous. Flowering period, June and July.

Rustyleaf occurs near the coast in a few localities in Humboldt and Del Norte counties (near Orick; Prairie Creek; Patricks Point; in redwood forest on Freshwater Creek; Holland Grade, 3 mi. out of Crescent City to Grants Pass, Ore.). It extends northward to British Columbia and Alaska and eastward to Idaho and Montana.

Menziesia ferruginea Smith, Pl. Ic. 3:pl. 56 (1791). Type locality: Western North America. Collected by *Menzies.*

8. **Leucothoe** D. Don

(Named for Leucothoe, daughter of Orchamur, King of Babylon.)

This genus contains about 32 species native to America. A single species is native to California.

1. **Leucothoe Davisiae** Torr. Black-laurel. Sierra-laurel. Fig. 501.

An erect evergreen shrub, 2 to 5 feet high, with glabrous or slightly puberulent branches. Leaves simple, alternate; the blades thick and somewhat leathery, oblong or oval, 3/4-inch to 2 3/4 inchs long, 3/8- to 5/8-inch wide, 1-veined from the base, deep green and shining above, paler and dull beneath, glabrous on both sides, serrulate to entire; petioles 1/4-inch or less long. Flowers bisexual, white, pendulous in terminal raceme-like panicles 2 to 4 inches long; calyx star-shaped, the 5 lobes longer than the tube; corolla ovate, 1/4- to 3/8-inch long, the 5 lobes much longer than the tube; stamens 10, included; ovary superior, 5-celled. Fruit a smooth glabrous broadly oval capsule about 1/4-inch long, somewhat depressed at summit. Flowering period, June and July.

Black-laurel occurs occasionally in wet meadows and springy ground in the Sierra Nevada from Madera County northward at scattered locations to Lassen Peak, Shasta County, westward to the Salmon Mountains, Trinity County, and in Siskiyou County (Hancock Lake; Whiskey Butte) from about 6000 to 8500 feet elevation. It extends northward into Oregon.

Leucothoe Davisiae Torr.; Gray, Proc. Am. Acad. 7:400 (1868). Type locality: Near Eureka, Nevada County, California. Collected by *Miss N. J. Davis.*

9. **Gaultheria** L.

(Named in honor of Dr. Gaultier, physician and botanist of Canada.)

Shrubs or subshrubs. Leaves simple, alternate, evergreen. Flowers bisexual, white or pink; calyx 5-cleft; corolla 5-toothed or -lobed, regular; stamens 10, the filaments dilated at base; ovary superior, 5-celled, 5-lobed, on a thin undulate-toothed disk. Fruit berry-like, consisting of a 5-celled pod enclosed by the persistent fleshy calyx.

This is a large genus consisting of about 100 species, chiefly American, extending from Canada through the United States and Mexico to the Andes of South America. A few species occur in the Himalayas, eastern Asia, Australia, and New Zealand. Three species occur in California.

KEY TO THE SPECIES

Leaves usually over 1 1/2 inches long; flowers in racemes; filaments hairy.
1. *G. shallon.*

Leaves less than 1 1/2 inches long; flowers solitary; filaments glabrous.

Leaves oval, about 1/2-inch long, entire or obscurely serrulate. . . 2. *G. humifusa.*

Leaves ovate, 3/4-inch to 1 1/2 inches long, distinctly serrulate. . . . 3. *G. ovatifolia.*

1. **Gaultheria shallon** Pursh. Salal. Fig. 502.

A spreading shrub, 1 to 6 feet high, with slender stems and stoutish glandular-pubescent branchlets. Leaf-blades ovate to nearly round, 1 3/4 to 4 inches long, 3/4-inch to 1 1/2 inches wide, slightly heart-shaped at base, shining and glabrous above, paler and glabrous or nearly so beneath, distinctly serrulate; petioles ⅛-inch or less long. Flowers in axillary or terminal racemes 3 to 6 inches long, glandular-pubescent; pedicels reflexed, bearing 2 bractlets below the middle or at the base; bracts reddish; calyx reddish; corolla white or pinkish, urn-shaped, ⅓- to nearly ½-inch long, 5-lobed at the narrow orifice, the lobes recurved; filaments hairy. Fruit globular, about ¼-inch in diameter, black, many-seeded. Flowering period, March to June.

Salal is a rather common shrub of the Redwood belt along the coast from Del Norte County southward to Monterey County and occasionally in the woods of the Santa Ynez Mountains of Santa Barbara County. It extends northward to British Columbia. Its glossy evergreen foliage is much used for Christmas decorations. The fruit has a spicy aromatic odor and is eaten by birds and livestock. The foliage is not very palatable.

Gaultheria shallon Pursh, Fl. Am. Sept. 1:283 (1814). Type locality: "Falls of the Columbia River." Collected by *Lewis* but first discovered by *Menzies*.

2. **Gaultheria humifusa** (Graham) Rydb. WESTERN WINTERGREEN. ALPINE WINTERGREEN. Fig. 503.

A low evergreen decumbent subshrub, 4 to 10 inches high, with sparingly pubescent creeping stems. Flowering period, June and July.

Western Wintergreen is a rare species in California. To my knowledge it has been collected only in the Kings River region, in the Granite Basin by Mrs. M. Clemens and at Grouse Meadows in Le Conte Canyon by Peirson. It extends northward to British Columbia and eastward to Colorado.

Gaultheria humifusa (Graham) Rydb. Mem. N. Y. Bot. Gard. 1:300 (1900). *Vaccinium humifusum* Graham. Type locality: "Rocky Mountains of British America." "Grown from seed in the botanical garden at Edinburgh."

3. **Gaultheria ovatifolia** Gray. OREGON WINTERGREEN. OVAL-LEAF GAULTHERIA. Fig. 504.

A low subshrub, 4 to 8 inches high, with procumbent stems and ascending or erect branches. Branchlets, petioles, and calyces pubescent with loosely spreading hairs. Flowering period, June to August.

Oregon Wintergreen occurs in the coniferous forests in a few locations in the higher mountains of Humboldt, Del Norte, and northwestern Siskiyou counties (Horse Mountain, *J. P. Tracy;* Bartlett Trail to Preston Peak, *Chester Dudley;* Bear Wallows, 2 miles north of Sanger Peak, *Doris Kildale;* head of Redwood Creek, *Chestnut* & *Drew;* near Putnam Peak, Klamath Range, *Jepson*). It extends northward to British Columbia and eastward to northern Idaho.

Gaultheria ovatifolia Gray, Proc. Am. Acad. 19:85 (1883). Type locality: Cascade Mountains from Oregon to British Columbia. Collected by *Lyall, E. Hall, S. Watson, W. N. Suksdorf.*

10. **Ledum** L.

(From the Greek *Ledon,* name of an oriental shrub, *Cistus.*)

This genus consists of 3 species of northern North America, one of which occurs also in northern Europe and Asia. Only one species is native to California.

1. **Ledum glandulosum** Nutt. WESTERN LABRADOR TEA. TRAPPERS TEA. Fig. 505.

An erect rigid shrub, 2 to 5 feet high. Leaves simple, alternate, evergreen, crowded near the ends of the branches; the blades oblong, ovate, or elliptic-ovate, rounded at base, acute or obtuse at apex, 1¼ to 2½ inches long, ½- to ¾-inch

FIG. 502 GAULTHERIA SHALLON

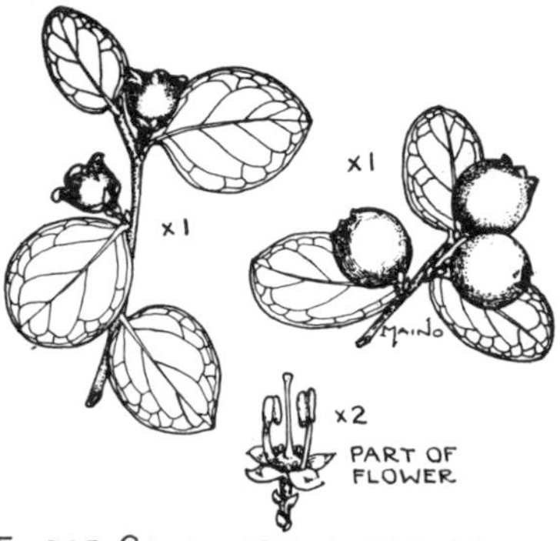

FIG. 503 GAULTHERIA HUMIFUSA

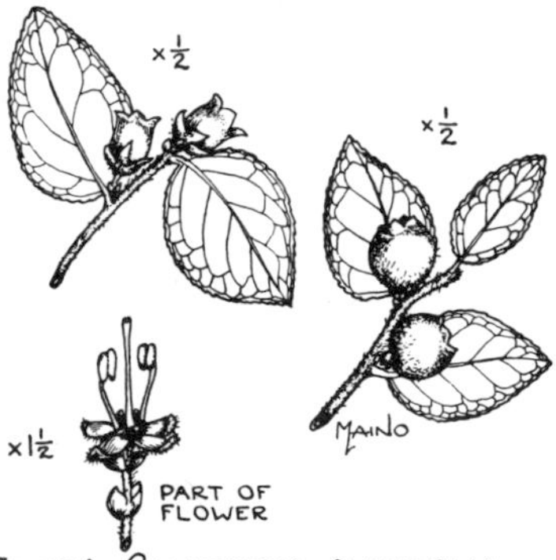

FIG. 504 GAULTHERIA OVATIFOLIA

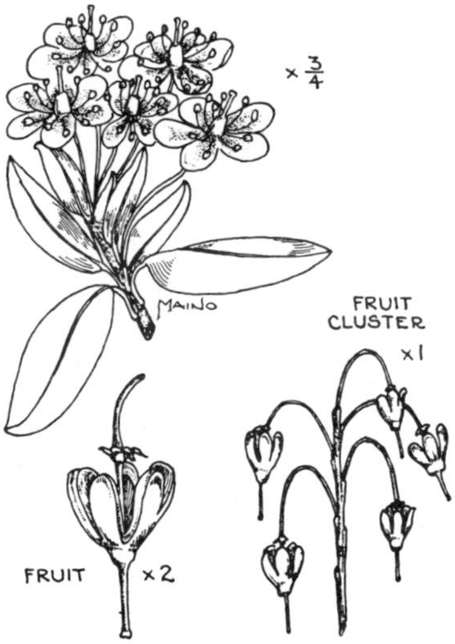

FIG. 505 LEDUM GLANDULOSUM

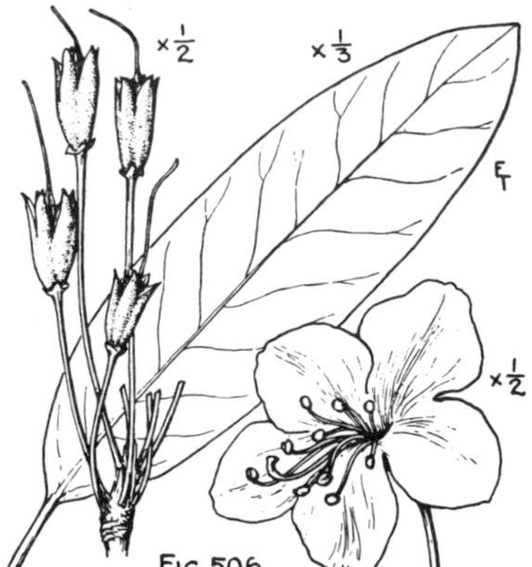

FIG. 506 RHODODENDRON MACROPHYLLUM

wide, dark green and glabrous above, pale, glaucous, and dotted with resin-glands beneath, entire; petioles 1/4- to 1/2-inch long. Flowers bisexual, white, numerous, crowded in terminal clusters; pedicels about 1 inch long; each flower nearly 1/2-inch broad; sepals 5, very small, somewhat glandular-pubescent, divided into linear divisions at apex; petals 5, oval, 1/4-inch long, almost distinct; stamens 10, distinct, longer than the petals, the filaments glandular-hairy below the middle; ovary superior, 5-celled, glandular. Fruit a 5-celled globose or oval capsule about 1/6-inch long. Flowering period, June to August.

Western Labrador Tea occurs in marshy places along the coast in the North Coast Ranges from Point Reyes, Marin County northward to Del Norte County and in the Sierra Nevada from about 5000 to 10,000 feet elevation. It extends northward to British Columbia and eastward to the Rocky Mountains. The leaves when bruised have a very characteristic odor resembling somewhat the odor of turpentine. Experimental work with the foliage shows it to be slightly toxic to livestock.

Ledum glandulosum Nutt. Trans. Am. Phil. Soc. 8:270 (1843). Type locality: "In the central chain of the Rocky Mountains on the side of mountains which close up Thornburg's ravine." Collected by *Nuttall.*

11. **Rhododendron** L.

(From the Greek *rhodos,* rose, and *dendron,* tree.)

Mostly shrubs or sometimes small trees. Leaves simple, alternate, deciduous or evergreen. Flowers bisexual, large and showy, in umbels or corymbs, from terminal buds; sepals 5, very small; petals 5, united to form a funnel- or bell-shaped corolla, this often somewhat irregular; stamens 5 or 10; ovary superior, 5-celled. Fruit a 5-valved capsule, splitting along the walls.

This is a large genus of 150 to 800 species (including *Azalea* and *Azaleastrum*), chiefly Asiatic in distribution, many species occurring in the Himalayas and the mountains of southwest China. Several species occur in Europe and North America. Only 2 species are native to California.

KEY TO THE SPECIES

Leaves thick and leathery, evergreen; stamens 10. . . . . 1. *R. macrophyllum.*
Leaves thin, ciliate on the margins, deciduous; stamens 5. . . . . . 2. *R. occidentale.*

1. **Rhododendron macrophyllum** G. Don. Coast Rhododendron. California Rose-bay. Fig. 506.

An evergreen shrub, 4 to 10 feet high, or sometimes nearly tree-like and up to 20 feet high. Leaf-blades oblong to elliptical, 2 1/2 to 6 inches long, 1 1/4 to 2 inches wide, thick and leathery, dark green and glabrous above, paler and sometimes rusty beneath, entire; petioles stout, about 1 inch long. Flowers rose-purple or rarely white, 1 1/4 to 1 1/2 inches long, the lobes wavy-margined; stamens 10; ovary densely reddish silky. Capsule about 3/4-inch long. Flowering period, May and June.

Coast Rhododendron occurs in the Redwood belt from Monterey County northward to Del Norte and Siskiyou counties. It is more abundant in Mendocino and Humboldt counties where it occurs in the peaty acid soils in the mountains along the coast. It extends northward to Washington and British Columbia. This is the state flower of Washington and is the only true *Rhododendron* in the western United States.

Fig. 507. Western Azalea. *Rhododendron occidentale* (T. & G.) Gray.
(Photograph by Sidney Gulick.)

Rhododendron macrophyllum G. Don, Hist. Dichl. Pl. 3:843 (1834). Type locality: Port Discovery, Washington, in Menzies' Journal page 20, May 4th, 1792. *R. californicum* Hook.

2. **Rhododendron occidentale** (T. & G.) Gray. WESTERN AZALEA. Fig. 507.

A loosely branched deciduous shrub, 3 to 10 feet high, with glabrous or soft-pubescent branchlets. Leaf-blades rather thin, elliptic to obovate, 1 to 4 inches long, $\frac{1}{2}$-inch to 1 inch wide, with short scattered hairs on both sides or almost glabrous, the margins ciliate, entire; petioles $\frac{1}{8}$- to $\frac{1}{4}$-inch long. Pedicels glandular-pubescent. Corolla white or pink-tinged, $1\frac{1}{4}$ to $1\frac{3}{4}$ inches long, slightly irregularly lobed, the upper lobe with a yellow splotch, the tube funnelform, glandular-viscid. Stamens 5, exserted. Capsules oblong, $\frac{3}{8}$- to $\frac{3}{4}$-inch long, pubescent. Flowering period, May to July.

Western Azalea occurs along stream banks and in other moist places, chiefly in coniferous woods of the outer and middle Coast Ranges from the Santa Cruz Mountains northward to Humboldt and Shasta counties, in the Sierra Nevada from Shasta and Lassen counties southward to Tulare County, and in the San Jacinto, Palomar, and Cuyamaca mountains of southern California, chiefly in the Humid Transition Life Zone.

This species is a very handsome and fragrant flowering shrub. It is sometimes known as Mountain-laurel, Sheep-laurel, and California Azalea. Since it is not related to the true laurel *(Laurus)* and since several other species of our mountain-inhabiting shrubs are called laurel it is best that common names including the word laurel be abandoned. The foliage is reported to be poisonous to sheep and cattle.

Rhododendron occidentale (T. & G.) Gray, Bot. Calif. 1:458 (1876). *Azalea occidentale* T. & G. *Azalea californica* T. & G. Type locality: "Hills along Deer Creek, Nevada County, California." Collected by *Henry Pratten*.

12. **Vaccinium** L. HUCKLEBERRY. BILBERRY

(The Latin name for bilberry.)

Mostly shrubs or subshrubs with simple alternate leaves. Flowers bisexual; sepals 5, united at their bases with the receptacle to form a receptocalyx surrounding the ovary; petals 5 (or 4), united to form a globular or urn-shaped corolla; stamens usually 10 (rarely 8); anthers, except in *V. ovatum,* with 2 awns; ovary inferior, 4- or 5-celled. Fruit a berry.

This is a large genus of about 100 species widely distributed in both the Old and New Worlds. Seven species occur in California. All seem to thrive in acid soils. Many of the species are used for their edible fruits and some are browsed by sheep and cattle.

The different species of *Vaccinium* have a mixed nomenclature of common names of which Huckleberry, Bilberry, Whortleberry, and Blueberry are the more common ones.

KEY TO THE SPECIES

Leaves thick and leathery, evergreen; flowers in racemes............1. *V. ovatum.*

Leaves thin, deciduous; flowers solitary or rarely 2 to 4 in the axils.

Calyx distinctly 4- or 5-lobed or parted; leaves entire; branchlets terete. 2. *V. occidentale.*

Calyx entire or slightly lobed.

Branchlets terete.................................3. *V. caespitosum.*

Branchlets angled.

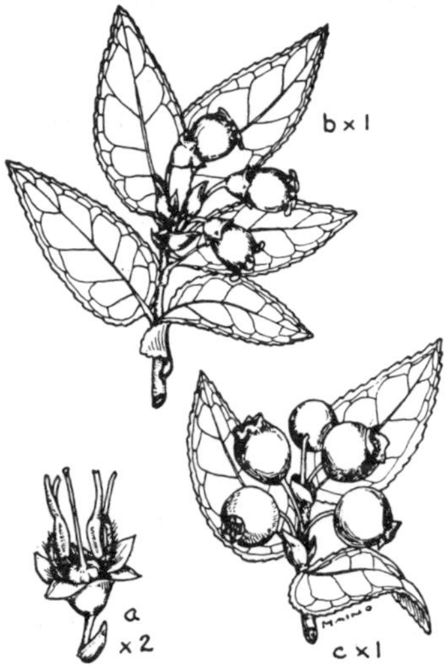

FIG. 508 V. OVATUM

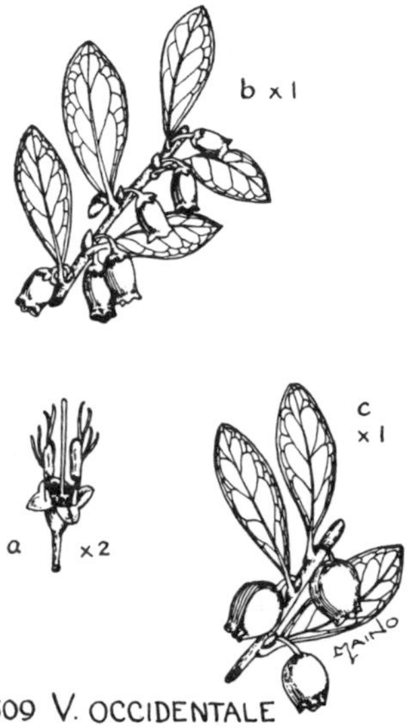

FIG. 509 V. OCCIDENTALE

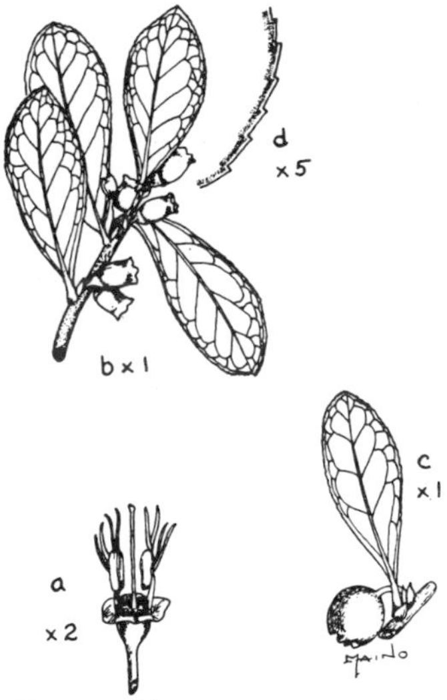

FIG. 510 V. CAESPITOSUM

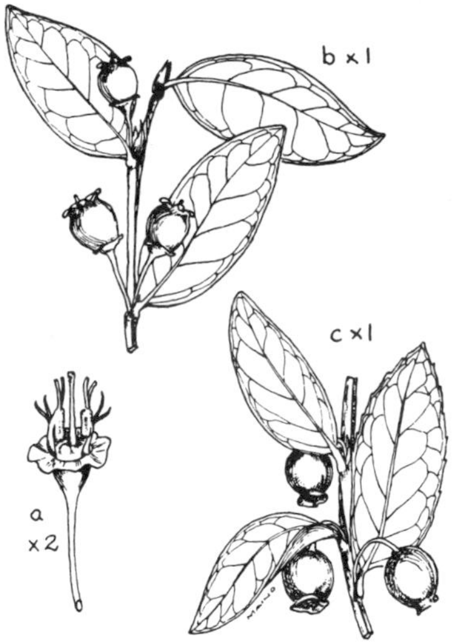

FIG. 511 V. PARVIFOLIUM

VACCINIUM. a, Flower. b, Flowering branchlet. c, Fruiting branchlet. d, Leaf-margin.

Leaves entire or rarely minutely serrulate............4. *V. parvifolium.*
Leaves serrulate or rarely almost entire.
Leaves ½-inch to 1½ inches long; plants over 1 foot high; fruit black. 5. *V. membranaceum.*
Leaves ¼- to ¾-inch long; plants less than 1 foot high; fruit red. 6. *V. scoparium.*

1. **Vaccinium ovatum** Pursh. CALIFORNIA HUCKLEBERRY. Fig. 508.

KEY TO THE SPECIES AND VARIETY

Fruit globose, without bloom..................................*V. ovatum.*
Fruit pear-shaped, with bloom............................1a. var. *saporosum.*

A tall stout erect shrub, 2 to 8 feet high, with alternate evergreen leaves. Leaf-blades thick and leathery, ovate or oblong-ovate, ½-inch to 1¼ inches long, ¼- to ½-inch wide, 1-veined from the base, glabrous and shining above, glabrous and paler beneath, serrate; petioles ⅛-inch or less long. Flowers pink, bell-shaped, about ¼-inch long, in 1- to 5-flowered racemes. Anthers without awns. Berry broadly ovoid, about ¼-inch long, black, without a glaucous bloom. Flowering period, April and May.

California Huckleberry occurs from sea level up to about 2500 feet elevation in the Coast Ranges from Santa Barbara County northward to Del Norte County. It is frequently the dominant shrub under the Redwood and Douglas Fir where it associates with Salal. It extends northward to British Columbia and occurs also on Santa Cruz and Santa Rosa islands. The foliage is used for Christmas decorations.

1a. Var. **saporosum** Jepson.

Berry pear-shaped, covered with a glaucous bloom. Flowering period, April.

This variety occurs occasionally with the species. I have observed specimens from Sail Rock Ranch, Mendocino County and near Redwood Peak, Alameda County. It has been reported from Gualala, Mendocino County *(R. Brandt)* and near the Big Basin in the Santa Cruz Mountains *(H. A. Dutton).* The berries have a sweeter flavor than in the species.

Vaccinium ovatum Pursh, Fl. Am. Sept. 1:290 (1814). Type locality: "On the Columbia River." Collected by *Lewis* near Astoria, Oregon.

Var. saporosum Jepson, Man. 751 (1925). Type locality: Gualala, Mendocino County. Collected by *Robert Brandt.*

2. **Vaccinium occidentale** Gray. WESTERN BLUEBERRY. Fig. 509.

A low compact shrub, 1 to 2½ feet high (sometimes almost prostrate), with smooth terete branches and thin deciduous leaves. Leaf-blades oblong-elliptic or oval to obovate, ⅜- to ¾-inch long, ⅛- to ⅜-inch wide, pale green and glabrous above, paler and glaucescent beneath, entire, slightly revolute, tapering to a petiole-like base or with a petiole 1/16-inch or less long. Flowers mostly solitary in the upper leaf-axils or in clusters of 2 to 4; calyx 4- or 5-lobed; corolla white or pinkish especially in bud, mostly 4-lobed at apex; anthers with awns. Berry elliptic, about ¼-inch long, blue-black, with a glaucous bloom. Flowering period, June and July.

Western Blueberry occurs along the borders of wet meadows and streams in the Canadian and Hudsonian Life Zones in the Sierra Nevada from Tulare County northward to Modoc and Siskiyou counties and westward to Trinity Summit, Humboldt County (McKay's Prairie, el. 5000 ft., *Doris Kildale*). It extends north-

FIG. 512 VACCINIUM MEMBRANACEUM

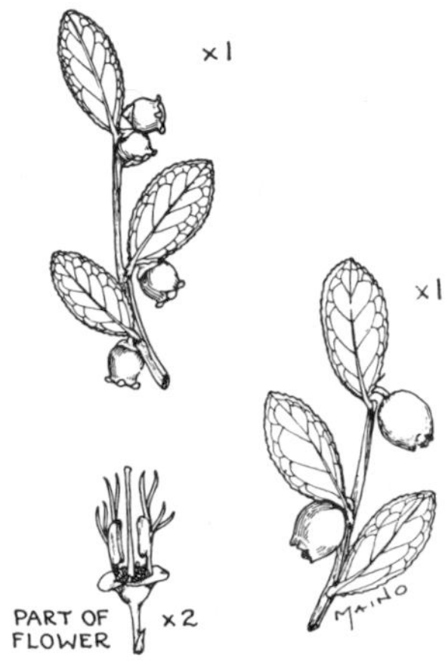

FIG. 513 VACCINIUM SCOPARIUM

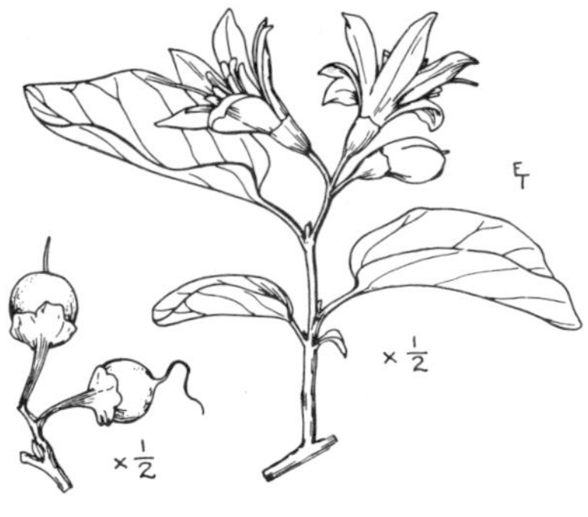

FIG. 514 STYRAX OFFICINALIS
VAR. CALIFORNICA

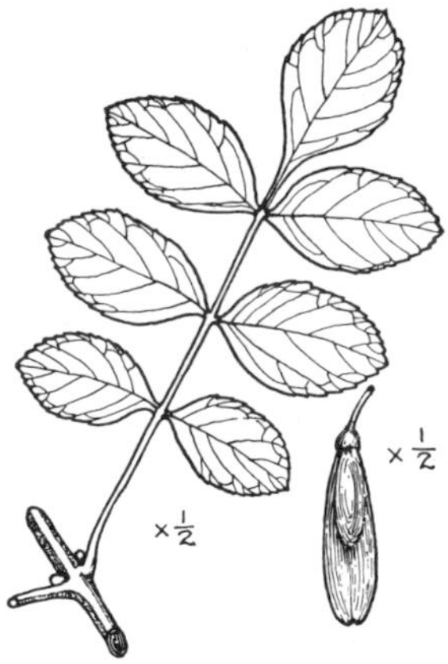

FIG. 515 FRAXINUS DIPETALA

ward to British Columbia and eastward to Utah and Montana. On the granite outcroppings along the river in Tuloumne Meadows and near Lake Tenaya this huckleberry grows nearly prostrate. The herbage is reported to be good browse for sheep and cattle.

Vaccinium occidentale Gray, Bot. Calif. 1:451 (1876). Type locality: "Sierra Nevada at six thousand or seven thousand feet, from Mariposa to Sierra Co." Collected by *Bolander* and others.

3. **Vaccinium caespitosum** Michx. DWARF BILBERRY. Fig. 510.

A low spreading subshrub, 3 to 10 inches high, with thin deciduous leaves mostly crowded at the ends of the terete branchlets. Flowering period, June and July.

Dwarf Bilberry is a rather common subshrub often forming a close ground-cover in moist places from 7000 to about 12,000 feet elevation in the Sierra Nevada from Tulare County northward to Lassen and Modoc counties, westward in Siskiyou County to Del Norte County, and southward in the Coast Ranges from 100 to 5000 feet elevation at scattered locations in Humboldt County and at Point Reyes P. O., Marin County *(Elmer)*. It extends northward to Alaska and eastward to Labrador, New York, and the New England States.

Vaccinium caespitosum Michx. Fl. Bor. Am. 1:234 (1803). Type locality: "In borealis Americae, praesertim circa sinum Hudsonis." Collected by *Michaux*.

4. **Vaccinium parvifolium** Smith. RED HUCKLEBERRY. Fig. 511.

Usually a tall straggly shrub, 4 to 12 feet (rarely up to 18 feet) high, with deep green very sharply angled branches and branchlets and thin deciduous leaves. Leaf-blades oval to elliptic, 1/2- to 3/4-inch long, 3/16- to 3/8-inch wide, light green and glabrous above, paler beneath, entire, almost sessile. Flowers greenish to whitish, solitary or in pairs in the leaf axils; calyx slightly 5-lobed; corolla globular, about 1/4-inch long, 5-lobed, the lobes slightly reflexed; anthers awned. Berry globose, about 1/4-inch in diameter, clear bright red. Flowering period, May and June.

Red Huckleberry occurs chiefly in the redwood region from the Santa Cruz Mountains northward in the Coast Ranges to Del Norte County, eastward in Siskiyou County, and southward in a few scattered localities in the Sierra Nevada to Fresno County (trail from Fresno Big Trees, *W. R. Dudley*), in the Humid Transition and Canadian Life Zones. It extends northward to Alaska. The red berries are eaten by birds and the young foliage is frequently browsed by cattle and sheep.

Vaccinium parvifolium Smith; Rees, Cycl. 36; no. 3 (1817). Type locality: On the west coast of North America. Collected by *Menzies*.

5. **Vaccinium membranaceum** Dougl. THINLEAF HUCKLEBERRY. Fig. 512.

An erect deciduous shrub, 1 to 4 feet high, with widely spreading branches and slightly angled branchlets. Leaf-blades membranous, usually ovate or obovate to broadly elliptic, 1 to 2 inches long, 3/8- to 3/4-inch wide, glabrous and pale green on both surfaces, finely serrulate, nearly sessile. Flowers solitary; calyx entire or only slightly lobed; corolla greenish white, subglobose, 1/8-inch long; anthers awned. Berry globose, 1/4-inch or more in diameter, black or wine-colored, sweet. Flowering period, May to July.

Thinleaf Huckleberry is rare in California, occurring to my knowledge only in a few localities in Humboldt and Siskiyou counties (Lily Pad Lake, near Hancock Lookout on trail to Marble Mt., *Doris Kildale;* "Lassen Creek, in Lodgepole Pine bog, associated with *Kalmia,* alt. 7000 ft.," *L. S. Smith*). It extends northward to British Columbia and Alaska and eastward to Idaho, Montana, and Michigan.

Vaccinium membranaceum Dougl.; Torr. Bot. Wilkes Exped. 377 (1878). Type locality: Northwest coast of America. Collected by *Menzies.*

6. **Vaccinium scoparium** Leiberg. LITTLELEAF HUCKLEBERRY. GROUSE WHORTLEBERRY. Fig. 513.

A low subshrub, 4 to 12 inches high, with sharply angled bright green branches and small thin deciduous leaves. Flowering period, June and July.

Littleleaf Huckleberry is rare in California, occurring to my knowledge only at a few locations in Siskiyou County (Salmon Mountains, *W. R. Dudley;* Hancock Lake, on trail to Marble Mt., *Doris Kildale*). Outside the state it has a wide range of distribution, extending northward to British Columbia and eastward to New Mexico.

This species appears to be a dwarf form of *V. parvifolium* with smaller more serrulate leaves. It is reported to be an important food plant for game birds and other wild life.

Vaccinium scoparium Leiberg, Mazama 1:196 (1897). *V. myrtillus* var. *microphyllum* Hook. Type locality: "Alpine Woods near the Height of Land and Columbia Portage." Collected by *Drummond.*

Styracaceae. Storax Family

This family contains 8 genera with about 120 species, distributed in the warmer parts of North and South America, eastern Asia, and the Mediterranean region.

1. **Styrax** L. STORAX. STYRAX

(The ancient Greek name for one of the species that produces storax, a fragrant gum resin.)

About 100 species belong to this genus, one of which has 2 varieties native to California.

KEY TO THE VARIETIES

Leaves glabrous in age or only slightly pubescent on the veins beneath; calyx-teeth scarcely visible............................1. *S. officinalis* var. *californica.*

Leaves densely stellate-tomentose beneath; petioles and peduncles gray or rusty-tomentose; calyx-teeth quite evident.........2. *S. officinalis* var. *fulvescens.*

1. **Styrax officinalis** var. **californica** (Torr.) Rehd. CALIFORNIA STYRAX. Fig. 514.

An erect deciduous shrub, 3 to 8 feet high, with grayish twigs. Leaves simple, alternate; the blades round-ovate, oval, or obovate, abrupt at both ends, 1 to 3½ inches long, ¾-inch to 3 inches wide, 1-veined from the base, minutely pubescent to densely soft-tomentose beneath when young, becoming glabrous in age, entire; petioles ¼- to ½-inch long, glabrous or rarely slightly tomentose. Flowers bisexual, regular, white, somewhat resembling orange blossoms, few in terminal clusters borne on peduncles ¼- to ½-inch long; sepals 5, united into a persistent often unequally toothed calyx, the teeth usually scarcely evident; petals 4 to 8, commonly 6, broadly elliptical to oblong, ½-inch to 1 inch long, united at base; stamens 10 to 16, united at base and forming a short tube adherent to the base of the corolla; ovary superior or partially inferior, 3- to 5-celled at base and 1-celled at top because of imperfect partitions. Fruit globose, about ½-inch in diameter, surrounded at base by the persistent calyx, usually splitting into 3 valves, with a single large bony seed which resembles a small nut. Flowering period, April to June.

California Styrax occurs in scattered localities in the inner North Coast Range from Lake County *(Abrams)* north in Glenn, Colusa, Tehama, and Shasta counties, thence southward in the dry foothills of the Sierra Nevada to Tulare County.

Styrax officinalis var. californica (Torr.) Rehd. Mit. Deutsch. Dendr. Ges. 1915:226 (1915). *Styrax californica* Torr. Type locality: "Hillsides and river banks, Mokelumne Hill, California." "Upper Sacramento." Collected by *Fremont.*

2. **Styrax officinalis** var. **fulvescens** (Eastw.) Munz & Johnst. SOUTHERN CALIFORNIA STYRAX.

Leaf-blades usually soft-pubescent above and densely stellate-tomentose beneath; petioles gray- or rusty-pubescent. Peduncles pubescent. Calyx-teeth prominent.

This variety occurs in southern California from San Luis Obispo County (1¼ mi. n.w. of Colwell Ranch, *H. C. Lee*), southward in the Santa Ynez, San Bernardino, and Santa Ana mountains, also in a few localities in the mountains of San Diego County ("4 miles below Hinshaw Dam, San Luis Rey River," *P. A. Munz;* east of Rainbow, San Luis Rey Quadrangle, *H. A. Jensen*).

Styrax officinalis var. fulvescens (Eastw.) Munz & Johnst. Bull. Torr. Club 51:297 (1924). *Styrax californica* var. *fulvescens* Eastw. Type locality: "Near the Painted Cave in the Santa Ynez Mountains back of Santa Barbara, California." Collected by *Eastwood.*

Oleaceae. Olive or Ash Family

The Olive Family consists of about 20 genera and 500 species of trees and shrubs widely distributed in the temperate and tropical regions of both the Old and New Worlds. The olive *(Olea)*, lilac *(Syringa)*, privet *(Ligustrum)*, and jasmine *(Jasminum)* belong to this family.

KEY TO THE GENERA

Leaves pinnately compound. . . . . 1. FRAXINUS.
Leaves simple.
  All leaves opposite.
    Branchlets 4-angled; leaves broadly ovate or round. . . 1. FRAXINUS ANOMALA.
    Branchlets terete; leaves oblong-lanceolate. . . . . 3. FORESTIERA.
  Leaves mostly alternate, the lower rarely opposite; fruit a capsule. 2. MENODORA.

1. **Fraxinus** L. ASH

(The Latin name of the ash tree.)

Trees or shrubs. Leaves odd-pinnately compound or rarely simple, opposite. Flowers inconspicuous, bisexual or unisexual, the staminate and pistillate flowers borne in clusters upon different plants; calyx 4-lobed, or wanting; petals (in ours) 2 or wanting; stamens 2, rarely 1, 3, or 4; ovary superior, 2-celled. Fruit a 1-seeded samara, winged at the apex or all around.

There are about 40 species of ashes, 4 of which are native to California, 2 being often shrub-like.

KEY TO THE SPECIES

Leaves compound, with 3 to 9 leaflets; flowers bisexual; foothill species.
1. *F. dipetala.*

Leaves simple or compound with 2 or 3 leaflets; flowers bisexual and unisexual; desert-mountain species . . . . 2. *F. anomala.*

1. **Fraxinus dipetala** H. & A. FOOTHILL ASH. FLOWERING ASH. Fig. 515.

A shrub or small tree, 6 to 18 feet high, with 4-angled branchlets. Leaves deciduous, 2 to 5½ inches long, with 3 to 9 leaflets (rarely 1); leaflets oblong-ovate, ½-inch to 1½ inches long, ⅜- to ¾-inch wide, glabrous on both surfaces, serrate or entire. Flowers bisexual, numerous, in compound clusters; petals 2, white, about ¼-inch long. Samara ¾-inch to 1 inch long, often notched at tip; pedicels ¼-inch or more long. Flowering period, March to June.

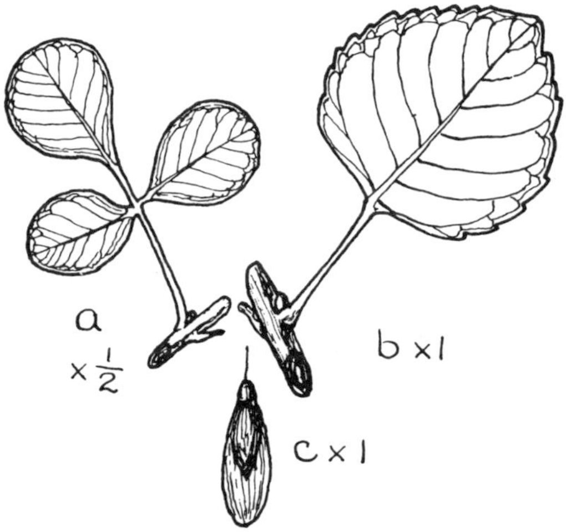

Fig. 516. FRAXINUS ANOMALA. a, Compound leaf. b, Simple leaf. c, Fruit.

Foothill Ash occurs in the canyons and on slopes of the foothills and lower mountains of the middle and inner North Coast Range, the Sierra Nevada, the inner South Coast Range, the mountains of Santa Barbara and Ventura counties, the San Bernardino Mountains, and in the Santa Ana River canyon. It also occurs in Lower California where it usually has simple or trifoliolate leaves. The large axillary clusters of white flowers appearing with the leaves are quite ornamental.

Fraxinus dipetala H. & A. Bot. Beechey 362 (1841). Type locality: Probably near Monterey, California. Collected by *Douglas.*

2. **Fraxinus anomala** Torr. SINGLELEAF ASH. DWARF ASH. Fig. 516.

A shrub or small tree, 6 to 30 feet high, with 4-angled branchlets. Leaves deciduous, simple, or compound with 2 or 3 leaflets; the blades broadly ovate or round, rarely cordate, ¾-inch to 2 inches long, about as wide, or the terminal leaflet larger, glabrous on both surfaces, serrate to crenate or some nearly entire; petioles ½-inch to 1½ inches long. Flowers inconspicuous, in axillary clusters, bisexual or some pistillate; calyx with 4 small teeth; petals none. Samara ½- to ¾-inch long, the wing surrounding the body; pedicels ¼-inch or less long. Flowering period, April and May.

Singleleaf Ash occurs on the eastern slope of the Providence Mountains of San Bernardino County and in the Panamint Mountains of Inyo County. It occurs also in Nevada, Arizona, Utah, Colorado, and Texas.

Fraxinus anomala Torr.; Bot. King's Expl. 5:283 (1871). Type locality: "First discovered by Newberry on Macomb's Expedition in 1859 in Labyrinth Cañon on the Colorado River, Utah."

2. **Menodora** H. & B. MENODORA

(From the Greek *menos,* force, and *doron,* gift, in reference to the force or strength it gave to animals.)

Shrubs or subshrubs, rarely herbs. Leaves simple, alternate or opposite. Flowers bisexual, regular; calyx with 5 to 15 linear lobes; corolla 5- or 6-lobed; stamens 2 or 3; ovary superior, 2-celled. Fruit a deeply 2-parted 2-celled capsule with 2 seeds in each cell.

This genus contains 9 species and 11 varieties of North America, 6 species and one variety of South America, and 2 species and one variety of Africa. Two species and 2 varieties are native to California.

KEY TO THE SPECIES

Plants distinctly spiny and shrubby; seeds 2 in each cell.........1. *M. spinescens.*
Plants not spiny, woody only at base; seeds 4 in each cell.
Foliage sparse towards the tips of the stems, the leaves here reduced to bracts or rudimentary..2. *M. scoparia.*
Foliage less sparse, all leaves more or less foliose.......3. *M. scabra* var. *laevis.*

1. **Menodora spinescens** Gray. SPINY MENODORA. GREENFIRE. Fig. 517.

KEY TO THE SPECIES AND VARIETY

Corolla 1/8- to 1/4-inch long...................................*M. spinescens.*
Corolla 3/8- to 1/2-inch long..........................1a. var. *mohavensis.*

A widely spreading spinescent shrub, 1 to 3 feet high, with gray or yellowish green minutely puberulent branches. Leaves alternate, linear-oblong, 1/4- to 1/2-inch long, or some reduced to scales, entire, sessile. Flowers white, tinged with purple, solitary or few in axillary clusters; calyx-lobes usually 5; corolla funnel-shaped, 1/8- to 1/4-inch long, the lobes oblong, about 1/3 the length of the tube. Fruit a capsule, distinctly 2-parted almost to the base, each half globose, membranous, about 1/4-inch in diameter. Flowering period, March to May.

Spiny Menodora occurs in the eastern part of the Mohave Desert in San Bernardino County, and north into Inyo County. (SAN BERNARDINO COUNTY: Barnwell, *K. Brandegee;* Providence Mts., *Cooper.* INYO COUNTY: Funeral Mts., *Coville* & *Funston;* western slope of Argus Mts., *Hall* & *Chandler;* head of Furnace Creek wash on Death Valley Junction road, *Ferris, Scott, Bacigalupi*). It extends eastward into Nevada.

1a. Var. **mohavensis** Steyermark. Fig. 518.

Corolla 3/8- to 1/2-inch long, the tube more broadly funnel-shaped and more open toward the orifice.

This variety has been collected from the Ord Mountains *(Hall* & *Chandler),* Funeral Mountains *(Jaeger),* Leastalk, Mohave Desert *(S. B. Parish),* Calico Mountains *(Jepson),* and in a few other localities in San Bernardino and Inyo counties.

Menodora spinescens Gray, Proc. Am. Acad. 7:388 (1867). Type locality: "Cañons and hillsides, southeastern part of the State of Nevada." Collected by *C. L. Anderson.*

Var. mohavensis Steyermark. Ann. Mo. Bot. Gard. 19:155 (1932). Type locality: "14 miles northeast of Barstow, Mohave Desert, San Bernardino Co." Collected by *S. B. Parish.*

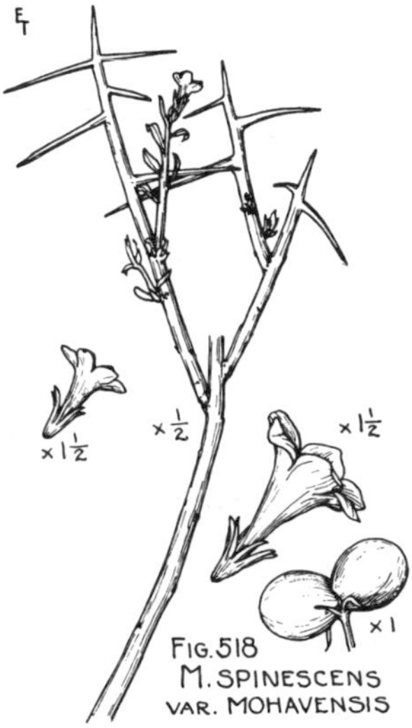

FIG. 517 MENODORA SPINESCENS

FIG. 519 MENODORA SCOPARIA

FIG. 520 MENODORA SCABRA VAR. LAEVIS

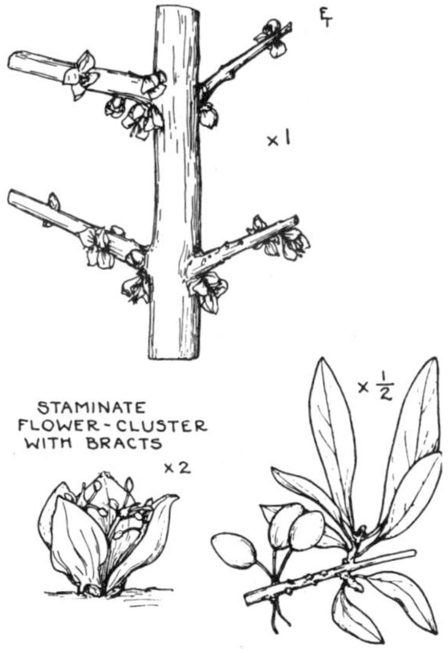

FIG. 521 FORESTIERA NEOMEXICANA

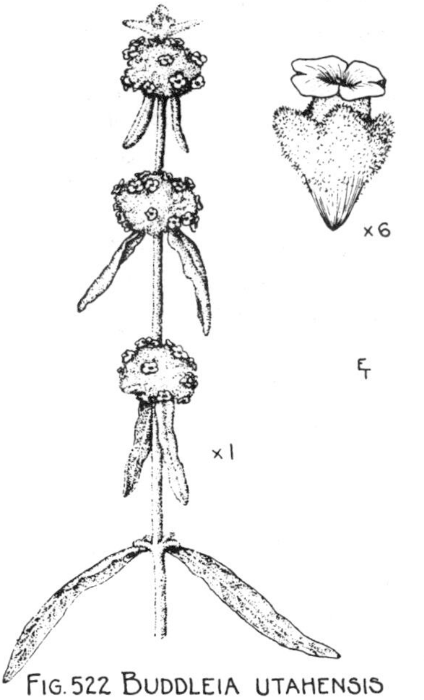

FIG. 522 BUDDLEIA UTAHENSIS

2. **Menodora scoparia** Engelm. BROOM MENODORA. Fig. 519.

An erect paniculately branched unarmed perennial, ½-foot to 2 feet high, with numerous slender mostly glabrous stems from a woody base. Flowering period, May and June.

Broom Menodora occurs in the Providence and New York mountains of eastern San Bernardino County and on the dry gravelly hills near Jacumba, San Diego County. It extends eastward to Arizona, New Mexico, and Texas and southward into Mexico.

Menodora scoparia Engelm. ex Gray; Bot. Calif. 1:471 (1876). Type locality: "On Mts. about Saltillo, Coahuila, Mexico." Collected by *Gregg*.

3. **Menodora scabra** var. **laevis** (Woot. & Standl.) Steyermark. SMOOTH MENODORA. Fig. 520.

An almost herbaceous perennial, 4 to 16 inches high, with numerous erect glabrous stems leafy almost to their tips. Flowering period, May to August.

Smooth Menodora is known in California from the New York Mountains of eastern San Bernardino County. It extends eastward to Texas and southward to Mexico. This species and the preceding one are very closely related, the evident difference being in the degree of leafiness of the stems.

Menodora scabra var. laevis (Woot. & Standl.) Steyermark, Ann. Mo. Bot. Gard. 19:137 (1932). *Menodora laevis* Woot. & Standl. Type locality: Organ Mountains of New Mexico. Collected by *G. R. Vasey*.

3. **Forestiera** Poir. ADELIA

(Named for Dr. M. Forestier, a French physician.)

This is a small genus of about 15 species occurring in North and South America, only one of which is native to California.

1. **Forestiera neomexicana** Gray. ADELIA. Fig. 521.

An erect stiffly branched shrub, 4 to 12 feet high, with smooth gray bark. Leaves simple, opposite and often with additional axillary ones on the short lateral spur-like branchlets, deciduous; the blades oblong-ovate or spatulate-oblong, ½-inch to 1¾ inches long, ¼- to ½-inch wide, grayish green and glabrous on both surfaces, crenate, or entire near the tapering base; petioles ⅛- to ¼-inch long. Flowers few, small, dioecious or polygamous, in sessile axillary clusters subtended by 4 small bracts; sepals 4 to 6, minute; petals none or rarely 1 or 2 and falling early, white; stamens 2 to 4; ovary superior, 2-celled. Fruit a blue-black ovoid drupe, about ¼-inch long. Flowering period, March to May, appearing before the leaves on stems of the previous year.

Adelia occurs in dry ravines, along intermittent streams, and on lower mountain flats in the more arid parts of California, extending from the Arroyo Mocho in the Mount Hamilton Range of Alameda and Santa Clara counties, southward in San Benito, Monterey, San Luis Obispo, Los Angeles, San Bernardino, and Riverside counties, and in Inyo County, in the Upper and Lower Sonoran Life Zones. It grows also in Arizona, Utah, New Mexico, Colorado, and western Texas. This shrub has some ornamental value when used in mixed planting. It can be propagated from cuttings or from seeds. It thrives in either light or heavy soil, and is suited for planting along streams.

Forestiera neomexicana Gray, Proc. Am. Acad. 12:63 (1876). Type locality: New Mexico. Collected by *Fendler*.

Loganiaceae. Logania Family

This family contains about 30 genera and about 300 species of herbs, shrubs, or trees, mostly of tropical distribution. A few species extend into temperate North America. A single genus occurs in California.

1. **Buddleia** L. BUTTERFLYBUSH

(Named in honor of Adam Buddle, an English botanist.)

This genus consists of about 70 species of woody plants, rarely herbs, native to the tropical, subtropical, and a few to the temperate regions of both the Old and New Worlds. A single species is native to California.

1. **Buddleia utahensis** Cov. PANAMINT BUTTERFLYBUSH. Fig. 522.

A low deciduous shrub, 1 to 2 feet high, 1 to 3 feet broad, with densely tomentose young branches, leaves, and calyces. Leaves simple, opposite; the blades linear-oblong, ½- to ¾-inch long, thick, irregularly crenate, with undulate revolute margins, nearly sessile. Flowers creamy-yellow, drying purple or brownish purple, bisexual, regular, borne in 2 to 4 dense clusters about ⅝-inch in diameter and about 1 inch apart in spike-like inflorescences terminating the branches; sepals 4 or 5, joined at their bases; petals 4 or 5, joined to a rotate-campanulate corolla, the corolla-tube tomentose without; stamens 4 or 5, adnate to the corolla-tube, alternate with the corolla-lobes; ovary superior, 2-celled. Fruit a globular or oblong capsule. Flowering period, June and July.

Panamint Butterflybush occurs on dry rocky slopes in a few localities in Titus Canyon, Grapevine Mountains, in Butte Valley in the Panamint Range, Inyo County *(M. F. Gilman),* and in the Kingston Mountains of San Bernardino County ("base of pass between Kingston and Francis Spring," *C. B. Wolf;* "1.4 miles northwest of Beck Spring." *C. B. Wolf* & *P. C. Everett),* in the Sonoran Life Zones. It extends eastward to Nevada and Utah.

Buddleia utahensis Cov. Proc. Biol. Soc. Wash. 7:69 (1892). Type locality: "Near St. George, southern Utah." Collected by *Palmer.*

Polemoniaceae. Phlox Family

The Phlox Family contains about 12 genera and 270 species of annual and perennial herbs and a few subshrubs. About 12 species are found in the Old World and the remainder in North and South America, but chiefly in the southwestern United States. Ten genera and about 100 species are native to California, 11 species of which are woody at the base.

KEY TO THE GENERA

Leaves opposite or those of the inflorescence alternate.
- Leaves not divided; stamens unequally inserted on the corolla-tube; corolla-tube definitely exserted beyond the calyx .... 1. PHLOX.
- Leaves palmately 3- to 7-lobed or -divided, or the lower entire; stamens equally inserted on the corolla-tube; corolla-tube shorter than or scarcely exserted from the calyx.
  - Leaves not prickly-pointed .... 2. LINANTHUS.
  - Leaves prickly-pointed .... 5. LEPTODACTYLON.

Leaves mostly alternate; stamens equally inserted on the corolla-tube.

Corolla scarlet, the limb somewhat irregularly cleft into 5 lobes, the lobes 3-toothed at apex; stamens exserted........................3. LOESELIA.
Corolla not scarlet, the limb regularly cleft into 5 lobes.
Leaves narrowly linear, entire or commonly with few short lateral lobes; flowers blue, in dense leafy-bracted terminal clusters; calyx and bracts enmeshed in a dense white-woolly tomentum..............4. HUGELIA.
Leaves 3- to 9-divided from near the base; flowers not blue; calyx and bracts not enmeshed in a woolly tomentum...............5. LEPTODACTYLON.

1. **Phlox** L. PHLOX

(The Greek name for flame, once applied to a species of *Lychnis* but transferred by Linnaeus to plants now known as *Phlox*.)

Low mostly perennial herbs, some woody at base. Leaves simple, opposite, or the upper ones and those of the inflorescences sometimes alternate, entire, sessile. Flowers bisexual, regular, or rarely slightly irregular, commonly in bright colors, in terminal cymes; calyx narrow-tubular, 5-ribbed and 5-cleft, scarious between the lobes; corolla-tube narrow-cylindrical, scarcely if at all broader at the summit, with 5 spreading obovate lobes; stamens 5, usually unequal in length or in points of attachment on the corolla-tube; ovary superior, 3-celled. Fruit a 3-valved capsule, ultimately rupturing the persistent calyx.

The genus *Phlox* contains about 50 species, chiefly of North America. Eight species and several varieties are native to California, 6 of which are often woody at the base.

KEY TO THE SPECIES

Leaves ovate or broadly elliptic, ½-inch to 1¾ inches long, ½-inch to 1½ inches broad; style longer than the calyx.........................1. *P. adsurgens.*
Leaves linear to narrowly lanceolate or lance-ovate.
Corolla-tube 3 to 5 times longer than the calyx, usually 1½ to 2 inches long; style longer than the calyx...........................2. *P. dolichantha.*
Corolla-tube not more than 2 times longer than the calyx.
Flowers long-pedicelled or subsessile in *P. hirsuta;* leaves sharp-pointed.
Style longer than the calyx; petals not usually notched at apex. 3. *P. Stansburyi.*
Style shorter than the calyx.
Plants 2 to 4 inches high; herbage glandular-hirsute; leaves lanceolate or ovate-oblong, ⅜- to ¾-inch long; petals not normally notched at apex...4. *P. hirsuta.*
Plants 6 to 20 inches high; herbage puberulent or glabrous; leaves linear or narrowly lanceolate, ½-inch to 1½ inches long; petals usually notched at apex.................................5. *P. speciosa.*
Flowers sessile or subsessile; low matted plants.
Leaves lanceolate, over 1/16-inch wide....................4. *P. hirsuta.*
Leaves linear, 1/16-inch or less wide....................6. *P. Douglasii.*

1. **Phlox adsurgens** Torr. NORTHERN PHLOX. Fig. 523.

A slender perennial, with diffuse or ascending branches 6 to 18 inches long from a woody base, glabrous herbage, and glandular-pubescent inflorescence. Flowering period, May to August.

Northern Phlox occurs in the mountains from 4000 to 6500 feet elevation from Mendocino County north to Siskiyou County and southwestern Oregon.

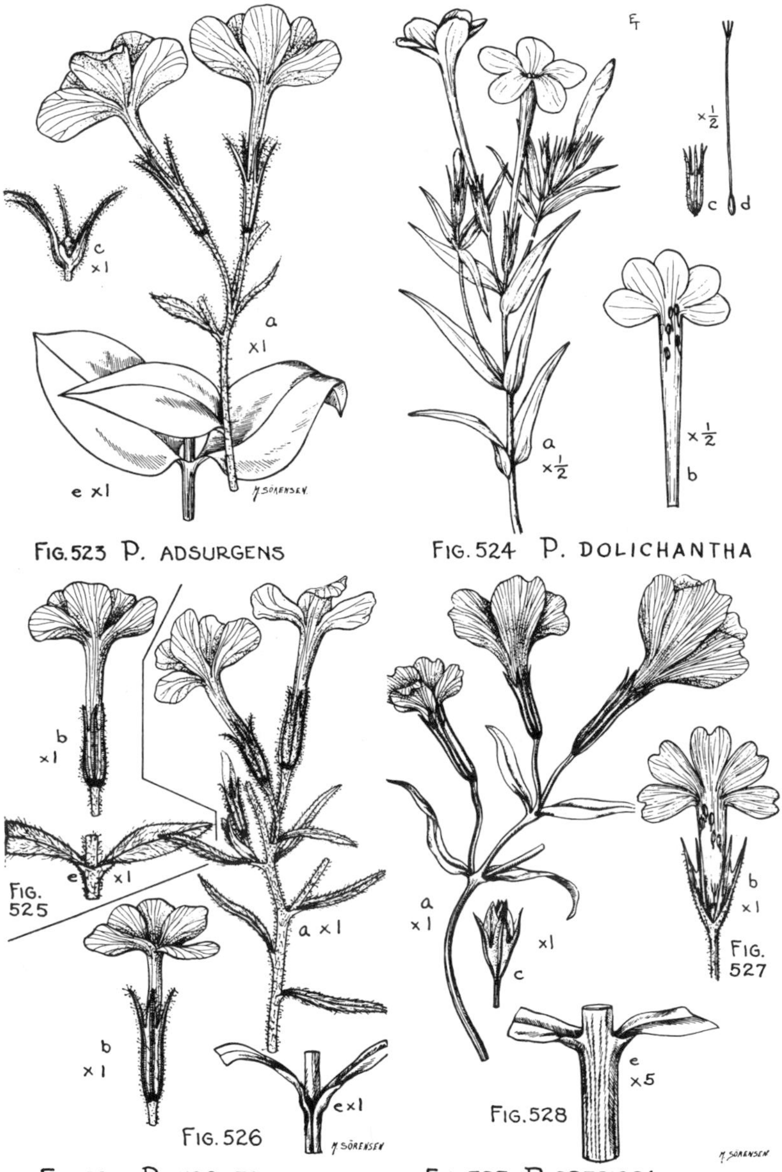

FIG. 523 P. ADSURGENS
FIG. 524 P. DOLICHANTHA
FIG. 525 P. HIRSUTA
FIG. 526 P. STANSBURYI
FIG. 527 P. SPECIOSA
FIG. 528 P. SPECIOSA VAR. NITIDA

PHLOX. a, Flowering branchlet. b, Single flower. c, Calyx. d, Pistil. e, Portion of stem with leaves.

Phlox adsurgens Torr.; Gray, Proc. Am. Acad. 8:256 (1870). Type locality: "Cañon Pass, Oregon." Collected by *A. Wood.*

2. **Phlox dolichantha** Gray. San Bernardino Phlox. Fig. 524.

A slender sparingly branched perennial, with erect or ascending branches 5 to 12 inches long from a woody base. Flowering period, May to July.

San Bernardino Phlox is known in California from the San Bernardino Mountains (Bear Valley region) from 4000 to 7000 feet elevation where it occurs on dry slopes or in open pine forests. It extends eastward into Nevada. Specimens from the Bishop Creek region of Inyo County have slightly shorter corolla-tubes and seem intermediate between *P. dolichantha* and *P. Stansburyi.* These specimens may belong to Brand's *P. superba.*

Phlox dolichantha Gray, Proc. Am. Acad. 22:310 (1887). Type locality: Southeastern Nevada in the Pahranagat Mountains. Collected by *Miss Searles. P. superba* of Jepson, not Brand. *P. bernardina* Munz & Johnst.

3. **Phlox Stansburyi** (Torr.) Heller. Desert Mountain Phlox. Fig. 526.

A low perennial, 4 to 12 inches high, with few to several erect slender commonly puberulent branches from a woody base. Flowering period, April to July.

Desert Mountain Phlox occurs on dry slopes and flats of the desert mountains in eastern San Bernardino and Inyo counties and also in the Warner Mountains of Modoc County, and south to Lassen County. It extends eastward to Nevada, Arizona, Utah, and New Mexico and northward to Idaho. Most of the Californian specimens have leaves about ½-inch to 1 inch long and ⅛- to 3/16-inch wide. These have been given the varietal name **brevifolia** by some authors.

Phlox Stansburyi (Torr.) Heller, Bull. Torr. Club 24:478 (1897). *P. speciosa* var. *Stansburyi* Torr. Type locality: Organ Mountains, New Mexico. Collected by *Bigelow. P. dolichantha* of Jepson's Manual, not Gray.

4. **Phlox hirsuta** E. Nels. Siskiyou Phlox. Fig. 525.

A caespitose perennial, 1 to 4 inches high, with numerous short branches from a woody base. Flowering period, March to June.

This is a rare species, known only from Siskiyou (dry hills near Yreka, *Butler*) and Lassen (vicinity of Doyle Station, *Eggleston*) counties, California.

Phlox hirsuta E. Nels. Rev. West. N. Am. Phloxes 28 (1899). Type locality: Near Yreka, California. Collected by *Greene.*

5. **Phlox speciosa** Pursh. Showy Phlox. Fig. 527.

KEY TO THE SPECIES AND VARIETY

Inflorescence glandular-puberulent . . . . *P. speciosa.*
Inflorescence glabrous . . . . 5a. var. *nitida.*

A suffrutescent perennial, 6 to 20 inches high, with erect or ascending branches and glabrous herbage or the upper parts pubescent. Flowering period, March to July.

Showy Phlox occurs on hill slopes from northern Sonoma County northward in the Coast Ranges of Mendocino, Tehama, Humboldt, Trinity, and Del Norte counties and in the Sierra Nevada from Fresno County northward to Lassen County. It extends northward to Oregon, Washington, and Idaho and eastward to Arizona.

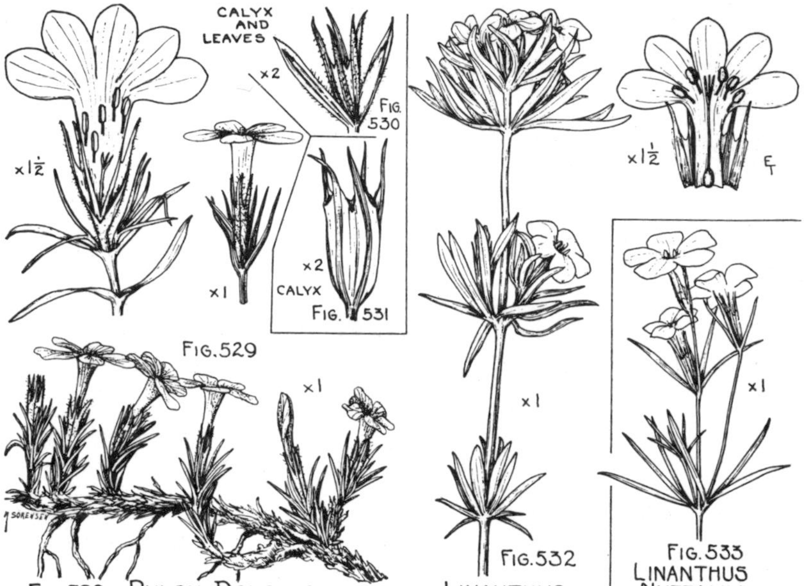

FIG. 529. PHLOX DOUGLASII
FIG. 530. P. DOUGLASII VAR. CAESPITOSA
FIG. 531 P. DOUGLASII VAR. AUSTROMONTANA

LINANTHUS NUTTALLII

FIG. 533
LINANTHUS NUTTALLII VAR. FLORIBUNDUS

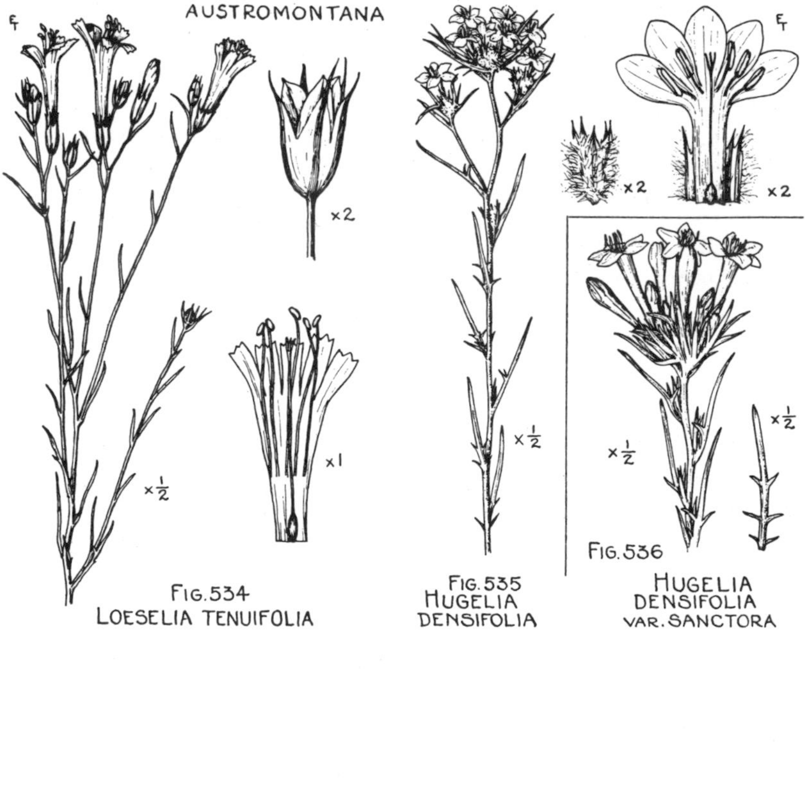

FIG. 534
LOESELIA TENUIFOLIA

FIG. 535
HUGELIA DENSIFOLIA

HUGELIA DENSIFOLIA VAR. SANCTORA

5a. Var. **nitida** Suksdorf. Fig. 528.

The entire plant glabrous. Flowers bright pink, fading in drying.

This variety is known from Siskiyou (Mt. Bradley near Shasta Retreat, *Condit*), Shasta (Anderson, *L. E. Smith*), Sonoma (Jensen Ranch 5 mi. west of Healdsburg, *Baker*), and Del Norte (in chaparral, north side of Middle Fork of Smith River on old Gasquet Toll Road, *Parks* & *Tracy*) counties and may be expected elsewhere in the North Coast Ranges. It extends northward to Washington, but is rarely collected.

Phlox speciosa Pursh, Fl. Am. Sept. 1:149 (1814). Type locality: On the plains of the Columbia. Collected by *Lewis*. *P. occidentalis* Dur.

Var. nitida Suksdorf; Deutsch. Bot. Monatsschr. 18:132 (1900). Type locality: Klickitat County, Washington. Collected by *Suksdorf*.

6. **Phlox Douglasii** Hook. GRANITE PHLOX. Fig. 529.

A low matted perennial with a woody base. Flowering period, May to August.

Granite Phlox grows on gravelly granite slopes, ridges, and summits above 5000 feet elevation in the Sierra Nevada from Fresno County northward to Modoc County and on Mount Piños, Ventura County. It extends northward to Washington and eastward to the Rocky Mountains. Some of its varieties occur in the mountains of Inyo County and in the mountains of southern California. It often forms dense mats several inches broad from which arise the erect flower-bearing stems.

The following key will aid in the identification of the more common variations which occur in this species.

Herbage and calyx-tube densely white-canescent or -lanate; style about as long as the calyx; Modoc County . . . . var. *canescens*.

Herbage not white-canescent or -lanate; style shorter than the calyx.

- Calyx glandular; leaves less than $\frac{1}{4}$-inch long; stems 1 to 2 inches high; alpine summits . . . . var. *caespitosa*. Fig. 530.
- Calyx not glandular.
  - Calyx folded into lengthwise folds in the sinuses; leaves $\frac{3}{8}$- to $\frac{3}{4}$-inch long; mountains of southern California . . . . var. *austromontana*. Fig. 531.
  - Calyx not folded lengthwise in the sinuses; leaves usually $\frac{1}{4}$- to $\frac{3}{8}$-inch long.
    - Plants with dense foliage; Mt. Piños and the Sierra Nevada . . . *P. Douglasii*.
    - Plants with less dense foliage; found with the species . . . . var. *diffusa*.

Phlox Douglasii Hook. Fl. Bor. Am. 2:73 (1838). Type locality: "N. W. America." Collected by *Douglas*. "Common on the limestone range of the Blue Mountains, and on the Rocky Mountains, near confines of snow."

2. **Linanthus** Benth.

(From the Greek *linon,* flax, and *anthos,* flower, in reference to the flax-like flower.)

This is a western American genus of about 35 species, mostly annuals but a few sometimes woody at the base. Some authors include this genus as a subgenus or section of the genus *Gilia*. One native Californian species is woody at the base.

KEY TO THE SPECIES AND VARIETY

Leaf-divisions or the simple leaves linear-spatulate, $\frac{1}{16}$- to $\frac{1}{8}$-inch broad.
1. *L. Nuttallii*.

Leaf-divisions or the simple leaves filiform, less than 1/16-inch broad.
1a. var. *floribundus.*

1. **Linanthus Nuttallii** (Gray) Greene. Bush-gilia. Fig. 532.

A low perennial, 4 to 12 inches high, with several puberulent or pubescent herbaceous stems from a woody base. Flowering period, June to August.

Bush-gilia grows on dry brushy slopes from the San Bernardino Mountains northward in the Sierra Nevada and the mountains of Inyo County, at elevations from 3000 to 12,000 feet, to Modoc County, westward in Siskiyou and Trinity counties to northern Humboldt County. It extends northward to Washington and eastward to Colorado, Idaho, Wyoming, and New Mexico. In the mountains of Inyo County the plants are usually much reduced in size and the herbage is grayish pubescent.

1a. Var. **floribundus** (Gray) n. comb. Fig. 533.

This variety occurs in the San Jacinto and Santa Ana mountains of Riverside and Orange counties, California. It extends southward in San Diego County to Lower California and eastward to Arizona, Utah, Colorado, and New Mexico.

Linanthus Nuttallii (Gray) Greene; Milliken, Rev. Calif. Polem. 54 (1904). *Gilia Nuttallii* Gray. Type locality: "Rocky Mountains of Colorado and Utah to the Sierra Nevada in California." Collected by *Nuttall, Fremont, Anderson, Brewer, Watson. Leptodactylon Nuttallii* (Gray) Rydb. *Gilia Nuttallii* var. *parviflora* (Nutt.) Brand.

Var. floribundus (Gray) McMinn. *Gilia floribunda* Gray. Type locality: Probably on the southern boundary of California. Collected by *Coulter. Gilia Nuttallii* var. *floribunda* (Gray) Munz. *Leptodactylon Nuttallii* var. *floribunda* (Gray) Jepson.

3. **Loeselia** L.

(Named in honor of John Loesel, an early Prussian botanist.)

This genus is very closely related to *Gilia* and by some authors included in that genus as a section or subgenus. As accepted by Brand there are 12 species occurring in southwestern United States, Lower California, and in Colombia and Venezuela. A single species native to California is slightly woody at the base.

1. **Loeselia tenuifolia** Gray. Jacumba-gilia. Fig. 534.

A low perennial, 4 to 16 inches high, much branched from a woody base, leafy throughout. Leaves alternate, narrowly linear, 3/8- to 3/4-inch long, entire or with few small teeth, sessile. Flowers bisexual, scarlet, few in clusters at the ends of the branches. Fruit a 3-valved capsule. Flowering period, April to June.

Jacumba-gilia is a local species growing on dry slopes in the vicinity of Jacumba and Campo, San Diego County. It extends southward into Lower California.

Loeselia tenuifolia Gray, Proc. Am. Acad. 11:86 (1876). Type locality: "Northern borders of Lower California, Tantillas Mountains." Collected by *W. Dunn* and *E. Palmer. Gilia tenuifolia* Gray.

4. **Hugelia** Benth.

(Named in honor of Baron Charles de Hugel of Vienna.)

This is a small genus with about 5 species and several varieties native to Pacific North America. Some authors consider *Hugelia* a section or subgenus of *Gilia.* One species with one well defined variety and 3 or 4 doubtful varieties is native to California.

KEY TO THE SPECIES AND VARIETY

Corolla ½- to ¾-inch long. . . . . 1. *H. densifolia.*
Corolla 1 to 1½ inches long. . . . . 1a. var. *sanctora.*

1. **Hugelia densifolia** Benth. Mesa-phlox. Fig. 535.

A bushy perennial, ½-foot to 2½ feet high, with several stems from a woody base. Herbage when young white-tomentose. Leaves simple, alternate, linear or with few pairs of small sharp lobes, ¼-inch to 2 inches long, white-woolly when young, becoming glabrate in age, sessile. Flowers deep blue, bisexual, regular, in compact terminal leafy-bracted clusters, white-woolly matted between the flowers and bracts. Fruit a 3-valved capsule. Flowering period, May to September.

Mesa-phlox inhabits dry mountain slopes or sandy hills and canyon washes in the South Coast Ranges from Santa Clara, San Benito, and Monterey counties southward to the Tehachapi, San Gabriel, San Bernardino, San Jacinto mountains and the mountains of San Diego County, and eastward to the southern Sierra Nevada in Tulare and Kern counties and in the Owens Valley, Inyo County. It extends southward into Lower California. Several varieties have been described in this species, all of which seem to intergrade to such an extent that they are very difficult to distinguish. The plants in Antelope Valley and elsewhere on the Mohave Desert north to Inyo County are usually less robust and more woolly-lanate than those in the coastal mountains. They are considered by some authors as **Gilia densifolia** var. **mohavensis** Craig.

1a. Var. **sanctora** (Milliken) Jepson. Fig. 536.

Entire plant densely white-woolly even in age. Flowers 1 to 1½ inches long.

This variety occurs in the San Bernardino Valley and in the Santa Ana River basin.

Hugelia densifolia Benth. Bot. Reg. 19, t. 1622 (1833). Type locality: "in Nova California." Collected by *Douglas*. *Gilia densifolia* Benth. *Gilia densifolia* var. *elongata* (Benth.) Gray. *Gilia densifolia* var. *austromontana* Craig.

Var. sanctora (Milliken) Jepson, Man. 792 (1925). *Gilia densifolia* var. *sanctora* Milliken. Type locality: Santa Ana River near Riverside, California. Collected by *Hall.*

5. **Leptodactylon** H. & A.

(From the Greek *leptus,* narrow, and *dactylon,* finger, in reference to the palmately divided leaves.)

Very leafy subshrubs or perennial herbs woody at the base. Leaves alternate (or the lower ones opposite), fascicled in the axils of larger more prominent leaves, palmately 3- to 9-parted, pungently pointed. Flowers bisexual, regular, in terminal few-flowered clusters or rarely solitary; calyx tubular, 5-lobed, membranous between the lobes; corolla salverform or widening at the summit, the tube usually longer than the calyx, the limb equally 5-lobed, the lobes entire; stamens 5, equally inserted on the corolla-tube or throat; ovary superior, 3-celled. Fruit a 3-valved capsule.

This is a small genus of about 6 species of woody perennials or subshrubs confined to southwestern North America. Two species are native to California.

KEY TO THE SPECIES

Plants 1 to 3½ feet high; corolla-tube as long as or shorter than the lobes; stamens inserted at or near the middle of the corolla-tube. . . . . 1. *L. californicum.*

Fig. 537. PRICKLY-PHLOX. *Leptodactylon californicum* H. & A.

Plants less than 1 foot high; corolla-tube 1¼ to nearly 2 times the length of the lobes; stamens inserted near the summit of the tube.........2. *L. pungens.*

1. **Leptodactylon californicum** H. & A. Prickly-phlox. Fig. 537.

A shrubby plant, 1 to 3½ feet high, with tomentose stems thickly set with clusters of prickly leaves in the axils of the main leaves. Leaves alternate or the lower ones sometimes opposite, falling the second season, palmately cleft into 5 to 9 (rarely 3) linear divisions ⅛- to ½-inch long. Flowers sessile, solitary or few in

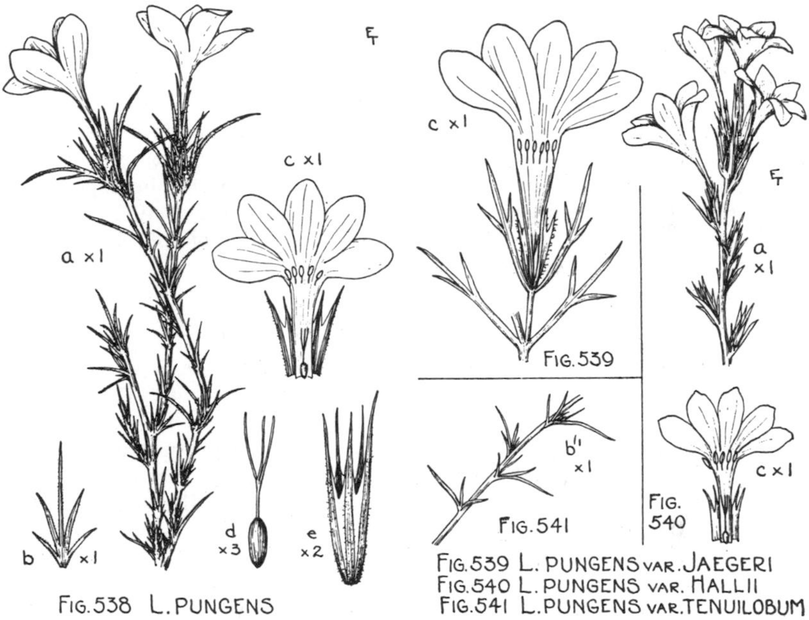

Leptodactylon. a, Flowering branchlet. b, Leaf. b', Leafy branchlet. c, Section of flower. d, Pistil. e, Calyx.

clusters terminating the branchlets; corolla bright pink or rose-color, the tube nearly cylindrical, ½- to ¾-inch long, shorter than or as long as the lobes; stamens included, inserted at or near the middle of the corolla-tube. Flowering period, February to July, or rarely to November.

Prickly-phlox grows on dry brushy hill slopes, sand hills, and along borders of intermittent streams from Monterey County southward in the Coast Range to the Santa Monica Mountains. It continues southward and eastward in the varietal form to the San Bernardino, San Jacinto, and Santa Ana mountains.

The profuse clusters of large bright pink flowers and leafy branches make this phlox-like plant one of the most ornamental of our native shrubs. Its habit of shedding leaves in late fall and its short life of 3 to 6 years make it unsuitable for perennial or shrub gardens.

1a. Var. **glandulosum** (Eastw.) Abrams.

Herbage more glandular-pubescent. This is the common form in the mountains of southern California.

Leptodactylon californicum H. & A. Bot. Beechey 369 t. 89 (1840). Type locality: "California." Probably near Santa Barbara or Monterey. Collected by *Douglas*. *Gilia californica* (H. & A.) Benth.

Var. glandulosum (Eastw.) Abrams, Bull. N. Y. Bot. Gard. 6:438 (1910). *Gilia californica* var. *glandulosa* Eastw. Type locality: Los Angeles County, California. Collected by *M. E. Jones*.

2. **Leptodactylon pungens** (Torr.) Nutt. GRANITE-GILIA. Fig. 538.

A low perennial, 4 to 12 inches high, with several stems from a branching woody base. Flowering period, May to August.

This low phlox-like perennial has a wide distribution in the Sierra Nevada and the mountains of southern California between 4000 and 13,000 feet elevation. It inhabits rocky and gravelly places where it often forms mats a foot in diameter. Outside of California it extends northward to British Columbia and eastward to the Rocky Mountains. Considerable variation in density of foliage, amount of pubescence, size and arrangement of leaves, and glandulosity of herbage occurs in this species and consequently several varieties have been described. The characters used, however, seem to break down when a large series of specimens collected throughout the range of the species is examined.

The following varieties, in their typical forms, are worthy of note.

KEY TO THE VARIETIES

Leaves usually opposite to the summit of the stems, simple or 3- to 5-parted; stamens commonly 6; caespitose glandular-pubescent plants; Tahquitz Peak, San Jacinto Mountains. . . . . .var. *Jaegeri*. Fig. 539.

Leaves usually alternate near the summit of the stems; plants usually not matted.

Stems tomentose, not glandular or only slightly so; leaves 3-parted, very rigid, the lateral divisions 1/4 to 1/2 the length of the middle one; Santa Rosa Mountains and southward in San Diego County. . . . . .var. *Hallii*. Fig. 540.

Stems glandular-pubescent.

Flowers yellowish, usually restricted to the summits of the branches, 1 inch or more long; leaves less rigid than in the preceding variety; San Jacinto, San Bernardino, Panamint, and Providence mountains. var. *tenuilobum*. Fig. 541.

Flowers white, pinkish, or rarely yellow, not restricted to the summit of the branches, 1/2-inch to 1 inch long; stems with long internodes; mountains of southern California and eastern slopes and summits of the Sierra Nevada, north to Oregon. . . . . .var. *Hookeri*.

Leptodactylon pungens (Torr.) Nutt. Jour. Phil. Acad. n. ser. 1:157 (1847). *Cantua pungens* Torr. Type locality: Valley of the Loup Fork. *Gilia pungens* (Torr.) Benth.

Hydrophyllaceae. Phacelia or Waterleaf Family

This family contains about 18 genera and 225 species of annual or perennial herbs or some shrubs, widely distributed but more abundant in North America. Thirteen genera and about 100 species are native to California; 2 genera with about 10 species are shrubby or woody at the base.

KEY TO THE GENERA

Plants distinctly shrubby; capsules leathery, 4-valved, 2- or 4-seeded. 1. ERIODICTYON.

Plants with herbaceous stems, often woody at the base; capsule membranous, 2-valved, 12- to many-seeded....................................2. NAMA.

1. **Eriodictyon** Benth. YERBA SANTA. MOUNTAIN BALM

(From the Greek *erion,* wool, and *diktuon,* network, in reference to the netted veins and woolliness of the underside of the leaves.)

Usually aromatic shrubs. Leaves simple, alternate, evergreen, 1-veined from the base, more or less leathery, short-petioled. Flowers bisexual, regular, borne in one-sided curved compound clusters; sepals 5, nearly distinct; petals 5, united into a funnel- or cylinder-shaped tube; stamens 5, inserted on the corolla-tube; ovary superior, 2-celled, composed of 2 carpels; styles 2, distinct to the base. Fruit a 4-valved capsule. Seeds few (less than 10).

This genus contains about 8 species with several varieties and many intermediate forms. All are limited to the western United States and adjacent Mexico. Seven species and 2 varieties are native to California.

In the field one meets two distinct types or groups, easily recognized by their foliage characters. One type has both surfaces of the leaves covered with gray or whitish tomentum in the form of a silky mat. *Eriodictyon crassifolium* is an example of this type. The second type, exemplified by *Eriodictyon californicum,* has a smooth usually glutinous upper leaf-surface, while the lower leaf-surface usually has a fine mesh-work of veins between which occurs a very short tomentum. Abrams and Smiley (see Bibl.) found that the leaves of the *Eriodictyon californicum* group possessed several rows of palisade tissue and that a single row was characteristic of the leaves of the *Eriodictyon crassifolium* type. Both are apparently well adapted to the dry habitats in which they usually occur. Intermediate forms between the two types are often found which seem to indicate a common origin. Some of these are included in the key and diagnoses which follow. For the more critical student, however, it seems best to recognize 7 Californian species and 2 varieties.

KEY TO THE SPECIES

Leaves narrowly linear; inflorescence usually head-like..........1. *E. capitatum.*
Leaves broader; inflorescence a panicle of one-sided cymes.
  Leaves glabrous and glutinous above.
    Leaves densely white-tomentose beneath, obscuring all but the main veins, commonly revolute; sepals densely white-hairy but not glandular; corolla tubular-conical, ¼- to ⅜-inch long...................2. *E. lanatum.*
    Leaves whitened or pale beneath between the evident reticulations, flat or rarely slightly revolute.
      Sepals densely hairy or rarely only sparsely hairy, not glandular; corolla funnelform, ¼- to ⅜-inch long....................3. *E. trichocalyx.*
      Sepals glabrous or rarely only sparsely hairy along the margins, more or less glutinous; corolla funnelform, ⅜- to ⅝-inch long. .4. *E. californicum.*
  Leaves not glutinous above (rarely glutinous in *E. crassifolium* var. *denudatum*), varying from densely white- and soft-tomentose to grayish or greenish tomentose or almost glabrate.
    Calyx and corolla hairy but not glandular without; corolla funnelform, ¼- to ⅝-inch long, not constricted near the summit.
      1. Leaves densely hoary- or silvery-tomentose above; corolla ⅜- to ⅝-inch long, pale bluish purple........................5. *E. crassifolium.*

2. Leaves dull gray-green above, with less dense tomentum; corolla ¼- to ⅜-inch long, white to very pale blue. 5a. *E. crassifolium* var. *nigrescens.*
3. Leaves greenish and glabrate and sometimes slightly glutinous above; corolla ¼- to ⅜-inch long, lavender.
5b. *E. crassifolium* var. *denudatum.*

Calyx glandular-hirsute, or hairy and with interspersed glands; corolla pubescent and glandular, tubular or a little urn-shaped, constricted near the summit of the tube.

Sepals dark-colored, with gland-bearing hairs, not densely silvery-tomentose; corolla about ¼-inch long, the lobes about ⅛-inch long. 6. *E. Traskiae.*

Sepals densely silvery-hairy and with interspersed glands; corolla ⅛- to 3⁄16-inch long, the lobes less than 1⁄16-inch long . . . . . 7. *E. tomentosum.*

1. **Eriodictyon capitatum** Eastw. LOMPOC YERBA SANTA. Fig. 542.

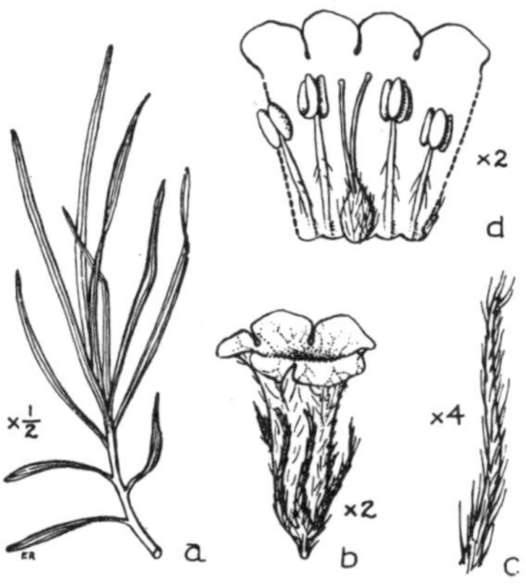

Fig. 542. ERIODICTYON CAPITATUM. a, Leaves. b, Flower. c, Sepal. d, Open corolla.

An erect openly branched shrub, 2 to 6 feet high, with glutinous branches and leaves. Leaves narrowly linear, 1 to 2½ inches long, about ⅛-inch broad, glabrous and usually glutinous above, white-tomentose beneath, the margins strongly revolute, sessile. Flowers usually crowded in head-like clusters terminating the branches; sepals linear, about ⅜-inch long, densely hirsute; corolla purplish, funnelform, ⅜- to ⅝-inch long, pubescent without, glabrous within. Flowering period, May to July.

Lompoc Yerba Santa is known only from the mesa region about 5 miles north of Lompoc, Santa Barbara County (ravine approaching Burton Mesa, *McMinn;* road to Casmalia, *Hoffman*). The extremely narrow leaves and head-like clusters of flowers easily distinguish this species from all other Californian species.

Eriodictyon capitatum Eastw. Leafl. West. Bot. 1:40 (1933). Type locality: North of Lompoc, Santa Barbara County, growing under *Pinus muricata.* Collected by *Ralph Hoffman.*

2. **Eriodictyon lanatum** (Brand) Abrams. SAN DIEGO YERBA SANTA. Fig. 543.

An erect shrub, 1½ to 5 feet high, with the branches more or less permanently tomentose. Leaf-blades narrow elliptical to linear-lanceolate, 1 to 3 inches long, ¼- to ¾-inch wide, glabrous and glutinous above, densely white-tomentose beneath, nearly obscuring the reticulations, the margins sinuate, entire or dentate, slightly revolute; petioles ¼- to ½-inch long, expanding gradually from the stem into the tapering base. Flowers crowded into the 1-sided branched cluster; sepals densely white-pubescent; corolla purplish, blue, or nearly white, tubular-conical, ¼- to ⅜-inch long, much exceeding the calyx. Flowering period, April to June.

San Diego Yerba Santa occurs in the chaparral on the desert slopes of the mountains of San Diego County, the Santa Rosa Mountains of Riverside County, and in northern Lower California. It is very closely related to *E. trichocalyx* but differs from that species in having revolute leaves and a much denser white tomentum on the lower leaf-surfaces.

Eriodictyon lanatum (Brand) Abrams, Bot. Gaz. 60:126 (1915). *E. californicum* var. *lanatum* Brand. Type locality: In the chaparral between Campo and Jacumba, San Diego County, California. Collected by *Abrams*. *E. trichocalyx* var. *lanatum* (Brand) Jepson.

3. **Eriodictyon trichocalyx** Heller. HAIRY YERBA SANTA. Fig. 544.

An open erect shrub, 1½ to 6 feet high, with usually glabrous and often glutinous branchlets. Leaf-blades linear-lanceolate to broadly lanceolate or rarely oblanceolate, tapering to both ends, 2 to 5 inches long, ½-inch to 1½ inches wide, glabrous and glutinous above, grayish or gray-green beneath with a fine dense tomentum between the prominent network of veins, the margins dentate, sometimes slightly revolute; petioles ¼- to ½-inch long. Branches of the flower-clusters pubescent. Sepals densely pubescent; corolla pale lilac or white, funnelform, ¼- to ⅜-inch long, densely pubescent without. Flowering period, May to August.

Hairy Yerba Santa inhabits stony or sandy soils of dry brushy slopes and sandy plains from the Santa Ynez Mountains of Santa Barbara County southward along the desert slopes of the mountains of Ventura, Los Angeles, San Bernardino, and Riverside counties, in the Upper Sonoran Life Zone. Some specimens from the Santa Ynez Mountains closely resemble *E. lanatum*. The older leaves of this species and of *E. californicum* are often black with the spores of a fungal growth.

Eriodictyon trichocalyx Heller, Muhlenbergia 1:108 (1904). Type locality: "Seven Oaks Camp, San Bernardino Mountains." Collected by *Mrs. G. B. Grant*. *E. angustifolium* var. *pubens* Gray.

4. **Eriodictyon californicum** (H. & A.) Torr. CALIFORNIA YERBA SANTA. MOUNTAIN BALM. Fig. 545.

An erect shrub, 2 to 8 feet high, usually with glabrous and glutinous branchlets. Leaf-blades lanceolate to elliptical or linear-lanceolate, 2 to 4 (or 8) inches long, ⅜-inch to 2 (or 3) inches wide, glabrous and usually glutinous above, grayish beneath with a fine felt between the prominent network of veins, the margins serrate and sometimes undulate; petioles ¼- to ½-inch long. Branches of the flower-cluster glabrous or slightly pubescent. Sepals linear, glabrous or sparsely hairy along the margins, more or less glutinous; corolla lavender, pale blue, or rarely almost white, tubular-funnelform, ⅜- to ⅝-inch long, weakly puberulent without. Flowering period, May to July.

California Yerba Santa occurs in dry habitats of the foothills and lower mountain slopes in the Upper Sonoran and lower Transition Life Zones in the Coast Ranges from northern San Luis Obispo County, California northward to the Siskiyou Mountains and to Jackson, Josephine, and Curry counties, Oregon; and in the Sierra Nevada foothills from Kern and Tulare counties northward to Plumas County. Much variation occurs in the size and shape of the leaves from plants collected throughout the range of the species. Some specimens from the Giant Forest of Tulare County have leaves 8 inches long and 3 inches wide, while specimens from very dry habitats of other localities have leaves which are only 1½ inches long and about ¼-inch wide. The plants are often attacked by a fungus, the fruiting spores of which turn the leaves nearly black, thus rendering the species unsuitable for ornamental planting.

Eriodictyon californicum (H. & A.) Torr. Bot. Mex. Bound. 148 (1859). *Wigan-*

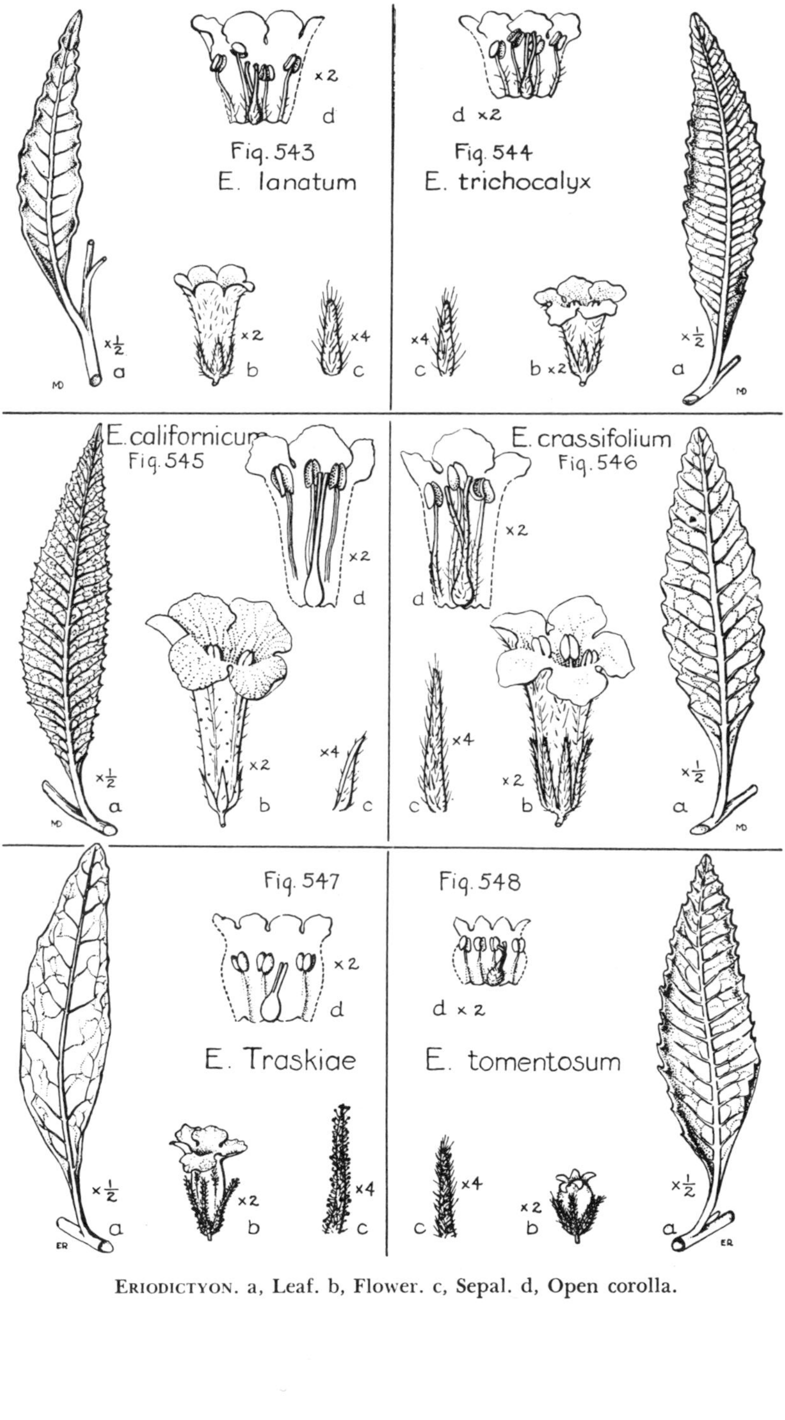

ERIODICTYON. a, Leaf. b, Flower. c, Sepal. d, Open corolla.

dia californica H. & A. Type locality: "In the coastal region of California, between Sonoma and Monterey." Collected by *Douglas.*

5. **Eriodictyon crassifolium** Benth. THICKLEAF YERBA SANTA. Fig. 546.

KEY TO THE SPECIES AND VARIETIES

Leaf-blades densely gray-tomentose on both surfaces; corolla 3/8- to 5/8-inch long, slightly hairy without.................................*E. crassifolium.*
Leaf-blades less tomentose above; corolla 1/4- to 3/8-inch long, densely pubescent without.
  Leaf-blades dull gray-green above.......................5a. var. *nigrescens.*
  Leaves greenish, glabrate, and sometimes slightly glutinous above. 5b. var. *denudatum.*

An erect shrub, 3 to 12 feet high, usually hoary-tomentose throughout. Leaf-blades oblong-lanceolate or broadly elliptical to oval, 2 to 6 inches long, 1/2-inch to 2 inches wide, densely gray- (or gray-green-) tomentose on both surfaces, the margins crenate-dentate, rarely entire or shallowly lobed; petioles about 1/4-inch long, gradually broadening upward to the leaf-blades. Branches of the flower-clusters densely tomentose. Sepals narrowly linear, silvery-hairy but not glandular; corolla pale bluish purple, broadly funnelform, not constricted near the summit, 3/8- to 5/8-inch long, 2 or 3 times longer than the sepals, slightly hairy without, not glandular. Flowering period, April to June.

Thickleaf Yerba Santa occurs on sandy or gravelly plains and foothills from San Diego County northward in the Santa Ana River canyon of Orange County to the eastern slope of the San Jacinto Mountains of Riverside County, thence northward and westward in the San Gabriel and Santa Monica mountains of Los Angeles County where the leaves are less hoary-tomentose. In Ventura, Santa Barbara, and western Kern counties, this species grades over into the following varieties.

5a. Var. **nigrescens** Brand.

Leaves dull gray-green above, with less dense tomentum. Corolla white to pale blue, 1/4- to 3/8-inch long, densely hairy without.

This variety occurs in the Liebre Mountains, in the San Fernando wash, the Arroyo Seco, and elsewhere in Los Angeles County; in Matilija Canyon, Ventura County, and on the "river road between Bakersfield and Bodfish, Kern County" *(Abrams);* and along the Ridge Route in the Tehachapi Mountains. It is apparently a derivative of *E. crassifolium* and may have given rise to *E. Traskiae* and probably *E. crassifolium* var. *denudatum.*

5b. Var. **denudatum** Abrams.

Leaves greenish, glabrate, and sometimes a little glutinous above. Corolla lavender, 1/4- to 3/8-inch long, densely pubescent without.

This variety occurs in the chaparral areas of the foothills and lower mountain slopes of Santa Barbara and Ventura counties. The glabrate and somewhat glutinous upper leaf-surfaces of some specimens relate this variety to *E. trichocalyx* which also occurs in a few localities in the same region.

Eriodictyon crassifolium Benth. Bot. Voy. Sulph. 35 (1844). Type locality: "San Diego." Collected by *Barclay. E. tomentosum* of various authors, not Benth.

Var. nigrescens Brand; Engler, Pflanzenreich 59:140 (1913). Type locality: Acton, Los Angeles County. Collected by *Elmer.*

Var. denudatum Abrams, Bot. Gaz. 60:129 (1915). Type locality: Red Reef Canyon, Topatopa Mountains, Ventura County, California. Collected by *Abrams* and *McGregor*.

6. **Eriodictyon Traskiae** Eastw. TRASK YERBA SANTA. Fig. 547.

An erect shrub, 2½ to 6 feet high, with grayish foliage. Leaf-blades oblanceolate to elliptic-ovate, 2 to 4½ inches long, ½-inch to 1½ inches wide, densely silvery-hairy on both surfaces, the margins sinuate-dentate; petioles ¼- to ½-inch long. Inflorescences pubescent, much branched, the flowers borne in congested clusters at the ends of the branches. Sepals narrowly linear, dark-colored, with glandular hairs; corolla purplish, tubular, constricted near the summit, about ¼-inch long, the upper part glandular-hairy without, the lobes about ⅛-inch long; stamens shorter than the tube, nearly sessile, inserted at the middle of the tube. Flowering period, April to July.

Trask Yerba Santa occurs in the Santa Ynez Mountains (trail to La Cumbre Peak; Painted Cave Ranch; Santa Ynez River), near the summit of Harriston Grade north of Lompoc, Santa Barbara County, in the Santa Lucia Mountains of San Luis Obispo County, and on Santa Catalina Island. It is related to *E. tomentosum* but differs from that species in the absence of silvery tomentum on the sepals, its longer corolla-lobes, and the insertion of the stamens.

Eriodictyon Traskiae Eastw. Proc. Calif. Acad. ser. 3, 1:131 (1898). Type locality: "On one volcanic upland on Santa Catalina Island, California." Collected by *Blanche Trask*. *E. crassifolium* var. *Traskiae* (Eastw.) Brand.

7. **Eriodictyon tomentosum** Benth. WOOLLY YERBA SANTA. Fig. 548.

An erect branching shrub, 2 to 6 feet high, with silvery- or white-tomentose foliage. Leaf-blades elliptic-ovate or obovate, 1½ to 3½ inches long, ½-inch to 1¼ inches wide, densely white-tomentose on both surfaces, the margins crenate-dentate or rarely entire or coarsely dentate; petioles about ¼-inch long, broadening upward into the leaf-blades. Branches of the flower-clusters tomentose. Sepals linear, densely silvery-hairy and with interspersed glands; corolla white or pale violet, tubular or slightly urn-shaped, constricted near the summit, ⅛- to 3/16-inch long, the lobes less than 1/16-inch long; stamens equalling the corolla-tube, inserted below the throat. Flowering period, April to June.

Woolly Yerba Santa inhabits gravelly flats and chaparral-covered areas of the eastern slopes of the South Coast Ranges from the northern boundary of Santa Barbara County northward in San Luis Obispo, Monterey, and San Benito counties. It has been confused with *E. crassifolium* but it inhabits a different geographical range and can be distinguished from that species by its more silvery herbage and its shorter tubular corolla which is constricted at the summit.

Eriodictyon tomentosum Benth. Bot. Voy. Sulph. 36 (1844). Type locality: "Probably in the vicinity of Mission San Antonio, Monterey County, California." Collected by *Douglas*. *E. niveum* Eastw.

2. Nama L.

(From the Greek *nama*, a spring, in reference to the habitat of the original species.)

Plants usually herbaceous throughout but a very few woody at the base. Leaves simple and alternate. Flowers bisexual, regular; sepals 5, joined at base, persistent in fruit; petals 5, united into a funnelform tube; stamens 5, shorter than the corolla-tube; ovary superior, 2-celled. Fruit a 2-valved capsule; seeds 12 to numerous.

The genus *Nama* contains about 15 species native to warm and tropical regions. About 10 species occur in California, 2 of which are often woody at the base.

KEY TO THE SPECIES

Leaves entire, of 2 types; stems usually procumbent, not more than 2 feet high; herbage white-woolly. . . . . 1. *N. Lobbii.*

Leaves toothed, of one kind; stems distinctly erect, 3 to 6 feet high; herbage ill-smelling, viscid. . . . . 2. *N. Parryi.*

Fig. 549 Nama Lobbii

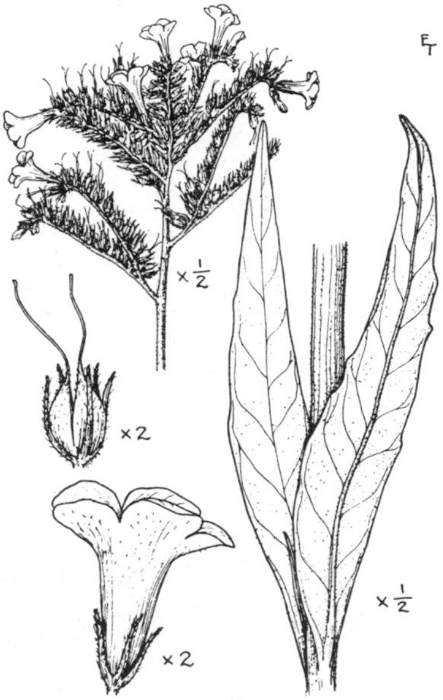

Fig. 550 Nama Parryi

1. **Nama Lobbii** Gray. Woolly Nama. Fig. 549.

A low perennial, ½-foot to 2 feet high, with few creeping or somewhat erect slightly woody stems and silky-woolly herbage. Flowering period, May to July.

Woolly Nama usually inhabits rocky or red clay soils, from 4000 to 7000 feet elevation, in the Sierra Nevada from Eldorado County (near Meeks Bay) northward to Mount Lassen in Shasta County, thence north and west to near Shasta Springs, Siskiyou County. It extends eastward to western Nevada.

Nama Lobbii Gray, Proc. Am. Acad. 6:37 (1864). Type locality: California. Collected by *Lobb.*

2. **Nama Parryi** Gray. Sticky Nama. Poodle-dog Bush. Figs. 550, 551.

A coarse perennial plant, 3 to 6 feet high, somewhat woody below, with several stems from the base and viscid-pubescent ill-smelling herbage. Flowering period, June to August.

Fig. 551. STICKY NAMA. *Nama Parryi* Gray.
(Photograph by A. E. Wieslander, courtesy California Forest and Range Experiment Station, U. S. Forest Service.)

Sticky Nama inhabits dry places in the open forests and adjacent brushy areas in the mountains of southern California from 1000 to 7000 feet elevation (Cuyamaca, Palomar, San Jacinto, Santa Ana, San Bernardino, San Gabriel, and Santa Monica mountains). It also occurs occasionally in the southern Sierra Nevada in Tulare County and in the Mount Piños region of Ventura County. It extends southward to Lower California.

Nama Parryi Gray, Bot. Calif. 1:621 (1876). Type locality: "On the Mohave slope of the San Bernardino Mts." Collected by *Parry*. *Eriodictyon Parryi* (Gray) Greene.

Boraginaceae. Borage Family

The Borage Family consists of about 85 genera and 1500 species of herbs or rarely shrubs or trees, widely distributed in the temperate and tropical regions, most abundant in western North America and the Mediterranean region. Sixteen genera and about 85 species are native to California, only 4 of which are somewhat woody at base.

KEY TO THE GENERA

Leaves linear; style unbranched. . . . . 1. CRYPTANTHA.
Leaves ovate, obovate, or lanceolate, style 2-cleft or -parted. . . . . 2. COLDENIA.

1. **Cryptantha** Lehm. WILD FORGET-ME-NOT

(From the Greek *kruptos,* hidden, and *anthos,* flower, in reference to the obscure corollas in the original species.)

This genus contains over 60 species, mostly herbaceous annuals native to western North America and Chile. A few are perennial and slightly woody at the base.

1. **Cryptantha racemosa** (Wats.) Greene. WHITE FORGET-ME-NOT. Fig. 552.

A profusely branched subshrub, ⅓-foot to 3 feet high, with very slender branchlets and hispid herbage. Flowering period, April to June.

This hispid subshrub occurs about rocks in the desert regions of Inyo, San Bernardino, Riverside, Imperial, and San Diego counties up to 4600 feet altitude. It extends eastward into Nevada and Arizona and southward to Lower California.

Cryptantha racemosa (Wats. ex Gray) Greene, Pitt. 1:115 (1887). *Eritrichium racemosum* Wats. ex Gray. Type locality: Mesquite Canyon near Mesquite Station, San Bernardino County, California. Collected by *S. B.* and *W. F. Parish.*

2. **Coldenia** L.

(Named in honor of Dr. Cadwallader Colden, Lieutenant-Governor of New York, and a botanical correspondent of Linnaeus.)

Herbs or small shrubs, mostly low-growing, usually with hoary-pubescent or often hispid herbage. Leaves small, simple, alternate, usually with conspicuous veins. Flowers small, bisexual, regular, sessile, solitary or usually clustered in the forks or at the ends of the branches and subtended by a few small leaves; calyx 5-lobed; corolla short-funnelform, with an erect or spreading 5-lobed limb; stamens 5, included and inserted on the corolla-tube; ovary superior, 2-carpelled but with 4 cells; style cleft or parted. Fruit splitting into 4 one-seeded nutlets.

This is a small genus of about 12 species, one in the Old World and 11 in the New World. Four species are native to California, 3 of which are somewhat woody at the base.

KEY TO THE SPECIES

Stems forking regularly by 2's; flowers borne in clusters; leaves distinctly veiny.
  Plants matted, the stems prostrate; leaves with about 6 pairs of deeply impressed veins. . . . . 1. *C. plicata.*
  Plants not matted, the stems trailing or erect; leaves with 2 or 3 pairs of shallowly impressed veins. . . . . 2. *C. Palmeri.*

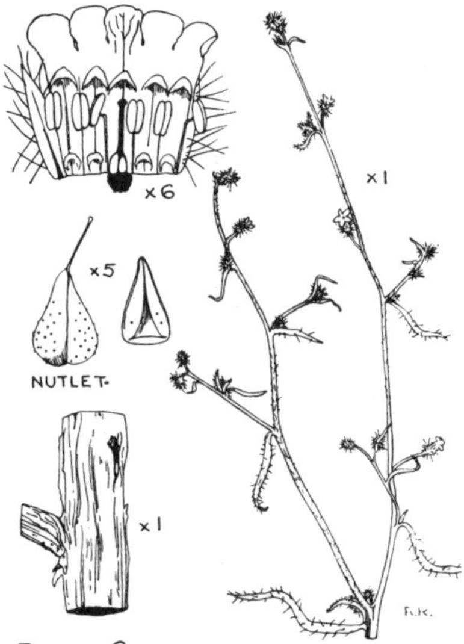

FIG. 552 CRYPTANTHA RACEMOSA

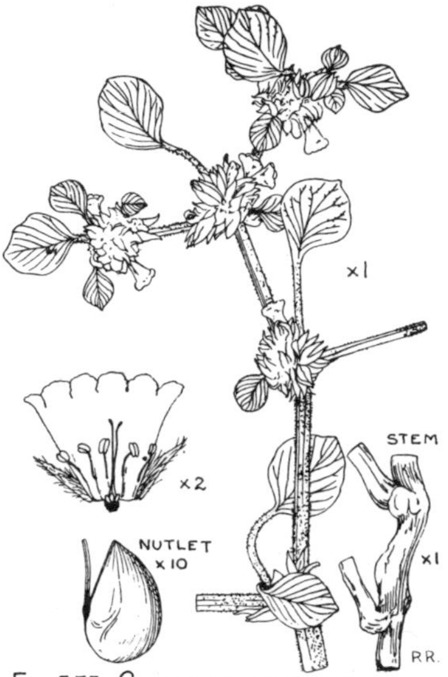

FIG. 553. COLDENIA PLICATA

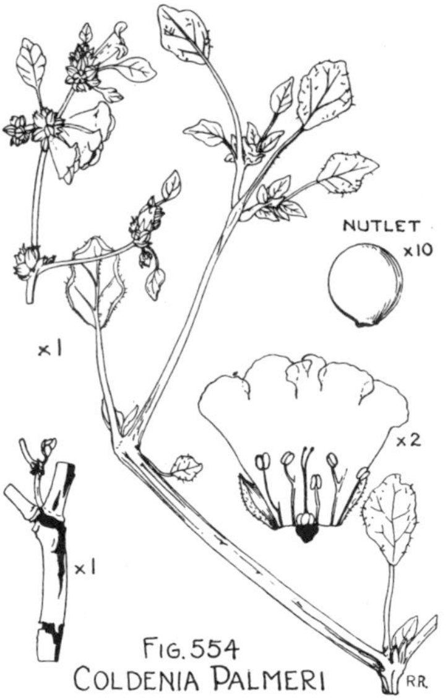

FIG. 554
COLDENIA PALMERI

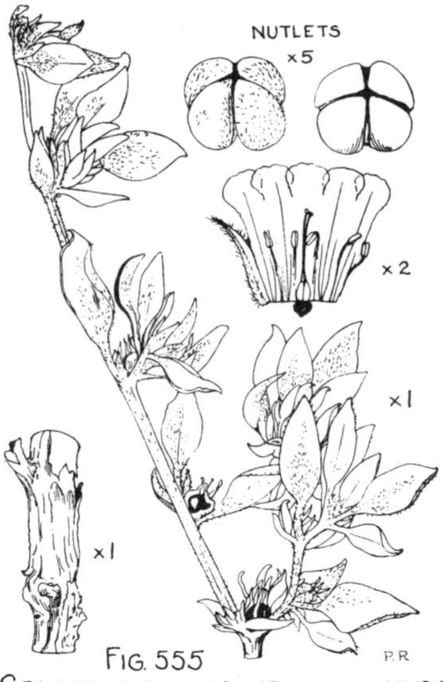

FIG. 555
COLDENIA CANESCENS VAR. SUBNUDA

Stems not forking regularly by 2's; flowers usually solitary; leaves obscurely veined.
3. *C. canescens* var. *subnuda*.

1. **Coldenia plicata** (Torr.) Cov. DESERT MAT. Fig. 553.

A prostrate matted plant, 4 to 20 inches broad, with mostly herbaceous branches spreading from a somewhat woody caudex or herbaceous throughout. Flowering period, April and May.

This species occurs in sandy places in the Colorado and Mohave deserts below 2600 feet elevation. It is more abundant on the Colorado Desert. It extends eastward to western Arizona and southern Nevada and southward to Lower California.

Coldenia plicata (Torr.) Cov. Contr. U. S. Nat. Herb. 4:163 (1893). *C. brevifolia* var. *plicata* Torr. *Tiquilia brevifolia* var. *plicata* Torr. Type locality: Colorado Desert, California. Collected by *Schott*. *Coldenia Palmeri* Wats., not Gray.

2. **Coldenia Palmeri** Gray. PALMER COLDENIA. Fig. 554.

A low slightly glutinous trailing perennial, 4 to 12 inches high and from 8 inches to nearly 3 feet broad, with 2-forked stems. Older branches somewhat suffrutescent and with white bark exfoliating in thin strips. Flowering period, March to May.

Palmer Coldenia inhabits sandy places below 500 feet elevation in the Colorado Desert and along the Colorado River to Needles. It extends eastward to western Arizona and southward to Lower California.

Coldenia Palmeri Gray, Proc. Am. Acad. 8:292 (1870). Type locality: "Lower Colorado River." Collected by *Palmer*. *Coldenia brevicalyx* Wats.

3. **Coldenia canescens** var. **subnuda** Johnst. COLDENIA. Fig. 555.

A low spreading or procumbent perennial, 2 to 6 inches high, with suffrutescent rough-barked stems from a gnarled usually much thickened woody base, and white-tomentose and hispid herbage. Flowering period, April and May.

This is a rare species of the eastern part of the Colorado Desert where it is known from rocky slopes and ridges in the Eagle, Chocolate, and Chuckawalla mountains. It extends eastward to Arizona and southward to Lower California.

Coldenia canescens var. subnuda Johnst. Proc. Calif. Acad. ser. 4, 12:1137 (1924). Type locality: "On a stony bench at San Nicholas Bay, Lower California." Collected by *I. M. Johnston*.

Verbenaceae. Verbena Family

This family contains about 65 genera and 750 species of herbs, shrubs, and trees, mainly of tropical and subtropical distribution. Two genera occur in California, one of which has a single woody species.

1. **Lippia** L.

(Named in honor of Dr. A. Lippi, a French traveler and naturalist.)

This genus consists of about 125 species, nearly all in tropical and subtropical America, 2 or 3 in Africa, and one or 2 widely scattered in warm countries.

1. **Lippia Wrightii** Gray. BUSH LIPPIA. Fig. 556.

An erect aromatic shrub, 2 to 4 feet high, with slender spreading branches. Leaves simple, opposite, evergreen; the blades broadly ovate to nearly round, $\frac{1}{4}$- to $\frac{1}{2}$-inch (or 1 inch) long, rugose and scabrous above, canescent-tomentose beneath, 3-veined from the base, crenate; petioles $\frac{1}{8}$- to $\frac{1}{4}$-inch long. Flowers small, white,

FIG. 556 LIPPIA WRIGHTII

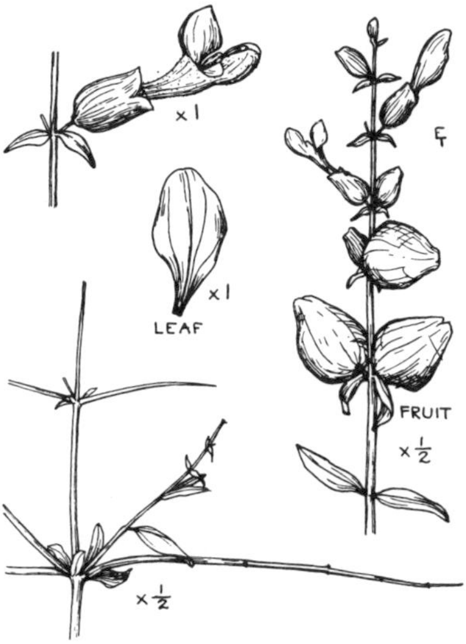

FIG. 557 SALAZARIA MEXICANA

FIG. 558
TRICHOSTEMA LANATUM

FIG. 559
TRICHOSTEMA PARISHII

bisexual, in bracteate axillary and terminal spikes 1 to 2½ inches long; bracts ovate-lanceolate, about the length of the calyx; calyx small, with 4 acute equal lobes, densely white-hirsute; petals 5, joined into a cylindrical tube bilabiate at summit; stamens 4, adnate to the corolla-tube; ovary superior, 2-celled. Fruit dry, composed of 2 nutlets separating at maturity. Flowering period, April and May.

Bush Lippia is known in California only from the Providence Mountains of San Bernardino County, at an elevation of about 3000 feet (acc. *Munz*). Its range extends eastward through Arizona and New Mexico to western Texas and southward into Mexico.

Lippia Wrightii Gray. (name only) Am. Jour. Sci. ser. 2, 16:98 (1853). *L. Wrightii* Gray; Torr. Bot. Mex. Bound. 2:126 (issued before April 21, 1859, acc. *A. Schott*). Type locality: New Mexico. Collected by *Wright*.

Menthaceae (Labiatae). Mint Family

The Mint Family contains about 170 genera and 3000 species of annual or perennial herbs, some shrubs, rarely trees or climbers, usually with 4-angled stems, opposite exstipulate leaves, and aromatic odor. The species occur mostly in warm and temperate regions. Seven genera and about 28 species of shrubs and subshrubs are native to California.

KEY TO THE GENERA

Flowers in heads terminating the branches and surrounded at base by broad bracts; corolla nearly regular or only slightly 2-lipped......1. MONARDELLA.
Flowers not in terminal heads (flower-clusters usually solitary in *Salvia Clevelandii,* but the corolla is distinctly irregular).
  Branches usually spinescent; calyx 2-lipped, conspicuously enlarged and thin in fruit, resembling an inflated bladder.....................2. SALAZARIA.
  Branches not spinescent; calyx not bladder-like in fruit (somewhat inflated in *Sphacele*).
    Flowers ½-inch or less long.
      Fertile stamens 2..7. SALVIA.
      Fertile stamens 4.
        Leaves linear-oblong or lanceolate, revolute, usually 1 inch or more long ....3. TRICHOSTEMA.
        Leaves ovate to round, usually less than 1 inch long.
          Flowers solitary or 2 to 4 in the leaf-axils; calyx only slightly 2-lipped. 4. SATUREIA.
          Flowers in axillary short-peduncled clusters which are often paniculate at the ends of the branchlets; calyx with 5 nearly equal teeth. 5. HYPTIS.
    Flowers usually more than ½-inch long.
      Leaves sessile, ¼-inch or less wide, usually revolute; ovary with 4 united nutlets..3. TRICHOSTEMA.
      Leaves petiolate, commonly over ¼-inch wide; ovary with 4 distinct or nearly distinct nutlets.
        Fertile stamens 4; calyx nearly equally 5-toothed...........6. SPHACELE.
        Fertile stamens 2; calyx 2-lipped, the upper lip entire or 3-toothed, the lower lip 2-cleft.................................7. SALVIA.

1. **Monardella** Benth.

(Named as a diminutive of *Monarda*, on account of its resemblance to that genus.)

Mostly annual or perennial herbs, some subshrubs, usually pleasantly fragrant. Leaves opposite, entire or serrate. Flowers borne in terminal globose heads subtended by broad more or less colored bracts; calyx narrow-tubular, 5-toothed, the teeth erect, triangular, nearly equal; corolla usually rose-purple or rarely almost dull white, very slightly 2-lipped, the upper lip 2-lobed, the lower lip 3-lobed; stamens 4, all fertile, distinct, not much exserted; ovary superior, 4-parted; style shortly and unequally bifid at apex. Fruit of 4 smooth nutlets.

The monardellas are confined to western North America, chiefly in the mountains and interior valleys of California, northern Lower California, southern Oregon, and the Great Basin region. Twelve species are here "keyed out" but not described.

KEY TO THE SPECIES

Calyx ½-inch to 1 inch long; corolla 1 to 2 inches long.
  Corolla 1 to 1¼ inches long, white or yellowish; calyx about ½-inch long and nearly as long as the corolla-tube..........................1. *M. nana*.
  Corolla 1½ to 2 inches long, scarlet or yellowish; calyx ¾-inch to 1 inch long, not as long as the corolla-tube........................2. *M. macrantha*.
Calyx less than ½-inch long; corolla less than 1 inch long.
  Leaves strongly wavy-margined or crisped, oblanceolate; corolla purple. 3. *M. crispa*.
  Leaves not wavy-margined or crisped.
    Leaves with a strongly developed white felt-like tomentum on the lower surface.
      Leaves strongly revolute (only slightly revolute or plane in *M. hypoleuca* var. *saxicola*).
        Leaves glabrous above............................4. *M. hypoleuca*.
        Leaves moderately lanate above.........................5. *M. lanata*.
      Leaves not revolute (rarely so in *M. viridis*).
        Dwarfish plants, 1 to 5 inches high; leaves round-ovate, all less than ½-inch long..................................6. *M. cinerea*.
        Erect plants, 1 to 3 feet high; leaves oblong, ½-inch to 1¼ inches long, bright green above.............................7. *M. viridis*.
    Leaves glabrous or pubescent or tomentose but not felt-like beneath.
      Leaves typically less than ½-inch long.
        Leaf-blades entire; corolla ⅜-inch long; plants 1 to 1½ feet high. 12. *M. Robisonii*.
        Leaf-blades usually denticulate.
          Leaves sessile, finely pubescent and with an ashy hue on both surfaces. 6. *M. cinerea*.
          Leaves petiolate, apparently glabrous above, purplish..9. *M. villosa*.
      Leaves typically ½-inch or more long.
        Stems erect, ½-foot to 2½ feet tall.
          Bracts subtending the flower-clusters usually foliaceous; leaves commonly more or less toothed or entire...............9. *M. villosa*.
          Bracts subtending the flower-clusters membranous or rarely foliaceous, purplish or pinkish (rarely whitish); leaves mostly entire.

Leaves sessile, linear or oblong or linear-lanceolate, silvery-white with a dense microscopic puberulence.........10. *M. linoides.*

Leaves petiolate, narrowly ovate to lanceolate, glandular-dotted, pale and often finely pubescent or glabrous. 11. *M. odoratissima.*

Stems decumbent, 2 to 6 inches high..................8. *M. australis.*

2. **Salazaria** Torr.

(Named in honor of Don José Salazar, member of the United States and Mexican Survey Commission.)

This genus contains a single species native to New Mexico, Arizona, Utah, Nevada, southern California, and Mexico.

1. **Salazaria mexicana** Torr. Bladder-sage. Fig. 557.

An intricately branched shrub, 1½ to 3½ feet high, with spinescent branchlets. Leaves simple, opposite; the blades oblong-ovate to broadly lanceolate, ¼- to ¾-inch long, ⅛- to ¼-inch wide, obscurely 1- or 3-veined from the base, entire or some irregularly toothed, glabrous; petioles less than ⅛-inch long. Flowers in loose spike-like clusters 2 to 4 inches long; calyx about ⅓-inch long, with 2 very short entire lips, in fruit becoming much enlarged and bladder-like; corolla purplish, 2-lipped, about ¾-inch long, pubescent outside with short reflexed hairs; stamens 4; ovary superior, 4-lobed. Fruit of 4 roughened nutlets surrounded by the inflated bladder-like persistent calyx, this ½- to ¾-inch long. Flowering period, April and May.

Bladder-sage grows in dry washes and rocky canyons of the northern Colorado and the Mohave deserts in the Lower Sonoran Life Zone of Imperial, Riverside, Los Angeles, San Bernardino, Inyo, and Kern counties. It extends eastward into Nevada, Arizona, and Utah and southward to northern Mexico. The peculiar bladder-like fruiting calyx easily distinguishes this plant from all other native shrubs.

Salazaria mexicana Torr. Bot. Mex. Bound. 133, t. 39 (1858). Type locality: "Ravines, Chihuahua, below Presidio del Norte, near the Rio Grande." Collected by *Parry*. First discovered by Fremont on "Rio de Los Angeles, a branch of the Rio Virgen, western New Mexico."

3. **Trichostema** L. Blue Curls

(From the Greek *trichos,* hair, and *stemon,* stamen, in reference to the hairy calyx and protruding stamens.)

Strong-scented herbs or shrubs. Leaves simple, opposite. Flowers bisexual, irregular, borne in axillary cymes or sometimes racemose to paniculate, or even spicate; calyx nearly equally 5-cleft; corolla with a slender tube exceeding the calyx, 2-lipped, the upper lip 2-lobed, the lower lip 2-lobed; stamens 4, long-exserted; ovary superior, 4-lobed, 4-celled. Fruit of 4 roughened nutlets.

This genus contains about 10 species native to North America. Two of the 7 Californian species are woody at the base.

KEY TO THE SPECIES

Inflorescence congested; corolla ⅜- to ⅝-inch long; stamens 1¼ to 1½ inches long..1. *T. lanatum.*

Inflorescence open-paniculate, the branches at right angles to the central axis; corolla about ⅜-inch long; stamens ¾-inch to 1 inch long....2. *T. Parishii.*

FIG. 560 SATUREIA CHANDLERI

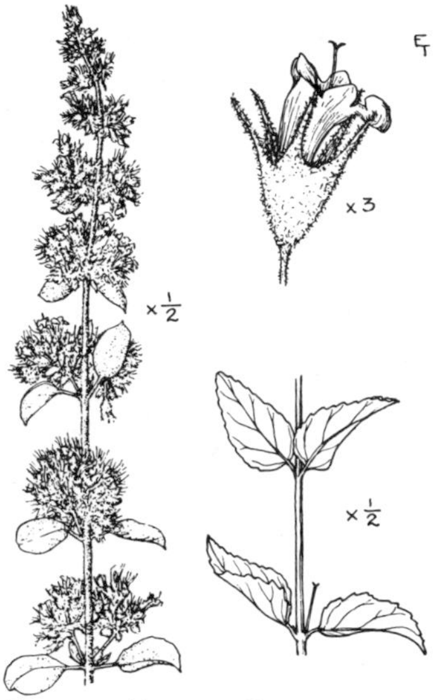

FIG. 561 HYPTIS EMORYI

FIG. 562
SPHACELE
CALYCINA

FIG. 563
SPHACELE CALYCINA
VAR. WALLACEI

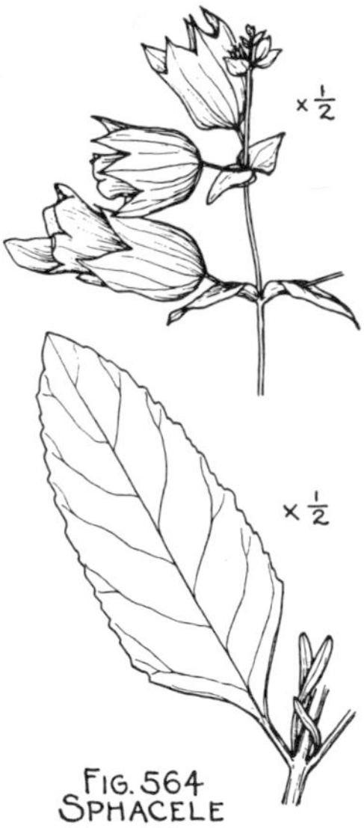

FIG. 564
SPHACELE
CALYCINA VAR.
GLABELLA

1. **Trichostema lanatum** Benth. WOOLLY BLUE CURLS. ROMERO. Fig. 558.

An erect very leafy bush, 1½ to 3½ feet high, with several brittle stems from the woody base. Flowering period, May and June.

Woolly Blue Curls occurs chiefly on dry chaparral slopes of the coastal mountains from San Benito (Chalone Creek, *Hall*) and Monterey counties southward to the ocean-facing slopes of the mountains of San Diego County and to northern Lower California. This is a very handsome shrub and is suited for cultivation in California gardens.

Trichostema lanatum Benth. Lab. Gen. et Sp. 659 (1835). Type locality: "Hab. in California septentrionale." Collected by *Douglas,* probably between Santa Barbara and Monterey.

2. **Trichostema Parishii** Vasey. MOUNTAIN BLUE CURLS. Fig. 559.

An erect perennial, 2 to 4 feet high, with herbaceous branches from woody stems. Flowering period, May and June.

Mountain Blue Curls inhabits dry slopes of the interior mountains of San Diego County and extends northward to the desert slopes of the San Jacinto, San Bernardino, San Antonio, and San Gabriel (Acton, Los Angeles County, *Elmer*) mountains. It extends southward to Lower California.

Trichostema Parishii Vasey, Bot. Gaz. 6:173 (1881). Type locality: San Diego County, California. Collected by *S. B. Parish* and *C. R. Vasey. T. lanatum* var. *denudatum* Gray.

4. **Satureia** L.

(The ancient Latin name.)

This genus contains about 130 species in the warmer regions of both hemispheres. A single species is native to California.

1. **Satureia Chandleri** (Brandg.) Druce. POTMINT. Fig. 560.

A spreading suffrutescent perennial, 1 to 3 feet high, with several branching square stems forming a rounded bush. Leaves simple, opposite; the blades thick, nearly round, ¼- to ⅜-inch long, gray-green and slightly pubescent above, paler and more pubescent beneath, entire or slightly irregularly crenulate; petioles about ¼-inch long. Flowers cream-white, bisexual, irregular, usually 2 to 4 in the axils of the upper leaves. Fruit of 4 nutlets. Flowering period, May and June.

Potmint is a rare subshrub, being known only from San Diego County on San Miguel Mountain *(Chandler)* and in a rocky canyon near Murretta in the Santa Ana Mountains *(Robinson & Crocker).*

Satureia Chandleri (Brandg.) Druce, Rep. Bot. Exch. Club Brit. Isles 1916:644 (1917). *Calamintha Chandleri* Brandg. Type locality: San Miguel Mountain, near San Diego, California. Collected by *Chandler.*

5. **Hyptis** Jacq.

(From the Greek *uptios,* turned back, referring to the lower lip of the corolla.)

This genus contains about 350 species of herbs or shrubs, chiefly Mexican and South American. A single species is native to California.

1. **Hyptis Emoryi** Torr. BEE-SAGE. EMORY BUSHMINT. DESERT-LAVENDER. Fig. 561.

An erect-spreading shrub, 3 to 10 feet high and sometimes with a spread of 12 feet, with numerous straight slender stems and whitish scurfy-tomentose fragrant foliage. Leaves simple, opposite; the blades ovate or rarely orbicular, ¼-inch to 1 inch long, 1/4- to 1/2-inch wide, gray-green above, paler beneath, crenulate to crenate-dentate; petioles 1/8- to 1/4-inch long. Flowers purple, bisexual, irregular, in short-peduncled axillary clusters at the ends of the branchlets; calyx narrowly turbinate, with 5 subequal teeth, white-woolly with branched hairs; corolla violet-purple, 1/8- to nearly 1/4-inch long, 2-lipped, the middle lobe of the lower lip saccate, the lateral lobes of the lower lip and the 2 lobes of the upper lip nearly alike; stamens 4, all fertile, included in the sac of the middle lower lobe, the upper pair shorter and their filaments densely hairy; ovary superior, early 4-celled, each cell with a single ovule. Fruit of 4 nutlets. Flowering period, March to May.

Bee-sage occurs on rocky and gravelly slopes and in ravines on the Colorado Desert and in the vicinity of Needles and elsewhere at scattered localities in the southern Mohave Desert, in the Lower Sonoran Life Zone. It extends eastward to Arizona and southward to Mexico. Goats and sheep sometimes browse upon the herbage.

Hyptis Emoryi Torr. Ives Rep. Col. River Bot. 20 (1860). Type locality: On the Lower Gila River, Arizona. Collected by *Major Emory.*

6. **Sphacele** Benth.

(From *Sphakos,* the name the Greeks applied to sage, the foliage of the plants of *Sphacele* being similar to that of the sage.)

This genus contains about 20 species of shrubs or subshrubs in South America, Hawaii, and California. A single species, with 2 varieties, occurs in California.

1. **Sphacele calycina** Benth. Pitcher-sage. Fig. 562.

KEY TO THE SPECIES AND VARIETIES

Herbage pubescent or somewhat woolly.
- Leaves rounded or cuneate or sometimes truncate at base; calyx usually broad at base when developed or some rather narrow, the segments triangular-lanceolate . . . . *S. calycina.*
- Leaves truncate or subcordate at base; calyx densely villous, narrow at base when developed, the segments linear-lanceolate . . . . 1a. var. *Wallacei.*

Herbage nearly glabrous; calyx broad at base when developed, the lobes triangular-lanceolate . . . . 1b. var. *glabella.*

An erect suffrutescent plant, 2 to 4 feet high, with prominently veined aromatic leaves and large white or pinkish flowers. Leaves simple, opposite; the blades oblong-ovate or broadly ovate, 2 to 4 1/2 inches long, 3/4-inch to 1 1/2 inches wide, rounded or cuneate or sometimes truncate at base (rarely subcordate to cordate), glabrate above, tomentose beneath, usually coarsely crenate-serrate except near the base, the upper blades sessile, the lower ones with petioles about 1/2-inch long. Flowers bisexual, irregular, solitary in the axils of the small upper leaves, thus forming a leafy raceme. Fruit of 4 black nutlets, finely pubescent. Flowering period, April to July.

Pitcher-sage occurs on dry exposed places of the hills and canyons of the Coast Ranges from Lake, Napa, and Marin counties southward to San Luis Obispo County, and in a few localities in the lower Sierra Nevada of Placer, Butte, and Eldorado counties. Considerable variation occurs in size, shape, margins, and pubescence of the leaves and in the characters of the calyces. The following varieties in their typical form are easily identified.

1a. Var. **Wallacei** Gray. Fig. 563.

This variety occurs occasionally in canyons of the San Gabriel and Santa Monica mountains, the San Antonio Mountains (Cucamonga Canyon), and on Santa Catalina, Santa Cruz, and Santa Rosa islands.

1b. Var. **glabella** Gray. Fig. 564.

This variety occurs in Ventura and Santa Barbara counties.

Sphacele calycina Benth. Lab. Gen. et Sp. 568 (1834). Type locality: "Hab. in California septentrionali." Collected by *Douglas*. *S. gracilis* Eastw. *S. Blochmanae* Eastw.

Var. Wallacei Gray, Bot. Calif. 1:598 (1876). Type locality: Santa Cruz Island, in the canyons of the south side. Collected by *Wallace*. *Lepechinia calycina* var. *Wallacei* (Gray) Epling.

Var. glabella Gray, Bot. Calif. 1:598 (1876). Type locality: Santa Barbara County, California. Collected by *Bridges* and *Peckham*. *Lepechinia calycina* var. *glabella* (Gray) Epling.

7. Salvia L. Sage

(From the Latin *salveo,* to save, to be well or healthy, referring to the medicinal properties of some species.)

Aromatic herbs or shrubs with clustered flowers, the clusters in spikes, racemes, panicles, or rarely in a single whorl. Leaves simple, opposite. Flowers bisexual, irregular; calyx tubular or turbinate, 2-lipped or rarely nearly equally 5-toothed, the upper lip entire or 3-toothed, the lower lip 2-cleft or -toothed; corolla-tube cylindrical, flaring somewhat toward the throat, usually strongly 2-lipped or the upper lip obsolete, the lower lip spreading and 3-lobed, the middle lobe often fringed; fertile stamens 2, inserted in the throat of the corolla or sometimes toward the middle of the tube or upon the base of the lower lip, the upper sterile pair wanting or represented by sterile filaments or vestiges; filaments continuous with 2 filament-like connectives, one or both of which bear anther-cells, sometimes one connective almost obsolete; ovary superior, 4-lobed, with 2 carpels, but with 4 cells, each cell with 1 ovule. Fruit of 4 nutlets, separating at maturity.

The genus *Salvia* contains about 500 species widely distributed in the temperate and warm regions of both hemispheres. About 17 species are native to California, 13 of which are shrubs or subshrubs.

The true sages belong to this genus, but many Californians apply the name "sage" to certain species of the genus *Artemisia,* which belongs to the family Asteraceae. Most of the true sages occur on the hot dry foothills and lower mountain slopes and in the desert regions. They are usually aromatic plants and are important bee-plants in California. Some of the species are browsed by animals and a few are used as ornamentals.

In southern California there is considerable hybridization among the species and this leads to much confusion in the identification of many specimens.

KEY TO THE SPECIES

Leaves spine-tipped and -toothed.
  Leaves greenish gray, with 3 to 6 spinescent teeth . . . . 1. *S. Greatae.*
  Leaves white-woolly, usually with 1 terminal spine but some with 1 to 4 lateral ones . . . . 2. *S. funerea.*
Leaves not spine-tipped or -toothed.

Flowers in long contracted panicles 1 to 4 feet long; leaves usually whitish on both surfaces..3. *S. apiana.*
Flowers in compact whorls, these usually forming interrupted spikes or the clusters solitary or spike-like.
Bracts beneath the flower-clusters thin and paper-like, often colored.
Leaves distinctly wrinkled, the margins crenulate.
Leaves of 2 kinds, those beneath the flower-clusters plane or eventually revolute and oblong-lanceolate, those on the short lateral branches revolute and fascicled; corolla about 3/4-inch long; bracts purplish or purple-green............................4. *S. eremostachya.*
Leaves of 1 kind, ovate to oblong-ovate, none revolute; corolla 1/2-inch or less long; bracts very thin, whitish, glandular, 1/2-inch to 1 inch long.......................................5. *S. mohavensis.*
Leaves not wrinkled on the upper surface, obovate or spatulate, the margins entire; bracts purplish.
Bracts 1/4- to 3/8-inch long; leaves usually less than 1 inch long. 6. *S. carnosa.*
Bracts about 1/2-inch long, leaves usually 1 inch or more long; flower-clusters very close together.....................7. *S. pachyphylla.*
Bracts beneath the flower-clusters not thin and papery but more foliaceous; leaves crenulate.
Calyx-teeth and bracts long-aristate; plants mostly whitish.....8. *S. Vaseyi.*
Calyx-teeth and bracts not long-aristate.
Bases of leaves truncate, broadly rounded, or some subcordate. 9. *S. leucophylla.*
Bases of leaves gradually tapering to the petiole.
Plants forming mats; flowering stalks almost leafless, 6 to 12 inches high....................................10. *S. sonomensis.*
Plants erect, distinctly shrubby.
Flower-clusters solitary or few and distantly placed (1 inch or more apart); corolla over 1/2-inch long; leaves pale, rarely over 1 1/4 inches long.............................11. *S. Clevelandii.*
Flower-clusters more numerous; corolla typically 1/2-inch or less long.
Leaves linear, revolute; stamens included within the corolla-tube; Santa Rosa Island.....................13. *S. Brandegei.*
Leaves oblong-elliptical or obovate, not revolute; stamens exserted beyond the corolla-tube.
Leaves usually oblong-elliptical, 1 to 3 1/2 inches long; anthers a little exceeding the upper lip...........14. *S. mellifera.*
Leaves mostly obovate or oblanceolate, usually 1/2- to 3/4-inch long; anthers not protruding beyond the upper lip. 12. *S. Munzii.*

1. **Salvia Greatae** Brandg. Dos Palmos Sage. Fig. 565.

A dense spreading shrub, 2 to 4 feet high, with tomentose branches. Leaf-blades broadly ovate, 1/2-inch to 1 inch long, 1/4- to 1/2-inch wide, 3- to 5-veined from the base, gray-green and with branched hairs on both surfaces, the margins with 3 to 6 long green spine-tipped teeth 1/2- to 3/4-inch long, sessile. Flowers pale bluish lavender, in 4 or 5 interrupted whorls of 6 to 10 flowers; calyx nearly 1/2-inch long; corolla nearly twice as long as the calyx; stamens seated nearly in the throat, both connectives with anthers. Flowering period, April and May.

Dos Palmos Sage is known only from the Orocopia Mountains of the Colorado Desert in Riverside County (Salt Creek wash, near Mecca; Canyon Spring wash; and probably in other canyons of the adjacent areas), in the Lower Sonoran Life Zone.

Salvia Greatae Brandg. Zoe 5:229 (1906). Type locality: "a wash about 4 miles northeast of Dos Palmos in the northern part of the Colorado Desert." Collected by *Hall* and *Greata.*

2. **Salvia funerea** Jones. DEATH VALLEY SAGE. FUNERAL SAGE. Fig. 566.

An intricately branched shrub, 2 to 3 feet high, with white woolly herbage. Leaf-blades ovate to lance-ovate, 1/4-inch to 1 inch long, 1/8- to 1/2-inch wide, ashy gray on both surfaces with branching hairs, with one terminal spine and sometimes with 2 to 4 lateral spiny teeth, sessile or with a petiole about 1/16-inch long. Flowers purplish, usually 3 in the leaf-axils, crowded into a foliose spike 1 to 3 inches long; calyx about 1/4-inch long, with 5 short about equal teeth hidden in tufts of woolly tomentum; corolla about 5/8-inch long, the lower lip almost as long as the tube; stamens inserted between the middle of the tube and the throat, both connectives with anthers. Flowering period, April and May.

Death Valley Sage occurs from about 1000 to 3000 feet elevation in the narrow canyons on the western slope of the Amargosa Range (Funeral, Black, and Granite mountains), in Titus Canyon of the Grapevine Mountains, and in the northern part of the Panamint Mountains, all in Inyo County.

Salvia funerea Jones, Contr. West. Bot. 12:71 (1908). Type locality: Funeral Mountains, Death Valley. Collected by *M. E. Jones. S. funerea* var. *fornacis* Jepson.

3. **Salvia apiana** Jepson. WHITE SAGE. Fig. 567.

An erect whitish shrub, 3 to 8 feet high, with few long straight almost herbaceous stems from a woody base. Leaf-blades oblong-lanceolate or oval, 1 to 4 inches long, 1/2-inch to 1 1/2 inches wide, whitened on both surfaces with minute appressed hairs, finely wrinkled above, crenulate; petioles 1/4-inch to 1 inch long. Flowers few, sessile in loose clusters, these usually arranged in branching spike-like panicles 1 to 4 feet long; calyx about 1/4-inch long, 2-lipped, whitened with minute appressed hairs; corolla white, often spotted with lavender, 1/2- to 3/4-inch long, the lower lip much enlarged and 3-lobed with the middle lobe cupped, rounded, and fringed, the upper lip very short or nearly absent; stamens long-exserted, inserted on the base of the lower lip, the connectives longer than and continuous with the filaments, the lower connective represented by a small tooth. Flowering period, May to September.

White Sage is very common and widespread on the mesas and in the canyons at the lower elevations of the mountains of southern California from Santa Barbara County southward to San Diego County and to Lower California. It extends inland as far as the western borders of the Colorado Desert and to Cajon Pass, San Bernardino County. It occurs also on Santa Catalina Island. Along the border of the Colorado Desert, the inflorescences are more compact (var. **compacta** Munz).

This sage is easily distinguished, except in some of its hybrid forms, by its white leaves and its flowers borne on long willow-like stems. Browsing animals feed upon the herbage, especially during the winter months. The flowers are an excellent source of honey materials. It may hybridize with *S. mellifera* (Black Sage), *S. leucophylla* (Purple Sage), *S. Clevelandii* (Cleveland Sage), *S. eremostachya* (Sand Sage), *S. Vaseyi* (Brittle Sage), and *S. Munzii.*

FIG. 565
S. GREATAE

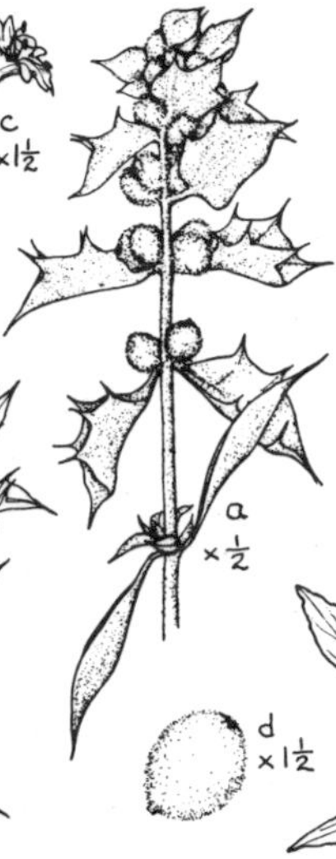

FIG. 566
S. FUNEREA

FIG. 567
S. APIANA

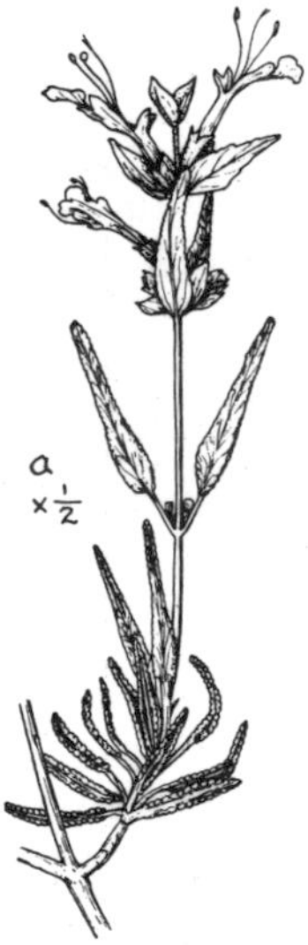

FIG. 568
S. EREMOSTACHYA

FIG. 569
S. MOHAVENSIS

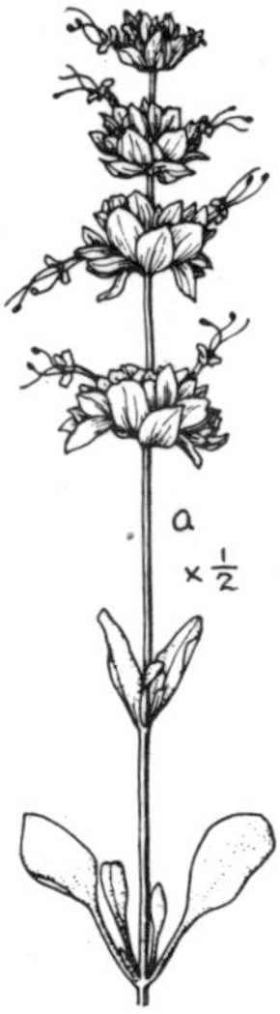

FIG. 570
S. CARNOSA

FIG. 571
S. PACHYPHYLLA

SALVIA. a, Flowering branchlet. b, Portion of branchlet with leaves. c, Flower. d, Calyx.

Salvia apiana Jepson, Muhlenbergia 3:144 (1908). *Audibertia polystachya* Benth. Type locality: California. Collected by *Douglas*. "Hab. in California septentrionali Douglas (h.s. sp. e.Mus.Soc.Hort.Lond.)"

4. **Salvia eremostachya** Jepson. SAND SAGE. Fig. 568.

An erect shrub, 2 to 3 feet high, with glandular-hairy branchlets. Leaves of 2 kinds; those of the flowering shoots oblong-lanceolate, 1 to 1⅜ inches long, obtuse at apex, truncate at base or narrowed to a broad short petiole ⅛- to ¼-inch long, the upper surface rugulose, the lower reticulate with raised veins, both surfaces hispidulous, the margins crenulate; leaves of the short axillary shoots fascicled, linear, ½-inch to 1 inch long, strongly revolute. Flowers few in whorled clusters, arranged in an interrupted spike of 2 or 3 whorls, subtended by purplish green thin round-ovate bracts; calyx ¼- to ⅜-inch long, glandular-hairy; corolla blue or rose-color or rarely nearly white, about ¾-inch long; stamens attached to the throat, one connective anther-bearing and the other represented by a short tooth at the union with the filament. Flowering period, April to November.

Sand Sage occurs only on the western edge of the Colorado Desert of Riverside and San Diego counties (Indian Canyon of Collins Valley, Rockhouse Canyon, and Martinez Canyon in the Santa Rosa Mountains; Coyote Canyon; Palms to Pines Highway from the base of the grade to the piñon pines).

Salvia eremostachya Jepson, Man. 870 (1925). Type locality: Indian Canyon, Collins Valley, western edge of the Colorado Desert. Collected by *Jepson*.

5. **Salvia mohavensis** Greene. MOHAVE SAGE. Fig. 569.

A low rounded shrub, 1 to 2 or rarely to 4 feeet high, with hispidulous branches and bright green puberulent foliage. Leaf-blades oblong-ovate to lance-ovate or ovate, ¼- to ¾-inch long, 3/16-to ⅜-inch wide, wrinkled above, distinctly veiny beneath, margins crenulate; petioles slender, ¼- to ¾-inch long. Flowers few in a subglobose terminal head, subtended by thin usually whitish glandular bracts ⅜- to ¾-inch long; calyx 2-lipped, ¼- to nearly ⅜-inch long; corolla pale blue or lavender, about ½-inch long, the lobes oblong; stamens inserted in the throat, only one connective anther-bearing, this shorter than the filament. Flowering period, April to July.

Mohave Sage occurs on rocky cliffs and canyon walls in the Little San Bernardino Mountains and it ranges eastward through the desert mountains of eastern San Bernardino and Riverside counties. It extends eastward to Arizona and Nevada and southward to Sonora, Mexico.

Salvia mohavensis Greene, Pitt. 2:235 (1892). *Audibertia capitata* Gray. Type locality: Providence Mountains, San Bernardino County, California. Collected by *Cooper*.

6. **Salvia carnosa** Dougl. ex Benth. DESERT SAGE. Fig. 570.

KEY TO THE SPECIES AND VARIETIES

Floral whorls usually 3 to 5.
  Leaf-blades mostly oval or elliptic, sometimes obovate or oblanceolate, ⅝-inch to 1¼ (or rarely 1½) inches long. . . . .*S. carnosa.*
  Leaf-blades usually orbicular, mostly less than ⅝-inch long; bracts pilose on the outer surfaces. . . . . .6a. var. *pilosa.*
Floral whorls usually 2 or 3, rarely solitary; bracts usually glabrate except for the ciliate margins.

Floral whorls about 5/8-inch in diameter; leaf-blades mostly about 1/4-inch long. 6b. var. *Gilmanii.*
Floral whorls 5/8-inch to 1 inch in diameter; leaf-blades mostly 1/2- to 5/8-inch long .... 6c. var. *argentea.*

A low compact shrub, 3/4-foot to 2 1/2 feet high and about as broad, with very leafy canescent branches. Leaf-blades broadly obovate or spatulate-oblong, 3/8- to 3/4-inch long, 1/8- to 1/4-inch wide, finely tomentulose, not at all wrinkled, entire or very slightly crenulate; petioles 1/4- to 1/2-inch long or none in the uppermost leaves. Flowers in dense clusters usually arranged in interrupted spikes, subtended by oval or rounded membranous bracts, these highly colored with rose or purple; calyx 2-lipped; corolla deep blue, its tube 3/16- to 7/16-inch long; stamens inserted in the throat, much exserted, only one connective anther-bearing, this somewhat shorter than the filament, the second connective represented by a small tooth at the junction with the filament. Flowering period, May to July.

The typical form of Desert Sage occurs on the rocky bluffs along the Klamath River, Siskiyou County *(G. D. Butler)*. Its range extends northward into Oregon, Washington, and Idaho.

6a. Var. **pilosa** (Gray) Jepson.

Branchlets and inflorescences usually villous-pubescent. Leaf-blades usually less than 5/8-inch long. Bracts more or less pilose on the outer surface.

This variety occurs with sagebrush *(Artemisia tridentata)* usually at the lower border of the juniper-piñon association from 2000 to 6800 feet elevation from Lassen County (Hot Springs Peak, acc. *Epling*) southward (Mono and Inyo counties) to Kern, Tulare (mouth of Long Canyon, 6800 feet, V. T. M.), Los Angeles, San Bernardino, and Riverside counties. It extends eastward to western Nevada.

6b. Var. **Gilmanii** (Epling) n. comb.

Leaf-blades mostly about 1/4-inch long. Bracts usually glabrate except for the ciliate margins.

This variety occurs in the Panamint and Argus mountains of Inyo County. It extends eastward into Nevada.

6c. Var. **argentea** (Rydb.) n. comb.

Leaf-blades mostly 1/2- to 5/8-inch long. Bracts usually glabrate except for the ciliate margins.

This variety occurs in Mono (Topaz, acc. *Epling*) and Inyo (Nelson Range, acc. *Epling*) counties, California. It extends eastward to Arizona, Nevada, and Utah and northward to Idaho.

Salvia carnosa Dougl. ex Benth. Bot. Reg. 17: t. 1469 (1831). Type locality: "on clayey banks of the Columbia and plains from Walla Walla to Spokane and on the south to the Sources of the Missouri." Collected by *Douglas.*

Var. pilosa (Gray) Jepson, Man. 870 (1925). *Audibertia incana* var. *pilosa* Gray. Type locality: "Northern base of San Bernardino Mts., on the border of the Mohave Desert." Collected by *Parish. Audibertia Dorrii* Kell.?

Var. Gilmanii (Epling) McMinn. *S. carnosa* subsp. *Gilmanii* Epling. Type locality: Piñon Mesa and Wild Rose Canyon, Panamint Mountains. Collected by *Epling* and *Gilman.*

Var. argentea (Rydb.) McMinn. *Audibertiella argentea* Rydb. Type locality: Mokiah Pass, Arizona. Collected by *Palmer.*

7. **Salvia pachyphylla** Epling ex Munz. MOUNTAIN DESERT SAGE. Fig. 571.

A compact rounded shrub, 1 to 2 feet high, with ascending or spreading branches and scurfy-puberulent whitened branchlets. Leaf-blades mostly obovate, 3/4-inch to 1 1/4 inches long, rounded at apex, narrowed at the base to petioles 1/8- to 1/2-inch long, whitened with minute appressed hairs on both surfaces, entire. Flowers in dense clusters usually arranged in a compact spike 2 to 4 inches long, subtended by showy usually purplish bracts 1/2- to 3/4-inch long, these more or less ciliate on the margins, usually glabrous or scarcely pilose on the surfaces; corolla dark violet-blue, rarely rose-color, its tube 5/8- to 7/8-inch long, cylindrical; stamens inserted in throat, the connective equalling the filament. Flowering period, July to September.

This species usually inhabits dry slopes and flats of the Arid Transition Life Zone in the Panamint, New York, San Bernardino, San Jacinto, and Santa Rosa mountains. It extends southward to Lower California. This salvia resembles in general appearance *Salvia carnosa* but the leaves are usually longer and more oblanceolate, the bracts larger, and the flowering period later. Epling has observed both species growing together in Wild Rose Canyon in the Panamint Mountains and on Cactus Flat in the San Bernardino Mountains but states that no hybrids are formed, "due presumably to the difference in flowering period."

Salvia pachyphylla Epling ex Munz, Man. S. Calif. Bot. 445 (1935). *Audibertia incana* var. *pachystachya* Gray. Type locality: Bear Valley in the San Bernardino Mountains. Collected by *S. B.* and *W. F. Parish*. *Salvia carnosa* var. *compacta* Hall.

8. **Salvia Vaseyi** (Porter) Parish. BRISTLE SAGE. Fig. 572.

An erect shrub, 3 to 5 feet tall, with long wand-like flowering branches. Leaf-blades round-ovate, 1 to 2 inches long, 1/2-inch to 1 inch wide, whitish pubescent, crenulate; petioles 1/4- to 3/4-inch long. Flowers many in compact clusters arranged in long-peduncled spikes 1 to 2 feet long, subtended by whitened bracts tipped by short bristles; calyx whitish with minute hairs, the lobes narrowed into a bristle; corolla white, its tube about 1/2-inch long; stamens inserted in the throat, only one connective anther-bearing. Flowering period, April to June.

Bristle Sage occurs along the western edge of the Colorado Desert in Riverside, Imperial, and San Diego counties and in Morongo Valley in the Little San Bernardino Mountains, in the Lower Sonoran Life Zone. It hybridizes with *S. apiana* and *S. eremostachya*.

Salvia Vaseyi (Porter) Parish, Muhlenbergia 3:126 (1907). *Audibertia Vaseyi* Porter. Type locality: Mountain Springs, San Diego County. Collected by *Vasey*.

9. **Salvia leucophylla** Greene. PURPLE SAGE. Fig. 573.

An upright shrub, 2 to 6 feet high, with many white-mealy stems from a woody base. Leaf-blades ovate to oblong-lanceolate, 1 to 3 inches long, 3/8- to 3/4-inch wide, finely wrinkled and grayish above, white-tomentulose beneath, crenulate; petioles 1/16- to 1/2-inch long. Flowers many in 3 to 5 compact whorled clusters, subtended by densely white-mealy floral bracts; corolla light purple, 1/2- to 5/8-inch long, the tube not much longer than the calyx; stamens inserted in the throat, only a single connective anther-bearing and this continuous with and shorter than the filament. Flowering period, May and June.

Purple Sage inhabits the dry foothills of the coastal mountains from San Luis Obispo County (Pismo Beach) southward to Santiago Canyon in Orange County, in the Upper Sonoran Life Zone. It hybridizes with *S. apiana* (Santa Monica Mountains) and with *S. mellifera*.

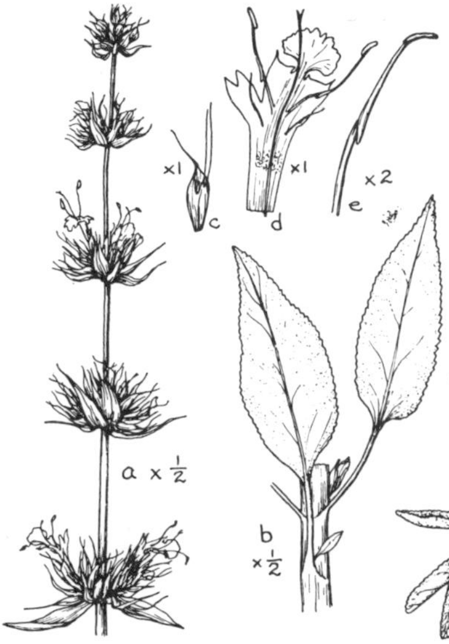

FIG. 572 S. VASEYI

FIG. 573 S. LEUCOPHYLLA

FIG. 574
S. CLEVELANDII

FIG. 575
X S. PALMERI

FIG. 576
S. MUNZII

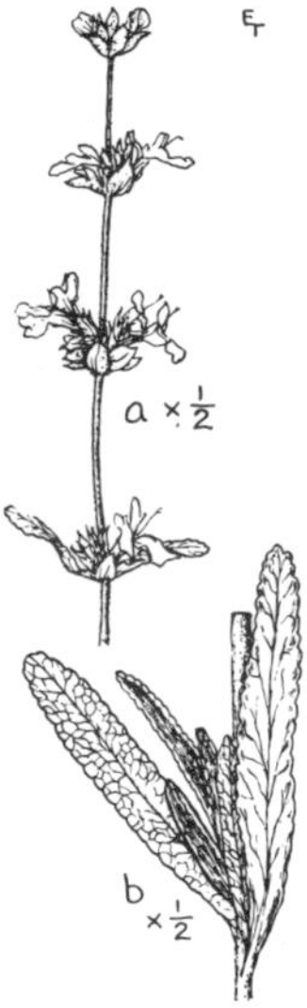

FIG. 577
S. BRANDEGEI

SALVIA. a, Flowering branchlet. b, Portion of branchlet with leaves. c, Calyx. d, Open corolla. e, Stamen with connective and anther.

Salvia leucophylla Greene, Pitt. 2:236 (1892). *Audibertia nivea* Benth. Type locality: California. Collected by *Douglas.*

10. **Salvia sonomensis** Greene. CREEPING SAGE.

A low creeping plant forming dense mats. Flowering stems herbaceous and almost leafless, ½-foot to 1 foot high, from a slightly woody base. Flowering period, May to July.

Creeping Sage occurs on dry mountain ridges and slopes in many widely scattered localities in California in the Upper Sonoran Life Zone, along the Sierra Nevada foothills from Shasta County southward to Calaveras County, in the mountains of Trinity and Siskiyou counties, in the Coast Ranges of Sonoma, Lake, Napa, San Benito, Monterey, and San Luis Obispo counties, and in the Cuyamaca Mountains of San Diego County.

Salvia sonomensis Greene, Pitt. 2:236 (1892). *Audibertia humilis* Benth. Type locality: California. Collected by *Douglas.*

11. **Salvia Clevelandii** (Gray) Greene. FRAGRANT SAGE. CLEVELAND SAGE. Fig. 574.

A low shrub, 1 to 2 feet high, with a very penetrating and persistent fragrance. Leaf-blades oblong-elliptical or oblanceolate, ¾-inch to 1¼ inches long, 3⁄16- to 5⁄16-inch wide, gray-green above, ashy below, crenulate to nearly entire. Flowers blue or rarely whitish, in solitary heads or the heads few and far apart, subtended by whitish pubescent floral bracts; calyx viscid-glandular; corolla about ¾-inch long, the tube well exserted beyond the calyx; stamens inserted toward the throat, well exserted. Flowering period, May to August.

Fragrant Sage occurs on the chaparral slopes from near sea level to 3000 feet elevation in the Upper Sonoran Life Zone of the mountains of middle and western San Diego County. It extends southward into Lower California. It apparently hybridizes with *S. apiana* to produce **S. Palmeri** (Gray) Greene (fig. 575), which has the general aspect of *S. Clevelandii* but with leaves more like those of *S. apiana.* The inflorescence is nearly intermediate between the two parents. The odor is less aromatic than that of *S. Clevelandii.*

Salvia Clevelandii (Gray) Greene, Pitt. 2:236 (1892). *Audibertia Clevelandii* Gray. Type locality: In the mountains near Potrero, east of San Diego, California. Collected by *Cleveland.*

× S. Palmeri (Gray) Greene, Pitt. 2:236 (1892). *Audibertia Palmeri* Gray. Type locality: Tighes Ranch in the southern part of San Diego County, California. Collected by *Palmer.*

12. **Salvia Munzii** Epling. SAN MIGUEL MOUNTAIN SAGE. Fig. 576.

This species is closely related to *S. mellifera* and perhaps should be considered a variety of that species. The leaves are usually obovate or oblanceolate and about ½- to ¾-inch long. The anthers do not exceed the upper lip. It is known in California only from San Miguel Mountain in southern San Diego County. It extends into Lower California. Flowering period, February and March.

Salvia Munzii Epling, Madroño 3:169 (1935). Type locality: Lower California. Collected by *Epling* and *Robison. S. mellifera* var. *Jonesii* Munz.

13. **Salvia Brandegei** Munz. ROLLEDLEAF SAGE. SANTA ROSA ISLAND SAGE. Fig. 577.

An erect shrub, 2 to 3½ feet high, with the habit and form of *S. mellifera.* Leaves linear-oblong to oblong, ¾-inch to 1½ inches long, the margins crenulate and strongly revolute, subsessile. Stamens not exserted beyond the corolla-tube. Flowering period, April to June.

Fig. 578. Black Sage. *Salvia mellifera* Greene.

This species is known only from the canyons of Santa Rosa Island.

Salvia Brandegei Munz, Bull. S. Calif. Acad. 31:69 (1932). *Audibertia stachyoides* var. *revoluta* Brandg. Type locality: Santa Rosa Island. Collected by *T. S. Brandegee.*

14. **Salvia mellifera** Greene. BLACK SAGE. Fig. 578.

An erect very aromatic shrub, 2 to 5 feet high, with puberulent more or less glandular herbaceous branches from woody stems. Leaf-blades oblong to oblong-elliptic, 1 to 3½ inches long, ¼- to ¾-inch wide, green and wrinkled above, paler and tomentulose beneath, the margins crenulate; petioles ¼- to ½-inch long. Flowers many in compact whorled clusters, these arranged in interrupted spicate inflorescences, subtended by ovate more or less glandular foliaceous bracts reflexed at maturity; calyx 2-lipped, about ¼-inch long; corolla pale blue or lilac or rarely white, ⅜- to ½-inch long, the tube exserted beyond the calyx; lower pair of stamens fertile, with a single connective continuous with the filament and with a rudiment of the second present as a small tooth at joint, exserted from the corolla-tube, the anthers exceeding the upper lip, upper pair of stamens sterile. Flowering period, April to June.

Black Sage is a common shrub in the coastal-sage *(Artemisia californica)* formation on the dry lower mountain slopes and foothills in the Upper Sonoran Life Zone from Mount Diablo, Contra Costa County southward in the Coast Ranges to San Diego County. It extends eastward as far as the San Jacinto Mountains and to Cajon Pass, San Bernardino County and southward into Lower California and is found on Santa Catalina and Santa Cruz islands. This shrub is considered by bee keepers to be one of the best sources of honey in California. Hybrids are often formed between this species and *S. apiana* and with *S. leucophylla.*

Salvia mellifera Greene, Pitt. 2:236 (1892). *Audibertia stachyoides* Benth. Type locality: California. Collected by *Douglas.*

Solanaceae. Nightshade Family

The Nightshade Family consists of about 80 genera and 2000 species of herbs, shrubs, vines, and a few small trees. They are widely distributed in the temperate and tropical regions of the world. About 20 species and varieties of shrubs or subshrubs are native to California. Potatoes, tomatoes, and tobacco belong to this family.

KEY TO THE GENERA

Shrubs with spines; fruit a berry.................................1. LYCIUM.

Shrubs, subshrubs, or one a small tree, without spines.

Large shrubs or rarely small trees; flowers yellow, long-tubular; fruit a capsule. 2. NICOTIANA.

Small shrubs or subshrubs; flowers blue or rarely white, rotate; fruit a berry. 3. SOLANUM.

1. **Lycium** L. DESERT THORN

(Named for the ancient country, Lycia, in Asia Minor.)

Erect or spreading shrubs, usually with spines. Leaves simple, alternate, entire, often with smaller ones clustered in their axils. Flowers bisexual, regular, solitary or in clusters of 2 to 4, rarely more; sepals usually 5, united at base into a bell-shaped tube which is normally broken by the growing fruit; petals usually 5 (rarely 4 or 6), united into a funnel-shaped or cylindrical corolla; stamens as many as the corolla-lobes, inserted on the corolla-tube; ovary superior, 2-celled. Fruit a fleshy or dry berry, 2- to many-seeded.

The genus *Lycium* contains over 100 species, widely distributed in temperate and tropical regions. Fourteen species are native to North America, 8 of which are native to the desert areas of California. One introduced species, *Lycium halimifolium,* has escaped and has become naturalized in a few localities in California.

The desert thorns are spiny shrubs characteristic of desert areas. A great many common names have been given to them, including boxthorn, wolfberry, squawthorn, buckthorn, bullberry, tomatilla, and rabbit thorn. Some of the species are a source of food for browsing animals when other and better forage plants are not available. Birds and desert rodents feed upon the berries.

KEY TO THE SPECIES AND VARIETIES

Calyx-lobes from 2/3 as long as to longer than the tubular portion, or at least 1/16-inch long.
 Corolla large, trumpet-shaped, 3/16-inch or more in diameter at summit; leaves glaucous-green........................1. *L. pallidum* var. *oligospermum.*
 Corolla smaller, more tubular or funnelform, less than 3/16-inch in diameter at summit; leaves not glaucous.
  Fruit constricted near the summit, the pericarp hardened; corolla nearly tubular..2. *L. Cooperi.*
  Fruit not constricted, fleshy; corolla funnelform.
   Corolla-lobes commonly 4 (5), at least 1/3 as long as the tube.
    Calyx-lobes usually shorter than the tube...............3. *L. brevipes.*
    Calyx-lobes longer than the tube............3a. *L. brevipes* var. *Hassei.*
   Corolla-lobes 5, less than 1/3 as long as the tube; calyx densely pubescent. 4. *L. Parishii.*
Calyx-lobes less than 2/3 as long as the tube, usually about 1/16-inch long.
 Leaves fleshy and spatulate.................................3. *L. brevipes.*
 Leaves not fleshy and spatulate, though they may be either fleshy or spatulate.
  Fruit 2-seeded; branches with numerous corky protuberances after leaf-fall; corolla-tube scarcely longer than the calyx; corolla-lobes 4, about equal to the tube; leaves fleshy.........................5. *L. californicum.*
  Fruit several- to many-seeded; corolla-tube decidedly longer than the calyx; corolla-lobes 5, rarely 4.
   Some or all leaves 1/8-inch or more broad.
    Herbage glabrate.
     Corolla-tube 3/8- to 5/8-inch long, the lobes 1/4 or less the length of the tube, their margins densely ciliate-lanate...........6. *L. Torreyi.*
     Corolla-tube 1/8- to 1/4-inch long, the lobes 1/3 to as long as the tube, their margins not ciliate....................9. *L. halimifolium.*
    Herbage densely pubescent.
     Calyx-tube 1/8- to 1/4-inch long, the lobes seldom over 1/3 the length of the tube; spines 3/8-inch to 1 inch long..........7. *L. Fremontii.*
     Calyx-tube 1/8-inch or less long, the lobes 1/2 the length of the tube or longer; spines 1/8- to 3/16-inch long...............4. *L. Parishii.*
   All leaves 1/8-inch or less broad.
    Leaves glabrous or nearly so; calyx sparsely pubescent or glabrous.

Leaves 1/8- to 5/8-inch long........................8. *L. Andersonii.*
Leaves 5/8-inch to 1 3/8 inches long. .8a. *L. Andersonii* forma *deserticola.*
Leaves densely pubescent; calyx pubescent.............4. *L. Parishii.*

1. **Lycium pallidum** var. **oligospermum** C. L. HITCHCOCK. RABBIT THORN. Fig. 579.

A densely branched spreading spiny shrub, 2 to 6 feet high, with somewhat flexuous glabrous or sparingly pubescent branches. Spines slender, 1/4- to 3/8-inch long. Leaf-blades ovate to broadly elliptic or oblanceolate, 3/8- to 3/4-inch (rarely 1 to 2 inches) long, 1/8- to 1/4-inch wide, glaucous-green and glabrous on both surfaces, 1-veined from the base or with 2 sublateral veins; petiole very short. Flowers solitary or in pairs; calyx 3/16- to 5/16-inch long, the 5 lobes as long as or longer than the tube; corolla white or lavender, trumpet-shaped, 1/2- to 3/4-inch long, the 5 lobes about 1/4 the length of the tube. Berry globular, about 1/4-inch in diameter, bluish, 4- to 8-seeded. Flowering period, March and April.

Rabbit Thorn occurs on the Mohave Desert from the vicinity of Barstow and Trona northward to the Panamint and Death valleys of Inyo County and eastward in adjacent Nevada, in the Lower Sonoran Life Zone. The large trumpet-shaped flowers and large glaucous leaves easily distinguish this variety from all other Californian species.

Lycium pallidum var. oligospermum C. L. Hitchcock, Ann. Mo. Bot. Gard. 19:304 (1932). Type locality: Barstow, San Bernardino County, California. Collected by *Jepson.*

2. **Lycium Cooperi** Gray. COOPER DESERT THORN. Fig. 580.

A stout densely branched spiny shrub, 2 to 6 feet tall, with rigid thick branches, densely pubescent when young. Spines short, thick, 1/8- to 3/8-inch long. Leaves 3 to 10 in a fascicle; the blades oblanceolate or oblong, 3/8-inch to 1 1/4 inches long, 1/8- to 3/8-inch wide, attenuate at base, glabrate to densely glandular-pubescent; petiole very short or almost obsolete. Flowers numerous, 1 to 3 in fascicles; calyx 1/4- to 9/16-inch long, usually glandular-hispidulous, the lobes from 1/2 as long as to equalling the tube; corolla greenish white with lavender veins, the tube 5/16- to 9/16-inch long, the lobes about 1/4 the length of the tube. Fruit ovoid, with a wedge-shaped apex, laterally constricted above the middle forming 2 compartments. Flowering period, March and April.

Cooper Desert Thorn occurs on the Mohave and Colorado deserts of California, in the Lower and Upper Sonoran Life Zones. It extends eastward to Arizona, Nevada, and southwestern Utah. The constricted fruit easily separates this species from all other Californian species.

Lycium Cooperi Gray, Proc. Am. Acad. 7:388 (June 11, 1867). Type locality: Eastern slope of Providence Mountains, San Bernardino County, California. Collected by *Cooper.*

3. **Lycium brevipes** Benth. DESERT THORN. Fig. 581.

An erect or spreading much branched shrub, 3 to 9 feet high, with slender usually flexuous spinescent branches and thick sharp spines. Leaf-blades thick and fleshy, elliptic, oblanceolate, or spatulate, 1/4- to 3/4-inch long, 1/8- to 3/8-inch wide, glabrate to densely pubescent on both surfaces; petioles 1/16-inch or less long. Flowers solitary or in groups of 2 to 4 in the axils of the fasciculate leaves; calyx glabrate or pubescent, 1/16- to 1/4-inch long, 2- to 4- or 6-lobed, the lobes quite variable, triangular and less than 1/2 as long as the tube, or linear or spatulate and as

FIG. 579 L. PALLIDUM VAR. OLIGOSPERMUM

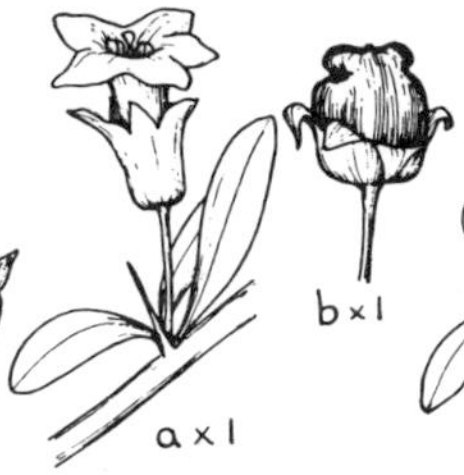

FIG. 580 L. COOPERI

FIG. 581 L. BREVIPES

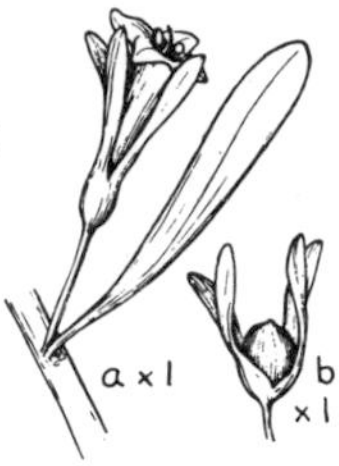

FIG. 582 L. BREVIPES VAR. HASSEI

FIG. 583 L. PARISHII

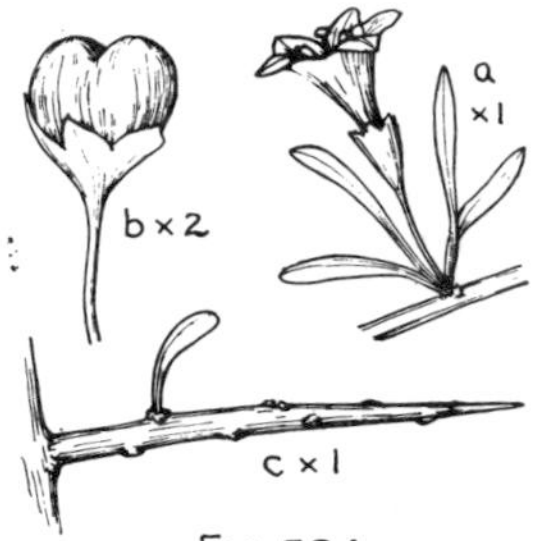

FIG. 584 L. CALIFORNICUM

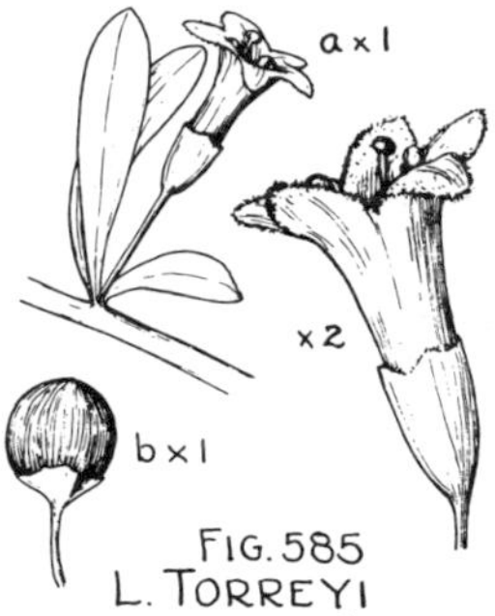

FIG. 585 L. TORREYI

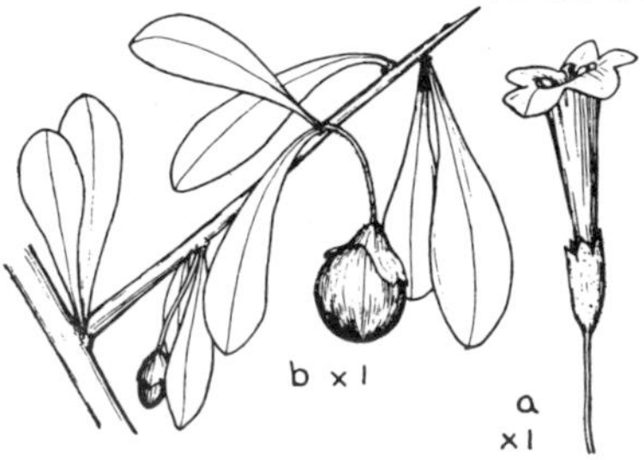

FIG. 586 L. FREMONTII

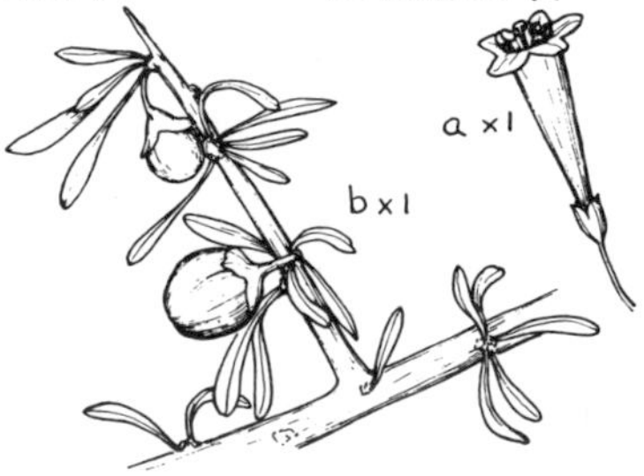

FIG. 587 L. ANDERSONII

FIG. 588 L. ANDERSONII VAR. DESERTICOLA

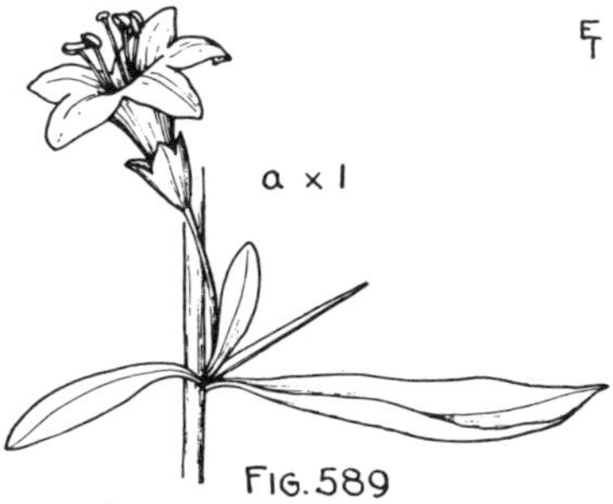

FIG. 589 L. HALIMIFOLIUM

LYCIUM. a, Flowering branchlet. b, Fruit.

long as or longer than the tube; corolla pink or violet, funnelform, sometimes with black stripes in the throat, the tube 1/8- to 3/8-inch long, the oval lobes spreading and 1/3 as long to nearly as long as the tube; stamens a little exserted. Fruit an ovoid red berry, about 3/16-inch long, 30- to 50-seeded. Flowering period, February to April.

Desert Thorn occurs on the Colorado Desert in Riverside, Imperial, and San Diego counties and on the island of San Clemente, in the Lower Sonoran Life Zone. It extends southward into Lower California and into Sonora, Mexico. Much variation occurs in the length of the calyx- and corolla-lobes and this usually causes considerable trouble in placing specimens in the proper species. However, the fleshy spatulate leaves and long oval corolla-lobes distinguish this species from the other Californian ones.

3a. Var. **Hassei** (Greene) C. L. Hitchcock. Fig. 582.

Plants almost spineless. Calyx-lobes 1 to 3 times as long as the tube.

This variety is known from the islands off the coast of southern California and from the coast of San Diego County. It has been collected also in Santa Barbara and Los Angeles where it occurs as a cultivated plant.

Lycium brevipes Benth. Bot. Voy. Sulph. 40 (1844). Type locality: Bay of Magdalena, Lower California. Collected by *Barclay*. *Lycium Richii* Gray.

Var. Hassei (Greene) C. L. Hitchcock, Leafl. West. Bot. 1:58 (1933). *L. Hassei* Greene. Type locality: Santa Catalina Island. Collected by *Hasse* and *Lyon*. *L. Richii* var. *Hassei* (Greene) Johnst.

4. **Lycium Parishii** Gray. PARISH DESERT THORN. Fig. 583.

A rigid much branched shrub, 3 to 8 feet high, armed with short sharp spines about 1/4-inch long. Leaves usually 1 to 4 in fascicles; the blades spatulate or elliptic, 1/8- to 1/2-inch long, 3/16-inch or less wide, or larger on young shoots, densely pubescent; petioles very short or none. Flowers solitary, on pedicels about 1/4-inch long; calyx 1/8- to 1/4-inch long, densely pubescent, the 5 lobes erect and 1/2 as long as to longer than the tube; corolla bright purple, the tube brownish, rather conspicuously contracted above the ovary, the 5 lobes 1/4 to 1/3 as long as the tube, their margins rather densely ciliolate. Fruit ovoid, about 1/4-inch long, red, 7- to 12-seeded. Flowering period, March to May.

Parish Desert Thorn is a rare shrub in California, being known only from Vallecito in the Colorado Desert and from a small canyon near Mountain Palm Spring, San Diego County *(Munz & Hitchcock)*, in the Upper Sonoran Life Zone. It was first collected from a mesa in the San Bernardino Valley by *S. B.* and *W. F. Parish*, but the plants from which the specimens were taken have been destroyed, according to a note (Aug. 1, 1918) by *S. B. Parrish* on the type collection sheet at the University of California Herbarium. It occurs more abundantly in southern Arizona and over the border in Sonora, Mexico.

Lycium Parishii Gray, Proc. Am. Acad. 20:305 (1885). Type locality: A mesa in the San Bernardino Valley. Collected by *S. B.* and *W. F. Parish*.

5. **Lycium californicum** Nutt. CALIFORNIA DESERT THORN. Fig. 584.

A spreading or decumbent densely branched shrub, 1 to 4 1/2 feet high, with knotty intertwined glabrous branches. Spines short, blunt, terminating the branchlets. Leaves 1 to 3 in a fascicle; the blades fleshy, ovoid, 1/4-inch or less long, glabrous or sparingly pubescent, sessile or with a very short petiole. Flowers solitary, pedicelled; calyx about 1/8-inch long, the tube 1/8- to 1/4-inch long, 2- to 4- (or rarely 5-) lobed, the lobes about 1/3 as long as the tube; corolla whitish or becoming purplish, the 4 lobes about equal to the tube, remotely ciliate. Fruit ovoid, about 3/16-inch long, the pericarp much hardened, 2-seeded, 2-carpelled, the carpels separating at maturity. Flowering period, March and April.

California Desert Thorn occurs chiefly along the coast of Los Angeles, Orange, and San Diego counties, in the Upper Sonoran Life Zone. It also has been collected from near San Bernardino and from Santa Catalina, San Clemente, and San Nicholas islands. It extends southward along the coast of Lower California and into Sonora, Mexico.

Lycium californicum Nutt. ex Gray, Bot. Calif. 1:542 (1876). Type locality: On clay hill slopes, near San Diego, California. Collected by *Nuttall.*

6. **Lycium Torreyi** Gray. TORREY DESERT THORN. SQUAWTHORN. Fig. 585.

An erect or spreading much branched shrub, 3 to 9 feet high, usually with thick stout spines 1/4- to almost 1/2-inch long, or sometimes almost unarmed. Leaf-blades oblong, elliptic, or oblanceolate, 3/8-inch to 2 inches long, 1/8- to 3/8-inch wide, tapering to a petiole-like base, glabrous; petioles very short or apparently none. Flowers 1 to 3 in a fascicle; calyx 3/16-inch or less long, sparsely pubescent to glabrate, the 5 lobes 1/4 to 1/2 the length of the tube; corolla lavender-purple or whitish, the tube 3/8- to 5/8-inch long, somewhat constricted at the top of the ovary; the 5 (or 4) spreading lobes about 1/4 the length of the tube, their margins densely woolly-ciliate and appearing as a tiny white fringe to the unaided eye. Fruit ovoid, 1/4- to 3/8-inch long, bright red, 8- to 20-seeded, very juicy and sweet. Flowering period, April to June.

Torrey Desert Thorn occurs on the Colorado and southwestern Mohave deserts of California, in the Lower and Upper Sonoran Life Zones. It extends eastward to Arizona, Utah, Nevada, New Mexico, and Texas and southward into Mexico.

Lycium Torreyi Gray, Proc. Am. Acad. 6:47 (1862). Type locality: Fort Yuma, California. Collected by *Thomas.* Gray cited no type but the collections cited were from Texas on the Rio Grande to Fort Yuma, California.

7. **Lycium Fremontii** Gray. FREMONT DESERT THORN. Fig. 586.

An erect or spreading freely branched shrub, 3 to 8 feet high, with somewhat pubescent glandular herbage and unarmed branches or the branches with few slender sharp spines 3/8- to 5/8-inch long. Leaves 4 to 5 in a fascicle; the blades usually spatulate, 3/8-inch to 1 inch long, 1/8- to 1/4-inch wide, pubescent or sometimes viscid-pubescent; petioles very short or apparently none. Flowers mostly 1 to 4 in a fascicle; calyx 3/16- to 5/16-inch long, the 5 lobes usually less than 1/3 the length of the tube; corolla violet or lavender to white with purple veins, 5/16- to 5/8-inch long, the 5 lobes about 1/4 the length of the tube. Fruit oblong-ovoid, 1/4- to 3/8-inch long, red, 40- to 60-seeded. Flowering period, January to March.

Fremont Desert Thorn occurs on the Colorado Desert of eastern San Diego and Imperial counties, in the Lower Sonoran Life Zone. It extends eastward to Arizona and southward into Lower California and Sonora, Mexico. It occurs also on Santa Rosa Island. The long calyx-tube easily distinguishes this species from all others here included.

Lycium Fremontii Gray, Proc. Am. Acad. 6:46 (1862). Type locality: "Interior of California or country east of it." Probably Boundary Monument, Colorado Desert. Collected by *Fremont.*

8. **Lycium Andersonii** Gray. ANDERSON DESERT THORN. Fig. 587.

An intricately branched rounded shrub, 1½ to 9 feet high, usually glabrous or sometimes scurfy with slender needle-like spines, or the older branches often unarmed. Leaves solitary or fascicled; the blades fleshy, spatulate, linear-terete, or ovoid, ⅛- to ⅝-inch long, about 1/16-inch broad, almost glabrous or sometimes scurfy, tapering to slender petioles about 1/16-inch or less long. Flowers solitary or in pairs, on pedicels ⅛- to ¼-inch long; calyx cup-shaped, 1/16- to ⅛-inch long, with 4 or 5 tooth-like lobes or sometimes 2-lipped, the lobes about ¼ as long as the tube; corolla white-lavender, fading to white, tubular-funnelform, the tube ¼- to ⅝-inch long, the 5 or 4 lobes about 1/16-inch long and finely ciliate or glabrous. Fruit ovoid or ellipsoid, ⅛- to almost ⅜-inch long, red, many-seeded. Flowering period, November to April.

Anderson Desert Thorn occurs from coastal southern California eastward in the Colorado and Mohave deserts and north to Mono County, in the Lower and Upper Sonoran Life Zones. It has been collected from Mono, Inyo, Kern, San Bernardino, Imperial, Riverside, San Diego, and Los Angeles counties. It extends eastward into Arizona and New Mexico, northward to Nevada and Utah, and southward to Lower California and Sonora, Mexico.

The fleshy somewhat pear-shaped leaves usually are sufficient to distinguish this species. It is sometimes confused with *L. Torreyi* but that species differs in having the margins of the corolla-lobes densely lanate-ciliate with white hairs instead of glabrous to ciliate as is characteristic of *L. Andersonii.*

8a. Forma **deserticola** C. L. Hitchcock. Fig. 588.

This is a form with leaves ¾-inch to 1½ inches long which resembles the species in other characteristics. It occurs in the vicinity of Palm Springs and elsewhere on the Colorado Desert. It has been collected also near Old Dad Mountain in the Providence Mountains on the Mohave Desert *(Hilend).*

Lycium Andersonii Gray, Proc. Am. Acad. 7:388 (1868). Type locality: Southeastern part of the State of Nevada. Collected by *Anderson.*

Forma deserticola C. L. Hitchcock, Ann. Mo. Bot. Gard. 19:280 (1932). Type locality: Palm Springs, desert base of Mount San Jacinto, Riverside County. Collected by *S. B. Parish. L. Torreyi* var. *Wrightii* (Gray) Jepson.

9. **Lycium halimifolium** Mill. European Desert Thorn. Fig. 589.

A sparingly branched spreading or climbing shrub, 3 to 15 feet high, with sharp slender spines about ⅜-inch long, or sometimes without spines. Leaves elliptic, ovate, lanceolate, or spatulate, ¾-inch to 2¼ inches long, ¼- to ¾ inch wide, tapering to a distinct petiole ⅛- to ⅜-inch long. Flowers lavender, borne in 2's or 3's or solitary, on pedicels ⅜- to ¾-inch long. Fruit ovoid, about ⅜-inch long, fleshy, salmon-red, 10- to 20-seeded.

This European species is cultivated throughout most of the United States. It has escaped and become naturalized in several localities. In California it is known from Tehama, Sierra, Alpine, and San Bernardino counties.

Lycium halimifolium Mill. Gard. Dict. ed. 8 (1768).

2. Nicotiana L. Tobacco

(Named in honor of Jean Nicot, French diplomat and author, who introduced tobacco into France from Portugal.)

This genus contains from 45 to 100 species of mostly herbs, native chiefly to tropical America and a few farther north and south. One shrubby or tree-like species, native to Argentina, has become naturalized in the warmer parts of California.

1. Nicotiana glauca Graham. TREE TOBACCO. Fig. 590.

A tall loosely branched shrub, 6 to 15 feet high, or sometimes tree-like, with long slender stems and glaucous foliage. Leaves simple, alternate, evergreen; the blades ovate, 2½ to 5 inches long, 1 to 2 inches wide, entire, glabrous and glaucous on both surfaces; petioles 1 to 2 inches long. Flowers bisexual, regular, yellow, numerous in terminal panicles; calyx unequally 5-toothed, about ½-inch long; corolla long-tubular, about 1½ inches long, dilated above the calyx, constricted just below the 5 short lobes; stamens 5, inserted on the corolla-tube; ovary superior, 2-celled. Fruit a small 2-celled oblong capsule about ½-inch long. Seeds numerous, very small. Flowering period, from April to August or almost throughout the year.

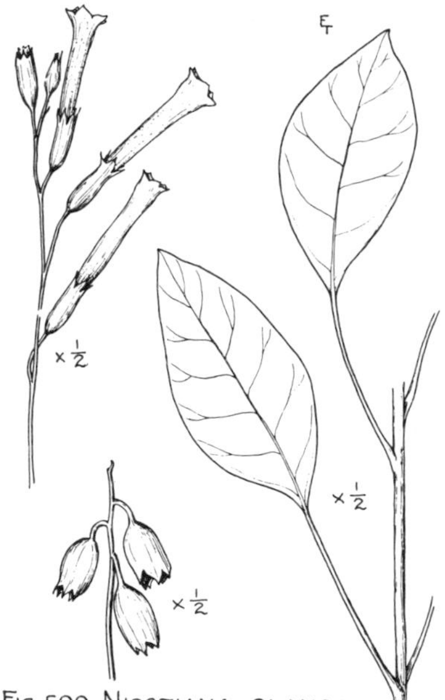

FIG. 590 NICOTIANA GLAUCA

Tree Tobacco is the only shrubby species of tobacco growing in the United States. It is native to Argentina and was introduced into California from Mexico during the period of the Spanish missions. It has become abundantly naturalized in waste places, stream-beds, and cultivated grounds in southern California. It extends northward through the interior coastal valleys and the Great Valley to Alameda, Contra Costa, and Butte counties. It spreads by means of the numerous small seeds and from offshoots of old plants.

Nicotiana glauca Graham, Edinb. Phil. Jour. 175 (1828). "It was raised in 1827 from seeds communicated, without specific name, to the Royal Botanic Garden, Edinburgh, by Mr. Smith at Monkwood, whose son sent them from Buenos Ayres."

3. Solanum L. NIGHTSHADE

(From the Latin *solamen,* quieting, referring to the supposed effect on the nerves.)

Erect or rarely climbing herbaceous or woody plants. Leaves simple, alternate. Flowers bisexual, regular, usually in umbels; calyx 5-cleft; corolla wheel-shaped (rotate), 5-angled or -lobed, with a very short tube; stamens 5, inserted on the corolla-tube, the filaments very short, the anthers somewhat connate into a cylinder around the style; ovary superior, 2-celled. Fruit a many-seeded berry.

This genus consists of about 1200 species of wide distribution in temperate and tropical regions. Eleven species have been described from California, 7 of which (with 5 varieties) are woody at least at the base.

KEY TO THE SPECIES AND VARIETIES

Corolla ¼- to ½-inch broad, deeply 5-cleft, whitish; peduncles longer than the pedicels..1. *S. Douglasii.*

Corolla ½-inch to 2 inches broad, 5-angled or -lobed, usually blue, violet, or purple (rarely whitish); peduncle shorter than the pedicels or nearly none.
Herbage nearly glabrous.
Leaves mostly with few linear lobes at base, linear to narrowly oblong. 2. *S. tenuilobatum.*
Leaves rarely lobed, ovate to elliptical.
Leaves obtuse or subcordate at base..........6a. *S. Xantii* var. *Hoffmannii.*
Leaves acute or tapering at base..........................3. *S. Parishii.*
Herbage distinctly pubescent to hirsute.
Stems only slightly pubescent with short simple non-glandular hairs interspersed with few branched hairs....4a. *S. umbelliferum* var. *glabrescens.*
Stems distinctly pubescent or hirsute.
Herbage not glandular-viscid; hairs branched.
Herbage white-tomentose; leaves lance-ovate or narrowly ovate to ovate. 5. *S. californicum.*
Herbage grayish green to green, only moderately pubescent, not tomentose ....4. *S. umbelliferum.*
Herbage more or less glandular-viscid; hairs unbranched.
Pedicels and calyx glabrous or nearly so; stems and branches with nearly uniform short gland-tipped hairs....6b. *S. Xantii* var. *intermedium.*
Pedicels and calyx definitely hirsute.
Herbage densely tawny-villous; leaves 1½ to 4 (or 6) inches long, thickish, crenate; fruit dark purple; corolla ¾-inch to 1¾ inches wide...................................7. *S. Wallacei.*
Herbage grayish or grayish green.
Leaves 1½ to 4 inches long, subcordate or truncate at base; fruit yellow (or white?). ....7a. *S. Wallacei* var. *Clokeyi.*
Leaves usually smaller; fruit greenish.................6. *S. Xantii.*

1. **Solanum Douglasii** Dunal. Douglas Nightshade. Fig. 591.

A spreading perennial bush-like plant, 1 to 6 feet high, with herbaceous angular stems and branches, often somewhat woody at base. Flowering period, almost throughout the year.

Douglas Nightshade occurs sparingly from San Francisco County southward along the coast to San Diego County, eastward to Arizona, south to Mexico, and on the islands off the coast of southern California. The berries are poisonous to browsing animals and slightly so to man.

Solanum Douglasii Dunal; DC. Prodr. 13, pt. 1:48 (1852). Type locality: "in Nova California." Collected by *Douglas.*

2. **Solanum tenuilobatum** Parish. San Diego Nightshade. Fig. 592.

A suffrutescent perennial, 1½ to 3 feet high, with slender slightly ridged or angled stems, glabrous or hirsutulous above, glabrescent below. Flowering period, February to May.

This is a rare and little-known nightshade. It occurs only in San Diego County (Carrizo Creek, *Brandegee;* near Campo, *Munz;* Mt. Tecate, *Wolf*) and in Lower California.

Solanum tenuilobatum Parish, Proc. Calif. Acad. ser. 3, 2:165 (1901). Type locality: "Lower California (probably near Ensenada)." Collected by *C. C. Parry.*

3. **Solanum Parishii** Heller. Parish Nightshade. Fig. 593.

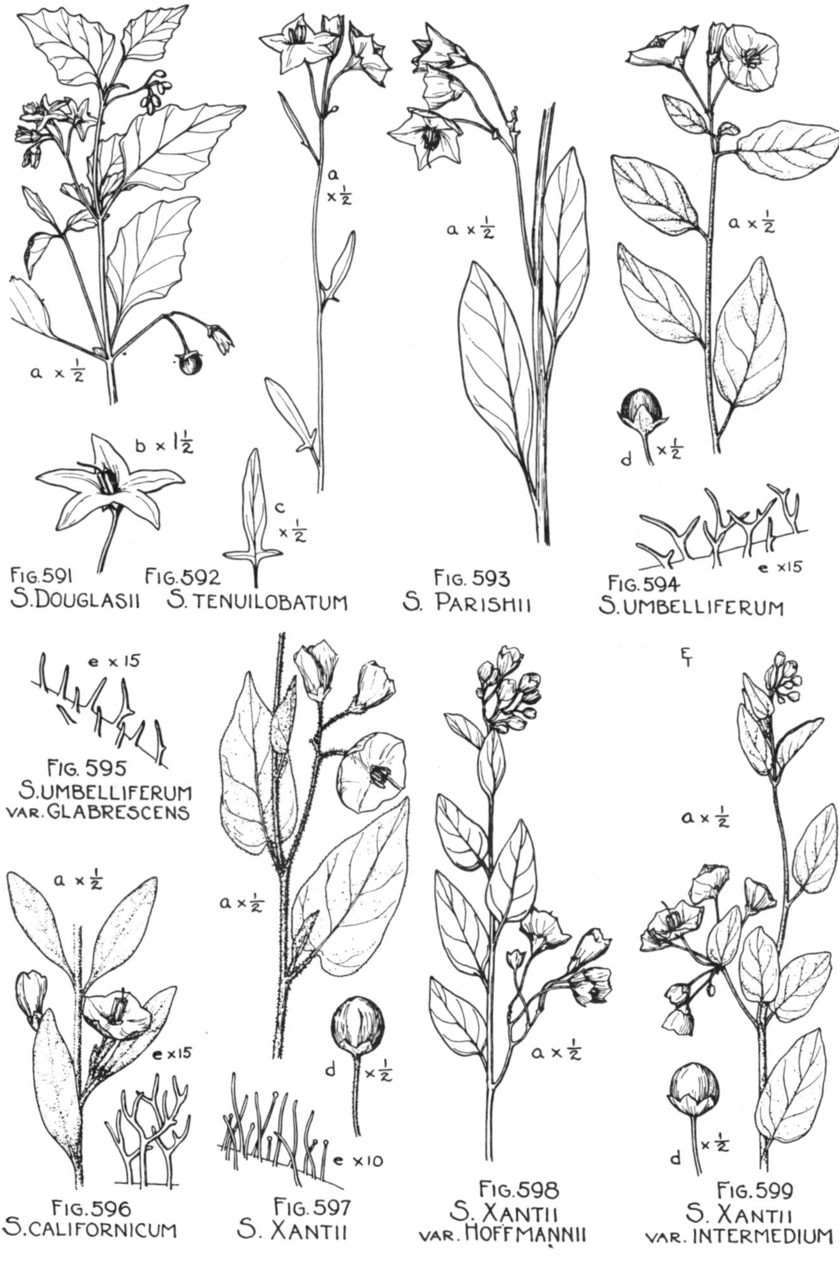

SOLANUM. a, Flowering branchlet. b, Flower. c, Leaf. d, Fruit. e, Hairs on leaf-blades.

An erect or ascending suffrutescent perennial with slender glabrous longitudinally ridged stems and branches. Flowering period, April to July.

Parish Nightshade apparently has two areas of distribution in California, one throughout northern California (north of Monterey Bay) and the other in the foothill area of Riverside and San Diego counties of southern California. It has usually passed under the name of *Solanum Xantii* var. *glabrescens* Parish, but Miss Osgood (see Bibl.) has shown that the specimens which Parish included in this variety can be separated into two well-marked groups—*S. umbelliferum* var. *glabrescens* Torr. and *S. Parishii* Heller. The latter species is glabrous and the former is minutely pubescent with short non-glandular hairs, mostly simple but also with longer branched hairs mixed with the unbranched ones.

Solanum Parishii Heller, Muhlenbergia 2:133 (1906). *S. Xantii* var. *glabrescens* Parish, in part. Type locality: Near Redding, Shasta County, California. Collected by *Heller*.

4. **Solanum umbelliferum** Esch. Blue Witch. Fig. 594.

An erect or spreading subshrub, 2 to 3½ feet high, with gray-green mostly 5-angled or -ridged herbaceous stems, woody at base. Herbage gray-green with non-glandular branched hairs. Flowering period, almost throughout the year but more abundantly from April to July.

Blue Witch is one of the most common species of nightshade in California. It occurs on brush covered slopes and in wooded canyons in the foothills of the Coast Ranges from Sonoma and Marin counties southward to northern Santa Barbara County, in the Upper Sonoran and Transition Life Zones. Its berries are said to yield an oil useful for the treatment of skin eruptions.

4a. Var. **glabrescens** Torr. Fig. 595.

Branches sparingly pubescent; the hairs short, unbranched, non-glandular, interspersed with few longer branched hairs.

This variety occurs in the foothills and on the lower mountain slopes of southern California from Santa Barbara County south to San Diego County. It extends eastward to Arizona where, according to Miss Osgood, the herbage is more pubescent and has more branched hairs.

Solanum umbelliferum Esch. Mem. Acad. Sci. St. Petersb. 10:283 (1826). Type locality: California.

Var. glabrescens Torr. Pacif. R. Rep. 7:17 (1857). *S. Xantii* var. *glabrescens* Parish, in part. Type locality: "Santa Ynez; also between San Bernardino and San Gabriel."

5. **Solanum californicum** Dunal. Hoary Nightshade. Fig. 596.

An erect or sprawling subshrub, 1 to 3 feet high, with densely white-tomentose herbage or the leaves less tomentose. Flowering period, April to July, or to November.

Hoary Nightshade inhabits the dry interior valleys and lower mountain slopes of the South Coast Range from Contra Costa County (Antioch, *Heller;* Oakley, *Keck*) southward to the Cuyama Valley and Frazier Mountain regions of Ventura County and to the Santa Monica Hills *(Summers)* of Los Angeles County. It has usually been classified with *S. umbelliferum* Esch. but the densely white-tomentose herbage and smaller more oblong to lance-ovate leaves separate it from that species.

Solanum californicum Dunal; DC. Prodr. 13:86 (1852). Type locality: "In Nova

Fig. 600. Catalina Nightshade. *Solanum Wallacei* (Gray) Parish.
(Photograph by Lustin E. Martindale)

California." Collected by *Douglas*. *S. umbelliferum* Esch. as given by Munz, Man. S. Calif. Bot.

6. **Solanum Xantii** Gray. Chaparral Nightshade. Purple Nightshade. Fig. 597.

An erect or spreading or almost prostrate plant with many herbaceous stems from a woody base. Herbage usually gray-pubescent, rarely green, with simple short usually spreading somewhat viscid hairs. Flowering period, May to July.

Chaparral Nightshade inhabits dry hillsides in the foothills and on mountain slopes from 100 to 7500 feet elevation nearly throughout California. It occurs more abundantly, however, in the mountains of Los Angeles, Ventura, Santa Barbara, Kern, and western San Bernardino counties. It intergrades with the following varieties.

6a. Var. **Hoffmannii** Munz. Fig. 598.

Plants glabrous throughout. Leaf-blades 1¼ to 2¾ inches long, thinnish, obtuse to subcordate at base.

This variety is known only from the Gaviota Pass region in Santa Barbara county.

6b. Var. **intermedium** Parish. Fig. 599.

Subshrubby plants with moderately pubescent herbage, the hairs uniformly short and gland-tipped. Pedicels and calyx glabrous or nearly so.

This variety has a wide distribution in the foothills and canyons of the mountains of California. It ranges from the San Bernardino Mountains northward in the Sierra Nevada to Placer County and in the Coast Ranges to Mendocino County. There apparently are numerous gaps in its distribution in the southern Sierra Nevada and in the South Coast Ranges but further collecting may eliminate these.

Solanum Xantii Gray, Proc. Am. Acad. 11:90 (1876). Type locality: Fort Tejon, California. Collected by *Xanthus de Vesey*.

Var. Hoffmannii Munz, Bull. S. Calif. Acad. 31:70 (1932). Type locality: Gaviota Pass, Santa Barbara County. Collected by *Munz*.

Var. intermedium Parish, Proc. Calif. Acad. ser. 3, 2:168 (1901). Type locality: San Bernardino County, California. Collected by *S. B. Parish*.

7. **Solanum Wallacei** (Gray) Parish. Catalina Nightshade. Fig. 600.

A spreading or ascending suffrutescent plant, 2 to 6 feet high, often forming rounded clumps. Herbage densely tawny-villous with long simple viscid-glandular hairs. Flowering period, February to July, or nearly throughout the year.

Catalina Nightshade occurs on Santa Catalina Island. Its berries are said to be poisonous to man and animals.

7a. Var. **Clokeyi** (Munz) n. comb.

Similar to the species but the foliage is less viscid and hairy. Corolla smaller in some Santa Rosa Island material. Berries described as yellow but said by Clokey to be white.

This variety is known from Santa Cruz and Santa Rosa (*McMinn* 2742) islands. Its characters closely relate it to *S. Wallacei* and to *S. Xantii*.

Solanum Wallacei (Gray) Parish, Proc. Calif. Acad. ser. 3, 2:166 (1901). *S. Xantii* var. *Wallacei* Gray. Type locality: Santa Catalina Island. Collected by *Wallace*.

Var. Clokeyi (Munz) McMinn. *S. Clokeyi* Munz. *S. arborescens* Clokey, not Moench. Type locality: Pelican Bay, Santa Cruz Island. Collected by *Clokey*.

Scrophulariaceae. Figwort Family

The Figwort Family consists of about 200 genera and 2600 species, mostly herbs and subshrubs, rarely shrubs and trees, of wide distribution but chiefly in the temperate regions of both hemispheres. Four genera native to California and adjacent islands have shrubby or subshrubby species.

KEY TO THE GENERA

Leaves alternate, sessile, commonly cut into narrow divisions.......1. CASTILLEIA.
Leaves opposite or 3 at a node (the upper sometimes alternate).
  Corolla with a sac at base................................2. ANTIRRHINUM.
  Corolla without a sac at base.
    Leaves commonly viscid-glandular or glutinous; flowers red or yellow, solitary (rarely 2) in the axils of the leaves; stamens 4, all with anthers. 3. DIPLACUS.
    Leaves not glutinous; flowers usually in clusters (racemes, panicles, or spikes); stamens 5, 4 with anthers and the fifth sterile............4. PENSTEMON.

1. **Castilleia** Mutis. PAINTBRUSH

(Named for D. Castillejo, a Spanish botanist.)

Usually herbs, sometimes partially parasitic on the roots of other plants, or sometimes suffrutescent plants. Leaves alternate, sessile, entire or often cut into narrow divisions. Flowers bisexual, irregular, in dense leafy-bracted terminal spikes, the bracts often highly colored and more conspicuous than the flowers; calyx tubular, laterally compressed, cleft at the apex on one side and also usually on the other side, the lobes or divisions scarlet, red, or yellow; corolla very irregular, the tube usually not longer than the calyx, the limb 2-lipped, the upper lip (galea) arched or straight, long and narrow, laterally compressed, enclosing the style and 4 unequal stamens, the lower lip short, 3-lobed; stamens usually 4, inserted on the corolla-tube in 2 pairs; ovary superior, 2-celled. Fruit a many-seeded capsule.

The genus *Castilleia* is represented in California and on the adjacent islands by 17 species, of which 2 are annuals and 15 are perennials. Only one is distinctly shrubby, but 4 others are sometimes slightly woody at the base and are therefore included in the following key.

KEY TO THE SPECIES

Plants usually densely white-woolly; calyx-lobes scarcely toothed at apex.
  Herbage densely covered with long simple woolly hairs; island species. 1. *C. hololeuca*.
  Herbage densely covered with compound star-shaped hairs; mainland species and Santa Catalina Island..............................2. *C. foliolosa*.
Plants not densely white-woolly.
  Galea scarcely exserted from the calyx, often included.
    Herbage hairy, not glandular; leaves linear or linear-lanceolate, often with linear lobes..........................3. *C. parviflora* var. *Douglasii*.
    Herbage viscid-pubescent; leaves oval or obovate............4. *C. latifolia*.
  Galea much exserted; herbage glandular-hairy; leaves usually entire, some trisected..5. *C. pinetorum*.

1. **Castilleia hololeuca** Greene. SHRUBBY PAINTBRUSH. Fig. 602.

A spreading shrub, 2 to 4 feet high, with herbage covered with a dense mat of white simple woolly hairs. Leaves linear, ½-inch to 1¼ inches long, the upper ones sometimes divided into 2 to 4 linear divisions. Tips of the floral bracts and calyx reddish. Galea distinctly exserted beyond the calyx. Flowering period, February to July.

Shrubby Paintbrush occurs on Anacapa, Santa Cruz, and Santa Rosa islands.

Castilleia hololeuca Greene, West Am. Sci. 3:3 (1886). Type locality: Santa Cruz Island. Collected by *Greene*.

2. **Castilleia foliolosa** H. & A. WOOLLY PAINTBRUSH. Fig. 601.

A bushy suffrutescent perennial, 1 to 1½ feet high, with herbage covered with a dense mat of compound star-shaped hairs. Flowering period, February to July.

Woolly Paintbrush occurs in dry rocky places in the hills and lower mountain slopes from San Diego County northward in the Coast Ranges to Napa and Mendocino counties and in the Sierra Nevada foothills of Eldorado, Amador, and Mariposa counties. It occurs also on Santa Catalina and San Clemente islands, at Hesperia on the Mohave Desert, and in Grapevine Canyon on the Colorado Desert.

Castilleia foliolosa H. & A. Bot. Beechey 154 (1833). Type locality: San Francisco or Monterey, California. Collected by *Collie*.

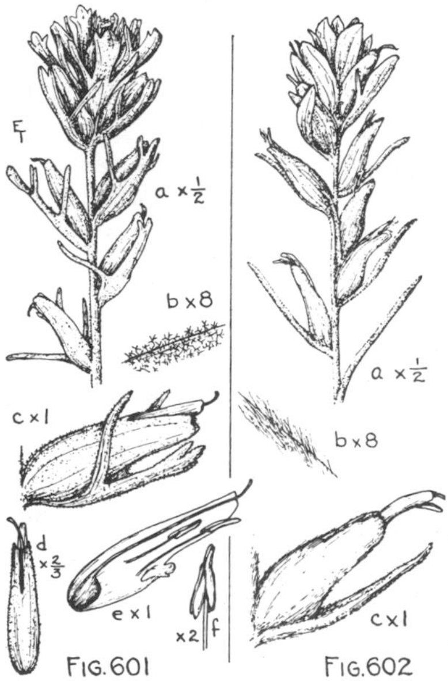

CASTILLEIA. a, Flowering branchlet. b, Hairs on leaf-margins. c, Flower with bract. d, Calyx. e, Section of flower. f, Anther.

3. **Castilleia parviflora** var. **Douglasii** (Benth.) Jepson. INDIAN PAINTBRUSH.

An herbaceous perennial, 1 to 2 feet high, sometimes woody at base, with villous-pubescent or hirsute herbage. Flowering period, April to July.

Indian Paintbrush is a common perennial inhabiting canyon slopes and hillsides among shrubs from San Diego County northward in the Coast Ranges to Humboldt County, thence eastward in Siskiyou County to Modoc County, and southward in the Sierra Nevada below 6000 feet elevation to Mariposa County. It also occurs on Santa Cruz Island.

Castilleia parviflora var. Douglasii (Benth.) Jepson. Fl. W. Mid. Calif. 412 (1901). *C. Douglasii* Benth. Type locality: "In Nova California." Collected by *Douglas*. *C. parviflora* var. *californica* (Abrams) Zeile, in Jepson's Manual.

4. **Castilleia latifolia** H. & A. SEASIDE PAINTED CUP.

A slender-stemmed perennial, ½-foot to 1½ feet high, often diffusely branched from a slightly woody base, with viscid-pubescent herbage. Flowering period, April to July.

Seaside Painted Cup occurs along the coast from Monterey to Mendocino County.

Castilleia latifolia H. & A. Bot. Beechey 154 (1833). Type locality: San Francisco, California. Collected by *Collie*.

5. **Castilleia pinetorum** Fer. PINE PAINTBRUSH.

An erect slender herbaceous perennial, ½-foot to 1 foot high, with glandular-pubescent herbage, sometimes from a woody base. Flowering period, April to July.

Pine Paintbrush occurs on dry slopes, usually among trees or bushes, in the mountains of southern California and in the Sierra Nevada from Tulare County to Butte and Plumas counties from 6000 to 9000 feet elevation. It also occurs in southern Oregon.

Castilleia pinetorum Fer. Erythea 6:50 (1898). Type locality: In pine woods, Swan Lake Valley, Klamath County, Oregon. Collected by *Applegate*.

2. **Antirrhinum** L. SNAPDRAGON

(From the Greek *anti,* like, and *rhinon,* nose, in reference to the snout-like flowers.)

Annual or perennial herbs, sometimes shrubby. Leaves simple, opposite, the upper ones usually alternate. Flowers bisexual, irregular; calyx 5-parted; corolla 2-lipped, swollen or distended on one side at base, the lower side of the throat of the corolla swollen and nearly closing the throat; fertile stamens 4; the fifth stamen represented by a gland; ovary superior, 2-celled. Fruit a capsule.

This genus contains about 40 species, mostly annual or perennial herbs, chiefly in North America. Fourteen species are native to California, of which one is distinctly shrubby and another is sometimes woody at the base.

KEY TO THE SPECIES

Leaves lanceolate; sessile; herbage glandular-pubescent; woody only at base. 1. *A. glandulosum.*

Leaves oblong or oval, short-petioled; herbage not glandular-pubescent; distinctly shrubby and bush-like . . . . 2. *A. speciosum.*

1. **Antirrhinum glandulosum** Lindl. STICKY SNAPDRAGON. WILD SNAPDRAGON. Fig. 603.

An erect herbaceous perennial, 3 to 5 feet high, sometimes slightly woody at the base, with glandular-pubescent herbage. Flowering period, May to August.

Sticky Snapdragon occurs on mountain slopes from about 1000 to 5000 feet elevation in the Santa Cruz, Santa Lucia, San Gabriel, and San Bernardino mountains and in the Sierra Nevada foothills of Calaveras County.

Antirrhinum glandulosum Lindl. Bot. Reg. n. ser. 9, t. 1893 (1836). Type locality: California. Seeds were sent to the London Horticultural Society by *Douglas*.

2. **Antirrhinum speciosum** Gray. CATALINA SNAPDRAGON. BUSH SNAPDRAGON. Fig. 604.

A spreading widely branched evergreen shrub, 2 to 6½ feet high, with glabrous or pubescent green branches. Leaves opposite or 3 at a node; the blades thick and leathery, oblong-ovate or oval, 1 to 1¼ inches long, ⅜- to ½-inch wide, dark green and pubescent or almost glabrous on both surfaces, entire; petioles very short. Flowers axillary and terminal; calyx 5-parted, the lobes nearly equal; corolla scarlet, about 1 inch long, the tube cylindrical, saccate at the base, the lips about equal; the projection in the throat of the corolla (palate) prominent but not closing the throat; 4 stamens attached near the base of the corolla-tube, in 2 pairs, hairy at the base, the fifth stamen represented by a lobed gland. Fruit a subglobose 2-celled capsule, opening below the apex by 2 or 3 irregular apertures. Flowering period, March to June or to November when in cultivation.

Catalina Snapdragon occurs on wooded hillsides and cliffs on Santa Catalina and San Clemente islands. Plants with either pubescent or glabrous herbage occur on both islands. The dark evergreen coriaceous leaves and large red flowers make

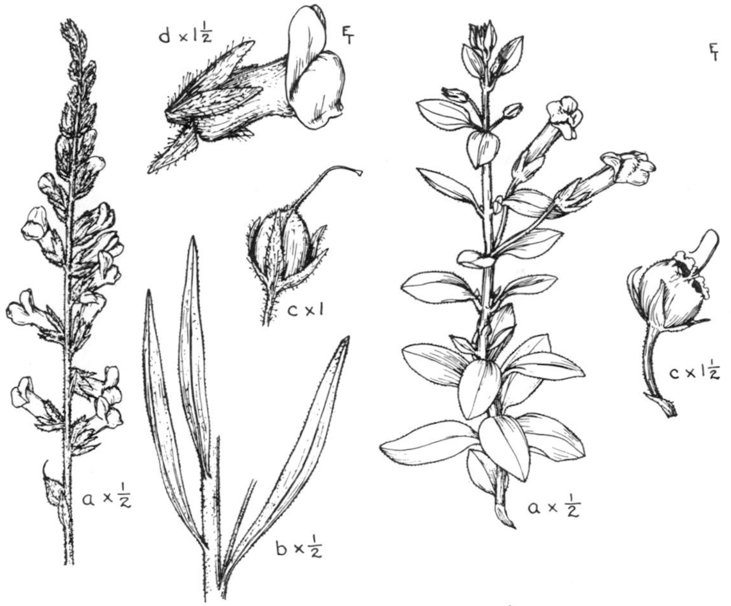

FIG. 603 A. GLANDULOSUM FIG. 604 A. SPECIOSUM

ANTIRRHINUM. a, Flowering branchlet. b, Leaves. c, Fruit. d, Flower.

this shrub very desirable for ornamental use. It can be easily propagated by sections taken at the base of the stem. Offshoots are rather common but do not spread out of control. It needs a moderate amount of water and rather well drained soil for its best development. This shrub deserves a much wider use in our gardens.

Antirrhinum speciosum (Nutt.) Gray, Proc. Am. Acad. 7:376 (1868). *Gambelia speciosa* Nutt. Type locality: Santa Catalina Island. Collected by *Gambell. Galvesia speciosa* (Nutt.) Gray.

3. **Diplacus** Nutt. MONKEYFLOWER

(From the Greek *di,* double, and *plakous,* a cake, in reference to the double swollen placenta.)

Evergreen shrubs with glabrous, viscid, or glandular-pubescent herbage. Leaves simple, opposite, entire or toothed or rarely lobed. Flowers bisexual, irregular, solitary and axillary, often disposed in open leafy racemes; calyx prismatic or tubular, with 5 unequal teeth (or rarely equal), 5-angled; corolla strongly 2-lipped, the tube funnelform, with a wide open throat and more or less spreading irregular lobes; stamens 4, without a vestige of the fifth; filaments mostly glabrous; ovary superior, 2-celled; stigmas mostly of 2 flat lobes. Fruit an oblong or linear 2-valved capsule.

The genus *Diplacus* contains about 8 species, occurring from southern Oregon southward to Lower California and on the islands off the coast of California and Lower California.

In southern California there is apparently much hybridization among the two common species, *D. longiflorus* and *D. puniceus*. The intermediate forms encountered are difficult of assignation to either species. Dr. Loye Miller has been able to produce forms by artificial hybridization which simulate those found growing wild. This fact gives evidence of the hybrid origin of many of the intermediate forms found in southern California. Most of the species are worthy of cultivation since their large irregular flowers are usually highly colored.

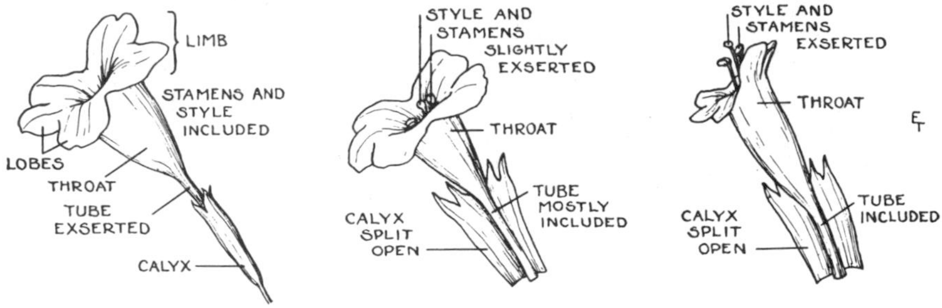

Fig. 605. Structure of flowers of DIPLACUS.

KEY TO THE SPECIES

Plants glandular-villous, not glutinous, mostly herbaceous from a woody base; corolla golden-yellow, the lobes nearly equal, the tube usually not projecting beyond the calyx.......................................1. *D. Clevelandii*.

Plants glutinous, distinctly shrubby; corolla-limb bilabiate, the lobes unequal.

Flowers yellow or salmon-yellow.

Calyces, pedicels, and upper part of stem white-woolly or villous-pubescent. 2. *D. longiflorus*.

Calyces, pedicels, and upper flowering branches not white-woolly or villous.

Corolla 1⅝ to 2½ inches long.

Calyx about 1¼ inches long; corolla-lobes rounded and slightly notched at apex; stamens exserted..........................3. *D. aridus*.

Calyx ¾-inch to 1 inch long; corolla-lobes deeply notched at apex; stamens included...............................4. *D. leptanthus*.

Corolla usually 1 to 1¾ inches long, the lobes rounded or slightly notched or gnawed at apex...............................5. *D. aurantiacus*.

Flowers red or at least shaded with red.

Leaves glabrous on both surfaces, less than 4 times longer than broad; corolla 1 to 1⅝ inches long...............................6. *D. parviflorus*.

Leaves more or less pubescent below, at least 4 times (usually 5 to 8 times) longer than broad.

FIG. 606
D. CLEVELANDII

FIG. 607
D. LONGIFLORUS

FIG. 608
D. LONGIFLORUS
VAR. CALYCINUS

FIG. 609
D. ARIDUS

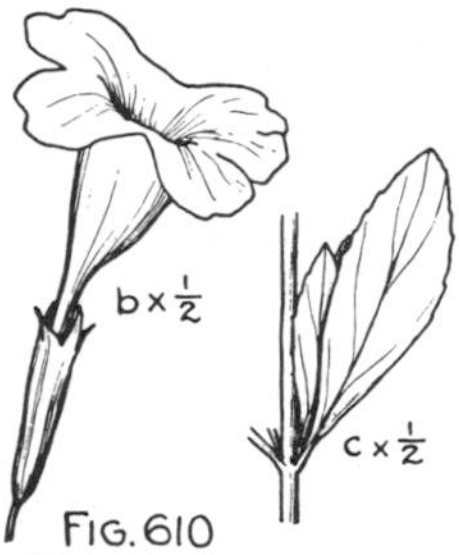

FIG. 610
D. LEPTANTHUS

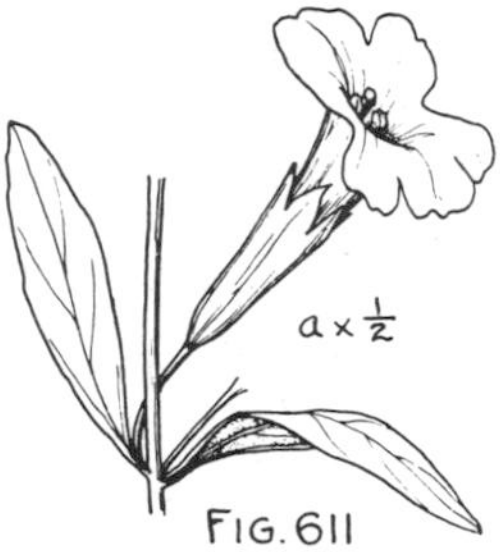

FIG. 611
D. AURANTIACUS

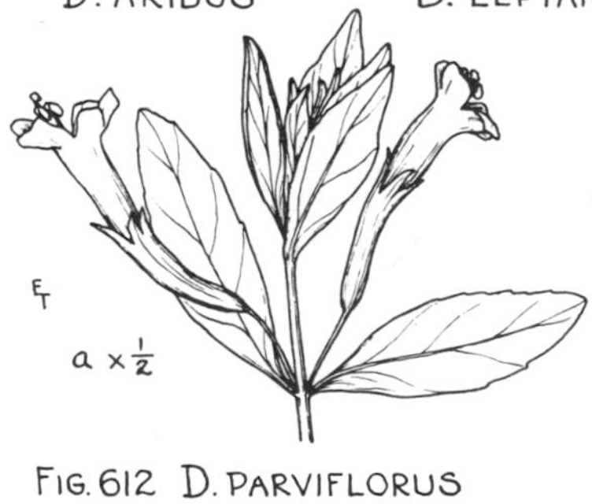

FIG. 612 D. PARVIFLORUS

FIG. 613 D. PUNICEUS

DIPLACUS. a, Portion of flowering branchlet. b, Flower. c, Leaves.

Corolla 1⅜ to 1⅝ inches long; style exserted; stamens (upper pair) usually slightly exserted . . . . 7. *D. puniceus.*

Corolla 1¾ to 2¼ inches long; style included; stamens included in lower part of throat of the corolla . . . . 2b. *D. longiflorus* var. *rutilus.*

1. **Diplacus Clevelandii** (Brandg.) Greene. CLEVELAND MONKEYFLOWER. Fig. 606. An erect freely branching subshrub, 1 to 2 feet high, with herbaceous villous-pubescent often glandular-hairy stems from a woody base. Leaf-blades oblong or lanceolate, 1 to 4 inches long, ⅜-inch to 1 inch wide, glandular-villous but not glutinous on both surfaces, entire or usually serrate along the upper half, the margins sometimes revolute, sessile. Flowers few, on the upper part of the stem

and branches; calyx campanulate, about 1 inch long, constricted just above the ovary, glandular-pubescent externally; corolla golden-yellow, about 1½ inches long, the tube pubescent, included, expanding gradually into a broad funnelform throat, the lobes rounded, nearly equal, entire; stamens included, attached to the lower part of the corolla-tube; style included. Capsule ⅜- to ½-inch long. Flowering period, May to July.

Cleveland Monkeyflower occurs on dry disturbed soil of ridges and peaks in the chaparral from about 4000 to 6000 feet elevation, in the Santa Ana, Cuyamaca, and Laguna mountains of San Diego and Riverside counties.

Diplacus Clevelandii (Brandg.) Greene, Erythea 4:22 (1896). *Mimulus Clevelandii* Brandg. Type locality: South side of Cuyamaca Peak, San Diego County. Collected by *T. S. Brandegee.*

2. **Diplacus longiflorus** Nutt. Southern Monkeyflower. Fig. 607.

A profusely branched shrub, 1 to 3 feet high, with densely pubescent glandular-hairy stems and branches. Leaf-blades lanceolate to linear-lanceolate or oblong, 1 to 3¼ inches long, ¼- to ⅝-inch wide, yellowish green, almost glabrous above, pubescent beneath, entire or more or less toothed, sessile or the lower leaf-blades sometimes petioled, with smaller leaves frequently fascicled in the axils. Pedicels, calyces, and upper part of stems and branches densely glandular-hairy or whitened by a woolly pubescence. Calyx 1 to 1¼ inches long, constricted near the middle and then expanding to a wide throat; corolla salmon-yellow or cream-color, 1¾ to 2¾ inches long, the tube narrow and sometimes distinctly exserted, the lobes broadly rounded and irregularly cut, gnawed, or wavy; stamens included, attached near the top of the tube; style slightly exserted. Capsule oblong, about ¾-inch long. Flowering period, April to July.

Southern Monkeyflower inhabits the foothills of the South Coast Range of San Luis Obispo County and extends southward throughout the lower mountain slopes of southern California and into Lower California. It also occurs on Santa Cruz Island where it apparently hybridizes with *D. parviflorus.*

2a. Var. **calycinus** (Eastw.) Jepson. Fig. 608.

This variety has broader and more oblong-ovate or obovate leaf-blades, densely viscid-woolly arachnoid pedicels and calyces, and broader somewhat foliaceous calyx-teeth. It occurs in rocky places of the foothills and lower mountain slopes of the Kern, Tule, Kaweah, and Kings river regions from Fresno County southward to the Tehachapi Mountains of Kern County.

2b. Var. **rutilus** (Grant) n. comb.

This variety has dark red or salmon-red flowers. The corolla-tube is about as long as the calyx. It occurs in the foothills of Ventura and Los Angeles counties.

2c. Var. **linearis** (Benth.) n. comb.

Herbage glabrate. Calyx not much expanded into the throat. This variety occurs on the lower and middle slopes of the mountains of San Diego and Riverside counties.

Diplacus longiflorus Nutt.; Taylor's Ann. Nat. Hist. I, 1:139 (1838). Type locality: "In rocky places by small streams, in the vicinity of Santa Barbara." Collected by *Nuttall. Mimulus longiflorus* (Nutt.) Grant.

Var. calycinus (Eastw.) Jepson, Man. 919 (1925). *Diplacus calycinus* Eastw. Type locality: South fork of the Kaweah River, Tulare County. Collected by *Culbertson.*

Var. rutilus (Grant) McMinn. *Mimulus longiflorus* var. *rutilus* Grant. Type locality: Santa Susanna Pass, Ventura County. Collected by *Adele L. Grant*.

Var. linearis (Benth.) McMinn. *Mimulus linearis* Benth. Type locality: California. Collected by *Douglas*.

3. **Diplacus aridus** Abrams. San Diego Monkeyflower. Fig. 609.

A low somewhat decumbent subshrub, 8 to 16 inches high, with glabrous glutinous herbage. Leaf-blades oblong, oblanceolate, or obovate, ½-inch to 1¾ inches long, ¼- to ⅜-inch wide, yellowish green, crowded together on the short yellow stems and branches, glabrous and glutinous on both surfaces, entire or slightly dentate, the smaller leaf-blades often revolute, sessile or short-petioled. Flowers numerous; calyx funnelform, spreading abruptly at the throat, about 1¼ inches long; corolla pale buff to yellow, 1¾ to 2¼ inches long, the tube slender and exserted, the lobes rounded and slightly notched at apex; stamens exserted; style exserted. Capsule about ½-inch long. Flowering period, June to August.

San Diego Monkeyflower is known only from the dry hills and ridges in the southeastern part of San Diego County (Jacumba and El Cajon).

Diplacus aridus Abrams, Bull. Torr. Club 32:540 (1905). Type locality: "Growing on dry rocky ridges at Jacumba near the boundary monument." Collected by *Abrams*. *Mimulus aridus* (Abrams) Grant.

4. **Diplacus leptanthus** Nutt. Slender Monkeyflower. Fig. 610.

A rather low shrub, ¾-foot to 1½ feet high, with slender puberulent stems and branches. Leaf-blades oblong to spatulate, the larger 1 to 2 inches long, 5/16- to ½-inch wide, glabrous, shining as though varnished but not glandular, entire or slightly toothed, commonly slightly revolute, with smaller leaves fascicled in the axils, sessile or very short-petioled. Flowers numerous; calyx tubular, ¾-inch to 1 inch long; corolla yellow to cream-color, 1¾ to 2½ inches long, the tube very slender and exserted, the lobes deeply cut and broad, often with a spread of 1¼ inches; stamens included; style somewhat exserted. Capsule ½-inch or less long. Flowering period, May to July.

Slender Monkeyflower occurs in the foothills of Plumas, Nevada, Butte, and Placer counties and in the Santa Lucia Mountains of Monterey and San Luis Obispo counties.

Diplacus leptanthus Nutt.; Taylor's Ann. Nat. Hist. I, 1:138 (1838). Type locality: Probably Monterey County. Collected by *Nuttall*. *D. longiflorus* var. *grandiflorus* (Greene) Jepson.

5. **Diplacus aurantiacus** (Curtis) Jepson. Northern Monkeyflower. Figs. 611, 614.

Usually an erect or slightly spreading shrub, 2 to 4 feet high, with puberulent or pubescent often glandular branchlets. Leaf-blades oblong-lanceolate or sometimes almost linear, 1 to 2 inches long, 3/16- to ½-inch wide, dark green, shining and nearly glabrous above, covered with numerous sessile glands, paler and pubescent beneath, usually with branched hairs, entire or denticulate to coarsely toothed, revolute, sessile, often with smaller leaves fascicled in the axils. Flowers usually numerous; calyx narrow, ¾-inch to 1⅛ inches long, not constricted at the middle, the teeth covered with sessile glands; corolla yellow or salmon-color, about 1½ inches long, the tube mostly included, expanding to a large broad funnelform throat; the lobes spreading, unequal, slightly notched or gnawed at the apex; stamens slightly exserted; style usually slightly exserted. Capsule linear-oblong,

Fig. 614. Northern Monkeyflower. *Diplacus aurantiacus* (Curtis) Jepson.

½-inch to 1 inch long. Flowering period, April to August, or for most of the year.

Northern Monkeyflower is a very common shrub of the dry hills and canyon slopes in the Sierra Nevada foothills from Tuolumne County to Eldorado County and in the Coast Ranges from Del Norte County southward to Santa Barbara County. This species is closely related to *D. longiflorus* but that species occurs chiefly in southern California whereas *D. aurantiacus* occurs north of Ventura County. Intermediate forms are frequently met with in the region of overlapping distribution.

Diplacus aurantiacus (Curtis) Jepson, Man. 919 (1925). *Mimulus aurantiacus* Curtis. Type locality: Collected by *Menzies,* probably at Monterey or San Francisco.

6. **Diplacus parviflorus** Greene. Island Monkeyflower. Fig. 612.

A very leafy rigid shrub, ¼-foot to 2 feet high, with nearly glabrous herbage. Leaf-blades obovate or rhombic-ovate, ¾-inch to 1¾ inches long, ¼- to ⅞-inch wide, glabrous and dark green above, paler and shining as though varnished beneath, entire or irregularly serrate, sometimes revolute, sessile. Flowers numerous; calyx tubular, ⅝- to ⅞-inch long, slightly spreading at the throat, covered with sessile glands; corolla brick-red, 1 to 1⅝ inches long, the tube slender and included, the lobes short and little spreading; stamens exserted; style exserted. Capsule about ¾-inch long. Flowering period, January to August.

Island Monkeyflower grows only on Santa Cruz and Santa Rosa islands.

Diplacus parviflorus Greene, Pitt. 1:36 (1887). Type locality: Santa Cruz Island. Collected by *Greene. Mimulus Flemingii* Munz. *M. parviflorus* (Greene) Grant, not Lindl.

7. **Diplacus puniceus** Nutt. Red Monkeyflower. Fig. 613.

A freely branched shrub, 1½ to 5 feet high, with glabrous or puberulent gultinous herbage. Leaf-blades thick, linear-lanceolate, ¾-inch to 2¼ inches long, ⅛- to ⅜-inch wide, dark green and glabrous above, paler and pubescent beneath, entire or denticulate, usually revolute, sessile and partly clasping the stem, with smaller leaves fascicled in the axils. Flowers several; calyx tubular, ¾-inch to 1 inch long; corolla brick-red or crimson, 1⅜ to 1¾ inches long, the tube included, the lobes narrow and notched or toothed; stamens inserted on the upper part of the tube, the longer pair slightly exserted; style exserted. Capsule cylindrical, about ¾-inch long. Flowering period, April to July.

Red Monkeyflower inhabits the dry hills of Ventura County and extends southward into Los Angeles, Riverside, Orange, and San Diego counties. It is found also on Santa Catalina, San Clemente, Santa Cruz, and Santa Rosa islands.

In the northern part of its range intermediate forms with *D. aurantiacus* and *D. longiflorus* are found.

Diplacus puniceus Nutt.; Taylor's Ann. Nat. Hist. I, 1:137 (1838). Type locality: Near San Diego, California. Collected by *Nuttall. Mimulus puniceus* (Nutt.) Steud.

4. **Penstemon** Mitch. Penstemon

(From the Greek *pente,* five, and *stemon,* stamen.)

Chiefly perennial herbs and subshrubby plants. Leaves opposite or the upper ones occasionally alternate, rarely verticillate, petioled or the upper ones sessile, entire or toothed. Flowers bisexual, irregular, rarely nearly regular, usually showy, in racemes, whorled clusters, corymbs, or panicles; calyx 5-parted, the segments imbricated; corolla-tube elongated, not spurred or saccate, more or less enlarged above, the limb 2-lipped, upper lip 2-lobed, lower lip 3-lobed; stamens 5, included, 4 of them with anthers and arranged in 2 pairs, the fifth present as a sterile filament which is often bearded or swollen; ovary superior, 2-celled. Fruit an ovoid or oblong capsule dehiscing along the septae, with numerous seeds.

This is a large genus consisting of about 150 species confined to North America, and attaining its best development in the western United States. Much variation occurs in the floral and vegetative characters, and consequently authors are at considerable variance in regard to the number of species and varieties. Probably 40 species occur in California, 7 of which are usually shrubs. About 25 others are often woody at the base.

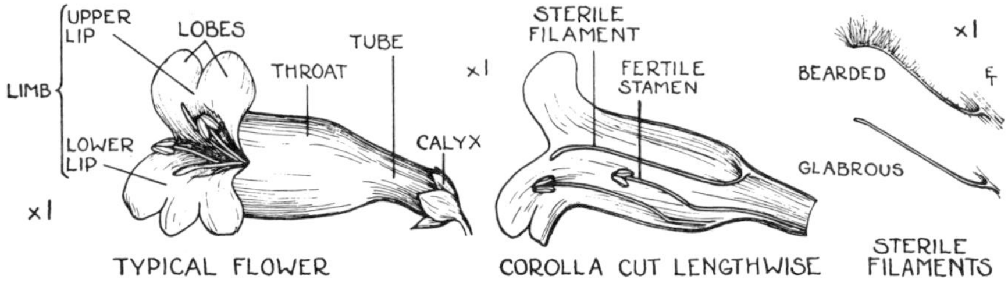

Fig. 615. Structure of the flower of PENSTEMON.

KEY TO THE SPECIES

I. Plants distinctly shrubby throughout or at least at base; leaves thick and leathery; corolla strongly bilabiate.
  Leaves chiefly in whorls of three, serrate; flowers scarlet. . . . . 1. *P. ternatus.*
  Leaves opposite.
    Flowers red.
      Leaves mostly subcordate at base; inflorescence a short leafy panicle with usually reflexed branches; sterile filament bearded at the tip. 2. *P. cordifolius.*
      Leaves acute or obtuse at base; inflorescence a terminal corymb with ascending branches; sterile filament densely bearded for its entire length. 3. *P. corymbosus.*
    Flowers yellowish or whitish, sometimes tinged with pink.
      Inflorescences spike-like; flowers solitary, sessile or subsessile. 4. *P. Rothrockii.*
      Inflorescences paniculate; flowers with distinct pedicels, these often longer than the calyces.
        Leaves serrulate to subentire; corolla-tube ¼-inch or less broad.
          Leaves ovate or ovate-lanceolate; sterile filament densely bearded above; flowers purplish brown or dull yellow. . . .5. *P. Lemmonii.*
          Leaves linear to oblong-lanceolate; sterile filament not bearded above; flowers white with pinkish markings. . . . . .6. *P. breviflorus.*
        Leaves usually entire, linear-oblanceolate; corolla-tube more than ¼-inch broad; flowers bright yellow with reddish lines without.
          Herbage green; sepals ovate, obtuse. . . . . .7. *P. antirrhinoides.*
          Herbage pallid; sepals more or less long-acuminate. 7a. *P. antirrhinoides* var. *microphyllus.*

II. Plants not distinctly shrubby but usually somewhat woody at base.
Flowers in varying shades of red (vermilion, scarlet, crimson) or flesh-colored in one var. of *P. Clevelandii.*
All leaves entire, more than 2 times longer than broad; sterile filament glabrous.
Stem leaves usually petiolate, or if sessile, then not clasping the stem; corolla decidedly 2-lipped; anthers dehiscent 1/2 to 3/4 their lengths. 8. *P. Bridgesii.*
Stem leaves sessile or subcordate-clasping; corolla not markedly 2-lipped, the lobes about equal; anthers dehiscent from 4/5 to almost their entire lengths. . . . . 9. *P. centranthifolius.*
Leaves mostly serrulate or denticulate or some entire.
Upper leaves commonly auriculate-clasping; flowers in panicles.
Corolla 3/4-inch to 1 inch long; sterile filament glabrous. . . . 10. *P. Parishii.*
Corolla 3/4-inch or less long; sterile filament usually hairy (glabrous in one variety). . . . . 11. *P. Clevelandii.*
Upper leaves not auriculate-clasping; flowers in short racemes; anthers densely woolly. . . . . 12. *P. Newberryi.*
Flowers not red. (May be purplish red, pink, blue, yellow, whitish or flesh-color.)
Leaves mostly serrulate or serrate, rarely entire.
Corolla 3/4-inch to 1 1/2 inches long.
Corolla-tube about as long as the calyx; sterile filament exserted.
Upper leaves usually connate-perfoliate; ovary glandular-pubescent. 13. *P. Palmeri.*
Upper leaves sessile but distinct; ovary glabrous. . . . . 14. *P. Grinnellii.*
Corolla-tube twice as long as the calyx; sterile filament included.
Upper leaves connate-perfoliate.
Corolla pink to rose-color, 3/4-inch to 1 inch long, the throat 3/16- to 5/16-inch wide. . . . . 18. *P. pseudospectabilis.*
Corolla lavender-purple with blue lobes, 1 to 1 3/8 inches long, the throat 3/8- to 1/4-inch wide. . . . . 15. *P. spectabilis.*
Upper leaves not connate-perfoliate, sometimes auriculate-clasping at base but distinct.
Sterile filament bearded for almost its entire length; inflorescence lax, the peduncles widely divaricate; leaves linear-lanceolate, mostly entire. . . . . 16. *P. incertus.*
Sterile filament glabrous; inflorescence straight and erect, the peduncles erect or suberect; leaves broadly lanceolate, mostly toothed. 17. *P. floridus.*
Corolla about 1/2-inch or less long. . . . . 19. *P. deustus.*
Leaves entire, rarely serrulate.
Flowers in head-like clusters, the clusters in whorls near the tops of the stems, blue to purple; sterile filament bearded or glabrous, fertile filaments not bearded at base. . . . . 20. *P. confertus.*
Flowers in loose panicles or racemes, rarely in spike-like panicles.
Leaves of two kinds; the basal ones with rotund blades and narrow petioles; the upper stem-leaves lanceolate to oblanceolate or orbicular, short-petiolate or sessile; low plants; branches decumbent or ascending.

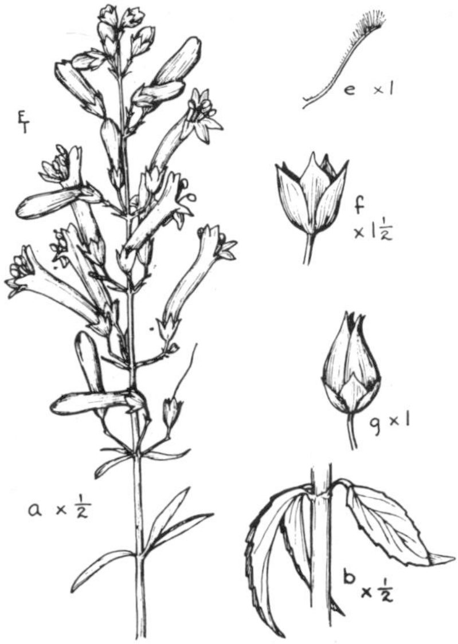

FIG. 616 P. TERNATUS

FIG. 617 P. CORDIFOLIUS

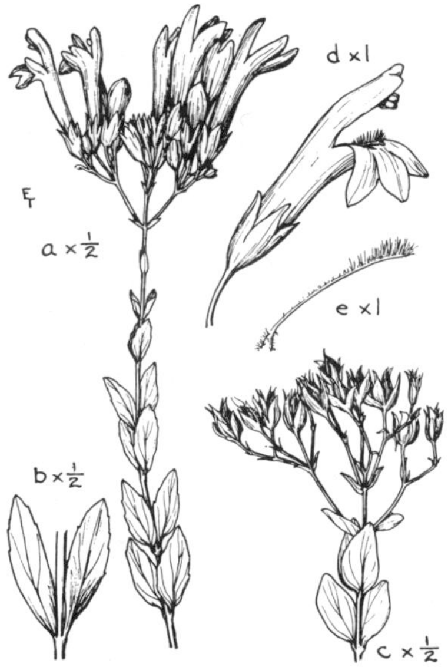

FIG. 618 P. CORYMBOSUS

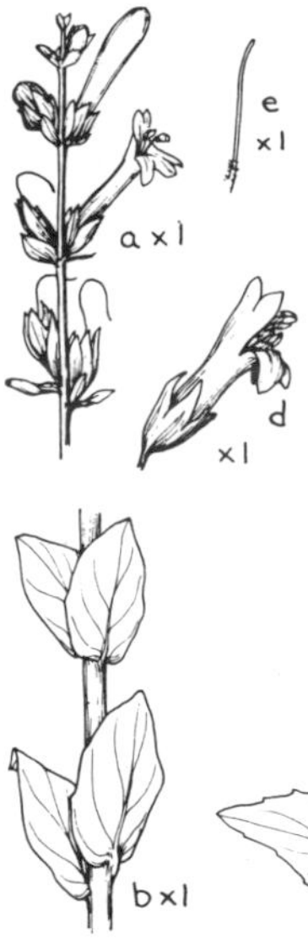

FIG. 619 P. ROTHROCKII

FIG. 620 P. LEMMONII

PENSTEMON. a, Flowering branchlet. b, Leaves. c, Fruit-cluster. d, Flower. e, Sterile filament. f, Calyx. g, Fruit.

Basal leaves densely white-canescent, not coriaceous.
Leaves mostly basal, usually 2 pairs of stem-leaves on the flowering stems; petioles of basal leaves once or twice as long as the blades; sterile filament bearded....................21. *P. scapoides.*
Leaves about equally distributed; petioles of basal leaves about ½ as long as the blades; sterile filament glabrous..22. *P. Purpusii.*
Basal leaves glabrous, coriaceous; corolla purplish blue.
Petioles of basal leaves about as long as the blades; upper stem-leaves in 1 or 2 pairs; corolla less than 1 inch long; sterile filament glabrous..................................23. *P. caesius.*
Petioles of basal leaves much shorter than the blades; upper stem-leaves in numerous pairs; corolla 1 inch or more long; sterile filament densely bearded at tip.24. *P. Menziesii* var. *Davidsonii.*
Leaves nearly all of one kind, or if dimorphic the basal leaves not rotund but oblanceolate or obovate; branches erect, usually 1 to 5 feet long (rarely 6 to 12 inches long); plants not caespitose.
Flowers pale pink, rose-colored, or white.
Leaves ½-inch to 1¼ inches long; stems very woody at base; plants 2 to 5 feet high; sterile filament glabrous; flowers rose-colored or pink.........................25. *P. ambiguus* var. *Thurberi.*
Leaves 1½ to 3 inches long (or the lower ones longer); stems scarcely woody at base; plants 1 to 3 feet high; sterile filament hairy, exserted; flowers white or pale pink........26. *P. fruticiformis.*
Flowers blue or purplish or tricolored.
Sterile filament hairy.
Flowers usually less than ⅔-inch long.
Leaves less than ¾-inch long...............27. *P. californicus.*
Leaves over ¾-inch long.................28. *P. gracilentus.*
Flowers 1 inch or more long....................16. *P. incertus.*
Sterile filament glabrous.
Inflorescence glandular-pubescent; peduncles usually divergent from the main axis.
Herbage blue-glaucous; flowers usually tricolored.
29. *P. neotericus.*
Herbage not blue-glaucous; flowers bluish purple.
30. *P. laetus.*
Inflorescence not glandular-pubescent; peduncles appressed to the main axis.
Leaves just below the inflorescence sessile, not noticeably widest at their bases......................31. *P. heterophyllus.*
Leaves just below the inflorescence with their bases clasping the stem, noticeably widest at their bases........32. *P. azureus.*

1. **Penstemon ternatus** Gray. WHORL-LEAF PENSTEMON. Fig. 616.

A straggly shrub, 3 to 6 feet high, with long slender straight flowering stems from a woody base. Leaves in whorls of 3, lanceolate or linear-lanceolate or some ovate, ¾-inch to 1½ inches long, ¼- to ⅜-inch wide, glabrous on both surfaces, serrulate, almost sessile. Flowers pale scarlet or terracotta-color, about 1 inch long, in an elongated terminal cluster. Pedicels and sepals glabrous. Sterile filament densely hairy along the entire upper side. Flowering period, July and August.

Whorl-leaf Penstemon occurs in the Laguna and Palomar mountains of San Diego County, in the San Gabriel, San Jacinto, and San Bernardino mountains of Los Angeles, Riverside, and San Bernardino counties, in the Upper Sonoran and Transition Life Zones. It extends southward into Lower California.

1a. Var. **septentrionalis** Munz & Johnst.

Sepals and pedicels glandular-pubescent.

This variety occurs in the Liebre Mountains of Los Angeles County and extends westward to Mount Piños and eastward in the Tehachapi Mountains into Kern County.

Penstemon ternatus Torr.; Gray, Bot. Mex. Bound. 115 (1859). Type locality: "Mountains east of San Diego." Collected by *Parry*.

Var. septentrionalis Munz & Johnst. Bull. S. Calif. Acad. 23:28 (1924). Type locality: Oakgrove Canyon, Liebre Mountains, Los Angeles County. Collected by *Abrams* and *McGregor*.

2. **Penstemon cordifolius** Benth. STRAGGLY PENSTEMON. CLIMBING PENSTEMON. HEART-LEAF PENSTEMON. Fig. 617.

A very bushy shrub climbing over other shrubs, with long straggling stems, 2 to 11 feet long. Leaf-blades very shiny, ovate to almost round, ¾-inch to 2¼ inches long, ½-inch to 1¼ inches wide, truncate or somewhat heart-shaped at base, glabrous, prominently veined below, serrate or some almost entire, sessile or with petioles ¼- to ¾-inch long. Flowers red or scarlet, 1¼ to 1½ inches long, in short leafy panicles. Sterile filament bearded along the upper side. Flowering period, April to June.

Straggly Penstemon occurs in canyons and on hill slopes in the coastal mountains of southern California from San Luis Obispo County to San Diego County and eastward to the San Jacinto and San Bernardino mountains. It also occurs on San Clemente, Santa Cruz, Santa Rosa, and Santa Catalina islands and in Lower California. It inhabits the Upper Sonoran Life Zone between 500 and 2000 feet elevation.

This plant does well under cultivation. Its glossy dark green foliage and large scarlet flowers render it attractive throughout the year. It does best in well-watered but well-drained soil.

Penstemon cordifolius Benth. Scroph. Ind. Introd. 7 (1835). Type locality: "New California." Collected by *Douglas*.

3. **Penstemon corymbosus** Benth. RED PENSTEMON. THYMELEAF PENSTEMON. Fig. 618.

A low shrub, ¾-foot to 1¼ feet high, with more or less glaucous stems from a woody base, often forming dense mats. Leaf-blades ovate to elliptic or oblong or the lower obovate, ½-inch to 1¼ inches long, ¼- to ⅜-inch wide, glabrous, entire or serrulate, sessile or with petioles about ¼-inch long. Flowers scarlet, 1 to 1¼ inches long, in terminal corymbs. Sterile filament hairy along the upper side. Flowering period, July and August.

Red Penstemon inhabits rocky slopes and cliffs of the Coast Ranges from Point Sur, Monterey County, northward to Mount Hamilton, Mount Tamalpais, and Mount Diablo, and thence more commonly through Sonoma, Lake, Mendocino, and Humboldt counties to Del Norte County. It extends eastward to Trinity, Shasta, and Siskiyou counties in its varietal form.

3a. Var. **puberulentus** Jepson.

Herbage puberulent to cinereous. Leaves narrowly elliptic to ovate.

This variety occupies the same geographical range as the species but is much less common.

Penstemon corymbosus Benth.; DC. Prodr. 10:593 (1846). Type locality: Probably in the Santa Lucia Mountains of Monterey County. Collected by *Coulter*.

Var. puberulentus Jepson, Man. 909 (1925). *P. intonsus* Heller. Type locality: Along the Eel River near Hullville, Lake County, California. Collected by *Heller*.

4. **Penstemon Rothrockii** Gray. ROTHROCK PENSTEMON. Fig. 619.

A loosely branched, rounded bushy shrub, 1 to 2 feet high, with erect slender stems from a woody base. Leaf-blades firm but rather thin, ovate to ovate-oblong, subcordate at base, 1/4- to 5/8-inch long, 1/8- to 1/4-inch wide, grayish with a short scabrous pubescence, slightly glandular above, entire or denticulate, often curled and wavy-margined, upper leaves sessile and much reduced, lower leaves subsessile. Flowers dull yellow, sometimes tinged with pink or purple, 3/8- to 1/2-inch long, sessile or on very short pedicels in the upper axils of the reduced leaves and forming a spike-like inflorescence. Sterile filament glabrous, pubescent at base. Flowering period, June and July.

Rothrock Penstemon occurs on mountain slopes from 6000 to 9100 feet elevation, in the southern part of the Sierra Nevada from Mono County to Tulare County and in the Panamint Mountains of Inyo County. It also occurs in western Nevada.

4a. Var. **jacintensis** (Abrams) Munz & Johnst.

Leaves green, nearly glabrous. Corolla about 5/8-inch long.

This variety occurs in the San Jacinto Mountains of Riverside County, between 7000 and 9000 feet elevation.

Penstemon Rothrockii Gray, Syn. Fl. 2:260 (1878). Type locality: "S. E. California, on Little Olanche Mountain, toward the sources of the Kern River, at 10,400 feet." Collected by *Rothrock*.

Var. jacintensis (Abrams) Munz & Johnst. Bull. S. Calif. Acad. 23:27 (1924). *P. jacintensis* Abrams. Type locality: San Jacinto Mountains, Riverside County. Collected by *Hall*.

5. **Penstemon Lemmonii** Gray. LEMMON BEARD-TONGUE. LEMMON PENSTEMON. Fig. 620.

A spreading bush-like shrub, 2 to 3 feet high, with several glaucous stems from a woody base. Leaf-blades ovate-lanceolate or oblong-ovate, 1/2-inch to 1 3/4 inches long, 1/4- to 3/4-inch wide, light green and glabrous above, paler beneath, serrulate or sometimes entire, the upper leaves sessile, the lower ones with petioles about 1/8-inch long or subsessile. Flowers small, dull yellow or purplish, about 1/2-inch long, in terminal rather narrow panicles. Sterile filament bearded on one side. Flowering period, July and August.

Lemmon Beard-tongue occurs in the canyons of the North Coast Ranges at 500 to about 5000 feet elevation from Solano and Sonoma counties northward to Humboldt County, thence eastward in Siskiyou, Trinity, and Shasta counties, and southward in the Sierra Nevada to Placer County. It extends eastward into Nevada.

Penstemon Lemmonii Gray, Bot. Calif. 1:557 (1876). Type locality: "Long Valley, Mendocino Co. *(Kellogg)*, Plumas Co. *(Lemmon)*."

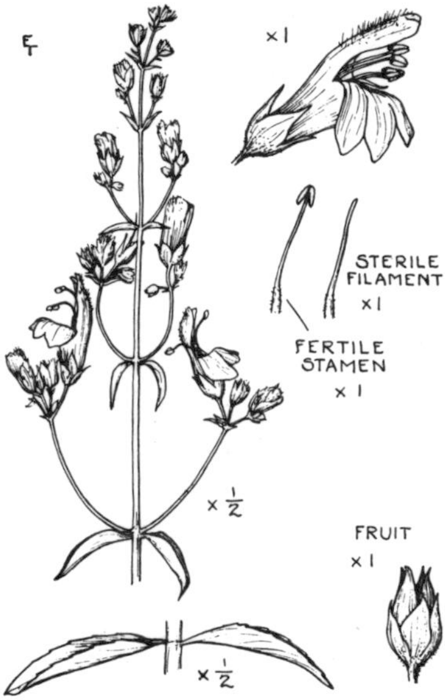

Fig. 621
Penstemon breviflorus

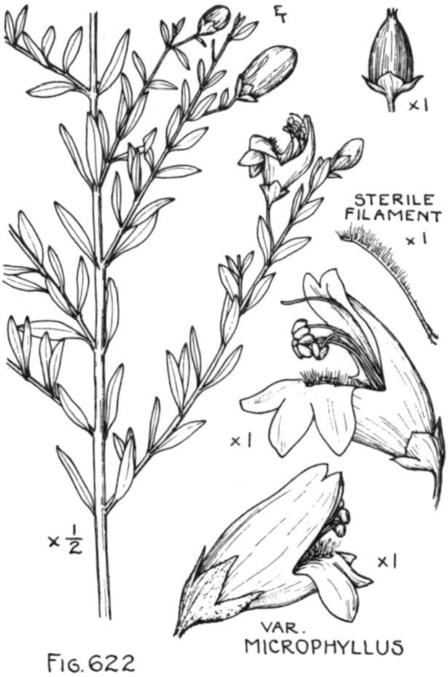

Fig. 622
Penstemon antirrhinoides

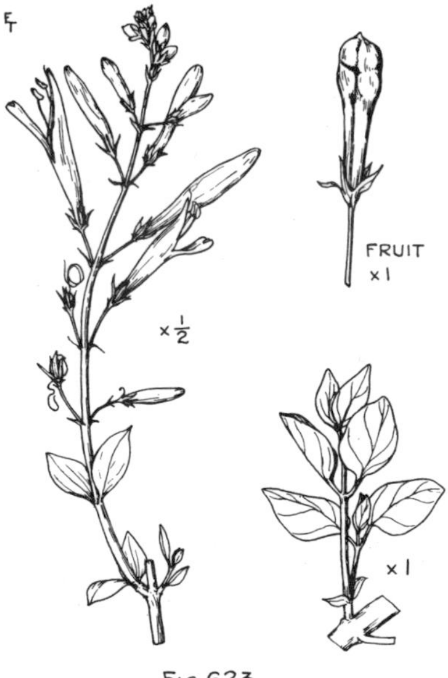

Fig. 623
Beloperone californica

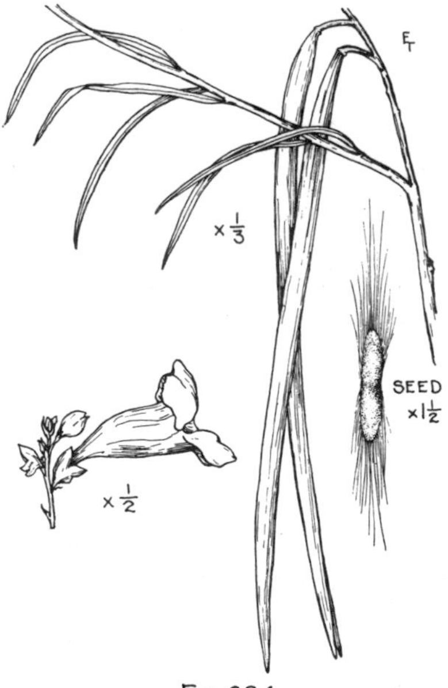

Fig. 624
Chilopsis linearis

6. **Penstemon breviflorus** Lindl. BUSH BEARD-TONGUE. STUBFLOWER PENSTEMON. Fig. 621.

A scraggly shrub, 1 to 3 feet high, with numerous glabrous and glaucous stems from a woody base. Leaf-blades oblong to oblong-lanceolate, or the upper ones narrowly lanceolate, ½-inch to 2 inches long, ⅛- to ½-inch wide, pale green and glabrous, serrulate, the upper ones almost entire, sessile, or the lower ones with petioles about ⅛-inch long. Flowers about ½-inch long, whitish or cream-color with pink or purple markings, yellowish in bud, borne in loose ample terminal panicles. Sterile filament glabrous except at base. Flowering period, June to August.

Bush Beard-tongue inhabits the dry rocky foothills and lower mountain slopes in the Upper Sonoran and Transition Life Zones in the inner Coast Range from Los Angeles and Ventura counties northward to Shasta County, thence southward in the Sierra Nevada through Plumas and Butte counties to Tulare County. It occurs on both sides of the Sierra Nevada and also in the mountains of Inyo County bordering the northern and western part of the Mohave Desert and in western Nevada. In the inner North Coast Range the flowers usually have glabrous sepals while in the South Coast Range the sepals are glandular-pubescent. In the Sierra Nevada the two forms intermingle and many intermediates are found. Keck (Madroño 3:207, 1936) segregates the form with glabrous sepals as the subspecies **glabrisepalus.**

Penstemon breviflorus Lindl. Bot. Reg. 23:1946 (1837). Type locality: The original description and drawing were made from a plant grown in England, from seeds taken from a herbarium specimen collected by *Douglas,* probably in Monterey County, California.

7. **Penstemon antirrhinoides** Benth. YELLOW PENSTEMON. SNAPDRAGON PENSTEMON. Fig. 622.

A bushy shrub-like plant, 2 to 8 feet high, with spreading stems and branches and green herbage, the young stems finely puberulent. Leaf-blades ovate to broadly elliptical or linear or some oblanceolate, ¼- to ¾-inch long, ⅛- to ¼-inch wide, glabrous or glandular-puberulent, entire or very slightly denticulate; petioles very short. Flowers yellow, ½- to ¾-inch long, about ½-inch broad, in ample leafy panicles. Sterile filament with a heavy yellow beard on one side near the apex. Flowering period, March to June.

Yellow Penstemon occurs on the chaparral-covered slopes of the mountains of San Bernardino, Riverside, Orange, and San Diego counties, in the Upper Sonoran Life Zone. It extends southward into Lower California. Its evergreen foliage and conspicuous yellow flowers make it a very desirable plant for ornamental use. It thrives as far north as the San Francisco Bay region.

7a. Var. **microphyllus** (Gray) Munz & Johnst. LITTLELEAF PENSTEMON.

Resembling the species but differing in the more pallid canescent herbage and the lance-oblong acuminate sepals.

This variety occurs in rocky places in the Upper Sonoran Life Zone in the Providence, Old Woman, Santa Rosa, Old Dad, and the Little San Bernardino mountains and along the western edge of the Colorado Desert. It extends southward to Lower California and eastward to Arizona.

Penstemon antirrhinoides Benth.; DC. Prodr. 10:594 (1846). Type locality: Southern California. Collected by *Coulter.*

Var. microphyllus (Gray) Munz & Johnst. Bull. Torr. Club 49:43 (1922). *P.*

microphyllus Gray. Type locality: "On Williams Fork of the Colorado, New Mexico." Probably Mohave or Yuma County, Arizona, acc. *Munz.*

8. **Penstemon Bridgesii** Gray. BRIDGES PENSTEMON.

A subshrub, 1 to 2½ feet high, with simple flowering stems from a woody base. Leaf-blades oblanceolate, oblong, or the lower ones spatulate, 1½ to 3 inches long, ¼- to ⅜-inch wide, glabrous on both surfaces, entire, almost sessile or the lower ones petiolate. Flowers scarlet, 1 to 1¼ inches long, numerous in a narrow panicle; sterile filament glabrous. Flowering period, June and July.

Bridges Penstemon occurs on arid slopes and in clearings of forests from 4500 to 10,000 feet elevation in the mountains of San Diego County, northward in the San Jacinto, San Bernardino, and San Gabriel mountains to the region of Mount Piños in Ventura County, eastward in the Tehachapi Mountains, northward in the Sierra Nevada to Mono and Tuolumne counties, and in the White Mountains of eastern Mono and Inyo counties. It extends eastward to Nevada and Arizona.

Penstemon Bridgesii Gray, Proc. Am. Acad. 7:379 (1868). Type locality: "California, somewhere in the Middle Sierras." Collected by *Bridges.*

9. **Penstemon centranthifolius** Benth. SCARLET BUGLER.

A glabrous and glaucous perennial, 1 to 4 feet high, with 1 to several slender simple stems from a woody base. Leaves opposite, thick, entire; the basal ones oblanceolate, ¾-inch to 3 inches long, gradually narrowed into a short petiole; stem-leaves ovate to elliptic or lanceolate, mostly sessile, the uppermost with subcordate clasping bases. Flowers scarlet, tubular, about 1 inch long, not markedly 2-lipped, in long straight slender panicles. Sterile filament glabrous. Flowering period, April to June.

Scarlet Bugler inhabits gravelly places below 6000 feet elevation in the mountains of San Diego County northward in the Coast Ranges to Lake County. It is rarely collected north of Monterey County. This plant extends southward to the Sierra San Pedro Martir, Lower California.

Its numerous tubular scarlet flowers mark this species as one of the most striking of the native penstemons. It should find greater use in our gardens as an ornamental perennial.

Penstemon centranthifolius Benth. Scroph. Ind. Introd. 7 (1835). Type locality: California. Collected by *Douglas.*

10. **Penstemon Parishii** Gray. PARISH PENSTEMON.

A subshrub, 2 to 3 feet high, with slender straight flowering stems from a woody base. Leaf-blades oblong to ovate or lanceolate, 1 to 2½ inches long, ¼- to ½-inch wide, glabrous, mostly serrulate or some entire, the upper ones auriculate-clasping, the lower very short-petioled. Flowers red, about 1 inch long, in terminal panicles. Flowering period, April to June.

Parish Penstemon occurs on dry flats and in valleys from about 1000 to 3000 feet elevation in San Diego County and northward along the western border of the Colorado Desert to the vicinity of the San Jacinto River Canyon and in the San Bernardino Valley. It is a very ornamental species, usually considered a hybrid between *P. spectabilis* and *P. centranthifolius.* It has the foliage and habit of the latter and inflorescence and flowers of the former.

Penstemon Parishii Gray, Proc. Am. Acad. 17:228 (1882). Type locality: "Southeastern California, in the Cucamonga Mountains and elsewhere." Collected by *Wallace.*

11. **Penstemon Clevelandii** Gray. Cleveland Penstemon.

A glabrous perennial, 2 to 6 feet high, with several straight slender stems from a woody base. Leaf-blades glabrous, usually thick and leathery, denticulate or entire, the lower ovate, 3/4-inch to 2 inches long, 3/8- to 3/4-inch wide, petioled; the upper ones smaller, oblong to ovate, sessile. Flowers red or purplish red (rarely bluish), about 3/4-inch long, many in a long slender panicle 4 to 16 inches long. Sterile filament somewhat hairy at the swollen apex or almost glabrous. Flowering period, April to June.

Cleveland Penstemon, in its typical form, apparently occurs only in the mountains of eastern San Diego County and in Lower California, in the Upper Sonoran Life Zone. To the north it is represented by three varieties.

KEY TO THE VARIETIES

Upper leaves joined around the stem by their bases.
  Sterile filament bearded..................................11a. var. *connatus*.
  Sterile filament glabrous..................................11b. var. *Stephensii*.
Upper leaves distinct; corolla contracted at orifice.........11c. var. *mohavensis*.

11a. Var. **connatus** Munz & Johnst.

Leaves blue-glaucous, strongly and finely serrate. Pedicels and calyces glabrous. Corolla not contracted at orifice. Sterile filament bearded.

This variety occurs in the Palm Springs region on the northwestern end of the Colorado Desert.

11b. Var. **Stephensii** (Brandg.) Munz & Johnst.

Leaves weakly glaucous, thin, finely and sharply denticulate. Corolla flesh-colored, not contracted at orifice. Sterile filament glabrous.

This variety is known only from the Providence Mountains of San Bernardino County.

11c. Var. **mohavensis** (Keck) n. comb.

Leaves bright green, strongly and coarsely serrate. Pedicels and calyces glandular-pubescent. Corolla contracted at orifice. Sterile filament bearded.

This variety occurs from the Little San Bernardino Mountains to the Sheephole Mountains, along the southern edge of the Mohave Desert (acc. *Keck*) in San Bernardino County.

Penstemon Clevelandii Gray, Proc. Am. Acad. 11:94 (1876). Type locality: Tantillas Canyon, Lower California. Collected in flower probably by *Dunn*, and in fruit by *Palmer*.

Var. connatus Munz & Johnst. Bull. Torr. Club 49:359 (1923). Type locality: "near Van Deventers, southeastern base of San Jacinto Mountains." Collected by *Hall*.

Var. Stephensii (Brandg.) Munz & Johnst. Bull. Torr. Club 49:41 (1922). *P. Stephensii* Brandg. Type locality: Providence Mountains of San Bernardino County. Collected by *T. S. Brandegee*.

Var. mohavensis (Keck) McMinn. *P. Clevelandii* subsp. *mohavensis* Keck. Type locality: Keys Ranch, Little San Bernardino Mountains. Collected by *M. F. Gilman*.

12. **Penstemon Newberryi** Gray. Mountain Pride.

A low subshrub, 3/4-foot to 1 1/2 feet high, with simple leafy flowering stems from a woody base. Leaf-blades thick and leathery, oblong-elliptical, round-ovate, or some almost round, 1/2-inch to 1 1/4 inches long, 1/8- to 1/2-inch wide, glabrous, somewhat glaucous, serrulate or entire, sessile or with a petiole up to 1/4-inch long. Flowers bright red or crimson, 1 to 1 1/4 inches long, in terminal racemes; anthers densely woolly. Flowering period, June and July.

Mountain Pride is a very common penstemon growing usually among the granite ledges from 4500 to 10,000 feet elevation. It occurs in the Sierra Nevada from Tulare County northward to Mount Shasta, Siskiyou County, thence westward and southward to Cobb Mountain and Hoods Peak in the North Coast Range. It extends eastward into Nevada and northward to Washington. This plant has a most appropriate common name as it certainly is the "pride of the mountain." In the vicinity of Silver Lake, Amador County, it grows abundantly among the granite crevices and ledges where it is associated with three or more species of *Eriogonum* and *Spiraea densiflora*.

Penstemon Newberryi Gray, Pacif. R. Rep. 6:82 pl. 14 (1857). Type locality: "on rocks, forming broad tufts near Mount St. Joseph's, N. California." Collected by *Newberry*.

13. **Penstemon Palmeri** Gray. PALMER PENSTEMON.

A perennial, sometimes subshrubby, with few straight stems 1 1/2 to 3 feet high, from a woody base, glabrous and often glaucous below, the peduncles and pedicels glandular-pubescent. Leaf-blades ovate to obovate or ovate-lanceolate, 1 3/4 to 4 inches long, 3/8- to 3/4-inch wide, thick and leathery, glaucous, serrate, the upper stem-leaves sessile and usually joined around the stem, the lower leaves with petioles 1/8-inch to 1 inch long, or rarely auriculate-clasping, the uppermost reduced to bracts. Flowers flesh-color or creamy-white, often streaked with pink or purple, 1 to 1 1/2 inches long, borne in a racemose one-sided branched cluster. Sterile filament densely yellow-hairy at apex. Flowering period, June and July.

Palmer Penstemon is known from desert washes and adjacent areas in the Argus, Coso, and Providence mountain regions of Inyo and San Bernardino counties. It extends eastward to Nevada, Arizona, and Utah.

Penstemon Palmeri Gray, Proc. Am. Acad. 7:379 (1868). Type locality: "Skull Valley, Arizona, and on Rio Verde, near Fort Whipple." Collected by *Coues* and *Palmer*.

14. **Penstemon Grinnellii** Eastw. GRINNELL PENSTEMON.

A branching perennial from a woody base, 1 to 3 feet high or sometimes the stems decumbent at base. Leaf-blades green, usually not glaucous, the lower ones broadly lanceolate, the stem-leaves lanceolate to ovate-oblong, the uppermost sessile but distinct, the largest up to 3 inches long, finely to coarsely dentate or the upper nearly entire. Flowers white or with a purplish or bluish tinge or blue, 3/4-inch to 1 1/4 inches long, in a glandular-pubescent loose panicle. Sterile filament densely bearded with yellow hairs on the upper side near the apex. Flowering period, June and July.

Grinnell Penstemon occurs on the dry slopes and ridges from 3000 to 9500 feet elevation in the South Coast Range from Santa Clara (San Antonio Valley between Livermore and Mt. Hamilton), San Benito, and Monterey counties southward to the Mount Piños, Tehachapi, San Gabriel, San Jacinto, San Bernardino, and Santa Rosa mountain areas, and in the southern Sierra Nevada of Tulare and Kern counties.

Penstemon Grinnellii Eastw. Bull. Torr. Club 32:207 (1905). Type locality: "Mt. Wilson." Collected by *Fordyce Grinnell Jr. P. Palmeri* of Jepson's Manual in part, not Gray. *P. Palmeri* var. *Grinnellii* Munz & Johnst.

15. **Penstemon spectabilis** Thurber. Showy Penstemon.

A glabrous perennial, 2 to 4 feet high, with several erect often slightly glaucous stems from a woody base. Leaf-blades somewhat thick and leathery, oblong to ovate, 3/4-inch to 3 1/2 inches long, 3/8-inch to 1 3/4 inches wide, sharply serrate, the lower ones sessile or short-petioled, the upper ones joined around the stem by their bases. Flowers blue or purplish, 3/4-inch to 1 1/4 inches long, many in an open much branched panicle. Pedicels and calyces glabrous. Corolla broadly funnelform, its throat 3/8- to 1/2-inch wide. Sterile stamen glabrous. Flowering period, April to June.

Showy Penstemon occurs on the dry hills and washes of the Upper Sonoran Life Zone from Los Angeles County southward and eastward in the mountains to San Diego County and Lower California. It reaches the edge of the Colorado Desert in the Santa Rosa Mountains.

15a. Var. **subviscosus** (Keck) n. comb.

Similar to the species but with glandular-pubescent pedicels and calyces.

This variety is the common form in the Liebre and Santa Monica mountains of Los Angeles County. It extends southeastward to the gravelly washes of the southern slopes of the San Gabriel and San Bernardino mountains where it occurs with the species.

The species and variety apparently hybridize with *P. centranthifolius* and *P. Palmeri*.

Penstemon spectabilis Thurber; Gray, Pacif. R. Rep. 4:119 (1857). Type locality: San Pasqual, San Diego County, California. Collected by *Thurber*.

Var. subviscosus (Keck) McMinn. *P. spectabilis* subsp. *subviscosus* Keck. Type locality: In a wash, Claremont, Los Angeles County, California. Collected by *P. A. Munz*.

16. **Penstemon incertus** Brandg. Argus Penstemon.

A glabrous and glaucous subshrub, often spreading, 1 to 3 feet broad and 1 to 2 feet high. Leaf-blades narrowly linear-lanceolate, 3/4-inch to 2 1/4 inches long, entire or serrulate, the upper sessile but not joined around the stem. Inflorescence lax, slightly glandular-pubescent. Corolla purplish or violet, 1 to 1 1/4 inches long. Sterile filament densely bearded with medium long yellow hairs for almost its whole length. Flowering period, May to July.

Argus Penstemon is a rare species occurring on the eastern side of the Sierra Nevada and in the Argus Mountains southward to Antelope Valley. An isolated station has been located by M. F. Gilman and S. B. Parish at Warren's Well in the southern Mohave Desert.

In vegetative characters this species is quite similar to *P. fruticiformis* but the two species differ in several floral characters. The corolla in *P. fruticiformis* is pale pink, glabrous without, and shorter and broader than that of *P. incertus,* the corolla of which is blue-purple and glandular-pubescent without.

Penstemon incertus Brandg. Bot. Gaz. 27:454 (1899). Type locality: "Walker Pass and sandy slopes of Argus mountains, California." Collected by *C. A. Purpus*. *P. fruticiformis* var. *incertus* (Brandg.) Munz & Johnst.

17. **Penstemon floridus** Brandg. Panamint Penstemon.

A bushy perennial, 2 to 3 1/2 feet high, sometimes woody at base, with gray-glaucous foliage. Leaf-blades at base of plant oblong-ovate, the stem-leaves lance-ovate, irregularly dentate or the uppermost entire, sessile or auriculate-clasping but distinct at base, the largest to 4 inches long. Flowers rose-pink, often yellowish in bud, 3/4-inch to 1 1/4 inches long, 2-lipped. Sterile filament glabrous. Flowering period, June and July.

This rare species grows in canyons and on dry plains of the White, Inyo, and Panamint mountain regions of Mono and Inyo counties. It extends eastward into Nevada.

Penstemon floridus Brandg. Bot. Gaz. 27:454 (1899). Type locality: "Mt. Magruder, Nevada." Collected by *C. A. Purpus.*

18. **Penstemon pseudospectabilis** M. E. Jones. DESERT PENSTEMON.

A tall perennial, 2 to 4 feet high, with glabrous and glaucous stems from a woody base. Leaf-blades ovate to lanceolate, 3/4-inch to 5 inches long, 3/8- to 3/4-inch wide, glabrous and glaucous, serrate, the upper ones sessile or joined around the stems by their bases, the lower ones distinctly petioled. Flowers purplish red or pinkish or rarely bluish, tubular-fullenform, 1 to 1 1/4 inches long, in a straight narrow glandular-puberulent panicle 4 inches to 1 1/2 feet long. Sterile filament glabrous. Flowering period, March to May.

Desert Penstemon is known in California only from the Sheephole, Mopas, and Chuckawalla mountains in the southeastern part of the Mohave Desert. It extends eastward into Arizona.

Penstemon pseudospectabilis M. E. Jones, Contr. West. Bot. 12:66 (1908). Type locality: "Chimihuevis Mts., northwestern Arizona." Collected by *M. E. Jones.*

19. **Penstemon deustus** Dougl. SCABLAND PENSTEMON.

A low perennial, 6 to 12 inches high, with several stems from a somewhat woody base and with glabrous herbage. Leaf-blades sharply serrate, sessile. Flowers yellowish to flesh-color, 1/2-inch or less long, in clusters in opposite leaf-axils, forming a spike-like panicle 3 to 6 inches long. Sterile filament glabrous. Flowering period, June to August.

Scabland Penstemon is a montane species occurring among rocks in the Sierra Nevada from Amador County (Thimble Peak) north to eastern Tehama and Modoc counties, westward to Siskiyou and Humboldt counties, and thence northward into Oregon and Washington to British Columbia and Montana.

Penstemon deustus Dougl.; Lindl. Bot. Reg. t. 1318 (1830). Type locality: Northwest America. Collected by *Douglas.*

20. **Penstemon confertus** Dougl. WHORLFLOWER PENSTEMON.

This species is represented in California by several varieties with blue to purplish flowers arranged in head-like clusters in whorls near the top of the stem. None is distinctly shrubby but occasionally some become slightly woody at the base. The plants vary from 4 to 20 inches high and they have few to several stems from a branching root-crown. The inflorescence is usually composed of 2 to 5 distinct whorls of flowers but may be reduced to a single whorl.

The various forms of this variable species occur in the Sierra Nevada, between 5000 and 12,000 feet elevation, from Modoc and Siskiyou counties southward to Tulare County, and also in the Yollo Bolly Mountains of the inner North Coast Range, and in the White Mountains of Mono County. The species or its varieties extend eastward to Nevada and northward to Washington.

Penstemon confertus Dougl.; Lindl. Bot. Reg. t. 1260 (1829). Type locality: Western North America. Collected by *Douglas.*

21. **Penstemon scapoides** Keck. INYO PENSTEMON.

A low tufted perennial, $\frac{3}{4}$-foot to $1\frac{1}{2}$ feet high, with grayish soft-canescent leaves. Basal leaves with blades ovate to orbicular, $\frac{1}{4}$- to $\frac{5}{8}$-inch long and almost as broad; petioles as long as or longer than the blades. Leaves on the flowering stems usually of 2 pairs, lanceolate, sessile. Flowers red-lilac to pale lilac, about 1 inch long; sterile filament bearded on one side. Flowering period, June and July.

This rare species has been collected by Keck at "Westgard Pass, 11.5 miles northeast of Big Pine, Inyo County, California, at 7000 feet altitude," in 1930 and by V. Duran in 1924 on "Wyman Creek, White Mountains, at 9500 feet altitude." According to Keck it grows "in a rock-bound desert canyon of the Upper Sonoran Zone on gravelly slopes with *Pinus monophylla, Artemisia tridentata, Ephedra viridis,* and *Penstemon Bridgesii.*"

Penstemon scapoides Keck, Univ. Calif. Publ. Bot. 16:379 (1932). Type locality: Westgard Pass, Inyo County, California. Collected by *Keck.*

22. **Penstemon Purpusii** Brandg. PURPUS PENSTEMON.

A low perennial, $\frac{1}{3}$- to $\frac{1}{2}$-foot high, with decumbent or ascending stems from a slightly woody base, densely white-canescent herbage, and glandular-pubescent inflorescences. Leaf-blades mostly entire or some serrulate, the basal ones nearly round, with petioles about $\frac{1}{2}$ as long as the blades, the upper ones lanceolate or oval, sessile. Flowers violet, shading to blue on the corolla-tube, $\frac{3}{4}$-inch to $1\frac{1}{4}$ inches long, in spike-like clusters; sterile filament glabrous. Flowering period, June and July.

Purpus Penstemon is restricted in its distribution to the high inner North Coast Range from Lake County north to Trinity County (South Yollo Bolly, Mt. Hull, Mt. Sanhedrin, and Snow Mt.)

Penstemon Purpusii Brandg. Bot. Gaz. 27:455 (1899). Type locality: Snow Mountain, Lake County, California. Collected by *C. A. Purpus.*

23. **Penstemon caesius** Gray. SAN BERNARDINO PENSTEMON.

A low perennial, 1 to $1\frac{1}{2}$ feet high, with erect stems from a woody base. Leaves of two kinds; blades of basal leaves orbicular, $\frac{1}{4}$- to $\frac{3}{4}$-inch long, with petioles about as long; stem-leaves in 1 or 2 pairs, their blades oblanceolate, sessile or tapering to a petiole up to $\frac{1}{2}$-inch long; both kinds entire, glabrous and glaucous. Flowers blue or purplish blue, $\frac{3}{4}$-inch to 1 inch long, in rather open panicles 4 to 8 inches long. Sterile filament glabrous. Flowering period, June and July.

San Bernardino Penstemon is a rather common caespitose perennial in the Sierra Nevada of Fresno and Tulare counties and in the San Gabriel and San Bernardino mountains of southern California. It grows on dry ridges and slopes from about 6000 to 10,000 feet elevation.

Penstemon caesius Gray, Proc. Am. Acad. 19:92 (1883). Type locality: San Bernardino Mountains, California. Collected by *Parry, Lemmon.*

24. **Penstemon Menziesii** var. **Davidsonii** (Greene) Piper. TIMBERLINE PENSTEMON.

A low prostrate perennial with 3 to 8 leafy-bracted flowering stalks arising from a basal mat of leafy often woody branches. Lower leaf-blades ovate to almost round, $\frac{1}{4}$- to $\frac{1}{2}$-inch long, thick and leathery, glabrous, entire, with short petioles; upper leaf-blades reduced and usually sessile. Flowers purplish blue, $1\frac{1}{4}$ to $1\frac{1}{2}$ inches long, 2 to 5 (or 1) on leafy-bracted peduncles forming a short raceme. Sterile filament bearded at apex. Anthers woolly. Flowering period, June to August.

Timberline Penstemon occurs on exposed rocky summits of the higher mountain peaks in the Sierra Nevada from Tulare County northward to Mount Lassen and Mount Shasta. It extends northward to Washington and east to Nevada.

Penstemon Menziesii var. Davidsonii (Greene) Piper. Contr. U. S. Nat. Herb. 11:499 (1906). *P. Davidsonii* Greene. Type locality: "On Mt. Conness, at an altitude of 12,300 feet" (Yosemite region), California.

25. **Penstemon ambiguus** var. **Thurberi** (Torr.) Gray. THURBER PENSTEMON.

An erect branching perennial, 2 to 5 feet high, with few glabrous stems, woody at the base. Leaves linear, 1 to 2 inches long, 1/16- to 1/8-inch wide, glabrous, entire, sessile, gradually reduced upward. Flowers pink or rose-color, about 1/2-inch long, in narrow panicles. Sterile filament glabrous.

I have seen only one collection of this species from California and that from near San Felipe, San Diego County. Munz reports that it occurs also at Keys Ranch in the Little San Bernardino Mountains. To my knowledge, it has not been found elsewhere in California. It occurs also in Arizona and New Mexico.

Penstemon ambiguus var. Thurberi (Torr.) Gray, Proc. Am. Acad. 6:65 (1862). *P. Thurberi* Torr. Type locality: "Burro Mts., N. Mex." Collected by *Thurber*.

26. **Penstemon fruticiformis** Cov. DESERT-MOUNTAIN PENSTEMON.

A much branched perennial, 1 to 3 feet high, with glabrous glaucous stems from a woody base. Leaves linear-lanceolate or oblong-elliptic, 3/4-inch to 2 1/4 inches (or the lowest up to 5 inches) long, 1/8- to 1/4-inch wide, glabrous and somewhat glaucous, entire or slightly denticulate, sessile or very short-petiolate. Flowers pale pink or white, the limb with some blue, 3/4-inch to 1 inch long, few in narrow open panicles. Pedicels and sepals glabrous. Sterile filament densely hairy near the apex, exserted. Flowering period, May and June.

Desert-mountain Penstemon is common in canyons of the Panamint and Argus mountains of the Death Valley region of Inyo County and on the east side of Walker Pass, near the summit, in Kern County.

Penstemon fruticiformis Cov. Contr. U. S. Nat. Herb. 4:170 (1893). Type locality: "Wild Rose Canyon, Panamint Mountains, Inyo County, California." Collected by *Coville* and *Funston*.

27. **Penstemon californicus** (Munz & Johnst.) Keck. SAN JACINTO PENSTEMON.

A low perennial, 2 to 8 inches high, from a woody base, densely leafy below, with densely cinereous-pubescent pallid herbage. Leaf-blades linear-lanceolate, 5/8-inch or less long, thick, entire. Corolla purplish blue, narrowly tubular-funnelform, 1/2- to 3/4-inch long, externally viscid. Sterile filament yellow-bearded. Flowering period, June and July.

San Jacinto Penstemon occurs locally in the San Jacinto Mountains of Riverside County and at Aguanga near the boundary between Riverside and San Diego counties. It extends southward to the San Pedro Martir Mountains of Lower California.

Penstemon californicus (Munz & Johnst.) Keck, Bull. Torr. Club 64:378 (1937). *P. linearioides* var. *californicus* Munz & Johnst. Type locality: "Kenworthy, Hemet Valley, San Jacinto Mts." Collected by *Munz* and *Johnston*.

28. **Penstemon gracilentus** Gray. SLENDER PENSTEMON.

A bright green perennial herb or subshrub, 1 to 1 1/2 feet high, with slender erect stems from a woody base. Leaf-blades oblong to lanecolate or linear, sometimes oblanceolate, 1 1/2 to 2 1/4 inches long, 1/4-inch to 1 1/8 inches wide, glabrous, sometimes glaucous, entire; petioles 1/4-inch to 1 inch long, or the blades sessile. Flowers blue to purple or reddish purple, ½- to ¾-inch long, in clusters forming a loose or compact panicle. Sterile filament with yellow hairs on one side toward the apex. Flowering period, July and August.

Slender Penstemon occurs in the northern Sierra Nevada, chiefly on the eastern slope, in the open forest regions from about 5000 to 8000 feet elevation. It ranges from Nevada County northward to Modoc and Siskiyou counties and eastward into Washoe and Ormsby counties, Nevada.

Penstemon gracilentus Gray, Pacif. R. Rep. 6:82 (1857). Type locality: "At the base of Lassen's Butte, N. California." Collected by *Newberry*.

29. **Penstemon neotericus** Keck. KECK PENSTEMON.

A slightly woody perennial, 8 inches to 2 feet high, with simple erect stems. Basal leaves oblanceolate to spatulate, ¾-inch to 3¼ inches long, ⅛- to ⅜-inch wide, blue-glaucous, entire, petiolate; upper stem-leaves narrowly ovate or linear, sessile. Flowers usually tricolored (blue, red, and violet) or nearly pure blue, 1 to 1⅜ inches long, in somewhat strict panicles; the inflorescence glandular-pubescent. Sterile filament glabrous. Flowering period, July and August.

Keck Penstemon is reported to be rather common in parts of Lassen, Tehama, Butte, and Plumas counties. Dr. Keck, who described the species, believes it to be of hybrid origin, the supposed parents being *P. laetus* and *P. azureus*. The inflorescence resembles that of the former and the stems and leaves are more like those of the latter. Clausen (see Bibl.) gives the chromosome number of this species as "n = 32," that of *P. laetus* "n = 8," and that of *P. azureus* "n = 24."

Penstemon neotericus Keck, Univ. Calif. Publ. Bot. 16:398 (1932). Type locality: "Plumas County, halfway between Chester and Westwood, Lassen County." Collected by *Keck*.

30. **Penstemon laetus** Gray. MOUNTAIN BLUE PENSTEMON. GAY PENSTEMON.

A low tufted perennial, 8 inches to 2½ feet high, from a woody base, with gray- or yellow-green minutely puberulent herbage, not glaucous. Leaf-blades linear to olbong or oblanceolate (rarely filiform), ⅝-inch to 3 inches long (rarely to 4½ inches), entire, sessile, or a few of the upper leaves clasping the stems by their bases. Flowers blue or bright bluish purple, ¾-inch to 1¼ inches long, in loose racemose glandular-pubescent panicles. Peduncles 1- to 4-flowered. Sterile filament glabrous. Flowering period, June and July.

Mountain Blue Penstemon inhabits dry slopes and flats on the western slope of the Sierra Nevada from Yuba and Eldorado counties southward to Tulare County, in the Tehachapi Mountains, on Mount Frazier and Mount Piños, and in the region of Old Fort Tejon in Kern County. It varies much in the shape and size of the leaves, size of the calyx and corolla, and in the shape of the anthers. The following varieties may be distinguished.

Leaves all filiform, the margins usually involute; corolla 9/16- to 13/16-inch long; anthers broadly oval or ovate .... 30a. var. *filiformis*.
Leaves linear or wider, the margins not involute.
  Corolla ¾-inch to 1¼ inches long.
    Anthers narrowly arrow-shaped .... 30b. var. *sagittatus*.
    Anthers broadly oval or ovate; calyx ¼- to 9/16-inch long; sepals linear-lanceolate .... 30c. var. *leptosepalus*.
  Corolla 9/16- to 13/16-inch long .... 30d. var. *Roezlii*.

30a. Var. **filiformis** (Keck) n. comb. Shasta County, "between Lamoine and Sims in the belt of *Pinus ponderosa* and *Quercus garryana* in open stony places along the highway grade." Also below Dunsmuir.

30b. Var. **sagittatus** (Keck) n. comb. In Shasta, Humboldt, Trinity, Siskiyou, and Del Norte counties, chiefly in the "Klamath mountain chains." It also occurs in Josephine County, Oregon.

30c. Var. **leptosepalus** Gray. On the western slope of the Sierra Nevada in Placer, Nevada, Yuba, and Plumas counties and in the Coast Ranges of Tehama County, from 2400 to about 5500 feet elevation.

30d. Var. **Roezlii** (Regel) Jepson. Chiefly in the northern Sierra Nevada from Inyo, Alpine, and Amador counties north to Lassen, Modoc, Siskiyou, and Trinity counties. It extends northward to south-central Oregon and eastward into Nevada about Lake Tahoe.

Penstemon laetus Gray, Proc. Bost. Soc. Nat. Hist. 7:147 (1859). Type locality: "Fort Tejon and vicinity." Collected by *L. J. Xantus.*

Var. filiformis (Keck) McMinn. *P. laetus* subsp. *filiformis* Keck. Type locality: Shasta County, between Lamoine and Sims. Collected by *Heller.*

Var. sagittatus (Keck) McMinn. *P. laetus* subsp. *sagittatus* Keck. Type locality: North side of Mt. Shasta, Siskiyou County. Collected by *H. E. Brown.*

Var. leptosepalus Gray, Syn. Fl. 2:442 (1886). Type locality: "Butte County, California." Collected by *Mrs. Austin.*

Var. Roezlii (Regel) Jepson, Man. 916 (1925). *P. Roezlii* Regel. Type locality: Sierra Nevada of California. Collected by *Roezl.*

31. **Penstemon heterophyllus** Lindl. FOOTHILL BLUE PENSTEMON. CHAPARRAL PENSTEMON.

A low tufted slightly woody perennial, 1 to 2 feet high, with many erect, often reddish stems and grayish, yellowish, or bluish green glabrous or puberulent herbage. Leaf-blades linear to lanceolate or the basal ones oblanceolate, 3/4-inch to 4 inches long, entire, sessile or the upper half clasping the stems by their bases. Inflorescence glabrous. Flowers rose-violet at base, the upper part of corolla-tube and -lobes blue, 3/4-inch to 1 3/8 inches long, solitary and pedunculate in the axils of the upper opposite bract-like leaves, forming a racemose panicle. Sterile filament glabrous. Anthers arrow-shaped. Flowering period, May to July.

Foothill Blue Penstemon is rather common in the foothills of the Coast Ranges from northern Lake County southward to Los Angeles County, in the foothills bordering the Sacramento-San Joaquin Valley, and is found occasionally in San Diego County.

The following varieties may be distinguished.

Leaves 1 1/4 to 2 1/2 (rarely to 3 1/2) inches long, 1/8- to 1/4- (rarely 3/8-) inch wide, only occasionally fascicled; sepals usually glabrous; herbage of inflorescence puberulent . . . . 31a. var. *Purdyi.*

Leaves 3/4-inch to 2 inches long, about 1/8-inch wide, usually fascicled; sepals usually glabrous; herbage puberulent throughout . . . . 31b. var. *australis.*

31a. Var. **Purdyi** (Keck) n. comb. In the Sierra Nevada foothills from Butte County southward to Madera County, and in the North Coast Ranges from Humboldt and Trinity counties southward to Santa Clara and San Benito counties.

31b. Var. **australis** Munz & Johnst. From southern Monterey County southward in the Coast Range to San Diego County. Usually in the chaparral belt from 300 to 6000 feet elevation.

Penstemon heterophyllus Lindl. Bot. Reg. 22:t. 1899 (1836). Type locality: California. Collected by *Douglas.*

Var. Purdyi (Keck) McMinn. *P. heterophyllus* subsp. *Purdyi* Keck. Type locality: Mount Hamilton, Santa Clara County, California. Collected by *Elmer.*

Var. australis Munz & Johnst. Bull. S. Calif. Acad. 23:40 (1924). Type locality: Claremont, California. Collected by *C. F. Baker.*

32. **Penstemon azureus** Benth. SKYBLUE PENSTEMON. AZURE PENSTEMON.

A low glabrous and blue-glaucous perennial, 8 inches to 2 feet high, with several stems from a woody base. Leaf-blades entire, of 2 kinds; the basal ones oblanceolate to obovate, 5/8-inch to 2 1/2 inches long, 1/4- to 3/4-inch wide, with a short petiole-like base; the upper stem-leaves narrowly lanceolate to oblong or ovate, 1/2-inch to 2 1/2 inches long, sessile or half-clasping by their wide bases. Flowers deep purple, 3/4-inch to 1 1/4 inches long, the corolla-tube lilac and the lobes azure-blue, solitary on peduncles in the axils of the upper bract-like leaves; peduncles appressed to the main axis forming a strict racemose or spike-like inflorescence. Sterile filament glabrous. Flowering period, June and July.

Skyblue Penstemon is a variable species occurring in Del Norte, Humboldt, Trinity, Siskiyou, and Modoc counties, and extending southward in the Sierra Nevada at middle altitudes to Placer, Madera, and Fresno counties.

The following varieties may be distinguished.

Corolla 1/2- to 3/4-inch long. . . . . .32a. var. *parvulus.*

Corolla 3/4-inch to 1 1/4 inches long; basal leaves lanceolate but tapering from the middle to the base and apex, 1/8- to 1/4-inch wide. . . . . .32b. var. *angustissimus.*

32a. Var. **parvulus** Gray. At high elevations in the southern Sierra Nevada (southern Fresno and Tulare counties) and in the Siskiyou Mountains between 4500 and 8000 feet elevation.

32b. Var. **angustissimus** Gray. Locally in the inner North Coast Range of Glenn County and in the Sierra Nevada from Madera County northward to eastern Butte County from about 1500 feet to 2600 feet elevation or rarely to 6000 feet.

Penstemon azureus Benth. Pl. Hartw. 327 (1849). Type locality: In dry stream beds of the Sacramento Valley. Collected by *Hartweg. P. Jeffreyanus* Hook. *P. heterophyllus* var. *azureus* Jepson.

Var. parvulus Gray, Syn. Fl. 2:272 (1878). Type locality: Siskiyou Mountains, "in mountains above Jackson Lake, at 8000 feet." Collected by *Greene. P. Jeffreyanus* var. *parvulus* (Gray) Jepson.

Var. angustissimus Gray, Syn. Fl. 2:272 (1878). Type locality: "Yosemite Valley, Etc."

Acanthaceae. Acanthus Family

The Acanthus Family is a large family of 220 genera and about 2000 species, mostly inhabiting tropical and subtropical regions. A single species is native to the Pacific Coast.

1. **Beloperone** Nees.

(From the Greek *belos,* an arrow, and *perone,* something pointed, in reference to the arrow-shaped connectives of the anthers.)

This genus consists of about 30 species of shrubs and subshrubs or herbaceous perennials native to tropical and subtropical America.

1. **Beloperone californica** Benth. CALIFORNIA BELOPERONE. Fig. 623.

A slender almost leafless shrub, 2 to 5 feet high, with greenish or whitish tomentulose branches. Leaves simple, opposite, soon falling; the blades ovate to ovate-lanceolate or round-oval, ¼-inch to 1 inch long, entire; petioles ¼-inch or less long. Flowers dull red, bisexual, solitary in the axils of small successive opposite bracts, in dense clusters; sepals 5, united at base, subtended by a pair of bractlets; petals 5, joined to form a tubular 2-lipped corolla 1 to 1¼ inches long; stamens 2, exserted from the tube; pistil 1, with a superior 2-celled ovary and a filiform style. Fruit a 2-celled tomentose club-shaped capsule with a stalk-like lower part longer than the seed-bearing part, each cell 2-seeded. Flowering period, February to April, but blossoms may be found during every month of the year, depending upon seasonal conditions.

California Beloperone occurs on the western and northern edges of the Colorado Desert in the Lower Sonoran Life Zone, usually near water courses. It extends southward to Lower California and eastward to Arizona.

Beloperone californica Benth. Bot. Voy. Sulph. 38 (1844). Type locality: "Cape San Lucas, Lower California." Collected by *Hinds.*

Bignoniaceae. Catalpa or Bignonia Family

The Catalpa Family contains about 100 genera and 600 species of trees, shrubs, and woody vines, widely distributed in tropical regions, a few extending into the north and south temperate zones. A single genus with one species is native to California.

1. **Chilopsis** D. Don. DESERT-WILLOW

(From the Greek *cheilos,* labium or lip, and *opsis,* resemblance, referring to the 2-lipped corolla.)

A single species and probably 1 or 2 varieties compose this genus.

1. **Chilopsis linearis** (Cav.) Sweet. DESERT-WILLOW. Fig. 624.

An erect or sprawling shrub or sometimes a small tree 10 to 20 feet high, with slender willow-like usually glabrous branchlets. Leaves simple, alternate or some rarely opposite or whorled, deciduous, linear or linear-lanceolate, often curving as a sickle, 2 to 5 inches long, about ¼-inch or less wide, sharply pointed at the attenuate apex, tapering to a narrow base, light green and glabrous, entire, sessile. Flowers large and showy, bisexual, irregular, in short terminal clusters; sepals 5, joined to form a 2-lipped calyx, the upper lip minutely 3-toothed, the lower lip 2-toothed; petals 5, joined and forming a funnel-shaped corolla 1 to 2 inches long bilabiately 5-lobed, pink or whitish with purplish marking; stamens 4, a fifth without anther, attached to the corolla-tube; ovary superior, 2-celled. Fruit a linear capsule, 4 to 10 inches long, the many seeds silky-hairy at both ends. Flowering period, April to July.

Desert-willow inhabits dry washes and stream-beds of the desert in San Diego, Imperial, Riverside, and San Bernardino counties of southern California. It extends eastward to Arizona, Nevada, New Mexico, and western Texas and southward into Mexico and Lower California.

Throughout the range of the species some variation occurs in the glabrous or pubescent and glutinous character of the leaves and branchlets. Most of the Californian plants have glabrous or almost glabrous sterile branchlets and their leaves are usually curved as a sickle. The young leaves are only occasionally glutinous.

The large sweet-scented bignonia-like flowers, long pendulous capsules, and slender willow-like branches make this shrub a desirable one for mixed plantings in regions with semi-desert conditions.

Chilopsis linearis (Cav.) Sweet, Hort. Brit. ed. 1, 283 (1827). *Bignonia linearis* Cav. Type locality: Unknown. *Chilopsis linearis* var. *arcuata* Fosberg.

Rubiaceae. Madder Family

The Madder Family contains about 340 genera and 4500 species of herbs, shrubs, and trees, mainly tropical. Four genera and 27 species are native to California, of which 2 genera with 14 species are somewhat woody. Beverages, quinine and other drugs, dyes, and flavoring are obtained from plants of this family.

KEY TO THE GENERA

Plants distinctly shrubby; leaves 2 inches or more long........1. CEPHALANTHUS.
Plants climbing, vine-like, woody only at base; leaves less than 1 inch long.
2. GALIUM.

1. **Cephalanthus** L. BUTTON BUSH

(From the Greek *kephale,* head, and *anthos,* flower, referring to the arrangement of the flowers in head-like clusters.)

Five or 6 species of *Cephalanthus* have been described from Asia and 2 from North America. Only one occurs in California.

1. **Cephalanthus occidentalis** L. BUTTON BUSH. BUTTON-WILLOW. Fig. 625.

A medium-sized or large shrub, 3 to 12 feet high, sometimes becoming a small tree, with gray or brown bark often furrowed on the older stems and branches. Young branches commonly in whorls of 3, with smooth green, yellow, or sometimes reddish bark. Leaves simple, opposite, or more commonly in whorls of 3, 4, or 5, deciduous; the blades ovate, elliptic, or oblong-elliptic, 3 to 6 inches long, 3/4-inch to 1 1/2 inches wide, acuminate or acute at apex, pale green, glabrous, entire, often wavy-margined; petioles usually 1/4-inch or less (rarely 1 inch) long. Flowers numerous, small, bisexual, sessile, in globose peduncled heads resembling the flower-clusters of the sycamore tree, 1/2-inch to 1 1/2 inches in diameter, 1 to 6 heads terminating the branches; sepals 4, minute, forming a tube about 1/8-inch long, adnate to the ovary; petals 4, united to form a narrow funnel-shaped corolla 1/4- to 1/2-inch long; stamens 4; ovary inferior, 2-celled; style very slender, much exserted. Fruit a dry hard capsule about 1/4-inch long, tardily dehiscent into 2 to 4 achene-like portions. Flowering period, July to September.

Button Bush inhabits living stream-beds of the Sacramento, San Joaquin, and adjacent valleys. It occurs from Siskiyou County southward in the inner Coast Range to Lake and Napa counties and to Tulare County in the Sierra Nevada foothills. It extends northward to Canada, eastward to New Brunswick, and southward to Florida. It is known also from Cuba. The glossy green foliage and clusters of white flowers make it a desirable shrub for ornamental use in moist places.

Cephalanthus occidentalis L. Sp. Pl. 95 (1753). Type locality: North America, "Habitat in America septentrionali."

Fig. 625. BUTTON BUSH. *Cephalanthus occidentalis* L.

2. Galium L. Bedstraw

(From the Greek *gala*, milk, certain species said to be used to curdle milk.)

Annual or perennial herbs, some woody at the base, usually sprawling, with 4-angled stems and branches. Leaves simple, apparently whorled but in reality opposite because the other leaf-like structures at the nodes are stipules. Flowers bisexual or unisexual, regular, solitary or in peduncled clusters; sepals 4, completely fused with the ovary, the calyx-limb nearly obsolete; petals 4, joined at the base; stamens 4; ovary inferior, 2-celled. Fruit of 2 like halves, dry or fleshy, separating when mature into distinct 1-seeded carpels.

This is a large genus of about 225 species widely distributed in various parts of the world. Twenty-four species and several varieties are native to California, 13 of which are somewhat woody at the base.

KEY TO THE SPECIES

Fruit glabrous when mature or slightly pubescent with short hairs.
  Plants with stems or branches 2 to 5 feet long; distinctly woody at least at base.
    Stems usually erect, 2 to 4 feet high; leaves on the main branches ½-inch to 1 inch long; fruit dry. . . . . .1. *G. catalinense*.
    Stems or branches usually climbing; leaves less than ½-inch long; fruit fleshy. 2. *G. Nuttallii*.
  Plants less than 2 feet high; scarcely woody.
    Flowers unisexual and dioecious; fruit sparsely hispid-pubescent; leaves on the main branches broadly oval, ¼- to ¾-inch long; fruit fleshy. 3. *G. pubens*.
    Flowers bisexual; leaves linear to oblong, less than ⅛-inch wide.
      Flowers purple; fruit fleshy. . . . . .4. *G. Bolanderi*.
      Flowers white; fruit dry. . . . . .5. *G. boreale*.
Fruit densely hispid when mature.
  Leaves linear or linear-lanceolate.
    Flowers reddish; stems not at all scabrous, ending in diffuse panicles. 6. *G. Rothrockii*.
    Flowers greenish white or white; panicles usually slender.
      Plants diffuse, with long woody branches, more or less scabrous-pubescent throughout; leaves linear-lanceolate to ovate; flowers white; deserts. 7. *G. stellatum* var. *eremicum*.
      Plants erect, 1 to 4 feet high; stems not scabrous; leaves linear; flowers greenish white. . . . . .8. *G. angustifolium*.
  Leaves ovate-lanceolate to broadly ovate or lanceolate.
    Herbage mostly glabrous.
      Leaves ¼-inch or less long, ovate-lanceolate. . . . . .9. *G. Matthewsii*.
      Leaves 5⁄16- to ¾-inch long, broadly ovate. . . . . .10. *G. multiflorum*.
    Herbage hispid-pubescent throughout.
      Flowers reddish; plants less than 12 inches high, tufted, erect. 11. *G. Parishii*.
      Flowers not red; plants usually decumbent or reclining or spreading, not tufted, sometimes with ascending branches.
        Fruit including hairs ⅛-inch or less broad.
          Leaves lanceolate, mucronate; plants definitely woody at base; stems intricately branched, 4 to 12 inches long; flowers white; panicles crowded. . . . . .7. *G. stellatum*.

Leaves broadly ovate to lance-ovate, not mucronate; plants scarcely woody at base; stems erect or decumbent, 4 to 16 inches tall; flowers brownish; panicles not densely flowered. . . . 12. *G. Munzii.*
Fruit including hairs over 1/8-inch broad; plants shrubby at base, with diffuse and spreading stems 1 to 2 feet long; flowers white; panicles loose, leafy, drooping at the tips. . . . . 13. *G. Hallii.*

1. **Galium catalinense** Gray, Syn. Fl. 1, pt. 2:445 (1886). CATALINA BEDSTRAW. Known only from the Santa Barbara Islands.

2. **Galium Nuttallii** Gray, Pl. Wright. 1:80 (1852). NUTTALL BEDSTRAW. Fig. 626. Rather common in the Coast Ranges from Siskiyou County to Monterey County, in the lower Sierra Nevada from Eldorado County to Fresno County, in the mountains of southern California, and on Santa Cruz and Santa Catalina islands. It extends northward into southern Oregon and southward into Lower California.

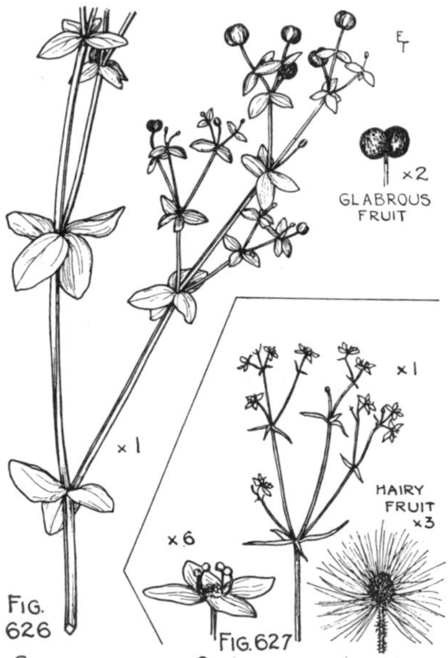

FIG. 626 GALIUM NUTTALLII
FIG. 627 GALIUM STELLATUM VAR. EREMICUM

3. **Galium pubens** Gray, Proc. Am. Acad. 7:350 (1868). HAIRY BEDSTRAW. In the Sierra Nevada from Kern County north to Plumas County, the North Coast Ranges of Napa and Lake Counties, and in the San Gabriel Mountains of Los Angeles County.

4. **Galium Bolanderi** Gray, Proc. Am. Acad. 7:350 (1868). BOLANDER BEDSTRAW. In the North Coast Ranges to Siskiyou County and south in the Sierra Nevada to Mariposa County.

5. **Galium boreale** L. Sp. Pl. 108 (1753). NORTHERN BEDSTRAW. Known in California only from Humboldt and Shasta counties. North to Alaska, east to New Jersey.

6. **Galium Rothrockii** Gray, Proc. Am. Acad. 17:203 (1882). ROTHROCK BEDSTRAW. Rare in California, known only from the Clark and Providence mountains of eastern San Bernardino County. East to Arizona and New Mexico.

7. **Galium stellatum** var. **eremicum** Hilend & Howell, Leafl. West. Bot. 1:137 (1934). DESERT BEDSTRAW. Fig. 627. On the Colorado and Mohave deserts of California, and eastward to Arizona and Nevada. The species in its typical form occurs only on Cedros Island.

8. **Galium angustifolium** Nutt.; T. & G. Fl. N. Am. 2:22 (1841). CHAPARRAL BEDSTRAW. In the foothills and on the lower mountain slopes from San Benito and Monterey counties southward to San Diego County.

9. **Galium Matthewsii** Gray, Proc. Am. Acad. 19:80 (1883). MATTHEWS BEDSTRAW. Known only from Inyo County and western Nevada.

10. **Galium multiflorum** Kell. Proc. Calif. Acad. 2:96 (1863). TUFTED BEDSTRAW. Occurs mostly in the northern Sierra Nevada, in Trinity and Siskiyou counties, and southward to Lake County.

11. **Galium Parishii** Hilend & Howell, Leafl. West. Bot. 1:136 (1934). PARISH BEDSTRAW. *G. multiflorum* var. *parvifolium* Parish. *G. parvifolium* (Parish) Jepson, not Gaud. On gravelly slopes and ridges from 6000 to 10,000 feet elevation in the San Gabriel, San Bernardino, San Jacinto, New York, and Santa Rosa mountains of southern California.

12. **Galium Munzii** Hilend & Howell, Leafl. West. Bot. 1:135 (1934). MUNZ BEDSTRAW. *G. Matthewsii* var. *scabridum* Jepson. Known from the White Mountains of Inyo County, from the northern base of the San Bernardino Mountains, and from the Providence Mountains of San Bernardino County. Also in the Charleston Mountains of Nevada.

13. **Galium Hallii** Munz & Johnst. Bull. Torr. Club 49:358 (1922). HALL BEDSTRAW. On dry slopes of the mountains bordering the western side of the Mohave Desert from 4000 to 7000 feet elevation (San Rafael Mountains of Santa Barbara County, Tehachapi Mountains, the southern Sierra Nevada of Kern County, and the San Bernardino Mountains).

Caprifoliaceae. Honeysuckle Family

The Honeysuckle Family contains 11 genera and about 350 species of trees, shrubs, vines, or rarely herbs, chiefly of the north temperate zone, a few in the tropical mountains, and some in South America and Australia. Five genera and 17 species are native to California. All are woody except one.

KEY TO THE GENERA

Leaves compound..1. SAMBUCUS.
Leaves simple.
  Leaves 3- to 5-veined from the base, coarsely dentate except at base . 2. VIBURNUM.
  Leaves 1-veined from the base, entire or lobed.
    Corolla regular; berry snow-white......................3. SYMPHORICARPOS.
    Corolla usually somewhat irregular; berry red or black.........4. LONICERA.

1. **Sambucus** L. ELDERBERRY

(From the Greek, *sambuke,* a musical instrument, made of elder wood.)

Shrubs or trees with usually very pithy branches. Leaves odd-pinnately compound, opposite, deciduous. Flowers small, whitish or cream-color, bisexual, regular, in terminal compound clusters; calyx-lobes generally 5, minute or almost absent; corolla saucer-shaped, 5-lobed; stamens 5, distinct, inserted on the base of the corolla and alternate with its lobes; ovary inferior, 3- to 5-celled; stigmas 3 to 5. Fruit a 3- to 5-celled berry-like drupe with 3 to 5 one-seeded nutlets.

This genus contains about 20 species and is most abundantly represented in the north temperate zone, but is found in almost all parts of the world. Two species and 3 varieties are native to California.

KEY TO THE SPECIES

Flowers in flat-topped clusters, the main axis not continuous; fruit blue-gray to nearly black, usually covered with a bloom.................1. *S. coerulea.*

Fig. 628. BLUE ELDERBERRY. *Sambucus coerulea* Raf.

Flowers in dome-shaped clusters, the main axis continuous........2. *S. racemosa.*

1. **Sambucus coerulea** Raf. BLUE ELDERBERRY. Fig. 628.

KEY TO THE SPECIES AND VARIETY

Leaflets usually glabrous.......................................*S. coerulea.*
Leaflets usually pubescent...................................1a. var. *velutina.*

A shrub, 4 to 10 feet high or developing into a small tree up to 30 feet high, with glabrous or soft-pubescent and often glaucous branchlets. Leaves 5 to 8 inches long; leaflets 5 to 9, firm, narrowly oblong or ovate-lanceolate to nearly orbicular, 1 to 6 inches long, ½-inch to 2 inches wide, the lateral ones usually unequal at base, varying from glabrous or soft-pubescent to short-hispid, sharply and finely serrate except at the abruptly acuminate apex, short-petiolulate or sessile, the lower leaflets sometimes 3-parted or pinnate. Flowers white or cream-color, numerous in flat-topped branched clusters 2 to 8 inches broad. Fruit subglobose, about ¼-inch in diameter, blue to nearly black, usually covered with a whitish bloom. Flowering period, April to August.

Blue Elderberry has a wide distribution in California. It usually inhabits moist places in the coastal and interior valleys, the lower and middle altitudes of the Sierra Nevada, the Coast Ranges, and the mountains of southern California. It extends northward to British Columbia, eastward to the Rocky Mountains from Alberta to Arizona, and southward to Lower California, Sonora, and Chihuahua, Mexico.

This species is quite variable in the size, shape, and pubescence of its leaflets. In the Coast Ranges and the Great Valley the leaflets are usually quite glabrous, though many plants occur with the pubescent leaflets which are characteristic of the shrubs of the higher Sierra Nevada and southern California.

1a. Var. **velutina** (D. & H.) Schwerin. Fig. 630.

Branchlets densely soft-pubescent or sometimes nearly glabrous. Leaflets usually very unequal at base and soft-pubescent or short-hispid and harsh to the touch. Flowering period, June to August.

This variety occurs in the Sierra Nevada and the mountains of southern California usually at higher elevations than the species. However, some specimens have nearly glabrous leaflets and therefore the retention of this form as a variety has been done with some reluctance.

Sambucus coerulea Raf. Alsog. Am. 48 (1838). Type locality: "Mentioned by Lewis and Clark trav. 2, p. 160, as growing near Oregon Mts." *S. glauca* Nutt.

Var. velutina (D. & H.) Schwerin, Mitt. Deutsch. Dendr. Ges. 1909:37 & 328 (1909). *S. velutina* D. & H. *S. mexicana* var. *velutina* Dur. Type locality: Poso Creek, Kern County, California. Collected by *Heermann*.

2. **Sambucus racemosa** L. RED ELDERBERRY. Fig. 631.

KEY TO THE SPECIES AND VARIETIES

Fruit red.
Leaflets usually glabrous.......................................*S. racemosa.*
Leaflets usually pubescent.............................2a. var. *callicarpa.*
Fruit black; leaflets usually glabrous....................2b. var. *melanocarpa.*

A shrub, 2 to 6 feet high, with the young stems and branches green, the pith brownish. Leaves 3 to 6 inches long; leaflets 5 or 7 (rarely 3), ovate to ovate-lanceo-

Fig. 629. Coast Red Elderberry. *Sambucus racemosa* var. *callicarpa* (Greene) Jepson.

late or elliptic, $1\frac{1}{2}$ to 5 inches long, $\frac{3}{4}$-inch to $1\frac{1}{2}$ inches wide, equal or only slightly unequal at base, long-acuminate at apex, glabrous or sometimes finely pubescent beneath, sharply serrate except at the very apex, sessile or short-petiolulate. Flowers cream-color to nearly white, in compound dome-shape clusters $1\frac{1}{2}$ to $2\frac{1}{2}$ inches broad. Fruit bright red, about $\frac{3}{16}$-inch in diameter. Flowering period, May to July.

Red Elderberry inhabits moist places in the Sierra Nevada from 6000 to 11,800 feet elevation from Tulare County north to Nevada County and in the San Bernardino Mountains (Dollar Lake, *Louis Wheeler*) of southern California. It extends northward to British Columbia, eastward to Newfoundland, and thence south to Georgia. It occurs also in Europe. Cattle and sheep browse upon the foliage. The bright red berries against the green foliage are very decorative from late July to October. They are reputed to be somewhat poisonous to humans but sheep eat them without ill effects.

2a. Var. **callicarpa** (Greene) Jepson. COAST RED ELDERBERRY. Figs. 629, 632.

A shrub or sometimes a small tree, 8 to 20 feet high. Leaflets pubescent beneath and often above, usually serrate to the very apex. Flower-clusters 2 to 5 inches broad. Fruit bright red.

This variety occurs in moist canyons and on flats in the outer Coast Range from San Mateo County northward to Del Norte County and eastward into western Siskiyou County. It extends northward to Washington. The large clusters of bright red berries from July to September make this shrub one of the attractive landscape features along the northern section of the Redwood Highway. It is easily propagated from cuttings.

2b. Var. **melanocarpa** (Gray) n. comb.

Leaflets glabrous or the younger slightly pubescent. Fruit black, without bloom, $\frac{1}{8}$- to $\frac{1}{4}$-inch in diameter.

This variety is rare in California. It has been collected in Tulare County (Olanche Mt.), Lake Tahoe region, and Siskiyou County. It occurs more commonly in the Rocky Mountains.

Sambucus racemosa L. Sp. Pl. 270 (1753). Type locality: "Habitat in Europa australis montosis." *S. pubens* Michx.

Var. callicarpa (Greene) Jepson, Fl. W. Mid. Calif. 471 (1901). *S. callicarpa* Greene. Type locality: "Coast Ranges," California.

Var. melanocarpa (Gray) McMinn. *S. melanocarpa* Gray. Type locality: "in New Mexico." Collected by *Fendler*.

2. **Viburnum** L.

(The Latin name of the Wayfaring Tree.)

This genus contains over 100 species, widely distributed throughout the north temperate zone, as well as in northern Africa and in Central and South America. Only one species is native to California.

1. **Viburnum ellipticum** Hook. WESTERN VIBURNUM. Fig. 633.

A slender shrub, 3 to 12 feet high, with cinnamon-brown bark on the young branchlets. Leaves simple, opposite, deciduous; the blades round to elliptical, 1 to 3 inches long, $\frac{3}{4}$-inch to 2 inches wide, 3- to 5-veined from the base, coarsely dentate except at the base, glabrous or sparingly pubescent above, paler and finely pubescent beneath; petioles $\frac{1}{4}$- to $\frac{1}{2}$-inch long. Flowers white, $\frac{1}{4}$- to $\frac{1}{3}$-inch wide,

FIG. 630 SAMBUCUS COERULEA VAR. VELUTINA

FIG. 632 S. RACEMOSA VAR. CALLICARPA

FIG. 631 SAMBUCUS RACEMOSA

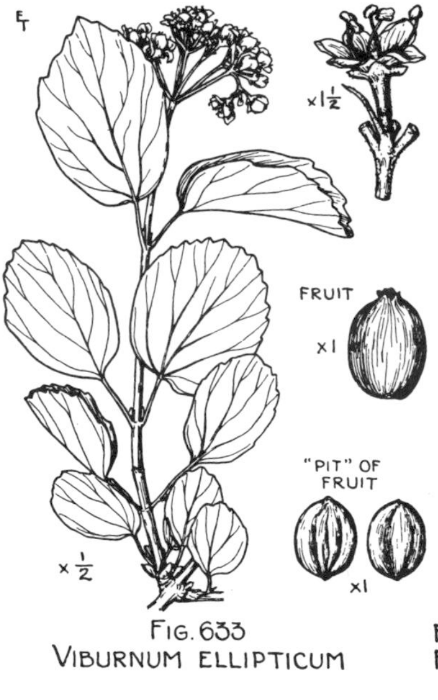

FIG. 633 VIBURNUM ELLIPTICUM

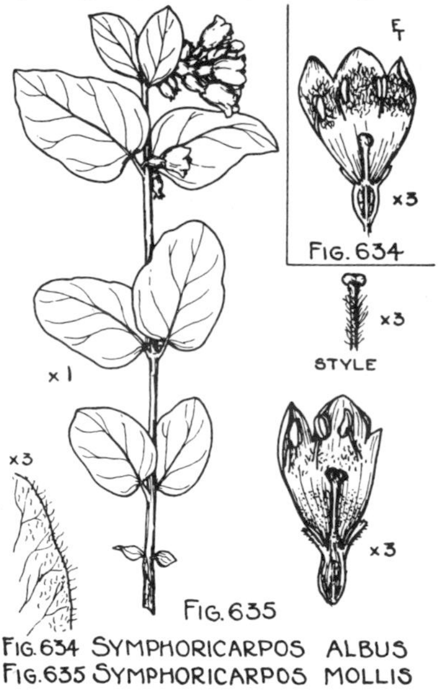

FIG. 634 SYMPHORICARPOS ALBUS
FIG. 635 SYMPHORICARPOS MOLLIS

jointed on the pedicels in terminal compound peduncled clusters; sepals 5, united at base; petals 5, joined to form a spreading tubular corolla 1/4- to 1/3-inch long; stamens 5; ovary inferior, 1-celled. Fruit a black ellipsoidal drupe, about 1/2-inch long; the stone with 5 grooves, 2 on one side and 3 on the other. Flowering period, April to June.

Western Viburnum is not a common shrub in California. It is known in the North Coast Ranges in Sonoma (El Cerrito Ranch, *Mrs. R. Kuhn*), Mendocino (Long Valley; Cummings Creek; near Blue Rock, *J. B. Davy*), Humboldt, and Glenn counties ("near the old sawmill site west of Bennett Spring on the Newville-Covelo Road, el. about 3000 ft. on a wooded N. slope in the Yellow Pine Belt," *Heller*). It has also been collected from near Placerville, Eldorado County and may be expected elsewhere on the western slope of the Sierra Nevada. The range extends northward to Oregon and Washington.

Viburnum ellipticum Hook. Fl. Bor. Am. 1:280 (1833). Type locality: "Common on the branches of the Columbia, near its confluence with the Pacific." Collected by *Douglas*.

3. **Symphoricarpos** L. WAXBERRY. SNOWBERRY

(From the Greek *sumphoreo,* to bear in clusters, and *karpos,* fruit, in reference to the fruit in clusters.)

Shrubs of low or medium height, with prostrate or upright stems, often spreading by suckers. Leaves simple, opposite, deciduous. Flowers bisexual, regular, pink or white, in small terminal or axillary clusters; receptocalyx surmounted by 4 or 5 calyx-teeth; corolla-tube usually bell-shaped, or tubular-funnelform, 4- or 5-lobed; stamens 4 or 5, adnate to the corolla-tube and alternate with its lobes; ovary 4-celled, 2 cells of which contain a single ovule, the other 2 cells bear abortive ovules which never mature. Fruit a globose or ovoid 4-celled 2-seeded berry.

This genus contains from 10 to 15 variable species, all of which are native to North America. Four species are here included as native to California.

KEY TO THE SPECIES

Corolla bell-shaped, 1/8- to 1/4-inch long, the tube hairy within near and above the insertion of stamens.

Plants erect, 2 to 6 feet high; leaves on fertile shoots 3/4-inch to 2 inches long, glabrous above, the margins not ciliate........................1. *S. albus*.

Plants low and diffuse or semi-prostrate, 6 to 18 inches high; leaves on fertile shoots 1/2- to 3/4-inch long, usually finely pubescent on both surfaces, the margins ciliate...2. *S. mollis*.

Corolla elongate-campanulate to tubular-funnelform, 1/4- to 5/8-inch long, the tube not hairy within above the insertion of stamens.

Corolla 1/4- to 3/8-inch long, the tube pubescent within below the stamens. 3. *S. rotundifolius*.

Corolla 3/8- to 5/8-inch long, the tube glabrous within.........4. *S. longiflorus*.

1. **Symphoricarpos albus** (L.) Blake. COMMON SNOWBERRY. Figs. 634, 636.

An erect or spreading shrub, 2 to 6 feet high, with slender branches, thin light brown bark on young growth and shreddy gray or dark brown bark on older branches. Leaf-blades ovate, oval, or broadly elliptical to almost round, 3/4-inch to 2 inches long (sometimes up to 4 inches on young sterile shoots growing in the shade), 1/2-inch to 1 1/2 (rarely 3) inches wide, dull green and glabrous above, paler

Fig. 636. COMMON SNOWBERRY. *Symphoricarpos albus* (L.) Blake.

and glabrous or somewhat pubescent beneath, entire or sinuately lobed on the same branch (leaves on young, sterile shoots more commonly lobed); petioles 1/8- to 1/4-inch long. Flowers several, in small clusters in the axils of the leaves or terminating the branchlets; calyx-teeth 4 or 5, minute; corolla pink, bell-shaped, 1/8- to 1/4-inch long, cleft nearly to the middle, the tube slightly distended on one side, glabrous without, the throat with numerous long white hairs; style glabrous. Fruit white, globose, 3/8- to 1/2-inch in diameter. Flowering period, May and June.

Common Snowberry inhabits slopes and valley bottoms of the foothills of the Coast Ranges, the Sierra Nevada, and the mountains of southern California, usually at elevations below 2000 feet. It extends northward to British Columbia and eastward to Pennsylvania and the New England states. The clusters of pink flowers in May and June, followed by the clusters of white berries which remain on the plants during late summer and fall, make this shrub very desirable for ornamental planting. It is easily propagated from cuttings or sections of old plants. As a browse plant in the West, it ranks among the best for cattle and sheep.

Symphoricarpos albus (L.) Blake, Rhodora 16:117 (1914). *Vaccinium album* L. Type locality: Pennsylvania. Collected by *Kalm*. *S. racemosus* Michx.

2. **Symphoricarpos mollis** Nutt. SPREADING SNOWBERRY. CREEPING SNOWBERRY. Fig. 635.

A low diffuse or decumbent straggling shrub, usually less than 18 inches high, but often with stems several feet long. Leaf-blades broadly oval or elliptical or nearly round, 1/2- to 3/4-inch long on the fertile shoots, usually larger on the sterile shoots, soft-pubescent on both surfaces or nearly glabrous above, usually more pubescent beneath and appearing whitish, entire or lobed or rarely toothed, usually ciliate on the margins; petioles 1/8- to 1/4-inch long. Flowers in short clusters, or rarely 1 or 2 in the leaf-axils; corolla pinkish, about 1/8-inch long, slightly to densely bearded within; style usually glabrous but sometimes hairy. Fruit usually globose, about 1/4-inch long. Flowering period, April to June.

Spreading Snowberry inhabits the wooded hills and mountain slopes of the Coast Ranges, the Sierra Nevada, and the mountains of southern California. It also occurs on Santa Catalina, Santa Cruz, and Santa Rosa islands. Its range extends north to Washington. In the Oakland hills, the hills of Santa Clara County, and in the Sierra Nevada, this species becomes nearly prostrate but in southern California it is a more straggling shrub and often approaches *S. albus* in habit of growth.

Specimens of *S. albus* and *S. mollis* transplanted to the experimental plot at Mills College have retained their respective differences for several years. The prostrate habit, earlier flowering period, fewer flowers, and smaller fruit easily distinguish *S. mollis* from *S. albus*.

Symphoricarpos mollis Nutt.; T. & G. Fl. N. Am. 2:4 (1841). Type locality: Santa Barbara, California. Collected by *Nuttall*. *S. ciliatus* Nutt. *S. albus* var. *mollis* (Nutt.) Keck.

3. **Symphoricarpos rotundifolius** Gray. MOUNTAIN SNOWBERRY. ROUNDLEAF SNOWBERRY. Fig. 637.

A straggling shrub, 1 to 4 feet high, with reddish brown bark on new growth and shreddy grayish or brown bark on older branches. Branchlets and foliage usually finely pubescent. Leaf-blades ovate, elliptical to broadly oval, or almost round, rounded or rarely acutish at base and apex, 1/2-inch to 1 inch long, 1/8- to 3/4-inch

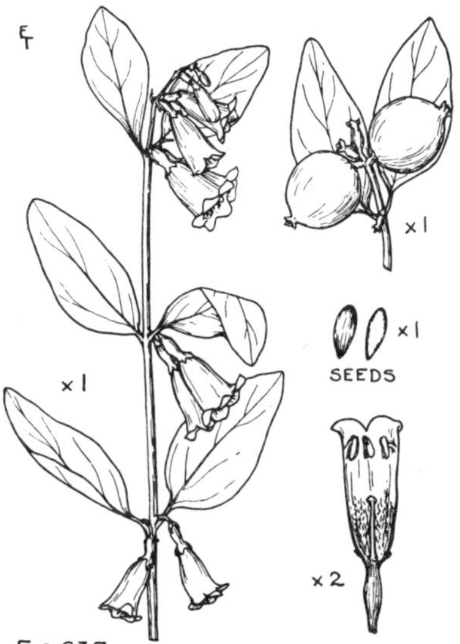

FIG. 637
SYMPHORICARPOS ROTUNDIFOLIUS

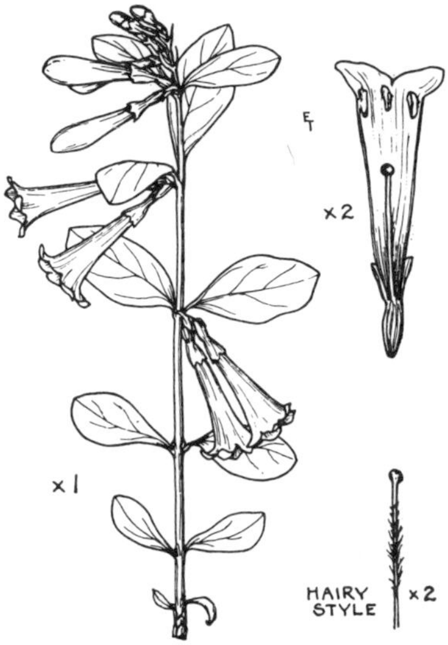

FIG. 638
SYMPHORICARPOS LONGIFLORUS

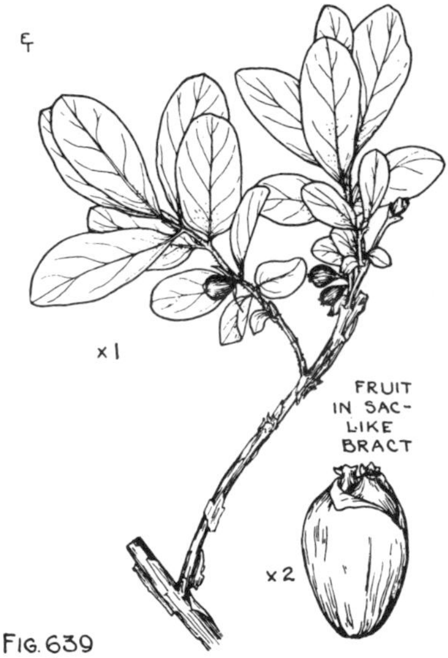

FIG. 639
LONICERA COERULEA

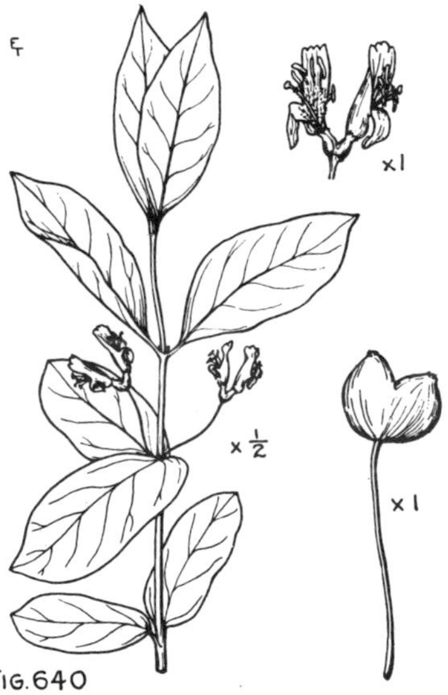

FIG. 640
LONICERA CONJUGIALIS

wide, usually dull green and finely pubescent above (rarely almost glabrous), paler and finely pubescent beneath, the margins entire, or rarely irregularly toothed or some slightly lobed; petioles 1/8-inch or less long. Flowers sessile, in pairs or in small clusters in the axils of the upper leaves, or terminating the branchlets; corolla white, yellowish, or pink, tubular-funnelform, 1/4- to 3/8-inch long, glabrous without, hairy within below the stamens, the tube about 4 times the length of the lobes; style glabrous. Fruit white, ovoid, about 3/8-inch long, enclosing 2 bony seeds which are either obtuse at both ends or very commonly acute at base. Flowering period, June and July.

Mountain Snowberry occurs in the higher mountain regions of the North Coast Range from northern Lake County to Humboldt, Shasta, and Siskiyou counties, eastward in Modoc County, southward in the Sierra Nevada, at 5000 to 10,000 feet elevation, to Tulare County, and in the higher mountains of southern California (San Jacinto, San Antonio, Santa Rosa, San Bernardino, San Gabriel, Laguna, and Topatopa mountains). It extends northward into Oregon and Washington and eastward to the Rocky Mountains. Throughout its range it undergoes much variation in thickness, shape, and pubescent character of leaves, size of corolla, pubescence within the corolla-tube, and size and shape of the bony seeds. Upon the basis of these variations many species and varieties have been described but since no constant character has been found to distinguish them it has seemed advisable to include them all under the earliest name, *Symphoricarpos rotundifolius*.

This snowberry, like most of the other species, is a valuable browse plant for livestock and deer on the western ranges.

Symphoricarpos rotundifolius Gray, Pl. Wright. 2:66 (1853). Type locality: "Sides of mountains around the copper mines, New Mexico." Collected by *C. Wright*. *S. oreophilus* Gray. *S. Parishii* Rydb. *S. parvifolius* Eastw. *S. acutus* Howell. *S. montanus* Gray. *S. Austinae* Eastw. *S. rotundifolius* var. *oreophilus* Jones.

4. **Symphoricarpos longiflorus** Gray. DESERT SNOWBERRY. Fig. 638.

An intricately branched shrub, 2 to 4 feet high, with glabrous or minutely pubescent branches. Leaf-blades oval to spatulate-oblong, or oblong-ovate to elliptic, 3/8- to 5/8-inch long, 1/8- to 3/8-inch wide, grayish, pubescent and very glaucous beneath, entire; petioles 1/8-inch or less long. Flowers sessile, 1, 2, or 3 in the axils of the upper leaves; corolla white, shading to pink, tubular-funnelform, 3/8- to 5/8-inch long, the tube glabrous within; style barbate or glabrous. Fruit white, ellipsoidal, about 3/8-inch long, with 2 oblong bony seeds. Flowering period, May and June.

In California, Desert Snowberry occurs in the Argus, Panamint, and Providence mountains, in the Upper Sonoran and Arid Transition Life Zones. It extends eastward into Nevada, Utah, Arizona, and Texas in the foothills and canyons of the *Artemisia,* Piñon Pine, and Yellow Pine belts.

This species is very closely related to *S. rotundifolius* which varies greatly in its characters in the dry mountain regions east of the Sierra Nevada and in the Great Basin area. The former can be distinguished by its longer corolla. The flowers examined on the type specimen have slightly barbate styles, but this character is not constant.

Symphoricarpos longiflorus Gray, Jour. Linn. Soc. 14:12 (1873). Type locality: Pahranagat Mountains in southeastern Nevada. Collected by *Miss Searles*. *Symphoricarpos fragrans* Nels. & Kennedy.

4. **Lonicera** L. Honeysuckle

(Named for Adam Lonitzer, a German herbalist of the 16th century.)

Erect shrubs or woody twining vines. Leaves simple, opposite, the uppermost pair sometimes joined at base. Flowers in interrupted terminal spikes, heads, or axillary clusters; receptocalyx ovoid or globose, surmounted by 5 minute calyx-teeth or none; corolla-tube funnel-, trumpet-, or bell-shaped, 5-lobed, distinctly 2-lipped or only slightly irregular, often more or less swollen or distended on one side at base; stamens 5, adnate to the corolla-tube and alternate with its lobes; ovary 2- or 3-celled. Fruit a fleshy 2- or 3-celled few-seeded berry.

This genus includes about 100 species, chiefly of the north temperate zone. Ten species are native to California.

KEY TO THE SPECIES

Flowers borne in pairs on a common peduncle in the leaf-axils; leaves deciduous; erect shrubs.
- Peduncles 1/4-inch or less long; the two ovaries and berries enclosed in sac-like juicy bractlets, the whole appearing as one fleshy berry; flowers yellowish. 1. *L. coerulea.*
- Peduncles 1/2- to 1 inch long; berries not enclosed in the juicy sac-like bractlets.
  - Flowers subtended by large broad bracts becoming reddish in age; corolla yellow or reddish, nearly regular. 2. *L. involucrata.*
  - Flowers subtended by very minute bractlets or the bractlets often absent; corolla 2-lipped.
    - Flowers purple-black; the two ovaries partially or totally joined. 3. *L. conjugialis.*
    - Flowers white to salmon-color; the two ovaries entirely distinct. 4. *L. utahensis.*

Flowers sessile, borne in whorls, in terminal spikes or panicles, sometimes in a single whorl.
- Flower-whorls single, rarely 2 or 3, terminal; leaves very glaucous beneath, the margins with hairs, deciduous; corolla 3/4-inch or more long. . . 5. *L. ciliosa.*
- Flower-whorls in terminal spikes or panicles, rarely single; leaves evergreen; corolla 3/4-inch or less long.
  - Leaves all distinct, rarely the upper pair slightly connate; inflorescence glandular-pubescent.
    - Leaf-blades linear-oblong to oblong, over twice as long as wide; corolla about 3/8-inch long. . . . . 7. *L. subspicata.*
    - Leaf-blades oblong-ovate to nearly orbicular, not over 2 times longer than broad; corolla about 1/2-inch long.
      - Leaves distinctly white-pubescent beneath. . . . . 6. *L. Johnstonii.*
      - Leaves yellowish and nearly glabrate beneath. . . . . 8. *L. denudata.*
  - Upper leaves connate or rarely all distinct; stems glaucous.
    - Leaves without stipules; inflorescence glabrous; corolla yellow or reddish-tinged, 3/8- to 1/2-inch long, glabrous without; woody trunk 1 foot or more high . . . . 9. *L. interrupta.*
    - Leaves, except the lower, usually with stipular appendages; inflorescence glandular-pubescent; corolla pinkish or purplish, 7/16- to 11/16-inch long, glandular-pubescent without; without an erect woody trunk. 10. *L. hispidula.*

1. **Lonicera coerulea** L. MOUNTAIN FLY HONEYSUCKLE. Fig. 639.

A low erect shrub, 1 to 3 feet high, with very shreddy light brown bark, and pubescent or nearly glabrous branchlets. Leaf-blades membranous, oval, elliptic, ovate or obovate, rounded at apex, rounded or narrowed at base, 3/4-inch to 2 inches long, 1/4- to 3/4-inch wide, the upper surface glabrous or pubescent, the lower surface paler and with long hairs, often glabrous in age, the margins entire and ciliate; petioles 1/4-inch or less long. Flowers in pairs in the axils of the leaves; peduncle about 1/4-inch long; the 2 bracts at base of ovaries awl-shaped; ovaries of the two flowers completely surrounded by the juicy cup-like bractlets, thus apparently united; calyx-border very minute, scarcely lobed; corolla yellow, funnelform, 1/4- to 1/2-inch long, the tube slightly sac-like on one side at base, the lobes nearly equal, about as long as the tube, hairy within. Fruit bluish-black, oval, about 1/4-inch in diameter, bearing scars of the two flowers near the summit. Flowering period, May and June.

This honeysuckle occurs in the Sierra Nevada where it is known in Tulare, Mariposa, Tuolumne, and Nevada counties between 5000 and 8000 feet elevation. It has a wide distribution outside California, extending around the world in the northern hemisphere.

Lonicera coerulea L. Sp. Pl. 174 (1753). Type locality: "Habitat in Helvetia."

2. **Lonicera involucrata** (Richardson) Banks. TWINBERRY. Fig. 641.

An upright deciduous shrub, 2 to 10 feet high, with the season's branches angled. Leaf-blades ovate, oval, or obovate, tapering at the apex, narrowed or rounded at the base, 2 to 5 inches long, 3/4-inch to 2 1/2 inches wide, dark green and glabrous above, paler and pubescent beneath or becoming glabrous in age, the margins entire, often ciliate; petioles 1/4- to 1/2-inch long. Flowers in pairs in the leaf-axils, on a peduncle 1/2-inch to 1 inch long; the two bracts at the summit of peduncle ovate or oblong, about 1/2-inch long, becoming reddish in age, subtending the united bractlets which enlarge and become fleshy and black with ripening of the fruit; corolla yellow or reddish-tinged, nearly cylindrical, about 1/2-inch long, viscid-pubescent, the tube enlarged on one side at base, the lobes nearly equal, about 1/3 as long as the tube; ovaries separated from each other. Fruit black, oval or globose, about 1/3-inch in diameter. Flowering period, March to July.

Twinberry occurs in moist shady places of canyon bottoms and flats, and along mountain streams of the Sierra Nevada and Coast Ranges, from sea level to 9500 feet elevation. It extends in the Sierra Nevada from Modoc County southward to Tulare County and in the Coast Ranges from Del Norte County southward to Santa Barbara County. This species is widely distributed across North America from Quebec westward to Alaska and British Columbia and southward into California, Colorado, Utah, and Arizona.

In the Sierra Nevada it is usually much smaller than in the Coast Ranges, the corolla rarely becomes tinged with red and the anthers are often slightly exserted. By some authors the plants of the Sierra Nevada are considered the typical form of the species, while others consider them to be *L. involucrata* var. *flavescens* Rehd.

In the Coast Ranges the plants grow from 4 to 10 feet high, the corolla often becomes tinged with red, and the anthers are included within the corolla. This form has been recognized as *L. Ledebourii* Esch. by some authors while others consider it *L. involucrata* var. *Ledebourii* (Esch.) Hort. Since these differences are too variable and of little consequence in so variable a genus, it seems best in this work to include the Sierra Nevada and Coast Range plants in one species.

Fig. 641. TWINBERRY. *Lonicera involucrata* (Richardson) Banks.

The plants are easily propagated from cuttings. They grow well in moist or semi-moist conditions and are very attractive when in flower and fruit. The berries have a bitter taste and are of no known economic value.

Lonicera involucrata (Richardson) Banks; Spreng. Syst. Veg. 1:759 (1825). *Xylosteum involucratum* Richardson. Type locality: "Wooded country from 54 deg. to 64 deg. north." British America. *L. Ledebourii* Esch. *L. involucrata* var. *Ledebourii* (Esch.) Hort.; Zabel.

3. **Lonicera conjugialis** Kell. Double Honeysuckle. Fig. 640.

A straggling slender deciduous shrub, 2 to 5 feet high, with soft-pubescent branchlets. Leaf-blades oval, oblong-ovate, elliptical, or obovate, commonly tapering at apex and base, or rounded at apex, 3/4-inch to 2 1/2 inches long, 1/2-inch to 1 1/2 inches wide, thin, light green, glabrous or sparingly pubescent above, lighter and more pubescent beneath, entire; petioles about 1/8-inch long. Flowers in pairs, on a common slender peduncle 3/4-inch to 1 inch long, the latter borne in the axils of the opposite leaves; bracts minute or nearly wanting; ovaries of the two flowers wholly or partially joined; corolla dull purple, 1/4- to 3/8-inch long, strongly 2-lipped, the upper lip barely 4-toothed, the lower lip deflexed, the throat of corolla with the base of the filaments and style soft white-hairy, the tube swollen below the lower lip. Fruit bright red, composed of the two joined ripened ovaries, about 1/4-inch long. Flowering period, June and July.

Double Honeysuckle occurs in the Sierra Nevada from Tulare County northward to Modoc County, westward to Siskiyou, Trinity, and Humboldt counties, in the Canadian Life Zone from 6500 to 10,000 feet elevation. It extends northward into Oregon and Washington and eastward into western Nevada. It is the most common honeysuckle in the Lake Tahoe and upper Yosemite regions.

Lonicera conjugialis Kell. Proc. Calif. Acad. 2:67 (1863). Type locality: Washoe, Nevada. Collected by *J. A. Veatch*.

4. **Lonicera utahensis** Wats. Utah Honeysuckle. Fig. 642.

A low deciduous shrub, 2 to 5 feet high, with wide-spreading slender branches. Leaf-blades oval or oblong-ovate, rounded or very blunt at apex, rounded or sometimes heart-shaped at base, 1 to 2 1/4 inches long, 1/2-inch to 1 1/4 inches wide, thin, glabrous on both surfaces, or sometimes slightly pubescent beneath, entire; petioles 1/4-inch or less long. Flowers in pairs on a common slender peduncle 1/2- to 3/4-inch long; the 2 bracts slender, about 1/2 as long to as long as the ovaries, the latter divergent at base and not joined; corolla white or light yellow, fading to a salmon-yellow, about 3/4-inch rarely 1 inch long, funnelform, with a distended swelling on one side at base, this tinged with pink, the lobes about equal in shape and size but arranged in a 2-lipped position. Fruit red, globular, about 1/4-inch in diameter. Flowering period, May and June.

Utah Honeysuckle has been found in California only in Siskiyou County, near Yreka. It is a plant of the Northwest, being found from British Columbia to Alberta and southward through Montana, Wyoming, Utah, Washington, Idaho, and Oregon (Union and Wallowa counties).

Lonicera utahensis Wats. Bot. King's Expl. 133 (1871). Type locality: "Wahsatch mountains, Utah, in Cottonwood Cañon: 9000 feet altitude." Collected by *Watson*.

5. **Lonicera ciliosa** (Pursh) Poir. Orange Honeysuckle. Fig. 643.

A low trailing vine-like deciduous shrub, 2 to 18 feet in length. Leaf-blades ovate or broadly elliptic, rounded or pointed at apex, rounded or broadly wedge-shaped

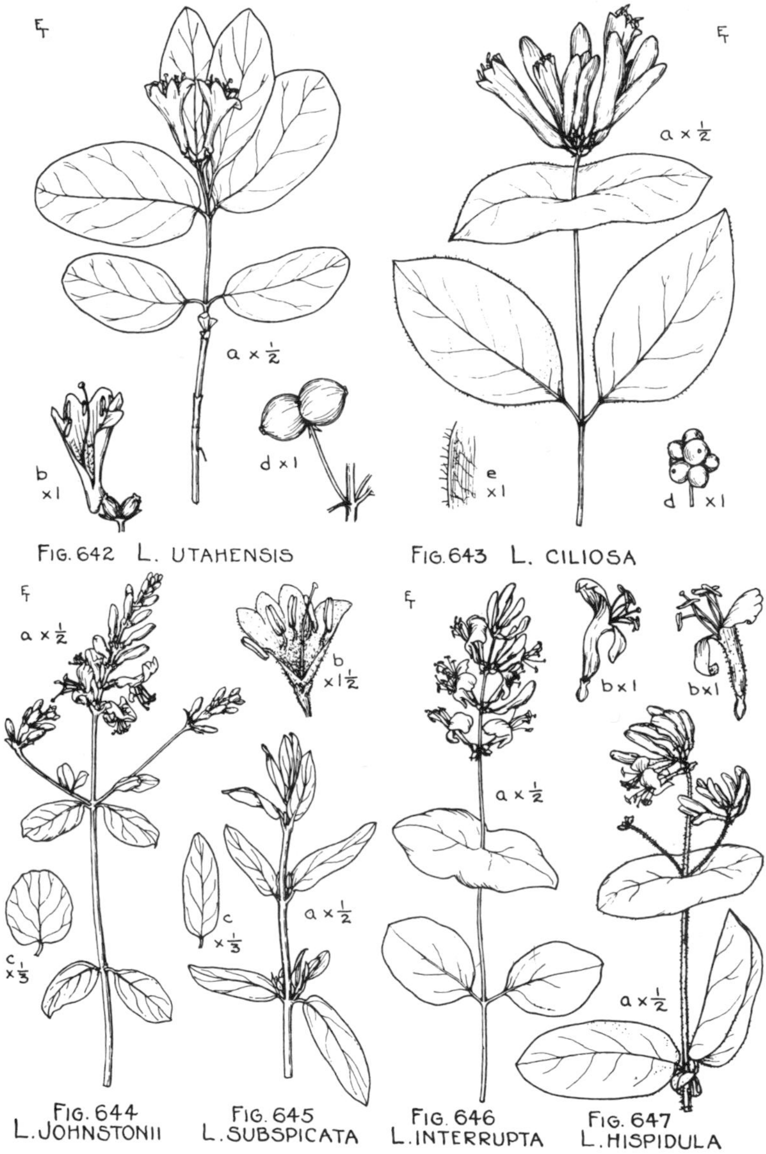

LONICERA. a, Flowering branchlet. b, Flower. c, Leaf. d, Fruit. e, Ciliate leaf-margin.

at base, 1½ to 3½ inches long, ¾-inch to 2 inches wide, the upper surface glabrous and green, the lower surface pale with a whitish bloom, the margins entire and ciliate; petioles usually less than ¼-inch long or absent in the upper 1 or 2 pairs, then the blades more or less united at the base forming an apparently single blade through which the stem passes. Flowers in a single terminal whorl or rarely in an interrupted spike of 2 whorls, sessile or short-peduncled; corolla reddish yellow or orange, trumpet-shaped, ¾-inch to 1¼ inches long, slightly 2-lipped, distended on one side at base, nearly glabrous. Fruit small, red, about ¼-inch or less in diameter. Flowering period, May to July.

Orange Honeysuckle is not common in California. It occurs in the mountains of northern Humboldt, Siskiyou, and Trinity counties and southward in Shasta and Butte counties, in the Upper Sonoran and Transition Life Zones. It extends northward to British Columbia, thence southward into Idaho, Montana, and Arizona. In general appearance this plant somewhat resembles *L. hispidula* from which it can be distinguished by its larger and usually single clusters of flowers terminating the branches and the absence of stipules on the stem. Too much reliance should not be placed upon the absence of pubescence on the surfaces of the leaves as some specimens apparently belonging to this species have short hairs on the surfaces as well as on the margins.

Lonicera ciliosa (Pursh) Poir.; Lam. Encycl. Suppl. 5:612 (1817). *Caprifolium ciliosum* Pursh. Type locality: "On the banks of the Kooskooski." Collected by *Lewis* on the banks of the Clearwater River, Idaho.

6. **Lonicera Johnstonii** (Keck) n. comb. SOUTHERN HONEYSUCKLE. Fig. 644.

A spreading suberect or climbing and reclining evergreen shrub, 3 to 8 feet high, with thin shredded brown or grayish bark on old twigs and smooth purplish-tinged bark on young twigs. Leaf-blades oblong-ovate to nearly orbicular, ½-inch to 1 inch long, ⅜- to ¾-inch wide, rounded at base and apex, finely pubescent above, grayish and lightly or densely pubescent beneath, rarely subglabrous, usually without stipular appendages, all distinct, entire; petioles ⅛- to ¼-inch long. Flowers few to several in whorls forming glandular-pubescent terminal leafy spikes often in open panicles; corolla yellowish or cream-colored, sometimes tinged with pink, ⅜- to ⅝-inch long, glandular-pubescent without and within, 2-lipped and often recurved, the lower lip not lobed, the upper lip 4-lobed. Fruit yellowish or red, ovoid, about ¼-inch long, with several seeds bearing 2 grooves on each surface. Flowering period, April to June.

Southern Honeysuckle occurs on dry mountain slopes, usually below 5000 feet elevation, in San Diego, Orange, western Riverside, Los Angeles, southwestern San Bernardino, Ventura, Santa Barbara, and western Kern counties. Several specimens collected from the inner South Coast Range from Santa Barbara County northward to Mount Diablo, Contra Costa County, appear to be intermediate between this species and *L. interrupta*.

Lonicera Johnstonii (Keck) McMinn. *L. subspicata* var. *Johnstonii* Keck. Type locality: Poppet Flat, Idyllwild Road, Riverside County. Collected by *Munz*.

7. **Lonicera subspicata** H. & A. SANTA BARBARA HONEYSUCKLE. Fig. 645.

A clambering evergreen shrub, 3 to 8 feet high, with thin shredded brownish or grayish bark on old branches and often purplish red on young shoots. Leaf-blades linear-oblong to oblong or narrow-elliptical, ½-inch to 1½ inches long, ¼- to ½-inch wide, rounded at apex and base, all distinct, leathery, dark green and

Fig. 648. CALIFORNIA HONEYSUCKLE. *Lonicera hispidula* Dougl.

glabrous above, densely white-pubescent beneath, without stipular appendages, entire; petioles 1/16- to 1/4-inch long. Flowers pale yellow, few, in compact whorls forming short leafy spikes 1 to 4 inches long, the whole inflorescence glandular-pubescent; corolla funnelform, 1/4- to 3/8-inch long, glandular-pubescent, the limb 2-lipped and often recurved; stamens equal, included or slightly exserted, the filaments pubescent at base. Fruit yellowish or red, ellipsoidal, about 1/4-inch long, with several shallowly pitted seeds. Flowering period, June to August.

Santa Barbara Honeysuckle is known only from the lower dry slopes of the mountains near Santa Barbara, California. It has long been confused with the broader-leaved honeysuckle, *L. Johnstonii,* more generally distributed over the cismontane regions of southern California.

Lonicera subspicata H. & A. Bot. Beechey 349 (1840). Type locality: Santa Barbara, California. Collected by *Douglas.*

8. **Lonicera denudata** (Rehd.) Dav. & Mox. San Diego Honeysuckle.

Like *L. Johnstonii,* but the leaf-blades yellowish and usually glabrous beneath.

San Diego Honeysuckle occurs in a few localities in southwestern Riverside County and in San Diego County, usually near the coast and at lower elevations than the closely related species *L. Johnstonii.* Specimens of these two species growing together at the Rancho Santa Ana Botanic Garden are quite distinct in the hue of their foliage. The foliage of *L. Johnstonii* is grayish and dull, while that of *L. denudata* is more green and shining.

Lonicera denudata (Rehd.) Dav. & Mox. Fl. S. Calif. 344 (1923). *L. subspicata* var. *denudata* Rehd. Type locality: San Diego. Collected by *Thurber.*

9. **Lonicera interrupta** Benth. Chaparral Honeysuckle. Fig. 646.

An evergreen bushy shrub with rigid woody and usually erect trunks 1 to 2 feet high, with branches twining or leaning on other plants. Young branchlets often purplish and glaucous. Leaf-blades elliptic-ovate, ovate, or almost round, obtuse or rounded at apex, rounded or tapering at base, 1/2-inch to 2 inches long, 3/8-inch to 1 inch wide, light green above, glaucous beneath, glabrous or rarely slightly puberulent, thick and somewhat leathery, usually without stipular appendages, the uppermost pair commonly joined at base forming an apparently single leaf through which the stem passes, the margins entire; petioles 1/4-inch or less long. Flowers in whorls in a terminal spike 2 to 6 inches long, often with additional spikes in the axils of the uppermost leaves, the whole forming an open glabrous panicle; corolla yellowish, funnel-shaped, somewhat swollen on one side at base, 3/8- to 1/2-inch long, glabrous without, 2-lipped, lower lip with a single lobe, the lobe almost 1/4-inch long, upper lip 4-lobed, the lobes about 1/16-inch long. Fruit red, subglobose, almost 1/4-inch long. Flowering period, May to July.

Chaparral Honeysuckle occurs on dry slopes of the middle and inner Coast Ranges, in the foothills of the Sierra Nevada, and in the mountains of Santa Barbara, Ventura, Los Angeles, and San Bernardino counties, in the Upper Sonoran Life Zone. This species may be easily confused with some variations of *L. hispidula* which occur in the drier parts of its distributional range. Both species, though usually having the upper leaves joined around the stem by their bases, may have some branches with all the leaves distinct. The inflorescence in this species is usually glabrous while in *L. hispidula* it is usually glandular-pubescent. Almost glabrous forms are not uncommon in the latter, however.

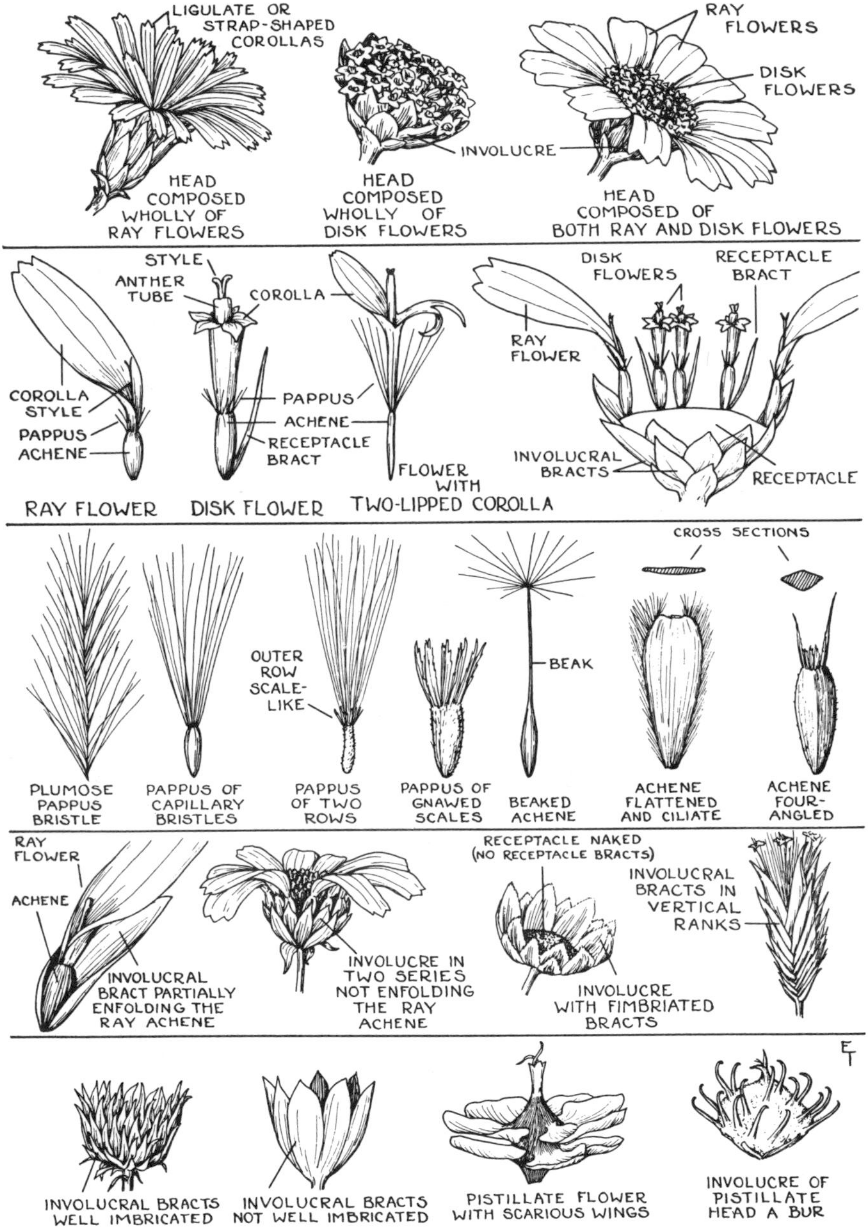

Fig. 649. Terminology of the ASTERACEAE (Compositae).

Lonicera interrupta Benth. Pl. Hartw. 313 (1849). Type locality: Near Carmel River, Monterey, California. Collected by *Hartweg*.

10. **Lonicera hispidula** Dougl. CALIFORNIA HONEYSUCKLE. Figs. 647, 648.

An evergreen climbing shrub or vine, 6 to 20 feet long, with glaucous purplish younger stems. Leaf-blades elliptical to ovate, rounded or often somewhat heart-shaped at base, obtuse at apex, 1¼ to 3 inches long, ½-inch to 1¾ inches wide, green and usually glabrous above, rarely pubescent, very glaucous and often puberulent or sometimes pilose beneath, thick and leathery or rarely thin, usually with stipular appendages on all but the lowest leaves, the uppermost leaves usually joined by their bases to form an apparently single leaf through which the stem passes, the margins entire, sometimes ciliate; petioles about ⅛-inch long on lower leaves. Flowers in many whorls, forming spikes, these arranged singly or more commonly in loose leafy panicles, the whole inflorescence usually glandular-pubescent; corolla purplish or pink, funnel-shaped, 7/16- to ¾-inch long, not expanded at base, usually glandular-hairy without, 2-lipped, lower lip with a single lobe about ⅜-inch long, upper lip 4-lobed, the lobes ⅛-inch or less long. Fruit red, subglobose, about ¼-inch long. Flowering period, April to July.

California Honeysuckle occurs in the canyons and along streams in the lower foothills of the Coast Ranges, the Sierra Nevada, and sparingly in the mountains of Santa Barbara, Los Angeles, and Riverside counties, also on Santa Cruz and Santa Catalina islands. It extends northward to Oregon, Washington, and British Columbia. Its bright red berries in large clusters are very attractive during the fall months.

Lonicera hispidula Dougl.; T. & G. Fl. N. Am. 2:8 (1841). *Caprifolium hispidulum* Dougl. Type locality: "On the subalpine slopes of Mount Hood. Sparingly at the Grand Rapids, and on steep rocks near 'Oak Point,' on the Columbia." Collected by *Douglas. L. hispidula* var. *vacillans* Gray. *L. californica* T. & G. *L. hispidula* var. *californica* (T. & G.) Rehd.

Asteraceae (Compositae). Sunflower Family

The Sunflower Family contains about 800 genera and over 10,000 species of herbs, shrubs, or sometimes trees, widely distributed all over the world. In California, there are 35 genera with 115 species and 66 varieties which are shrubs or subshrubs.

KEY TO THE GENERA

Flowers distinctly 2-lipped . . . . 1. TRIXIS.
Flowers not 2-lipped.
  Flowers all strap-shaped (ligulate or ray-flowers), white, pink, or rose; receptacle naked; plants with milky juice.
    Pappus of plumose bristles . . . . 2. STEPHANOMERIA.
    Pappus of capillary bristles . . . . 3. MALACOTHRIX.
  Flowers not all strap-shaped (ray-flowers).
    A. Heads composed of both ray- and disk-flowers.
      Ray-flowers blue, violet, lavender, or purple.
        Pappus of disk-flowers reddish brown; pappus of ray-flowers much reduced or wanting . . . . 4. CORETHROGYNE.
        Pappus of disk-flowers white; pappus of ray-flowers not reduced . 5. ASTER.

Ray-flowers yellow.
Receptacle with chaffy bracts.
Involucre of one series of equal bracts partially enfolding the ray-achenes; ray-flowers less than 1/4-inch long........15. HEMIZONIA.
Involucre of 2 or 3 series of bracts not enclosing the ray-achenes; ray-flowers 1/4-inch to 1 1/4 inches long.
Leaves twice- or thrice-divided....................16. COREOPSIS.
Leaves simple or only once-divided.
Leaves not distinctly scabrous, all alternate; disk-achenes strongly flattened and ciliate; pappus none or rarely of 2 slender awns.
17. ENCELIA.
Leaves distinctly scabrous, at least the lower ones opposite; disk-achenes 4-angled or only slightly flattened, not winged; pappus present.................................18. VIGUIERA.
Receptacle without chaffy bracts, usually naked.
Bracts of the involucre imbricated.
Ray-flowers 1 or 2.
Disk-flowers 3 to 6...........................6. AMPHIPAPPUS.
Disk-flowers 1 or 2.....................7. GUTIERREZIA LUCIDA.
Ray-flowers more than 2.
1. Pappus of 5 to 8 deciduous awns; heads large and gummy.
8. GRINDELIA.
2. Pappus of 4 to 15 short gnawed scales; heads small.
7. GUTIERREZIA.
3. Pappus of numerous persistent bristles or awns.
Involucral bracts fringed; heads solitary.
9. ACAMPTOPAPPUS SHOCKLEYI.
Involucral bracts not fringed.
Pappus usually in 2 rows, the outer row linear and scale-like.
10. CHRYSOPSIS VILLOSA.
Pappus in a single row of straight capillary bristles.
12. HAPLOPAPPUS.
Bracts of the involucre rarely much imbricated.
Leaves pinnately divided into 3 to several linear lobes or divisions, or only slightly lobed, or the upper ones linear and entire.
Pappus paleaceous........................20. ERIOPHYLLUM.
Pappus of many white soft hairs..................32. SENECIO.
Leaves not pinnately divided or lobed.
Leaves ovate, crenate, dentate, 2 to 7 inches long; pappus wanting ....21. VENEGASIA.
Leaves linear to narrow-spatulate, 1/2-inch to 2 inches long.
Pappus of 4 to 6 transparent paleae.........22. PSILOSTROPHE.
Pappus of 9 to 12 paleae..................20. ERIOPHYLLUM.

B. Heads composed of all disk-flowers or rarely with some inconspicuous ray-flowers.
1. Receptacle with chaffy bracts (in at least those of the staminate or bisexual heads in *Hymenoclea*).
Heads unisexual.
Plants monoecious; pappus none.

Involucre of pistillate heads bur-like...............24. FRANSERIA.
Involucre of pistillate heads with broad scarious wings.
25. HYMENOCLEA.
Plants dioecious; pappus present..........13. BACCHARIS SERGILOIDES.
Heads not unisexual; flowers unisexual or bisexual.
Leaves pinnately parted or the upper ones entire; pappus none.
Involucral bracts 4 to 6; bracts of the receptacle slender, not surrounding the flowers.......................26. OXYTENIA.
Involucral bracts more than 6; bracts of the receptacle scale-like and surrounding many of the flowers......28. ARTEMISIA PALMERI.
Leaves entire or rarely toothed.
Leaves ovate to oblong, ⅓-inch to 1 inch long; achenes flat and ciliate..............................17. ENCELIA FRUTESCENS.
Leaves lance-ovate or spatulate-oblong to linear or linear-oblanceolate, ¾-inch to 2 inches long.
Involucral bracts about 5; pappus none.......27. IVA HAYESIANA.
Involucral bracts more than 5, in 3 rows.
Pappus of 15 to 20 long-plumose bristles....19. BEBBIA JUNCEA.
Pappus of 5 to 8 unequal persistent paleae....11. EASTWOODIA.

2. Receptacle naked.
a. Flowers not yellow.
Flowers purplish.
Herbage glabrous, ill-scented; involucres dotted with oil-glands.
23. POROPHYLLUM.
Herbage canescent or silvery.
Herbage mostly bitter and aromatic, with odor of sage.
28. ARTEMISIA.
Herbage not aromatic; leaves linear to lanceolate, entire.
29. PLUCHEA.
Flowers white or whitish.
Petioles ¾-inch to 2 inches long; leaf-blades ⅓-inch or less long.
30. HOFMEISTERIA.
Petioles less than ¾-inch long or the leaves sessile.
Herbage ill-scented; leaves filiform or linear, entire; branches sparingly leafy, somewhat rush-like......23. POROPHYLLUM.
Herbage not ill-scented, often glandular-dotted and viscid; leaves usually broader, often toothed.
Plants dioecious............................13. BACCHARIS.
Plants not dioecious........................31. BRICKELLIA.
b. Flowers yellow.
Herbage aromatic with odor of sage; pappus none.....28. ARTEMISIA.
Herbage without odor of sage; pappus present.
Bracts of the involucre usually well imbricated.
Plants dioecious............................13. BACCHARIS.
Plants not dioecious.
Involucral bracts with fringed margins.
9. ACAMPTOPAPPUS SPHAEROCEPHALUS.
Involucral bracts without fringed margins.
Involucral bracts in distinct vertical rows of 3 to 5 each and forming an angled involucre......14. CHRYSOTHAMNUS.

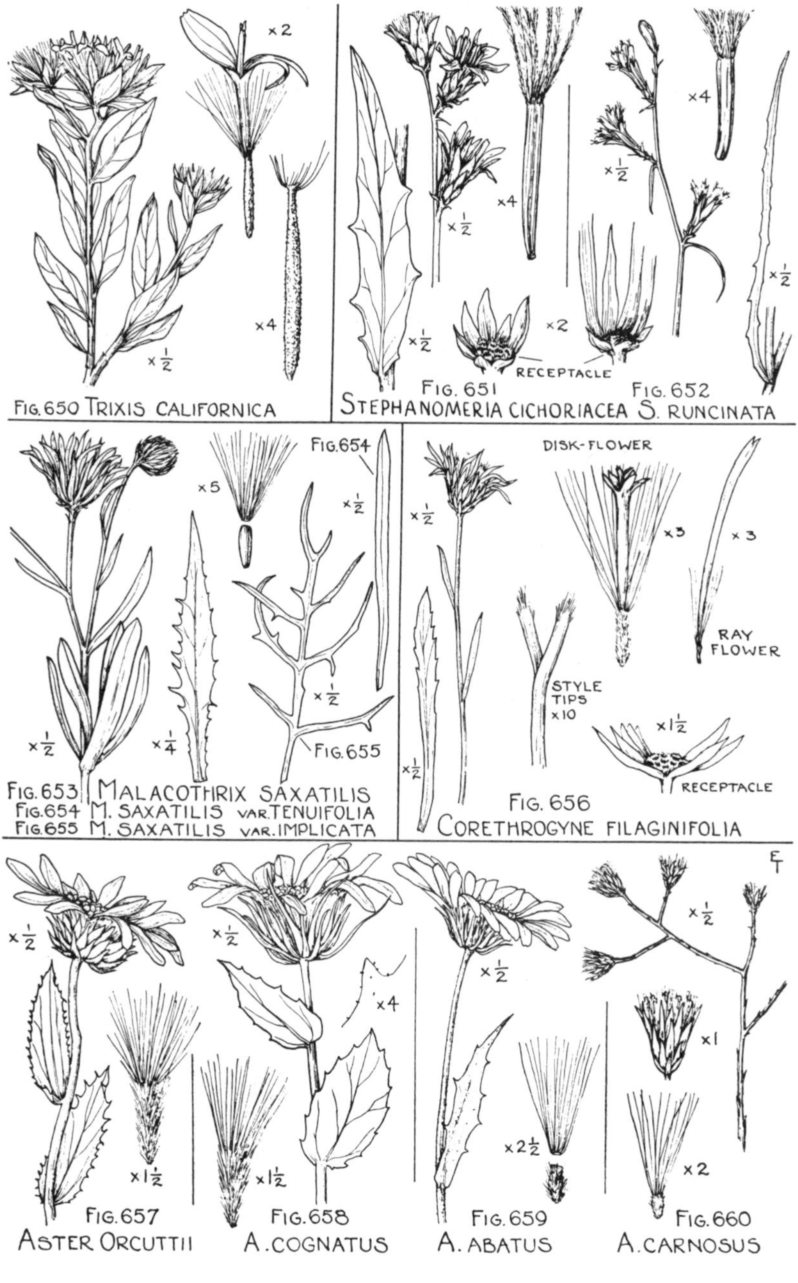

FIG. 650 TRIXIS CALIFORNICA

FIG. 651 STEPHANOMERIA CICHORIACEA

FIG. 652 S. RUNCINATA

FIG. 653 MALACOTHRIX SAXATILIS

FIG. 654 M. SAXATILIS VAR. TENUIFOLIA

FIG. 655 M. SAXATILIS VAR. IMPLICATA

FIG. 656 CORETHROGYNE FILAGINIFOLIA

FIG. 657 ASTER ORCUTTII

FIG. 658 A. COGNATUS

FIG. 659 A. ABATUS

FIG. 660 A. CARNOSUS

Involucral bracts not in distinct vertical rows.
Plants almost leafless; lower leaves linear, fleshy, ½-inch to 1 inch long, upper leaves reduced to scales; heads solitary............................5. ASTER CARNOSUS.
Plants distinctly leafy.
Achenes flattened.............10. CHRYSOPSIS OREGANA.
Achenes not flattened...............12. HAPLOPAPPUS.
Bracts of the involucre not much imbricated, in 1 to 2 few series.
Leaves pinnately parted into 3 to 7 narrowly linear divisions. 20. ERIOPHYLLUM.
Leaves not pinnately parted, entire.
Leaves reduced and scale-like; involucral bracts in 3 or 4 series. 33. LEPIDOSPARTUM.
Leaves conspicuous.
Herbage glabrous, balsamic; involucral bracts numerous, in 2 series, bright green; heads solitary..34. PEUCEPHYLLUM.
Herbage tomentose; involucral bracts 4 to 6, concave; heads usually in corymbs or racemes.........35. TETRADYMIA.

MUTISIEAE. MUTISIA TRIBE

1. **Trixis** P. Br.

(From the Greek *trixos,* three-fold, in reference to the 3-cleft lower lip of the corolla.)

This genus contains about 35 species of shrubs or rarely herbs of the tropical and subtropical regions of America. A single species is native to California.

1. **Trixis californica** Kell. CALIFORNIA TRIXIS. Fig. 650.

An erect bushy shrub, 1 to 2 or 3 feet high, leafy up to the heads, with minutely glandular-puberulent herbage. Leaves simple, alternate, sessile, the blades lanceolate, narrowed to the base, ¾-inch to 1½ inches long, ⅜- to ⅝-inch wide, entire or sparingly dentate. Heads cymose or solitary at the ends of short branchlets. Flowers yellow, all alike, bisexual and fertile; corolla 2-lipped, the upper lip deeply 2-lobed, the lower one 3-toothed. Involucre little if at all imbricated, subtended by leafy bracts; the proper bracts firm, straw-color, 8 to 12 in a single series, about ½-inch high. Receptacle mostly pilose. Achenes slender, tapering to the apex or beaked, glandular. Pappus soft, copious. Flowering period, March and April.

California Trixis occurs in canyons and on dry stony slopes from the western borders of the Colorado Desert of Riverside, San Diego, and Imperial counties eastward to Arizona and New Mexico and southward to Lower California and Mexico.

Trixis californica Kell. Proc. Calif. Acad. 2:182 (1863). Type locality: Cedros Island, Lower California. Collected by *J. A. Veatch. T. suffruticosa* Wats. *T. angustifolia* var. *latiuscula* Gray.

CICHORIEAE. CHICORY TRIBE

2. **Stephanomeria** Nutt.

(From the Greek *stephane,* a wreath, and *meros,* a division, the reference obscure.)

Usually tall and slender annual or perennial herbs with milky juice, a few sometimes woody at the base, paniculately branching above. Leaves simple, alternate, the upper ones reduced to herbaceous bracts. Heads usually small, 3- to 14-flowered in ours. Flowers all ligulate, pink or flesh-color, open in the early morning, the ligules all equal. Involucre cylindric or rarely campanulate. Receptacle flat, naked or rarely hirsute. Achenes oblong, truncate at both ends, strongly angled, glabrous, often rugose, the broad base hollowed at the insertion. Pappus plumose, at least above the middle.

This genus contains about 15 species which occur mainly in western North America. Two species and 2 varieties native to California are often woody at the base.

KEY TO THE SPECIES AND VARIETIES

Heads 9- to 14-flowered; involucre imbricated; receptacle deeply pitted, hirsute; herbage woolly when young; leaves entire to remotely and saliently toothed.
1. *S. cichoriacea.*

Heads 3- to 6-flowered; involucres not imbricated; receptacle naked.

Herbage glabrous.

Branches rigid, mostly divaricate; lower leaves runcinate-pinnatifid with narrow divisions; upper leaves entire, often reduced to scales.
2. *S. runcinata.*

Branches very slender, ascending; leaves linear-filiform.
2a. *S. runcinata* var. *myrioclada.*

Herbage grayish, hispidulous-tomentose..........2b. *S. runcinata* var. *Parishii.*

1. **Stephanomeria cichoriacea** Gray. TEJON MILK-ASTER. Fig. 651.

A tall perennial, from a large woody root-crown.

This species occurs on rocky slopes and canyons in the foothills and lower mountains from the vicinity of Tejon Pass, Kern County and the mountains of Santa Barbara County, southward in the San Gabriel, San Bernardino, and Santa Ana mountains. It occurs also on the Santa Barbara Islands.

Stephanomeria cichoriacea Gray, Proc. Am. Acad. 6:552 (1865). Type locality: Near Fort Tejon, Kern County, California. Collected by *Van Horn.*

2. **Stephanomeria runcinata** Nutt. DESERT MILK-ASTER. Fig. 652.

A rounded bushy plant, 1 to 2 feet high, with stems woody at the base and nearly leafless branches. Flowering period, April to June.

Desert Milk-aster occurs in washes and flats of the Colorado and Mohave deserts and adjacent mountains. It extends northward into Inyo County and eastward to Arizona, Nevada, and Texas.

2a. Var. **myrioclada** (D. C. Eaton) Jepson.

This variety occurs in the eastern part of the Mohave Desert. It extends eastward to Nevada and Arizona.

2b. Var. **Parishii** Jepson.

This variety is known from the vicinity of Victorville on the Mohave Desert. It may be only a form of *S. runcinata* which retains its tomentum.

Stephanomeria runcinata Nutt. Trans. Am. Phil. Soc. ser. 2, 7:427 (1841). Type locality: "Big Sandy Creek, a rivulet of the Colorado." Collected by *Nuttall. S. pauciflora* (Torr.) Nels.

Var. myrioclada (D. C. Eaton) Jepson, Man. 998 (1925). *S. myrioclada* D. C.

Eaton. Type locality: Nevada. Collected by *Watson,* acc. Eaton. *S. pauciflora* var. *myrioclada* (D. C. Eaton) Munz.

Var. Parishii Jepson, Man. 998 (1925). Type locality: Victorville, San Bernardino County, California. Collected by *Parish.*

3. **Malacothrix** DC.

(From the Greek *malakos,* soft, and *thrix,* hair, in reference to the long wool on one species.)

This genus contains about 25 species of herbaceous plants, a few of which are rarely woody at the base. They are native to the warmer parts of western North America. About 10 species occur in California, only one of which is frequently woody at the base.

1. **Malacothrix saxatilis** (Nutt.) T. & G. CLIFF-ASTER. Fig. 653.

KEY TO THE SPECIES AND VARIETIES

Herbage somewhat succulent; leaves lanceolate to spatulate, mostly obtuse, entire to dentate, or the lower ones toothed or pinnatifid. . . . . *M. saxatilis.*
Herbage not succulent.
Leaves all linear to filiform, entire, the upper ones much reduced.
1a. var. *tenuifolia.*
Lower leaves pinnatifid or twice-pinnate.
Lower leaves pinnatifid, the segments and upper leaves linear-filiform.
1b. var. *tenuissima.*
Leaves twice-pinnately divided into linear segments. . . . . . 1c. var. *implicata.*

Leaves simple or pinnate, alternate, usually sessile. Heads small or medium-sized, solitary or panicled, never sessile, commonly nodding in the bud. Flowers white or pinkish, all ligulate. Involucral bracts linear-attenuate, about ½-inch high, only slightly if at all imbricated, in 3 or 4 series, the outer ones very short. Receptacle naked. Achenes short, truncate at apex, crowned with a minute denticulate white border, 10- to 15-ribbed, 5 of the ribs stronger than the others. Pappus-bristles soft, more or less united at the base and falling early as a ring.

Cliff-aster occurs on sea-bluffs and exposed road-cuts from Santa Barbara west to the region of Gaviota Pass.

1a. Var. **tenuifolia** (Nutt.) Gray. Fig. 654.

This variety occurs on hillsides and in canyons near the coast from Santa Barbara southward to Laguna Beach, Orange County and inland to Whittier and Redlands, and also on Santa Catalina Island.

1b. Var. **tenuissima** Munz.

This variety is known from the Santa Ana Mountains on the boundary of Orange and Riverside counties.

1c. Var. **implicata** (Eastw.) Hall. Fig. 655.

This variety occurs on Santa Rosa, Santa Cruz, San Nicholas, and San Miguel islands.

Malacothrix saxatilis (Nutt.) T. & G. Fl. N. Am. 2:486 (1842). *Leucoseris saxatilis* Nutt. Type locality: "St. Barbara, on shelving rocks near the sea." Collected by *Nuttall.*

Var. tenuifolia (Nutt.) Gray, Syn. Fl. 1:423 (1884). *Leucosyris tenuifolia* Nutt. Type locality: Santa Barbara, California. Collected by *Nuttall.*

Var. tenuissima Munz, Man. S. Calif. Bot. 591 (1935). Type locality: Santiago Peak, Santa Ana Mountains. "Altitude of 3000 ft. on trail from Glen Ivy to Santiago Peak." Collected by *Munz.*

Var. implicata (Eastw.) Hall, Univ. Calif. Publ. Bot. 3:269 (1907). *M. implicata* Eastw. Type locality: San Nicholas Island. Collected by *Blanche Trask.*

ASTEREAE. ASTER TRIBE

4. **Corethrogyne** Nutt.

(From the Greek *korethron,* tuft, and *gune,* style, in reference to the tuft of hairs on the style.)

This is a small genus of 3 species of perennial herbs native to California. One species with several varieties is often more or less suffrutescent at the base.

1. **Corethrogyne filaginifolia** (H. & A.) Nutt. CUDWEED-ASTER. Fig. 656.

A somewhat suffrutescent perennial, with several erect slender stems from a decumbent base and usually white-tomentose herbage, the tomentum often deciduous. Flowering period, May to September.

This is a variable species with many described varieties, occurring mostly along the coast from Monterey County southward to San Diego, but also on the lower and middle mountain slopes, foothills, and plains of southern California, and on the Santa Barbara Islands.

Corethrogyne filaginifolia (H. & A.) Nutt. Trans. Am. Phil. Soc. ser. 2, 7:290 (1841). *Aster ? filaginifolia* H. & A. Type locality: Monterey, California. Collected by *Collie* and *Lay.*

5. **Aster** L. ASTER

(From the Greek *astere,* a star, in reference to the star-like heads of flowers.)

Usually late summer or autumn herbs, or rarely spring- and summer-flowering shrubs, with leafy stems. Leaves simple, alternate. Heads showy, with ray- and disk-flowers or the ray-flowers absent. Involucres turbinate, hemispheric, or campanulate, the bracts usually imbricated in several series. Receptacle naked, pitted. Ray-flowers pistillate, blue, purple, or violet. Disk-flowers bisexual, yellow, often changing to purple or brown. Achenes somewhat flattened. Pappus copious, of simple capillary bristles.

The genus Aster contains about 250 species distributed in Europe, Asia, Africa, and America. They are most abundant in North America. About 20 species occur in California, 4 of which are shrubby or at least woody at the base.

KEY TO THE SPECIES

Ray-flowers none..1. *A. carnosus.*
Ray-flowers present.
  Leaves and branches glabrous; leaves obovate to oblong, spinulose-toothed. 2. *A. Orcuttii.*
  Leaves and branchlets pubescent or glandular.
    Leaves linear or lanceolate to oblong, $1\frac{1}{2}$ to 3 inches long; peduncles elongate, naked or with a few much reduced leaves...........3. *A. abatus.*
    Leaves oblong or obovate, $\frac{3}{4}$-inch to $1\frac{1}{4}$ inches long; peduncles short, leafy. 4. *A. cognatus.*

1. **Aster carnosus** Gray. DESERT ASTER. Fig. 660.

A rigidly much branched shrub, 2 to 3 feet high, with pale slender branches and inconspicuous scale-like leaves. Lower leaves linear, fleshy, up to 3/4-inch long, entire, the upper leaves linear or scale-like. Heads solitary, terminating the branches. Involucres about 1/4-inch high, the imbricated bracts with a greenish midrib. Ray-flowers none. Achenes pubescent. Flowering period, June to October.

Desert Aster occurs on alkaline plains of the Mohave Desert of Kern, Los Angeles, and San Bernardino counties. It extends northward into the head of the San Joaquin Valley of Kern County (10 mi. w. of Delano), into Tulare County (Visalia), and into Inyo County, southward into the San Bernardino Valley (Colton, Riverside, and vicinity), and eastward to Nevada and Arizona, mainly in the Lower Sonoran Life Zone. It occurs also in Mexico.

Aster carnosus Gray, Syn. Fl. 1:202 (1884). *Linosyris carnosa* Gray. Type locality: "Low, subsaline valley, west of the Chiricahui Mountains, Sonora, Mexico." (Now Chiricahua Mountains, Arizona.) Collected by *Wright.*

2. **Aster Orcuttii** Vasey & Rose. ORCUTT ASTER. Fig. 657.

A very leafy bushy perennial, 1 to 3 feet high, woody below, with glabrous herbage and pearly-white bark. Flowering period, March and April.

Orcutt Aster occurs in rocky places along the western border of the Colorado Desert of Riverside, San Diego, and Imperial counties, in the Lower Sonoran Life Zone.

Aster Orcuttii Vasey & Rose, Bot. Gaz. 16:113 (1891). Type locality: Cariso Creek wash, San Diego and Imperial counties. Collected by *Orcutt.*

3. **Aster abatus** Blake. MOHAVE ASTER. Fig. 659.

A low leafy perennial, 1 to 2 feet high, more or less branched from a woody base, with whitish bark and tomentose-pubescent herbage. Flowering period, April and May.

Mohave Aster is common in stony soil in the Lower Sonoran Life Zone of the Mohave Desert and the northern border of the Colorado Desert. It extends north into Inyo County and east to Arizona, Nevada, and Utah.

Aster abatus Blake, Contr. U. S. Nat. Herb. 25:556, 562 (1925). *A. tortifolius* (T. & G.) Gray, not Michx. *Aplopappus tortifolius* T. & G. Type locality: "On the Wind River Chain of the Rocky Mountains." Collected by *Fremont. A. mohavensis* Cov.

4. **Aster cognatus** Hall. COLORADO DESERT ASTER. Fig. 658.

Much like *A. Orcuttii,* but with broader leaves and pubescent or stipitate-glandular herbage. Involucral bracts much elongated, up to 1 inch long, glandular, only the inner ones ciliate. Flowering period, May and June.

This species occurs in a few scattered locations on the northerly borders of the Colorado Desert (Mecca, Hidden Spring, Shavers Well, Indio, Red Canyon near Mecca).

Aster cognatus Hall, Univ. Calif. Publ. Bot. 6:173 (1915). Type locality: "North of Indio, along the northerly side of Coachella Valley, Riverside County." Collected by *Hall.*

6. **Amphipappus** T. & G.

(From the Greek *amphi,* double, and *pappos,* pappus, in reference to a double pappus-row in some species.)

This genus contains the following species.

1. **Amphipappus Fremontii** T. & G. FREMONT CHAFFBUSH. Fig. 661.

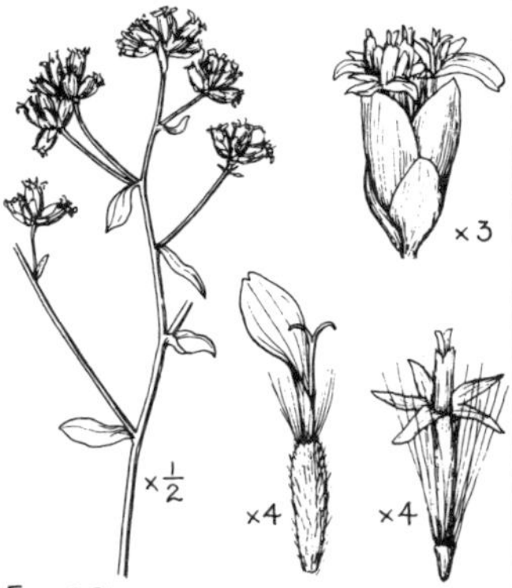

Fig. 661 Amphipappus Fremontii

Fig. 662 Gutierrezia californica

Fig. 663 G. Sarothrae

Fig. 664 G. lucida

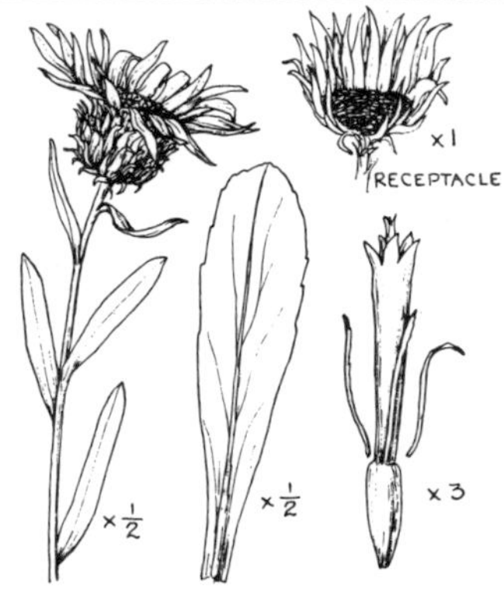

Fig. 665 Grindelia humilis

Fig. 666 Acamptopappus Schockleyi

Fig. 667 A. sphaerocephalus

Fig. 668 Chrysopsis villosa

Fig. 669 C. oregana

Fig. 670 Eastwoodia elegans

A low rounded shrub, 1 to 2 feet high, with rigid divaricate branches and glabrous herbage. Leaves simple, alternate, obovate or elliptic, 1/4- to 1/2-inch long, acute, entire, sessile or short-petioled. Heads numerous, clustered in compound terminal leafy-bracted cymes, nearly sessile, with yellow ray- and disk-flowers. Involucres ovoid, about 1/8-inch high, the 7 to 9 bracts thin, closely imbricated. Ray-flowers 1 or 2, less than 1/8-inch long, pistillate, fertile. Disk-flowers 3 to 6, bisexual, sterile. Pappus of ray-flowers of few short bristles, coalesced at base into 2 or 3 lanciniate scales. Pappus of disk-flowers of 5 to 20 weak bristles, united at base, nearly as long as the corolla, some dilated at base. Ray-achenes pubescent. Flowering period, April to June.

Fremont Chaffbush occurs on rocky mountain slopes in the Death Valley region and northern Mohave Desert (Slate Range and Panamint Mts. acc. *Hall* & *Chandler;* Argus Mts., *Purpus;* Funeral Range acc. *Jepson;* Providence Mts., acc. *Munz*), in the Lower Sonoran Life Zone. It extends eastward to Arizona, Nevada, and Utah.

Amphipappus Fremontii T. & G. Jour. Bost. Soc. Nat. Hist. 5:108 (1845). Type locality: "several places along the Mohave River, etc., somewhere between California and the Rocky Mountains." Collected by *Fremont. Amphiachyris Fremontii* (T. & G.) Gray.

7. **Gutierrezia** Lag.

(Named for a Spanish family, Gutierrez.)

Low suffrutescent or herbaceous plants, nearly glabrous but resinous. Leaves simple, alternate. Heads with yellow ray- and disk-flowers, numerous and small, in branched clusters at the summit of the stems. Involucral bracts thickened, with green tips, closely imbricated. Receptacle naked, flat in the Californian species. Achenes pubescent, angled or striate. Pappus of 4 to 15 oblong or linear unequal erose paleae.

This genus contains about 20 species native mostly to western North America. Three species are native to California.

KEY TO THE SPECIES

Ray-flowers 7 to 11, disk-flowers 6 to 14........................1. *G. californica.*
Ray- and disk-flowers 3 to 7 each..............................2. *G. Sarothrae.*
Ray- and disk-flowers 1 or 2 each; herbage yellowish green, very resinous.
3. *G. lucida.*

1. **Gutierrezia californica** (DC.) T. & G. MATCHWEED. CALIFORNIA SNAKEWEED. Fig. 662.

A loosely branched subshrub, 3/4-foot to 2 feet high. Flowering period, June to October.

Matchweed inhabits dry slopes and plains of the Upper San Joaquin Valley, the South Coast Ranges, cismontane southern California, and the western borders of the Colorado Desert. It extends southward into Lower California and eastward to Arizona and Nevada.

1a. Var. **bracteata** (Abrams) Hall.

Branchlets strongly divaricate with numerous bract-like leaves. Heads solitary on the peduncles, less numerous than in the species.

This variety occurs in the limited area from San Gorgonio Pass to Palm Springs.

Gutierrezia californica (DC.) T. & G. Fl. N. Am. 2:193 (1842). *Brachyris californica* DC. Type locality: California. Collected by *Douglas.*

Var. bracteata (Abrams) Hall, Univ. Calif. Publ. Bot. 3:36 (1907). *G. bracteata* Abrams. Type locality: "Desert slopes of San Bernardino County, between Banning and Seven Palms." Collected by *Orcutt.*

2. **Gutierrezia Sarothrae** (Pursh) Britt. & Rusby. BROOM SNAKEWEED. Fig. 663.

A bushy plant, 1 to 2 feet high, with numerous erect stems from a woody base. Flowering period, May to July or to October.

Broom Snakeweed occurs on arid plains and rocky hills almost throughout southern California from Los Angeles County southward to San Diego County and eastward in the San Bernardino Mountains to the New York Mountains of the Mohave Desert. It extends nearly throughout the Rocky Mountain states north to Canada, eastward to Texas, and south to Mexico.

Gutierrezia Sarothrae (Pursh) Britt. & Rusby, Trans. N. Y. Acad. 7:10 (1887). *Solidago Sarothrae* Pursh. Type locality: "From the plains of the Missouri." Collected by *Lewis.*

3. **Gutierrezia lucida** Greene. STICKY SNAKEWEED. Fig. 664.

A many-stemmed straggly bush, 1 to 2 feet high, with very resinous herbage. Flowering period, June to September.

Sticky Snakeweed occurs in the mountains of Inyo County, 2000 to 6000 feet altitude, and southward in the mountain valleys of the Mohave Desert of Kern and San Bernardino counties. It extends eastward to Arizona, New Mexico, and Texas and southward to Mexico.

Gutierrezia lucida Greene, Fl. Fr. 361 (1897). *Xanthocephalum lucidum* Greene. Type locality: Mohave Desert. Probably first collected by *Berlandier. G. Euthamiae* var. *microcephala* Gray, in part.

8. **Grindelia** Willd.

(Named in honor of Hieronymus Grindel, a Russian botanist.)

This genus consists of about 25 species of coarse perennial herbs, sometimes woody at the base, mostly native to the United States west of the Mississippi River. Six species occur in California, one of which is often woody at the base.

1. **Grindelia humilis** H. & A. MARSH GRINDELIA. Fig. 665.

A semi-shrubby perennial, the stems woody up to 2 or 3 feet, with 1 to several furrowed woody branches giving rise each season, mostly from the upper part, to subherbaceous flowering shoots, the lower part usually producing short leafy shoots. Leaves simple, alternate; the blades of the vegetative shoots oblong-oblanceolate or spatulate-oblong, ½-inch to 4 inches long, ⅛- to ½-inch wide, thick and leathery, dark or pale green, glabrous, mostly remotely serrulate to crenate-serrulate or subentire, sessile by a broad base, those of the flowering shoots much reduced. Heads 1 to 1½ inches broad, solitary on corymbosely or paniculately branched flower-bearing branchlets, with ray- and disk-flowers. Ray-flowers 16 to 34, bright yellow, mostly ½- to ¾-inch long. Involucres campanulate, moderately resinous; the bracts usually erect and appressed, but sometimes strongly reflexed, in 5 or 6 series. Receptacle naked. Achenes glabrous, about ¼-inch long, grayish to brown. Pappus of 5 to 8 deciduous awns. Flowering period, July and August.

Marsh Grindelia occurs in salt marshes, tidal flats, and borders of estuaries in the San Francisco Bay region, Bolinas Bay, and north to Tomales Bay.

Grindelia humilis H. & A. Bot. Beechey 147 (1833). Type locality: San Francisco Bay region. Collected by *Lay* and *Collie. G. cuneifolia* of most authors, not Nutt.

9. **Acamptopappus** Gray

(From the Greek *akamptos,* unbending, and *pappos,* pappus, in reference to the rather stiff pappus.)

Small rounded desert shrubs with slender rigid stems and nearly glabrous herbage. Leaves simple, alternate, entire. Heads solitary, terminating the branches, or in loose terminal clusters, with 12 to 36 yellow flowers, discoid or radiate. Flowers all bisexual. Involucral bracts closely imbricated, in about 3 series, very broad and obtuse, pale, the margins thin-scarious, irregularly fringed. Achenes short-turbinate, densely villous. Pappus of 30 to 40 persistent silvery awns, some flattened, others bristle-like and shorter.

This genus contains 2 species native to the desert regions of Nevada, Utah, Arizona, and California.

KEY TO THE SPECIES

Heads radiate .... 1. *A. Shockleyi.*
Heads discoid .... 2. *A. sphaerocephalus.*

1. **Acamptopappus Shockleyi** Gray. SHOCKLEY GOLDENHEAD. Fig. 666.

Similar in appearance to *A. sphaerocephalus.* Leaf-blades narrowly obovate to oblanceolate, 1/4- to 3/4-inch long, sessile. Heads solitary. Involucres about 1/4-inch high. Ray-flowers 10 to 12, bright yellow, 1/3- to 1/2-inch long. Flowering period, April to June.

Shockley Goldenhead occurs in the mountains of the Death Valley region of Inyo County and southward to northern San Bernardino County (Baker, Mohave Desert). It extends eastward to Nevada.

Acamptopappus Shockleyi Gray, Proc. Am. Acad. 17:208 (1882). Type locality: Western Nevada, near Candelaria, Esmeralda County. Collected by *Shockley.*

2. **Acamptopappus sphaerocephalus** (Harv. & Gray) Gray. GOLDENHEAD. Fig. 667.

A low round-topped shrub, 8 inches to 1 1/2 feet high, with numerous striate stems and pale nearly glabrous herbage. Leaf-blades linear or linear-spatulate, 1/4- to 3/4-inch long, acute, sessile, sometimes fascicled. Heads solitary or in loose terminal clusters. Involucres 1/4- to 1/3-inch high, the bracts coriaceous, commonly with a subapical greenish spot. Ray-flowers none. Flowering period, April to June.

Goldenhead is common in the Larrea belt below 4000 feet elevation, on the western border of the Colorado Desert and occasionally on the Mohave Desert where it is replaced by the variety *hirtellus.* It extends eastward to Arizona and Utah.

2a. Var. **hirtellus** Blake. Stems and leaves scabrous-puberulent. Widely distributed on the Mohave Desert in the Yucca and Larrea belts.

Acamptopappus sphaerocephalus (Harv. & Gray) Gray, Proc. Am. Acad. 8:634 (1873). *Aplopappus sphaerocephalus* Harv. & Gray. Type locality: California. Collected by *Coulter.*

Var. hirtellus Blake, Jour. Wash. Acad. Sci. 19:270 (1929). Type locality: Near Lone Pine, Inyo County, California. Collected by *Coville* and *Funston.*

10. **Chrysopsis** Nutt.

(From the Greek *chrusos,* golden, and *opsis,* likeness, in reference to the color of the flowers.)

Perennial herbs sometimes suffrutescent, with alternate entire leaves. Heads either with disk-flowers or with ray- and disk-flowers. Involucral bracts well imbricated. Receptacle naked. Achenes villous. Pappus of numerous persistent capillary bristles.

This genus contains about 20 species occurring from Mexico northward to Canada. Four species occur in California, 2 of which are occasionally woody at the base.

KEY TO THE SPECIES

Heads with yellow ray-flowers.......................................1. *C. villosa.*
Heads without ray-flowers.......................................2. *C. oregana.*

1. **Chrysopsis villosa** (Pursh) Nutt. HAIRY GOLDEN-ASTER. Fig. 668.

This species, with several varieties and numerous forms, is widely distributed throughout California below 7000 feet elevation.

Chrysopsis villosa (Pursh) Nutt. Gen. Pl. 2:151 (1818). *Amellus villosus* Pursh. Type locality: On the Missouri. Collected, probably, by *Lewis.*

2. **Chrysopsis oregana** (Nutt.) Gray. OREGON GOLDEN-ASTER. Fig. 669.

This species with 2 or 3 varieties occurs in sand or gravel along streams, from Monterey County northward in the Coast Ranges to Del Norte and Siskiyou counties and in the Sierra Nevada in Plumas and Tulare counties. It extends northward to Oregon.

Chrysopsis oregana (Nutt.) Gray, Proc. Am. Acad. 6:543 (1865). *Ammodia oregana* Nutt. Type locality: "On the sand and gravel bars of the Oregon and its tributary streams." Collected by *Nuttall.*

11. **Eastwoodia** Brandg.

(Named in honor of Miss Alice Eastwood, curator of the herbarium of the California Academy of Sciences.)

This genus contains a single species.

1. **Eastwoodia elegans** Brandg. YELLOW MOCK ASTER. Fig. 670.

A suffrutescent nearly glabrous perennial, 1½ to 3 feet high, with striate stems and whitish bark becoming shreddy in age. Leaves simple, alternate, linear-oblanceolate, ¾-inch to 1½ inches long, 1-veined, minutely and sparsely scabrous, somewhat fleshy, entire, sessile. Flowers discoid, bisexual, yellow, many in solitary heads, or the heads loosely cymose at the ends of slender branches. Involucral bracts whitish, firm, narrow, imbricated in 3 or 4 series forming a short campanulate involucre. Receptacle hemispherical, with chaffy hard bracts subtending the flowers. Achenes short-turbinate, somewhat 3- or 4-angled, densely upwardly pubescent. Pappus of 5 to 8 unequal linear-lanceolate white persistent paleae, longer than the achenes. Flowering period, May to July.

This species occurs in the dry canyons along the western border of the San Joaquin Valley from the region of Corral Hollow, San Joaquin County southward to the Maricopa Hills of Kern County, and also in San Luis Obispo County 4½ miles southeast of Chimeneas Ranch.

Eastwoodia elegans Brandg. Zoe 4:397 (1894). Type locality: Cariso Plains of eastern San Luis Obispo County, California. Collected by *L. Jared* on the Cariso Plains; by *Eastwood,* near Alcade; by *W. L. Watts* on the hills west of Bakersfield.

12. **Haplopappus** Cass. GOLDENBUSH

(From the Greek *haploos,* simple, and *pappos,* down, in reference to the simple pappus-ring.)

Annual and perennial herbs and shrubs, usually with resinous or glandular herbage. Leaves simple, alternate (or the lower ones rarely opposite), entire to variously lobed. Heads small to large, variously clustered or solitary, with ray- and disk-flowers or the ray-flowers wanting. Involucres hemispheric to obconic; bracts numerous, from nearly equal to closely and regularly imbricated in several lengths, never in vertical rows, varying from herbaceous to chartaceous or coriaceous, the tips usually greenish; receptacle alveolate, without scales or bracts. Ray-flowers 1 to numerous, pistillate or neutral or wanting, fertile or sterile, usually yellow, sometimes purple. Disk-flowers few to numerous, bisexual, usually fertile. Achenes terete or angled, cylindric to turbinate, pubescent to glabrous. Pappus simple, of numerous capillary scabrous bristles in one or more series, unequal in length.

The genus *Haplopappus,* as here treated, includes the genera *Stenotopsis, Macronema, Isocoma, Hazardia,* and *Ericameria* of some authors. It consists of about 150 species and many varieties confined to North America and western and south ern South America. Hall states that "all of the available evidence suggests the Mexican region as the ancestral home of the genus *Haplopappus.* In past geologic time, however, there came about a separation into two groups, or subgenera, one now confined to North America, the other to western South America, with the tropics forming an impassable barrier between them." (See Bibl.)

Twenty species and 15 varieties of shrubs and subshrubs belonging to this genus are native to California. They usually occur on dry slopes, interior cismontane valleys, deserts, gravelly washes, and sandy areas along the coast. Since most of the species have numerous heads of golden-yellow flowers, the name goldenbush seems appropriate. Goldenweed, goldenfleece, rayless goldenrod, and yellowbrush are other common names sometimes given to species of this genus. Some of the species are used medicinally by the Indians and Mexicans, while some are of slight forage value, a few are reputedly poisonous, and most are highly ornamental when in full bloom.

KEY TO THE SPECIES

Heads with ray-flowers (some heads on a plant may lack ray-flowers).
- Ray-flowers 11 to 25.
  - Ray-flowers 15 to 25; stems nearly leafless; leaves toothed, without resin-pits. 1. *H. junceus.*
  - Ray-flowers 11 to 18; stems densely leafy; leaves entire, with resin-pits. 2. *H. linearifolius.*
- Ray-flowers 1 to 10 (or rarely none or up to 30 in the spring heads of *H. pinifolius*).
  - Leaves and branches with distinct resin-pits.
    - Leaves obovate or oblanceolate; inflorescence cymose; ray-flowers 1 to 3 (or 5) or usually absent . . . . 3. *H. cuneatus.*
    - Leaves filiform to linear or narrowly oblanceolate.
      - Disk-flowers 20 to 25; ray-flowers 1 or 2 or none in some heads. 4. *H. Eastwoodae.*
      - Disk-flowers 5 to 20.
        - Inflorescence cymose; ray-flowers 1 or 2 or none; disk-flowers 5 to 9. 5. *H. Cooperi.*
        - Inflorescence paniculate or corymbose.
          - Leaves about ½-inch to 1½ inches long.

Fig. 671. Narrowleaf Goldenbush. *Haplopappus linearifolius* DC.
(Photograph by Sidney Gulick.)

Ray-flowers 5 to 10 (or in the spring heads 25 to 30); disk-flowers 12 to 18 (or more numerous in the spring heads); achenes sparsely and lightly pubescent..............6. *H. pinifolius.*

Ray-flowers 1 to 8; disk-flowers 5 to 20; achenes densely appressed-pubescent with long hairs..................7. *H. Palmeri.*

Leaves less than ½-inch (usually about ⅛-inch) long; ray-flowers 2 to 6; disk-flowers 8 to 12; achenes glabrous........8. *H. ericoides.*

Leaves and branches without resin-pits, often more or less glandular and viscid.

Leaves densely white-tomentose.

Leaves obovate to oblanceolate, 1½ to 4½ inches long; ray-flowers 4 to 6, inconspicuous or absent...........................12. *H. canus.*

Leaves narrowly linear, ¾-inch to 1½ inches long; ray-flowers 1 to 5 or absent............................15b. *H. Bloomeri* var. *Sonnei.*

Leaves not white-tomentose, less than 1½ inches long or to 2¼ inches in *H. Bloomeri* and then filiform to linear or oblong-linear.

1. Disk-flowers 4 to 12; leaves 1-nerved.

Leaves ⅜- to ⅝-inch long..........................14. *H. nanus.*

Leaves ¾-inch to 2¼ inches long..................15. *H. Bloomeri.*

2. Disk-flowers 7 to 20; leaves with a prominent mid-vein and often with 2 additional veins from the base..................16. *H. Greenei.*

3. Disk-flowers 20 to 40; leaves 1-nerved............17. *H. suffruticosus.*

Heads without ray-flowers.

Leaves and branches with resin-pits.

Disk-corollas with slender tube dilated to a much broader throat.

Stems white, glabrous and shining; involucral bracts with conspicuous thickenings or glands or resin-pockets near their tips; desert plants. 19. *H. acradenius.*

Stems pale brown or darker; involucral bracts with thin greenish tips; cismontane plants..........................20. *H. venetus* varieties.

Disk-corollas gradually widening upward.

Leaves oblanceolate to obovate, the apex obtuse or retuse...3. *H. cuneatus.*

Leaves filiform to linear or narrowly oblanceolate.

Flowers 20 to 25................................9. *H. arborescens.*

Flowers 5 to 12.

Flowers 5 to 8 (rarely 10); sometimes with 1 or 2 ray-flowers. 5. *H. Cooperi.*

Flowers 9 to 12.

Principal leaves 1 to 2¼ inches long, ⅛- to ¼-inch wide. 10. *H. Parishii.*

Principal leaves ⅜- to ¾-inch long, less than 1⁄16-inch wide. 11. *H. propinquus.*

Leaves without resin-pits but often glandular.

Leaves densely white-tomentose, at least beneath.

Leaves 1½ to 4½ inches long; disk-flowers 40 or more.......12. *H. canus.*

Leaves ¾-inch to 1½ inches long; disk-flowers 4 to 12. 15b. *H. Bloomeri* var. *Sonnei.*

Leaves not white-tomentose, none more than 2½ inches long; disk-flowers 30 or less.

FIG. 672
HAPLOPAPPUS JUNCEUS

FIG. 673
H. LINEARIFOLIUS

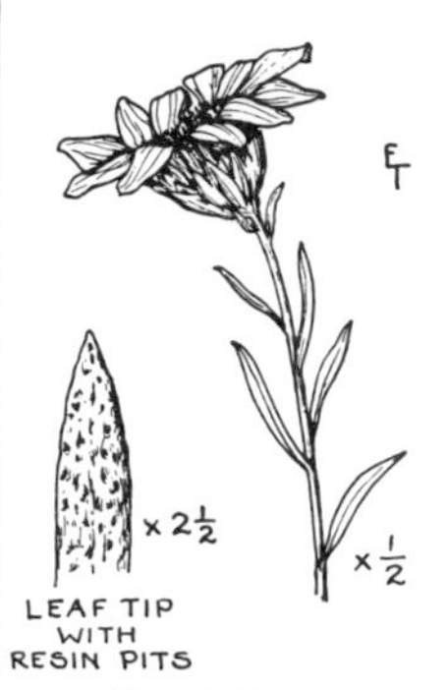

FIG. 674
H. LINEARIFOLIUS
VAR. INTERIOR

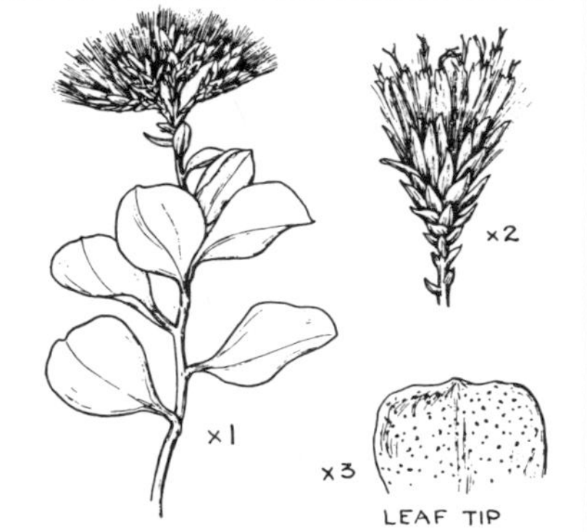

FIG. 675 H. CUNEATUS

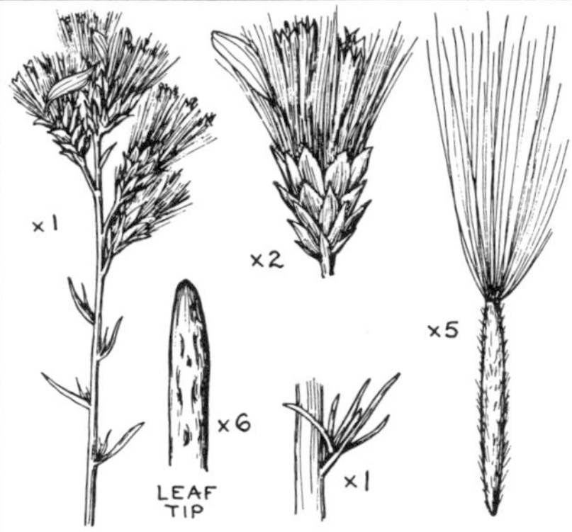

FIG. 676 H. EASTWOODAE

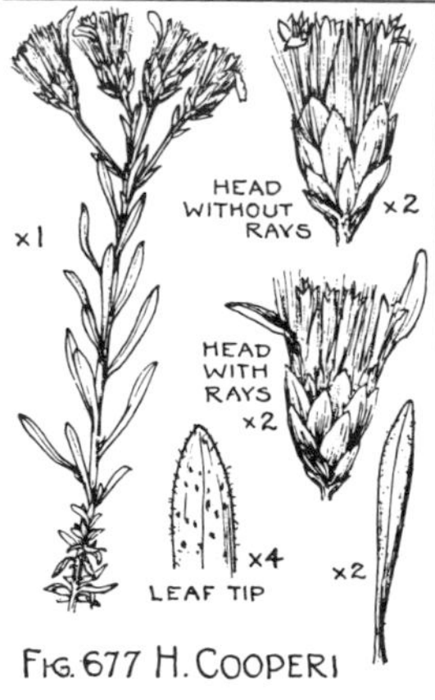

FIG. 677 H. COOPERI

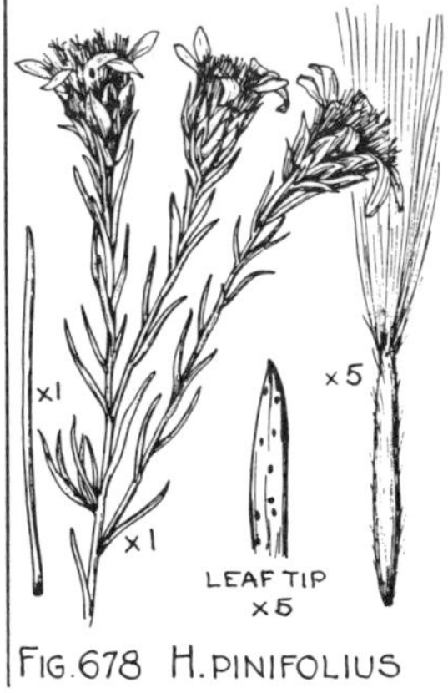

FIG. 678 H. PINIFOLIUS

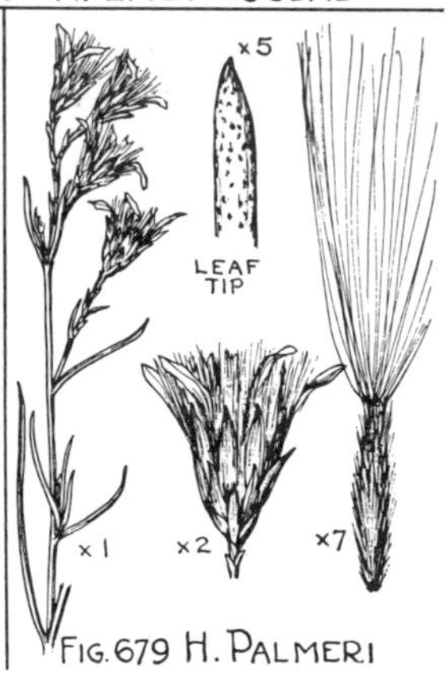

FIG. 679 H. PALMERI

Leaves usually ⅜- to ¾-inch wide, sharply serrate throughout.
13. *H. squarrosus.*

Leaves usually less than ⅜-inch wide, rarely up to ½-inch in width.

Branches densely white-tomentose, the tomentum usually sparse or wanting near the heads.......................... 18. *H. Macronema.*

Branches not white-tomentose.

Principal leaves usually with secondary fascicled leaves in their axils.

Stems white, glabrous and shining; involucral bracts with conspicuous thickenings or glands or resin-pockets near their tips; desert plants.................................. 19. *H. acradenius.*

Stems pale brown or darker; involucral bracts with thin greenish tips; cismontane plants..............20. *H. venetus* varieties.

Principal leaves without secondary fascicled leaves in their axils.

Leaves entire.................................15. *H. Bloomeri.*

Leaves spinosely toothed...................21. *H. brickellioides.*

1. **Haplopappus junceus** Greene. Rush Goldenbush. Fig. 672.

A subshrub, woody only at base, 1 to 3 feet high, with slender wiry erect to widely spreading stems, nearly glabrous but slightly glandular or scabrid striate branches, and yellow flowers. Flowering period, late summer and autumn.

Rush Goldenbush is known in California only from southern San Diego County in very arid locations, usually in the Lower Sonoran Life Zone (near Valley Center, *Chandler;* Descanso, *Brandegee;* Cottonwood Grade, *Cleveland*). It extends into northern Lower California and Sonora, Mexico.

Haplopappus junceus Greene, Bull. Calif. Acad. 4:190 (1885). Type locality: San Diego County, California.

2. **Haplopappus linearifolius** DC. Narrowleaf Goldenbush. Figs. 671, 673.

KEY TO THE SPECIES AND VARIETY

Leaves usually ¾-inch to 1⅝ inches long; involucres ⅜- to ½-inch high.
H. linearifolius.

Leaves ⅜- to ¾-inch long; involucres ⁵⁄₁₆- to ⅜-inch high........2a. var. *interior.*

A rounded bushy shrub, 1½ to 5 feet high, with many stout woody branches, nearly erect and usually striate and resinous branchlets, and yellow flowers. Leaves crowded; the blades nearly linear but broader at or above the middle, acute, usually ¾-inch to 1⅝ inches long, thick, glabrous, resinous and conspicuously impressed-punctate, entire, sessile or tapering to a petiole-like base. Heads numerous, large, solitary on leafy peduncles or nearly naked above, the numerous erect peduncles extending the flowers far beyond the leafy twigs. Involucral bracts numerous in 2 or 3 irregular series, broadly lanceolate to linear, ⅜- to ½-inch long, thin, greenish, scarious-margined. Ray-flowers 11 to 18, the ligules ⅜- to ¾-inch long. Disk-flowers numerous. Achenes compressed, densely silky-pubescent. Pappus soft, white, more or less deciduous. Flowering period, March and April.

Narrowleaf Goldenbush inhabits arid regions on mountain slopes, interior cismontane valleys, and desert borders below 5000 feet elevation from San Diego County north in the Coast Ranges to Mount Diablo and the Marysville Buttes. It is usually a shrub but in the desert areas it is often reduced to a subshrub. This is a very ornamental species with numerous large heads of bright yellow flowers extending beyond the glabrous green foliage.

2a. Var. **interior** (Cov.) Jones. INTERIOR GOLDENBUSH. DESERT GOLDENBUSH. Fig. 674.

Leaves commonly shorter than in the species, 3/8- to 3/4-inch long. Heads smaller; ligules 1/4- to 1/2-inch long.

Interior Goldenbush occurs on desert ranges and around the borders of the Mohave and Colorado deserts, but more commonly on the Mohave Desert. It extends westward from the Mohave Desert to eastern Ventura County where the conditions of the Lower Sonoran Life Zone prevail.

Transplants of the species and the variety have been grown together at Mills College and the characters of each were maintained for five years.

Haplopappus linearifolius DC. Prodr. 5:347 (1836). Type locality: California, probably on Mount Diablo. Collected by *Douglas*. *Stenotopsis linearifolius* (DC.) Rydb.

Var. interior (Cov.) Jones, Proc. Calif. Acad. ser. 2, 5:697 (1895). *Haplopappus interior* Cov. Type locality: Darwin Mesa, Inyo County, California. Collected by *Coville* and *Funston*. *Stenotopsis linearifolius* var. *interior* Macbr.

3. **Haplopappus cuneatus** Gray. WEDGELEAF GOLDENBUSH. Fig. 675.

A dwarf intricately branched shrub, 1/2-foot to 2 (or rarely 4) feet high, with glabrous and resinous-punctate foliage and yellow flowers. Leaves rather crowded; the blades oblanceolate or obovate, 1/4- to 3/4-inch long, 1/8- to 3/8-inch wide, thick, obtuse, often retuse and commonly mucronate at apex, narrowed to a cuneate or spatulate petiole-like base, glabrous, entire but often undulate. Heads in small compact cymes, rarely solitary. Involucral bracts 20 to 30, imbricated in about 5 series, narrow, chartaceous, the inner with white membranous margins, glabrous, the outermost passing into the bracts of the peduncle. Ray-flowers 1 to 5 or none, the ligules less than 3/16-inch long. Disk-flowers 9 to 20. Achenes prismatic, appressed-pubescent, 4-angled. Flowering period, September to December.

Wedgeleaf Goldenbush inhabits rocky slopes and summits of mountains in the Upper Sonoran Life Zone of eastern San Diego County and extends northward to Riverside, San Bernardino, Kern, Los Angeles, and Santa Barbara counties, and in the Sierra Nevada to Sierra County and into Inyo and Mono counties. Some authors consider the form without ray-flowers as var. *spathulata* (Gray) Blake, but the reduction of ray-flowers, according to Hall, "has taken place over most of the area covered by the species, but . . . it still is incomplete in some localities, especially in the outlying districts toward the north."

Haplopappus cuneatus Gray, Proc. Am. Acad. 8:635 (1873). Type locality: "Calif., in Bear Valley, alt. 4500 ft." Collected by *Bolander*. *Ericameria cuneata* (Gray) McCl.

4. **Haplopappus Eastwoodae** Hall. MONTEREY GOLDENBUSH. Fig. 676.

A dense round-topped shrub, 1 to 3 feet high, with several main stems and ascending branches, densely leafy erect short striate branchlets, glabrous resinous foliage, and yellow flowers. Leaves heather-like, the alternate ones with fascicled ones in their axils; the blades filiform, 3/8- to 3/4-inch long, the fascicled leaves much shorter, terete or slightly flattened, grooved on the back except when very narrow, resinous-punctate, sessile. Heads solitary or cymose to subracemose on leafy-bracted peduncles 1/8- to 3/4-inch long. Involucral bracts 22 to 26, loosely but regularly imbricated in 4 or 5 series, much shorter than the disk, scarious and pale yellow, resinous. Ray-flowers 1 or 2, apparently wanting in some heads, the ligules about

¼-inch or less long. Disk-flowers about 20 to 25. Achenes subcylindric, densely covered with long silky white upwardly appressed hairs. Flowering period, August to November.

Monterey Goldenbush is apparently restricted to the sand dunes of Monterey and Carmel bays. It is sometimes associated and confused with *H. ericoides* but can be distinguished by the fascicled leaves which are much shorter than the primary ones, few ray-flowers (1 or 2), more numerous disk-flowers (20 to 25), and pubescent achenes.

Haplopappus Eastwoodae Hall, Carnegie Inst. Publ. 389:259 (1928). *Chrysoma fasciculata* Eastw. Type locality: Along the coast near Monterey. Collected by *Abbott. Ericameria fasciculata* Macbr.

5. **Haplopappus Cooperi** (Gray) Hall. Cooper Goldenbush. Fig. 677.

Usually a low much branched shrub, 1 to 4 feet high (rarely 6 feet), with short leafy more or less striate resinous-punctate puberulent branchlets, and yellow flowers. The alternate leaves sometimes with fascicled smaller ones in their axils; the blades linear or linear-spatulate, ¼- to ¾-inch long, thick, straight, usually impressed-punctate, minutely puberulent. Heads small, in open rounded cymes, on peduncles ⅛- to ½-inch long. Involucral bracts 10 to 14, loosely imbricated, in about 3 series, much shorter than the disk, with a greenish middle portion and white-scarious border, puberulent. Ray-flowers 1 or 2, or none in some heads, the ligules about 3/16-inch long. Disk-flowers 5 to 9. Achenes obtusely 4-angled, densely villous. Flowering period, April to June.

Cooper Goldenbush is a common shrub of the desert borders in the upper part of the Lower Sonoran Life Zone. It extends from Inyo County southward through Kern to San Bernardino and Los Angeles counties, eastward to Nevada, and southward to Lower California.

Haplopappus Cooperi (Gray) Hall, Carnegie Inst. Publ. 389:275 (1928). *Bigelovia Cooperi* Gray. Type locality: Southeastern California, on the eastern slope of the Providence Mountains. Collected by *Cooper. Ericameria monactis* (Gray) McCl. of Jepson's Manual.

6. **Haplopappus pinifolius** Gray. Pine Goldenbush. Pine-bush. Fig. 678.

A stout spreading bushy shrub, 1½ to 10 feet high, often with trunk-like main stems, densely leafy glabrous fastigiately crowded branchlets, and yellow flowers. Leaves alternate, filiform or linear, ½-inch to 1⅜ inches long, often curved, mucronate, obscurely resinous-punctate, usually with secondary much shorter fascicled leaves in their axils. Spring heads few and solitary on short leafy branchlets, with 15 to 30 ray-flowers and numerous disk-flowers. Involucres hemispheric, surrounded by long slender acuminate leaves resembling an outer involucre. Autumn heads numerous, in dense racemose or loose paniculate clusters, on leafy bracteate peduncles. Involucres turbinate, the bracts 20 to 26, imbricated, in about 4 series, slightly shorter than the disk, thin and chartaceous, the outer with green tips, the margins mostly membranous and woolly-ciliolate. Ray-flowers 5 to 10, the ligules ⅛- to 3/16-inch long. Disk-flowers 12 to 18. Achenes subcylindric, striate or ribbed, subglabrous or hairy at summit. Disk-pappus reddish. Yearly flowering periods two, one in early spring and the other from September to December.

Pine Goldenbush is an important shrub in the coastal sagebrush areas of southern California. It occurs in washes and foothills of the San Gabriel, San Bernardino, San Jacinto, and the Laguna mountains, in the Upper Sonoran Life Zone.

Haplopappus pinifolius Gray, Proc. Am. Acad. 8:636 (1873). Type locality: "Near Los Angeles, in a dry river bed." Collected by *Nevin*. *Ericameria pinifolia* (Gray) Hall.

7. **Haplopappus Palmeri** Gray. PALMER GOLDENBUSH. Fig. 679.

KEY TO THE SPECIES AND VARIETY

Leaves mostly 3/4-inch to 1 1/2 inches long; ray-flowers 4 to 8 . . . . *H. Palmeri*.
Leaves mostly 3/8- to 3/4-inch or rarely to 1 1/8 inches long; ray-flowers 1 to 6.
7a. var. *pachylepis*.

A tall much branched shrub, 3 to 9 feet high, with leafy resinous ascending or spreading nearly glabrous branchlets and yellow flowers. Leaves narrowly linear to filiform, 3/4-inch to 1 1/2 inches long, often curved, thick, resinous and impressed-punctate, usually with shorter fascicled leaves in their axils. Heads numerous, in elongated panicles or some racemose, the ultimate peduncles scaly-bracteate. Involucral bracts 18 to 24, imbricated, in 4 or 5 series, much shorter than the disk, chartaceous, with resinous-thickened yellowish green midrib and white-scarious margins. Ray-flowers 4 to 8, the ligules 1/8- to nearly 1/4-inch long. Disk-flowers 9 to 20. Achenes subcylindric, about 5-angled, appressed-pubescent with long hairs. Flowering period, March to October or to December.

Palmer Goldenbush inhabits gravelly and alluvial soils of dry slopes in southwestern San Diego County in the Lower Sonoran Life Zone. It extends into Lower California.

7a. Var. **pachylepis** (Hall) Munz.

A bushy shrub, 1 1/2 to 5 feet high, with the principal stems mainly erect. Leaves mostly 3/8- to 3/4-inch (rarely 1 1/8 inches) long, nearly straight. Bracts of the involucre 16 to 18. Ray-flowers 1 to 6. Disk-flowers 5 to 15.

This variety occurs on the dry coastal slopes of the foothills and on the plains west of the mountains in Riverside, Orange, and Los Angeles counties. Reported north to Santa Barbara County, acc. Munz.

Haplopappus Palmeri Gray, Proc. Am. Acad. 11:74 (1876). Type locality: Tecate Mountains, Lower California. Collected by *Palmer*. *Ericameria Palmeri* (Gray) Hall.

Var. pachylepis (Hall) Munz, Man. S. Calif. Bot. 522 (1935). *H. Palmeri* subsp. *pachylepis* Hall. Type locality: Summit of Box Springs Grade, near Riverside, California. Collected by *Keck*.

8. **Haplopappus ericoides** (Less) H. & A. HEATHER GOLDENBUSH. MOCK HEATHER. Fig. 680.

A compact heather-like shrub, 1 to 3 feet high, with numerous crowded densely leafy resinous striate branchlets and yellow flowers. Leaves filiform, 3/16- to nearly 1/2-inch long, curved or straight, deflexed in age, usually grooved on the back, resinous-punctate, with secondary fascicled leaves in their axils about as long as the alternate leaves. Heads cymose-paniculate, the ultimate peduncles 1/16-inch to 1 1/8 inches long and closely bracted. Involucral bracts 16 to 22, regularly imbricated, in 3 or 4 series, much shorter than the disk, scarious and yellowish but with a green tinge, tomentulose-ciliolate. Ray-flowers 2 to 6, the ligules about 3/16-inch long. Disk-flowers 8 to 12. Achenes subcylindric, 8- to 10-ribbed, glabrous. Flowering period, August to November.

Heather Goldenbush occurs on the sand dunes and sandy flats in the immediate proximity of the ocean from Bolinas, Marin County southward to Los Angeles County.

Haplopappus ericoides (Less) H. & A. Bot. Beechey 146 (1833). *Diplopappus ericoides* Less. Type locality: California. *Ericameria ericoides* (Less) Jepson.

9. **Haplopappus arborescens** (Gray) Hall. GOLDENFLEECE. Fig. 681.

An erect fastigiately branched shrub, 3 to 12 feet high, with slender leafy striate branchlets, yellow flowers, and often with trunk-like main stems. Leaves alternate, narrowly linear or closely revolute and becoming filiform, 1 to 2½ inches long, straight, glabrous, impressed-punctate, usually crowded, some with few shorter fascicled leaves in their axils. Heads regularly cymose, terminating the branches, the ultimate peduncles 1/16- to 3/8-inch long and more or less bracteate. Involucral bracts 20 to 25, very loosely imbricated, in 3 or 4 series, much shorter than the disk, thin, with a brown midrib, glabrous or slightly puberulent. Ray-flowers wanting. Disk-flowers 20 to 25. Achenes obtusely about 5-angled, densely appressed-pubescent. Flowering period, July to October.

Goldenfleece inhabits open dry slopes in the chaparral areas of the Coast Ranges from Del Norte County south to Santa Barbara County and on the western slope of the Sierra Nevada, in the Upper Sonoran Life Zone.

Haplopappus arborescens (Gray) Hall, Univ. Calif. Publ. Bot. 7:273 (1919). *Linosyris arborescens* Gray. Type locality: California. *Ericameria arborescens* (Gray) Greene.

10. **Haplopappus Parishii** (Greene) Blake. PARISH GOLDENBUSH. Fig. 682.

An erect branched shrub, 3 to 12 feet high, often arborescent, with densely leafy stout erect glabrous striate more or less resinous branchlets and yellow flowers. Leaves alternate, oblanceolate to linear-oblong, 1 to 2¼ inches long, 1/8- to 1/4-inch wide, thick, glabrous, resinous-punctate, rather crowded but without secondary fascicled leaves in their axils. Heads regularly cymose, terminating the branches, the ultimate peduncles 1/4-inch or less long and with bracts similar to those of the involucre. Involucral bracts about 20, well imbricated, in 4 series, a little shorter than the disk, chartaceous, with a thick brown midrib, glabrous or slightly puberulent. Ray-flowers wanting. Disk-flowers 9 to 12. Achenes turbinate, slightly angled, densely appressed-pubescent. Flowering period, August to October.

Parish Goldenbush is a rare evergreen shrub on hot dry hillslopes in the Upper Sonoran Life Zone in the coastal sagebrush association of the San Gabriel and San Bernardino mountains, southward in the San Jacinto and Santa Ana ranges to the Cuyamaca Mountains of San Diego County. It extends southward to the San Pedro Martir Mountains, Lower California.

Haplopappus Parishii (Greene) Blake, Contr. U. S. Nat. Herb. 23:1491 (1926). *Bigelovia Parishii* Greene. Type locality: San Bernardino Mountains. Collected by *Parish*. *Ericameria Parishii* (Greene) Hall.

11. **Haplopappus propinquus** Blake. CHAPARRAL GOLDENBUSH. Fig. 683.

A rigidly branched shrub, 3 to 9 feet high, with short densely leafy glabrous resinous-punctate branchlets and yellow flowers. Leaves alternate, filiform, 3/8- to 3/4-inch long, grooved on the back, glabrous, resinous-punctate, with shorter fascicled leaves in their axils. Heads racemose or narrowly paniculate, the peduncles short and scaly-bracted. Involucral bracts 16 to 22, loosely imbricated, in about 3 series, glabrous, much shorter than the disk, with a brown resinous median ridge

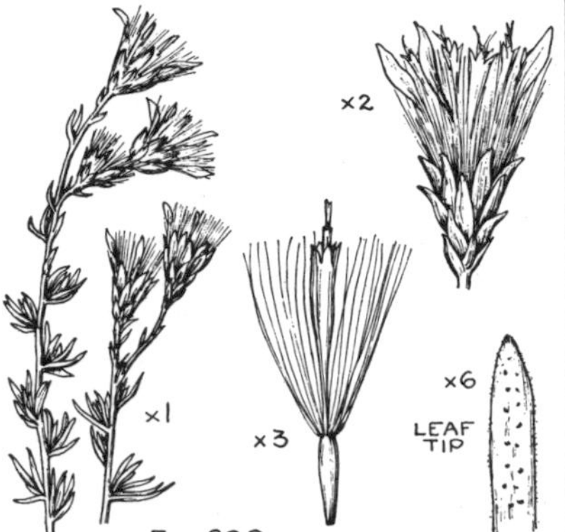

FIG. 680
HAPLOPAPPUS ERICOIDES

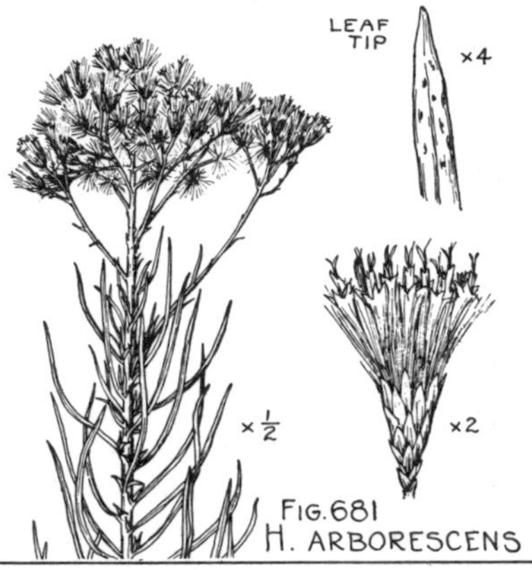

FIG. 681
H. ARBORESCENS

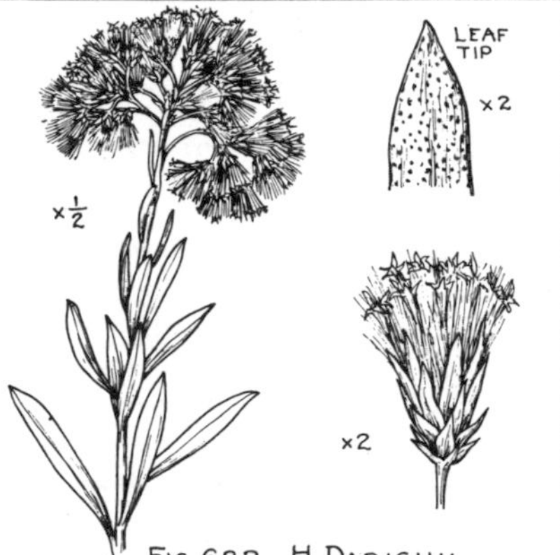

FIG. 682 H. PARISHII

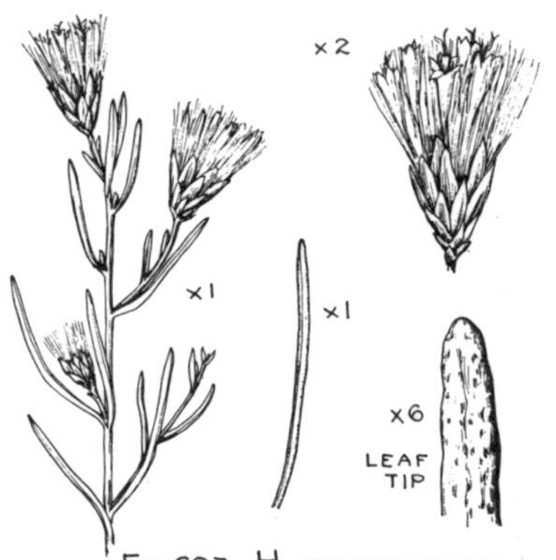

FIG. 683 H. PROPINQUUS

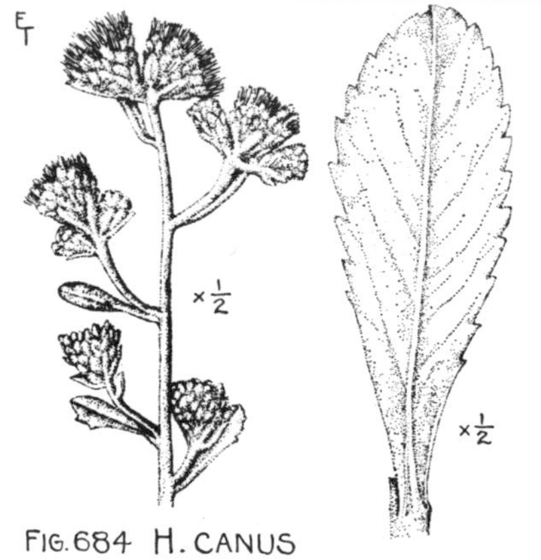

FIG. 684 H. CANUS

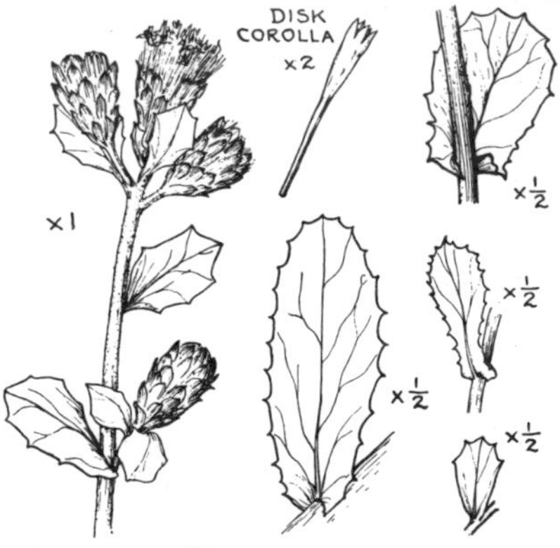

FIG. 685 H. SQUARROSUS

and white scarious margins. Ray-flowers wanting. Disk-flowers 8 to 12. Achenes linear, densely villous. Flowering period, late fall and early winter.

Chaparral Goldenbush occupies a very limited area in the chaparral of southern San Diego County in the Upper Sonoran Life Zone, usually between the desert scrub and the coastal chaparral.

Miss Alice Eastwood has named a form closely related to this species, but with 4 or 5 ray-flowers and sparingly hairy achenes, *Haplopappus illinitus.* It occurs at Warner's Hot Springs, San Diego County. According to Hall, the specific name *illinitus* was given to a South American species in 1856 by Philippi, and therefore this specific name is untenable.

Haplopappus propinquus Blake, Contr. U. S. Nat. Herb. 23:1490 (1926). *Bigelovia brachylepis* Gray, not *H. brachylepis* Philippi. Type locality: "Larkens' Station [now Jacumba], 80 miles east by north of San Diego." Collected by *Palmer*. *Ericameria brachylepis* (Gray) Hall.

12. **Haplopappus canus** (Gray) Blake. HAZARDIA. HOARY GOLDENBUSH. Fig. 684.

A loosely branched shrub, 2 to 4 feet high, with densely white-woolly herbage and yellow flowers turning purple. Leaves alternate, obovate to oblanceolate, 1½ to 4½ or rarely 8 inches long, ½-inch to 1¼ inches wide, densely white-tomentose or the upper surface becoming free of tomentum, sharply serrate or nearly entire, tapering to a narrow petiole-like base or half-clasping. Heads usually cymose, or racemose. Involucral bracts numerous, regularly imbricated, usually in 6 series, white-tomentose. Ray-flowers 4 to 6 or none, the ligules very short. Disk-flowers numerous (40 or more). Achenes usually 4-angled, prominently nerved, canescent. Flowering period, June to September.

Hazardia does not occur in the wild state on the mainland but occurs on rocky slopes on the islands off the coast of southern and Lower California (Santa Rosa, Santa Cruz, San Clemente, and Guadalupe islands). It is cultivated in southern California for its white-woolly herbage and numerous flower-heads.

Haplopappus canus (Gray) Blake, Contr. U. S. Nat. Herb. 24:86 (1922). *Diplostephium canum* Gray. Type locality: Guadalupe Island. *Hazardia cana* Greene.

13. **Haplopappus squarrosus** H. & A. SAWTOOTH GOLDENBUSH. Fig. 685.

KEY TO THE SPECIES AND VARIETIES

Flowers 9 to 30.
  Involucral bracts acute, with green tips. . . . . *H. squarrosus.*
  Involucral bracts very obtuse or truncate but with a short cusp. 13a. var. *obtusus.*
Flowers 4 to 6. . . . . 13b. var. *stenolepis.*

A low freely branched subshrub, 1 to 3 feet high, of bushy habit, with minutely roughish erect stems, strongly striate tomentulose to scabrid or rarely glabrous viscid brittle branchlets, and yellow flowers. Leaves alternate, obovate to oblanceolate, ¾-inch to 2 inches long, ⅜- to ¾-inch wide, obtuse or rounded at apex, sharply serrate, glutinous or glandular-dotted, stiffly chartaceous, with a sessile and somewhat clasping base, some with 1 to 4 smaller leaves in their axils. Heads racemosely paniculate or in close terminal racemes. Involucral bracts numerous, acute, regularly imbricated, in 6 to 8 series, shorter than the disk, with conspicuous minutely glandular green tips. Ray-flowers wanting. Disk-flowers 9 to 30. Achenes fusiform, 5-nerved, glabrous or sparsely pubescent. Flowering period, September and October.

FIG. 686 HAPLOPAPPUS BLOOMERI

FIG. 687 H. BLOOMERI VAR. ANGUSTATUS

FIG. 688 H. GREENEI

FIG. 689 H. SUFFRUTICOSUS

FIG. 690 H. SUFFRUTICOSUS VAR. TENUIS

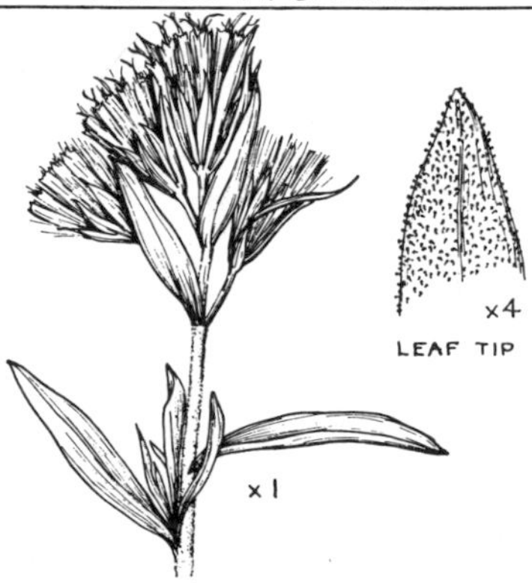

FIG. 691 H. MACRONEMA

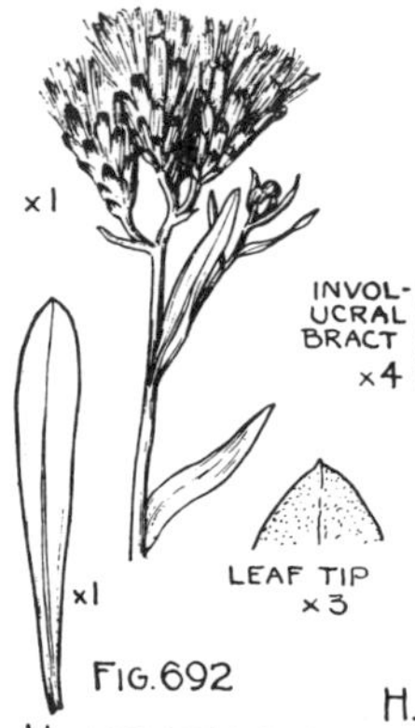

FIG. 692 H. ACRADENIUS

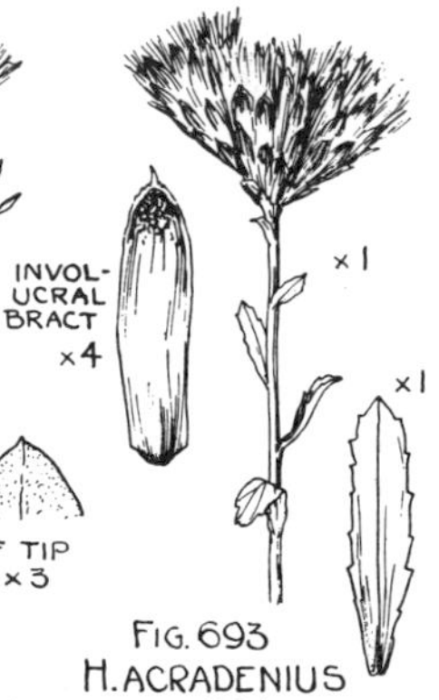

FIG. 693 H. ACRADENIUS VAR. BRACTEOSUS

FIG. 694 H. VENETUS VAR. VERNONIOIDES

FIG. 695 H. VENETUS VAR. OXYPHYLLUS

Sawtooth Goldenbush is a rather common half-shrub in the open chaparral of the coastal mountains from Monterey County southward to San Diego County, eastward to the foothills near San Bernardino, and on Santa Cruz and Santa Catalina islands.

13a. Var. **obtusus** (Greene) n. comb.

An openly branched shrub mostly broader than high. Leaves obovate to broadly oblong, 3/4-inch to 1 inch long. Heads in close terminal racemes. Involucral bracts very obtuse, with a short cusp, resinous-glandular. Flowers 18 to 25. Achenes glabrous.

This variety occurs in a very limited area of the inner South Coast Ranges in Kern County (San Emigdio Canyon, *Eastwood;* near mouth of Grapevine Canyon, *Hall*).

13b. Var. **stenolepis** (Hall) n. comb.

A low compact leafy shrub, often broader than high, forming green tufts on overgrazed hillsides, with stems very woody at base. Leaves oblong to oblong-spatulate, 5/8-inch to 1 inch long. Heads in spikes or some in clusters of 2 or 3 heads each, these in narrow spikes. Involucral bracts linear, loosely imbricated, acuminate or mucronately acute, glabrous but slightly viscid. Flowers 4 to 6. Achenes glabrous.

According to Hall, this variety grows on "serpentine soil on the eastern slope of Parkfield Grade, inner South Coast Ranges of Fresno County . . . same district but on westerly slope, in Monterey County."

Haplopappus squarrosus H. & A. Bot. Beechey 146 (1833). "Probably vicinity of Monterey." Collected on Beechey's voyage. *Hazardia squarrosa* Greene.

Var. obtusus (Greene) McMinn. *Hazardia obtusa* Greene. Type locality: San Emigdio Canyon, Kern County. Collected by *Eastwood. Hazardia squarrosa* var. *obtusa* (Greene) Jepson.

Var. stenolepis (Hall) McMinn. *H. squarrosus* subsp. *stenolepis* Hall. Type locality: "Eastern slope of Parkfield Grade, inner South Coast Ranges of Fresno County." Collected by *Hall.*

14. **Haplopappus nanus** (Nutt.) D. C. Eaton. DWARF GOLDENBUSH.

A dwarf subshrub, 1/3-foot to 1 1/2 feet high, with numerous thick gnarled branches, brittle leafy glabrous resinous branchlets, and yellow flowers. Flowering period, July to October.

Dwarf Goldenbush is known in California only from Mono County (Benton Range, *Hall*) and Inyo County (Death Valley region, *M. F. Gilman*). It occurs in the hills and mountains of the Great Basin region in Nevada, Utah, Idaho, Washington, and eastern Oregon. Hall suggests that this plant may be utilized as a source of rubber if brought into cultivation. Tests made by Hall and Goodspeed showed 5 to 10 per cent of rubber.

Haplopappus nanus (Nutt.) D. C. Eaton, Bot. King's Expl. 159 (1871). *Ericameria nana* Nutt. Type locality: Blue Mountains of Oregon. Collected by *Nuttall.*

15. **Haplopappus Bloomeri** Gray. BLOOMER GOLDENBUSH. Fig. 686.

KEY TO THE SPECIES AND VARIETIES

Herbage green and glandular.

Leaves about 1/8-inch wide, usually straight. . . . . *H. Bloomeri.*

Leaves about $\frac{1}{16}$-inch or less wide, usually curved.........15a. var. *angustatus.*
Herbage gray- or white-tomentose...........................15b. var. *Sonnei.*

A low compact subshrub, 1 to 2 (or 4) feet high, with many ascending stems freely branching to form a rounded bush, brittle densely leafy branchlets, and yellow flowers. Flowering period, July to September.

Bloomer Goldenbush occurs in the mountains from Lake County northward in the inner Coast Range around the head of the Sacramento Valley and thence southward in the Sierra Nevada to the Yosemite region. It extends northward into Oregon and Washington and eastward into Nevada.

15a. Var. **angustatus** Gray. Fig. 687.

This variety occurs in the San Bernardino Mountains (near Baldwin Lake, *Peirson*), and in the foothills and on the lower slopes of the Sierra Nevada from Fresno County northward to Modoc and Siskiyou counties, thence northward to Oregon and southeastern Washington.

15b. Var. **Sonnei** Greene.

This variety is known in California from near Donner Lake. It extends northward into Oregon and Washington.

Haplopappus Bloomeri Gray, Proc. Am. Acad. 6:540 (1865). Type locality: "Near Virginia City, Nevada." Collected by *Bloomer. Chrysothamnus Bloomeri* (Gray) Greene, of Jepson's Manual.

Var. angustatus Gray, Proc. Am. Acad. 7:354 (1868). Type locality: Mount Shasta, California. Collected by *Brewer.*

Var. Sonnei Greene, Pitt. 2:17 (1889). Type locality: "Sandy soil about Donner Lake, in the Sierra Nevada." Collected by *Sonne.*

16. **Haplopappus Greenei** Gray. NORTHERN GOLDENBUSH. Fig. 688.

KEY TO THE SPECIES AND VARIETY

Herbage green, minutely glandular or viscid.......................*H. Greenei.*
Herbage gray with a close fine tomentum......................16a. var. *mollis.*

A low subshrub, 1 foot or less high, with spreading woody branches, erect leafy flowering branchlets, and yellow flowers. Flowering period, August to October.

Northern Goldenbush occurs in the mountains of northern California (Yollo Bolly Mts. to Scott Mts.; Modoc Co., acc. *Jepson*). It extends northward to Oregon and Washington.

16a. Var. **mollis** Gray.

This variety has been collected in the Warner Mountains of Modoc County and in the mountains about the headwaters of the Sacramento River *(Pringle),* acc. Hall.

Haplopappus Greenei Gray, Proc. Am. Acad. 16:80 (1880). Type locality: "Scott Mountains, Siskiyou County." Collected by *Greene. Macronema Greenei* (Gray) Greene.

Var. mollis Gray, Syn. Fl. 1:135 (1884). *H. mollis* Gray. Type locality: "High mountains of Union County, Oregon." Collected by *Cusick. Macronema Greenei* var. *mollis* (Gray) Jepson.

17. **Haplopappus suffruticosus** (Nutt.) Gray. SINGLEHEAD GOLDENBUSH. Fig. 689.

KEY TO THE SPECIES AND VARIETY

Leaves oblong to oblanceolate.................................*H. suffruticosus.*
Leaves filiform-linear...17a. var. *tenuis.*

A bushy subshrub, 1/3-foot to 1 foot high, with numerous spreading branches forming a compact bush often broader than high, glandular-puberulent brittle branchlets, and yellow flowers. Flowering period, July to October.

Singlehead Goldenbush occurs in the subalpine regions of the Sierra Nevada, in the Hudsonian Life Zone. (White Mts., Mono Co., *Shockley;* near Farewell Gap, southern Sierra Nevada, *Hopping;* Pyramid Peak, *Brewer;* ridge s. of Donner Pass, *Heller,* acc. *Hall;* Mt. Guyot, Mt. Goddard, and Castle Peak, acc. *Jepson.*) It extends northward to Oregon and eastward into Nevada, Idaho, Wyoming, and Montana.

17a. Var. **tenuis** (Hall) n. comb. Fig. 690.

This variety has been collected from Mount Guyot, eastern Tulare County *(Hall),* borders of meadows near Black Mountain, Fresno County *(Hall & Chandler),* and Mount Hoffman, Yosemite National Park *(Hall).*

Haplopappus suffruticosus (Nutt.) Gray, Proc. Am. Acad. 6:542 (1865). *Macronema suffruticosa* Nutt. Type locality: "Banks of the Malade, a tributary of the Columbia River, near the Blue Mountains." Collected by *Nuttall.*

Var. tenuis (Hall) McMinn. *H. suffruticosus* subsp. *tenuis* Hall. Type locality: "Near Big Creek in the Black Mountain district of Fresno County, California." Collected by *Hall & Chandler.*

18. **Haplopappus Macronema** Gray. WHITESTEM GOLDENBUSH. Fig. 691.

A low compact subshrub, 6 inches to 1½ feet high, with numerous short branches covered with a dense white tomentum except near the heads. Flowering period, July to September.

Whitestem Goldenbush occurs in a narrow belt in the higher parts of the Sierra Nevada from Tulare County northward to Eldorado County. It extends eastward to Nevada, Utah, and Colorado and northward to Oregon and Idaho. It is rather a common plant near timber-line.

Haplopappus Macronema Gray, Proc. Am. Acad. 6:542 (1866). Type locality: "Banks of the Lewis River and other streams of the Oregon." Collected by *Nuttall. Macronema discoidea* Nutt.

19. **Haplopappus acradenius** (Greene) Blake. PALELEAF GOLDENBUSH. Fig. 692.

KEY TO THE SPECIES AND VARIETIES

Leaves entire; flowers 6 to 13.................................*H. acradenius.*
Leaves mostly denticulate or dentate; flowers 15 to 20 or more.
  Leaves 1 to 2 inches long; Colorado Desert.............19a. var. *eremophilus.*
  Leaves usually less than 1 inch long; San Joaquin Valley..19b. var. *bracteosus.*

An erect subshrub, 1 to 3 feet high, with many woody branches from the base forming a rounded bush. Bark smooth, white or straw-color. Flowering period, September and October.

Paleleaf Goldenbush occurs in alkaline soils of the Mohave Desert, in the Lower Sonoran Life Zone. It extends eastward into Nevada.

19a. Var. **eremophilus** (Greene) Munz.

This variety occurs on the Colorado Desert and at Box "S" Ranch on the Mohave Desert, acc. *Munz.* It extends eastward to Arizona and southward into Lower California.

19b. Var. **bracteosus** (Greene) n. comb. Fig. 693.

This variety occurs at the southern end of the San Joaquin Valley in Kern and Tulare counties.

Haplopappus acradenius (Greene) Blake, Contr. U. S. Nat. Herb. 25:546 (1925). *Bigelovia acradenia* Greene. Type locality: Mohave Desert, California. Collected probably by *Parry. Isocoma veneta* var. *acradenia* Hall.

Var. eremophilus (Greene) Munz, Man. S. Calif. Bot. 523 (1935). *Isocoma eremophila* Greene. Type locality: "Southwestern part of the Colorado Desert, California." Collected by *Orcutt.*

Var. bracteosus (Greene) McMinn. *Isocoma bracteosa* Greene. Type locality: Tulare County. Collected by *Sheldon.*

20. **Haplopappus venetus** var. **vernonioides** (Nutt.) Munz. COAST GOLDENBUSH. Fig. 694.

The species *H. venetus* (H. B. K.) Blake in its typical form does not occur in California, but the 2 following varieties and numerous forms are common in western California from the San Francisco Bay southward.

KEY TO THE VARIETIES

Leaves mostly dentate, lobed or incised. . . . . var. *vernonioides.*
Leaves mostly entire. . . . . 20a. var. *oxyphyllus.*

An erect or sometimes a low and decumbent shrub, up to 4 feet high, with nearly glabrous to villous herbage and yellow flowers. Principal leaves spatulate-oblong, somewhat acute and mucronate, varying to obtuse, 3/8-inch to 1 1/4 inches long, 1/8- to 3/8-inch wide, spinulose-dentate to almost lobed, sometimes entire, with petiole-like bases, with secondary fascicled leaves in their axils. Heads in rounded terminal cymes, these either compact or the lower branches elongated. Involucral bracts regularly imbricated, in about 4 series of different lengths, glabrous and resinous or rarely pubescent, with green acutish tips, the margins often erose. Ray-flowers none. Disk-flowers 15 to 25 or 30. Achenes very slender, about 1/8-inch long, about 4-angled, silky-villous. Flowering period, late summer and early fall.

This variety is a common bushy shrub in the coastal areas and adjacent valleys in California from San Francisco Bay southward to San Diego County and on the islands off the coast of southern California. It is an exceedingly variable entity.

20a. Var. **oxyphyllus** (Greene) Munz. Fig. 695.

An erect robust plant, 3 to 6 feet high, with loosely villous to nearly glabrous herbage. Principal leaves oblanceolate, mostly 1 1/4 to 2 inches long, decidedly acute to acuminate, mostly all entire. Heads numerous in rounded cymes, these open-paniculate.

This variety occurs along the coast and in the adjacent valleys of southwestern San Diego County. It extends southward into Lower California.

Haplopappus venetus var. vernonioides (Nutt.) Munz, Man. S. Calif. Bot. 522 (1935). *Isocoma vernonioides* Nutt. Type locality: Marshes near the sea, Santa Barbara, California. Collected by *Nuttall. Isocoma veneta* var. *vernonioides* Jepson.

Var. oxyphyllus (Greene) Munz, Man. S. Calif. Bot. 523 (1935). *Isocoma oxyphylla* Greene. Type locality: Jamul Valley, east of San Diego, California. Collected by *Palmer*.

21. **Haplopappus brickellioides** Blake. BRICKELL GOLDENBUSH.

Characters of the key.

This is a little-known species occurring at the type locality, "Rocks, Ash Meadows, Sheep Mountain, Nevada." Ash Meadows is southeast of Death Valley on the California-Nevada boundary.

Haplopappus brickellioides Blake, Proc. Biol. Soc. Wash. 35:173 (1922).

13. **Baccharis** L.

(Name from Bacchus, the Greek god of vegetation, later of wine.)

Usually shrubs but some herbaceous perennials, commonly resinous or glutinous, sometimes pubescent. Leaves simple and alternate. Flowers whitish or yellowish, all discoid, unisexual, the staminate and pistillate borne in separate heads on different plants. Involucral bracts well imbricated. Receptacle naked or rarely with chaffy bracts. Achenes slightly compressed, 5- or 10-nerved, not beaked. Pappus in staminate flowers of scanty capillary bristles, in the fertile (i.e. pistillate) flowers copious and usually rather long.

The genus *Baccharis* contains about 300 species native to America, mostly in South America. Nine species occur in California, all of which are shrubs or subshrubs.

KEY TO THE SPECIES

Plants prostrate to decumbent, 6 to 12 inches high. . . . . 1. *B. pilularis.*
Plants erect, over 1 foot high.
  Leaves willow-like, 1 to 6 inches long; achenes 5-nerved.
    Heads terminating lateral branchlets from a woody stem; involucral bracts golden-brown or tinged with pink when young; herbage not glutinous. 2. *B. viminea.*
    Heads terminating the main branches, these herbaceous; mature involucral bracts straw-colored, often pink-tinged when young; herbage often glutinous. . . . . 3. *B. glutinosa.*
  Leaves not willow-like.
    Leaves commonly obovate or oblanceolate.
      Leaves usually irregularly sinuately and coarsely toothed; heads sessile, in small clusters in a densely leafy panicle; receptacle without chaffy bracts. . . . . 1a. *B. pilularis* var. *consanguinea.*
      Leaves usually entire or rarely few-toothed; heads pedunculate, in nearly leafless panicles; receptacle with chaffy bracts. . . . . 4. *B. sergiloides.*
    Leaves linear or lanceolate to ovate or oblong.
      Plants woody only at or near the base.
        Leaves linear or linear-oblong, 2 inches or less long; herbage pubescent.
          Leaves entire, less than ¾-inch long, acute, the upper ones scale-like. . . . . 5. *B. brachyphylla.*
          Leaves sharply serrate, ¾-inch to 2 inches long, obtuse. 6. *B. Plummerae.*
        Leaves lanceolate or ovate-lanceolate, 2½ to 4 inches long, glutinous. 7. *B. Douglasii.*

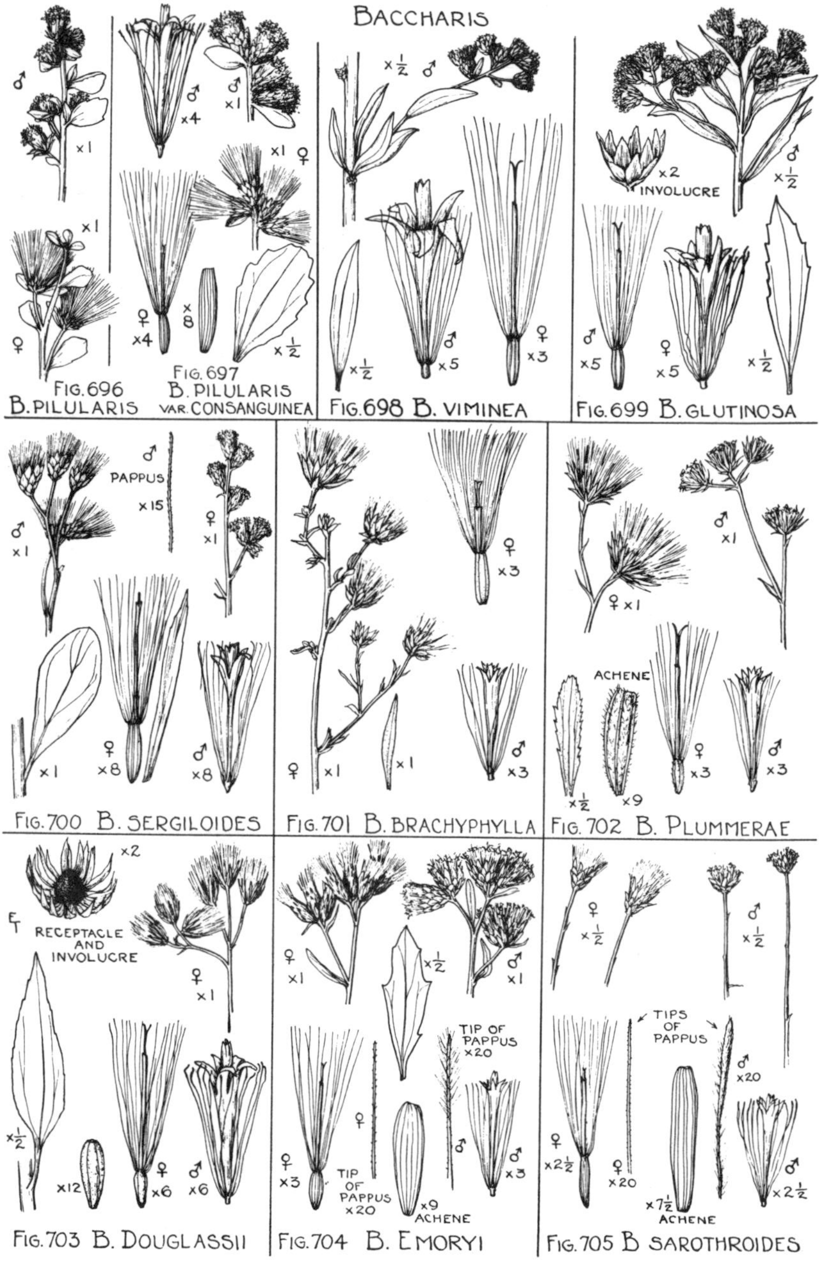
BACCHARIS
FIG. 696 B. PILULARIS
FIG. 697 B. PILULARIS VAR. CONSANGUINEA
FIG. 698 B. VIMINEA
FIG. 699 B. GLUTINOSA
INVOLUCRE
FIG. 700 B. SERGILOIDES
PAPPUS
FIG. 701 B. BRACHYPHYLLA
FIG. 702 B. PLUMMERAE
ACHENE
RECEPTACLE AND INVOLUCRE
FIG. 703 B. DOUGLASSII
TIP OF PAPPUS
ACHENE
FIG. 704 B. EMORYI
TIPS OF PAPPUS
ACHENE
FIG. 705 B SAROTHROIDES

Plants distinctly shrubby; achenes 10-nerved.
Heads in sessile or subsessile clusters in a leafy panicle; leaves 3-nerved or the upper ones 1-nerved.
Panicles densely leafy.............1a. *B. pilularis* var. *consanguinea.*
Panicles sparingly leafy.............................8. *B. Emoryi.*
Heads usually solitary on the branches of the broom-like leafless or nearly leafless panicle; leaves 1-nerved or rarely inconspicuously 3-nerved.
Receptacle with a few chaffy bracts; pappus of matured pistillate flowers about 1/8-inch long....................4. *B. sergiloides.*
Receptacle without chaffy bracts; pappus of matured pistillate flowers 1/4- to 1/3-inch long, brownish................9. *B. sarothroides.*

1. **Baccharis pilularis** DC. DWARF BACCHARIS. DWARF CHAPARRAL BROOM. Fig. 696.

KEY TO THE SPECIES AND VARIETY

Plants prostrate to decumbent, 6 to 12 inches high..................*B. pilularis.*
Plants erect, 2 to 10 feet high..........................1a. var. *consanguinea.*

A prostrate or decumbent evergreen shrub, 6 to 12 inches high and with a spread of 2 to 10 feet. Leaves cuneate-obovate, 1/4- to 1/2-inch long, tapering to a petiole-like base, dark green and glabrous, coarsely or sinuately few-toothed, or sometimes entire. Heads about 1/4-inch long, mostly solitary in the axils or terminal on the leafy branchlets. Pistillate flowers whitish. Staminate flowers yellowish. Involucral bracts narrowly oblong, acutish. Achenes 10-nerved. Pappus of the pistillate flowers abundant, becoming 3/8-inch long, that of the staminate flowers about half as long, minutely scabrous. Flowering period, July to September.

Dwarf Baccharis occurs on open hill slopes, sand dunes, and sandy bluffs near the ocean from Sonoma County (near the mouth of the Russian River) southward to Point Sur, Monterey County. Plants grown from seed collected in Marin County retain their prostrate habit. This plant should make a good ground-cover because of its natural spreading habit.

1a. Var. **consanguinea** (DC.) Ktze. CHAPARRAL BROOM. Fig. 697.

An erect compactly branched evergreen shrub, 2 to 10 feet high, with green angular branchlets in new growth. Leaves obovate or oblanceolate or rarely oblong-elliptical, 1/2-inch to 1 1/2 inches long, 1-nerved or somewhat 3-nerved from the cuneate base, leathery in texture, coarsely and irregularly toothed or sometimes nearly entire, dark green and glabrous, tapering below to a petiole-like base. Heads solitary or commonly several in the axils or in terminal clusters on the leafy branches. Involucral bracts obtuse, the outer bracts broadly oblong to ovate, the inner ones narrowly oblong. Flowering period, August to October.

Chaparral Broom is a common shrub on open low hills and lower mountain slopes from Monterey County northward in the coastal counties to southern Oregon. It extends southward, but is much less abundant, to northern San Diego County and occurs also in scattered locations on the western slope of the Mount Hamilton Range, in the foothills of the central Sierra Nevada counties, and on the islands off the coast of southern California.

A satisfactory hedge can be grown from this variety if proper pruning is practised.

Baccharis pilularis DC. Prodr. 5:407 (1836). Type locality: "In California." Collected by *Douglas,* probably at Monterey.

Var. consanguinea (DC.) Ktze. Rev. Gen. 1:319 (1891). *B. consanguinea* DC. Type locality: "In California." Collected by *Douglas,* probably at San Francisco.

2. **Baccharis viminea** DC. MULE FAT. Fig. 698.

An erect-spreading very leafy and loosely branched evergreen shrub, 6 to 12 feet high, with usually numerous short lateral flowering branchlets and scarcely glutinous herbage. Leaves narrowly lanceolate to oblong, willow-like, 1 to 3½ inches long, tapering to a sessile base, 1-nerved or inconspicuously 3-nerved, pale green, entire or slightly denticulate. Heads rather numerous, in close corymbose clusters on the ends of the lateral branchlets. Involucral bracts firm, oblong or ovate, with scarious margins, erose and mostly ciliate, pinkish when young. Receptacle flat, without bracts. Achenes 5-nerved. Pappus of pistillate flowers apparently smooth but minutely scabrous as seen under a lens. Flowering period, May to July.

Mule Fat is a common willow-like shrub along water courses and moist waste places of the Lower and Upper Sonoran Life Zones from the Sacramento and adjacent valleys and occasionally in the valleys of Napa and Lake counties, southward in the warm coast valleys, the San Joaquin Valley, and the lower valleys of the Sierra Nevada foothills to the coastal and cismontane areas of southern California.

Baccharis viminea DC. Prodr. 5:400 (1836). Type locality: "In California." Collected by *Douglas.*

3. **Baccharis glutinosa** Pers. STICKY BACCHARIS. SEEPWILLOW. WATER WALLY. Fig. 699.

An erect or straggling evergreen shrub, 3 to 9 feet high, with several slender leafy stems in a cluster, usually herbaceous above and woody at the base. Leaves lanceolate, willow-like, 1½ to 4 inches (or to 6 inches) long, bright green and usually glutinous, 3-nerved from the base or the upper leaves 1-nerved, tapering at base to a short petiole, remotely denticulate or entire. Heads in terminal cymes or panicles, the staminate heads about ⅛-inch high, the pistillate ones about ¼-inch high. Involucral bracts straw-colored, with narrow scarious margins, the outer bracts ovate, the inner ones oblong-lanceolate. Achenes 5-nerved. Pappus-bristles minutely scabrous. Flowering period, February to May.

Sticky Baccharis occurs along streams and in moist ground in the Upper and Lower Sonoran Life Zones throughout southern California northward through the Mohave Desert to Owens Valley, Inyo County. It extends eastward to Texas and southward to Mexico and occurs also in Chile. It resembles *B. viminea* in general appearance but in that species the stems are usually woody to near the summit, the leaves are rarely glutinous, and the inflorescences are normally lateral.

Baccharis glutinosa Pers. Syn. 2:425 (1807). Type locality: "In Regni Chilensis ruderatis."

4. **Baccharis sergiloides** Gray. SQUAW BACCHARIS. SQUAW WATERWEED. Fig. 700.

An erect glabrous shrub, 3 to 6 feet high, with mostly 4-sided striate slender branchlets and glutinous herbage. Leaves obovate or spatulate, ½-inch to 1¼ inches long or rarely longer on the sterile shoots, usually more sparse and smaller on the flowering shoots, entire or rarely few-toothed. Heads solitary on short bractless peduncles, these numerous in dense nearly leafless broom-like panicles. Involucral bracts firm, oblong-ovate. Receptacle with a few chaffy bracts among the flowers. Achenes glabrous, 10-nerved. Pappus of staminate flowers rather stiff and sparse, broadening upward. Pappus of pistillate flowers more abundant, filiform throughout, about 1/8-inch long when mature. Flowering period, April to June.

Squaw Baccharis occurs in washes and canyons along the base of the mountains bordering the western side of the Colorado Desert and extends eastward and northward in the Colorado and Mohave deserts to the Panamint Mountains of Inyo County and to Nevada, Arizona, and Utah.

Baccharis sergiloides Gray, Bot. Mex. Bound. 83 (1859). Type locality: "Along the Gila or Colorado," *Emory;* "Dry arroyos, 50 miles west of the Colorado," *Bigelow.*

5. **Baccharis brachyphylla** Gray. SHORTLEAF BACCHARIS. Fig. 701.

A diffusely much branched evergreen perennial, 2 to 3 1/2 feet high, with slender herbaceous stems woody at the base and with pubescent herbage. Flowering period, July to September.

Shortleaf Baccharis occurs in southern San Diego County and in Morongo wash, 0.3 mile south of the San Bernardino County line in Riverside County *(Wolf),* in the Lower Sonoran Life Zone. It extends eastward to Arizona and Utah and southward to Mexico.

Baccharis brachyphylla Gray, Pl. Wright. 2:83 (1853). Type locality: "Between Conde's camp and the Chiricahui Mountains, in stony soil," Mexico. (Now Chiricahua Mountains, Arizona.) Collected by *Wright.*

6. **Baccharis Plummerae** Gray. PLUMMER BACCHARIS. Fig. 702.

A loosely much branched deciduous perennial from a woody base, 2 to 3 1/2 feet high, with viscid-pubescent herbage and inflorescences. Flowering period, July to September.

Plummer Baccharis inhabits dry bluffs and canyons near the sea from the Santa Monica Mountains of Los Angeles County northward to the Santa Ynez Mountains of Santa Barbara County and on Santa Cruz Island, in the Upper Sonoran Life Zone.

Baccharis Plummerae Gray, Proc. Am. Acad. 15:48 (1879). Type locality: "Along a stream in Glen Lock ravine, in the mountains near Sta. Barbara, California." Collected by *Sara Plummer.*

7. **Baccharis Douglasii** DC. DOUGLAS BACCHARIS. Fig. 703.

A tall perennial, 3 to 6 feet high, woody at the bsae, with stems simple up to the inflorescence and with glutinous herbage. Flowering period, July to September.

Douglas Baccharis occurs in moist places in the Upper Sonoran Life Zone from San Diego County northward through cismontane southern California and the Coast Ranges to the San Francisco Bay counties and in scattered localities in San Joaquin, Amador (vicinity of Ione), and Humboldt (Van Duzen River) counties. It probably occurs elsewhere in northern and central California.

Baccharis Douglasii DC. Prodr. 5:400 (1836). Type locality: "In California." Collected by *Douglas.*

8. **Baccharis Emoryi** Gray. EMORY BACCHARIS. Fig. 704.

An erect loosely branched evergreen shrub, 3 to 12 feet high, with striate-angled branchlets. Lower leaves broadly to narrowly oblong, 3/4-inch to 1 1/2 inches long, 3-nerved from the base, commonly with few to several short broad teeth, upper leaves usually smaller, linear, 1-nerved, and entire. Heads in small compact clusters terminating short nearly naked peduncles, the whole inflorescence forming a large rather loose sparsely leafy panicle. Involucral bracts closely imbricated, the outer oval, the inner narrower and thinner. Receptacle naked. Achenes glabrous, 10-nerved. Pappus of pistillate flowers abundant, filiform throughout, nearly ½-inch long, very showy in fruit, that of the staminate flowers bearded at the apex. Flowering period, June to September.

Emory Baccharis occurs in moist habitats in the Lower and Upper Sonoran Life Zones from Los Angeles County southward to San Diego County and Lower California, and eastward to the Colorado Desert, Arizona, and Utah.

Baccharis Emoryi Gray, Bot. Mex. Bound. 83 (1859). Type locality: "Very common on the Gila," Arizona. Collected by *Emory;* and at Fort Yuma, eastern California by *Major Thomas.*

9. **Baccharis sarothroides** Gray. Broom Baccharis. Fig. 705.

A much branched nearly leafless shrub, 2 to 6 feet high, with numerous slender 4-sided and strongly striate twigs. Leaves few, linear, ¼- to ¾-inch long, 1-nerved, entire. Heads mostly solitary on naked wiry peduncles, these numerous and forming a dense broom-like panicle. Outer involucral bracts oval, very firm, the inner bracts thin and narrow. Receptacle flat, without bracts. Achenes glabrous, 10-nerved. Pappus of pistillate flowers soft and abundant, brownish, ¼- to ⅓-inch long when mature, that of the staminate flowers scant and dilated at the tip. Flowering period, August and September.

Broom Baccharis occurs in southern San Diego County (Sweetwater Dam; Mission Valley) and extends southward to Lower California. One specimen collected by E. E. Schellenger from the Chuckawalla Bench on the Colorado Desert and filed in the University of California herbarium apparently belongs to this species. It also occurs in Arizona.

Baccharis sarothroides Gray, Proc. Am. Acad. 17:211 (1882). Type locality: Southern borders of California. Collected by *Sutton Hayes, Palmer.*

14. **Chrysothamnus** Nutt. Rabbitbrush

(From the Greek *chrysos,* gold, and *thamnos,* shrub, in reference to the brilliant golden-yellow flowers.)

Shrubs and subshrubs with glabrous to tomentose often resinous and aromatic herbage. Leaves simple, alternate, entire. Ray-flowers none. Disk-flowers 4 to 20 in each head, bisexual, fertile. Heads in various clusters or rarely solitary, usually in panicles or cymes. Involucral bracts firm, often leathery, well imbricated in more or less distinct vertical ranks. Receptacle naked. Achenes slender, round in cross section or slightly angled, glabrous to densely pubescent. Pappus of soft capillary bristles, dull white or brownish.

The genus *Chrysothamnus* contains about 12 species with many subspecies or varieties native to the arid regions of western North America. Five species and 22 varieties occur in California. This genus is closely related to the genus *Haplopappus* from which it differs in its narrower heads and the more or less distinctly vertical ranks of involucral bracts. The latex of a few species of this genus has been found to yield rubber.

Key to the Species

Herbage resinous-punctate.

Leaves nearly round in cross section.

Heads in short terminal spikes, these apparently cymose or thyrsoid; bracts of the involucre 16 to 20 . . . . 1. *C. teretifolius.*

Heads in terminal panicles or reduced to racemes; bracts of the involucre 13 to 17 . . . . 2. *C. paniculatus.*

Leaves at first flat but drying to filiform; heads in terminal corymbose clusters . . . . 3. *C. albidus.*

Herbage not resinous-punctate.

Branches covered with felt-like tomentum.

Inflorescence spike-like or racemose; bracts of the involucre 10 to 20. 4. *C. Parryi* varieties.

Inflorescence not spike-like or racemose; bracts of the involucre 20 to 25. 5. *C. nauseosus* varieties.

Branches glabrous, or pubescent but without a felt-like tomentum.

Bracts of the involucre 20 to 25, strongly keeled . . . . 6. *C. depressus.*

Bracts of the involucre about 15, not strongly keeled . . . . . . 7. *C. viscidiflorus.*

1. **Chrysothamnus teretifolius** (D. & H.) Hall. Rabbitbrush. Fig. 707.

An irregularly branched rounded shrub, 1 to 4 feet high, with brittle glabrous resinous-punctate branches, these very leafy. Leaves linear, round in cross section, 3/8- to 3/4-inch long, glabrous but conspicuously dotted with impressed resin-glands. Heads in short terminal spikes. Involucral bracts 16 to 20, in 5 vertical ranks, straw-colored, with a thickened green spot near the apex. Flowers 5 or 6. Achenes 5-angled, densely villous. Flowering period, August to October.

Rabbitbrush occurs on gravelly hillsides and in rocky canyons of the mountains of Inyo County and along the eastern borders of the southern Sierra Nevada, southward and westward in the Tehachapi Mountains, and in San Gorgonio Pass and the Santa Rosa Mountains. It extends eastward to Nevada and Arizona.

Chrysothamnus teretifolius (D. & H.) Hall, Univ. Calif. Publ. Bot. 3:57 (1907). *Linosyris teretifolia* D. & H. Type locality: "All over the mountains around Tejon Valley, California." Collected by *Heermann. Ericameria teretifolia* Jepson.

2. **Chrysothamnus paniculatus** (Gray) Hall. Sticky Rabbitbrush. Fig. 708.

A broad rounded shrub, 2 to 6 feet high, with leafy brittle twigs, glabrous but resinous and viscid. Leaves linear, round in cross section, 3/4-inch to 1 1/4 inches long, glabrous, marked with impressed resin-dots. Heads in profuse panicles or rarely subracemose. Involucral bracts 13 to 17, in 5 vertical ranks, straw-colored, without a green apical spot. Flowers 5 to 8. Achenes 5-angled, appressed-villous. Flowering period, May to October.

Sticky Rabbitbrush occurs occasionally in gravelly washes of the Colorado and Mohave deserts from the region of Chuckawalla Bench and Whitewater, Riverside County northward to the eastern slope of the Tehachapi Mountains and to Inyo County. It extends eastward to Nevada, Arizona, and southwestern Utah.

Chrysothamnus paniculatus (Gray) Hall, Univ. Calif. Publ. Bot. 3:58 (1907). *Bigelovia paniculata* Gray. Type locality: Probably in the southeastern part of California. Collected by *Schott. Ericameria paniculata* (Gray) Rydb.

3. **Chrysothamnus albidus** (Jones) Greene. Alkali Rabbitbrush. Fig. 709.

A fastigiately branched shrub, 1 to 3 feet high, with very leafy, glabrous, resinous-viscid branches. Leaves at first flat but drying to filiform through enrolling of the margins, 3/4-inch to 1 1/2 inches long, glabrous, resinous-pitted. Involucral bracts about 15, in obscure vertical ranks. Flowers 5 or 6. Achenes densely villous. Flowering period, June to August.

Fig. 706. Rubber Rabbitbrush. *Chrysothamnus nauseosus* var. *gnaphalodes* (Greene) Hall. (*Photograph by Hugh P. Dearing.*)

To my knowledge this shrub has been collected in California only in the Owens Valley (*Kellogg,* acc. *Hall.*) It is a shrub of the Great Basin area to the east of California.

Chrysothamnus albidus (Jones) Greene, Erythea 3:107 (1895). *Bigelovia albida* Jones. Type locality: "In alkaline soils, Wells, Nevada." Collected by *M. E. Jones.*

4. **Chrysothamnus Parryi** (Gray) Greene. PARRY RABBITBRUSH.

A low shrub, 1 to 2 feet high, with numerous ascending flexible branches and branchlets closely covered with a whitish tomentum. Leaves narrowly to broadly linear, 3/4-inch to 3 inches long, green and viscid-glandular or gray and tomentulose. Heads in leafy terminal racemes, these sometimes branching. Involucral bracts 10 to 20. Flowers 4 to 20. Achenes 4-angled, densely appressed-villous.

This species apparently does not occur in its typical form in California, but is represented by the following varieties.

KEY TO THE VARIETIES

Racemes reduced to 1 or 2 heads; heads with 5 or 6 flowers. 4a. var. *monocephalus.*
Racemes or panicles with few to numerous heads.
  Heads few, peduncled in a reduced raceme, with 11 to 15 flowers; plants less than 6 inches high.................................... 4b. var. *imulus.*
  Heads few to numerous, with 4 to 11 flowers.
    Leaves more than 1/8-inch wide.
      Leaves thick and rigid; heads with 5 to 7 flowers........... 4c. var. *latior.*
      Leaves thinner and soft; heads with 8 to 11 or rarely 7 flowers. 4d. var. *Bolanderi.*
    Leaves less than 1/8-inch wide.
      Bracts of involucre 13 to 20, strongly keeled; flowers 4 to 6. 4e. var. *nevadensis.*
      Bracts of involucre 8 to 12, not strongly keeled.
        Leaves with sessile resin glands; flowers 5 to 7........ 4f. var. *vulcanicus.*
        Leaves with stalked glands; flowers 5 to 10.............. 4g. var. *asper.*

4a. Var. **monocephalus** (Nels. & Ken.) Jepson, Man. 1033 (1925). *C. monocephalus* Nels. & Ken. Type locality: Summit of Mount Rose, Washoe County, Nevada. Collected by *Kennedy.* Distribution in California: Vicinity of Mono Pass and east side of Mount Dana, 8000 to 9000 feet elevation, Mono County; about "2½ miles northwest of Sonora Pass, Tuolumne County," *W. A. Peterson.* Flowering period, August and September.

4b. Var. **imulus** (Hall) Jepson, Man. 1033 (1925). *C. Parryi* subsp. *imulus* Hall. Type locality: Bear Valley, San Bernardino Mountains, California. Collected by *M. E. Jones.* Distribution: Known only from the San Bernardino Mountains, California.

4c. Var. **latior** (Hall) Jepson, Man. 1033 (1925). Fig. 711. *C. Parryi* subsp. *latior* Hall. Type locality: Mount Eddy, Siskiyou County, California. Collected by *Heller.* Distribution: Mountains of Siskiyou and Modoc counties, California. Flowering period, July and August.

4d. Var. **Bolanderi** (Gray) Jepson, Man. 1033 (1925). *Linosyris Bolanderi* Gray. Type locality: Mono Pass, Mono County, California. Collected by *Bolander.* Dis-

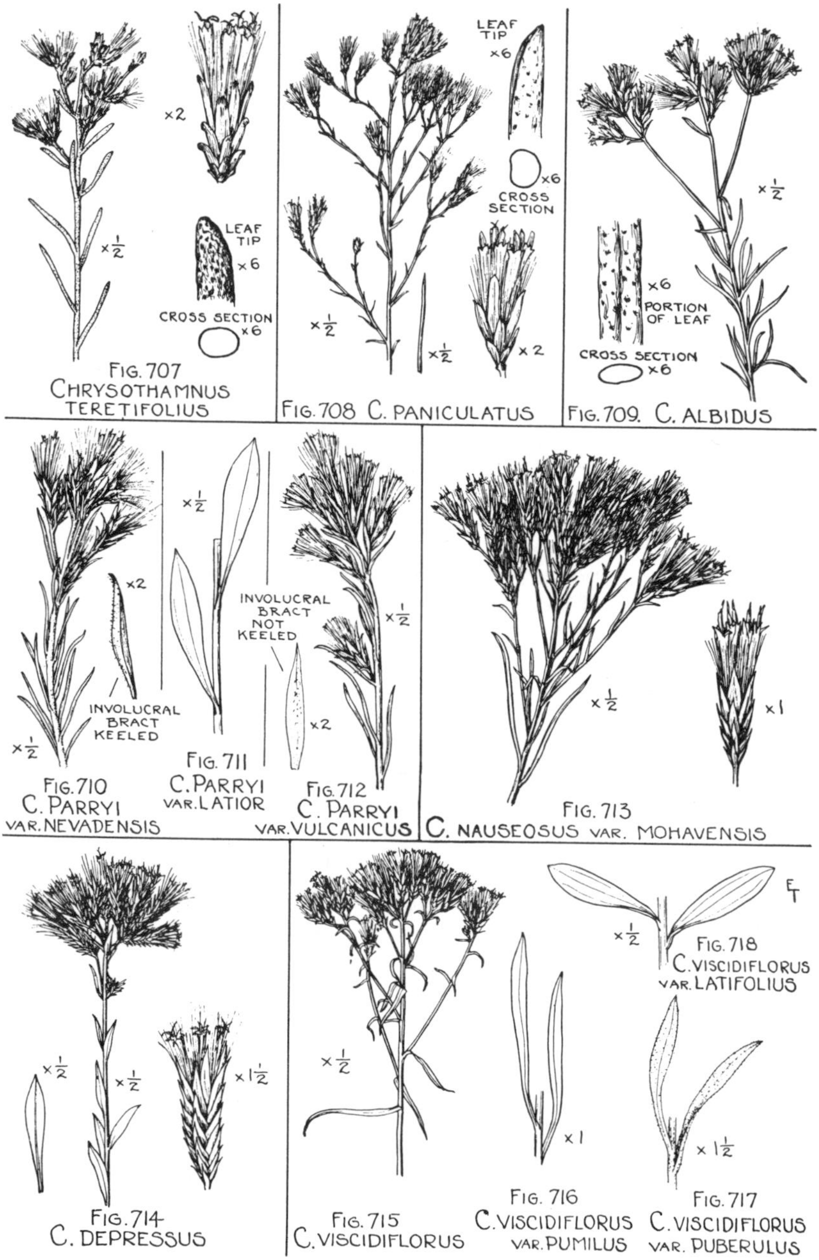

FIG. 707 CHRYSOTHAMNUS TERETIFOLIUS

FIG. 708 C. PANICULATUS

FIG. 709. C. ALBIDUS

FIG. 710 C. PARRYI VAR. NEVADENSIS

FIG. 711 C. PARRYI VAR. LATIOR

FIG. 712 C. PARRYI VAR. VULCANICUS

FIG. 713 C. NAUSEOSUS VAR. MOHAVENSIS

FIG. 714 C. DEPRESSUS

FIG. 715 C. VISCIDIFLORUS

FIG. 716 C. VISCIDIFLORUS VAR. PUMILUS

FIG. 717 C. VISCIDIFLORUS VAR. PUBERULUS

FIG. 718 C. VISCIDIFLORUS VAR. LATIFOLIUS

tribution: Known to the writer only from the type locality at 8500 to 10,000 feet elevation. In Tuolumne, Mono, and Tulare counties, acc. *Jepson*.

4e. Var. **nevadensis** (Gray) Jepson, Man. 1032 (1925). Fig. 710. *Linosyris Howardii* var. *nevadensis* Gray. Type locality: "Mount Davidson, Nevada, about Virginia City." Collected by *Bloomer*. Distribution in California: High mountains to nearly timber-line in the eastern Sierra Nevada from Plumas County to Alpine County and at the western edge of Honey Lake Valley, Lassen County. Flowering period, August and September.

4f. Var. **vulcanicus** (Greene) Jepson, Man. 1033 (1925). Fig. 712. *C. vulcanicus* Greene. Type locality: Volcano Creek, above Volcano Falls, Tulare County, California. Collected by *Culbertson*. Distribution: Southern Sierra Nevada of California, in Mono, Inyo, and Tulare counties. Flowering period, August and September.

4g. Var. **asper** (Greene) Munz, Man. S. Calif. Bot. 524 (1935). *C. asper* Greene. Type locality: Hockett Trail, in the valley of Little Cottonwood Creek, eastern slope of the Sierra Nevada in Inyo County, California. Collected by *Coville*. Distribution in California: Inyo, Mono, Tulare, and Ventura (Alamo Mountain, *Hall*) counties.

5. **Chrysothamnus nauseosus** (Pall.) Britt. RUBBER RABBITBRUSH. Fig. 706.
A shrub, usually 1 to 7 feet high, with several stems erect from the base and flexible moderately leafy branchlets, these closely covered with a gray-green or white felt-like tomentum. Leaves nearly filiform or broadly linear, 3/4-inch to 2 1/2 inches long, more or less tomentulose. Heads in terminal rounded cymes, these sometimes compound. Involucral bracts usually 20 to 25, without herbaceous tips. Flowers usually 5 or 6. Achenes 5-angled, glabrous to densely villous.

This species is represented in California by the following varieties.

KEY TO THE VARIETIES

Involucre puberulent to densely woolly; foliage mostly gray or white.
  Tomentum loose, copious, and nearly pure white on the twigs and leaves.
    Style-appendage longer than the stigmatic part; corolla-lobes lanceolate. 5a. var. *albicaulis*.
    Style-appendage shorter than the stigmatic part; corolla-lobes short-ovate. 5b. var. *hololeucus*.
  Tomentum close, compact, smooth, and gray or white on the twigs, the leaves gray or greenish.
    Involucres 1/4- to 3/8-inch high.
      Style-appendage longer than the stigmatic part.
        Bracts acuminate to mostly acute....................5c. var. *speciosus*.
        Bracts abruptly acute..........................5d. var. *occidentalis*.
      Style-appendage shorter than the stigmatic part......5e. var. *gnaphalodes*.
    Involucres 3/8- to nearly 1/2-inch high; corolla-lobes villous, less than 1/16-inch long..5f. var. *bernardinus*.
Involucres glabrous, sometimes glandular; foliage mostly greenish.
  Achenes glabrous or nearly so.........................5g. var. *leiospermus*.
  Achenes densely pubescent.

Involucral bracts with slender recurved tips...........5h. var. *ceruminosus.*
Involucral bracts with obtuse to acute erect tips.
Involucre sharply 5-angled, the strongly keeled bracts in very distinct rows..5i. var. *mohavensis.*
Involucre not sharply angled, the bracts only moderately keeled.
Corolla $\frac{5}{16}$-inch or less long; branches slender........5j. var. *consimilis.*
Corolla $\frac{5}{16}$- to $\frac{3}{8}$-inch long; branches stout..........5k. var. *viridulus.*

5a. Var. **albicaulis** (Nutt.) Rydb. Mem. N. Y. Bot. Gard. 1:385 (1900). *C. speciosus* β *albicaulis* Nutt. Type locality: Probably in the valley of the Snake River. Collected by *Nuttall.* Distribution in California: Eastern side of the Sierra Nevada from Modoc County southward to Mono County.

5b. Var. **hololeucus** (Gray) Hall, Univ. Calif. Publ. Bot. 7:166 (1919). *Bigelovia graveolens* var. *hololeuca* Gray. Type locality: Owens Valley, California. Collected by *Horn.* Distribution: Eastern side of the Sierra Nevada from Mono County southward in Inyo County, and southwestward to Antelope Valley in the western part of the Mohave Desert. Flowering period, October and November.

5c. Var. **speciosus** (Nutt.) Hall, Univ. Calif. Publ. Bot. 7:169 (1919). *C. speciosus* Nutt. Type locality: "In the Rocky Mountain plains, near Lewis River." Collected by *Nuttall.* Distribution in California: Eastern side of the Sierra Nevada from Mono County northward and westward to Siskiyou County.

5d. Var. **occidentalis** (Greene) Hall, Univ. Calif. Publ. Bot. 3:60 (1907). *C. occidentalis* Greene. Type locality: "In the Coast Ranges of California, from Humboldt County southward and in the mountains of southern California." Distribution: Inner North Coast Ranges, Sierra Nevada, San Bernardino, and San Jacinto mountains. Flowering period, August to October.

5e. Var. **gnaphalodes** (Greene) Hall, Univ. Calif. Publ. Bot. 7:167 (1919). Fig. 706. *C. speciosus* var. *gnaphalodes* Greene. Type locality: Pyramid Lake, Nevada. Collected by *Curran.* Distribution in California: Eastern side of the Sierra Nevada from Mono County southward in Inyo County to western Mohave Desert and occasionally on the western edge of the Colorado Desert (Banning, *Toumey*), and on the mesas near Colton, San Bernardino County *(Parish).* Flowering period, August to October.

5f. Var. **bernardinus** Hall, Univ. Calif. Publ. Bot. 7:171 (1919). Type locality: Hillsides, Bluff Lake, San Bernardino Mountains, California. Collected by *Grinnell.* Distribution: San Bernardino, San Jacinto, and San Gabriel mountains of southern California between 4000 and 9500 feet elevation. Flowering period, August and September.

5g. Var. **leiospermus** (Gray) Hall, Univ. Calif. Publ. Bot. 7:173 (1919). *Bigelovia leiosperma* Gray. Type locality: Saint George, southwestern Utah. Collected by *Palmer.* Distribution in California: Providence and Clark mountains, San Bernardino County. Flowering period, June to September.

5h. Var. **ceruminosus** (D. & H.) Hall, Univ. Calif. Publ. Bot. 7:175 (1919). *Linosyris ceruminosa* D. & H. Type locality: Tejon Pass, California. Collected by *Heermann.* Distribution: Rare in the western Mohave Desert and in the vicinity of Tejon Pass.

5i. Var. **mohavensis** (Greene) Hall, Univ. Calif. Publ. Bot. 7:179 (1919). Fig. 713. *Bigelovia mohavensis* Greene. Type locality: Mohave Desert, California. Collected by *Greene, Parry, Pringle*. Distribution: Western Mohave Desert, northward in the inner South Coast Ranges to the Mount Hamilton Range. Flowering period, July to October.

5j. Var. **consimilis** (Greene) Hall, Univ. Calif. Publ. Bot. 7:176 (1919). *C. consimilis* Greene. Type locality: Deeth, Elko County, Nevada. Collected by *Greene*. Distribution in California: Alkaline areas in northern California from Siskiyou County east to Modoc County and south on the eastern side of the Sierra Nevada to Mono County. Flowering period, September and October.

5k. Var. **viridulus** Hall, Univ. Calif. Publ. Bot. 7:177 (1919). Type locality: Benton, Mono County, California. Collected by *Hall*. Distribution in California: Alkaline flats east of the Sierra Nevada from Mono County south to the desert side of the San Bernardino Mountains.

6. **Chrysothamnus depressus** Nutt. Dwarf Rabbitbrush. Fig. 714.

A low subshrub, 4 to 12 inches high, forming dense clumps, with brittle striate pubescent branchlets. Leaves oblanceolate to spatulate, 5/16- to 3/4-inch long, green, finely puberulent. Heads in small compact terminal cymes. Involucral bracts 20 or 25, in 5 well-defined vertical ranks. Flowers 5. Achenes 4-angled to nearly equally 8-ribbed, obscurely pubescent. Flowering period, August to October.

Dwarf Rabbitbrush occurs in California in the Providence, Clark *(M. E. Jones)*, and New York (near Keystone Springs, acc. *Munz*) mountains of eastern San Bernardino County between 5000 and 7000 feet elevation. It extends eastward to Arizona, Nevada, Utah, New Mexico, and Colorado.

Chrysothamnus depressus Nutt. Jour. Phil. Acad. 2, 1:171 (1847). Type locality: According to Hall, the type specimen is labelled "Rocky Mountains" although Nuttall states, "in the Sierra of Upper California." Collected by *Nuttall*.

7. **Chrysothamnus viscidiflorus** (Hook.) Nutt. Rabbitbrush. Fig. 715.

A shrub of exceedingly diverse habit and variable foliage characters, 6 inches to 8 feet high, with leafy glabrous or puberulent branchlets. Leaves narrowly linear to oblong or lanceolate, often twisted, 3/4-inch to 2 1/4 inches long, 1- to 5-nerved, glabrous or pubescent, usually viscidulous. Heads in terminal rounded or flat-topped cymes. Involucral bracts about 15, in poorly defined vertical ranks. Flowers about 5. Achenes 5-angled, densely to sparsely villous.

This polymorphic species has had many of its forms described as species, subspecies, and varieties. The following key will aid in the identification of some of the more common forms.

KEY TO THE SPECIES AND VARIETIES

Plants mostly 1 1/2 to 8 feet high.
  Leaves 1- to 3-nerved, less than 3/16-inch wide . . . . 7. *C. viscidiflorus*.
  Leaves 3- to 5-nerved, 3/16- to nearly 1/2-inch wide . . . . 7a. var. *latifolius*.
Plants mostly 4 inches to 1 1/2 feet, rarely to 3 feet, high.
  Herbage glabrous.
    Leaves bright green . . . . 7b. var. *pumilus*.
    Leaves pale green, 1/16-inch or less wide . . . . 7c. var. *stenophyllus*.
  Herbage densely puberulent.

Fig. 719. GIANT COREOPSIS. *Coreopsis gigantea* (Kell.) Hall.
Photograph taken in a canyon on Santa Rosa Island.

Leaves narrowly linear, 1/16-inch or less wide............7d. var. *puberulus*.
Leaves linear or linear-oblanceolate, many over 1/16-inch wide.7e. var. *humilis*.

C. viscidiflorus (Hook.) Nutt. Trans. Am. Phil. Soc. 2, 7:324 (1840). *Crinitaria viscidiflora* Hook. Type locality: "Northwest America on the plains of the Columbia, from the Great Falls to the mountains, and along the Salmon River." Collected by *Douglas*. Distribution in California: Santa Rosa and San Jacinto mountains, northward to the eastern side of the Sierra Nevada.

7a. Var. **latifolius** (D. C. Eaton) Greene, Erythea 3:96 (1895). Fig. 718. *Linosyris viscidiflora* var. *latifolia* D. C. Eaton. Type locality: "Mountains at the head of the Humboldt River, Nevada." Collected by *Watson*. Distribution in California: Modoc County *(M. F. Gilman)*.

7b. Var. **pumilus** (Nutt.) Jepson, Man. 1031 (1925). Fig. 716. *C. pumilus* Nutt. Type locality: "on the borders of Lewis River and the Rocky Mountain Plains." Collected by *Nuttall*. Distribution in California: San Bernardino Mountains, Mount Piños, and on the eastern side of the Sierra Nevada.

7c. Var. **stenophyllus** (Gray) Hall, Univ. Calif. Publ. Bot. 3:59 (1907). *Bigelovia Douglasii* var. *stenophylla* Gray. Type locality: Northwestern Nevada. Collected by *Watson*. Distribution in California: Eastern end of Bear Valley, San Bernardino Mountains *(Grinnell)* and in the Santa Rosa Mountains of Riverside County.

7d. Var. **puberulus** (D. C. Eaton) Jepson, Man. 1031 (1925). Fig. 717. *Linosyris viscidiflora* var. *puberula* D. C. Eaton. Type locality: "Near the Truckee and on the Hot Springs Mountains in western Nevada." Collected by *W. W. Bailey*. Distribution in California: Mono County, near Benton *(Hall)*, "1/4-mile s.e. of County Farm, alt. 6700 ft." *(A. D. Gifford)*, and along the north shore of Mono Lake *(Peirson)*; Inyo County, White Mountains *(V. Duran)*.

7e. Var. **humilis** (Greene) Jepson, Man. 1031 (1925). *C. humilis* Greene. Type locality: "Plains of the Truckee River, Nevada County, California." Collected by *Sonne*. Distribution in California: Eastern Nevada County, Martis Valley, near Truckee *(Sonne)* and in Mono County (s. slope of Sherwin Hill, *Wolf*).

MADIEAE. TARWEED TRIBE

15. **Hemizonia** DC. Tarweed

(From the Greek *hemi*, half, and *zonia*, zone, in reference to the bracts which half enclose the achenes.)

This genus contains about 30 species of annual and perennial herbs native to western North America, a few of which are slightly woody at the base.

1. **Hemizonia clementina** Brandg. Island Hemizonia. Island Tarweed. Fig. 720.

A semi-shrubby perennial, 1 to 2 feet high, with densely leafy branching stems and sparsely hirsute and slightly glandular herbage. Flowering period, April to July.

Island Hemizonia occurs on San Clemente, Santa Barbara, Santa Catalina, San Nicholas, and Anacapa islands.

Hemizonia clementina Brandg. Erythea 7:70 (1899). Type locality: San Clemente Island. Collected by *T. S. Brandegee*.

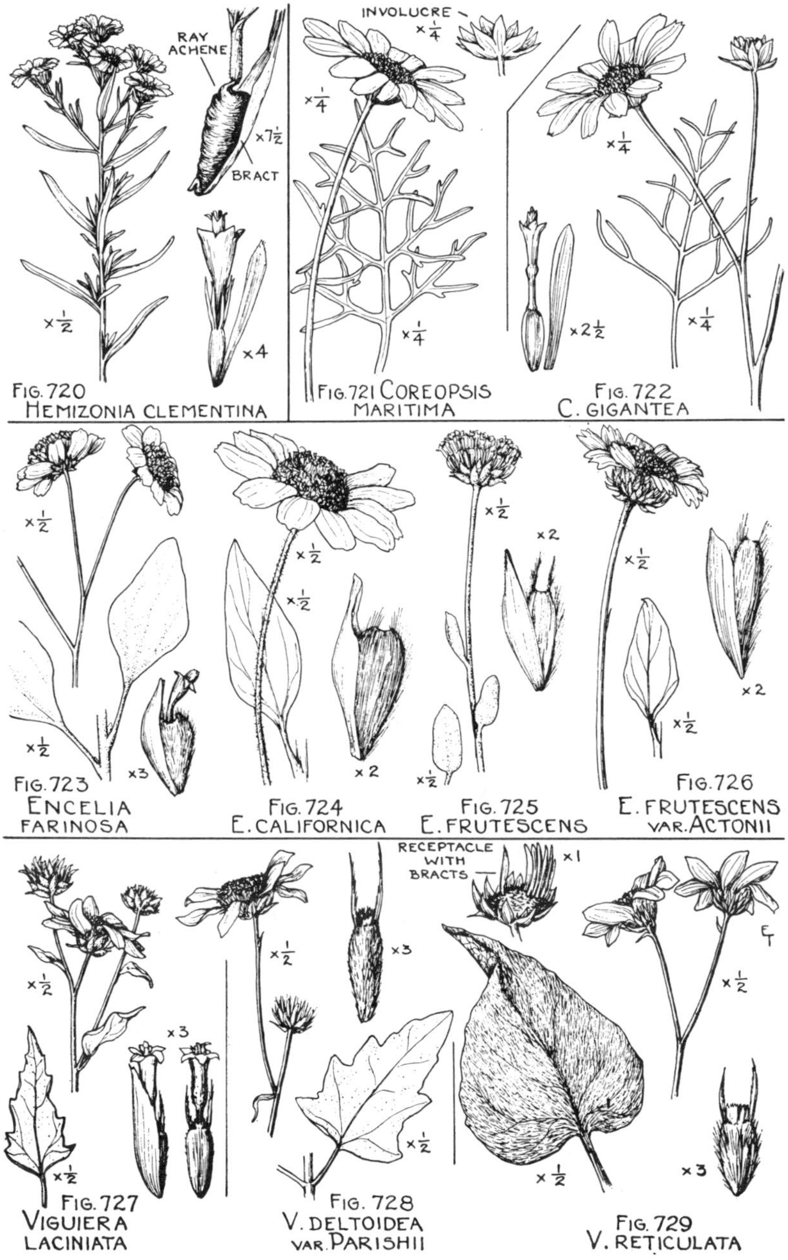

FIG. 720 HEMIZONIA CLEMENTINA

FIG. 721 COREOPSIS MARITIMA

FIG. 722 C. GIGANTEA

FIG. 723 ENCELIA FARINOSA

FIG. 724 E. CALIFORNICA

FIG. 725 E. FRUTESCENS

FIG. 726 E. FRUTESCENS VAR. ACTONII

FIG. 727 VIGUIERA LACINIATA

FIG. 728 V. DELTOIDEA VAR. PARISHII

FIG. 729 V. RETICULATA

HELIANTHEAE. SUNFLOWER TRIBE

16. **Coreopsis** L. Coreopsis

(From the Greek *koris,* a bug, and *opsis,* likeness, in reference to the achenes of some species.)

Mostly annual or perennial herbs, a few shrubby. Leaves (in ours) alternate, dissected into linear or filiform lobes. Heads (in ours) with yellow ray- and disk-flowers, long-peduncled, solitary or in loose clusters. Involucral bracts in 2 series; those of the outer series 5 to 8, narrow, loose, and foliaceous; those of the inner series 8 to 12, erect, membranous. Receptacle flat, with chaffy bracts falling with the achenes. Achenes flattened, linear-oblong to oval, the margins smooth or ciliate and winged. Pappus none or of bristles, scales, or teeth proceeding from the angles of the achene.

About 70 species belong to this genus. They are mostly native to eastern North America. Six species are native to California, 2 of which are often shrub-like.

KEY TO THE SPECIES

Heads solitary on scattered peduncles 6 to 12 inches long . . . . 1. *C. maritima.*
Heads many on peduncles 3 to 6 inches long forming a branched cluster.
2. *C. gigantea.*

1. **Coreopsis maritima** (Nutt.) Hook. f. Sea-dahlia. Coast Coreopsis. Fig. 721.

A somewhat shrubby perennial, 1 to 2½ feet high, with a stout much branched stem from a woody base and somewhat fleshy glabrous herbage. Leaves 2 or 3 times pinnately divided into linear lobes, 2½ to 5 inches long. Heads large, 2 to 3½ inches broad, on peduncles 6 to 12 inches long. Ray-flowers 16 to 20, ¾-inch to 1¼ inches long. Pappus mostly none. Flowering period, March to June.

Sea-dahlia occurs along the coast of San Diego County and extends into Lower California. It is sometimes grown for its showy flowers and fern-like foliage.

Coreopsis maritima (Nutt.) Hook. f. Bot. Mag. t. 6241 (1876). *Tuckermannia maritima* Nutt. Type locality: San Diego, California. Collected by *Nuttall.*

2. **Coreopsis gigantea** (Kell.) Hall. Giant Coreopsis. Figs. 719, 722.

A robust erect shrub-like plant, 1 to 4 or up to 10 feet high, with a fleshy woody trunk irregularly branched into ascending or horizontal branches leafy only towards the ends. Leaves 2 or 3 times pinnately divided into narrowly linear or filiform divisions, 3 to 12 inches long. Heads 2 to 3 inches broad, on cymosely clustered peduncles 6 inches or less long. Ray-flowers 10 to 16, about 1 inch long. Pappus none. Flowering period, March to July.

Giant Coreopsis occurs near the coast from Los Angeles County northward to southern San Luis Obispo County and on the islands off the coast of southern California. Its feathery foliage and large yellow flowers make this plant very attractive in cultivation. Like the preceding species, it is a short-lived plant, living in cultivation for only about six years.

Coreopsis gigantea (Kell.) Hall, Univ. Calif. Publ. Bot. 3:142 (1907). *Leptosyne gigantea* Kell. Type locality: "Cuyler Harbor, San Miguel Island." Collected by *Harford.*

17. **Encelia** Adans.

(Named for Christopher Encel, who wrote on oak-galls in 1577.)

Herbs and low shrubs. Leaves simple, alternate in ours. Heads with ray- and disk-flowers or the ray-flowers absent. Ray-flowers yellow; disk-flowers yellow or purple. Involucral bracts in 2 or 3 series. Receptacle with chaffy bracts which embrace the achenes and fall with them. Disk-achenes flat, obovate, black, with conspicuously ciliate margins, notched or truncate at summit. Pappus none or rarely with 2 slender awns.

This genus contains about 30 species native to the western part of North and South America. Three species and one variety are native to California.

KEY TO THE SPECIES

Heads numerous in cymose panicles; leaves white-mealy. . . . . 1. *E. farinosa.*
Heads solitary; leaves not white-mealy.
  Ray-flowers usually absent; disk-flowers yellow. . . . . 2. *E. frutescens.*
  Ray-flowers present.
    Disk-flowers yellow; leaves whitened, soft-pubescent.
      2a. *E. frutescens* var. *Actonii.*
    Disk-flowers purplish; leaves green, appressed-pubescent. . . . . 3. *E. californica.*

1. **Encelia farinosa** Gray. INCIENSO. MEALY ENCELIA. DESERT ENCELIA. Fig. 723.

A roundish bush, 1 to 3 feet high, usually with a distinct trunk-like stem branching into numerous short branches very leafy at the ends from which arise the long-stemmed cymes. Leaf-blades broadly ovate to lanceolate, 3/4-inch to 2 or even 4 inches long, 1/2-inch to 1 inch wide, densely white- or silvery-tomentose, entire or somewhat toothed, 3-veined from the base; petioles 1/4- to 3/4-inch long. Ray-flowers 8 to 18, 3/8- to 5/8-inch long. Disk-flowers yellow. Pappus none. Flowering period, April to June.

Incienso occurs chiefly in the Lower Sonoran Life Zone on benches and the lower mountain slopes of the Colorado and Mohave deserts. It extends westward into the San Bernardino Valley and region about Lake Elsinore, southward into western San Diego County and Lower California, northward to Inyo County, and eastward to Arizona. The name Incienso has been given to this plant because of the custom among the inhabitants of Lower California of collecting and burning the resinous exudation as an incense in churches. (T. S. Brandegee, Zoe 1:83. 1890.)

Encelia farinosa Gray; Torr. in Emory Rep. 143 (1848). Type locality: Vicinity of Carrizo Creek, San Diego and Imperial counties. Collected by *Coulter*.

2. **Encelia frutescens** Gray. BUSH ENCELIA. Fig. 725.

A round-topped bushy shrub, 2 to 4 feet high, commonly with whitish stems and greenish leaves. Leaf-blades oblong to ovate or elliptic, 3/8-inch to 1 inch long, more or less scabrous, entire, narrowed to a short petiole. Peduncles rather long, terminating leafy branchlets, with a single head about 1/2-inch broad. Involucres whitish hispid. Ray-flowers usually absent. Disk-flowers yellow, with pubescent teeth. Pappus of 2 delicate long villous awns or wanting. Flowering period, April to June.

Bush Encelia is rather common in the Lower Sonoran Life Zone on the dry hills and lower mountain slopes and in the washes of the Colorado and Mohave deserts. It extends eastward to Arizona and Nevada. It is a variable species and seems to form intergrades with the following variety and the other species here described.

2a. Var. **Actonii** (Elmer) Blake. Fig. 726.

Leaves usually broadly ovate, whitened by a soft pubescence. Ray-flowers 8 to 18, 1/4- to 1/2-inch long. Flowering period, March to June.

This variety occurs in the Lower Sonoran Life Zone from Acton, Los Angeles County northeast through the Mohave Desert to the Greenhorn Mountains of Kern County and to Inyo County, southward to the western borders of the Colorado desert and to the San Jacinto and Palomar mountains.

Encelia frutescens Gray, Proc. Am. Acad. 8:657 (1873). *Simsia frutescens* Gray. Type locality: "Agua Caliente, on the Gila." Collected by *Emory*.

Var. Actonii (Elmer) Blake, Proc. Am. Acad. 49:365 (1913). *E. Actonii* Elmer. Type locality: Acton, Los Angeles County. Collected by *Elmer*.

3. **Encelia californica** Nutt. CALIFORNIA ENCELIA. Fig. 724.

A much branched bushy perennial, 2 to 4 feet high, with slender stems woody only at the base. Leaf-blades ovate to lanceolate, 3/4-inch to 2 1/2 inches long, 1/2-inch to 1 1/4 inches broad, 3-veined from the rounded or tapering base, green, minutely scabrous or glabrate, entire or repand-dentate; petioles 1/8- to 1/2-inch long. Heads solitary, terminating elongated nearly naked pubescent peduncles. Involucres tomentose, about 1/2-inch high. Ray-flowers 16 to 30, 1/2-inch to 1 1/4 inches long. Disk-flowers purple. Flowering period, March to June.

California Encelia is rather common on hillsides and in canyons of the Upper Sonoran Life Zone from Santa Barbara southward to San Diego and Lower California, and inland as far as Riverside.

Encelia californica Nutt. Trans. Am. Phil. Soc. ser. 2, 7:357 (1841). Type locality: On dry hills, near Santa Barbara. Collected by *Nuttall*.

18. **Viguiera** H. B. K.

(Named in honor of Dr. A. Viguier, a French botanist.)

Herbs or shrubs with slender brittle stems and scabrous alternate or opposite petioled leaves. Heads with yellow ray- and disk-flowers. Involucral bracts imbricated in 2 or 3 series, herbaceous. Receptacle with chaffy bracts embracing the 4-angled or slightly compressed disk-achenes. Pappus of 2 or more short erose or laciniate scales and of 2 longer paleaceous awns or narrow paleae, one at each angle of the achene, or pappus none.

This genus contains about 70 species in the warmer parts of the world, especially in America. Five species are native to California, 3 of which are shrubs or subshrubs.

KEY TO THE SPECIES

Leaves lanceolate, 3/4-inch to 2 inches long, the lower usually pinnatifid. 1. *V. laciniata*.

Leaves ovate.

Leaves green above, 1/2-inch to 1 1/4 (rarely 1 1/2) inches long, coarsely serrate to entire, scabrous..............................2. *V. deltoidea* var. *Parishii*.

Leaves densely pubescent above, 1 to 4 inches long, entire, not scabrous. 3. *V. reticulata*.

1. **Viguiera laciniata** Gray. SAN DIEGO-SUNFLOWER. Fig. 727.

A round-topped bush, 2 to 4 feet high, with numerous branching stems leafy to the summit and woody at the base, and with scabrous-pubescent resinous herbage. Flowering period, March to June.

San Diego-sunflower occurs on dry slopes in the Lower Sonoran Life Zone of southwestern San Diego County. It extends into Lower California.

Viguiera laciniata Gray, Bot. Mex. Bound. 89 (1859). Type locality: "Rancho Gamacho, east of San Diego, California." Collected by *Schott*.

Fig. 730. GOLDEN-YARROW. *Eriophyllum confertiflorum* (DC.) Gray.

2. **Viguiera deltoidea** var. **Parishii** (Greene) Vasey & Rose. DESERT-SUNFLOWER. Fig. 728.

A compact much branched shrub, 1 to 2½ feet high, with several densely and harshly tuberculate-hispidulous stems from the base. Flowering period, April to June.

Desert-sunflower occurs in rocky gullies and canyons of the Lower Sonoran Life Zone from the eastern Mohave Desert southward through the Colorado Desert to western San Diego County. It extends eastward to Arizona and Nevada and southward to Lower California.

Viguiera deltoidea var. Parishii (Greene) Vasey & Rose, Contr. U. S. Nat. Herb. 1:72 (1890). *V. Parishii* Greene. Type locality: San Luis Rey, San Diego County. Collected by *Parish*.

3. **Viguiera reticulata** Wats. DEATH VALLEY-SUNFLOWER. Fig. 729.

An erect bushy plant, 2 to 4 feet high, with many white-barked stems loosely branched from a woody base. Flowering period, April to June.

Death Valley-sunflower occurs in rocky places of the Lower Sonoran Life Zone in the Death Valley region of Inyo County and southward into northwestern San Bernardino County (canyon below Salt Wells). It extends eastward into Nevada.

Viguiera reticulata Wats. Am. Nat. 7:301 (1873). Type locality: "Telescope Mountain, Nevada." Collected by *Wheeler*.

19. **Bebbia** Greene

(Named after M. S. Bebb, a distinguished American student of willows.)

This is a genus of one or probably 2 species of subshrubby plants native to the arid southwestern part of North America. A single species and one variety occur in California.

1. **Bebbia juncea** (Benth.) Greene. RUSH BEBBIA. Fig. 731.

KEY TO THE SPECIES AND VARIETY

Herbage gabrous except on the involucre. . . . . *B. juncea*.
Herbage more or less hispidulous with upturned white hairs or pustules.
1a. var. *aspera*.

A rounded bushy strong-scented subshrub, 1 to 4 feet high, with green and nearly leafless intricately much branched stems and often rush-like branches. Leaves simple, the lower ones opposite, the upper ones alternate, linear or rarely oblong, ¼-inch to 1 inch (rarely to 2 inches) long, entire or with 1 or 2 pairs of teeth near the middle. Flowers yellow, all discoid, bisexual. Flowering period, May to July.

Rush Bebbia occurs on dry slopes and in washes from western San Bernardino County southward to Orange and Riverside counties, in the Lower Sonoran Life Zone. It extends southward to Lower California. On the Mohave and Colorado deserts this species is replaced by the following variety.

1a. Var. **aspera** Greene.

Herbage more or less hispidulous with upturned white hairs or these deciduous, leaving only the pustule-like bases.

This variety is common in stony and sandy washes and flats on the Colorado Desert. It extends northward to the Mohave Desert and to Inyo County where it is much less common. It extends eastward to Nevada and Arizona.

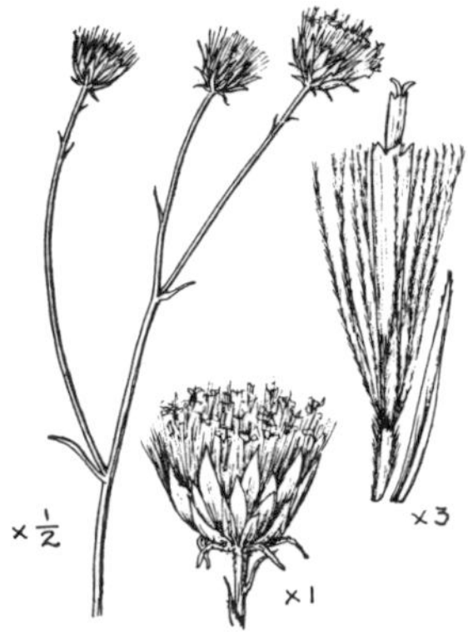

FIG. 731 BEBBIA JUNCEA

FIG. 732 ERIOPHYLLUM LANATUM VAR. GRANDIFLORUM

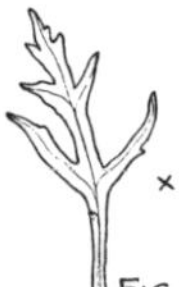

FIG. 733 E. LANATUM VAR. ACHILLAEOIDES

FIG. 734 E. LANATUM VAR. ARACHNOIDEUM

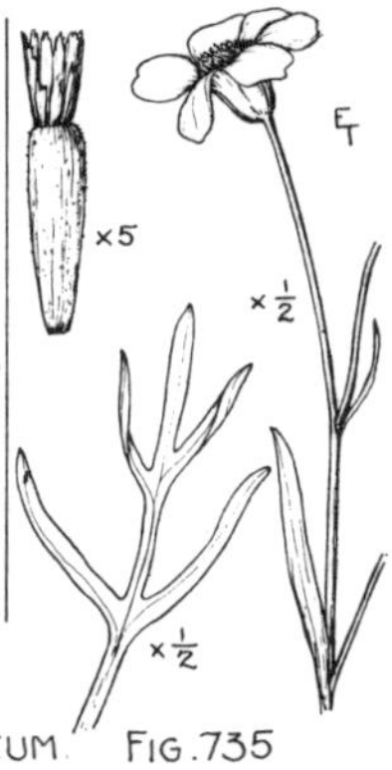

FIG. 735 E. JEPSONII

FIG. 736 ERIOPHYLLUM CONFERTIFLORUM

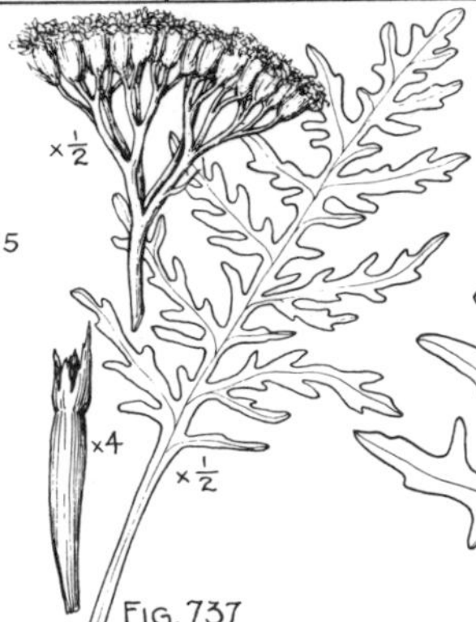

FIG. 737 E. NEVINII

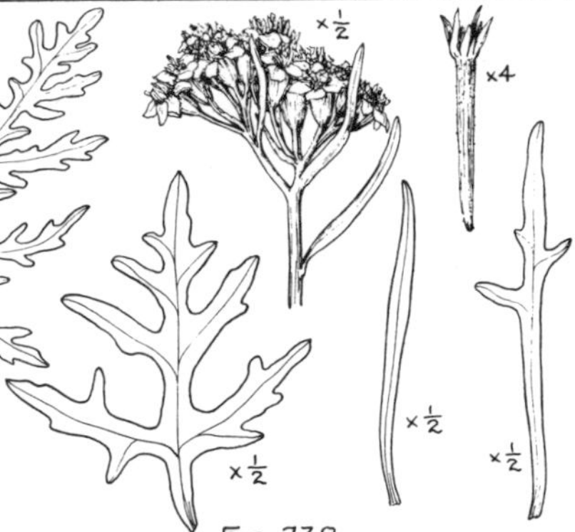

FIG. 738 E. STAECHADIFOLIUM

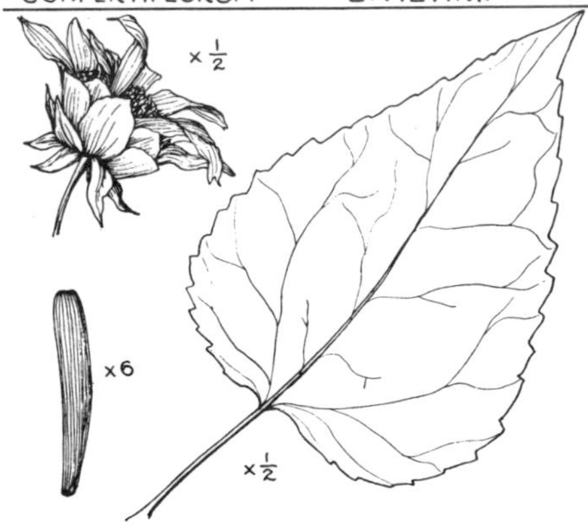

FIG. 739 VENEGASIA CARPESIOIDES

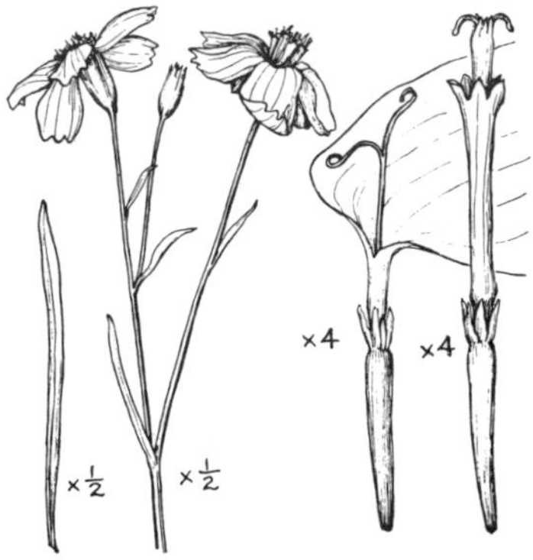

FIG. 740 PSILOSTROPHE COOPERI

Bebbia juncea (Benth.) Greene, Bull. Calif. Acad. 1:180 (1885). *Carphephorus junceus* Benth. Type locality: Magdalena Bay, Lower California. Collected by *Hinds.*

Var. aspera Greene, Bull. Calif. Acad. 1:180 (1885). Type locality: "Southeastern borders of California and adjacent Arizona."

HELENIEAE. SNEEZEWEED TRIBE

20. **Eriophyllum** Lag.

(From the Greek *erion,* wool, and *phullon,* leaf, in reference to the woolly herbage.)

Annual and perennial herbs or shrubs and subshrubs usually with tomentose herbage. Leaves simple, alternate, rarely opposite on young shoots, sometimes entire but commonly variously toothed, lobed, or divided. Heads with ray- and disk-flowers or the ray-flowers wanting. Involucres campanulate or hemispheric, the bracts rigid and permanently erect, in 1 or rarely 2 series. Receptacle naked. Achenes slender, 4-angled. Pappus of firm hyaline or opaque usually erose or fimbriate paleae.

This is a small genus of 11 species (or as many as 45, by one author) and 12 varieties occurring in temperate western North America. Ten species and 11 varieties are native to California, 5 species of which are woody.

KEY TO THE SPECIES

Heads including the rays ½-inch to 1¼ inches broad, on long peduncles.
  Plants woody only at base, usually less than 20 inches high; heads often solitary; leaves entire, toothed, or lobed. . . . . 1. *E. lanatum.*
  Plants shrubby throughout, over 20 inches high; heads in loose corymbs; leaves pinnately divided into 5 to 7 narrowly linear lobes. . . . . 2. *E. Jepsonii.*
Heads less than ½-inch broad, sessile or very short-peduncled, usually in dense compound clusters.
  Ray-flowers 5 or less, rarely none; involucral bracts 4 to 7. . . 3. *E. confertiflorum.*
  Ray-flowers 6 to 10; involucral bracts 8 to 12.
    Leaves white-tomentose on both surfaces, once- or twice-pinnately parted; island species. . . . . 4. *E. Nevinii.*
    Leaves white-tomentose beneath, green above; mainland and island species. 5. *E. staechadifolium.*

1. **Eriophyllum lanatum** (Pursh) Forbes. Woolly-yarrow. Figs. 732, 733, 734.

This species apparently does not occur in its typical form in California. It is a very plastic species and, according to Constance, no less than 75 names have been assigned to its variations. The description which follows is generalized sufficiently to include the numerous variations.

Low to medium-sized perennials, 4 inches to 2½ feet high, with simple or branching herbaceous stems from a woody base and with conspicuous tomentum. Leaves variable, ⅜-inch to 3 inches long, usually more or less toothed or divided. Heads ½-inch to 1¼ inches broad, long-peduncled, terminal, solitary to many and loosely corymbose. Involucral bracts 5 to 15, lanceolate to ovate, sharply ridged on the back. Ray-flowers 5 to 15, yellow, notched or toothed at apex. Disk-flowers numerous. Achenes 4-angled, variously hairy, glandular or bald. Pappus of 6 to 12 hyaline scales of diverse shape and size or wanting. Flowering period, May to July.

Eriophyllum lanatum (Pursh) Forbes, Hort. Woburn. 183 (1833). *Actinella lanata* Pursh. Type locality: "Uplands on the Kooskooskee River." Collected by *Lewis*. *Eriophyllum caespitosum* Dougl.

2. **Eriophyllum Jepsonii** Greene. BUSH-YARROW. Fig. 735.

A shrubby perennial, 1½ to 3 feet high, with white-tomentose stems. Leaves ovate in outline, 1¼ to 2½ inches long, pinnately parted into 5 to 7 linear obtuse lobes, white-tomentose on both surfaces but soon becoming glabrous and green above, the margins revolute. Heads loosely corymbose, on peduncles 2 to 4 inches long. Ray-flowers 6 to 8, yellow. Achenes slightly hispidulous. Pappus-palea about 8, in 2 unequal series. Flowering period, May and June.

Bush-yarrow occurs in a few localities in the Mount Hamilton Range and on Mount Diablo, Contra Costa County.

Eriophyllum Jepsonii Greene, Pitt. 2:165 (1891). Type locality: Hills between Arroyo Mocho and Arroyo Valle, south of Livermore, California. Collected by *Jepson*.

3. **Eriophyllum confertiflorum** (DC.) Gray. GOLDEN-YARROW. Figs. 730, 736.

Low perennials, ¾-foot to 2½ feet high, usually woody below, the flowering branchlets mostly herbaceous, the herbage closely tomentose, the tomentum more or less deciduous. Flowering period, May to July.

Golden-yarrow is rather common in the dry foothills and mountains of the Coast Ranges from Mendocino County southward to San Diego County and Lower California, in the mountains of southern California, northward in the Sierra Nevada foothills to Calaveras County, and on the islands off the coast of southern California. It occurs from near sea level to about 10,000 feet elevation. In Mariposa and Calaveras counties, the plants usually have a more shrubby habit, larger heads, leaves, ray- and disk-flowers, and more numerous bracts. These plants are included by most writers in the variety *tanacetiflorum* (Greene) Jepson, but since the above characters are quite variable it has not seemed necessary in this work to retain the variety.

In Marin and Sonoma counties and occasionally throughout the range of the species, plants occur which have heads without ray-flowers. These plants have frequently been referred to var. *discoideum* Greene. I accept the treatment of Constance, who states, "In view of the wide discontinuity in range of the reduced, discoid forms, the sporadic occurrence of the eradiate condition throughout the species-population and its common occurrence in *E. lanatum* and *E. staechadifolium*, and the existence of radiate plants side by side with the discoid (with which they agree in every important character), this segregate is considered unworthy of retention." (See Bibl.)

Eriophyllum confertiflorum (DC.) Gray, Proc. Am. Acad. 19:25 (1883). *Bahia confertiflora* DC. Type locality: California. Collected by *Douglas*.

4. **Eriophyllum Nevinii** Gray. CATALINA SILVER LACE. NEVIN GOLDEN-YARROW. Fig. 737.

An evergreen perennial, 1 to 3 feet high, with ascending stems white-woolly and woody below. Leaves alternate, 3 to 7 inches long, once- or twice-pinnately parted into numerous oblong lobes, white-tomentose on both surfaces, the margins revolute. Heads numerous, densely crowded into naked-pedunculate broad flat-topped cymes. Involucral bracts 8 to 12, rather loose, scarcely overlapping. Ray-flowers

6 to 10, yellow, scarcely longer than the bracts. Pappus of 3 to 6 erose often unequal paleae. Flowering period, May to August.

Catalina Silver Lace occurs on the bluffs of San Clemente and Santa Catalina islands. It is a beautiful yellow-flowering shrub, worthy of cultivation in the warmer coastal regions of California.

Eriophyllum Nevinii Gray, Syn. Fl. ed. 2, 1:452 (1886). Type locality: San Clemente Island. Collected by *Nevin* and *Gray*.

5. **Eriophyllum staechadifolium** Lag. LIZARD TAIL. Fig. 738.

A much branched shrubby perennial, 1 to 5 feet high, covered with a close tardily deciduous tomentum. Leaves alternate, rarely some opposite, 1 to 2¾ inches long, once- or twice-pinnately parted into 5 to 7 lobes, or the upper ones on some plants often simple, linear-oblong, entire or few-toothed or -lobed, all persistently white-tomentose beneath, usually soon glabrate and green above, the margins revolute. Heads numerous, short-peduncled, in dense but loose corymbs. Involucral bracts 8 to 12, scarcely overlapping, carinate. Ray-flowers 6 to 9 or rarely wanting, yellow. Pappus of 8 to 12 unequal obtuse paleae, those on the angles usually longer. Flowering period, April to July.

Lizard Tail occurs near the coast from Santa Barbara County northward to Coos County, Oregon. It usually inhabits sandy beaches and bluffs from sea level to about 300 feet elevation. It occurs also on Anacapa, Santa Cruz, and Santa Rosa islands. This species is quite variable in habit of growth and foliage charcters. Some plants are often decumbent and trailing and others more bushy and erect. The plants growing at Pacific Grove northward to Santa Cruz usually have a larger proportion of the leaves undivided.

Eriophyllum staechadifolium Lag. Gen. & Sp. 28 (1816). Type locality: Monterey, California. Collected by the Malaspina Expedition. *E. staechadifolium* var. *artemisiaefolium* (Less.) Jepson.

21. **Venegasia** DC.

(Named in honor of Michael Venegas, a Jesuit missionary.)

This genus contains two species, one native to southern California and the other to Lower California.

1. **Venegasia carpesioides** DC. CANYON-SUNFLOWER. Fig. 739.

An erect perennial suffrutescent herb, 3 to 8 feet high, with leafy sparingly branched stems. Leaves simple, alternate; the blades thin, ovate, 2 to 6 inches long, 1 to 4 inches broad, cordate or truncate at base, glabrous or slightly pubescent, serrate or nearly entire; petioles ¾-inch to 2 inches long. Heads large, few, in the upper leaf-axils and terminal, short-pedunculate, with ray- and disk-flowers. Involucral bracts mostly membranous, oval, and erect, in 2 or 3 series. Receptacle flat, naked. Ray-flowers 13 to 20, about 1 inch long, yellow. Corollas of disk-flowers yellow, glandular-bearded at base. Achenes about 12-nerved, roughened. Pappus none. Flowering period, March to June.

Canyon-sunflower occurs in moist shady places of the coastal region from Santa Barbara County southward to northern San Diego County, inland to western Riverside County, and on Santa Cruz and Santa Rosa islands. This plant somewhat resembles the wild sunflower, *Helianthus,* in its habit of growth and general appearance of the heads of yellow flowers.

Venegasia carpesioides DC. Prodr. 6:43 (1837). Type locality: California. Collected by *Douglas.*

22. **Psilostrophe** DC.

(From the Greek *psilos,* bare, and *strophe,* to turn.)

This is a small genus of 3 species native to the southwestern United States and adjacent Mexico. A single species is native to California.

1. **Psilostrophe Cooperi** (Gray) Greene. WHITESTEM PAPERFLOWER. Fig. 740.

A low rounded shrub, 1 to 2 feet high, with densely white-woolly stems and young growth. Leaves simple, alternate, narrowly linear, 3/8-inch to 2 inches long, white-tomentulose, becoming green and glabrous in age, entire, sessile. Heads with yellow ray- and disk-flowers, solitary or cymose. Involucral bracts 15 to 30, little imbricated in 1 to 3 series, the inner ones soft, the outer ones rigid. Receptacle small, naked. Ray-flowers 4 to 8, 1/2- to 3/4-inch long, 3-toothed at the apex, becoming papery in age. Disk-flowers 5 to 12, bisexual, regular, with 5 short glandular lobes. Achenes narrow, round in cross section, glabrous. Pappus of 4 to 6 lanceolate or oblong hyaline paleae. Flowering period, April to October.

Whitestem Paperflower occurs in California in the Chuckawalla Mountains along the northern border of the Colorado Desert and in the Providence and Clark mountains on the eastern Mohave Desert of San Bernardino County. It extends eastward to Nevada, Arizona, New Mexico, and Utah.

Psilostrophe Cooperi (Gray) Greene, Pitt. 2:176 (1891). *Riddellia Cooperi* Gray. Type locality: Fort Mohave. Collected by *Cooper.*

23. **Porophyllum** Vaill.

(From the Greek *poros,* a passage, and *phullon,* leaf, in reference to the involucral bracts (leaves) with translucent oil-glands.)

This genus contains about 25 species native to the warmer parts of America.

1. **Porophyllum gracile** Benth. PORELEAF. Fig. 741.

A slender much branched suffrutescent herb, 1/2-foot to 2 feet high, with ill-scented glabrous herbage and with involucres punctate with oil-glands. Flowering period, April and May.

Poreleaf is a common plant on dry plains and slopes below 3500 feet elevation in coastal San Diego and Orange counties.

Porophyllum gracile Benth. Bot. Voy. Sulph. 29 (1844). Type locality: Bay of Magdalena, Lower California. Collected by *Hinds.*

AMBROSIEAE. RAGWEED TRIBE

24. **Franseria** Cav. BURSAGE

(Named in honor of Ant. Franser, Spanish physician and botanist.)

Herbs or shrubs. Leaves usually alternate. Flowers inconspicuous, all discoid, unisexual, the staminate and pistillate borne in separate heads usually in the same cluster. Staminate heads nodding, in terminal catkin-like racemes or spikes, the involucres bowl-shaped. Pistillate heads below or rarely among the staminate, 1- to 4-flowered, the involucre closed, 1- to 4-celled and 1- to 4-beaked or -pointed, armed with several rows of spines and becoming a bur in fruit. Receptacle with chaffy bracts. Pappus none.

This genus contains about 20 species native to arid western North America. Nine species are native to California, 5 of which are shrubs or subshrubs.

KEY TO THE SPECIES

Leaves coarsely spinose-toothed, sessile. . . . . 1. *F. ilicifolia.*
Leaves not spinose, petioled or rarely nearly sessile.
Spines on fruit very numerous (100 or more); fruit 3/8-inch to 1 1/4 inches long; leaves simple, lanceolate to narrow-ovate, irregularly dentate. 2. *F. ambrosioides.*
Spines on fruit less than 30; fruit less than 3/8-inch long.
Bur with straight spines.
Leaves once- to thrice-pinnately parted, silvery-canescent on both sides. 3. *F. dumosa.*
Leaves dentate to once-pinnate, greenish above . . . . 4. *F. eriocentra.*
Bur with hooked spines woolly at base; leaves round-ovate, subentire to crenate. . . . . 5. *F. chenopodiifolia.*

1. **Franseria ilicifolia** Gray. HOLLYLEAF BURSAGE. Fig. 746.

A much branched shrubby perennial, 1 to 3 feet high and with a spread of 5 feet, with hirsute or glandular-hispid branches, leafy to the summit or to the inflorescence. Flowering period, February to April.

Hollyleaf Bursage occurs in sandy washes in the mountains of the Colorado Desert (Signal Mt.; Chuckawalla Mts.; Maria Mts., *E. E. Schellenger*). It extends southward to Lower California and eastward to Arizona.

Franseria ilicifolia Gray, Proc. Am. Acad. 11:77 (1876). Type locality: "Great Cañon of the Tantillas Mountains, near the border of Lower California." Collected by *Palmer*.

2. **Franseria ambrosioides** Cav. AMBROSIA BURSAGE. Fig. 745.

A tall shrubby perennial, 3 to 6 feet high, with grayish hirsute branches. Flowering period, April to July.

Ambrosia Bursage is rare in California. It is known from the vicinity of San Diego southward to Lower California and Sonora, Mexico and from Arizona.

Franseria ambrosioides Cav. Ic. 2:79 (1793). Type locality: Mexico.

3. **Franseria dumosa** Gray. SANDBUR. WHITE BURSAGE. Fig. 742.

A low spreading rounded shrub, 1 to 2 feet high, with many rigid and brittle branches and with the herbage whitened with a close fine pubescence. Leaves 3/8- to 3/4-inch long, rarely to 1 1/2 inches, once- to thrice-pinnately parted into rounded short lobes. Involucre of the pistillate heads usually 2-flowered. Bur about 3/16-inch long, glandular-puberulent, the spines straight and tapering from a broad flat base to a sharp tip. Flowering period, March to May or sometimes throughout the year.

Sandbur is a common shrub on the Colorado and Mohave deserts usually in the Lower Sonoran Life Zone. It extends eastward to Arizona and Utah and southward to Mexico. Its most abundant associate is the Creosote Bush *(Larrea divaricata).*

Franseria dumosa Gray; Torr. in Frem. 2nd. Rep. Calif. 316 (1845). Type locality: "Sandy uplands of the Mohave River." Collected by *Fremont.*

4. **Franseria eriocentra** Gray. WOOLLY BURSAGE. Fig. 743.

A rigidly branched spreading shrub, 1 to 3 feet high, with the herbage whitened with a minute tomentum, the leaves soon becoming glabrous and green above. Leaves cuneate-oblong to lanceolate, 1/2-inch to 1 inch long, sinuately few-toothed or -lobed, nearly sessile by a tapering attenuate base. Involucre of pistillate heads

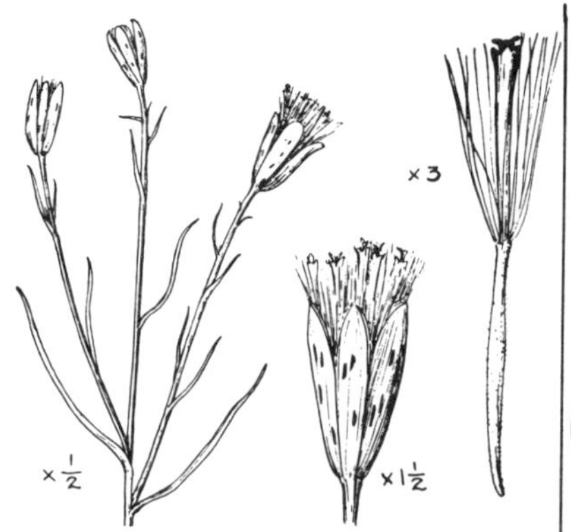

FIG. 741 POROPHYLLUM GRACILE

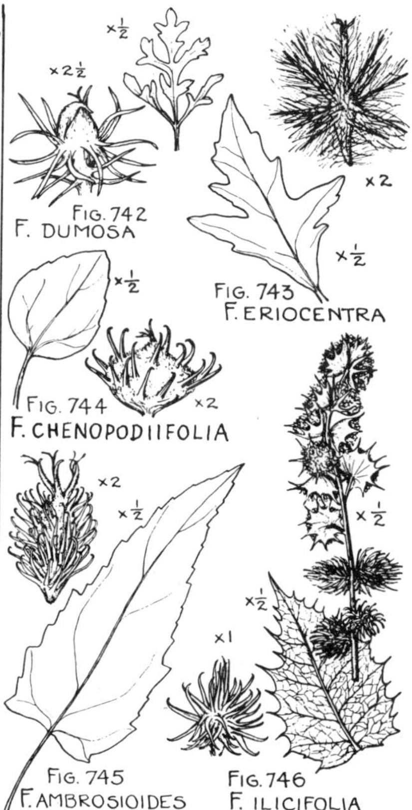

FIG. 742 F. DUMOSA

FIG. 743 F. ERIOCENTRA

FIG. 744 F. CHENOPODIIFOLIA

FIG. 745 F. AMBROSIOIDES

FIG. 746 F. ILICIFOLIA

FRANSERIA

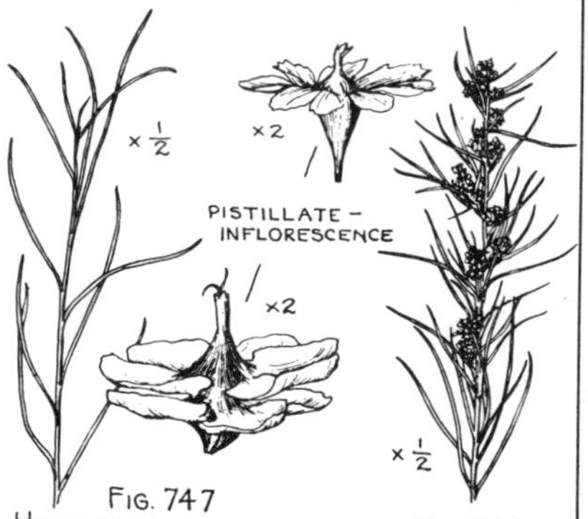

FIG. 747 HYMENOCLEA SALSOLA

FIG. 748 H. MONOGYRA

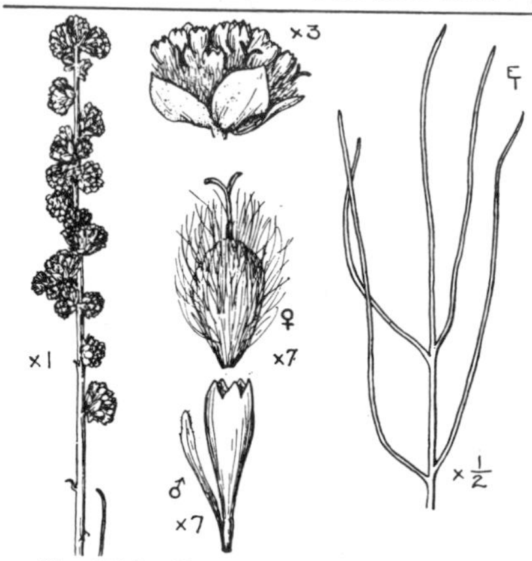

FIG. 749 OXYTENIA ACEROSA

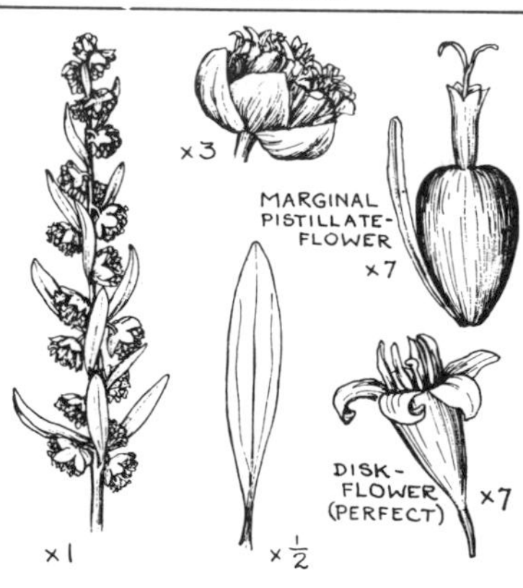

FIG. 750 IVA HAYESIANA

1-flowered. Bur about 5/16-inch long, white-woolly, the spines straight and rigid and almost equalled by the wolly hairs, the beak subulate, about as long as the body. Flowering period, April and May.

Woolly Bursage is known in California from the Providence and New York mountains of the eastern Mohave Desert in San Bernardino County. It extends eastward to Arizona, Nevada, and Utah.

Franseria eriocentra Gray, Proc. Am. Acad. 7:355 (1868). Type locality: "East slope of the Providence Mountains, Arizona," (probably California). Collected by *J. G. Cooper*.

5. **Franseria chenopodiifolia** Benth. San Diego Bursage. Fig. 744.

A low much branched perennial, woody only at the base, 6 to 12 inches high, with white-tomentose herbage. Flowering period, March to June.

San Diego Bursage has been collected in California only south of San Diego to near Tia Juana. It extends southward in Lower California.

Franseria chenopodiifolia Benth. Bot. Voy. Sulph. 26 (1844). Type locality: Bay of Magdalena, Lower California. Collected by *Hinds*.

25. **Hymenoclea** T. & G. Burrobrush

(From the Greek *humen*, membrane, and *kleio*, to enclose, in reference to the membranous winged involucral bracts enlosing the flower.)

Diffusely branched shrubs with glabrous or minutely pubescent herbage. Leaves simple, alternate, narrowly linear to filiform. Flowers inconspicuous, all discoid, unisexual, the staminate and pistillate borne in separate heads on the same plant, the heads small and numerous, the two kinds either intermixed in the panicles or the pistillate borne in the lower axils. Staminate heads nodding, several-flowered; the involucre saucer-shaped, usually 4- to 6-lobed. Pistillate heads erect, with a single flower; the involucre ovoid, beaked at apex and winged with broad scarious wings or scales.

This is a small genus, related to the ragweeds *(Ambrosia)*, containing 2 or 3 species native to the arid southwestern part of North America.

KEY TO THE SPECIES

Leaves sparse, reduced to 1/4- to 3/4-inch long near the ends of the branchlets, not more than 20 on the last 6 inches of the branch; wings of the fruit in several spirally arranged series. 1. *S. Salsola*.

Leaves numerous to the ends of the branches, at least 50 on the last 6 inches of the branch; wings of the fruit in a single radiating series from near the middle of the body. 2. *S. monogyra*.

1. **Hymenoclea Salsola** T. & G. White Burrobrush. Fig. 747.

An erect-spreading bushy shrub, 3 to 6 feet high, with grayish bark. Leaves filiform, 3/4-inch to 2 inches long, becoming shorter and sparser near the inflorescence, often resinous. Fruit with several orbicular wing-like scales spirally arranged from the base to the middle, the margins usually erose. Flowering period, March to May.

White Burrobrush is common in sandy washes in the Colorado and Mohave deserts and northward to the Sierra Nevada foothills south of Bishop in Inyo County, to the Buena Vista Hills near Bakersfield, and to the Cuyama Valley of Santa Barbara County. It extends eastward to Arizona, Nevada, and Utah and southward to Lower California.

Hymenoclea Salsola T. & G. Pl. Fendl. 79 (1849). Type locality: "Uplands near the Mohave River, California." Collected by *Fremont.*

2. **Hymenoclea monogyra** T. & G. Singlewhorl Burrobrush. Fig. 748.

An erect bushy shrub, 2 to 6 feet high, with straw-colored or gray bark. Leaves filiform or the lower ones with filiform divisions, 1 to 3 inches long, numerous to the ends of the branches. Fruit with 7 to 9 spreading scale-wings in a single series from the middle. Flowering period, March to June.

This species is known to occur in California at Needles and near Rialto *(Wheeler),* San Bernardino County and in Mission Canyon near San Diego. It occurs also in Arizona, eastward to Texas, and southward to Mexico.

Hymenoclea monogyra T. & G. Pl. Fendl. 79 (1849). Type locality: Valley of the Gila, Arizona. Collected by *Emory.*

26. **Oxytenia** Nutt.

(From the Greek *oxytenes,* pointed, in reference to the narrow pointed leaves.)

This genus contains a single species.

1. **Oxytenia acerosa** Nutt. Oxytenia. Fig. 749.

An erect shrubby perennial, 3 to 6 feet high, with stems sometimes leafless and rush-like or sometimes with numerous leaves. Flowering period, July to September.

Oxytenia occurs occasionally in the Death Valley region of Inyo County. It extends eastward to Arizona, Utah, and southwestern Colorado.

Oxytenia acerosa Nutt. Jour. Phil. Acad. 2,1:172 (1847). Type locality: "Southeastern borders of California and adjacent parts of Arizona, in a desert region." Collected by *Gambel, Lieut. Wheeler.*

27. **Iva** L.

(Named after *Ajuga iva,* a species of the Mint Family, in reference to its similar odor.)

This is a small genus of about 12 species of perennial herbs or shrubs native to America. Two species are native to California, one of which has stems woody below.

1. **Iva Hayesiana** Gray. Poverty Weed. Fig. 750.

A coarse perennial, 2 to 3 feet high, with ascending branches from a branched woody base. Flowering period, May to July.

Poverty Weed inhabits alkaline soils in western San Diego County. It extends southward into Lower California.

Iva Hayesiana Gray, Proc. Am. Acad. 11:78 (1876). Type locality: San Diego, California. Collected by *Hayes.*

ANTHEMIDEAE. MAYWEED TRIBE

28. **Artemisia** L. Sagebrush

(Named after Artemisia, wife of Mausolus, king of Caria.)

Herbs and shrubs, usually with bitter and aromatic herbage. Leaves simple, alternate, entire to variously lobed or dissected. Flowers all tubular, yellow or purplish, the marginal ones pistillate or sometimes bisexual, the disk-flowers bisexual, fertile or sterile. Heads small, nodding or erect, in panicled spikes or racemes, apparently with all disk-flowers but the marginal flowers in some are irregular ray-flowers. Receptacle slightly convex, naked or rarely chaffy. Involucral bracts well-imbricated, in 2 to 4 series, dry and scarious. Achenes obovoid or oblong to nearly prismatic, usually glabrous, rounded at the summit to a disk. Pappus none.

This is a large genus including about 250 species of both hemispheres but mostly in arid regions of the northern hemisphere. About 14 species and several varieties are native to California, of which 6 species and 7 varieties are shrubs or subshrubs.

The sagebrushes are usually well-known gray bushes of the arid mountain and hill slopes and alkaline areas of the Great Basin area of western North America. Some species are known as wormwood or mugwort, or sometimes as "sage." Their flowers yield an abundance of light wind-blown pollen which is an important factor in causing hay-fever throughout the range of distribution. Several species are of great importance as browse plants for cattle, sheep, and other livestock.

KEY TO THE SPECIES

Plants very spiny; usually not more than 1 foot high............1. *A. spinescens.*
Plants not spiny.
  Receptacle chaffy with scarious bracts; plants usually with herbaceous stems from a slightly woody base...............................2. *A. Palmeri.*
  Receptacle not chaffy; plants normally distinct shrubs.
    Ray-flowers present.
      Leaves linear-cuneate, 3-toothed at the truncate apex or many entire; ray-flowers 1 or 2, or rarely none; disk-flowers 1 to 3........3. *A. Bigelovii.*
      Leaves mostly once- or twice-divided into linear segments or the upper ones entire; ray-flowers 6 to 10; disk-flowers 15 to 40.......4. *A. californica.*
    Ray-flowers absent.
      Leaves mostly toothed or parted, or the upper ones entire...5. *A. tridentata.*
      Leaves linear, entire or a few rarely with a few teeth or lobes...6. *A. cana.*

1. **Artemisia spinescens** D. C. Eaton. BUD SAGEBRUSH. BUD-SAGE. Fig. 751.

An intricately branched rounded spiny shrub, 4 to 12 inches high, with white-tomentose or short-villous herbage. Leaves palmately 3- to 5-divided or -parted, the divisions again divided into linear-spatulate lobes, 1/4- to 3/4-inch long including the petiole, densely villous. Heads few, in short lateral spikes or racemes, the rachis transformed into a rigid spine after the fall of the heads. Ray-flowers 2 to 6, fertile. Disk-flowers 5 to 13, sterile. Achenes densely hairy. Flowering period, March to June.

Bud Sagebrush occurs in California from the Mohave Desert slopes of the San Bernardino Mountains northward through Inyo County and on the eastern side of the Sierra Nevada to Lassen County. It extends northward into eastern Oregon and Idaho and eastward to Montana, Colorado, and New Mexico.

This is considered by stockmen to be a valuable browse plant in spite of its spiny nature. It is known on the range as Bud-sage.

Artemisia spinescens D. C. Eaton; Bot. King's Expl. 180 (1871). *Picrothamnus desertorum* Nutt. Type locality: "Rocky Mountain plains, in arid deserts, toward the north sources of the Platte River." Collected by *Nuttall.*

2. **Artemisia Palmeri** Gray. TALL SAGEBRUSH. Fig. 752.

A perennial, usually with straight wand-like herbaceous stems 1 1/2 to 6 feet high, from a slightly woody base. Leaves pinnately parted into 3 to 5 linear lobes, or

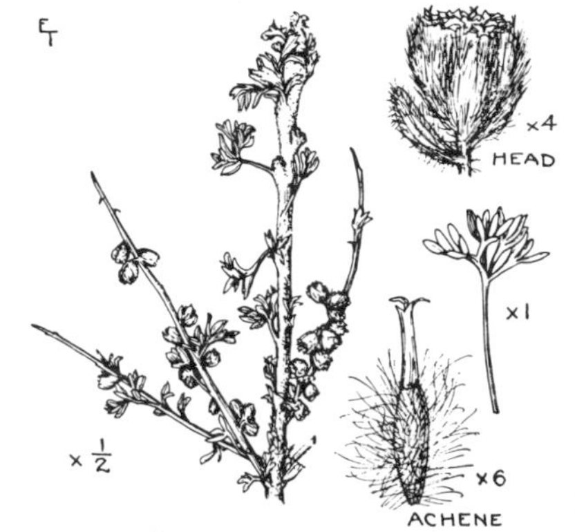

FIG. 751 ARTEMISIA SPINESCENS

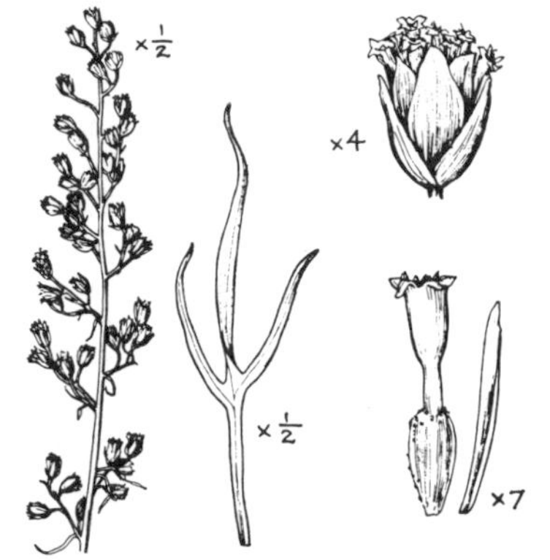

FIG. 752 A. PALMERI

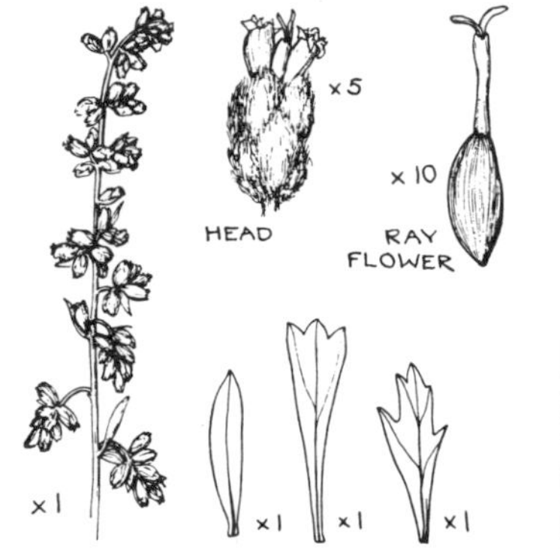

FIG. 753 A. BIGELOVII

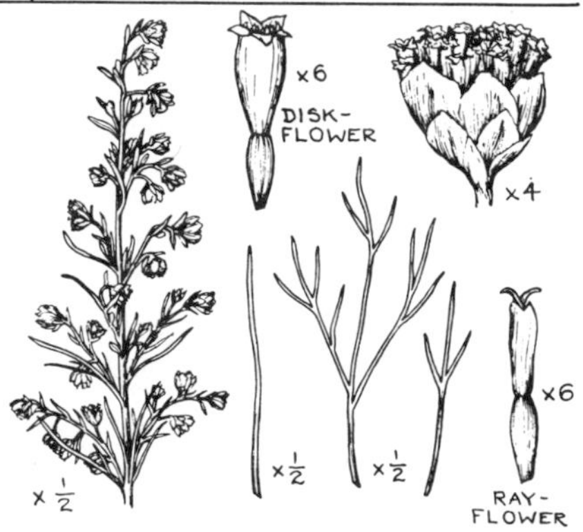

FIG. 754 A. CALIFORNICA

FIG. 755 A. TRIDENTATA

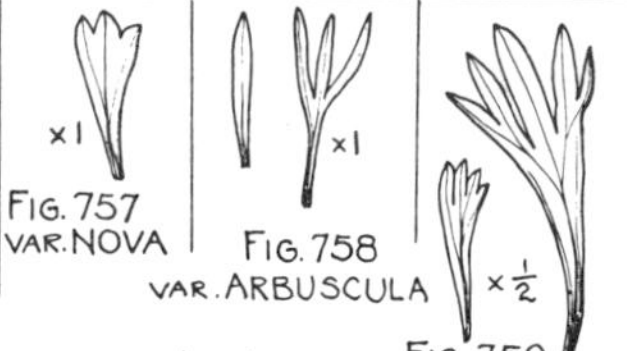

FIG. 757 VAR. NOVA

FIG. 758 VAR. ARBUSCULA

FIG. 759 VAR. ROTHROCKII

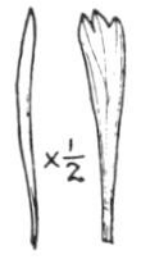

FIG. 756 VAR. PARISHII

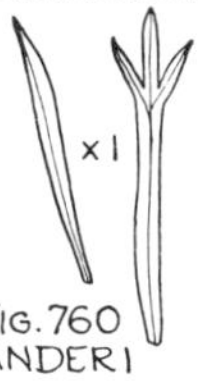

FIG. 760 VAR. BOLANDERI

FIG. 761 A. CANA

linear and entire, 2 to 4 inches long, green and nearly glabrous above, densely white-tomentose beneath, petioled or sessile, the margins revolute. Heads numerous in open panicles. Ray-flowers none. Disk-flowers 12 to 25. Receptacle chaffy with scarious bracts. Achenes 4-angled, granuliferous. Flowering period, July and August.

Tall Sagebrush occurs occasionally in moist ravines in southwestern San Diego County from the canyons near La Jolla southward into Lower California.

Artemisia Palmeri Gray, Proc. Am. Acad. 11:79 (1876). Type locality: In Jamul Valley about 20 miles east of San Diego. Collected by *Palmer*.

3. **Artemisia Bigelovii** Gray. FLAT SAGEBRUSH. BIGELOW SAGEBRUSH. Fig. 753.

A low shrub, 8 to 18 inches high, with many slender erect flowering branches. Leaves narrowly cuneate, 1/4- to 3/4-inch long, sharply 3-toothed at the truncate apex or some entire, silvery-canescent. Heads many in an elongated narrow panicle or sometimes in nearly spike-like inflorescences. Ray-flower usually 1. Disk-flowers 1 to 3. Achenes of both ray- and disk-flowers glabrous, about 5-ribbed. Flowering period, September and October.

Flat Sagebrush occurs in California only "in a narrow canyon at 5500 ft. elevation on Clark Mountain, eastern Mohave Desert," *Munz*. Outside of California it occurs in the southern Rocky Mountains, from southern Colorado and southeastern Utah to Arizona and New Mexico and northwestern Texas.

Artemisia Bigelovii Gray, Pacif. R. Rep. 4:110 (1857). Type locality: "On the Upper Canadian, Texas." Collected by *Bigelow*.

4. **Artemisia californica** Less. COAST SAGEBRUSH. CALIFORNIA SAGEBRUSH. OLD MAN. Fig. 754.

A densely bushy gray shrub, 2 to 5 feet high, with a pungent sage-like odor. Leaves mostly once- or twice-divided into linear or filiform lobes or segments, or the upper ones linear and entire, 3/4-inch to 3 inches long, minutely gray-canescent, often with smaller leaves fascicled in their axils. Heads many, nodding, in racemose panicles 4 to 12 inches long. Ray-flowers 6 to 10 or up to 15, the corolla tubular and nearly regular, usually 4-toothed. Disk-flowers 15 to 30 or up to 40, the corolla campanulate, 5-toothed. Achenes of both ray- and disk-flowers 5-angled, resinous-granuliferous. Flowering period, July to September.

Coast Sagebrush is a common shrub on exposed slopes and dry hills in California from the north and east sides of San Francisco Bay southward in the Coast Ranges from near sea level to 2500 feet elevation to the Tehachapi Mountains and the mountains of coastal southern California, and eastward to the borders of the Colorado Desert. It occurs also on the islands off the coast of southern California and in Lower California. In the Tehachapi Pass area, Coast Sagebrush is associated with the true sagebrush *(Artemisia tridentata)*.

Artemisia californica Less. Linnaea 6:523 (1831). Type locality: San Francisco, California. Collected by *Chamisso*.

5. **Artemisia tridentata** Nutt. SAGEBRUSH. Fig. 755.

KEY TO THE SPECIES AND VARIETIES

Leaves deeply 3-cleft into linear or spatulate divisions, these often 3-cleft, or the upper leaves linear and entire; flowers 5 to 8................5b. Var. *trifida*.

Leaves 3- or rarely 5- to 7-dentate at apex, or entire.

Shrubs 1 1/2 to 15 feet high; inflorescences 3/4-inch to 4 inches broad.

Achenes glabrous, often resinous-granuliferous.
Leaves narrowly cuneate, 3/8- to 3/4-inch long. . . . . *A. tridentata.*
Leaves narrowly linear, 3/4-inch to 1 1/4 inches long. . . .5a. var. *angustifolia.*
Achenes villous. . . . . .5c. var. *Parishii.*
Shrubs usually less than 1 1/2 feet high; inflorescences less than 1 1/4 inches broad.
Flowers 3 to 6; heads about 1/16-inch broad; involucre greenish yellow.
5d. var. *nova.*
Flowers 5 to 9; heads 1/8- to 1/4-inch broad; leaves mostly 1/2-inch or less long.
5e. var. *arbuscula.*
Flowers 8 to 20 (rarely as few as 6).
Leaves narrowly cuneate, commonly viscid; pubescence gray, appressed.
5f. var. *Rothrockii.*
Leaves narrowly linear, not viscid; pubescence white and loose.
5g. var. *Bolanderi.*

A much branched shrub with erect branches 1 1/2 to 15 feet high, usually with a definite trunk and with gray-canescent foliage emitting an aromatic odor. Leaves narrowly cuneate, 3/8- to 3/4-inch or rarely to 1 1/2 inches long, 3- or rarely 4- to 7-toothed at the apex, or the upper leaves linear or oblanceolate and entire. Heads ovoid, numerous, in dense leafy panicles. Ray-flowers none. Disk-flowers 4 to 6. Achenes resinous-granuliferous. Flowering period, late July to November.

Sagebrush is a common shrub of the Great Basin area of western North America. In California, the typical form occurs from Siskiyou County eastward to Modoc County and southward on the eastern dry slopes and flats of the Sierra Nevada to Inyo County, westward in the Tehachapi Mountains to the desert slopes of the mountains of Ventura County.

5a. Var. **angustifolia** Gray.

This is the common form on the desert slopes of the San Gabriel and San Bernardino mountains southward to Lower California.

5b. Var. **trifida** (Nutt.) n. comb.

This variety occurs near Lancaster on the Mohave Desert, according to Parish, Munz, and Hall.

5c. Var. **Parishii** (Gray) Jepson. Fig. 756.

According to Hall, this variety occurs in California in the southwestern part of the Mohave Desert and extends westward toward the coast along the Santa Clara River.

5d. Var. **nova** (Nels.) n. comb. Fig. 757.

This variety is known in California from Bear Valley in the San Bernardino Mountains, on Clark Mountain, in the Panamint Mountains (acc. *Munz*), and in Silver Canyon in the Inyo Range (acc. *Hall*).

5e. Var. **arbuscula** (Nutt.) n. comb. Fig. 758.

Hall cites this variety from the following locations in California: Near Olancha Peak, southern Sierra Nevada; Mono County; ridge northwest of Donner Pass; divide between American and Rubicon rivers, Eldorado County.

5f. Var. **Rothrockii** (Gray) n. comb. Fig. 759.

This variety usually occurs at higher elevations in the San Bernardino Mountains (east end of Bear Lake) and in the southern Sierra Nevada northward to

Placer County. (Little Cottonwood Creek, Inyo County; Olancha Mountain, Volcano and Monache meadows, Tulare County; Soda Springs of the Tuolumne, Mono Pass, Tuolumne Pass, and Mount Dana, Tuolumne County; Angora Peak near Fallen Leaf Lake, Eldorado County; Bear Valley on the Truckee River, Placer County.)

5g. Var. **Bolanderi** (Gray) n. comb. Fig. 760.

This variety is known only from the vicinity of Mono Lake, Mono County, California.

Artemisia tridentata Nutt. Trans. Am. Phil. Soc. 2, 7:398 (1841). Type locality: "Plains of the Columbia River." Collected by *Nuttall.*

Var. angustifolia Gray, Proc. Am. Acad. 19:49 (1883). Type locality: Southern Idaho.

Var. trifida (Nutt.) McMinn. *A. trifida* Nutt. Type locality: Plains of the Rocky Mountains. Collected by *Nuttall. A. tripartita* Rydb.

Var. Parishii (Gray) Jepson, Man. 1140 (1925). *A. Parishii* Gray. Type locality: Newhall, Los Angeles County, California. Collected by *Parish.*

Var. nova (Nels.) McMinn. *A. nova* Nels. Type locality: Medicine Bow, Wyoming. Collected by *Nelson.*

Var. arbuscula (Nutt.) McMinn. *A. arbuscula* Nutt. Type locality: Arid plains of the Snake River. Collected by *Nuttall.*

Var. Rothrockii (Gray) McMinn. *A. Rothrockii* Gray. Type locality: Sierra Nevada of Tulare County, California. Collected by *Rothrock.*

Var. Bolanderi (Gray) McMinn. *A. Bolanderi* Gray. Type locality: Mono Pass in the Sierra Nevada of California. Collected by *Bolander.*

6. **Artemisia cana** Pursh. HOARY SAGEBRUSH. Fig. 761.

A low rounded shrub, usually 1 to 3 feet high, with silky-canescent herbage emitting a pungent turpentine-like odor when crushed. Leaves linear, ¾-inch to 2 inches long, entire or rarely with 1 or 2 irregular teeth or lobes. Heads erect, mostly sessile in small head-like clusters, forming a narrow leafy panicle. Ray-flowers none. Disk-flowers 6 to 15 or rarely to 20. Achenes angled or with 4 or 5 evident ribs, granuliferous. Flowering period, August and September.

Hoary Sagebrush occurs in California on the eastern side of the Sierra Nevada from north of Bridgeport, Mono County northward to Nevada County. It extends northward to Canada and eastward to New Mexico and Nebraska.

Artemisia cana Pursh, Fl. Am. Sept. 521 (1814). Type locality: On the Missouri River. Collected by *Lewis.*

INULEAE. EVERLASTING TRIBE

29. **Pluchea** Cass.

(Named in honor of N. A. Pluche, a Parisian naturalist of the 18th century.)

This genus contains about 30 species of warm temperate and tropical regions. Two species, one of which is a shrub, are native to California.

1. **Pluchea sericea** (Nutt.) Cov. ARROW-WEED. Fig. 762.

A slender willow-like shrub, 3 to 12 feet high, with silvery-silky herbage. Leaves simple, alternate, linear-lanceolate, ¾-inch to 1½ inches long, acute at apex, tapering below to a petiole-like base, entire. Flowers purplish, discoid, in heads clustered in corymb-like terminal cymes. Marginal flowers of the head pistillate and fertile, the central flowers bisexual but sometimes sterile, with tubular 5-cleft corollas. Involucral bracts imbricated, in 2 or 3 series, pubescent, the outer ones firm, brown or purplish, the inner ones thinner, straw-colored to white. Receptacle flat, naked. Achenes about 5-ribbed, glabrous, not beaked. Pappus of a single circle of capillary bristles. Flowering period, May and June.

Arrow-weed inhabits river bottoms, ditches, stream borders, and washes of the Colorado and Mohave deserts.

Pluchea sericea (Nutt.) Cov. Contr. U. S. Nat. Herb. 4; 128 (1893). *Polypappus sericeus* Nutt. Type locality: California.

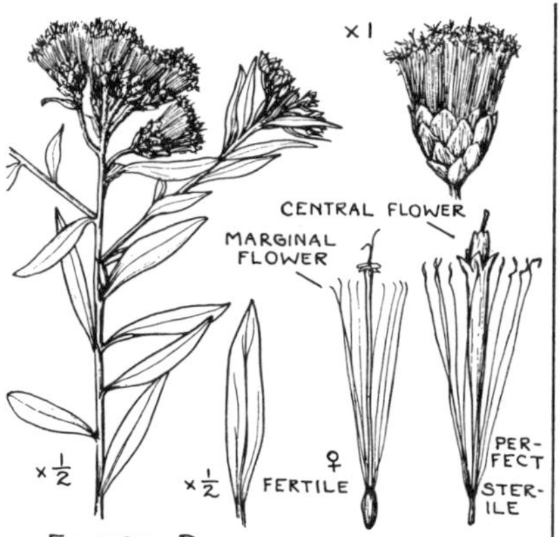

FIG. 762 PLUCHEA SERICEA

FIG. 763 HOFMEISTERIA PLURISETA

EUPATORIEAE. EUPATORY TRIBE

30. **Hofmeisteria** Walp.

(Named in honor of W. Hofmeister, a German botanist.)

This is a small genus of about 4 species native to the southwestern United States and northwestern Mexico. A single species occurs in California.

1. **Hofmeisteria pluriseta** Gray. ARROW-LEAF. Fig. 763.

An intricately much branched bushy shrub, 1 to 2½ feet high, with usually glandular-pubescent herbage. Leaves simple, the lower ones opposite, the upper ones alternate; the blades deltoid-lanceolate to linear, $\frac{3}{16}$- to ⅜-inch long, entire or with 1 or 2 small teeth; petioles ¾-inch to 1½ inches long. Flowers whitish, discoid, bisexual and fertile, in long-pedunculate or nearly sessile heads, these about 20-flowered. Involucral bracts narrow, 3-striated, imbricated, the outer ones shorter. Receptacle flat, naked. Achenes 5-angled, with a thick callous at base. Pappus of 10 to 12 scabrous bristles and with additional short thin paleae. Flowering period, April and May.

Arrow-leaf is a rather common shrub in the rocky canyons of the desert ranges below 4000 feet elevation from the Inyo Mountains southward throughout the Mohave and Colorado deserts. It extends eastward to Arizona and Utah and southward to northern Lower California (acc. *Paul C. Standley*).

Hofmeisteria pluriseta Gray, Pacif. R. Rep. 4:96 (1857). Type locality: "Bill Williams Fork, Arizona." Collected by *Bigelow*.

31. **Brickellia** Ell. Brickellbush

(Named in honor of Dr. J. Brickell, early botanist of Georgia.)

Herbs or small shrubs or subshrubs. Leaves simple, alternate or opposite. Flowers whitish or flesh-colored, bisexual, all discoid, 5 to 50 in small or medium-sized heads. Involucral bracts well imbricated in several series, striated. Receptacle naked. Achenes 10-ribbed. Pappus of numerous scabrous or plumose capillary bristles, usually in a single whorl.

The genus *Brickellia* consists of about 40 species native to the warmer parts of the United States, Mexico, Central America, and northern South America. Fourteen species are native to California, 13 of which are woody, at least at the base.

The brickellbushes of California are usually low woody-stemmed perennials or sometimes distinctly shrubby. They are of little ornamental value and are not usually cultivated.

KEY TO THE SPECIES

Heads 3- to 7-flowered.
- Leaves linear . . . . 1. *B. longifolia.*
- Leaves lanceolate to ovate.
  - Leaves entire or denticulate; heads 3- to 5-flowered in racemosely arranged clusters . . . . 2. *B. multiflora.*
  - Leaves usually serrate; heads 5- to 7-flowered, in compact head-like cymes. 3. *B. Knappiana.*

Heads with more than 7 flowers.
- Herbage very viscid and hairy up to the heads . . . . 4. *B. Greenei.*
- Herbage not viscid or hairy.
  - Herbage distinctly white-tomentose.
    - Heads solitary, terminating the branchlets, 30- to 40-flowered; leaves ovate-oblong to linear . . . . 5. *B. incana.*
    - Heads 1 to 3 at the ends of the branches of the panicle; leaves ovate to subcordate . . . . 6. *B. Nevinii.*
  - Herbage not white-tomentose.
    - Heads less than 20-flowered, clustered on the ends of the branchlets.
      - Leaves 3-nerved, triangular-ovate, ½-inch to 2 inches long, crenate-serrate. 7. *B. californica.*
      - Leaves 1-nerved.
        - Leaves and young stems somewhat viscid, very aromatic; heads 15- to 18-flowered . . . . 8. *B. Watsonii.*
        - Leaves and young stems puberulent, not viscid; heads 8- to 12-flowered. 9. *B. desertorum.*
    - Heads with 20 or more flowers.
      - Heads solitary at the ends of the branchlets.
        - Branchlets somewhat spinose; leaves ⅛- to ½-inch long. 10. *B. frutescens.*
        - Branchlets not spinose; leaves ⅜-inch to 1 inch long.
          - Leaves ovate, saliently toothed to entire . . . . 11. *B. arguta.*
          - Leaves ovate-oblong to linear, entire or with 1 or 2 teeth. 12. *B. oblongifolia* var. *linifolia.*
      - Heads in clusters of 1 to 3 on the branches of the panicle; leaves round-ovate to oblong, subcordate or truncate at base, ¼- to ¾-inch long. 13. *B. microphylla.*

1. **Brickellia longifolia** Wats. Longleaf Brickellbush.

A glabrous much branched shrub, 1 to 2½ feet high. Leaves alternate, linear, 1 to 4 inches long, entire, nearly sessile. Heads 3- to 5-flowered, in small clusters which are racemosely arranged.

This species has been reported from the Panamint Mountains of Inyo County *(M. F. Gilman).* It extends eastward to Arizona and Utah.

Brickellia longifolia Wats. Am. Nat. 7:301 (1873). Type locality: Southern Nevada. Collected by *Wheeler.*

2. **Brickellia multiflora** Kell. Inyo Brickellbush.

An erect shrub, 3 to 6 feet high, with white stems and branches. Leaves alternate, ovate-lanceolate, 1 to 3 inches long, 3-nerved, entire or denticulate, very gummy, nearly sessile. Heads 3- to 5-flowered, in racemosely arranged clusters, these often compound and ½-foot to 1¼ feet long.

Inyo Brickellbush occurs in sandy washes in the Panamint and Inyo ranges of Inyo County. It extends eastward to Nevada.

Brickellia multiflora Kell. Proc. Calif. Acad. 7:49 (1877). Type locality: Kings River region, southern Sierra Nevada. Collected by *Kellogg.*

3. **Brickellia Knappiana** Drew. Willow Brickellbush.

A slender willow-like shrub, 3 to 8 feet high, the branches with a smooth white bark which tends to become shreddy in age. Leaves alternate, ovate-lanceolate, 1 to 1½ inches long, sharply serrate or the upper ones entire, narrowed to a very short but distinct petiole. Heads 5- to 7-flowered, in clusters terminating lateral branchlets of the open leafy panicle. Flowering period, August and September.

Willow Brickellbush is a rare shrub known only in the Panamint Mountains of Inyo County and near the Mohave River.

Brickellia Knappiana Drew, Pitt. 1:260 (1888). Type locality: "In the neighborhood of the Mohave River." Collected by *M. A. Knapp.*

4. **Brickellia Greenei** Gray. Mountain Brickellbush.

A low very leafy perennial, ½-foot to 1½ feet high, with many erect or ascending stems from a woody base, and very viscid herbage. Flowering period, June to August.

Mountain Brickellbush occurs in the northern Sierra Nevada from Placer County northward to Lassen Peak, Shasta County, in the Yollo Bolly and Scott mountains, and on Mount Shasta, from 6000 to 9000 feet elevation. It extends northward to Oregon.

Brickellia Greenei Gray, Proc. Am. Acad. 12:58 (1876). Type locality: Siskiyou County, California on the south fork of Scott River. Collected by *Greene.*

5. **Brickellia incana** Gray. White Brickellbush.

A globose white-tomentose bush, 2 to 4 feet high, loosely branched from a woody base, the tomentum deciduous from the stems and exposing the white bark. Flowering period, May and June.

White Brickellbush occurs in sandy washes and in flats below 4000 feet elevation on the northern edge of the Colorado Desert, on the southern Mohave Desert, and in Death Valley. It extends eastward to southern Nevada.

Brickellia incana Gray, Proc. Am. Acad. 7:350 (1868). Type locality: Providence Mountains, in the Mohave Desert. Collected by *J. G. Cooper.*

6. **Brickellia Nevinii** Gray. Nevin Brickellbush.

A loosely branched but dense shrub, 1 to 1½ feet high, with white-tomentose herbage, the tomentum becoming loose and scurfy. Leaves alternate, ovate to subcordate, ¼- to ⅝-inch long, coarsely few-toothed or entire, sessile or short-petioled. Heads about 25-flowered, solitary or in clusters of 2 or 3, terminating the short branchlets of an open panicle. Flowering period, August and September.

Nevin Brickellbush inhabits dry slopes and washes of the Santa Ynez Mountains and the south slopes of the San Gabriel and Santa Monica mountains.

Brickellia Nevinii Gray, Proc. Am. Acad. 20:297 (1885). Type locality: Near Newhall, Los Angeles County, California. Collected by *J. C. Nevin*.

7. **Brickellia californica** (T. & G.) Gray. CALIFORNIA BRICKELLBUSH. Fig. 764.

A straggly rounded aromatic bush, 1½ to 3½ feet high, with many stems from a woody base and with roughish puberulent herbage. Leaves alternate, triangular-ovate, mostly ½-inch to 2 inches long, 3-nerved, crenate-serrate, short-petioled (1/16- to ¼-inch). Heads 10- to 15-flowered, in small clusters terminating lateral branchlets of a leafy panicle or the branchlets of the panicle much reduced and the inflorescence becoming spicate. Flowering period, June to November.

California Brickellbush inhabits dry gravelly stream beds and dry slopes of the Upper Sonoran Life Zone in the mountains of coastal southern California, northward in the Coast Ranges to Siskiyou County, in the Sierra Nevada foothills from Amador County northward to Shasta County, and occasionally on the Mohave Desert (Cushenberry Springs and Clark Mt.). It extends southward to Mexico and eastward to Texas.

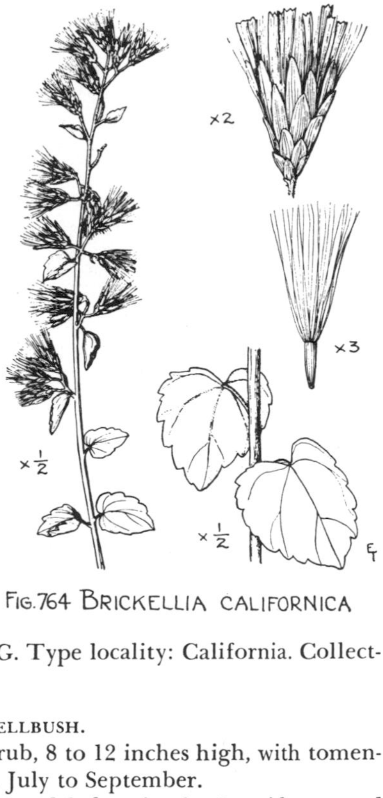

FIG. 764 BRICKELLIA CALIFORNICA

Brickellia californica (T. & G.) Gray, Pl. Fendl. 64 (1849). *Bulbostylis californica* T. & G. Type locality: California. Collected by *Douglas*.

8. **Brickellia Watsonii** Rob. WATSON BRICKELLBUSH.

A very aromatic intricately branched subshrub, 8 to 12 inches high, with tomentulose-puberulent herbage. Flowering period, July to September.

Watson Brickellbush occurs on rocky walls and ledges in the Providence and Clark mountains of eastern San Bernardino County and in the Amargosa Mountains of Inyo County. It extends eastward to Utah.

Brickellia Watsonii Rob. Mem. Gray Herb. 1:42 (1917). Type locality: "East Humboldt Mountains, Nevada, and mouth American Cañon, Utah." Collected by *Watson*. *B. microphylla* Wats., not Gray.

9. **Brickellia desertorum** Cov. DESERT BRICKELLBUSH.

An intricately branched shrubby perennial, 2 to 3 feet high, with white-tomentulose herbage, the branches becoming glabrous and white-barked. Flowering period, October and November.

Desert Brickellbush is a rare plant in rocky places between 1000 and 4000 feet elevation on the western edge of the Colorado Desert and occasionally on the Mohave Desert north to the Panamint Mountains of Inyo County. It extends eastward to Nevada and Arizona.

Brickellia desertorum Cov. Proc. Biol. Soc. Wash. 7:68 (1892). Type locality: Between Banning and Seven Palms, on the Southern Pacific Railroad, California. Collected by *C. R. Orcutt*.

10. **Brickellia frutescens** Gray. RIGID BRICKELLBUSH.

An intricately branched rigid shrub, 1 to 2 feet high, with divaricate often spinose branches and glandular-pubescent herbage. Leaves alternate, linear-spatulate to oblong-obovate, 1/8- to 1/2-inch long, pale green, entire, short-petioled. Heads 20- to 35-flowered, solitary and terminal on the corymbose branchlets. Flowering period, April and May.

Rigid Brickellbush occurs in dry rocky places along the western border of the Colorado Desert in the Lower Sonoran Life Zone. It extends southward to Lower California.

Brickellia frutescens Gray, Proc. Am. Acad. 17:207 (1882). Type locality: "Tantillas Cañon, near the borders of San Diego Co., but within Lower California." Collected by *Palmer* and others.

11. **Brickellia arguta** Rob. PUNGENT BRICKELLBUSH.

A much branched shrub, 8 inches to 1 1/2 feet high, with zigzag stems and glandular-hairy herbage. Leaves alternate, ovate, 3/8-inch to 1 inch long, bright green, prominently veined, saliently toothed to entire, nearly sessile. Heads 35- to 50-flowered, solitary and terminating the branchlets. Flowering period, April to June.

This species occurs in rocky places in the desert mountain ranges from Inyo County southward in the Mohave Desert to the Colorado Desert and into Lower California.

11a. Var. **odontolepis** Rob. Similar to the species but the outer involucral bracts conspicuously foliaceous and dentate.

This variety occurs occasionally on the western part of the Colorado Desert.

Brickellia arguta Rob. Mem. Gray Herb. 1:102 (1917). *Coleosanthus atractyloides* Cov. Type locality: Not given. Probably collected by *Coville* and *Funston*. *Brickellia atractyloides* Hall, not Gray. *B. atractyloides* var. *arguta* (Rob.) Jepson.

Var. odontolepis Rob. Mem. Gray Herb. 1:103 (1917). Type locality: Colorado Desert. Collected by *C. R. Orcutt*.

12. **Brickellia oblongifolia** var. **linifolia** (D. C. Eaton) Rob. MOHAVE BRICKELLBUSH.

A low round-topped bush, 8 to 16 inches high, with numerous leafy stems from a woody base and with cinereous-pubescent and often somewhat glandular herbage. Flowering period, April to June.

Mohave Brickellbush inhabits dry rocky places below 6500 feet elevation in the mountains of the western Colorado Desert northward to the southern Mohave Desert and probably to Inyo County. It extends eastward to Arizona and Utah.

Brickellia oblongifolia var. linifolia (D. C. Eaton) Rob. Mem. Gray Herb. 1:104 (1917). *B. linifolia* D. C. Eaton. Type locality: "Sandy bottoms of American Fork, Jordan Valley, Utah." Collected by *Watson*. *B. mohavensis* Gray.

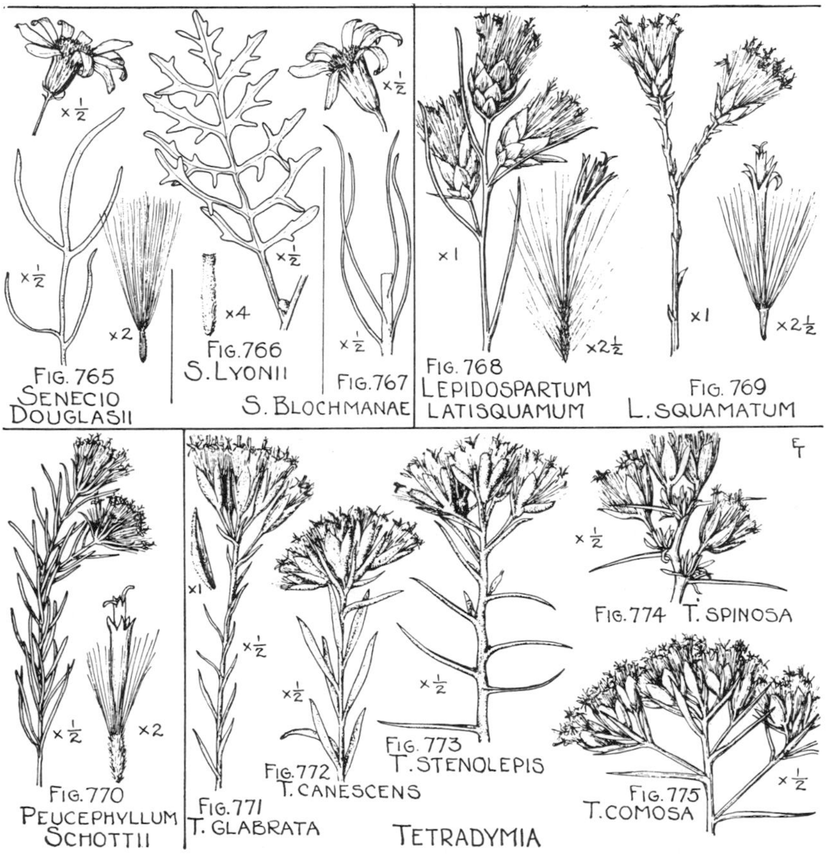

13. **Brickellia microphylla** (Nutt.) Gray. LITTLELEAF BRICKELLBUSH.

A much branched shrubby perennial, 1 to 2 feet high, with glandular-villous herbage. Flowering period, August to October.

Littleleaf Brickellbush occurs in dry sandy canyons on the eastern side of the Sierra Nevada in Inyo and Mono counties and in San Antonio Canyon of the San Gabriel Mountains. It extends eastward to Nevada and Colorado and northward to Oregon and Idaho.

Brickellia microphylla (Nutt.) Gray, Pl. Wright. 1:85 (1852). *Bulbostylis microphylla* Nutt. Type locality: Blue Mountains of Oregon. Collected by *Nuttall.*

SENECIONEAE. GROUNDSEL TRIBE

32. Senecio L. GROUNDSEL

(From the Latin *senex,* old man, in reference to the white pappus hairs.)

Herbs or shrubs. Leaves alternate, simple, and entire to pinnatifid. Heads with yellow ray- and disk-flowers or with disk-flowers only. Involucres cylindrical to campanulate, mostly with 1 or 2 rows of equal bracts and sometimes with additional bracteoles at their bases. Receptacle flat, naked. Achenes round in cross-section. Pappus of abundant white soft bristles.

This genus contains about 1200 species widely distributed all over the world. Over 30 species have been described from California, 3 of which are shrubs or sub-shrubs.

KEY TO THE SPECIES

Leaves once- or twice-divided; ray-flowers 10 to 13.
  Leaf-lobes 3 to 9, linear or filiform, acute; mainland...........1. *S. Douglasii.*
  Leaf-lobes numerous, obtuse; insular............................2. *S. Lyonii.*
Leaves simple, linear-filiform; ray-flowers 5 to 8................3. *S. Blochmanae.*

1. **Senecio Douglasii** DC. Bush Senecio. Bush Groundsel. Creek Senecio. Fig. 765.

A bushy perennial, 2 to 5 feet high, with erect striate stems woody at the base and leafy up to the inflorescence. Flowering period, July to September.

Bush Senecio occurs in dry stream-beds and in gravelly and sandy washes throughout cismontane southern California, northward mostly in the inner Coast Ranges to Lake County, in the Sierra Nevada foothills, and east of the Sierra Nevada to Mono County, in the Upper Sonoran Life Zone from near sea level to about 5000 feet elevation. It occurs also on Santa Catalina and Santa Cruz islands.

1a. Var. **monoensis** (Greene) Jepson. Mono Senecio.

A much branched bush, less woody than the species, with bright green glabrous herbage.

This variety occurs in the mountain valleys of Mono and Inyo counties.

Senecio Douglasii DC. Prodr. 6:429 (1837). Type locality: California. Collected by *Douglas.*

Var. monoensis (Greene) Jepson. *S. monoensis* Greene, Leaflets 1:221 (1906).

2. **Senecio Lyonii** Gray. Island Senecio. Fig. 766.

A somewhat shrubby perennial, 2 to 3 feet high, freely branching and leafy throughout. Herbage at first white-tomentose, becoming glabrate except for persistent tufts of short woolly tomentum in the leaf-axils. Flowering period, March to July.

Island Senecio occurs on San Clemente and Santa Catalina islands and in Lower California.

Senecio Lyonii Gray, Syn. Fl. N. Am. 1:456 (1886). Type locality: San Clemente Island. Collected by *Nevin* and *Lyon.*

3. **Senecio Blochmanae** Greene. Coast Senecio. Fig. 767.

A tufted perennial, 2 to 4 feet high, with simple very leafy stems and glabrous heavy-scented herbage. Leaves linear-filiform, 2 to 4 inches long, recurved or deflexed, entire. Heads cylindrical, about ½-inch high. Ray-flowers 5 to 8. Achenes white-tomentose. Pappus copious, very white and soft. Flowering period, July to November.

This species is a local endemic restricted to the Santa Maria River basin of San Luis Obispo and Santa Barbara counties (acc. *Greene*) and the coast of Santa Barbara County southward to Surf.

Senecio Blochmanae Greene, Erythea 1:7 (1893). Type locality: Santa Maria River, San Luis Obispo County, California. Collected by *Mrs. Blochman.*

33. **Lepidospartum** Gray.

(From the Greek *lepis,* scale, and *sparton,* the name of the broom shrub, in reference to the scale-like leaves on the broom-like branches.)

Broom-like shrubs with simple alternate leaves, all but the earliest of these reduced to scales. Heads with disk-flowers only, these pale yellow, bisexual, and fertile. Involucral bracts regularly imbricated, in 3 or 4 series. Receptable naked. Achenes round in cross section, 8- to 10-nerved. Pappus of numerous minutely scabrous capillary bristles.

This is a small genus of 2 species native to the southwestern United States.

KEY TO THE SPECIES

Heads 4- or 5-flowered; achenes villous; branches persistently tomentose. 1. *L. latisquamum.*

Heads 10- to 15-flowered; achenes glabrous; branches glabrate. .2. *L. squamatum.*

1. **Lepidospartum latisquamum** Wats. GREENBROOM. Fig. 768.

An erect-spreading shrub, 4 to 7 feet high and sometimes with a spread of 12 feet, with strongly striate stems and persistently tomentose branches. Leaves numerous, filiform, $\frac{3}{4}$-inch to $1\frac{1}{4}$ inches long, entire, sessile. Heads 4- or 5-flowered. Involucre about $\frac{3}{8}$-inch high. Achenes silky. Flowering period, July and August.

Greenbroom is known in California from Payson Canyon in the White Mountains of Inyo County *(V. Duran),* 5 miles east of summit of Westgard Pass, Inyo Mountains *(Wolf),* and from Swartout Valley in the northern part of the San Gabriel Mountains *(M. E. Jones).* It extends eastward to Nevada.

Lepidospartum latisquamum Wats. Proc. Am. Acad. 25:133 (1890). Type locality: "Soda Spring Cañon, Esmeralda County, Nevada, at 6,000 feet altitude." Collected by *W. H. Shockley. L. striatum* Cov.

2. **Lepidospartum squamatum** Gray. SCALEBROOM. Fig. 769.

A rigid broom-like shrub, 3 to 6 feet high, with ascending virgate branches, the young shoots tomentose and densely leafy with obovate entire leaves $\frac{1}{4}$- to $\frac{1}{2}$-inch long, the older stems and branches glabrate, green, with the leaves reduced to ovate-acute scales. Heads 10- to 15-flowered, solitary, terminating the short lateral branches and appearing racemose or spicate. Achenes glabrous. Flowering period, June to December.

Scalebroom is a common shrub in sandy washes and gravelly places in cismontane southern California below 5000 feet elevation and mostly inland from the immediate coast. It occurs occasionally also on the Colorado and Mohave deserts, in the dry inner South Coast Ranges as far northward as the Arroyo Mocho, Alameda County, in the upper San Joaquin Valley, and in the southern Sierra Nevada of Kern and Tulare counties. It extends eastward to Nevada and Arizona and southward to Lower California.

Lepidospartum squamatum Gray, Proc. Am. Acad. 19:50 (1883). *Linosyris squamata* Gray, and var. *Breweri* Gray. Type locality: "Low Hills of the Sierra Santa Monica, Los Angeles County, California." Collected by *Brewer. L. squamatum* var. *obtectum* Jepson. *Baccharis sarothroides* var. *pluricephala* Jepson.

34. **Peucephyllum** Gray

(From the Greek *peuke,* the fir, and *phullon,* leaf, in reference to the fir-like foliage.)

This genus contains a single species native to California, Arizona, Nevada, and Lower California.

1. **Peucephyllum Schottii** Gray. PIGMY-CEDAR. Fig. 770.

An erect much branched evergreen shrub, 1 to 9 feet high, with crowded resinous-punctate terete leaves exuding a balsamic odor. Leaves simple, alternate, crowded near the ends of the branches, 1/4-inch to 1 inch long, green, sessile. Flowers yellowish, all discoid, bisexual and fertile, in nearly sessile solitary heads, these scattered. Involucral bracts green, linear-subulate, in about 2 series, forming a campanulate involucre. Receptacle flat, naked. Achenes turbinate or oblong, obscurely 8- to 10-nerved, densely hirsute. Pappus of numerous unequal rather roughish bristles, shorter than the corolla, the inner ones sometimes flattened. Flowering period, March to June.

Pigmy-cedar occurs in dry canyons and foothills of the mountains of Inyo County and on the Mohave and Colorado deserts. It extends southward to Lower California and eastward to Arizona and Nevada.

Peucephyllum Schottii Gray, Bot. Mex. Bound. 74 (1859). Type locality: "On the banks of the Colorado, Sonora," Mexico. Collected by *Schott.*

35. Tetradymia DC.

(From the Greek *tetra,* four, and *dymos,* together, in reference to the 4-flowered heads of the first species described.)

Low rigid shrubs with the herbage covered with a dense matted tomentum. Leaves simple, alternate, entire, often modified into spines. Flowers discoid, yellow, bisexual, regular, 4 to 9 in each head. Involucral bracts 4 to 6, firm, concave, overlapping, often enlarged and thickened at the base. Receptacle flat, naked. Achenes round in cross section, faintly 5-nerved. Pappus of soft fine capillary bristles, usually whitish.

This is a small genus of about 6 species native to the arid regions of western North America. Five species occur in California.

KEY TO THE SPECIES

Heads 4-flowered: branches not spiny.
  Leaves early glabrate, the primary ones 1/4- to 1/2-inch long, early deciduous. 1. *T. glabrata.*
  Leaves permanently tomentose, 1/2- to 7/8-inch long, not early deciduous. 2. *T. canescens.*
Heads 5-flowered; plants spiny.............................3. *T. stenolepis.*
Heads 6- to 9-flowered.
  Heads on short axillary peduncles..........................4. *T. spinosa.*
  Heads nearly sessile, in close terminal corymbs..................5. *T. comosa.*

1. **Tetradymia glabrata** Gray. LITTLELEAF HORSEBRUSH. Fig. 771.

A rounded bushy shrub, 1 to 3 feet high, with ascending or arched and more or less white-tomentose branches. Leaves early glabrate and greenish; primary leaves rigid-subulate, 1/4- to 1/2-inch long, early deciduous; axillary leaves 3 to 6 in a fascicle, linear-oblanceolate, 1/4- to 1/2-inch long, soft, persistent; leaves of sterile shoots linear-subulate, appressed, without fascicled ones in their axils. Heads in small terminal clusters, 4-flowered. Involucral bracts 4 or 5, carinate. Achenes densely villous. Flowering period, May to July.

Littleleaf Horsebrush occurs in the Lower and Upper Sonoran Life Zones from the western Mohave Desert northward on the eastern side of the Sierra Nevada to Lassen County. It extends northward to eastern Oregon, Idaho, and Montana and eastward to Nevada and Utah.

Tetradymia glabrata Gray, Pacif. R. Rep. 11, pt. 1, 122 (1855). Type locality: "On the Sierra Nevada." Collected by *James A. Snyder.*

2. **Tetradymia canescens** DC. GRAY HORSEBRUSH. Fig. 772.

An unarmed freely branched shrub, 4 to 12 inches high, with white-tomentose herbage. Leaves linear or linear-lanceolate, ½- to ⅞-inch long, crowded but rarely if at all fascicled, permanently tomentose, not early deciduous. Heads in short-peduncled cymose clusters terminating the short branchlets, 4-flowered. Involucral bracts 4 or 5, carinate. Achenes glabrous to villous. Flowering period, June to August.

Gray Horsebrush has a wide distribution on dry slopes in the Upper Sonoran and Transition Life Zones from the San Bernardino and San Gabriel mountains northward east of the Sierra Nevada crest to Modoc and Siskiyou counties. It extends northward to British Columbia, Idaho, Montana, and Wyoming, and eastward to Arizona, Nevada, and Utah.

Along Clark Creek, about 10 miles from San Luis Obispo, specimens have been collected by E. Palmer which have shorter leaves and involucres. This has been described as var. **inermis** (Nutt.) Gray. It is apparently the common form in the Rocky Mountains.

Tetradymia canescens DC. Prodr. 6:440 (1837). Type locality: Columbia River. Collected by *Douglas.*

Var. inermis (Nutt.) Gray, Bot. Calif. 1:408 (1876). *T. inermis* Nutt.

3. **Teradymia stenolepis** Greene. MOHAVE HORSEBRUSH. Fig. 773.

A spiny much branched shrub, 1½ to 2½ feet high, with permanently white-tomentose herbage. Lower primary leaves oblanceolate, about ¾-inch long, the upper primary leaves modified into spreading rigid spines ¾-inch to 1¼ inches long, often with secondary leaves fascicled in their axils. Heads in close terminal clusters, 5-flowered. Involucral bracts 5, very thick and rigid. Achenes canescent but glabrate. Flowering period, May to July.

Mohave Horsebrush occurs occasionally in the Lower and Upper Sonoran Life Zones of the western and central Mohave Desert north to the southern Sierra Nevada and the mountains of Inyo County.

Tetradymia stenolepis Greene, Bull. Calif. Acad. 1:92 (1885). Type locality: "Between Cameron and Mohave stations." *K. Brandegee.* Collected by *K. Brandegee.*

4. **Tetradymia spinosa** H. & A. COTTONTHORN. SHORTSPINE HORSEBRUSH. Fig. 774.

A rigidly branched white-tomentose shrub, 2 to 4 feet high, with the primary leaves modified into rigid spines and bearing secondary fascicled leaves in their axils. Spines either straight or recurved, ½-inch to 1¾ inches long, tomentose or glabrate. Secondary leaves green, ¼- to ½-inch long. Heads on short stout axillary peduncles, 6- or 7-flowered. Involucral bracts 5 or 6, short-woolly. Achenes with soft white hairs nearly as long as the pappus bristles. Flowering period, April to June.

Cottonthorn inhabits arid slopes and flats in the southwestern part of the Mohave Desert and along the desert east slopes of the Sierra Nevada northward to

Lassen County. It extends northward to eastern Oregon and eastward to Nevada and Utah. The spines are said to be used for tattoo needles.

Tetradymia spinosa H. & A. Bot. Beechey 360 (1840). Type locality: "Snake County." The vicinity of the Snake River in Oregon. Collected by *Tolmie*.

5. **Tetradymia comosa** Gray. HAIRY HORSEBRUSH. Fig. 775.

An erect bush, 2 to 4 feet high, with many virgate branches and permanently white-tomentose herbage. Primary leaves linear, 1 to 2 inches long, the earlier ones soft, the later rigid and spine-tipped. The secondary fascicled leaves when present linear, ½-inch or less long. Heads nearly sessile, in close terminal corymbs, 6- to 9-flowered. Involucral bracts 5 or 6, oblong, woolly. Achenes with long soft wool concealing the true pappus. Flowering period, July and August.

Hairy Horsebrush occurs in arid places below 5000 feet elevation in interior cismontane southern California north to Newhall and occasionally on the Mohave Desert. It extends eastward to Nevada.

Tetradymia comosa Gray, Proc. Am. Acad. 12:60 (1876). Type locality: "W. Nevada," *Lemmon;* "S.E. borders of California," *E. Palmer;* "Potrero, San Diego Co.," *D. Cleveland.*

ADDENDA

×**Eriogonum Blissianum** Mason, Madroño 4:290 (1938). (*E. giganteum* Wats. × *E. arborescens* Greene.)

This hybrid *Eriogonum* is a rounded compact shrub, 2 to 4 feet high, which resembles *E. arborescens* in its growth form and inflorescence and *E. giganteum* in the size and shape of the floral bracts. The leaves are intermediate in shape between those of the two parents.

This hybrid is a desirable shrub for use as an ornamental in California gardens. The specimen selected by Mason as the type appeared as a volunteer in the Santa Barbara Botanic Garden. To my knowledge this *Eriogonum* does not occur in the wild.

The following species are sometimes slightly woody at the base.

POLYGONACEAE. Polygonum Bolanderi Brew. BOLANDER KNOTWEED. **Polygonum Paronychia** C. & S. ROLLEDLEAF KNOTWEED.

NYCTAGINACEAE. Acleisanthes longiflora Gray. YERBA DE LA RABIA. **Hermidium alipes** Wats. MESSENGER BUSH. **Mirabilis laevis** (Benth.) Curran. WISHBONE BUSH. CALIFORNIA FOUR-O'CLOCK. **Mirabilis tenuiloba** Wats. SLENDER FOUR-O'CLOCK.

BATIDACEAE. Batis maritima L. SALTWORT.

BRASSICACEAE. Arabis Breweri Wats. BREWER ROCK-CRESS. **Arabis dispar** M. E. Jones. CANYON ROCK-CRESS. **Arabis glaucovalvula** M. E. Jones. MESA ROCK-CRESS. **Arabis Lemmonii** Wats. LEMMON ROCK-CRESS. **Arabis maxima** Greene. CURLY ROCK-CRESS. **Arabis perennans** Wats. NEVADA ROCK-CRESS. **Arabis platysperma** Gray. PIONEER ROCK-CRESS. **Arabis pulchra** M. E. Jones. DESERT ROCK-CRESS. **Arabis suffrutescens** Wats. PURPLE ROCK-CRESS. **Erysimum insulare** Greene. ISLAND WALLFLOWER.

EMPETRACEAE. Empetrum nigrum L. BLACK CROWBERRY.

GLOSSARY OF BOTANICAL TERMS

Acaulescent. Apparently stemless, the leaves all borne at the surface of the ground and the flowers sessile or borne on a leafless stalk from the ground.

Achene. A one-seeded dry fruit from a simple or compound ovary which does not open.

Acorn. A nut partly surrounded by a fibrous or woody cup; the fruit of an oak.

Acuminate. Gradually diminishing to the apex.

Acute. Terminating in an angle, usually less than a right angle, but not prolonged.

Adherent. Growing fast to or united with another body or organ of a different kind, as the stamens to the petals.

Adnate. Adherent.

Adventitious. Applied to buds produced abnormally, as from the internode of the stem instead of at the node in the axils of the leaves.

Aerial. Pertaining to parts of plants living above the surface of the ground or water.

Alternate. Said of a single leaf or branch at a node.

Alveolate. Marked as though honeycombed.

Angiospermous. Having the seeds borne in an ovary, as in Angiosperms.

Angiosperms. Plants having their seeds enclosed in an ovary.

Annual. A plant flowering and fruiting in the first year or season and then dying.

Anther. The pollen-bearing pouch at the top of the stamen.

Apetalous. Without petals.

Apex. The end or summit, as the end of a leaf.

Apical. Pertaining to or occurring at the point of any structure.

Apiculate. Ending in a short-pointed tip.

Appressed. Pressed close to the stem or other organ.

Arachnoid. Like a cobweb, from an entanglement of fine whitish hairs.

Arborescent. Tree-like.

Arctic-alpine Life Zone. The zone above timber-line.

Areole. A specialized organ or area from which spines, flowers, and other organs develop, as in the Cataceae.

Arid Transition Life Zone. The zone above the Humid Transition Zone with less rainfall, hotter summers, and colder winters.

Aril. An appendage or extra growth associated with the seed.

Arillate. Furnished with an aril.

Aristate. Furnished with an arista or awn, like the beard or bristle of barley.

Armed. Bearing spines, thorns, or similar structures.

Aromatic. With a pleasant odor.

Assurgent. Rising or curving upwards from the base.

Attenuate. Gradually narrowed or prolonged.

Auriculate. With small ear-shaped lobes or appendages.

Autophyte. A plant which synthesizes its food from inorganic substances; one possessing chlorophyll (green pigment).

Awl-shaped. Narrow and tapering to a point like a shoemaker's awl; subulate.

Awn. A bristle, like the beard of barley.

Awned. Provided with a bristle.

Axil. The angle between a leaf and stem.

Axillary. Occurring in an axil or angle, as a bud in the axil formed by the leaf and stem.

Axis. The part of the stem or branch upon which the flowers are borne.

Banner. The largest petal or standard of a papilonaceous flower, as in lupine.

Barbate. With hairs or bristles.

Beaked. Said of fruits which end in a long point.

Bearded. Having tufts of hairs.

Berry. A fleshy fruit from a compound ovary with a fleshy pulp throughout.

Biennial. A plant requiring two years to complete its life cycle, growing one year, and flowering and fruiting the second.

Bifid. Divided halfway into two.

Bilabiate. Divided into two lips, as are many sympetalous corollas.

Bipinnate. Twice pinnate.

Bisexual. Having both stamens and pistils; possessing perfect flowers.

Bloom. The white waxy or powdery covering on many fruits and leaves.

Bract. A modified or undeveloped leaf associated with the flower or flower-cluster; a narrow structure subtending the cone-scales in cone-bearing trees.

Bracteole. A bractlet.
Bractlet. A bract of the last grade, as one inserted on a pedicel or ultimate flower-stalk, instead of subtending it.
Bristle. A stiff hair.
Bur. A prickly fruit like that of a chestnut or beech.
Burl. A swollen growth at the junction of roots and stems from which sprouts may arise.
Caespitose. Growing in tufts like grass.
Callous. An abnormally thickened part.
Calyces. Plural of calyx.
Calyx. The sepals collectively; the outermost series of floral envelopes.
Campanulate. Bell-shaped.
Canadian Life Zone. The zone between the Hudsonian and Transition Life Zones.
Canescent. Growing gray or hoary.
Capillary. Slender, comparable to a hair.
Capitate. Growing in heads.
Capsule. A dry fruit from a compound ovary, splitting along three or more lines.
Carinate. Keeled.
Carpel. A simple pistil or an element of a compound pistil; a modified leaf constituting a pistil.
Caruncle. A "wart" or protuberance on one side of some seeds.
Catkin. A slender compact cluster of unisexual flowers, as in the willow.
Caudate. With a tail-like appendage.
Caudex. A short stem or trunk.
Chaparral. Shrubs with usually thick, leathery, stiff, and evergreen leaves.
Chartaceous. Papery.
Choripetalous. Having the petals separate; not sympetalous.
Ciliate. Having the margin fringed with hairs.
Ciliolate. The diminutive of ciliate.
Cinerous. Gray as wood ashes.
Cismontane. West of the Sierra Nevada crest and the desert areas in California.
Clavate. Club-shaped; thickened towards the apex.
Claw. The petiole-like base of petals and sepals.
Cleft. Cut halfway down.
Coalesced. Said of united organs of the same kind, as the union of petals.
Composite head. An inflorescence composed of many small flowers in a compact cluster surrounded by an involucre, as in Asteraceae.
Compound. Composed of more than one similar part united into a single organ.
Compressed. Flattened.
Cone. A collection of ovule-bearing scales, bracts, or carpels, usually applied to the fruits of pines, firs, and other Coniferae, but also to those of alders, birches, etc.
Confluent. Blended into one.
Conical. Cone-shaped.
Coniferous. Producing or bearing cones.
Connate. United, congenitally or subsequently.
Connate-perfoliate. United at the base in pairs around the supporting axis.
Cordate. Heart-shaped, with a broad and notched base.
Coriaceous. Leathery.
Corky. Of the texture or quality of cork.
Corolla. The interior perianth, composed of petals, free or united.
Corymb. A type of inflorescence in which the lower divisions or pedicels are elongated so as to form a flat-topped cluster.
Corymbose. Arranged in corymbs.
Cotyledon. A leaf of the embryo within the seed-coat.
Crenate. Notched with rounded teeth.
Crenulate. Crenate, but the toothings themselves small.
Crest. An elevation or ridge upon the summit of an organ.
Crown-sprout. A sprout growing from the burl or root-crown.
Cruciferous. Cross-bearing, said of the corollas of Brassicaceae, which have four petals.
Cuneate. Wedge-shaped.
Cusp. A sharp, rigid point.
Cuspidate. Tipped with a cusp.
Cyclic. Arranged in whorls; relating to a cycle.
Cyme. A flower cluster in which the terminating or central flower blooms first.
Cymose. Bearing or relating to cymes.
Deciduous. Said of leaves that drop off before winter.
Decumbent. Reclining, but with the summit ascending.
Decurrent. Running down, as when leaves extend down the stem beyond the point of attachment.
Decussate. In opposite pairs alternately arranged at right angles.
Deflexed. Bent outward and downward; the opposite of inflexed.

Dehiscent. Splitting open naturally at maturity.
Deltoid. Shaped like an equilateral triangle.
Dentate. Toothed with the teeth directed outward.
Denticulate. Minutely dentate.
Depressed. Sunk down, as if flattened from above.
Diadelphous. With two groups of united stamens.
Dichotomous. Forked; parted by pairs.
Dicotyledons. Plants having two seed-leaves or cotyledons in their seeds.
Dimorphic. Occurring under two forms.
Dioecious. Staminate and pistillate flowers borne upon separate plants, as in the willow.
Discoid. Said of heads with disk-flowers only, as in Asteraceae.
Disk-achene. An achene borne by the disk-flower.
Disk-flower. A flower occurring on the central portion of the heads of Asteraceae, not of the ray (or margin), usually tubular.
Dissected. Deeply divided or cut into many segments.
Distant. Not close together on the axis.
Distinct. Separate from; not united.
Divaricate. Extremely divergent.
Dominant. Said of a species which is the most prominent in or controls a plant community.
Dorsal. Relating to the back, or attached thereto.
Drupaceous. Resembling a drupe.
Drupe. A stone fruit, such as a plum.
Drupelets. Small drupes, as the sections of a blackberry.
Edaphic. Said of ecological factors pertaining to the soil.
Ellipsoid. An elliptic solid.
Ellipsoidal. Shaped like an ellipsoid; that is, a solid bounded by a surface all plane sections of which are ellipses.
Elliptic. Like an ellipse; longer than broad and with regularly curving margins and rounded ends.
Elliptical. Elliptic.
Emarginate. With a notch cut out, usually at the tip.
Endemic. Confined to a given region, as an island or country.
Entire. With an even margin; not toothed.
Epidermis. The outer covering of a plant part.
Eradiate. Without ray-flowers.
Erose. Having the margin irregularly notched as if gnawed.
Even-pinnate. Said of a pinnate leaf ending in a pair of leaflets.
Evergreen. Having leaves throughout the year.
Exfoliating. Peeling off in scales or flakes.
Exotic. Not native; introduced from abroad.
Exserted. Produced beyond, as stamens beyond the tube of the corolla.
Exstipulate. Wanting stipules.
Falcate. Sickle-shaped.
Fascicle. A close cluster or bundle of flowers, leaves, stems, or roots.
Fascicled. In clusters, as the needles of pine.
Fasciculate. Fascicled.
Fastigiate. Said of clustered, parallel, ascending branches.
Feather-veined. With the veins of the leaf arising from the sides of the midrib.
Fertile. Capable of producing fruit.
Fibrovascular. Tissue of mixed vessels and fibers.
Filament. A thread-like structure; the stalk of the stamen.
Filiform. Thread-shaped.
Fimbriate. With the margin bordered by long slender processes; fringed.
Flexuous. Bent alternately in opposite directions; more or less zigzag.
Floccose. Bearing locks of soft hair or wool.
Floret. A small flower, one of a cluster, as in the family Asteraceae.
Foliaceous. Having the texture or shape of a leaf.
Foliar. Leafy or leaf-like.
Foliolate. Having leaflets, as 3-foliolate.
Foliose. Closely clothed with leaves.
Follicle. A dry fruit from a simple pistil, splitting along one line.
Fruit. The matured ovary and its contents, with any external part which is an integral portion of it.
Fusiform. Thick, but tapering toward each end.
Galea. A petal shaped like a helmet, placed next to the axis.
Glabrate. Nearly glabrous or becoming glabrate in age.
Glabrescent. Becoming glabrous, or slightly so.
Glabrous. Not hairy; bald.

Gland. A definite secreting structure on the surface, embedded, or ending in a hair.

Glandular. Possessing glands.

Glaucescent. Nearly glaucous, or becoming so.

Glaucous. Covered with a whitish or grayish bloom which easily rubs off.

Globose. Spherical in form.

Globular. Globose.

Glochid. A barbed hair or bristle, as in Cactaceae.

Glutinous. Covered with a sticky exudation.

Granuliferous. Granule bearing.

Gymnospermous. Having seeds not enclosed in an ovary.

Gymnosperms. Plants with their seeds not enclosed in an ovary.

Habitat. The environment of the plant.

Halophytic. Said of plants (halophytes) growing in saline habitats.

Hastate. Halberd-shaped; sagittate, with the basal lobes turned outward.

Haustoria. Absorbing structures in parasitic plants.

Head. A type of inflorescence, as in the sunflower.

Herbaceous. With the texture, color, and properties of an herb.

Hirsute. Hairy; with long, tolerably distinct hairs.

Hirsutulous. Minutely hirsute.

Hispid. Having stiff hairs.

Hispidulous. Minutely hispid.

Horn. An appendage shaped like an animal's horn.

Hudsonian Life Zone. The highest zone in which trees are found.

Humid Transition Life Zone. A zone above the Arid Transition Zone with moist climate, rather uniform temperature, and luxuriant forests.

Hyaline. Colorless or translucent.

Hybrid. A cross between two nearly related species.

Hypanthium. An enlargement or development of the receptacle; receptocalyx.

Hypogynous. Free from and inserted beneath the pistil.

Imbricated. Overlapping like shingles on a roof.

Impressed. Marked with slight depressions.

Impressed-punctate. Marked with dots, depressions, or translucent glands.

Incised. Cut sharply into the margin.

Indehiscent. Not breaking open at maturity.

Indument. A covering, as hairiness.

Inferior. Said of an ovary when grown to the calyx or receptacle; below the other floral parts.

Inflorescence. The arrangement of flowers on the stem.

Integument. The covering of a body or an organ.

Internode. The portion of a stem or branch between two nodes.

Involucel. A secondary partial involucre.

Involucre. A circle of bracts subtending a flower-cluster or some fruits.

Involute. Having the edges of the leaves rolled inward.

Irregular. Wanting in regularity of form.

Joint. An articulation, as a node in grasses or other plants.

Keeled. Having a central ridge or keel on the back of an organ.

Keel-petal. One of the two lower slightly joined petals in a papilionaceous flower.

Laciniate. Slashed; cut into narrow lobes.

Lanate. Clothed with woolly and intergrown hairs.

Lanceolate. Lance-shaped; about four to six times as long as wide and broader below the middle.

Latex. The milky juice of such plants as spurge or lettuce.

Leaf-blade. The expanded part of the leaf.

Leaflet. A division of a compound leaf.

Leaf-rachis. The central axis of a pinnately compound leaf; the continuation of the petiole.

Legume. A dry fruit from a simple pistil, splitting along two lines.

Lenticels. Lenticular corky spots on young bark, corresponding to epidermal stomata.

Life Zones. Regions determined by temperature, water, altitude, latitude, and other factors, in which plants and animals live.

Lignified tissue. Woody tissue.

Ligulate. Furnished with a ligule; having strap-shaped florets.

Ligule. A strap-shaped body, such as the limb of a ray-flower in Asteraceae.

Linear. Long and narrow with parallel sides.

Lip. One of the two divisions of a bilabiate corolla or calyx.

Lobe. Any division of an organ, often rounded.

Lower Sonoran Life Zone. The lowest, driest, and hottest Life Zone.

Margin. The edge or boundary line of a body.

Mealy. Farinaceous; of the nature of starch.

Medial. Belonging to the middle.

Membranaceous. Membranous.

Membranous. Thin and rather soft, like an animal membrane.

-merous. Used as a suffix to denote parts or numbers, as 3-merous.

Mesophytic. Said of plants (mesophytes) growing in places with an average amount of water; most land plants.

Midrib. The central vein or rib of a leaf.

Monadelphous. Having stamens united by their filaments into a single tube.

Monoecious. Having staminate and pistillate flowers borne on the same plant.

Monocotyledons. Plants that have seeds with one seed-leaf, the foliage leaves usually parallel-veined.

Montane. Growing in the mountains.

Mucronate. Tipped with a short abrupt point.

Mucronulate. Diminutive of mucronate.

Nerve. A simple or unbranched vein or slender rib.

Netted-veined. Reticulated; with any system of closely interwoven cross veins.

Neutral. Pertaining to neither sex.

Node. The place of attachment of leaves on the stem.

Nut. A dry fruit from a compound ovary, with a hard wall not splitting open.

Nutlet. A small nut.

Ob-. A Latin prefix, signifying an inversion.

Obconic. Conical, but attached at the narrower end.

Obcordate. Inversely heart-shaped, the notch being apical.

Oblanceolate. Inversely lanceolate, the broadest part beyond the middle.

Oblique. Unequal-sided.

Oblong. About three or four times as long as wide and with nearly parallel sides.

Obovate. Inversely ovate.

Obovoid. Solidly obovate.

Obsidian. Volcanic glass-like rock, usually dark colored.

Obtuse. Blunt or rounded.

Odd-pinnate. Said of a pinnate leaf ending in a single leaflet.

Opposite. Set against, as leaves with two at one node.

Orbicular. Circular in outline.

Orifice. An opening by which spores, etc., escape.

Oval. Broad-elliptic, with rounded ends.

Ovary. The part of the pistil bearing the ovules.

Ovate. Of the shape of a longitudinal section of a hen's egg, with the broad end basal.

Ovoid. Egg-shaped; solid ovate, or less correctly solid oval.

Ovulate. Bearing ovules; said of the female flowers of Gymnosperms because they have no pistils.

Ovule. The structure in the ovary which when matured becomes the seed.

Palate. The prominent lower lip of a gaping corolla; the projection in the throat in some sympetalous corollas.

Palea. The chaffy scales on the receptacle of many Asteraceae.

Paleaceous. Chaffy; furnished with paleae, or chaff-like in texture.

Palisade tissue. Tissue of a leaf composed of perpendicular elongated parenchyma cells.

Palmate. Radiately lobed or divided, like the fingers from the palm of the hand.

Palmately compound. With the leaflets all borne at the summit of the petiole.

Palmately lobed. Radiately lobed.

Palmately veined. With the primary veins radiating from the summit of the petiole.

Panicle. A compound flower-cluster.

Paniculate. Said of an inflorescence which forms a panicle.

Papilionaceous. Having flowers similar to those of the sweet pea; that is, having a large upper petal (banner), two smaller lateral petals (wings), and two lower slightly joined petals forming a keel.

Papilla. A small nipple-shaped protuberance.

Papillate. Having papillae.

Papillose. Covered with papillae.

Pappus. Thistledown; the various tufts of hairs on achenes or fruits.

Parietal. Borne on or belonging to a wall.

Pedicel. The stalk of the individual flowers in a cluster.

Pedicellate. Borne on a pedicel.

Peduncle. The general term for the stalk of a flower; also applied to a stalk bearing a cluster of single flowers.

Pedunculate. Furnished with a stalk.

Pendulous. Hanging; pendent.

Perennial. A plant which lives several years; usually not perishing after once flowering and fruiting.

Perfoliate. Said of a stem which apparently passes through a leaf.

Perianth. Collectively the corolla and calyx; the floral envelopes.

Pericarp. The wall of a fructified ovary.

Perigynous. Literally, around the ovary; usually said of organs adnate to the perianth.

Petiolate. Having a petiole.

Petiole. The stalk of a leaf.

Petiolule. The stalk of a leaflet.

Pilose. Hairy; with any kind of pilosity, usually pertaining to soft and distinct hairs.

Pinna. A division of a compound leaf.

Pinnate. With the divisions of a compound leaf arranged along the sides of the central axis or rachis.

Pinnately compound. Pinnate.

Pinnately veined. With the veins arising from the sides of the midrib.

Pinnatifid. Pinnately cleft.

Pistil. The female organ of a flower, consisting when complete of ovary, style, and stigma.

Pistillate. Said of flowers with pistils but without stamens.

Placenta. The organ which bears the ovules in an ovary; often the margin of the carpellary leaves.

Plane. Flat and even.

Plicate. Folded into plaits, usually lengthwise.

Plumose. With long branched hairs; feathery.

Pod. A dry fruit that splits open.

Polygamo-dioecious. With perfect, staminate, and pistillate flowers on different plants.

Polygamo-monoecious. With perfect, staminate, and pistillate flowers on the same plant.

Polygamous. Polygamo-monoecious.

Polymorphic. Occurring in several or various forms; variable as to habit.

Pome. A fleshy fruit from a compound ovary, with papery or cartilaginous carpels surrounded by a fleshy adherent calyx and receptacle, as in the apple.

Procumbent. Lying along the ground.

Propagule. Any part of a plant such as a bulb, seed, etc., which is capable of producing a new plant.

Puberulent. Minutely pubescent.

Pubescent. Having soft or downy hairs.

Punctate. Marked with dots, depressions, or translucent glands.

Pungent. Terminating in a rigid sharp point; pertaining to a sharp odor.

Pustule. A pimple or blister.

Pyramidal. Pyramid-shaped.

Pyriform. Resembling a pear in shape.

Raceme. A type of inflorescence with a central elongating axis giving off pedicels of about equal length.

Racemose. Having racemes; raceme-like.

Rachis. The central axis of a compound leaf; the continuation of the petiole; the axis of a raceme or panicle; the continuation of the peduncle.

Radiate. Spreading from or arranged around a common center, as the circumference of a circle; bearing ray-flowers, as in Asteraceae.

Rank. A row, especially a vertical row.

Ray. A ray-flower.

Ray-achene. An achene borne by the ray-flower.

Ray-flower. An outer floret, ligulate or tubular, of Asteraceae.

Receptacle. The summit of the stalk that bears the parts of a flower; the enlarged summit of the stem bearing flowers, as in the Sunflower Family.

Receptocalyx. The structure formed by the continuation of the receptacle into the calyx.

Reflexed. Abruptly bent or turned downward or backward.

Regular. Uniform or symmetrical in shape or structure.

Remote. Scattered; not close together on the axis.

Reniform. Kidney-shaped.

Repand. With a slightly uneven margin, less so than "sinuous."

Reticulate. Netted, as the mass of veins in a leaf.

Retrorse. Directed backward or downward.

Retuse. With a shallow notch at a rounded apex.

Revolute. Rolled back from the margins.

Rhombic. Shaped like a rhomb, an equilateral oblique-angled figure.

Rhomboidal. More or less rhombic, but with three dimensions.

Root-crown. An enlarged often woody structure formed at the junction of the root with the stem.

Rotate. Wheel-shaped; circular and flat.

Rotund. Rounded in outline; somewhat orbicular, but a little inclined towards oblong.

Rugose. Covered with or thrown into wrinkles.

Rugulose. Somewhat wrinkled.

Saccate. Bag-shaped.

Sagittate. Enlarged at the base into two acute straight lobes, like the barbed head of an arrow.

Salverform. Having an expanded part or rim spreading at right angles to a slender tube, as in the corolla of the primrose.

Samara. A winged nut, achene, or any other indehiscent fruit, as in the ash and maple.

Scaberulose. Only slightly rough.

Scabrid. Somewhat rough.

Scabrous. Rough to the touch.

Scale. A small thin structure, usually a degenerate leaf.

Scarious. Thin, dry, and membranous; not green.

Schizocarp. A pericarp (wall of the fruit) which splits into one-seeded portions (mericarps or "split-fruits").

Sclerophyllous. Having hard and stiff leaves, as in manzanita.

Scurfy. With small bran-like scales on the epidermis.

Seed. The structure developed from the ovule.

Segment. One of the divisions into which a plant organ, as a leaf, may be cleft.

Sepal. One of the segments composing a calyx.

Serpentine. A rock consisting of hydrous magnesium silicate, and having usually a dull green color.

Serrate. Saw-toothed, with the teeth directed forward or upward.

Serrulate. Minutely serrate.

Sessile. Without a stalk.

Sheath. An enrolled part of an organ, as the lower part of a leaf-blade or expanded petiole enclosing the stem for some distance; the tissue surrounding the cluster of pine needles.

Simple. Of one part; not branched.

Sinuate. With a wavy or recessed margin.

Sinus. A recess or re-entering angle.

Solitary. Single; only one from the same place.

Spatulate. Oblong, with the basal end attenuated like a druggist's spatula.

Spicate. Like a spike; disposed in a spike.

Spike. A cluster of flowers without pedicels and set along a central axis.

Spine. A sharp-pointed and hardened or woody structure.

Spinescent. Ending in a spine or sharp point.

Spinose. Having spines.

Spiny. Beset with spines; resembling a spine.

Spur. A hollow and slender extension of some part of the flower, usually nectariferous as the calyx of larkspur or the corolla of the violet.

Stamen. One of the essential organs of a flower, bearing pollen in the anther.

Staminate. Said of flowers with stamens but without pistils.

Staminodia. Sterile or abortive stamens.

Stellate. Star-shaped or radiating like the points of a star.

Sterile. Barren, as a flower destitue of pistil, or a stamen wanting the anther.

Stigma. That part of the pistil or style which receives the pollen.

Stipe. A support such as that of a carpel.

Stipitate. Having a stipe or special stalk.

Stipular. Having stipules, or relating to them.

Stipule. A small appendage borne in pairs at the base of the petiole of a leaf.

Stolon. A sucker, runner, or any basal branch which is disposed to root.

Stomata. Plural of stoma, an aperture in the epidermis of leaves for gas exchange.

Striate. Marked with fine longitudinal parallel lines, as grooves or ridges.

Strigose. Beset with sharp-pointed appressed straight and stiff hairs or bristles; hispid.

Style. The usually narrowed part of the pistil between the ovary and stigma.

Sub-. A Latin prefix, meaning somewhat, nearly, under, or below.

Subtended. Extended under; opposite to.

Subulate. Awl-shaped.

Succulent. Juicy.

Suffrutescent. Obscurely shrubby.
Suffruticose. Somewhat shrubby.
Superior. Growing or placed above.
Suture. A junction or seam of union.
Sympetalous. With united petals.
Terete. Round in cross section.
Ternate. In threes, as three in a whorl or cluster.
Thorn. A sharp and hardened or woody structure, usually a modified branch.
Throat. The orifice of a sympetalous corolla or calyx.
Thyrsoid. Like a thyrse; in a close or contracted panicle.
Timber-line. The upper limit of tree growth on mountains.
Tomentose. With dense, short, soft hairs of matted wool.
Tomentulose. Slightly tomentose.
Tomentum. Pubescence.
Transition Life Zone. See Arid and Humid Transition Life Zones.
Trifoliolate. Having three leaflets.
Trisected. Divided into three; three-cleft to the base.
Truncate. Cut off squarely at the end.
Tubercle. A little tuber; a wart-like structure.
Tufted. Caespitose.
Turbinate. Shaped like a top.
Type locality. The locality or station where the type or original specimen was collected.
Umbel. A flower-cluster with the divisions arising from the summit of a common peduncle.
Umbellate. Having the flowers in umbels.
Umbellet. A small or simple umbel.
Umbo. A protuberance or point at the center of the enlarged terminal portions of cone-scales.
Unarmed. Without spines, prickles, or thorns.
Undulate. Wavy-margined.
Unifoliolate. With one leaflet only.
Unisexual. Of one sex; having stamens or pistils only, or their representatives.
Upper Sonoran Life Zone. The zone occupying warm dry areas below the Transition Life Zone.
Utricle. A fruit with a small bladder-like pericarp, as in Atriplex.
Valve. A piece into which a capsule naturally separates at maturity.
Varnished. Shiny, as though varnished.
Vein. A division or branch of the midrib; a strand of vascular tissue.
Venation. The mode of veining.
Verrucose. Warty.
Verticillate. Whorled.
Villous. With long weak hairs.
Virgate. Wand-shaped; twiggy.
Viscid. Sticky with a tenacious secretion.
Whorl. The arrangement of organs in a circle around an axis.
Wing. Any membranous expansion attached to an organ.
Wing-petal. The lateral petal, as in lupine.
Xerophytic. Said of plants (xerophytes) growing in areas with little water, as in the desert.

INDEX TO NAMES OF SPECIES AND VARIETIES OF CALIFORNIA SHRUBS

BY DANIEL DEWEY

DEPARTMENT OF CLASSICAL LANGUAGES IN MILLS COLLEGE

This index includes all names of species and varieties of native California shrubs used in this book, with the exception of those derived from names of persons and genera, i.e., those beginning with capital letters. All geographical names have been included and are translated as nouns for ease of locating. These forms are theoretically adjectives, but nouns in place of adjectives are sometimes found. For the sake of convenience a brief list of explanations is given. Unless otherwise specified, the words are of Latin origin. The geographical names are modern adaptations to Latin forms. The masculine singular ending is used. The species names are divided into the following classes.

a. Nouns:

1) -cola, this is a noun suffix appended to a word and means inhabitant of, e.g. saxicola, living in rocks.

2) Found in genitive case; a descriptive noun used in an adjectival manner to explain the species; e.g. Ceanothus pinetorum, of the pines.

b. Adjectives:

1) Adjectives of the first and second Latin declensions, ending in -us or -er, masculine; -a or -ra, feminine; -um or -rum, neuter. The endings -osus, -a, -um, imply fulness. The superlatives -issimus, -a, -um, or -errimus, -a, -um, are included with the positive form.

2) Adjectives of the third Latin declension, ending in -is, masculine; -is, feminine; -e, neuter. Comparative forms of the adjective ending in -ior, masculine; -ior, feminine; -us, neuter are also included with the positive with some exceptions which are noted.

c. Participles:

1) Present participles end in -ans or -ens, masculine, feminine, and neuter. Often the ending -scens is used, thus giving a meaning of increase to the verb, e.g. virescens, growing green.

2) Perfect participles are passive and end in -us, -a, -um, and are translated like English participles, e.g. fusus, scattered, spread abroad.

The Latin suffix -formis, and the Greek suffix -oides, mean similar to, or in the form or shape of.

Abbreviations:

Fr. French	Sp. Spanish	gen. genitive
Gr. Greek	comp. comparative	pl. plural
	dim. diminutive	sup. superlative

abatus Beaten down; lowly, humble.
aboriginus Aboriginal, native.
acantho- Gr. akantha, thorn.
acanthocladus With thorny shoots.
acanthodes Thorn-like.
acerosus Sharp, keen; mingled with chaff.
acradenius Resembling Acradenia.
-adenius Gr. aden, gland.
adsurgens Rising up, erect.
agrifolius. Probably a printer's error for aquifolius, sharp-leaved.
alatus Winged.
albi-, albidus, albus White.
albicaulis White-stemmed.
albifrons White-leaved.
alni- Alnus, alder.
alnifolius Alder-leaved.
alpinus Alps; alpine.
alternans Alternate.
alyssoides Gr. alysson, Alyssum; resembling Alyssum.
amarus Bitter.
ambiguus Doubtful, uncertain.
ambrosioides Gr. ambrosia, Ambrosia; like Ambrosia.
americanus America.
angustatus, angustissimus, angustus Narrow.
angustifolius Narrow-leaved.
aniso- Gr. anisos, unequal.
anisophyllus Unequal leaflets.
annulatus Annulus, ring, band; ringed.
anomalus Gr. anomalos, deviating from the rule; anomalous.
-anthos Gr. anthos, flower.
antirrhinoides Gr. antirrhon, Antirrhinum, snapdragon; like Antirrhinum.
apianus Pertaining to bees.
aqui- Acus, sharp.
aquifolius Sharp-leaved.
arborescens Becoming a tree; tree-like.
arboreus Arbor, tree; pertaining to a tree.
arbusculus Arbuscula, dim. of arbor; little tree, shrub.
arbuti- Arbutus, arbutus.
arbutifolius Arbutus-leaved.
arcuatus Curved.
argenteus Silver.
argo- Gr. argos, bright, shiny.
argophyllus Shiny-leaved.
argutus Sharp, pungent.
armatus Armed.
aridus Dry, arid.
asper Rough, sharp.
assurgens Rising up, erect.
assurgentiflorus With erect flowers.
aurantiacus Orange-colored; Citrus aurantium, the orange.
aureus Golden.
auriculatus Dim. auris, ear; with auricles.
australis Auster, south wind; southern.
baccatus Bacca, berry; with berries.
bernardinus San Bernardino Mountains.
betuloides Betula, birch; like Betula.
bi-, bis Twice.
bicolor Two-colored.
binominatus Twice-named.
brachy- Gr. brachus, short, small, few.
brachyphyllus Short-leaved.
bracteatus, bracteosus Provided with bracts.
brevi-, brevialatus Brevis, short.
breviflorus Short-flowered.
brevifolius Short-leaved.
brevipes Short-stemmed.
brickellioides Like Brickellia.
-bundus Intensive adj. suffix.
buxi- Buxus, box-wood tree.
buxifolius Leaf as in boxwood.
caespitosus Caespes, turf, sod; growing on the ground.
californicus California.
calli- Gr. kalos, beautiful.
callicarpus With beautiful fruit.
calycinus Gr. kalux, calyx; predicated of a flower in which the calyx is prominent.
-calyx Gr. kalux, calyx..
camelorum Gen. pl. camelus, camel; of camels.
campestris Campestris, pertaining to a field, flat, of the field.
canariensis Canary Islands.
canescens Growing white; with gray or white pubescence.
canthari- Gr. kantharos, drinking vessel, cup.
cantheriformis Cup-shaped.
canus White, gray, ash-colored.
capitatus Caput, head; provided with a head.
carnosus Fleshy.
carpesioides Like Carpesium.
-carpus Gr. karpos, fruit.
catalinensis Santa Catalina Island.
caudatus Cauda, tail; with a tail.
-caulis Gr. kaulis, stem, trunk.
-cephalus Gr. kephale, head.
cerasi- Gr. keras, horn.
cerasiformis Shaped like a horn.
cerco- Gr. kerkos, tail.
cercophorus Bearing a tail.
cereus Waxen.
ceruminosus Cera, wax; full of wax-like secretion.
chenopodifolius Leaf like Chenopodium.
chenopodii- Gr. chen, goose; pous, foot; chenopod, goosefoot.
chilensis Chile.
chinensis China.
chryso- Gr. chrusos, gold.
chrysolepis With golden scales.
chrysophyllus With golden leaf.
cibatus Food.
cichoriacea Like Cichorium.
ciliosus Cilium, eyelash.
cinereus Ash-colored.
circinatus Round, circinate.
-cladus Gr. klados, young shoot.
clementinus San Clemente Island.

coeruleus, coerulus Dark-colored, often green or blue.
cognatus Related.
-cola Colere, to inhabit, to cultivate; a derivative word.
collinus Collis, hill; relating to hills.
-color Color.
coloradensis Colorado.
columbianus Columbia River country.
communis Common, general.
commutatus Changed, altered.
comosus Hairy.
con- With; idea of likeness; intensive.
concinnus Beautiful, shapely.
conferti- Pressed close together.
confertiflorus Clustered flowers.
confertifolius Clustered leaves.
confusus Poured together; confused.
conjugialis Conjugium, marriage; joined together.
consanguineus Blood-colored.
consimilis Related.
cordatus, cordulatus Cor, cordis, heart; heart-shaped.
cordi- Cor, heart.
cordifolius With heart-shaped leaves.
cornutus Horned.
corymbosus Gr. korumbos, cluster of flowers.
crassi- Crassus, thick.
crassifolius Thick-leaved.
crenulatus Crena, notch; with margins cut into rounded teeth.
crinitus Provided with hairs; having long hairs.
crispus Curly, wavy.
croceus Yellow.
cruentus Stained with blood, bloody.
crustaceus Crusta, shell, rind, bark; brittle.
cuneatus Cuneus, wedge; wedge-shaped.
cyaneus Gr. kuaneos, dark blue.
dasy- Gr. dasus, thick.
dasypodus Thick-stemmed.
decumbens Lying down; decumbent, low.
delnortensis Del Norte County.
deltoideus Gr. deltoeides, triangle-shaped.
demissus Sent down; lowly, humble.
dendroideus Gr. dendron, tree; tree-like.
densi- Densus, dense.
densiflorus With closely set flowers.
densifolius With closely set leaves.
dentatus, denticulatus Dens, tooth; toothed, dentate, denticulated.
denudatus Naked.
depressus Pressed down; growing near the ground.
-dermis Gr. derma, skin.
deserti- Desertus, desert.
deserticola Living in the desert.
di-, dis Apart, asunder.
di-, dis Gr. twice; cf. Lat. bis.
dictyotus Gr. dictyotos, made as a net, reticulated.
dioicus Gr. oikos, house, plants male or female.
dipetalus Gr. petalon, petal; with two petals.
discolor Of different colors, not necessarily of two colors.
distans Standing apart; distant.
divaricatus Stretched apart; widely diverging.
divergens Turning in opposite directions.
diversifolius Leaves variable.
diversilobus Diversified lobes or leaf-segments.
diversus, diversi- Deviating from each other; diverse, separate.
dolic- Gr. dolichos, long.
dolicanthus With long flowers.
drupaceus Gr. druppa, an over ripe olive; like a drupe (a stone fruit), drupaceous.
dubius Doubtful.
dumosus Shrubby.
duratus Hardened.
elatus Tall.
elegans Elegant; mostly applied to slender strict plants.
ellipiticus Gr. elleiptikos, elliptical.
emarginatus The margin taken away; notched.
empetri- Gr. empetron, Empetrum, a rock plant.
empetriformis Shaped like Empetrum.
eremicus, eremo- Gr. eremos, lonely, desert.
eremophilus Fond of the desert.
eremostachys Desert Stachys.
ericoides Gr. ereike, Erica, heather; like heather.
erinaceus Hedgehog.
erio- Gr. erion, wool.
eriocentrus Woolly thorns.
eriophyllus Woolly-leaved.
europaeus Europe.
exaltatus Raised, elevated, tall.
excubitus Excubitor, watchman, sentinel.
exiguus Small, diminutive.
extimus Sup. exter, outside; outermost.
falcatus Shaped like a scythe, curved.
farinosus Mealy.
fasciculatus Fasces; fasciculate; with fasciculated leaves.
ferrugineus Of the color of iron rust.
-ferus Verbal adj. from ferre, to bear; bearing.
filaginfolius Thread-like leaf, leaf like Filago.
fili-, filum Thread.
flavescens Growing yellow.
floribundus Freely flowering.
floridus Flowery, florid.
-florus Flora, flower.
foliolosus, foliosus Leafy, abounding in leaves.
-folius Folium, leaf.
fontanalis Fons, spring, fountain.
-formis Similar to, like.
fresnensis Fresno County.
-frons Frons, foliage.
frutescens, fruticosus Frutex, shrub; shrubby, bushy.
fulvescens Fulvus, reddish yellow, tawny.
funereus Funeral Mountains in Death Valley.
-furcus Furcus, fork; forked.
fuscus Dark-colored, mostly in red shades.
-fusus Poured, spread, scattered.

gallicus French.
giganteus Gigans, giant, large.
glabellus, glaber, glabratus Without hairs, bald.
glabrescens Becoming bald.
glanduli- Glandulae, glands.
glanduliferus With glands.
glandulosus Provided with glands.
glauco-, glaucus Gr. glaukos, whitened with a bloom.
globosus Globus, globe, sphere.
gloriosus Glorious, renowned.
glutinosus Glutinous, viscous, sticky.
gnaphalodes Gr. gnaphalion, Gnaphalium, cudweed; like Gnaphalium.
gracilentus, gracilis Slender, thin.
grandi-, grandis Large.
grandifolius With large leaves.
griseus Fr. gris, gray.
gymno- Gr. gumnos, naked, lightly clad.
gymnocarpus With uncovered fruits.
-gyrus Gr. gyros, whorl, whirl.
halimi- Gr. halimon, a plant.
halimifolium Leaves like Halimum.
hebe- Gr. hebe, youth, puberty; pubescent.
hebecladus With hairy branches.
hesperius Hesperus, evening star; western.
hirsutus, hirtellus Rough, hairy, hirsute.
hispidulus, hispidus Rough, shaggy, bristly.
holo- Gr. holos, all.
hololeucus All white.
humi- Humus, ground.
humifusus Spread on the ground.
humilis Lowly, lying near the ground.
hymenelytrus Gr. hymen, membrane; elytron, cover; covered with a membrane.
hypo- Gr. hupo, under, less; cf. sub-.
hypoleucus Somewhat white.
hystricinus, hystrix Gr. hustrix, porcupine; plants with spines.
ilici- Ilex, holly.
ilicifolius Holly-like leaves.
imbricatus Formed like a gutter tile; closely put together, overlapping.
implicatus Folded in.
impressus Pressed upon, imprinted.
imulus Dim. form of imus, sup. of inferus; lowest.
incanus Quite gray, hoary.
indecorus Unbecoming, unsightly.
inermis Unarmed, without spines.
insularis Of an island, insular.
integer, integerrimus, integri- Whole.
integrifolius Entire leaf-margin.
interior Interior; not coastal.
intermedius Intermediate as between other forms.
interruptus Broken into pieces; not close together.
intricatus Entangled, perplexed.
involucratus Involucrum, wrapper; provided with an involucre.
ixo- Gr. ixos, bird lime; sticky, viscid.
ixodermis With sticky covering.
jacitensis Mount San Jacinto.
junceus Juncus, a rush; rush-like.
klamathensis Klamath River country.
laciniatus Lacinia, edge, flap; with jagged edges.
lacustris Lacus, lake; pertaining to lakes.
laetus Gay, happy.
laevigatus, laevis Smooth.
lanatus Woolly.
lanceolatus Lance-like.
lasianthus Hairy or woolly flower.
lasio- Gr. lasios, shaggy, hairy, woolly.
lasiolepis With hairy scales.
lati-, latior (Comp.) Latus, wide, broad.
latifolius With broad leaves.
latisquamus With broad scales.
laurinus Laurel.
laxi- Laxus, wide, open, loose.
laxiflorus With loose-flowering clusters.
ledi- Ledum glandulosum, Labrador Tea.
ledifolius Leaves like Ledum.
leio- Gr. leios, smooth.
leiospermus With smooth seeds.
lenti- Lens, lentil.
lentiformis Shaped like a lentil.
-lepis Gr. lepis, scale.
lept- Gr. leptos, thin, fine, delicate.
leptanthus With delicate flowers.
leptosmus With delicate fragrance.
leuco- Gr. leukos, white.
leucodermis With white or grayish bark.
leucophyllus White-leaved.
ligatus Bound together.
ligustici- Ligusticum.
ligusticifolius Leaves like Ligusticum.
lineari-, linearis Linear.
linearifolius With linear leaves.
linoides Gr. linon, Linum, flax; like Linum.
lobatus, lobus Gr. lobos, lobe, a leaf-segment; lobed.
longi- Longus, long.
longiflorus With long flowers.
longifolius With long leaves.
lucidus Shiny, bright.
luteus Reddish yellow.
lycioides Like Lycium.
macilentus Thin.
macr-, macro- Gr. makros, long, large.
macranthos With large or long flowers.
macrophyllus With large leaves.
macrourus With long tails.
malaco- Gr. malakos, soft.
malacophyllus With soft leaves.
malvaceus Belonging to mallows, like mallow (Malva).
manzanita Sp. manzanita, little apple.
mariposus Mariposa County.
maritimus Of the sea.
marrubioides Marrubium-like.
mega-, meion (Comp.) Gr. megas, great, large.
megacarpus With large fruit.
melan- Gr. melas, black, dark.

melanocarpus With dark or black fruit.
melanopsis Dark-appearing.
melli- Mel, mellis, honey.
melliferus Honey-bearing.
membranaceus Of membrane; membranaceous.
mertensianus Like Mertensia.
mewukka Indian name.
mexicanus Mexico.
micro- Gr. mikros, small.
microphyllus With small leaves.
mille- Mille, thousand, many.
millefolius With many leaves.
minor (Comp.) Less, small.
minuti- Minutus, smaller, small.
minutiflorus With small flowers.
miser Poor, miserable, unfortunate.
mississippensis Mississippi Valley.
modestus Modest, unassuming.
modocensis Modoc County.
mohavensis Mohave Desert.
mollis Soft, tender, flexible.
monicus Mono County.
mono- Gr. monos, one, alone.
monocephalus One-headed.
monogyrus One-whorled.
montanus Mons, mountain; of the mountain.
montigenus Mountain-born.
Morehus Abram's oak, named from the encampment in the groves of Moreh.
morroensis Morro Bay.
multi- Multus, much, many.
multiflorus With many flowers.
myricae- Gr. murika, Myrica, a shrub.
myricaefolius Leaves like Myrica.
myrio- Gr. murios, ten thousand, numberless.
myriocladus With numberless branches.
myrsinites Gr. mursine, murtos, myrtle; referring to myrtle.
myrti- Gr. murtos, myrtle.
myrtifolius Leaves like myrtle, Myrtus.
nanus Gr. nanos, dwarf.
napensis Napa County.
nauseosus Nauseous.
neomexicanus New Mexico.
nervosus Nerved, veined.
nesioticus Gr. nesiotikos, of an island, insular.
nevadensis Nevada.
niger, nigrescens Black.
nissenanus Indian name.
nitidus Shining.
nivalis, niveus Snowy.
-nominatus Named.
novus New.
-nudus Bare, naked.
nummularius Money-like, round.
nutkanus Nootka.
obispoensis San Luis Obispo County.
oblongi- Oblongus, oblong.
oblongifolius With oblong leaves.
obtusi-, obtusissimus, obtusus Flattened, obtuse.
obtusifolius With flattened leaves, usually at the apex or base.
occidentalis Western.
odonto- Gr. odous, odontos, tooth.
odontolepis Tooth-like scales.
odoratissimus Sup. odoratus, sweet-smelling.
officinalis Officina, workshop; officinal drugs as sold by apothecaries.
-oides Similar to, like.
oliganthus With few flowers.
oligo- Gr. oligos, few.
oligocarpus With few fruits.
oligospermus With few seeds.
olivaceus Oliva, olive; like the olive.
-opsis Gr. appearance, with noun prefix translate "like."
orbiculatus Rounded, circular.
oreganus Oregon.
orestrus Gr. orestes, mountaineer.
ornitho- Gr. ornis, ornithos, a bird.
ornithopus Like a bird's foot.
-osmus Gr. osme, scent.
otayensis Otay Mountain, San Diego County.
-ourus Gr. oura, tail; with a tail.
ovatifolius Leaves ovate.
ovatus, ovati- Ovatus, ovate.
oxy- Gr. oxus, sharp.
oxyphyllus Sharp-leaved.
pachy- Gr. pachus, thick.
pachyphyllus With thick leaves.
pajaroensis Pajaro Valley.
pallidus Pallid, pale.
panamintensis Panamint Mountains.
paniculatus Panicula, tuft, panicle; flowers in a panicle.
papillosus Papilla, teat; papillate; with raised bumps.
paradoxus Gr. paradoxos, contrary to belief.
parvi-, parvus Parvus, small.
parviflorus With small flowers.
parvifolius With small leaves.
patulus Spreading.
pauci-, paucus Paucus, few, little.
pauciflorus With few flowers.
paucifolius With few leaves.
pechoensis Pecho Mountain.
pectinatus Combed, comb-like, with projecting teeth.
peduncularis, pedunculatus Provided with peduncles, stalks.
perplexans Making confusion, causing perplexity.
-pes Pes, pedis, foot.
petiolaris Petiolus, stem, stalk; petioled.
petro- Gr. petros, rock.
petrophilus Of the rocks.
-philus Gr. philos, loving.
-phyllus Gr. phullon, leaf.
pilosulus, pilosus Pilosus, hairy; with short shaggy hairs.
pilularis In the shape of a pill; flower-heads in the shape of round pills.
pinetorum Gen. pl. Pinus, pine; of the pines.
pini- Pinus, pine.

pinifolius With leaves thin, like a pine.
pinnatus Pinna, feather; leaflets arranged on opposite sides of the rachis.
piso- Pisum, pea.
pisocarpus Fruit like Pisum.
planus Level, flat, plane.
plicatus Folded as in a fan, with pleats.
plurisetus Plus, pluris, much; saeta, thistle; very bristly.
-podus Gr. pous, podos, foot.
poli- Gr. polios, gray.
polifolius With gray leaves.
poly- Gr. polus, many.
polyadenius With many glands.
polycarpus With many fruits.
-pous Gr. pous, podos, foot.
propinquus Near by; growing in patches.
prostratus Thrown down; growing prostrate.
pseudo- Gr. pseudos, falsehood; false.
pseudomyrsinites False myrtle.
pubens, puberulentus, puberulus, pubescens Pubes, puberty; pubescent, hairy.
pumilus Dwarfish, small.
punctatus Punctum, a dot; marked with dots.
pungens Pricking; sharp, pointed.
puniceus Reddish, red, purple-colored.
purpureus. Purple.
pusillus Very small, puny, insignificant.
quercetorum Gen. pl. quercetus, oak wood; of the oaks.
racemosus Flowers in a raceme.
ramosissimus, ramosus, ramulosus Ramus, branch; with many branches; branchy.
recurvans Curving backward.
repens Creeping, crawling.
reticulatus Made like a net, reticulated.
rigidus Stiff, rigid.
rostratus Rostrum, beak; beaked.
rotundi- Rotundus, round.
rotundifolius With round leaves.
ruber, rubescens Red.
rubicundus Ruddy, red.
rubiginosus Rusty.
rudis Rough, shaggy.
runcinatus Planed off; pinnae with turned down lobes.
rutilus Red.
sanctorus Sacred.
sanguineus Sanguis, blood; blood-colored.
saporosus Of good flavor.
sarothr- Gr. sarothron, broom.
sarothroides Broom-like.
saxatilis Found among rocks.
saxi- Saxum, rock.
saxicola Growing in rocks.
scaber Rough, scabrous.
schidigerus Gr. schidia, little splinters.
scoparius Sweeper; like a broom.
semper- Always, eve..
sempervirens Evergreen.
senilis Old, aged, white-haired.
sensitivus Sensus, feeling; sensitive.
-sepalus Derivation obscure; used with qualifying adjective; sepal.
septentrionalis Northern.
sergiloides Sergilus, old name for Baccharis; Baccharis-like.
sericatus, sericeus Serica, silken garments; silken.
serpylli- Serpyllum vulgare, the wild thyme of England.
serpyllifolius Leaves like Serpyllum.
serrulatus Serrulus, a small saw; serrated.
sessilis Low, dwarf; without a stalk.
shallon Indian name for salal (Gaultheria).
shastensis Mount Shasta region.
sibiricus Siberia.
silvi- Silva, forest.
silvicola Forest dweller.
sinuatus Bent, curved; leaf-margin curved.
sitchensis Sitka.
sonomensis Sonoma County.
sorediatus Having soredia or something resembling them.
sparsi- Few, scattered.
sparsifolius With scattered leaves.
spatulatus Shaped like a spatula; spatulate.
speciosus Showy, handsome.
spectabilis Remarkable, spectacular, showy.
-spermus Gr. sperma, spermatos, seed.
sphaerocephalus Gr. sphaira, ball; round-headed.
-spicatus Spicatus, spiked.
spinescens, spinosus Spiny, thorny.
spini- Spina, thorn.
spiniferus Spine-bearing.
spithameus Gr. spithame, span, distance one can embrace between the thumb and little finger; about 7½ inches.
splendens Shining.
squamatus, squamus Squama, a scale; scaly.
squarrosus Scabby, scaly.
-stachys Gr. stachus, ear of corn.
staechadi- Gr. Stoichas, an aromatic plant.
staechadifolius Leaves like Stoichas.
steno- Gr. stenos, narrow.
stenolepis With narrow scales.
stenophyllus With narrow leaves.
stoloni- Stolo, stolonis, shoot, branch.
stoloniferus With stolons underground.
sub- Under; modifies or makes less the meaning of the adj.; somewhat.
subcoerulus Bluish.
subcordatus Almost heart-shaped.
subnudus Almost uncovered.
subspicatus Almost spike-like.
subspinosus Somewhat thorny.
suffrutescens, suffruticosus Slightly shrubby.
tenui- Tenuis, thin, slender.
tenuiflorus With slender flowers.
tenuifolius With slender leaves.
tenuilobatus, tenuilobus With slender lobes.
tenuissimus Sup. tenuis, thin.
tereti- Teres, rounded.

teretifolius Leaf round in cross section.
ternatus Terni, by threes.
-thecus Gr. theke, box, chest.
thyrsi- Gr. thursos, stalk.
thyrsiflorus Flowers in a thyrse, cluster.
tomentellus, tomentosus Tomentum, stuffing of wool; woolly.
tri- Gr. & Lat. Tri, three.
tricho- Gr. thrix, trichos, hair.
trichocalyx With hairy calyx.
tridentatus Three-toothed.
trifidus Cut into three parts.
trifurcus Three-forked.
ultramontanus Ultra, beyond, on the other side of the mountain.
umbelliferus Umbella, parasol, little shade; umbellate.
urens Burning, stinging as in nettle.
ursinus Ursus, a bear.
utahensis Utah.
vaccinifolius Leaves like Vaccinium.
velutinus Vellus, fleece; covered with a silky pubescence.
venetus Venum, vein; veined.
vermiculatus Worm-shaped.
vernonioides Like Vernonia.
verrucosus Full of warts or wart-like protuberances, warty.
vespertinus Of the evening.
vestitus Clothed, covered.
viburnifolius Leaves like Viburnum.
villosus Rough, hairy, villous.
vimineus Of wicker-work; pliable.
virens, viridissimus, viridulus Green.
virgatus Made of osiers; willow-like; twiggy.
virginianus Virginia.
viridescens Becoming green.
viscidi-, viscosissimus Viscidus, viscid, sticky.
viscidiflorus With viscid flowers.
viti- Vitis, genus of the grape.
vitifolius Leaves like Vitis.
vulcanicus Volcanus, god of fire; pertaining to volcanic soil.
yosemitanus Yosemite Valley.
zacaensis Zaca Lake.

NOMENCLATORIAL CHANGES MADE IN THIS BOOK

Atriplex lentiformis var. Torreyi (Wats.) McMinn, n. comb. *Obione Torreyi* Wats.

Atriplex lentiformis var. Breweri (Wats.) McMinn, n. comb. *Atriplex Breweri* Wats.

Berberis Sonnei (Abrams) McMinn, n. comb. *Mahonia Sonnei* Abrams.

Berberis Piperiana (Abrams) McMinn, n. comb. *Mahonia Piperiana* Abrams.

Ribes divaricatum var. inerme (Rydb.) McMinn, n. comb. *Ribes inerme* Rydb.

Ribes divaricatum var. klamathense (Cov.) McMinn, n. comb. *Grossularia klamathense* Cov.

Dalea Fremontii var. californica (Wats.) McMinn, n. comb. *Dalea californica* Wats.

Halliophytum fasciculatum var. Hallii (Brandg.) McMinn, n. comb. *Tetracoccus Hallii* Brandg.

Ceanothus Greggii var. vestitus (Greene) McMinn, n. comb. *Ceanothus vestitus* Greene.

Rhamnus rubra var. modocensis (Wolf) McMinn, n. comb. *Rhamnus rubra* subsp. *modocensis* Wolf.

Rhamnus rubra var. yosemitana (Wolf) McMinn, n. comb. *Rhamnus rubra* subsp. *yosemitana* Wolf.

Rhamnus californica var. ursina (Greene) McMinn, n. comb. *Rhamnus ursina* Greene.

Malvastrum Palmeri var. involucratum (Rob.) McMinn, n. comb. *Malvastrum involucratum* Rob.

Malvastrum Fremontii var. Helleri (Eastw.) McMinn, n. comb. *Malvastrum Helleri* Eastw.

Malvastrum Fremontii var. niveum (Eastw.) McMinn, n. comb. *Malvastrum niveum* Eastw.

Malvastrum marrubioides var. viscidum (Abrams) McMinn, n. comb. *Malvastrum viscidum* Abrams.

Malvastrum fasciculatum var. nesioticum (Rob.) McMinn, n. comb. *Malvastrum nesioticum* Rob.

Malvastrum fasciculatum var. catalinense (Eastw.) McMinn, n. comb. *Malvastrum catalinense* Eastw.

Malvastrum fasciculatum var. Nuttallii (Abrams) McMinn, n. comb. *Malacothamnus Nuttallii* Abrams.

Fremontia californica var. napensis (Eastw.) McMinn, n. comb. *Fremontia napensis* Eastw.

Arctostaphylos nummularia var. sensitiva (Jepson) McMinn, n. comb. *Arctostaphylos sensitiva* Jepson.

Arctostaphylos viscida var. oblongifolia (Howell) Adams ex McMinn, n. comb. *Arctostaphylos oblongifolia* Howell.

Arctostaphylos columbiana var. Tracyi (Eastw.) Adams ex McMinn, n. comb. *Arctostaphylos Tracyi* Eastw.

Arctostaphylos canescens var. sonomensis (Eastw.) Adams ex McMinn, n. comb. *Arctostaphylos sonomensis* Eastw.

Arctostaphylos tomentosa var. hebeclada (DC.) Adams ex McMinn, n. comb. *Andromeda bracteosa* var. *hebeclada* DC.

Arctostaphylos tomentosa var. crinita Adams ex McMinn, n. var.

Arctostaphylos crustacea var. Rosei (Eastw.) McMinn, n. comb. *Arctostaphylos Rosei* Eastw.

Arctostaphylos glandulosa var. zacaensis (Eastw.) Adams ex McMinn, n. comb. *Arctostaphylos zacaensis* Eastw.

Arctostaphylos glandulosa var. Howellii (Eastw.) Adams ex McMinn, n. comb. *Arctostaphylos Howellii* Eastw.

Arctostaphylos glandulosa var. Campbellae (Eastw.) Adams ex McMinn, n. comb. *Arctostaphylos Campbellae* Eastw.

Arctostaphylos glandulosa var. Cushingiana (Eastw.) Adams ex McMinn, n. comb. *Arctostaphylos Cushingiana* Eastw.

Arctostaphylos Andersonii var. imbricata (Eastw.) Adams ex McMinn, n. comb. *Arctostaphylos imbricata* Eastw.

Arctostaphylos Andersonii var. pallida (Eastw.) Adams ex McMinn, n. comb. *Arctostaphylos pallida* Eastw.

Arctostaphylos Andersonii var. pajaroensis Adams ex McMinn, n. var.

Arctostaphylos viridissima (Eastw.) McMinn, n. comb. *Arctostaphylos pechoensis* var. *viridissima* Eastw.

Linanthus Nuttallii var. floribundus (Gray) McMinn, n. comb. *Gilia floribunda* Gray.

Salvia carnosa var. Gilmanii (Epling) McMinn, n. comb. *Salvia carnosa* subsp. *Gilmanii* Epling.

Salvia carnosa var. argentea (Rydb.) McMinn, n. comb. *Audibertiella argentea* Rydb.

Solanum Wallacei var. Clokeyi (Munz) McMinn, n. comb. *Solanum Clokeyi* Munz.

Diplacus longiflorus var. rutilus (Grant) McMinn, n. comb. *Mimulus longiflorus* var. *rutilus* Grant.

Diplacus longiflorus var. linearis (Benth.) McMinn, n. comb. *Mimulus linearis* Benth.

Penstemon Clevelandii var. mohavensis (Keck) McMinn, n. comb. *Penstemon Clevelandii* subsp. *mohavensis* Keck.

Penstemon heterophyllus var. Purdyi (Keck) McMinn, n. comb. *Penstemon heterophyllus* subsp. *Purdyi* Keck.

Penstemon laetus var. filiformis (Keck) McMinn, n. comb. *Penstemon laetus* subsp. *filiformis* Keck.

Penstemon laetus var. saggitatus (Keck) McMinn, n. comb. *Penstemon laetus* subsp. *saggitatus* Keck.

Penstemon spectabilis var. subviscosus (Keck) McMinn, n. comb. *Penstemon spectabilis* subsp. *subviscosus* Keck.

Sambucus racemosa var. melanocarpa (Gray) McMinn, n. comb. *Sambucus melanocarpa* Gray.

Lonicera Jonstonii (Keck) McMinn, n. comb. *Lonicera subspicata* var. *Johnstonii* Keck.

Cornus stolonifera var. californica (C. A. Mey.) McMinn, n. comb. *Cornus californica* C. A. Mey.

Haplopappus squarrosus var. obtusus (Greene) McMinn, n. comb. *Hazardia obtusa* Greene.

Haplopappus squarrosus var. stenolepis (Hall) McMinn, n. comb. *Haplopappus squarrosus* subsp. *stenolepis* Hall.

Haplopappus suffruticosus var. tenuis (Hall) McMinn, n. comb. *Haplopappus suffruticosus* subsp. *tenuis* Hall.

Haplopappus acradenius var. bracteosus (Greene) McMinn, n. comb. *Isocoma bracteosa* Greene.

Artemisia tridentata var. trifida (Nutt.) McMinn, n. comb. *Artemisia trifida* Nutt.

Artemisia tridentata var. nova (Nels.) McMinn, n. comb. *Artemisia nova* Nels.

Artemisia tridentata var. arbuscula (Nutt.) McMinn, n. comb. *Artemisia arbuscula* Nutt.

Artemisia tridentata var. Rothrockii (Gray) McMinn, n. comb. *Artemisia Rothrockii* Gray.

Artemisia tridentata var. Bolanderi (Gray) McMinn, n. comb. *Artemisia Bolanderi* Gray.

BIBLIOGRAPHY

ABRAMS, LE ROY

1910. "A Phytogeographic and Taxonomic Study of Southern California Trees and Shrubs," *Bulletin of the New York Botanical Garden,* Vol. VI, No. 21.

1923. *Illustrated Flora of the Pacific States,* Vol. I. Stanford University Press.

1934. "The Mahonias of the Pacific States," *Phytologia,* Vol. I, No. 2, pp. 89-94. New York Botanical Garden, Bronx Park, New York.

ABRAMS, LE ROY AND SMILEY, F. J.

1915. "Taxonomy and Distribution of Eriodictyon," *The Botanical Gazette,* Vol. LX, No. 2, pp. 115-133.

ADAMS, JOSEPH E.

1935. "A Systematic Study of the Genus Arctostaphylos." *Thesis submitted for the degree of Doctor of Philosophy,* Graduate Division, University of California.

BALL, G. R.

1934. "New or Little Known West American Willows," *University of California Publications in Botany,* Vol. XVII, No. 14, pp. 399-435.

1938. "New Varieties and Combinations in Salix," *Journal of the Washington Academy of Sciences,* Vol. XXVIII, No. 10, pp. 443-452.

BARKLEY, F. A.

1937. "A Monographic Study of Rhus and Its Immediate Allies in North and Central America, Including the West Indies," *Annals of the Missouri Botanical Gardens,* Vol. XXIV, pp. 265-498.

BENSON, GILBERT T.

1930. "The Trees and Shrubs of Western Oregon," *Contributions from the Dudley Herbarium,* Vol. II, Stanford University Press.

BLAKE, S. F.

1924. "Polygalaceae," *North American Flora,* Vol. XXV, Pt. 5, pp. 341-343.

BRANDEGEE, T. S., AND BRANDEGEE, K.

1890-1904. (ed.) *Zoe, A Journal of Biology,* Vols. I to V.

BREWER, W. H.; WATSON, SERENO, AND GRAY, A.

1876-1880. *Geological Survey of California, Botany,* Vols. I and II. University Press, Cambridge, Mass.

BRIQUET, JOHN

1935. *International Rules of Botanical Nomenclature.* Verlag von Gustav Fischer in Jena.

BRITTON, N. L.

1930. "Krameriaceae." *North American Flora,* Vol. XXIII, Pt. 4, pp. 195-200.

CANBY, MARGARET L.

1927. "The Genus Corethrogyne in Southern California," *Bulletin of the Southern California Academy of Sciences,* Vol. XXVI, Pt. 1, pp. 8-16.

CLAUSEN, JENS

1933. "Cytological Evidence for the Hybrid Origin of Pentstemon neotericus Keck," *Hereditas,* Vol. XVIII, p. 5.

CLEMENTS, F. E.

1920. "Plant Indicators," *Carnegie Institution of Washington,* No. 290. Washington, D.C.

CONSTANCE, LINCOLN

1937. "A Systematic Study of the Genus Eriophyllum," *University of California Publications in Botany,* Vol. XVIII, No. 5, pp. 69-136.

COOPER, W. S.
1922. "The Broad-sclerophyll Vegetation of California," *Carnegie Institution of Washington,* No. 319, Washington, D.C.

COVILLE, F. V.
1893. "Botany of the Death Valley Expedition," *Contributions from the United States National Herbarium,* Vol. IV, Government Printing Office, Washington, D.C.

COVILLE, F. V., AND BRITTON, N. L.
1908. "Grossulariaceae," *North American Flora,* Vol. XXII, Pt. 3, pp. 193-225.

DAVIDSON, A., AND MOXLEY, G. L.
1923. *Flora of Southern California,* Times-Mirror Press, Los Angeles.

DAYTON, WM. A.
1931. "Important Western Browse Plants," *Miscellaneous Publications,* No. 101, United States Department of Agriculture, Washington, D.C.
1937. *Range Plant Handbook.* Prepared by Forest Service United States Department of Agriculture. Government Printing Office, Washington, D.C.

DE DALLA TORRE, C. G., AND HARMS, H.
1900-1907. *Genera Siphonogamarum.*

DU RIETZ, G. EINAR
1931. *Life-Forms of Terrestrial Flowering Plants* I. Almquist & Wiksells Boktryckeri-A.-B. Uppsala.

EASTWOOD, ALICE
1902. "A Flora of the South Fork of Kings River," *Publications of the Sierra Club,* No. 27, San Francisco.
1934. "A Revision of Arctostaphylos with Key and Descriptions," *Leaflets of Western Botany,* Vol. I, No. 11, pp. 105-127.
1936. "The Shrubby Malvastrums of California," *Leaflets of Western Botany,* Vol. I, No. 18, pp. 213-220.
1938. "The Perennial Lupines of California I," *Leaflets of Western Botany,* Vol. II, No. 6, pp. 81-86.

EPLING, C. C.
1925. "Monograph of the Genus Monardella," *Annals of the Missouri Botanical Garden,* Vol. XII, No. 1, pp. 1-106.
1938. "The California Salvias," *Annals of the Missouri Botanical Garden,* Vol. XXV, pp. 95-188.

ESTES, F. E.
1925. "The Shrubby Malvastrums of Southern California," *Bulletin of the Southern California Academy of Sciences,* Vol. XXIV, Pt. 3, pp. 81-87.

FOREST SERVICE, UNITED STATES DEPARTMENT OF AGRICULTURE
1937. *Range Plant Handbook,* Government Printing Office, Washington, D.C. Prepared under the immediate supervision of W. A. Dayton.

GILKEY, HELEN M.
1936. *Handbook of Northwest Flowering Plants.* Metropolitan Press, Portland, Oregon.

GRANT, A. L.
1924. "A Monograph of the Genus Mimulus," *Annals of the Missouri Botanical Garden,* Vol. XI, pp. 99-388.

GRAY, A., AND OTHERS
1884-1897. *Synoptical Flora of North America.* Vols. I and II. Published by the Smithsonian Institution, Washington, D.C.

GREENE, E. L.

1887-1905 (ed.) Pittonia, *A Series of Botanical Papers,* Vols. I to V. (Can be purchased from the Department of Botany, Notre Dame University, South Bend, Indiana.)

1891-1892. *Flora Franciscana.* Parts I, II, III. Cubery and Company, San Francisco.

1894. *Manual of the Botany of the Region of San Francisco Bay.* Cubery and Company, San Francisco.

GROFF, G. W., AND CLARK, G. W.

1928. "The Botany of Ephedra in Relation to the Yield of Physiologically Active Substances," *University of California Publications in Botany,* Vol. XIV, pp. 247-282.

HALL, H. M.

1902. "A Botanical Survey of San Jacinto Mountain," *University of California Publications in Botany,* Vol. I, pp. 1-140.

1907. "Compositae of Southern California," *University of California Publications in Botany,* Vol. III, No. 1, pp. 1-302.

1919. "Chrysothamnus nauseosus and Its Varieties," *University of California Publications in Botany,* Vol. VII, No. 6, pp. 159-181.

1928. "The Genus Haplopappus," *Carnegie Institution of Washington,* No. 389, Washington, D.C.

HALL, H. M., AND CLEMENTS, F. E.

1923. "The Phylogenetic Method in Taxonomy. The North American Species of Artemisia, Chrysothamnus, and Atriplex," *Carnegie Institution of Washington,* No. 326. Washington, D.C.

HALL, H. M., AND HALL, C. C.

1912. *A Yosemite Flora.* Paul Elder and Company, San Francisco.

HILEND, MARTHA, AND HOWELL, J. T.

1935. "The Genus Galium in Southern California," *Leaflets of Western Botany,* Vol. I, No. 13, pp. 145-168.

HITCHCOCK, CHARLES L.

1932. "A Monographic Study of the Genus Lycium of the Western Hemisphere," *Annals of the Missouri Botanical Garden,* Vol. XIX, pp. 179-374.

JAEGER, EDMUND C.

1933. *The California Deserts.* Stanford University Press.

JEPSON, W. L.

1893-1938. (ed.) *Erythea, A Journal of Botany West American and General,* Vols. I to VIII.

1909-1936. *A Flora of California.* Vol. I and Vol. II, Pts. 1, 2, 3. Associated Students' Store, University of California, Berkeley.

1916-1934. (ed.) *Madroño, Journal of the California Botanical Society,* Vols. I and II.

1925. *Manual of the Flowering Plants of California.* Associated Students' Store, University of California, Berkeley.

JOHNSTON, I. M.

1924. "Expedition of the California Academy of Sciences to the Gulf of California in 1921," *Proceedings of the California Academy of Sciences,* Ser. 4, Vol. XII, No. 30, pp. 951-1218.

KEARNEY, T. H.

1935. "The North American Species of Sphaeralcea, Subgenus Eusphaeralcea," *University of California Publications in Botany,* Vol. XIX, No. 1, pp. 1-128.

KECK, D. D.

1926. "Lonicera and Symphoricarpos in Southern California," *Bulletin of the Southern California Academy of Sciences,* Vol. XXV, Pt. 2, pp. 28-35.

1932. "Studies in Penstemon, a Systematic Treatment of the Section Saccanthera," *University of California Publications in Botany,* Vol. XVI, No. 11, pp. 367-426.
1936. "Studies in Penstemon. The Section Hesperothamnus," *Madroño,* Vol. III, No. 5, pp. 200-219.
1936. "Studies in Penstemon III. The Section Cryptostemon," *Madroño,* Vol. III, No. 6, pp. 248-250.
1937. "Studies in Penstemon IV. The Section Ericopsis," *Bulletin of the Torrey Botanical Club,* Vol. LXIV, pp. 357-381.
1937. "Studies in Penstemon V. The Section Peltanthera," *The American Midland Naturalists,* Vol. XVIII, No. 5, pp. 790-824. The University Press, Notre Dame, Indiana.
1938. "Studies in Penstemon VI. The Section Aurator," *Bulletin of the Torrey Botanical Club,* Vol. LXV, pp. 233-255.

KIRKWOOD, J. E.
1930. *Northern Rocky Mountain Trees and Shrubs,* Stanford University Press.

MASON, H. L.
1935-1939 (ed.) *Madroño, Journal of the California Botanical Society.*

MCKELVEY, SUSAN DELANO
1938. *Yuccas of the Southwestern United States,* Part I. Published by the Arnold Arboretum.

MCMINN, H. E.
1930. "A Geographic and Taxonomic Study of the California Species of the Genus Ceanothus," *Contributions from the Dudley Herbarium of Stanford University,* Vol. I, No. 4. Stanford University Press.
1935. "Notes on Western Leatherwood, Dirca occidentalis Gray," *Madroño,* Vol. III, No. 3, pp. 117-120.

MILLIKEN, JESSIE
1904. "A Review of California Polemoniaceae," *University of California Publications in Botany,* Vol. II, pp. 1-71.

MUNZ, P. A.
1927. "The Southern California Species of Salvia," *Bulletin of the Southern California Academy of Sciences,* Vol. XXVI, Pt. 1, pp. 17-29.
1935. *Manual of Southern California Botany.* J. W. Stacey, Inc. Distributor, San Francisco, California.

MUNZ, P. A., AND JOHNSTON, I. M.
1924. "The Penstemons of Southern California," *Bulletin of the Southern California Academy of Sciences,* Vol. XXIII, Pt. 1, pp. 21-40.

OSGOOD, M. ELSIE
1937. "A Study of the California Species of the Genus Solanum," *Thesis for the M.A. Degree,* University of California, Berkeley.

OTTLEY, A. M.
1923. "A Revision of the Californian Species of Lotus," *University of California Publications in Botany,* Vol. X, No. 3, pp. 180-305.

PARISH, S. B.
1901. "A Group of Western American Solanums," *Proceedings of the California Academy of Sciences,* Ser. 3, Vol. II, No. 5.

PIPER, C. V.
1906. "Flora of the State of Washington," *Contributions from the United States National Herbarium,* Vol. XI. Government Printing Office, Washington, D.C.

PIPER, C. V., AND BEATTIE, R. K.
1915. *Flora of the Northwest Coast.* State College of Washington, Pullman.

ROBINSON, B. L.
1917. "A Monograph of the Genus Brickellia," *Memoirs of the Gray Herbarium* of Harvard University.

SAUNDERS, C. F.
1920. *Useful Wild Plants of the United States and Canada.* Published by Robert M. McBride & Company.

ST. JOHN, H.
1937. *Flora of Southeastern Washington and Adjacent Idaho.* Student Book Corporation, Pullman, Washington.

SMALL, J. K.
1914. "Ericaceae," *North American Flora,* Vol. XXIX, Pt. 1, pp. 33-102.

SMILEY, F. J.
1921. "Flora of the Sierra Nevada of California," *University of California Publications in Botany,* Vol. IX.

STANDLEY, P. C.
1916. "Chenopodiaceae," *North American Flora,* Vol. XXI, Pt. 1, pp. 3-92.
1920-1926. "Trees and Shrubs of Mexico," *Contributions from the United States National Herbarium,* Vol. XXIII, Government Printing Office, Washington, D.C.

THORNBER, J. J.
1910. "The Grazing Ranges of Arizona," *Arizona Agriculture Experiment Station Bulletin,* Vol. LXV, p. 245.

TIDESTROM, I.
1925. "Flora of Utah and Nevada," *Contributions from the United States National Herbarium,* Vol. XXV. Government Printing Office, Washington, D.C.

TRELEASE, WM.
1924. "The American Oaks," *Memoirs of the National Academy of Sciences,* Vol. XX. Government Printing Office, Washington, D.C.

VAN DERSAL, WILLIAM R.
1938. "Native Woody Plants of the United States," *United States Department of Agriculture, Miscellaneous Publication* No. 303.

WEAVER, JOHN E., AND CLEMENTS, F. E.
1929. *Plant Ecology.* McGraw-Hill Book Company.

WIGGINS, IRA L.
1934. "A Report on Several Species of Lycium from the Southwestern Deserts." *Contributions from the Dudley Herbarium of Stanford University,* Vol. I, No. 6. Stanford University Press.

WOLF, CARL B.
1938. *The North American Species of Rhamnus.* Monographs, Botanical Series, No. 1, Rancho Santa Ana Botanic Garden, Orange County, California.

WOOTON, E. O., AND STANDLEY, PAUL C.
1915. "Flora of New Mexico," *Contributions from the United States National Herbarium,* Vol. XIX. Government Printing Office, Washington, D.C.

INDEX

(The italicized words are synonyms.)

C